Handbook of Pediatric Brain Imaging

Advances in Magnetic Resonance Technology and Applications

Handbook of Pediatric Brain Imaging

Methods and Applications

Volume 2

Edited By

Hao Huang

Department of Radiology, Children's Hospital of Philadelphia, Philadelphia, PA, United States

Department of Radiology, Perelman School of Medicine, University of Pennsylvania, Philadelphia, PA, United States

Timothy P.L. Roberts

Department of Radiology, Children's Hospital of Philadelphia, Philadelphia, PA, United States

Department of Radiology, Perelman School of Medicine, University of Pennsylvania, Philadelphia, PA, United States

Series Editors

In-Young Choi, PhD

Department of Neurology, Department of Radiology, Department of Molecular & Integrative Physiology, Hoglund Biomedical Imaging Center, University of Kansas Medical Center, Kansas City, KS, United States

Peter Jezzard, PhD

Wellcome Centre for Integrative Neuroimaging, Nuffield Department of Clinical Neurosciences, University of Oxford, Oxford, United Kingdom

Brian Hargreaves, PhD

Department of Radiology, Department of Electrical Engineering, Department of Bioengineering, Stanford University, Stanford, CA, United States

Greg Zaharchuk, MD, PhD

Department of Radiology, Stanford University, Stanford, CA, United States

Academic Press is an imprint of Elsevier
125 London Wall, London EC2Y 5AS, United Kingdom
525 B Street, Suite 1650, San Diego, CA 92101, United States
50 Hampshire Street, 5th Floor, Cambridge, MA 02139, United States
The Boulevard, Langford Lane, Kidlington, Oxford OX5 1GB, United Kingdom

Notices

Knowledge and best practice in this field are constantly changing. As new research and experience broaden our understanding, changes in research methods, professional practices, or medical treatment may become necessary.

Practitioners and researchers must always rely on their own experience and knowledge in evaluating and using any information, methods, compounds, or experiments described herein. In using such information or methods they should be mindful of their own safety and the safety of others, including parties for whom they have a professional responsibility.

To the fullest extent of the law, neither the Publisher nor the authors, contributors, or editors, assume any liability for any injury and/or damage to persons or property as a matter of products liability, negligence or otherwise, or from any use or operation of any methods, products, instructions, or ideas contained in the material herein.

Library of Congress Cataloging-in-Publication Data
A catalog record for this book is available from the Library of Congress

British Library Cataloguing-in-Publication Data
A catalogue record for this book is available from the British Library

ISBN : 978-0-12-816633-8

For information on all Academic Press publications
visit our website at https://www.elsevier.com/books-and-journals

Publisher: Mara Conner
Acquisitions Editor: Tim Pitts
Editorial Project Manager: Emily Thomson
Production Project Manager: Vijayaraj Purushothaman
Cover Designer: Matthew Limbert

Typeset by STRAIVE, India

List of other books in series

1. Seiberlich et al: *Quantitative Magnetic Resonance Imaging*, ISBN: 978-0-12-817057-1, November 2020
2. Huang and Roberts: *Pediatric Brain Imaging*, ISBN: 978-0-12-816633-8, May 2021

Contents

SECTION 2 MRI Postprocessing

Contributors

Banu Ahtam
Department of Pediatrics, Harvard Medical School; Fetal-Neonatal Neuroimaging and Developmental Science Center, Division of Newborn Medicine, Boston Children's Hospital, Boston, MA, United States

Bharat B. Biswal
Department of Biomedical Engineering, New Jersey Institute of Technology, Newark, NJ, United States

Miao Cao
Institute of Science and Technology for Brain-Inspired Intelligence, Fudan University; Key Laboratory of Computational Neuroscience and Brain-Inspired Intelligence, Fudan University, Ministry of Education, Shanghai, China

Kim M. Cecil
Department of Radiology, University of Cincinnati College of Medicine, Cincinnati Children's Hospital Medical Center, Cincinnati, OH, United States

Donna Y. Chen
Department of Biomedical Engineering, New Jersey Institute of Technology; Department of Biomedical Engineering, Rutgers Biomedical and Health Sciences, Newark, NJ, United States

Douglas C. Dean, III
Department of Pediatrics; Department of Medical Physics, University of Wisconsin-Madison, School of Medicine & Public Health; Waisman Center, University of Wisconsin-Madison, Madison, WI, United States

Sara DeMauro
Division of Neonatology, Children's Hospital of Philadelphia; University of Pennsylvania Perelman School of Medicine, Philadelphia, PA, United States

Sean C.L. Deoni
Maternal, Newborn, and Child Health Discovery & Tools, Bill & Melinda Gates Foundation, Seattle, WA; Advanced Baby Imaging Lab, Rhode Island Hospital; Department of Pediatrics, Warren Alpert Medical School at Brown University, Providence, RI, United States

Jessica Dubois
University of Paris, NeuroDiderot Unit UMR1141, Inserm, Paris; Paris-Saclay University, NeuroSpin/UNIACT, CEA, Gif-sur-Yvette, France

M. Dylan Tisdall
Radiology, Perelman School of Medicine, University of Pennsylvania, Philadelphia, PA, United States

David A. Edmondson
Department of Radiology, University of Cincinnati College of Medicine, Cincinnati Children's Hospital Medical Center, Cincinnati, OH, United States

Kun Gao
Department of Radiology and Biomedical Research Imaging Center, University of North Carolina at Chapel Hill, Chapel Hill, NC, United States

P. Ellen Grant
Department of Pediatrics, Harvard Medical School; Fetal-Neonatal Neuroimaging and Developmental Science Center, Division of Newborn Medicine, Boston Children's Hospital, Boston, MA, United States

Heather L. Green
Department of Radiology, Children's Hospital of Philadelphia, Philadelphia, PA, United States

Rakibul Hafiz
Department of Biomedical Engineering, New Jersey Institute of Technology; Department of Biomedical Engineering, Rutgers Biomedical and Health Sciences, Newark, NJ, United States

Yong He
State Key Laboratory of Cognitive Neuroscience and Learning; Beijing Key Laboratory of Brain Imaging and Connectomics; IDG/McGovern Institute for Brain Research, Beijing Normal University, Beijing, China

Hao Huang
Department of Radiology, Children's Hospital of Philadelphia; Department of Radiology, Perelman School of Medicine, University of Pennsylvania, Philadelphia, PA, United States

Kiho Im
Department of Pediatrics, Harvard Medical School; Fetal Neonatal Neuroimaging and Developmental Science Center, Division of Newborn Medicine, Boston Children's Hospital, Boston, MA, United States

Jens H. Jensen
Department of Neuroscience, Medical University of South Carolina, Charleston, SC, United States

Katherine C. Ji
Department of Biomedical Engineering, New Jersey Institute of Technology, Newark, NJ, United States

Sandy Johng
Division of Neonatology, Children's Hospital of Philadelphia; University of Pennsylvania Perelman School of Medicine, Philadelphia, PA, United States

Mitsuru Kikuchi
Research Center for Child Mental Development, Kanazawa University, Kanazawa, Japan

Emily Kilroy
Department of Occupational Therapy and Occupational Science; Brain and Creativity Institute, University of Southern California, Los Angeles, CA, United States

Rachel E. Lean
Department of Psychiatry, Washington University School of Medicine, St. Louis, MO, United States

Gang Li
Department of Radiology and Biomedical Research Imaging Center, University of North Carolina at Chapel Hill, Chapel Hill, NC, United States

Daniel Licht
University of Pennsylvania Perelman School of Medicine; Divisions of Neurology and Pediatrics, Children's Hospital of Philadelphia, Philadelphia, PA, United States

Weili Lin
Department of Radiology and Biomedical Research Imaging Center, University of North Carolina at Chapel Hill, Chapel Hill, NC, United States

Scott Lorch
Division of Neonatology, Children's Hospital of Philadelphia; University of Pennsylvania Perelman School of Medicine, Philadelphia, PA, United States

Jeffrey Neil
Department of Neurology; Department of Pediatrics; Department of Radiology, Washington University School of Medicine; St. Louis Children's Hospital, St. Louis, MO, United States

Jeffrey J. Neil
Department of Neurology; Department of Pediatrics; Department of Radiology, Washington University School of Medicine, St. Louis, MO, United States

Charles A. Nelson
Boston Children's Hospital; Harvard Medical School, Boston; Harvard Graduate School of Education, Cambridge, MA, United States

Sijie Niu
Department of Radiology and Biomedical Research Imaging Center, University of North Carolina at Chapel Hill, Chapel Hill, NC, United States

Kenichi Oishi
The Russell H. Morgan Department of Radiology and Radiological Science, The Johns Hopkins University School of Medicine, Baltimore, MD, United States

Yusuf Osmanlıoğlu
DiCIPHR (Diffusion & Connectomics In Precision Healthcare Research) Lab, Department of Radiology, Perelman School of Medicine, University of Pennsylvania, Philadelphia, PA, United States

Minhui Ouyang
Department of Radiology, Children's Hospital of Philadelphia, Philadelphia, PA, United States

Christos Papadelis
Division of Newborn Medicine, Boston Children's Hospital, Harvard Medical School, Boston, MA; Jane and John Justin Neurosciences Center, Cook Children's Health Care System, Fort Worth; School of Medicine, Texas Christian University and University of North Texas Health Science Center; Department of Bioengineering, University of Texas at Arlington, Arlington, TX, United States

Timothy P.L. Roberts
Department of Radiology, Children's Hospital of Philadelphia; Department of Radiology, Perelman School of Medicine, University of Pennsylvania, Philadelphia, PA, United States

Joni N. Saby
Department of Radiology, Children's Hospital of Philadelphia, Philadelphia, PA, United States

Xingfeng Shao
Laboratory of FMRI Technology (LOFT), USC Mark & Mary Stevens Neuroimaging and Informatics Institute, Keck School of Medicine, University of Southern California, Los Angeles, CA, United States

Dinggang Shen
Department of Radiology and Biomedical Research Imaging Center, University of North Carolina at Chapel Hill, Chapel Hill, NC, United States; The Department of Research and Development, Shanghai United Imaging Intelligence Co., Ltd., Shanghai, China

Christopher D. Smyser
Department of Neurology; Department of Pediatrics; Department of Radiology, Washington University School of Medicine; St. Louis Children's Hospital, St. Louis, MO, United States

Marina Solti
Department of Pediatrics, Harvard Medical School; Fetal-Neonatal Neuroimaging and Developmental Science Center, Division of Newborn Medicine, Boston Children's Hospital, Boston, MA, United States

Susan Sotardi
Department of Radiology, Children's Hospital of Philadelphia, Philadelphia, PA, United States

Yue Sun
Department of Radiology and Biomedical Research Imaging Center, University of North Carolina at Chapel Hill, Chapel Hill, NC, United States

Shruti Varshney
Department of Biomedical Engineering, New Jersey Institute of Technology, Newark, NJ, United States

Ragini Verma
DiCIPHR (Diffusion & Connectomics In Precision Healthcare Research) Lab, Department of Radiology, Perelman School of Medicine, University of Pennsylvania, Philadelphia, PA, United States

Arastoo Vossough
Department of Radiology, Children's Hospital of Philadelphia; University of Pennsylvania Perelman School of Medicine, Philadelphia, PA, United States

Danny JJ Wang
Laboratory of FMRI Technology (LOFT), USC Mark & Mary Stevens Neuroimaging and Informatics Institute; Department of Neurology, Keck School of Medicine, University of Southern California, Los Angeles, CA, United States

Fan Wang
Department of Radiology and Biomedical Research Imaging Center, University of North Carolina at Chapel Hill, Chapel Hill, NC, United States

Li Wang
Department of Radiology and Biomedical Research Imaging Center, University of North Carolina at Chapel Hill, Chapel Hill, NC, United States

Zhengwang Wu
Department of Radiology and Biomedical Research Imaging Center, University of North Carolina at Chapel Hill, Chapel Hill, NC, United States

Wanze Xie
School of Psychological and Cognitive Sciences; PKU-IDG/McGovern Institute for Brain Research, Peking University, China

Yuko Yoshimura
Research Center for Child Mental Development, Kanazawa University, Kanazawa, Japan

Fenqiang Zhao
Department of Radiology and Biomedical Research Imaging Center, University of North Carolina at Chapel Hill, Chapel Hill, NC, United States

Tianjia Zhu
Department of Radiology, Perelman School of Medicine; Department of Bioengineering, University of Pennsylvania, Philadelphia, PA, United States

SECTION

MRI methods

1

CHAPTER 1

Special considerations for acquisition of pediatric MRI of high spatial and temporal resolution

Timothy P.L. Roberts[a,b], Tianjia Zhu[b,c], and Hao Huang[a,b]

Department of Radiology, Children's Hospital of Philadelphia, Philadelphia, PA, United States[a] Department of Radiology, Perelman School of Medicine, University of Pennsylvania, Philadelphia, PA, United States[b] Department of Bioengineering, University of Pennsylvania, Philadelphia, PA, United States[c]

1. Background

Why do we need *pediatric* neuroimaging?

In addition to the obvious clinical answer of diagnostic evaluation in the cases of pediatric disease of the central nervous system (CNS), and to rule out neurologic components (e.g., brain tumor) in the setting of sudden onset physical or mental status change, it should be considered that many diagnoses made later in life may have their biological onset in childhood (or earlier, in utero) and that early identification of such biological departures from typical development might provide an option for earlier patient management (particularly in children at high risk of subsequent diagnosis, through family history and/or genetic screening). Examples of this can be found in prodromal schizophrenia or familial risk for autism spectrum disorder (ASD). Research is ongoing in the early prediction of neuropsychiatric disorders, such as ASD, with promising results reported from structural, microstructural, and functional magnetic resonance imaging (MRI) approaches (Ouyang et al., 2020; Hazlett et al., 2017; Rosenberg et al., 2018; Adeli et al., 2019).

Moreover, there are so many microstructural, organizational and specialization changes occurring throughout the brain and at various stages of development that understanding of the dynamics of brain development are imperative for our understanding of human brain neuroscience in both health and disease: outcome(s) depends on trajectory(ies). The nature of brain development in childhood varies with age as well as systems. In infants, the priority is establishing sensory systems and myelinating the thalamo-cortical connections to improve the speed with which the brain can "experience" its sensory environment, the world. Later integrative and cognitive systems assume priority. Longer range connectivities become established. On an ongoing basis, "use it or lose it" principles governing synaptic plasticity define brain development through modulation by experience. Ultimately, we arrive at the "adult" brain. Pediatric neuroimaging allows us to glimpse into "how we get there."

Handbook of Pediatric Brain Imaging. https://doi.org/10.1016/B978-0-12-816633-8.00019-3

Modern neuroimaging boasts an impressive armory of multimodal techniques, including variants of MRI such as diffusion-MRI (dMRI), perfusion-MRI, functional-MRI (fMRI) and magnetic resonance spectroscopy (MRS) as well as electrophysiological techniques (such as EEG and MEG). Each type of imaging technique rapidly evolves, providing ever more accurate and clinically informative measurements. For instance, novel diffusion MRI models that account for non-Gaussian diffusion like diffusion kurtosis imaging (DKI) (Jensen et al., 2005) show unprecedented sensitivity to the underlying neurocytoarchitecture (Zhu et al., 2021), and have been applied in both developmental (Ouyang et al., 2019a, b; Paydar et al., 2014; Falangola et al., 2008) and disease studies (Helpern et al., 2011; Gong et al., 2013), particularly in brain regions inappropriate for Gaussian approaches such as diffusion tensor imaging (DTI). Similarly, advances in other imaging techniques such as functional connectome mapping from resting-state functional MRI (rs-fMRI), perfusion MRI, myelin water fraction (MWF), quantitative susceptibility mapping (QSM), and magnetic resonance spectroscopy (MRS), as well as advanced diffusion MRI tractography all offer powerful new tools for pediatric neuroimaging. These tools are proving vital in meeting the above goals of characterizing the brain in health and disease. However, the majority of these tools have been developed for use in the adult population. While their application to the pediatric brain might appear trivial, several concerns becoming quickly apparent and much of the focus of pediatric neuroimaging is to mitigate these concerns so as to maximize the value opportunity of these techniques in the critically-needed study of brain development. In a nutshell, these concerns stem from the following generalizations:

- Children (and their brains) are smaller than adults (and theirs)
- Children are less likely to understand and cooperate with the need to remain motionless during scanning
- Children are less likely to be able to tolerate lengthy examinations
- Children are less likely to understand and perform complex instructions and behavioral paradigms
- Children's brains are still a "works-in-progress" and so standard adult expectations (e.g., of tissue contrast secondary to myelination) may not apply.
- Children may exhibit greater anxiety than adults in an unfamiliar hospital/technical environment.

It should be noted that in general, many of these concerns are more significant in younger children and, by extension, most significant in infants.

The overall goal of this book is to address the opportunities and obstacles in pediatric neuroimaging, to assess the commonalities with adult imaging and the nuanced adjustments that must be made to optimize acquisitions and analyses in infants, toddlers, children and adolescents allowing definition of trajectories from conception to adulthood. This chapter, as an introduction to the book, highlights some of the opportunities, challenges and mitigation strategies that are explored in subsequent domain-specific contributions, providing an outline of common themes and setting the stage for the comprehensive exposition to follow.

2. Challenges in pediatric neuroimaging and approaches to their mitigation

While in general there are many challenges in pediatric neuroimaging research and clinical practice shared with adult imaging (such as considerations of optimal study design and choice of appropriate controls/reference images), there are some additional or exacerbated challenges in the pediatric setting.

These are briefly introduced below and considered in more detail in subsequent methodological chapters as they pertain to advanced imaging approaches.

2.1 Study design—Subject selection and characterization

The first step toward a successful pediatric neuroimaging study is setting a clear goal for the study. While comparing "atypical" against "typical" development seems like a universal, unequivocal theme, many complexities arise from the intricate relationship between single symptoms and disorders or syndromes, comorbid conditions, and heterogeneity within both typically and atypically developing populations (Greene et al., 2016). A study aiming to understand a specific symptom of a disease would benefit more from restrictive inclusion criteria while a study aiming to understand a disorder as a whole would benefit from including a wide range of common co-occurring conditions and medication status and subsequent subgroup level analysis. In fact, in many brain disorders, patients with comorbidity/co-occurring symptoms/phenotypes outnumber patients with a "pure" condition. A simple "not medicated" label may mean "never taken any medication for the condition," "have been on medication but are currently off-medication" or "continuously taking medicine but did not take it for the scan day." Each type of medication history may affect the subject's brain differently and must be considered. Recruiting only a nonmedicated sample may bias the study toward a rarified subpopulation, not in fact representative of the whole. In addition, in the typically developing control group, subclinical symptoms, behavior-based subgroups, and imaging-based subgroups (e.g., fMRI-based subgroups) jointly cause within-group heterogeneity. Comparisons within *subgroups* of both the atypical and typical populations would hence be more desirable than a simple comparison between an atypically developing population and a "typically developing" population. In some studies, group-level analysis may belie the unique patterns of activity present in the individual central to understanding brain structure, function, and disorders. Individual-level analyses have therefore been developed to identify individual differences in development (Dubois and Adolphs, 2016; Miller and Van Horn, 2007; Van Horn et al., 2008; Xu et al., 2019). Posthoc inclusion/exclusion criteria (after the scan) also weigh in since excluding subjects with severe motion may bias the study population and violate the commonly used "missing at random" statistical model.

In sum, once the prescan and postscan inclusion criteria have been identified to suit the goal of the study, study design becomes a trade-off between data quality and cost, specificity, and generalizability. Clearly, useful data yielding sufficient statistical power to address the study hypotheses should be collected. When scanner-time and subject cooperation permits, scans can be repeated on the same individual to increase scan-wise success rate. Subgroup and individual level analysis should be conducted as much as possible and limitations should be mentioned (Greene et al., 2016). In subsequent sections, we will introduce the challenges and technical methods for improving the acquisition of adequate, high-quality pediatric imaging data.

2.2 Scanner environment

The MRI scanner environment will be unfamiliar to most pediatric subjects and can cause varying degrees of excitement and anxiety, especially in children. Such changes in the subject's cognitive and affective states will likely increase head motion and change brain activity and physiologic measures like respiratory motion, heart rate, and muscle tension. Moreover, an unpleasant scanner experience will make the subjects reluctant to come back for longitudinal scans (Greene et al., 2016). A common method for familiarizing the participants with the scanner environment is using "mock" scanners, which are replicas of the MRI scanner without the safety restrictions of the high field magnet itself. To simulate the actual scan environment, audio recordings of MRI noise can be played through speakers in the mock scanner (Greene et al., 2016; de Bie et al., 2010; Raschle et al., 2009; Barnea-Goraly et al., 2014). Since mock scanners are somewhat expensive, having the parents play the audio of MRI noise to children in the days and weeks before the scan may be a cost-effective alternative approach to de-sensitization. Mock scanners can also be equipped with effective head motion control training systems (such as systems to pause a watched video whenever head movement exceeds a desired threshold). Cognitive paradigms for functional MRI can also be tested behaviorally prior to scanning, and especially in the mock MRI environment, as needed.

2.3 Acquisition challenges—Motion

Typical MRI scans (with differing contrasts obtained via pulse sequence choice and parameters) are characterized by acquisition times ranging from seconds to minutes. Even the ultrafast (e.g., echo planar imaging, EPI) sequences (themselves captured in ~50 ms per slice and ~2–3 s per multi-slice volume) are often acquired as a part of a "dynamic" scan extending over several minutes. Thus, a fundamental consideration in pediatric MRI is maintaining a motionless head position during such an extended period. Failing to do so introduces motion "artifacts" in extended acquisitions (often characterized by blurring or ghost images) and/or motion-related "mis-registration" in dynamic series (e.g., contrast-enhanced studies of perfusion, or functional MRI). While, in part, volume to volume (*inter*scan) motion in dynamic acquisitions can be "corrected" by posthoc, or retrospective, realignment of images, usually with a rigid-body registration, *intra*scan motion presents additional challenges with artifact nature depending on the choice of acquisition strategy (in particular, k-space trajectory). Motion problems are typically more pronounced for pediatric populations, especially children with psychiatric disorders like attention deficit hyperactivity disorder, ADHD. Most major public datasets for brain development and high-quality dataset acquired by leading groups (Howell et al., 2019; Harms et al., 2018; Makropoulos et al., 2018; Volkow et al., 2018; Satterthwaite et al., 2016; Yu et al., 2014, 2016, 2020; Ouyang et al., 2015, 2016, 2019a,b, 2020; Zhao et al., 2019a,b; Feng et al., 2019; Cao et al., 2017; Huang et al., 2015; Mishra et al., 2013) exploit cutting-edge motion correction techniques to obtain optimal scan results. Popular techniques employed in these large-scale studies are listed in Table 1, "primary difference from adults" column. Of note, in population studies commonly encountered in MRI research, such "group differences" (typically between diagnostic groups or contrasting patient population vs controls) in motion performance may confound interpretation of apparent "group differences" in signal. This requires careful mitigation to avoid ascribing "connectivity differences" or "functional activity differences" to a population, where a fundamental difference in motion characteristics was co-observed (Power et al., 2015).

2.4 Mitigation of motion problems

Generally, two classes of methods are effective in mitigating motion-related artifacts: *reducing* head movement and *accounting for* head movement. To reduce head movement, games like the "statue game" (http://cibsr.stanford.edu/participating/Games.html) may be helpful. Physical restraints like bite bars, masks, and cushions can be adjusted to fit the smaller size of children. Furthermore, strategies to

Table 1 Age-specific tissue relaxation properties and T1w, T2w, acquisition sequences and parameters summarized from major brain development public datasets.

Age group	Age range	T1 (GM/WM)	T2 (GM/WM)	Sequence	Type of head coil	TR/TE	FOV	Resolution	Thickness	Primary difference from sequence for adults	References
FAST		N/A	N/A	HASTE, PROPELLER	32-ch	PROPELLER: TR > 3600 ms, TE = 92 ms. HASTE: TR = 4300 ms, TE = 60 ms	256 × 256	1.3 mm		Modified pulse sequence and/or k-space trajectories to reduce scan time, motion estimation and correction.	Patel et al. (1997) and Pipe (1999)
Young adult	22–35 years	800–1000 ms/550–600 ms	800–1000 ms/550–600 ms	3D MPRAGE for T1w; 3D T2-SPACE for T2w	32-ch	TR = 2400 ms, TE = 2.14 ms for T1w; TR = 3200 ms, TE = 565 ms for T2w.	224 × 224 mm	0.7 mm isotropic	0.7 mm	Same as adults	Harms et al. (2018) (HCP-YA protocol)
Children	2–21 years	800–1000 ms/550–600 ms	60–70 ms/50–60 ms	Conventional MPRAGE or multiecho MPRAGE for T1w; variable-flip-angle TSE for T2w.	32-ch for 8–21 years; 32-ch pediatric coil with smaller diameter for younger children.	TR = 2500 ms, TE = 1.8/3.6/5.4/7.2 ms. (multiecho) for T1w; TR/TE = 3200/564 ms, turbo factor = 314 for T2w	256 × 240 ×166 mm	0.8 × 0.8 mm	1.2 mm	Multiecho MPRAGE to reduce susceptibility-induced distortions and improve SNR. Use of volumetric navigators (vNavs) for prospective motion correction.	Harms et al. (2018) (HCP-D protocol); Howell et al. (2019) (BCP protocol); Holland et al. (1986) (T1, T2 values)
Infant	0–2 years	2 years: 820 ± 25 ms/ 505 ± 55 ms 1.5 years: 840 ± 90 ms/570 ±40 ms 1 year: 890 ± 75 ms/580 ±50 ms 0.5 years.: 1300 ±70 ms/1150 ±60 ms	2 years: 69 ± 4 ms/56 ± 4 ms 1.5 years: 68 ± 6 ms/59 ± 5 ms 1 year: 68 ± 3 ms/57 ±5 ms 0.5 year:67 ±7 ms/64 ± 6 ms	MPRAGE for T1w; 3D variable flip angle turbo spin-echo sequence (Siemens-Space) was used for T2 weighted images	32-ch	TR = 2400/1060 ms, TE = 2.24 ms for T1w; TR = 3200 ms, TE = 564 ms for T2w.	256 × 256 mm	0.8 mm isotropic	0.8 mm	Subject put to natural sleep. Motion reduction and correction techniques applied.	Howell et al. (2019) (BCP protocol)

Continued

Table 1 Age-specific tissue relaxation properties and T1w, T2w, acquisition sequences and parameters summarized from major brain development public datasets—cont'd

Age group	Age range	T1 (GM/WM)	T2 (GM/WM)	Sequence	Type of head coil	TR/TE	FOV	Resolution	Thickness	Primary difference from sequence for adults	References
Neonate	29–45 gw	1590 ± 60 ms/1615 ± 120 ms	GM:88 ± 8 ms, WM:91 ± 6 ms	Inversion Recovery (IR) TSE sequence for T1w; TSE for T2w	32-ch, dedicated neonatal coil with positioning device (Hughes et al., 2017)	TR = 4800 ms, TE = 8.7 ms for T1w; TR = 12,000 ms, TE = 156 ms for T2w	145 × 145 ×101.5 mm	0.8 × 0.8 mm	1.6 mm	Subject put to natural sleep. Dedicated neonate coil. Positioning device allows placement of infant's head deep into the coil to maximize SNR; Dedicated slim immobilization pieces to reduce motion; transport trolley for putting infant to sleep before transferring to the scanner; modified scanner software to enable slow ramp-up for gradients and the continuation of gradient noise to avoid stop-start noise pattern.	Hughes et al. (2017)

Fetal	Before birth	/	/	2D GRE for T1w; HASTE for T2w	32-ch phased-array torso surface coil	/	200–300 mm	256 × 256	>3 mm	Single-shot fast protocols to reduce scan time; fetal white matter contains more water, long TE allows better gray-white matter contrast difference	Weisstanner et al. (2017) and Gholipour et al. (2014)

Abbreviations: BCP, *Baby Connectome Project;* FOV, *field of view;* GM, *gray matter;* GRE, *gradient recalled echo;* HASTE, *HAlf fourier Single-shot Turbo spin-Echo;* HCP-D, *Human Connectome Project Development;* HCP-YA, *Human Connectome Project Young Adult;* MPRAGE, *magnetization prepared rapid acquisition with gradient echoes;* PROPELLER, *Periodically Rotated Overlapping ParallEL Lines with Enhanced Reconstruction;* SNR, *signal to noise ratio;* T1w, *T1-weighted;* T2w, *T2-weighted;* TE, *echo time;* TR, *repetition time;* TSE, *turbo spin echo;* WM, *white matter.*

acquire adequate imaging information in less time will reduce the sensitivity to involuntary motion (as motion-free head positioning is easier to briefly *attain than to maintain* for an extended period). To account for head movement, participants with severe head motion should be excluded from the study by expert visual inspection or estimating errors in automated segmentation software like Freesurfer (Fischl, 2012). Exclusion criteria for popular large-scale datasets can often be found in the release notes. Prospective motion correction (PMC) techniques like optical guidance, spiral navigator scans, and online motion tracking track the motion during the scan and "correct for" the motion either in real-time or during image reconstruction (Brown et al., 2010). Pipelines like PROspective Motion correction (PROMO) (White et al., 2010) and Prospective Acquisition Correction (PACE) (Hirokawa et al., 2008) combine advanced PMC techniques to achieve optimal acquisition. Incorporating additional "navigator" echoes into the pulse sequence (borrowing from *cardiac* MRI) has been widely used in high-quality public datasets for brain development such as the Human Connectome Project-Development (HCP-D) (Harms et al., 2018). Recently, optically-guided PMC with in-scanner motion-recording cameras have been developed and commercialized by companies such as Kineticor (KinetiCor, HI, United States). Optical PMC has been shown to improve precision of quantitative metrics from MRI in both structural (Callaghan et al., 2015) and functional (Todd et al., 2015) MRI. PMC can also be achieved by applying new MRI sequences. For example, navigator scans can be incorporated into in dMRI and fMRI to estimate motion such that the data acquired right after the navigator echo is accepted only if motion at a given moment is smaller than a threshold limit (White et al., 2010). Cardiac-related pulsatility artifacts in fMRI can also be corrected by acquiring fMRI signal at the same cardiac phase (Zhang et al., 2006; Napadow et al., 2008). "Online" motion tracking modifies the sequences during acquisition according to navigator motion-tracking results in real-time (Hirokawa et al., 2008; White et al., 2010). Alternatively (and possibly in addition) retrospective motion correction (RMC) techniques divide a high-resolution 3D MRI scan into multiple shorter acquisitions to turn harder-to-correct *intra*scan motions into *inter*scan motions and have been validated, for example, on children with ADHD (Kochunov et al., 2006). In simple cases where motion is random about the origin, averaging multiple acquisitions will diminish the motion artifacts at the cost of increasing scan time. New sequences that help RMC have also been developed in multimodal MRI. For structural MRI, radial sampling of k-space allows sampling the center of k-space multiple times to estimate the motion in low-frequency content of the image corresponding to large structures. Radial sampling also avoids discrete ghosts along a single phase-encode direction and produces more evenly distributed noise (Feng et al., 2014; Pipe, 1999). For fMRI, a novel sequence called multiecho echo-planar imaging (EPI) was developed to differentiate neuronally related Blood Oxygen Level-Dependent (BOLD) signals from motion and physiology artifacts using the unique echo time (TE) dependence of BOLD signals (Kundu et al., 2012). Advanced PMC and RMC techniques can often be combined into optimized pipelines like PROPELLER (Pipe, 1999) to synergize advantages of each technique.

To reduce scan time, well-tested faster sequences such as turbo (fast) spin echo (TSE/FSE) (Hennig et al., 1986) for T2w, single-shot EPI for dMRI, and (more recently) multiband-accelerated EPI for fMRI are widely used in popular public datasets and other high quality datasets (see Table 1, sequence column and Yu et al., 2014, 2016, 2020; Ouyang et al., 2015, 2016, 2019a,b, 2020; Zhao et al., 2019a,b; Feng et al., 2019; Cao et al., 2017; Huang et al., 2015; Mishra et al., 2013). In addition, for fetal scans requiring minimal scan time and highest resolution, HAlf fourier Single-shot Turbo spin-Echo (HASTE) (Semelka et al., 1996), PROPELLER (Pipe, 1999) and segmented EPI (Holdsworth et al., 2008) for dMRI have been adapted to reduce scan time.

2.5 Resolution and FOV considerations

Apart from motion, the smaller size and unique physical properties of the pediatric brain also pose unique challenges. The small size of pediatric brain structures demands higher spatial resolution (to achieve comparable "anatomic" resolution to adult MRI) which comes at a price of diminished signal to noise ratio, SNR, typically resulting in longer scan times (to partially compensate for the SNR loss associated with smaller voxels); yet children are generally less able to tolerate longer scans. As an alternative strategy to improve SNR, dedicated pediatric radiofrequency, RF, head coils can be built for each age group (Keil et al., 2011) with improved filling factor, coil element proximity and, hence, sensitivity. For instance, the European dHCP (developing human connectome) study for neonates employed a dedicated neonatal coil with a positioning device (See Table 1, Hughes et al., 2017). For children younger than 8 years old, HCP-D (the human connectome project development) used a pediatric coil with smaller diameter (Harms et al., 2018). In large public datasets as well as advanced studies by leading groups, spatial resolution, and field of view (FOV) are optimized according to the size of brain structures (equivalent "anatomic" resolution) at each age and age-related limitations on scan time (see Table 1 for optimal resolution and FOV for each age and modality, Howell et al., 2019; Harms et al., 2018; Makropoulos et al., 2018; Satterthwaite et al., 2016; Yu et al., 2014, 2016, 2020; Ouyang et al., 2015, 2016, 2019a,b, 2020; Zhao et al., 2019a,b; Feng et al., 2019; Cao et al., 2017; Huang et al., 2015; Mishra et al., 2013).

2.6 Age-specific optimization of sequences

In addition to size and morphology changes, MRI related physico-chemical properties of the brain undergo dynamic change during development (Ouyang et al., 2019a,b). T1 and T2 relaxation times both decrease sharply during the first 2 years of life and diffusion and functional MRI metrics continue to change throughout development (Holland et al., 1986; Howell et al., 2019; Greene et al., 2016; Ouyang et al., 2019a,b). Consequently, acquisition parameters such as sequence echo time and repeat time, TE/TR (Dean et al., 2014; Harms et al., 2018), and dMRI *b*-values and gradient tables for age-specific brain microstructures (Howell et al., 2019; Hutter et al., 2018; Harms et al., 2018; Feng et al., 2019; Ouyang et al., 2015) should be optimized for each age. Optimization of sequence parameters heavily depends on the goals of the study, and often boils down to maximizing contrast between specific tissues or between age-groups. For example, to optimize the TE/TR for structural MRI, simulations can be performed to find the TE and TR combination that maximizes the contrast between white matter, WM, and gray matter, GM, on T1-weighted (T1w) or T2-weighted (T2w) images, and the final optimized sequence is a trade-off between maximizing contrast difference and reducing scan time (Jones, 2004). To optimize *b*-value for diffusion tensor imaging (DTI), the *b*-value that yields the maximum contrast in the DTI-derived parameters such as FA for the target topic of the study is usually selected (Hui et al., 2010). Jones showed using simulations and experiments that at least 30 gradient directions should be acquired to obtain robust DTI fitting, and that the optimal gradients are uniformly distributed on a sphere (Jones, 2004). A rule-of-thumb for *b*-value choice is that the product of *b*-value and tissue apparent diffusion coefficient, ADC, should be $\sim$1, leading to lower *b*-values in pediatric applications ($\sim$700 s/mm^2), where tissue apparent diffusion coefficients are greater compared to adults ($\sim$1000 s/mm^2).

2.7 Fetal MRI

In fetal imaging, there are even more pronounced challenges. The fetus moves a lot more than children or infants, and there is no technique to hold the fetus still inside the womb. Generally, pharmaceutical sedation of the mother is not preferred, because of unknown risk to the fetus. Consequently, fetal MRI requires yet faster (and, generally, single shot) scans, and typically torso or cardiac coils with associated poorer sensitivity are used, although recently the sensitivity has been improved with multitransmit systems, multichannel coils, and parallel imaging (Gholipour et al., 2014). Fetal brain structures are, of course, even smaller, and thus demand even higher spatial resolution. A few studies have explored optimizing sequences for fetal MRI (Weisstanner et al., 2017; Gholipour et al., 2014) and state-of-the-art acquisition parameters, relatively consistent across studies, are summarized in Table 1. There are currently no large-scale public datasets for fetal MRI and acquiring high-quality fetal MRI images remains a challenge and an active area of research.

2.8 Optimized parameters table: A starting point for high-quality pediatric MRI

To this date, no reviews or textbooks have summarized a comprehensive table for age-specific optimized pediatric MRI acquisition parameters. In the following section, we provide a suggested table of parameters based on major public datasets (Howell et al., 2019; Harms et al., 2018; Makropoulos et al., 2018; Satterthwaite et al., 2016) with cutting-edge acquisition techniques for each age group and existing reviews (Ouyang et al., 2019a,b; Tarui et al., 2018). In sum, protocol development and parameter choice for pediatric MRI is a trade-off between obtaining high-quality images, and for multisite large datasets, availability of advanced hardware or pulse sequences across sites. Our Tables 2 and 3 offered as a reliable starting point for obtaining high quality pediatric MRI data. Advanced sequences and optimization strategies will be discussed in detail in later chapters.

Table 2 Age-specific diffusion MRI acquisition sequences and parameters summarized from major brain development public datasets.

Age group/ acquisition	Fetal	Neonates	Infants	Children	Young adults	FAST
Sequence	Single shot DW-SE-EPI	Single shot DW-SE-EPI	Single shot DW-SE-EPI	Single shot DW-SE-EPI	DW-SE-EPI	Segmented EPI
Type of coil	Body	32-ch head	32-ch head	32-ch head	32-ch head	–
TR/TE	–	TR = 3800 ms, TE = 90 ms; Delta = 42.5 ms, delta = 14 ms	TR = 2640 ms, TE = 89–100 ms	TR = 3230 ms, TE = 89.2 ms	TR = 5520 ms, TE = 89.5 ms	TR = 1800–3000 ms, TE = 68 ms
FOV	300–350 mm	150–168 mm	170–220 mm	220–256 mm	210 × 180 mm	260 mm

Table 2 Age-specific diffusion MRI acquisition sequences and parameters summarized from major brain development public datasets—cont'd

Age group/ acquisition	Fetal	Neonates	Infants	Children	Young adults	FAST
Resolution	2–3 mm	1.5 × 1.5 mm	1.3–2.2 mm	1.7–2 mm	1.2 × 1.2 mm	0.9 mm
Thickness	2–4 mm	1.6–3 mm	1.5 mm	1.5 mm	1.2 mm	4 mm
***b*-Value**	700–1000 s/mm^2	700–1000 s/mm^2	700–1000 s/mm^2	1000 s/mm^2	1000 s/mm^2	1000 s/mm^2
Diffusion gradient strategy	6–15 directions; suboptimal but reduces scan time	30–98 gradient directions; uniformly spaced on sphere	30–98 gradient directions; uniformly spaced on sphere	30–98 gradient directions; uniformly spaced on sphere	30–98 gradient directions; uniformly spaced on sphere	30–98 gradient directions; uniformly spaced on sphere
Primary difference from sequence for adults	Coil choice; resolution; lower *b*-value because of higher tissue ADC (higher water content)	Coil choice; resolution; lower *b*-value because of higher tissue ADC (higher water content); need for natural sleep during scan	Coil choice; resolution; lower *b*-value because of higher tissue ADC (higher water content); need for natural sleep during scan	Coil choice; resolution; increased motion	Same as adults	–
References	Weisstanner et al. (2017) and Gholipour et al. (2014)	Hutter et al. (2018) (dHCP); Ouyang et al. (2019a, b) and Jones et al. (2004)	Howell et al. (2019) (BCP)	Harms et al. (2018) (HCP-D)	Harms et al. (2018) (HCP-YA)	Holdsworth et al. (2008)

Abbreviations: ADC, *apparent diffusivity coefficient;* BCP, *Baby Connectome Project;* dHCP, *Developing Human Connectome Project;* DW-SE-EPI, *diffusion-weighted spin-echo echo planar imaging;* FOV, *field of view;* HCP-D, *Human Connectome Project Development;* HCP-YA, *Human Connectome Project Young Adult;* TE, *echo time;* TR, *repetition time.*

In summary, pediatric neuroimaging presents unprecedented opportunities for studying the most critical period of brain development. Along with that come a variety of constraints that prohibit simple translation of adult approaches. That said, with judicious consideration of the idiosyncrasies of pediatric imaging, we should be able to capitalize on recent advances in physiologic and anatomic imaging, generally pioneered in adults, but often so relevant to the child. Mostly, incorporation of these advances into our clinical and research protocols requires special considerations and ingenious innovations, but as the chapters of this book illustrate, when these can be implemented, new avenues open to study the neuroscience of the developing brain in health and disease.

Table 3 Age-specific functional MRI acquisition sequences and parameters summarized from major brain development public datasets.

Age group	Sequence	Type of head coil	TR/TE	FOV	Resolution	Thickness	Number of dynamics	Primary difference from sequences for adults	References
Fetal	/	Body	/	230 × 230 mm	2..4 mm	4 mm	/	No task-based, advanced motion correction methods	Weisstanner et al. (2017) and Gholipour et al. (2014)
Neonate	Multiband 9× accelerated EPI	32-ch	TR = 392 ms, TE = 38 ms	145 × 145 mm	2.15 mm isotropic	2.15 mm	/	No task-based, advanced motion correction methods	Hutter et al. (2018) (dHCP)
Infant	2D multiband GRE-EPI	32-ch	TR = 800 ms, TE = 37 ms	208 × 208 mm	2 mm isotropic	2 mm	/	No task-based, advanced motion correction methods	Howell et al. (2019) (BCP)
Children	2D multiband GRE-EPI	32-ch	TR = 800 ms, TE = 37 ms	not recorded in HCP-D paper	2 mm isotropic	2 mm	/	Shorter task-based paradigms. Age-appropriate materials	Harms et al. (2018) (HCP-D)
Young Adult	2D multiband GRE-EPI	32-ch	TR = 720 ms, TE = 33.1 ms	208 × 180 mm	2 mm isotropic	2 mm	/	Same as adults	Harms et al. (2018) (HCP-YA)

Abbreviations: BCP, *Baby Connectome Project;* dHCP, *Developing Human Connectome Project;* FOV, *field of view;* GRE-EPI, *gradient recalled echo echo planar imaging;* HCP-D, *Human Connectome Project Development;* HCP-YA, *Human Connectome Project Young Adult;* TE, *echo time;* TR, *repetition time.*

References

Adeli, E., Meng, Y., Li, G., Lin, W., Shen, D., 2019. Multi-task prediction of infant cognitive scores from longitudinal incomplete neuroimaging data. NeuroImage 185, 783–792.

Barnea-Goraly, N., Weinzimer, S.A., Ruedy, K.J., Mauras, N., Beck, R.W., Marzelli, M.J., Mazaika, P.K., Aye, T., White, N.H., Tsalikian, E., Fox, L., 2014. High success rates of sedation-free brain MRI scanning in young children using simple subject preparation protocols with and without a commercial mock scanner–the Diabetes Research in Children Network (DirecNet) experience. Pediatr. Radiol. 44 (2), 181–186.

Brown, T.T., Kuperman, J.M., Erhart, M., White, N.S., Roddey, J.C., Shankaranarayanan, A., Han, E.T., Rettmann, D., Dale, A.M., 2010. Prospective motion correction of high-resolution magnetic resonance imaging data in children. NeuroImage 53 (1), 139–145.

Callaghan, M.F., Josephs, O., Herbst, M., Zaitsev, M., Todd, N., Weiskopf, N., 2015. An evaluation of prospective motion correction (PMC) for high resolution quantitative MRI. Front. Neurosci. 9, 97.

Cao, M., He, Y., Dai, Z., Liao, X., Jeon, T., Ouyang, M., Chalak, L., Bi, Y., Rollins, N., Dong, Q., Huang, H., 2017. Early development of functional network segregation revealed by connectomic analysis of the preterm human brain. Cereb. Cortex 27 (3), 1949–1963.

de Bie, H.M., Boersma, M., Wattjes, M.P., Adriaanse, S., Vermeulen, R.J., Oostrom, K.J., Huisman, J., Veltman, D.J., Delemarre-Van de Waal, H.A., 2010. Preparing children with a mock scanner training protocol results in high quality structural and functional MRI scans. Eur. J. Pediatr. 169 (9), 1079–1085.

Dean, D.C., Dirks, H., O'Muircheartaigh, J., Walker, L., Jerskey, B.A., Lehman, K., Han, M., Waskiewicz, N., Deoni, S.C., 2014. Pediatric neuroimaging using magnetic resonance imaging during non-sedated sleep. Pediatr. Radiol. 44 (1), 64–72.

Dubois, J., Adolphs, R., 2016. Building a science of individual differences from fMRI. Trends Cogn. Sci. 20 (6), 425–443.

Falangola, M.F., Jensen, J.H., Babb, J.S., Hu, C., Castellanos, F.X., Di Martino, A., Ferris, S.H., Helpern, J.A., 2008. Age-related non-Gaussian diffusion patterns in the prefrontal brain. J. Magn. Reson. Imaging 28 (6), 1345–1350.

Feng, L., Grimm, R., Block, K.T., Chandarana, H., Kim, S., Xu, J., Axel, L., Sodickson, D.K., Otazo, R., 2014. Golden-angle radial sparse parallel MRI: combination of compressed sensing, parallel imaging, and golden-angle radial sampling for fast and flexible dynamic volumetric MRI. Magn. Reson. Med. 72 (3), 707–717.

Feng, L., Li, H., Oishi, K., Mishra, V., Song, L., Peng, Q., Ouyang, M., Wang, J., Slinger, M., Jeon, T., Lee, L., 2019. Age-specific gray and white matter DTI atlas for human brain at 33, 36 and 39 postmenstrual weeks. NeuroImage 185, 685–698.

Fischl, B., 2012. FreeSurfer. NeuroImage 62 (2), 774–781.

Gholipour, A., Estroff, J.A., Barnewolt, C.E., Robertson, R.L., Grant, P.E., Gagoski, B., Warfield, S.K., Afacan, O., Connolly, S.A., Neil, J.J., Wolfberg, A., 2014. Fetal MRI: a technical update with educational aspirations. Concept. Mag. Reson. A 43 (6), 237–266.

Gong, N.J., Wong, C.S., Chan, C.C., Leung, L.M., Chu, Y.C., 2013. Correlations between microstructural alterations and severity of cognitive deficiency in Alzheimer's disease and mild cognitive impairment: a diffusional kurtosis imaging study. Magn. Reson. Imaging 31 (5), 688–694.

Greene, D.J., Black, K.J., Schlaggar, B.L., 2016. Considerations for MRI study design and implementation in pediatric and clinical populations. Dev. Cogn. Neurosci. 18, 101–112.

Harms, M.P., Somerville, L.H., Ances, B.M., Andersson, J., Barch, D.M., Bastiani, M., Bookheimer, S.Y., Brown, T.B., Buckner, R.L., Burgess, G.C., Coalson, T.S., 2018. Extending the human connectome project across ages: imaging protocols for the lifespan development and aging projects. NeuroImage 183, 972–984.

Hazlett, H.C., Gu, H., Munsell, B.C., Kim, S.H., Styner, M., Wolff, J.J., Elison, J.T., Swanson, M.R., Zhu, H., Botteron, K.N., Collins, D.L., 2017. Early brain development in infants at high risk for autism spectrum disorder. Nature 542 (7641), 348–351.

Helpern, J.A., Adisetiyo, V., Falangola, M.F., Hu, C., Di Martino, A., Williams, K., Castellanos, F.X., Jensen, J.H., 2011. Preliminary evidence of altered gray and white matter microstructural development in the frontal lobe of adolescents with attention-deficit hyperactivity disorder: a diffusional kurtosis imaging study. J. Magn. Reson. Imaging 33 (1), 17–23.

Hennig, J., Nauerth, A., Friedburg, H., 1986. RARE imaging: a fast imaging method for clinical MR. Magn. Reson. Med. 3 (6), 823–833.

Hirokawa, Y., Isoda, H., Maetani, Y.S., Arizono, S., Shimada, K., Togashi, K., 2008. MRI artifact reduction and quality improvement in the upper abdomen with PROPELLER and prospective acquisition correction (PACE) technique. Am. J. Roentgenol. 191 (4), 1154–1158.

Holdsworth, S.J., Skare, S., Newbould, R.D., Guzmann, R., Blevins, N.H., Bammer, R., 2008. Readout-segmented EPI for rapid high resolution diffusion imaging at 3T. Eur. J. Radiol. 65 (1), 36–46.

Holland, B.A., Haas, D.K., Norman, D., Brant-Zawadzki, M., Newton, T.H., 1986. MRI of normal brain maturation. Am. J. Neuroradiol. 7 (2), 201–208.

Howell, B.R., Styner, M.A., Gao, W., Yap, P.T., Wang, L., Baluyot, K., Yacoub, E., Chen, G., Potts, T., Salzwedel, A., Li, G., 2019. The UNC/UMN baby connectome project (BCP): an overview of the study design and protocol development. NeuroImage 185, 891–905.

Huang, H., Shu, N., Mishra, V., Jeon, T., Chalak, L., Wang, Z.J., Rollins, N., Gong, G., Cheng, H., Peng, Y., Dong, Q., 2015. Development of human brain structural networks through infancy and childhood. Cereb. Cortex 25 (5), 1389–1404.

Hughes, E.J., Winchman, T., Padormo, F., Teixeira, R., Wurie, J., Sharma, M., Fox, M., Hutter, J., Cordero-Grande, L., Price, A.N., Allsop, J., 2017. A dedicated neonatal brain imaging system. Magn. Reson. Med. 78 (2), 794–804.

Hui, E.S., Cheung, M.M., Chan, K.C., Wu, E.X., 2010. B-value dependence of DTI quantitation and sensitivity in detecting neural tissue changes. NeuroImage 49 (3), 2366–2374.

Hutter, J., Tournier, J.D., Price, A.N., Cordero-Grande, L., Hughes, E.J., Malik, S., Steinweg, J., Bastiani, M., Sotiropoulos, S.N., Jbabdi, S., Andersson, J., 2018. Time-efficient and flexible design of optimized multishell HARDI diffusion. Magn. Reson. Med. 79 (3), 1276–1292.

Jensen, J.H., Helpern, J.A., Ramani, A., Lu, H., Kaczynski, K., 2005. Diffusional kurtosis imaging: the quantification of non-gaussian water diffusion by means of magnetic resonance imaging. Magn. Reson. Med. 53 (6), 1432–1440.

Jones, D.K., 2004. The effect of gradient sampling schemes on measures derived from diffusion tensor MRI: a Monte Carlo study. Magn. Reson. Med. 51 (4), 807–815.

Jones, R.A., Palasis, S., Grattan-Smith, J.D., 2004. MRI of the neonatal brain: optimization of spin-echo parameters. Am. J. Roentgenol. 182 (2), 367–372.

Keil, B., Alagappan, V., Mareyam, A., McNab, J.A., Fujimoto, K., Tountcheva, V., Triantafyllou, C., Dilks, D.D., Kanwisher, N., Lin, W., Grant, P.E., 2011. Size-optimized 32-channel brain arrays for 3 T pediatric imaging. Magn. Reson. Med. 66 (6), 1777–1787.

Kochunov, P., Lancaster, J.L., Glahn, D.C., Purdy, D., Laird, A.R., Gao, F., Fox, P., 2006. Retrospective motion correction protocol for high-resolution anatomical MRI. Hum. Brain Mapp. 27 (12), 957–962.

Kundu, P., Inati, S.J., Evans, J.W., Luh, W.M., Bandettini, P.A., 2012. Differentiating BOLD and non-BOLD signals in fMRI time series using multi-echo EPI. NeuroImage 60 (3), 1759–1770.

Makropoulos, A., Robinson, E.C., Schuh, A., Wright, R., Fitzgibbon, S., Bozek, J., Counsell, S.J., Steinweg, J., Vecchiato, K., Passerat-Palmbach, J., Lenz, G., 2018. The developing human connectome project: a minimal processing pipeline for neonatal cortical surface reconstruction. NeuroImage 173, 88–112.

Miller, M.B., Van Horn, J.D., 2007. Individual variability in brain activations associated with episodic retrieval: a role for large-scale databases. Int. J. Psychophysiol. 63 (2), 205–213.

Mishra, V., Cheng, H., Gong, G., He, Y., Dong, Q., Huang, H., 2013. Differences of inter-tract correlations between neonates and children around puberty: a study based on microstructural measurements with DTI. Front. Hum. Neurosci. 7, 721.

Napadow, V., Dhond, R., Conti, G., Makris, N., Brown, E.N., Barbieri, R., 2008. Brain correlates of autonomic modulation: combining heart rate variability with fMRI. NeuroImage 42 (1), 169–177.

Ouyang, A., Jeon, T., Sunkin, S.M., Pletikos, M., Sedmak, G., Sestan, N., Lein, E.S., Huang, H., 2015. Spatial mapping of structural and connectional imaging data for the developing human brain with diffusion tensor imaging. Methods 73, 27–37.

Ouyang, M., Cheng, H., Mishra, V., Gong, G., Mosconi, M.W., Sweeney, J., Peng, Y., Huang, H., 2016. Atypical age-dependent effects of autism on white matter microstructure in children of 2–7 years. Hum. Brain Mapp. 37 (2), 819–832.

Ouyang, M., Dubois, J., Yu, Q., Mukherjee, P., Huang, H., 2019a. Delineation of early brain development from fetuses to infants with diffusion MRI and beyond. NeuroImage 185, 836–850.

Ouyang, M., Jeon, T., Sotiras, A., Peng, Q., Mishra, V., Halovanic, C., Chen, M., Chalak, L., Rollins, N., Roberts, T.P., Davatzikos, C., 2019b. Differential cortical microstructural maturation in the preterm human brain with diffusion kurtosis and tensor imaging. Proc. Natl. Acad. Sci. 116 (10), 4681–4688.

Ouyang, M., Peng, Q., Jeon, T., Heyne, R., Chalak, L., Huang, H., 2020. Diffusion-MRI-based regional cortical microstructure at birth for predicting neurodevelopmental outcomes of 2-year-olds. elife 9, e58116.

Patel, M.R., Klufas, R.A., Alberico, R.A., Edelman, R.R., 1997. Half-fourier acquisition single-shot turbo spin-echo (HASTE) MR: comparison with fast spin-echo MR in diseases of the brain. Am. J. Neuroradiol. 18 (9), 1635–1640.

Paydar, A., Fieremans, E., Nwankwo, J.I., Lazar, M., Sheth, H.D., Adisetiyo, V., Helpern, J.A., Jensen, J.H., Milla, S.S., 2014. Diffusional kurtosis imaging of the developing brain. Am. J. Neuroradiol. 35 (4), 808–814.

Pipe, J.G., 1999. Motion correction with PROPELLER MRI: application to head motion and free-breathing cardiac imaging. Magn. Reson. Med. 42 (5), 963–969.

Power, J.D., Schlaggar, B.L., Petersen, S.E., 2015. Recent progress and outstanding issues in motion correction in resting state fMRI. NeuroImage 105, 536–551.

Raschle, N.M., Lee, M., Buechler, R., Christodoulou, J.A., Chang, M., Vakil, M., Stering, P.L., Gaab, N., 2009. Making MR imaging child's play-pediatric neuroimaging protocol, guidelines and procedure. J. Vis. Exp. 29, e1309.

Rosenberg, M.D., Casey, B.J., Holmes, A.J., 2018. Prediction complements explanation in understanding the developing brain. Nat. Commun. 9 (1), 1–13.

Satterthwaite, T.D., Connolly, J.J., Ruparel, K., Calkins, M.E., Jackson, C., Elliott, M.A., Roalf, D.R., Hopson, R., Prabhakaran, K., Behr, M., Qiu, H., 2016. The Philadelphia neurodevelopmental cohort: a publicly available resource for the study of normal and abnormal brain development in youth. NeuroImage 124, 1115–1119.

Semelka, R.C., Kelekis, N.L., Thomasson, D., Brown, M.A., Laub, G.A., 1996. HASTE MR imaging: description of technique and preliminary results in the abdomen. J. Magn. Reson. Imaging 6 (4), 698–699.

Tarui, T., Madan, N., Farhat, N., Kitano, R., Ceren Tanritanir, A., Graham, G., Gagoski, B., Craig, A., Rollins, C. K., Ortinau, C., Iyer, V., 2018. Disorganized patterns of sulcal position in fetal brains with agenesis of corpus callosum. Cereb. Cortex 28 (9), 3192–3203.

Todd, N., Josephs, O., Callaghan, M.F., Lutti, A., Weiskopf, N., 2015. Prospective motion correction of 3D echo-planar imaging data for functional MRI using optical tracking. NeuroImage 113, 1–12.

Van Horn, J.D., Grafton, S.T., Miller, M.B., 2008. Individual variability in brain activity: a nuisance or an opportunity? Brain Imaging Behav. 2 (4), 327–334.

Volkow, N.D., Koob, G.F., Croyle, R.T., Bianchi, D.W., Gordon, J.A., Koroshetz, W.J., Pérez-Stable, E.J., Riley, W.T., Bloch, M.H., Conway, K., Deeds, B.G., 2018. The conception of the ABCD study: from substance use to a broad NIH collaboration. Dev. Cogn. Neurosci. 32, 4–7.

Weisstanner, C., Gruber, G.M., Brugger, P.C., Mitter, C., Diogo, M.C., Kasprian, G., Prayer, D., 2017. Fetal MRI at 3T—ready for routine use? Br. J. Radiol. 90 (1069), 20160362.

White, N., Roddey, C., Shankaranarayanan, A., Han, E., Rettmann, D., Santos, J., Kuperman, J., Dale, A., 2010. PROMO: real-time prospective motion correction in MRI using image-based tracking. Magn. Reson. Med. 63 (1), 91–105.

Xu, Y., Cao, M., Liao, X., Xia, M., Wang, X., Jeon, T., Ouyang, M., Chalak, L., Rollins, N., Huang, H., He, Y., 2019. Development and emergence of individual variability in the functional connectivity architecture of the preterm human brain. Cereb. Cortex 29 (10), 4208–4222.

Yu, Q., Peng, Y., Mishra, V., Ouyang, A., Li, H., Zhang, H., Chen, M., Liu, S., Huang, H., 2014. Microstructure, length, and connection of limbic tracts in normal human brain development. Front. Aging Neurosci. 6, 228.

Yu, Q., Ouyang, A., Chalak, L., Jeon, T., Chia, J., Mishra, V., Sivarajan, M., Jackson, G., Rollins, N., Liu, S., Huang, H., 2016. Structural development of human fetal and preterm brain cortical plate based on population-averaged templates. Cereb. Cortex 26 (11), 4381–4391.

Yu, Q., Peng, Y., Kang, H., Peng, Q., Ouyang, M., Slinger, M., Hu, D., Shou, H., Fang, F., Huang, H., 2020. Differential white matter maturation from birth to 8 years of age. Cereb. Cortex 30 (4), 2674–2690.

Zhang, W.T., Mainero, C., Kumar, A., Wiggins, C.J., Benner, T., Purdon, P.L., Bolar, D.S., Kwong, K.K., Sorensen, A.G., 2006. Strategies for improving the detection of fMRI activation in trigeminal pathways with cardiac gating. NeuroImage 31 (4), 1506–1512.

Zhao, T., Mishra, V., Jeon, T., Ouyang, M., Peng, Q., Chalak, L., Wisnowski, J.L., Heyne, R., Rollins, N., Shu, N., Huang, H., 2019a. Structural network maturation of the preterm human brain. NeuroImage 185, 699–710.

Zhao, C., Ouyang, M., Slinger, M.A., Huang, H., 2019b. Delineation of White Matter Microstructural Maturation of Infant Brain With DKI. ISMRM. abstract number 3555.

Zhu, T., Peng, Q., Ouyang, A., Huang, H., 2021. Neuroanatomical underpinning of diffusion kurtosis measurements in the cerebral cortex of healthy macaque brains. Magn. Reson. Med. 85 (4), 1895–1908.

CHAPTER

Frontiers of microstructural imaging with diffusion MRI

2

Jens H. Jensen

Department of Neuroscience, Medical University of South Carolina, Charleston, SC, United States

You've got to be very careful if you don't know where you are going, because you might not get there

— **Yogi Berra**

1. Introduction

The spatial resolution of conventional human MRI is limited to about 1 mm^3 due to hardware and time constraints. It is nevertheless possible to extract information from an MRI signal about tissue structure on the much smaller scale of microns (1 μm = 0.001 mm). This is comparable to the dimensions of most cells, the realm of histology, and the scale at which pathological changes are often most evident.

Micron-level information is encoded by MRI signals because they mainly originate from randomly moving water molecules. This motion is referred to as diffusion, and the root-mean-square distance water molecules move during a given time interval is the diffusion length (Grebenkov, 2007; Yablonskiy and Sukstanskii, 2010; Kiselev, 2017; Novikov et al., 2019). For a typical MRI pulse sequence, the echo time is about 10–100 ms, which corresponds to a diffusion length of about 5–25 μm. As a consequence, microstructural features of comparable size, such as cells and organelles, can substantially alter the signal. While water diffusion influences image contrast for a variety of MRI pulse sequences, some are designed to be especially sensitive to diffusion. These are known as diffusion MRI (dMRI) sequences and have been widely applied to characterize tissue microstructure (Yablonskiy and Sukstanskii, 2010; Kiselev, 2017; Novikov et al., 2019; Jones, 2010; Le Bihan and Johansen-Berg, 2012).

Although dMRI has been successfully used in a number of body regions, the vast majority of dMRI studies have focused on brain. This is in part for technical reasons, such as the brain's relatively long T2 relaxation rate, that make implementation of dMRI easier in brain than in most other organs, but also because brain microstructure is significantly altered in several neuropathologies, including stroke and brain trauma, and because the unmatched complexity of brain cytoarchitecture is of great fundamental scientific interest. In this chapter, much of the discussion will therefore be framed with the brain in mind as the target organ. Nonetheless, it should be appreciated that many of the concepts and techniques described here can be extended to other areas of the body (Taouli, 2010).

The numerous dMRI methods that have been developed can be placed into two principal categories. The first consists of those that aim to explicitly quantify only water diffusion properties. The best of such methods have solid theoretical underpinnings and broad generality. Diffusion properties are sensitive to differences in tissue microstructure, due to disease, development, or aging, and they can thus

Handbook of Pediatric Brain Imaging. https://doi.org/10.1016/B978-0-12-816633-8.00007-7

serve as biomarkers. The most well-known technique of this type is diffusion tensor imaging (DTI) which estimates several different diffusion measures including mean diffusivity and fractional anisotropy (Basser et al., 1994; Le Bihan et al., 2001). However, a disadvantage of pure diffusion properties is that their precise biological meaning is often unclear. For this reason, a second category of dMRI methods that seek to establish direct connections between the dMRI signal and specific biophysical quantities has been rapidly gaining in popularity. The price for this is a diminishment of generality and robustness due to tissue-dependent assumptions and simplifying idealizations needed to attain an increased specificity. The most prominent examples from this second category are white matter fiber tractography methods that allow structural connectivity within the brain to be assessed noninvasively (Lazar, 2010).

The goal of this chapter is to both review the basic concepts and techniques that form the foundation of dMRI and to describe some of the more recently developed approaches that seem most promising to this author. Regarding the latter, a substantial degree of subjectivity must be acknowledged as dMRI is a dynamic field of research with a good share of controversy. A rather large number of distinct dMRI methods have been proposed over the past 30 years, and the ones highlighted here represent only a small fraction of these. Undoubtedly, some that have been overlooked will, with time, prove their value. It is hoped that this chapter provides the reader with a clear grasp of the main principles of dMRI, a flavor of the current research, and a sense of where the field may be heading.

2. Diffusion weighted MRI sequences

The roots of dMRI can be traced back to early studies of diffusion in liquids using nuclear magnetic resonance. Initial approaches for measuring diffusivities were developed by Hahn (Hahn, 1950) and by Carr and Purcell (Carr and Purcell, 1954), while the pulsed-field-gradient sequence technique, pioneered by Stejskal and Tanner (Stejskal and Tanner, 1965), still forms the foundation of many modern dMRI sequences. The pulse sequence proposed by Stejskal and Tanner is depicted in Fig. 1. It consists

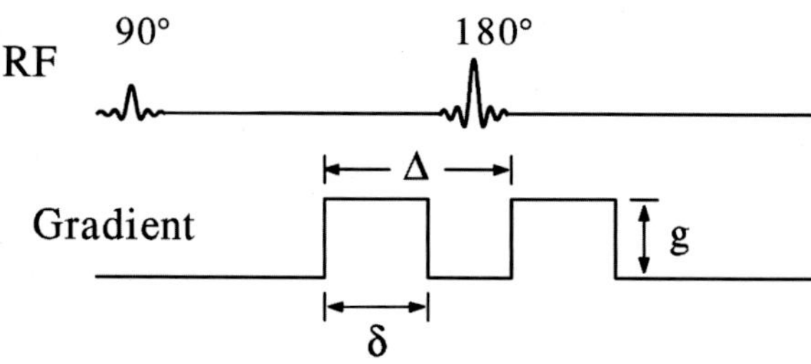

FIG. 1

Pulse sequence diagram for the Stejskal-Tanner sequence. The first line shows the radiofrequency (RF) pulses that excite and refocus the nuclear spins (e.g., proton spins in the case of water). The second line shows the gradient pulses that sensitize the signal to molecular diffusion. The gradient pulses have an amplitude g, a diffusion time Δ, and a pulse duration δ. The Stejskal-Tanner sequence is the prototype for many diffusion weighted sequences used in dMRI.

of a classic spin echo sequence augmented by a pair of gradient pulses, one on each side of a 180° refocusing pulse. For stationary water molecules, the gradient pulses do not affect the signal since the dephasing caused by the first pulse is flipped by the refocusing pulse and then rephased by the second gradient pulse. However, for water molecules that move during the sequence, the rephasing by the second gradient pulse may be imperfect because the molecules are at different locations than for the first gradient pulse and hence experience a different magnetic field. As a consequence, the MRI signal is reduced by an amount related to how far the molecules diffuse.

The gradient pulse has a spatial orientation that is under experimental control, and the signal is only affected by diffusion that is parallel to the gradient. Hence, the gradient orientation is also called the diffusion encoding direction. For isotropic media, the diffusion encoding direction is inconsequential. But for anisotropic media, the choice of diffusion encoding directions is crucial. Typically, multiple diffusion encoding directions will be employed for anisotropic media in order to obtain a comprehensive description of the diffusion dynamics in three-dimensions. A prominent example of this is dMRI in white matter for which the number of directions is usually at least 3 and often 100 or more.

The simplest type of diffusion is when the molecular displacements follow a Gaussian probability distribution. This is known as Gaussian diffusion and is realized for homogeneous liquids, as Einstein famously showed in 1905 (Chowdhury, 2005). For Gaussian diffusion, the MRI signal obtained with the Stejskal-Tanner sequence is simply

$$S(b) = S_0 \exp(-bD) \tag{1}$$

where D is the diffusivity, S_0 is the signal when no diffusion weighting is applied, and b is the b-value (Yablonskiy and Sukstanskii, 2010). The b-value is a standard parameter for indicating the strength of the diffusion weighting, and it is related to the Stejskal-Tanner pulse sequence parameters by

$$b = (\gamma g \delta)^2 \left(\Delta - \frac{\delta}{3} \right) \tag{2}$$

where g is the amplitude of the gradient pulses, Δ is the diffusion time, δ is the pulse duration, and γ is the gyromagnetic ratio for water protons. Thus for Gaussian diffusion, the diffusivity is easily obtained by fitting the MRI signal for two or more different b-values to the monoexponential form of Eq. (1). If one has data for just two b-values, b_1 and b_2, then Eq. (1) implies

$$D = \frac{1}{b_2 - b_1} \ln \left[\frac{S(b_1)}{S(b_2)} \right]. \tag{3}$$

In practice, the diffusion weighted pulse sequences used on MRI scanners are a bit more complicated than the Stejskal-Tanner sequence. They incorporate finite gradient rise times and additional pulses needed to generate images. Sometimes they also include extra pulses to reduce imaging artifacts (Reese et al., 2003) or to acquire more refined diffusion information (Shemesh et al., 2016). As a consequence, the b-value is generally given by a more complicated formula than Eq. (2) (Price and Kuchel, 1991; Nezamzadeh, 2012). But the essential principles are the same as those illustrated by the Stejskal-Tanner sequence.

3. Q-space and diffusion displacement probability distribution function

In complex diffusive media, such as biological tissues, diffusion is usually not Gaussian, so Eq. (1) will be at best an approximation. In fact, the experimental signature of non-Gaussian diffusion is precisely a b-value dependence of the MRI signal that deviates from a monoexponential decay (Yablonskiy and Sukstanskii, 2010). In many cases, non-Gaussian diffusion is caused by barriers (e.g., cell membranes) that hinder water diffusion. Thus, there is a close link between diffusional non-Gaussianity and microstructural complexity.

To quantify non-Gaussian diffusion, it is useful to introduce the notion of q-space (King et al., 1994; Cohen and Assaf, 2002). This is an abstract space of "q-vectors" defined (for a Stejskal-Tanner sequence) by

$$\mathbf{q} = \frac{\gamma \delta g}{2\pi}\mathbf{n} \tag{4}$$

where $\mathbf{n}$ is a unit vector that specifies the diffusion encoding direction. Thus a point in q-space can be associated with the MRI signal acquired for a given gradient amplitude and orientation. This allows us to consider the signal as a function of the vector $\mathbf{q}$. In the limit of short pulse durations, Stejskal demonstrated the remarkable relationship (Stejskal, 1965; Tanner and Stejskal, 1968)

$$S(\mathbf{q}) = S_0 \int d^3 s P(\mathbf{s}) e^{-2\pi i \mathbf{q}\cdot\mathbf{s}} \tag{5}$$

so that the signal is a Fourier transform of the diffusion displacement probability distribution function (dPDF), $P(\mathbf{s})$, where $\mathbf{s}$ is the displacement vector for the diffusing water molecules. Eq. (5) is known as Stejskal's formula and provides an explicit link between MRI measurements and diffusion dynamics (Callaghan, 2011; Jensen, 2015). Although only exact in the limit of small δ, it is often a good approximation and provides crucial insights that underlie several important dMRI methods.

The most direct way to employ Stejskal's formula is to invert the Fourier transform to yield

$$P(\mathbf{s}) = \frac{1}{S_0} \int d^3 q S(\mathbf{q}) e^{2\pi i \mathbf{q}\cdot\mathbf{s}} \tag{6}$$

Thus, given dMRI data for many different q-vectors, it is possible, in principle, to calculate the dPDF. Usually these would be chosen to lie on a Cartesian grid which allows one to apply the same discrete Fourier techniques used in MRI for reconstructing images from k-space data (Wedeen et al., 2005; Mohanty et al., 2018). The grid spacing and maximum q-vector magnitude then determine the displacement field of view and spatial resolution for the dPDF according to the formulae

$$L = \frac{1}{\Delta q} \tag{7}$$

and

$$a = \frac{1}{2q_{\max}} \tag{8}$$

where L is the field of view, Δq is the q-space grid spacing, a is the spatial resolution, and $q_{\max}$ is the maximum q-vector amplitude. Hence a dense q-space grid is needed to obtain a large field of view, and a large $q_{\max}$ is needed to obtain a high resolution. For a pulse duration of $\delta = 30$ ms and a maximum gradient amplitude of $g = 40$ mT/m, Eq. (8) yields a resolution of 9.8 μm, which is typical of what can be achieved on many clinical MRI scanners. A fundamental property of the dPDF is that it has antipodal symmetry so that $P(-\mathbf{s}) = P(\mathbf{s})$. This follows from Eq. (6) and the fact that the signal generally has antipodal symmetry in q-space.

Various implementations of q-space imaging have been proposed (Cohen and Assaf, 2002; Wedeen et al., 2005; Mohanty et al., 2018; Chin et al., 2004; Lätt et al., 2008; Kuo et al., 2008). Often one just considers a single diffusion encoding direction in order to reduce the data acquisition burden. However, full three-dimensional q-space imaging is possible, with the most popular approach being diffusion spectrum imaging (DSI) (Wedeen et al., 2005; Kuo et al., 2008), although the acquisition times tend to be long.

4. Diffusion and kurtosis tensors

Because of time constraints, three-dimensional q-space imaging is rarely employed for human studies, particularly in clinical settings, and the commonly used dMRI methods require data for a more manageable number of q-space vectors. Two of the most prominent dMRI methods are based on a cumulant expansion of the diffusion weighted MRI signal (Grebenkov, 2007; Yablonskiy and Sukstanskii, 2010; Kiselev, 2017; Novikov et al., 2019). This corresponds to a power series for the logarithm of the signal in terms of the q-vector. To leading order, one has

$$\ln[S(\mathbf{q})] = S_0 + \sum_{i,j=1}^{3} C_{ij}^{(1)} q_i q_j + O(q^4) \tag{9}$$

where q_i is a component of $\mathbf{q}$, q is the magnitude of $\mathbf{q}$, and $C_{ij}^{(1)}$ are the components a symmetric tensor $\mathbf{C}^{(1)}$. Terms with odd powers of the q-vector are excluded here since these vanish as a consequence of symmetry considerations. The apparent diffusion tensor is defined by

$$\mathbf{D} = -\frac{q^2}{b}\mathbf{C}^{(1)} \tag{10}$$

which allows Eq. (9) to be recast as

$$\ln[S(\mathbf{q})] = S_0 - b\mathbf{n}^T\mathbf{D}\mathbf{n} + O(q^4). \tag{11}$$

If the order q^4 terms are dropped, then we have the approximation

$$S(\mathbf{q}) \approx S_0 \exp(-b\mathbf{n}^T\mathbf{D}\mathbf{n}) \tag{12}$$

which is the signal model used for DTI (Basser et al., 1994; Le Bihan et al., 2001). Since it is symmetric, the diffusion tensor has 6 independent components. For this reason, data from at least 6 different diffusion encoding directions are needed in order to apply DTI. Because S_0 also has to be determined, DTI requires data from a minimum of 7 q-space points, one of which is usually chosen as $\mathbf{q} = 0$.

By applying Stejskal's formula, one can show, for small pulse durations, that

$$D_{ij} = \frac{1}{2\Delta}\int d^3 s P(\mathbf{s}) s_i s_j \tag{13}$$

where s_i is a component of $\mathbf{s}$ and D_{ij} is a component of $\mathbf{D}$. The right side of Eq. (13) is precisely the definition of the exact diffusion tensor (Basser, 2002). Thus the apparent diffusion tensor measured with DTI approaches the exact diffusion tensor as δ is taken to zero.

Since DTI is based on the cumulant expansion, its accuracy also requires q to be small enough to justify neglecting the higher order terms. From Eqs. (2) and (4), we see that

$$b = (2\pi q)^2\left(\Delta - \frac{\delta}{3}\right) \tag{14}$$

so restricting the size of q also limits the size of b. Empirically, it is found that DTI works quite well in brain for b-values up to about 1000 s/mm^2. The accuracy of DTI improves as the b-value is reduced, but then the effect of diffusion weighting on the signal is also diminished relative to signal noise, which results in a lower precision for the estimated diffusion tensor. Hence the choice of b-values is generally a trade-off between accuracy and precision, and it should be considered carefully in the design of any DTI experiment.

The diffusivity in a direction $\mathbf{n}$ is given by

$$D(\mathbf{n}) = \mathbf{n}^T\mathbf{D}\mathbf{n}. \tag{15}$$

This allows Eq. (12) to be rewritten as

$$S(\mathbf{q}) \approx S_0 \exp[-bD(\mathbf{n})] \tag{16}$$

which is precisely the same monoexponential form of Eq. (1) for Gaussian diffusion. Thus the DTI signal model is exact for Gaussian diffusion, and it is sometimes said that DTI is based on a Gaussian approximation. This fact is one reason for preferring the cumulant expansion of Eq. (9) over a power series expansion for the signal itself.

The DTI signal model of Eqs. (12) and (16) usually provides a good description of dMRI data in brain for low b-values. But as the b-value is increased much above 1000 s/mm^2, deviations from monoexponential decay often become apparent, as non-Gaussian diffusion effects begin to manifest (Clark and Le Bihan, 2000; Mulkern et al., 2001). A natural way to accommodate this is to simply extend the cumulant expansion to the next order as

$$\ln[S(\mathbf{q})] = S_0 + \sum_{i,j=1}^{3} C_{ij}^{(1)} q_i q_j + \sum_{i,j,k,l=1}^{3} C_{ijkl}^{(2)} q_i q_j q_k q_l + O(q^6) \tag{17}$$

where $C_{ijkl}^{(2)}$ are the components of a symmetric tensor $\mathbf{C}^{(2)}$. Since $\mathbf{C}^{(2)}$ has 4 indices, it is referred to as a rank 4 tensor, in contrast to $\mathbf{C}^{(1)}$ which is a rank 2 tensor. Because $\mathbf{C}^{(2)}$ is symmetric, only 15 of its 81 components are independent.

It is convenient to define an apparent kurtosis tensor by

$$\mathbf{W} = \frac{6q^4}{b^2\overline{D}^2}\mathbf{C}^{(2)} \tag{18}$$

where

$$\overline{D} = \frac{1}{4\pi}\int d\Omega_{\mathbf{n}} D(\mathbf{n}) \tag{19}$$

is the mean diffusivity. With this and Eq. (10), the cumulant expansion takes on the form

$$\ln[S(\mathbf{q})] = S_0 - b\mathbf{n}^T\mathbf{D}\mathbf{n} + \frac{1}{6}b^2\overline{D}^2 \sum_{i,j,k,l=1}^{3} W_{ijkl} n_i n_j n_k n_l + O(q^6) \tag{20}$$

with W_{ijkl} being a component of $\mathbf{W}$ and n_i a component of $\mathbf{n}$. If we drop the order q^6 terms, then one is led to the approximation

$$S(\mathbf{q}) \approx S_0 \exp\left(-b\mathbf{n}^T\mathbf{D}\mathbf{n} + \frac{1}{6}b^2\overline{D}^2 \sum_{i,j,k,l=1}^{3} W_{ijkl}n_in_jn_kn_l\right) \tag{21}$$

which is the signal model for diffusional kurtosis imaging (DKI) and generalizes the DTI signal model of Eq. (12) (Jensen et al., 2005; Lu et al., 2006; Jensen and Helpern, 2010; Wu and Cheung, 2010; Poot et al., 2010). This model can fit signal decays that are not necessarily monoexponential in b and thereby allows non-Gaussian diffusion effects to be quantified. Since $\mathbf{W}$ has 15 independent components, DKI requires at least 15 different diffusion encoding directions, and since Eq. (21) has 22 unknowns, data for at least 22 distinct q-space points must be acquired.

Just as for the apparent diffusion tensor, a physical interpretation for the apparent kurtosis tensor can be found by invoking Stejskal's formula. One finds that

$$W_{ijkl} = -\frac{1}{\overline{D}^2}\left(D_{ij}D_{kl} + D_{ik}D_{jl} + D_{il}D_{jk}\right) + \frac{1}{\left(2\Delta\overline{D}\right)^2}\int d^3s P(\mathbf{s}) s_i s_j s_k s_l \tag{22}$$

where again this is exact in the limit of small δ. From this, it can further be shown that the kurtosis of the dPDF in the direction $\mathbf{n}$ is

$$K(\mathbf{n}) = \frac{\overline{D}^2}{[D(\mathbf{n})]^2} \sum_{i,j,k,l=1}^{3} W_{ijkl}n_in_jn_kn_l. \tag{23}$$

The kurtosis was first introduced by Pearson in 1905 as generic index of non-Gaussianity for probability distributions (Pearson, 1905). For Gaussian diffusion, the kurtosis vanishes in all directions. Using Eqs. (15) and (23), the DKI signal model can also be expressed as

$$S(\mathbf{q}) \approx S_0 \exp\left\{-bD(\mathbf{n}) + \frac{1}{6}[bD(\mathbf{n})]^2 K(\mathbf{n})\right\}. \tag{24}$$

Because of the added kurtosis term, Eqs. (21) and (24) are able to satisfactorily fit dMRI data in brain up to b-values of about 2000 s/mm^2 (Jensen and Helpern, 2010). However, the choice of b-values is again a trade-off between accuracy and precision – a higher maximum b-value improves precision but at the price of a lower accuracy (Mohanty et al., 2018). A typical DKI experiment in brain would use b-values of 0, 1000, and 2000 s/mm^2 together with 30 or more diffusion encoding directions (Jensen and Helpern, 2010).

From the diffusion and kurtosis tensors, one can calculate a number of diffusion properties. In analogy with the aforementioned mean diffusivity, the mean kurtosis is defined by

$$\overline{K} = \frac{1}{4\pi}\int d\Omega_{\mathbf{n}} K(\mathbf{n}) \tag{25}$$

which provides a useful overall measure of diffusional non-Gaussianity. In white matter, quantifying diffusion anisotropy is of great interest. The most commonly used metric for this is the fractional anisotropy defined by Basser and Pierpaoli (1996) as

$$\mathrm{FA} = \sqrt{\frac{3}{2}} \cdot \frac{\|\mathbf{D} - \overline{D}\mathbf{I}\|}{\|\mathbf{D}\|} \tag{26}$$

with **I** being the identity tensor and the symbol ||...|| indicating the Frobenius norm. From the kurtosis tensor, one may similarly define the kurtosis fractional anisotropy as (Glenn et al., 2015a; Hansen and Jespersen, 2016)

$$\mathrm{KFA} = \frac{\|\mathbf{W} - \overline{W}\mathbf{I}^{(4)}\|}{\|\mathbf{W}\|} \tag{27}$$

where $\mathbf{I}^{(4)}$ is a rank 4 generalization of **I** and

$$\overline{W} = \frac{1}{4\pi\overline{D}^2} \int d\Omega_{\mathbf{n}} K(\mathbf{n}) [D(\mathbf{n})]^2. \tag{28}$$

While the FA and KFA are conceptually similar, each quantifies different aspects of diffusion anisotropy.

Parametric maps of $\overline{D}$, $\overline{K}$, FA, and KFA are shown in Fig. 2 for a healthy subject. The mean diffusivity indicates the amplitude of the diffusion process and is proportional to the square of the diffusion length. The mean kurtosis, in contrast, is related to the complexity of diffusion. Unrestricted diffusion has zero kurtosis, while the mean kurtosis in the brain is about one, with somewhat higher

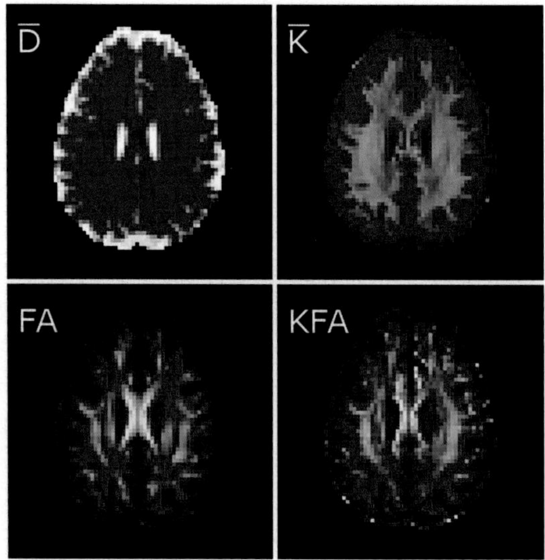

FIG. 2

Maps of pure diffusion parameters as estimated with DKI. All the maps are for the same anatomical brain slice from a healthy subject. The mean diffusivity ($\overline{D}$) quantifies the amplitude of diffusion, the mean kurtosis ($\overline{K}$) quantifies the non-Gaussianity of diffusion, the fractional anisotropy (FA) quantifies the anisotropy of the diffusion tensor, and the kurtosis fractional anisotropy (KFA) quantifies the anisotropy of the kurtosis tensor. Diffusion in complex media, such as biological tissues, has many physical aspects that are characterized by a variety of distinct measures.

values occurring in white matter than in gray matter. Both the FA and KFA are high in most white matter regions and low in gray matter regions. However, there are some white matter regions with crossing fibers that have low FA and high KFA. Other useful diffusion properties that can be constructed from the diffusion and kurtosis tensors include the axial diffusivity, radial diffusivity, axial kurtosis, and radial kurtosis (Jensen and Helpern, 2010).

5. Diffusion orientation distribution function

In order to describe the directional dependence of water diffusion, several quantities have been proposed. The most familiar of these is the diffusion ellipsoid which is given by (Basser et al., 1994)

$$r(\mathbf{n}) = \sqrt{\frac{2\Delta}{\mathbf{n}^T \mathbf{D}^{-1} \mathbf{n}}}. \tag{29}$$

However, this mathematical function has only a single distinct maximum and thus a limited ability to characterize diffusion directionality. (There are technically two maxima but these are simply related by reflection symmetry, so we just count them here as a single peak. There are also exceptional cases when the ellipsoid is either a sphere or an oblate spheroid for which the maximum value is attained at an infinity of points, but this is unlikely to occur with real MRI data).

To provide a more detailed representation of diffusion directionality, one can use the diffusion orientation distribution function (dODF) defined by

$$\psi_\alpha(\mathbf{n}) = \frac{1}{Z} \int_0^\infty ds P(s\mathbf{n}) s^\alpha \tag{30}$$

where Z is a normalization constant and the power α controls the relative weighting for displacements of different lengths (Canales-Rodríguez et al., 2010). The dODF is a much more flexible mathematical function than the diffusion ellipsoid with the capability of exhibiting an arbitrary number of distinct peaks. But they again come in reflection symmetric pairs due to the dPDF's antipodal symmetry. The dODF fits well with q-space imaging techniques as these provide estimates for the dPDF. In particular, a central element of DSI is the calculation of the dODF with $\alpha = 2$ (Wedeen et al., 2005).

One can also formulate approximations for the dODF using other dMRI approaches that require less comprehensive q-space sampling than DSI. A notable one is q-ball imaging, which only requires data lying on a single spherical shell in q-space (and thus for a single b-value). It is based on the approximation

$$\psi_0(\mathbf{n}) \approx T_F[S, \mathbf{n}] \tag{31}$$

where T_F represents the Funk (or Funk-Radon) transform (Tuch, 2004). The Funk transform is a linear transformation that maps a function defined on a spherical surface onto another function on a sphere. For the dMRI signal, it can be calculated according to

$$T_F(S, \mathbf{n}) = \frac{1}{q_0} \int d^3 q S(\mathbf{q}) \delta(\mathbf{q} \cdot \mathbf{n}) \delta(|\mathbf{q}| - q_0) \tag{32}$$

where q_0 is the radius of the q-space sphere and $\delta(x)$ represents the Dirac delta function (not to be confused with the δ used to indicate the Stejskal-Tanner sequence pulse duration). This corresponds to integrals over the great circles of the q-space sphere. As the choice for q_0 (or b) is increased, the resolving power of the q-ball estimate for the dODF improves (Jensen and Helpern, 2016). It is possible to extend q-ball imaging to obtain approximations for the dODF with $\alpha = 2$, but the mathematical formulation of this is somewhat more complicated (Aganj et al., 2010).

The diffusion and kurtosis tensors can also be used to construct an approximation of the dODF for any value of α (Jensen et al., 2014). This is called the kurtosis dODF. Its performance varies significantly with α, and $\alpha = 4$ has been suggested as an optimum choice (Glenn et al., 2015b). The kurtosis dODF can support up to 4 distinct peaks. An advantage of the kurtosis dODF is that it only requires the relatively low b-value data used with DKI. In vivo experiments have shown that the kurtosis dODF in white matter is remarkably similar to the dODF obtained using DSI (Glenn et al., 2016).

6. Fiber orientation density function

In applications to white matter, the dODF peaks are often regarded as indicating the directions of axonal fiber bundles. While it is true that water diffusion tends to be less hindered parallel to axonal fiber bundles than in perpendicular directions (Beaulieu, 2002), the imprint axons leave on the dODF is a blurred one, so peaks of the dODFs do not always correspond exactly to the orientations of axonal fiber bundles (Jensen and Helpern, 2016). Moreover, even the notion of distinct fiber bundle directions is an idealization as imaging voxels can contain as many as a million individual axons whose arrangement is more properly described by a continuous "fiber orientation density function" (fODF) that directly gives the angular density of fiber directions. For these reasons, considerable effort has been made to develop dMRI methods for determining the fODF within individual white matter voxels.

The most straightforward approach for estimating an fODF is to assume a multiple Gaussian compartment signal model of the form

$$S(\mathbf{q}) = S_0 \left[\sum_{m=1}^{N} w_m \exp\left(-b\mathbf{n}^T \mathbf{D}^{(m)} \mathbf{n} \right) \right] \tag{33}$$

where $\mathbf{D}^{(m)}$ is the diffusion tensor for the mth compartment, w_m is the fractional weight of the mth compartment, and N is the total number of compartments (Alexander et al., 2002). The corresponding fODF is then

$$F(\mathbf{n}) = \frac{1}{2\pi} \sum_{m=1}^{N} w_m \left\{ \delta\left[\mathbf{n} \cdot \mathbf{e}_1^{(m)} - 1 \right] + \delta\left[\mathbf{n} \cdot \mathbf{e}_1^{(m)} + 1 \right] \right\} \tag{34}$$

where $\mathbf{e}_1^{(m)}$ is the principal eigenvector for $\mathbf{D}^{(m)}$ normalized to unit magnitude. Here we have again utilized the Dirac delta function. It is easy to verify the reflection property

$$F(-\mathbf{n}) = F(\mathbf{n}) \tag{35}$$

and the normalization property

$$1 = \int d\Omega_{\mathbf{n}} F(\mathbf{n}) \tag{36}$$

which one can always require of any fODF without loss of generality. The physical picture underlying Eq. (33) is that water diffusion within an individual fiber bundle is approximately Gaussian and the orientation of the bundle is parallel to the bundle's principal diffusion tensor eigenvector since this is the direction of least hindered diffusion.

As a sum of Dirac delta functions, Eq. (34) still represents the presumably continuous exact fODF in terms of distinct fiber bundle directions. One way of converting this into a continuous distribution is by smoothing, for example, using a truncated spherical harmonics expansion. Another approach is to take the limit $N \to \infty$ and treat the fractional weights as a continuous function, in which case constraints must be imposed to keep the number of free parameters finite.

When fitting Eq. (33) to experimental data, one encounters, however, two difficulties. First, the number of adjustable parameters is $7N$, and so even with just two bundles, there are 14 separate parameters to estimate. Because fitting with Eq. (33) is a nonlinear optimization problem, determining the best values for so many variables is often difficult in practice. This is in sharp contrast with DTI and DKI for which the parameter estimation can be reduced to linear (or nearly linear) problems that are easily handled by conventional numerical methods (Basser et al., 1994; Tabesh et al., 2011; Veraart et al., 2013). Cost functions for nonlinear optimization problems frequently have multiple local minima that make finding the global minimum problematic, especially if one wishes to do this in thousands of voxels in an efficient and reliable manner. Second, voxels with complex geometrical arrangements of axonal fibers are not well represented by an fODF of the form of Eq. (34) unless a prohibitively large number of compartments is assumed. In order to reduce these difficulties, additional assumptions are frequently imposed – for example, that the bundles are axially symmetric (Anderson, 2005) or that the distribution of diffusion tensor eigenvectors can be parameterized in a simple way (Zhang et al., 2012). Although such constraints make the fitting more numerically tractable, they can also result in less physically realistic solutions.

Such obstacles are largely avoided by an approach called constrained spherical deconvolution (CSD) developed by Tournier and coworkers (Tournier et al., 2004, 2007; Dell'Acqua and Tournier, 2019). Here one models the signal as

$$S(\mathbf{q}) = \overline{S}_q \int d\Omega_{\mathbf{n}} F(\mathbf{n}) R(\mathbf{q}, \mathbf{n}) \tag{37}$$

where $R(\mathbf{q}, \mathbf{n})$ is a single fiber response function that gives the signal for an individual axon oriented in the direction $\mathbf{n}$ and

$$\overline{S}_q = \frac{1}{4\pi} \int d\Omega_{\mathbf{q}} S(\mathbf{q}) \tag{38}$$

Eq. (37) is normalized so that

$$1 = \frac{1}{4\pi} \int d\Omega_{\mathbf{q}} R(\mathbf{q}, \mathbf{n}). \tag{39}$$

as long as Eq. (36) holds. The response function is assumed to have antipodal and axial symmetry and to be the same in every white matter voxel. Thus if there is a voxel for which

$$F(\mathbf{n}) = \frac{1}{2\pi} \{\delta[\mathbf{n} \cdot \mathbf{n}' - 1] + \delta[\mathbf{n} \cdot \mathbf{n}' + 1]\}, \tag{40}$$

one finds from Eq. (37) that

$$R(\mathbf{q},\mathbf{n}') = \frac{S(\mathbf{q})}{\bar{S}_q} \tag{41}$$

The response function can then be measured assuming there are voxels for which the axons are all unidirectional, which is approximately true in some white matter regions with high fractional anisotropy. If $R(\mathbf{q},\mathbf{n})$ is known for one direction $\mathbf{n}$, it can be computed for any other direction by applying a rotation. Thus a single voxel or region of interest is sufficient to determine the response function for the entire white matter.

Treating the response function as a given, Eq. (37) then represents a linear relationship between the signal and the fODF, which is straightforward to solve numerically provided dMRI data are available for a sufficient number of q-space points. In practice, this is usually accomplished by using spherical harmonics as basis functions. A key advantage of CSD is that data for q-space points all lying on a single b-value shell are adequate to estimate the fODF. However, the straightforward inversion of Eq. (37) often leads to fODFs that take on unphysical negative values in some directions (Tournier et al., 2004). As a consequence, CSD imposes constraints to suppress these via a Tikhonov regularization scheme (Tournier et al., 2007). This substantially reduces undesired negative lobes, but does not entirely eliminate them in all voxels.

More recently, it has been shown that the fODF can be estimated from the inverse Funk transform according to (Jensen et al., 2016)

$$F(\mathbf{n}) = \frac{1}{2\bar{S}_q} T_F^{-1}(S,\mathbf{n}). \tag{42}$$

This approach, known as fiber ball imaging (FBI), requires data on a single b-value shell with $b \geq 4000\ \text{s/mm}^2$ to be accurate (Moss et al., 2019). The inverse Funk transform is linear and easily calculated using a spherical harmonics basis (Jensen et al., 2016; Moss et al., 2019; Funk, 1913). Key advantages of FBI are that it completely avoids the need for numerical fitting and for a response function. The fact FBI does not require a globally defined response function might be especially important for applications to white matter pathology with focal changes in tissue microstructure. A comparison of the q-ball imaging dODF, the CSD fODF, and the FBI fODF for a single white matter voxel is shown in Fig. 3.

7. White matter fiber tractography

A primary motivation for calculating dODFs and fODFs is their use as building blocks in constructing white matter fiber tractography (Lazar, 2010; Jeurissen et al., 2019). A variety of algorithms for this have been devised which can be divided into two main categories – deterministic and probabilistic. Both approaches generate a collection of "fiber tracks" that reflect the geometrical organization of white matter pathways.

It should be appreciated, however, that these tracks are not guaranteed to coincide with actual axonal fiber bundles. Instead, they are more properly regarded as streamlines that delineate the global structure of either diffusion or fiber directionality. These may deviate from true axonal fiber bundles since distinct axon configurations can generate identical dMRI data. In other words, the problem of inferring the geometrical arrangement of axons from dMRI data is ill-posed. Fiber tracks are therefore

FIG. 3

The q-ball imaging (QBI) dODF, the constrained spherical deconvolution (CSD) fODF, and the fiber ball imaging (FBI) fODF for the same white matter voxel. Identical dMRI data were used in all three cases. The *b*-value was 6000 s/mm^2, and 128 uniformly distributed diffusion encoding directions were employed. The CSD fODF additionally required that a response function be determined from data in other voxels with high fractional anisotropy. All three methods detect three major peak directions, indicating a fiber crossing, although the fODF peaks are much sharper. The two fODFs also detect several smaller peaks that are not apparent in the dODF. These smaller peaks could represent true fine structure, but they could also be spurious due, for example, to noise or imaging artifacts.

surrogates for the true axon paths, but nonetheless of great value as a noninvasive means of assessing white matter organization.

Deterministic fiber tractography uses either the diffusion ellipsoid, dODF or fODF to determine a small number of peak directions in each voxel. These are then stitched together to create fiber tracks, with the peak directions being parallel to the tracks' tangent vectors. The details of the tracks are strongly affected by how the peaks are determined. If the diffusion ellipsoid is employed, only a single peak direction per voxel is identified. This is called DTI fiber tractography and is adequate for depicting the major white matter tracts, but performs poorly in regions where tracts intersect (Lazar, 2010; Jeurissen et al., 2019; Mori and Van Zijl, 2002). Therefore, it is recommended that a dODF or fODF be used if sufficient data for this has been acquired. Both dODFs and fODFs can generate satisfactory fiber tractography, and one should choose an approach based on the available data and the intended application. An advantage of fODFs is that they often identify more peaks and have a better resolving power for detecting fiber crossings with small intersection angles than dODFs (Jeurissen et al., 2019; Jones et al., 2013). On the other hand, fODFs are also more prone to display spurious peaks due, for example, to noise or imaging artifacts (Parker et al., 2013). No single method can be considered best in all circumstances. Fig. 4 gives examples of DTI tractography and tractography based on the FBI fODF.

A common problem encountered in generating long tracks with deterministic fiber tractography is that even a small amount of signal noise may be sufficient to substantially alter their course as small errors in peak directions accumulate over distance. In order to account for such deviations, a noise model can be incorporated into the calculation so that each voxel has an associated distribution of peak directions reflecting their statistical uncertainty (Lazar, 2010; Jeurissen et al., 2019; Behrens et al., 2003). This is one example of probabilistic fiber tractography. In calculating fiber tracks, the distribution of peak directions may be sampled many times resulting in fuller and denser sets of tracks than for deterministic fiber tractography. But the interpretation of probabilistic tracks is quite different than for

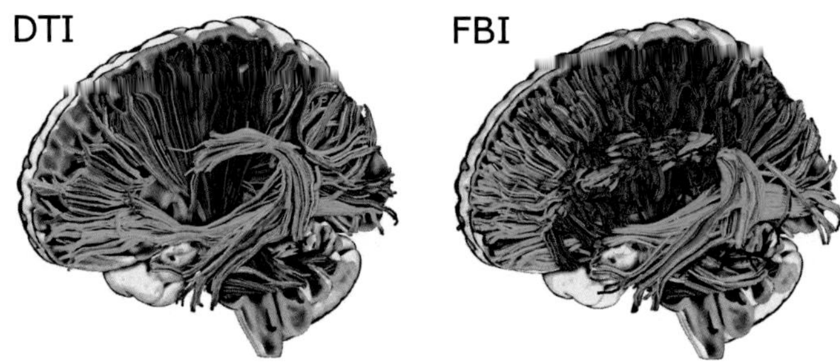

FIG. 4

Whole brain deterministic fiber tractography as calculated with DTI and FBI. Even though identical seed points and tracking algorithms were used in both cases, the FBI tractography is substantially more comprehensive. This reflects the FBI fODF's ability to detect fiber crossings that are missed by the diffusion ellipsoid.

deterministic tracks as they represent a broad array possible white matter pathways consistent with the data rather than just the most likely ones.

Several types of probabilistic fiber tractography have been proposed (Lazar, 2010; Jeurissen et al., 2019). Their defining feature is that directions for each voxel are obtained from random sampling of some type of probability distribution. These do not necessarily have to describe signal noise. For example, some versions of probabilistic fiber tractography treat the fODF itself as a probability distribution in order to take advantage of the full functional form of the fODF rather than just its peak directions (Descoteaux et al., 2008). In general, the proper interpretation of tracks obtained with probabilistic fiber tractography is subtle and dependent on a good understanding of the actual algorithm utilized.

There are at least three ways in which fiber tractography can be useful. First, it provides a qualitative representation of the white matter organization that can be helpful, for example, in presurgical planning (Potgieser et al., 2014). Second, it allows for tract-based segmentation of white matter that can be applied in assessing how different white matter regions are affected by the disease (Jones et al., 2005; Yeatman et al., 2012). Third, it can be employed to calculate the structural connectivity between two gray matter regions (Lazar, 2010; Jeurissen et al., 2019; Hagmann et al., 2007; Sotiropoulos and Zalesky, 2019). Regarding the latter, an important caveat is that the calculated connectivity can vary substantially among the different tractography methods and should not be expected to closely match structural connectivity as determined from chemical tracer experiments (Donahue et al., 2016). Nevertheless, structural connectivity obtained with fiber tractography holds promise as a noninvasive means of characterizing abnormal brain organization in neuropathologies.

8. Other dMRI tissue modeling methods

White matter fiber tractography is an example of dMRI tissue modeling since dMRI data is combined with tissue-specific assumptions in order to extract biophysical information in the form of fiber tracks and structural connectivity. Methods for estimating the fODF are also classified as tissue modeling, because their validity is dependent on certain biological properties. In contrast, dODF methods reflect just the diffusion dynamics and have no such restrictions. They are thus pure dMRI methods, as are DTI and DKI.

Broadly speaking, pure dMRI methods are more reliable and have greater generality than tissue modeling methods since they are based solely on the principles of diffusion physics. Their main limitation is that they do not give explicit information about tissue microstructure, even while being sensitive to microstructural alterations due to disease, development, or aging. Tissue modeling methods have been introduced, mainly for brain, to quantify specific microstructural features. The cost, however, of greater specificity is often a lesser degree of confidence in estimated tissue modeling parameters due to uncertainty in the assumed biological properties (which are often highly idealized for the sake of simplicity). For this reason, it is good practice to clearly distinguish pure dMRI measures, such as the fractional anisotropy, from tissue modeling measures, such as structural connectivity, when reporting dMRI results even if they are derived from identical data. An enlightening review of the challenges associated with tissue modeling is given by Novikov and coworkers (Novikov et al., 2018a).

Tissue modeling for dMRI is easier in white matter than in gray matter. This is both because the diffusion anisotropy in white matter encodes considerable microstructural information and because the exchange time for water inside myelinated axons is usually long in comparison to the pulse sequence diffusion time (Nilsson et al., 2013; Brusini et al., 2019). The long exchange time allows for separate quantification of intra-axonal and extra-axonal diffusion properties as well as estimation of the axonal water fraction (Novikov et al., 2019, 2018b; Assaf et al., 2004; Jelescu and Budde, 2017; McKinnon et al., 2018; Veraart et al., 2018). One parameter that has been particularly challenging to pin down is the intra-axonal diffusivity (Jelescu et al., 2016; Kunz et al., 2018), but recent work utilizing multiple diffusion encoding MRI is encouraging in this regard (Jensen and Helpern, 2018; Dhital et al., 2019; Ramanna et al., 2020). In gray matter, the anisotropy is low, and myelinated axons are scarce. As a result, methods for extracting specific microstructural information from dMRI data that work well for white matter are less effective. Improved approaches for tissue modeling in gray matter are still needed (Novikov et al., 2019; McKinnon et al., 2017), and this is an important topic of current research.

Most dMRI experiments obtain data for a single diffusion time. This is typically the shortest diffusion time allowed by the scanner hardware, consistent with the desired diffusion weighting, since this maximizes the single-to-noise ratio. However, the time dependence of the dMRI signal contains valuable microstructural information that is exploited by several different methods (Novikov et al., 2019, 2014, 2011; Does et al., 2003; Xu et al., 2009; Novikov and Kiselev, 2010; Aggarwal et al., 2012; Burcaw et al., 2015; Veraart et al., 2018). Some of these have attempted to quantify axon diameter, although their accuracy has been a matter of some controversy (Burcaw et al., 2015; Nilsson et al., 2017). The majority of axons in brain have diameters of about a micron which, for most practical experiments on clinical scanners, is small in comparison to the spatial resolution calculated from Eq. (8). As a consequence, the axon diameter is difficult to accurately determine in human brain using MRI technology commonly available to imaging scientists.

9. Applications of dMRI to disease and development

The major clinical applications of dMRI are to ischemic stroke, assessment of tumors, and presurgical planning in the brain. For acute ischemic stroke, the diffusivity inside a lesion drops by as much as a factor of two and is a key diagnostic marker (Fung et al., 2011). Recently, the utility of the kurtosis in helping to predict which tissue is salvageable has been investigated (Cheung et al., 2012; Wang et al., 2017). Since diffusion is often more restricted in tumors than in surrounding tissues, dMRI provides a useful contrast mechanism for tumor identification (Tang and Zhou, 2019). While low *b*-value (i.e., ≤ 2000 s/mm^2) dMRI has most often been applied, the conspicuity of smaller tumors may sometimes be enhanced with higher *b*-values. In planning for brain surgery, it is often helpful to map out the major white matter tracts with fiber tractography, so damage to the most functionally important tracts can be minimized (Potgieser et al., 2014). To date, DTI fiber tractography has predominated for this purpose, although the potential value of more advanced techniques is being actively explored (Abhinav et al., 2014).

An emerging application of dMRI is the characterization of microstructural changes in brain that occur during development (Ouyang et al., 2019; Shi et al., 2019). Pure diffusion measures, such as the fractional anisotropy and kurtosis, change substantially during childhood and may provide benchmarks for assessing brain trauma (Mayer et al., 2012), autism (Travers et al., 2012), and attention-deficit/hyperactivity disorder (Adisetiyo et al., 2014). Tissue modeling has also been used to assess microstructure during development (Jelescu et al., 2015; Mah et al., 2017), although modeling assumptions that are reasonable for adult brain may not be as well justified in children. In particular, myelination of most white matter tracts is low during infancy and early childhood, which could have a substantial impact on the water exchange time for axons (Brusini et al., 2019).

10. Conclusion

In the over 30 years since the initial experiments were conducted, dMRI has established itself as a versatile and informative imaging modality with important applications to both basic research and clinical practice. It is distinguished from other MRI techniques in being uniquely suited to quantifying microstructural properties of tissues, particularly in the brain and in tumors throughout the body. It continues to develop at a remarkable rate fueled by a combination of improving scanner hardware, new theoretical insights, and more effective numerical algorithms for signal processing. At the moment, there is little indication of this progress slowing, and dMRI is likely to play an increasingly prominent role in MRI practice.

Acknowledgments

The author is grateful to Hunter Moss and Sid Dhiman for assistance in preparing the figures.

References

Abhinav, K., Yeh, F.C., Pathak, S., Suski, V., Lacomis, D., Friedlander, R.M., Fernandez-Miranda, J.C., 2014. Advanced diffusion MRI fiber tracking in neurosurgical and neurodegenerative disorders and neuroanatomical studies: a review. Biochim. Biophys. Acta (BBA)—Mol. Basis Dis. 1842 (11), 2286–2297.

Adisetiyo, V., Tabesh, A., Di Martino, A., Falangola, M.F., Castellanos, F.X., Jensen, J.H., Helpern, J.A., 2014. Attention-deficit/hyperactivity disorder without comorbidity is associated with distinct atypical patterns of cerebral microstructural development. Hum. Brain Mapp. 35 (5), 2148–2162.

Aganj, I., Lenglet, C., Sapiro, G., Yacoub, E., Ugurbil, K., Harel, N., 2010. Reconstruction of the orientation distribution function in single-and multiple-shell q-ball imaging within constant solid angle. Magn. Reson. Med. 64 (2), 554–566.

Aggarwal, M., Jones, M.V., Calabresi, P.A., Mori, S., Zhang, J., 2012. Probing mouse brain microstructure using oscillating gradient diffusion MRI. Magn. Reson. Med. 67 (1), 98–109.

Alexander, D.C., Barker, G.J., Arridge, S.R., 2002. Detection and modeling of non-Gaussian apparent diffusion coefficient profiles in human brain data. Magn. Reson. Med. 48 (2), 331–340.

Anderson, A.W., 2005. Measurement of fiber orientation distributions using high angular resolution diffusion imaging. Magn. Reson. Med. 54 (5), 1194–1206.

Assaf, Y., Freidlin, R.Z., Rohde, G.K., Basser, P.J., 2004. New modeling and experimental framework to characterize hindered and restricted water diffusion in brain white matter. Magn. Reson. Med. 52 (5), 965–978.

Basser, P.J., 2002. Relationships between diffusion tensor and q-space MRI. Magn. Reson. Med. 47 (2), 392–397.

Basser, P.J., Pierpaoli, C., 1996. Microstructural and physiological features of tissues elucidated by quantitative-diffusion-tensor MRI. J. Magn. Reson.B 111 (3), 209–219.

Basser, P.J., Mattiello, J., LeBihan, D., 1994. MR diffusion tensor spectroscopy and imaging. Biophys. J. 66 (1), 259–267.

Beaulieu, C., 2002. The basis of anisotropic water diffusion in the nervous system–a technical review. NMR Biomed. 15 (7–8), 435–455.

Behrens, T.E., Woolrich, M.W., Jenkinson, M., Johansen-Berg, H., Nunes, R.G., Clare, S., Matthews, P.M., Brady, J.M., Smith, S.M., 2003. Characterization and propagation of uncertainty in diffusion-weighted MR imaging. Magn. Reson. Med. 50 (5), 1077–1088.

Brusini, L., Menegaz, G., Nilsson, M., 2019. Monte Carlo simulations of water exchange through myelin wraps: implications for diffusion MRI. IEEE Trans. Med. Imaging 38 (6), 1438–1445.

Burcaw, L.M., Fieremans, E., Novikov, D.S., 2015. Mesoscopic structure of neuronal tracts from time-dependent diffusion. NeuroImage 114, 18–37.

Callaghan, P.T., 2011. Translational Dynamics and Magnetic Resonance: Principles of Pulsed Gradient Spin Echo NMR. Oxford University Press.

Canales-Rodríguez, E.J., Lin, C.P., Iturria-Medina, Y., Yeh, C.H., Cho, K.H., Melie-García, L., 2010. Diffusion orientation transform revisited. NeuroImage 49 (2), 1326–1339.

Carr, H.Y., Purcell, E.M., 1954. Effects of diffusion on free precession in nuclear magnetic resonance experiments. Phys. Rev. 94 (3), 630–638.

Cheung, J.S., Wang, E., Lo, E.H., Sun, P.Z., 2012. Stratification of heterogeneous diffusion MRI ischemic lesion with kurtosis imaging: evaluation of mean diffusion and kurtosis MRI mismatch in an animal model of transient focal ischemia. Stroke 43 (8), 2252–2254.

Chin, C.L., Wehrli, F.W., Fan, Y., Hwang, S.N., Schwartz, E.D., Nissanov, J., Hackney, D.B., 2004. Assessment of axonal fiber tract architecture in excised rat spinal cord by localized NMR q-space imaging: simulations and experimental studies. Magn. Reson. Med. 52 (4), 733–740.

Chowdhury, D., 2005. 100 years of Einstein's theory of Brownian motion: from pollen grains to protein trains–1. Resonance 10 (9), 63–78.

Clark, C.A., Le Bihan, D., 2000. Water diffusion compartmentation and anisotropy at high b values in the human brain. Magn. Reson. Med. 44 (6), 852–859.

Cohen, Y., Assaf, Y., 2002. High b-value q-space analyzed diffusion-weighted MRS and MRI in neuronal tissues–a technical review. NMR Biomed. 15 (7–8), 516–542.

Dell'Acqua, F., Tournier, J.D., 2019. Modelling white matter with spherical deconvolution: how and why? NMR Biomed. 32 (4), e3945.

Descoteaux, M., Deriche, R., Knosche, T.R., Anwander, A., 2008. Deterministic and probabilistic tractography based on complex fibre orientation distributions. IEEE Trans. Med. Imaging 28 (2), 269–286.

Dhital, B., Reisert, M., Kellner, E., Kiselev, V.G., 2019. Intra-axonal diffusivity in brain white matter. NeuroImage 189, 543–550.

Does, M.D., Parsons, E.C., Gore, J.C., 2003. Oscillating gradient measurements of water diffusion in normal and globally ischemic rat brain. Magn. Reson. Med. 49 (2), 206–215.

Donahue, C.J., Sotiropoulos, S.N., Jbabdi, S., Hernandez-Fernandez, M., Behrens, T.E., Dyrby, T.B., Coalson, T., Kennedy, H., Knoblauch, K., Van Essen, D.C., Glasser, M.F., 2016. Using diffusion tractography to predict cortical connection strength and distance: a quantitative comparison with tracers in the monkey. J. Neurosci. 36 (25), 6758–6770.

Fung, S.H., Roccatagliata, L., Gonzalez, R.G., Schaefer, P.W., 2011. MR diffusion imaging in ischemic stroke. Neuroimaging Clin. 21 (2), 345–377.

Funk, P., 1913. Über Flächen mit lauter geschlossenen geodätischen Linien. Math. Ann. 74 (2), 278–300.

Glenn, G.R., Helpern, J.A., Tabesh, A., Jensen, J.H., 2015a. Quantitative assessment of diffusional kurtosis anisotropy. NMR Biomed. 28 (4), 448–459.

Glenn, G.R., Helpern, J.A., Tabesh, A., Jensen, J.H., 2015b. Optimization of white matter fiber tractography with diffusional kurtosis imaging. NMR Biomed. 28 (10), 1245–1256.

Glenn, G.R., Kuo, L.W., Chao, Y.P., Lee, C.Y., Helpern, J.A., Jensen, J.H., 2016. Mapping the orientation of white matter fiber bundles: a comparative study of diffusion tensor imaging, diffusional kurtosis imaging, and diffusion spectrum imaging. Am. J. Neuroradiol. 37 (7), 1216–1222.

Grebenkov, D.S., 2007. NMR survey of reflected Brownian motion. Rev. Mod. Phys. 79 (3), 1077–1137.

Hagmann, P., Kurant, M., Gigandet, X., Thiran, P., Wedeen, V.J., Meuli, R., Thiran, J.P., 2007. Mapping human whole-brain structural networks with diffusion MRI. PLoS One 2 (7), e597.

Hahn, E.L., 1950. Spin echoes. Phys. Rev. 80 (4), 580–594.

Hansen, B., Jespersen, S.N., 2016. Kurtosis fractional anisotropy, its contrast and estimation by proxy. Sci. Rep. 6, 23999.

Jelescu, I.O., Budde, M.D., 2017. Design and validation of diffusion MRI models of white matter. Front. Phys. 5, 61.

Jelescu, I.O., Veraart, J., Adisetiyo, V., Milla, S.S., Novikov, D.S., Fieremans, E., 2015. One diffusion acquisition and different white matter models: how does microstructure change in human early development based on WMTI and NODDI? NeuroImage 107, 242–256.

Jelescu, I.O., Veraart, J., Fieremans, E., Novikov, D.S., 2016. Degeneracy in model parameter estimation for multi-compartmental diffusion in neuronal tissue. NMR Biomed. 29 (1), 33–47.

Jensen, J.H., 2015. Stejskal's formula for multiple-pulsed diffusion MRI. Magn. Reson. Imaging 33 (9), 1182–1186.

Jensen, J.H., Helpern, J.A., 2010. MRI quantification of non-Gaussian water diffusion by kurtosis analysis. NMR Biomed. 23 (7), 698–710.

Jensen, J.H., Helpern, J.A., 2016. Resolving power for the diffusion orientation distribution function. Magn. Reson. Med. 76 (2), 679–688.

Jensen, J.H., Helpern, J.A., 2018. Characterizing intra-axonal water diffusion with direction-averaged triple diffusion encoding MRI. NMR Biomed. 31 (7), e3930.

Jensen, J.H., Helpern, J.A., Ramani, A., Lu, H., Kaczynski, K., 2005. Diffusional kurtosis imaging: the quantification of non-Gaussian water diffusion by means of magnetic resonance imaging. Magn. Reson. Med. 53 (6), 1432–1440.

Jensen, J.H., Helpern, J.A., Tabesh, A., 2014. Leading non-Gaussian corrections for diffusion orientation distribution function. NMR Biomed. 27 (2), 202–211.

Jensen, J.H., Glenn, G.R., Helpern, J.A., 2016. Fiber ball imaging. NeuroImage 124, 824–833.

Jeurissen, B., Descoteaux, M., Mori, S., Leemans, A., 2019. Diffusion MRI fiber tractography of the brain. NMR Biomed. 32 (4), e3785.

Jones, D.K. (Ed.), 2010. Diffusion MRI. Oxford University Press.

Jones, D.K., Travis, A.R., Eden, G., Pierpaoli, C., Basser, P.J., 2005. PASTA: pointwise assessment of streamline tractography attributes. Magn. Reson. Med. 53 (6), 1462–1467.

Jones, D.K., Knösche, T.R., Turner, R., 2013. White matter integrity, fiber count, and other fallacies: the do's and don'ts of diffusion MRI. NeuroImage 73, 239–254.

King, M.D., Houseman, J., Roussel, S.A., Van Bruggen, N., Williams, S.R., Gadian, D.G., 1994. Q-space imaging of the brain. Magn. Reson. Med. 32 (6), 707–713.

Kiselev, V.G., 2017. Fundamentals of diffusion MRI physics. NMR Biomed. 30 (3), e3602.

Kunz, N., da Silva, A.R., Jelescu, I.O., 2018. Intra-and extra-axonal axial diffusivities in the white matter: which one is faster? NeuroImage 181, 314–322.

Kuo, L.W., Chen, J.H., Wedeen, V.J., Tseng, W.Y.I., 2008. Optimization of diffusion spectrum imaging and q-ball imaging on clinical MRI system. NeuroImage 41 (1), 7–18.

Lätt, J., Nilsson, M., Wirestam, R., Johansson, E., Larsson, E.M., Ståhlberg, F., Brockstedt, S., 2008. In vivo visualization of displacement-distribution-derived parameters in q-space imaging. Magn. Reson. Imaging 26 (1), 77–87.

Lazar, M., 2010. Mapping brain anatomical connectivity using white matter tractography. NMR Biomed. 23 (7), 821–835.

Le Bihan, D., Johansen-Berg, H., 2012. Diffusion MRI at 25: exploring brain tissue structure and function. NeuroImage 61 (2), 324–341.

Le Bihan, D., Mangin, J.F., Poupon, C., Clark, C.A., Pappata, S., Molko, N., Chabriat, H., 2001. Diffusion tensor imaging: concepts and applications. J. Magn. Reson. Imaging 13 (4), 534–546.

Lu, H., Jensen, J.H., Ramani, A., Helpern, J.A., 2006. Three-dimensional characterization of non-Gaussian water diffusion in humans using diffusion kurtosis imaging. NMR Biomed. 19 (2), 236–247.

Mah, A., Geeraert, B., Lebel, C., 2017. Detailing neuroanatomical development in late childhood and early adolescence using NODDI. PLoS One 12 (8), e0182340.

Mayer, A.R., Ling, J.M., Yang, Z., Pena, A., Yeo, R.A., Klimaj, S., 2012. Diffusion abnormalities in pediatric mild traumatic brain injury. J. Neurosci. 32 (50), 17961–17969.

McKinnon, E.T., Jensen, J.H., Glenn, G.R., Helpern, J.A., 2017. Dependence on *b*-value of the direction-averaged diffusion-weighted imaging signal in brain. Magn. Reson. Imaging 36, 121–127.

McKinnon, E.T., Helpern, J.A., Jensen, J.H., 2018. Modeling white matter microstructure with fiber ball imaging. NeuroImage 176, 11–21.

Mohanty, V., McKinnon, E.T., Helpern, J.A., Jensen, J.H., 2018. Comparison of cumulant expansion and q-space imaging estimates for diffusional kurtosis in brain. Magn. Reson. Imaging 48, 80–88.

Mori, S., Van Zijl, P.C., 2002. Fiber tracking: principles and strategies–a technical review. NMR Biomed. 15 (7–8), 468–480.

Moss, H.G., McKinnon, E.T., Glenn, G.R., Helpern, J.A., Jensen, J.H., 2019. Optimization of data acquisition and analysis for fiber ball imaging. NeuroImage 200, 690–703.

Mulkern, R.V., Vajapeyam, S., Robertson, R.L., Caruso, P.A., Rivkin, M.J., Maier, S.E., 2001. Biexponential apparent diffusion coefficient parametrization in adult vs newborn brain. Magn. Reson. Imaging 19 (5), 659–668.

Nezamzadeh, M., 2012. Diffusion time dependence of magnetic resonance diffusion signal decays: an investigation of water exchange in human brain in vivo. MAGMA 25 (4), 285–296.

Nilsson, M., Lätt, J., van Westen, D., Brockstedt, S., Lasič, S., Ståhlberg, F., Topgaard, D., 2013. Noninvasive mapping of water diffusional exchange in the human brain using filter-exchange imaging. Magn. Reson. Med. 69 (6), 1572–1580.

Nilsson, M., Lasič, S., Drobnjak, I., Topgaard, D., Westin, C.F., 2017. Resolution limit of cylinder diameter estimation by diffusion MRI: the impact of gradient waveform and orientation dispersion. NMR Biomed. 30 (7), e3711.

Novikov, D.S., Kiselev, V.G., 2010. Effective medium theory of a diffusion-weighted signal. NMR Biomed. 23 (7), 682–697.

Novikov, D.S., Fieremans, E., Jensen, J.H., Helpern, J.A., 2011. Random walks with barriers. Nat. Phys. 7 (6), 508.

Novikov, D.S., Jensen, J.H., Helpern, J.A., Fieremans, E., 2014. Revealing mesoscopic structural universality with diffusion. Proc. Natl. Acad. Sci. 111 (14), 5088–5093.

Novikov, D.S., Kiselev, V.G., Jespersen, S.N., 2018a. On modeling. Magn. Reson. Med. 79 (6), 3172–3193.

Novikov, D.S., Veraart, J., Jelescu, I.O., Fieremans, E., 2018b. Rotationally-invariant mapping of scalar and orientational metrics of neuronal microstructure with diffusion MRI. NeuroImage 174, 518–538.

Novikov, D.S., Fieremans, E., Jespersen, S.N., Kiselev, V.G., 2019. Quantifying brain microstructure with diffusion MRI: theory and parameter estimation. NMR Biomed. 32 (4), e3998.

Ouyang, M., Dubois, J., Yu, Q., Mukherjee, P., Huang, H., 2019. Delineation of early brain development from fetuses to infants with diffusion MRI and beyond. NeuroImage 185, 836–850.

Parker, G.D., Marshall, D., Rosin, P.L., Drage, N., Richmond, S., Jones, D.K., 2013. A pitfall in the reconstruction of fibre ODFs using spherical deconvolution of diffusion MRI data. NeuroImage 65, 433–448.

Pearson, K., 1905. Das Fehlergesetz und Seine Verallgemeiner-ungen durch Fechner und Pearson. A Rejoinder. Biometrika 4 (1–2), 169–212.

Poot, D.H., Arnold, J., Achten, E., Verhoye, M., Sijbers, J., 2010. Optimal experimental design for diffusion kurtosis imaging. IEEE Trans. Med. Imaging 29 (3), 819–829.

Potgieser, A.R., Wagemakers, M., van Hulzen, A.L., de Jong, B.M., Hoving, E.W., Groen, R.J., 2014. The role of diffusion tensor imaging in brain tumor surgery: a review of the literature. Clin. Neurol. Neurosurg. 124, 51–58.

Price, W.S., Kuchel, P.W., 1991. Effect of nonrectangular field gradient pulses in the Stejskal and Tanner (diffusion) pulse sequence. J. Magn. Reson. 94 (1), 133–139.

Ramanna, S., Moss, H.G., McKinnon, E.T., Yacoub, E., Helpern, J.A., Jensen, J.H., 2020. Triple diffusion encoding MRI predicts intra-axonal and extra-axonal diffusion tensors in white matter. Magn. Reson. Med. 83 (6), 2209–2220.

Reese, T.G., Heid, O., Weisskoff, R.M., Wedeen, V.J., 2003. Reduction of eddy-current-induced distortion in diffusion MRI using a twice-refocused spin echo. Magn. Reson. Med. 49 (1), 177–182.

Shemesh, N., Jespersen, S.N., Alexander, D.C., Cohen, Y., Drobnjak, I., Dyrby, T.B., Finsterbusch, J., Koch, M.A., Kuder, T., Laun, F., Lawrenz, M., Lundell, H., Mitra, P.P., Nilsson, M., Özarslan, E., Topgaard, D., Westin, C. F., 2016. Conventions and nomenclature for double diffusion encoding NMR and MRI. Magn. Reson. Med. 75 (1), 82–87.

Shi, J., Yang, S., Wang, J., Huang, S., Yao, Y., Zhang, S., Zhu, W., Shao, J., 2019. Detecting normal pediatric brain development with diffusional kurtosis imaging. Eur. J. Radiol. 108690.

Sotiropoulos, S.N., Zalesky, A., 2019. Building connectomes using diffusion MRI: why, how and but. NMR Biomed. 32 (4), e3752.

Stejskal, E.O., 1965. Use of spin echoes in a pulsed magnetic-field gradient to study anisotropic, restricted diffusion and flow. J. Chem. Phys. 43 (10), 3597–3603.

Stejskal, E.O., Tanner, J.E., 1965. Spin diffusion measurements: spin echoes in the presence of a time-dependent field gradient. J. Chem. Phys. 42 (1), 288–292.

Tabesh, A., Jensen, J.H., Ardekani, B.A., Helpern, J.A., 2011. Estimation of tensors and tensor-derived measures in diffusional kurtosis imaging. Magn. Reson. Med. 65 (3), 823–836.

Tang, L., Zhou, X.J., 2019. Diffusion MRI of cancer: from low to high b-values. J. Magn. Reson. Imaging 49 (1), 23–40.

Tanner, J.E., Stejskal, E.O., 1968. Restricted self-diffusion of protons in colloidal systems by the pulsed-gradient, spin-echo method. J. Chem. Phys. 49 (4), 1768–1777.

Taouli, B. (Ed.), 2010. Extra-Cranial Applications of Diffusion-Weighted MRI. Cambridge University Press.

Tournier, J.D., Calamante, F., Gadian, D.G., Connelly, A., 2004. Direct estimation of the fiber orientation density function from diffusion-weighted MRI data using spherical deconvolution. NeuroImage 23 (3), 1176–1185.

Tournier, J.D., Calamante, F., Connelly, A., 2007. Robust determination of the fibre orientation distribution in diffusion MRI: non-negativity constrained super-resolved spherical deconvolution. NeuroImage 35 (4), 1459–1472.

Travers, B.G., Adluru, N., Ennis, C., Tromp, D.P., Destiche, D., Doran, S., Bigler, E.D., Lange, N., Lainhart, J.E., Alexander, A.L., 2012. Diffusion tensor imaging in autism spectrum disorder: a review. Autism Res. 5 (5), 289–313.

Tuch, D.S., 2004. Q-ball imaging. Magn. Reson. Med. 52 (6), 1358–1372.

Veraart, J., Rajan, J., Peeters, R.R., Leemans, A., Sunaert, S., Sijbers, J., 2013. Comprehensive framework for accurate diffusion MRI parameter estimation. Magn. Reson. Med. 70 (4), 972–984.

Veraart, J., Novikov, D.S., Fieremans, E., 2018. TE dependent diffusion imaging (TEdDI) distinguishes between compartmental T2 relaxation times. NeuroImage 182, 360–369.

Wang, E., Wu, Y., Cheung, J.S., Zhou, I.Y., Igarashi, T., Zhang, X., Sun, P.Z., 2017. pH imaging reveals worsened tissue acidification in diffusion kurtosis lesion than the kurtosis/diffusion lesion mismatch in an animal model of acute stroke. J. Cereb. Blood Flow Metab. 37 (10), 3325–3333.

Wedeen, V.J., Hagmann, P., Tseng, W.Y.I., Reese, T.G., Weisskoff, R.M., 2005. Mapping complex tissue architecture with diffusion spectrum magnetic resonance imaging. Magn. Reson. Med. 54 (6), 1377–1386.

Wu, E.X., Cheung, M.M., 2010. MR diffusion kurtosis imaging for neural tissue characterization. NMR Biomed. 23 (7), 836–848.

Xu, J., Does, M.D., Gore, J.C., 2009. Quantitative characterization of tissue microstructure with temporal diffusion spectroscopy. J. Magn. Reson. 200 (2), 189–197.

Yablonskiy, D.A., Sukstanskii, A.L., 2010. Theoretical models of the diffusion weighted MR signal. NMR Biomed. 23 (7), 661–681.

Yeatman, J.D., Dougherty, R.F., Myall, N.J., Wandell, B.A., Feldman, H.M., 2012. Tract profiles of white matter properties: automating fiber-tract quantification. PLoS One 7 (11), e49790.

Zhang, H., Schneider, T., Wheeler-Kingshott, C.A., Alexander, D.C., 2012. NODDI: practical in vivo neurite orientation dispersion and density imaging of the human brain. NeuroImage 61 (4), 1000–1016.

CHAPTER

Structural connectomics: Where we are and where we should be?

3

Ragini Verma and Yusuf Osmanlıoğlu

DiCIPHR (Diffusion & Connectomics In Precision Healthcare Research) Lab, Department of Radiology, Perelman School of Medicine, University of Pennsylvania, Philadelphia, PA, United States

1. What is connectomics?

The human brain is a complex system containing $\sim 10^{11}$ neurons, with each making thousands of synaptic connections (Bullmore et al., 2009). While region-specific analyses have yielded insight about their specific role in the brain, the interconnected structure of the brain makes it necessary to model the *connectivity* of individual regional processing units to understand the mechanism of how the brain functions (Friston, 2011). Although we are far from investigating the connectivity at a cellular level for the human brain, in vivo noninvasive imaging techniques developed within the last few decades, provide insights into brain organization at a macroscale (Craddock et al., 2013) in order of magnitude of mm^3 voxels that contain roughly 10^6 neurons. It is also a common practice to cluster voxels that share common features into regions of interest, and investigate connectivity of these regions. Connectivity maps obtained at this scale are called "connectomes" (Sporns et al., 2005).

We can consider the brain as an interconnected system of highways, with mechanisms in place to manage a smooth flow of traffic through this network, which is disrupted by pathology. Different imaging modalities can be used to explain the various aspects of this network. dMRI (diffusion MRI) provides an insight into the roads (both their integrity, as well as the connectivity), fMRI (functional MRI) through its activation maps elucidates whether traffic reached from point A to B, and MEG/EEG aid in determining the timing of the traffic. Connectomes derived from these modalities are called structural and functional connectomes, respectively. This chapter focuses on structural connectomes that capture the underlying anatomical white matter pathways that connect gray matter regions (Hagmann et al., 2008). Considering the brain as an information processing system, functional connectivity can be regarded as the influx of information exchange while structural connectivity would represent the data pathways that the information travels through.

2. How are structural connectomes generated?

Structural connectomes are derived from diffusion MRI (dMRI) scans. dMRI captures the random (Brownian) motion of water molecules in the tissue (Stejskal and Tanner, 1965) such that, water constrained within or between tightly packed axons would diffuse along the axons (anisotropic diffusion),

Handbook of Pediatric Brain Imaging. https://doi.org/10.1016/B978-0-12-816633-8.00011-9

while water with little or no constraint (such as in dendrites and CSF, respectively) would demonstrate a random (isotropic) diffusion (Jones, 2008a). Connectomes represent the networks of the brain, and consist of computational units (or regions) that interact with each other through communication channels. In order to model this network systematically, abstract representations called *graphs* are used, where computational units in the brain are represented as nodes, and the connectivity between these units are represented as edges (Sporns et al., 2005). In order to create a connectome, the brain is parcellated into regions, and connectivity between these regions is obtained by tractography between these regions, by exploiting the anisotropic diffusion of the water molecules (Basser et al., 2000). The brain regions form the nodes of the graph, and the edges of the graph are weighted by some measure derived from the connectivity (Fig. 1).

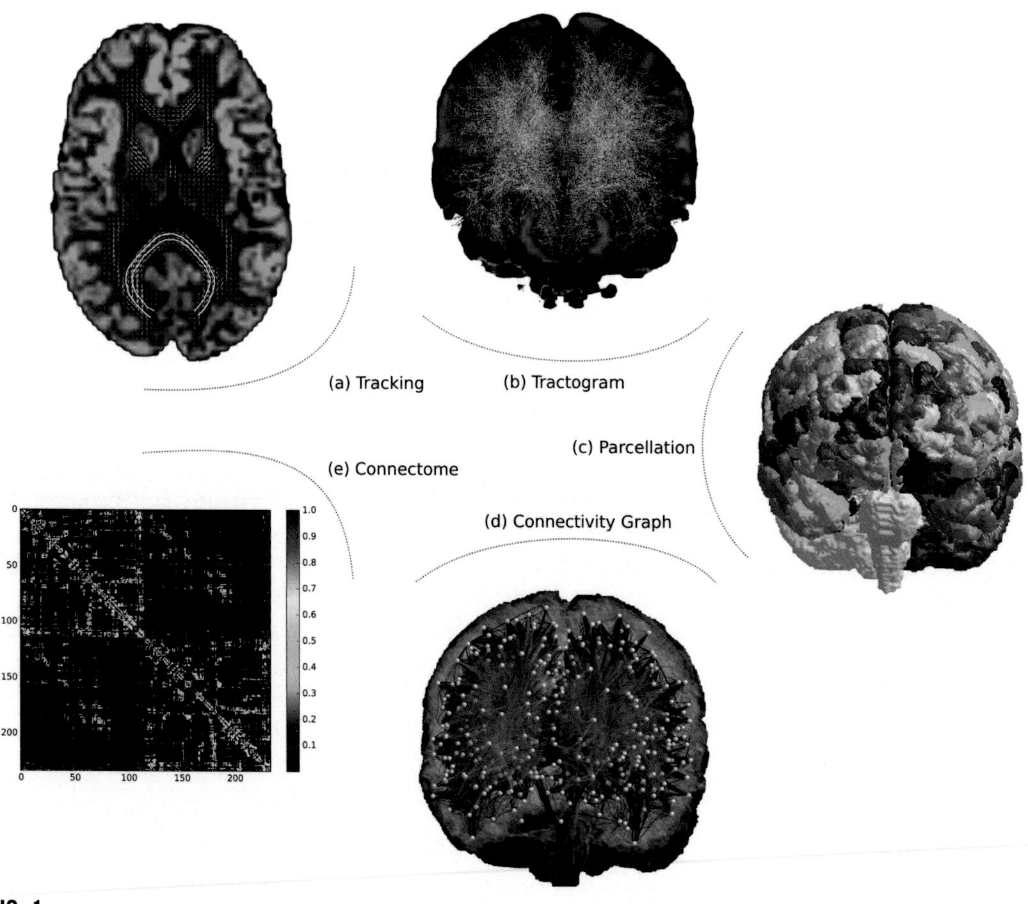

FIG. 1

Various steps in creating a connectome.

2.1 Defining nodes of the brain network: Parcellation schemes

Since connectomics evaluates connectivity of the brain at a macroscale, nodes represent gray matter voxels sharing common anatomical or functional features that are clustered together into regions of interest (ROI), which is also known as parcellation. It is a common practice in connectomics to generate parcellation templates called *atlases*, that delineate the brain into regions (Catani and de Schotten, 2008). Brain parcellation could be anatomical (Desikan et al., 2006), or functional (Yeo et al., 2011, 2014). The size of the connectome depends on the resolution of the parcellation that is adopted. The aim of using these parcellation atlases in generating connectomes is to create a standardized connectivity map, such that the connectomes and their derived measures are comparable across the population(s) being investigated.

2.2 Defining edges of the brain network: Tractography

Once the brain is parcellated into regions using one of the atlases, tractography is used to generate connections between these regions. Tractography involves (i) fitting a *tissue model* per voxel characterizing the underlying fibers; (ii) constructing streamlines that represent white matter fiber trajectories by starting from random *seed points* located inside a voxel and *tracking* the main orientation of anisotropic water diffusion across voxels until a stopping criterion is reached (Jeurissen et al., 2019); and (iii) deriving the connectivity-based weight for each of the edges.

2.2.1 Fitting the tissue model

There are various means of fitting a model to the data, which is intricately linked to how the data are acquired. Every such selection affects the connectome (Qi et al., 2015). Orientation of fibers in a given voxel can be reconstructed using various methods, each making certain assumptions and affected by how the data are acquired (Fig. 2). The most common model is a tensor (denoted DTI to represent diffusion tensor imaging), which is an ellipsoid with three principal directions and magnitudes associated with these directions (Conturo et al., 1999). Tensors can be fitted to any single shell dMRI acquisition and at least 6 gradient directions, with more directions providing higher accuracy (Lebel et al., 2012). Although successful in reconstructing streamlines for several tracts, the diffusion tensor model is vulnerable to the cases where a voxel contains multiple fibers, as observed in "kissing" or crossing fibers (Tournier et al., 2011; Farquharson et al., 2013). Higher Angular Resolution Diffusion Imaging (HARDI) (Descoteaux, 1999) partially overcomes the limitations of DTI, by fitting a higher order model in each voxel, allowing for the modeling of multiple fibers, with various HARDI models being developed over the years (Tournier et al., 2008). This requires acquisitions with higher b values (e.g., $b > 1800$ s/mm^2) with denser angular sampling (generally 45 or more gradient directions), either in a single or multishell format. The tensor and HARDI models, do not allow for multicompartments, which has been rectified in the recent years in which each voxel is modeled as a combination of two or more compartments associated with extra- and intracellular aspects of the voxel. A popular form of this model separates the tissue from the extracellular free water, with the tissue compartment being modeled by a tensor (Parker et al., 2020; Pasternak et al., 2009). In the presence of pathology, the free water captures edema, and in the absence of it, it models the partial voluming and creates a cleaner tissue model.

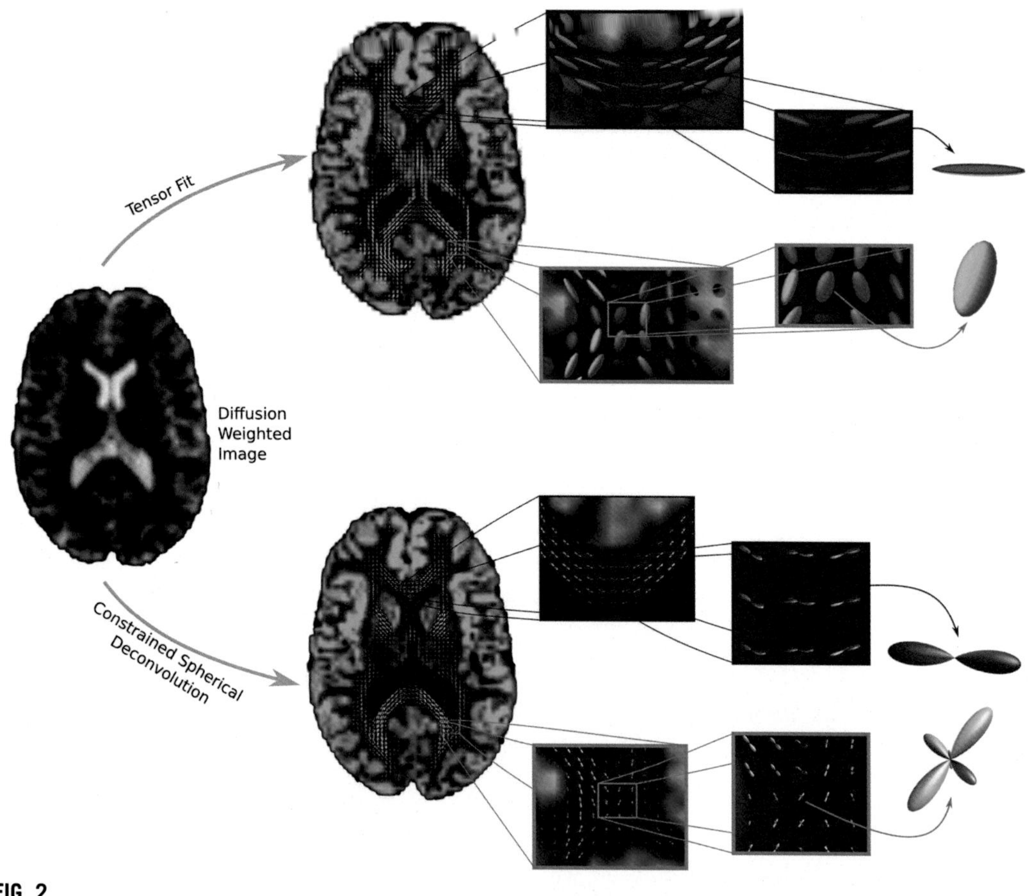

FIG. 2

Estimation of underlying fiber orientations. *(Top)* tensor fit *(Bottom)* higher order model.

2.2.2 Tracking

Once local fiber orientations are estimated at each voxel, streamlines representing the white matter fibers are constructed by linking the neighboring voxels by utilizing the calculated fiber orientations, a process known as tracking. Starting from a seed voxel, the gist of tracking is to choose the neighboring voxel to be visited next, until a stopping condition is reached. Thus, tracking consists of three main components:

(i) Seeding: The starting point of tracking for a streamline is called a seed, which is a randomly selected point inside a voxel. The seeding strategy for tracking involves choosing (i) the location of the seeding, and (ii) the number of seeds to be generated. Location-wise, seeding can be done in three main tissue types: gray matter (GM) (Johansen-Berg et al., 2004), whole brain white matter

(WM) (Conturo et al., 1999; Tournier et al., 2011) or gray matter-white matter interface (GMWMI) (Li et al., 2012). Location of seeding is known to have an impact on the topology of the ensuing network due to inherent biases of these approaches (Girard et al., 2014), such as GM seeding leading to sparse connectivity on account of favoring short range connections and WM seeding leading to inflated connectivity strength in longer streamlines (Zajac et al., 2017). Seeding from GMWMI with anatomically constrained tracking has been shown to perform relatively better in overcoming these biases (Smith et al., 2012). Also, the number of seeds to be generated plays an important role in obtaining stable and reproducible brain networks. Seeding can be done by either generating a constant number of seeds per voxel (such as 5000 seeds per voxel) (Cheng et al., 2012) or by generating seeds until a globally set number of streamlines are successfully generated (such as 10 million streamlines) (Roine et al., 2019).

(ii) **Rules for traversal:** The decision regarding the next voxel to visit in tracking is made either deterministically or probabilistically (Descoteaux et al., 2009). In deterministic tracking, a single choice of direction is made at each voxel, along the principal direction of the underlying tensor (Basser et al., 2000). With probabilistic tracking, on the other hand, a distribution of fiber orientations is estimated for each voxel, and a random sample is drawn from this distribution for each streamline that is being tracked through a voxel (Behrens et al., 2007). Both algorithms have pros and cons. Deterministic tracking is criticized for being too sensitive to the principal direction of fiber orientations, being susceptible to noise, and not accounting for the inherent uncertainty in orientation estimations. These factors lead to a lower sensitivity, that is, certain streamlines, especially those that are passing through voxels containing crossing or kissing fibers, couldn't be identified (Sarwar et al., 2019). On the other hand, it has high specificity in that the streamlines that are identified by deterministic approaches are representatives of real underlying fiber tracts, leading to connectomes with higher reproducibility (Sarwar et al., 2019). In contrast to deterministic methods, probabilistic tractography handles kissing or crossing fibers better which leads to a higher sensitivity. The probabilistic nature of the algorithm becomes a liability when it comes to the false positive streamlines, as the approach has low specificity (Jones, 2008b). Thus, the trade-off between sensitivity and specificity needs to be considered carefully when choosing the tracking algorithm. We also note that, tracking bias correction methods (which we will explore later in the text) can alleviate the specificity problem of the probabilistic tracking, possibly making it the more favorable of the two approaches.

(iii) **Stopping criteria:** Tracking of a streamline is finalized when one or more of certain conditions are met. One of the most commonly utilized stopping criteria is to set a minimum FA or fiber orientation distribution function (ODF) amplitude value threshold, where the tracking ends if the FA or ODF of the projected subsequent voxel is below that threshold. The rationale behind this criterion is twofold. First, the high level of uncertainty in the anisotropy of water diffusion in such voxels would potentially lead to propagating to an incorrect direction (Girard et al., 2014). Second, lower FA or ODF values is a characteristic of gray matter regions where the tracking is expected to end. Setting a maximum curvature constraint is another common stopping criterion, which prevents reconstructing streamlines that would take a sharp turn within a voxel, in order to respect the anatomical structure of the underlying white matter fiber tracts that constitute smooth trajectories (Tournier et al., 2011).

2.2.3 Defining the edge weights

On completion of tracking, there are streamlines between any two pairs of regions. The edges of the connectome can either be unweighted or weighted. *Unweighted connectomes* model connectivity as binary, where the presence of streamlines between two nodes regardless of their count is considered as an edge with unit weight, and the lack of streamlines is represented as an edge with zero weight (Sotiropoulos and Zalesky, 2019). Although commonly used in early stages of connectomics research due to limitations of the data acquisition, use of binary connectomes is in decline relative to their weighted counterparts as they discard valuable information (Civier et al., 2019). *Weighted connectomes*, on the other hand, represent the strength of connectivity between regions as edge weights. Connectivity strength in weighted connectomes is most commonly represented as the number of streamlines between two ROIs, since it allows a relatively straightforward interpretation. Edges can also be represented by DTI driven *diffusion scalars* such as FA or MD, where connectivity strength is calculated as the average FA (or MD) of voxels that the streamlines between two ROIs pass through. Despite being an indirect measure of connectivity that is hard to interpret, such connectivity maps are reported as efficient biomarkers for diseases such as traumatic brain injury (TBI) (Hulkower et al., 2013) or, outside the realm of pediatric imaging, Alzheimer's (Contreras et al., 2015).

3. Refining connectomes of underlying biases

As described above, connectome creation involves many steps, each associated with tradeoffs and inherent biases, introducing noise in the ensuing connectome that makes "clean up" a necessity (Girard et al., 2014), for which there are several filtering techniques.

3.1 Spurious fibers and thresholding

Due to the uncertainty that is inherent in the fiber orientation estimation and tractography, tracking might lead to spurious streamlines that connect two regions which are in fact disconnected. Since such errors are expected to be irregular and relatively rare, the spurious streamlines would sum to make weak connections between regions. Leveraging this observation, thresholding of weak edges has been a common practice, especially in the early stages of connectomics research. In its most basic form, thresholding involves setting the weight of edges that have a value below a threshold to zero, which can be applied in both unweighted and weighted connectomes (Rubinov and Sporns, 2010). An alternative thresholding approach involves removing weaker edges until the density of the network, that is, the ratio of existing edges to the possible number of edges, is reduced to a certain percentage (Colon-Perez et al., 2016). In both thresholding approaches, spurious edges are assumed to be among the weakest exclusively. Considering that this assumption might fail as some of the weak edges might constitute real connections, consistency thresholding is proposed. In this scheme, edges that appear consistently across the sample are retained even if they are weak, while inconsistent edges are discarded regardless of their strength (Roberts et al., 2017). A main criticism about thresholding is the arbitrariness of the threshold value, which is generally addressed by doing experiments over a range of thresholds (Vasa et al., 2018). Recently, there has been conflicting reports regarding the efficacy of thresholding, with some studies highlighting that thresholding is inconsequential in graph theoretical analysis unless done aggressively (Civier et al., 2019; Osmanlioglu et al., 2020), while others suggest that thresholded connectomes respect underlying biology more (such as offering more age-sensitive measures) relative to unthresholded connectomes (Drakesmith et al., 2015).

3.2 Distance bias

The uncertainty inherent in tracking gets compounded and error gets accumulated as tracking of a streamline proceeds across voxels. This implies that long range connections have a higher probability of getting terminated before reaching an ROI, rendering it an invalid streamline. Consequently, long range connections are relatively underrepresented in a connectome (Jbabdi and Johansen-Berg, 2011). Scaling edge weights according to the geodesic length of streamlines is a simple fix to this bias (Hagmann et al., 2008), albeit being incomplete in eradicating the problem (Yeh et al., 2016).

3.3 Seeding bias

The choice of seeding scheme can cause various biases, leading to an over or under sampling of certain connections. One type of bias occurs when the seeding is done per voxel rather than a fixed number of seeds across the brain, where subjects with larger brain volumes would get stronger connectivity between any two regions relative to subjects with smaller brain volumes (Cheng et al., 2012). Such a bias could lead to incorrect conclusions especially if the sample being investigated consists of participants with varying brain sizes, as in developmental cohorts. Another bias occurs when seeding is done across the whole brain white matter, where longer white matter tracts will be over sampled as more seeds will be located on them, leading to an inflated connectivity strength in long range connections (Hagmann et al., 2008). Normalizing streamline counts by total brain volume or volume of ROIs is a simple way to partially address the problem (Osmanlioglu et al., 2020).

3.4 Tractography filtering techniques

Fundamentally, the seeding as well as distance bias happen due to the inconsistency between density of streamlines at the voxel level and the underlying fiber density (Smith et al., 2013; Calamante, 2019). A family of rigorous methods named *tractography filtering techniques* aims to tackle this inconsistency problem by utilizing a basic observation related to underlying data. Specifically, in modeling HARDI data with CSD, for example, the magnitude of FOD in a certain direction is proportional to local intracellular volume, implying that the magnitude of FOD should also be proportional to the streamline density (Raffelt et al., 2012). SIFT (Smith et al., 2013), SIFT2 (Smith et al., 2015a), COMMIT (Daducci et al., 2015), COMMIT2 (Schiavi et al., 2020), and LiFE (Pestilli et al., 2014) are some of the methods that reduce streamline density biases using this observation, each making different assumptions about the data. Although refining connectomes by removing these biases is necessary to obtain a robust and reproducible brain network (Smith et al., 2015b), the use of aforementioned tractography filtering techniques can introduce further distortions to the reconstructed network. It was recently shown that filtering streamlines using SIFT2 or COMMIT leads to significant alterations in the brain network topology of healthy subjects as well as traumatic brain injury patients relative to unfiltered structural connectomes, regardless of the data acquisition being at clinical or research quality (Frigo et al., 2020). The same study further highlighted that graph theoretical measures derived from connectomes that are filtered using SIFT2 and COMMIT have significant nonnegligible differences relative to each other. Both results underline the importance of being cautious when using such tools.

4. Enhanced connectomes

In its basic yet most frequently used form, connectomes are represented as weighted matrices, where edges are numerical values encoding a single connectivity type (such as structural or functional connectivity) while nodes are the rows and columns of the matrix where no explicit information regarding the ROIs is evaluated except their pairwise connectivity. Although these types of connectomes allow a robust network-level analysis of the brain, various neuroimaging techniques provide a plethora of additional information regarding local features of ROIs, as well as various connectivity related information that can further improve our understanding of the brain. By encoding this information into more complex graph representations, more elaborate structures which are referred to as enhanced or enriched connectomes were proposed (Osmanlioglu et al., 2017; Lariviere et al., 2019).

Connectivity among brain regions can be defined using various modalities such as EEG, MEG, functional MRI, and structural MRI. While each connectivity type can be analyzed on its own, a combination of these connectivity types is increasingly being considered. Each imaging modality offers various information for connectivity between regions. Diffusion weighted imaging, for example, provides measures quantifying water diffusion such as fractional anisotropy (FA) and mean diffusivity (MD) for each streamline, where average of such values across streamlines connecting two regions is commonly evaluated as alternative connectivity types. In defining functional connectivity of the brain, correlation between the fMRI signals of regions in multiple time frames define various connectivity maps for the same set of nodes, which is referred to as dynamic functional connectivity (Preti et al., 2017). Combining various types of relationship between functional activations such as cross-correlation, coherence, wavelet coherence, and mutual information, to achieve a composite and multimetric definition is recently shown to better characterize functional connectivity relative to the conventional use of correlation of BOLD signals alone (Mohanty et al., 2020). A further elaboration of enhanced edges in functional connectivity involves the employment of hyper graphs where multiple nodes that have highly correlated activation signals are connected together with a single (hyper) edge (Davison et al., 2016).

In enriching connectomes with nodal information, annotated graphs are used to represent brain networks where nodes consist of feature vectors encoding local information (Khambhati et al., 2018). Recently, we considered network topological measures of nodes such as degree, strength, participation coefficient, centrality, and efficiency as the node features, which are calculated over structural connectivity (Osmanlioglu et al., 2018a). We demonstrated that enriching connectomes with nodal information provides a more distinctive representation in classification of traumatic brain injury (TBI) patients relative to using conventional connectomes that lack nodal features. Alternative features coming from anatomy such as gray matter density, cortical thickness, or cytoarchitectural characteristics have also been suggested as nodal features (van den Heuvel et al., 2015). In functional imaging modalities, average of regional activation signals are commonly used in describing nodes.

5. Harmonization of connectomes

With the growing large sample size studies, and the demands of "big data," connectomic analysis increasingly requires pooling connectomes created from multiple sites. dMRI is highly sensitive to acquisition protocol variation (magnet strength, scanning protocol parameters, coils, scanner software versions, etc.), with the effect being variable regionally across the brain, as well as across different dMRI measures of tissue microstructure and connectivity. This complex effect of dMRI acquisition parameters on the data prevents the combination of existing data across sites by simply treating site as a statistical covariate. It is particularly challenging for multisite studies, where despite best efforts, inadvertent changes in protocols between (or even within) sites could render large parts of the data incomparable between sites. Additionally, postprocessing for artifact alleviation, like motion correction, may introduce more changes in the data. It therefore precludes the use of methods that harmonize the raw data. Traditional batch effect removal techniques used in gene expression studies (Fortin et al., 2014; Leek and Storey, 2007) do not preserve the underlying biology, except ComBat (Johnson et al., 2007). ComBat has been adapted in the context of neuroimaging studies (Fortin et al., 2016), to harmonize the measures of fidelity. However, diffusion measures of connectivity have different distributions, with the fidelity measures being normally distributed, and the connectomes demonstrating zero-inflation and more complex distributions (Ismail et al., 2018). Hence, new tools are needed to harmonize connectomes, with the research in this area being still in its infancy.

6. Communication paradigms in the brain

The brain can be considered as an information processing network with special characteristics such as small worldness, existence of hub regions, and community structure (Bassett and Sporns, 2017). In this setup, the anatomic connections of the brain can be regarded as the roads while the functional interactions among brain regions would be considered as the traffic flow over these pathways, suggesting an explanation to the indirect connectivity. Several traffic patterns have been proposed to characterize the nature of the information exchange in the brain, with shortest path being the most popular as it complies with the established theory of efficiency of brain networks (Bullmore and Sporns, 2012). Alternative traffic patterns, such as search information, path transitivity, and communicability, on the other hand, model information to flow through diverse routes (Estrada and Naomichi, 2008; Goni et al., 2014). Our comprehensive evaluation of various traffic patterns of the brain at the network as well as systems level, demonstrated that information flow in the brain is explained better with communicability, which considers the communication as a diffusion process with the communication between regions occurring through multiple pathways simultaneously (Fig. 3) (Osmanlioglu et al., 2019).

In our analysis of a large cohort of 641 participants of age range 8–22 years, we demonstrated that visual and somatomotor systems achieve the highest structure-function coupling while having the lowest participation coefficient among all functional systems. We also showed that the structure-function coupling is inversely proportional to the participation coefficient at node level across all systems. These results highlight that the functional interactions in modular systems, which have high intraconnectedness and lower interactions with the rest of the brain, can be explained with their structural connectivity using communicability as the traffic pattern. These findings are notable

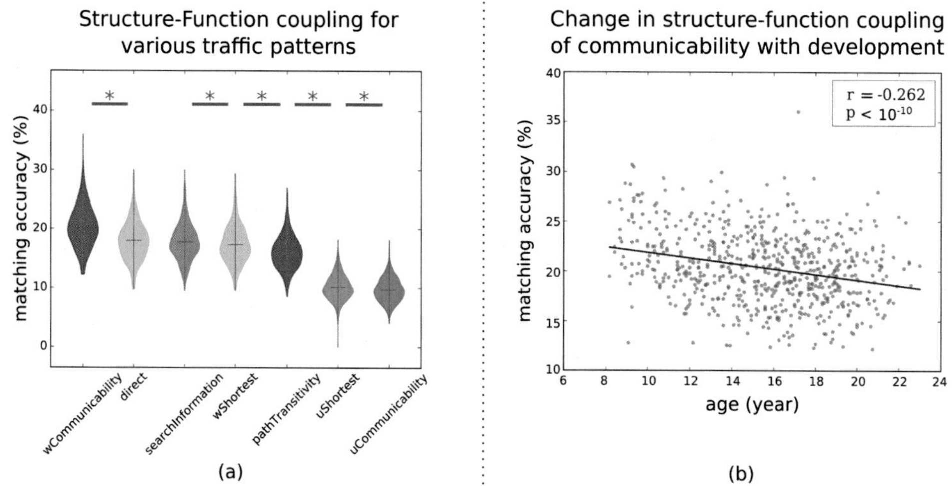

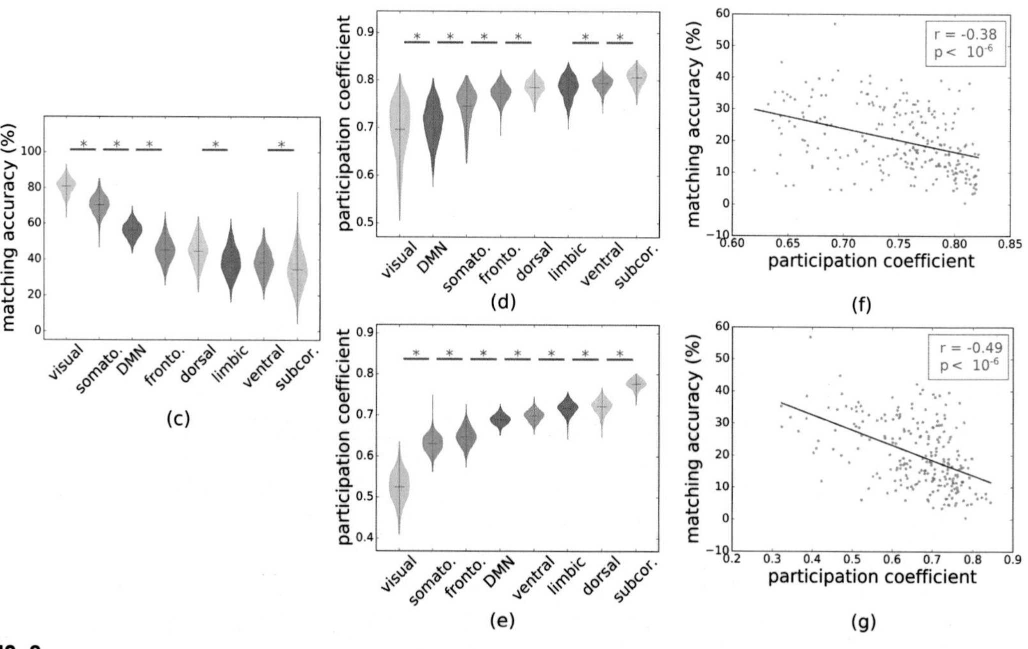

FIG. 3

Structure-function coupling at connectome and system level: (A) Structure-function coupling was observed to be highest in weighted communicability, a traffic pattern that considers communication to happen through parallel pathways simultaneously. (B) Coupling between weighted communicability-based connectivity and actual functional connectivity decreases with age, possibly indicating that the brain adopts more complex traffic patterns with the development. (C) Coupling is observed to be higher in visual, somato-motor, and DMN systems. These systems are observed to be highly modular due to their lower participation coefficient (D) functionally and (E) structurally. A negative correlation was observed between structure-function coupling and participation coefficient of (F) functional and (G) structural connectomes, implying that communicability might be insufficient in explaining the interactions of systems with more intramodular connectivity.

considering commonly suggested lower cognitive roles of motor and visual systems (Gur et al., 2012), further supporting their being sensory modules. Our analysis further revealed that the structure-function coupling decreases with age in our developmental cohort, pointing to an uneven rate of change in the structural and functional connectivity during development. The negative correlation that we observed between structure-function coupling and age may also indicate that communicability as the traffic pattern becomes insufficient in explaining how the functional connectivity arises from structural pathways in later stages of development. This might further suggest that the traffic pattern adopted by the brain is dynamic and develops with age, possibly becoming more complex during adolescence. Interestingly, our results indicated a lack of significant difference in structure-function coupling between sexes, with regard to both the kind of relationship between structural and functional connectivity (that is, communicability) and the strength of this relationship. Despite many reported differences both in the structural and functional connectivity between sexes, when studied separately, our result seems to suggest that the underlying mechanism of information processing in the brain is consistent between sexes.

7. Can structural connectomes be a fingerprint of a group or an individual: Connectomic consistency?

Within the last decade, several studies have demonstrated the presence of a relationship between structure and function of the brain, by using various approaches to quantify the magnitude of similarity between the two connectivity types. Pearson's correlation, for example, has been a frequently used measure that takes values between $[-1,1]$, where magnitudes closer to zero indicate dissimilarity while magnitudes closer to 1 indicate higher similarity, with the positive and negative signs indicating direct or inverse relationship, respectively. Structure-function coupling studies mainly demonstrated a correlation in the 0.3–0.65 range (Goni et al., 2014; Honey et al., 2010). Taking a positive attitude, these results indicate the presence of a moderate relationship between the two modalities. On the other hand, it also shows that the glass is half empty: structure cannot predict function fully. As mentioned in the previous section, this imperfection can be due to the limitations of proposed communication models in predicting function from structure, as certain traffic patterns (such as communicability) outperforms others, while still being incapable of predicting function perfectly. This partial success of currently available communication models makes one question whether a model that can fully predict function from structure exists, or whether the inherent difference between the nature of the two modalities is another limiting factor. Therefore, it is necessary to explore how much variation should be expected in structure and function.

Despite sharing several common features across people, connectomes are shown to be unique for individuals. This concept, which is referred to as connectome fingerprinting (Mars et al., 2018), has been evaluated on structural (Osher et al., 2016) and functional (Finn et al., 2015) connectomes, separately. These results have demonstrated that the two connectomes of a subject obtained from scans at different time points resemble each other more than they resemble the connectomes of other subjects, potentially identifying individuals. Since these studies have evaluated the structure and function of the brain separately, however, they do not provide a comparative answer to how much variation one should

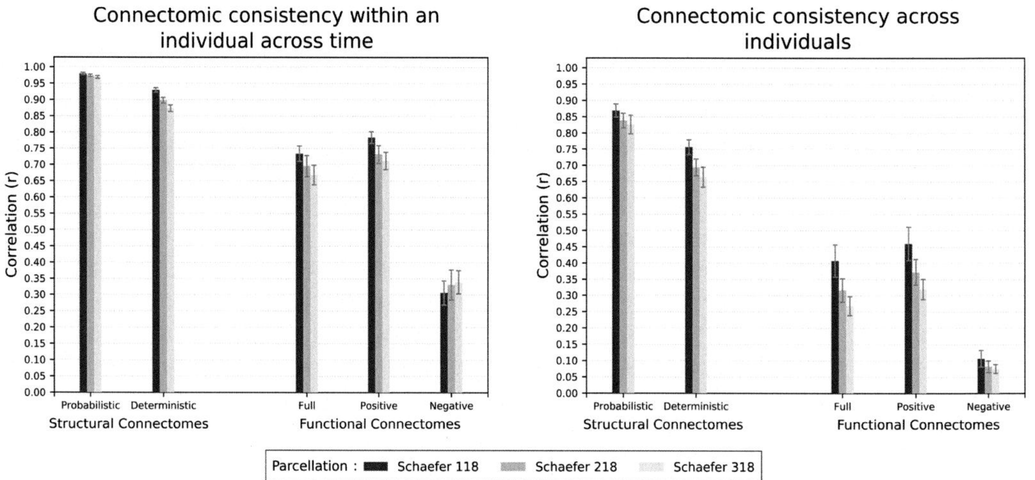

FIG. 4

Connectomic consistency: Structural connectomes demonstrated a higher consistency than functional connectomes both within an individual over time and between individuals. Consistency of both connectivity types were higher within an individual relative to across individuals. Interestingly, structural connectivity obtained via probabilistic tracking was observed to have higher consistency. Among all connectivity types, negative functional connectivity was observed to have the lowest consistency. This discrepancy of consistency highlights a potential source of imperfection for the structure-function coupling studies.

expect from each modality. Defining this concept of variation across connectomes as consistency, we recently made a comprehensive assessment of variation in structural and resting state functional connectomes that are derived from clinical dMRI and rs-fMRI scans in various flavors, both between people and within a single person across scans (Osmanlioglu et al., 2020).

We showed that structural connectomes are more consistent relative to functional connectomes (Fig. 4). Evaluating a longitudinal dataset on a single person and a cross-sectional dataset across a population, we further showed that the connectomic consistency of a single subject across time is higher than the consistency across a set of subjects. Lower consistency of function even for the same individual across time in contrast to the very high consistency of structural connectivity might indicate that, at the macroscale analysis of connectomics, a perfect prediction of function from structure might not be possible due to the dynamic nature of functional connectivity. In an analysis of structural connectomes, probabilistic tracking yielded more consistent structural connectomes relative to deterministic tracking. These results further highlight that consistency of connectomes also depends on how they are generated.

8. Measures derived from connectomes

Various measures have been derived from connectomes (Brain Connectivity Tool box (Rubinov and Sporns, 2010) and BRAPH (Mijalkov et al., 2017)) and have gained wide appeal because of the ease of computation. However, these do not account for topological differences in the network, that can only be

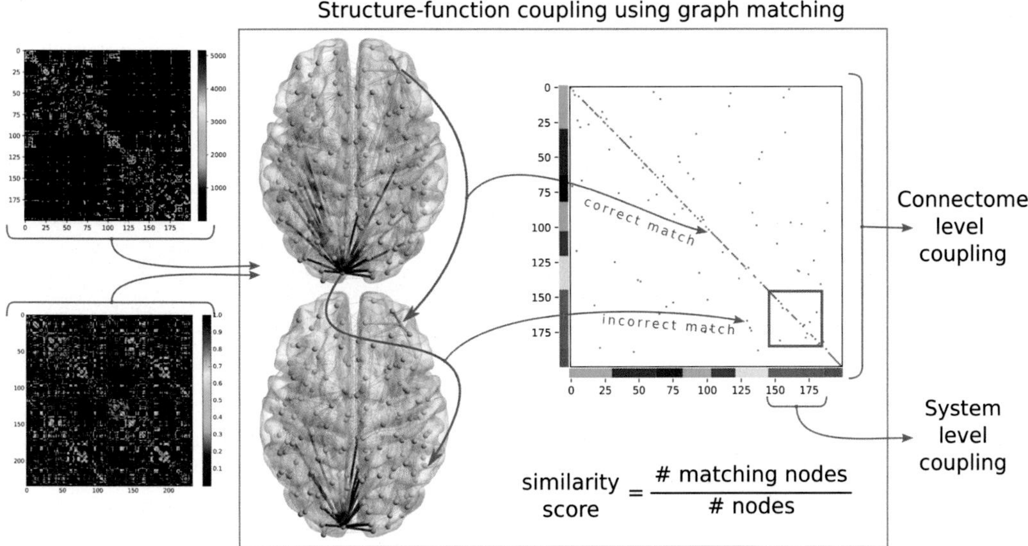

FIG. 5

A connectomic similarity measure evaluating topological properties of the brain networks: Given a structural and a functional connectome that are generated using the same parcellation, we considered them as graphs and calculated a matching between nodes that have similar connectivity signatures. We then calculated a connectome level coupling score as the fraction of the number of correctly matched nodes over the total number of nodes. We also calculated a system level coupling score by applying the same formula over subsets of nodes comprising functional systems.

elucidated when the brain is treated as a graph. In doing so, we have proposed a measure to evaluate structure-function coupling of the brain which considers the topological similarity among the two networks, in contrast to the most frequently used correlation approach that considers the similarity locally at the edge level (Fig. 5). This measure can be used to quantify the network rewiring of the brain.

9. Connectomics in action

Connectomic analysis of the brain has led to several breakthroughs in neuroscience and broadened our understanding of the most complex organ. Connectomes can be analyzed at the level of edges, using measures derived from connectomes and using graph theory constructs. The following provide an idea of the expansive possibilities that connectomes present, in terms of analysis, that can provide insight into the brain.

9.1 Population analysis using connectomes: Sex differences

Population based analysis using connectomes could be undertaken at various levels—statistical comparison at the level of each edge (edge-based analysis), on connectomic measures (as described in Section 8), and on subnetworks. Presented here are different approaches to investigating the sex

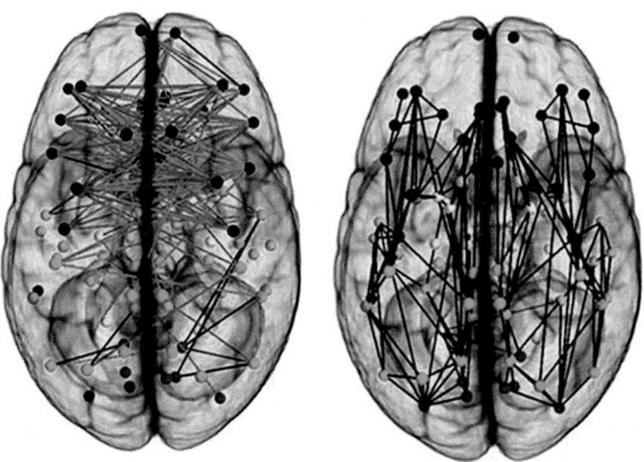

FIG. 6

Sex differences in the brain interrogated at the level of each edge. *The solid lines* indicate those that are statistically significant. *Orange lines* represent significantly higher connectivity in females and *blue edges* are significantly higher in males. As can be seen, females connect interhemispherically on average and males connect intrahemispherically.

Figure courtesy Ingalhalikar, M., et al., 2014. Sex differences in the structural connectome of the human brain. Proc. Natl. Acad. Sci. U. S. A. 111(2), 823–8.

differences during development, using connectomes. In addition to the actual results of the analysis, also presented are the interpretation of the findings with the aim of demonstrating the immense potential of connectomes.

The *first* question that a network-based investigation attempts to answer is whether there is a sex difference in the connectome. Using edge-based analysis on a large cross-sectional developmental samples of ~950 children, adolescents and young adults (ages 8–21 years) (Ingalhalikar et al., 2014), we showed that on average, there are significant differences between the sexes in their structural connectomes, indicating that the brain is wired differently. Additionally, there was increased interhemispheric connectivity in women and increased intrahemispheric connectivity in men (Fig. 6). The sex differences were found to be most prominent in the period of adolescence. A higher proportion of myelinated fibers within hemispheres in males compared with an equal or larger volume of WM in the callosum suggests that male brains are optimized for communicating within the hemispheres, whereas female brains are optimized for interhemispheric communication, although the opposite was observed in the cerebellum. Combining this with the results of the behavioral tasks performed by the subjects in the study, a greater intrahemispheric connectivity seemed to facilitate spatial processing in men (who outperform women, on average, in complex spatial tasks), and a greater interhemispheric connectivity seemed to facilitate the better average performance of women in verbal tasks. This study further emphasizes that although social factors may play a role, developmental sex differences suggest that some of the differences in symptom onset and severity may be due to differential vulnerabilities of maturing brain circuitry. From the perspective of developmental disorders, this raises a very interesting point. The differences in the developmental trajectories of the sexes, may be the reasons that, for example, autism is more prevalent in males, and the brain wiring of females may be neuro-protective.

Identification of such extensive connection-wise differences in structural networks, led to the investigation of topological properties of the network. Investigation of the properties of segregation and integration can reveal how the complex human behavioral repertoire emerges from simultaneous processes of segregated neuronal clusters and their integration during complicated cognitive tasks (Schwarz et al., 2008; Tononi et al., 1994). We measured the modularity of the network (Rubinov and Sporns, 2010), a measure of structural/functional segregation that quantifies the degree to which the network can be subdivided into densely interconnected groups of regions. A higher modularity means increased segregation of such groups of regions, as well as increased integration inside the groups, possibly pertaining to the functional specialization of neuronal clusters. Males showed significantly higher modularity compared with females, evident in all age ranges, indicating that this was not due to an effect of hormonal differences between the sexes. The high modularity in the males could be due to either increased intramodular or decreased intermodular connectivity in males. Simultaneously, increased intermodular connectivity in females could be possibly consequent to increased interhemispheric connectivity since the modular structure of the human brain is predominantly shaped by the hemispheres.

Finally, sex differences in the meso-scale architecture, specifically in *subnetworks*, of the connectome was investigated. A subnetwork is a collection of brain regions (nodes) and their connections (edges) that interact in order to perform a function (Ghanbari et al., 2014; Tunç et al., 2015). It was found that the alliance of brain regions forming the subnetworks does not differ significantly between males and females, indicating similar functional associations for the regions or that the same regions were recruited by the sexes in performing a function. This finding is crucial as it indicates that the network organization of male and female brains does not differ despite the significant difference in volume between the sexes. The bigger question is whether there is a difference in how these regions are recruited to perform a function. Analysis of these subnetworks revealed several functionally related differences between male and female groups. Consistent with the behavioral findings on sex differences (Moreno-Briseño et al., 2010; Gur et al., 2012), males had increased connectivity between motor and sensory (auditory) systems, along with increased connectivity in the fronto-parietal and cingulo-opercular systems that are traditionally associated with complex reasoning and control. Furthermore, males had higher connectivity in the integration of the default mode network (DMN) with subcortical and sensory (visual) systems. DMN has been associated with self-related and internal processes such as stimulus-independent thoughts and introspection, and in the integration of cognitive processes (Greicius et al., 2003). On the other hand, females had increased connectivity with subcortical regions, attention (both dorsal and ventral) systems and sensory (both visual and auditory) systems. The subcortical regions including amygdala, hypothalamus, hippocampus, dorsal striatum (caudate and putamen), ventral striatum (nucleus accumbens), thalamus and pallidum have been mainly associated with emotion processing, social cognition, and motivation. In agreement with these connectivity findings, improved socially relevant skills have been reported in females (Erwin et al., 1992; Williams et al., 2009). The integration between attention systems and sensory systems being stronger in females, was also consistent with behavioral literature (Gur et al., 2012). On investigating subnetworks based on their behavioral domains, males had higher connectivity between motor, executive functions and sensory (auditory) systems, and females had higher connectivity between reward, memory and sensory (auditory) systems. Higher memory performance in females has been extensively reported (Hedges and Nowell, 1995; Ramanan et al., 2012).

This body of work demonstrates the various ways connectomes can be used to interrogate a problem, in this case sex differences. However, the same combination of edge-based, network measures-based, and subnetwork-based analysis can be used to investigate any pathology-based effects.

9.2 Connectomic biomarkers of disease(s)

Connectomic analysis on patient populations (through the various ways discussed in Section 9.1) have revealed connectivity patterns characterizing several neuropsychiatric diseases and disorders (Kaiser, 2011). However, group-based analyses do not provide insight at the level of the individual, which is essential for precision medicine. This has led to the development of biomarkers. Connectomic biomarkers have been reported for various conditions include lowered connectivity in schizophrenia (Skudlarski et al., 2010), stronger local connectivity in Autism Spectrum Disorder (ASD) (Roine et al., 2015) and increased shortest path length and decreased global efficiency in Alzheimer's disease (Lo et al., 2010).

However, identifying connectomic biomarkers to assess disease severity of individuals is a task that is relatively more challenging than demonstrating group differences between patients and controls, especially for conditions with high heterogeneity across the patient population, and when the connectivity changes are not straightforward and involve rewiring of some form. Traumatic Brain Injury (TBI), a white matter disorder arising from axonal injuries due to causes such as falling, traffic accidents, or sports concussions, is a prime example of such heterogeneous diseases due to the variation of its potential cause across people (Johnson et al., 2013). Injury of axons in TBI causes disruptions in structural connectivity of the brain, interrupting neural communication, eventually leading to psychological, cognitive, and emotional disturbances (Schultz and Tate, 2013). Despite the TBI being a connectivity disorder (Hayes et al., 2016), connectomic measures that effectively quantify the injury burden of patients have only recently started to emerge (Imms et al., 2019; Solmaz et al., 2017; Kim et al., 2013).

Using matching accuracy (described above in Section 8), as the connectomic biomarker, we quantified the dissimilarity of the brain network of a TBI patient from that of healthy controls (Osmanlioglu et al., 2018b, 2021). Unlike traditional approaches that consider differences locally at individual edges, our graph matching based approach evaluates connectivity disruptions globally by evaluating the differences in the network topology. Over a cohort of 39 moderate-to-severe TBI patients and 35 healthy controls with longitudinal DTI acquired at 3, 6 and 12 months post injury (controls scanned once), we demonstrated that proposed measure distinguishes patients from controls (Fig. 7). We also showed that the structural dissimilarity score quantifies injury severity of individuals, as it significantly correlates with posttraumatic amnesia score of TBI patients. Our proposed measure also correlates with processing speed and executive functioning scores of the TBI patients, highlighting the ability of imaging to inform about cognitive outcomes of network disruptions in the disease.

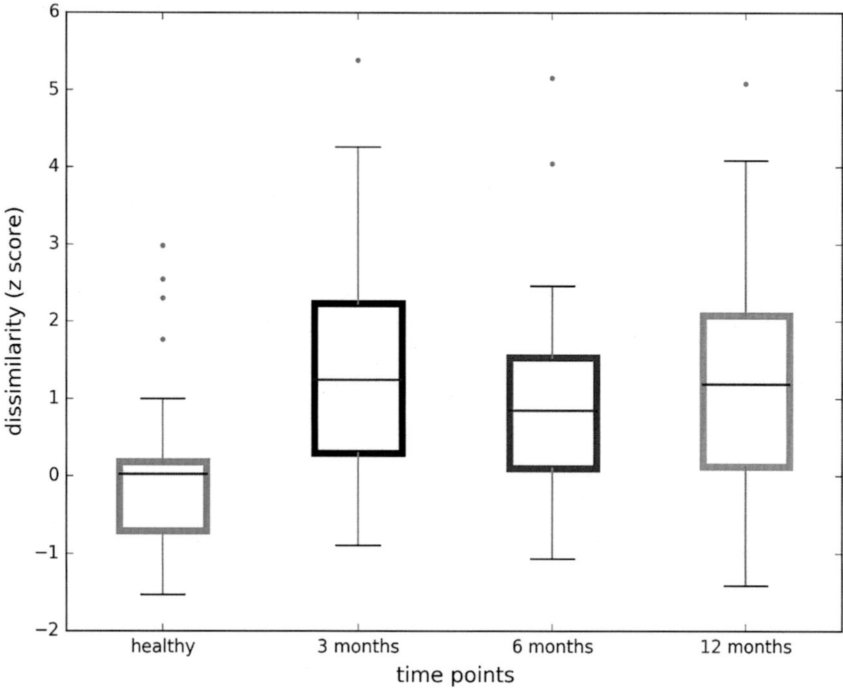

FIG. 7

Z-score of graph dissimilarity of subjects relative to healthy controls. Structural connectomic dissimilarity scores of patients are significantly different than controls at 3, 6 and 12 months post injury. Variation of dissimilarity was larger among patients relative to controls, highlighting the fact the marker was able to capture the heterogeneous nature of the disease.

9.3 Connectomics of brain tumors

In the previous two sections, we have discussed cases in which the brain is topologically intact, with only connections being rewired. In the case of tumors, its presence and later its absence after resection, makes the process of creating a connectome immensely challenging (Verma et al., 2018). Creating a connectome for tumors will revolutionize neuro-oncology. An enriched connectome with information from tissue microstructure and fMRI, will enable the surgeon to take a connectomic approach to surgery in which the effect of the resection of tumor and healthy tissue around the tumor region, can be known beforehand, enabling maximal resection with minimal current and future deficit, structurally, functionally, and behaviorally. Such a connectome will help understand the mechanism of plasticity as the tumor grows, or recurs, suggesting therapeutic intervention. This is expected to improve the quality of life considerably. However, creating such a connectome in the presence of tumors is challenging as the presence of tumor will affect the registration and hence the parcellation which is the primary step to creating the connectome. The methods that avoid registration to an atlas by obtaining subject specific parcellation (Honnorat et al., 2017), still fail around the tumor. Hence, tracking based on edema invariant tractography (Parker et al., 2020), using it to create a connectivity map of the brain, is an open area of research. Success of graph matching in identifying anomalies in TBI (Osmanlioglu et al., 2018a, b), suggests it as a promising tool to overcome the registration problem through mapping regions from a healthy brain into a brain with tumor. Once such a connectome is created, measures of injury like matching accuracy (described in Section 9.2), can be used to quantify the effect of WM removal, and that of radiation on the rest of the brain. Analysis at the subnetwork level of eloquent (motor, visual and language) and behavioral (executive functioning, working memory and other cognitive networks) subnetworks will pave the way of quantifying cognitive changes temporally. Surgical and radiation planning will improve with such a connectome, as it will be possible to know how the surgical path will affect the brain postsurgery, as well as determine a radiation plan that is least invasive. It also has the potential to predict functional outcome, which can be used as a prognostic tool to improve the quality of life of a patient.

10. Future of connectomics

From the perspective of systems neuroscience level, connectomics has great promise (Petersen and Sporns, 2015). Connectomics (Hagmann et al., 2010; Sporns, 2013) has also revolutionized brain research in the past decade, enabling research in sex differences (Ingalhalikar et al., 2014; Tunc et al., 2016), development (Fair et al., 2009) and psychopathology (van den Heuvel et al., 2013). However, its use in the clinic has been faced with many challenges. The primary one being that validating connectomes is not easy, and even though part of the blame can be ascribed to the lack of comprehensive validation of the tractography, it goes beyond that in connectomes. A comprehensive validation would require an edge-wise test of the connectome, which is practically impossible. As alternatives, the following can be undertaken: (i) validate any biomarker that has been created from the connectome by correlating with clinical scores. This will also establish their clinical meaningfulness; (ii) repeat the analysis using different ways of creating the connectome to demonstrate the robustness of the results; and (iii) test the hypothesis using multiple connectomic analyses, such as edge-wise, topological, and subnetwork-based, in order to assess the replicability of the result. Ideally, structural connectomes should be combined with functional connectomes to get a full picture of the disease.

References

Basser, P.J., et al., 2000. In vivo fiber tractography using DT-MRI data. Magn. Reson. Med. 44 (4), 625–632.

Bassett, D.S., Sporns, O., 2017. Network neuroscience. Nat. Neurosci. 20 (3), 353–364.

Behrens, T.E., et al., 2007. Probabilistic diffusion tractography with multiple fibre orientations: what can we gain? NeuroImage 34 (1), 144–155.

Bullmore, E., Sporns, O., 2012. The economy of brain network organization. Nat. Rev. Neurosci. 13 (5), 336–349.

Bullmore, E., et al., 2009. Generic aspects of complexity in brain imaging data and other biological systems. NeuroImage 47 (3), 1125–1134.

Calamante, F., 2019. The seven deadly sins of measuring brain structural connectivity using diffusion MRI streamlines fibre-tracking. Diagnostics 9 (3).

Catani, M., de Schotten, M.T., 2008. A diffusion tensor imaging tractography atlas for virtual in vivo dissections. Cortex 44 (8), 1105–1132.

Cheng, H., et al., 2012. Optimization of seed density in DTI tractography for structural networks. J. Neurosci. Methods 203 (1), 264–272.

Civier, O., et al., 2019. Is removal of weak connections necessary for graph-theoretical analysis of dense weighted structural connectomes from diffusion MRI? NeuroImage 194, 68–81.

Colon-Perez, L.M., et al., 2016. Small worldness in dense and weighted connectomes. Front. Phys. 4.

Contreras, J.A., et al., 2015. The structural and functional connectome and prediction of risk for cognitive impairment in older adults. Curr. Behav. Neurosci. Rep. 2 (4), 234–245.

Conturo, T.E., et al., 1999. Tracking neuronal fiber pathways in the living human brain. Proc. Natl. Acad. Sci. 96 (18), 10422–10427.

Craddock, R.C., et al., 2013. Imaging human connectomes at the macroscale. Nat. Methods 10 (6), 524–539.

Daducci, A., et al., 2015. COMMIT: convex optimization Modeling for microstructure informed tractography. IEEE Trans. Med. Imaging 34 (1), 246–257.

Davison, E.N., et al., 2016. Individual differences in dynamic functional brain connectivity across the human lifespan. PLoS Comput. Biol. 12 (11).

Descoteaux, M., 1999. High angular resolution diffusion imaging (HARDI). In: Encyclopedia of Electrical and Electronics Engineering. Wiley, pp. 1–25.

Descoteaux, M., et al., 2009. Deterministic and probabilistic tractography based on complex fibre orientation distributions. IEEE Trans. Med. Imaging 28 (2), 269–286.

Desikan, R.S., et al., 2006. An automated labeling system for subdividing the human cerebral cortex on MRI scans into gyral based regions of interest. NeuroImage 31 (3), 968–980.

Drakesmith, M., et al., 2015. Overcoming the effects of false positives and threshold bias in graph theoretical analyses of neuroimaging data. NeuroImage 118, 313–333.

Erwin, R.J., et al., 1992. Facial emotion discrimination: I. Task construction and behavioral findings in normal subjects. Psychiatry Res. 42, 231–240.

Estrada, E., Naomichi, H., 2008. Communicability in complex networks. Phys. Rev. 77, 036111.

Fair, D.A., et al., 2009. Functional brain networks develop from a "local to distributed" organization. PLoS Comput. Biol. 5 (5).

Farquharson, S., et al., 2013. White matter fiber tractography: why we need to move beyond DTI. J. Neurosurg. 118 (6), 1367–1377.

Finn, E.S., et al., 2015. Functional connectome fingerprinting: identifying individuals using patterns of brain connectivity. Nat. Neurosci. 18 (11), 1664–1671.

Fortin, J.P., et al., 2014. Functional normalization of 450k methylation array data improves replication in large cancer studies. Genome Biol. 15 (12), 503.

Fortin, J.P., et al., 2016. Removing inter-subject technical variability in magnetic resonance imaging studies. NeuroImage 132, 198–212.

Frigo, M., et al., 2020. Diffusion MRI tractography filtering techniques change the topology of structural connectomes. J. Neural Eng.

Friston, K.J., 2011. Functional and effective connectivity: a review. Brain Connect. 1 (1), 13–36.

Ghanbari, Y., et al., 2014. Identifying group discriminative and age regressive sub-networks from DTI-based connectivity via a unified framework of non-negative matrix factorization and graph embedding. Med. Image Anal. 18 (8), 1337–1348.

Girard, G., et al., 2014. Towards quantitative connectivity analysis: reducing tractography biases. NeuroImage 98C, 266–278.

Goni, J., et al., 2014. Resting-brain functional connectivity predicted by analytic measures of network communication. Proc. Natl. Acad. Sci. U. S. A. 111 (2), 833–838.

Greicius, M.D., et al., 2003. Functional connectivity in the resting brain: a network analysis of the default mode hypothesis. Proc. Natl. Acad. Sci. U. S. A. 100, 253–258.

Gur, R.C., et al., 2012. Age group and sex differences in performance on a computerized neurocognitive battery in children age 8-21. Neuropsychology 26 (2), 251–265.

Hagmann, P., et al., 2008. Mapping the structural core of human cerebral cortex. PLoS Biol. 6 (7), e159.

Hagmann, P., et al., 2010. MR connectomics: principles and challenges. J. Neurosci. Methods 194 (1), 34–45.

Hayes, J.P., Bigler, E.D., Verfaellie, M., 2016. Traumatic brain injury as a disorder of brain connectivity. J. Int. Neuropsychol. Soc. 22 (2).

Hedges, L.V., Nowell, A., 1995. Sex differences in mental test scores, variability, and numbers of high-scoring individuals. Science (New York, N.Y.) 269, 41–45.

Honey, C.J., Thivierge, J.-P., Sporns, O., 2010. Can structure predict function in the human brain? NeuroImage 52, 766–776.

Honnorat, N., Parker, D., Tunç, B., Davatzikos, C., Verma, R., 2017, September. Subject-specific structural parcellations based on randomized AB-divergences. In: International Conference on Medical Image Computing and Computer-Assisted Intervention. Springer, Cham, pp. 407–415.

Hulkower, M.B., et al., 2013. A decade of DTI in traumatic brain injury: 10 years and 100 articles later. AJNR Am. J. Neuroradiol. 34, 2064–2074.

Imms, P., et al., 2019. The structural connectome in traumatic brain injury: a meta-analysis of graph metrics. Neurosci. Biobehav. Rev. 99, 128–137.

Ingalhalikar, M., et al., 2014. Sex differences in the structural connectome of the human brain. Proc. Natl. Acad. Sci. U. S. A. 111 (2), 823–828.

Ismail, A.O., et al., 2018. Are Brain Networks Reproducible across Sites? In: ISMRM. Paris, France.

Jbabdi, S., Johansen-Berg, H., 2011. Tractography: where do we go from here? Brain Connect. 1 (3), 169–183.

Jeurissen, B., et al., 2019. Diffusion MRI fiber tractography of the brain. NMR Biomed. 32 (4).

Johansen-Berg, H., et al., 2004. Changes in connectivity profiles define functionally distinct regions in human medial frontal cortex. Proc. Natl Acad. Sci. USA 101 (36), 13335–13340.

Johnson, W.E., Li, C., Rabinovic, A., 2007. Adjusting batch effects in microarray expression data using empirical Bayes methods. Biostatistics 8 (1), 118–127.

Johnson, V.E., Stewart, W., Smith, D.H., 2013. Axonal pathology in traumatic brain injury. Exp. Neurol. 246, 35–43.

Jones, D.K., 2008a. Studying connections in the living human brain with diffusion MRI. Cortex 44 (8), 936–952.

Jones, D.K., 2008b. Tractography gone wild: probabilistic fibre tracking using the wild bootstrap with diffusion tensor MRI. IEEE Trans. Med. Imaging 27 (9), 1268–1274.

Kaiser, M., 2011. A tutorial in connectome analysis: topological and spatial features of brain networks. NeuroImage 57 (3), 892–907.

Khambhati, A.N., et al., 2018. Modeling and interpreting mesoscale network dynamics. NeuroImage 180, 337–349.

Kim, N., et al., 2013. Whole brain approaches for identification of microstructural abnormalities in individual patients: comparison of techniques applied to mild traumatic brain injury. PLoS ONE 8, e59382.

Lariviere, S., et al., 2019. Microstructure-informed connectomics: enriching large-scale descriptions of healthy and diseased brains. Brain Connect. 9 (2), 113–127.

Lebel, C., Benner, T., Beaulieu, C., 2012. Six is enough? Comparison of diffusion parameters measured using six or more diffusion-encoding gradient directions with deterministic tractography. Magn. Reson. Med. 68 (2), 474–483.

Leek, J.T., Storey, J.D., 2007. Capturing heterogeneity in gene expression studies by surrogate variable analysis. PLoS Genet. 3 (9), 1724–1735.

Li, L.C., et al., 2012. The effects of connection reconstruction method on the interregional connectivity of brain networks via diffusion tractography. Hum. Brain Mapp. 33 (8), 1894–1913.

Lo, C.Y., et al., 2010. Diffusion tensor tractography reveals abnormal topological organization in structural cortical networks in Alzheimer's disease. J. Neurosci. 30, 16876–16885.

Mars, R.B., Passingham, R.E., Jbabdi, S., 2018. Connectivity fingerprints: from areal descriptions to abstract spaces. Trends Cogn. Sci. 22 (11), 1026–1037.

Mijalkov, M., et al., 2017. BRAPH: a graph theory software for the analysis of brain connectivity. PLoS ONE 12 (8).

Mohanty, R., et al., 2020. Rethinking measures of functional connectivity via feature extraction. Sci. Rep. 10 (1).

Moreno-Briseño, P., et al., 2010. Sex-related differences in motor learning and performance. Behav. Brain Funct. 6, 74.

Osher, D.E., et al., 2016. Structural connectivity fingerprints predict cortical selectivity for multiple visual categories across cortex. Cereb. Cortex 26 (4), 1668–1683.

Osmanlioglu, Y., et al., 2017. A graph Based representation and similarity measure for multi-feature brain networks. In: OHBM. Vancouver, Canada.

Osmanlioglu, Y., et al., 2018a. A graph representation and similarity measures for brain networks with nodal features. In: Graphs in Biomedical Image Analysis and Integrating Medical Imaging and Non-Imaging Modalities, p. 1423.

Osmanlioglu, Y., et al., 2018b. A graph based similarity measure for assessing altered connectivity in traumatic brain injury. In: MICCAI. Brainlesion Workshop, to appear, Granada, Spain.

Osmanlioglu, Y., et al., 2019. System-level matching of structural and functional connectomes in the human brain. NeuroImage 199, 93–104.

Osmanlioglu, Y., et al., 2020. Connectomic consistency: a systematic stability analysis of structural and functional connectivity. J. Neural Eng. 17 (4), 045004.

Osmanlioglu, Y., Parker, D., Alappatt, J.A., Gugger, J.J., Diaz-Arrastia, R.R., Whyte, J., Kim, J.J., Verma, R., 2021. Connectomic assessment of injury burden and longitudinal structural network alterations in moderate-to-severe traumatic brain injury. bioRxiv. Submitted for publication.

Parker, D., et al., 2020. Freewater EstimatoR using iNtErpolated iniTialization (FERNET): characterizing peritumoral edema using clinically feasible diffusion MRI data. PLoS ONE.

Pasternak, O., et al., 2009. Free water elimination and mapping from diffusion MRI. Magn. Reson. Med. 62, 717–730.

Pestilli, F., et al., 2014. Evaluation and statistical inference for human connectomes. Nat. Methods 11 (10), 1058–1063.

Petersen, S.E., Sporns, O., 2015. Brain networks and cognitive architectures. Neuron 88 (1), 207–219.

Preti, M.G., Bolton, T.A., Van De Ville, D., 2017. The dynamic functional connectome: state-of-the-art and perspectives. NeuroImage 160, 41–54.

Qi, S.L., et al., 2015. The influence of construction methodology on structural brain network measures: a review. J. Neurosci. Methods 253, 170–182.

Raffelt, D., et al., 2012. Apparent fibre density: a novel measure for the analysis of diffusion-weighted magnetic resonance images. NeuroImage 59 (4), 3976–3994.

Ramanan, V.K., et al., 2012. Pathway analysis of genomic data: concepts, methods, and prospects for future development. Trends Genet. 28 (7), 323–332.

Roberts, J.A., et al., 2017. Consistency-based thresholding of the human connectome. NeuroImage 145, 118–129.

Roine, U., et al., 2015. Abnormal wiring of the connectome in adults with high-functioning autism spectrum disorder. Mol. Autism. 6 (1), 65.

Roine, T., et al., 2019. Reproducibility and intercorrelation of graph theoretical measures in structural brain connectivity networks. Med. Image Anal. 52, 56–67.

Rubinov, M., Sporns, O., 2010. Complex network measures of brain connectivity: uses and interpretations. NeuroImage 52 (3), 1059–1069.

Sarwar, T., Ramamohanarao, K., Zalesky, A., 2019. Mapping connectomes with diffusion MRI: deterministic or probabilistic tractography? Magn. Reson. Med. 81 (2), 1368–1384.

Schiavi, S., et al., 2020. A new method for accurate in vivo mapping of human brain connections using microstructural and anatomical information. Sci. Adv. 6 (31).

Schultz, R., Tate, R.L., 2013. Methodological issues in longitudinal research on cognitive recovery after traumatic brain injury: evidence from a systematic review. Brain Impair. 14 (3), 450–474.

Schwarz, A.J., Gozzi, A., Bifone, A., 2008. Community structure and modularity in networks of correlated brain activity. Magn. Reson. Imaging 26 (7), 914–920.

Skudlarski, P., et al., 2010. Brain connectivity is not only lower but different in schizophrenia: a combined anatomical and functional approach. Biol. Psychiatry 68 (1), 61–69.

Smith, R.E., et al., 2012. Anatomically-constrained tractography: improved diffusion MRI streamlines tractography through effective use of anatomical information. NeuroImage 62 (3), 1924–1938.

Smith, R.E., et al., 2013. SIFT: spherical-deconvolution informed filtering of tractograms. NeuroImage 67, 298–312.

Smith, R.E., et al., 2015a. SIFT2: enabling dense quantitative assessment of brain white matter connectivity using streamlines tractography. NeuroImage 119, 338–351.

Smith, R.E., et al., 2015b. The effects of SIFT on the reproducibility and biological accuracy of the structural connectome. NeuroImage 104, 253–265.

Solmaz, B., et al., 2017. Assessing connectivity related injury burden in diffuse traumatic brain injury. Hum. Brain Mapp. 38 (6), 2913–2922.

Sotiropoulos, S.N., Zalesky, A., 2019. Building connectomes using diffusion MRI: why, how and but. NMR Biomed. 32 (4).

Sporns, O., 2013. The human connectome: origins and challenges. NeuroImage 80, 53–61.

Sporns, O., Tononi, G., Kötter, R., 2005. The human connectome: a structural description of the human brain. PLoS Comput. Biol. 1 (4), e42.

Stejskal, E.O., Tanner, J.E., 1965. Spin diffusion measurements: spin echoes in the presence of a time-dependent field gradient. J. Chem. Phys. 42 (1), 288–292.

Tononi, G., Sporns, O., Edelman, G.M., 1994. A measure for brain complexity: relating functional segregation and integration in the nervous system. Proc. Natl. Acad. Sci. U. S. A. 91 (11), 5033–5037.

Tournier, J.D., et al., 2008. Resolving crossing fibres using constrained spherical deconvolution: validation using diffusion-weighted imaging phantom data. NeuroImage 42 (2), 617–625.

Tournier, J.-D., Mori, S., Leemans, A., 2011. Diffusion tensor imaging and beyond. Magn. Reson. Med. 65, 1532–1556.

Tunç, B., et al., 2015. Towards a quantified network portrait of a population. In: Information Processing in Medical Imaging (IPMI). Springer Lecture Notes Computer Science: Isle of Skye, Scotland.

Tunc, B., et al., 2016. Establishing a link between sex-related differences in the structural connectome and behaviour. Philos. Trans. R. Soc. Lond. Ser. B Biol. Sci. 371 (1688).

van den Heuvel, M.P., et al., 2013. Abnormal rich club organization and functional brain dynamics in schizophrenia. JAMA Psychiat. 70 (8), 783–792.

van den Heuvel, M.P., et al., 2015. Bridging cytoarchitectonics and connectomics in human cerebral cortex. J. Neurosci. 35 (41), 13943–13948.

Vasa, F., Bullmore, E.T., Patel, A.X., 2018. Probabilistic thresholding of functional connectomes: application to schizophrenia. NeuroImage 172, 326–340.

Verma, R., Osmanlioglu, Y., Ismail, A.A.O., 2018, September. Multimodal patho-connectomics of brain injury. In: International MICCAI Brainlesion Workshop. Springer, Cham, pp. 3–14.

Williams, L.M., et al., 2009. Explicit identification and implicit recognition of facial emotions: I. Age effects in males and females across 10 decades. J. Clin. Exp. Neuropsychol. 31, 257–277.

Yeh, C.H., et al., 2016. Correction for diffusion MRI fibre tracking biases: the consequences for structural connectomic metrics. NeuroImage 142, 150–162.

Yeo, B.T.T., et al., 2011. The organization of the human cerebral cortex estimated by intrinsic functional connectivity. J. Neurophysiol. 106 (3), 1125–1165.

Yeo, B.T.T., et al., 2014. Functional Specialization and Flexibility in Human Association Cortex. Cereb. Cortex.

Zajac, L., et al., 2017. Seed location impacts whole-brain structural network comparisons between healthy elderly and individuals with Alzheimer's disease. Brain Sci. 7 (4).

CHAPTER

Resting state functional connectivity in pediatric populations

4

Donna Y. Chen[a,b,*], Katherine C. Ji[a,*], Shruti Varshney[a], Rakibul Hafiz[a,b], and Bharat B. Biswal[a]
Department of Biomedical Engineering, New Jersey Institute of Technology, Newark, NJ, United States[a] Department of Biomedical Engineering, Rutgers Biomedical and Health Sciences, Newark, NJ, United States[b]

1. Introduction

The exploration and development of various neuroimaging methods in previous decades has promoted the emergence of research on normal and abnormal cognitive function, particularly in adult volunteers. However, neuroimaging research in pediatric populations is still lacking. An understanding of brain development in the pediatric population, including infants and children, is critical to understanding normal brain development and the prognosis of developmental diseases such as ADHD, ASD, and juvenile diabetes. Despite the various neuroimaging modalities used, functional magnetic resonance imaging (fMRI) is often preferred due to its high contrast and spatial resolution. One method of fMRI, resting state fMRI (rs-fMRI), has made it easier to study neural development of pediatric groups for the advantages it offers in eliminating methodological issues of scanning infants and children. rs-fMRI has been critical to developing the pediatric functional connectome, or an understanding of connections in the brain through different stages of development.

2. Pediatric brain imaging

Brain development in pediatric populations is marked by explosive growth and postnatal plasticity associated with epigenetic modifications. Thus, imaging pediatric populations through such critical stages of early development offers unprecedented opportunities to understand normal brain development and expansion of skills, such as language, motor, processing, communication, and musical skills (Overy et al., 2005). This is invaluable to understanding the developmental trajectory and prognosis of developmental disorders and may lead to more accurate diagnosis and treatment of diseases/disorders (Raschle et al., 2012). Early brain development in infants and children is characterized by the highest level of plasticity after childbirth, such that most neuropsychiatric disorders, such as schizophrenia, have been found to have been at least partially manifested from a milieu of various modifications related to a child's environment (Insel, 2010). Thus, examining plasticity in early brain development is

*These authors contributed equally to this work.

Handbook of Pediatric Brain Imaging. https://doi.org/10.1016/B978-0-12-816633-8.00005-3

crucial for identification of early risks that have the potential to alter a child's future development at the exact time when such neuropsychiatric and mental disorders may still be preventable (Gao et al., 2017; Beardslee et al., 2011).

Despite this, research in pediatric groups is less common than in adults, due in part to the practical challenges posed by pediatric imaging sessions as well as improper analysis of data (Raschle et al., 2012; Bookheimer, 2000). While adults can be instructed to stay still and follow task-based instructions, children may not be as compliant, and may be more anxious to enter scanners or perform tasks for long periods of time. Additionally, young populations are more prone to head motion that causes artifacts in data and can be difficult to correct in a standardized manner (Poldrack et al., 2002; Power et al., 2012). Due to distinct anatomical differences through a child's development, acquiring clear images of pediatric groups as well as pre and post analyses of data in pediatric groups has proven difficult. For example, results of previous studies indicate significant variability in gray and white matter development in children, such that segmentation cannot be standardized among pediatric populations (Wilke and Holland, 2003).

These challenges are especially important to consider when evaluating infant populations or children with brain disorders. Researchers must take particular care in devising exact comparisons and control conditions between samples of pediatric groups because the previously mentioned variables compound upon the experimental design in young children and infants (Bookheimer, 2000). Additionally, little is yet known regarding intra-regional functional connections that make up pediatric functional brain networks. Patient motion and other previously mentioned confounding variables related to experimental stimuli have precluded significant results regarding functional connectivity in the pediatric brain using fMRI (Mongerson et al., 2017). Resting-state functional magnetic resonance imaging (rs-fMRI), which collects data during restful-wake states or physiological, pharmacological, and clinically-induced unconscious states (Heine et al., 2012), offers a solution to this problem as it moves away from typical task-based fMRI studies in pediatric populations. Indeed, resting state networks (RSNs) produced from rs-fMRI, which describe patterns of large-scale intrinsic functional brain networks (Biswal et al., 1995), have been linked and exhibit similar functional networks that are activated or deactivated during task-based fMRI (Smith et al., 2009).

3. Resting state fMRI

3.1 What is resting state fMRI?

In order to better study the pediatric brain, various neuroimaging techniques including fMRI, positron emission tomography (PET), and functional near-infrared spectroscopy (fNIRS) have been used (Nagamitsu et al., 2012; Stanescu et al., 2013). In pediatric neuroimaging, functional MRI has emerged as the method of choice because of its nonionizing radiation in addition to its high contrast and spatial resolution (Ho et al., 2017). rs-fMRI focuses on the spontaneous low frequency blood-oxygen-level-dependent (BOLD) signal fluctuations of the resting brain (<0.1 Hz), which is used as a neurophysiological measure (Biswal et al., 1995; Fox and Raichle, 2007). Initially believed to be noise that contained no useful information, it was removed prior to any analysis. However, the low frequency signals of the brain at rest were found to be correlated between functionally related regions of the brain, which led to the increased attention for rs-fMRI (Biswal, 2012). Resting state fMRI is different from the more traditional task-based fMRI technique, in that the subject being scanned does not have to perform any tasks to induce neural activation and the subject can simply lay down in the scanner, essentially at rest while in an awake state. This is favorable for pediatric populations, since children may not perform well on or understand certain task paradigms, especially if the tasks require great cognitive demands, or the children may be more comfortable and prefer to be at rest. Another advantage of rs-fMRI over task-based fMRI is that the measurements provide insight on the brain in a more neutral environment, since there is no specific task-based activation, where a response is expected based on the task given (Hohenfeld et al., 2018). In other words, instead of focusing on the extrinsic organization of the brain, or the response to an external stimulus, rs-fMRI focuses on the intrinsic organization of the brain, which reflects baseline neuronal activity.

Several methods are used in collecting rs-fMRI data, where subjects either have their eyes closed, eyes open, or eyes fixated on a crosshair, while in a rested state. Greater reliability in connectivity has been found in the method of fixation on a crosshair, within various networks such as the default-mode, attention, and auditory networks, which will be discussed later; however, the primary visual network showed greatest reliability in subjects that had their eyes open and not fixated on a crosshair (Patriat et al., 2013). The standard rs-fMRI scan duration for which subjects are at rest is 5–7 min; however, increasing the duration to 9–13 min or longer has been shown to improve reliability measures in functional connectivity, which is not due to the increased number of time points, but rather the scan length itself, to reach steady-state (Birn et al., 2013). Therefore, in choosing the ideal rs-fMRI data collection method, one must consider the rest condition in addition to scan duration for greatest reliability. Furthermore, regions of the brain exhibiting high levels of functional connectivity have been shown to exhibit the highest degree of reliability, showing the fundamental organization of the brain, being reliable not only intra-session, but also inter-session (Shehzad et al., 2009; ,Chou et al., 2012). The reproducible and reliable rs-fMRI results allow for the ongoing and increasing usage of rs-fMRI in various studies ranging from the adult to pediatric population, greatly enhancing our understanding of the brain in neurologically diseased and healthy populations.

3.2 Resting state networks

Using multivariate statistical methods, such as independent component analysis (ICA), allows for the grouping of brain regions into networks and consequently, various resting state networks (RSNs) (Fig. 1). One of the first resting state networks identified was the sensorimotor network (Biswal et al., 1995). There are various RSNs, such as the visual, language, and motor, but in certain regions of the brain, the BOLD activities have been found to be higher in rest than in the task state (Damoiseaux et al., 2006). Thus, there exists regions of the brain with correlated activity during rest, as well as regions with higher levels of activity during rest than in task, such as the default mode network (DMN), which is not only active during rest, but deactivated during periods of specific goal-oriented tasks (Raichle et al., 2001).

3.2.1 Sensorimotor network

The sensorimotor network (SMN), as its name suggests, includes the somatosensory and motor regions of the brain. The SMN was one of the earliest RSNs defined, where functional connectivity was observed in opposite sensorimotor cortices of the brain at rest (Ho et al., 2017). More specifically, the SMN is comprised of the primary and secondary somatosensory cortices (S1,S2), premotor cortex

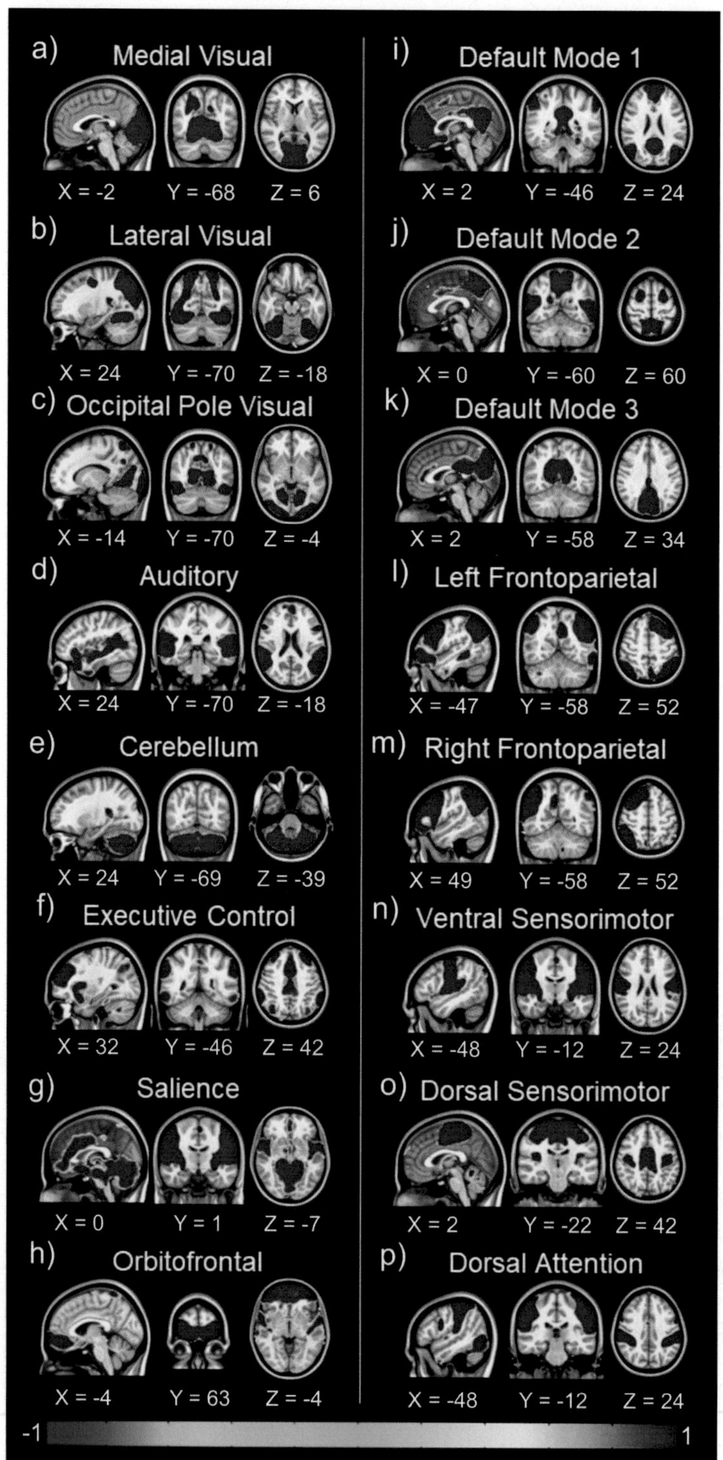

FIG. 1

Independent component analysis (ICA) performed on a dataset from Autism Brain Imaging Data Exchange (ABIDE) initiative. SPM12 and AFNI were used for preprocessing on 115 subjects, and then ICA analysis performed using FSL's MELODIC. The RSNs were subject to a threshold of 0.95. (A), (B), and (C) represent three common visual networks;

(Continued)

(PMC), primary motor cortex (M1), and supplementary motor area (SMA) (Zhang et al., 2017). The SMN of pediatric populations, among other networks, shows high spatial concordance with the SMN seen in adults (Thornburgh et al., 2017). Changes in connectivity have been demonstrated in both sensory and motor areas obtained during resting state conditions, just after 1 h of force-field learning, where robotic forces are applied to movement-based learning (Vahdat et al., 2011). The SMN includes both the sensory and motor regions of the brain, as motor activities often occur in response to a sensory input. Thus, not only do RSNs interact with each other, but the regions associated within an RSN often behave in a coupled manner, further supporting the dynamic nature of the brain.

3.2.2 Default mode network

The default mode network (DMN) is considered a very prominent RSN, first discovered by using positron emission tomography (PET), and later with fMRI, being linked to stimulus-independent thoughts and mind-wandering (Raichle et al., 2001; Shulman et al., 1997; Mason et al., 2007; Greicius et al., 2003). Major regions often associated with the DMN include the ventral medial prefrontal cortex (vMPFC), the dorsal medial prefrontal cortex (dMPFC), the posterior cingulate cortex (PCC), and the inferior parietal lobule (IPL) (Raichle, 2015; Buckner et al., 2008). In attention deficit hyperactivity disorder (ADHD), there is a positive correlation between ADHD severity and connectivity in the DMN nodes (van Rooij et al., 2015). In addition to ADHD, major depressive disorder (MDD) patients have been shown to have increased functional connectivity in the DMN at rest, which correlated with behavioral measures of rumination (Berman et al., 2011). Therefore, although the DMN is associated with the reflective states of oneself, it is also associated with the more negative ruminations that may occur. The DMN also plays a role in working memory, emotional processing, and cognitive functions (Mohan et al., 2016). Moreover, the DMN is incompletely developed at 2-weeks of age, but at 2 years of age, the DMN in healthy pediatric populations closely resembles the DMN of healthy adults (Gao et al., 2009).

3.2.3 Executive control network

The executive control network (ECN) consists of the following regions of the brain: the bilateral middle, inferior and superior frontal cortices, bilateral inferior parietal lobules, anterior cingulate cortex (ACC)/supplementary motor area (SMA), and bilateral insular cortices (Heine et al., 2012). While the DMN is associated with more internal thoughts, the ECN is associated with more externally demanded thoughts (Ng et al., 2016). Studies have found that in addition to the functional connectivity being altered in the DMN of patients with MDD, altered functional connectivity is also found in the ECN of patients with MDD, where the anterior cingulate cortex and thalamus show increased functional connectivity, and the superior frontal gyrus of the ECN shows decreased functional connectivity (Zhao et al., 2019). Thus, altered functional connectivity is not only found in single brain networks, but often multiple in the case of neurological disorders. The brain is a highly dynamic system where a single network is not solely activated in many cases, such as in divergent thinking, or creative thinking,

FIG. 1, CONT'D (D) is the auditory network; (E) is the cerebellum network; (F) shows the executive control network, bilaterally; (G) is the salience network; (H) is the orbitofrontal network; (I, J, K) shows three main default mode networks that consist of the anterior and posterior cingulate cortex, medial prefrontal cortex, and angular gyrus, respectively; (L) left and (M) right frontoparietal networks are shown; (N) is the ventral and (O) dorsal sensorimotor networks; and lastly, (P) is the dorsal attention network.

where the coupling of both the DMN and ECN occur (Beaty et al., 2015). The executive control network has been found in children and adolescents, with stable ECN maps over the course of 2–3 years showing high levels of reliability (Thomason et al., 2011).

3.2.4 Salience network

The salience network (SN) is mainly composed of the dorsal anterior cingulate cortex (dACC) and the orbital fronto-insula (FI), which activates in response to tasks of personal salience or importance, either cognitive, homeostatic, or emotional (Seeley et al., 2007). The dACC is involved in cognitive control, whereas the anterior right insula (aRI) plays a role in detecting errors, both working coactively (Ham et al., 2013). Furthermore, there is a significant interaction between negative moods and memory modulation in the SN, which is consistent with studies showing that post-traumatic stress disorder (PTSD) patients have greater functional connectivity in the SN, where a negative experience or mood elicits strong painful memories (Rabinak et al., 2011; Andreano et al., 2017). Thus, higher levels of functional connectivity in the SN allows for stronger memory consolidation, however, those memories may have negative associations with them.

3.2.5 Auditory network

The main regions of the auditory network include the Heschl gyrus, primary and associative auditory cortices, superior temporal, and insular cortices (Damoiseaux et al., 2006; Maudoux et al., 2012a). In patients suffering from tinnitus, the perception of sound in the absence of sound input, modified functional connectivity has been observed in the auditory resting state network, where tinnitus patients have increased functional connectivity between the auditory cortices and left parahippocampal region (Maudoux et al., 2012b). By studying the functional connectivity in the resting brain's auditory network, the intrinsic basis of tinnitus or hearing-loss is better understood. Hearing loss is difficult to study extrinsically because the input of a sound to a subject may go unnoticed due to the subject's hearing condition. Thus, this is an area where resting-state fMRI is advantageous in studying the intrinsic brain functions of those with hearing loss, since the subjects are simply scanned at rest.

3.2.6 Visual network

The visual network is comprised of the following regions of the brain: the peristriate, lateral, and superior occipital gyrus (Damoiseaux et al., 2006). Interestingly, a study found that alcohol administration increases the resting state functional connectivity strength of the visual network, where other RSNs did not exhibit the same increase, suggesting the visual cortex being selectively and primarily targeted in acute alcohol administration (Esposito et al., 2010). Furthermore, in children aged 8–12 years old with reading difficulties who were trained through a computerized training program—the Reading Acceleration Program, training resulted in increases in resting state functional connectivity between visual and cognitive-control networks (Horowitz-Kraus et al., 2015). Thus, the study of RSNs can also be applied to evaluations of the effectiveness of certain acceleration programs, such as reading training programs.

3.2.7 Frontoparietal network

The frontoparietal network (FPN) is regarded as a functional hub, in that it engages strongly with other functional brain networks, with studies showing significant positive correlation between the integration of the FPN and overall cognitive ability (Marek and Dosenbach, 2018). The FPN is involved in attention, executive, and cognitive control and includes the bilateral dorsolateral prefrontal gyri, inferior parietal lobule, and superior parietal lobule (Dixon et al., 2018). In children with ADHD, there is aberrant functional connectivity in the FPN, which is associated with impulsivity and defiance (Lin et al., 2015).

3.2.8 Cerebellar network

The cerebellar network is comprised of the cerebellum, as its name suggests. It carries a diverse range of functions, from motor and coordination skills, to working memory, executive functions, emotional learning, and feeding behavior (Amianto et al., 2013; Bernard et al., 2012; D'Angelo et al., 2011). Connectivity within the cerebellum of healthy infants is greater than that of healthy adults, with similarities in the intra- and cortico-cerebellar functional connectivity existing between both groups (Herzmann et al., 2019). The same study showed that in premature infants, reduced functional connectivity in the cerebellar network is apparent. Furthermore, in children and adolescents with autism spectrum disorder (ASD), aberrant connectivity is observed in the cerebellum, when compared with typically developing (TD) children and adolescents (Hanaie et al., 2018). Thus, cerebellar network connectivity is important in the study of normally and abnormally developing pediatric brains.

3.3 Resting state functional connectivity

Functional connectivity (FC) is typically defined as the temporal correlation between neurophysiological activities in different regions of the brain that are anatomically separate, while resting state functional connectivity (RSFC) is FC obtained from rs-fMRI data (Friston et al., 1993; Friston, 1994). Essentially, the brain recruits different regions which functionally communicate with each other. To measure functional connectivity, various methods for analysis and quantification can be used, such as correlation, mutual information, coherence, Granger causality, transfer entropy, and generalized synchronization, among many other different types of methods (Wang et al., 2014). Based on the data at hand, different methods of analysis can be chosen. Applying various methods to rs-fMRI data allows one to obtain multiple RSFC metrics, where the brain connectivity in subjects at rest can be more comprehensively studied, and ultimately a functional connectivity map of the whole brain or specific regions of the brain can be obtained. On the other hand, task-fMRI studies mostly focus on specific regions of the brain and seldomly the whole brain. RSFC maps have also been shown to reveal more activated areas related to the primary motor cortex than the functional connectivity maps from task-fMRI (Xiong et al., 1999).

3.4 The functional connectome

The idea of collecting all the functional connections of the human brain gave rise to the term, "functional connectome". The 1000 Functional Connectomes Project has pooled rs-fMRI data from many different brain imaging centers across the world (Biswal et al., 2010). By pooling such a large dataset, the presence of a commonly shared architecture of the functional connectome could be established, in addition to seeing the differences that may arise between different functional connectomes. Variability between individuals' functional connectivity maps have been shown, particularly in the frontal, temporal, and parietal association cortex areas, which are associated with reasoning and language (Mueller et al., 2013). With variability existing between individuals, it is advantageous to create specific personalized identifications of the functional connectomes of different individuals. This sort of fingerprinting of an individual's functional connectome led to the term, "connectotype", with individual functional connectome variability also being found in nonhuman primates (Finn et al., 2015; Miranda-Dominguez et al., 2014).

Similar to the 1000 Functional Connectomes Project, other large public data repositories include the Human Connectome Project (HCP), Brain Genomics Superstruct project (GSP), IMAGEN, and the Chinese Color Nest project (CCNP), which aim to compare individual brain circuits, behavior, and genetics, using various adult populations (Van Essen et al., 2013; Yang et al., 2017; Schumann et al., 2010; Holmes et al., 2015). Thus, the emergence of large public data repositories of fMRI data has allowed for greater study of functional connectivity, not only on a group-level, but also on a more specific subject-level. The optimization of identifying specific individuals based on their functional connectomes is also a matter of interest, in order to develop individualized treatments or study individual differences (Dubois and Adolphs, 2016), which has been shown to be stable within an individual over months to years (Amico and Goni, 2018; Horien et al., 2019). The goal of these studies is to eventually translate to the clinical realm, where the identification of various distinct functional connectomes can be used as biomarkers for neurological and psychiatric illnesses, with the following properties being of high importance: validity, reliability, sensitivity, and specificity (Castellanos et al., 2013). Additionally, studies on the functional connectome can start as early as in the womb, in prenatal rs-fMRI scans, with one study showing the alteration of the functional connectome in developing brains from prenatal stress exposure (Scheinost et al., 2017).

3.5 Processing methods in resting state fMRI

3.5.1 Preprocessing of rs-fMRI data

From rs-fMRI scans, raw data is obtained. In order to accurately analyze the data, preprocessing must first be performed, since the raw data is usually noisy due to unwanted artifacts. Preprocessing steps may vary from study to study, but certain core traits are shared between different preprocessing pipelines in rs-fMRI. A general preprocessing scheme will usually contain the following parameters: removal of the first few volumes for T1 stabilization, slice time correction to account for any temporal delays, head motion correction, intensity normalization, coregistration, nuisance variable removal, temporal filtering, and spatial smoothing (Park et al., 2019). The steps of the preprocessing pipeline each aim to improve signal detection for accurate scan results (Ge et al., 2017). Variations in preprocessing pipelines may be due to differences in experimental conditions, magnetic field strength, and pulse sequence type, such as: echo planar imaging or spiral imaging (Strother, 2006). Therefore, it is crucial to choose the correct preprocessing pipeline based on those parameters. Available software packages exist to perform processing of fMRI data, such as SPM, AFNI, FSL, DPARSF, and REST.

After the first few time points have been removed, the functional and anatomical images are aligned to a predetermined origin, commonly the anterior commissure in the white matter tract. Post reorientation, motion correction aims to reduce the effects of any head motion, including three translational motions and three rotational motions. These motion parameters are determined using a least-squares approach and are later removed during nuisance regression. Then, the realigned functional image is coregistered to the anatomical image by first aligning a mean of the functional images to the anatomical image to generate a matrix, which can then be applied to the original functional dataset.

Once the images are aligned, the anatomical image is segmented into probability maps containing gray matter (GM), white matter (WM), cerebrospinal fluid (CSF), blood vessels, and nonbrain tissue. All functional images and segmented anatomical images are normalized, or deformed, into the same 3D space defined by a brain template. There are a few existing templates that can be used to normalize these datasets, such as the Montreal Neurological Institute (MNI) adult template used to generate Figs. 1–3. Pediatric datasets cannot use templates such as the MNI template because of the changes in brain connectivity and structure during adolescence. Thus, many studies often use either a study-specific template that is generated during preprocessing or use study-specific templates created by other research groups, such as the Japanese and Chinese children templates (Weng et al., 2015). The motion parameters from realignment are used to create a total of 24 parameters: 6 head motion parameters, 6 head motion parameters from a previous time point, and 12 corresponding quadratic parameters. Additionally, the first five principal components from the CSF and WM can be used as regressors to remove high frequency and physiological noises. The final step in preprocessing is typically filtering and smoothing all datasets (Fig. 2). A bandpass filter restricts the signal to frequencies between 0.01 and 0.1 Hz; these signals are generally of interest in rs-fMRI. Then, spatial smoothing of the

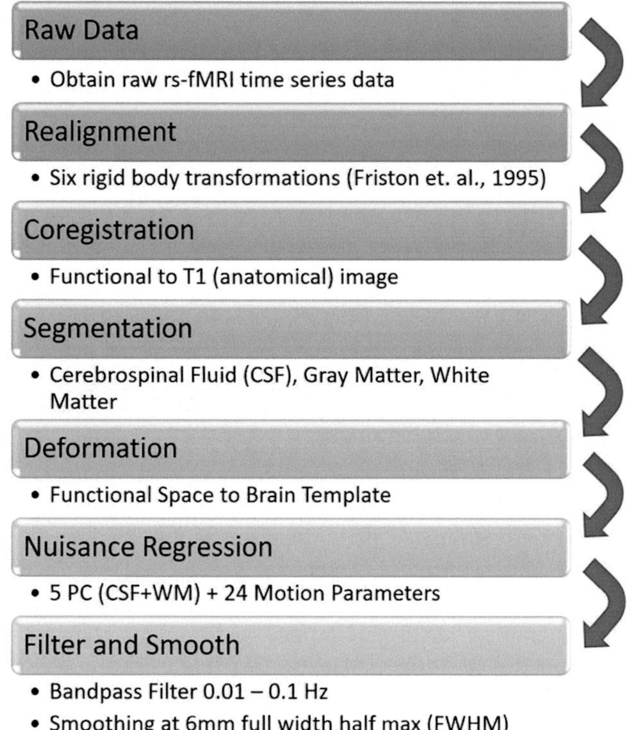

FIG. 2

Preprocessing pipeline of rs-fMRI data, covering the following steps in order: obtaining raw data, realignment, coregistration, segmentation, deformation, nuisance regression, and filtering and smoothing.

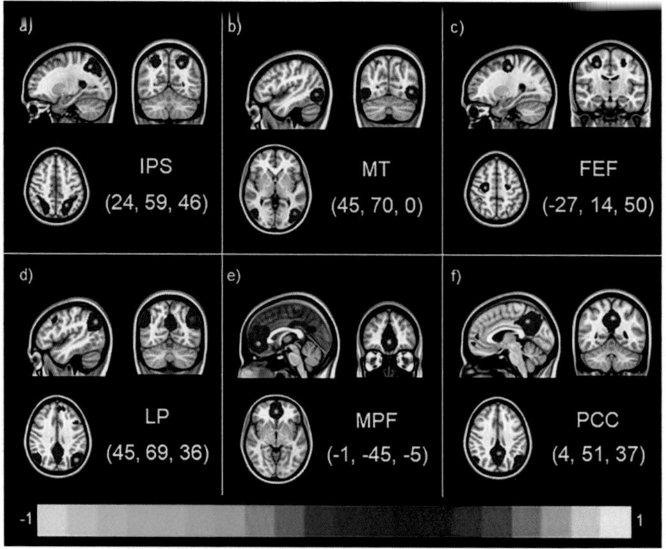

FIG. 3

115 Control subjects from the Autism Brain Imaging Data Exchange (ABIDE) initiative were preprocessed using SPM12 and AFNI. Seed correlation analysis was performed using AFNI at six regions of interest (ROIs): (A) the intraparietal sulcus, (B) the middle temporal region, (C) the right frontal eye field, (D) the left lateral parietal cortex, (E) the medial prefrontal cortex, and (F) the posterior cingulate cortex. MNI coordinates are shown.

images blurs the images, in which the degree of blurring can be adjusted depending on the experiment, and the information retrieved at each voxel produces a smooth image of the brain that can be analyzed without interference from the signal-to-noise ratio (Karunakaran et al., 2020).

3.5.2 RSFC analysis methods

After preprocessing all the rs-fMRI images across multiple subjects in an identical fashion, various RSFC analysis methods can be applied. These methods include, but are not limited to: seed-based analysis, frequency based analysis including ALFF and fALFF, multivariate analysis including principal component analysis (PCA), independent component analysis (ICA), and clustering (van den Heuvel and Hulshoff Pol, 2010). One of the first methods used to test for RSFC was the use of seed-based analysis, where a specific region of interest (ROI) or "seed" is chosen on the brain and the activity of that particular seed is correlated with all the other voxels of the brain (Fig. 3) (Biswal et al., 1995). However, since the user is choosing the seed, an a priori hypothesis is needed, making the ROI dependent on the user's choice. This yields a seed-based FC map, which shows regions that are highly correlated (Biswal, 2012). A seed-based analysis can be difficult to apply to the functional connectome of the whole brain, and selection of the ROI may require prior training in neuroanatomy (Azeez and Biswal, 2017).

Alternatively, voxel based analyses can be used to quantify the amplitude of low frequency fluctuations (ALFF) and the fractional amplitude of low frequency fluctuations (fALFF) (Smitha et al.,

2017). ALFF is used to determine the relationship between low-frequency fluctuations and functional connectivity. However, it is often corrupted by background noise and has a tendency to display false results at the edge of the brain; fALFF was developed to solve these issues (Zou et al., 2008). Resting state physiological fluctuation of amplitude (RSFA) on the other hand, calculates the standard deviation of the low frequency BOLD signal (Kannurpatti and Biswal, 2008). Another method of voxel-based analysis focuses on the similarities in the time series of a particular voxel with that of its neighbors (Smitha et al., 2017). This is referred to as regional homogeneity, also known as ReHo, which assumes that a voxel is temporally correlated with its surrounding voxels and that any changes to this pattern are significant (Fig. 4) (Zang et al., 2004). Kendall's correlation coefficient, sometimes referred to as the Kendall coefficient of concordance, is used in ReHo to determine the similarity between the time series of multiple voxels. It is important to note that while extensive smoothing during preprocessing can affect the results from this method, ReHo is generally robust against influences from background noise (Azeez and Biswal, 2017).

Another method for analyzing RSFC is using ICA (Fig.1), which is a multivariate data-driven approach, unlike seed-based analysis which is a hypothesis-driven approach. The benefit of ICA being a data-driven approach is that it does not require an a priori hypothesis targeting an unknown or unpredictable brain activity region of interest, therefore a data-driven approach is sometimes preferred (McKeown et al., 2003). An ICA algorithm decomposes the fMRI data into various separate independent components, with each independent component consisting of a spatial map and the time course of activation (McKeown et al., 1998). Using these maps, one is able to see which components contribute to the fMRI data.

4. Resting state fMRI in pediatrics

Due to a large area of clinical research being focused on pediatrics, rs-fMRI quickly transitioned from being used in the adult population to the pediatric population. Functional connectivity has been shown to exist not only in adult populations, but also in pediatric populations where various pediatric resting state networks have been defined. The resting state networks of an infant include the visual, sensorimotor, and auditory regions, which share similarities with the patterns of adult resting state networks (Fransson et al., 2007). Yet despite the similarities in the resting state networks in both pediatric and adult populations, differences are also apparent, specifically in the default mode network, where children have a more fragmented default mode network, which becomes more integrated over time due to development (Fair et al., 2008). Investigating the resting state networks of the pediatric brain may provide us with insight into the different brain networks and functions of the pediatric population, and can also allow us to study the development of various brain regions over time, starting from a very young age. The brain regions of children communicate in a more localized manner, but over the course of development, these brain regions begin to communicate in a more distributed manner, with longer-range functional connections (Fair et al., 2009).

The use of ICA in obtaining the RSNs of children has shown to be robust, with the RSNs typically found in adults also being present in children aged 6–10 years old, and certain areas such as parts of the brainstem showing up over 98% of the time in repeated ICA (Muetzel et al., 2016). Alternatively, seed-based analyses have also been used in rs-fMRI studies on epileptic pediatric patients, where connectivity in the temporal lobe seeds was analyzed and showed significant differences (Grassia et al., 2018). Another study focusing on children with epilepsy, or more specifically, infantile spasms (IS),

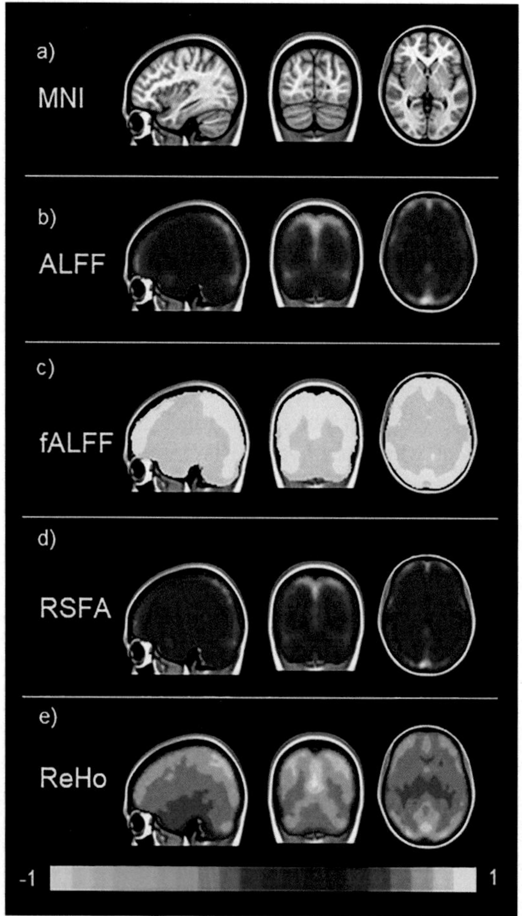

FIG. 4

Images taken from the Autism Brain Imaging Data Exchange (ABIDE) initiative, at the MNI coordinates (36,78,0) without thresholding, show (A) the anatomical image derived from an MNI template, (B) the amplitude of low frequency fluctuations (ALFF), (C) the fractional amplitude of low frequency fluctuations (fALFF), (D) the resting state fluctuation amplitude (RSFA), and (E) regional homogeneity (ReHo) analyses performed using AFNI. The results from AFNI were statistically analyzed using SPM12's *t*-test function. The dataset represents 115 control subjects and were preprocessed using SPM12 and AFNI.

performed ALFF to discover the driving mechanism behind IS, where lower ALFF signals within the DMN of pediatric patients with IS was found (Wang et al., 2017). ReHo has also been examined in pediatric populations, such as pediatric bipolar disorder (PBD), where patients with PBD showed alterations in ReHo measures in the bilateral hippocampus and anterior cingulate gyrus (Xiao et al., 2013). Many different rs-fMRI analyses have been incorporated into pediatric studies, showing reliable results.

4.1 Resting state fMRI for pediatric brain disorders

The goal of many studies related to pediatric imaging with rs-fMRI techniques, beyond analyzing differences between pediatric brains and adult brains, is to identify biomarkers for specific neurological and psychiatric illnesses to serve as clinical diagnostic tools. These disorders alter functional connectivity and can be recognized during processing. These neurological and psychiatric disorders include attention deficit hyperactivity disorder (ADHD), autism spectrum disorder (ASD), type 1 diabetes, fetal alcohol syndrome (FAS), etc. While there are many pediatric disorders that have been examined using rs-fMRI, a few of the prominent focuses of this field are highlighted in this section. Each of these conditions have been shown to affect the resting state functional connectivity patterns of the patient in different ways.

4.1.1 Attention deficit hyperactivity disorder

Attention deficit hyperactivity disorder (ADHD) is a commonly diagnosed pediatric disorder that results in unsuitable levels of attention, organization, activity, and impulse. ADHD heavily affects vigilant attention, a neurological function that maintains focus during uninteresting or trivial situations. A research study compared the vigilant attention resting state functional network of patients with ADHD with a healthy control group and determined that there are several connections in this network that are significantly different as a result of this disorder. The network appears as a collection of sub-networks rather than a single functional connection (Zepf et al., 2019). Other research studies have focused primarily on the default mode network (DMN), cognitive control networks, and salience network. These networks are critical portions of the functional connectome that work in tandem during attention-requiring tasks. Irregularities within either of these networks or their ability to work together has been correlated with fluctuating attention and lapses in attention. Comparison between ADHD patients and control group participants show that those with this disorder demonstrate difficulty with tasks that require the DMN to work with the other networks. Therefore, ADHD is often termed as a DMN disorder (Kaboodvand et al., 2020).

4.1.2 Autism Spectrum disorder

Autism spectrum disorder (ASD) is a neurological condition that develops early in childhood and affects the individual throughout his or her life. Patients with this condition often exhibit difficulties with social interaction, motor coordination, obsessive, or repetitive behaviors but exact symptoms vary from person to person. Resting state fMRI studies have shown aberrant connectivity within the cortico-cortical networks that support language, working memory, visual attention, and social cognition in patients with ASD compared to individuals with typical connectivity. This research has also shown increased functional connectivity between sensory networks and subcortical networks, and the strength of this connection was found to be correlated with the severity of the symptoms caused by ASD. These results suggest that atypical sensory processing caused by ASD could be the result of the increased influence of environmental sensory features on information processing that could possibly overwrite some cognitive processes (Cerliani et al., 2015). Another study concentrated on repetitive behaviors in infants at risk for this disorder, and found that these behaviors are associated with anomalous connectivity between the default mode networks and the visual network at 12 months and then the control network at 24 months. These results are the earliest known markers for autism spectrum disorder (McKinnon et al., 2019).

4.1.3 Type 1 diabetes

Diabetes is a condition where the pancreas in the body is unable to produce any or enough insulin to break down the sugar digested. Type 1 diabetes is a juvenile disorder that is linked to altered brain anatomy and connectivity. Research with rs-fMRI techniques show increased connectivity in the prefrontal cortex, insula, cingulate gyrus, thalamus, and dorsal attention network in pediatric cases of this condition. Some researchers have designated this increased connectivity as a result of reorganization of the brain to compensate for lacking or malfunctioning regions. While this has not been confirmed, the correlation between this high connectivity and behavioral analysis has been observed. However, the functional networks that are affected from type 1 diabetes, and therefore cause this reorganization to occur, have not yet been determined using rs-fMRI techniques (Saggar et al., 2017).

4.1.4 Fetal alcohol syndrome

Fetal alcohol syndrome (FAS), also known as fetal alcohol spectrum disorder (FASD), refers to the condition that occurs with prenatal alcohol exposure. When expectant mothers consume high levels of alcohol, the child can suffer from long-term brain damage and growth issues. MRI scans have shown that the white matter portion of the brain is directly impacted from the exposure, and rs-fMRI studies have aimed to determine how this damage translates to abnormalities in functional connectivity (Wozniak et al., 2017). It has been determined that children with FAS demonstrate lower connectivity in the following regions: postcentral gyrus in the anterior default mode network, middle frontal gyrus in the salience network, precentral gyrus in the ventral attention network, the precentral gyrus in the dorsal attention network, and portions of the executive control network. Overall, these affected networks are responsible for higher order cognitive processes, emotional regulation, and attention. On the other hand, networks responsible for sensory processing appeared very similar to the control group and relatively unaffected by FAS. The lower connectivity within the anterior default mode network and the salience network can be associated with difficulty in social perception and interaction (Fan et al., 2017).

4.1.5 Tourette's syndrome

Tourette's syndrome is a disorder that presents uncontrollable repetitive behaviors, referred to as tics, that generally range between specific movements or phrases. Some examples of tics are unusual sounds, offensive words, uncontrollable shrugging, excessive blinking, etc. The Yale Global Tic Severity Scale (YGTSS) is often used as a clinical tool to determine the severity of the disorder, where 50 represents severe impairment while 0 indicates no impairment. Research studies have compared patients with Tourette's syndrome to a control group and have found that decreased connectivity within the internal globus pallidus (GPi) negatively correlates to the score achieved from YGTSS testing. In other words, the lower the functional connectivity in the GPi, the more severe the tic (Ji et al., 2016). There also appears to be atypical connectivity within the frontoparietal network and the salience network, which are responsible for task control and maintenance. This information, combined with some variance found within cortical networks, is the basis for development of an rs-fMRI method for Tourette's syndrome identification. A team has attempted to use these differences in functional connectivity to diagnose patients as healthy control or with Tourette's syndrome. Results indicate that the researchers could identify this disorder with 74% accuracy, 76% sensitivity, and 71% specificity (Greene et al., 2016).

4.1.6 Premature birth

Premature birth is a major public health issue that affects around 500,000 newborns every year in the United States. While high mortality is the main issue concerning these newborn babies, advances in neonatal and pediatric medicine have allowed survival rates to increase. However, impaired neural development is still a complication that these patients face. Children born with less than 32 weeks of gestation face developmental disability, with a negative correlation between length of gestation and severity of the disability. Current research into the functional connectome of preterm children concentrates on several domains: motor, cognitive, language, and socio-emotional. rs-fMRI studies have shown that there are irregularities within the motor network of children with premature birth, with the total amount of differences corresponding to the severity of motor impairment; the same trend is found between language impairment and the language functional networks. Further, abnormalities within cognitive processes are linked to deficits in functional networks including the thalamus, hippocampus, paracentral lobule, posterior cingulate, parietal and occipital cortices, and frontal and temporal gyri. Studies into the socio-emotional domain of preterm children show that their functional connectivity patterns are similar to that of patients suffering from ADHD, anxiety, and ASD. These results suggest that premature birth may increase the risk of developing these disorders, or similar socio-emotional disorders. Although plenty of research has been conducted due to these difficulties, treatment for premature birth and its consequent disabilities is still lacking to help these children or improve their neural development (Rogers et al., 2018).

5. Discussion

Research in adult populations often cannot be extrapolated to child populations due to the distinct anatomical differences in size and development, as well as the differences in the progression of diseases and disabilities in children. Additionally, several genetic conditions such as Tay Sachs disease are exclusive to children populations; or, proper treatment of certain genetic conditions such as phenylketonuria, are dependent on early and proper diagnosis in infanthood or childhood. Diseases occurring in both pediatric and adult populations may vary significantly in severity, the exact causes or physiology, and proper and safe treatment. Evidently, conducting biomedical and neurological research in pediatric populations to understand the progression and treatment of pediatric diseases is a necessity for a number of reasons (Bull Med Ethics., 2004). The necessity of studying brain development in pediatric populations can also provide significant information regarding early development and the effects of epigenetic modifications. Understanding normal brain development is essential to developing early treatment for developmental and neuropsychiatric disorders, which may be heavily affected by childhood (Insel, 2010; Gao et al., 2017; Beardslee et al., 2011).

Despite this identified need to study pediatric populations, a vast majority of neuroimaging research is still conducted in adult populations due to the various challenges that present themselves in imaging infants and children. First, children are more prone to head motion, which may be difficult to correct for. Efforts have been made to ensure that children remain as motionless as possible. Restraint-based approaches, such as bite bars and disposable head restraints have demonstrated success (Vaidya et al., 1998; Temple et al., 2001). However, such approaches also prove difficult because restraint-based approaches may cause discomfort and anxiety in children (Poldrack et al., 2002). Additionally, the use of sedation would alter the blood flow and oxygenation in children, which should be carefully considered and often requires heavier consideration by human research committees (Abdelhalim and Alberico, 2009; Barkovich et al., 2019). Children may be anxious or nervous to enter scanners to begin with, so it can be more difficult to ensure cooperation in performing tasks or comfort with completing a scan session. This requires further care for the comfort of the individual (Poldrack et al., 2002). Techniques to acclimate the child to the scanner, such as mock scanners and MR compatible video goggles, have been used as an alternative to sedation and anesthesia methods (McGuirt, 2016). Additionally, sessions of shorter duration that help account for discomfort or anxiety also lead to a decrease in statistical power, especially for task-based studies, which often last longer than 40 min (Raschle et al., 2012). Novel pulse sequences that utilize echo planar imaging and multiple coil detection in fMRI that increase the speed of acquiring images and allow for much higher temporal resolution may be useful to increase success and statistical power in imaging pediatric groups (Feinberg et al., 2010).

Acquiring clear images of pediatric groups pose difficulties because of differences in shape and size across age, brain contrast, baseline blood flow, baseline diffusivity, and the strength of the hemodynamic response function (Raschle et al., 2012). Another challenge in applying neuroimaging methods to pediatric groups involves the pre and post analysis of data. For example, the most commonly used MNI and Talairach spaces, which are extremely useful for spatial normalization and eliminating artifacts from images, are templates for normal adult brains. However, these templates account for neither size nor developmental differences in infants and children, and have been a point of concern in pediatric research (Muzik et al., 2000; Burgund et al., 2002). Results of previous studies also indicate significant variability in gray and white matter development in children, such that segmentation cannot be standardized among pediatric populations (Wilke and Holland, 2003). To combat this, more pediatric brain templates are becoming available to account for such age-related changes (Altaye et al., 2008; Fonov et al., 2011; Sanchez et al., 2012). With a range of varying brain templates, several labs have developed techniques such as surface-based registration that allows better alignment for comparison between different age groups (Ghosh et al., 2010).

6. Conclusion

Studies on functional brain connectivity of pediatric populations have come a long way since its beginnings. A large part of this momentum has been due to the reliability and ease-of-use of rs-fMRI, in which subjects are not restrained to perform specific tasks and can simply be at rest. This fMRI technique is well suited for the pediatric population, where children and adolescents do not often feel inclined to perform cognitive tasks in a tight space or may not be able to comprehend the tasks given at hand, especially for infants and toddlers. Moreover, pediatric populations with neurological diseases or impairments benefit greatly from rs-fMRI, due to the ease of the scanning procedure. From rs-fMRI, functional connectivity measures and resting state networks can be obtained, ultimately allowing for the compilation of the resting state functional connectome of the pediatric population. By studying the functional connectome in pediatric populations using rs-fMRI, we are better able to assess pediatric brain function, development, and connectivity, not only in healthy groups, but also in groups with various pediatric disorders such as ADHD, ASD, type 1 diabetes, FAS, Tourette's syndrome, and premature birth. The future of pediatric brain imaging is a very open field and as more studies seek to improve rs-fMRI, the pediatric brain imaging community also benefits. Specifically, one future direction of increasing interest is the incorporation of naturalistic viewing paradigms such as movie-watching in rs-fMRI studies, where the subject does not have to perform any task, but simply watches a movie at rest (Vanderwal et al., 2019; Di and Biswal, 2020). It may be difficult or feel unnaturally forced for the pediatric population to just simply be at rest, but to rest and watch a movie is quite different and more enjoyable for a child. With better rs-fMRI approaches geared toward the pediatric population, not only does a stronger understanding of the pediatric functional connectome ensue, but the road to greater clinical applicability also becomes more apparent, thus allowing for better treatment of pediatric brain disorders.

References

Abdelhalim, A.N., Alberico, R.A., 2009. Pediatric neuroimaging. Neurol. Clin. 27 (1), 285–301. x https://doi.org/10.1016/j.ncl.2008.09.005.

Altaye, M., Holland, S.K., Wilke, M., Gaser, C., 2008. Infant brain probability templates for MRI segmentation and normalization. NeuroImage 43 (4), 721–730. https://doi.org/10.1016/j.neuroimage.2008.07.060.

Amianto, F., D'Agata, F., Lavagnino, L., et al., 2013. Intrinsic connectivity networks within cerebellum and beyond in eating disorders. Cerebellum 12 (5), 623–631. https://doi.org/10.1007/s12311-013-0471-1.

Amico, E., Goni, J., 2018. The quest for identifiability in human functional connectomes. Sci. Rep. 8 (1), 8254. https://doi.org/10.1038/s41598-018-25089-1.

Andreano, J.M., Touroutoglou, A., Dickerson, B.C., Barrett, L.F., 2017. Resting connectivity between salience nodes predicts recognition memory. Soc. Cogn. Affect. Neurosci. 12 (6), 948–955. https://doi.org/10.1093/scan/nsx026.

Azeez, A.K., Biswal, B.B., 2017. A review of resting-state analysis methods. Neuroimaging Clin. N. Am. 27 (4), 581–592. https://doi.org/10.1016/j.nic.2017.06.001.

Barkovich, M.J., Li, Y., Desikan, R.S., Barkovich, A.J., Xu, D., 2019. Challenges in pediatric neuroimaging. NeuroImage 185, 793–801. https://doi.org/10.1016/j.neuroimage.2018.04.044.

Beardslee, W.R., Chien, P.L., Bell, C.C., 2011. Prevention of mental disorders, substance abuse, and problem behaviors: a developmental perspective. Psychiatr. Serv. 62 (3), 247–254. https://doi.org/10.1176/ps.62.3.pss6203_0247.

Beaty, R.E., Benedek, M., Kaufman, S.B., Silvia, P.J., 2015. Default and executive network coupling supports creative idea production. Sci. Rep. 5, 10964. https://doi.org/10.1038/srep10964.

Berman, M.G., Peltier, S., Nee, D.E., Kross, E., Deldin, P.J., Jonides, J., 2011. Depression, rumination and the default network. Soc. Cogn. Affect. Neurosci. 6 (5), 548–555. https://doi.org/10.1093/scan/nsq080.

Bernard, J.A., Seidler, R.D., Hassevoort, K.M., et al., 2012. Resting state cortico-cerebellar functional connectivity networks: a comparison of anatomical and self-organizing map approaches. Front. Neuroanat. 6, 31. https://doi.org/10.3389/fnana.2012.00031.

Birn, R.M., Molloy, E.K., Patriat, R., et al., 2013. The effect of scan length on the reliability of resting-state fMRI connectivity estimates. NeuroImage 83, 550–558. https://doi.org/10.1016/j.neuroimage.2013.05.099.

Biswal, B.B., 2012. Resting state fMRI: a personal history. NeuroImage 62 (2), 938–944. https://doi.org/10.1016/j.neuroimage.2012.01.090.

Biswal, B., Yetkin, F.Z., Haughton, V.M., Hyde, J.S., 1995. Functional connectivity in the motor cortex of resting human brain using echo-planar MRI. Magn. Reson. Med. 34 (4), 537–541. https://doi.org/10.1002/mrm.1910340409.

Biswal, B.B., Mennes, M., Zuo, X.N., et al., 2010. Toward discovery science of human brain function. Proc. Natl. Acad. Sci. U. S. A. 107 (10), 4734–4739. https://doi.org/10.1073/pnas.0911855107.

Bookheimer, S.Y., 2000. Methodological issues in pediatric neuroimaging. Ment. Retard. Dev. Disabil. Res. Rev. 6 (3), 161–165. https://doi.org/10.1002/1098-2779(2000)6:3<161::AID-MRDD2>3.0.CO;2-W.

Buckner, R.L., Andrews-Hanna, J.R., Schacter, D.L., 2008. The brain's default network: anatomy, function, and relevance to disease. Ann. N. Y. Acad. Sci. 1124, 1–38. https://doi.org/10.1196/annals.1440.011.

Anon., 2004. Ethical conduct of clinical research involving children. Bul.l Med. Ethics 201, 8–11.

Burgund, E.D., Kang, H.C., Kelly, J.E., et al., 2002. The feasibility of a common stereotactic space for children and adults in fMRI studies of development. NeuroImage 17 (1), 184–200. https://doi.org/10.1006/nimg.2002.1174.

Castellanos, F.X., Di Martino, A., Craddock, R.C., Mehta, A.D., Milham, M.P., 2013. Clinical applications of the functional connectome. NeuroImage 80, 527–540. https://doi.org/10.1016/j.neuroimage.2013.04.083.

Cerliani, L., Mennes, M., Thomas, R.M., Di Martino, A., Thioux, M., Keysers, C., 2015. Increased functional connectivity between subcortical and cortical resting-state networks in autism Spectrum disorder. JAMA Psychiatry. 72 (8), 767–777. https://doi.org/10.1001/jamapsychiatry.2015.0101.

Chou, Y.H., Panych, L.P., Dickey, C.C., Petrella, J.R., Chen, N.K., 2012. Investigation of long-term reproducibility of intrinsic connectivity network mapping: a resting-state fMRI study. AJNR Am. J. Neuroradiol. 33 (5), 833–838. https://doi.org/10.3174/ajnr.A2894.

Damoiseaux, J.S., Rombouts, S.A., Barkhof, F., et al., 2006. Consistent resting-state networks across healthy subjects. Proc. Natl. Acad. Sci. U. S. A. 103 (37), 13848–13853. https://doi.org/10.1073/pnas.0601417103.

D'Angelo, E., Mazzarello, P., Prestori, F., et al., 2011. The cerebellar network: from structure to function and dynamics. Brain Res. Rev. 66 (1–2), 5–15. https://doi.org/10.1016/j.brainresrev.2010.10.002.

Di, X., Biswal, B.B., 2020. Intersubject consistent dynamic connectivity during natural vision revealed by functional MRI. NeuroImage 116698. https://doi.org/10.1016/j.neuroimage.2020.116698.

Dixon, M.L., De La Vega, A., Mills, C., et al., 2018. Heterogeneity within the frontoparietal control network and its relationship to the default and dorsal attention networks. Proc. Natl. Acad. Sci. U. S. A. 115 (7), E1598–E1607. https://doi.org/10.1073/pnas.1715766115.

Dubois, J., Adolphs, R., 2016. Building a science of individual differences from fMRI. Trends Cogn. Sci. 20 (6), 425–443. https://doi.org/10.1016/j.tics.2016.03.014.

Esposito, F., Pignataro, G., Di Renzo, G., et al., 2010. Alcohol increases spontaneous BOLD signal fluctuations in the visual network. NeuroImage 53 (2), 534–543. https://doi.org/10.1016/j.neuroimage.2010.06.061.

Fair, D.A., Cohen, A.L., Dosenbach, N.U., et al., 2008. The maturing architecture of the brain's default network. Proc. Natl. Acad. Sci. U. S. A. 105 (10), 4028–4032. https://doi.org/10.1073/pnas.0800376105.

Fair, D.A., Cohen, A.L., Power, J.D., et al., 2009. Functional brain networks develop from a "local to distributed" organization. PLoS Comput. Biol. 5 (5). https://doi.org/10.1371/journal.pcbi.1000381, e1000381.

Fan, J., Taylor, P.A., Jacobson, S.W., et al., 2017. Localized reductions in resting-state functional connectivity in children with prenatal alcohol exposure. Hum. Brain Mapp. 38 (10), 5217–5233. https://doi.org/10.1002/hbm.23726.

Feinberg, D.A., Moeller, S., Smith, S.M., et al., 2010. Multiplexed echo planar imaging for sub-second whole brain FMRI and fast diffusion imaging. PLoS One 5 (12). https://doi.org/10.1371/journal.pone.0015710, e15710.

Finn, E.S., Shen, X., Scheinost, D., Rosenberg, M.D., Huang, J., Chun, M.M., Papademetris, X., Constable, R.T., 2015. Functional connectome fingerprinting: identifying individuals using patterns of brain connectivity. Nat. Neurosci. 18 (11), 1664–1671. https://doi.org/10.1038/nn.4135.

Fonov, V., Evans, A.C., Botteron, K., et al., 2011. Unbiased average age-appropriate atlases for pediatric studies. NeuroImage 54 (1), 313–327. https://doi.org/10.1016/j.neuroimage.2010.07.033.

Fox, M.D., Raichle, M.E., 2007. Spontaneous fluctuations in brain activity observed with functional magnetic resonance imaging. Nat. Rev. Neurosci. 8 (9), 700–711. https://doi.org/10.1038/nrn2201.

Fransson, P., Skiold, B., Horsch, S., et al., 2007. Resting-state networks in the infant brain. Proc. Natl. Acad. Sci. U. S. A. 104 (39), 15531–15536. https://doi.org/10.1073/pnas.0704380104.

Friston, K.J., 1994. Functional and effective connectivity in neuroimaging: a synthesis. Hum. Brain Mapp. 2, 56–78.

Friston, K.J., Frith, C.D., Liddle, P.F., Frackowiak, R.S., 1993. Functional connectivity: the principal-component analysis of large (PET) data sets. J. Cereb. Blood Flow Metab. 13 (1), 5–14. https://doi.org/10.1038/jcbfm.1993.4.

Gao, W., Zhu, H., Giovanello, K.S., et al., 2009. Evidence on the emergence of the brain's default network from 2-week-old to 2-year-old healthy pediatric subjects. Proc. Natl. Acad. Sci. U. S. A. 106 (16), 6790–6795. https://doi.org/10.1073/pnas.0811221106.

Gao, W., Lin, W., Grewen, K., Gilmore, J.H., 2017. Functional connectivity of the infant human brain: plastic and modifiable. Neuroscientist 23 (2), 169–184. https://doi.org/10.1177/1073858416635986.

Ge, Y., Pan, Y., Dou, W., 2017. Analysis of BOLD fMRI signal preprocessing pipeline on different datasets while reducing false positive rates. Proc. Int. Conf. Biol. Inf. Biomed. Eng. (BIBE) 1, 8.

Ghosh, S.S., Kakunoori, S., Augustinack, J., et al., 2010. Evaluating the validity of volume-based and surface-based brain image registration for developmental cognitive neuroscience studies in children 4 to 11 years of age. NeuroImage 53 (1), 85–93. https://doi.org/10.1016/j.neuroimage.2010.05.075.

Grassia, F., Poliakov, A.V., Poliachik, S.L., et al., 2018. Changes in resting-state connectivity in pediatric temporal lobe epilepsy. J. Neurosurg. Pediatr. 22 (3), 270–275. https://doi.org/10.3171/2018.3.PEDS17701.

Greene, D.J., Church, J.A., Dosenbach, N.U., et al., 2016. Multivariate pattern classification of pediatric Tourette syndrome using functional connectivity MRI. Dev. Sci. 19 (4), 581–598. https://doi.org/10.1111/desc.12407.

Greicius, M.D., Krasnow, B., Reiss, A.L., Menon, V., 2003. Functional connectivity in the resting brain: a network analysis of the default mode hypothesis. Proc. Natl. Acad. Sci. U. S. A. 100 (1), 253–258. https://doi.org/10.1073/pnas.0135058100.

Ham, T., Leff, A., de Boissezon, X., Joffe, A., Sharp, D.J., 2013. Cognitive control and the salience network: an investigation of error processing and effective connectivity. J. Neurosci. 33 (16), 7091–7098. https://doi.org/10.1523/JNEUROSCI.4692-12.2013.

Hanaie, R., Mohri, I., Kagitani-Shimono, K., et al., 2018. Aberrant cerebellar-cerebral functional connectivity in children and adolescents with autism Spectrum disorder. Front. Hum. Neurosci. 12, 454. https://doi.org/10.3389/fnhum.2018.00454.

Heine, L., Soddu, A., Gomez, F., et al., 2012. Resting state networks and consciousness: alterations of multiple resting state network connectivity in physiological, pharmacological, and pathological consciousness states. Front. Psychol. 3, 295. https://doi.org/10.3389/fpsyg.2012.00295.

Herzmann, C.S., Snyder, A.Z., Kenley, J.K., Rogers, C.E., Shimony, J.S., Smyser, C.D., 2019. Cerebellar functional connectivity in term- and very preterm-born infants. Cereb. Cortex 29 (3), 1174–1184. https://doi.org/10.1093/cercor/bhy023.

Ho, M.L., Campeau, N.G., Ngo, T.D., Udayasankar, U.K., Welker, K.M., 2017. Pediatric brain MRI part 1: basic techniques. Pediatr. Radiol. 47 (5), 534–543. https://doi.org/10.1007/s00247-016-3776-7.

Hohenfeld, C., Werner, C.J., Reetz, K., 2018. Resting-state connectivity in neurodegenerative disorders: is there potential for an imaging biomarker? Neuroimage Clin. 18, 849–870. https://doi.org/10.1016/j.nicl.2018.03.013.

Holmes, A.J., Hollinshead, M.O., O'Keefe, T.M., et al., 2015. Brain genomics Superstruct project initial data release with structural, functional, and behavioral measures. Sci. Data. 2, 150031. https://doi.org/10.1038/sdata.2015.31.

Horien, C., Shen, X., Scheinost, D., Constable, R.T., 2019. The individual functional connectome is unique and stable over months to years. NeuroImage 189, 676–687. https://doi.org/10.1016/j.neuroimage.2019.02.002.

Horowitz-Kraus, T., DiFrancesco, M., Kay, B., Wang, Y., Holland, S.K., 2015. Increased resting-state functional connectivity of visual- and cognitive-control brain networks after training in children with reading difficulties. Neuroimage Clin. 8, 619–630. https://doi.org/10.1016/j.nicl.2015.06.010.

Insel, T.R., 2010. Rethinking schizophrenia. Nature 468 (7321), 187–193. https://doi.org/10.1038/nature09552.

Ji, G.J., Liao, W., Yu, Y., et al., 2016. Globus pallidus interna in Tourette syndrome: decreased local activity and disrupted functional connectivity. Front. Neuroanat. 10, 93. https://doi.org/10.3389/fnana.2016.00093.

Kaboodvand, N., Iravani, B., Fransson, P., 2020. Dynamic synergetic configurations of resting-state networks in ADHD. NeuroImage 207, 116347. https://doi.org/10.1016/j.neuroimage.2019.116347.

Kannurpatti, S.S., Biswal, B.B., 2008. Detection and scaling of task-induced fMRI-BOLD response using resting state fluctuations. Neuroimage 40 (4), 1567–1574. https://doi.org/10.1016/j.neuroimage.2007.09.040.

Karunakaran, K.D., Yuan, R., He, J., et al., 2020. Resting-state functional connectivity of the thalamus in complete spinal cord injury. Neurorehabil. Neural Repair 34 (2), 122–133. https://doi.org/10.1177/1545968319893299.

Lin, H.Y., Tseng, W.Y., Lai, M.C., Matsuo, K., Gau, S.S., 2015. Altered resting-state frontoparietal control network in children with attention-deficit/hyperactivity disorder. J. Int. Neuropsychol. Soc. 21 (4), 271–284. https://doi.org/10.1017/S135561771500020X.

Marek, S., Dosenbach, N.U.F., 2018. The frontoparietal network: function, electrophysiology, and importance of individual precision mapping. Dialogues Clin. Neurosci. 20 (2), 133–140.

Mason, M.F., Norton, M.I., Van Horn, J.D., Wegner, D.M., Grafton, S.T., Macrae, C.N., 2007. Wandering minds: the default network and stimulus-independent thought. Science 315 (5810), 393–395. https://doi.org/10.1126/science.1131295.

Maudoux, A., Lefebvre, P., Cabay, J.E., et al., 2012a. Auditory resting-state network connectivity in tinnitus: a functional MRI study. PLoS One 7 (5). https://doi.org/10.1371/journal.pone.0036222, e36222.

Maudoux, A., Lefebvre, P., Cabay, J.E., et al., 2012b. Connectivity graph analysis of the auditory resting state network in tinnitus. Brain Res. 1485, 10–21. https://doi.org/10.1016/j.brainres.2012.05.006.

McGuirt, D., 2016. Alternatives to sedation and general anesthesia in pediatric magnetic resonance imaging: a literature review. Radiol. Technol. 88 (1), 18–26.

McKeown, M.J., Makeig, S., Brown, G.G., et al., 1998. Analysis of fMRI data by blind separation into independent spatial components. Hum. Brain Mapp. 6 (3), 160–188.

McKeown, M.J., Hansen, L.K., Sejnowsk, T.J., 2003. Independent component analysis of functional MRI: what is signal and what is noise? Curr. Opin. Neurobiol. 13 (5), 620–629. https://doi.org/10.1016/j.conb.2003.09.012.

McKinnon, C.J., Eggebrecht, A.T., Todorov, A., et al., 2019. Restricted and repetitive behavior and brain functional connectivity in infants at risk for developing autism Spectrum disorder. Biol. Psychiatry. Cogn. Neurosci. Neuroimaging. 4 (1), 50–61. https://doi.org/10.1016/j.bpsc.2018.09.008.

Miranda-Dominguez, O., Mills, B.D., Carpenter, S.D., et al., 2014. Connectotyping: model based fingerprinting of the functional connectome. PLoS One 9 (11). https://doi.org/10.1371/journal.pone.0111048, e111048.

Mohan, A., Roberto, A.J., Mohan, A., et al., 2016. The significance of the default mode network (DMN) in neurological and neuropsychiatric disorders: a review. Yale J. Biol. Med. 89 (1), 49–57.

Mongerson, C.R.L., Jennings, R.W., Borsook, D., Becerra, L., Bajic, D., 2017. Resting-state functional connectivity in the infant brain: methods, pitfalls, and potentiality. Front. Pediatr. 5, 159. https://doi.org/10.3389/fped.2017.00159.

Mueller, S., Wang, D., Fox, M.D., et al., 2013. Individual variability in functional connectivity architecture of the human brain. Neuron 77 (3), 586–595. https://doi.org/10.1016/j.neuron.2012.12.028.

Muetzel, R.L., Blanken, L.M., Thijssen, S., et al., 2016. Resting-state networks in 6-to-10 year old children. Hum. Brain Mapp. 37 (12), 4286–4300. https://doi.org/10.1002/hbm.23309.

Muzik, O., Chugani, D.C., Juhasz, C., Shen, C., Chugani, H.T., 2000. Statistical parametric mapping: assessment of application in children. NeuroImage 12 (5), 538–549. https://doi.org/10.1006/nimg.2000.0651.

Nagamitsu, S., Yamashita, Y., Tanaka, H., Matsuishi, T., 2012. Functional near-infrared spectroscopy studies in children. Biopsychosoc. Med. 6, 7. https://doi.org/10.1186/1751-0759-6-7.

Ng, K.K., Lo, J.C., Lim, J.K.W., Chee, M.W.L., Zhou, J., 2016. Reduced functional segregation between the default mode network and the executive control network in healthy older adults: a longitudinal study. NeuroImage 133, 321–330. https://doi.org/10.1016/j.neuroimage.2016.03.029.

Overy, K., Norton, A., Cronin, K., Winner, E., Schlaug, G., 2005. Examining rhythm and melody processing in young children using FMRI. Ann. N. Y. Acad. Sci. 1060, 210–218. https://doi.org/10.1196/annals.1360.014.

Park, B.Y., Byeon, K., Park, H., 2019. FuNP (fusion of neuroimaging preprocessing) pipelines: a fully automated preprocessing software for functional magnetic resonance imaging. Front. Neuroinform. 13, 5. https://doi.org/10.3389/fninf.2019.00005.

Patriat, R., Molloy, E.K., Meier, T.B., et al., 2013. The effect of resting condition on resting-state fMRI reliability and consistency: a comparison between resting with eyes open, closed, and fixated. NeuroImage 78, 463–473. https://doi.org/10.1016/j.neuroimage.2013.04.013.

Poldrack, R.A., Pare-Blagoev, E.J., Grant, P.E., 2002. Pediatric functional magnetic resonance imaging: progress and challenges. Top. Magn. Reson. Imaging 13 (1), 61–70. https://doi.org/10.1097/00002142-200202000-00005.

Power, J.D., Barnes, K.A., Snyder, A.Z., Schlaggar, B.L., Petersen, S.E., 2012. Spurious but systematic correlations in functional connectivity MRI networks arise from subject motion. Neuroimage 59 (3), 2142–2154. https://doi.org/10.1016/j.neuroimage.2011.10.018.

Rabinak, C.A., Angstadt, M., Welsh, R.C., et al., 2011. Altered amygdala resting-state functional connectivity in post-traumatic stress disorder. Front. Psychiatry. 2, 62. https://doi.org/10.3389/fpsyt.2011.00062.

Raichle, M.E., 2015. The brain's default mode network. Annu. Rev. Neurosci. 38, 433–447. https://doi.org/10.1146/annurev-neuro-071013-014030.

Raichle, M.E., MacLeod, A.M., Snyder, A.Z., Powers, W.J., Gusnard, D.A., Shulman, G.L., 2001. A default mode of brain function. Proc. Natl. Acad. Sci. U. S. A. 98 (2), 676–682. https://doi.org/10.1073/pnas.98.2.676.

Raschle, N., Zuk, J., Ortiz-Mantilla, S., et al., 2012. Pediatric neuroimaging in early childhood and infancy: challenges and practical guidelines. Ann. N. Y. Acad. Sci. 1252, 43–50. https://doi.org/10.1111/j.1749-6632.2012.06457.x.

Rogers, C.E., Lean, R.E., Wheelock, M.D., Smyser, C.D., 2018. Aberrant structural and functional connectivity and neurodevelopmental impairment in preterm children. J. Neurodev. Disord. 10 (1), 38. https://doi.org/10.1186/s11689-018-9253-x.

Saggar, M., Tsalikian, E., Mauras, N., et al., 2017. Compensatory hyperconnectivity in developing brains of young children with type 1 diabetes. Diabetes 66 (3), 754–762. https://doi.org/10.2337/db16-0414.

Sanchez, C.E., Richards, J.E., Almli, C.R., 2012. Neurodevelopmental MRI brain templates for children from 2 weeks to 4 years of age. Dev. Psychobiol. 54 (1), 77–91. https://doi.org/10.1002/dev.20579.

Scheinost, D., Sinha, R., Cross, S.N., et al., 2017. Does prenatal stress alter the developing connectome? Pediatr. Res. 81 (1–2), 214–226. https://doi.org/10.1038/pr.2016.197.

Schumann, G., Loth, E., Banaschewski, T., et al., 2010. The IMAGEN study: reinforcement-related behaviour in normal brain function and psychopathology. Mol. Psychiatry 15 (12), 1128–1139. https://doi.org/10.1038/mp.2010.4.

Seeley, W.W., Menon, V., Schatzberg, A.F., et al., 2007. Dissociable intrinsic connectivity networks for salience processing and executive control. J. Neurosci. 27 (9), 2349–2356. https://doi.org/10.1523/JNEUROSCI.5587-06.2007.

Shehzad, Z., Kelly, A.M., Reiss, P.T., et al., 2009. The resting brain: unconstrained yet reliable. Cereb. Cortex 19 (10), 2209–2229. https://doi.org/10.1093/cercor/bhn256.

Shulman, G.L., Fiez, J.A., Corbetta, M., et al., 1997. Common blood flow changes across visual tasks: II. Decreases in cerebral cortex. J. Cogn. Neurosci. 9 (5), 648–663. https://doi.org/10.1162/jocn.1997.9.5.648.

Smith, S.M., Fox, P.T., Miller, K.L., et al., 2009. Correspondence of the brain's functional architecture during activation and rest. Proc. Natl. Acad. Sci. U. S. A. 106 (31), 13040–13045. https://doi.org/10.1073/pnas.0905267106.

Smitha, K.A., Akhil Raja, K., Arun, K.M., et al., 2017. Resting state fMRI: a review on methods in resting state connectivity analysis and resting state networks. Neuroradiol. J. 30 (4), 305–317. https://doi.org/10.1177/1971400917697342.

Stanescu, L., Ishak, G.E., Khanna, P.C., Biyyam, D.R., Shaw, D.W., Parisi, M.T., 2013. FDG PET of the brain in pediatric patients: imaging spectrum with MR imaging correlation. Radiographics 33 (5), 1279–1303. https://doi.org/10.1148/rg.335125152.

Strother, S.C., 2006. Evaluating fMRI preprocessing pipelines. IEEE Eng. Med. Biol. Mag. 25 (2), 27–41. https://doi.org/10.1109/memb.2006.1607667.

Temple, E., Poldrack, R.A., Salidis, J., et al., 2001. Disrupted neural responses to phonological and orthographic processing in dyslexic children: an fMRI study. Neuroreport 12 (2), 299–307. https://doi.org/10.1097/00001756-200102120-00024.

Thomason, M.E., Dennis, E.L., Joshi, A.A., et al., 2011. Resting-state fMRI can reliably map neural networks in children. NeuroImage 55 (1), 165–175. https://doi.org/10.1016/j.neuroimage.2010.11.080.

Thornburgh, C.L., Narayana, S., Rezaie, R., et al., 2017. Concordance of the resting state networks in typically developing, 6-to 7-year-old children and healthy adults. Front. Hum. Neurosci. 11, 199. https://doi.org/10.3389/fnhum.2017.00199.

Vahdat, S., Darainy, M., Milner, T.E., Ostry, D.J., 2011. Functionally specific changes in resting-state sensorimotor networks after motor learning. J. Neurosci. 31 (47), 16907–16915. https://doi.org/10.1523/JNEUROSCI.2737-11.2011.

Vaidya, C.J., Austin, G., Kirkorian, G., et al., 1998. Selective effects of methylphenidate in attention deficit hyperactivity disorder: a functional magnetic resonance study. Proc. Natl. Acad. Sci. U. S. A. 95 (24), 14494–14499. https://doi.org/10.1073/pnas.95.24.14494.

van den Heuvel, M.P., Hulshoff Pol, H.E., 2010. Exploring the brain network: a review on resting-state fMRI functional connectivity. Eur. Neuropsychopharmacol. 20 (8), 519–534. https://doi.org/10.1016/j.euroneuro.2010.03.008.

Van Essen, D.C., Smith, S.M., Barch, D.M., et al., 2013. The WU-Minn human connectome project: an overview. NeuroImage 80, 62–79. https://doi.org/10.1016/j.neuroimage.2013.05.041.

van Rooij, D., Hartman, C.A., Mennes, M., et al., 2015. Altered neural connectivity during response inhibition in adolescents with attention-deficit/hyperactivity disorder and their unaffected siblings. Neuroimage Clin. 7, 325–335. https://doi.org/10.1016/j.nicl.2015.01.004.

Vanderwal, T., Eilbott, J., Castellanos, F.X., 2019. Movies in the magnet: naturalistic paradigms in developmental functional neuroimaging. Dev. Cogn. Neurosci. 36, 100600. https://doi.org/10.1016/j.dcn.2018.10.004.

Wang, H.E., Benar, C.G., Quilichini, P.P., Friston, K.J., Jirsa, V.K., Bernard, C., 2014. A systematic framework for functional connectivity measures. Front. Neurosci. 8, 405. https://doi.org/10.3389/fnins.2014.00405.

Wang, Y., Li, Y., Wang, H., Chen, Y., Huang, W., 2017. Altered default mode network on resting-state fMRI in children with infantile spasms. Front. Neurol. 8, 209. https://doi.org/10.3389/fneur.2017.00209.

Weng, J., Dong, S., He, H., Chen, F., Peng, X., 2015. Reducing individual variation for fMRI studies in children by minimizing template related errors. PLoS One 10 (7). https://doi.org/10.1371/journal.pone.0134195, e0134195.

Wilke, M., Holland, S.K., 2003. Variability of gray and white matter during normal development: a voxel-based MRI analysis. Neuroreport 14 (15), 1887–1890. https://doi.org/10.1097/00001756-200310270-00001.

Wozniak, J.R., Mueller, B.A., Mattson, S.N., et al., 2017. Functional connectivity abnormalities and associated cognitive deficits in fetal alcohol spectrum disorders (FASD). Brain Imaging Behav. 11 (5), 1432–1445. https://doi.org/10.1007/s11682-016-9624-4.

Xiao, Q., Zhong, Y., Lu, D., et al., 2013. Altered regional homogeneity in pediatric bipolar disorder during manic state: a resting-state fMRI study. PLoS One 8 (3). https://doi.org/10.1371/journal.pone.0057978, e57978.

Xiong, J., Parsons, L.M., Gao, J.H., Fox, P.T., 1999. Interregional connectivity to primary motor cortex revealed using MRI resting state images. Hum. Brain Mapp. 8 (2–3), 151–156. https://doi.org/10.1002/(sici)1097-0193(1999)8:2/3<151::aid-hbm13>3.0.co;2-5.

Yang, N., He, Y., Zhang, Z., et al., 2017. Chinese color nest project: growing up in China. Chin. Sci. Bull. 62, 3008–3022. https://doi.org/10.1360/N972017-00362.

Zang, Y., Jiang, T., Lu, Y., He, Y., Tian, L., 2004. Regional homogeneity approach to fMRI data analysis. Neuroimage 22 (1), 394–400. https://doi.org/10.1016/j.neuroimage.2003.12.030.

Zepf, F.D., Bubenzer-Busch, S., Runions, K.C., et al., 2019. Functional connectivity of the vigilant-attention network in children and adolescents with attention-deficit/hyperactivity disorder. Brain Cogn. 131, 56–65. https://doi.org/10.1016/j.bandc.2017.10.005.

Zhang, J., Su, J., Wang, M., et al., 2017. The sensorimotor network dysfunction in migraineurs without aura: a resting-state fMRI study. J. Neurol. 264 (4), 654–663. https://doi.org/10.1007/s00415-017-8404-4.

Zhao, Q., Swati, Z.N.K., Metmer, H., Sang, X., Lu, J., 2019. Investigating executive control network and default mode network dysfunction in major depressive disorder. Neurosci. Lett. 701, 154–161. https://doi.org/10.1016/j.neulet.2019.02.045.

Zou, Q.-H., Zhu, C.-Z., Yang, Y., Zuo, X.-N., Long, X.-Y., Cao, Q.-J., Wang, Y.-F., Zang, Y.-F., 2008. An improved approach to detection of amplitude of low-frequency fluctuation (ALFF) for resting-state fMRI: fractional ALFF. J. Neurosci. Methods 172 (1), 137–141. https://doi.org/10.1016/j.jneumeth.2008.04.012.

CHAPTER

Advanced pCASL pediatric perfusion MRI

5

Emily Kilroy[a,b], Xingfeng Shao[c], and Danny JJ Wang[c,d]

Department of Occupational Therapy and Occupational Science, University of Southern California, Los Angeles, CA, United States[a] Brain and Creativity Institute, University of Southern California, Los Angeles, CA, United States[b] Laboratory of FMRI Technology (LOFT), USC Mark & Mary Stevens Neuroimaging and Informatics Institute, Keck School of Medicine, University of Southern California, Los Angeles, CA, United States[c] Department of Neurology, Keck School of Medicine, University of Southern California, Los Angeles, CA, United States[d]

1. Perfusion and brain development

1.1 Brain development during childhood to adolescence

The developmental period from infancy to young adulthood is marked by both great potential and vulnerability (Christie and Viner, 2005; Heller and Casey, 2016; Paus et al., 2008). Paralleling biological changes, such as surges in sex hormones, is the buildup of cognitive capabilities with age (Heller and Casey, 2016; Steinberg, 2005). Alternatively, atypical neurodevelopment can lead to a reduction or delay in cognitive capacities and the emergence of neuropsychiatric disorders. Understanding typical development provides a window in which to better understand the mechanisms that contribute to neurodevelopmental disorders. Advances in neuroimaging technology continuously provide a more accurate understanding of these mechanisms which help to inform prevention therapies and treatment.

One such technology is arterial spin labeled (ASL) perfusion MRI. ASL provides noninvasive and quantitative measurements of cerebral blood flow (CBF) using magnetically labeled arterial blood water as an endogenous tracer. Since CBF is normally coupled to glucose metabolism and neuronal activity (Akgören et al., 1994; Hoge and Pike, 2001), it is a surrogate marker of brain function. ASL CBF measurements have been validated using ^{15}O-water PET (Feng et al., 2004; Heijtel et al., 2014; Kilroy et al., 2014; Ye et al., 2000; Zhang et al., 2014), and have been shown to provide comparable information as FDG PET measurement of cerebral glucose metabolism (Cha et al., 2013; Chen et al., 2011; Dolui et al., 2019; Newberg et al., 2005; Roman et al., 2017). The main limitations of ASL have been the relatively low signal-to-noise ratio (SNR) due to the small arterial blood fraction ($\sim$1%), as well as the arterial-transit effects if the postlabeling delay (PLD; the time between labeling and image acquisition) is not long enough to allow labeled blood to reach tissue. Nevertheless, several physiological properties of the pediatric brain make ASL an ideal tool for perfusion imaging in developing populations (Wang and Licht, 2006). For example, blood flow rates are generally higher in children compared with adults (except in newborns), which increases perfusion contrast, and the water content of the brain

Handbook of Pediatric Brain Imaging. https://doi.org/10.1016/B978-0-12-816633-8.00013-2

is also higher in children than adults, which yields a greater concentration and half-life of the tracer (blood water). As a result, a 70% increase in the SNR of ASL images has been reported in children compared to adults (Wang et al., 2003).

2. ASL perfusion MRI for neurodevelopmental studies

2.1 Accuracy and reliability of ASL for developmental studies

Among various ASL techniques, pseudo-continuous ASL (pCASL) has recently emerged as the technique of choice for brain perfusion studies as it combines the advantages of pulsed ASL, including hardware compatibility with current MRI scanners, and the higher tagging efficiency of continuous ASL, which includes a longer tagging bolus and thus higher SNR (Dai et al., 2008; Wu et al., 2007). In order to reliably apply ASL for tracking the developmental trajectory of CBF, the accuracy and longitudinal repeatability of ASL perfusion MRI needs to be established in children. Jain et al. (2012) performed pCASL perfusion MRI in 22 healthy children aged 7–17 using repeated scans 2–4 weeks apart. By taking into account developmental changes of key physiological parameters (e.g., blood T1 and ATT), the accuracy of pCASL against the reference standard of phase contrast (PC) MRI measured by intraclass correlation coefficient (ICC) was 0.65. CBF measurements using pCASL demonstrated a good level of longitudinal repeatability (ICC = 0.65, within-subject Coefficient of Variance/wsCV = 14%). This study laid a solid foundation for quantitative CBF mapping in typically developing children and adolescents.

2.2 Arterial blood T1 in children

Age-dependent variations in blood T1 is a potential confounding factor affecting the accuracy of perfusion quantification. Previous studies reported that T1 of neonatal arterial blood decreases with hematocrit (Hct) ($1/T1 = 0.59Hct + 0.30$) (De Vis et al., 2014; Liu et al., 2016). Rapid body growth of neonates results in hemodilution and an approximate linear decrease in hematocrit was found in neonates during the first 28 days after birth (Jopling et al., 2009). As a result, blood T1 in neonates and infants was found to be longer and more variable (around 1.8–2.0 s at 3T) (De Vis et al., 2014; Varela et al., 2015) than in adults (around 1.6–1.7 s) (Lu et al., 2004). Pediatric ASL has benefited from higher SNR due to the prolonged blood T1. However, assuming an incorrect blood T1 in the quantification model can cause an overestimation of perfusion up to 30% (De Vis et al., 2014). It has been recommended to use Hct corrected blood T1 and/or a population dependent T1 value for neonatal and pediatric ASL (De Vis et al., 2014; Liu et al., 2016).

2.3 Arterial transit time in perfusion quantification

The importance of ATT in perfusion quantification cannot be ignored. For example, low ASL signals can be ambiguous, reflecting either low blood flow or alternatively a prolonged ATT. ATT shows an increasing trend with age and varies considerably across brain regions in typically developing children ($ATT = 13.6 \times \text{age (years)} + 1383.7$ ms) (Jain et al., 2012). To account for age-related changes in ATT, multidelay ASL methods have recently been introduced and are becoming increasingly used in clinical settings (Hu et al., 2019). With ASL images acquired from multiple PLDs, quantitative maps of ATT as well as ATT-corrected CBF maps can be obtained simultaneously (i.e., use a weighted-delay approach or curve fitting), as demonstrated in Fig. 1. CBF computed from weighted-delay and curve-fitting methods agreed strongly, with Pearson correlation coefficients ranging from 0.97–0.99 across the measured regions ($P < 0.05$). Correlation coefficients for ATT ranged from 0.87–0.96 ($P < 0.05$) (Hu et al., 2019).

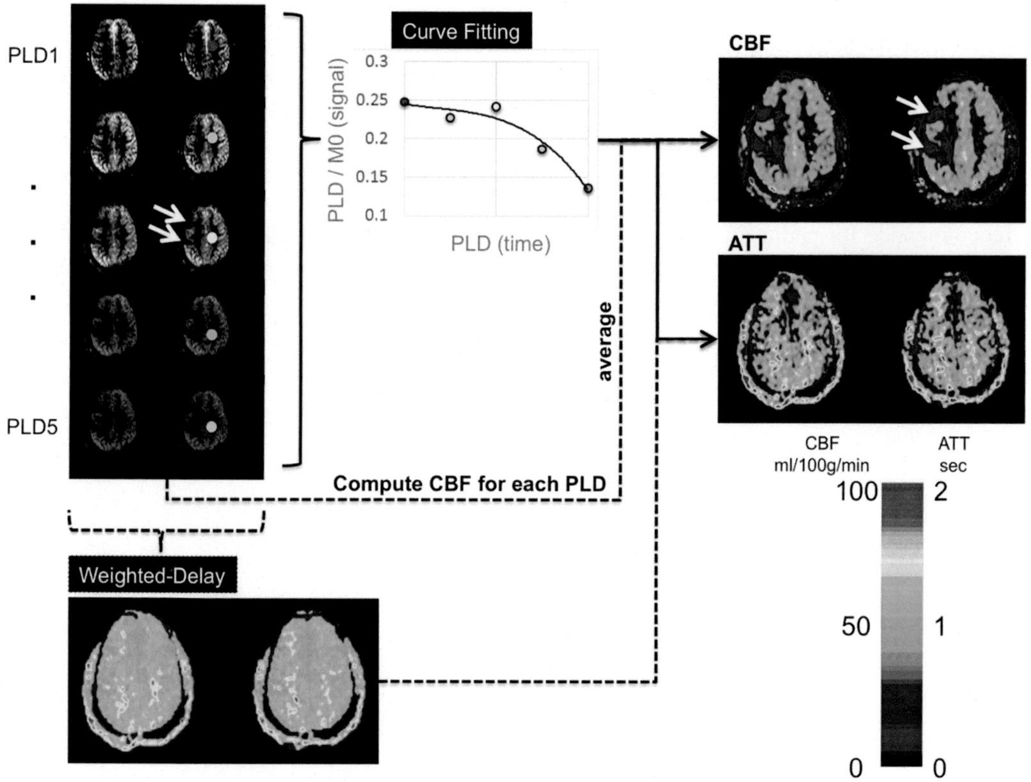

FIG. 1

Exemplary multidelay ASL data from a 17-year female patient with a history of stroke. There are two perfusion deficits in the posterior right frontal lobe, which corresponds to foci of cystic encephalomalacia (*arrows*). Left top panel shows individual PLD data for two slices (from top to bottom: PLD = 500 ms + 500 ms increments). Remainder of figure shows the flow chart of how a weighted-delay routine (*dashed arrow path*) and an iterative curve fitting routine (*solid arrow path*) are used to generate CBF and ATT maps. CBF and ATT are shown using the same colorbar, but from 0 to 100 ml/100 g/min or 0–2 s, respectively. The weighted-delay is computed from the individual PLD data and is also in units of time (*s*), shown on the same color scale as the ATT map. In the weighted-delay approach, individual CBFs are also computed for each PLD, and the final CBF is the group mean of the five estimated CBFs at each of the five PLDs.

Figure adapted from Hu, H.H., Rusin, J.A., Peng, R., Shao, X., Smith, M., Krishnamurthy, R., . . . Wang, D.J., 2019. Multi-phase 3D arterial spin labeling brain MRI in assessing cerebral blood perfusion and arterial transit times in children at 3T. Clin. Imaging. 53, 210–220.

2.4 Blood flow velocity and labeling efficiency

Labeling efficiency of pCASL is highly dependent on the blood flow velocities at the carotid arteries. According to a study with 82 subjects aged from 7 month to 61 years (Wu et al., 2016), internal carotid artery peak velocities maintain relatively high levels in children (83–85 cm/s in infants (age < 1 year), 83–95 cm/s in toddlers and school age (age = 1–11 years), and 65–89 cm/s in adolescents (age = 12–18 years)), and decline with age in adults (~40–60 cm/s (Dai et al., 2008)). For sufficient labeling efficiency, the flow-driven adiabatic condition needs to be met (Maccotta et al., 1997). Higher RF amplitude is necessary to maintain sufficient labeling efficiency for higher blood flow velocity in children. Bloch equation simulations can be used to estimate the labeling efficiency. Fig. 2 shows the pCASL labeling efficiency as a function of peak velocity in teenagers and adults. Increasing FA (or B1) shifts the range of high-efficiency response toward higher velocities, however, specific-absorption-rate (SAR) would also increase quadratically as B1 increases. While FA of 25 degree (or B1 = 7 uT) is typically used for adults, a higher FA of 30 degree (or B1 = 8.4 uT) would be recommended for pediatric ASL for sufficient labeling efficiency (>90%). Increasing FA from 25–30 degrees causes 44% more SAR, and a longer repetition time might be required to avoid exceeding the SAR limit.

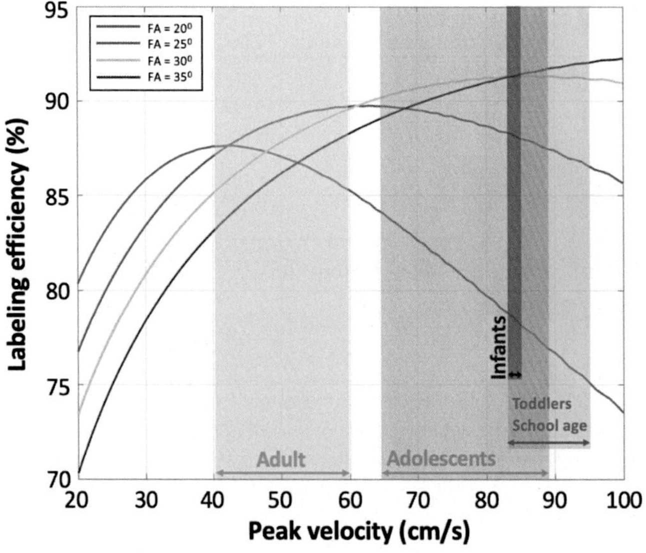

FIG. 2

Plot of labeling efficiency as a function of peak velocity at the carotid artery with four pCASL RF flip angles (FAs): 20, 25, 30 and 35 degree. *Red, blue, orange, and green shadows* represent the range of peak velocities in infants (<1 year), toddlers and school age (1–11 years), adolescents (12–18 years) and adults (>18 years), respectively. Other pCASL parameters used for the Bloch equation simulation were: Hann-window shaped RF pulse, Gave = 0.6 mT/m, Gmax/Gave ratio = 10, RF duration = 500 us, RF gap = 920 μs, no B0 off-resonance.

3. Perfusion of typical brain development

The developing brain is a highly dynamic system undergoing radical changes in neural function, connectivity, and other physiological changes that can be evaluated by CBF measures. In this section, we discuss current research on perfusion across typical brain development. We specifically focus on neonatal perfusion patterns, the effects of gender on perfusion, and how perfusion correlates with cognition and sensory processing.

Across development, pediatric ASL studies demonstrate an age-related increase of CBF from neonates to toddlers, followed by tapering of CBF from childhood to adulthood (Biagi et al., 2007; Miranda et al., 2006; Wang et al., 2003; Wang et al., 2009). This developmental trajectory of CBF is generally consistent with existing literature based on nuclear medicine approaches (Chiron et al., 1992; Chugani, 1998). Avants and colleagues have recently published the Pediatric Template of Brain Perfusion that includes pCASL and other MRI modalities in 120 children 7–18 years of age (Avants et al., 2015). Furthermore, a number of studies have shown that development effects in brain structure and perfusion can be differentiated by employing gray matter density (GMD) adjusted regional CBF as well as by decomposing ASL CBF into perfusion information that can be predicted by anatomical features and a residual perfusion image (Kandel et al., 2015; Taki et al., 2011a,b). These studies showed that the relationship between GMD adjusted CBF and age can be characterized by an inverted U-shape followed by a U-shaped trajectory in most brain regions throughout childhood and adolescence, with a greater prominence of an inverted u-shaped pattern in many higher-order frontal and parietal regions (Taki et al., 2011a,b).

3.1 Neonatal perfusion

Brain physiology changes occur rapidly during the neonatal/infant stage of development. CBF continuously increases in the first 18 months of life, exceeding adult levels by 12 months (Liu et al., 2019; Lu et al., 2011; Peng et al., 2014). This increase is likely to reflect the fast brain development in both brain structure and function at this early stage of life. These rapid changes also result in greater inter-subject variation in blood flow velocity as measured by Phase-contrast (PC) MRI (4.5–56.0 cm/s) (Liu et al., 2019). In the few studies that have been conducted in healthy full-term infants, global CBF measured by ASL is estimated to be between 11 and 29 mL/100 g/min (Kehrer et al., 2002; Massaro et al., 2013; Miranda et al., 2006; Wong et al., 2019). This estimate is slightly lower than estimated CBF measurements using PET (between 18 and 24 mL/100 g/min). The underestimation is thought to be due to the use of a very short PLD time used in the studies (Bouyssi-Kobar et al., 2018) or intrinsically low signal-to-noise ratio of the neonatal brain on ASL imaging (Liu et al., 2019). Based on these findings, future research should consider a longer PLD or multidelay approach when scanning neonatal populations (Alsop et al., 2015).

While development from infancy to adulthood perfusion follows a U-shaped trajectory, within infancy, whole-brain perfusion follows a cubic model (Wong et al., 2019). In a study measuring perfusion in typically developing infants and toddlers, researchers applied a mathematical model fitting technique that indicated perfusion at this time fits a cubic model for the regression between whole-brain CBF and age. Whole-brain CBF was observed to increase with age before 90 weeks, plateaued from 90 to 160 weeks, and increased with increasing age thereafter (Fig. 3). Researchers demonstrated that the cubic model was the best fit for all cerebral cortical regions.

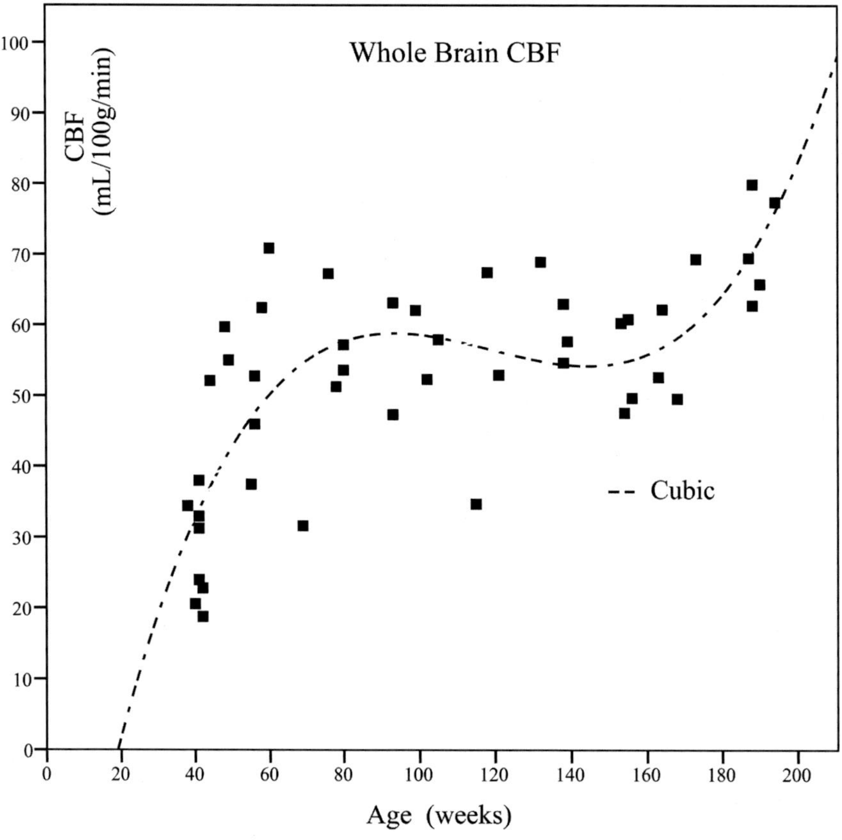

FIG. 3

Graph of whole-brain CBF as a function of postmenstrual age in weeks. The *line* represents the correlation adopting the best-fitting mathematical model (Wong et al., 2019).

At a cortical region-specific level, perfusion during infancy varies across the cerebral cortical areas. In a recent ASL study comparing full-term and preterm infants, researchers reported that the insula was one of the most perfused cerebral cortical areas during infancy (Bouyssi-Kobar et al., 2018). In addition to the insula, the sensorimotor cortex and the ACC also had greater CBF compared to other cerebral cortical areas (Bouyssi-Kobar et al., 2018; Camacho et al., 2019). Similar to findings from other studies (Børch and Greisen, 1998; Jill et al., 2013), the lateral frontal gray matter demonstrated low perfusion at term-equivalent age. Taken together, these findings highlight the early development of the insula, sensorimotor cortex, and ACC. These areas are important for sensorimotor processing, emotion formation and processing, learning, and memory. These regions are also known to be atypical in several disorders such as Autism Spectrum Disorder (ASD), Attention Deficit Disorders (Lopez-Larson et al., 2012), and depression (Sprengelmeyer et al., 2011). How perfusion develops in infants who go on to develop neurodevelopmental and or psychiatric disorders is unknown.

3.2 Gender effect on perfusion

In addition to age-related changes, gender influences brain development patterns and trajectories in children and adolescents. The influx of hormones during puberty, including testosterone and estrogen, results in divergent, sex-specific neural maturation in males and females. The influences of puberty have previously been shown to be reflected in both functional and structural brain trajectories (Blanton et al., 2012; Giedd et al., 1999, 2006; Neufang et al., 2009; Peper et al., 2009; Raznahan et al., 2010). As mentioned above, patterns of cerebral perfusion change throughout development (Taki et al., 2011a,b) and these patterns can vary depending on the gender of the individual. During early childhood, both sexes have similar patterns of increasing CBF (Paniukov et al., 2020) but during adolescence, CBF becomes markedly different in males and females (Satterthwaite et al., 2014).

The age in which peak CBF occurs in males and females is unclear. In a recent large longitudinal study, Paniukov et al. (2020) investigated CBF trajectories in healthy children ($n = 96$; 279 scans) before the onset of puberty. CBF was measured in children starting between age 2 and 3 years old and followed up to age 7 years old. Researchers demonstrated CBF continues to increase linearly (mean increase of 29% over baseline values, or approximately 3.20 mL/100 g/min per year, in areas with significant changes) with age across the cortex and cerebellum in early childhood. This data suggests that CBF continues to increase during childhood, with peak values obtained sometime after age 7 years. Females showed slightly lower CBF than males throughout the brain, however, these differences were not significant. These findings suggest that sex differences in CBF become more prominent later in childhood or adolescents. In a large cross-sectional study of over 1000 children and adolescents by Satterthwaite et al. (2014), researchers used data from the Philadelphia Neurodevelopmental Cohort to investigate age-related differences in CBF measured by pCASL in males and females. Researchers reported age by gender interactions in several brain regions important for intrinsic activity, executive function, and emotional processing (Fig. 4A). During early puberty (8–12 years) CBF values in males

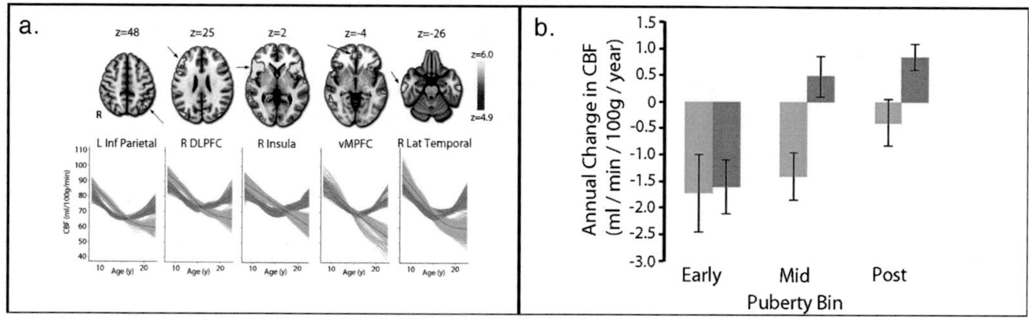

FIG. 4

(A) Developmental pattern of CBF change between males (*blue*) and females (*pink*) in multiple regions within heteromodal association cortex. Whereas CBF values declined in males until late adolescence, CBF in females declined until mid-adolescence but increased thereafter. Images thresholded at $z > 4.9$ (Bonferroni corrected $P < 0.05$), $k > 100$; age plots in bottom row depict general additive model fit for each voxel in a specified cluster, stratified by sex and adjusted for model covariates. (B) Impact of puberty on sex-specific patterns of CBF change. Age-related differences in CBF diverge in males (*blue*) and females (*pink*) with advancing pubertal development. Error bars represent SEs.

and females were more similar and declined with age at the same rate, however by the mid-pubertal period (determined by a puberty measure; (Tanner (1971)) stage 4), females showed increased rates of CBF (U-shaped trajectory) while CBF in males continued to decline (Fig. 4B). Decreased perfusion in adolescents has since been replicated in other studies (Avants et al., 2015).

3.3 Correlation with IQ and cognition

A growing body of literature is using ASL to explore the relationships between CBF and cognitive functioning. While most studies focus on older and clinical populations (Buschkuehl et al., 2014; Hshieh et al., 2017), a few have investigated healthy pediatric populations (Jog et al., 2016; Kilroy et al., 2011; Schmithorst et al., 2015). Kilroy et al. (2011) investigated the relationship between IQ and pCASL CBF in 39 children and adolescents aged 7 to 17. After adjusting for age, sex, global mean CBF, and gray matter density (GMD), a positive correlation between CBF and IQ scores was observed in the subgenual/anterior cingulate, right orbitofrontal, superior temporal and right inferior parietal regions. An inverse relationship between CBF and IQ was mainly observed in bilateral posterior temporal regions. These findings support the Parieto-Frontal Integration Theory of intelligence (P-FIT) which suggests that individual differences in intelligence result from differences in a distributed network that processes information through a network of regions where the anterior cingulate is implicated in response selection.

One gap in neurocognitive development research is understanding how neuronal–vascular coupling changes across development, since the BOLD signal is known to be influenced by CBF and cerebral metabolic rate of oxygen (CMRO2) (Buxton, 2013; Buxton et al., 2014; Uludağ et al., 2009). Two studies have recently investigated perfusion and BOLD response during different cognitive tasks in different age groups of children. In one study, Schmithorst et al. (2015) observed significant age-related increases in the ratio of BOLD signal to relative CBF change in children aged 3–18 performing a narrative comprehension task. In contrast, a similar study reported no variation with age in CBF or BOLD in a cohort of children and adolescents aged 7–17 while performing a verbal working memory n-back task (Jog et al., 2016). Interestingly, in both studies, a decrease in relative oxygen metabolism with age during task-performance was observed. Specifically, (Schmithorst et al., 2015) reported decreased relative oxygen metabolism with age in task-related regions (middle temporal gyri and the left inferior frontal gyrus), while Jog et al. (2016), observed this pattern (significant decline of the fractional CMRO2 with age) only in detailed voxel wise analyses in sub-regions of the task-engaged fronto-parietal regions.

Two additional studies compared CBF levels and BOLD contrast in children and adults during different tasks, an auditory and a finger-tapping task. Here, researchers observed that CBF significantly differed between the age groups in task-related brain regions, despite BOLD response remaining consistent across age (Moses et al., 2014a,b). These results are seemingly incongruent with the current understanding of how physiology and cerebrovascular dynamics give rise to BOLD signal. While Moses and colleagues (Moses et al., 2014a,b) proposed several potential explanations for this, such as elevated metabolic processes in younger children, more research is needed to better understand this interplay between CBF and BOLD signal.

Overall, these findings suggest that the ratio of BOLD signal to CBF changes across childhood and that caution should be taken when interpreting the relationship between BOLD signal and neuronal activity in developing populations. Indeed, not all developmental changes may be detectable by BOLD imaging alone, and future studies can benefit from investigating CBF patterns across development while performing different cognitive tasks. Here, techniques such as dual-echo EPI pCASL can prove useful, providing the capability of concurrently mapping cerebral blood flow and blood oxygenation. These concurrent measurements can be used to estimate CMRO2 (Buxton, 2013; Buxton et al., 2014; Uludağ et al., 2009), thereby providing a means to identify neurocognitive changes across development.

4. Perfusion of neurodevelopmental disorders

Accumulating data demonstrates that ASL MRI is a promising imaging biomarker for assessing brain function in developmental disorders. ASL has been applied to characterize neurobiological changes in children with disorders such as Autism Spectrum Disorder (ASD) (Jann et al., 2015), adolescent depression (Ho et al., 2013), Attention-Deficit/Hyperactivity Disorder (ADHD) (Schrantee et al., 2017) and substance use (Rao et al., 2007). Below we focus on recent findings from ASD studies.

4.1 Autism spectrum disorder

ASD is a heterogeneous neurodevelopmental disorder characterized by social communication and interaction deficits as well as restrictive and repetitive behaviors (Association, 2013) The Centers for Disease Control and Prevention (CDC) estimate nearly 1 in 59 children in the US have ASD. Broadly, several imaging biomarkers have been explored in ASD: altered activation and functional connectivity (FC) patterns during tasks and at rest (Just et al., 2004; Müller et al., 2011), as well as, abnormal structural patterns (Carper et al., 2002) have all been identified in ASD. However, neuroimaging research has yet to come to a consensus regarding neurological biomarkers of ASD. While atypical neurofunction has been identified in ASD compared to TD controls, they are often aberrant and inconsistent (Katuwal et al., 2016; Lau et al., 2019). Understanding how baseline perfusion correlates with other neuroimaging findings can provide meaningful information about aberrant brain activity patterns in clinical populations by potentially resolving ambiguity in previous findings (Jann et al., 2015).

Recent pCASL studies (Jann et al., 2015; Saitovitch et al., 2019; Yerys et al., 2018) have begun to investigate perfusion patterns in ASD compared to typically developing (TD) peers. There is accumulating evidence to suggest that hypoperfusion plays an important role in the pathophysiology of ASD and that this hypoperfusion is related to autism symptom severity (Bjørklund et al., 2018). Over the last few decades, several ASD perfusion imaging studies have reported attenuated CBF in individuals with ASD compared to controls, especially in the temporal cortices (Burroni et al., 2008; Critchley et al., 2000; Gendry Meresse et al., 2005; George et al., 1992; Ohnishi et al., 2000; Starkstein et al., 2000; Wen-han et al., 2011; Zilbovicius et al., 2000). Temporal cortices are important for language development, as well as, social perception and have been consistently found to be related to ASD pathology (Carper and Courchesne, 2005; Dinstein et al., 2011; Eyler et al., 2012; Hazlett et al., 2011; Schumann et al., 2010). For example, previous research has shown that temporal cortices are $\sim$13% greater in volume in children with ASD relative to peers (Carper et al., 2002), and more recent work has shown decreased temporal cortical thickness in large samples of ASD (Van Rooij and Buitelaar, 2016). The basic cause of hypoperfusion in ASD is unknown but may involve genetic and/or environmental factors.

4.2 Perfusion studies in children and adolescents with ASD

In an ASL reproducibility study by Yerys et al. (2018), 58 adolescents ages 12–17 with and without ASD were scanned twice 8 weeks apart. Consistent hypoperfusion in the temporal lobes compared to typical peers was observed during a passive video watching task. Specifically, they found hypoperfusion in the fusiform gyrus, a region critical to social perception and cognition. Moreover, CBF in this region was positively correlated with more normative facial recognition performance in children with ASD. This finding is congruent with other research indicating that individuals with ASD have reduced activation in the fusiform during the processing of faces and is in line with the social reward theory of ASD (Dawson et al., 2005; Schultz, 2005). However, other research studies have not replicated this finding (Demurie et al., 2016). One possible reason for this discrepancy is the vast symptom heterogeneity in the population.

4.3 Perfusion and functional connectivity in children and adolescents with ASD

More recently, research on network analysis suggests that ASD is a disorder of atypical network functioning as opposed to a single specific brain region abnormality. Intrinsic functional connectivity (the temporal correlation between the time series of different brain regions) derived from resting-state fMRI is one method of measuring brain connectivity and network function. Previous resting-state research has found hyper- and hypo-functional connectivity in ASD relative to TD controls. ASD symptomatology has been correlated with these differences in connectivity and has been used to predict an ASD diagnosis (Plitt et al., 2015; Uddin et al., 2013; Yerys et al., 2015). However, the direction of these patterns is inconsistent. It has been proposed that in addition to the heterogeneity of symptom presentation in ASD, age-dependent differences in ASD may explain some of the discrepant findings (Lawrence et al., 2019). Measuring absolute quantitative measurement of CBF may help to delineate specific ASD connectivity patterns.

The relationship between regional FC and CBF represents the minimum metabolic demand to efficiently process information (Passow et al., 2015; Riedl et al., 2014; Tomasi et al., 2013), and increased FC requires increased metabolic demand (Liang et al., 2013; Tomasi et al., 2013). This is thought to be true for both healthy individuals and those with ASD. Consistent with PET and SPECT studies investigating children with ASD, ASL resting-state connectivity studies reported hypoperfusion in the temporal cortices (Jann et al., 2015; Saitovitch et al., 2019). In a recent resting-state study, 18 children with ASD and 36 typical controls underwent an ASL scan. Significant hypoperfusion was found in the ASD group in superior temporal regions (Saitovitch et al., 2019). The superior temporal sulcus and gyrus are important for biological motion and social perception (Georgescu et al., 2013; Gervais et al., 2004). CBF was found to be negatively correlated with autism severity scores in the right superior temporal gyrus suggesting that autism severity is associated with lower CBF. Whole-brain correlation analysis also revealed a relationship between symptom severity and the cerebellum such that fewer ASD symptoms were related to higher CBF values. Hypoperfusion in the superior temporal regions is consistent with previous PET and SPECT findings (Ohnishi et al., 2000; Zilbovicius et al., 2000). Future research with increased sample sizes will help us to understand the interactions between CBF and FC in ASD and may indicate which patterns network connectivity are the most accurate biomarkers for ASD.

Networks considered to be important for intrinsic awareness and social perception have also been investigated in ASD. One such network is the default mode network (DMN). The DMN is an intrinsic neural relevant for self-referential thought, social and emotional processes, and theory of mind (ToM) (Buckner et al., 2008). In a resting-state study by Jann et al. (2015), authors used pCASL with 3D GRASE to simultaneously investigate patterns of resting perfusion and FC of the DMN in children with ASD as compared to age, gender and IQ matched TD children. Jann and colleagues found widespread hyperperfusion in frontal and temporal cortices as well as hypoperfusion in the dorsal anterior cingulate cortex (ACC) of children with ASD. Changes in the connectivity of the DMN were also detected and characterized by locally increased FC within the dorsal ACC and reduced long-range FC between anterior and posterior modules of the DMN. These findings are consistent with existing BOLD literature (Assaf et al., 2010; Hernandez et al., 2015; Monk et al., 2009; Rudie and Dapretto, 2013; Washington et al., 2014). Perfusion data from other intrinsic networks (i.e., salience network) that have been found to be related to ASD have yet to be investigated. Future studies are needed to understand CBF patterns in other networks in this population.

4.4 Ongoing ASD perfusion research in ASD perfusion research

In the last decade, neuroimaging research studies have begun to utilize large multisite datasets and are applying statistical analyses that are less dependent on generating hypotheses for specific feature selections to identify ASD biomarkers, such as deep learning algorithms. To date, machine learning techniques have been applied to perfusion data collected on clinical populations such as depression and Alzheimer's disease and mild cognitive impairment (Brown et al., 2018; Collij et al., 2016), however, to the best of our knowledge, no published study has utilized quantitative perfusion data to classify ASD among TD controls or other disorders. Using BOLD signal, classification accuracy across different techniques can range between 66% and $<$90% when differentiating ASD from TD controls (Aghdam et al., 2018; Heinsfeld et al., 2018; Just et al., 2014). A recent study found that underconnectivity between the anterior and posterior areas of the ASD brains that contributed the most to the present classification (Heinsfeld et al., 2018). Since perfusion studies are also reliable in detecting abnormal CBF in ASD (Jann et al., 2015), including perfusion measures in feature selections may increase classification accuracy (Xie et al., 2019).

5. Limitations and future directions

Currently, pCASL with background suppressed 3D acquisitions such as GRASE (a hybrid of gradient and spin echo) and Stack-of-Spirals is recommended as the preferred common strategy for clinical applications (Alsop et al., 2015). However, there remain significant challenges for making 3D pCASL an impactful tool in pediatric neurodevelopment studies: (1) The spatial resolution of existing 3D pCASL is generally on the order of $4 \times 4 \times 4$ mm^3. In particular, there is considerable spatial blurring along the slice direction due to the modulation of k-space signals by the transverse (T_2) relaxation during the long readout time (half width of the point-spread function on the order of 1.5 voxels) (Vidorreta et al., 2013). This blurring effect makes it very challenging to accurately quantify perfusion of small brain structures such as hippocampus and amygdala as well as the cerebral cortex with a thickness of a few mm. This issue is potentially problematic given that the cortex continues to thin with development

(Tamnes et al., 2017). (2) To reduce the blurring effect, long readout trains must be broken down into a few segments. However, the segmented 3D acquisition is susceptible to (inter-segment) head motion that is frequently present in pediatric populations. In the following, we summarize two recent trends in 3D and 2D ASL to address the above challenges (see Fig. 5 for pulse sequence diagram).

5.1 Accelerated perfusion imaging with 3D accelerated ASL

The 2D-CAIPIRINHA (controlled aliasing in parallel imaging results in higher acceleration) technique (Breuer et al., 2006) was proposed as an under-sampling strategy to achieve robust high resolution and/or highly accelerated 3D imaging by more efficiently exploiting coil sensitivity variations along both phase and slice dimensions (lower coil g-factor) to achieve reliable parallel imaging reconstruction. Several groups (Boland et al., 2018; Shao and Wang, 2017; Spann et al., 2020) have recently developed single-shot 3D GRASE pCASL sequences using 2D-CAIPI accelerations (see Fig. 5B). A time-dependent 2D-CAIPI sampling pattern can be further implemented to increase the temporal incoherence between measurements or PLDs (Fig. 5B), which has been combined with a novel image reconstruction method employing both spatial and temporal total-generalized-variation (TGV) regularization (Spann et al., 2020). The ASL-TGV method generates reliable high resolution (iso-3 mm) perfusion images from each under-sampled measurement and improves the motion robustness of 3D ASL data. Another advantage of ASL-TGV method is the de-noising effect, which improves the image quality of the CBF maps compared to those acquired by a standard segmented approach.

Fig. 6 shows CBF maps acquired from a standard 3D acquisition with 6 segments and single-shot 2D-CAIPI acquisition. The single-shot CBF maps reconstructed with the ASL-TGV method shows improved image quality compared to fully sampled but segmented acquisition. In the presence of

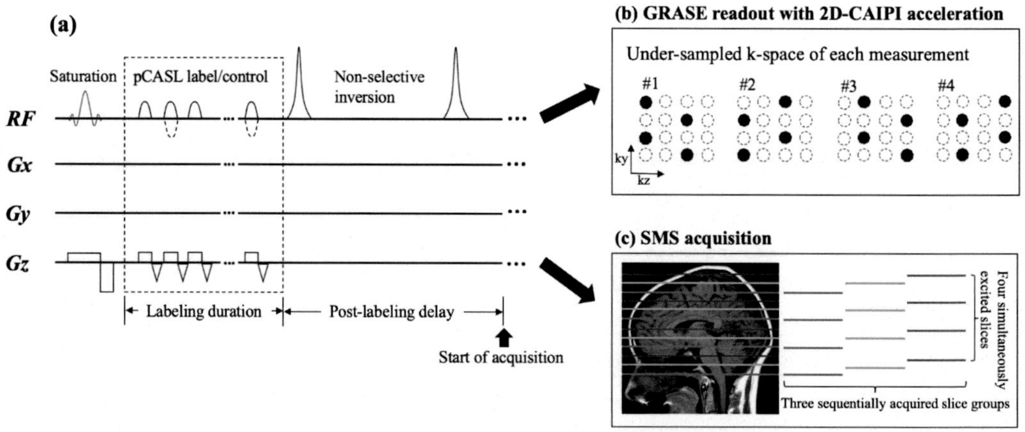

FIG. 5

Diagram of pCASL (A) with accelerated 3D GRASE (B) and 2D SMS acquisition (C). The background suppression consists of a presaturation and two nonselective inversion pulses. (B) illustrates a fourfold accelerated GRASE readout with CAIPIRINHA under-sampling pattern along phase (ky) and partition (kz) directions, which shifts between subsequent label/control pairs. This time-dependent under-sampling pattern increases the temporal incoherence between the measurements. (C) illustrates the 2D acquisition with fourfold SMS acceleration. In this example, four slices were excited simultaneously and three slice groups were acquired sequentially.

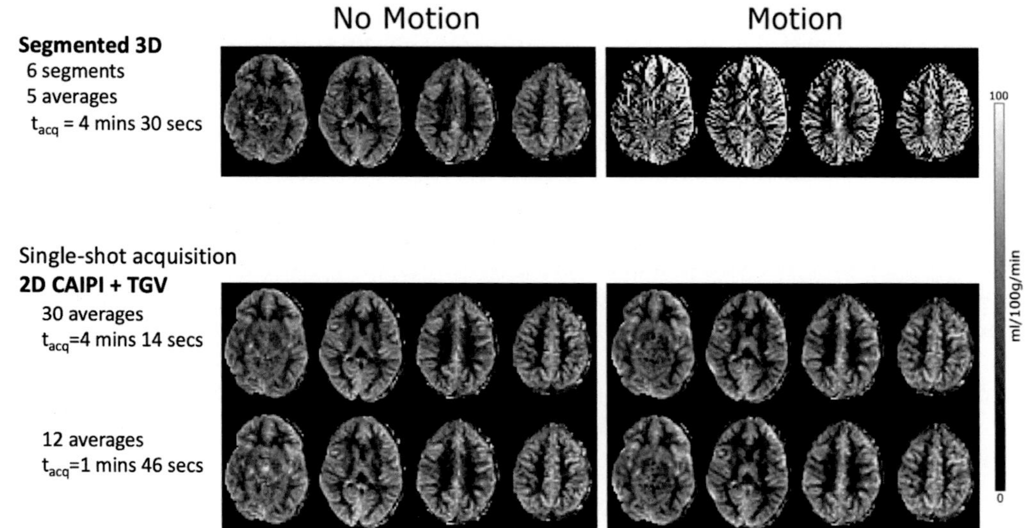

FIG. 6

Four-slice of CBF maps from standard segmented 3D acquisition and proposed single-shot acquisition. Six segments were acquired for standard 3D acquisition. Single-shot acquisition was achieved by 2D-CAIPI under-sampling pattern and spatio-temporal TGV-regularized reconstruction. The single-shot CBF maps reconstructed with the TGV approach shows an improved image quality compared to fully sampled but segmented acquisition (left column). In the presence of subject head movement (right column), inter-segment motion cannot be corrected for segmented acquisition, and as a result, the CBF maps of the standard segmented 3D acquisition are not interpretable. For the single-shot method, the motion can be corrected retrospectively, which results in CBF maps with a good image quality. With 2D-CAIPI and TGV, similar image quality is achieved with fewer averages or shorter scan time (bottom row).

Figure adapted from Spann, S.M., Shao, X., Wang, D.J., Aigner, C.S., Schloegl, M., Bredies, K., Stollberger, R., 2020. Robust single-shot acquisition of high resolution whole brain ASL images by combining time-dependent 2D CAPIRINHA sampling with spatio-temporal TGV reconstruction. NeuroImage. 206, 116337.

subject movement (right column), inter-segment motion (~45 s acquisition window) cannot be corrected for segmented acquisition, resulting in severely corrupted CBF maps of the standard segmented 3D acquisition. The single-shot method is immune to the head motion due to the short acquisition time of each measurement (<0.3 s), and the inter-volume motion can be corrected retrospectively. The right column of Fig. 6 shows the CBF maps acquired with head motion, which is often present in pediatric scans, and the single-shot acquisition still generates high quality CBF maps. Additionally, similarly high image quality can be achieved with the ASL-TGV method in a reduced scan time due to the denoising effect (Fig. 6 bottom row).

5.2 Highly efficient perfusion imaging with 2D simultaneous multislice (SMS) ASL

2D SMS or multiband (MB) is a new accelerated imaging technology that simultaneously excites multiple slices and recovers each slice with parallel imaging techniques (Feinberg et al., 2010; Setsompop et al., 2012), as shown in Fig. 5C. Preliminary studies combining SMS with ASL showed that SMS can reduce T1 relaxation of the label, improve spatial coverage, and/or resolution compared to those of standard 2D ASL (Kim et al., 2013; Li et al., 2015; Wang et al., 2015). SMS imaging may overcome the limitation of 3D ASL acquisitions in terms of head motion and spatial blurring. However, the SNR of existing SMS ASL techniques is inferior to that of 3D ASL partly due to the suboptimal background suppression (BS), as multiple SMS excitations are required, and the background signal recovers with sequential slice acquisitions. Recently, a constrained slice-dependent background suppression (CSD-BS) scheme was developed to improve the SNR of 2D MB pCASL to be comparable to that of 3D pCASL (Shao et al., 2018). Slice-dependent premodulation pulses were used and the timing of BS inversion pulses was optimized to achieve effective BS across SMS slice groups. Recently, a super-resolution 2D pCASL method was developed by combining the Slice Dithered Enhanced Resolution (SLIDER) with 2D MB pCASL with CSD-BS (Shao et al., 2018; Shou et al., 2020) and a MB factor of 4 to enhance both the resolution and SNR. As shown in Fig. 7, the reconstructed images achieve a resolution of isotropic $2 \times 2 \times 2\ \text{mm}^3$, and show increased spatial and temporal SNR compared to standard high-resolution pCASL images.

5.3 Layer dependent perfusion measurement at ultra-high field

Brain development during childhood is a dynamic process and usually involves changes in cortical volumes and thickness. In the first a few years of life, cortical volume, surface area and thickness all increase over time (Gilmore et al., 2012; Lyall et al., 2015). Continuous thinning of cortical volume and thickness was observed from early or mid-childhood (Walhovd et al., 2016), with accelerated thinning during adolescence (Raznahan et al., 2011; Shaw et al., 2007, 2008; Tamnes et al., 2017). Although the structural changes from infancy to childhood have been well studied, underlying

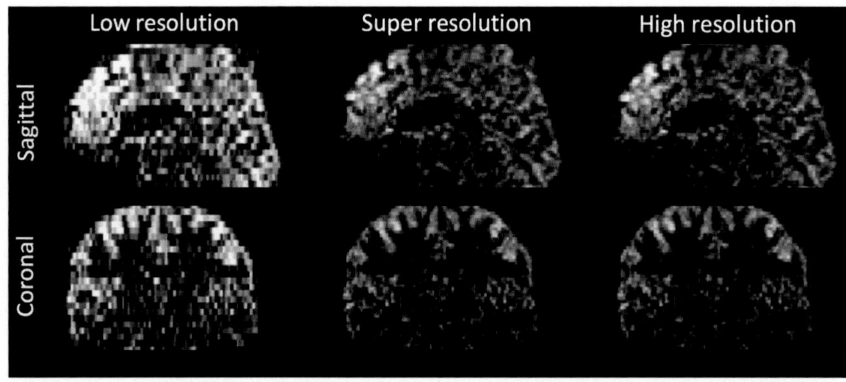

FIG. 7

Sagittal and Coronal view of the super-resolution and reference images. The reconstructed super-resolution images have a spatial resolution of $2 \times 2 \times 2\ \text{mm}^3$, where the reference low-resolution images have a spatial resolution of $2 \times 2 \times 4\ \text{mm}^3$.

Figure adapted from Shou, Q., Shao, X., Wang, D.J., 2020. Super-resolution multi-band ASL using slice dithered enhanced resolution (SLIDER) technique. Proc. Intl. Soc. Mag. Reson.

physiological changes associated with neurodevelopment, especially in different cortical layers, await more investigation.

Spatial resolution of clinical ASL scan at 1.5T or 3T is typically in the range of 3–5 mm (Alsop et al., 2015). Because of the thin cerebral cortex (thickness is usually less than 3 mm) (Tamnes et al., 2017), sub-millimeter spatial resolution of ASL is required to separate multiple layers in the cerebral cortex in order to study layer dependent physiological changes. Ultra-high field ASL has benefitted from significantly higher SNR due to longer longitudinal relaxation time of arterial blood (Wang et al., 2002; Zuo et al., 2013) and super-linearly increased SNR with field strength (Pohmann et al., 2016). Shao and Wang et al., recently demonstrated that pCASL labeling scheme combined with efficient 3D inner-volume gradient and spin echo (GRASE) readout and background suppression has the capability of revealing layer dependent CBF at Ultra-high field (7T) (Shao et al., 2019).

Fig. 8B shows sub-millimeter CBF maps acquired from one healthy young subject (Male, 27 years old) at 7T. In-plane resolution is 0.5 mm after interpolation. Three layers of gray matter (superficial, middle, deep) were manually segmented based on coregistered T1w MP-RAGE images. Average CBF was 42.1, 49.4, and 40.3 mL/100 g/min in superficial, middle and deep layers, respectively (Fig. 8C). CBF was significantly higher in the middle layer (~20%), which corresponds to the highest capillary density in the middle layers reported in anatomical studies in animals and specimens of human brain tissue (Lauwers et al., 2008). Separation of CBF in cortical layers allows many opportunities to understand the regional blood supply and neurovascular coupling in a laminar fashion associated with the neurodevelopment in childhood. With increasing availability of ultrahigh field MR at 7T, we expect research on laminar perfusion in typical and atypical neurodevelopment will emerge and grow.

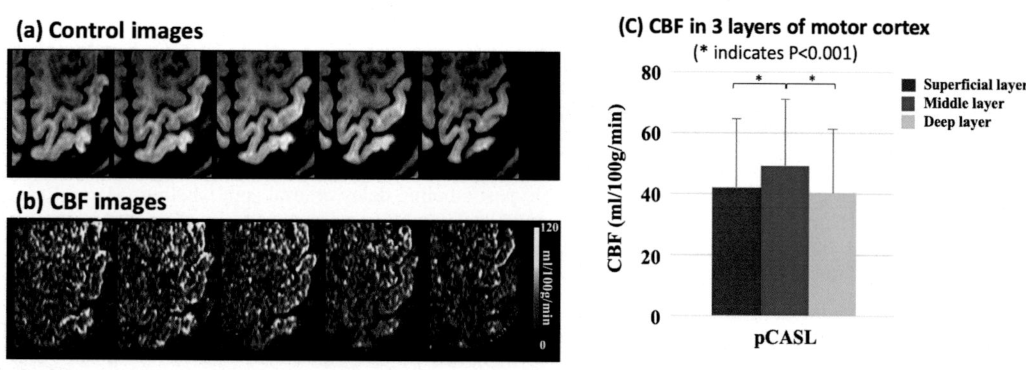

FIG. 8

Five slices of CBF maps with sub-millimeter in-plane resolution (0.5 mm, after interpolation) acquire at 7T (B). Corresponding control images are shown in (A). Small FOV was acquired with inner-volume acquisition to shorten the acquisition window and increase SNR. (C) shows the bar plot of CBF in three layers of motor cortex. CBF in the middle layer is significantly higher than the CBF in the superficial and deep layer.

Figure adapted from Shao, X., Wang, K., Wang, D.J., 2019. 7T high-resolution arterial spin labeling reveals layer dependent cerebral blood flow. Proc. Intl. Soc. Mag. Reson. Med.

6. Conclusion

ASL perfusion MRI is an appealing imaging tool to study brain development due to its entirely non-invasive nature and several physiological properties of a child brain. ASL has already shown promising results in both typical and atypical neurodevelopment, and new technical developments will allow improved spatial resolution, quantification accuracy and robust to motion.

References

Aghdam, M.A., Sharifi, A., Pedram, M.M., 2018. Combination of rs-fMRI and sMRI data to discriminate autism spectrum disorders in young children using deep belief network. J. Digit. Imaging 31 (6), 895–903.

Akgören, N., Fabricius, M., Lauritzen, M., 1994. Importance of nitric oxide for local increases of blood flow in rat cerebellar cortex during electrical stimulation. Proc. Natl. Acad. Sci. 91 (13), 5903–5907.

Alsop, D.C., Detre, J.A., Golay, X., Günther, M., Hendrikse, J., Hernandez-Garcia, L., Smits, M., 2015. Recommended implementation of arterial spin-labeled perfusion MRI for clinical applications: a consensus of the ISMRM perfusion study group and the European consortium for ASL in dementia. Magn. Reson. Med. 73 (1), 102–116.

Assaf, M., Jagannathan, K., Calhoun, V.D., Miller, L., Stevens, M.C., Sahl, R., Pearlson, G.D., 2010. Abnormal functional connectivity of default mode sub-networks in autism spectrum disorder patients. NeuroImage 53 (1), 247–256.

Association, D.-A. P, 2013. Diagnostic and Statistical Manual of Mental Disorders. American Psychiatric Publishing, Arlington.

Avants, B.B., Duda, J.T., Kilroy, E., Krasileva, K., Jann, K., Kandel, B.T., Smith, R., 2015. The pediatric template of brain perfusion. Scientific Data 2 (1), 1–17.

Biagi, L., Abbruzzese, A., Bianchi, M.C., Alsop, D.C., Del Guerra, A., Tosetti, M., 2007. Age dependence of cerebral perfusion assessed by magnetic resonance continuous arterial spin labeling. Magn. Reson. Med. 25 (4), 696–702.

Bjørklund, G., Kern, J.K., Urbina, M.A., Saad, K., ElHoufey, A.A., Geier, D.A., Aaseth, J., 2018. Cerebral hypoperfusion in autism spectrum disorder. Acta Neurobiol. Exp. 78 (21), 9.

Blanton, R.E., Cooney, R.E., Joormann, J., Eugène, F., Glover, G.H., Gotlib, I.H., 2012. Pubertal stage and brain anatomy in girls. Neuroscience 217, 105–112.

Boland, M., Stirnberg, R., Pracht, E.D., Kramme, J., Viviani, R., Stingl, J., Stöcker, T., 2018. Accelerated 3D-GRASE imaging improves quantitative multiple post labeling delay arterial spin labeling. Magn. Reson. Med. 80 (6), 2475–2484.

Børch, K., Greisen, G., 1998. Blood flow distribution in the normal human preterm brain. Pediatr. Res. 43 (1), 28–33.

Bouyssi-Kobar, M., Murnick, J., Brossard-Racine, M., Chang, T., Mahdi, E., Jacobs, M., Limperopoulos, C., 2018. Altered cerebral perfusion in infants born preterm compared with infants born full term. J. Pediatr. 193, 54. 61. e52.

Breuer, F.A., Blaimer, M., Mueller, M.F., Seiberlich, N., Heidemann, R.M., Griswold, M.A., Jakob, P.M., 2006. Controlled aliasing in volumetric parallel imaging (2D CAIPIRINHA). Magn. Reson. Med. 55 (3), 549–556.

Brown, E., Forkert, N.D., Marcil, L., Talai, A.S., Ramasubbu, R., 2018. S116. The use of arterial spin labeling perfusion MRI for automated classification of major depression disorder. Biol. Psychiatry 83 (9), S392.

Buckner, R.L., Andrews-Hanna, J.R., Schacter, D.L., 2008. The brain's Default Network: Anatomy, Function, and Relevance to Disease.

Burroni, L., Orsi, A., Monti, L., Hayek, Y., Rocchi, R., Vattimo, A.G., 2008. Regional cerebral blood flow in childhood autism: a SPET study with SPM evaluation. Nucl. Med. Commun. 29 (2), 150–156.

Buschkuehl, M., Hernandez-Garcia, L., Jaeggi, S.M., Bernard, J.A., Jonides, J., 2014. Neural effects of short-term training on working memory. Cogn. Affect. Behav. Neurosci. 14 (1), 147–160.

Buxton, R.B., 2013. The physics of functional magnetic resonance imaging (fMRI). Rep. Prog. Phys. 76 (9), 096601.

Buxton, R.B., Griffeth, V.E., Simon, A.B., Moradi, F., 2014. Variability of the coupling of blood flow and oxygen metabolism responses in the brain: a problem for interpreting BOLD studies but potentially a new window on the underlying neural activity. Front. Neurosci. 8, 139.

Camacho, M.C., King, L.S., Ojha, A., Garcia, C.M., Sisk, L.S., Cichocki, A.C., Gotlib, I.H., 2019. Cerebral blood flow in 5-to 8-month-olds: regional tissue maturity is associated with infant affect. Dev. Sci., e12928.

Carper, R.A., Courchesne, E., 2005. Localized enlargement of the frontal cortex in early autism. Biol. Psychiatry 57 (2), 126–133.

Carper, R.A., Moses, P., Tigue, Z.D., Courchesne, E., 2002. Cerebral lobes in autism: early hyperplasia and abnormal age effects. NeuroImage 16 (4), 1038–1051.

Cha, Y.-H.K., Jog, M.A., Kim, Y.-C., Chakrapani, S., Kraman, S.M., Wang, D.J., 2013. Regional correlation between resting state FDG PET and pCASL perfusion MRI. J. Cereb. Blood Flow Metab. 33 (12), 1909–1914.

Chen, Y., Wolk, D., Reddin, J., Korczykowski, M., Martinez, P., Musiek, E., Greenberg, J., 2011. Voxel-level comparison of arterial spin-labeled perfusion MRI and FDG-PET in Alzheimer disease. Neurology 77 (22), 1977–1985.

Chiron, C., Raynaud, C., Mazière, B., Zilbovicius, M., Laflamme, L., Masure, M.-C., Syrota, A., 1992. Changes in regional cerebral blood flow during brain maturation in children and adolescents. J. Nucl. Med. 33 (5), 696–703.

Christie, D., Viner, R., 2005. Adolescent development: ABC of adolescence. BMJ 330, 301–304.

Chugani, H.T., 1998. A critical period of brain development: studies of cerebral glucose utilization with PET. Prev. Med. 27 (2), 184–188.

Collij, L.E., Heeman, F., Kuijer, J.P., Ossenkoppele, R., Benedictus, M.R., Möller, C., van der Flier, W.M., 2016. Application of machine learning to arterial spin labeling in mild cognitive impairment and Alzheimer disease. Radiology 281 (3), 865–875.

Critchley, H.D., Daly, E.M., Bullmore, E.T., Williams, S.C., Van Amelsvoort, T., Robertson, D.M., Howlin, P., 2000. The functional neuroanatomy of social behaviour: changes in cerebral blood flow when people with autistic disorder process facial expressions. Brain 123 (11), 2203–2212.

Dai, W., Garcia, D., De Bazelaire, C., Alsop, D.C., 2008. Continuous flow-driven inversion for arterial spin labeling using pulsed radio frequency and gradient fields. Magnetic Resonance in Medicine: An Official Journal of the International Society for Magnetic Resonance in Medicine 60 (6), 1488–1497.

Dawson, G., Webb, S.J., McPartland, J., 2005. Understanding the nature of face processing impairment in autism: insights from behavioral and electrophysiological studies. Dev. Neuropsychol. 27 (3), 403–424.

De Vis, J., Hendrikse, J., Groenendaal, F., De Vries, L., Kersbergen, K., Benders, M., Petersen, E., 2014. Impact of neonate haematocrit variability on the longitudinal relaxation time of blood: implications for arterial spin labelling MRI. NeuroImage: Clinical 4, 517–525.

Demurie, E., Roeyers, H., Wiersema, J.R., Sonuga-Barke, E., 2016. No evidence for inhibitory deficits or altered reward processing in ADHD: data from a new integrated monetary incentive delay go/no-go task. J. Atten. Disord. 20 (4), 353–367.

Dinstein, I., Pierce, K., Eyler, L., Solso, S., Malach, R., Behrmann, M., Courchesne, E., 2011. Disrupted neural synchronization in toddlers with autism. Neuron 70 (6), 1218–1225.

Dolui, S., Li, Z., Nasrallah, I., Detre, J., Wolk, D., 2019. Multimodal Magnetic Resonance Imaging Versus 18F-FDG-PET to Identify Mild Cognitive Impairment (P5. 1–022). AAN Enterprises, In.

Eyler, L.T., Pierce, K., Courchesne, E., 2012. A failure of left temporal cortex to specialize for language is an early emerging and fundamental property of autism. Brain 135 (3), 949–960.

Feinberg, D.A., Moeller, S., Smith, S.M., Auerbach, E., Ramanna, S., Glasser, M.F., Yacoub, E., 2010. Multiplexed echo planar imaging for sub-second whole brain FMRI and fast diffusion imaging. PLoS One 5 (12).

Feng, C.-M., Narayana, S., Lancaster, J.L., Jerabek, P.A., Arnow, T.L., Zhu, F., Gao, J.-H., 2004. CBF changes during brain activation: fMRI vs PET. Neuroimage 22 (1), 443–446.

Gendry Meresse, I., Zilbovicius, M., Boddaert, N., Robel, L., Philippe, A., Sfaello, I., Mouren, M.C., 2005. Autism severity and temporal lobe functional abnormalities. Ann. Neurol. 58 (3), 466–469.

George, M.S., Costa, D.C., Kouris, K., Ring, H.A., Ell, P.J., 1992. Cerebral blood flow abnormalities in adults with infantile autism. J. Nerv. Ment. Dis. 180 (7), 413–417.

Georgescu, A.L., Kuzmanovic, B., Schilbach, L., Tepest, R., Kulbida, R., Bente, G., Vogeley, K., 2013. Neural correlates of "social gaze" processing in high-functioning autism under systematic variation of gaze duration. NeuroImage: Clin. 3, 340–351.

Gervais, H., Belin, P., Boddaert, N., Leboyer, M., Coez, A., Sfaello, I., Zilbovicius, M., 2004. Abnormal cortical voice processing in autism. Nat. Neurosci. 7 (8), 801–802.

Giedd, J.N., Blumenthal, J., Jeffries, N.O., Castellanos, F.X., Liu, H., Zijdenbos, A., Rapoport, J.L., 1999. Brain development during childhood and adolescence: a longitudinal MRI study. Nat. Neurosci. 2 (10), 861–863.

Giedd, J.N., Clasen, L.S., Lenroot, R., Greenstein, D., Wallace, G.L., Ordaz, S., Stayer, C., 2006. Puberty-related influences on brain development. Mol. Cell. Endocrinol. 254, 154–162.

Gilmore, J.H., Shi, F., Woolson, S.L., Knickmeyer, R.C., Short, S.J., Lin, W., Shen, D., 2012. Longitudinal development of cortical and subcortical gray matter from birth to 2 years. Cereb. Cortex 22 (11), 2478–2485.

Hazlett, H.C., Poe, M.D., Gerig, G., Styner, M., Chappell, C., Smith, R.G., Piven, J., 2011. Early brain overgrowth in autism associated with an increase in cortical surface area before age 2 years. Arch. Gen. Psychiatry 68 (5), 467–476.

Heijtel, D.F., Mutsaerts, H.J., Bakker, E., Schober, P., Stevens, M.F., Petersen, E.T., van Osch, M.J., 2014. Accuracy and precision of pseudo-continuous arterial spin labeling perfusion during baseline and hypercapnia: a head-to-head comparison with 15O H2O positron emission tomography. NeuroImage 92, 182–192.

Heinsfeld, A.S., Franco, A.R., Craddock, R.C., Buchweitz, A., Meneguzzi, F., 2018. Identification of autism spectrum disorder using deep learning and the ABIDE dataset. NeuroImage: Clin. 17, 16–23.

Heller, A.S., Casey, B., 2016. The neurodynamics of emotion: delineating typical and atypical emotional processes during adolescence. Dev. Sci. 19 (1), 3–18.

Hernandez, L.M., Rudie, J.D., Green, S.A., Bookheimer, S., Dapretto, M., 2015. Neural signatures of autism spectrum disorders: insights into brain network dynamics. Neuropsychopharmacology 40 (1), 171–189.

Ho, T.C., Wu, J., Shin, D.D., Liu, T.T., Tapert, S.F., Yang, G., Wolkowitz, O., 2013. Altered cerebral perfusion in executive, affective, and motor networks during adolescent depression. J. Am. Acad. Child Adolesc. Psychiatry 52 (10), 1076. 1091. e1072.

Hoge, R.D., Pike, G.B., 2001. Oxidative metabolism and the detection of neuronal activation via imaging. J. Chem. Neuroanat. 22 (1–2), 43–52.

Hshieh, T.T., Dai, W., Cavallari, M., Guttmann, C.R., Meier, D.S., Schmitt, E.M., Jones, R.N., 2017. Cerebral blood flow MRI in the nondemented elderly is not predictive of post-operative delirium but is correlated with cognitive performance. J. Cereb. Blood Flow Metab. 37 (4), 1386–1397.

Hu, H.H., Rusin, J.A., Peng, R., Shao, X., Smith, M., Krishnamurthy, R., Wang, D.J., 2019. Multi-phase 3D arterial spin labeling brain MRI in assessing cerebral blood perfusion and arterial transit times in children at 3T. Clin. Imaging 53, 210–220.

Jain, V., Duda, J., Avants, B., Giannetta, M., Xie, S.X., Roberts, T., Wang, D.J., 2012. Longitudinal reproducibility and accuracy of pseudo-continuous arterial spin–labeled perfusion MR imaging in typically developing children. Radiology 263 (2), 527–536.

Jann, K., Hernandez, L.M., Beck-Pancer, D., McCarron, R., Smith, R.X., Dapretto, M., Wang, D.J., 2015. Altered resting perfusion and functional connectivity of default mode network in youth with autism spectrum disorder. Brain Behav. 5 (9), e00358.

Jill, B., Petersen, E.T., De Vries, L.S., Groenendaal, F., Kersbergen, K.J., Alderliesten, T., Benders, M.J., 2013. Regional changes in brain perfusion during brain maturation measured non-invasively with arterial spin labeling MRI in neonates. Eur. J. Radiol. 82 (3), 538–543.

Jog, M.A., Yan, L., Kilroy, E., Krasileva, K., Jann, K., LeClair, H., Wang, D.J., 2016. Developmental trajectories of cerebral blood flow and oxidative metabolism at baseline and during working memory tasks. NeuroImage 134, 587–596.

Jopling, J., Henry, E., Wiedmeier, S.E., Christensen, R.D., 2009. Reference ranges for hematocrit and blood hemoglobin concentration during the neonatal period: data from a multihospital health care system. Pediatrics 123 (2), e333–e337.

Just, M.A., Cherkassky, V.L., Keller, T.A., Minshew, N.J., 2004. Cortical activation and synchronization during sentence comprehension in high-functioning autism: evidence of underconnectivity. Brain 127 (8), 1811–1821.

Just, M.A., Cherkassky, V.L., Buchweitz, A., Keller, T.A., Mitchell, T.M., 2014. Identifying autism from neural representations of social interactions: neurocognitive markers of autism. PLoS One 9 (12).

Kandel, B.M., Wang, D.J., Detre, J.A., Gee, J.C., Avants, B.B., 2015. Decomposing cerebral blood flow MRI into functional and structural components: a non-local approach based on prediction. NeuroImage 105, 156–170. https://doi.org/10.1016/j.neuroimage.2014.10.052.

Katuwal, G.J., Baum, S.A., Cahill, N.D., Dougherty, C.C., Evans, E., Evans, D.W., Michael, A.M., 2016. Inter-method discrepancies in brain volume estimation may drive inconsistent findings in autism. Front. Neurosci. 10, 439.

Kehrer, M., Goelz, R., Krägeloh-Mann, I., Schöning, M., 2002. Measurement of volume of cerebral blood flow in healthy preterm and term neonates with ultrasound. Lancet 360 (9347), 1749–1750.

Kilroy, E., Liu, C.Y., Yan, L., Kim, Y.C., Dapretto, M., Mendez, M.F., Wang, D.J., 2011. Relationships between cerebral blood flow and IQ in typically developing children and adolescents. J. Cogn. Sci. 12 (2), 151.

Kilroy, E., Apostolova, L., Liu, C., Yan, L., Ringman, J., Wang, D.J., 2014. Reliability of two-dimensional and three-dimensional pseudo-continuous arterial spin labeling perfusion MRI in elderly populations: comparison with 15o-water positron emission tomography. J. Magn. Reson. Imaging 39 (4), 931–939.

Kim, T., Shin, W., Zhao, T., Beall, E.B., Lowe, M.J., Bae, K.T., 2013. Whole brain perfusion measurements using arterial spin labeling with multiband acquisition. Magn. Reson. Med. 70 (6), 1653–1661.

Lau, W.K., Leung, M.-K., Lau, B.W., 2019. Resting-state abnormalities in autism Spectrum disorders: a meta-analysis. Sci. Rep. 9 (1), 1–8.

Lauwers, F., Cassot, F., Lauwers-Cances, V., Puwanarajah, P., Duvernoy, H., 2008. Morphometry of the human cerebral cortex microcirculation: general characteristics and space-related profiles. NeuroImage 39 (3), 936–948.

Lawrence, K.E., Hernandez, L.M., Bookheimer, S.Y., Dapretto, M., 2019. Atypical longitudinal development of functional connectivity in adolescents with autism spectrum disorder. Autism Res. 12 (1), 53–65. https://doi.org/10.1002/aur.1971.

Li, X., Wang, D., Auerbach, E.J., Moeller, S., Ugurbil, K., Metzger, G.J., 2015. Theoretical and experimental evaluation of multi-band EPI for high-resolution whole brain pCASL imaging. NeuroImage 106, 170–181.

Liang, X., Zou, Q., He, Y., Yang, Y., 2013. Coupling of functional connectivity and regional cerebral blood flow reveals a physiological basis for network hubs of the human brain. Proc. Natl. Acad. Sci. U. S. A. 110 (5), 1929–1934. https://doi.org/10.1073/pnas.1214900110.

Liu, P., Chalak, L.F., Krishnamurthy, L.C., Mir, I., Peng, S.l., Huang, H., Lu, H., 2016. T1 and T2 values of human neonatal blood at 3 tesla: dependence on hematocrit, oxygenation, and temperature. Magn. Reson. Med. 75 (4), 1730–1735.

Liu, P., Qi, Y., Lin, Z., Guo, Q., Wang, X., Lu, H., 2019. Assessment of cerebral blood flow in neonates and infants: a phase-contrast MRI study. NeuroImage 185, 926–933.

Lopez-Larson, M.P., King, J.B., Terry, J., McGlade, E.C., Yurgelun-Todd, D., 2012. Reduced insular volume in attention deficit hyperactivity disorder. Psychiatry Res. Neuroimaging 204 (1), 32–39.

Lu, H., Clingman, C., Golay, X., Van Zijl, P.C., 2004. Determining the longitudinal relaxation time (T1) of blood at 3.0 tesla. Magn. Reson. Med. 52 (3), 679–682.

Lu, H., Xu, F., Rodrigue, K.M., Kennedy, K.M., Cheng, Y., Flicker, B., Park, D.C., 2011. Alterations in cerebral metabolic rate and blood supply across the adult lifespan. Cereb. Cortex 21 (6), 1426–1434.

Lyall, A.E., Shi, F., Geng, X., Woolson, S., Li, G., Wang, L., Gilmore, J.H., 2015. Dynamic development of regional cortical thickness and surface area in early childhood. Cereb. Cortex 25 (8), 2204–2212.

Maccotta, L., Detre, J.A., Alsop, D.C., 1997. The efficiency of adiabatic inversion for perfusion imaging by arterial spin labeling. NMR Biomed. 10 (4–5), 216–221.

Massaro, A.N., Bouyssi-Kobar, M., Chang, T., Vezina, L., Du Plessis, A.J., Limperopoulos, C., 2013. Brain perfusion in encephalopathic newborns after therapeutic hypothermia. Am. J. Neuroradiol. 34 (8), 1649–1655.

Miranda, M.J., Olofsson, K., Sidaros, K., 2006. Noninvasive measurements of regional cerebral perfusion in preterm and term neonates by magnetic resonance arterial spin labeling. Pediatr. Res. 60 (3), 359–363.

Monk, C.S., Peltier, S.J., Wiggins, J.L., Weng, S.-J., Carrasco, M., Risi, S., Lord, C., 2009. Abnormalities of intrinsic functional connectivity in autism spectrum disorders. NeuroImage 47 (2), 764–772.

Moses, P., DiNino, M., Hernandez, L., Liu, T.T., 2014a. Developmental changes in resting and functional cerebral blood flow and their relationship to the BOLD response. Hum. Brain Mapp. 35 (7), 3188–3198.

Moses, P., Hernandez, L.M., Orient, E., 2014b. Age-related differences in cerebral blood flow underlie the BOLD fMRI signal in childhood. Front. Psychol. 5, 300.

Müller, R.-A., Shih, P., Keehn, B., Deyoe, J.R., Leyden, K.M., Shukla, D.K., 2011. Underconnected, but how? A survey of functional connectivity MRI studies in autism spectrum disorders. Cereb. Cortex 21 (10), 2233–2243.

Neufang, S., Specht, K., Hausmann, M., Güntürkün, O., Herpertz-Dahlmann, B., Fink, G.R., Konrad, K., 2009. Sex differences and the impact of steroid hormones on the developing human brain. Cereb. Cortex 19 (2), 464–473.

Newberg, A.B., Wang, J., Rao, H., Swanson, R.L., Wintering, N., Karp, J.S., Detre, J.A., 2005. Concurrent CBF and CMRGlc changes during human brain activation by combined fMRI–PET scanning. NeuroImage 28 (2), 500–506.

Ohnishi, T., Matsuda, H., Hashimoto, T., Kunihiro, T., Nishikawa, M., Uema, T., Sasaki, M., 2000. Abnormal regional cerebral blood flow in childhood autism. Brain 123 (9), 1838–1844.

Paniukov, D., Lebel, R.M., Giesbrecht, G., Lebel, C., 2020. Cerebral blood flow increases across early childhood. NeuroImage 204, 116224.

Passow, S., Specht, K., Adamsen, T.C., Biermann, M., Brekke, N., Craven, A.R., Hugdahl, K., 2015. A close link between metabolic activity and functional connectivity in the resting human brain. EJNMMI Phys. 2 (Suppl 1), A78. https://doi.org/10.1186/2197-7364-2-S1-A78.

Paus, T., Keshavan, M., Giedd, J.N., 2008. Why do many psychiatric disorders emerge during adolescence? Nat. Rev. Neurosci. 9 (12), 947–957.

Peng, S.-L., Dumas, J.A., Park, D.C., Liu, P., Filbey, F.M., McAdams, C.J., Lu, H., 2014. Age-related increase of resting metabolic rate in the human brain. NeuroImage 98, 176–183.

Peper, J.S., Brouwer, R.M., Schnack, H.G., van Baal, G.C., van Leeuwen, M., van den Berg, S.M., Pol, H.E.H., 2009. Sex steroids and brain structure in pubertal boys and girls. Psychoneuroendocrinology 34 (3), 332–342.

Plitt, M., Barnes, K.A., Martin, A., 2015. Functional connectivity classification of autism identifies highly predictive brain features but falls short of biomarker standards. NeuroImage: Clin. 7, 359–366.

Pohmann, R., Speck, O., Scheffler, K., 2016. Signal-to-noise ratio and MR tissue parameters in human brain imaging at 3, 7, and 9.4 tesla using current receive coil arrays. Magn. Reson. Med. 75 (2), 801–809.

Rao, H., Wang, J., Giannetta, J., Korczykowski, M., Shera, D., Avants, B.B., Hurt, H., 2007. Altered resting cerebral blood flow in adolescents with in utero cocaine exposure revealed by perfusion functional MRI. Pediatrics 120 (5), e1245–e1254.

Raznahan, A., Lee, Y., Stidd, R., Long, R., Greenstein, D., Clasen, L., Giedd, J.N., 2010. Longitudinally mapping the influence of sex and androgen signaling on the dynamics of human cortical maturation in adolescence. Proc. Natl. Acad. Sci. 107 (39), 16988–16993.

Raznahan, A., Shaw, P., Lalonde, F., Stockman, M., Wallace, G.L., Greenstein, D., Giedd, J.N., 2011. How does your cortex grow? J. Neurosci. 31 (19), 7174–7177.

Riedl, V., Bienkowska, K., Strobel, C., Tahmasian, M., Grimmer, T., Förster, S., Drzezga, A., 2014. Local activity determines functional connectivity in the resting human brain: a simultaneous FDG-PET/fMRI study. J. Neurosci. 34 (18), 6260–6266. https://doi.org/10.1523/JNEUROSCI.0492-14.2014.

Roman, G., Fung, S., Daza, M.A., Faridar, A., Dulay, M., Pascual, B., Fisher, R., 2017. Comparative Value of ASL-MRI and FDG-PET Imaging in Neurodegenerative Diseases: Cerebral Blood Flow vs. Glucose Metabolism (P4. 097). AAN Enterprises.

Rudie, J.D., Dapretto, M., 2013. Convergent evidence of brain overconnectivity in children with autism? Cell Rep. 5 (3), 565–566.

Saitovitch, A., Rechtman, E., Lemaitre, H., Tacchella, J.-M., Vinçon-Leite, A., Douard, E., Chabane, N., 2019. Superior temporal sulcus hypoperfusion in children with autism spectrum disorder: an arterial spin-labeling magnetic resonance study. bioRxiv, 771584.

Satterthwaite, T.D., Shinohara, R.T., Wolf, D.H., Hopson, R.D., Elliott, M.A., Vandekar, S.N., Gennatas, E.D., 2014. Impact of puberty on the evolution of cerebral perfusion during adolescence. Proc. Natl. Acad. Sci. 111 (23), 8643–8648.

Schmithorst, V.J., Vannest, J., Lee, G., Hernandez-Garcia, L., Plante, E., Rajagopal, A., Consortium, C.A., 2015. Evidence that neurovascular coupling underlying the BOLD effect increases with age during childhood. Hum. Brain Mapp. 36 (1), 1–15.

Schrantee, A., Mutsaerts, H.-J.M., Bouziane, C., Tamminga, H.G., Bottelier, M.A., Reneman, L., 2017. The age-dependent effects of a single-dose methylphenidate challenge on cerebral perfusion in patients with attention-deficit/hyperactivity disorder. NeuroImage: Clin. 13, 123–129.

Schultz, R.T., 2005. Developmental deficits in social perception in autism: the role of the amygdala and fusiform face area. Int. J. Dev. Neurosci. 23 (2–3), 125–141.

Schumann, C.M., Bloss, C.S., Barnes, C.C., Wideman, G.M., Carper, R.A., Akshoomoff, N., Lord, C., 2010. Longitudinal magnetic resonance imaging study of cortical development through early childhood in autism. J. Neurosci. 30 (12), 4419–4427.

Setsompop, K., Gagoski, B.A., Polimeni, J.R., Witzel, T., Wedeen, V.J., Wald, L.L., 2012. Blipped-controlled aliasing in parallel imaging for simultaneous multislice echo planar imaging with reduced g-factor penalty. Magn. Reson. Med. 67 (5), 1210–1224.

Shao, X., Wang, D., 2017. Single Shot High Resolution 3D Arterial Spin Labeling Using 2D CAIPI and ESPIRiT Reconstruction. (Paper presented at the Proc Int Soc Magn Reson Med).

Shao, X., Wang, Y., Moeller, S., Wang, D.J.J., 2018. A constrained slice-dependent background suppression scheme for simultaneous multislice pseudo-continuous arterial spin labeling. Magn. Reson. Med. 79 (1), 394–400. https://doi.org/10.1002/mrm.26643.

Shao, X., Wang, K., Wang, D.J., 2019. 7T high-resolution arterial spin labeling reveals layer dependent cerebral blood flow. Proc. Intl. Soc. Mag. Reson. Med. 27.

Shaw, P., Eckstrand, K., Sharp, W., Blumenthal, J., Lerch, J., Greenstein, D., Rapoport, J., 2007. Attention-deficit/hyperactivity disorder is characterized by a delay in cortical maturation. Proc. Natl. Acad. Sci. 104 (49), 19649–19654.

Shaw, P., Kabani, N.J., Lerch, J.P., Eckstrand, K., Lenroot, R., Gogtay, N., Rapoport, J.L., 2008. Neurodevelopmental trajectories of the human cerebral cortex. J. Neurosci. 28 (14), 3586–3594.

Shou, Q., Shao, X., Wang, D.J., 2020. Super-resolution multi-band ASL using slice dithered enhanced resolution (SLIDER) technique. Proc. Intl. Soc. Mag. Reson. Med.

Spann, S.M., Shao, X., Wang, D.J., Aigner, C.S., Schloegl, M., Bredies, K., Stollberger, R., 2020. Robust single-shot acquisition of high resolution whole brain ASL images by combining time-dependent 2D CAPIRINHA sampling with spatio-temporal TGV reconstruction. NeuroImage 206, 116337.

Sprengelmeyer, R., Steele, J.D., Mwangi, B., Kumar, P., Christmas, D., Milders, M., Matthews, K., 2011. The insular cortex and the neuroanatomy of major depression. J. Affect. Disord. 133 (1–2), 120–127.

Starkstein, S.E., Vazquez, S., Vrancic, D., Nanclares, V., Manes, F., Piven, J., Plebst, C., 2000. SPECT findings in mentally retarded autistic individuals. J. Neuropsychiatr. Clin. Neurosci. 12 (3), 370–375.

Steinberg, L., 2005. Cognitive and affective development in adolescence. Trends Cogn. Sci. 9 (2), 69–74.

Taki, Y., Hashizume, H., Sassa, Y., Takeuchi, H., Wu, K., Asano, M., Kawashima, R., 2011a. Correlation between gray matter density-adjusted brain perfusion and age using brain MR images of 202 healthy children. Hum. Brain Mapp. 32 (11), 1973–1985.

Taki, Y., Hashizume, H., Sassa, Y., Takeuchi, H., Wu, K., Asano, M., Kawashima, R., 2011b. Gender differences in partial-volume corrected brain perfusion using brain MRI in healthy children. NeuroImage 58 (3), 709–715.

Tamnes, C.K., Herting, M.M., Goddings, A.-L., Meuwese, R., Blakemore, S.-J., Dahl, R.E., Crone, E.A., 2017. Development of the cerebral cortex across adolescence: a multisample study of inter-related longitudinal changes in cortical volume, surface area, and thickness. J. Neurosci. 37 (12), 3402–3412.

Tanner, J.M., 1971. Sequence, tempo, and individual variation in the growth and development of boys and girls aged twelve to sixteen. Daedalus, 907–930.

Tomasi, D., Wang, G.J., Volkow, N.D., 2013. Energetic cost of brain functional connectivity. Proc. Natl. Acad. Sci. U. S. A. 110 (33), 13642–13647. https://doi.org/10.1073/pnas.1303346110.

Uddin, L.Q., Supekar, K., Lynch, C.J., Khouzam, A., Phillips, J., Feinstein, C., Menon, V., 2013. Salience network–based classification and prediction of symptom severity in children with autism. JAMA Psych. 70 (8), 869–879.

Uludağ, K., Müller-Bierl, B., Uğurbil, K., 2009. An integrative model for neuronal activity-induced signal changes for gradient and spin echo functional imaging. NeuroImage 48 (1), 150–165.

Van Rooij, D., Buitelaar, J., 2016. Subcortical brain volume development over age in autism spectrum disorder: results from the ENIGMA-ASD working group. Eur. Neuropsychopharmacol. 2 (26), S711.

Varela, M., Petersen, E.T., Golay, X., Hajnal, J.V., 2015. Cerebral blood flow measurements in infants using look–locker arterial spin labeling. J. Magn. Reson. Imaging 41 (6), 1591–1600.

Vidorreta, M., Wang, Z., Rodríguez, I., Pastor, M.A., Detre, J.A., Fernández-Seara, M.A., 2013. Comparison of 2D and 3D single-shot ASL perfusion fMRI sequences. NeuroImage 66, 662–671.

Walhovd, K.B., Fjell, A.M., Giedd, J., Dale, A.M., Brown, T.T., 2016. Through thick and thin: a need to reconcile contradictory results on trajectories in human cortical development. Cereb. Cortex 27 (2), bhv301.

Wang, J., Licht, D.J., 2006. Pediatric perfusion MR imaging using arterial spin labeling. Neurol. Clin. 16 (1), 149–167.

Wang, J., Alsop, D.C., Li, L., Listerud, J., Gonzalez-At, J.B., Schnall, M.D., Detre, J.A., 2002. Comparison of quantitative perfusion imaging using arterial spin labeling at 1.5 and 4.0 tesla. Magn. Reson. Med. 48 (2), 242–254.

Wang, J., Licht, D.J., Jahng, G.H., Liu, C.S., Rubin, J.T., Haselgrove, J., Detre, J.A., 2003. Pediatric perfusion imaging using pulsed arterial spin labeling. J. Magn. Reson. Imaging 18 (4), 404–413.

Wang, J., Rao, H., Detre, J., 2009. Arterial spin labeling perfusion MRI in developmental neuroscience. In: Neuroimging in Developmental Clinical Neuroscience. Cambridge University Press, Cambridge, pp. 326–343.

Wang, Y., Moeller, S., Li, X., Vu, A.T., Krasileva, K., Ugurbil, K., Wang, D.J., 2015. Simultaneous multi-slice turbo-FLASH imaging with CAIPIRINHA for whole brain distortion-free pseudo-continuous arterial spin labeling at 3 and 7 T. NeuroImage 113, 279–288.

Washington, S.D., Gordon, E.M., Brar, J., Warburton, S., Sawyer, A.T., Wolfe, A., Mbwana, J., 2014. Dysmaturation of the default mode network in autism. Hum. Brain Mapp. 35 (4), 1284–1296.

Wen-han, Y., Jin, J., Li-juan, X., Mu-hua, C., Xin, W., Peng, B., Qing-xiong, W., 2011. Regional cerebral blood flow in children with autism spectrum disorders: a quantitative 99mTc-ECD brain SPECT study with statistical parametric mapping evaluation. Chin. Med. J. 124 (9), 1362–1366.

Wong, A.M.-C., Liu, H.-L., Tsai, M.-L., Schwartz, E.S., Yeh, C.-H., Wang, H.-S., Lin, C.-Y., 2019. Arterial spin-labeling magnetic resonance imaging of brain maturation in early childhood: mathematical model fitting to assess age-dependent change of cerebral blood flow. Magn. Reson. Imaging 59, 114–120.

Wu, W.C., Fernández-Seara, M., Detre, J.A., Wehrli, F.W., Wang, J., 2007. A theoretical and experimental investigation of the tagging efficiency of pseudocontinuous arterial spin labeling. Magn. Reson. Med. 58 (5), 1020–1027.

Wu, C., Honarmand, A.R., Schnell, S., Kuhn, R., Schoeneman, S.E., Ansari, S.A., Shaibani, A., 2016. Age-related changes of normal cerebral and cardiac blood flow in children and adults aged 7 months to 61 years. J. Am. Heart Assoc. 5 (1), e002657.

Xie, D., Li, Y., Yang, H., Song, D., Shang, Y., Ge, Q., Wang, Z., 2019. BOLD fMRI-Based Brain Perfusion Prediction Using Deep Dilated Wide Activation Networks. (Paper presented at the International Workshop on Machine Learning in Medical Imaging).

Ye, F.Q., Berman, K.F., Ellmore, T., Esposito, G., Van Horn, J.D., Yang, Y., Weinberger, D.R., 2000. H215O PET validation of steady-state arterial spin tagging cerebral blood flow measurements in humans. Magn. Reson. Med. 44 (3), 450–456.

Yerys, B.E., Gordon, E.M., Abrams, D.N., Satterthwaite, T.D., Weinblatt, R., Jankowski, K.F., Vaidya, C.J., 2015. Default mode network segregation and social deficits in autism spectrum disorder: evidence from non-medicated children. NeuroImage: Clin. 9, 223–232.

Yerys, B.E., Herrington, J.D., Bartley, G.K., Liu, H.-S., Detre, J.A., Schultz, R.T., 2018. Arterial spin labeling provides a reliable neurobiological marker of autism spectrum disorder. J. Neurodev. Disord. 10 (1), 32.

Zhang, K., Herzog, H., Mauler, J., Filss, C., Okell, T.W., Kops, E.R., Sturm, W., 2014. Comparison of cerebral blood flow acquired by simultaneous [15O] water positron emission tomography and arterial spin labeling magnetic resonance imaging. J. Cereb. Blood Flow Metab. 34 (8), 1373–1380.

Zilbovicius, M., Boddaert, N., Belin, P., Poline, J.-B., Remy, P., Mangin, J.-F., Samson, Y., 2000. Temporal lobe dysfunction in childhood autism: a PET study. Am. J. Psychiatr. 157 (12), 1988–1993.

Zuo, Z., Wang, R., Zhuo, Y., Xue, R., Lawrence, K.S.S., Wang, D.J., 2013. Turbo-FLASH based arterial spin labeled perfusion MRI at 7 T. PLoS One 8 (6).

CHAPTER

Advanced fetal MRI

6

Kiho Im

Department of Pediatrics, Harvard Medical School, Boston, MA, United States; Fetal Neonatal Neuroimaging and Developmental Science Center, Division of Newborn Medicine, Boston Children's Hospital, Boston, MA, United States

1. Fetal brain MRI

Magnetic resonance imaging (MRI) is now widely used during the fetal period to observe the structure and function of the developing brain in utero, detect brain injury and malformations and provide prognostic information. Since ultrasonography is cost-efficient, easily accessible, and safe, it has traditionally been the primary imaging method for fetal body and brain assessment during pregnancy. Ultrasonography is routinely performed in the first trimester to look for major developmental abnormalities. A further detailed ultrasonography screening is offered in the second trimester to acquire a series of fetal measurements and evaluate fetal anatomy (Jarvis and Griffiths, 2019).

Fetal MRI is usually performed as a supplementary examination when fetal abnormalities are identified, or diagnostic doubts remain after prenatal ultrasonography. It may also be performed if there is a familial genetic syndrome or a known disorder that predisposes the fetus to harm. Fetal MRI can complement ultrasonography by providing multiplanar capabilities, a large field of view, the superior tissue contrast of the brain, and high resolution that cannot be obtained by any other imaging modality (Kline-Fath, 2019). Therefore, fetal MRI can improve the diagnostic accuracy for fetal brain abnormalities, leading to better prenatal counseling and clinical management (Griffiths et al., 2017). Griffiths et al. recently demonstrated that in fetuses with abnormal ultrasonography and brain malformations, fetal MRI provided additional diagnostic information in 50% of cases, changed prognostic information in 20% of cases, and changed clinical management in more than one-third of cases (Griffiths et al., 2017). This finding could lead us to propose that any fetus with a suspected brain abnormality on ultrasonography should have a fetal MRI to better provide counseling and management decisions.

The procedures for fetal brain MRI examinations are well-established at many institutions. However, MRI of the fetus in utero may be one of the most difficult imaging challenges due to the non-predictable and extreme movement, small brain size, and low tissue contrast. Especially, fetal motion disrupts the spatial encoding needed for 3D image acquisition. Therefore, it is highly important to use fine-tuned sequence parameters in fetal MRI. To date single-shot fast spin echo T2-weighted (SST2W, aka SSFSE or HASTE) imaging is the most common technique for structural MRI because it is less susceptible to fetal motion and shows relatively excellent tissue contrast. Despite the

Handbook of Pediatric Brain Imaging. https://doi.org/10.1016/B978-0-12-816633-8.00004-1

significant challenges involved, the other techniques commonly employed in conventional brain MRI are also of interest for fetal MRI. Diffusion-weighted and functional MRI can be used for quantitative microstructural evaluation and examination of structural and functional connectivity development in the fetal brain. This chapter introduces structural, diffusion, and functional MRI for the fetal brain in utero; fetal MRI postprocessing and analysis techniques; and the major findings of recent fetal brain MRI studies.

2. Fetal structural MRI

2.1 Single-shot T2-weighted imaging

To minimize the artifact caused by unconstrained fetal motion, fast fetal MRI is performed using a T2 weighted sequence. Since the human fetal brain has a high-water and low-lipid content, resulting in different image contrast to that observed in the myelinated adult brain, heavy T2-weighted sequences provide the best detail of brain anatomy. The majority of fetal brain anatomical information and interpretation have been extracted by the use of SST2W imaging. This sequence has been the primary method for clinical evaluation of most fetal organs, including the fetal brain, by minimizing the motion and providing excellent T2-weighted contrast. The SST2W sequence is run with specific names of different vendors (Single-Shot Fast Spin Echo (SSFSE): General Electric Medical systems; HAlf-fourier Single-shot Turbo spin Echo (HASTE): Siemens; Single-Shot half-Fourier Turbo Spin Echo (SShTSE): Philips; Rapid Acquisition with Relaxation Enhancement (RARE): Bruker Instruments). Other sequences for structural imaging include inversion recovery T1-weighted MRI to detect hemorrhage, unspoiled gradient echo steady state free precession (SSFP) for structural surveys such as midline brain, sulcation, bright blood, and cinematographic imaging (Gholipour et al., 2014). It is often necessary to perform multiple scans in the sagittal, axial, and coronal planes for obtaining diagnostic images.

2.2 Fetal brain MRI examinations

Most fetal MRI examinations are performed in the second and third trimester, typically after 18 gestational weeks (GW), at which time brain structures are large enough to be evaluated by MRI. It is needed to check fetal brain structures and measure important brain metrics such as ventricular morphology and size, cerebral biparietal and cerebellar transverse, anteroposterior vermian diameters, degree of sulcation, gray matter and white matter volume, and formation of the inter-hemispheric commissures (Barkovich and Barkovich, 2019). However, the changes in these brain structures are often too subtle to identify by qualitative visual MRI inspection. Recently, advanced fetal MRI processing techniques have been developed and used for quantitative analysis and sensitive detection of these subtle changes. To perform quantitative fetal MRI analysis, we need several postprocessing steps. One of the greatest challenges of quantitative fetal MRI analysis is to remove fetal head motion artifacts. Although fast fetal MRI is performed using T2 weighted sequence, we still need an image postprocessing technique for head motion correction in most cases. Another important step is brain tissue and region segmentation for quantitative volumetric and surface-based shape analysis.

2.3 Head motion correction

Fast 2D scans like SST2W MRI largely freeze fetal motion at about a few hundred milliseconds for each slice acquisition. However, the motion artifact shown between slices cannot be removed, and inter-slice head motion results in a discrepancy between slice positions and disrupted 3D volume image (Fig. 1). It affects any 3D image postprocessing and analysis that rely on high-quality volume data. Prospective motion correction has been used in fetal MRI through navigator echoes, but the nonrigid nature and the extent and complexity of fetal motion has made this approach challenging (Gholipour

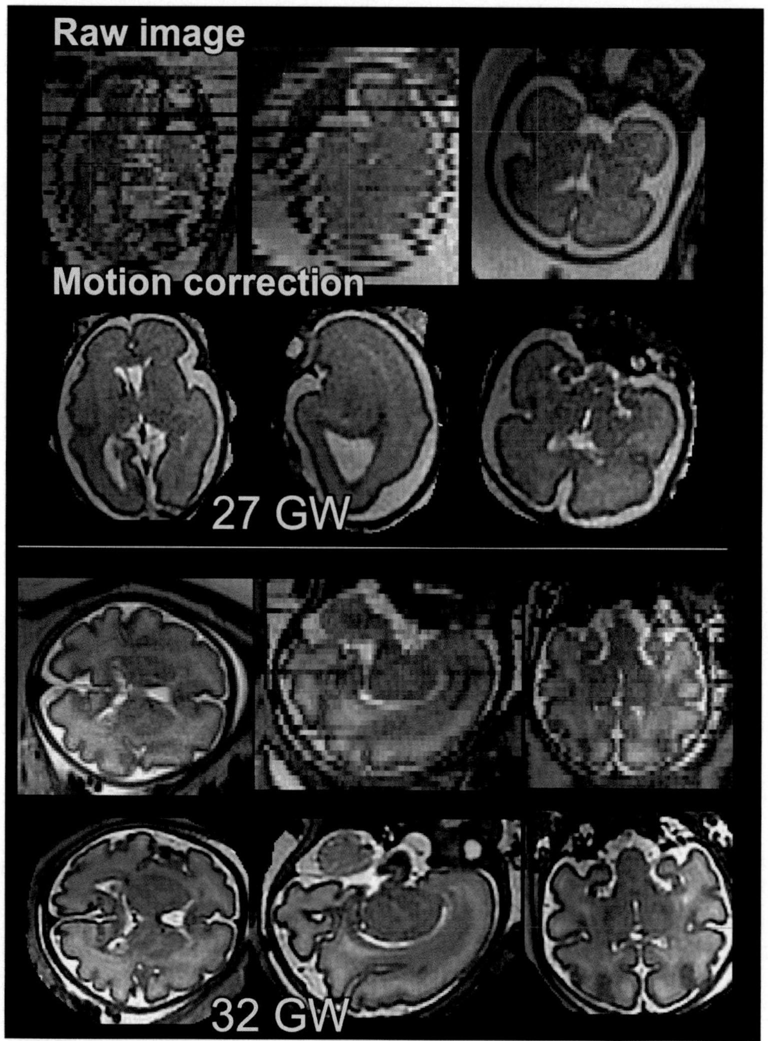

FIG. 1

Example of raw SST2W fetal imaging (27 and 32 GW) and head motion correction.

et al., 2014; Klessen et al., 2005; Cetin et al., 2011). In practice, retrospective inter-slice motion correction using image postprocessing techniques has been developed and considered to be a more successful and efficient approach for 3D volumetric image reconstruction (Fig. 1). To observe and analyze the structural image of fetal brains, multiple sets of images in the sagittal, axial, and coronal views are usually acquired. Most of the motion correction techniques are based on slice-to-volume registration and are applied to these multi-view images for inter-slice motion correction and super-resolution volume reconstruction (Gholipour et al., 2010; Kim et al., 2010; Kuklisova-Murgasova et al., 2012; Uus et al., 2020; Rousseau et al., 2013). The methods of slice-to-volume rigid registration and scattered data interpolation for the volumetric reconstruction of fetal brain MRI from multiple sets of thick-slice SST2W scans were first proposed by Rousseau et al. (Rousseau et al., 2006) and Jiang et al. (Jiang et al., 2007). In a more systematic approach, Gholipour et al. introduced a physical forward model of slice acquisition incorporating motion, slice profile, and sampling, and then solved an inverse problem to reconstruct a high-resolution volume from multiple image sets (Gholipour et al., 2010). Kuklisova-Murgasova et al. developed novel intensity matching of acquired 2D slices and expectation-maximization (EM)-based robust statistics which completely excludes identified misregistered or corrupted voxels and slices (Kuklisova-Murgasova et al., 2012). More recently, a hierarchical deformable slice-to-volume registration, a novel approach for non-rigid motion correction of fetal MRI has been proposed (Uus et al., 2020). These inter-slice motion correction techniques have been shown to enable super-resolution volume image reconstruction and advanced volumetric and morphometric analysis of early brain development.

2.4 Brain tissue and region segmentation

A fundamental process for the quantitative analysis of fetal MRI data is brain segmentation in terms of brain extraction, tissue segmentation (e.g., gray matter, white matter, and cerebrospinal fluid), and specific region-of-interest (ROI) segmentation. Accurate and automated brain segmentation is necessary for various volume- and surface-based morphometric analyses. Previous several fetal studies performed manual or semiautomatic brain tissue and ROI segmentation (Im et al., 2017; Tarui et al., 2018, 2020). However, manual or semiautomatic segmentation is a highly time-consuming and challenging task that is subject to high inter- and intra-rater variability. Over the past decade, several algorithms for brain segmentation from fetal MRI have been proposed. The atlas-based and EM segmentation methods have been employed for fetal brain tissue segmentation (Habas et al., 2010; Wright et al., 2014). The anatomical label map and probability map of brain tissues or regions of an atlas can be propagated to an unlabeled individual subject by using linear or nonlinear registration between the atlas (source) and the image of the subject (target). The EM algorithm estimates a mixture of tissue probability and classified the tissues on the individual brain image using a composition of a spatial prior term and an intensity term. The spatial prior knowledge is usually derived based on atlases. Recently, reports on deep learning in the field of image segmentation claimed superior performance compared to traditional methods. The convolutional neural network (CNN) has been widely used for brain tissue and region segmentation in postnatal MRI data (Guha Roy et al., 2019; Chen et al., 2018; Zhang et al., 2015). One deep learning study proposed fetal brain tissue segmentation using a 2D semantic CNN model that can segment seven brain tissues, including the cerebellum, basal ganglia and thalami, ventricular cerebrospinal fluid, white matter, brain stem, cortical gray matter and extracerebral cerebrospinal fluid (Khalili et al., 2019).

Despite the development of automatic brain segmentation methods, it is still needed to include a larger dataset of fetal brain MRIs across a wide gestational age range and improve the segmentation accuracy with more advanced technical development, because brain size; cortical folding morphology; transient cellular compartments (ventricular, subventricular, intermediate, and subplate zones); and tissue contrast in fetal MRI dynamically change with gestational age. A reliable and accurate automatic segmentation method will help reduce the data processing time and perform an accurate quantitative brain structural analysis.

2.5 Fetal brain volumetric analysis

On the segmented volume image, we can compute the volumes of the total brain and specific tissues and regions such as cortex, white matter, basal ganglia, and cerebellum in the normal fetal brain. The volumes of major fetal brain zones including cortical plate, subplate, and intermediate zones, germinal matrix, deep gray nuclei, and ventricles were calculated from automatic segmentation of motion-corrected, 3D reconstructed in utero MRI (Scott et al., 2011). Growth trajectories of the fetal brain tissues were estimated by the fitting of temporal linear, quadratic, and exponential models with age between 20.57 and 31.14 GW (Clouchoux et al., 2012b). The cerebellum demonstrated the greatest maturation rate, with a fourfold increase (384%) in volume between 25.4 and 36.6 weeks, and a relative growth rate of 12.87% per week. Both total brain and cerebral volumes increased by 230% and brain stem volume by 134% over the same gestational age period (Clouchoux et al., 2012b). Another fetal volumetric study calculated the rate of growth for the left and right cortical gray matter, fetal white matter, deep subcortical structures, and the cerebellum according to gestational age and described patterns of hemispheric growth (Andescavage et al., 2017). Each brain structure demonstrated major increases in volume during the second half of gestation. In that study, the cerebellum also showed the most prominent volumetric growth. More recently, spatiotemporal patterns, hemispheric asymmetries, and sexual dimorphism of the regional cortical plate and subplate volume growth (22 cortical regions) have been examined in healthy fetuses using fetal brain MRI (Vasung et al., 2020a,b).

Brain regional volumes have been compared between healthy fetuses and fetuses with brain abnormalities. Volumetric analysis of the ventricles and supratentorial brain structures was performed on 3D motion-corrected and reconstructed volume data in fetuses with isolated ventriculomegaly. Age-related volumetric changes of the brain structures were examined with linear and nonlinear regression models and compared between ventriculomegaly and control subjects. Fetuses with isolated ventriculomegaly had increased volumes of brain parenchyma, extra cerebral cerebrospinal fluid, and third and fourth ventricles when compared with the control cohort (Kyriakopoulou et al., 2014; Scott et al., 2013). Atypical brain volumetric growth during fetal life was shown in congenital heart disease (CHD). CHD is one of the most common major congenital malformations identified in utero, affecting about 1% of all live births and associated with a significant risk for neurodevelopmental disabilities (Marelli et al., 2016). Prior in vivo MRI studies have reported that abnormalities in brain structure are present before birth. During the third trimester, there were progressive and significant declines in gestational age-adjusted volumes of total brain, cortical gray and white matter, subcortical gray matter, and the intracranial cavity in CHD fetuses when compared to controls from 25 to 37 GW (Limperopoulos et al., 2010; Clouchoux et al., 2013). Recently, quantitative MRI analyses of regional brain volumetric growth were performed in living fetuses with Down syndrome, which is the most common liveborn autosomal chromosomal anomaly and is a major cause of developmental disability.

The fetal MRI volumetric study revealed decreased volumetric growth trajectories of the cortical plate, the subcortical parenchyma, and the cerebellar hemispheres in Down syndrome subjects compared to controls (Tarui et al., 2020).

2.6 Surface-based shape analysis

Cortical growth and folding in the human brain are associated with our capacity for high-order cognitive abilities and are under strong genetic controls. During fetal development, cortical areal expansion and folding occur through the proliferation and expansion of neural stem cells and progenitors in the ventricular and subventricular zones (Sun and Hevner, 2014). Defects in neuronal proliferation, migration, and differentiation cause atypical cortical folding pattern, which is associated with neurocognitive impairment in many brain malformations and disorders (Rakic, 2009, 2004). Furthermore, there is a region-specific timing of the emergence of primary cortical folding during the fetal stage (Habas et al., 2012; Garel et al., 2001). Therefore, several techniques have been used to assess global and regional cortical growth and folding in the developing fetal brain using a surface model that consists of triangular meshes.

Cortical surface area and global gyrification index (GI) are measured to estimate the overall amount of cortical areal growth and folding during fetal life (Im et al., 2017; Tarui et al., 2018; Clouchoux et al., 2013; Lefevre et al., 2016; Ortinau et al., 2019). The GI is a metric that is widely used and defined as the ratio of the whole cortical surface to their outer, convex hull surface area (Zilles et al., 1988). It quantifies the amount of cortex buried within the sulcal folds as compared with the amount of cortex on the outer visible cortex. The temporal changes of cortical surface area and GI were observed during fetal life between 21 and 36 GW in healthy fetuses and early imaged preterm newborns. Preterm newborns showed the significantly higher cortical surface area and global GI compared to healthy fetuses (Lefevre et al., 2016). Clouchoux et al. compared the cortical folding state between healthy fetuses and fetuses with CHD (Clouchoux et al., 2013). The cortical surface area and GI were found to be significantly lower in the CHD group, and the difference between the two groups became progressively greater with increasing gestational age.

To quantify the shape and degree of cortical folding, cortical surface curvatures and sulcal depth have been measured on the cortical surface model. Wright et al. computed several curvature-based folding measures including mean and Gaussian curvatures at a global and lobar regional level in healthy normal subjects between 21.7 and 38.0 GW (Wright et al., 2014). These were strongly correlated with gestational age, which allowed an age-dependent non-linear model to be accurately fitted to the folding measures. Since regional cortical surface growth and folding are associated with the development of specific functional areas (Fischl et al., 2008), examining regional cortical folding has provided more information about region-specific functional development that is not captured by whole-brain global analysis. Regional cortical curvature and sulcal folding depth at the vertex level (Fig. 2) have been observed on the 3D cortical surface in healthy normal fetal brains (20–35 GW) for the entire cortical area using surface-based registration technique (Habas et al., 2012; Clouchoux et al., 2012). These studies provided the 3D whole-brain map of cortical folding temporal changes and identified cortical regions that undergo significant folding changes during this developmental period. The emergence of inter-hemispheric asymmetries in early cortical folding was also revealed (Habas et al., 2012). Scott et al., performed vertex-based curvature analysis in the whole cortical area and detected reduced cortical folding and curvature near the parieto-occipital areas in

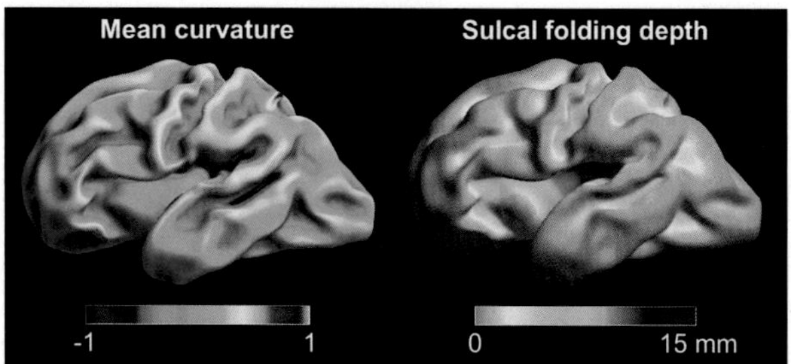

FIG. 2

Cortical mean curvature and folding depth maps (32 GW) on the 3D cortical surface model.

fetuses with isolated ventriculomegaly (Scott et al., 2013). While tissue volume appeared to be preserved in brains with ventriculomegaly, cortical folding was affected in regions where ventricles were enlarged. A quantitative and regional analysis of cortical folding in fetuses with developmental disorders may lead to a better understanding of early abnormalities in brain development, the mechanisms underlying pathological changes, and specific neurocognitive impairment.

2.7 Global sulcal pattern analysis

The primary pattern of sulcal folds, which means the global patterns of arrangement, number, and size of sulcal folds, is already noticeable during the radial growth of the cerebral cortex before the third trimester and fully determined before birth (Fig. 3). The human-specific stereotyped sulcal pattern has been hypothesized to be strongly under genetic control (Sun and Hevner, 2014; O'Leary et al., 2007). Recent transcriptomic analyses of cortical germinal layers identified distinct modules or blocks of high and low gene expression that faithfully mapped the location of sulcal and gyral folds in the gyrencephalic ferret and the human fetal cortex (de Juan Romero et al., 2015; Elsen et al., 2013). Sulcal pattern has been hypothesized to relate to optimal organization and arrangement of cortical functional areas and their connectivity predetermined from genetic protomap of ventricular zone (Rakic, 2004; Fischl et al., 2008; Klyachko and Stevens, 2003; Van Essen, 1997). Based on the protomap hypothesis, cortical neurons originated in the proliferative zones carry intrinsic programs for cortical functional regionalization and migrate to their proper laminar and areal positions (Rakic, 2009). Defective neuronal migration might affect the organization of cortical areas and their underlying connections. Altered gene expression patterns may also directly affect the genetic protomap of cortical areas. These factors may result in atypical patterning and connectivity of cortical functional areas, possibly causing disrupted sulcal pattern.

A quantitative sulcal pattern analysis technique using a graph structure has been developed to examine the interrelated arrangement and global patterning of early primary cortical folds in human fetal brains (Im et al., 2017; Im et al., 2011). The sulcal pattern was represented as a graph structure with sulcal pits and catchment basins as nodes. Sulcal pattern graphs between different individuals were optimally matched and automatically compared using a spectral-based matching algorithm based on a similarity measure (Im et al., 2011). The sulcal pattern comparison was performed using not only geometric features of sulcal folds themselves (position, depth, and size of sulcal pits and basins) but also their inter-sulcal geometric and topological relationships, emphasizing the interrelated arrangement and patterning of sulcal folds. This graph-based sulcal pattern method has been applied to fetal brains and revealed early differences of sulcal patterns in fetuses with brain abnormalities. Each fetal brain was quantitatively compared with normal template brains and the sulcal pattern similarities to the templates were measured. The sulcal pattern similarities to the template brains were compared between healthy fetuses and fetuses with brain malformations such as polymicrogyria and Chiari II, with similarities significantly reduced in all abnormal individual fetuses compared to normal fetuses (Im et al., 2017) (Fig. 3). Furthermore, in some abnormal cases, this quantitative analysis identified an abnormal sulcal pattern that was confirmed postnatally which was not detected in a qualitative fetal MRI assessment, showing higher sensitivity than qualitative visual assessment (Im et al., 2017). The same fetal sulcal pattern analysis was applied on another brain malformation, isolated agenesis of corpus callosum, ACC, clinically diagnosed to have no cortical malformations, and no other abnormalities (Tarui et al., 2018). Disorganized patterns of early sulcal position in fetuses with ACC were found compared to healthy fetuses, showing significant alterations in absolute sulcal positions and relative inter-sulcal positional relationship (Fig. 3). More recently, differences in early sulcal patterns between fetuses with CHD and healthy control fetuses were published (Ortinau et al., 2019). Significantly lower sulcal pattern similarity to the normal templates was revealed in CHD on the left hemispheric regions. CHD sulcal pattern features appeared to be lower than the normal range in early fetal stage

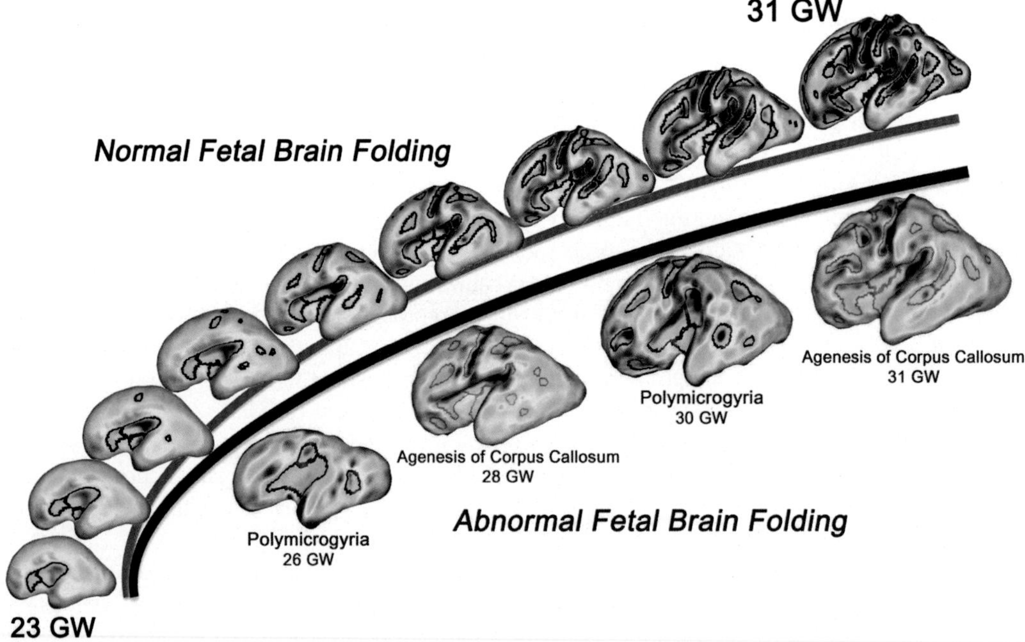

FIG. 3

Normal and abnormal cortical folding pattern development from 23 to 31 GW. Sulcal folding basins are represented with black lines on the cortical surface. Cortical surface shape and spatial patterning and arrangement of sulcal basins appear to be atypical in fetal brains with polymicrogyria and agenesis of corpus callosum compared to normal fetal brains.

before the third trimester. This innovative sulcal pattern analysis has been effective for characterizing the early cortical development and detecting subtle alterations in individual patients that emerge early and are difficult to detect via visual inspection.

3. Fetal diffusion MRI

Diffusion MRI measures the displacement of water molecules within tissues by applying strong gradient pulses either side of the 180 degree RF refocusing pulse in the three orthogonal axes during an echo planar imaging spin echo sequence (Bammer, 2003; Beaulieu, 2002). The apparent diffusion coefficient (ADC) measure can estimate the magnitude of this diffusion process (mean displacement of a water molecule during the application of the diffusion gradients) and varies across different tissues (Bammer, 2003). From a clinical standpoint, the ADC has been the most useful diffusion MRI parameter, showing acute and subacute tissue injury. In cerebrospinal fluid, the displacement of water molecules is equal in all directions (isotropic diffusion). However, in white matter, water diffusion is impeded by axonal membranes and is directionally dependent on the orientation of the underlying white matter fibers (anisotropic diffusion). Diffusion tensor imaging (DTI) is commonly used to characterize anisotropic diffusion in the brain, and the most common measure of DTI is fractional anisotropy (FA) on a voxel-wise basis, which is the fraction of the magnitude of diffusion that can be attributed to anisotropic diffusion. Also, DTI-based tractography techniques are widely used to study the 3D anatomy and architecture of white matter fiber tracts.

The importance of diffusion MRI assessment in the fetal brain is self-evident, and several studies have attempted to perform fetal brain diffusion imaging. The ADC values in healthy fetal brains have been successfully measured and reported (Cannie et al., 2007). Kasprian et al. showed the potential of in utero fetal DTI and tractography to visualize the main projection and commissural pathways in living, non-sedated human fetuses between 18 and 37 GW (Kasprian et al., 2008). Mitter et al. reconstructed and visualized major association fiber tracts and the fornix in utero using DTI tractography in healthy fetuses between 20 and 34 GW (Mitter et al., 2015). In this study, the uncinate fasciculus and inferior fronto-occipital fasciculus were detected as early as 20 GW. Reconstruction and visualization of the inferior longitudinal fasciculus, cingulum, and fornix were successful in older fetuses during the third trimester. (Mitter et al., 2015). Another previous study examined white matter fiber connectivity among 90 brain regions using DTI and streamline tractography in normally developing fetuses and fetuses with ACC (Jakab et al., 2015). Fetal brains with ACC showed disrupted global organization of connectivity network structure compared to normal. This study shows that DTI-based tractography analysis can detect abnormal connectivity pathways that are already present during at early stages of fetal brain development. Khan et al. recently constructed the first DTI atlas of the fetal brain computed from in utero diffusion MRI acquired from 67 healthy fetuses between 21 and 39 GW (Khan et al., 2019) (Fig. 4). This DTI atlas of the fetal brain is useful for reliable detection of major neuronal fiber bundle pathways and for characterization of the fetal brain reorganization that occurs in utero. The most recent study first performed a longitudinal analysis of DTI fiber tractography in the third trimester and examined white matter development in normal fetuses (Hooker et al., 2020). Knowledge of the normal fiber tract development at different stages throughout gestation may serve as a reference for improved understanding of growth and development and detection and characterization of pathology.

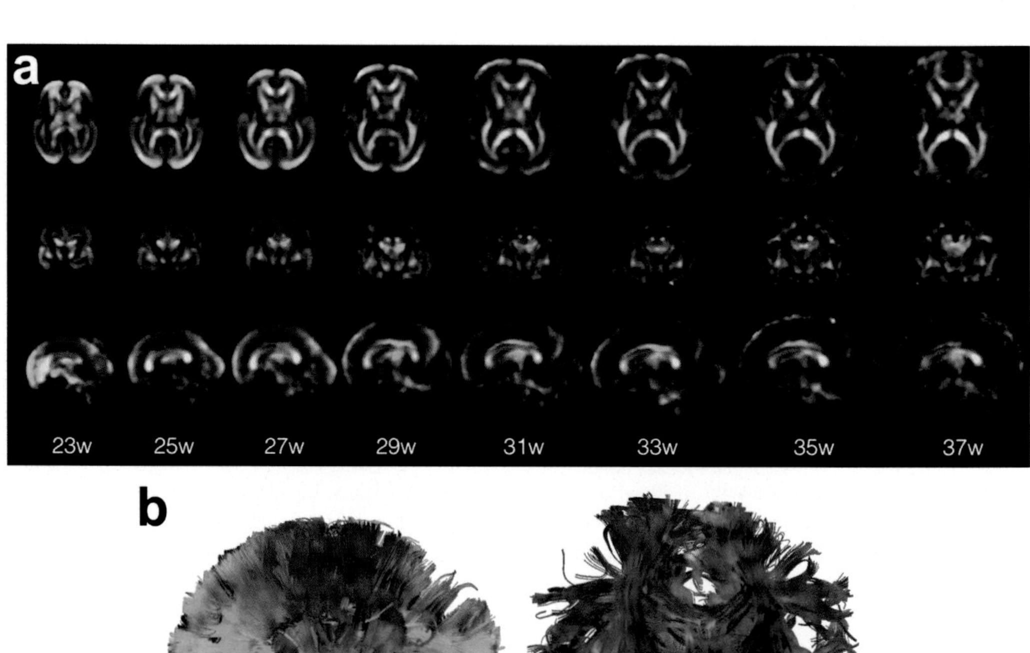

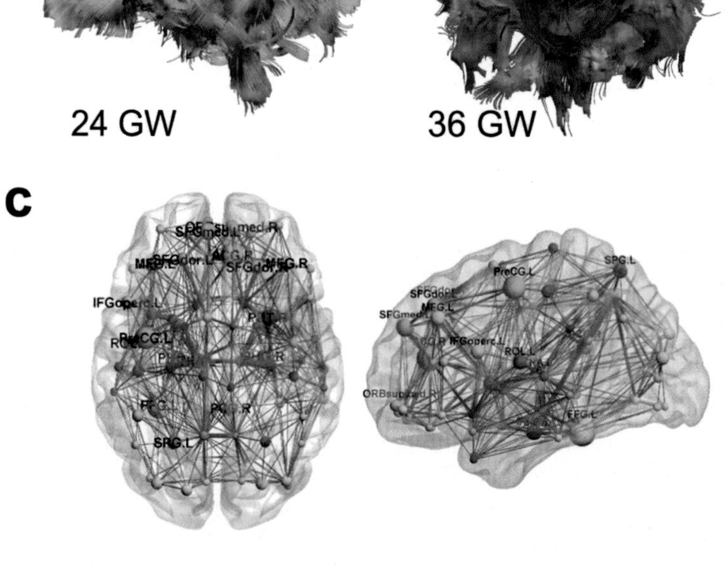

FIG. 4

(A) Axial, coronal, and sagittal views of color FA templates from the in utero DTI atlas (23–37 GW). (B) Example of DTI tractography of fetal brains at 24 and 36 GW. (C) Group averaged structural connectivity network from healthy fetuses.

This figure is reproduced from Khan, S., et al., 2019. Fetal brain growth portrayed by a spatiotemporal diffusion tensor MRI atlas computed from in utero images. NeuroImage. 185, 593–608; Marami, B., et al., 2017. Temporal slice registration and robust diffusion-tensor reconstruction for improved fetal brain structural connectivity analysis. NeuroImage. 156, 475–488.

However, much of this in utero research has been limited to studies of older fetuses or cases where the fetal head is engaged in the maternal pelvis, where fetal motion was constrained, Even with sedation and/or fetal head engagement, residual motion artifacts due to maternal breathing and small fetal movements can significantly degrade fetal diffusion MRI. Fetal head motion affects not only the intended anatomical location but also the anatomical orientation of the diffusion measurement. As a consequence, fetal diffusion MRI study is not yet feasible for general clinical imaging or larger-scale studies. For reliable white matter structure and connectivity analysis in the fetal brain, diffusion MRI data should be processed for motion correction and reconstruction. There are valuable recent studies that performed inter-slice motion correction for fetal diffusion MRI (Oubel et al., 2012; Jiang et al., 2009; Fogtmann et al., 2014). More recently, Marami et al. introduced a novel robust algorithm to reconstruct in vivo DTI of the moving fetal brain for improved fetal brain structural connectivity analysis (Marami et al., 2017). The proposed algorithm involved multiple steps of image registration incorporating a dynamic registration-based motion tracking algorithm to restore the spatial correspondence of diffusion imaging data at the slice level and reconstruct DTI of the fetal brain in the standard coordinate space. By using motion correction techniques, it has been possible to detect and visualize whole-brain white matter fiber tracts and connectivity network structure from in vivo fetal diffusion MRI (Fig. 4).

4. Fetal functional MRI

Functional MRI (fMRI) provides indirect information about neural activity by measuring temporal changes in the blood oxygenation level dependent (BOLD) contrast (Kwong et al., 1992; Ogawa et al., 1990). Relative increases and decreases of the BOLD signal can be interpreted as changes in neural activity (Logothetis et al., 2001). Such changes are temporally correlated with the timing of an explicit stimulus or task to infer regional brain function (task-based fMRI) (Bandettini et al., 1993). Even when seemingly at rest, the human brain is spontaneously active with a rich intrinsic dynamic structure, which can be modulated by external stimuli. The intrinsic neural activity can be detected as continuous low-frequency fluctuations of the BOLD signal, which occur in a highly correlated fashion across spatially distinct regions of the brain (resting-state fMRI) (Biswal et al., 1995). The gross topography of these resting-state networks has been reproducibly identified across populations and behavioral states (Smith et al., 2009).

Recently, fMRI has been applied to in utero fetal brain. Early fetal fMRI studies have shown that it is possible to apply stimulus-driven methods to study response to auditory stimuli (Hykin et al., 1999) and visual stimuli (Fulford et al., 2003; Born et al., 1998) in cases of limited fetal motion. Fetal resting-state fMRI connectivity studies have revealed the order and timing of functional connectivity development in the human brain. Those studies have demonstrated that the strength of long-range connectivity linearly increases with gestational age, interhemispheric connections show sigmoidal growth, and cross-hemispheric homotopy follows overlaid posterior-to-anterior and medial-to-lateral gradients (Thomason et al., 2013; Jakab et al., 2014; Thomason et al., 2015). Van den Heuvel et al. identified fetal resting-state functional connectivity hubs within the brain network in several areas of the temporal lobe, the precentral gyrus, and the cerebellum (van den Heuvel et al., 2018). A recent study by Turk et al. (2019) compared the overall brain network structure between adults and fetuses and observed a considerable network overlap of 61.66%. The fetal functional networks included four functional modules, compared with five in the adult group (Turk et al., 2019). Additional fetal resting-state functional connectivity studies using network approaches have shown that modularity decreases and efficiency increases in the fetal brain network with gestational age (Turk et al., 2019; Thomason et al., 2014). These studies demonstrate the presence of brain functional connectivity structure before birth that may be foundational to future brain health.

All fMRI processing and analysis depend on the detection of subtle temporal variations in the signal at each voxel location in the brain across many repeated scans. Therefore, fMRI analysis results are highly sensitive to head motion. In adults, even small head motions need to be corrected by using motion correction techniques because the presence of motion biases correlation measures in resting-state connectivity analysis (Saad et al., 2013). In the previous fetal fMRI study, Schopf et al. reported a 75% subject dropout rate due to head motion (Schopf et al., 2012). Thus, it is highly necessary to correct for fetal motion effects and motion-induced artifacts for unbiased fetal fMRI studies.

5. Conclusions

This chapter reviewed advanced in utero fetal neuroimaging and postprocessing methods to study the early development of brain structure and structural and functional connectivity. Many technical and clinical advances in fetal structural, diffusion, and functional MRI have been made and are summarized in this review. The use of fetal brain MRI during pregnancy, as a noninvasive diagnostic imaging technique, has become an established part of antenatal care. Fast imaging methods and data processing and analysis algorithms including head motion correction, brain tissue/region segmentation, and surface-based morphometry have been developed. These technical developments have enabled the quantitative assessment of brain volumetric growth; cortical surface areal growth and folding; global sulcal folding pattern; tissue microstructure; white matter structural connectivity; and functional connectivity and networks in healthy normal and abnormal fetuses. Thus, in vivo fetal MRI has great potential to not only help us better understand normal and abnormal brain development but also improve the management of high-risk pregnancies and the diagnosis and treatment of congenital anomalies. It is a still top priority to improve the spatial resolution and contrast of fetal MRI, decrease its sensitivity to motion, reduce the total acquisition time, and develop cutting-edge image processing and analysis technologies. Since neurodevelopmental disabilities associated with abnormal brain development may have a prenatal origin, it will be a highly important future study to explain a significant component of postnatal neurodevelopmental outcomes and create a predictive model for neurodevelopmental disability risk in developmental brain disorders from early fetal life using fetal MRI.

References

Andescavage, N.N., et al., 2017. Complex trajectories of brain development in the healthy human fetus. Cereb. Cortex 27 (11), 5274–5283.

Bammer, R., 2003. Basic principles of diffusion-weighted imaging. Eur. J. Radiol. 45 (3), 169–184.

Bandettini, P.A., et al., 1993. Processing strategies for time-course data sets in functional MRI of the human brain. Magn. Reson. Med. 30 (2), 161–173.

Barkovich, M.J., Barkovich, A.J., 2019. MR imaging of Normal brain development. Neuroimaging Clin. N. Am. 29 (3), 325–337.

Beaulieu, C., 2002. The basis of anisotropic water diffusion in the nervous system - a technical review. NMR Biomed. 15 (7–8), 435–455.

Biswal, B., et al., 1995. Functional connectivity in the motor cortex of resting human brain using echo-planar MRI. Magn. Reson. Med. 34 (4), 537–541.

Born, P., et al., 1998. Visual activation in infants and young children studied by functional magnetic resonance imaging. Pediatr. Res. 44 (4), 578–583.

Cannie, M., et al., 2007. A diffusion-weighted template for gestational age-related apparent diffusion coefficient values in the developing fetal brain. Ultrasound Obstet. Gynecol. 30 (3), 318–324.

Cetin, I., et al., 2011. Lactate detection in the brain of growth-restricted fetuses with magnetic resonance spectroscopy. Am. J. Obstet. Gynecol. 205 (4). 350 e1–7.

Chen, H., et al., 2018. VoxResNet: deep voxelwise residual networks for brain segmentation from 3D MR images. NeuroImage 170, 446–455.

Clouchoux, C., et al., 2012a. Quantitative in vivo MRI measurement of cortical development in the fetus. Brain Struct. Funct. 217 (1), 127–139.

Clouchoux, C., et al., 2012b. Normative fetal brain growth by quantitative in vivo magnetic resonance imaging. Am. J. Obstet. Gynecol. 206 (2). 173 e1–8.

Clouchoux, C., et al., 2013. Delayed cortical development in fetuses with complex congenital heart disease. Cereb. Cortex 23 (12), 2932–2943.

de Juan Romero, C., et al., 2015. Discrete domains of gene expression in germinal layers distinguish the development of gyrencephaly. EMBO J. 34 (14), 1859–1874.

Elsen, G.E., et al., 2013. The protomap is propagated to cortical plate neurons through an Eomes-dependent intermediate map. Proc. Natl. Acad. Sci. U. S. A. 110 (10), 4081–4086.

Fischl, B., et al., 2008. Cortical folding patterns and predicting cytoarchitecture. Cereb. Cortex 18 (8), 19731980.

Fogtmann, M., et al., 2014. A unified approach to diffusion direction sensitive slice registration and 3-D DTI reconstruction from moving fetal brain anatomy. IEEE Trans. Med. Imaging 33 (2), 272–289.

Fulford, J., et al., 2003. Fetal brain activity in response to a visual stimulus. Hum. Brain Mapp. 20 (4), 239–245.

Garel, C., et al., 2001. Fetal cerebral cortex: normal gestational landmarks identified using prenatal MR imaging. AJNR Am. J. Neuroradiol. 22 (1), 184–189.

Gholipour, A., Estroff, J.A., Warfield, S.K., 2010. Robust super-resolution volume reconstruction from slice acquisitions: application to fetal brain MRI. IEEE Trans. Med. Imaging 29 (10), 1739–1758.

Gholipour, A., et al., 2014. Fetal MRI: a technical update with educational aspirations. Concepts Magn. Reson. Part A Bridg. Educ. Res. 43 (6), 237–266.

Griffiths, P.D., et al., 2017. Use of MRI in the diagnosis of fetal brain abnormalities in utero (MERIDIAN): a multicentre, prospective cohort study. Lancet 389 (10068), 538–546.

Guha Roy, A., et al., 2019. QuickNAT: a fully convolutional network for quick and accurate segmentation of neuroanatomy. NeuroImage 186, 713–727.

Habas, P.A., et al., 2010. Atlas-based segmentation of developing tissues in the human brain with quantitative validation in young fetuses. Hum. Brain Mapp. 31 (9), 1348–1358.

Habas, P.A., et al., 2012. Early folding patterns and asymmetries of the normal human brain detected from in utero MRI. Cereb. Cortex 22 (1), 13–25.

Hooker, J.D., et al., 2020. Third-trimester in utero fetal brain diffusion tensor imaging fiber tractography: a prospective longitudinal characterization of normal white matter tract development. Pediatr. Radiol. 50 (7), 973–983.

Hykin, J., et al., 1999. Fetal brain activity demonstrated by functional magnetic resonance imaging. Lancet 354 (9179), 645–646.

Im, K., et al., 2011. Quantitative comparison and analysis of sulcal patterns using sulcal graph matching: a twin study. NeuroImage 57 (3), 1077–1086.

Im, K., et al., 2017. Quantitative folding pattern analysis of early primary sulci in human fetuses with brain abnormalities. AJNR Am. J. Neuroradiol. 38 (7), 1449–1455.

Jakab, A., et al., 2014. Fetal functional imaging portrays heterogeneous development of emerging human brain networks. Front. Hum. Neurosci. 8, 852.
Jakab, A., et al., 2015. Disrupted developmental organization of the structural connectome in fetuses with corpus callosum agenesis. NeuroImage 111, 277–288.
Jarvis, D.A., Griffiths, P.D., 2019. Current state of MRI of the fetal brain in utero. J. Magn. Reson. Imaging 49 (3), 632–646.
Jiang, S., et al., 2007. MRI of moving subjects using multislice snapshot images with volume reconstruction (SVR): application to fetal, neonatal, and adult brain studies. IEEE Trans. Med. Imaging 26 (7), 967–980.
Jiang, S., et al., 2009. Diffusion tensor imaging (DTI) of the brain in moving subjects: application to in-utero fetal and ex-utero studies. Magn. Reson. Med. 62 (3), 645–655.
Kasprian, G., et al., 2008. In utero tractography of fetal white matter development. NeuroImage 43 (2), 213–224.
Khalili, N., et al., 2019. Automatic brain tissue segmentation in fetal MRI using convolutional neural networks. Magn. Reson. Imaging 64, 77–89.
Khan, S., et al., 2019. Fetal brain growth portrayed by a spatiotemporal diffusion tensor MRI atlas computed from in utero images. NeuroImage 185, 593–608.
Kim, K., et al., 2010. Intersection based motion correction of multislice MRI for 3-D in utero fetal brain image formation. IEEE Trans. Med. Imaging 29 (1), 146–158.
Klessen, C., et al., 2005. Magnetic resonance imaging of the upper abdomen using a free-breathing T2-weighted turbo spin echo sequence with navigator triggered prospective acquisition correction. J. Magn. Reson. Imaging 21 (5), 576–582.
Kline-Fath, B.M., 2019. Ultrasound and MR imaging of the Normal fetal brain. Neuroimaging Clin. N. Am. 29 (3), 339–356.
Klyachko, V.A., Stevens, C.F., 2003. Connectivity optimization and the positioning of cortical areas. Proc. Natl. Acad. Sci. U. S. A. 100 (13), 7937–7941.
Kuklisova-Murgasova, M., et al., 2012. Reconstruction of fetal brain MRI with intensity matching and complete outlier removal. Med. Image Anal. 16 (8), 1550–1564.
Kwong, K.K., et al., 1992. Dynamic magnetic resonance imaging of human brain activity during primary sensory stimulation. Proc. Natl. Acad. Sci. U. S. A. 89 (12), 5675–5679.
Kyriakopoulou, V., et al., 2014. Cortical overgrowth in fetuses with isolated ventriculomegaly. Cereb. Cortex 24 (8), 2141–2150.
Lefevre, J., et al., 2016. Are developmental trajectories of cortical folding comparable between cross-sectional datasets of fetuses and preterm newborns? Cereb. Cortex 26 (7), 3023–3035.
Limperopoulos, C., et al., 2010. Brain volume and metabolism in fetuses with congenital heart disease: evaluation with quantitative magnetic resonance imaging and spectroscopy. Circulation 121 (1), 26–33.
Logothetis, N.K., et al., 2001. Neurophysiological investigation of the basis of the fMRI signal. Nature 412 (6843), 150–157.
Marami, B., et al., 2017. Temporal slice registration and robust diffusion-tensor reconstruction for improved fetal brain structural connectivity analysis. NeuroImage 156, 475–488.
Marelli, A., et al., 2016. Brain in congenital heart disease across the lifespan: the cumulative burden of injury. Circulation 133 (20), 1951–1962.
Mitter, C., et al., 2015. In vivo tractography of fetal association fibers. PLoS One 10 (3), e0119536.
Ogawa, S., et al., 1990. Oxygenation-sensitive contrast in magnetic resonance image of rodent brain at high magnetic fields. Magn. Reson. Med. 14 (1), 68–78.
O'Leary, D.D., Chou, S.J., Sahara, S., 2007. Area patterning of the mammalian cortex. Neuron 56 (2), 252–269.
Ortinau, C.M., et al., 2019. Early-emerging Sulcal patterns are atypical in fetuses with congenital heart disease. Cereb. Cortex 29 (8), 3605–3616.
Oubel, E., et al., 2012. Reconstruction of scattered data in fetal diffusion MRI. Med. Image Anal. 16 (1), 28–37.

Rakic, P., 2004. Neuroscience. Genetic control of cortical convolutions. Science 303 (5666), 1983–1984.

Rakic, P., 2009. Evolution of the neocortex: a perspective from developmental biology. Nat. Rev. Neurosci. 10 (10), 724–735.

Rousseau, F., et al., 2006. Registration-based approach for reconstruction of high-resolution in utero fetal MR brain images. Acad. Radiol. 13 (9), 1072–1081.

Rousseau, F., et al., 2013. BTK: an open-source toolkit for fetal brain MR image processing. Comput. Methods Prog. Biomed. 109 (1), 65–73.

Saad, Z.S., et al., 2013. Correcting brain-wide correlation differences in resting-state FMRI. Brain Connect 3 (4), 339–352.

Schopf, V., et al., 2012. Watching the fetal brain at 'rest'. Int. J. Dev. Neurosci. 30 (1), 11–17.

Scott, J.A., et al., 2011. Growth trajectories of the human fetal brain tissues estimated from 3D reconstructed in utero MRI. Int. J. Dev. Neurosci. 29 (5), 529–536.

Scott, J.A., et al., 2013. Volumetric and surface-based 3D MRI analyses of fetal isolated mild ventriculomegaly: brain morphometry in ventriculomegaly. Brain Struct. Funct. 218 (3), 645–655.

Smith, S.M., et al., 2009. Correspondence of the brain's functional architecture during activation and rest. Proc. Natl. Acad. Sci. U. S. A. 106 (31), 13040–13045.

Sun, T., Hevner, R.F., 2014. Growth and folding of the mammalian cerebral cortex: from molecules to malformations. Nat. Rev. Neurosci. 15 (4), 217–232.

Tarui, T., et al., 2018. Disorganized patterns of Sulcal position in fetal brains with agenesis of Corpus callosum. Cereb. Cortex 28 (9), 3192–3203.

Tarui, T., et al., 2020. Quantitative MRI analyses of regional brain growth in living fetuses with down syndrome. Cereb. Cortex 30 (1), 382–390.

Thomason, M.E., et al., 2013. Cross-hemispheric functional connectivity in the human fetal brain. Sci. Transl. Med. 5 (173), 173ra24.

Thomason, M.E., et al., 2014. Intrinsic functional brain architecture derived from graph theoretical analysis in the human fetus. PLoS One 9 (5), e94423.

Thomason, M.E., et al., 2015. Age-related increases in long-range connectivity in fetal functional neural connectivity networks in utero. Dev. Cogn. Neurosci. 11, 96–104.

Turk, E., et al., 2019. Functional connectome of the fetal brain. J. Neurosci. 39 (49), 9716–9724.

Uus, A., et al., 2020. Deformable slice-to-volume registration for motion correction of fetal body and placenta MRI. IEEE Trans. Med. Imaging.

van den Heuvel, M.I., et al., 2018. Hubs in the human fetal brain network. Dev. Cogn. Neurosci. 30, 108–115.

Van Essen, D.C., 1997. A tension-based theory of morphogenesis and compact wiring in the central nervous system. Nature 385 (6614), 313–318.

Vasung, L., et al., 2020a. Quantitative in vivo MRI assessment of structural asymmetries and sexual dimorphism of transient fetal compartments in the human brain. Cereb. Cortex 30 (3), 1752–1767.

Vasung, L., et al., 2020b. Spatiotemporal differences in the regional cortical plate and subplate volume growth during fetal development. Cereb. Cortex 30 (8), 4438–4453.

Wright, R., et al., 2014. Automatic quantification of normal cortical folding patterns from fetal brain MRI. NeuroImage 91, 21–32.

Zhang, W., et al., 2015. Deep convolutional neural networks for multi-modality isointense infant brain image segmentation. NeuroImage 108, 214–224.

Zilles, K., et al., 1988. The human pattern of gyrification in the cerebral cortex. Anat. Embryol. (Berl) 179 (2), 173–179.

CHAPTER 7

Special MRI (MWI, MTI, G-ratio) methods sensitive to age and development

Sean C.L. Deoni[a,b,c] and Douglas C. Dean, III[d,e,f]

Maternal, Newborn, and Child Health Discovery & Tools, Bill & Melinda Gates Foundation, Seattle, WA, United States[a] Advanced Baby Imaging Lab, Rhode Island Hospital, Providence, RI, United States[b] Department of Pediatrics, Warren Alpert Medical School at Brown University, Providence, RI, United States[c] Department of Pediatrics, University of Wisconsin-Madison, School of Medicine & Public Health, Madison, WI, United States[d] Department of Medical Physics, University of Wisconsin-Madison, School of Medicine & Public Health, Madison, WI, United States[e] Waisman Center, University of Wisconsin-Madison, Madison, WI, United States[f]

1. Introduction

The first 1000 days of a child's life are widely recognized as a sensitive window of development (Johnson, 2001), during which the structural and functional architecture of the brain develops (Clouchoux et al., 2012; Lyall et al., 2015; Makropoulos et al., 2016; Gao et al., 2017) and lifelong patterns of physical, cognitive, and socio-emotional health are established (Hofman et al., 2004). Across this prenatal and early postnatal period, a child's brain increases almost threefold in volume, and its eloquent neuroarchitecture matures through processes that include neurogenesis and migration, synaptogenesis and dendritic arborization, and myelination (Fig. 1). These structural and functional changes support nearly all emerging cognitive and behavioral skills and functioning (Clouchoux et al., 2012; Lyall et al., 2015; Makropoulos et al., 2016; Gao et al., 2017). This remarkable transformation is fueled by the mother and child's nutritional and energy resources, and shaped by integrated cascades of genetic and environmental interactions that are modulated through psychosocial and caregiving relationships (Rice and Barone, 2000; Stiles and Jernigan, 2010; Fields, 2015). Although the brain retains an exceptional capacity for change throughout adolescence and adulthood, the period from conception through toddlerhood represents a period of peak growth, maximal plasticity, and, by consequence, heightened sensitivity to environmental insult or injury (Rice and Barone, 2000; Choi et al., 2019).

A unique aspect of the human brain is its prolonged developmental timeline (Hrvoj-Mihic et al., 2013; Sousa et al., 2017). Infants are born with relatively immature brains that, like them, are simultaneously competent and vulnerable. Infants are inherently competent in their ability to initiate relationships, explore, seek meaning, and learn; but are vulnerable and depend entirely on caregivers for their survival, emotional security, modeling of behaviors, and the nature and rules of the physical and socio-cultural world that they inhabit. The infant brain is likewise born with immense capacity to learn,

Handbook of Pediatric Brain Imaging. https://doi.org/10.1016/B978-0-12-816633-8.00006-5

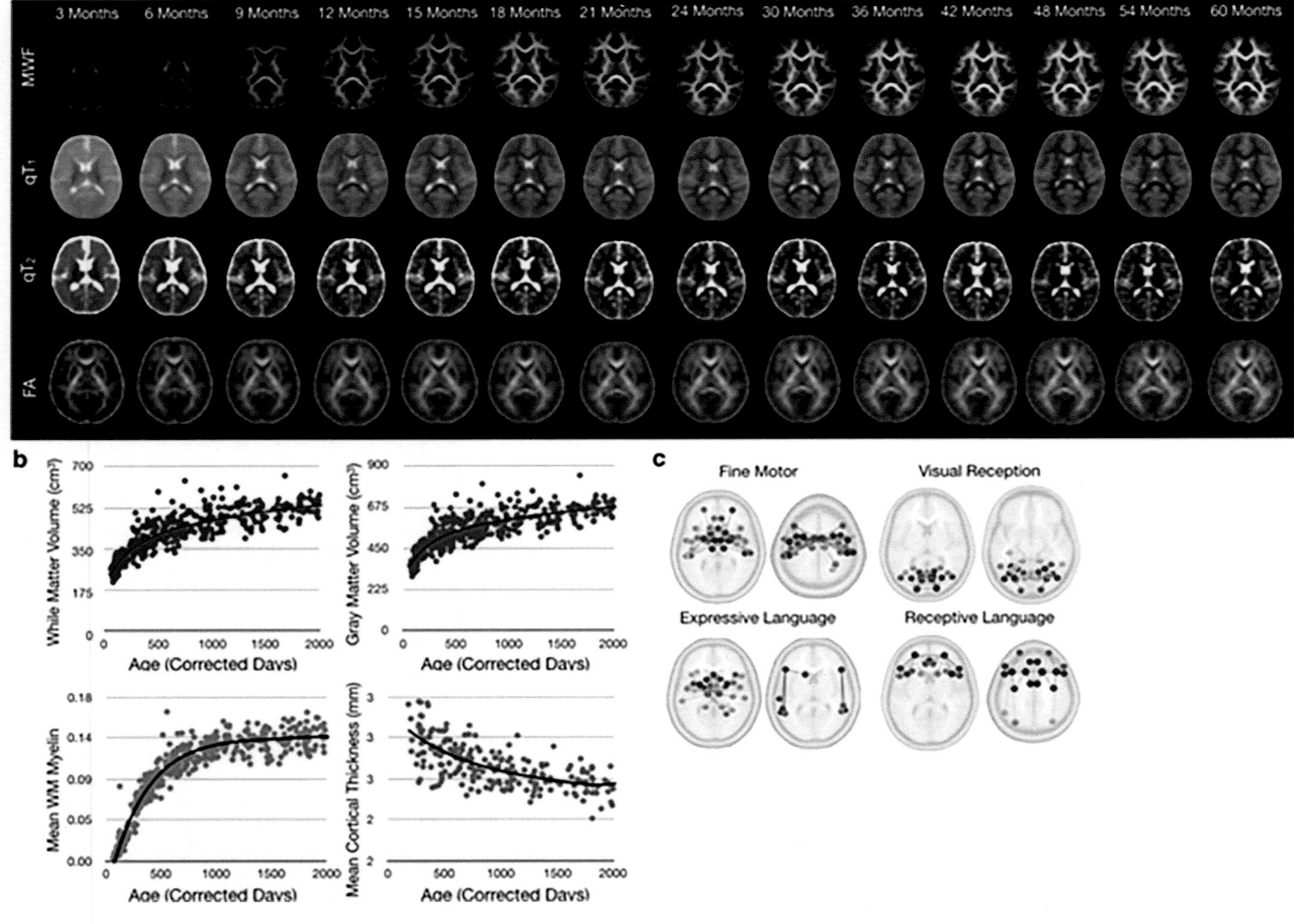

FIG. 1

(A) General multimodal MRI patterns of brain maturation, including indices of anatomy, myelination, and functional connectivity across the first 5 years of life. (B) Curated and condensed trajectories of white and gray matter volume, myelination, and mean cortical thickness showing the changing rate of development, with most developmental processes and changes occurring rapidly over the first 1000 days and the slowing throughout the remainder of childhood. (C) Networks of functional connectivity change associated with emerging fine motor, language, and visual processing skill.

remodel, and adapt, but is sensitive and vulnerable to neglect and environmental exposures that begin even before birth (Fulford et al., 2003; Bock et al., 2015; Vohr et al., 2017). Optimal brain development, therefore, depends on secure and trusting relationships with knowledgeable caregivers who are responsive to the infant's needs and interests. Myelination and synaptogenesis, for example, are stimulated by external cues and experiences like maternal interaction, and physical skin-to-skin "kangaroo" care, touch, and warmth (Kolb, 2009; Ismail et al., 2017; Choi et al., 2019). The brain's adaptive plasticity, however, is a double-edged sword. While positive and enriching environments can promote healthy brain development (Dobbing, 1964; Bradley and Corwyn, 2002; Noble et al., 2005; Farah et al., 2006; Georgieff, 2007; Swain et al., 2007), neglect and abuse can impair maturing brain systems and disrupt cognitive and behavioral outcomes (Rees and Inder, 2005).

As a result of their prolonged maturation timeline, responsiveness to environmental, genetic, and hormonal stimuli, and central role in brain communication and function (Hofman et al., 2004; Houston et al., 2014; Gao et al., 2017), myelination and synaptogenesis are of particular relevance to the studies of cognitive and behavioral development (Kisilevsky et al., 2009; Bock et al., 2015; Krebs et al., 2017; Vohr et al., 2017). The elaboration of the myelin sheath around neuronal axons (myelination) begins in mid-to-late gestation (~20 weeks) and plays an increasingly important role in brain communication (Hrvoj-Mihic et al., 2013). Myelination advances rapidly over the first 2–3 years of life in a carefully choreographed caudal-cranial, posterior-to-anterior arc (Brody et al., 1987; Barkovich et al., 1988; Paus et al., 2001). This ontogenic pattern is tightly regulated by neural activity (Demerens et al., 1996; Fields, 2005; Ishibashi et al., 2006) and spatio-temporally coincides with the emergence of cognitive skills and abilities (Nagy et al., 2004; Casey et al., 2005; Fields, 2008). That is, cognitive functions appear to mature at the same time that the subserving brain regions and neural systems are myelinated. Animal models demonstrate the importance of myelination to learning and skill development (McKenzie et al., 2014), and de- and dys-myelinating disorders (such as multiple sclerosis and leukodystrophies) confirm the importance of myelin to normative brain functioning. The maturation of the cortical myeloarchitecture also advances rapidly in association with evolving neurobehavioral functions (Peters and Sethares, 2002) and contributing developmental plasticity (McGee et al., 2005). Myelination continues at a slower rate into adulthood, reaching a maximum in the 2nd or 3rd decade of life depending on brain region (Bartzokis et al., 2010).

Preceding myelination, the growth of new synaptic connections (synaptogenesis) begins by the 5th week of gestation and drives the enlargement of the fetal and infant brain, which reaches 80% of its adult size by age 2 years (Knickmeyer et al., 2008; Gilmore et al., 2012). The increasing pace of synaptogenesis throughout the latter half of pregnancy results in an excess of synapses at birth (LaMantia and Rakic, 1990, 1994). Synaptic pruning throughout childhood and adolescence eliminates many of these connections (Huttenlocher, 1979), with synapses that receive constant input preserved while disused connections are eliminated. While pruning continues throughout the lifespan (Shankle et al., 1998), peaking during the transitions from child-to-adolescence and adolescence-to-adulthood (Levitt, 2003), the pattern of axonal connections remains relatively constant after age 2 (Innocenti and Price, 2005; Luo and O'Leary, 2005).

Magnetic resonance imaging, more so that other neuroimaging techniques (electroencephalography, EEG, near infrared spectroscopy, NIRS, and magnetoencephalography, MEG), offers compelling insight into the functional, structural, physiological, and biochemical changes that occur alongside and in coordination with myelination and synaptogenesis. Many of these changes, and the available methods to measure them, have been detailed in the prior chapters, and demonstrate the unique sensitivity and utility of MRI to the study of neurodevelopment. In this chapter, we turn our attention to quantitative methods, including quantitative relaxometry (qT_1 and qT_2 imaging), multicomponent relaxometry and myelin water imaging (MCR and MWI), magnetization transfer imaging (MT and qMT), and the combination of these techniques to explore developing brain microstructure.

2. Quantitative relaxometry (qT_1 & qT_2) methods

The exquisite soft tissue contrast provided by magnetic resonance imaging arises principally from differences in the intrinsic relaxation properties, T_1 and T_2, and proton density (representing water content). In conventional clinical MRI, tissue contrast is created by weighting the acquired MRI signal to one or more of these effects through the choice of pulse sequence and acquisition parameters. However, this weighted signal remains a complex function of these underlying features, as well as other patient and hardware-specific effects, such as patient position, field strength, and receiver coil geometry. This complex mixture, however, can mask subtle tissue maturation and makes it difficult to easily interpret observed imaging change. To gain improved sensitivity to microstructure development, specifically changes in lipid content as would accompany myelination, or water content potentially associated with changing neuronal cell size, packing, and density, or increasing protein content, an alternative approach involves the direct quantification of the relaxation and water content properties.

But what governs the longitudinal (T_1) and transverse (T_2) relaxation properties? And what physiological processes underlie them? And how can these be used to monitor and examine neurodevelopment? Intrinsically, the T_1 and T_2 relaxation processes are processes of molecular motion, interaction, and energy exchange. The first theoretical description that related the relaxation processes to molecular motion was presented by Bloembergen, Purcell and Pound (BPP) in the late 1940s (Bloembergen et al., 1947). In particular, T_1 relaxation involves an exchange of energy between water protons and protons attached to other surrounding lipids, proteins, and macromolecules (collectively termed the "lattice"). Acknowledging these interactions, T_1 relaxation is also commonly referred to as spin-lattice relaxation. In contrast, T_2 relaxation results from interactions between the water protons themselves and, accordingly, is also termed spin-spin relaxation. An important distinction between T_1 and T_2 processes is that while T_1 is an energy-loss process (with energy transferred from the water protons to the bulk lattice), T_2 is an energy-conserving process, resulting solely from the de-phasing of the individual spin magnetic moments in an ensemble without loss of energy.

Structural and compositional changes, resulting from disease pathology, development, learning, or plasticity, therefore, will likely result in measurable T_1, T_2 and/or PD changes. For example, the establishment of the lipid rich myelin sheath during early neurodevelopment, along with associated proteins, cholesterol, iron containing oligodendrocytes and glial cells, results in rapid and substantial T_1 and T_2 changes over the first 2 years of life (Brody et al., 1987; Deoni et al., 2012). Likewise, the reduced T_1 and T_2 of white matter compared to gray matter primarily derives from the different concentration of myelin. Similarly, differing concentrations of ferritin may underlie the T_1, T_2 and T_2* variations observed between deep gray matter structures.

However, adoption of quantitative imaging in clinical and research imaging studies has been slow. This may, in part, be due to the lengthy acquisition times, relatively poor spatial resolution, or limited brain coverage that may be associated with conventional measurement methods, such as multiple inversion time inversion recovery (or multiple repetition time saturation recovery) spin echo for T_1, and multiple echo time spin or gradient echo for T_2 and T_2*. While accelerated readout methods, such as multiple spin-echo (i.e., fast or turbo spin-echo, FSE or TSE) or gradient refocused echo-planar imaging (EPI), can substantially reduce acquisition times to the order of seconds or minutes, they do so at the expense of reduced maximal spatial resolution, reduced signal-to-noise ratio (SNR), and image degradation driven by off-resonance effects, signal drop-outs, and geometric distortions. Exemplary work by several research groups over the past decade, however, has led to the development of several accelerated methods that afford acquisition times and spatial resolutions on par with more conventional T_1, T_2 and PD-weighted images, and can be combined with motion correction techniques and/or noise-derated to make them more suitable for infant and pediatric imaging.

2.1 The look-locker method

The main limitation of conventional "gold-standard" approaches to qT_1 and qT_2 imaging is the excessive time between successive RF pulses that is spent allowing the system magnetization to fully recover to equilibrium. To increase imaging time efficiency, the first approach to acceleration is to acquire more than just a single line of the image after each pulse. This can be accomplished using echo-planar readouts, parallel imaging methods, or other ingenious schemes. Perhaps one of the most widely used rapid T_1 mapping approaches is the method of Look and Locker (LL) (Zhang et al., 1992), which makes the efficient use of the dead-time between successive inversion pulses in the IR sequence to comprehensively and continuously sample the full T_1 recovery curve using a series of small angle (α typically less than 40 degrees) RF pulses separated by a short time delay. In an imaging setting, each of these samples comprises a k_y line in a different image. Thus, the experiment is repeated N times, where N is the number of k_y lines in the final map image (i.e., $N = 128$ in a 128×128 matrix image). Due to the disturbing effect of the α RF pulses, the magnetization recovers to an effective equilibrium (that differs from the thermal equilibrium) via an *apparent* T_1 relaxation rate ($T_{1,e}$) that is related to a known way to the true T_1.

The LL method and variants thereof are fast enough for cardiac and dynamic contrast applications (Karlsson and Nordell, 2000; Messroghli et al., 2004), while retaining the accuracy and reproducibility of conventional qT_1 techniques (Roujol et al., 2014). To accelerate further from a 2-dimensional (D) to 3D sequence, Henderson and colleagues (Henderson et al., 1999) proposed a binning approach that grouped sets of k_y lines into different images. In this way, they could quickly loop through repeated prep-pulse + readout train cycles to fill multiple images simultaneously.

2.2 MP-N-RAGE

Simplistically, the MP-2 (Marques et al., 2010) and MP-N (Kecskemeti et al., 2016) RAGE techniques can be considered additional variants of the 3D Look-Locker approach (Henderson et al., 1999; Wade et al., 2014). The basic MP-RAGE sequence is similar to LL in that it involves a preparation pulse (usually an inversion or saturation pulse) followed by a series of low angle readout pulses after which a single line of the image is acquired. The readout is performed such that a full image slice (or plane in k-space) is acquired after each preparation pulse, starting from the bottom of the slice to the top and timed such that "effective" inversion time corresponds to the collection of the center line. In MP-N-RAGE, this is adjusted such that after each preparation pulse, an under-sampled radial readout collects a single image slice rather than just a single line. Again, through appropriate binning and reconstruction, similar to (Henderson et al., 1999; Wade et al., 2014), an almost unlimited series of image volumes can be reconstructed with differing effective inversion timings. From these discrete images, a qT_1 image can be calculated. The use of an under sample radial readout allows intrinsic corrections for field biases and reduces motion sensitivity, which appear as radial blurring rather than ghosting as in a standard Cartesian collection.

2.3 Method of variable flip angles

The methods presented above retain the principal of sampling the recovery of the longitudinal magnetization in some form following an initial preparation pulse. However, an alternative approach does away with this central tenet and instead uses a series of tightly-spaced small-angle pulses to establish a steady-state magnetization. By selectively spoiling (or eliminating) the transverse magnetization before each pulse, or not, the resulting signal can be made sensitive to T_1 only (spoiled) or a combination of T_1 and T_2 (fully balanced) as:

$$S_{\text{spoiled}} = M_0 \frac{1 - E_1 \sin(\alpha)}{1 - E_1 \cos(\alpha)} E_2^* \quad (1)$$

and

$$S_{\text{balanced}} = M_0 \frac{(1 - E_1) E_2 \sin(\alpha)}{1 - E_1 E_2 - (E_1 - E_2 \cos(\alpha))} \quad (2)$$

where $E_1 = \exp(-TR/T_1)$, $E_2 = \exp(-TR/T_2)$ and $E_2{}^* = \exp(-TE/T_2{}^*)$.

Repeating this over a set of different flip angles provides the opportunity to calculate proton density, T_1, and/or T_2. Adding an additional spoiled scan with a different TE can also allow calculation of $T_2{}^*$. An attractive feature of this approach is that, while not directly obvious, the spoiled and balanced signal equations can be rewritten in a linear form, allowing calculation of all four parameters from as few as 5 images.

As with the Look-Locker method, however, the method of variable flip angels (also termed DESPOT) requires accurate knowledge of the transmitted flip angle for accurate parameter quantification. Further, incomplete spoiling of the transverse magnetization can result in residual coherent transverse magnetization (Denolin et al., 2005; Lin and Song, 2009) reducing the accuracy of the T_1 estimates. Similarly, off-resonance effects, such as due to inhomogeneity in the applied magnetic field, or tissue susceptibility effects, will disrupt the balanced steady state signal and lead to reduced T_2 accuracy. These effects can be addressed through an accurate flip angle (B_1+) measurement and calibration (Deoni, 2011), as well as through B_0 field mapping. An approach for reducing off-resonance effects for T_2 mapping proposed by Deoni (2011) involves collection of balanced images with different phase angle offsets, allowing simultaneous T_2 and B_0 calculation.

2.4 MR fingerprinting

MR fingerprinting offer a novel departure from the above-mentioned techniques in that it does not specifically fit a well-defined single model to a set of imaging data but rather uses a pattern-recognition classifier to determine T_1 and T_2, as well as other quantitative parameters (Ma et al., 2013). In this approach, heterogeneous MR data (that is, from different acquisition sequences and/or different acquisition parameters) are acquired. Within each voxel, this set of signals represents a unique signature, or fingerprint. Theoretical signals corresponding to the applied acquisition strategy are then calculated for a wide range of T_1, T_2, T_2*, ρ and off-resonance values, creating a reference database of signal models (e.g., the fingerprint library). Correlations are then calculated between the measured signal fingerprint and each reference print in the library to determine the most appropriate match and, therefore, corresponding quantitative values. In preliminary reports, the method shows good reliability even in the presence of motion and other artifacts.

3. Quantitative relaxometry in pediatric imaging

Regardless of the method used, changes in the T_1 and T_2 relaxation parameters across infant and early child development provides insight into the maturing brain microstructure and changing biochemical and biophysical composition. Fig. 2 displays representative qT_1 images acquired from age 3 months to 8 years, with mean regional trajectories shown in Fig. 3. The logarithmically decreasing tissue relaxation properties has been ascribed to decreasing water content, increasing lipid content, changing fiber density and neural cell packing, as well as the arrival of other proteins and macromolecules involved in myelination, synaptogenesis, and synapse functioning. Such images can be used to examine differences in development across different brain regions, as well as used to explore differences in tissue

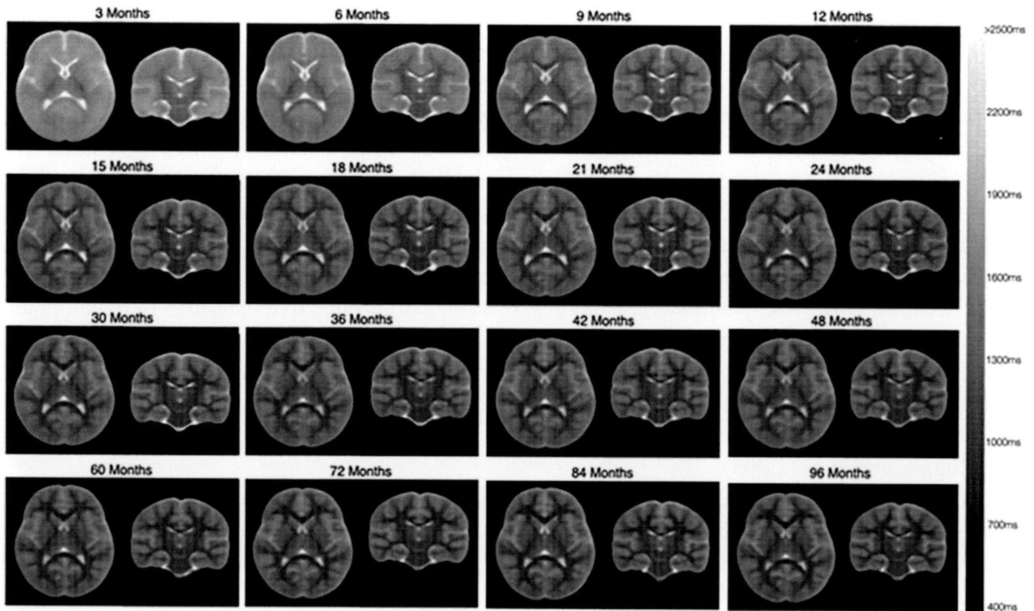

FIG. 2

Representative mean qT_1 images acquired across the first 9 years of life, showing the expected decrease in T_1 relaxation times with age and associated with changing lipid, myelin, and water content, fiber density, and other aspects of tissue maturation.

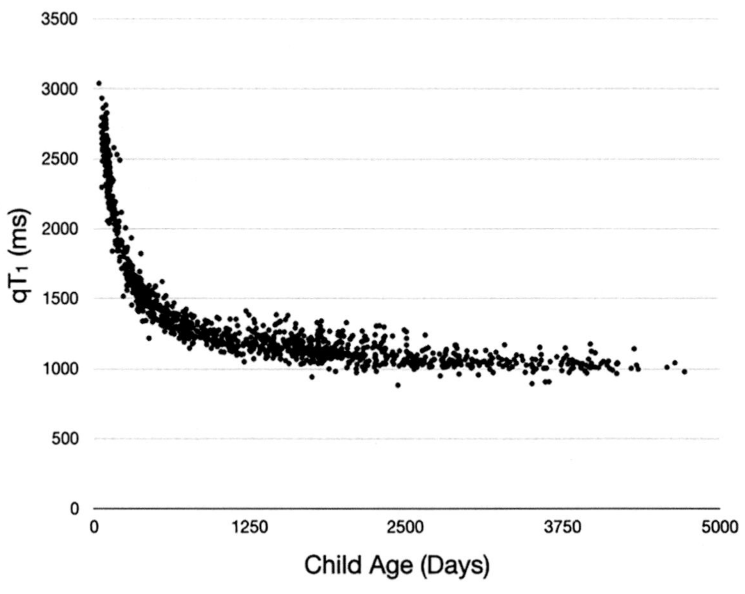

FIG. 3

Mean whole-brain white matter qT_1 vs age trajectories, following approximate logarithmic patterns across early life.

microstructure associated with environmental exposures, injury, prematurity, or other developmental influences; and their ultimate associations with cognitive, behavioral, and intellectual outcomes.

Although quantitative neuroimaging is not routinely performed in clinical settings, various clinical reports do point to its potential utility for identifying early developmental differences associated with de- and dys-myelinating disorders. Hypomyelinating leukodystrophies, for example, are difficult to readily identify and discern within the first 6–12 months of life due to paucity of gray-white matter contrast in the brain (Dreha-Kulaczewski et al., 2012; Pouwels et al., 2014; Steenweg et al., 2016). Likewise, lesions associated with pediatric multiple sclerosis (MS) are also difficult to identify for the same reason. However, quantitative T_1 and/or T_2 values offer objective measures of development that can be compared against normative population controls (such as described here for adults; (Dvorak et al., 2021)) to identify areas of significantly elevated values (indicative of reduced development and myelination). Alternations in T_1 and/or T_2 have further been associated with temporal lobe epilepsy (Khan et al., 2014; Woermann et al., 1998) and to potentially identify seizure foci (Liao et al., 2018; Rugg-Gunn et al., 2005).

In addition to these more direct and clinically-focused applications, quantitative relaxometry has found use in research studies of neurodevelopment, brain maturation, and aging. The relative independence of T_1 and T_2 on hardware, scanner manufacturer, and even acquisition parameters, as well as the high intra and intersite reliability of relaxometry measures, lends relaxometry to multicenter and longitudinal studies. This is demonstrated in Fig. 4, which shows the reproducibility values of qT_1 and qT_2 values acquired across different imaging centers and time-points.

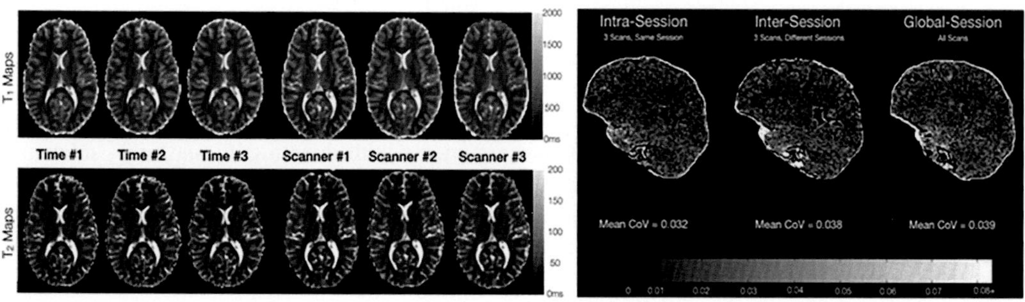

FIG. 4

Intra and intersite reproducibility of qT_1 and qT_2 values calculated from the variable flip angle method. Repeated images were acquired of the same set of volunteers on three separate occasions, and across three different imaging centers. Overall variation was less than 4%. One of the intrinsic advantages of quantitative imaging is its robustness and independence to scanner manufacturer, acquisition parameters, and other hardware effects. This allows for easier integration of data across multiple imaging centers or timepoints.

4. Myelin water and magnetization transfer imaging

The maturation and elaboration of the myelinated white matter is one of the most visible changes apparent on brain MR images across the first year of life, and underlies the functional development of the brain. On conventional T_1 and T_2-weighted images, myelination is observed as the appearance of hyper-intense signal throughout the white matter, and the gradual increase in white-gray matter image contrast to near adult levels by the end of the first year of life. qT_1 and qT_2 imaging can also provide insight into this important process (as shown in Fig. 2), as the increase lipid and macromolecule content of the lipid myelin sheath leads to reductions in T_1 and T_2, alongside reductions in water content, and potential increase in iron concentration associated with oligodendrocytes. Improved sensitivity to myelination and quantitative measures of myelin content can, however, be garnered by myelin-specific imaging using either magnetization transfer or myelin water imaging.

The conventional approach to magnetization transfer imaging—calculation of the semiquantitative magnetization transfer ratio (MTR) involves the acquisition of two T_1-weighted images, with and without the inclusion of an off-resonance preparation pulse. The off-resonance pulse excites water protons attached to macromolecules and lipid membranes, such as the myelin sheath. These protons then exchange with nonbound aqueous protons and contribute to the overall signal. The ratio of the two images provides the MTR measure, and is elevated in areas of increased myelin content.

MTR, therefore, provides information related to the relative fraction of bound protons. A separate and complementary, but not necessarily equivalent, approach to quantifying myelin content is myelin water imaging (MWI). Like MT, MWI has seen a proliferation of methods development over the past decade, ranging from qualitative myelin-sensitive techniques to quantitative multicomponent relaxometry (MRC) techniques.

5. Multicomponent relaxometry

Exploiting the sensitivity of the T_1 and T_2 relaxation properties to the local biophysical and biochemical environment, the aim of multicomponent relaxometry is to decompose the measured MRI signal into contributions from subvoxel tissue pools or components with differing T_1 and/or T_2 relaxation characteristics. In almost any biological tissue, and in brain parenchyma in particular, water is highly compartmentalized into anatomical subdomains, each with unique biophysical and biochemical properties. These differing characteristics impart unique T_1, T_2 and T_2* relaxation properties onto the water protons residing within them and, as a result, each has a distinct MR signal signature. The overall measured signal, therefore, represents the powder-average of these individual anatomical contributions. The result of this complexity is that signal decay is poorly described by a single T_1 and T_2 value. But, this complexity also provides a path toward identifying and quantifying these individual contributions.

The "classic" approach to examining tissue complexity via relaxometry was presented by MacKay et al. (1994) and involves the collection of multiple T_2-weighted spin-echo images over an extended range of echo times (for example, from 10 to 320 ms in 10 ms increments). Fitting a multiexponential model,

$$S(\mathrm{TE}) = M_o\left(\sum_{n=1}^{\infty} f_n \exp\left(-\frac{\mathrm{TE}}{T_{2,n}}\right)\right) \tag{3}$$

where f_n and $T_{2,n}$ are the relative volume fraction and the transverse relaxation time of component n, respectively, has consistently revealed the presence of at least 2 water species: a fast relaxing species ascribed to water trapped between the lipid bilayers of the myelin sheath; and a slower relaxing species associated with the intra and extra-cellular water (MacKay and Laule, 2016). Various groups have further demonstrated the ability to resolve the intra and extra-cellular water signals, particularly within disease or pathology.

MWI has proved extremely useful in studies of de-myelinating disorders, including multiple sclerosis (MS) and amyotrophic lateral sclerosis (ALS) (Minty et al., 2009; Vavasour et al., 2009), with high reproducibility and multicenter compatibility (Meyers et al., 2009, 2013). Further, the results agree strongly with histological assessments of myelin content (Laule et al., 2006, 2008), validating the approach as a myelin specific and sensitive technique, in comparison with other techniques, including diffusion and magnetization transfer imaging (Vavasour et al., 2011; Mancini et al., 2020). The use of accelerated imaging techniques [i.e., GRASE or parallel readouts (Dvorak et al., 2020; Piredda et al., 2021)] have further increased the potential clinical utility of the multi-TE technique by allowing whole-brain acquisitions in clinically-feasible timeframes. Alternative approaches, based on T_2*, have been proposed that also offer clinically acceptable acquisition times (Nguyen et al., 2016).

A further alternative approach to MWI is an extension of the variable flip angle T_1 and T_2 techniques presented above (Deoni et al., 2008, 2013). This approach aims to extract multicomponent information from a series of T_1 and T_1/T_2-weighted images. However, although this method allows potentially faster image acquisitions with high spatial resolutions, it also involves more complicated processing. A basic assumption that underlies the multiecho approach is that the relaxation rates of the individual compartments are fast relative to the rate of exchange of water between them. This allows the signal equation to reduce to the multiexponential model presented in Eq. (3). While this assumption appears to hold true for T_2, it is not the case of T_1 and, as a result, observation of multicomponent T_1 has been inconsistent and challenging (Deoni et al., 2007). Extension of multicomponent relaxation to the spoiled gradient and fully-balanced steady-state signal equations (Eqs. 1, 2) is nontrivial (Deoni et al., 2007) and accurate fitting is challenging (Deoni and Kolind, 2015), but possible.

5.1 Myelin sensitive imaging

If an image sensitive to myelin, and not a direct measure of myelin content, is desired, a variety of less complicated myelin-sensitive techniques may be preferable. Double-echo inversion imaging, ultrashort echo time imaging, and other image subtraction and manipulation techniques have been shown to successfully highlight and improve contrast of myelin-containing tissues. While expedient, results from these approaches are sensitive to acquisition parameters. In the context of pediatric imaging, this need to tailor the sequence adds an important challenge since the T_1 and T_2 properties change rapidly with a child age (Deoni et al., 2012). The semiquantitative T_1/T_2 approach (Glasser and Van Essen, 2011) is similarly sensitive to acquisition parameters and derives from basic assumptions: 1. T_1 is reduced by only increased myelination; and 2. T_2 decreases as a result of only iron accumulation in oligodendrocytes, that are not always valid in general (Bottomley et al., 1984, 1987), and may not be true in the case of the developing brain.

6. Imaging myelination throughout development

With the development of rapid and whole-brain methods for robust myelin sensitive imaging (MTR, MWI, etc.) that can be performed in sleeping infants, awake toddlers and children, and adolescents, recent studies have sought to investigate and map the trajectory of brain myelination throughout childhood, associate changes with evolving cognition and behavior, and understand the impact of child environmental exposures. With success in research, these methods may ultimately prove useful in clinical settings, specifically with respect to conditions affecting white matter, such as Leukodystrophies, ischemia, and other injury.

Fig. 5, for example provides the visualization of the stages of myelination throughout the brain across infancy and early childhood, with an example whole brain MWF vs. Age trajectory shown in Fig. 6, with a characteristic sigmoidal or modified Gompertz growth curve (Dean et al., 2014). Qualitatively, these data align with the histologically-established pattern (Brody et al., 1987; Girard et al., 1991) that evolves from center-out, deep brain to superficial, and back-to-front, in a topographical arc that temporally mirrors with the maturational progression of function (Van der Knaap et al., 1991). Of note, while various reports have used qT_1 as a proxy for myelin content (Glasser and Van Essen, 2011), given the partial dependence of longitudinal relaxation on lipid content (Bottomley et al., 1984), Fig. 6 *right* shows the relationship between measured MWF and qT_1 in the same group of children from birth to 13 years of age, and clearly demonstrates a nonlinear relationship. Examining the development and the maturation of the myelination white matter, Fig. 7, for example, displays myelination patterns from brain regions associated a priori with fine and gross motor function, visual processing, and expressive and receptive language, showing clear distinctions in myelination onset, development rate, and overall mature myelin content. Building from this, techniques more typically employed for functional imaging processing can be used to investigate the dynamic development of structural systems (Dai et al., 2019).

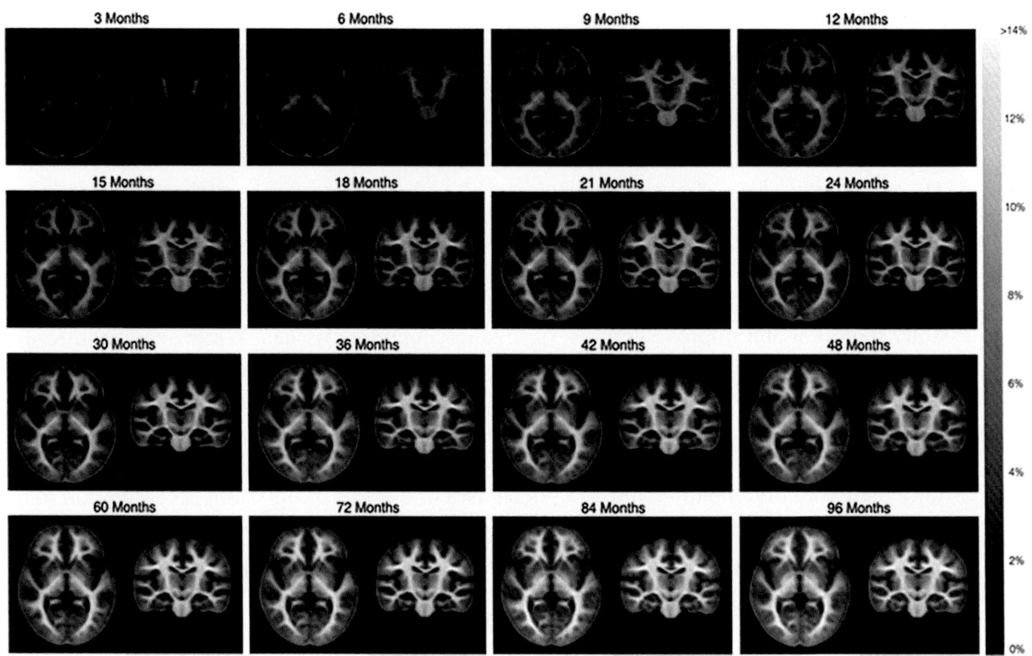

FIG. 5

Representative mean MWF images acquired across the first 8 years of life. Images reproduce the histologically-established pattern of myelination, beginning in the center of the brain and moving outwards and in a back-to-front arc. Note the rapid increase in myelination across the first 2 years of life that then slows and continues throughout the remainder of childhood.

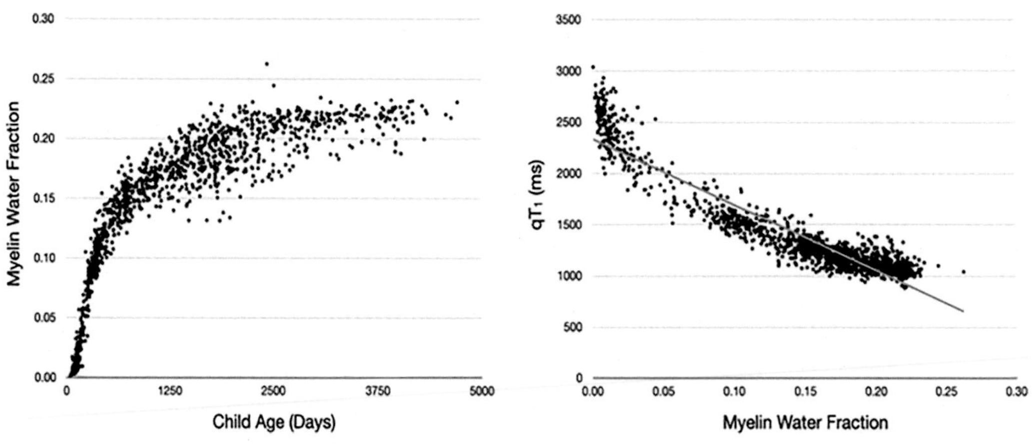

FIG. 6

(*Left*) Mean trajectory of whole white matter myelin water fraction across early childhood. (*Right*) Plot of myelin water fraction vs. qT_1. While T_1 relaxation is often assumed to closely reflect lipid and myelin content, this plot demonstrates that MWF and qT_1, while complementary, are not the same.

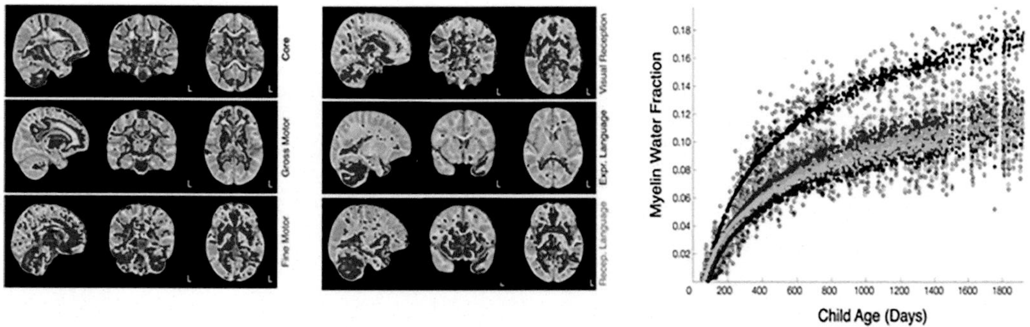

FIG. 7

Mean myelination trajectories calculated for different brain networks associated with individual functions, as well as a "core" brain network that overlaps with all functions. Brain "networks" were first identified using independent component analysis to isolate regions with shared developmental trajectories, and mixed modeling used to relate those developmental patterns to developing function.

Combined with nutritional information, such as the impact of breastfeeding vs formula milk (Deoni et al., 2013, 2014, 2018), or data on specific nutrient consumption (Deoni, Dean et al., 2018), delivery type (Deoni et al., 2019), or other birth outcome or early exposure (Dobbing, 1964; Georgieff, 2007; Dreha-Kulaczewski et al., 2012; Mercer et al., 2018), myelin imaging can provide important insight into factors that contribute to brain and cognitive development.

Although techniques for more rapid acquisitions are a focus of innovation, the ultimate research and clinical utility of myelin imaging rests heavily on the time required to acquire data for robust and accurate calculation. One way to address this is to exploit recent development in "synthetic MRI," the calculation of conventional appearing anatomical images from quantitative images (Deoni et al., 2006), and popularized by commercial on-scanner and cloud-based software services (e.g., Caliber MRI (https://qmri.com), Synthetic MRI (https://syntheticmr.com), and Olea Medical (https://olea-medical.com)). One such approach, detailed in Fig. 8, involves the acquisition of high resolution qT_1 and qT_2 images, which can be used to generate the convention T_1 and T_2 weighted images, and then a set of lower resolution images that allow more complete myelin modeling.

7. G-ratio imaging

As we've seen, the maturation of the central nervous system's white matter is driven, in large part, by the establishment of the myelin sheath around neuronal axons. The thickness of the myelin sheath plays an important role in determining the relative efficiency and conduction velocity of an axon, with thicker myelin sheaths enabling faster conduction for an axon of fixed diameter (Waxman, 1980). However, this conduction speed is also dependent on the axon's diameter (Berthold et al., 1983; Graf von Keyserlingk and Schramm, 1984), and therefore the amount of myelin wrapped around an axon needs to be carefully balanced with its diameter in order to maximize efficiency (Rushton, 1951; Chomiak and Hu, 2009). This is particularly true in central nervous system where myelination aims to reduce conduction delays and promote conduction fidelity while minimizing energy consumption and space

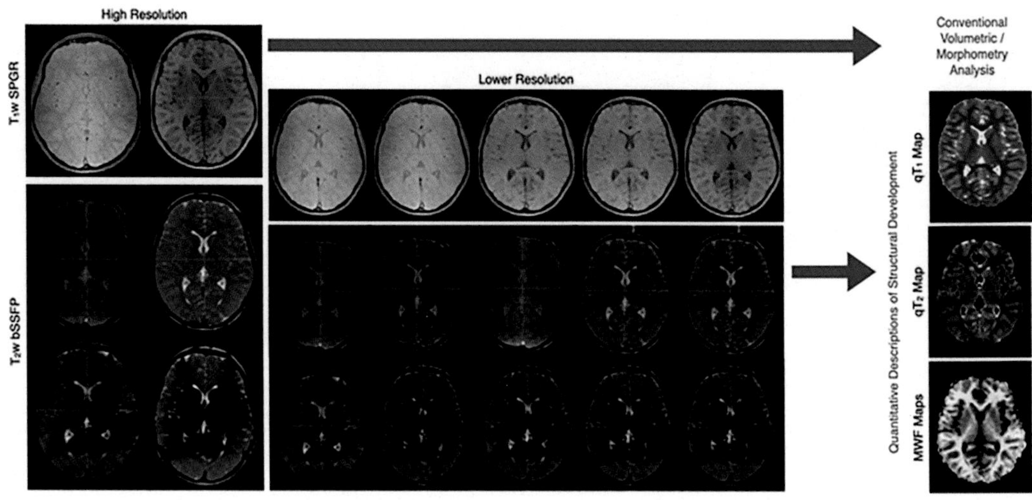

FIG. 8

One approach for incorporating quantitative relaxometry into a standard neuroimaging research protocol without substantively increasing scanner time. High resolution multiangle T_1-weighted spoiled and T_1/T_2-weighted balanced steady-state images are acquired to reconstruct high resolution qT_1 and qT_2 maps, which can then be used for standard volumetric and morphometric analysis and anatomical localization. In addition, lower-resolution data is acquired to allow full fitting for MWF (and T_2*) providing a thorough characterization of developing brain structure.

(Chomiak and Hu, 2009). The *g*-ratio, defined as the ratio between the axon diameter and total fiber diameter (i.e., axon diameter plus myelin thickness), is a fundamental property of white matter microstructure that captures the relationship between myelin thickness and axon diameter. Theoretical models have proposed a *g*-ratio of approximately 0.6–0.8 yields optimum fiber conduction (Rushton, 1951; Chomiak and Hu, 2009), while deviations from this optimal range are suspected to have significant functional consequences and may underly certain neurodevelopmental and "dysconnection" disorders (Uranova et al., 2001; Paus and Toro, 2009; Du et al., 2013).

The measurement of the *g*-ratio has historically been restricted to ex vivo and invasive methodologies, such as electron microscopy, thus having limited applicability to studying and tracking brain development (Schröder et al., 1988). Recently, Stikov et al. (2011, 2015a,b) proposed a tissue model in which an aggregate *g*-ratio could be estimated at the voxel level by combining quantitative MRI measures of myelin volume fraction (MVF) and fiber volume fraction (FVF) through a simple geometric relationship (Stikov et al., 2011, 2015a,b):

$$g = \sqrt{1 - \frac{\text{MVF}}{\text{FVF}}} \tag{4}$$

The term aggregate *g*-ratio is used to denote that the framework assumes a constant *g*-ratio of all axons in the imaging voxel and that the resulting estimate is a summary measure that is not necessarily representative of the underlying distribution of axon *g*-ratios. Stikov et al. (2015b) went on to further show that MRI derived aggregate g-ratio estimates were consistent with histological estimates in the macaque corpus callosum (Stikov et al., 2015a,b). West et al. (2016) extended this framework to show both theoretically and histologically that MRI derived aggregate *g*-ratio provides an axon-area-weighted measure of the *g*-ratio from all individual axons in a voxel. Furthermore, as suggested by Campbell et al. (2018), the more accurate the MRI measure is to the MVF and FVF, the more the aggregate *g*-ratio will be weighted by the underlying microscopic *g*-ratio.

Thus, the ability to map the aggregate *g*-ratio becomes a question of how best to measure the MVF and AVF with MRI. For estimating MVF, several quantitative MRI techniques that have been previously discussed have been also used in the computation of the aggregate *g*-ratio, including MWI via multicomponent relaxometry (MacKay et al., 1994; Deoni et al., 2008, 2013; Alonso-Ortiz et al., 2015), MTR and MTI, macromolecule tissue volume imaging (Mezer et al., 2013), and multiparametric quantitative MRI (Weiskopf et al., 2013). On the other hand, diffusion imaging techniques, such as Diffusion Tensor Imaging (DTI) (Basser and Pierpaoli, 1996), Neurite Orientation Dispersion and Density Imaging (NODDI) (Zhang et al., 2012), Tract Fiber Density (TFD) imaging (Reisert et al., 2013), Composite Hindered And Restricted Model of Diffusion (CHARMED) (Assaf and Basser, 2005), the White Matter Tissue Integrity (WMTI) model (Fieremans et al., 2011), and the multicompartment Spherical Mean Technique (mcSMT) (Kaden et al., 2016) have all been utilized to estimate the FVF. Here, the reader is referred to recent reviews by Campbell et al. (2018) and Mohammadi and Callaghan (2021) for further details about using these quantitative imaging approaches in measuring the *g*-ratio.

Imaging the *g*-ratio in infancy and early childhood can provide insight into the neurodevelopmental process of myelination and, given association between the *g*-ratio and fiber conduction speed, has the potential to offer new understanding about the interdependent development of brain structure and function. However, while several studies have examined age related changes in adolescence and adults (Mohammadi et al., 2015; Cercignani et al., 2017; Berman et al., 2018; Ellerbrock and Mohammadi, 2018; Mancini et al., 2018; Kamagata et al., 2019), studies in pediatric populations have been limited to date. Fig. 9 displays representative mean *g*-ratio images approximately 3, 12, 24, and 60 months of age, demonstrating a rapid decrease of the aggregate *g*-ratio over the course of the first 5 years of life. Similar to trajectories of qT_1 and qT_2 above, age-related changes of the aggregate *g*-ratio begin to appear as early as the late stages of prenatal development (Melbourne et al., 2016) and follow a decreasing logarithmic trajectory during early childhood (Dean et al., 2016). Approaching values that are in agreement with the theoretical predictions of the optimal *g*-ratio (Rushton, 1951; Chomiak and Hu, 2009). These changes seem to indicate the underlying increases in myelin thickness and fiber conduction efficiency that occur with early postnatal brain development and can be used in combination with other quantitative imaging measures already described to more fully characterize the development of the tissue microstructure. Larger and longitudinal imaging studies of the *g*-ratio will be informative for examining how myelination is guided and/or altered by genetic, environmental, and other developmental influences.

Declaration of interests

S.C. Deoni receives grant funding and consulting salary from Nestle SA, Wyeth Nutrition, and Mead-Johnson Nutrition. D.C. Dean has nothing to declare.

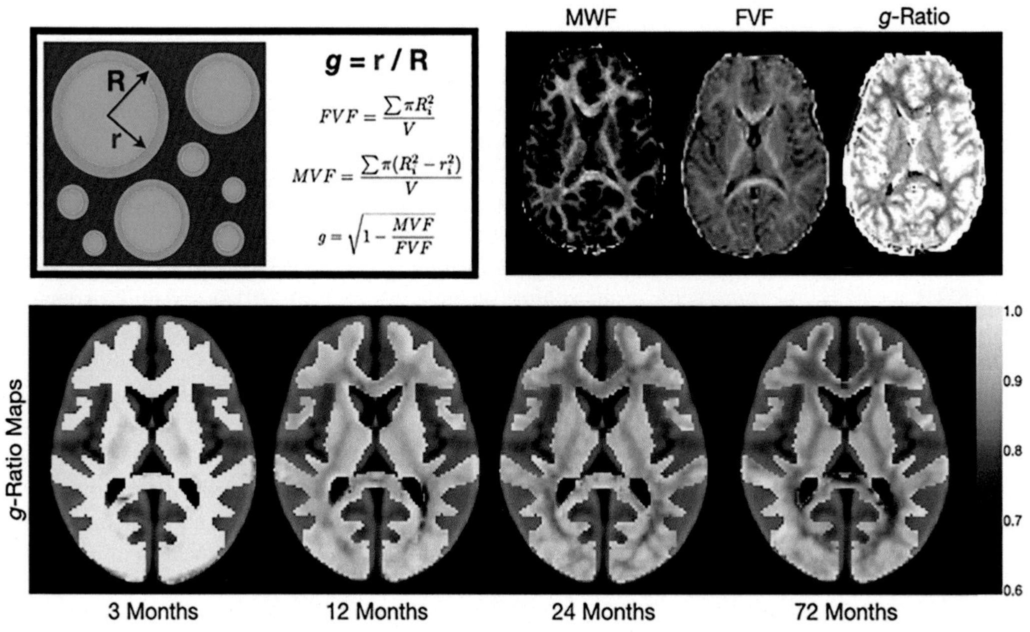

FIG. 9

(A) Schematic illustrating the *g*-ratio tissue model of (Stikov et al., 2015a,b). Myelinated axons are represented *green* (axon) and *orange* (myelin sheath) concentric circles and extracellular and free water space is represented by the background. The myelin volume fraction (MVF) corresponds to the ratio of the volume of myelin to the volume of the entire voxel (V), while the fiber volume fraction (FVF) is the ratio of the fiber volume to that of the entire voxel. Together, MVF and FVF are combined to estimate the aggregate *g*-ratio. (B) Representative MWF, FVF and aggregate *g*-ratio map from a single subject. As in Dean et al. (2016), mcDESPOT-derived MWF was used a surrogate measure of MVF and FVF was computed from NODDI based metrics. (C) Representative mean aggregate *g*-ratio images at 3, 12, 24, and 60 months overlaid on a T_1-weighted template. At the earliest ages, the *g*-ratio is near 1.0 for much of the white matter but decreases with increasing age toward a theoretical optimal range of 0.6–0.8, highlighting the progressive thickening of the myelin sheath.

References

Alonso-Ortiz, E., Levesque, I.R., Pike, G.B., 2015. MRI-based myelin water imaging: a technical review. Magn. Reson. Med. 73 (1), 70–81. https://doi.org/10.1002/mrm.25198.

Assaf, Y., Basser, P.J., 2005. Composite hindered and restricted model of diffusion (CHARMED) MR imaging of the human brain. NeuroImage 27 (1), 48–58. https://doi.org/10.1016/j.neuroimage.2005.03.042.

Barkovich, A.J., Kjos, B.O., Jackson Jr., D.E., Norman, D., 1988. Normal maturation of the neonatal and infant brain: MR imaging at 1.5 T. Radiology 166 (1 Pt 1), 173–180. https://doi.org/10.1148/radiology.166.1.3336675.

Bartzokis, G., Lu, P.H., Tingus, K., Mendez, M.F., Richard, A., Peters, D.G., Mintz, J., 2010. Lifespan trajectory of myelin integrity and maximum motor speed. Neurobiol. Aging 31 (9), 1554–1562. https://doi.org/10.1016/j.neurobiolaging.2008.08.015.

Basser, P.J., Pierpaoli, C., 1996. Microstructural and physiological features of tissues elucidated by quantitative-diffusion-tensor MRI. J. Magn. Reson. B *111* (3), 209–219. Retrieved from https://www.ncbi.nlm.nih.gov/pubmed/8661285.

Berman, S., West, K.L., Does, M.D., Yeatman, J.D., Mezer, A.A., 2018. Evaluating g-ratio weighted changes in the corpus callosum as a function of age and sex. NeuroImage 182, 304–313. https://doi.org/10.1016/j.neuroimage.2017.06.076.

Berthold, C.H., Nilsson, I., Rydmark, M., 1983. Axon diameter and myelin sheath thickness in nerve fibres of the ventral spinal root of the seventh lumbar nerve of the adult and developing cat. J. Anat. *136* (Pt. 3), 483–508. Retrieved from https://www.ncbi.nlm.nih.gov/pubmed/6885614.

Bloembergen, N., Purcell, E.M., Pound, R.V., 1947. Nuclear magnetic relaxation. Nature 160 (4066), 475. https://doi.org/10.1038/160475a0.

Bock, J., Wainstock, T., Braun, K., Segal, M., 2015. Stress in utero: prenatal programming of brain plasticity and cognition. Biol. Psychiatry 78 (5), 315–326. https://doi.org/10.1016/j.biopsych.2015.02.036.

Bottomley, P.A., Foster, T.H., Argersinger, R.E., Pfeifer, L.M., 1984. A review of normal tissue hydrogen NMR relaxation times and relaxation mechanisms from 1-100 MHz: dependence on tissue type, NMR frequency, temperature, species, excision, and age. Med. Phys. 11 (4), 425–448. https://doi.org/10.1118/1.595535.

Bottomley, P.A., Hardy, C.J., Argersinger, R.E., Allen-Moore, G., 1987. A review of 1H nuclear magnetic resonance relaxation in pathology: are T1 and T2 diagnostic? Med. Phys. 14 (1), 1–37. https://doi.org/10.1118/1.596111.

Bradley, R.H., Corwyn, R.F., 2002. Socioeconomic status and child development. Annu. Rev. Psychol. 53, 371–399. https://doi.org/10.1146/annurev.psych.53.100901.135233.

Brody, B.A., Kinney, H.C., Kloman, A.S., Gilles, F.H., 1987. Sequence of central nervous system myelination in human infancy. I. An autopsy study of myelination. J. Neuropathol. Exp. Neurol. 46 (3), 283–301. Retrieved from https://www.ncbi.nlm.nih.gov/pubmed/3559630.

Campbell, J.S.W., Leppert, I.R., Narayanan, S., Boudreau, M., Duval, T., Cohen-Adad, J., Stikov, N., 2018. Promise and pitfalls of g-ratio estimation with MRI. Neuroimage 182, 80–96. https://doi.org/10.1016/j.neuroimage.2017.08.038.

Casey, B.J., Galvan, A., Hare, T.A., 2005. Changes in cerebral functional organization during cognitive development. Curr. Opin. Neurobiol. 15 (2), 239–244. https://doi.org/10.1016/j.conb.2005.03.012.

Cercignani, M., Giulietti, G., Dowell, N.G., Gabel, M., Broad, R., Leigh, P.N., Bozzali, M., 2017. Characterizing axonal myelination within the healthy population: a tract-by-tract mapping of effects of age and gender on the fiber g-ratio. Neurobiol. Aging 49, 109–118. https://doi.org/10.1016/j.neurobiolaging.2016.09.016.

Choi, E.H., Blasiak, A., Lee, J., Yang, I.H., 2019. Modulation of neural activity for myelination in the central nervous system. Front. Neurosci. 13, 952. https://doi.org/10.3389/fnins.2019.00952.

Chomiak, T., Hu, B., 2009. What is the optimal value of the g-ratio for myelinated fibers in the rat CNS? A theoretical approach. PLoS One 4 (11), e7754. https://doi.org/10.1371/journal.pone.0007754.

Clouchoux, C., Guizard, N., Evans, A.C., du Plessis, A.J., Limperopoulos, C., 2012. Normative fetal brain growth by quantitative in vivo magnetic resonance imaging. Am. J. Obstet. Gynecol. 206 (2), 173 e171–178. https://doi.org/10.1016/j.ajog.2011.10.002.

Dai, X., Müller, H.G., Wang, J.L., Deoni, S.C., 2019. Age-dynamic networks and functional correlation for early white matter myelination. Brain Struct. Funct. 224 (2), 535–551. https://doi.org/10.1007/s00429-018-1785-z.

Dean 3rd, D.C., O'Muircheartaigh, J., Dirks, H., Travers, B.G., Adluru, N., Alexander, A.L., Deoni, S.C.L., 2016. Mapping an index of the myelin g-ratio in infants using magnetic resonance imaging. NeuroImage 132, 225–237. https://doi.org/10.1016/j.neuroimage.2016.02.040.

Dean III, D.C., O'Muircheartaigh, J., Dirks, H., Waskiewicz, N., Lehman, K., Walker, L., Han, M., Deoni, S.C., 2014. Modeling healthy male white matter and myelin development: 3 through 60 months of age. Neuroimage 84, 742–752. https://doi.org/10.1016/j.neuroimage.2013.09.058.

Demerens, C., Stankoff, B., Logak, M., Anglade, P., Allinquant, B., Couraud, F., Lubetzki, C., 1996. Induction of myelination in the central nervous system by electrical activity. Proc. Natl. Acad. Sci. USA 93 (18), 9887–9892. https://doi.org/10.1073/pnas.93.18.9887.

Denolin, V., Azizieh, C., Metens, T., 2005. New insights into the mechanisms of signal formation in RF-spoiled gradient echo sequences. Magn. Reson. Med. 54 (4), 937–954. https://doi.org/10.1002/mrm.20652.

Deoni, S.C., 2011. Correction of main and transmit magnetic field (B0 and B1) inhomogeneity effects in multicomponent-driven equilibrium single-pulse observation of T1 and T2. Magn. Reson. Med. 65 (4), 1021–1035. https://doi.org/10.1002/mrm.22685.

Deoni, S.C., Dean III, D.C., Piryatinsky, I., O'Muircheartaigh, J., Waskiewicz, N., Lehman, K., Han, M., Dirks, H., 2013. Breastfeeding and early white matter development: a cross-sectional study. Neuroimage 82, 77–86. https://doi.org/10.1016/j.neuroimage.2013.05.090.

Deoni, S.C., Dean III, D.C., Walker, L., Dirks, H., O'Muircheartaigh, J., 2014. Nutritional influences on early white matter development: response to Anderson and Burggren. Neuroimage 100, 703–705. https://doi.org/10.1016/j.neuroimage.2014.07.016.

Deoni, S.C., Kolind, S.H., 2015. Investigating the stability of mcDESPOT myelin water fraction values derived using a stochastic region contraction approach. Magn. Reson. Med. 73 (1), 161–169. https://doi.org/10.1002/mrm.25108.

Deoni, S.C., Rutt, B.K., Jones, D.K., 2007. Investigating the effect of exchange and multicomponent T(1) relaxation on the short repetition time spoiled steady-state signal and the DESPOT1 T(1) quantification method. J. Magn. Reson. Imaging 25 (3), 570–578. https://doi.org/10.1002/jmri.20836.

Deoni, S.C., Rutt, B.K., Arun, T., Pierpaoli, C., Jones, D.K., 2008. Gleaning multicomponent T1 and T2 information from steady-state imaging data. Magn. Reson. Med. 60 (6), 1372–1387. https://doi.org/10.1002/mrm.21704.

Deoni, S.C., Adams, S.H., Li, X., Badger, T.M., Pivik, R.T., Glasier, C.M., Ramakrishnaiah, R.H., Rowell, A.C., Ou, X., 2019. Cesarean delivery impacts infant brain development. Am. J. Neuroradiol. 40 (1), 169–177. https://doi.org/10.3174/ajnr.A5887.

Deoni, S., Dean III, D., Joelson, S., O'Regan, J., Schneider, N., 2018. Early nutrition influences developmental myelination and cognition in infants and young children. Neuroimage 178, 649–659. https://doi.org/10.1016/j.neuroimage.2017.12.056.

Deoni, S.C., Dean 3rd, D.C., O'Muircheartaigh, J., Dirks, H., Jerskey, B.A., 2012. Investigating white matter development in infancy and early childhood using myelin water faction and relaxation time mapping. NeuroImage 63 (3), 1038–1053. https://doi.org/10.1016/j.neuroimage.2012.07.037.

Deoni, S.C., Matthews, L., Kolind, S.H., 2013. One component? Two components? Three? The effect of including a nonexchanging "free" water component in multicomponent driven equilibrium single pulse observation of T1 and T2. Magn. Reson. Med. 70 (1), 147–154. https://doi.org/10.1002/mrm.24429.

Deoni, S.C., Rutt, B.K., Peters, T.M., 2006. Synthetic T1-weighted brain image generation with incorporated coil intensity correction using DESPOT1. Magn. Reson. Imaging 24 (9), 1241–1248. https://doi.org/10.1016/j.mri.2006.03.015.

Dobbing, J., 1964. The influence of early nutrition on the development and myelination of the brain. Proc. R. Soc. Lond. B Biol. Sci. 159, 503–509. https://doi.org/10.1098/rspb.1964.0016.

Dreha-Kulaczewski, S.F., Brockmann, K., Henneke, M., Dechent, P., Wilken, B., Gärtner, J., Helms, G., 2012. Assessment of myelination in hypomyelinating disorders by quantitative MRI. J. Magn. Reson. Imaging 36 (6), 1329–1338. https://doi.org/10.1002/jmri.23774.

Du, F., Cooper, A.J., Thida, T., Shinn, A.K., Cohen, B.M., Ongür, D., 2013. Myelin and axon abnormalities in schizophrenia measured with magnetic resonance imaging techniques. Biol. Psychiatry 74 (6), 451–457. https://doi.org/10.1016/j.biopsych.2013.03.003.

Dvorak, A.V., Swift-LaPointe, T., Vavasour, I.M., Lee, L.E., Abel, S., Russell-Schulz, B., Graf, C., Wurl, A., Liu, H., Laule, C., Li, D.K., 2021. An atlas for human brain myelin content throughout the adult life span. Sci. Rep. 11 (1), 1–13. https://doi.org/10.1038/s41598-020-79540-3.

Dvorak, A.V., Wiggermann, V., Gilbert, G., Vavasour, I.M., MacMillan, E.L., Barlow, L., Kolind, S.H., 2020. Multi-spin echo T2 relaxation imaging with compressed sensing (METRICS) for rapid myelin water imaging. Magn. Reson. Med. 84 (3), 1264–1279. https://doi.org/10.1002/mrm.28199.

Ellerbrock, I., Mohammadi, S., 2018. Four in vivo g-ratio-weighted imaging methods: comparability and repeatability at the group level. Hum. Brain Mapp. 39 (1), 24–41. https://doi.org/10.1002/hbm.23858.

Farah, M.J., Shera, D.M., Savage, J.H., Betancourt, L., Giannetta, J.M., Brodsky, N.L., Hurt, H., 2006. Childhood poverty: specific associations with neurocognitive development. Brain Res. 1110 (1), 166–174. https://doi.org/10.1016/j.brainres.2006.06.072.

Fields, R.D., 2005. Myelination: an overlooked mechanism of synaptic plasticity? Neuroscientist 11 (6), 528–531. https://doi.org/10.1177/1073858405282304.

Fields, R.D., 2008. White matter in learning, cognition and psychiatric disorders. Trends Neurosci. 31 (7), 361–370. https://doi.org/10.1016/j.tins.2008.04.001.

Fields, R.D., 2015. A new mechanism of nervous system plasticity: activity-dependent myelination. Nat. Rev. Neurosci. 16 (12), 756–767. https://doi.org/10.1038/nrn4023.

Fieremans, E., Jensen, J.H., Helpern, J.A., 2011. White matter characterization with diffusional kurtosis imaging. Neuroimage *58* (1), 177–188. https://doi.org/10.1016/j.neuroimage.2011.06.006.

Fulford, J., Vadeyar, S.H., Dodampahala, S.H., Moore, R.J., Young, P., Baker, P.N., Gowland, P.A., 2003. Fetal brain activity in response to a visual stimulus. Hum. Brain Mapp. 20 (4), 239–245. https://doi.org/10.1002/hbm.10139.

Gao, W., Lin, W., Grewen, K., Gilmore, J.H., 2017. Functional connectivity of the infant human brain: plastic and modifiable. Neuroscientist 23 (2), 169–184. https://doi.org/10.1177/1073858416635986.

Georgieff, M.K., 2007. Nutrition and the developing brain: nutrient priorities and measurement. Am. J. Clin. Nutr. 85 (2), 614S–620S. https://doi.org/10.1093/ajcn/85.2.614S.

Gilmore, J.H., Shi, F., Woolson, S.L., Knickmeyer, R.C., Short, S.J., Lin, W., Shen, D., 2012. Longitudinal development of cortical and subcortical gray matter from birth to 2 years. Cereb. Cortex 22 (11), 2478–2485. https://doi.org/10.1093/cercor/bhr327.

Girard, N., Raybaud, C., Du Lac, P., 1991. MRI study of brain myelination. J. Neuroradiol. 18 (4), 291–307.

Glasser, M.F., Van Essen, D.C., 2011. Mapping human cortical areas in vivo based on myelin content as revealed by T1- and T2-weighted MRI. J. Neurosci. 31 (32), 11597–11616. https://doi.org/10.1523/JNEUROSCI.2180-11.2011.

Graf von Keyserlingk, D., Schramm, U., 1984. Diameter of axons and thickness of myelin sheaths of the pyramidal tract fibres in the adult human medullary pyramid. Anat. Anz. 157 (2), 97–111.

Henderson, E., McKinnon, G., Lee, T.Y., Rutt, B.K., 1999. A fast 3D look-locker method for volumetric T1 mapping. Magn. Reson. Imaging 17 (8), 1163–1171. https://doi.org/10.1016/s0730-725x(99)00025-9.

Hofman, A., Jaddoe, V.W., Mackenbach, J.P., Moll, H.A., Snijders, R.F., Steegers, E.A., Buller, H.A., 2004. Growth, development and health from early fetal life until young adulthood: the generation R study. Paediatr. Perinat. Epidemiol. 18 (1), 61–72. https://doi.org/10.1111/j.1365-3016.2003.00521.x.

Houston, S.M., Herting, M.M., Sowell, E.R., 2014. The neurobiology of childhood structural brain development: conception through adulthood. Curr. Top. Behav. Neurosci. 16, 3–17. https://doi.org/10.1007/7854_2013_265.

Hrvoj-Mihic, B., Bienvenu, T., Stefanacci, L., Muotri, A.R., Semendeferi, K., 2013. Evolution, development, and plasticity of the human brain: from molecules to bones. Front. Hum. Neurosci. 7, 707. https://doi.org/10.3389/fnhum.2013.00707.

Huttenlocher, P.R., 1979. Synaptic density in human frontal cortex—developmental changes and effects of aging. Brain Res. 163 (2), 195–205. https://doi.org/10.1016/0006-8993(79)90349-4.

Innocenti, G.M., Price, D.J., 2005. Exuberance in the development of cortical networks. Nat. Rev. Neurosci. 6 (12), 955–965. https://doi.org/10.1038/nrn1790.

Ishibashi, T., Dakin, K.A., Stevens, B., Lee, P.R., Kozlov, S.V., Stewart, C.L., Fields, R.D., 2006. Astrocytes promote myelination in response to electrical impulses. Neuron 49 (6), 823–832. https://doi.org/10.1016/j.neuron.2006.02.006.

Ismail, F.Y., Fatemi, A., Johnston, M.V., 2017. Cerebral plasticity: windows of opportunity in the developing brain. Eur. J. Paediatr. Neurol. 21 (1), 23–48. https://doi.org/10.1016/j.ejpn.2016.07.007.

Johnson, M.H., 2001. Functional brain development in humans. Nat. Rev. Neurosci. 2 (7), 475–483. https://doi.org/10.1038/35081509.

Kaden, E., Kelm, N.D., Carson, R.P., Does, M.D., Alexander, D.C., 2016. Multi-compartment microscopic diffusion imaging. NeuroImage 139, 346–359. https://doi.org/10.1016/j.neuroimage.2016.06.002.

Kamagata, K., Zalesky, A., Yokoyama, K., Andica, C., Hagiwara, A., Shimoji, K., Aoki, S., 2019. MR g-ratio-weighted connectome analysis in patients with multiple sclerosis. Sci. Rep. 9 (1), 13522. https://doi.org/10.1038/s41598-019-50025-2.

Karlsson, M., Nordell, B., 2000. Analysis of the look-locker T(1) mapping sequence in dynamic contrast uptake studies: simulation and in vivo validation. Magn. Reson. Imaging 18 (8), 947–954. https://doi.org/10.1016/s0730-725x(00)00193-4.

Kecskemeti, S., Samsonov, A., Hurley, S.A., Dean, D.C., Field, A., Alexander, A.L., 2016. MPnRAGE: a technique to simultaneously acquire hundreds of differently contrasted MPRAGE images with applications to quantitative T1 mapping. Magn. Reson. Med. 75 (3), 1040–1053. https://doi.org/10.1002/mrm.25674.

Khan, A.R., Goubran, M., de Ribaupierre, S., Hammond, R.R., Burneo, J.G., Parrent, A.G., Peters, T.M., 2014. Quantitative relaxometry and diffusion MRI for lateralization in MTS and non-MTS temporal lobe epilepsy. Epilepsy Res 108 (3), 506–516. https://doi.org/10.1016/j.eplepsyres.2013.12.012.

Kisilevsky, B.S., Hains, S.M., Brown, C.A., Lee, C.T., Cowperthwaite, B., Stutzman, S.S., Wang, Z., 2009. Fetal sensitivity to properties of maternal speech and language. Infant Behav. Dev. 32 (1), 59–71. https://doi.org/10.1016/j.infbeh.2008.10.002.

Knickmeyer, R.C., Gouttard, S., Kang, C., Evans, D., Wilber, K., Smith, J.K., Gilmore, J.H., 2008. A structural MRI study of human brain development from birth to 2 years. J. Neurosci. 28 (47), 12176–12182. https://doi.org/10.1523/JNEUROSCI.3479-08.2008.

Kolb, B., 2009. Brain and behavioural plasticity in the developing brain: neuroscience and public policy. Paediatr. Child Health 14 (10), 651–652. https://doi.org/10.1093/pch/14.10.651.

Krebs, N.F., Lozoff, B., Georgieff, M.K., 2017. Neurodevelopment: the impact of nutrition and inflammation during infancy in low-resource settings. Pediatrics 139 (Suppl. 1), S50–S58. https://doi.org/10.1542/peds.2016-2828G.

LaMantia, A.S., Rakic, P., 1990. Axon overproduction and elimination in the corpus callosum of the developing rhesus monkey. J Neurosci 10 (7), 2156–2175. Retrieved from https://www.ncbi.nlm.nih.gov/pubmed/2376772.

LaMantia, A.S., Rakic, P., 1994. Axon overproduction and elimination in the anterior commissure of the developing rhesus monkey. J. Comp. Neurol. 340 (3), 328–336. https://doi.org/10.1002/cne.903400304.

Laule, C., Leung, E., Lis, D.K., Traboulsee, A.L., Paty, D.W., MacKay, A.L., Moore, G.R., 2006. Myelin water imaging in multiple sclerosis: quantitative correlations with histopathology. Mult. Scler. 12 (6), 747–753. https://doi.org/10.1177/1352458506070928.

Laule, C., Kozlowski, P., Leung, E., Li, D.K., Mackay, A.L., Moore, G.R., 2008. Myelin water imaging of multiple sclerosis at 7 T: correlations with histopathology. NeuroImage 40 (4), 1575–1580. https://doi.org/10.1016/j.neuroimage.2007.12.008.

Levitt, P., 2003. Structural and functional maturation of the developing primate brain. J. Pediatr. 143 (4 Suppl), S35–S45. https://doi.org/10.1067/s0022-3476(03)00400-1.

Liao, C., Wang, K., Cao, X., Li, Y., Wu, D., Ye, H., Ding, Q., He, H., Zhong, J., 2018. Detection of lesions in mesial temporal lobe epilepsy by using MR fingerprinting. Radiology 288 (3), 804–812. https://doi.org/10.1148/radiol.2018172131.

Lin, W., Song, H.K., 2009. Improved signal spoiling in fast radial gradient-echo imaging: applied to accurate T(1) mapping and flip angle correction. Magn. Reson. Med. 62 (5), 1185–1194. https://doi.org/10.1002/mrm.22089.

Luo, L., O'Leary, D.D., 2005. Axon retraction and degeneration in development and disease. Annu. Rev. Neurosci. 28, 127–156. https://doi.org/10.1146/annurev.neuro.28.061604.135632.

Lyall, A.E., Shi, F., Geng, X., Woolson, S., Li, G., Wang, L., Gilmore, J.H., 2015. Dynamic development of regional cortical thickness and surface area in early childhood. Cereb. Cortex 25 (8), 2204–2212. https://doi.org/10.1093/cercor/bhu027.

Ma, D., Gulani, V., Seiberlich, N., Liu, K., Sunshine, J.L., Duerk, J.L., Griswold, M.A., 2013. Magnetic resonance fingerprinting. Nature 495, 187–192.

MacKay, A.L., Laule, C., 2016. Magnetic resonance of myelin water: an in vivo marker for myelin. Brain Plast. 2 (1), 71–91. https://doi.org/10.3233/BPL-160033.

MacKay, A., Whittall, K., Adler, J., Li, D., Paty, D., Graeb, D., 1994. In vivo visualization of myelin water in brain by magnetic resonance. Magn. Reson. Med. *31* (6), 673–677. Retrieved from https://www.ncbi.nlm.nih.gov/pubmed/8057820.

Makropoulos, A., Aljabar, P., Wright, R., Huning, B., Merchant, N., Arichi, T., Rueckert, D., 2016. Regional growth and atlasing of the developing human brain. NeuroImage 125, 456–478. https://doi.org/10.1016/j.neuroimage.2015.10.047.

Mancini, M., Giulietti, G., Dowell, N., Spanò, B., Harrison, N., Bozzali, M., Cercignani, M., 2018. Introducing axonal myelination in connectomics: a preliminary analysis of g-ratio distribution in healthy subjects. Neuroimage 182, 351–359. https://doi.org/10.1016/j.neuroimage.2017.09.018.

Mancini, M., Karakuzu, A., Cohen-Adad, J., Cercignani, M., Nichols, T.E., Stikov, N., 2020. An interactive meta-analysis of MRI biomarkers of myelin. Elife 9. https://doi.org/10.7554/eLife.61523.

Marques, J.P., Kober, T., Krueger, G., van der Zwaag, W., Van de Moortele, P.F., Gruetter, R., 2010. MP2RAGE, a self bias-field corrected sequence for improved segmentation and T1-mapping at high field. NeuroImage 49 (2), 1271–1281. https://doi.org/10.1016/j.neuroimage.2009.10.002.

McGee, A.W., Yang, Y., Fischer, Q.S., Daw, N.W., Strittmatter, S.M., 2005. Experience-driven plasticity of visual cortex limited by myelin and Nogo receptor. Science 309 (5744), 2222–2226. https://doi.org/10.1126/science.1114362.

McKenzie, I.A., Ohayon, D., Li, H., de Faria, J.P., Emery, B., Tohyama, K., Richardson, W.D., 2014. Motor skill learning requires active central myelination. Science 346 (6207), 318–322. https://doi.org/10.1126/science.1254960.

Melbourne, A., Eaton-Rosen, Z., Orasanu, E., Price, D., Bainbridge, A., Cardoso, M.J., Ourselin, S., 2016. Longitudinal development in the preterm thalamus and posterior white matter: MRI correlations between diffusion weighted imaging and T2 relaxometry. Hum. Brain Mapp. 37 (7), 2479–2492. https://doi.org/10.1002/hbm.23188.

Mercer, J.S., Erickson-Owens, D.A., Deoni, S.C., Dean III, D.C., Collins, J., Parker, A.B., Wang, M., Joelson, S., Mercer, E.N., Padbury, J.F., 2018. Effects of delayed cord clamping on 4-month ferritin levels, brain myelin content, and neurodevelopment: a randomized controlled trial. J. Pediatrics 203, 266–272. https://doi.org/10.1016/j.jpeds.2018.06.006.

Messroghli, D.R., Radjenovic, A., Kozerke, S., Higgins, D.M., Sivananthan, M.U., Ridgway, J.P., 2004. Modified look-locker inversion recovery (MOLLI) for high-resolution T1 mapping of the heart. Magn. Reson. Med. 52 (1), 141–146. https://doi.org/10.1002/mrm.20110.

Meyers, S.M., Laule, C., Vavasour, I.M., Kolind, S.H., Madler, B., Tam, R., MacKay, A.L., 2009. Reproducibility of myelin water fraction analysis: a comparison of region of interest and voxel-based analysis methods. Magn. Reson. Imaging 27 (8), 1096–1103. https://doi.org/10.1016/j.mri.2009.02.001.

Meyers, S.M., Vavasour, I.M., Mädler, B., Harris, T., Fu, E., Li, D.K., Laule, C., 2013. Multicenter measurements of myelin water fraction and geometric mean T2: intra- and intersite reproducibility. J. Magn. Reson. Imaging 38 (6), 1445–1453. https://doi.org/10.1002/jmri.24106.

Mezer, A., Yeatman, J.D., Stikov, N., Kay, K.N., Cho, N.-J., Dougherty, R.F., Wandell, B.A., 2013. Quantifying the local tissue volume and composition in individual brains with magnetic resonance imaging. Nat. Med. 19 (12), 1667–1672. https://doi.org/10.1038/nm.3390.

Minty, E.P., Bjarnason, T.A., Laule, C., MacKay, A.L., 2009. Myelin water measurement in the spinal cord. Magn. Reson. Med. 61 (4), 883–892. https://doi.org/10.1002/mrm.21936.

Mohammadi, S., Callaghan, M.F., 2021. Towards in vivo g-ratio mapping using MRI: unifying myelin and diffusion imaging. J. Neurosci. Methods *348*, 108990. https://doi.org/10.1016/j.jneumeth.2020.108990.

Mohammadi, S., Carey, D., Dick, F., Diedrichsen, J., Sereno, M.I., Reisert, M., Weiskopf, N., 2015. Whole-brain in-vivo measurements of the axonal G-ratio in a group of 37 healthy volunteers. Front. Neurosci. 9 (441). https://doi.org/10.3389/fnins.2015.00441.

Nagy, Z., Westerberg, H., Klingberg, T., 2004. Maturation of white matter is associated with the development of cognitive functions during childhood. J. Cogn. Neurosci. 16 (7), 1227–1233. https://doi.org/10.1162/0898929041920441.

Nguyen, T.D., Deh, K., Monohan, E., Pandya, S., Spincemaille, P., Raj, A., Gauthier, S.A., 2016. Feasibility and reproducibility of whole brain myelin water mapping in 4 minutes using fast acquisition with spiral trajectory and adiabatic T2prep (FAST-T2) at 3T. Magn. Reson. Med. 76 (2), 456–465. https://doi.org/10.1002/mrm.25877.

Noble, K.G., Norman, M.F., Farah, M.J., 2005. Neurocognitive correlates of socioeconomic status in kindergarten children. Dev. Sci. 8 (1), 74–87. https://doi.org/10.1111/j.1467-7687.2005.00394.x.

Paus, T., Toro, R., 2009. Could sex differences in white matter be explained by g ratio? Front. Neuroanat. 3 (14). https://doi.org/10.3389/neuro.05.014.2009.

Paus, T., Collins, D.L., Evans, A.C., Leonard, G., Pike, B., Zijdenbos, A., 2001. Maturation of white matter in the human brain: a review of magnetic resonance studies. Brain Res. Bull. 54 (3), 255–266. https://doi.org/10.1016/s0361-9230(00)00434-2.

Peters, A., Sethares, C., 2002. Aging and the myelinated fibers in prefrontal cortex and corpus callosum of the monkey. J. Comp. Neurol. 442 (3), 277–291. https://doi.org/10.1002/cne.10099.

Piredda, G.F., Hilbert, T., Canales-Rodriguez, E.J., Pizzolato, M., von Deuster, C., Meuli, R., Kober, T., 2021. Fast and high-resolution myelin water imaging: accelerating multi-echo GRASE with CAIPIRINHA. Magn. Reson. Med. 85 (1), 209–222. https://doi.org/10.1002/mrm.28427.

Pouwels, P.J., Vanderver, A., Bernard, G., Wolf, N.I., Dreha-Kulczewksi, S.F., Deoni, S.C., Bertini, E., Kohlschütter, A., Richardson, W., Ffrench-Constant, C., Köhler, W., 2014. Hypomyelinating leukodystrophies: translational research progress and prospects. Ann. Neurol. 76 (1), 5–19. https://doi.org/10.1002/ana.24194.

Rees, S., Inder, T., 2005. Fetal and neonatal origins of altered brain development. Early Hum. Dev. 81 (9), 753–761. https://doi.org/10.1016/j.earlhumdev.2005.07.004.

Reisert, M., Mader, I., Umarova, R., Maier, S., Tebartz van Elst, L., Kiselev, V.G., 2013. Fiber density estimation from single q-shell diffusion imaging by tensor divergence. NeuroImage 77, 166–176. https://doi.org/10.1016/j.neuroimage.2013.03.032.

Rice, D., Barone Jr., S., 2000. Critical periods of vulnerability for the developing nervous system: evidence from humans and animal models. Environ. Health Perspect. 108 (Suppl. 3), 511–533. https://doi.org/10.1289/ehp.00108s3511.

Roujol, S., Weingartner, S., Foppa, M., Chow, K., Kawaji, K., Ngo, L.H., Nezafat, R., 2014. Accuracy, precision, and reproducibility of four T1 mapping sequences: a head-to-head comparison of MOLLI, ShMOLLI, SASHA, and SAPPHIRE. Radiology 272 (3), 683–689. https://doi.org/10.1148/radiol.14140296.

Rugg-Gunn, F.J., Boulby, P.A., Symms, M.R., Barker, G.J., Duncan, J.S., 2005. Whole-brain T2 mapping demonstrates occult abnormalities in focal epilepsy. Neurology 64 (2), 318–325. https://doi.org/10.1212/01.WNL.0000149642.93493.F4.

Rushton, W.A.H., 1951. A theory of the effects of fibre size in medullated nerve. J. Physiol. 115 (1), 101–122. https://doi.org/10.1113/jphysiol.1951.sp004655.

Schröder, J.M., Bohl, J., von Bardeleben, U., 1988. Changes of the ratio between myelin thickness and axon diameter in human developing sural, femoral, ulnar, facial, and trochlear nerves. Acta Neuropathol. 76 (5), 471–483. https://doi.org/10.1007/BF00686386.

Shankle, W.R., Landing, B.H., Rafii, M.S., Schiano, A., Chen, J.M., Hara, J., 1998. Evidence for a postnatal doubling of neuron number in the developing human cerebral cortex between 15 months and 6 years. J. Theor. Biol. 191 (2), 115–140. https://doi.org/10.1006/jtbi.1997.0570.

Sousa, A.M.M., Meyer, K.A., Santpere, G., Gulden, F.O., Sestan, N., 2017. Evolution of the human nervous system function, structure, and development. Cell 170 (2), 226–247. https://doi.org/10.1016/j.cell.2017.06.036.

Stikov, N., Perry, L.M., Mezer, A., Rykhlevskaia, E., Wandell, B.A., Pauly, J.M., Dougherty, R.F., 2011. Bound pool fractions complement diffusion measures to describe white matter micro and macrostructure. NeuroImage 54 (2), 1112–1121. https://doi.org/10.1016/j.neuroimage.2010.08.068.

Steenweg, M.E., Wolf, N.I., van Wieringen, W.N., Barkhof, F., van der Knaap, M.S., Pouwels, P.J., 2016. Quantitative MRI in hypomyelinating disorders: correlation with motor handicap. Neurology 87 (8), 752–758. https://doi.org/10.1212/WNL.0000000000003000.

Stikov, N., Campbell, J.S., Stroh, T., Lavelée, M., Frey, S., Novek, J., Pike, G.B., 2015a. Quantitative analysis of the myelin g-ratio from electron microscopy images of the macaque corpus callosum. Data Brief 4, 368–373. https://doi.org/10.1016/j.dib.2015.05.019.

Stikov, N., Campbell, J.S.W., Stroh, T., Lavelée, M., Frey, S., Novek, J., Pike, G.B., 2015b. In vivo histology of the myelin g-ratio with magnetic resonance imaging. Neuroimage *118*, 397–405. https://doi.org/10.1016/j.neuroimage.2015.05.023.

Stiles, J., Jernigan, T.L., 2010. The basics of brain development. Neuropsychol. Rev. 20 (4), 327–348. https://doi.org/10.1007/s11065-010-9148-4.

Swain, J.E., Lorberbaum, J.P., Kose, S., Strathearn, L., 2007. Brain basis of early parent-infant interactions: psychology, physiology, and in vivo functional neuroimaging studies. J. Child Psychol. Psychiatry 48 (3–4), 262–287. https://doi.org/10.1111/j.1469-7610.2007.01731.x.

Uranova, N., Orlovskaya, D., Vikhreva, O., Zimina, I., Kolomeets, N., Vostrikov, V., Rachmanova, V., 2001. Electron microscopy of oligodendroglia in severe mental illness. Brain Res. Bull. 55 (5), 597–610. https://doi.org/10.1016/s0361-9230(01)00528-7.

Van der Knaap, M.S., Valk, J., Bakker, C.J., Schooneveld, M., Faber, J.A.J., Willemse, J., Gooskens, R.H.J.M., 1991. Myelination as an expression of the functional maturity of the brain. Dev. Med. Child Neurol. 33 (10), 849–857. https://doi.org/10.1111/j.1469-8749.1991.tb14793.x.

Vavasour, I.M., Laule, C., Li, D.K., Oger, J., Moore, G.R., Traboulsee, A., MacKay, A.L., 2009. Longitudinal changes in myelin water fraction in two MS patients with active disease. J. Neurol. Sci. 276 (1–2), 49–53. https://doi.org/10.1016/j.jns.2008.08.022.

Vavasour, I.M., Laule, C., Li, D.K., Traboulsee, A.L., MacKay, A.L., 2011. Is the magnetization transfer ratio a marker for myelin in multiple sclerosis? J. Magn. Reson. Imaging 33 (3), 713–718. https://doi.org/10.1002/jmri.22441.

Vohr, B.R., Poggi Davis, E., Wanke, C.A., Krebs, N.F., 2017. Neurodevelopment: the impact of nutrition and inflammation during preconception and pregnancy in low-resource settings. Pediatrics 139 (Suppl. 1), S38–S49. https://doi.org/10.1542/peds.2016-2828F.

Wade, T., McKenzie, C.A., Rutt, B.K., 2014. Flip angle mapping with the accelerated 3D look-locker sequence. Magn. Reson. Med. 71 (2), 591–598. https://doi.org/10.1002/mrm.24697.

Waxman, S.G., 1980. Determinants of conduction velocity in myelinated nerve fibers. Muscle Nerve 3 (2), 141–150. https://doi.org/10.1002/mus.880030207.

Weiskopf, N., Suckling, J., Williams, G., Correia, M.M., Inkster, B., Tait, R., Lutti, A., 2013. Quantitative multi-parameter mapping of R1, PD(*), MT, and R2(*) at 3T: a multi-center validation. Front. Neurosci. 7, 95. https://doi.org/10.3389/fnins.2013.00095.

West, K.L., Kelm, N.D., Carson, R.P., Does, M.D., 2016. A revised model for estimating g-ratio from MRI. NeuroImage 125, 1155–1158. https://doi.org/10.1016/j.neuroimage.2015.08.017.

Woermann, F.G., Barker, G.J., Birnie, K.D., Meencke, H.J., Duncan, J.S., 1998. Regional changes in hippocampal T2 relaxation and volume: a quantitative magnetic resonance imaging study of hippocampal sclerosis. J. Neurol. Neurosurg. Psychiatry 65 (5), 656–664. https://doi.org/10.1136/jnnp.65.5.656.

Zhang, Y.T., Yeung, H.N., Carson, P.L., Ellis, J.H., 1992. Experimental analysis of T1 imaging with a single-scan, multiple-point, inversion-recovery technique. Magn. Reson. Med. 25 (2), 337–343. https://doi.org/10.1002/mrm.1910250212.

Zhang, H., Schneider, T., Wheeler-Kingshott, C.A., Alexander, D.C., 2012. NODDI: practical in vivo neurite orientation dispersion and density imaging of the human brain. NeuroImage 61 (4), 1000–1016. https://doi.org/10.1016/j.neuroimage.2012.03.072.

CHAPTER

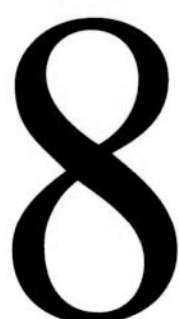

Multimodal MRI: Applications to early brain development in infants

Jessica Dubois[a,b]

University of Paris, NeuroDiderot Unit UMR1141, Inserm, Paris, France[a] *Paris-Saclay University, NeuroSpin/UNIACT, CEA, Gif-sur-Yvette, France*[b]

Abbreviations

AD	axial diffusivity
ASL	arterial spin labeling
BOLD	blood oxygen level dependent
CHARMED	composite hindered and restricted model of diffusion
DARTEL	diffeomorphic anatomical registration using exponentiated Lie algebra
DIAMOND	distribution of 3D anisotropic microstructural environments in diffusion compartment imaging
DISCO	diffeomorphic sulcal-based cortical registration
DKI	diffusion kurtosis imaging
DTI	diffusion tensor imaging
EEG	electroencephalography
fMRI	functional MRI
GMM	gaussian mixture model
MD	mean diffusivity
MEG	magnetoencephalography
MRI	magnetic resonance imaging
MTI	magnetization transfer imaging
MTR	magnetization transfer ratio
NODDI	neurite orientation dispersion and density imaging
pCASL	pseudo-continuous ASL
PC-MRA	phase-contrast MR angiography
QSM	quantitative susceptibility mapping
RD	radial diffusivity
rs-fMRI	resting-state fMRI
SPANGY	spectral analysis of gyrification
T1	longitudinal relaxation time
T1/T2w	T1/T2-weighted
T2	transverse relaxation times
w PMA	weeks of postmenstrual age

Handbook of Pediatric Brain Imaging. https://doi.org/10.1016/B978-0-12-816633-8.00017-X

1. Introduction

During the last trimester of pregnancy and the first postnatal year, the brain grows dramatically and matures intensely (Kostović et al., 2019), allowing newborns and infants to develop sophisticated perceptions of their environment and to acquire complex motor and cognitive skills according to the multiple experiences and learnings they are exposed to (Dehaene-Lambertz and Spelke, 2015). Early alterations in normal neural development can lead to a variety of behavioral disorders that manifest in childhood. It is therefore important to gain a better understanding of these phenomena, which requires linking brain and behavioral changes in vivo. This is why the use of noninvasive neuroimaging methods such as Magnetic Resonance Imaging (MRI) has revolutionized our knowledge in this field over the last 20 years.

Before describing these recent advances, it is important to remember that MRI measurements only indirectly reflect the complex series of dynamic and intertwined mechanisms observed throughout development at the molecular, cellular and network levels, which occur within a highly constrained but constantly evolving context (Stiles and Jernigan, 2010; Kostović et al., 2019). The main lines of cerebral architecture are set up early *in utero*, and then prolonged maturation phenomena are observed, with the growth of connections between neurons, synaptogenesis and pruning mechanisms, myelination, neurochemical maturation, etc. (Dubois et al., 2021). These changes in the brain tissue microstructure lead to intense macroscopic changes, with exponential increases in brain size and surface, and increasing morphological complexity with the formation of gyri and the folding of primary, secondary and tertiary sulci (Dubois and Dehaene-Lambertz, 2015). An elaborate structural and functional connectivity gradually develops between brain regions, relying on both long- and short-range connections (Dubois et al., 2015; Kostović et al., 2019). In addition to increasing the conduction speed of nerve fibers, the process of myelination may play a role in stabilizing connections that are functionally relevant. Most of these complex mechanisms occur over different time periods and at different rates in different in different regions of the brain and functional networks (Flechsig, 1920; Yakovlev and Lecours, 1967; Kostović et al., 2019), with the primary, unimodal and transmodal associative ones showing staggered trajectories of maturation.

Different MRI modalities make it possible to explore some of these mechanisms, with varying precision and specificity depending on the method. This requires addressing the main methodological challenges posed by an MRI of newborns and infants: sensitivity to movements, scanner noise, size of the brain structures in relation to the spatial resolution of images, incomplete tissue maturation involving specific MR characteristics and contrasts, all of which lead to the implementation of dedicated image acquisition sequences and postprocessing tools (Dubois et al., 2021).

In recent years, several groups of researchers and clinicians have turned to so-called "multimodal" approaches, aimed at coupling several imaging modalities, in order to improve the sensitivity and specificity of MRI in neonates or infants for the integrated study of brain development. With this in mind, this chapter is organized in four parts. First, we present a summary of the main MRI modalities and developmental changes observed in "univariate" studies of the baby brain (part 2), with more details in the chapters devoted to each of these modalities. We then describe the multimodal studies performed to assess the early maturation of brain tissues (part 3), to relate the complementary aspects of structural development (part 4), and finally to compare the structural and functional brain development (part 5). In addition to MRI, this last part includes studies that have used "electro- and magnetoencephalography" (EEG/MEG) to provide the complementary measures of neurophysiological maturation.

2. Overview of age-related changes in MRI modalities

2.1 Anatomical and relaxometry MRI

In anatomical MRI, the signal intensities of brain images are weighted by longitudinal or transverse relaxation times (T1, T2) that depend on water and fat contents and microenvironment, and decrease with maturation processes (Dubois et al., 2014, 2021). Contrasts between brain tissues thus evolve during development, and successive stages are generally described during infancy since T1 and T2 times decrease more strongly in white matter than in gray matter because of myelination processes. Changes in contrasts are observed on T1-weighted (T1w) images before T2w images because the change in water molecules compartmentalization (leading mostly to T1 shortening during the premyelinating state) occurs before the increase of protein and lipid contents with the chemical maturation of the myelin sheath (leading mostly to T2 shortening). To compare the maturation between brain regions or between infants, measuring T1 and T2 relaxation times quantitatively is a more relevant approach than the observation of T1w and T2w images.

2.2 Diffusion MRI

Because of the high-water content and the low myelination, the diffusion properties are also very different in the brains of neonates and infants compared with children and adults (Dubois et al., 2014, 2021). During the preterm period, different groups have observed an early anisotropy in cortical gray matter and a radial orientation of the main tensor eigenvector as measured with "diffusion tensor imaging" (DTI) (Ouyang et al., 2019b), which possibly relies on the early presence of radial glia fibers and apical dendrites of pyramidal neurons. Subsequently, diffusion within the cortical plate becomes isotropic with elongation and complex branches of neural connections (e.g., basal dendrites of pyramidal neurons, thalamocortical fibers). This decrease of DTI anisotropy in the cortex appears to stabilize around term equivalent age whereas diffusivity indices continue to decrease, due to several competitive microstructural mechanisms (Kostović et al., 2019). To better disentangle the progression of these mechanisms during development, recent studies have highlighted the potential of more complex diffusion models such as "diffusion kurtosis imaging" (DKI) and "neurite orientation dispersion and density imaging" (NODDI) (Batalle et al., 2019; Ouyang et al., 2019a; Dubois et al., 2021).

Diffusion MRI parameters also evolve in developing white matter, as axonal fibers gradually become mature and functional through the process of myelination (Dubois et al., 2014, 2016a, 2021). During the preterm period, DTI diffusivities decrease while anisotropy increases in most white matter regions except at cross-roads locations (Nossin-Manor et al., 2013; Kersbergen et al., 2014). During infancy and childhood, "radial diffusivity" (RD) decreases more than "axial diffusivity" (AD) in bundles, leading to anisotropy increase. Diffusion parameters might be sensitive to the proliferation of glial cell bodies, the extension of oligodendroglial processes, and their wrapping around axons.

2.3 Other quantitative MRI methods

Several other MRI parameters can be measured to quantify brain maturation (Dubois et al., 2021). The "magnetization transfer ratio" (MTR) is thought to reflect mostly the myelin amount as it increases from birth to 2 years of age, at different rates, in the main white matter regions and in the central gray matter nuclei. Nevertheless, in the preterm brain, this technique appears to be sensitive not only to myelin-associated macromolecules, but also to the macromolecular density of axonal cytoskeleton components such as microtubules and neurofilaments (Nossin-Manor et al., 2013). "Quantitative susceptibility mapping" (QSM) provides information on iron, myelin and macromolecular contents. It shows age-related increase in susceptibility in deep gray matter nuclei in infants, with differences between nuclei (Ning et al., 2019), compared to decrease in white matter bundles following a posterior-anterior spatial and temporal pattern (Zhang et al., 2019). Finally, "phase-contrast MR angiography" (PC-MRA), "arterial spin labeling" (ASL) and "pseudo-continuous ASL" (pCASL) have been used to estimate cerebral blood flow in the developing brain (Ouyang et al., 2017b; Dubois et al., 2021), showing age-related increases in infancy and early childhood that reflects brain maturation.

2.4 Multicompartmental methods

Recently, different modeling approaches based on relaxometry or diffusion MRI data have been proposed to better characterize the brain tissue microstructure by distinguishing different pools of water molecules inside each voxel, based on their distinct characteristics (Dubois et al., 2021). The analysis of multicomponent relaxation assumes that at least two or three pools of water contribute to the MR signal sensitized to T1 and T2 relaxometries (Spader et al., 2013), including water located within the myelin sheath (with relatively short T1 and T2 relaxation times). This provides an estimation of the volume fraction of water related to myelin, which drastically increases with age in the white matter. On the other hand, different multicomponent approaches [e.g., "composite hindered and restricted model of diffusion" CHARMED (Assaf and Basser, 2005) or NODDI (Zhang et al., 2012)] have been proposed to analyze the MR diffusion signal acquired with multiple shells (i.e., sensitized to multiple b-values) and with multiple gradient directions. The provided parameters also show intense age-related changes during infancy, both in the gray and white matter (Ouyang et al., 2019b; Dubois et al., 2021).

2.5 Functional MRI

Brain responses detected with task-based "functional MRI" (fMRI) also evolve throughout the development, because of progressive functional specialization and of physiological maturation processes leading to changes in cerebral blood flow, in oxygen consumption, and thus in the "blood oxygen level dependent" (BOLD) response characteristics (i.e., time-course, amplitude) (Dubois et al., 2021). Estimating the location of activated regions in a reliable way in newborns therefore requires measuring an accurate model of the hemodynamic response function, in a region-specific manner as the neurovascular coupling might differ between functional systems that are at different stages of maturation. "Resting-state fMRI" (rs-fMRI) studies have also shown some convergences but also some specific developmental patterns in the early architecture of brain networks (Dubois et al., 2021).

2.6 Methodological considerations for multimodal MRI

Therefore, the parameters measured by the different MRI modalities provide different, and complementary, information on the multiple maturation mechanisms that take place during early brain development. Nevertheless, it is important to note that MRI parameters vary across brains regions including in the adult brain, depending on tissue microstructure: the clearest example is in the white matter where the geometry, compactness and crossings of fibers have a considerable impact on diffusion parameters. The study of the interregional variability of maturation therefore requires dissociating it from the variability related to microstructure, which is observed throughout development and at the mature stage, in a more or less consistent manner. This can be taken into account by considering developmental trajectories to assess maturational asymptotes, or by normalizing infant measurements with adult references (Dubois et al., 2014), making it possible to differentiate maturation and microstructure patterns.

Coupling MRI measurements seems an interesting approach to provide an integrative view of brain development during infancy. However, correlating parameters that vary over the course of development requires considering this dependence on the age of the babies. This can for example be done with a partial correlation method. The first pan of research we aim to describe in the chapter is the use of multimodal MRI to attempt to quantify brain tissue maturation more reliably than univariate approaches.

3. Multimodal MRI to assess the early maturation of brain tissues

3.1 Differentiating brain tissues during early development

In neonates and infants below ~6–8 months of age, T2w images are generally preferred for delineating the immature white matter and the cortical and subcortical gray matter, whereas T1w images are useful for distinguishing the myelinated white matter. Therefore, multimodal approaches have proposed the combined use of T1w and T2w images to better distinguish between brain tissues and between regions with different maturation, and thus to provide more precise segmentations. But so far the benefit in infants does not seem so obvious (Dean et al., 2018).

Based on T1w and T2w images of a large cohort of premature and full-term neonates, a multioutput Bayesian regression technique has been used to model the typical changes in brain contrasts and local tissue shape, according to age at scan, degree of prematurity and sex (O'Muircheartaigh et al., 2020). And then it was able to detect focal white matter injury by calculating voxel-wise deviations of a neonate's observed MRI from that predicted by the model, suggesting a clear potential for clinical use.

In the continuity of recent studies conducted in adults, the T1w/T2w ratio has also been proposed as a marker of myelination. In preterm newborns between 36 and 44 weeks of postmenstrual age (w PMA), this measure increases in most cortical regions, suggesting intense maturation and differences between sensorimotor and associative regions (Bozek et al., 2018). This approach has also allowed the improvement of the contrast of early myelinating white matter structures (e.g., posterior limb of the internal capsule, corticospinal tract, optic radiations) in neonates (Soun et al., 2017).

3.2 Quantifying gray matter maturation

Multiparametric MRI approaches have been proposed recently to quantify the maturation of cortical and subcortical gray matter by integrating the complementary information provided by parameters from relaxometry MRI, diffusion MRI, and/or multicompartment methods. For instance, the microstructural properties of the cortex have been evaluated in preterm infants scanned at term equivalent age (Friedrichs-Maeder et al., 2017), showing that the values of T1 and DTI "mean diffusivity" (MD) were lower in the primary sensorimotor cortices than in secondary processing areas, which in turn were lower than in higher-order tertiary areas. This suggested differential patterns of microstructural maturation between functional regions. In typical infants between 1 and 5 months of age, we have mapped the maturational progression of the developing cortex without any hypothesis a priori on their anatomical location (Lebenberg et al., 2019), with the goal to consider jointly changes related to various maturation mechanisms, including changes in cell and membrane density, in water and iron content, in relation with the development of dendritic arborization, synaptogenesis, intra-cortical fiber myelination, etc. We used a clustering approach to group voxels with similar properties, based on relaxometry (T1) and DTI diffusivity (AD) characteristics (Fig. 1). The resulting maps showed different microstructural patterns between cortical regions at the individual level, as well as strong progression according to the infants' age. This confirmed the early maturation of primary sensorimotor regions, followed by adjacent unimodal associative regions, and finally by higher-order transmodal associative regions. Nevertheless, this study should be reproduced at different ages, especially after 1 year of age, when the developmental patterns observed with T1 and with the fraction of water related to myelin still varying between primary and associative cortical regions (Deoni et al., 2015).

Multiparametric MRI has also been used to explore the maturation of central gray nuclei, where the intense proliferation of glial cells and membranes, and fiber myelination are observed over the preterm period and infancy. While univariate studies have highlighted marked microstructural changes with age, such as decrease in T1, T2, DTI diffusivities, and an increase in anisotropy (Dubois et al., 2021), recent comparisons between multiple parameters have allowed us to disentangle maturational mechanisms (e.g., concentration of myelin-associated macromolecules, water content). In premature infants, measuring T1, DTI and MTR were relevant to fully characterize the microstructural properties and the maturational patterns of the globus pallidus, putamen, thalamus and ventrolateral thalamic nucleus (Nossin-Manor et al., 2013). For instance, this latter structure is already myelinated in the preterm period, which was confirmed by low T1 values, low DTI MD and RD diffusivities and high MTR, suggesting a high concentration of myelin-associated macromolecules and a low water content with high restriction, but this structure showed no specific directionality and coherence (low DTI anisotropy and AD) contrary to white matter structures. Another study, combining T2, NODDI measures and the fraction of water related to the myelin, further highlighted that microstructural changes observed in the thalamus during the preterm period are not solely due to myelination (Melbourne et al., 2016).

3.3 Quantifying white matter maturation

Although some studies have suggested developmental relationships such as inverse correlations between MTR and T1 or T2 (Dubois et al., 2014, 2021), different MRI parameters seem highly relevant to capture different properties of white matter maturation, which encourages combining or integrating these parameters. In a cuprizone mouse model of demyelination, a study has shown that the bound pool fraction from "magnetization transfer imaging" (MTI) is the best indicator of the myelin sheath fraction, while T1 relates to the fraction of myelinated axons, and DTI AD to the fraction of nonmyelinated cells (Thiessen et al., 2013). Compared with T1 and T2, the fraction of water related to myelin also seems to provide complementary sensitivity to the white matter maturation (Deoni et al., 2012; Chen et al., 2019).

On the one hand, multiparametric studies have been considered on the basis of diffusion MRI only, with the hypothesis that sequential changes in DTI parameters rely on the successive steps of white matter maturation (Dubois et al., 2008a, 2014; Nossin-Manor et al., 2015; Ouyang et al., 2019b). First, early changes in microstructure related to the fibers premyelination would mainly lead to a decrease in

a. Average maps of quantitative parameters over the cortex of infants

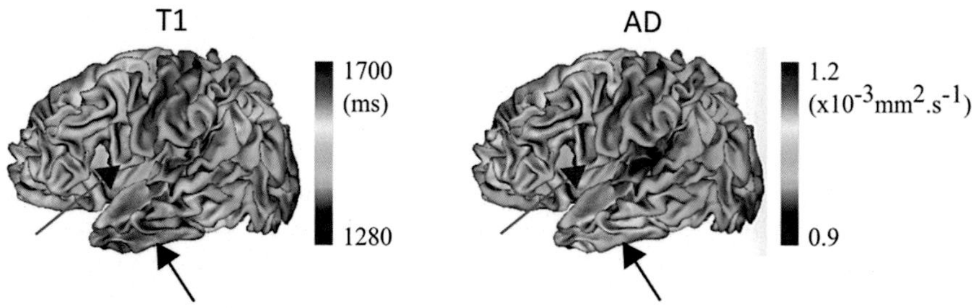

b. Individual parameters in each cortical cluster

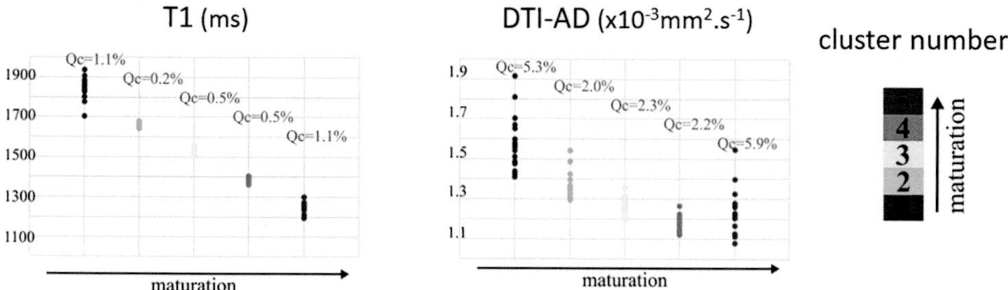

c. Average map of the clusters identified in the cortex

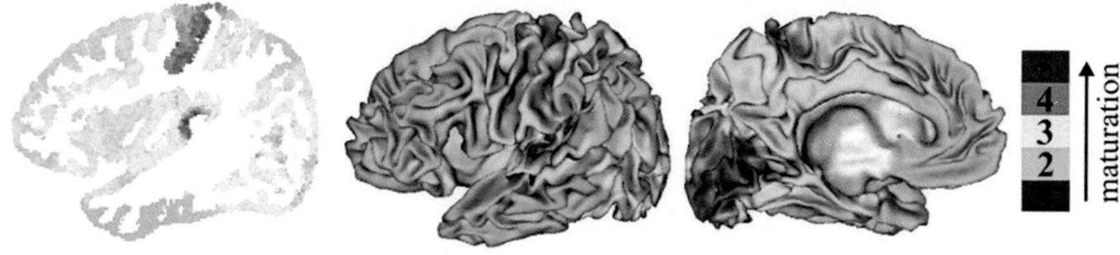

FIG. 1

Multimodal MRI to quantify the maturation of cortical regions. (A) T1 and DTI axial diffusivity (AD) vary between brain regions according to their different maturation and microstructure patterns, as shown here on average maps obtained from a group of typical infants aged 1–5 months. Higher maturation and a more complex microstructure correspond to lower T1 and AD values. (B) A clustering approach based on a "Gaussian mixture model" (GMM) algorithm applied to T1 and AD values of all infants allowed us to identify 5 clusters of cortical voxels. Although we were not able to compare these results with equivalent measurements obtained in the mature brain, we could extrapolate the microstructure properties and the maturation order of these clusters according to T1 and AD values in infants, from the least mature (highest values, in *blue*) to the most mature (lowest values, in *red*). (C) The spatial distribution of these clusters was highly meaningful. While the individual maps showed that immature clusters were observed in the youngest infants, and conversely for mature clusters (not shown), the average maps on the infant group highlighted the heterogeneities in maturation and microstructure in the cortical regions. The most mature clusters (in *red*) were localized in the primary regions (around the central sulcus for sensorimotor regions, in Heschl gyrus for auditory regions, around the calcarine fissure for visual regions), whereas the intermediate (in *yellow-green*) and the least mature clusters (in *green-blue*) were observed in unimodal and transmodal associative regions respectively.

Modified from Lebenberg, J., Mangin, J. F., Thirion, B., Poupon, C., Hertz-Pannier, L., Leroy, F., Adibpour, P., Dehaene-Lambertz, G., Dubois, J., 2019. Mapping the asynchrony of cortical maturation in the infant brain: a MRI multi-parametric clustering approach. NeuroImage 185, 641–653.

AD and RD. The subsequent wrapping of myelin sheaths around axons would not modify axial diffusivity but would decrease radial diffusivity, implying an additional increase in anisotropy. With such a DTI model, we were able to identify relevant differences in maturation between white matter bundles in infants (Dubois et al., 2008a). With a clustering approach based on DTI parameters, we showed different microstructural characteristics between bundles of the language network, as well as maturational asynchrony (Dubois et al., 2016b): the ventral pathways (uncinate, fronto-occipital, middle and inferior longitudinal fascicles) appeared more mature than the dorsal ones (arcuate and superior longitudinal fascicles), although this difference decreased during infancy. Maturational differences between white matter bundles were also highlighted between birth and 2 years of age by combining the age trajectories of DTI parameters, and evaluating their asymptotes, delays, and speeds (Sadeghi et al., 2013, 2017). Beyond DTI, NODDI studies in newborns and infants have shown differences between white matter regions in terms of intra-neurite volume fraction (informing on the axonal fibers maturation) and orientation dispersion index (reflecting the presence of fiber crossings and fanning) (Kunz et al., 2014; Jelescu et al., 2015; Dean et al., 2017). Thus comparing these parameters may help distinguish between bundles with similar cellular structure but different myelination (e.g., posterior vs anterior limb of the internal capsule), or reciprocally with similar maturation but different fiber microstructural organization (e.g., external capsule vs periventricular crossroads) (Kunz et al., 2014).

Diffusion parameters were also combined with other quantitative parameters to highlight maturation patterns of white matter regions, notably in premature infants. The comparison of T1, DTI parameters and MTR showed the high organization and packing of corpus callosum fibers during the preterm period despite their low myelination (Nossin-Manor et al., 2013). And voxel-wise analyses further highlighted the lamination pattern in the cerebral wall, as well as different maturation mechanisms in the brain compartments (e.g., intermediate zone, subplate) (Nossin-Manor et al., 2015). In the posterior white matter, T2 and NODDI changes were related over the same period and early infancy, but were not related to the fraction of water related to myelin, which suggested that the two former parameters rely on axonal and glial proliferation rather than on the myelin water content (Melbourne et al., 2016).

In a recent study of typical infants, we also proposed to combine T1, T2 and DTI diffusivities in white matter bundles, to provide an original measure of maturation based on the computation of the Mahalanobis distance comparing infants' individual data with a group of adults, while taking into account the possible correlations between MRI measurements (Kulikova et al., 2015). This revealed more maturational relationships between bundles than univariate approaches, and it allowed us to quantify their relative delays of maturation. The results confirmed the intense changes during the first postnatal year, as well as the maturational asynchrony, notably with early maturation of the spino-thalamic tract, optic radiations, cortico-spinal tract and fornix, and delayed maturation of associative bundles such as the superior longitudinal and arcuate fasciculi (Fig. 2). In the same group of infants, the clustering approach of voxels described in previous section for the cortex led us to uncover four white matter regions with different compactness, maturation and anatomically relevant spatial distribution (Lebenberg et al., 2015).

The last multiparametric method that can be mentioned concerning the assessment of white matter maturation is the one that aims to quantify the so called "g-ratio" (i.e., the ratio of the axon diameter to the outer fiber diameter including the myelin sheath) (Stikov et al., 2015). This composite marker can be estimated using diffusion MRI data (e.g., NODDI indices) and MTR or the fraction of water related to myelin. Studies in premature infants (Melbourne et al., 2014) and young children (Dean et al., 2016) have shown that this marker decreases with age in the white matter, because of the myelination process.

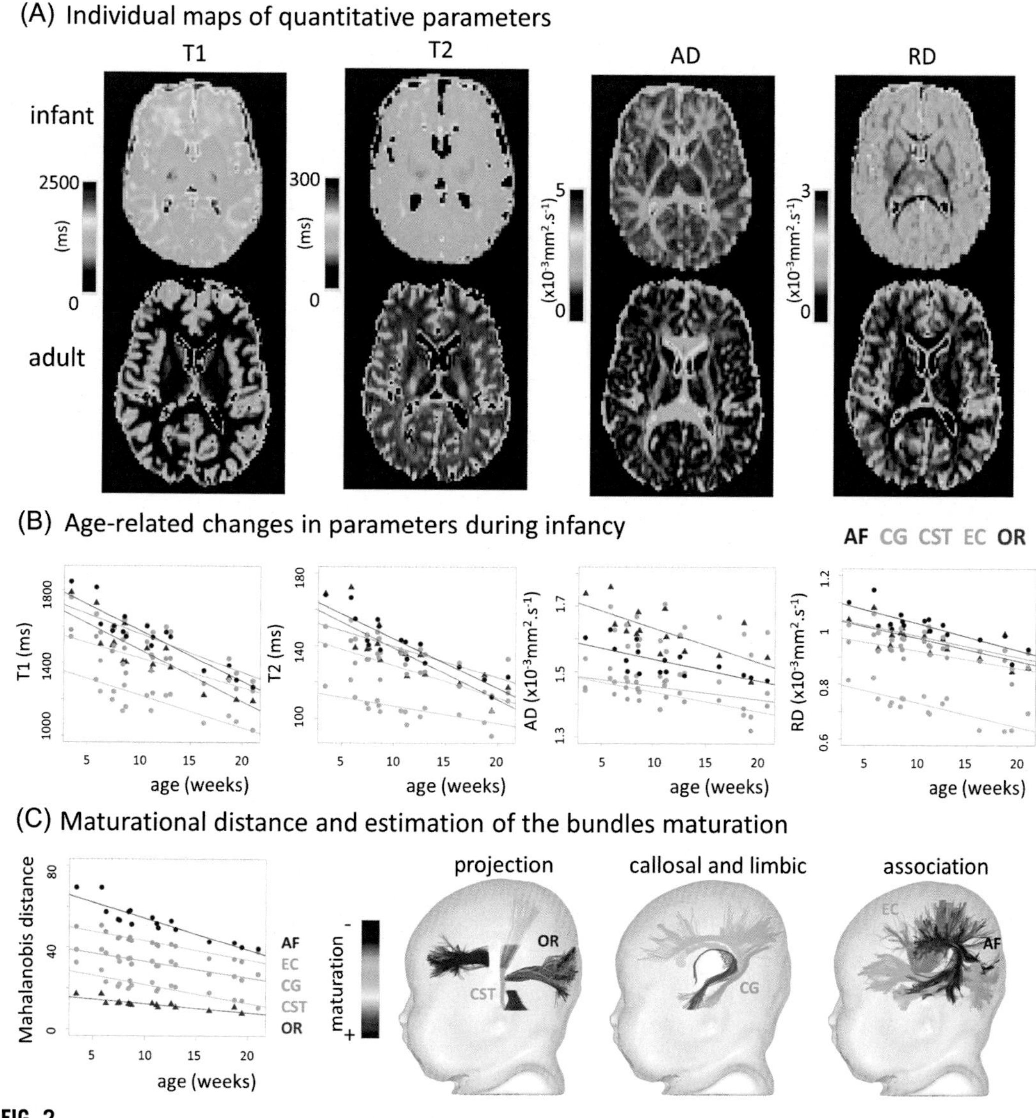

FIG. 2

Multimodal MRI to quantify the maturation of white matter bundles. (A) Maps of quantitative parameters (T1 and T2 relaxation times, DTI diffusivities: axial AD and radial RD) show different contrasts and developmental changes in the white matter, as illustrated here for a 2-month-old infant and an adult. (B) Strong decreases of these four parameters are observed in the white matter between 1 and 5 months of age (the *lines* show significant correlations with age). This is illustrated for bundles of different functional networks: projection bundles like the optic radiations (OR) and the inferior portion of the cortico-spinal tract (CST), limbic bundles like the inferior branch of the cingulum (CG), associative bundles like the external capsule (EC) and arcuate fasciculus (AF). The lower the parameters are, the more the bundle has a complex microstructure (with high compactness or myelination) or the more mature it is. But the order between bundles is not reproducible between parameters.

(Continued)

This index might provide relevant information on the efficiency of neural information transfer and on the conduction velocity of white matter pathways, but it remains difficult to estimate and interpret in the developing brain (Dubois et al., 2016a).

Therefore, these studies in newborns and infants have shown that multiparametric MRI approaches provide a more accurate description of maturation patterns in the developing brain, by considering complementary mechanisms through the white matter, and also the cortical and deep gray regions. Multimodal MRI can also be used to relate the different aspects of structural development, including morphological and microstructural properties of the brain tissues.

4. Multimodal MRI to relate complementary aspects of structural development

4.1 Relating morphometry, morphology, and microstructure during early development

During the last trimester of pregnancy and infancy, the cortical surface area dramatically increases [from ~150 cm^2 at 27w PMA (Makropoulos et al., 2016) to ~700 and ~2000 cm^2 at 1 and 24 postnatal months respectively (Lyall et al., 2015)], and the brain morphology becomes increasingly complex with the formation of gyri, primary, secondary and tertiary sulci (Dubois et al., 2019). Although underlying mechanisms are still widely discussed (Welker, 1990; Llinares-Benadero and Borrell, 2019), this folding process might support the enormous increase in cortical volume while maintaining reasonable connection distances (and thus information transmission times) between brain regions. So these intense macroscopic changes are probably the visible markers of changes in the microstructure of the cortical plate (the future cortex), over preterm and early postterm periods marked by synaptic outburst and pruning, modifications in dendritic branching and fiber myelination (Kostović et al., 2019).

Recent multimodal MRI studies, combining anatomical and diffusion MRI, have aimed to relate these morphological and microstructural features in the newborn brain. It was first proposed to compute a "radiality index" measuring the local directional coherence between the direction normal to the cortical surface and the main orientation of diffusion in the cortex, estimated with DTI model or "distribution of 3D anisotropic microstructural environments in diffusion-compartment imaging" (DIAMOND) (Eaton-Rosen et al., 2017). This showed strong age-related decrease during the preterm period, as well as fastest changes in the occipital lobe and slowest changes in the frontal and temporal

FIG. 2, CONT'D (C) A multiparametric approach combining these four parameters in each infant compared to a group of adults allowed us to estimate the maturation of white matter bundles in a more reliable way. The resulting Mahalanobis distance decreases with the infants' age and shows strong heterogeneities in maturation across projection, callosal, limbic and association bundles (the color codes for maturation: from *blue* in the least mature bundles to *red* in the most mature ones).

Modified from Dubois, J., Dehaene-Lambertz, G., Kulikova, S., Poupon, S., Hüppi, P.S., Hertz-Pannier, L., 2014. The early development of brain white matter: a review of imaging studies in fetuses, newborns and infants. Neuroscience 276, 48–71; Dubois, J., Kostovic, I., Judas, M., 2015. Development of structural and functional connectivity. Brain Mapping: An Encyclopedic Reference, vol. 2, 423-437; Kulikova, S., Hertz-Pannier, L., Dehaene-Lambertz, G., Buzmakov, A., Poupon, C., Dubois, J., 2015. Multi-parametric evaluation of the white matter maturation. Brain Struct. Funct. 220(6), 3657–3672.

lobes. This decrease in radiality index paralleled the decreases in diffusion anisotropy and MD observed in the cortex, but correlations between these parameters were not evaluated beyond the effects of age. Note that this study preferred not to include sulcal regions in the analysis for methodological reasons, while previous observations described more intense age-related DTI changes in gyri than in sulci (Ball et al., 2013; Ouyang et al., 2019b). Another study in premature infants compared changes in cortical volume, surface curvature, and microstructural characteristics of the cortex as measured with DTI and NODDI parameters (Batalle et al., 2019). While important correlations were reported between these morphological and microstructural measures mainly during the period between 25 and 38 week PMA and to a lesser extent during the 38–47 week period, no correlations between cortical volume and diffusion parameters were observed when age dependencies were taken into account. However, some partial correlations were observed between mean curvature and diffusion parameters in several cortical regions: negative correlations with DTI anisotropy, as well as positive correlations with NODDI orientation dispersion index.

These studies suggested that changes in cortical microstructure might be at least partially related to the gyrification process. To test this hypothesis, we investigated whether different stages of microstructural maturation could be detected in cortical regions that fold successively, in preterm infants imaged longitudinally at around 30 and 40w PMA (Hertz et al., 2018). We used anatomical MRI to perform a spectral analysis of gyrification (SPANGY) allowing us to detail the spatial-frequency structure of cortical patterns (Dubois et al., 2019), and we combined these measures with DTI information at the two ages (Fig. 3). We first highlighted that the proxies of primary folds had an advanced microstructural maturation at 30w PMA (i.e., lowest DTI anisotropy and AD values) (Hertz et al., 2018). Furthermore, the progression until term-equivalent age was lowest in these already well-developed regions, whereas it was most intense in the secondary fold proxies which grew considerably during this period. These findings were in agreement with a recent study in developing macaques which showed that cortical structural differentiation is coupled to the sulci formation rather than surface expansion (Wang et al., 2017). Nevertheless, this still did not allow to decipher whether the folding process induces microstructural maturation, or conversely if regions with an advanced microstructure become folded.

Few other studies have aimed to compare cortical thickness and microstructural properties during early brain development. From 1 to 6 years of age, there is almost no relationship between the thickness and the intra-cortical fraction of water related to myelin (Deoni et al., 2015). In infants in the first postnatal year, estimating changes in cortical thickness with MRI is difficult because the contrast between gray and white matter evolves on T1w and T2w images due to myelination of intra- and subcortical fibers. A dedicated pipeline of longitudinal data was recently used to characterize the temporal evolution of cortical thickness from 1 to 24 months of age (Wang et al., 2019). Nevertheless, the interpretation of thickness changes is subject to discussion given that this MRI measure is sensitive to the subject's motion and to the ongoing maturation of tissues (Ducharme et al., 2016; Walhovd et al., 2017; Dubois et al., 2021). Therefore, it would be informative to couple this information with measurements of the cortical microstructure.

4.2 Considering morphological patterns to assess brain tissue maturation

In order to study the maturation of tissues, especially the cortex, reliably between infants, it is necessary to consider similar regions between individuals, as adjacent regions may be at different stages of maturation. This is even more critical when a voxel-wise method is used, rather than a method based on

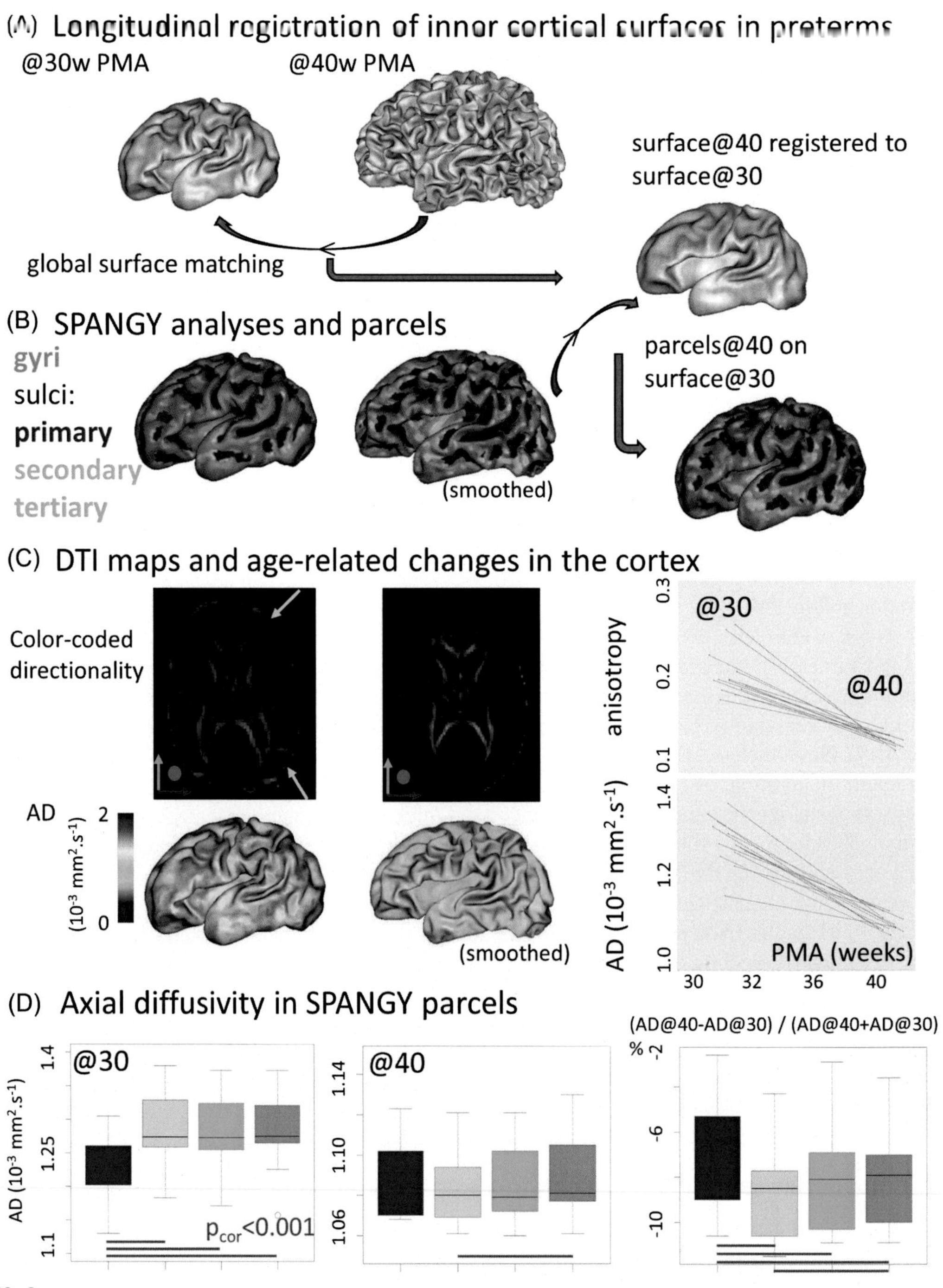

FIG. 3

See figure legend on next page.

(Continued)

regions of interest. And this is particularly challenging for studies of premature newborns and infants because the brain shows significant age-related growth in size and folding. Aligning brains in a common space through the procedures of registration and spatial normalization therefore requires specific methods in this population of subjects (Dubois et al., 2021).

Recently, a 2-step landmark-based strategy allowed us to register the brains of preterm newborns, infants and various databases of adults (Lebenberg et al., 2018). The DISCO method (for "diffeomorphic sulcal-based cortical registration") was used to embed sulcal constraints in a registration framework used to initialize the DARTEL step (for "diffeomorphic anatomical registration using exponentiated Lie algebra") which provided an accurate registration of cortical ribbons. This methodology allowed us to project an individual parcellation of cortical regions (Kabdebon et al., 2014) on a group of newborns. By coupling this anatomical framework with a precise mapping of diffusion parameters (DTI and NODDI), we were able to detail the developing microstructure of several motor and sensory regions (Chauvel et al., 2020). We highlighted important differences along the pre- and postcentral gyri, which might be related to the progressive functional specialization for the different parts of the body.

Comparing the microstructure of similar cortical regions across the left and right hemispheres also requires taking into account the asymmetries that are observed from an early age in the shape and folding of the hemispheres (e.g., at the level of the petalias, the Sylvian fissure, the superior temporal sulcus) (Dubois and Dehaene-Lambertz, 2015; de Vareilles et al., 2020). Using a similar DISCO-DARTEL framework to register left and right hemispheres of infants aged 1–5 months, we were able to compensate for morphological asymmetries and evaluate microstructural asymmetries based on voxel-wise analyses of DTI cortical maps (Rolland et al., 2019). This study highlighted asymmetrical microstructural organization in specific sensorimotor and language regions of infants, suggesting a structural basis for functional lateralization.

FIG. 3, CONT'D Multimodal MRI to relate the folding process and cortical microstructure. (A) In preterm newborns imaged longitudinally at around 30w PMA [29–32w PMA] and at term equivalent age [40–42w PMA], individual registration of inner cortical surfaces at the two ages was performed using a spectral-based algorithm with global surface matching. (B) Spectral analysis of gyrification (SPANGY) on surface curvature was used to identify proxies of the developmentally defined parcels (primary, secondary and tertiary folds) at the two ages. (C) DTI color-coded directionality map showed the early radial organization of the cortex at ~30w PMA (arrows) but not at term equivalent age. We observed a strong decrease in the DTI parameters measured in the cortical ribbon (anisotropy, axial diffusivity AD) with the age of the infants. (D) ANCOVA-Tukey analyses were performed to evaluate differences in DTI parameters between SPANGY parcels (*red bars*: $P<.001$ after correction for multiple comparisons). Proxies of primary folds (in *dark blue*) showed the lowest DTI parameters (AD shown here) at ~30w PMA and the smallest changes up to term-equivalent age, suggesting an early complex microstructure and an advanced maturation pattern. Secondary folds (in *light blue*), and tertiary folds to a lesser extent (in *green*), showed lower DTI indices than gyri and the most significant changes between ~30 and ~40w PMA, suggesting that regions that are folding have a changing microstructure.

Modified from Hertz, A., Pepe, A., Lefèvre, J., Zomeno, M., Leroy, F., Lebenberg, J., de Vries, L., Groenendaal, F., Germanaud, D., Benders, M., Dubois, J., 2018. Is cortical microstructure related to folding during development? A longitudinal MRI study in preterms. In: Proceedings of ISMRM.

4.3 Linking the maturation patterns of different brain tissues

Previous studies have shown the value of linking anatomical MRI and quantitative MRI modalities such as diffusion MRI to better understand some aspects of brain development. Other multimodal studies have aimed to link the maturation of different tissues. As detailed in part 3, spatial gradients of maturation have been described in both gray and white matter. But these changes are not taking place independently since synchronous development between cortical and adjacent white matter regions were observed in primary motor, primary visual, visual association, and prefrontal regions (Smyser et al., 2016). This again suggested that maturation in the primary motor and sensory regions precedes maturation in the association areas. Another study showed that the development of thalamic substructures around term age is synchronized with the maturation of their respective thalamo-cortical connections, to the frontal, precentral, postcentral, temporal and parieto-occipital cortices (Poh et al., 2015). More generally, the advancement of gray and white matter maturation seemed interrelated and dependent on the underlying brain connectivity architecture, as corresponding maturation levels were found in cortical regions and their incident connections in newborns, and also in connected regions (Friedrichs-Maeder et al., 2017). From 1 to 6 years of age, regional measures of cortical thickness were found to be partially driven by changes in adjacent white matter myelination, suggesting that cortical and white matter maturation reflect distinct, but complementary, neurodevelopmental processes (Croteau-Chonka et al., 2016). In older children (5–18 years old), covariation patterns were observed for different cortical shape measures and subcortical gray matter volumes, and considering this multimodal information provided an accurate prediction of a person's age, sex and general cognitive ability (Zhao et al., 2019). But this type of study remains to be done in the infant's brain. Finally, multimodal studies go beyond exploring the structural development of the brain, linking it to its functional development.

5. Multimodal imaging to compare structural and functional development

5.1 Relating functional specialization, morphometry, and microstructure

To date, the relationship between functional specialization and structural properties of the brain has been little explored during development. Yet it is an important question, as some recent studies in adults are beginning to show, particularly for the sensorimotor network. Following on from the observations made for the hand knob, studies combining anatomical MRI and task-based fMRI have outlined that functional representations of distinct parts of the body in the primary motor and somatosensory cortex (somatotopic arrangement) have a precise spatial correspondence with the morphological features of the regions, as shown for the sulcal segments of the central sulcus (Germann et al., 2019) and postcentral sulcus (Zlatkina et al., 2016). For instance, the transverse postcentral sulcus, when present, appeared to be functionally related to the oral sensorimotor representation (mouth and tongue). This indicates that exploring the sulcal morphology may inform functional specialization. Functional representations of body parts have also been linked to patterns of cortical myelination and to the topography of functional connections (connectopies) measured with T1w/T2w ratio and rs-fMRI respectively (Kuehn et al., 2017; Haak et al., 2018). These studies raise fundamental questions regarding the interplay between functional specialization, morphological growth, development of connections and maturation of cortical microstructure. Further studies in newborns and infants are needed to investigate this complex issue in the future.

5.2 Linking structural and functional connectivity patterns

In the recent years, the combined evaluation of structural and functional connectivity has been made possible by the acquisition of diffusion MRI and rs-fMRI data in the same individuals. A recent study in children and adolescents has suggested that the coupling between connectivity patterns might support the development of functional specialization and cognition (Baum et al., 2020). However, it is important to note that the mechanisms linking these measures are still poorly understood even in adults (Smyser et al., 2011): the strength of structural connections seems to predict the strength of functional connections, whereas strong functional connections exist between regions with no direct structural connections. And some have suggested that structural approaches could primarily reflect monosynaptic connections while functional approaches could also be sensitive to polysynaptic connections.

In the developing brain, a few multimodal studies have reported hierarchical structural maturation from primary to higher-order cortices, which is partially paralleled by functional development (Cao et al., 2017). In newborns, the similarities and dissimilarities between structural and functional connectivity patterns depend on the systems, with greater overlap in primary sensory networks than in higher-order transmodal ones where divergence in spatial patterns are observed (van den Heuvel et al., 2015; Ferradal et al., 2019; Larivière et al., 2020). This might be due to differences in maturation between systems, leading to technical biases in diffusion MRI (i.e., more reliable tractography reconstructions of mature structural connections) (Dubois et al., 2016a). Others have suggested that the structural network might remain ahead and pave the way for the development of the functional brain network (Zhao et al., 2018). Despite already established structural connections, associative regions might show delayed functional integration and segregation, and this might contribute to the observation of increased long-range functional connectivity and decreased short-range connectivity during development (Fair et al., 2009; Ouyang et al., 2017a). Although still incomplete, overall these studies suggested that the broad outlines of the brain network architecture are in place at an early stage.

5.3 Relating white matter maturation and EEG responses

While several MRI modalities have detailed the progressive maturation of white matter networks, the functional efficiency of neural communication has been evaluated with EEG and MEG recordings for sensory modalities. These techniques enable to measure the latency of evoked responses (i.e., the averaged responses over multiple trials following successive stimulations) and show drastic decreases in response latencies during development (Dubois et al., 2016a). Although the role played by of cortical maturation and synaptogenesis cannot be overlooked, white matter myelination is one of the key mechanisms that decreases the response latency, as it is known to significantly increase the conduction velocity of nerve impulses along axonal fibers (Baumann and Pham-Dinh, 2001). At constant pathway length, it leads to a decrease in response latency during development. Conversely, as brain size increases with age, mainly during the first 2 years, it may be necessary to further increase conduction velocity by prolonging myelination just to maintain constant latency (Salami et al., 2003). As with structural changes, these functional changes occur at different times and speeds depending on cerebral regions and functions involved (Dubois et al., 2016a). A few recent studies have sought to link decreased latency, increased conduction, and fibers myelination in a network by combining investigations with complementary MRI and EEG/MEG techniques in the same children. Again, the assessment of reliable anatomo-functional relationships required consideration of the age of the infants, which is the main factor explaining the developmental changes.

Some studies have investigated this issue for the visual modality that develops intensively after birth. Successive EEG/MEG visual evoked responses are recorded in occipital regions. At term birth, the first EEG positive component P1 (~P100 in adults) is detected at a latency that decreases strongly and quickly with age (Taylor et al., 1987; Harding et al., 1989; McCulloch and Skarf, 1991), from around 260 ms in neonates to around 110–120 ms at 12–14 weeks of age, depending on the patterns size (McCulloch et al., 1999). In infants, we related the increase in P1 conduction speed to the maturation of the optic radiations (the lower the radial diffusivity measured with DTI, the higher the speed) (Adibpour et al., 2018a; Dubois et al., 2008b) (Fig. 4A). This relation was specific (i.e., not observed for other white matter bundles) and not explained by intra-individual differences in infants' age. Recently, this observation has been further extended to cortico-cortical connections. When visual stimuli were presented laterally (i.e., in a single hemifield), visual responses were first observed in the contralateral hemisphere, then in the ipsilateral hemisphere of infants. And the speed of the interhemispheric transfer of responses was related to the maturation of visual callosal fibers connecting the occipital regions (Adibpour et al., 2018a) (Fig. 4B).

These anatomo-functional relationships have seemed less clear for the auditory system, suggesting more complex interaction mechanisms in which the environment may play a more important role. Indeed, the auditory modality is already functional *in utero*, but its development is more prolonged during early childhood than the visual and somatosensory modalities. Evoked responses show extended developmental changes throughout the early postnatal years (Dubois et al., 2016a), which may make comparison with white matter maturation in infants more difficult. Recently, we have observed early P2 responses in infants following monaural auditory stimulations (i.e., in one ear at a time), both on the contralateral and ipsilateral sides of the brain. Response latencies decreased with age, and ipsilateral responses were significantly longer in the left hemisphere than in the right (Adibpour et al., 2020), which was not the case in infants with agenesis of the corpus callosum (Adibpour et al., 2018b). These results suggested that left ipsilateral responses might include a transfer of right contralateral responses via the callosal fibers, while the reverse (left-to-right transfer) would not be observed. We further related the speed of left ipsilateral responses to the microstructure of the auditory callosal fibers connecting the temporal regions of the two hemispheres (Adibpour et al., 2020) (Fig. 4C). Such functional asymmetries relying on callosal fibers could influence the emergence of early lateralization of the language network and reinforce an initial bias during development.

To date, no studies have linked anatomical and functional maturation in the somatosensory modality, despite intense changes in electrophysiological responses during the preterm period and infancy (Dubois et al., 2016a). Additional studies are therefore needed to confirm the findings for the visual modality in infants. And comparison of anatomo-functional changes between modalities in the same subjects would make it possible to characterize the asynchronous development of brain networks and explore their sensitivity to distinct critical periods and various environmental stimulations. In addition to the latency of evoked responses, several other EEG/MEG parameters (e.g., evolution in peaks morphology and amplitude, complexity measures) could be compared to the brain anatomical changes during development (Dubois et al., 2016a).

(A) Visual responses to central stimuli

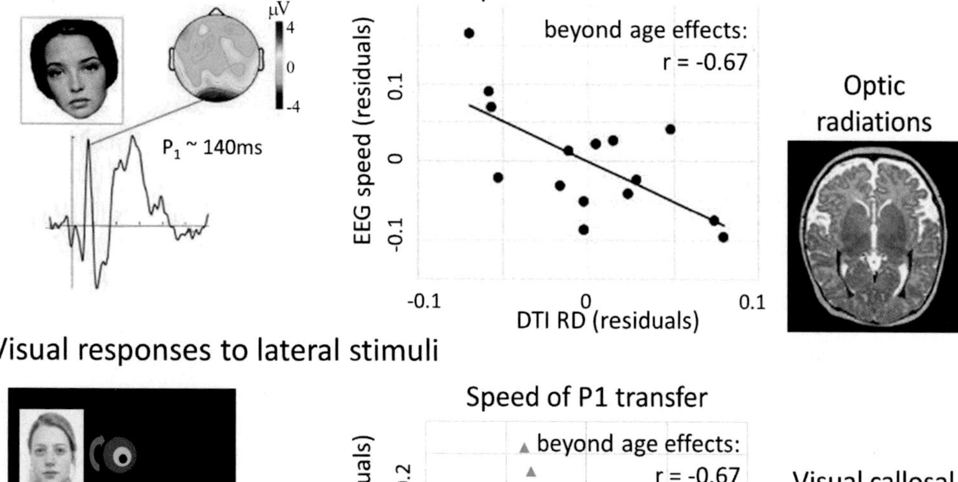

(B) Visual responses to lateral stimuli

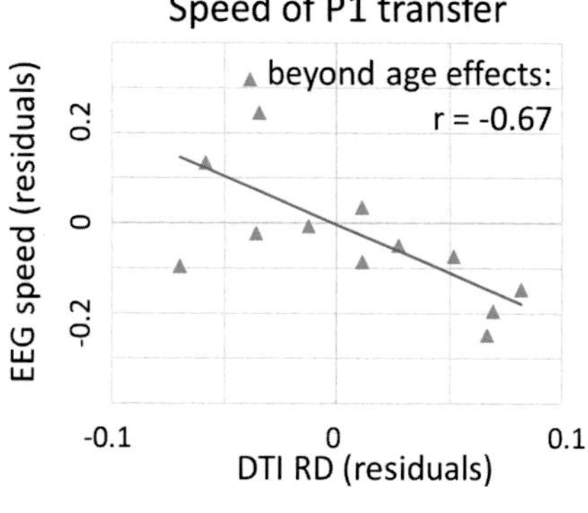

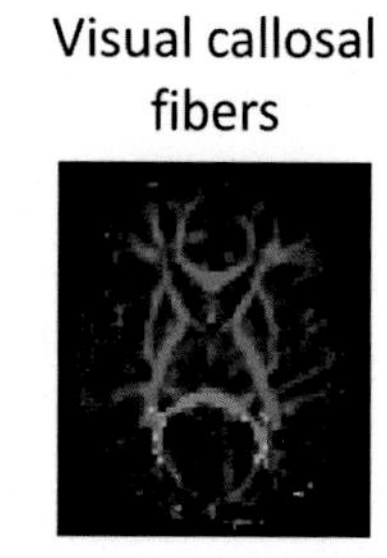

(C) Auditory responses to lateral stimuli

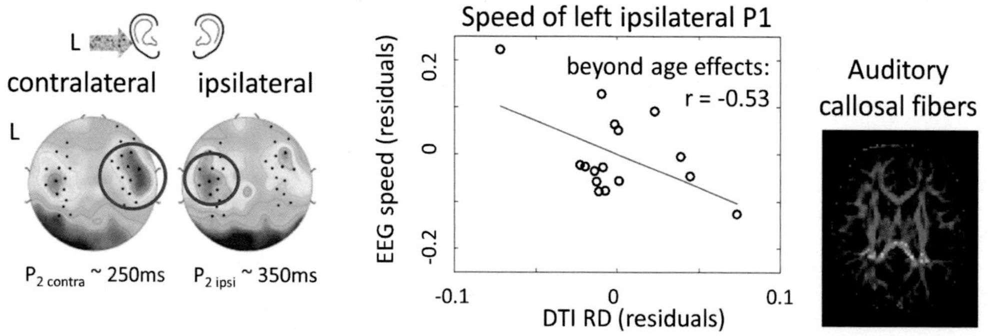

FIG. 4

Multimodal neuroimaging to relate structural and functional development. (A) During infancy, the speed of P1 responses to visual stimuli increases with age, while the visual pathways become myelinated, resulting in a decrease in DTI radial diffusivity in the optic radiations. For the visual system, these functional and structural markers of maturation have been related beyond age dependencies.

(Continued)

5.4 Comparing fMRI and EEG responses

Since EEG and functional MRI do not reflect the same mechanisms (neural vs. hemodynamic activity), it is important to compare the measures and responses provided by these methods in order to better understand their changes and significance during development. Nevertheless, to our knowledge, only two multimodal studies have used both EEG and fMRI in newborns so far. The first one considered simultaneous EEG-fMRI in preterm infants aged 32–36w PMA to localize the source of spontaneous neuronal bursts that are critical for brain maturation (the so-called "delta brush") (Arichi et al., 2017). It revealed that the insula, a densely connected hub of the developing brain, is a major source of transient bursting events in both the left and right hemispheres. It is interesting to note that this spontaneous activity, measured in preterm newborns shortly after birth, may be a good marker of brain development, as increased activity has been linked to more rapid growth of the brain and subcortical gray matter up to term-equivalent age (Benders et al., 2015).

The second study investigated voice perception in newborns using two independent paradigms with high-density EEG and fMRI (Adam-Darque et al., 2020). Results from both modalities suggested that the main components of the adult voice-processing networks are present early on and that preterm infants at term-equivalent age have enhanced processing for voices than full-term newborns. More studies are needed in the future to better understand how maturational changes in responses measured in EEG and fMRI are related during infancy.

6. Conclusion and perspectives

In recent years, a wide variety of new MRI methods have been proposed and implemented to allow precise exploration of the developing brain in newborns and infants, targeting multiple mechanisms ranging from morphological to microstructural changes in grey and white matter, in addition to metabolic and functional changes. Nevertheless, such studies remain limited in several aspects due to inherent methodological and experimental challenges. Research is still needed to improve the

FIG. 4, CONT'D (B) Similar relationships have been observed for responses to visual stimuli presented laterally (in one hemifield at a time). The speed of the responses transfer, from the contralateral to the ipsilateral hemisphere, have been related to the maturation of callosal fibers connecting visual regions. (C) Although such relationships are more difficult to demonstrate for the auditory system, we observed that the speed of ipsilateral responses measured in the left hemisphere following stimuli presented in the left ear, is related to the maturation of callosal fibers connecting auditory regions. This suggests that early structural biases might lead to the functional lateralization for speech processing in the left hemisphere.

Modified from (A) Dubois, J., Dehaene-Lambertz, G., Perrin, M., Mangin, J.F., Cointepas, Y., Duchesnay, E., Le Bihan, D., Hertz-Pannier, L., 2008a. Asynchrony of the early maturation of white matter bundles in healthy infants: quantitative landmarks revealed noninvasively by diffusion tensor imaging. Hum. Brain Mapp. 29(1), 14–27; Dubois, J., Dehaene-Lambertz, G., Soares, C., Cointepas, Y., Le Bihan, D., Hertz-Pannier, L., 2008b. Microstructural correlates of infant functional development: example of the visual pathways. J. Neurosci. 28(8), 1943–1948; (B) Adibpour, P., Dubois, J., Dehaene-Lambertz, G., 2018a. Right but not left hemispheric discrimination of faces in infancy. Nat. Hum. Behav. 2(1), 67–79; Adibpour, P., Dubois, J., Moutard, M.L., Dehaene-Lambertz, G., 2018b. Early asymmetric inter-hemispheric transfer in the auditory network: insights from infants with corpus callosum agenesis. Brain Struct. Funct. 223(6), 2893–2905; (C) Adibpour, P., Lebenberg, J., Kabdebon, C., Dehaene-Lambertz, G., Dubois, J., 2020. Anatomo-functional correlates of auditory development in infancy. Dev. Cogn. Neurosci. 42, 100752.

reproducibility of acquired data and quality control. A major issue in the coming years will be to link the different scales and facets of developmental processes, and to relate molecular, cellular and network changes in a comprehensive integrative model to be compared with the cognitive development of infants. Multimodal MRI has a key role to play in this regard, as well as to better characterize early deviations from neurodevelopmental trajectories due to pre- or perinatal disturbances. Because MRI examinations can be performed well before the child's behavior and clinical outcome are known, it is an essential investigative method for evaluating the efficiency of early neuroprotective interventions or remediation strategies to avoid long-term disability in children. Of course, the diverse information provided by this technique is complementary to the many other factors responsible for interindividual variability, such as intrauterine growth, gestational age at birth, socio-economic status, etc. For this reason, the multimodality of research and clinical studies should far exceed that of MRI brain exploration, by including complementary neurophysiological, behavioral, and clinical evaluations.

Acknowledgments

The research was supported by grants from the Médisite Foundation (2018), the Fondation de France (call Neurodevelopment 2012 and 2020), the Fyssen Foundation (2009), the European Union's Horizon 2020 Research and Innovation Programme (HBP 2013). This study contributed to the IdEx Université de Paris (ANR-18-IDEX-0001).

References

Adam-Darque, A., Pittet, M.P., Grouiller, F., Rihs, T.A., Leuchter, R.H., Lazeyras, F., Michel, C.M., Hüppi, P.S., 2020. Neural correlates of voice perception in newborns and the influence of preterm birth. Cereb. Cortex 30 (11), 5717–5730.

Adibpour, P., Dubois, J., Dehaene-Lambertz, G., 2018a. Right but not left hemispheric discrimination of faces in infancy. Nat. Hum. Behav. 2 (1), 67–79.

Adibpour, P., Dubois, J., Moutard, M.L., Dehaene-Lambertz, G., 2018b. Early asymmetric inter-hemispheric transfer in the auditory network: insights from infants with corpus callosum agenesis. Brain Struct. Funct. 223 (6), 2893–2905.

Adibpour, P., Lebenberg, J., Kabdebon, C., Dehaene-Lambertz, G., Dubois, J., 2020. Anatomo-functional correlates of auditory development in infancy. Dev. Cogn. Neurosci. 42, 100752.

Arichi, T., Whitehead, K., Barone, G., Pressler, R., Padormo, F., Edwards, A.D., Fabrizi, L., 2017. Localization of spontaneous bursting neuronal activity in the preterm human brain with simultaneous EEG-fMRI. Elife 6, e27814.

Assaf, Y., Basser, P.J., 2005. Composite hindered and restricted model of diffusion (CHARMED) MR imaging of the human brain. NeuroImage 27 (1), 48–58.

Ball, G., Srinivasan, L., Aljabar, P., Counsell, S.J., Durighel, G., Hajnal, J.V., Rutherford, M.A., Edwards, A.D., 2013. Development of cortical microstructure in the preterm human brain. Proc. Natl. Acad. Sci. USA 110 (23), 9541–9546.

Batalle, D., O'Muircheartaigh, J., Makropoulos, A., Kelly, C.J., Dimitrova, R., Hughes, E.J., Hajnal, J.V., Zhang, H., Alexander, D.C., David Edwards, A., Counsell, S.J., 2019. Different patterns of cortical maturation before and after 38 weeks gestational age demonstrated by diffusion MRI in vivo. NeuroImage 185, 764–775.

Baum, G.L., Cui, Z., Roalf, D.R., Ciric, R., Betzel, R.F., Larsen, B., Cieslak, M., Cook, P.A., Xia, C.H., Moore, T. M., Ruparel, K., Oathes, D.J., Alexander-Bloch, A.F., Shinohara, R.T., Raznahan, A., Gur, R.E., Gur, R.C.,

Bassett, D.S., Satterthwaite, T.D., 2020. Development of structure-function coupling in human brain networks during youth. Proc. Natl. Acad. Sci. USA 117 (1), 771–778.

Baumann, N., Pham-Dinh, D., 2001. Biology of oligodendrocyte and myelin in the mammalian central nervous system. Physiol. Rev. 81 (2), 871–927.

Benders, M.J., Palmu, K., Menache, C., Borradori-Tolsa, C., Lazeyras, F., Sizonenko, S., Dubois, J., Vanhatalo, S., Huppi, P.S., 2015. Early brain activity relates to subsequent brain growth in premature infants. Cereb. Cortex 25 (9), 3014–3024.

Bozek, J., Makropoulos, A., Schuh, A., Fitzgibbon, S., Wright, R., Glasser, M.F., Coalson, T.S., O'Muircheartaigh, J., Hutter, J., Price, A.N., Cordero-Grande, L., Teixeira, R., Hughes, E., Tusor, N., Baruteau, K.P., Rutherford, M.A., Edwards, A.D., Hajnal, J.V., Smith, S.M., Rueckert, D., Jenkinson, M., Robinson, E.C., 2018. Construction of a neonatal cortical surface atlas using multimodal surface matching in the developing human connectome project. NeuroImage 179, 11–29.

Cao, M., Huang, H., He, Y., 2017. Developmental connectomics from infancy through early childhood. Trends Neurosci. 40, 494–506.

Chauvel, M., Rheault, F., Rolland, C., Aubrain, K., Leroy, F., de Vareilles, H., Girard, G., Rivière, D., Hertz-Pannier, L., Mangin, J.F., Descoteaux, M., Dubois, J., 2020. Exploring the Microstructural Properties of the Newborn Sensorimotor Network With Diffusion MRI. Organization for Human Brain Mapping, Virtual meeting.

Chen, Y., Chen, M.H., Baluyot, K.R., Potts, T.M., Jimenez, J., Lin, W., Consortium, U.U.B.C.P., 2019. MR fingerprinting enables quantitative measures of brain tissue relaxation times and myelin water fraction in the first five years of life. NeuroImage 186, 782–793.

Croteau-Chonka, E.C., Dean 3rd, D.C., Remer, J., Dirks, H., O'Muircheartaigh, J., Deoni, S.C., 2016. Examining the relationships between cortical maturation and white matter myelination throughout early childhood. NeuroImage 125, 413–421.

de Vareilles, H., Rivière, D., Benders, M., Sun, Z.Y., Fischer, C., Leroy, F., Dubois, J., Mangin, J.F., 2020. Folding Dynamics of the Sylvian Fissure: A Longitudinal Study on Preterms. Organization for Human Brain Mapping.

Dean 3rd, D.C., O'Muircheartaigh, J., Dirks, H., Travers, B.G., Adluru, N., Alexander, A.L., Deoni, S.C., 2016. Mapping an index of the myelin g-ratio in infants using magnetic resonance imaging. NeuroImage 132, 225–237.

Dean 3rd, D.C., Planalp, E.M., Wooten, W., Adluru, N., Kecskemeti, S.R., Frye, C., Schmidt, C.K., Schmidt, N.L., Styner, M.A., Goldsmith, H.H., Davidson, R.J., Alexander, A.L., 2017. Mapping white matter microstructure in the one month human brain. Sci. Rep. 7 (1), 9759.

Dean 3rd., D.C., Planalp, E.M., Wooten, W., Schmidt, C.K., Kecskemeti, S.R., Frye, C., Schmidt, N.L., Goldsmith, H.H., Alexander, A.L., Davidson, R.J., 2018. Investigation of brain structure in the 1-month infant. Brain Struct. Funct. 223 (4), 1953–1970.

Dehaene-Lambertz, G., Spelke, E.S., 2015. The infancy of the human brain. Neuron 88 (1), 93–109.

Deoni, S.C., Dean 3rd, D.C., O'Muircheartaigh, J., Dirks, H., Jerskey, B.A., 2012. Investigating white matter development in infancy and early childhood using myelin water faction and relaxation time mapping. NeuroImage 63 (3), 1038–1053.

Deoni, S.C., Dean 3rd, D.C., Remer, J., Dirks, H., O'Muircheartaigh, J., 2015. Cortical maturation and myelination in healthy toddlers and young children. NeuroImage 115, 147–161.

Dubois, J., Alison, M., Counsell, S.J., Hertz-Pannier, L., Hüppi, P.S., Benders, M.J.N.L., 2021. MRI of the neonatal brain: a review of methodological challenges and neuroscientific advances. J. Magn. Reson. Imaging 53 (5), 1318–1343.

Dubois, J., Dehaene-Lambertz, G., 2015. Fetal and postnatal development of the cortex: insights from MRI and genetics. In: Toga, A. (Ed.), Brain Mapping: An Encyclopedic Reference. vol. 2. Academic Press: Elsevier, London, UK, pp. 11–19.

Dubois, J., Dehaene-Lambertz, G., Perrin, M., Mangin, J.F., Cointepas, Y., Duchesnay, E., Le Bihan, D., Hertz-Pannier, L., 2008a. Asynchrony of the early maturation of white matter bundles in healthy infants: quantitative landmarks revealed noninvasively by diffusion tensor imaging. Hum. Brain Mapp. 29 (1), 14–27.

Dubois, J., Dehaene-Lambertz, G., Soares, C., Cointepas, Y., Le Bihan, D., Hertz-Pannier, L., 2008b. Microstructural correlates of infant functional development: example of the visual pathways. J. Neurosci. 28 (8), 1943–1948.

Dubois, J., Dehaene-Lambertz, G., Kulikova, S., Poupon, C., Hüppi, P.S., Hertz-Pannier, L., 2014. The early development of brain white matter: a review of imaging studies in fetuses, newborns and infants. Neuroscience 276, 48–71.

Dubois, J., Kostovic, I., Judas, M., 2015. Development of structural and functional connectivity. In: Toga, A. (Ed.), Brain Mapping: An Encyclopedic Reference. vol. 2. Academic Press: Elsevier, London, UK, pp. 423–437.

Dubois, J., Adibpour, P., Poupon, C., Hertz-Pannier, L., Dehaene-Lambertz, G., 2016a. MRI and M/EEG studies of the white matter development in human fetuses and infants: review and opinion. Brain Plast. 2 (1), 49–69.

Dubois, J., Poupon, C., Thirion, B., Simonnet, H., Kulikova, S., Leroy, F., Hertz-Pannier, L., Dehaene-Lambertz, G., 2016b. Exploring the early organization and maturation of linguistic pathways in the human infant brain. Cereb. Cortex 26 (5), 2283–2298.

Dubois, J., Lefevre, J., Angleys, H., Leroy, F., Fischer, C., Lebenberg, J., Dehaene-Lambertz, G., Borradori-Tolsa, C., Lazeyras, F., Hertz-Pannier, L., Mangin, J.F., Huppi, P.S., Germanaud, D., 2019. The dynamics of cortical folding waves and prematurity-related deviations revealed by spatial and spectral analysis of gyrification. NeuroImage 185, 934–946.

Ducharme, S., Albaugh, M.D., Nguyen, T.V., Hudziak, J.J., Mateos-Pérez, J.M., Labbe, A., Evans, A.C., Karama, S., B. D. C. Group, 2016. Trajectories of cortical thickness maturation in normal brain development—the importance of quality control procedures. NeuroImage 125, 267–279.

Eaton-Rosen, Z., Scherrer, B., Melbourne, A., Ourselin, S., Neil, J.J., Warfield, S.K., 2017. Investigating the maturation of microstructure and radial orientation in the preterm human cortex with diffusion MRI. NeuroImage 162, 65–72.

Fair, D.A., Cohen, A.L., Power, J.D., Dosenbach, N.U., Church, J.A., Miezin, F.M., Schlaggar, B.L., Petersen, S. E., 2009. Functional brain networks develop from a "local to distributed" organization. PLoS Comput. Biol. 5 (5), e1000381.

Ferradal, S.L., Gagoski, B., Jaimes, C., Yi, F., Carruthers, C., Vu, C., Litt, J.S., Larsen, R., Sutton, B., Grant, P.E., Zollei, L., 2019. System-specific patterns of thalamocortical connectivity in early brain development as revealed by structural and functional MRI. Cereb. Cortex 29 (3), 1218–1229.

Flechsig, P., 1920. Anatomie des Menschlichen Gehirn und Rückenmarks, auf myelogenetischer grundlage. G. Thieme, Stuttgart, Germany.

Friedrichs-Maeder, C.L., Griffa, A., Schneider, J., Huppi, P.S., Truttmann, A., Hagmann, P., 2017. Exploring the role of white matter connectivity in cortex maturation. PLoS One 12 (5), e0177466.

Germann, J., Chakravarty, M.M., Collins, L.D., Petrides, M., 2019. Tight coupling between morphological features of the central sulcus and somatomotor body representations: a combined anatomical and functional MRI study. Cereb. Cortex 30 (3), 1843–1854.

Haak, K.V., Marquand, A.F., Beckmann, C.F., 2018. Connectopic mapping with resting-state fMRI. NeuroImage 170, 83–94.

Harding, G.F., Grose, J., Wilton, A., Bissenden, J.G., 1989. The pattern reversal VEP in short-gestation infants. Electroencephalogr. Clin. Neurophysiol. 74 (1), 76–80.

Hertz, A., Pepe, A., Lefèvre, J., Zomeno, M., Leroy, F., Lebenberg, J., de Vries, L., Groenendaal, F., Germanaud, D., Benders, M., Dubois, J., 2018. Is cortical microstructure related to folding during development? A longitudinal MRI study in preterms. In: Proceedings of ISMRM.

Jelescu, I.O., Veraart, J., Adisetiyo, V., Milla, S., Novikov, D.S., Fieremans, E., 2015. One diffusion acquisition and different white matter models: how does microstructure change in human early development based on WMTI and NODDI? NeuroImage 107, 242–256.

Kabdebon, C., Leroy, F., Simmonet, H., Perrot, M., Dubois, J., Dehaene-Lambertz, G., 2014. Anatomical correlations of the international 10-20 sensor placement system in infants. NeuroImage 99, 342–356.

Kersbergen, K.J., Leemans, A., Groenendaal, F., van der Aa, N.E., Viergever, M.A., de Vries, L.S., Benders, M.J., 2014. Microstructural brain development between 30 and 40week corrected age in a longitudinal cohort of extremely preterm infants. NeuroImage 103, 214–224.

Kostović, I., Sedmak, G., Judaš, M., 2019. Neural histology and neurogenesis of the human fetal and infant brain. NeuroImage 188, 743–773.

Kuehn, E., Dinse, J., Jakobsen, E., Long, X., Schafer, A., Bazin, P.L., Villringer, A., Sereno, M.I., Margulies, D.S., 2017. Body topography parcellates human sensory and motor cortex. Cereb. Cortex 27 (7), 3790–3805.

Kulikova, S., Hertz-Pannier, L., Dehaene-Lambertz, G., Buzmakov, A., Poupon, C., Dubois, J., 2015. Multiparametric evaluation of the white matter maturation. Brain Struct. Funct. 220 (6), 3657–3672.

Kunz, N., Zhang, H., Vasung, L., O'Brien, K.R., Assaf, Y., Lazeyras, F., Alexander, D.C., Huppi, P.S., 2014. Assessing white matter microstructure of the newborn with multi-shell diffusion MRI and biophysical compartment models. NeuroImage 96, 288–299.

Lebenberg, J., Poupon, C., Thirion, B., Leroy, F., Mangin, J.-F., Dehaene-Lambertz, G., Dubois, J., IEEE, 2015. Clustering the infant brain tissues based on microstructural properties and maturation assessment using multiparametric MRI. In: IEEE International Symposium on Biomedical Imaging (12th ISBI 2015), pp. 148–151.

Larivière, S., Vos de Wael, R., Hong, S.J., Paquola, C., Tavakol, S., Lowe, A.J., Schrader, D.V., Bernhardt, B.C., 2020. Multiscale structure-function gradients in the neonatal connectome. Cereb. Cortex 30 (1), 47–58.

Lebenberg, J., Labit, M., Auzias, G., Mohlberg, H., Fischer, C., Riviere, D., Duchesnay, E., Kabdebon, C., Leroy, F., Labra, N., Poupon, F., Dickscheid, T., Hertz-Pannier, L., Poupon, C., Dehaene-Lambertz, G., Huppi, P., Amunts, K., Dubois, J., Mangin, J.-F., 2018. A framework based on sulcal constraints to align preterm, infant and adult human brain images acquired in vivo and post mortem. Brain Struct. Funct. 223 (9), 4153–4168.

Lebenberg, J., Mangin, J.F., Thirion, B., Poupon, C., Hertz-Pannier, L., Leroy, F., Adibpour, P., Dehaene-Lambertz, G., Dubois, J., 2019. Mapping the asynchrony of cortical maturation in the infant brain: a MRI multi-parametric clustering approach. NeuroImage 185, 641–653.

Llinares-Benadero, C., Borrell, V., 2019. Deconstructing cortical folding: genetic, cellular and mechanical determinants. Nat. Rev. Neurosci. 20 (3), 161–176.

Lyall, A.E., Shi, F., Geng, X., Woolson, S., Li, G., Wang, L., Hamer, R.M., Shen, D., Gilmore, J.H., 2015. Dynamic development of regional cortical thickness and surface area in early childhood. Cereb. Cortex 25 (8), 2204–2212.

Makropoulos, A., Aljabar, P., Wright, R., Hüning, B., Merchant, N., Arichi, T., Tusor, N., Hajnal, J.V., Edwards, A.D., Counsell, S.J., Rueckert, D., 2016. Regional growth and atlasing of the developing human brain. NeuroImage 125, 456–478.

McCulloch, D.L., Skarf, B., 1991. Development of the human visual system: monocular and binocular pattern VEP latency. Invest. Ophthalmol. Vis. Sci. 32 (8), 2372–2381.

McCulloch, D.L., Orbach, H., Skarf, B., 1999. Maturation of the pattern-reversal VEP in human infants: a theoretical framework. Vis. Res. 39 (22), 3673–3680.

Melbourne, A., Eaton-Rosen, Z., De Vita, E., Bainbridge, A., Cardoso, M.J., Price, D., Cady, E., Kendall, G.S., Robertson, N.J., Marlow, N., Ourselin, S., 2014. Multi-modal measurement of the myelin-to-axon diameter g-ratio in preterm-born neonates and adult controls. Med. Image Comput. Comput. Assist. Interv. 17 (Pt 2), 268–275.

Melbourne, A., Eaton-Rosen, Z., Orasanu, E., Price, D., Bainbridge, A., Cardoso, M.J., Kendall, G.S., Robertson, N.J., Marlow, N., Ourselin, S., 2016. Longitudinal development in the preterm thalamus and posterior white matter: MRI correlations between diffusion weighted imaging and T2 relaxometry. Hum. Brain Mapp. 37 (7), 2479–2492.

Ning, N., Liu, C., Wu, P., Hu, Y., Zhang, W., Zhang, L., Li, M., Gho, S.M., Kim, D.H., Guo, H., Yang, J., Jin, C., 2019. Spatiotemporal variations of magnetic susceptibility in the deep gray matter nuclei from 1 month to 6 years: a quantitative susceptibility mapping study. J. Magn. Reson. Imaging 49 (6), 1600–1609.

Nossin-Manor, R., Card, D., Morris, D., Noormohamed, S., Shroff, M.M., Whyte, H.E., Taylor, M.J., Sled, J.G., 2013. Quantitative MRI in the very preterm brain: assessing tissue organization and myelination using magnetization transfer, diffusion tensor and T(1) imaging. NeuroImage 64, 505–516.

Nossin-Manor, R., Card, D., Raybaud, C., Taylor, M.J., Sled, J.G., 2015. Cerebral maturation in the early preterm period—a magnetization transfer and diffusion tensor imaging study using voxel-based analysis. NeuroImage 112, 30–42.

O'Muircheartaigh, J., Robinson, E., Pietsch, M., Wolfers, T., Aljabar, P., Grande, L.C., Teixeira, R.P.A.G., Bozek, J., Schuh, A., Makropoulos, A., Batalle, D., Hutter, J., Vecchiato, K., Steinweg, J.K., Fitzgibbon, S., Hughes, E., Price, A., Marquand, A., Reuckert, D., Rutherford, M., Hajnal, J., Counsell, S.J., Edwards, A.D., 2020. Modelling brain development to detect white matter injury in term and preterm born neonates. Brain 143 (2), 467–479.

Ouyang, M., Kang, H., Detre, J.A., Roberts, T.P.L., Huang, H., 2017a. Short-range connections in the developmental connectome during typical and atypical brain maturation. Neurosci. Biobehav. Rev. 83, 109–122.

Ouyang, M., Liu, P., Jeon, T., Chalak, L., Heyne, R., Rollins, N.K., Licht, D.J., Detre, J.A., Roberts, T.P., Lu, H., Huang, H., 2017b. Heterogeneous increases of regional cerebral blood flow during preterm brain development: preliminary assessment with pseudo-continuous arterial spin labeled perfusion MRI. NeuroImage 147, 233–242.

Ouyang, M., Jeon, T., Sotiras, A., Peng, Q., Mishra, V., Halovanic, C., Chen, M., Chalak, L., Rollins, N., Roberts, T.P.L., Davatzikos, C., Huang, H., 2019a. Differential cortical microstructural maturation in the preterm human brain with diffusion kurtosis and tensor imaging. Proc. Natl. Acad. Sci. USA 116 (10), 4681–4688.

Ouyang, M.H., Dubois, J., Yu, Q.L., Mukherjee, P., Huang, H., 2019b. Delineation of early brain development from fetuses to infants with diffusion MRI and beyond. NeuroImage 185, 836–850.

Poh, J.S., Li, Y., Ratnarajah, N., Fortier, M.V., Chong, Y.S., Kwek, K., Saw, S.M., Gluckman, P.D., Meaney, M.J., Qiu, A., 2015. Developmental synchrony of thalamocortical circuits in the neonatal brain. NeuroImage 116, 168–176.

Rolland, C., Lebenberg, J., Leroy, F., Moulton, E., Adibpour, P., Rivière, D., Poupon, C., Hertz-Pannier, L., Mangin, J.F., Dehaene-Lambertz, G., Dubois, J., 2019. Exploring microstructure asymmetries in the infant brain cortex: a methodological framework combining structural and diffusion MRI. IEEE ISBI, https://doi.org/10.1109/ISBI.2019.8759421.

Sadeghi, N., Prastawa, M., Fletcher, P.T., Wolff, J., Gilmore, J.H., Gerig, G., 2013. Regional characterization of longitudinal DT-MRI to study white matter maturation of the early developing brain. NeuroImage 68, 236–247.

Sadeghi, N., Gilmore, J.H., Gerig, G., 2017. Twin-singleton developmental study of brain white matter anatomy. Hum. Brain Mapp. 38 (2), 1009–1024.

Salami, M., Itami, C., Tsumoto, T., Kimura, F., 2003. Change of conduction velocity by regional myelination yields constant latency irrespective of distance between thalamus and cortex. Proc. Natl. Acad. Sci. USA 100 (10), 6174–6179.

Smyser, C.D., Snyder, A.Z., Neil, J.J., 2011. Functional connectivity MRI in infants: exploration of the functional organization of the developing brain. NeuroImage 56 (3), 1437–1452.

Smyser, T.A., Smyser, C.D., Rogers, C.E., Gillespie, S.K., Inder, T.E., Neil, J.J., 2016. Cortical gray and adjacent white matter demonstrate synchronous maturation in very preterm infants. Cereb. Cortex 26, 3370–3378.

Soun, J.E., Liu, M.Z., Cauley, K.A., Grinband, J., 2017. Evaluation of neonatal brain myelination using the T1- and T2-weighted MRI ratio. J. Magn. Reson. Imaging 46 (3), 690–696.
Spader, H.S., Ellermeier, A., O'Muircheartaigh, J., Dean 3rd, D.C., Dirks, H., Boxerman, J.L., Cosgrove, G.R., Deoni, S.C., 2013. Advances in myelin imaging with potential clinical application to pediatric imaging. Neurosurg. Focus. 34 (4), E9.
Stikov, N., Campbell, J.S., Stroh, T., Lavelee, M., Frey, S., Novek, J., Nuara, S., Ho, M.K., Bedell, B.J., Dougherty, R.F., Leppert, I.R., Boudreau, M., Narayanan, S., Duval, T., Cohen-Adad, J., Picard, P.A., Gasecka, A., Cote, D., Pike, G.B., 2015. In vivo histology of the myelin g-ratio with magnetic resonance imaging. NeuroImage 118, 397–405.
Stiles, J., Jernigan, T.L., 2010. The basics of brain development. Neuropsychol. Rev. 20 (4), 327–348.
Taylor, M.J., Menzies, R., MacMillan, L.J., Whyte, H.E., 1987. VEPs in normal full-term and premature neonates: longitudinal versus cross-sectional data. Electroencephalogr. Clin. Neurophysiol. 68 (1), 20–27.
Thiessen, J.D., Zhang, Y., Zhang, H., Wang, L., Buist, R., Del Bigio, M.R., Kong, J., Li, X.M., Martin, M., 2013. Quantitative MRI and ultrastructural examination of the cuprizone mouse model of demyelination. NMR Biomed. 26 (11), 1562–1581.
van den Heuvel, M.P., Kersbergen, K.J., de Reus, M.A., Keunen, K., Kahn, R.S., Groenendaal, F., de Vries, L.S., Benders, M.J., 2015. The neonatal connectome during preterm brain development. Cereb. Cortex 25 (9), 3000–3013.
Walhovd, K.B., Fjell, A.M., Giedd, J., Dale, A.M., Brown, T.T., 2017. Through thick and thin: a need to reconcile contradictory results on trajectories in human cortical development. Cereb. Cortex 27 (2), 1472–1481.
Wang, X., Studholme, C., Grigsby, P.L., Frias, A.E., Cuzon Carlson, V.C., Kroenke, C.D., 2017. Folding, but not surface area expansion is associated with cellular morphological maturation in the fetal cerebral cortex. J. Neurosci. 37 (8), 1971–1983.
Wang, F., Lian, C., Wu, Z., Zhang, H., Li, T., Meng, Y., Wang, L., Lin, W., Shen, D., Li, G., 2019. Developmental topography of cortical thickness during infancy. Proc. Natl. Acad. Sci. USA 116 (32), 15855–15860.
Welker, W., 1990. Why does cerebral cortex fissure and fold? A review of determinants of gyri and sulci. In: Jones, E., Peters, A. (Eds.), Comparative Structure and Evolution of Cerebral Cortex. Part II, vol. 8B. Plenum, New York, pp. 3–136.
Yakovlev, P.I., Lecours, A.R., 1967. The myelogenetic cycles of regional maturation in the brain. In: Minowski, A. (Ed.), Regional Development of the Brain in Early Life. Blackwell, Oxford, pp. 3–69.
Zhang, H., Schneider, T., Wheeler-Kingshott, C.A., Alexander, D.C., 2012. NODDI: practical in vivo neurite orientation dispersion and density imaging of the human brain. NeuroImage 61 (4), 1000–1016.
Zhang, Y., Shi, J., Wei, H., Han, V., Zhu, W.Z., Liu, C., 2019. Neonate and infant brain development from birth to 2 years assessed using MRI-based quantitative susceptibility mapping. NeuroImage 185, 349–360.
Zhao, T., Xu, Y., He, Y., 2018. Graph theoretical modeling of baby brain networks. NeuroImage 185, 711–727.
Zhao, Y., Klein, A., Castellanos, F.X., Milham, M.P., 2019. Brain age prediction: cortical and subcortical shape covariation in the developing human brain. NeuroImage 202, 116149.
Zlatkina, V., Amiez, C., Petrides, M., 2016. The postcentral sulcal complex and the transverse postcentral sulcus and their relation to sensorimotor functional organization. Eur. J. Neurosci. 43 (10), 1268–1283.

CHAPTER

Pediatric magnetic resonance spectroscopy

9

Kim M. Cecil and David A. Edmondson

Department of Radiology, University of Cincinnati College of Medicine, Cincinnati Children's Hospital Medical Center, Cincinnati, OH, United States

1. Introduction

The magnetic resonance spectroscopy (MRS) of the brain technique provides the clinician along with the research scientist a complementary probe of neurochemistry within the magnetic resonance imaging (MRI) setting. State-of-the-art commercial MRI scanner systems are equipped with "proton" MRS capabilities, as this method is approved by the United States Food and Drug Administration (US FDA) for clinical reimbursement. Proton MRS requires no additional hardware for acquisition; other nuclei, such as phosphorus, carbon, etc., require additional hardware. Proton MRS measures the hydrogen protons within molecules, specifically neurochemicals of "sufficient" concentration and mobility in the brain (Fig. 1A). The key neurochemicals routinely detected by the proton MRS technique inform us regarding neuronal health, cellular energetics, cellular membrane status, glial cell involvement and other cellular conditions such as anerobic glycolysis (Table 1). Newer MRS approaches improve the detection of low concentration neurochemical signals, such as γ-aminobutyric acid (GABA) and glutathione, which appear on the spectrum masked by more dominant signals (Fig. 1B). These measurements often afford coveted specificity to the MRI setting in the clinic and valued insight into research questions pertaining to brain metabolism when characterizing disease and injury, evaluating treatment response and prognosticating outcome. While proton MRS provides value for both adult and pediatric indications, the utility within the developing brain coupled with the often early appearance of metabolic diseases and congenital conditions make this technique very useful in narrowing the diagnostic differential and capturing time-sensitive information for the pediatric population including infant, toddler, child and adolescent.

As with adults, the questions being addressed with MRS are influenced by technical aspects as well as some practical concerns relevant primarily for pediatric populations. This chapter approaches the topic from the standpoint of a clinician or scientist wanting to develop a program employing MRS in a pediatric population. This chapter provides an overview of key topics for consideration. Magnetic field strength, pediatric sized head coils, water suppression techniques, localization pulse sequences, postprocessing methods, analysis, and interpretation all require special consideration for the immature brain. The reader is directed to a variety of textbooks and articles for further in-depth discussions of pertaining to mathematical theory and implementation of MRS (De Graaf, 2018; Drost et al., 2002; Stagg and Rothman, 2014). To ultimately synthesize the significance of pediatric proton MRS, a selection of interesting findings derived from clinical MRS is presented with suggestions for future MRS practice.

Handbook of Pediatric Brain Imaging. https://doi.org/10.1016/B978-0-12-816633-8.00009-0

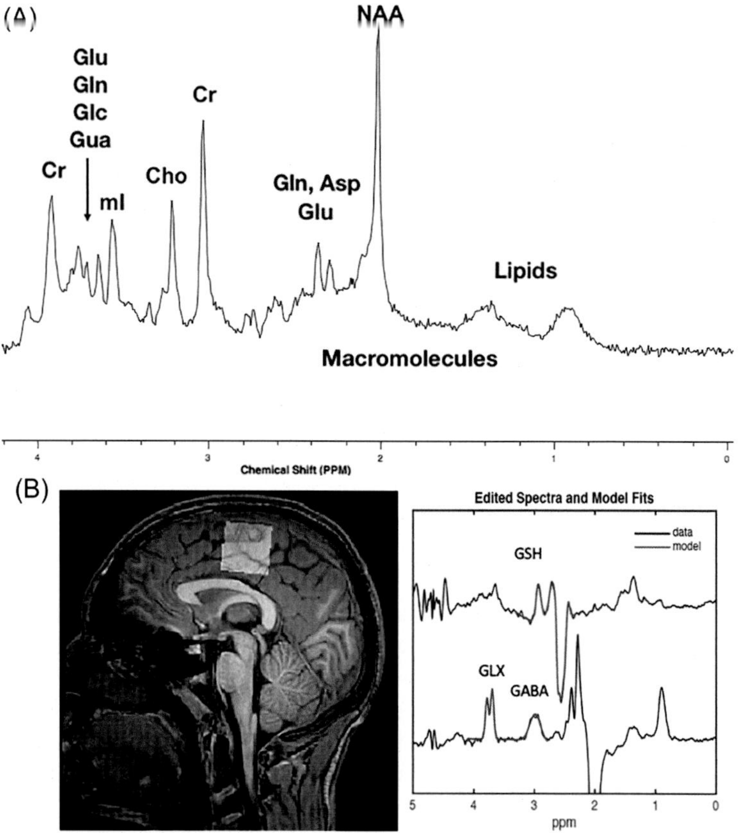

FIG. 1

Standard magnetic resonance spectroscopy. (A) An example of a short echo (35 milliseconds (ms)) proton spectrum acquired within the perigenual anterior cingulate cortex at 3 Tesla (T) field strength. Abbreviations: Gln-glutamine, Asp-aspartate, Glu-glutamate, Cr-creatine, and phosphocreatine, Cho-cholines, ml-myoinositol, Glc-glucose and Gua-guanidinoacetate. (B) **Spectral Editing**. An example from a child with acquisition of the HERMES: Hadamard Encoding and Reconstruction of MEGA-Edited Spectroscopy (MEGA: MEschler GArwood Point RESolved Spectroscopy). On the left, voxel localization within the motor cortex. On the right, the box shows two edited spectral data plots and the modeled fitting for glutathione (GSH), glutamate and glutamine (GLX) and γ-aminobutyric acid (GABA).

1.1 General considerations: Evaluating children, anesthesia, medications

Evaluating children requires some considerations of human factors along with the specific technical aspects relating to MRS. As with any imaging modality applied for clinical or research purposes, the child must remain motionless for the session. Only in special circumstances, such as for rare diseases, will an institutional review board permit sedation exclusively for MRI/MRS research purposes. For the infant, approaches to enhance natural sleep during the session (feed and swaddle) are often successful, especially when performed within the setting which includes implementing a desensitization protocol,

Table 1 Neurochemical and metabolite characteristics for proton MRS of the brain.

Neurochemical/ metabolite	Abbreviation	Key resonance (ppm)	Source, primary role
Lipids (CH_3)	Lip09	0.9	Membrane metabolism
β-Hydroxybutyrate	β-OHB	1.2	Ketogenic metabolite
Lipids (CH_2)n	Lip13	1.3	Membrane metabolism
Propylene Glycol[a]	PG	1.1	Exogenous compound
Lactate	Lac	1.3	Anerobic glycolysis
Alanine	Ala	1.4	Meningioma, abscess, anerobic glycolysis
Acetate	Ac	1.9	Abscess metabolite
γ-Aminobutyric Acid	GABA	1.9, 2.3, 3.0	Inhibitory neurotransmitter
N-Acetyl Aspartate[b]	NAA	2.02	Marker for integrity of neurons, axons
Glutamate	Glu	2.1, 2.3, 3.7	Excitatory neurotransmitter
Glutamine	Gln	2.1, 2.4, 3.8	Precursor for neurotransmitters
Glutathione	GSH	2.1, 2.5, 2.9, 3.8	Endogenous antioxidant
Acetone	Ace	2.22	Ketogenic metabolite
Acetoacetate	AcAc	2.27, 3.43	Ketogenic metabolite
Pyruvate	Pyr	2.35	Abscess metabolite
Succinate	Suc	2.39	Abscess metabolite
Aspartate	Asp	2.6, 2.8, 3.9	Excitatory neurotransmitter
Citrate	Cit	2.6	Cellular energetics
Creatine	Cr	3.0, 3.9	Cellular energetics
Methylsulfonylmethane[a]	MSM	3.1	Exogenous compound
Choline[b]	Cho	3.2	Membrane metabolism
Scyllo-inositol	sI	3.3	Isomer of inositol
Taurine[b]	Tau	3.4	Inhibitory neurotransmitter, osmolyte
Glucose[b]	Glu	3.4, 3.8	Cellular energetics
Myo-inositol	mI	3.5	Glial marker, osmolytic marker
Glycine	Gly	3.5	Inhibitory neurotransmitter
Mannitol[a]	–	3.8	Exogenous compound
Guanidinoacetate	Gua	3.8	Creatine synthesis precursor

Commonly observed neurochemicals/metabolites identified with pediatric brain magnetic resonance spectroscopy including nominal resonance assignments are listed. The endogenous neurochemicals/metabolites appear at normative levels in healthy conditions, however, abnormal (increased or decreased) levels represent pathologic conditions.

[a]*Some noted metabolites do not occur naturally, but are exogenous compounds often administered as medications or solvents for medications.*

[b]*Primary resonance assignment observed is noted with secondary resonance assignments omitted.*

appropriately trained staff and scanner availability with flexibility for extended session time (Vannest et al., 2014). However, the age period from toddler to preschooler (9 months to 5 years) generally requires anesthesia or sedation for the child. Children of all ages with cognitive impairments or conditions prohibiting them from holding still will also require some forms of sedation or anesthesia. For these instances, only clinical or combined clinical/research examinations will be permitted.

There is also concern regarding adverse neurodevelopment from the exposure to sedation and anesthetic agents especially in infants and young children (McCann and Soriano, 2019). From a more immediate standpoint, solutions associated with anesthetic, sedative and therapeutic agents may influence the spectra, typically by introducing a novel resonance to the spectrum. These exogenous agents include Ringer's lactate, propylene glycol as a solvent in barbiturate medications (Fig. 2), mannitol as a therapeutic treating elevated intracranial pressures (Fig. 3) and dietary supplements such as methylsulfonylmethane (Fig. 4).

1.2 General considerations: Magnetic resonance hardware

The selection of magnetic field strength is typically a choice between 1.5 Tesla (T) versus 3 T for clinical or research purposes as these systems are the ones most commonly available in hospitals and university settings. The repeated usage of these systems for children is viewed as safe (Holland et al., 2014). The FDA permits exposure up to 8 T in children at least 1 month old (Anon, 2014).

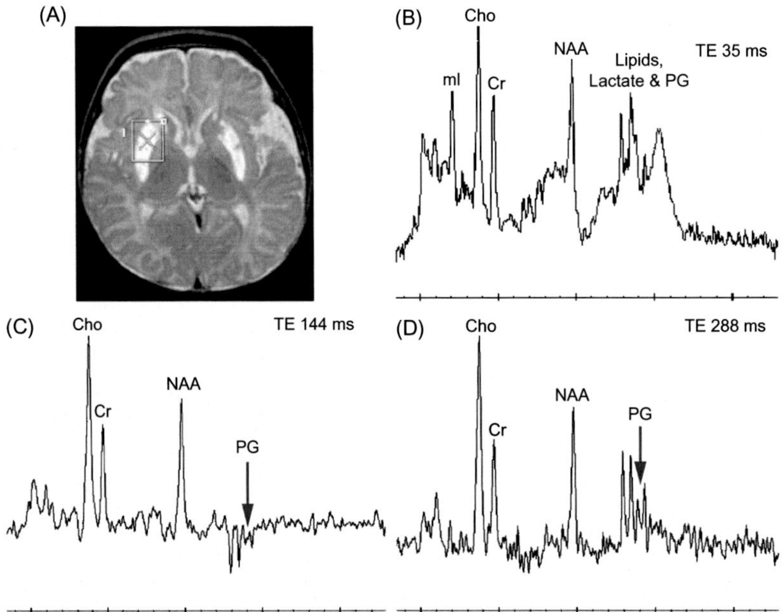

FIG. 2

Exogenous agents: Propylene glycol. An example of spectra displaying propylene glycol (PG) as a solvent from an infant treated with an anticonvulsant. (A) Voxel location for all spectra shown on an axial T2 weighted image within the basal ganglia of a male infant with Leigh Syndrome. (B) Short echo (35 milliseconds (ms)) proton spectrum shows a composite of lipids, lactate and PG that is simplified with (C) and the doublet resonance (*red arrow*) at 1.1 ppm on the intermediate echo (144 ms) which along with lactate (1.3 ppm) is inverted, but upright on the (D) long echo (288 ms) spectrum. Abbreviations: *Cho*: cholines, *Cr*: creatine and phosphocreatine, *ml*: myoinositol, *NAA*: *N*-acetylaspartate.

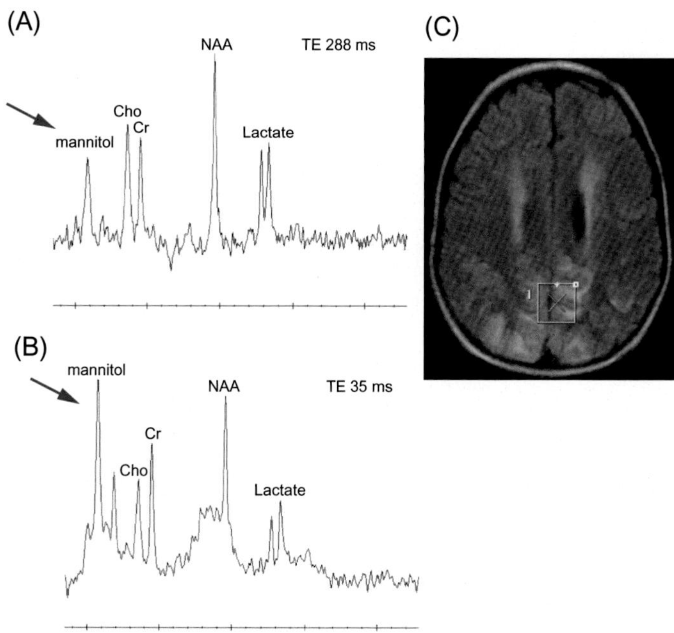

FIG. 3

Exogenous agents: Mannitol. An example of spectra displaying mannitol as a therapeutic for decreasing intracranial pressure. (A) Short echo (35 milliseconds (ms)) proton spectrum shows a single resonance (*red arrow*) at 3.8 ppm which persists on (B) the long echo (288 ms) spectrum. (C) Illustration of the voxel placement within the midline posterior cortex, a region with blood brain barrier breakdown of a child with a myelodysplastic syndrome. Abbreviations: *Cho*: cholines, *Cr*: creatine and phosphocreatine, *NAA*: *N*-acetylaspartate.

In 2017, the FDA cleared the first 7 T system for clinical usage (Press Release, 2017). However, only a few groups with research 7 T MRI systems have studied children, because of practical concerns about the ability of pediatric participants to remain motionless as sedation is typically not employed in these settings. There is also the issue of scanner acoustic noise and sound pressure levels being harmful, particularly for infants (Chou et al., 2014; Tocchio et al., 2015). The more mundane issue of scanner field strength selection often depends on the system availability at a given site. A 1.5 T system that is more flexible in scheduling, perhaps with less clinical demand, and available in the evenings to perform MRI/MRS research studies for nonsedated infants may be preferred over a 3 T unit employed 12 h a day for clinical service. However, there are some questions which may require the improved signal to noise ratio (SNR), increased chemical shift dispersion (this provides increased distance between resonances) afforded from 3 T field strength, especially for spectral editing approaches to determine GABA and glutathione (GSH) concentrations (Mescher et al., 1998; Edden and Barker, 2007; Choi et al., 2005a, b; Bielicki et al., 2004; Du et al., 2004; Rothman et al., 1993; Henry et al., 2001; Saleh et al., 2016). In contrast, the reduced chemical shift dispersion afforded at 1.5 T, often makes the detection of the spectroscopic glial marker myo-inositol (mI) easier as it demonstrates higher signal intensity with four

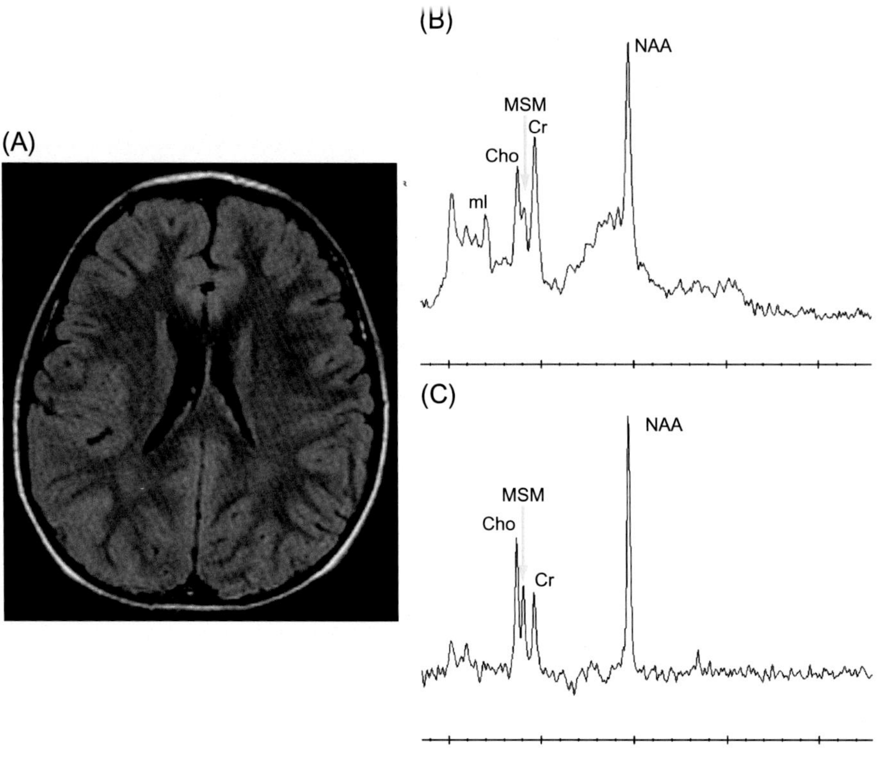

FIG. 4

Exogenous agents: Methylsulfonylmethane. An example of spectra displaying methylsulfonylmethane (MSM), used as a dietary supplement in a 5-year-old male with autism spectrum disorder. (A) Voxel location within left parietal white matter localized on an axial fluid attenuated inversion recovery (FLAIR) image. (B) Short echo (35 milliseconds (ms)) proton spectrum shows a resonance for MSM at 3.1 ppm (*yellow arrow*), located between the creatine (Cr) and choline (Cho) resonances. (C) This resonance persists on long echo (288 ms).

protons contributing to the single appearing resonance. From a technical standpoint, the benefits of higher field strength require an understanding of factors which are proportional to field strength and thus, intrinsically altered.

Higher field strengths influence spectra by changing the SNR, chemical shift dispersion, relaxation times, main magnetic field (B_0) homogeneity, excitation radiofrequency (RF) field (B_1) homogeneity and specific absorption rate (SAR) (De Graaf, 2018; Stagg and Rothman, 2014; Dydak and Schar, 2006). The increased field strength at 3 T improves spectral resolution via chemical shift dispersion which can also improve metabolite quantification and provide higher spatial resolution. Higher field strength enables higher spectral quality, but only if higher order shimming is conducted (Dydak and Schar, 2006). Higher field strength also requires RF pulses within localization sequences to be adapted to overcome metabolite signal misregistration and signal loss due to shorter T2 and longer T1 relaxation with increased field inhomogeneities from the B_0 and the B_1 field created by an RF pulse oriented at 90° to the main magnetic field (Dydak and Schar, 2006). As these RF pulses within a pulse sequence deposit energy, higher SAR is produced and increases with the square of the magnetic field strength. Children are particularly sensitive to RF-induced heating from pulses due to the relatively immature systems for controlling body temperature, especially infants and premature neonates (Tocchio et al., 2015). For most MRS techniques, SAR is naturally minimized as there are only a few RF pulses employed over relatively long repetition times (e.g., 1500, 2000 or 3000 milliseconds (ms)). However, temperature monitoring, particularly for the swaddled infant, employing multichannel transmit phased-array coils as opposed to body coils, and maintaining cool scanner rooms can mitigate the effects of SAR.

Commercial head coils designed for adults, including head arrays with 32 elements or quadrature knee coils, are not optimal for infants, toddlers, and children (Keil et al., 2011). With differences in shape, size and composition, the dielectric properties influence the coil loading upon placing pediatric heads in adult coils that adversely impact SNR and the performance of parallel imaging techniques. While the small size of the pediatric brain and the proximity to the surface are appealing for close fitting arrays with multiple small elements, the wide gap between the pediatric head and elements of the array reduces the effective coupling between tissue and coil (Keil et al., 2011). Decreased signal and increased noise sources also degrade the SNR. The benefits of acceleration afforded with parallel imaging are diminished as spatial frequencies within the coil sensitivity profiles are reduced in the central region of the adult array which is the location of the pediatric head (Keil et al., 2011).

2. Proton magnetic resonance spectroscopy essentials: Water suppression approaches

Water is the most abundant molecule in the human brain with the two protons producing an MRS signal at 4.65–4.7 ppm (ppm; the x-axis reflecting the frequency scale). While modern analog-to-digital converters could amply digitize the metabolite signals (on the order of 1–10 millimolar) from the signal of water (approximately 50–80 M), the baseline distortion and vibration-induced signal modulation that produces sidebands from water interferes with metabolite signal detection, thus requiring water signal suppression techniques to be implemented (De Graaf, 2018; Clayton et al., 2001; Serrai et al., 2001; Nixon et al., 2008; van Der Veen et al., 2000). Other factors to consider when selecting a water suppression technique include the experimental conditions for RF homogeneity, water signal magnetization recovery due to T1 relaxation, the detection of metabolite signal near the water resonance, how the technique perturbs metabolite signals and the ability to phase spectra (De Graaf, 2018).

Commonly implemented on commercial MRI scanners is the chemical shift selective (CHESS) saturation technique (Haase et al., 1985). CHESS typically employees three, nominally 90 degree, Gaussian-shaped excitation RF pulses, which are attractive due to their relatively low R value (product of bandwidth and pulse length), and well-defined frequency selectivity (De Graaf, 2018). The CHESS module with RF pulses and dephasing gradients produce minimal effects on measured metabolite signals distant from the water signal (de Graaf et al., 1999). CHESS can be applied before the localization sequence and repeated multiple times to minimize imperfect suppression that occurs from T1 relaxation effects, inhomogeneities in the RF magnetic field and the spread of water frequencies. When T1 relaxation effects result in strong residual water signal, the water suppression enhanced through T1 effects (WET) technique provides better performance than CHESS in removing water signal

(Ogg et al., 1994). With WET, the nutation angle of the four RF pulses are optimized. Another method, variable pulse powers and optimized relaxation delays (VAPOR) demonstrates insensitivity to B_1-inhomogeneity and T1 relaxation with seven (or eight) frequency-selective RF pulses interspersed with optimized T1 recovery delays and providing a range of nutation angles (Tkac et al., 1999). Mescher Garwood (MEGA) is another frequency-selective refocusing technique that can be employed for water suppression as well as incorporated into J-difference editing MRS (Mescher et al., 1998, 1996). When used for water suppression, MEGA generates a stimulated echo or a Hahn spin-echo to dephase transverse water signal with minimal spectral distortions (Mescher et al., 1998, 1996). MEGA water suppression differs from CHESS, WET and VAPOR, as it can be interposed between the 180 localization pulses.

For most pediatric applications, the water suppression approaches do not differ from those applied in adults. However, it is important to consider the effects of maturation and myelination. The greatest degree of myelination occurs in the first 2 years of life. Water populations in the brain include those within the myelin sheath, possessing short T1 and T2 relaxation times, and those of free water not bound to macromolecules, having longer T1 and T2 relaxation times arising from water outside the myelin sheath in interstitial and intraaxonal compartments (Barkovich, 2000). Determining the percentage increase of water for the "wet" brain of the infant relative to the toddler, child or adult is a difficult endeavor. The immature brain may have very low concentrations of select metabolites (especially *N*-acetyl-aspartate and creatine), thus, optimizing water suppression via the suppression sequence while minimizing inhomogeneity of the static and transmit fields, is essential for obtaining diagnostic quality MR spectra in the infant (Bluml et al., 2014).

3. Common aspects: Outer volume suppression

Conventional localization approaches with voxel selection can often successfully avoid (in three dimensions) excitation sources of lipid signals, such as the scalp, especially in single voxel spectroscopy of children. However, for some cases, the diagnostic quality of the spectrum requires assurance that any detected lipid signal reflects the pathology and not a source from outside of the voxel. For example, grading pediatric neoplasms often requires assessing lesion lipid concentrations. Outer Volume Suppression (OVS) prevents unwanted signals, primarily lipids, from contaminating the acquired MRS region of interest. As with water, elevated lipids distort spectral baselines and interfere with quantification. Clinical MR systems provide several options for implementing saturation pulse modules ranging from single saturation bands to a scheme often used for spectroscopic imaging with a minimum of eight OVS slices positioned in an elliptical shape encompassing the circumference of the skull in the axial plane. These approaches implement slice-selective excitation of the lipid rich regions, then dephase the transverse magnetization via spoiling them with a magnetic field crusher gradient (Duyn et al., 1993). OVS is applied prior to localization with subsequent localization of the voxel yielding metabolite signals arising from the region of interest without contamination. The success of OVS depends on accounting for T1 relaxation and RF magnetic field inhomogeneity. The application of the OVS slice order and timing impacts the completeness of the saturation. Variations in the interpulse timings and the nutation angles can improve the results (De Graaf, 2018). A variety of pulses have been implemented for OVS including pure or modified Gaussian waveforms, hyperbolic secant waveforms (Smith et al., 2005), doubly modulated excitations (Singh et al., 1996), asymmetric 180 dual-frequency waveforms (BASING) (Star-Lack et al., 1998, 1997), and dual-frequency BISTRO (Henning et al., 2008). For infants, the addition of OVS may produce increases in SAR, especially with spectroscopic imaging, so a balance between diagnostic quality and OVS implementation must be achieved.

4. Common aspects: Shimming

Within the static magnetic field, interfaces between brain tissue, air, eyes and bone within the human head distort the magnetic field and produce susceptibility artifacts. Fortunately, the pediatric brain is relatively more homogeneous than the adult brain due to the more spherical shape of the skull and the lack of developed bony and air-filled structures such as the frontal sinus and nose. Reduced voxel sizes prescribed in the frontal lobe can continue to be problematic in terms of SNR and the placement proximity to the orbits produces susceptibility artifacts within the spectrum. Iron deposition within the globus pallidus does not occur until later childhood, thereby, allowing MRS sampling within the basal ganglia without metabolite and water signal broadening as observed in adults. Thus, shimming remains an essential element of proton MRS. Optimal water suppression, SNR, and metabolite signal lineshapes depend upon the level of homogeneity created by shimming to counter the effects of differing magnetic susceptibilities within tissue, air and bone. If homogeneity is poor, this will also adversely impact defining where signal from one metabolite begins and ends along with quantification.

Passive shimming occurs during scanner installation and achieves field correction by positioning ferromagnetic materials, such as steel or iron, in patterns at specific locations along the inner bore of the magnet (Wilson et al., 2002). Field mapping guides the service engineer to adjust the shims to achieve the optimal level of B_0 homogeneity. This process can achieve excellent static homogeneity, however, it is hampered when bore heating results in field shifts and the shims themselves become magnetized over time. Also, the passive shimming process is performed without a patient/participant within the magnet. An individual patient/participant creates additional, unique field distortions from diamagnetic susceptibility effects (Wilson et al., 2002). Therefore, a dynamic, active shimming process is also required to adjust for individual variations. This is achieved by generating a corrective magnetic field by placing currents through specialized shim coils which have designs similar to gradient coils. These coils are either resistive or superconducting. Each vendor provides distinct software for their systems to implement the adjustments. In effect, a mathematical model can be generated with solutions from mixtures of static plus linear first order terms (x-, y- and z-), second order terms (xy, zx, zy, xyz, x^2-y^2, and z^2), etc., in various directions (Juchem and de Graaf, 2017; Gruetter, 1993). While MRI is sensitive to magnetic field homogeneity, MRS is hypersensitive to it.

5. Localization

For voxel localization, MRS pulse sequences use a combination of gradients and RF pulses to isolate the signal in space, as well as optimize the signal for reliable analysis. Localization is achieved using slice-selective RF pulses with gradients to isolate a single volume of interest (voxel), what is commonly referred to as single-voxel spectroscopy (SVS). Phase-encoding can also be introduced to provide a signal from multiple voxels as a time, or magnetic resonance spectroscopic imaging (MRSI), a process similar to imaging but with less spatial resolution. Because MRS is used for the quantification of metabolite signals which are orders smaller in concentration than water, an optimized localization sequence providing good SNR and linewidth is essential for optimal postprocessing and interpretation.

5.1 Single voxel spectroscopy

SVS acquires metabolite signals in a specific region of interest. A spectrum is acquired from the intersection of three spatially-selective slices using frequency-selective RF pulses, producing a voxel with spatial resolution equal to the thickness of all three slices. For most commercial scanner systems, a user-friendly software interface for positioning a 3D cubic voxel on an anatomical image, typically a T1-weighted sequence, guides the acquisition site of the vendor-tailored SVS sequences. The most commonly used sequences are described below.

5.1.1 STEAM

STimulated Echo Acquisition Mode (STEAM) uses three 90-degree pulses which excite three orthogonal slices and localize the signal for the spectrum to a cubic region of interest as defined by the voxel placement in the scanner. This sequence can allow for very short TE acquisitions and thus can acquire a signal from short-lived metabolites reliably, however with relatively low SNR compared to other methods. This may be beneficial for subjects that are prone to movement and fetal scanning. Increasing the number of acquisitions can increase the signal, however this will lead to a longer acquisition time, which may render the potential benefits obsolete. Historically, this sequence was used as the 90-degree pulses demanded less power from the RF amplifier. For modern MR systems, STEAM is typically used for 7 T MRS acquisitions due to SAR considerations and demand for precise localization.

5.1.2 PRESS

Point-resolved spectroscopy (PRESS) differentiates itself from STEAM by using one 90-degree pulse followed by two 180-degrees pulses. The acquired signal is a spin echo and thus has higher SNR (nearly twice) than STEAM (Wilson et al., 2019). Due to the longer frequency-selective RF pulses, PRESS cannot achieve echo times as short as with STEAM, but the increase in signal is beneficial to processing. However, due to the two 180-degree RF pulses, PRESS suffers from chemical shift displacement artifact (CSDA) which impacts the composition of tissue sampled with a contribution from outside of the voxel and thus, the interpretation of results.

Due to the small bandwidth of the 180-degree RF pulses, CSDA occurs more readily in PRESS than in STEAM. While the RF pulses are set at a single, center frequency, metabolite signals are slightly off-resonant of this frequency, thus leading to excitation of signal outside of the region of interest. Therefore, unwanted metabolite signals inevitably contribute to the spectrum. This displacement of metabolite signal can be further exaggerated with higher field strengths. However, because PRESS can achieve an echo time of around 30 ms with better SNR than STEAM, PRESS became the preferred choice at 1.5 T and 3 T, largely due to the increase in acquired signal.

5.1.3 LASER and semi-LASER

The large presence of CSDA from PRESS can be overcome by using adiabatic pulses which are effectively a series of shorter RF pulses that have virtually the same localization effect as a single pulse, but greatly reduce the CSDA due the larger bandwidth of each single pulse (Garwood and DelaBarre, 2001). LASER (Localization by Adiabatic Selective Refocusing) uses adiabatic pulses to replace all three pulses in PRESS with six adiabatic pulses, but this leads to long acquisition times. To minimize scan time, another sequence, known as semi-LASER, only replaces the two 180 degree pulses with four adiabatic pulses, thus giving the advantages of LASER, but without a large impact on scan-time (Deelchand et al., 2019). Semi-LASER has been shown to be provide more precise localization and is robust to subject movement (Wilson et al., 2019). Due to these advantages, semi-LASER has been recommended for localization in all research MRS studies, when possible (Wilson et al., 2019). However, SAR increases with Semi-LASER due to the use of adiabatic pulses, which may not be reasonable for some pediatric populations.

5.1.4 General considerations for SVS

While the selection of the localization sequence can influence SNR and linewidth, particularly in the case of semi-LASER, two other adjustments may be done to increase SNR: increase voxel size and acquire more spectral averages. Increasing voxel size effectively increases the amount of signal obtained during the acquisition. Obtaining more spectral averages allows for more information to be obtained and thus allows more reliable separation of metabolite signal from the noise, but at the expense of increased acquisition time.

5.2 Multivoxel spectroscopy

If a clinician or researcher is interested in multiple regions of interest, SVS can be used in different locations, but this will increase the overall examination time. Multivoxel spectroscopy, or MRSI, provides a way to acquire spectra from many regions in a single acquisition. Conceptually, MRSI is the combination of a SVS sequence and phase-encoding which allows for multiple regions of interest to be measured during a sequence. This method is more challenging than SVS because it is difficult to account for B_0 inhomogeneity across the entire region and intervoxel contamination due to off-resonant excitation. Additionally, MRSI typically has longer acquisition times than SVS and there is a larger amount of data for analysis, which may require substantial expertise for processing. A variety of fast MRSI techniques have been developed incorporating echo-planar, spiral, turbo and parallel imaging techniques (Al-Iedani et al., 2017; Zhu and Barker, 2011; Schar et al., 2016).

Another alternative to MRSI is the use of parallel reconstruction in accelerated multivoxel (PRIAM) spectroscopy (Boer et al., 2015). Using a similar encoding scheme, PRIAM can be used in studies that wish to acquire two separate regions of interest that are orthogonal to one another, such as right and left thalami or anterior and posterior cingulate cortices. This technique can also be combined with spectral editing to acquire novel metabolite signals, as will be addressed in the following section.

6. Spectral editing approaches

While signals for nearly 15 different metabolites appear within the standard proton spectrum, many more are also inherent, but are unable to be resolved due to signal overlap from metabolites with higher concentrations. Metabolites such as GABA, the primary inhibitory neurotransmitter in the CNS, or glutathione (GSH) are hidden by the more abundant NAA and Cr signal resonances. Using spectral editing, these metabolites can be measured.

One technique for parsing out hidden signals is J-difference editing. This approach can be used in combination with localization to acquire spectra capable of measuring select metabolite signals. A common method was adapted from the MEGA suppression technique, which uses a selective frequency RF editing pulse to extract information from the acquired spectra (Mescher et al., 1998). The method requires interleaved acquisition of two spectra: one with the selective editing RF pulse and one without. When the selective editing RF pulse is applied to the first spectrum, signal is suppressed at that frequency which also affects signal in other frequencies due to intrinsic scalar coupling within a molecule. The second spectrum is acquired without the editing pulse. The two spectra are subtracted from one another to yield a difference spectrum that only contains signals not influenced by the editing pulse, specifically, the edited metabolite signal of interest.

MEGA can be implemented with PRESS and semi-LASER for acquiring GABA, aspartate, GSH and lactate (Harris et al., 2017). Unfortunately, because two spectra are being acquired and the target metabolite signal is often of lower concentration, voxel sizes are relatively large and acquisition times can be significantly longer than standard localization methods due to increased number of averages necessary to obtain adequate SNR. However, a couple of recent advancements allow for acquiring more than one edited metabolite signal during one acquisition. HERMES (Hadamard Encoding and Reconstruction of MEGA-edited Spectroscopy) extends the MEGA approach to allow for simultaneous acquisitions for two low concentration, overlapped metabolite signals such as GABA and GSH (Saleh et al., 2016). HERMES employs four distinct acquisitions: one with two editing pulses, two with one editing pulse each, and one without editing pulses. Subtraction between the four acquired spectra yield two difference spectra, one for each edited metabolite. An example of the output is shown in Fig. 1B.

7. Postprocessing

Given the time constraints of operating an MRI scanner system in a clinical environment, metabolite signal ratios are usually employed both for SVS or MRSI rather than determining metabolite concentrations with corrections accounting for partial volume effects from mixtures of gray and white matter with cerebrospinal fluid, and altered signal characteristics due to water and metabolite relaxation properties. Typically, the creatine signal area is regarded as the reference metabolite, as both creatine and phosphocreatine are measured as a single resonance on proton MRS at typical MR field strengths. However, many pathologies (neoplasms, metabolic diseases, hypoxia, and ischemia) *do* alter the composite creatine signal and concentration. Yet, from among the primary three metabolites (*N*-acetyl aspartate, creatine, and choline), creatine is the most constant for the majority of conditions due to the measured pool combining creatine and phosphocreatine.

Clinically acquired proton spectra can be postprocessed with vendor-supplied scanner-installed software by the MR technologist with appropriate training. These software packages are acceptable for postprocessing clinical MRS. The packages range from fully automated with no selection of parameters or semiautomated requiring an operator to select a postprocessing protocol with parameters that mathematically treat the raw spectra and are readily modified by the technologist, physicist or radiologist based upon their preferences. These are adequate for an individual patient examination producing a basic integration of the signal area underneath each metabolite resonance. These signal areas can be referenced to one another to form ratios, which are often reported by the neuroradiologist within their overall interpretation of an MRI examination for a patient.

For clinical operations, users of MRS should define a specific protocol and routinely apply it in a consistent manner. While it may be the first inclination to sample a lesion, the first spectra acquired when developing a clinical MRS service should be healthy tissue in a region with either pure white matter or pure gray matter. For example, the standard locations for sampling in a pediatric population are typically the basal ganglia, frontal or parietal white matter, and parasagittal cortex either in the parietal or occipital lobe. The nominal single voxel dimension is 2 cm per side of the cubic region for a total voxel volume of 8 cm^3 (cc) in children 3 years and older. For infants and toddlers, this voxel can be too large, so reductions to produce a total 3–4 cc volume are acceptable. While voxel dimensions of 1 cm per cubic side are achievable, this selection rarely generates high quality spectra in routine clinical practice. Moving away from a cubic volume towards a rectangular prism is a way to maintain voxel volume with one side approaching 2 cm or more. The voxel shape can vary from the cube with different lengths to best match either the pathology or the structure. However, ideally, the total volume should remain consistent for relative quantification across patients/participants. It is very important to recognize that for a pediatric clinical MRS service employing ratios, the actual values obtained are not only age and sampling location specific, but also the technique specific (localization technique, water suppression technique, with or without OVS, voxel volume, etc.). With ongoing structural development and especially myelination, there will be age and maturation effects on the metabolic spectral profile. For children and adults, tissue type, specifically, whether the sample is mostly gray, mostly white or mixed contributions, influences the spectral metabolite profile. The technical factors influencing the ratios include the scanner type (as a vendor may have variation within their models or software platform), field strength, sampling conditions such as pulse sequence, water suppression, outer volume saturation, echo time, repetition time, voxel size and number of averages. Consistency in approach and voxel placement can alleviate technical variations allowing for the desired developmental and pathological features to be appreciated in the interpretation.

When more rigorous determinations of metabolite concentration are desired in either the clinical or research setting, there are several widely recognized software packages that read in data from the major clinical MRI vendors. LCModel (Provencher, 2001) and the Java-based Magnetic Resonance User Interface (jMRUI) (Ratiney et al., 2004) are among the most commonly used, independent spectral processing software packages. These software packages allow concentration estimates to be generated rapidly, but usually require extra off-line processing including extraction of the raw spectral data and transfer to a separate workstation.

LCModel is commercially available (now open source/freely available), off-line to the scanner software that compares a library of model spectra of known concentrations with the user's proton MRS data in the frequency domain. Model spectra within the LCModel library were constructed from either in vitro solutions of individual metabolites using the same field strength, pulse sequence and other general parameters or via computer simulations to produce the basis sets (Provencher, 1993). LCModel software enables all of the signals from metabolites across the entire spectrum to be modeled simultaneously. In addition, this approach accounts for multiple proton signals within an individual metabolite. In contrast, the MR system vendor software typically performs fitting on individual resonances independent of the relationship that one resonance has with another from the same molecule within the spectrum. With the known concentrations from the model metabolite solutions, LCModel software essentially iterates on various combinations of pure metabolite spectra via the basis sets to fit the user's spectral data and produce concentration estimates. Novel metabolites can be added to the basis sets to better characterize and quantitate spectra (Fig. 5) (Cecil et al., 2015; Wisnowski et al., 2016).

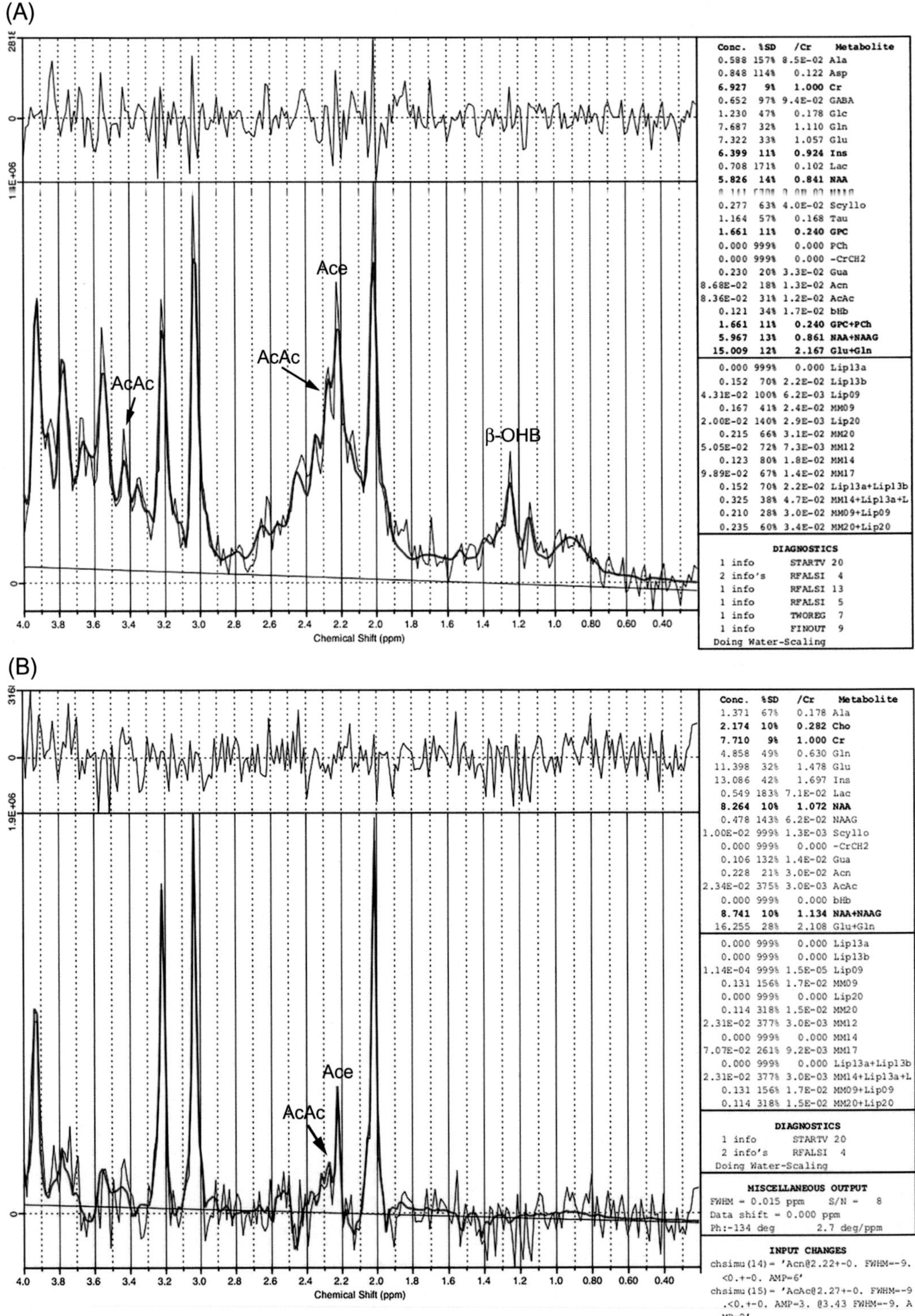

FIG. 5

see figure legend on opposite page

jMRUI (http://www.jmrui.eu) provides an advanced software package for processing MRS data within the time domain without user interventions employing black box quantitation algorithms based on singular-value decomposition. This tackles problems with the analyses by minimizing approximations and assumptions. jMRUI is made freely available to registered users.

Another open source MRS software package for research, known as Tarquin (tarquin.sourceforge.net), appears in several publications (Wilson et al., 2009, 2011; Gill et al., 2014; Manias et al., 2018). This program allows users to input raw spectroscopy data, postprocess, quantify and export output from the data to produce metabolite units of concentration.

Within an institution, these methods can be reliably used for research participant comparisons; however, further corrections are necessary, such as accounting for water and metabolite signal relaxation rates, tissue and cerebrospinal fluid compositions within the voxel, and the internal water concentration to convert the institutional unit to a measure of concentration such as millimolar units useful for comparisons across investigators using various scanner systems at multiple institutions. Details regarding these and additional corrections for proton MRS quantification have been reported (Barantin et al., 1997; Henriksen, 1995; Soher et al., 1996a, b; Kreis et al., 1993).

For postprocessing of spectral editing, LCModel software can be employed. However, Gannet (www.gabamrs.com) is software designed for user-friendly analysis of edited MRS data (Edden et al., 2014). The software was constructed to run without user intervention to help eliminate variance from quantification. Gannet processes the time domain data, conducts the appropriate subtractions and additions of edited and unedited spectra, performs coregistration of T1 anatomical imaging with the determination of gray matter, white matter and CSF voxel fractions, provides fitting of the edited spectrum and calculates tissue-corrected concentrations (Fig. 6).

8. Interpretation

Many studies have recognized early developmental patterns associated with brain maturation (Zhu and Barker, 2011; Kreis et al., 1993; Huppi et al., 1991; Kok et al., 2002a, 2002b; Heerschap et al., 2003; Girard et al., 2006a, 2006b, 2006c; Cetin et al., 2011.; Charles-Edwards et al., 2010; Limperopoulos et al., 2014; Story et al., 2011, 2013; Xu et al., 2011; Xu and Vigneron, 2010;

FIG. 5, cont'd

LCModel software with ketogenic metabolites. An example of LCModel software output is shown with spectra of a child treated with a ketogenic diet. (A) The raw processed short echo (35 milliseconds (ms)) proton spectrum is plotted in *black* with the spectral fitting overlay plotted in *red*. The difference between the raw data and the fitting is shown at the top of the figure as the line which should resemble noise. In this example, the fitting for several metabolites was incomplete with some narrow lines standing out in the difference spectrum. Additional parameters were added to the basis set to account for ketogenic metabolites, noted as beta-hydroxybutyrate (β-OHB), acetone (Ace) and acetoacetonate (AcAc). On the right hand side of the figure, the concentration estimated from the fitting, the percent standard deviation (also known as the Cramer-Rao bounds), the ratio of the concentration of the metabolite to creatine and the metabolite name are listed in the table. Lipids and Macromolecules are also estimated in this basis set. Diagnostics of the process are coded. For (B) additional outputs for the full width half maximum width (FWHM) of water is shown along with the signal to noise (S/N) and other items on the intermediate echo (TE 144 ms) spectrum with the Ace and AcAc labelled.

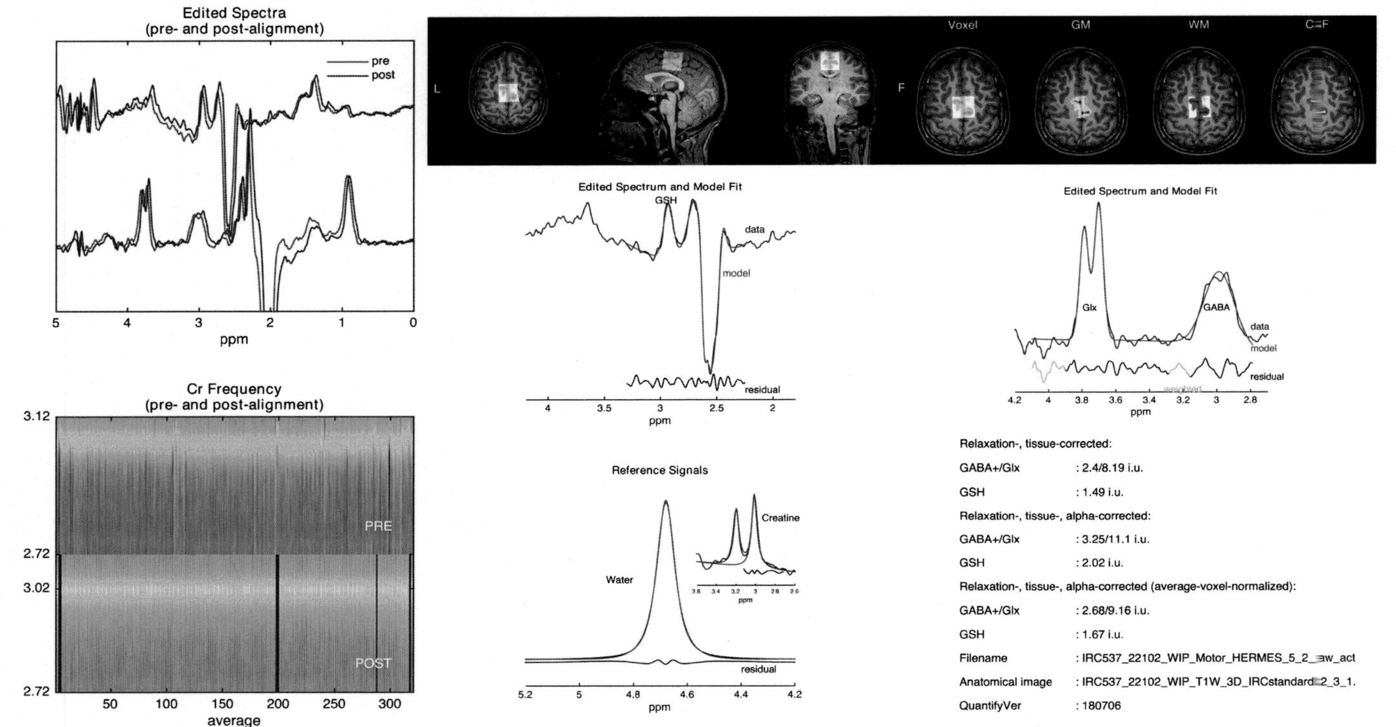

FIG. 6

Gannet software output for spectral editing. The raw spectra are loaded into Gannet software for automatic conversion to the edited spectra (top left). A correction for frequency drift based on the creatine signal is performed with an illustration showing the effect displayed in the bottom left of the figure. The spectral voxel is coregistered with the anatomical three dimensional (3D) T1 images (top middle). Segmentation of the voxel to account for gray matter (GM), white matter (WM) and cerebrospinal fluid (CSF) is featured in the top right. Center and right middle of the figure show the edited spectra for glutathione (GSH) and glutamate with glutamine (GLX) and γ-aminobutyric acid (GABA) noted on the raw and fitted spectra along with the residual difference. Middle bottom reference signals plot the water resonance and with the insert, the creatine and choline for the unedited spectra. Bottom right provides the quantitative output with corrections for the metabolites.

Kimura et al., 1995; Hart et al., 2014; Augustine et al., 2008; Roelants-van Rijn et al., 2004; Vigneron et al., 2001; Vigneron, 2006). Recognizing the point on the developmental curve is essential to properly evaluating metabolite concentrations as age and brain location influences normative levels of a metabolite signal within a patient or participant spectrum. MRS detected metabolite concentrations demonstrate significant changes from the fetal period, through birth and into the early postnatal period. NAA and Cr concentrations are initially very low during the fetal period, as evidenced from very preterm studies, but increase with age and appear to stabilize around 4 years of age (Kreis et al., 1993). The fetal brain features high concentrations of Cho prior to birth, which are thought to be stable in the first 3 months of life, however, these decrease with age (Story et al., 2013, 2011; Sone et al., 2017). The decrease is attributed to incorporation of phosphocholines into cellular membranes, which occur with myelination and maturation (Zhu and Barker, 2011; Xu et al., 2011). For example, regions such as cortical spinal tracts, which are recognized as among the fastest to mature, demonstrate increases in NAA and Cr with declines in Cho (Zhu and Barker, 2011; Xu et al., 2011). At 22 weeks gestational age, mI is also a prominent resonance that remains high at birth then declines over the first month of life (Girard et al., 2006a).

Bluml et al. observed that prematurity impacted the developmental time courses in parietal white matter for NAA, Cr, and Cho in preterm infants without evidence of structural injury (Bluml et al., 2014). Synchronization of white and gray matter maturation relevant for developmental processes was altered in preterm infants, especially those born before 28 weeks, compared to term born infants. Preterm parietal white matter NAA and Cr concentrations were initially higher than those born at term. However, the rate of increase with age for NAA and Cr concentrations those born preterm was significantly slower compared with term born infants with levels becoming comparable at approximately 350 postconceptual days. The Bluml et al. study results were consistent with the findings by Viola et al. that found premature neonates demonstrated higher NAA and Cr levels compared with fetuses (Bluml et al., 2014; Viola et al., 2011). This elevation could represent a “false start” in parietal white matter for maturational processes and/or increased higher energy demands due to the premature transition from the intrauterine to the oxygen-rich postnatal environment (Bluml et al., 2014).

NAA is localized primarily in neurons and axons and regarded as a biomarker of neuronal health and integrity (Moffett et al., 2007). NAA levels may reflect axonal outgrowth in white matter during development (Bluml et al., 2014; Moffett et al., 2007). After maturation, the concentration of NAA remains stable until later in life and reduces following neuronal injury and loss. High amounts of phosphocreatine, and creatine kinase are observed in glial cells (Wyss and Kaddurah-Daouk, 2000). Creatine transporter activity is high in astroglial cells in tissue cultures from embryonic or newborn rats (Wyss and Kaddurah-Daouk, 2000; Moller and Hamprecht, 1989). Creatine and phosphocreatine help regulate high-energy phosphate metabolism exerting a key role in the storage and transport of cellular energy (Wyss and Kaddurah-Daouk, 2000; Clark and Cecil, 2015).

MRS detects the trimethylammonium residues of choline and mobile choline-containing compounds to produce a signal appearing at 3.2 ppm. Mobile choline-containing compounds contribute to the net choline signal; immobile sources do not. Choline-containing compounds within the brain include choline, acetylcholine, phosphocholine, cytidine diphosphate choline and glycerophosphocholine (Cecil and Jones, 2001). While phosphatidylcholine is a major membrane constituent produced in all cells, it does not contribute significantly to the observable Cho signal (Cohen et al., 1995). Those contributing primarily include the intracellular pools of the membrane precursor phosphocholine (PC), membrane breakdown product glycerophosphocholine (GPC) and a small portion ($\sim$5%) of free choline for an approximate total observable choline concentration estimated between 1 and 2 mM. However,

Bluml reports that in the newborn, approximately 25% of the signal has been estimated to arise from phosphorylethanolamine and glycerolphosphorylethanolamine (Bluml et al., 1999). The study also observed phosphocholine was observed as initially high with phosphorus MRS in the newborn brain and subsequently decreases (Bluml et al., 1999). In contrast, glycerolphosphocholine is initially low but then rises in the newborn brain. Changes in the Cho level are intrinsically connected to membrane biochemistry. Elevations of the resonance can either reflect the precursors of myelin synthesis or the degradation products upon myelin degradation and/or destruction. Thus, the interpretation of changes associated with Cho can be complex as multiple processes may be occurring with regional variation across the developing brain.

9. Significant discoveries afforded from proton MRS

Within the course of clinical MRS practice, proton MRS significantly contributed to the discovery (creatine deficiency syndromes including GAMT deficiency and creatine transporter deficiency, Leukoencephalopathy with Brainstem and Spinal Cord Involvement and Lactate Elevation), characterization (Canavan's Disease) and management of several pediatric diseases (nonketotic hyperglycinemia). Illustrative spectra and images are featured in Figs. 7–11.

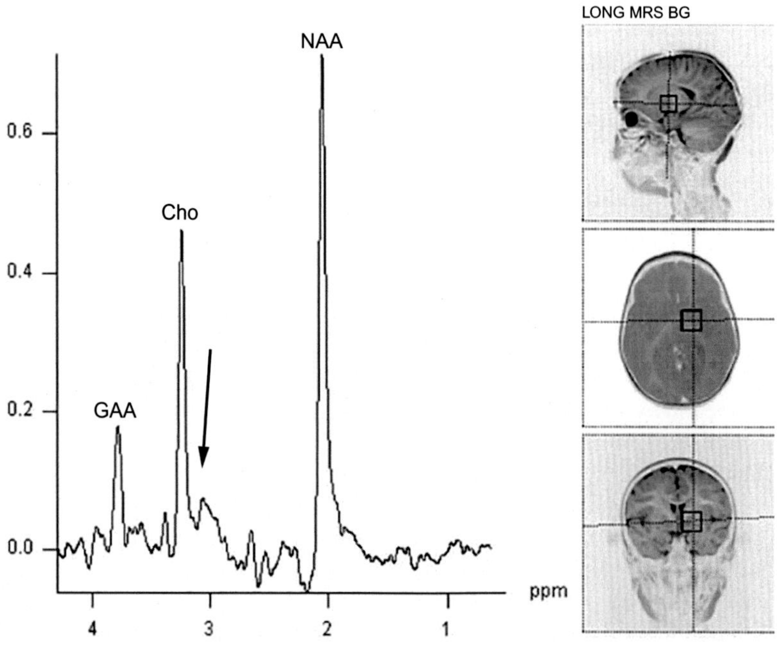

FIG. 7

Guanidinoacetate methyltransferase deficiency (creatine synthesis defect). Long echo (288 milliseconds (ms)) proton spectrum acquired at 1.5 Tesla field strength within the basal ganglia of a 5 year old female patient with guanidinoacetate methyltransferase (GAMT) deficiency. The defect results in the accumulation of guanidinoacetate (GAA) noted at 3.8 ppm and the absence of creatine, noted with the black arrow at 3.0 ppm. Levels of *N*-acetyl aspartate (NAA) and Cholines (Cho) are within normal limits.

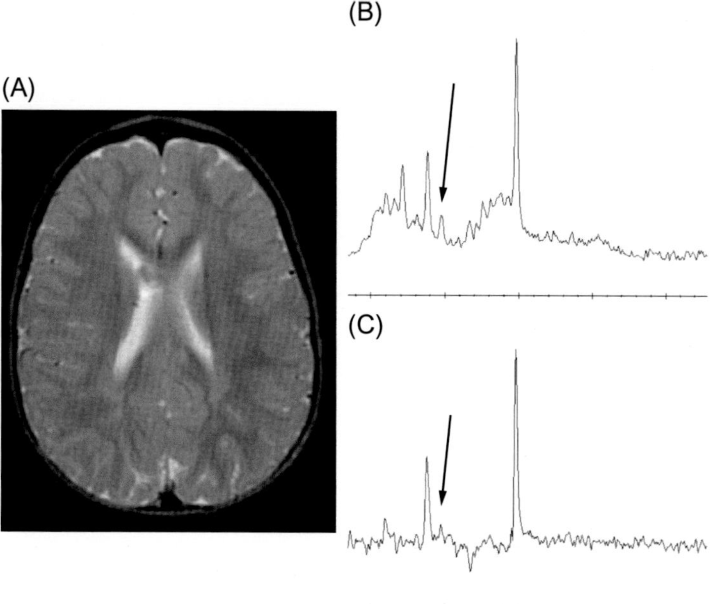

FIG. 8

Creatine Transporter Deficiency. (A) Voxel location within left parietal white matter for all spectra shown on an axial T2 weighted image. (B) Short echo (35 milliseconds (ms)) proton spectrum shows a diminished resonance at 3.0 ppm (*black arrow*) for what should be creatine and phosphocreatine (Cr). (C) The Cr resonance remains reduced (*black arrow*) on long echo (288 ms).

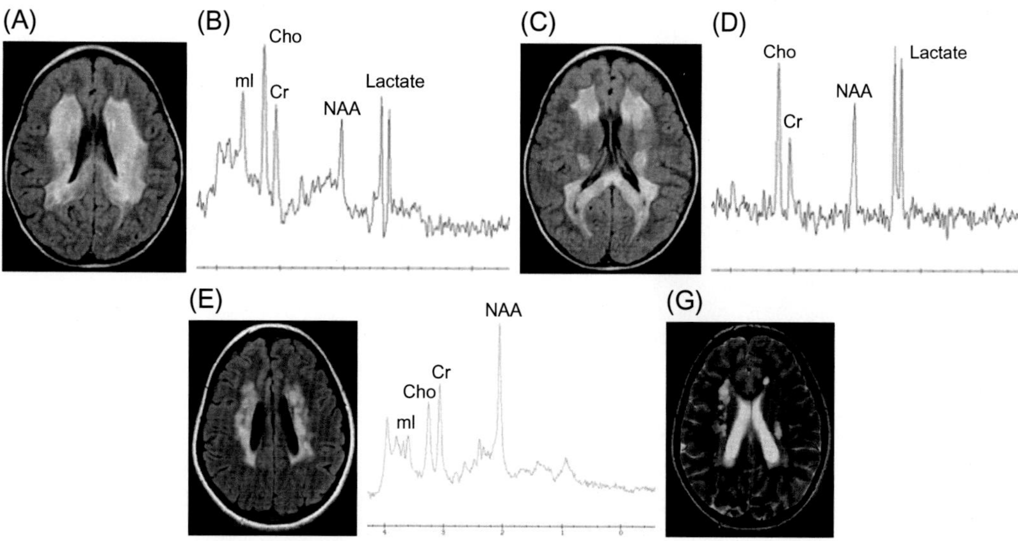

FIG. 9

Leukoencephalopathy with brainstem and spinal cord involvement and elevated lactate (LBSL). In a 2-year-old female patient with LBSL, axial fluid attenuated inversion recovery (FLAIR) images (A and C), short echo (35 milliseconds (ms)) and long echo 288 ms) (B and D) for a voxel positioned within the parietal white matter reveal dramatic elevations of lactate, marked elevations for choline (Cho) and myoinositol (ml) with reductions of *N*-acetyl aspartate (NAA). At 17 years of age, the imaging (E and G) show less confluent signal abnormality with resolution of the lactate signal and normalization of primary metabolites (NAA, creatine and phosphocreatine (Cr), Cho and ml).

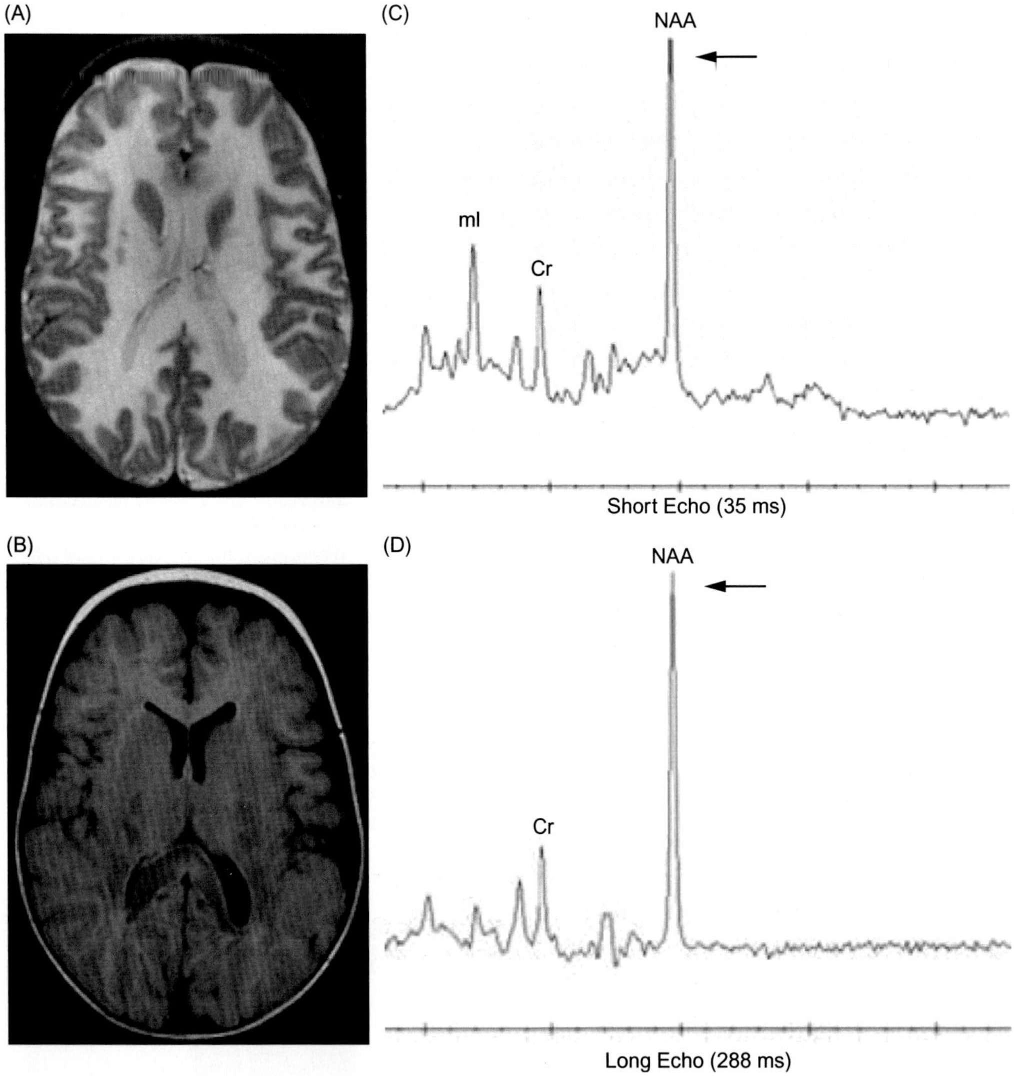

FIG. 10

Canavan's disease. (A) Axial T2 weighted and (B) fluid attenuated inversion recovery (FLAIR) images of a 12-month-old female diagnosed with Canavan's Disease. (B) Short echo (35 milliseconds (ms)) proton spectrum acquired within the frontal white matter revealed a dramatically elevated *N*-acetyl aspartate (NAA) resonance (*black arrow*), mildly increased myoinositol (mI) relative to creatine and phosphocreatine (Cr). C) The NAA resonance (*black arrow*) on long echo (288 ms) confirms the striking elevation relative to all other metabolite signals.

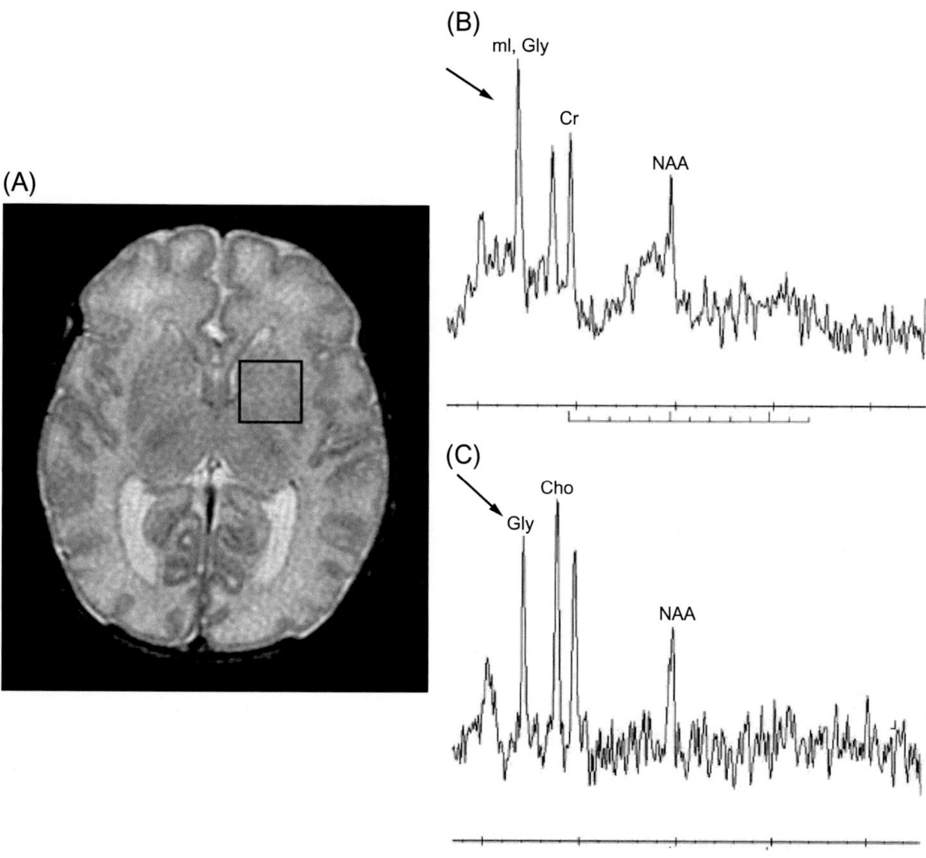

FIG. 11

Nonketotic hyperglycinemia. (A) Axial T2 weighted image with voxel localization within the basal ganglia (*black square*) of a neonate with nonketotic hyperglycinemia. (B) Short echo (35 milliseconds (ms)) proton spectrum reveals a significant elevation of the combined resonance of glycine (Gly) and myoinositol (ml) at 3.5 ppm (*black arrow*). (C) Intermediate echo (144 ms) spectrum features the Gly resonance (*black arrow*) as the ml contribution is minimized with T2 relaxation effects. Both spectra feature relatively low NAA levels which are appropriate for age.

10. Summary/future directions

In some instances, MRS provides novel and unique information leading to disease discovery and individual diagnoses. However, the routine implementation of MRS within clinical and research settings has a distinct purpose that typically provides support for a given diagnosis, enhanced characterization and monitors therapeutic response for various conditions and diseases. Understanding the principles behind MRS described in this chapter and optimizing them with further innovation and technique development, especially spectral editing, will augment the usage of MRS. Future progress with software that supports radiologist interpretation, particularly within pediatrics, will be transformative for clinical practice. Finally, better multidisciplinary integration to unravel disease mechanisms with genetic investigations, functional imaging and MRS are needed to advance care.

References

Al-Iedani, O., et al., 2017. Fast magnetic resonance spectroscopic imaging techniques in human brain—applications in multiple sclerosis. J. Biomed. Sci. 24 (1), 17.

Anon, 2014. Criteria for Significant Risk Investigations of Magnetic Resonance Diagnostic Devices–Guidance for Industry and Food and Drug Administration Staff. United States Health and Human Services, Food and Drug Administration, Rockville, MD.

Augustine, E.M., et al., 2008. Can magnetic resonance spectroscopy predict neurodevelopmental outcome in very low birth weight preterm infants? J. Perinatol. 28 (9), 611–618.

Barantin, L., Le Pape, A., Akoka, S., 1997. A new method for absolute quantitation of MRS metabolites. Magn. Reson. Med. 38 (2), 179–182.

Barkovich, A.J., 2000. Concepts of myelin and myelination in neuroradiology. AJNR Am. J. Neuroradiol. 21 (6), 1099–1109.

Bielicki, G., et al., 2004. Brain GABA editing by localized in vivo (1)H magnetic resonance spectroscopy. NMR Biomed. 17 (2), 60–68.

Bluml, S., Seymour, K.J., Ross, B.D., 1999. Developmental changes in choline- and ethanolamine-containing compounds measured with proton-decoupled (31)P MRS in in vivo human brain. Magn. Reson. Med. 42 (4), 643–654.

Bluml, S., et al., 2014. Metabolic maturation of white matter is altered in preterm infants. PLoS One 9 (1), e85829.

Boer, V.O., et al., 2015. Parallel reconstruction in accelerated multivoxel MR spectroscopy. Magn. Reson. Med. 74 (3), 599–606.

Cecil, K.M., Jones, B.V., 2001. Magnetic resonance spectroscopy of the pediatric brain. Top. Magn. Reson. Imaging 12 (6), 435–452.

Cecil, K.M., et al., 2015. Brain ketones detected by proton magnetic resonance spectroscopy in an infant with Ohtahara syndrome treated with ketogenic diet. Pediatr. Radiol. 45 (1), 133–137.

Cetin, I., et al., 2011. Lactate detection in the brain of growth-restricted fetuses with magnetic resonance spectroscopy. Am. J. Obstet. Gynecol. 205 (4), 350 e1–350 e7.

Charles-Edwards, G.D., et al., 2010. Non-invasive detection and quantification of human foetal brain lactate in utero by magnetic resonance spectroscopy. Prenat. Diagn. 30 (3), 260–266.

Choi, I.Y., Lee, S.P., Shen, J., 2005a. Selective homonuclear Hartmann-Hahn transfer method for in vivo spectral editing in the human brain. Magn. Reson. Med. 53 (3), 503–510.

Choi, I.Y., Lee, S.P., Shen, J., 2005b. In vivo single-shot three-dimensionally localized multiple quantum spectroscopy of GABA in the human brain with improved spectral selectivity. J. Magn. Reson. 172 (1), 9–16.

Chou, I.J., et al., 2014. Subjective discomfort in children receiving 3 T MRI and experienced adults' perspective on children's tolerability of 7 T: a cross-sectional questionnaire survey. BMJ Open 4 (10), e006094.

Clark, J.F., Cecil, K.M., 2015. Diagnostic methods and recommendations for the cerebral creatine deficiency syndromes. Pediatr. Res. 77 (3), 398–405.

Clayton, D.B., et al., 2001. 1H spectroscopy without solvent suppression: characterization of signal modulations at short echo times. J. Magn. Reson. 153 (2), 203–209.

Cohen, B.M., et al., 1995. Decreased brain choline uptake in older adults. An in vivo proton magnetic resonance spectroscopy study. JAMA 274 (11), 902–907.

de Graaf, R.A., van Kranenburg, A., Nicolay, K., 1999. Off-resonance metabolite magnetization transfer measurements on rat brain in situ. Magn. Reson. Med. 41 (6), 1136–1144.

Deelchand, D.K., et al., 2019. Across-vendor standardization of semi-LASER for single-voxel MRS at 3T. NMR Biomed., e4218.

Drost, D.J., et al., 2002. Proton magnetic resonance spectroscopy in the brain: report of AAPM MR task group #9. Med. Phys. 29 (9), 2177–2197.

Du, F., et al., 2004. In vivo GABA detection with improved selectivity and sensitivity by localized double quantum filter technique at 4.1T. Magn. Reson. Imaging 22 (1), 103–108.

Duyn, J.H., et al., 1993. Multisection proton MR spectroscopic imaging of the brain. Radiology 188 (1), 277–282.

Dydak, U., Schar, M., 2006. MR spectroscopy and spectroscopic imaging: comparing 3.0 T versus 1.5 T. Neuroimaging Clin. N. Am. 16 (2), 269–283 (x).

Edden, R.A., Barker, P.B., 2007. Spatial effects in the detection of gamma-aminobutyric acid: improved sensitivity at high fields using inner volume saturation. Magn. Reson. Med. 58 (6), 1276–1282.

Edden, R.A., et al., 2014. Gannet: a batch-processing tool for the quantitative analysis of gamma-aminobutyric acid-edited MR spectroscopy spectra. J. Magn. Reson. Imaging 40 (6), 1445–1452.

Garwood, M., DelaBarre, L., 2001. The return of the frequency sweep: designing adiabatic pulses for contemporary NMR. J. Magn. Reson. 153 (2), 155–177.

Gill, S.K., et al., 2014. Diagnosing relapse in children's brain tumors using metabolite profiles. Neuro-Oncology 16 (1), 156–164.

Girard, N., et al., 2006a. Assessment of normal fetal brain maturation in utero by proton magnetic resonance spectroscopy. Magn. Reson. Med. 56 (4), 768–775.

Girard, N., et al., 2006b. Magnetic resonance imaging and the detection of fetal brain anomalies, injury, and physiologic adaptations. Curr. Opin. Obstet. Gynecol. 18 (2), 164–176.

Girard, N., et al., 2006c. MRS of normal and impaired fetal brain development. Eur. J. Radiol. 57 (2), 217–225.

Gruetter, R., 1993. Automatic, localized in vivo adjustment of all first- and second-order shim coils. Magn. Reson. Med. 29 (6), 804–811.

Haase, A., et al., 1985. 1H NMR chemical shift selective (CHESS) imaging. Phys. Med. Biol. 30 (4), 341–344.

Harris, A.D., Saleh, M.G., Edden, R.A., 2017. Edited (1) H magnetic resonance spectroscopy in vivo: methods and metabolites. Magn. Reson. Med. 77 (4), 1377–1389.

Hart, A.R., et al., 2014. Diffusion-weighted imaging and magnetic resonance proton spectroscopy following preterm birth. Clin. Radiol. 69 (8), 870–879.

Heerschap, A., Kok, R.D., van den Berg, P.P., 2003. Antenatal proton MR spectroscopy of the human brain in vivo. Childs Nerv. Syst. 19 (7–8), 418–421.

Henning, A., et al., 2008. SELOVS: brain MRSI localization based on highly selective T1- and B1-insensitive outer-volume suppression at 3T. Magn. Reson. Med. 59 (1), 40–51.

Henriksen, O., 1995. In vivo quantitation of metabolite concentrations in the brain by means of proton MRS. NMR Biomed. 8 (4), 139–148.

Henry, P.G., et al., 2001. Brain GABA editing without macromolecule contamination. Magn. Reson. Med. 45 (3), 517–520.

Holland, S.K., et al., 2014. Data on the safety of repeated MRI in healthy children. Neuroimage Clin. 4, 526–530.

Huppi, P.S., et al., 1991. Magnetic resonance in preterm and term newborns: 1H-spectroscopy in developing human brain. Pediatr. Res. 30 (6), 574–578.

Juchem, C., de Graaf, R.A., 2017. B0 magnetic field homogeneity and shimming for in vivo magnetic resonance spectroscopy. Anal. Biochem. 529, 17–29.

Keil, B., et al., 2011. Size-optimized 32-channel brain arrays for 3 T pediatric imaging. Magn. Reson. Med. 66 (6), 1777–1787.

Kimura, H., et al., 1995. Metabolic alterations in the neonate and infant brain during development: evaluation with proton MR spectroscopy. Radiology 194 (2), 483–489.

Kok, R.D., et al., 2002a. Maturation of the human fetal brain as observed by 1H MR spectroscopy. Magn. Reson. Med. 48 (4), 611–616.

Kok, R.D., et al., 2002b. MR spectroscopy in the human fetus. Radiology 223 (2), 384 (author reply 384-5).

Kreis, R., Ernst, T., Ross, B.D., 1993. Development of the human brain: in vivo quantification of metabolite and water content with proton magnetic resonance spectroscopy. Magn. Reson. Med. 30 (4), 424–437.

Limperopoulos, C., et al., 2014. Injury to the premature cerebellum: outcome is related to remote cortical development. Cereb. Cortex 24 (3), 728–736.

Manias, K., et al., 2018. Evaluation of the added value of (1)H-magnetic resonance spectroscopy for the diagnosis of pediatric brain lesions in clinical practice. Neurooncol. Pract. 5 (1), 18–27.

McCann, M.E., Soriano, S.G., 2019. Does general anesthesia affect neurodevelopment in infants and children? BMJ 367, l6459.

Mescher, M., et al., 1996. Solvent suppression using selective Echo Dephashing. J. Magn. Reson. Ser. A 123, 226–229.

Mescher, M., et al., 1998. Simultaneous in vivo spectral editing and water suppression. NMR Biomed. 11 (6), 266–272.

Moffett, J.R., et al., 2007. N-Acetylaspartate in the CNS: from neurodiagnostics to neurobiology. Prog. Neurobiol. 81 (2), 89–131.

Moller, A., Hamprecht, B., 1989. Creatine transport in cultured cells of rat and mouse brain. J. Neurochem. 52 (2), 544–550.

Nixon, T.W., et al., 2008. Compensation of gradient-induced magnetic field perturbations. J. Magn. Reson. 192 (2), 209–217.

Ogg, R.J., Kingsley, P.B., Taylor, J.S., 1994. WET, a T1- and B1-insensitive water-suppression method for in vivo localized 1H NMR spectroscopy. J. Magn. Reson. B 104 (1), 1–10.

De Graaf, R.A., 2018. In Vivo NMR Spectroscopy: Principles and Techniques. third ed. (online resource) https://onlinelibrary.wiley.com/doi/book/10.1002/9781119382461.

Press Release. United States Health and Human Services, Food and Drrug Administration. October 12, 2017. 2017 https://www.fda.gov/news-events/press-announcements/fda-clears-first-7t-magnetic-resonance-imaging-device. Accessed 27 June 2020.

Provencher, S.W., 1993. Estimation of metabolite concentrations from localized in vivo proton NMR spectra. Magn. Reson. Med. 30 (6), 672–679.

Provencher, S.W., 2001. Automatic quantitation of localized in vivo 1H spectra with LCModel. NMR Biomed. 14 (4), 260–264.

Ratiney, H., et al., 2004. Time-domain quantitation of 1H short echo-time signals: background accommodation. MAGMA 16 (6), 284–296.

Roelants-van Rijn, A.M., et al., 2004. Cerebral structure and metabolism and long-term outcome in small-for-gestational-age preterm neonates. Pediatr. Res. 56 (2), 285–290.

Rothman, D.L., et al., 1993. Localized 1H NMR measurements of gamma-aminobutyric acid in human brain in vivo. Proc. Natl. Acad. Sci. U. S. A. 90 (12), 5662–5666.

Saleh, M.G., et al., 2016. Simultaneous edited MRS of GABA and glutathione. NeuroImage 142, 576–582.

Schar, M., Strasser, B., Dydak, U., 2016. CSI and SENSE CSI. In: eMagRes. 5, pp. 1291–1306.

Serrai, H., et al., 2001. Water modeled signal removal and data quantification in localized MR spectroscopy using a time-scale postacquistion method. J. Magn. Reson. 149 (1), 45–51.

Singh, S., et al., 1996. Simultaneous multislice rapid (SMR) FLASH MRI with hard pulse excitation. J. Magn. Reson. B 111 (3), 289–295.

Smith, M.A., et al., 2005. Simultaneous water and lipid suppression for in vivo brain spectroscopy in humans. Magn. Reson. Med. 54 (3), 691–696.

Soher, B.J., et al., 1996a. Quantitation of automated single-voxel proton MRS using cerebral water as an internal reference. Magn. Reson. Med. 36 (3), 335–339.

Soher, B.J., et al., 1996b. Quantitative proton MR spectroscopic imaging of the human brain. Magn. Reson. Med. 35 (3), 356–363.

Sone, D., et al., 2017. Noninvasive detection of focal brain hyperthermia related to continuous epileptic activities using proton MR spectroscopy. Epilepsy Res. 138, 1–4.

Stagg, C., Rothman, D.L. (Eds.), 2014. Magnetic Resonance Spectroscopy, first ed. Elsevier, p. 398.

Star-Lack, J., et al., 1997. Improved water and lipid suppression for 3D PRESS CSI using RF band selective inversion with gradient dephasing (BASING). Magn. Reson. Med. 38 (2), 311–321.

Star-Lack, J., et al., 1998. In vivo lactate editing with simultaneous detection of choline, creatine, NAA, and lipid singlets at 1.5 T using PRESS excitation with applications to the study of brain and head and neck tumors. J. Magn. Reson. 133 (2), 243–254.

Story, L., et al., 2011. Brain metabolism in fetal intrauterine growth restriction: a proton magnetic resonance spectroscopy study. Am. J. Obstet. Gynecol. 205 (5), 483 e1–483 e8.

Story, L., et al., 2013. Myo-inositol metabolism in appropriately grown and growth-restricted fetuses: a proton magnetic resonance spectroscopy study. Eur. J. Obstet. Gynecol. Reprod. Biol. 170 (1), 77–81.

Tkac, I., et al., 1999. In vivo 1H NMR spectroscopy of rat brain at 1 ms echo time. Magn. Reson. Med. 41 (4), 649–656.

Tocchio, S., et al., 2015. MRI evaluation and safety in the developing brain. Semin. Perinatol. 39 (2), 73–104.

van Der Veen, J.W., et al., 2000. Proton MR spectroscopic imaging without water suppression. Radiology 217 (1), 296–300.

Vannest, J., et al., 2014. Factors determining success of awake and asleep magnetic resonance imaging scans in nonsedated children. Neuropediatrics 45 (6), 370–377.

Vigneron, D., 2006. Magnetic resonance spectroscopic imaging of human brain development. Neuroimaging Clin. N. Am. 16 (1), 75–85.

Vigneron, D.B., et al., 2001. Three-dimensional proton MR spectroscopic imaging of premature and term neonates. AJNR Am. J. Neuroradiol. 22 (7), 1424–1433.

Viola, A., et al., 2011. Is brain maturation comparable in fetuses and premature neonates at term equivalent age? AJNR Am. J. Neuroradiol. 32 (8), 1451–1458.

Wilson, J.L., Jenkinson, M., Jezzard, P., 2002. Optimization of static field homogeneity in human brain using diamagnetic passive shims. Magn. Reson. Med. 48 (5), 906–914.

Wilson, M., et al., 2009. A quantitative comparison of metabolite signals as detected by in vivo MRS with ex vivo 1H HR-MAS for childhood brain tumours. NMR Biomed. 22 (2), 213–219.

Wilson, M., et al., 2011. A constrained least-squares approach to the automated quantitation of in vivo (1)H magnetic resonance spectroscopy data. Magn. Reson. Med. 65 (1), 1–12.

Wilson, M., et al., 2019. Methodological consensus on clinical proton MRS of the brain: review and recommendations. Magn. Reson. Med. 82 (2), 527–550.

Wisnowski, J.L., et al., 2016. The effects of therapeutic hypothermia on cerebral metabolism in neonates with hypoxic-ischemic encephalopathy: an in vivo 1H-MR spectroscopy study. J. Cereb. Blood Flow Metab. 36 (6), 1075–1086.

Wyss, M., Kaddurah-Daouk, R., 2000. Creatine and creatinine metabolism. Physiol. Rev. 80 (3), 1107–1213.

Xu, D., Vigneron, D., 2010. Magnetic resonance spectroscopy imaging of the newborn brain—a technical review. Semin. Perinatol. 34 (1), 20–27.

Xu, D., et al., 2011. MR spectroscopy of normative premature newborns. J. Magn. Reson. Imaging 33 (2), 306–311.

Zhu, H., Barker, P.B., 2011. MR spectroscopy and spectroscopic imaging of the brain. Methods Mol. Biol. 711, 203–226.

CHAPTER

Distortion, motion artifacts and how to address them

10

M. Dylan Tisdall

Radiology, Perelman School of Medicine, University of Pennsylvania, Philadelphia, PA, United States

1. Introduction

Distortions arising from imaging system imperfections and artifacts arising from motion are the major sources of errors in almost all MRI studies. As key limiting factors on the quality of neuroimaging data, these are the topics of intense interest to both the physicists and engineers who develop MRI methods, and the neuroscience community who uses them for quantitative studies. Many excellent reviews are available, addressing motion and/or imperfections in specific contexts, along with strategies for minimizing them (Jezzard and Clare, 1999; Pierpaoli, 2010; Maclaren et al., 2013; Zaitsev et al., 2015, 2017). While these technical surveys apply equally well to pediatric imaging, the particular challenges of mitigating motion in pediatric subjects are far larger than in many adult populations. While age-specific strategies have been developed to reduce subject motion (see Section 5.1), these are not completely effective. As a result, studies often assume a high failure rate for pediatric neuroimaging acquisitions, scheduling additional time for data reacquisition, or simply recruiting more subjects to account for data loss (Mathur et al., 2008; O'Shaughnessy et al., 2008; Barkovich et al., 2018).

While we strongly encourage readers to refer to the existing surveys for greater depth in specific sequences and artifacts, this chapter specifically: (1) provides a unified survey of the most common mechanisms through which motion and system imperfections produce artifacts across the common pediatric neuroscience MRI sequences; (2) makes clear the interactions between motion and system imperfections that impede correction of any individual component without considering the entirety of artifact sources; (3) highlights that these effects are not just an issue of "data quality," but in fact produce consistent biases in quantitative analyses of neuroimaging data; and (4) present an account of the most recent advances in correcting these artifacts, both in images and in subsequent quantitative analyses, emphasizing methods used in pediatric neuroimaging studies.

Toward these aims, we begin by discussing distortions of the image signal caused by system imperfections. We then consider how, in the absence of motion, these effects can be corrected using contemporary methods. We follow this with a discussion of how motion induces further imaging artifacts and also interacts with the system imperfections. Finally, we consider strategies for reducing motion artifacts, including mitigating their effects on quantitative analyses of group-level differences. Recognizing that this topic covers decades of advances in MRI and image analysis methods, we will direct readers to both the original works on these topics, and the most recent technologies being adopted in the field.

Handbook of Pediatric Brain Imaging. https://doi.org/10.1016/B978-0-12-816633-8.00002-8

2. Sources of distortion and "drop-out"

Spatial distortion in MRI occurs when imperfections in the imaging system lead to signal intensity being modulated and shifted from its "true" location in the image to an incorrect one. In addition, "drop-out" occurs when anatomy fails to generate a measurable signal, most frequently due to rapid, localized decay of the MRI signal before it can be imaged. In extreme cases, the result of these effects can be observed as "stretching" or "bunching" of the image, or "holes" where signal is suppressed. In more subtle cases, the anatomy is slightly warped or shaded, which can produce visually acceptable images but lead to errors in subsequent quantitative analyses. The magnitude of distortions is highly dependent on the MRI sequence and protocol used, but the general principles underlying the signal displacement are shared by the vast majority of pulse sequences.

Distortions directly impact quantitative morphometric analyses, producing images with incorrect shapes, thicknesses, volumes, etc. (van der Kouwe et al., 2008). However, other quantitative analyses can be similarly corrupted by distortions. In particular, differences in distortions between anatomical scans and subsequent BOLD or diffusion scans can lead to errors in localizing the observed functional and microstructural features within the brain (Saad et al., 2009).

Before considering strategies to mitigate the effects of distortion, we begin by describing three major sources of distortion in MRI: gradient nonlinearity, B_0 inhomogeneity, and eddy currents.

2.1 Gradient nonlinearity

The standard image-formation model for MRI assumes that linear gradients are used for spatial encoding. This is embedded in the definition of k-space, where we use the Fourier transform to represent the relationship between the spatial-domain signal and the measured signal at k-space location $\boldsymbol{k}$ (Ljunggren, 1983; Twieg, 1983). To express this formally, we start by letting $\Delta B(\boldsymbol{x},\tau)$ represents the time- and space-dependent variation in the main magnetic field induced by the encoding gradients. Under the assumption that $\Delta B(\boldsymbol{x},\tau)$ is spatially linear with no constant term, this simplifies to

$$\Delta B(\boldsymbol{x},\tau) = \Delta \boldsymbol{B}(\tau)\cdot \boldsymbol{x}. \tag{1}$$

If we now define $\boldsymbol{k}(t) = \gamma \int_0^t \Delta \boldsymbol{B}(\tau)d\tau$, with γ being the gyromagnetic ratio, we can write our signal equation as

$$F(\boldsymbol{k}(t)) = \int_{\Omega} f(\boldsymbol{x})e^{-i\,\boldsymbol{k}(t)\cdot\boldsymbol{x}}d\boldsymbol{x}, \tag{2}$$

which is the expected Fourier transform relationship of k-space ($f(\boldsymbol{x})$ defined within the region $\boldsymbol{x} \in \Omega$).

In practice, gradient coil designs must trade-off linearity against other desirable properties, such as switching speed (supporting rapid imaging methods) and peripheral nerve stimulation (Hidalgo-Tobon, 2010). Thus, Eq. (1) generally only represents a good approximation in a restricted region around a scanner's isocenter. To represent this formally, instead of assuming linearity of $\Delta B(\boldsymbol{x},\tau)$, assume there is a spatial transformation $\boldsymbol{x}' = \boldsymbol{g}(\boldsymbol{x})$, such that Eq. (1) instead holds in the transformed space,

$$\Delta B(\boldsymbol{x}',\tau) = \Delta \boldsymbol{B}(\tau)\cdot \boldsymbol{x}'. \tag{3}$$

Further assuming $\boldsymbol{g}(\boldsymbol{x})$ is invertible (which is generally true near scanner isocenter), substituting this into Eq. (2), and applying an inverse-Fourier transform produces a new, distorted image

$$\hat{f}(y) = f(g^{-1}(y))\left|\frac{dg^{-1}(y)}{dy}\right|, \tag{4}$$

where $\left|\frac{dg^{-1}(x')}{dx}\right|$ is the determinant of the Jacobian of the inverse coordinate transformation, representing the amount of "stretch" applied at each point in space by the nonlinear encoded gradient.

A graphical representation of this result is shown for a simulation applying a single nonlinear gradient direction applied to a 2D image in Fig. 1. Note that, as the effect of the sublinear gradient in the y axis is to both stretch the image and reduce the image intensity in the stretched regions.

Fortunately, gradient nonlinearity has high day-to-day reproducibility for a given scanner (barring scanner recalibration or hardware replacement) (Gunter et al., 2009). As such, the true spatial gradient functions can be computed, stored, and applied without the need for recalibration during individual scan sessions, which we will revisit in Section 3.1.

2.2 B_0 inhomogeneity

B_0 inhomogeneity results, in large part, from the interaction of the subject's tissue with the magnetic field. All substances have a magnetic susceptibility χ that quantifies the relationship between an imposed magnetic field (e.g., the scanner's main magnetic field) and the induced field within the object (Lüdeke et al., 1985). Moreover, boundaries between materials with very different magnetic susceptibilities (e.g., air and human tissue in the sinuses) cause distortions in the induced magnetic field that extend beyond just the boundary itself and into surrounding space (Lüdeke et al., 1985; Li et al., 1996). Therefore, even though the scanner's main field is carefully calibrated to be spatially homogenous, once a subject is loaded into the scanner, the local magnetic field becomes highly variable within the brain (or other tissues).

Unlike gradient nonlinearity, which is stable across subjects and generally represents smooth distortions of image space, B_0 inhomogeneity induced by the sample is both subject-dependent and can vary substantially over short distances. To mitigate this, scanners have automatic processes for

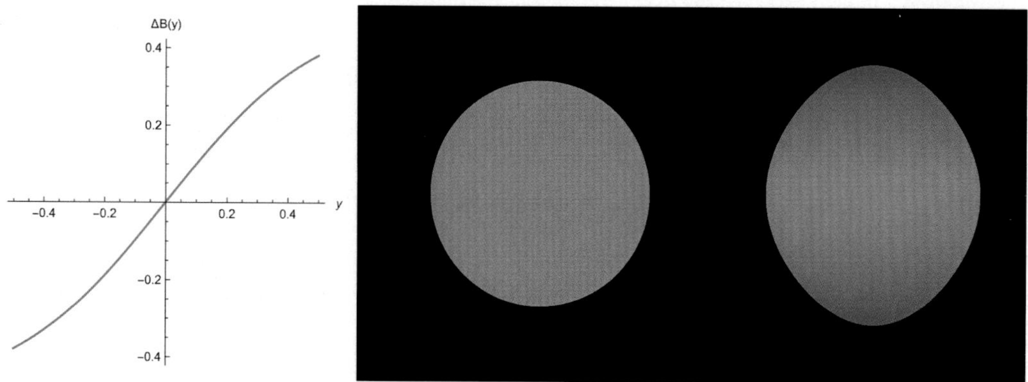

FIG. 1

Effect of a nonlinear encoding gradient applied in the *y*-axis. *Left:* Plot of the nonlinear encoding gradient applied along the *y*-axis. *Middle:* Image depicting the true signal, a homogeneous circle. *Right:* Distorted image resulting from applying the nonlinear encoding gradient on the *y*-axis and an ideal linear encoding gradient on the *x*-axis.

"shimming" the magnetic field based on measurements taken with the subject in position. This process generally consists of first measuring a field map (more on this in Section 3.2), fitting a low-order model describing the spatial variation in B_0 induced by the subject, and then applying current to shim coils, creating static magnetic fields to compensate for the measured inhomogeneity (Schneider and Glover, 1991; Webb and Macovski, 1991; Wen and Jaffer, 1995; Wilson et al., 2002).

While the built-in shimming process of modern scanners can correct for B_0 distortions that vary slowly in space, residual local errors around the sinuses and ear canals can still be significant (Ericsson et al., 1995; Li et al., 1996). Moreover, B_0 inhomogeneity increases with main field strength, and so these effects are much more visible at 3T than at 1.5T. These residual inhomogeneities cause two separate effects: spatial distortion and "drop-out."

2.2.1 Spatial distortion

Similar to the results for gradient nonlinearity shown in Section 2.1, B_0 inhomogeneity results in spatial distortions of the image. If the inhomogeneity is viewed as an additive magnetic field, $\Delta B_0(\boldsymbol{x})$, superimposed on the background homogenous B_0, then we can see that $\Delta B_0(\boldsymbol{x})$ will act as yet another encoding gradient. Note that its effects are different from that of gradient nonlinearities, in that $\Delta B_0(\boldsymbol{x})$ is "always on" and does not scale with applied encoding gradient fields (Lüdeke et al., 1985).

This can be made clear formally by modifying Eq. (2) to include a spatially varying but time-constant inhomogeneity term, $\Delta B_0(\boldsymbol{x})$, thus

$$\Delta B(\boldsymbol{x}, \tau) = \Delta \boldsymbol{B}(\tau) \cdot \boldsymbol{x} + \Delta B_0(\boldsymbol{x}). \tag{5}$$

Substituting this into our definition of k-space then gives $\boldsymbol{k}(t) = \gamma \int_0^t \Delta \boldsymbol{B}(\tau) d\tau$

$$F(\boldsymbol{k}(t)) = \int_{\Omega} f(\boldsymbol{x}) e^{-i\,[\boldsymbol{k}(t)\cdot \boldsymbol{x} + \gamma\, t \Delta B_0(\boldsymbol{x})]} d\boldsymbol{x}. \tag{6}$$

From this equation, we can see that, in an idealized sequence where all points in k-space are acquired at the same time t, the net effect of the off-resonance term is simply a spatially varying phase modulation of the resulting image. However, all practical sequences acquire different parts of k-space at different times and so we need to further understand how this time-varying phase in k-space will affect the final image.

In the frequency-encoded (i.e., readout) direction, we can see that our inhomogeneity term will result in each point in space resonating at the "wrong" frequency relative to what is anticipated based on the applied gradient. However, this "wrong" frequency will be constant at all measurement times. Thus, we can see that our inverse-Fourier transform in the frequency-encoded direction will simply map each point to the spatial location encoded by its "wrong" frequency. The exact size of the displacement in pixels can be computed from the total receiver bandwidth per pixel, BWpp—the observed displacement, in units of pixels, is then

$$\Delta \boldsymbol{x} = \frac{\gamma \Delta B_0(\boldsymbol{x})}{\text{BWpp}}. \tag{7}$$

The specific effect of this distortion on the resulting image requires further consideration of the specific encoding pattern employed by a given sequence. The simplest (and perhaps most-common) encoding pattern is Cartesian imaging, employed in high-resolution structural sequences like MPRAGE (*a.k.a.*, IR-SPGR or TFE). In these scans, one readout is acquired per TR, and it is acquired in the same readout direction every time, just with different phase-encoding gradients applied initially. Due to the identical timings, the distortions in the readout direction are identical for all samples. Moreover, since the timing of each TR is identical, there is no accumulated phase difference due to inhomogeneity between the various phase-encoding steps. Thus, Cartesian imaging will generally show a distortion exclusively in the readout direction. Note that, because readout bandwidths are generally quite high for structural sequences, these distortions are small except in regions of pronounced inhomogeneity (e.g., near sinuses or ear canals) (van der Kouwe et al., 2008).

EPI scans are somewhat unique, in that they extend the effective readout train, while allowing the phase due to inhomogeneity to accumulate across the phase-encoding steps. The time between phase-encoding steps is called the *echo spacing*, which we will denote ΔE. We can then see that each step will accumulate an additional phase of $\gamma \Delta B_0(\boldsymbol{x})\ \Delta E$. This will produce a linear phase-roll across the sequential phase-encoded k-space samples, which, when inverse-Fourier transformed, is the equivalent of a translation in image-space. The size of the distortion, in pixels, is given by

$$\Delta \boldsymbol{x} = \gamma \Delta B_0(\boldsymbol{x}) \Delta E\, n, \tag{8}$$

where n is the number encoding "steps" in the phase-encoded direction (i.e., the EPI acceleration factor).

Radial and spiral scans, by contrast, do not have a consistent frequency-encoded direction. As such, off-resonance distortions will manifest in the resulting images as blurring. This blur is spatially varying and locally proportional to $\Delta B_0(\boldsymbol{x})$, similar to the distortion in Cartesian and EPI scans (Noll et al., 1992).

As we can see from Eq. (6), the accumulated phase from the B_0 inhomogeneity is simply a function of time. Therefore, reversing the time-order of a readout in k-space (e.g., switching from positive to negative readout polarities, or reversing phase-encode blips in EPI) will, in turn, reverse the effective distortion from field inhomogeneities. This effect is best seen in EPI data, where reversing the phase-encode blip polarity reverses the direction of the distortions (Jezzard and Balaban, 1995) (see Fig. 2). Note that spin-echo acquisitions cannot correct for these errors, as the spatial distortions relate to the additional inhomogeneity "encoding gradient" during the readout train itself, which is the same in both spin- or gradient-echo EPI (see Figs. 2 and 3). While less obvious than the distortions in EPI-based acquisitions, even high-resolution structural scans, which generally rely on shorter readouts, are sensitive to this effect, as can be seen by reversing the polarity of the readout gradient (van der Kouwe et al., 2008).

2.2.2 Drop-out and blurring

B_0 inhomogeneity also leads to "drop-out" in regions with more severe gradient. This occurs when the inhomogeneity is significant within voxels, leading to dephasing of the signal before the echo is acquired (the rate of this exponential signal decay is denoted T_2^*) (Farzaneh et al., 1990; Johnson and Hutchison, 1985; Lipschutz et al., 2001; Ojemann et al., 1997). In general, this effect is most visible in gradient-echo scans; acquiring a spin-echo allows the effect of the inhomogeneity to be refocused, mitigating drop-out. Note, however, that many nominal spin-echo sequences (e.g., spin-echo EPI) do in fact still have some T_2^*-induced effects due to their readout occurring over a finite duration and not just at the instant of full signal-refocusing (see blue line in Fig. 3). This generally manifests as blurring in the phase-encode direction and a small amount of residual T_2^*-weighting, due to the variable amount of

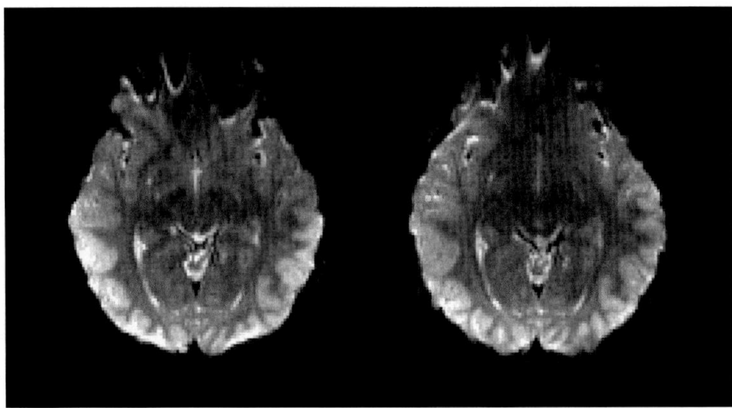

FIG. 2

Two spin-echo EPI images acquired with negative (left) and positive (right) polarity for the phase-encoding gradients, which were applied in the anterior-posterior direction. We can see that in regions of low B_0 inhomogeneity (e.g., the posterior region), there is little distortion and both images show similar anatomy. In regions with high B_0 inhomogeneity (e.g., orbitofrontal) there is substantial distortion in both images, just in opposite directions. Note that these are spin-echo images, showing that the effect of B_0 inhomogeneity on image distortion is not corrected due to errors accumulated over the readout itself. However, the spin-echo does allow us to recover some signal in the orbitofrontal cortex that would be lost to T_2^* in a gradient-echo EPI sequence.

refocusing over the readout duration, with the artifact becoming more apparent as the EPI echo train becomes longer (Duong et al., 2002; Farzaneh et al., 1990).

To understand the source of this blur more formally, we can add a term for T_2^* to our previous signal Eq. (2), producing

$$F(\boldsymbol{k}(t)) = \int_{\Omega} f(\boldsymbol{x}) e^{-\frac{t}{T_2^*} - i\,\boldsymbol{k}(t)\cdot\boldsymbol{x}} d\boldsymbol{x}. \tag{9}$$

Assuming $\boldsymbol{k}(t)$ advances linearly in time with sampling interval Δt and encoding step size $\Delta \boldsymbol{k}$, and performing an inverse-Fourier transform on this results in the observed image $\hat{f}(\boldsymbol{x})$ being defined by

$$\hat{f}(\boldsymbol{x}) = f(\boldsymbol{x}) \circledast L(\boldsymbol{x}), \tag{10}$$

where $\circledast$ represents convolution, and $L(\boldsymbol{x}) = \left(\frac{\Delta t}{\Delta \boldsymbol{k}\, T_2^*} + i\,\boldsymbol{x}\right)^{-1}$ is a Lorentzian function extending in the direction in which $\boldsymbol{k}(t)$ was moving through time (i.e., in EPI we would be interested in the blur in the phase-encoded direction, and the sample time would be the echo spacing), and whose width is inversely proportional to T_2^* (Farzaneh et al., 1990; Johnson and Hutchison, 1985).

2.3 Eddy currents

Eddy currents, induced in components of the MRI scanner by the switching of the encoding gradients, in turn produce their own magnetic fields that are both spatially and temporally variable, overlaid on the background B_0 inhomogeneity and further distorting the image. Eddy currents are minimized by design of the physical hardware as well as real-time modifications of the gradient waveforms to compensate for the resulting eddy-current fields (Boesch et al., 1991). The result of these improvements is that, in

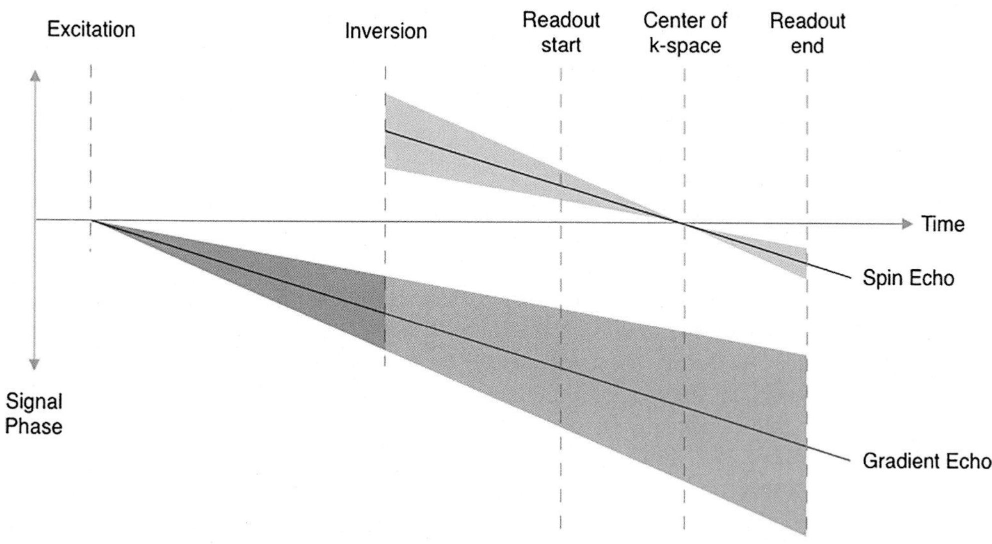

FIG. 3

Schematic of signal phase error evolution in spin-echo *(blue)* and gradient-echo *(red)* readouts due to background inhomogeneity. We depict the evolution of a single point as *solid lines*, while we show the evolution of all spins in a voxel via the shaded triangles. Both spin- and gradient-echo sequences start with no accumulated phase at the time of excitation, and then proceed to accumulate phase errors linearly with time *(purple region)*. The two signal paths diverge at the inversion time, as the gradient-echo has no inversion pulse and continues along the red line, while the spin-echo sequence inverts the spins and thus the accumulated phase errors, before proceeding along the blue line. We note that, for each individual point, the difference in phase between the start and end of the readout is the same for both spin- and gradient-echo sequences—therefore they both exhibit the same distortion due to this additional "encoding gradient." However, the spin-echo sequence has 0 phase error within the voxel at the center of *k*-space, regardless of the magnitude of the inhomogeneity, while the gradient-echo sequence accumulates a local phase error—thus gradient-echo is sensitive to drop-out due to large local dispersion of phases within the voxel, while spin-echo is largely immune.

modern scanners, eddy currents are negligible in many common imaging sequences. However, their effects are still acute in most DWI protocols, due to the large diffusion-encoding gradients employed, particularly at higher *b*-values used for more advanced diffusion analysis methods. As each volume of a DWI sequence is encoded with a different orientation and duration for the gradient, so too do the induced eddy-current fields vary with each diffusion-encoding step (Jezzard et al., 1998; Rohde et al., 2004). The outcome is a series of volumes with unique spatial distortions that must be corrected before quantification of diffusion parameters, to ensure that voxel locations in each volume truly correspond to the same anatomy.

3. Mitigating distortion

Depending on the source of the distortion, a variety of techniques have been developed for their mitigation, either by minimizing their size in the initial data, or by undistorting data using postprocessing approaches. In many cases, small changes to imaging protocols can have substantial effects on these artifacts, and so careful optimization of acquisition is always the first opportunity to ensure high-quality data. To that end, in this section, we will consider specific strategies to mitigate each of the distortions outlined in Section 2.

3.1 Gradient unwarping

The majority of scanners sold today have vendor-provided 3D unwarping algorithms that are highly effective, run nearly instantaneously on the scanner console itself, and thus minimize the need for custom postprocessing in routine structural imaging. Fig. 4 shows an example of an image acquired with and without applying the vendor-supplied gradient unwarping algorithm.

However, these algorithms are generally implemented as interpolations in the image domain, and thus introduce unavoidable blurring (Tao et al., 2015). When multiple geometric transformations are to be applied to an image as part of a processing pipeline, this compounding of the blurring can further reduce image quality. Instead, it may be preferable to start from a "raw" image volume without vendor-provided unwarping, and apply a single interpolation based on the composition of the various geometric transforms relevant for a particular analysis (Glasser et al., 2013).

3.2 Off-resonance maps

Given that the major source of B_0 inhomogeneity is the susceptibility of the tissue, which does not vary with time, we can map the inhomogeneity and use it as part of a subsequent correction algorithms. As the distortions due to off-resonance are generally most-pronounced in EPI, most work has focused on correcting these scans. Most popular strategies for mapping the field inhomogeneity rely on either:

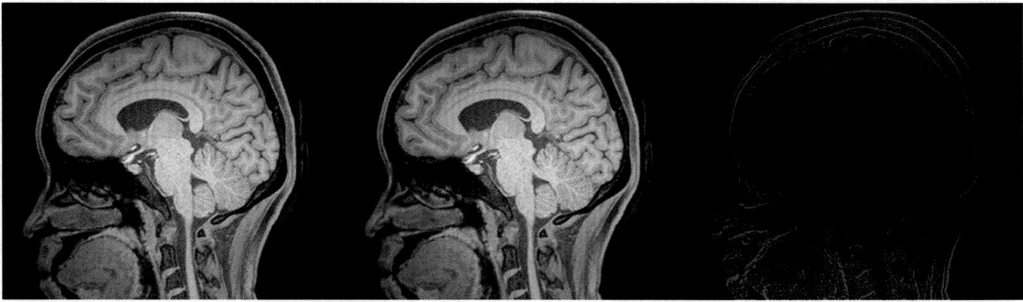

FIG. 4

Effect of the vendor-supplied 3D gradient unwarping algorithm on a T_1-weighted structural scan. *Left*: image acquired without gradient unwarping. *Middle:* identical slice location, with gradient unwarping applied. *Right:* normalized difference image, with *blue* indicating voxels that were brighter in the distorted image, and *red* indicating voxels that were brighter in the undistorted image. As this subject was well-positioned at isocenter, the effects in the brain are relatively small, although notable discrepancies are still present at the most dorsal and frontal parts of the brain.

(1) a separate scan specifically sensitized to the local phase-evolution due to inhomogeneity (Ericsson et al., 1995; Hutton et al., 2002); or
(2) reversing the polarity of the readout and relying on the reversal of distortions to localize inhomogeneity (Bowtell et al., 1994; Chang and Fitzpatrick, 1992; Andersson et al., 2003; Holland et al., 2010).

In general, acquiring a separate field map can be performed in a matter of minutes at high resolution (e.g., 1 mm isotropic) using a multiecho gradient-echo sequence, with echo times chosen to match the phase difference between fat and water at both echo times (Jezzard and Balaban, 1995; Funai et al., 2008). This provides a distortion-free reference for the true field inside the brain and is often taken as the "gold standard" for off-resonance maps.

Critically, it has been shown that, even when given a "perfect" field map, the undistortion of EPI data acquired with a single phase-encode polarity is ill-posed, resulting in noise amplification and artifacts in undistorted images if care is not taken (Andersson et al., 2003). Conceptually, this is the result of signal from several voxels "bunching" into a single voxel in the measured image—it is then impossible to accurately "unmix" this signal back into the original voxels. These negative effects of undistortion from a single-polarity image can be reduced through careful regularization of the undistortion map, enabling approximate correction of single-polarity time-series (e.g., EPI-based BOLD fMRI) without the need for matched opposite-polarity image pairs (Holland et al., 2010).

Moreover, it has been found that the off-resonance map itself can be extracted from careful analysis of matched spin-echo EPI scans with reversed phase-encoding polarity (Andersson et al., 2003; Holland et al., 2010). Due to their time-efficiency and demonstrated efficacy, these methods have been incorporated in several large multicenter imaging studies (Casey et al., 2018; Harms et al., 2018) and become de facto standards across many smaller studies as well.

3.3 Increasing encoding gradient amplitudes

In the context of 3D-encoded high-resolution structural scans, inhomogeneity is generally only an issue relative to the size of the readout gradient. Increasing the readout gradient in these sequences implies increasing the receiver bandwidth and more rapidly traversing *k*-space in the readout direction. Referring to Eq. (7), we can see that, all else being equal, increasing the bandwidth per pixel will indeed reduce distortion. While this reduces distortions, it has the negative consequence of also reducing SNR. Acquiring multiple high-bandwidth echoes, in the place previously filled by a single low-bandwidth echo, gains back SNR, while retaining the low-distortion benefit of larger encoding gradients (Macovski, 1996; van der Kouwe et al., 2008).

In EPI, we are generally concerned with the scale of inhomogeneity relative to the effective phase-encoding gradient (i.e., the time-average of the phase-encoding blips over the duration of the entire readout). Simply increasing the readout bandwidth has only a marginal effect, as the dominant factor in the total EPI readout duration is the number of phase-encoding steps and the echo spacing. Considering Eq. (9), and assuming a fixed resolution and echo spacing (as EPI echo spacing is normally minimized to the limits of the hardware), the number of phase-encoding steps is then the last quantity that can be reduced to minimize distortion. The number of steps, and thus total readout duration, can be reduced by

(1) acquiring asymmetric coverage of *k*-space ("partial Fourier") (Jesmanowicz et al., 1998);

(2) using parallel acceleration (e.g., GRAPPA or SENSE) to reduce the number of phase-encoding steps (de Zwart et al., 2002); or

(3) segmenting the readout across multiple excitations (*a.k.a.*, multishot), reducing the effective duration for any single readout train (Hoogenraad et al., 2000).

3.4 Eddy-current compensation

Beyond the built-in scanner features to minimize eddy currents, the use of bipolar gradients for diffusion-encoding, either with a single refocusing pulse or spread around two refocusing pulses, has been widely studied (Alexander et al., 1997; Finsterbusch, 2009; Reese et al., 2003), and can have the benefit of also reducing motion sensitivity (which we discuss in Section 4.3) (Norris, 2001). For a specific protocol and scanner, it is possible to alter the relative durations of the four pulses in this scheme to compensate specific eddy currents (Reese et al., 2003). However, the cost of this approach is a significant increase in echo time and concomitant decrease in SNR, relative to monopolar acquisition. Therefore, there is a strong incentive to use monopolar sequences with worse eddy currents, and address the resulting distortion during the quantitative analysis stage, which we will discuss in Section 5.6.

Eddy currents are not significantly impacted by the subject in the scanner. Thus, an alternative to compensation is to instead fully measure the induced eddy-current fields, using either a prescan or separate field-monitoring hardware attached to the scanner, and then include them in a more advanced reconstruction algorithm (Horsfield, 1999; Wilm et al., 2011).

4. Sources of motion artifacts

Motion artifacts are a nearly unavoidable aspect of pediatric neuroimaging as many subjects are developmentally unable to fully cooperate and remain still for the complete MRI study. Subject head motion causes several distinct types of errors, all of which interact with choices in the design of the particular protocol. To start, we will highlight four major sources of error, as they arise from separate mechanisms, although in practice they all are superimposed to create the appearance of motion artifacts in images.

4.1 Inconsistencies in spatial encoding

Likely the most intuitive and readily apparent artifact due to motion is the inconsistent location of the anatomy in the resulting images. In rapid single-shot slice-selective sequences (e.g., EPI or HASTE), motion is generally "frozen" within each image slice, as each slice is acquired so quickly that little motion can occur during the measurement itself. However, over the duration of the entire scan, the subject can move considerably, with the general effect of producing position inconsistencies between neighboring slices. This effect is most pronounced when slices are acquired in an interleaved order (i.e., even slices first, then odd), as the time elapsed between neighboring slices can be a second or more, depending on the TR of the sequence (Zaitsev et al., 2017).

This artifact also arises in a second form in sequences that acquire multiple volumes, either to detect time-varying signals (e.g., BOLD) or to weight the contrast of each volume by different modulation (e.g., diffusion weighting). In these contexts, while the volumes themselves may look consistent, discrepancies in position across volumes corrupt subsequent quantitative analyses, a problem we will consider further in Section 5.6.

4.2 Inconsistencies in *k*-space

While motion between slices or volumes results in spatial-encoding discrepancies, errors can also occur during the time required to encode *k*-space. Particularly in high-resolution 3D-encoded sequences where the encoding duration stretches to minutes, and often proceeds sequentially from one "side" of *k*-space to the other—effectively line-scanning in *k*-space—we can produce data where the different regions of *k*-space are measured when the object is in different positions.

We can begin to predict the effects of these discrepancies using the Fourier duality for rigid motion: translations in the image-space are simply phase-rolls in *k*-space, and rotations in image-space are identical rotations of *k*-space. Formally, denoting a translation by $\Delta \boldsymbol{x}$ and a rotation by $\boldsymbol{R}$,

$$F(\boldsymbol{k})e^{-i\boldsymbol{k}\cdot\Delta\boldsymbol{x}} = \int_{\Omega} f(\boldsymbol{x}-\Delta\boldsymbol{x})e^{-i\boldsymbol{k}(t)\cdot\boldsymbol{x}}d\boldsymbol{x}, \tag{11}$$

$$F(\boldsymbol{Rk}) = \int_{\Omega} f(\boldsymbol{Rx})e^{-i\boldsymbol{k}(t)\cdot\boldsymbol{x}}d\boldsymbol{x}. \tag{12}$$

We can then observe that, with translations, we will apply discrepant phases across *k*-space depending on the direction of translation. Rotations, by contrast, lead to us sampling completely different parts of *k*-space pre and postrotation, due to the transformation of $\boldsymbol{k}$ coordinate. We must emphasize that, unlike optical methods where we would expect a superposition of the object states, and thus blurring, as a result of motion, the structure of artifacts resulting from *k*-space discrepancies is more complicated when transformed back to the image domain. An example of the effects this produces are shown in Fig. 5.

4.3 Spin history

Many MRI pulse sequences use spatially selective RF pulses, most commonly slice-selective pulses used as part of the spatial-encoding process. However, human brain tissues have T_1 relaxation times on the order of 1 s or longer, meaning that the "memory" of each RF pulse in the spin state of brain tissue can be quite long (often approximated as $2\times$ or $3\times T_1$). In general pulse sequences are designed to apply RF pulses to each slice of tissue with at a fixed frequency (i.e., the repetition time, TR), and this ensures that a consistent spin state is created by each repetition of the RF pulse. However, if the tissue moves between pulses, then the assumption of a constant TR is violated—a given region of the brain might experience one excitation pulse, then move and experience a second excitation pulse meant for a different location.

In general, this produces a "saturation" effect, where regions of the brain that experience two pulses during a TR appear darker until they return to steady state (we show an example of this in Fig. 6). A key result of spin-history effects is that, for sequences acquiring multiple volumes in rapid succession (e.g., fMRI or diffusion-weighted imaging), retrospective realignment of data does not suffice—the tissue's magnetization state is truly a function of previous head positions over several seconds. This problem

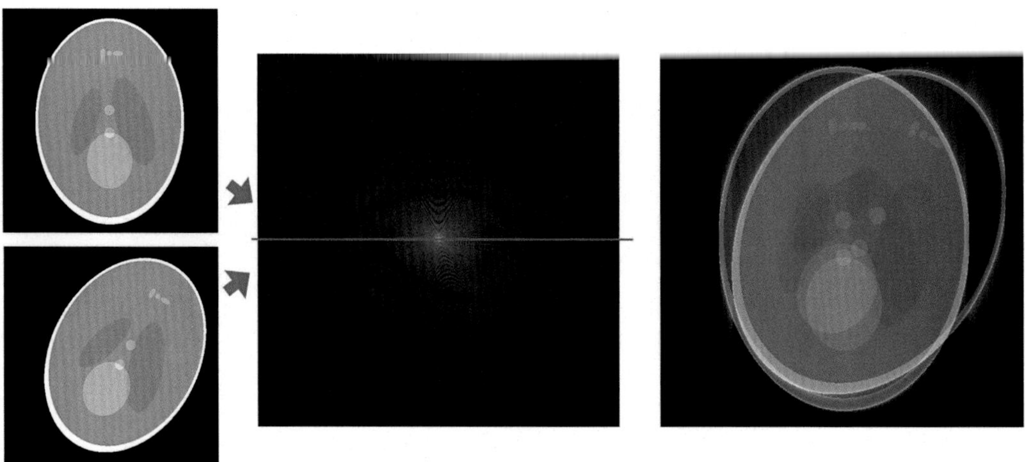

FIG. 5

Synthetic example of the effect of a rotation and translation during the encoding of *k*-space. The two left-most images represent the two positions in which the object was imaged. The top half of *k*-space (middle column) was acquired with the object in the first position, with the bottom half of *k*-space was acquired with the object in the second position. For our synthetic example, we assume this motion was instantaneous and occurred immediately after acquiring the middle-most line of *k*-space. The resulting image is shown on the right. We note that, although there is clearly the gross superposition of the two images, there are also significant vertical streaking artifacts, and high-frequency errors (e.g., the white outer edge of the phantom have developed additional "fringes" not present in the original images).

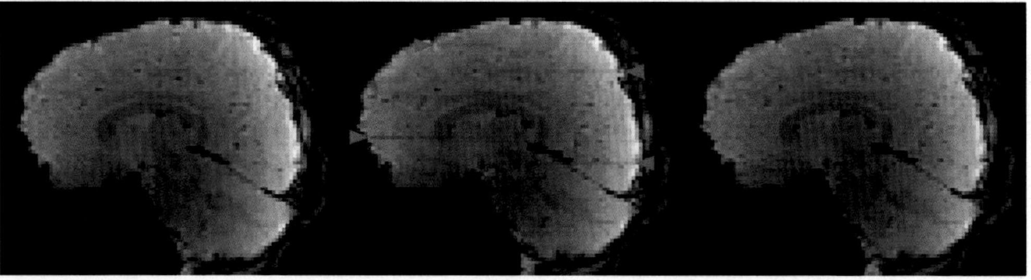

FIG. 6

Example of the effect of a small through-plane motion on spin history in 2D EPI. In this case, the subject made a small nodding motion during the second volume, resulting in some regions being excited twice and thus appearing dark (horizontal stripes indicated by red arrowheads). As this data was acquired with a TR of 2 s, the effect is largely dissipated by the time the third volume is acquired. Note that this data was not realigned, demonstrating that, even though the nodding motion was very small and the spatial inconsistencies are small, the spin history effect on the data is obvious in a sagittal projection that "cuts across" the slices.

has been well-studied in the context of BOLD fMRI (Friston et al., 1996; Yancey et al., 2011), and we will return to it in Section 5.6 were we consider the effects of motion on quantitative analyses.

A unique form of spin-history effect arises in the context of DWI, where motion can lead to complete loss of the signal in specific slices. This arises because the diffusion-encoding portion of the sequence, played before each slice is read out, is designed to reduce signal proportional to the incoherent microscopic motion of the signal source. However, even small rotations of the head (large displacements compared to tissue water diffusion pathlengths) can lead to complete cancelation of the signal (Andersson et al., 2016; Norris, 2001).

Spin history is less of an issue in sequences based on 3D-encoded gradient-echo readouts (e.g., MPRAGE), as the pulses are designed to excite all tissues within the FOV identically, and so movement of the tissue does not notably modulate the experienced RF pulse at 1.5 or 3T. Interestingly, 3D-encoded sequences that use variable-flip-angle spin-echo trains to produce specific contrast (e.g., SPACE) are more sensitive to spin-history effects induced by motion during their echo trains (Frost et al., 2019; Herbst et al., 2012b).

4.4 Interactions between motion and distortions

While the effects described to this point can be thought of as directly arising from motion, it is important to also recognize that subject motion interacts with the sources of distortion previously described in Section 2. These interactions can in turn negate the effects of the correction strategies outlined in Section 3, in addition to causing their own artifacts. Three excellent surveys delve into these and other interaction effects of motion in great detail (Maclaren et al., 2013; Zaitsev et al., 2015, 2017). However, here we will highlight the key findings most important for pediatric neuroimaging studies.

While gradient nonlinearity and eddy currents are the fixed features of the scanner's coordinates, and thus not directly affected by subject motion, each position of the subject's head will be distorted differently by these nonlinearities. Thus, motion that is rigid in the real world may appear nonrigid in sequential images due to the different distortions applied. This problem becomes pronounced in the context of DWI scans, where eddy currents produce significant time-varying distortions (Andersson and Skare, 2002; Andersson and Sotiropoulos, 2016), a problem we will return to when discussing quantitative analyses in Section 5.6. These interactions also increase the magnitude of motion artifacts in high-resolution 3D-encoded structural scans, as the distortions lead to local discrepancies between data acquired in different poses (Yarach et al., 2015).

B_0 inhomogeneity has a significant interaction with motion, due to the inhomogeneity itself arising from the geometry of the head relative to the main magnetic field. Thus both the spatial distortions and the observed T_2^* at each voxel are modulated by head position (Friston et al., 1996; Graham et al., 2017; Jezzard and Clare, 1999; Maclaren et al., 2013; Wu et al., 1997). In the context of applying field maps to correct for B_0-induced distortions, this interaction is very important—a field map acquired with the subject's head in one position cannot be easily applied to subsequent data when the subject changes position. Moreover, simply rotating the field map to follow the subject's head, while perhaps better than performing no update, is not sufficient. The position-dependent change in observed T_2^* is also an important effect to consider in time-series analyses, which we will touch on in more detail in Section 5.6.

Finally, although we did not discuss them above as a distortion, receive coil sensitivity profiles are also fixed in scanner coordinates, and so interact with the signal when the subject moves. Anatomy that is close to a receive coil is initially measured as producing "brighter signal" in the resulting images, due to the spatially varying scaling applied by the receive coils (this is often corrected in normalization steps during image reconstruction). Motion during a scan will cause the anatomy to move relative to this receive bias fields and thus effectively modulate signal intensity. This effect is most significant in time-series analyses, where it can combine with the change B_0 inhomogeneity as another motion-correlated source of temporal signal variation (Friston et al., 1996; Zaitsev et al., 2017).

5. Mitigating motion artifacts

A vast set of strategies have been developed for reducing the effects of motion in neuroimaging studies. As we can see from Section 5, motion can impact signals in a variety of ways, and interactions with other artifacts are often dependent on the specific protocol or pulse sequence employed. As such, there are opportunities to mitigate motion artifacts at several places within the acquisition and analysis pipeline, and we will consider these different strategies in this section.

5.1 Keeping subjects still

The most obvious strategy to mitigate motion artifacts is to not have subjects move in the first place. Critically, in clinical practice, motion is often addressed by the use of sedation. However, this is not without risk to the subject, both due to adverse events under sedation (Cravero et al., 2009) and the potential developmental side-effects of the sedative drugs themselves, which resulted in the US Food and Drug Administration mandating a change to labeling for sedative use in children under 3 years old (Andropoulos and Greene, 2017). As such, sedation is very rarely considered ethical in pediatric research studies, and alternative strategies must be employed.

Unfortunately, this is difficult for many pediatric populations, simply due to participants' limited capacity for following directions and remaining still for the durations required in MRI. However, even if complete compliance cannot be achieved with every subject, techniques that can measurably reduce motion are an important part of pediatric neuroimaging. To this end, a variety of age-specific strategies are routinely employed with significant success.

For neonates, a "feed-and-wrap" strategy is routinely employed, which uses the natural sleep schedule of the neonate, along with swaddling to minimize the chance of waking (Barkovich et al., 2018; Mathur et al., 2008). In infants and toddlers, this strategy generally shifts to scanning at night, when children will more reliably sleep, with a significant emphasis on preparing the environment and minimizing scanner noise (Dean et al., 2014).

The scanning environment can be anxiety-inducing for pediatric subjects, and this in turn reduces subject compliance in the scanner. In children who are old enough that sleep-scanning is not an option or when awake functional data is of interest, a variety of strategies have shown success in helping acclimate subjects to the environment, including simulations with "mock scanners" (de Bie et al., 2010; Raschle et al., 2009; Rosenberg et al., 1997). In addition to presession training methods, groups have also explored using movie-watching as an in-scanner activity to help distract children (Vanderwal et al., 2015). As an additional strategy, using real-time motion feedback (e.g., by pausing or occluding a movie) has been found to further reduce children's in-scanner motion (Greene et al., 2018).

In general head restraint in awake subjects has been found to be counter-productive, with discomfort during longer scan sessions potentially inducing greater subject motion. However, recent work with subject-specific 3D-milled Styrofoam molds demonstrated success in reducing motion in an older pediatric cohort (Power et al., 2019).

5.2 Measuring motion information

Despite best efforts to minimize subject head motion, it is still the case that most pediatric neuroimaging studies will observe some amount of head motion in many of their subjects. Before we consider strategies to correct for motion (the topic of the rest of this chapter), we must first determine how we will measure motion. In general, we describe head motion as a time-series of rigid transforms, each time-point having six degrees of freedom—three rotations and three translations. A variety of methods have been developed to estimate these motion time-series over the history of MRI, representing different trade-offs between ease-of-use, applicability across imaging sequences, and tracking accuracy. To date, there is no clear "best method" that is universally accepted across neuroimaging studies. Instead, motion measurement technologies remain an active area of work, with very few actually commercialized. It is likely that individual methods may show greater success in certain populations or pulse sequences. As such, this section will provide a survey of both the historical development of motion measurement technologies, as well as recent developments that may be of interest to neuroimaging researchers.

5.2.1 Self-navigation

Among the first concepts proposed for motion measurement, self-navigating readouts are pulse sequences that, due to their repeated sampling of the center of k-space, can extract motion information from subsamples of the complete imaging data. This method is elegant, in that it requires no additional motion-tracking hardware, but suffers from the need to redesign pulse sequences to use these sorts of redundant trajectories. Over time, the number of sequences that have been redeveloped with redundant readouts has expanded, and remains an active area of work.

Perhaps the most widely adopted example of this method is PROPELLER (alternatively marketed as BLADE and MultiVane imaging), which most commonly used for 2D-encoded turbo-spin-echo sequences, including T_2- and diffusion-weighted protocols (Pipe, 1999; Pipe et al., 2002). The core idea of PROPELLER is to sample 2D strips of k-space (commonly called a "blade"), centered around the center of k-space, extending to the entire bandwidth in the readout direction, but having limited coverage in the phase-encode direction. Each blade is generally acquired in a one or more shots, and then subsequent blades are each rotated around the origin of k-space. When all the overlapping blades are visualized in k-space, the visual effect is akin to a propeller, hence the method's name. As all of the "blades" overlap in a circular region at the center of k-space, data in this region can be used to generate low-resolution images and estimate in-plane motion. Unfortunately, due to the inherently 2D nature of the method, through-plane motion remains difficult to estimate. As such, an active area of work is the expansion core intuition has also been expanded to 3D-encoded acquisitions, with approaches suggesting either rotating EPI "planes" to cover the 3D k-space volume (McNab et al., 2009), or 3D "bricks" that are filled over several shots and then rotated (Holdsworth et al., 2008).

Radial acquisitions also offer the ability to be made self-navigating, depending on the order in which spokes are acquired. If the set of radial spokes acquired in short time windows all have roughly equal coverage of k-space, then subsects of the data can be used to reconstruct low-resolution images. This time-series of images can then be registered to estimated subject motion; in the case of 2D acquisitions this can detect in-plane motion (Schaffter et al., 1999), and in 3D can fully estimate rigid head motion (Anderson et al., 2013; Kecskemeti et al., 2016). In general these methods have been applied to radial gradient-echo sequence (e.g., FLASH, SPGR, or FFE) (Anderson et al., 2013; Schaffter et al., 1999), but have also been expanded to inversion prepared gradient-echo sequences (e.g., MPRAGE, IR-SPGR, or TFE) (Kecskemeti et al., 2016).

Some sequences are, by their nature, effectively self-navigated. BOLD fMRI is perhaps the canonical example of this; most fMRI acquisitions are designed to provide whole-brain coverage with a very short volume-repetition time to maximize sensitivity to the hemodynamics of the brain, but this also inherently captures information about the motion of the brain. Many analysis tools can be used to extract motion data retrospectively, and these are generally built into standard fMRI analysis software packages (e.g., Cox, 1996; Friston et al., 1996; Jenkinson et al., 2002). However, estimating motion information from fMRI data in real time is also possible, but requires efficient image registration algorithms to be full practical (Dosenbach et al., 2017; Thesen et al., 2000).

Extending similar approaches to diffusion-weighted data is somewhat more difficult, as the variable directional-sensitivity of the diffusion weighting between volumes produces signal variations that can confound motion estimation. Moreover, at high b-values, there may be a little residual signal to use for motion-tracking. One approach is to continuously update an estimate of the "average" image expected for each b-value, which can then be used as the reference image for 3D volume registration with each new volume acquired at the same b-value. This method has been found to produce acceptable estimates of head motion in real time at the lower b-values common in clinical imaging (Benner et al., 2011). An alternative approach is to reorder the diffusion vectors such that each contiguous subset of three vectors is nearly orthogonal. This allows an approximate trace-weighted image to be generated for each set of three vectors, which can then be used as the basis for real-time volume registration to estimate subject motion (Hoinkiss and Porter, 2017).

In summary, while a wide-variety of self-navigated sequence have been developed over the years, many of them require modifications to the underlying sequence readout that may affect the final image output in subtle ways (e.g., switching from Cartesian to PROPELLER readouts), or limit the range of possible protocols (e.g., reordering diffusion directions). While the incremental cost of using these technologies is low, essentially no different from any other pulse sequence, the choice to transition from an established sequence always needs careful evaluation, to ensure the new data will be acceptable for use in specific image analysis pipelines.

5.2.2 Navigators

As an alternative to the trade-offs inherent in the design of self-navigated sequences, it is also possible to interleave two pulse sequences together: (1) a standard imaging sequence and (2) a second small sequence explicitly sensitized to motion, *a.k.a.*, a navigator. This approach has the advantage that the imaging sequence's design is minimally disturbed, providing the output that users are accustomed to. However, the challenge is then deciding both what navigator subsequence gives sufficient information and how to interleave it into the "parent" imaging sequence.

Early work in the design of navigators focused on the use of the Fourier duality for rigid motion. Eqs. (11) and (12) suggest that, when the whole FOV moves rigidly, only a small subset of k-space to estimate the transform. From these equations we can see that a circular k-space trajectory in 2D, or a spherical trajectory in 3D will ensure that rigid motions in image space can be fully estimated—translations in image-space will be phase rolls across our k-space shell, while rotations in image-space will rotate k-space samples along our k-space shell. These methods were first explored in 2D and called orbital navigators (Fu et al., 1995), and then expanded to 3D and called spherical navigators (Welch et al., 2002).

While spherical navigators are well-suited to estimating rigid motion of the FOV, they require a relatively long period to acquire, which can make interleaving them into some "parent" sequences more challenging. In an effort to produce a shorter navigator, the cloverleaf trajectory was introduced, consisting of three orthogonal straight segments and three orthogonal curved segments to extract translation and rotation information, and reducing the navigator duration to 4.2 ms (van der Kouwe et al., 2006).

Eqs. (11), (12) only hold if the motion of the entire FOV is rigid. In practice, this is not the case for true head motion. First, the jaw and neck move independently of the brain. Second, the complex signal measured in k-space is also influenced by off-resonance effects that are motion-sensitive themselves, as discussed in Section 5.4 above. This suggests that, while they make a good approximation, they may not suffice for highly accurate navigator-based motion tracking. To address this shortcoming, and taking advantage of the rapid increase in both gradient performance and image reconstruction computing power of more modern MRI scanners, navigators based on acquiring whole images and tracking motion in image space were introduced.

The first of these methods, named PROMO, uses three orthogonal 2D-encoded spiral images with FOV covering the whole head. The motion of the brain is then tracked directly via image registration. In the initial implementation, five repetitions of the 3-plane navigator were played, producing a complete navigator block requiring approximately 500 ms, although this could be shortened by playing fewer repetitions with a commensurate reduction in tracking accuracy (White et al., 2010).

The volumetric navigators (vNavs) method opted to use a 3D-encoded EPI readout with FOV covering the whole head, acquired in approximately 275 ms. Similar to PROMO, motion estimates are then generated via 3D volume-to-volume registration (Hess et al., 2011; Tisdall et al., 2012). By expanding this navigator to include two EPI volumes with two TEs, field maps can also be computed on-the fly, to help account for some of the interaction effects described in Section 5.4 (Hess et al., 2011; Alhamud et al., 2016; Liu et al., 2019). Fig. 7 shows a motion path acquired with the vNavs system during an MPRAGE scan.

Clearly the navigator durations for both PROMO and vNavs are quite long relative to the TRs of many MRI sequences. However, these methods were both initially developed for use in the high-resolution 3D structural sequences most commonly employed in neuroimaging studies: MPRAGE and T2 SPACE. These sequences have the interesting property that they have long deadtimes that are used to allow relaxation to generate their desired contrasts. These deadtimes make ideal locations for the PROMO and vNav navigator blocks, and because both navigators use very small flip angles, the effective disruption of the final images' contrast is quite small (Tisdall et al., 2012).

In an effort to shorten an image-based navigator and make it more generally applicable, authors have suggested taking advantage of the spatially sparse fat signal in the head (located around the skull) for both projection (Avventi et al., 2020; Engström et al., 2015) and highly accelerated (Gallichan et al., 2016) readouts. Both these methods achieve their speed by using high undersampling factors, enabled by the fact that the fat signal is not only sparse, but generally located close to individual coil elements, making head-fat images ideally suited for GRAPPA- or SENSE-based reconstructions.

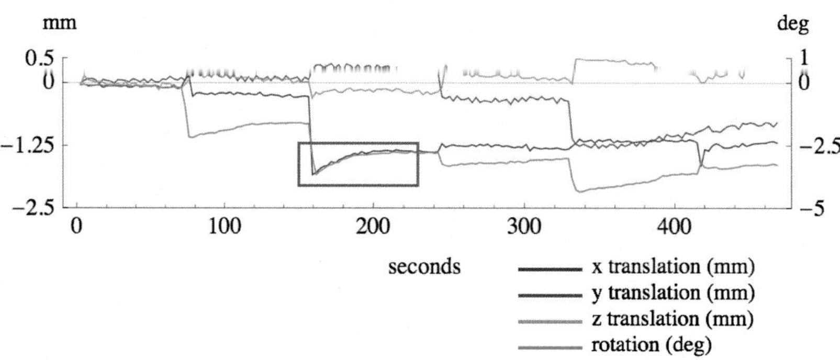

FIG. 7

Motion path recorded with vNavs during an MPRAGE scan. Subject was asked to move their head to a new location every 90 s and then remain still. The *red box* highlights an apparent "drift" in position after these directions—this was determined to be the result of the subject gradually relaxing their neck and rolling their head to a more neutral position.

Taking this approach to its limit, FID navigators eschew any gradient-based spatial encoding, in favor of using the modulation of the signal within the receive coil sensitivity profiles to estimate subject motion (Kober et al., 2011; Wallace et al., 2019). When inserted after an existing nonselective excitation pulse (e.g., in 3D-encoded structural sequences) a FID navigator can be acquired in as little as 100 μs, making it likely the shortest-possible motion navigator. The challenge with this method is using the limited quantity of data to fully extract motion information. Initial development of the method focused simply on detecting motion (Kober et al., 2011). However, more recent work has shown that with a minimal calibration scan (often acquired as part of standard image reconstructions anyway) full rigid motion estimates can be generated efficiently and at high temporal frequency (Wallace et al., 2019).

Navigator-based methods are still an active area of research, particularly in the development of novel strategies to shorten readouts of interleave them within specific imaging sequences. Despite their long history of use in body imaging, navigator-based methods for neuroimaging have seen limited commercialization. However, in part due to the cross-scanner-vendor availability of the related PROMO and vNavs methods, these structural sequence have seen adoption in some large multicenter imaging studies, including the Adolescent Brain Cognitive Development study (Casey et al., 2018), and the Human Connectome Aging and Development studies (Harms et al., 2018).

5.2.3 External motion-tracking hardware

Rather than using the MRI scanner itself to detect motion, it is also possible to add external motion-tracking hardware to the system. This approach has a number of advantages: it poses fewer requirements on the pulse sequence (no requirements in the case of optical trackers), and can usually estimate head motion at far higher temporal resolution than can be achieved using MRI-based methods.

One of the earliest and most well-developed optical tracking methods operates by attaching reflective markers to the subject. Using multiple markers with a known geometry, the displacement of the head can be determined from a pair of sensors providing stereoscopic measurements (Eviatar et al., 1999; Zaitsev et al., 2006). However, attaching these markers in such a way that multiple cameras outside the bore proved challenging due to complicated line-of-sight issues. Moving the camera-pair in-bore solves this problem, but generally requires a more-informative, and thus larger, marker to ensure enough features are within both cameras' narrower field of view (which is necessarily reduced by mounting in-bore and close to the head) (Qin et al., 2009; Aksoy et al., 2011).

To address some of these practical issues and further improve tracking accuracy, a Moiré phase tracking marker was introduced, that can be used to estimate all 6 degrees of rigid motion from a single camera (Weinhandl et al., 2010). In fact, the spatial and temporal resolution of this system is so high that it can reliably detect the ballistocardiogram of the head, and could potentially be used for cardiac synchronization in addition to motion tracking (Maclaren et al., 2012).

As an alternative to attaching fiducial markers to subjects, structured infrared light can be used to create a map of the subject's face while they are in the scanner (see Fig. 8). While the lack of the marker is a practical advantage, this substantially increases the challenge of motion tracking, as the facial surface can distort nonrigidly, and these distortions must be separated from the rigid movement of the whole head. However, using structured light has the additional benefit that little hardware needs to be in the scanner bore itself, which has led to its application for head motion tracking in both PET and MRI (Olesen et al., 2012; Andersen et al., 2019b; Frost et al., 2019).

All optical systems require line-of-sight between a sensor and the subject or reflector, introducing an inherent design challenge within the tight confines of the scanner bore and head coil. This constraint

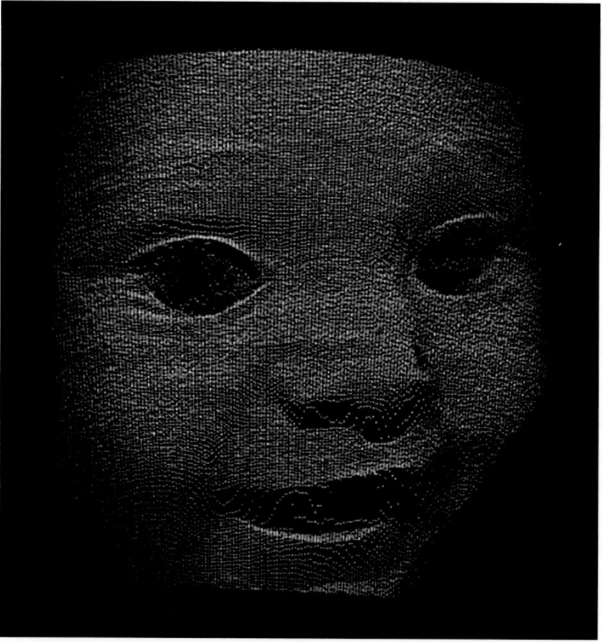

FIG. 8

Example of a 3D point cloud generated by a structured infrared light system. Each point represents a 3D sample estimating the location of the subject's face. Taken together, these point clouds can be registered to estimate subject motion.

Courtesy of TracInnovations.

can be lifted, however, by moving from optical-based methods to other sensors that can be attached to the subject. An early approach used three small water samples, each wrapped in a miniature receive coil and affixed rigidly to a headband. The water samples where then excited and a crude projection image made using the MRI scanner itself, effectively combining fiducial markers with MRI-based motion measurement (Ooi et al., 2009).

The idea of using NMR probes has been further refined to minimize the overhead required in the sequence. First, through the use of separate transmit hardware and probes whose resonance frequency is far off from water. Second, through overlying continuous, high-frequency gradient "tones" over an arbitrary pulse sequence's gradient waveforms, providing spatial information without notably disrupting sequence timing or limiting sequence design (Haeberlin et al., 2015). Unfortunately, in commercial MRI systems, the introduction of these tones is generally nontrivial, and so the system was further refined to use the existing gradient waveforms of product pulse sequences, although this required careful inspection of the gradient waveforms in advance to ensure sample timing for motion tracking (Aranovitch et al., 2018).

Finally, detecting the slew of predefined gradient pulses via small, subject-mounted pickup coils can also allow estimation of the head position. While initial devices used a system precalibration method to account for imperfections in the gradients (van der Kouwe et al., 2009), recent work has produced subject-mountable wireless sensor packages that can directly account for the majority of system imperfections and produce high-quality motion estimates (van Niekerk et al., 2019).

Clearly, there are many advantages to using additional hardware for motion tracking: both in reducing the demands on the pulse sequence—no demands at all when using optical systems—and in improving the accuracy and temporal resolution of motion estimates. However, all of these systems encounter their own challenges in practice: either the requirement to attach markers to subjects' heads and faces, or achieving line-of-sight between cameras and the subjects. Despite these challenges, external motion trackers remain an active area of both research and commercialization.

5.3 Summarizing motion

Although rigid brain motion between two instantaneous observations of head position is well-expressed as a 6-degree-of-freedom transform, it is often useful to summarize the "amount of motion" during a scan, or subsection of a scan. This can be useful both for reporting motion levels in a population, and also as a subject- or scan-level regressor in subsequent analyses. This reduction of a high-dimensional trajectory to a single number necessitates the loss of much information, and unfortunately there is little consensus on standardized summary measures throughout the neuroimaging literature, making it sometimes difficult to compare the scale of motion described in one study to that in another.

Motion time-courses can be quantified as the 6 degree-of-freedom transform either between each position observation (i.e., the discrete derivative of the head displacement), or using the reference position for comparison (i.e., the displacement from the reference position). For BOLD fMRI and DWI, "Framewise Displacement" is a commonly-reported metric, with the "frame" being a single volume. Computing the framewise displacement involves using the derivative series, converting the angular rotation estimates to displacements on the surface of a sphere, and then taking the 1-norm of the resulting 6-vector (Power et al., 2012). A related metric, root-mean-squared motion within a sphere centered on the head, is also used to aggregate the effects of translations and rotations (Jenkinson, 1999). Other groups discard the rotation components and report the 2-norm of the translation components alone

(Satterthwaite et al., 2012; Van Dijk et al., 2012). Still others report and analyze the translation and rotation components separately (Yendiki et al., 2014). Of course, these metrics are not limited to motion estimated from image "frames" and can be applied more generally to any motion time-course (e.g., Reuter et al., 2015).

While a variety of related metrics can be generated at each "sample" along the motion time-course, one additional source of ambiguity in the reporting of motion measures arises from how they are averaged over time to produce a single summary measure for an entire scan. The discrete derivatives underlying these measures are not generally divided by the time between position samples when they are reported. This means that there is a variable scaling across the reported measures—the average motion in each 2 s block of a scan should reasonably be higher than the average motion in each 1 s block, even when describing the "same motion." While for a given study, generally acquired with a fixed protocol and thus fixed sampling frequency for motion, this scaling will be constant and thus not impact between-subject comparisons, it can make between-study comparisons more challenging, particularly when comparing the scale of regressed motion effects across studies. For example, although both studies used the same root-mean-squared motion metric (Couvy-Duchesne et al., 2016) does not account for the between sample time in their "average" motion measure (reporting RMS/sample-window), while (Reuter et al., 2015) does (reporting RMS/minute).

5.4 Applying motion information retrospectively

Retrospective motion correction is the process of taking the acquired data and measured motion trajectory, and attempting to synthesize new data that removes the influence of motion. This strategy has much to recommend it: the pulse sequence itself can potentially be left unmodified, and there is always the option of analyzing both the "raw" and "corrected" data separately, to evaluate the impact of the motion-correction algorithms.

5.4.1 Addressing image- and k*-space inconsistencies*

In the context of single-shot 2D scans (e.g., EPI or spiral BOLD fMRI), where motion is often assumed to be "frozen" within the slice, retrospective correction then focuses primarily on realigning data in image space to account for motion (Cox, 1996; Friston et al., 1996; Jenkinson et al., 2002). These algorithms all operate on the level of volumes, assuming that a single estimate of position can be applied to all the data within a volume and performing 3D interpolation to resample data into a consistent coordinate space. While motion-correction at the level of individual slices has been demonstrated to improve accuracy of motion correction (Kim et al., 1999), it is less-commonly applied, and within-volume motion is generally left to be accounted for in the analysis step (see Section 5.6).

While single-shot scans can perform realignment in image space, sequences where *k*-space is acquired over multiple TRs generally require that retrospective correction be applied in *k*-space directly. From Eq. (11) we can see that correcting translations is equivalent to applying phase-rolls to our existing *k*-space samples, while Eq. (12) shows that correcting rotations requires interpolating new sampling locations to correct for the rotation applied in *k*-space by the rigid motion. This interpolation is often performed using the nonuniform fast Fourier transform (Fessler and Sutton, 2003), which can be combined with motion information to determine the acquired *k*-space sampling locations for eventual image reconstruction (Bammer et al., 2007; Gallichan et al., 2016; Gallichan, 2020).

A similar retrospective re-gridding process has been demonstrated for 3D radially sampled k-space data. Radial data is generally interpolated to a Cartesian sampling grid as part of its reconstruction; thus, retrospectively rotating radial spokes is particularly easy, since it simply represents changing the assumed angle at which each spoke was sampled (Anderson et al., 2013).

5.4.2 Addressing interactions with distortions

While the retrospective techniques described so far can account for sampling inconsistencies in image- and k-space, they do not fully compensate for interactions with, for example, B_0 inhomogeneity and the resulting position-dependent spatial distortions. In the context of BOLD fMRI, approaches to addressing this interaction include the use of dual-echo EPI readouts either throughout the scan (Roopchansingh et al., 2003; Visser et al., 2012) or as a reference (Dymerska et al., 2018), triple-echo EPI with alternating phase-encoding directions (Weiskopf et al., 2005), and spiral in-out readouts (Sutton et al., 2004). In the context of diffusion-weighted imaging with spin-echo EPI, a similar approach using two echoes with reversed polarity blips has also been demonstrated (Gallichan et al., 2010).

The majority of distortion correction work has been applied in the context of EPI imaging, where the artifact is most apparent, while 3D-encoded structural data is generally assumed to be relatively immune due to its higher effective bandwidth. However, it is often underappreciated that, when retrospective motion correction is applied to high-resolution images from any sequence, the interaction between motion and gradient nonlinearity becomes a significant source of error, and should likely be accounted for in retrospective motion-correction pipelines (Yarach et al., 2015).

Finally, retrospective time-varying "linear shim" correction can be applied to partially compensate time-varying changes in B_0 inhomogeneity. When dynamic field mapping data is available, the effects of both motion and spatially linear B_0 inhomogeneity can be expressed as phase corrections and re-gridding operations in k-space, which can then be included in a generalized NUFFT reconstruction. While this approach is not sufficient to compensate for the local distortions prevalent in EPI-based readouts, it has demonstrated substantial improvements in high-resolution 3D-encoded data, particularly T_2^*-weighted sequences (Gretsch et al., 2018; Liu et al., 2019).

5.5 Applying motion information prospectively

Prospective correction strategies attempt to modify the acquisition itself to dynamically compensate for subject motion. While retrospective methods can use substantial computational power to estimate motion-free data off-line, prospective methods must process real-time motion and field estimates to respond immediately as data is acquired. However, despite these engineering challenges, the greatest benefit of prospective methods is their relatively transparency for users—in the ideal case, the data that are produced by the scanner requires no further processing to correct for motion. Of course, in practice not all motion-induced artifacts can be corrected this way, and in this section, we will evaluate the prospective strategies that have been developed.

5.5.1 Moving the encoding axes

Perhaps the most intuitive solution to address rigid motion, given a real-time source of motion information, is to simply update the imaging axes to follow the subject's head. By keeping the k-space axes consistently aligned with the anatomy, and applying the necessary k-space phase corrections to correct for image-space translations, we can avoid the need to re-grid k-space data before reconstruction. This has the significant benefit of enabling standard on-scanner image reconstruction pipelines to be applied to the data, producing output very similar to that of standard vendor-supplied pulse sequences. Additionally, in cases of large subject motions, re-gridding alone may not be able to correct for missing data due to gaps in the resultant irregular sampling locations (Bammer et al., 2007)—prospective methods avoid this problem by enforcing a regular sampling grid (Maclaren et al., 2013; Zaitsev et al., 2015).

However, the details of how these updates are applied have a substantial impact on the quality of the motion-correction that results. One of the earliest examples of this approach was applied to BOLD EPI data, with updates occurring after each complete volume (Thesen et al., 2000), and was subsequently extended to diffusion-weighted imaging (Alhamud et al., 2012; Benner et al., 2011). While this will correct for infrequent motion, its update frequency is too slow to correct data from subjects who move often, even if the motion amplitudes are small.

Image-based navigator systems in 3D-encoded imaging sequences have generally opted to perform one update per echo train, as that is the frequency with which navigators can be successfully interleaved into the imaging sequences (Andersen et al., 2019a; Tisdall et al., 2012; White et al., 2010).

At the extreme end, updates from optical systems can be applied much more rapidly, on the order of once per EPI slice (Aksoy et al., 2011; Ooi et al., 2011; Zaitsev et al., 2006), or once per echo in 3D-encoded sequences (Frost et al., 2019; Herbst et al., 2012b; Zaitsev et al., 2006). In the context of spoiled-gradient-echo sequences, increasing the update frequency has been demonstrated to show marked improvements in image quality, while the effect is less pronounced in turbo-spin-echo sequences, perhaps due to the increased motion sensitivity of the refocused spin-echo train (Frost et al., 2019). In contrast, it has been shown that diffusion-weighted EPI experiments can benefit from even more frequent updates: dynamically updating the diffusion-encoding gradients themselves to remain aligned with the subject anatomy at a 2 ms update frequency (Herbst et al., 2012a).

One major concern with prospective correction methods is that, should the estimated motion path be incorrect, the "correction" may introduce "pseudo-motion" by shifting the encoding axes relative to the anatomy. Since no estimated motion path is perfect, we must consider what degree of accuracy is sufficient to provide benefit for prospective correction. Limits on accuracy have been estimated based on the goal of reducing motion artifacts due to "noise" in the motion estimates below the thermal noise floor of a scan, suggesting that precision should be several times higher than the imaging resolution (Maclaren et al., 2010). However, in practice, when subjects are moving, even a moderately precise and accurate correction is superior to having no correction at all. As such, this often produces a tradeoff in using practical prospective systems, where subjects who are near-perfectly still may produce slightly degraded image quality due to motion-tracking errors, while data from subjects who move is substantially improved. As is the case with any imaging protocol, it is good practice to pilot prospective motion-correction systems in the population of interest, to ensure that the results are in favor of its application in a full study.

5.5.2 Automatic reacquisition

No matter how rapidly the imaging coordinates are prospectively updated, there will likely always be motion effects that are not fully corrected. As such, it is often useful to reacquire subparts of sequences that are impacted by the motion. In its most naïve form, this can be accomplished by simply acquiring more scans than are needed (e.g., acquiring two structural scans and keeping the best one, or acquiring more diffusion directions than needed and discarding degraded ones). However, automated reacquisition allows the on-scanner image reconstruction software to determine which subparts of a scan need reacquisition and direct the scanner to reschedule them, saving time and reducing the odds of acquiring, e.g., two bad scans and keeping none.

In the context of 3D-encoded structural scanning, automatic reacquisition has been generally implemented at the level of the echo train (Andersen et al., 2019a; Tisdall et al., 2012; White et al., 2010). While the details of each implementation differ slightly, in general all of these sequences use the real-time motion information they receive to produce a single "motion score" for each TR. They then compare this against a threshold, and, once the initial scan is complete, continuing replaying the motion-damaged TRs until they have all been successfully reacquired (or some time limit expires). A similar method has been demonstrated for DWI, with the addition of a test to ensure that "drop-outs" due to motion during the diffusion-encoding gradients are also flagged for reacquisition (Benner et al., 2011).

5.5.3 Dynamic shimming

As linear shimming can be performed by simply updating the applied gradients, this can be used prospectively to at least partially correct for B_0 inhomogeneity due to changes in subject position. An early example of this in the context of EPI, used projection navigators to estimate the linear shim term along each gradient axis (Ward et al., 2002). However, this has the limitation of shimming over the entire region of receive coil sensitivity, which may be significantly larger than the anatomy of interest (e.g., shimming the neck is undesirable for brain imaging). An extreme example of this is single-voxel spectroscopy (SVS), where the shim is to be optimized over a small volume within the brain—in this context dual-echo vNavs have been employed to create a field map during each TR which is then used to dynamically update the linear shim terms to optimize just the voxel of interest (Hess et al., 2011). A similar approach has also been applied in EPI-based DWI with vNavs, where the shim is optimized just to the DWI region of interest (Alhamud et al., 2016).

5.5.4 Combining prospective and retrospective methods

While prospective methods can significantly reduce the need for retrospective motion-correction, shimming and axis realignment cannot compensate for all motion-induced errors we have described above. As such, it is often useful to follow prospective methods with further retrospective corrections. For example, prospective correction can address the gross spatial discrepancies in EPI data and minimize spin-history artifacts, while retrospective correction is better suited to resolving the residual distortions due to changing B_0 inhomogeneity (Ooi et al., 2013). Similarly, retrospective correction for gradient nonlinearity has been demonstrated in high-resolution 3D sequences after prospective motion correction (Yarach et al., 2015).

One major strength of retrospective methods is that the "uncorrected" data is always available, while prospective methods necessarily only provide the "corrected" result. To address this problem, "reverse correction" has been proposed for 3D-encoded structural images, where the estimated motion path is applied to the prospectively corrected data, with the goal of simulating the data that would have been acquired without prospective correction (Zahneisen et al., 2016).

5.6 Addressing motion artifacts in quantitative analyses

To this point, we have considered the sources of, and means of addressing, distortions and motion artifacts at the level of the individual subject. However, in many neuroimaging studies, the goal is group-level comparison quantitative measures derived from imaging data. One might expect that motion artifacts simply increase variability in the downstream measures, and thus reduce study power. However, a large body of work has shown that motion induces particular biases in all of the major quantitative measures used in neuroimaging studies. Moreover, motion in the scanner is heritable (Couvy-Duchesne et al., 2016; Engelhardt et al., 2017; Hodgson et al., 2017), and highly correlated with age (Blumenthal et al., 2002; Satterthwaite et al., 2012; Pardoe et al., 2016), behavior (Kong et al., 2014; Couvy-Duchesne et al., 2016; Siegel et al., 2016; Bolton et al., 2020), clinical diagnosis (Pardoe et al., 2016), and body mass index (Siegel et al., 2016; Hodgson et al., 2017; Ekhtiari et al., 2019; Bolton et al., 2020). Thus, motion-induced biases can represent a substantial confound for group-difference analyses.

A key issue across all group-level analyses of neuroimaging data arises when considering the inclusion of motion as a nuisance regressor. Since it is highly correlated with measures of interest, its inclusion may lead to reduced detection power, and potentially lower effect size estimates for other explanatory variables. While matching subjects between groups by individual motion levels may help reduce motion biases, as suggested in (Yendiki et al., 2014), this is challenging when groups exhibit different levels of motion and may lead to the exclusion of important subpopulations from analyses. Additionally, it is unclear exactly how to "match" motion, as summary scores may not account for the relevant features of subject motion (Bolton et al., 2020). Instead, it is likely necessary to, as much as possible, address the effects of motion within each analysis pipeline itself, based on the knowledge of motion's effects that we have outlined above. While a complete survey of the methods for addressing these biases is an active area of work and beyond the scope of this chapter, we will introduce both descriptions of the common errors caused by motion, and widely used methods to mitigate them.

5.6.1 BOLD fMRI

BOLD fMRI's extreme sensitivity to motion was apparent from early in its development (Hajnal et al., 1994; Friston et al., 1996). While prospective and retrospective motion-correction methods can mitigate some of these effects, they are generally not sufficient to completely eliminate it. In the context of task-based analyses, it is common to generate nuisance regressors based on the estimated motion during the scan, separating motion-correlated artifacts from residual task-correlated activation (Friston et al., 1996).

The propensity of motion to bias results has been further noted in the context of functional connectivity analyses, where motion appears to reduce long-range correlation while increasing short-range correlation (Power et al., 2012; Satterthwaite et al., 2012; Van Dijk et al., 2012). To address this, strategies for removing or reducing the impact of motion-degraded subwindows of data are routinely used—either simply removing them from analyses ("scrubbing") (Power et al., 2012), and/or using a larger number of motion-derived nuisance regressors (including derivatives and lagged versions of the motion) (Satterthwaite et al., 2013). For more details, we direct readers to two recent and exhaustive evaluations of processing pipelines to control motion artifacts (Ciric et al., 2017; Parkes et al., 2018).

5.6.2 Diffusion-weighted imaging

Following the description of motion effects in functional connectivity analyses, similar findings of motion-induced biases were reported in DWI (Yendiki et al., 2014). Motion correction in DWI is complicated by the fact that most image volumes are also encoded with a unique diffusion-encoding vector, which is fixed inscanner coordinates, and so care must be taken when images are retrospectively motion-corrected to similarly rotate the diffusion vectors used in quantitative analyses (Leemans and Jones, 2009; Pierpaoli, 2010). Due to the strong interactions of motion, distortions due to eddy currents and B_0 inhomogeneity, and drop outs due to motion during diffusion encoding, a unified DWI-specific analysis framework for correcting these effects in parallel has been an active area of work (Rohde et al., 2004; Andersson et al., 2016; Andersson and Sotiropoulos, 2016); this approach has been widely adopted in recent studies (Casey et al., 2018; Harms et al., 2018).

5.6.3 Morphometry

Despite one early report of motion-induced biases in MRI-based morphometry (Blumenthal et al., 2002), this effect has only recently been explored in detail, finding reproducible spatial distributions of motion-induced bias across the brain using a variety of pulse sequences and analysis software packages (Reuter et al., 2015; Alexander-Bloch et al., 2016; Pardoe et al., 2016; Savalia et al., 2017). One key finding from this work was that even very aggressive quality control and discarding of motion-degraded structural data did not reduce the effect size of motion on morphometry, suggesting this effect is latent in even apparently high-quality imaging data (Reuter et al., 2015).

To date, only image-based navigators have been directly demonstrated to improve quantitative morphometry, and only in the context of directed-motion studies in healthy volunteers (Tisdall et al., 2016; Sarlls et al., 2018). However, this result strongly suggests that other motion-correction systems should offer similar improvements in similar directed-motion studies. An open question remains exactly how effective individual motion-correction technologies will be for specific study populations. Regardless, the strong suggestion of benefit has led to their inclusion in recent multicenter pediatric studies (Casey et al., 2018; Harms et al., 2018), and subsequent replication of these established protocols in many smaller studies.

6. Conclusion

In this chapter, we have evaluated many of the common sources of artifact in pediatric neuroimaging studies. A great deal of research over more than three decades has resulted in both a very good understanding of the physical causes of data degradation due to distortion and motion, and strategies for mitigating them either through modified acquisitions or data postprocessing. Moreover, as the impacts of these artifacts on quantitative analyses have become clear, new technologies have been developed and evaluated to further mitigate these spurious sources of group difference. However, it is also apparent that these artifacts are still a source of significant concern in studies, both due to their propensity for reducing study power and biasing quantitative results. As such, this remains an active area of work, both for engineers and physicists developing novel imaging technologies, and also for neuroscientists, improving study designs and analysis strategies to isolate artifactual effects from the true parameters of interest.

Acknowledgments

The author would like to thank Anne Park, who assisted the preparation of imaging data for Figs. 2, 4, and 6, and TracInnovations, for providing the point cloud image in Fig. 8.

References

Aksoy, M., Forman, C., Straka, M., Skare, S., Holdsworth, S., Hornegger, J., Bammer, R., 2011. Real-time optical motion correction for diffusion tensor imaging. Magn. Reson. Med. 66, 366–378. https://doi.org/10.1002/mrm.22787.

Alexander, A.L., Tsuruda, J.S., Parker, D.L., 1997. Elimination of eddy current artifacts in diffusion-weighted echo-planar images: the use of bipolar gradients. Magn. Reson. Med. 38, 1016–1021. https://doi.org/10.1002/mrm.1910380623.

Alexander-Bloch, A., Clasen, L., Stockman, M., Ronan, L., Lalonde, F., Giedd, J., Raznahan, A., 2016. Subtle in-scanner motion biases automated measurement of brain anatomy from in vivo MRI. Hum. Brain Mapp. 37, 2385–2397. https://doi.org/10.1002/hbm.23180.

Alhamud, A., Tisdall, M.D., Hess, A.T., Hasan, K.M., Meintjes, E.M., van der Kouwe, A.J.W., 2012. Volumetric navigators for real-time motion correction in diffusion tensor imaging. Magn. Reson. Med. 68, 1097–1108. https://doi.org/10.1002/mrm.23314.

Alhamud, A., Taylor, P.A., van der Kouwe, A.J.W., Meintjes, E.M., 2016. Real-time measurement and correction of both B0 changes and subject motion in diffusion tensor imaging using a double volumetric navigated (DvNav) sequence. NeuroImage 126, 60–71. https://doi.org/10.1016/j.neuroimage.2015.11.022.

Andersen, M., Björkman-Burtscher, I.M., Marsman, A., Petersen, E.T., Boer, V.O., 2019a. Improvement in diagnostic quality of structural and angiographic MRI of the brain using motion correction with interleaved, volumetric navigators. PLoS One 14, e0217145. https://doi.org/10.1371/journal.pone.0217145.

Andersen, J.B., Lindberg, U., Olesen, O.V., Benoit, D., Ladefoged, C.N., Larsson, H.B., Højgaard, L., Greisen, G., Law, I., 2019b. Hybrid PET/MRI imaging in healthy unsedated newborn infants with quantitative rCBF measurements using ^{15}O-water PET. J. Cereb. Blood Flow Metab. 39, 782–793. https://doi.org/10.1177/0271678X17751835.

Anderson, A.G., Velikina, J., Block, W., Wieben, O., Samsonov, A., 2013. Adaptive retrospective correction of motion artifacts in cranial MRI with multicoil three-dimensional radial acquisitions. Magn. Reson. Med. 69, 1094–1103. https://doi.org/10.1002/mrm.24348.

Andersson, J.L.R., Skare, S., 2002. A model-based method for retrospective correction of geometric distortions in diffusion-weighted EPI. NeuroImage 16, 177–199. https://doi.org/10.1006/nimg.2001.1039.

Andersson, J.L.R., Sotiropoulos, S.N., 2016. An integrated approach to correction for off-resonance effects and subject movement in diffusion MR imaging. NeuroImage 125, 1063–1078. https://doi.org/10.1016/j.neuroimage.2015.10.019.

Andersson, J.L.R., Skare, S., Ashburner, J., 2003. How to correct susceptibility distortions in spin-echo echo-planar images: application to diffusion tensor imaging. NeuroImage 20, 870–888. https://doi.org/10.1016/S1053-8119(03)00336-7.

Andersson, J.L.R., Graham, M.S., Zsoldos, E., Sotiropoulos, S.N., 2016. Incorporating outlier detection and replacement into a non-parametric framework for movement and distortion correction of diffusion MR images. NeuroImage 141, 556–572. https://doi.org/10.1016/j.neuroimage.2016.06.058.

Andropoulos, D.B., Greene, M.F., 2017. Anesthesia and developing brains—implications of the FDA warning. N. Engl. J. Med. 376 (10), 905–907.

Aranovitch, A., Haeberlin, M., Gross, S., Dietrich, B.E., Wilm, B.J., Brunner, D.O., Schmid, T., Luechinger, R., Pruessmann, K.P., 2018. Prospective motion correction with NMR markers using only native sequence elements. Magn. Reson. Med. 79, 2046–2056. https://doi.org/10.1002/mrm.26877.

Avventi, E., Ryden, H., Norbeck, O., Berglund, J., Sprenger, T., Skare, S., 2020. Projection-based 3D/2D registration for prospective motion correction. Magn. Reson. Med. 84, 1534–1542. https://doi.org/10.1002/mrm.28225.

Bammer, R., Aksoy, M., Liu, C., 2007. Augmented generalized SENSE reconstruction to correct for rigid body motion. Magn. Reson. Med. 57, 90–102. https://doi.org/10.1002/mrm.21106.

Barkovich, M.J., Xu, D., Desikan, R.S., Williams, C., Barkovich, A.J., 2018. Pediatric neuro MRI: tricks to minimize sedation. Pediatr. Radiol. 48, 50–55. https://doi.org/10.1007/s00247-017-3785-1.

Benner, T., van der Kouwe, A.J.W., Sorensen, A.G., 2011. Diffusion imaging with prospective motion correction and reacquisition. Magn. Reson. Med. 66, 154–167. https://doi.org/10.1002/mrm.22837.

Blumenthal, J.D., Zijdenbos, A., Molloy, E., Giedd, J.N., 2002. Motion artifact in magnetic resonance imaging: implications for automated analysis. NeuroImage 16, 89–92. https://doi.org/10.1006/nimg.2002.1076.

Boesch, C., Gruetter, R., Martin, E., 1991. Temporal and spatial analysis of fields generated by eddy currents in superconducting magnets: optimization of corrections and quantitative characterization of magnet/gradient systems. Magn. Reson. Med. 20, 268–284. https://doi.org/10.1002/mrm.1910200209.

Bolton, T.A.W., Kebets, V., Glerean, E., Zöller, D., Li, J., Yeo, B.T.T., Caballero-Gaudes, C., Van De Ville, D., 2020. Agito ergo sum: correlates of spatio-temporal motion characteristics during fMRI. NeuroImage 209, 116433. https://doi.org/10.1016/j.neuroimage.2019.116433.

Bowtell, R., McIntyre, D., Commandre, M., Glover, P., Mansfield, P., 1994. Correction of geometric distortion in echo planar images. Soc. Magn. Res. Abstr. 2, 411.

Casey, B.J., Cannonier, T., Conley, M.I., Cohen, A.O., Barch, D.M., Heitzeg, M.M., Soules, M.E., Teslovich, T., Dellarco, D.V., Garavan, H., Orr, C.A., Wager, T.D., Banich, M.T., Speer, N.K., Sutherland, M.T., Riedel, M.C., Dick, A.S., Bjork, J.M., Thomas, K.M., Chaarani, B., Mejia, M.H., Hagler, D.J., Daniela Cornejo, M., Sicat, C.S., Harms, M.P., Dosenbach, N.U.F., Rosenberg, M., Earl, E., Bartsch, H., Watts, R., Polimeni, J.R., Kuperman, J.M., Fair, D.A., Dale, A.M., 2018. The adolescent brain cognitive development (ABCD) study: imaging acquisition across 21 sites. Dev. Cogn. Neurosci. 32, 43–54. https://doi.org/10.1016/j.dcn.2018.03.001.

Chang, H., Fitzpatrick, J.M., 1992. A technique for accurate magnetic resonance imaging in the presence of field inhomogeneities. IEEE Trans. Med. Imaging 11, 319–329. https://doi.org/10.1109/42.158935.

Ciric, R., Wolf, D.H., Power, J.D., Roalf, D.R., Baum, G.L., Ruparel, K., Shinohara, R.T., Elliott, M.A., Eickhoff, S.B., Davatzikos, C., Gur, R.C., Gur, R.E., Bassett, D.S., Satterthwaite, T.D., 2017. Benchmarking of participant-level confound regression strategies for the control of motion artifact in studies of functional connectivity. NeuroImage 154, 174–187. https://doi.org/10.1016/j.neuroimage.2017.03.020.

Couvy-Duchesne, B., Ebejer, J.L., Gillespie, N.A., Duffy, D.L., Hickie, I.B., Thompson, P.M., Martin, N.G., de Zubicaray, G.I., McMahon, K.L., Medland, S.E., Wright, M.J., 2016. Head motion and inattention/hyperactivity share common genetic influences: implications for fMRI studies of ADHD. PLoS One 11, e0146271. https://doi.org/10.1371/journal.pone.0146271.

Cox, R.W., 1996. AFNI: software for analysis and visualization of functional magnetic resonance neuroimages. Comput. Biomed. Res. 29, 162–173. https://doi.org/10.1006/cbmr.1996.0014.

Cravero, J.P., Beach, M.L., Blike, G.T., Gallagher, S.M., Hertzog, J.H., 2009. The incidence and nature of adverse events during pediatric sedation/anesthesia with propofol for procedures outside the operating room: a report from the pediatric sedation research consortium. Anesthesia and Analgesia 108, 795–804. https://doi.org/10.1213/ane.0b013e31818fc334.

de Bie, H.M.A., Boersma, M., Wattjes, M.P., Adriaanse, S., Vermeulen, R.J., Oostrom, K.J., Huisman, J., Veltman, D.J., Delemarre-Van de Waal, H.A., 2010. Preparing children with a mock scanner training protocol results in high quality structural and functional MRI scans. Eur. J. Pediatr. 169, 1079–1085. https://doi.org/10.1007/s00431-010-1181-z.

de Zwart, J.A., van Gelderen, P., Kellman, P., Duyn, J.H., 2002. Application of sensitivity-encoded echo-planar imaging for blood oxygen level-dependent functional brain imaging. Magn. Reson. Med. 48, 1011–1020. https://doi.org/10.1002/mrm.10303.

Dean, D.C., Dirks, H., O'Muircheartaigh, J., Walker, L., Jerskey, B.A., Lehman, K., Han, M., Waskiewicz, N., Deoni, S.C.L., 2014. Pediatric neuroimaging using magnetic resonance imaging during non-sedated sleep. Pediatr. Radiol. 44, 64–72. https://doi.org/10.1007/s00247-013-2752-8.

Dosenbach, N.U.F., Koller, J.M., Earl, E.A., Miranda-Dominguez, O., Klein, R.L., Van, A.N., Snyder, A.Z., Nagel, B.J., Nigg, J.T., Nguyen, A.L., Wesevich, V., Greene, D.J., Fair, D.A., 2017. Real-time motion analytics during brain MRI improve data quality and reduce costs. NeuroImage 161, 80–93. https://doi.org/10.1016/j.neuroimage.2017.08.025.

Duong, T.Q., Yacoub, E., Adriany, G., Hu, X., Ugurbil, K., Vaughan, J.T., Merkle, H., Kim, S.-G., 2002. High-resolution, spin-echo BOLD, and CBF fMRI at 4 and 7 T. Magn. Reson. Med. 48, 589–593. https://doi.org/10.1002/mrm.10252.

Dymerska, B., Poser, B.A., Barth, M., Trattnig, S., Robinson, S.D., 2018. A method for the dynamic correction of B 0-related distortions in single-echo EPI at 7 T. NeuroImage 168, 321–331. https://doi.org/10.1016/j.neuroimage.2016.07.009.

Ekhtiari, H., Kuplicki, R., Yeh, H., Paulus, M.P., 2019. Physical characteristics not psychological state or trait characteristics predict motion during resting state fMRI. Sci. Rep. 9. https://doi.org/10.1038/s41598-018-36699-0.

Engelhardt, L.E., Roe, M.A., Juranek, J., DeMaster, D., Harden, K.P., Tucker-Drob, E.M., Church, J.A., 2017. Children's head motion during fMRI tasks is heritable and stable over time. Dev. Cogn. Neurosci. 25, 58–68. https://doi.org/10.1016/j.dcn.2017.01.011.

Engström, M., Mårtensson, M., Avventi, E., Norbeck, O., Skare, S., 2015. Collapsed fat navigators for brain 3D rigid body motion. Magn. Reson. Imaging 33, 984–991. https://doi.org/10.1016/j.mri.2015.06.014.

Ericsson, A., Weis, J., Hemmingsson, A., Wikström, M., Sperber, G.O., 1995. Measurements of magnetic field variations in the human brain using a 3D-FT multiple gradient Echo technique. Magn. Reson. Med. 33, 171–177. https://doi.org/10.1002/mrm.1910330205.

Eviatar, H., Schattka, B., Sharp, J., Rendell, J., Alexander, M.E., 1999. Real time head motion correction for functional MRI. In: Proceedings of the International Society for Magnetic Resonance in Medicine, p. 269.

Farzaneh, F., Riederer, S.J., Pelc, N.J., 1990. Analysis of T2 limitations and off-resonance effects on spatial resolution and artifacts in echo-planar imaging. Magn. Reson. Med. 14, 123–139. https://doi.org/10.1002/mrm.1910140112.

Fessler, J.A., Sutton, B.P., 2003. Nonuniform fast Fourier transforms using min-max interpolation. IEEE Trans. Signal Process. 51, 560–574. https://doi.org/10.1109/TSP.2002.807005.

Finsterbusch, J., 2009. Eddy-current compensated diffusion weighting with a single refocusing RF pulse. Magn. Reson. Med. 61, 748–754. https://doi.org/10.1002/mrm.21899.

Friston, K.J., Williams, S., Howard, R., Frackowiak, R.S.J., Turner, R., 1996. Movement-Related effects in fMRI time-series. Magn. Reson. Med. 35, 346–355. https://doi.org/10.1002/mrm.1910350312.

Frost, R., Wighton, P., Karahanoğlu, F.I., Robertson, R.L., Grant, P.E., Fischl, B., Tisdall, M.D., van der Kouwe, A., 2019. Markerless high-frequency prospective motion correction for neuroanatomical MRI. Magn. Reson. Med. 82, 126–144. https://doi.org/10.1002/mrm.27705.

Fu, Z.W., Wang, Y., Grimm, R.C., Rossman, P.J., Felmlee, J.P., Riederer, S.J., Ehman, R.L., 1995. Orbital navigator echoes for motion measurements in magnetic resonance imaging. Magn. Reson. Med. 34, 746–753. https://doi.org/10.1002/mrm.1910340514.

Funai, A.K., Fessler, J.A., Yeo, D.T.B., Olafsson, V.T., Noll, D.C., 2008. Regularized field map estimation in MRI. IEEE Trans. Med. Imaging 27, 1484–1494. https://doi.org/10.1109/TMI.2008.923956.

Gallichan, D., 2020. retroMoCoBox. WWW document https://github.com/dgallichan/retroMoCoBox.

Gallichan, D., Andersson, J.L.R., Jenkinson, M., Robson, M.D., Miller, K.L., 2010. Reducing distortions in diffusion-weighted echo planar imaging with a dual-echo blip-reversed sequence. Magn. Reson. Med. https://doi.org/10.1002/mrm.22318.

Gallichan, D., Marques, J.P., Gruetter, R., 2016. Retrospective correction of involuntary microscopic head movement using highly accelerated fat image navigators (3D FatNavs) at 7T: 3D FatNavs for high-resolution retrospective motion correction. Magn. Reson. Med. 75, 1030–1039. https://doi.org/10.1002/mrm.25670.

Glasser, M.F., Sotiropoulos, S.N., Wilson, J.A., Coalson, T.S., Fischl, B., Andersson, J.L., Xu, J., Jbabdi, S., Webster, M., Polimeni, J.R., Van Essen, D.C., Jenkinson, M., 2013. The minimal preprocessing pipelines for the human connectome project. NeuroImage 80, 105–124. https://doi.org/10.1016/j.neuroimage.2013.04.127.

Graham, M.S., Drobnjak, I., Jenkinson, M., Zhang, H., 2017. Quantitative assessment of the susceptibility artefact and its interaction with motion in diffusion MRI. PLoS One 12, e0185647. https://doi.org/10.1371/journal.pone.0185647.

Greene, D.J., Koller, J.M., Hampton, J.M., Wesevich, V., Van, A.N., Nguyen, A.L., Hoyt, C.R., McIntyre, L., Earl, E.A., Klein, R.L., Shimony, J.S., Petersen, S.E., Schlaggar, B.L., Fair, D.A., Dosenbach, N.U.F., 2018. Behavioral interventions for reducing head motion during MRI scans in children. NeuroImage 171, 234–245. https://doi.org/10.1016/j.neuroimage.2018.01.023.

Gretsch, F., Marques, J.P., Gallichan, D., 2018. Investigating the accuracy of FatNav-derived estimates of temporal B_0 changes and their application to retrospective correction of high-resolution 3D GRE of the human brain at 7T: FatNav-derived estimates of temporal B_0 changes. Magn. Reson. Med. 80, 585–597. https://doi.org/10.1002/mrm.27063.

Gunter, J.L., Bernstein, M.A., Borowski, B.J., Ward, C.P., Britson, P.J., Felmlee, J.P., Schuff, N., Weiner, M., Jack, C.R., 2009. Measurement of MRI scanner performance with the ADNI phantom: measurement ADNI phantom. Med. Phys. 36, 2193–2205. https://doi.org/10.1118/1.3116776.

Haeberlin, M., Kasper, L., Barmet, C., Brunner, D.O., Dietrich, B.E., Gross, S., Wilm, B.J., Kozerke, S., Pruessmann, K.P., 2015. Real-time motion correction using gradient tones and head-mounted NMR field probes: real-time motion correction using gradient tones and NMR Field probes. Magn. Reson. Med. 74, 647–660. https://doi.org/10.1002/mrm.25432.

Hajnal, J.V., Myers, R., Oatridge, A., Schwieso, J.E., Young, I.R., Bydder, G.M., 1994. Artifacts due to stimulus correlated motion in functional imaging of the brain. Magn. Reson. Med. 31, 283–291. https://doi.org/10.1002/mrm.1910310307.

Harms, M.P., Somerville, L.H., Ances, B.M., Andersson, J., Barch, D.M., Bastiani, M., Bookheimer, S.Y., Brown, T.B., Buckner, R.L., Burgess, G.C., Coalson, T.S., Chappell, M.A., Dapretto, M., Douaud, G., Fischl, B., Glasser, M.F., Greve, D.N., Hodge, C., Jamison, K.W., Jbabdi, S., Kandala, S., Li, X., Mair, R.W., Mangia, S., Marcus, D., Mascali, D., Moeller, S., Nichols, T.E., Robinson, E.C., Salat, D.H., Smith, S.M., Sotiropoulos, S.N., Terpstra, M., Thomas, K.M., Tisdall, M.D., Ugurbil, K., van der Kouwe, A., Woods, R.P., Zöllei, L., Van Essen, D.C., Yacoub, E., 2018. Extending the human connectome project across ages: imaging protocols for the lifespan development and aging projects. NeuroImage 183, 972–984. https://doi.org/10.1016/j.neuroimage.2018.09.060.

Herbst, M., Maclaren, J., Weigel, M., Korvink, J., Hennig, J., Zaitsev, M., 2012a. Prospective motion correction with continuous gradient updates in diffusion weighted imaging. Magn. Reson. Med. 67, 326–338. https://doi.org/10.1002/mrm.23230.

Herbst, M., Maclaren, J., Weigel, M., Zaitsev, M., 2012b. Investigation and continuous correction of motion during turbo spin echo sequences. In: Proceedings 20th Scientific Meeting, International Society for Magnetic Resonance in Medicine, Melbourne.

Hess, A.T., Tisdall, M.D., Andronesi, O.C., Meintjes, E.M., van der Kouwe, A.J.W., 2011. Real-time motion and B0 corrected single voxel spectroscopy using volumetric navigators. Magn. Reson. Med. 66, 314–323. https://doi.org/10.1002/mrm.22805.

Hidalgo-Tobon, S.S., 2010. Theory of gradient coil design methods for magnetic resonance imaging. Concepts Magn. Reson. Part A 36A, 223–242. https://doi.org/10.1002/cmr.a.20163.

Hodgson, K., Poldrack, R.A., Curran, J.E., Knowles, E.E., Mathias, S., Göring, H.H., Yao, N., Olvera, R.L., Fox, P.T., Almasy, L., Duggirala, R., Barch, D.M., Blangero, J., Glahn, D.C., 2017. Shared genetic factors influence head motion during MRI and body mass index. Cereb. Cortex 27, 5539–5546. https://doi.org/10.1093/cercor/bhw321.

Hoinkiss, D.C., Porter, D.A., 2017. Prospective motion correction in diffusion-weighted imaging using intermediate pseudo-trace-weighted images. NeuroImage 149, 1–14. https://doi.org/10.1016/j.neuroimage.2016.12.055.

Holdsworth, S., Skare, S., Nordell, A., Newbould, R., Bammer, R., 2008. 3D SAP-EPI for self-navigated T1w spoiled gradient echo imaging. Proc. Int. Soc. Magn. Reson. Med. Tor. Can. 1352.

Holland, D., Kuperman, J.M., Dale, A.M., 2010. Efficient correction of inhomogeneous static magnetic field-induced distortion in echo planar imaging. NeuroImage 50, 175–183. https://doi.org/10.1016/j.neuroimage.2009.11.044.

Hoogenraad, F.G.C., Pouwels, P.J.W., Hofman, M.B.M., Rombouts, S.A.R.B., Lavini, C., Leach, M.O., Haacke, E.M., 2000. High-resolution segmented EPI in a motor task fMRI study. Magn. Reson. Imaging 18, 405–409. https://doi.org/10.1016/S0730-725X(00)00127-2.

Horsfield, M.A., 1999. Mapping eddy current induced fields for the correction of diffusion-weighted echo planar images. Magn. Reson. Imaging 17, 1335–1345. https://doi.org/10.1016/S0730-725X(99)00077-6.

Hutton, C., Bork, A., Josephs, O., Deichmann, R., Ashburner, J., Turner, R., 2002. Image distortion correction in fMRI: a quantitative evaluation. NeuroImage 16, 217–240. https://doi.org/10.1006/nimg.2001.1054.

Jenkinson, M., 1999. Measuring transformation error by RMS deviation (technical report no. TR99MJ1). FMRIB Technical Report, FMRIB, Oxford.

Jenkinson, M., Bannister, P., Brady, M., Smith, S., 2002. Improved optimization for the robust and accurate linear registration and motion correction of brain images. NeuroImage 17, 825–841. https://doi.org/10.1006/nimg.2002.1132.

Jesmanowicz, A., Bandettini, P.A., Hyde, J.S., 1998. Single-shot half k-space high-resolution gradient-recalled EPI for fMRI at 3 tesla. Magn. Reson. Med. 40, 754–762. https://doi.org/10.1002/mrm.1910400517.

Jezzard, P., Balaban, R.S., 1995. Correction for geometric distortion in echo planar images from B0 field variations. Magn. Reson. Med. 34, 65–73. https://doi.org/10.1002/mrm.1910340111.

Jezzard, P., Clare, S., 1999. Sources of distortion in functional MRI data. Hum. Brain Mapp. 8, 80–85. https://doi.org/10.1002/(SICI)1097-0193(1999)8:2/3<80::AID-HBM2>3.0.CO;2-C.

Jezzard, P., Barnett, A.S., Pierpaoli, C., 1998. Characterization of and correction for eddy current artifacts in echo planar diffusion imaging. Magn. Reson. Med. 39, 801–812. https://doi.org/10.1002/mrm.1910390518.

Johnson, G., Hutchison, J.M.S., 1985. The limitations of NMR recalled-echo imaging techniques. J. Magn. Reson. 1969 (63), 14–30. https://doi.org/10.1016/0022-2364(85)90149-0.

Kecskemeti, S., Samsonov, A., Hurley, S.A., Dean, D.C., Field, A., Alexander, A.L., 2016. MPnRAGE: a technique to simultaneously acquire hundreds of differently contrasted MPRAGE images with applications to quantitative T1 mapping. Magn. Reson. Med. 75, 1040–1053. https://doi.org/10.1002/mrm.25674.

Kim, B., Boes, J.L., Bland, P.H., Chenevert, T.L., Meyer, C.R., 1999. Motion correction in fMRI via registration of individual slices into an anatomical volume. Magn. Reson. Med. 41, 964–972. https://doi.org/10.1002/(SICI)1522-2594(199905)41:5<964::AID-MRM16>3.0.CO;2-D.

Kober, T., Marques, J.P., Gruetter, R., Krueger, G., 2011. Head motion detection using FID navigators. Magn. Reson. Med. 66, 135–143. https://doi.org/10.1002/mrm.22797.

Kong, X., Zhen, Z., Li, X., Lu, H., Wang, R., Liu, L., He, Y., Zang, Y., Liu, J., 2014. Individual differences in impulsivity predict head motion during magnetic resonance imaging. PLoS One 9, e104989. https://doi.org/10.1371/journal.pone.0104989.

Leemans, A., Jones, D.K., 2009. The B-matrix must be rotated when correcting for subject motion in DTI data. Magn. Reson. Med. 61, 1336–1349. https://doi.org/10.1002/mrm.21890.

Li, S., Dardzinski, B.J., Collins, C.M., Yang, Q.X., Smith, M.B., 1996. Three-dimensional mapping of the static magnetic field inside the human head. Magn. Reson. Med. 36, 705–714. https://doi.org/10.1002/mrm.1910360509.

Lipschutz, B., Friston, K.J., Ashburner, J., Turner, R., Price, C.J., 2001. Assessing study-specific regional variations in fMRI signal. NeuroImage 13, 392–398. https://doi.org/10.1006/nimg.2000.0687.

Liu, J., van Gelderen, P., de Zwart, J.A., Duyn, J.H., 2019. Reducing motion sensitivity in 3D high-resolution T2*-weighted MRI by navigator-based motion and nonlinear magnetic field correction. NeuroImage, 116332. https://doi.org/10.1016/j.neuroimage.2019.116332.

Ljunggren, S., 1983. A simple graphics representation of Fourier-based imaging methods. J. Magn. Reson. 54, 338–343.

Lüdeke, K.M., Röschmann, P., Tischler, R., 1985. Susceptibility artefacts in NMR imaging. Magn. Reson. Imaging 3, 329–343. https://doi.org/10.1016/0730-725X(85)90397-2.

Maclaren, J., Speck, O., Stucht, D., Schulze, P., Hennig, J., Zaitsev, M., 2010. Navigator accuracy requirements for prospective motion correction. Magn. Reson. Med. 63, 162–170.

Maclaren, J., Armstrong, B.S.R., Barrows, R.T., Danishad, K.A., Ernst, T., Foster, C.L., Gumus, K., Herbst, M., Kadashevich, I.Y., Kusik, T.P., Li, Q., Lovell-Smith, C., Prieto, T., Schulze, P., Speck, O., Stucht, D., Zaitsev, M., 2012. Measurement and correction of microscopic head motion during magnetic resonance imaging of the brain. PLoS One 7, e48088. https://doi.org/10.1371/journal.pone.0048088.

Maclaren, J., Herbst, M., Speck, O., Zaitsev, M., 2013. Prospective motion correction in brain imaging: a review. Magn. Reson. Med. 69, 621–636. https://doi.org/10.1002/mrm.24314.

Macovski, A., 1996. Noise in MRI. Magn. Reson. Med. 36, 494–497.

Mathur, A.M., Neil, J.J., McKinstry, R.C., Inder, T.E., 2008. Transport, monitoring, and successful brain MR imaging in unsedated neonates. Pediatr. Radiol. 38, 260–264. https://doi.org/10.1007/s00247-007-0705-9.

McNab, J.A., Gallichan, D., Miller, K.L., 2009. 3D steady-state diffusion-weighted imaging with trajectory using radially batched internal navigator echoes (TURBINE). Magn. Reson. Med. https://doi.org/10.1002/mrm.22183.

Noll, D.C., Pauly, J.M., Meyer, C.H., Nishimura, D.G., Macovskj, A., 1992. Deblurring for non-2D Fourier transform magnetic resonance imaging. Magn. Reson. Med. 25, 319–333. https://doi.org/10.1002/mrm.1910250210.

Norris, D.G., 2001. Implications of bulk motion for diffusion-weighted imaging experiments: effects, mechanisms, and solutions. J. Magn. Reson. Imaging 13, 486–495. https://doi.org/10.1002/jmri.1072.

O'Shaughnessy, E.S., Berl, M.M., Moore, E.N., Gaillard, W.D., 2008. Pediatric functional magnetic resonance imaging (fMRI): issues and applications. J. Child Neurol. 23, 791–801. https://doi.org/10.1177/0883073807313047.

Ojemann, J.G., Akbudak, E., Snyder, A.Z., McKinstry, R.C., Raichle, M.E., Conturo, T.E., 1997. Anatomic localization and quantitative analysis of gradient refocused echo-planar fMRI susceptibility artifacts. NeuroImage 6, 156–167. https://doi.org/10.1006/nimg.1997.0289.

Olesen, O.V., Paulsen, R.R., Hojgaard, L., Roed, B., Larsen, R., 2012. Motion tracking for medical imaging: a nonvisible structured light tracking approach. IEEE Trans. Med. Imaging 31, 79–87. https://doi.org/10.1109/TMI.2011.2165157.

Ooi, M.B., Krueger, S., Thomas, W.J., Swaminathan, S.V., Brown, T.R., 2009. Prospective real-time correction for arbitrary head motion using active markers. Magn. Reson. Med. 62, 943–954. https://doi.org/10.1002/mrm.22082.

Ooi, M.B., Krueger, S., Muraskin, J., Thomas, W.J., Brown, T.R., 2011. Echo-planar imaging with prospective slice-by-slice motion correction using active markers. Magn. Reson. Med. 66, 73–81. https://doi.org/10.1002/mrm.22780.

Ooi, M.B., Muraskin, J., Zou, X., Thomas, W.J., Krueger, S., Aksoy, M., Bammer, R., Brown, T.R., 2013. Combined prospective and retrospective correction to reduce motion-induced image misalignment and geometric distortions in EPI. Magn. Reson. Med. 69, 803–811. https://doi.org/10.1002/mrm.24285.

Pardoe, H.R., Kucharsky Hiess, R., Kuzniecky, R., 2016. Motion and morphometry in clinical and nonclinical populations. NeuroImage 135, 177–185. https://doi.org/10.1016/j.neuroimage.2016.05.005.

Parkes, L., Fulcher, B., Yücel, M., Fornito, A., 2018. An evaluation of the efficacy, reliability, and sensitivity of motion correction strategies for resting-state functional MRI. NeuroImage 171, 415–436. https://doi.org/10.1016/j.neuroimage.2017.12.073.

Pierpaoli, C., 2010. Artifacts in diffusion MRI. In: Jones, D.K. (Ed.), Diffusion MRI. Oxford University Press, pp. 303–318, https://doi.org/10.1093/med/9780195369779.003.0018.

Pipe, J.G., 1999. Motion correction with PROPELLER MRI: application to head motion and free-breathing cardiac imaging. Magn. Reson. Med. 42, 963–969. https://doi.org/10.1002/(SICI)1522-2594(199911)42:5<963::AID-MRM17>3.0.CO;2-L.

Pipe, J.G., Farthing, V.G., Forbes, K.P., 2002. Multishot diffusion-weighted FSE using PROPELLER MRI. Magn. Reson. Med. 47, 42–52. https://doi.org/10.1002/mrm.10014.

Power, J.D., Barnes, K.A., Snyder, A.Z., Schlaggar, B.L., Petersen, S.E., 2012. Spurious but systematic correlations in functional connectivity MRI networks arise from subject motion. NeuroImage 59, 2142–2154. https://doi.org/10.1016/j.neuroimage.2011.10.018.

Power, J.D., Silver, B.M., Silverman, M.R., Ajodan, E.L., Bos, D.J., Jones, R.M., 2019. Customized head molds reduce motion during resting state fMRI scans. NeuroImage 189, 141–149. https://doi.org/10.1016/j.neuroimage.2019.01.016.

Qin, L., van Gelderen, P., Derbyshire, J.A., Jin, F., Lee, J., de Zwart, J.A., Tao, Y., Duyn, J.H., 2009. Prospective head-movement correction for high-resolution MRI using an in-bore optical tracking system. Magn. Reson. Med. 62, 924–934. https://doi.org/10.1002/mrm.22076.

Raschle, N.M., Lee, M., Buechler, R., Christodoulou, J.A., Chang, M., Vakil, M., Stering, P.L., Gaab, N., 2009. Making MR imaging child's play-pediatric neuroimaging protocol, guidelines and procedure. J. Vis. Exp., e1309.

Reese, T.G., Heid, O., Weisskoff, R.M., Wedeen, V.J., 2003. Reduction of eddy-current-induced distortion in diffusion MRI using a twice-refocused spin echo. Magn. Reson. Med. 49, 177–182. https://doi.org/10.1002/mrm.10308.

Reuter, M., Tisdall, M.D., Qureshi, A., Buckner, R.L., van der Kouwe, A.J.W., Fischl, B., 2015. Head motion during MRI acquisition reduces gray matter volume and thickness estimates. NeuroImage 107, 107–115. https://doi.org/10.1016/j.neuroimage.2014.12.006.

Rohde, G.K., Barnett, A.S., Basser, P.J., Marenco, S., Pierpaoli, C., 2004. Comprehensive approach for correction of motion and distortion in diffusion-weighted MRI. Magn. Reson. Med. 51, 103–114. https://doi.org/10.1002/mrm.10677.

Roopchansingh, V., Cox, R.W., Jesmanowicz, A., Ward, B.D., Hyde, J.S., 2003. Single-shot magnetic field mapping embedded in echo-planar time-course imaging. Magn. Reson. Med. 50, 839–843. https://doi.org/10.1002/mrm.10587.

Rosenberg, D.R., Sweeney, J.A., Gillen, J.S., Kim, J., Varanelli, M.J., O'Hearn, K.M., Erb, P.A., Davis, D., Thulborn, K.R., 1997. Magnetic resonance imaging of children without sedation: preparation with simulation. J. Am. Acad. Child Adolesc. Psychiatry 36, 853–859. https://doi.org/10.1097/00004583-199706000-00024.

Saad, Z.S., Glen, D.R., Chen, G., Beauchamp, M.S., Desai, R., Cox, R.W., 2009. A new method for improving functional-to-structural MRI alignment using local Pearson correlation. NeuroImage 44, 839–848. https://doi.org/10.1016/j.neuroimage.2008.09.037.

Sarlls, J.E., Lalonde, F., Rettmann, D., Shankaranarayanan, A., Roopchansingh, V., Talagala, S.L., 2018. Effectiveness of navigator-based prospective motion correction in MPRAGE data acquired at 3T. PLoS One 13, e0199372. https://doi.org/10.1371/journal.pone.0199372.

Satterthwaite, T.D., Wolf, D.H., Loughead, J., Ruparel, K., Elliott, M.A., Hakonarson, H., Gur, R.C., Gur, R.E., 2012. Impact of in-scanner head motion on multiple measures of functional connectivity: relevance for studies of neurodevelopment in youth. NeuroImage 60, 623–632. https://doi.org/10.1016/j.neuroimage.2011.12.063.

Satterthwaite, T.D., Elliott, M.A., Gerraty, R.T., Ruparel, K., Loughead, J., Calkins, M.E., Eickhoff, S.B., Hakonarson, H., Gur, R.C., Gur, R.E., Wolf, D.H., 2013. An improved framework for confound regression and filtering for control of motion artifact in the preprocessing of resting-state functional connectivity data. NeuroImage 64, 240–256. https://doi.org/10.1016/j.neuroimage.2012.08.052.

Savalia, N.K., Agres, P.F., Chan, M.Y., Feczko, E.J., Kennedy, K.M., Wig, G.S., 2017. Motion-related artifacts in structural brain images revealed with independent estimates of in-scanner head motion. Hum. Brain Mapp. 38, 472–492. https://doi.org/10.1002/hbm.23397.

Schaffter, T., Rasche, V., Carlsen, I.C., 1999. Motion compensated projection reconstruction. Magn. Reson. Med. 41, 954–963. https://doi.org/10.1002/(SICI)1522-2594(199905)41:5<954::AID-MRM15>3.0.CO;2-J.

Schneider, E., Glover, G., 1991. Rapid in vivo proton shimming. Magn. Reson. Med. 18, 335–347. https://doi.org/10.1002/mrm.1910180208.

Siegel, J.S., Mitra, A., Laumann, T.O., Seitzman, B.A., Raichle, M., Corbetta, M., Snyder, A.Z., 2016. Data quality influences observed links between functional connectivity and behavior. Cereb. Cortex. https://doi.org/10.1093/cercor/bhw253.

Sutton, B.P., Noll, D.C., Fessler, J.A., 2004. Dynamic field map estimation using a spiral-in/spiral-out acquisition. Magn. Reson. Med. 51, 1194–1204. https://doi.org/10.1002/mrm.20079.

Tao, S., Trzasko, J.D., Shu, Y., Huston, J., Bernstein, M.A., 2015. Integrated image reconstruction and gradient nonlinearity correction: integrated image reconstruction and GNL correction. Magn. Reson. Med. 74, 1019–1031. https://doi.org/10.1002/mrm.25487.

Thesen, S., Heid, O., Mueller, E., Schad, L.R., 2000. Prospective acquisition correction for head motion with image-based tracking for real-time fMRI. Magn. Reson. Med. 44, 457–465. https://doi.org/10.1002/1522-2594(200009)44:3<457::AID-MRM17>3.0.CO;2-R.

Tisdall, M.D., Hess, A.T., Reuter, M., Meintjes, E.M., Fischl, B., van der Kouwe, A.J.W., 2012. Volumetric navigators for prospective motion correction and selective reacquisition in neuroanatomical MRI. Magn. Reson. Med. 68, 389–399. https://doi.org/10.1002/mrm.23228.

Tisdall, M.D., Reuter, M., Qureshi, A., Buckner, R.L., Fischl, B., van der Kouwe, A.J.W., 2016. Prospective motion correction with volumetric navigators (vNavs) reduces the bias and variance in brain morphometry induced by subject motion. NeuroImage 127, 11–22. https://doi.org/10.1016/j.neuroimage.2015.11.054.

Twieg, D.B., 1983. The k-trajectory formulation of the NMR imaging process with applications in analysis and synthesis of imaging methods. Med. Phys. 10, 610–621.

van der Kouwe, A.J.W., Benner, T., Dale, A.M., 2006. Real-time rigid body motion correction and shimming using cloverleaf navigators. Magn. Reson. Med. 56, 1019–1032. https://doi.org/10.1002/mrm.21038.

van der Kouwe, A.J.W., Benner, T., Salat, D.H., Fischl, B., 2008. Brain morphometry with multiecho MPRAGE. NeuroImage 40, 559–569. https://doi.org/10.1016/j.neuroimage.2007.12.025.

van der Kouwe, A., Fetics, B., Polenur, D., Roth, A., Nevo, E., 2009. Real-time prospective rigid-body motion correction with the endo scout gradient-based tracking system. In: Proc. 17th Scientific Meeting ISMRM, p. 4623.

Van Dijk, K.R.A., Sabuncu, M.R., Buckner, R.L., 2012. The influence of head motion on intrinsic functional connectivity MRI. NeuroImage 59, 431–438. https://doi.org/10.1016/j.neuroimage.2011.07.044.

van Niekerk, A., Meintjes, E., van der Kouwe, A., 2019. A wireless radio frequency triggered acquisition device (WRAD) for self-synchronised measurements of the rate of change of the MRI gradient vector Field for motion tracking. IEEE Trans. Med. Imaging 38, 1610–1621. https://doi.org/10.1109/TMI.2019.2891774.

Vanderwal, T., Kelly, C., Eilbott, J., Mayes, L.C., Castellanos, F.X., 2015. Inscapes: a movie paradigm to improve compliance in functional magnetic resonance imaging. NeuroImage 122, 222–232. https://doi.org/10.1016/j.neuroimage.2015.07.069.

Visser, E., Poser, B.A., Barth, M., Zwiers, M.P., 2012. Reference-free unwarping of EPI data using dynamic off-resonance correction with multiecho acquisition (DOCMA). Magn. Reson. Med. 68, 1247–1254. https://doi.org/10.1002/mrm.24119.

Wallace, T.E., Afacan, O., Waszak, M., Kober, T., Warfield, S.K., 2019. Head motion measurement and correction using FID navigators. Magn. Reson. Med. 81, 258–274. https://doi.org/10.1002/mrm.27381.

Ward, H.A., Riederer, S.J., Jack, C.R., 2002. Real-time autoshimming for echo planar timecourse imaging. Magn. Reson. Med. 48, 771–780. https://doi.org/10.1002/mrm.10259.

Webb, P., Macovski, A., 1991. Rapid, fully automatic, arbitrary-volume in vivo shimming. Magn. Reson. Med. 20, 113–122. https://doi.org/10.1002/mrm.1910200112.

Weinhandl, J.T., Armstrong, B.S.R., Kusik, T.P., Barrows, R.T., O'Connor, K.M., 2010. Validation of a single camera three-dimensional motion tracking system. J. Biomech. 43, 1437–1440. https://doi.org/10.1016/j.jbiomech.2009.12.025.

Weiskopf, N., Klose, U., Birbaumer, N., Mathiak, K., 2005. Single-shot compensation of image distortions and BOLD contrast optimization using multi-echo EPI for real-time fMRI. NeuroImage 24, 1068–1079. https://doi.org/10.1016/j.neuroimage.2004.10.012.

Welch, E.B., Manduca, A., Grimm, R.C., Ward, H.A., Jack Jr., C.R., 2002. Spherical navigator echoes for full 3D rigid body motion measurement in MRI. Magn. Reson. Med. 47, 32–41. https://doi.org/10.1002/mrm.10012.

Wen, H., Jaffer, F.A., 1995. An in vivo automated shimming method taking into account shim current constraints. Magn. Reson. Med. 34, 898–904. https://doi.org/10.1002/mrm.1910340616.

White, N., Roddey, C., Shankaranarayanan, A., Han, E., Rettmann, D., Santos, J., Kuperman, J., Dale, A., 2010. PROMO: real-time prospective motion correction in MRI using image-based tracking. Magn. Reson. Med. 63, 91–105. https://doi.org/10.1002/mrm.22176.

Wilm, B.J., Barmet, C., Pavan, M., Pruessmann, K.P., 2011. Higher order reconstruction for MRI in the presence of spatiotemporal field perturbations: higher order reconstruction for MRI. Magn. Reson. Med. 65, 1690–1701. https://doi.org/10.1002/mrm.22767.

Wilson, J.L., Jenkinson, M., de Araujo, I., Kringelbach, M.L., Rolls, E.T., Jezzard, P., 2002. Fast, fully automated global and local magnetic field optimization for fMRI of the human brain. NeuroImage 17, 967–976. https://doi.org/10.1006/nimg.2002.1172.

Wu, D.H., Lewin, J.S., Duerk, J.L., 1997. Inadequacy of motion correction algorithms in functional MRI: role of susceptibility-induced artifacts. J. Magn. Reson. Imaging 7, 365–370. https://doi.org/10.1002/jmri.1880070219.

Yancey, S.E., Rotenberg, D.J., Tam, F., Chiew, M., Ranieri, S., Biswas, L., Anderson, K.J.T., Nicole Baker, S., Wright, G.A., Graham, S.J., 2011. Spin-history artifact during functional MRI: potential for adaptive correction: spin-history artifact and adaptive correction during fMRI. Med. Phys. 38, 4634–4646. https://doi.org/10.1118/1.3583814.

Yarach, U., Luengviriya, C., Danishad, A., Stucht, D., Godenschweger, F., Schulze, P., Speck, O., 2015. Correction of gradient nonlinearity artifacts in prospective motion correction for 7T MRI: correction of gradient nonlinearity. Magn. Reson. Med. 73, 1562–1569. https://doi.org/10.1002/mrm.25283.

Yendiki, A., Koldewyn, K., Kakunoori, S., Kanwisher, N., Fischl, B., 2014. Spurious group differences due to head motion in a diffusion MRI study. NeuroImage 88, 79–90. https://doi.org/10.1016/j.neuroimage.2013.11.027.

Zahneisen, B., Keating, B., Singh, A., Herbst, M., Ernst, T., 2016. Reverse retrospective motion correction: reverse retrospective motion correction. Magn. Reson. Med. 75, 2341–2349. https://doi.org/10.1002/mrm.25830.

Zaitsev, M., Dold, C., Sakas, G., Hennig, J., Speck, O., 2006. Magnetic resonance imaging of freely moving objects: prospective real-time motion correction using an external optical motion tracking system. NeuroImage 31, 1038–1050. https://doi.org/10.1016/j.neuroimage.2006.01.039.

Zaitsev, M., Maclaren, J., Herbst, M., 2015. Motion artifacts in MRI: a complex problem with many partial solutions. J. Magn. Reson. Imaging 42, 887–901.

Zaitsev, M., Akin, B., LeVan, P., Knowles, B.R., 2017. Prospective motion correction in functional MRI. NeuroImage 154, 33–42. https://doi.org/10.1016/j.neuroimage.2016.11.014.

SECTION

MRI Postprocessing

2

CHAPTER

Pediatric brain atlases and parcellations

11

Kenichi Oishi

The Russell H. Morgan Department of Radiology and Radiological Science, The Johns Hopkins University School of Medicine, Baltimore, MD, United States

1. Introduction

The purpose of this chapter is to discuss the anatomical landmarks used for brain atlas parcellation, focusing particularly on the structures seen in pediatric brains. In this chapter, a brain atlas is defined as a set of anatomical images and the corresponding parcellation maps, in which various types of regional brain features, described in a standardized terminology, based on anatomy, function, metabolism, neurotransmitters, or gene expression, are assigned to each parcel. Three-dimensional digital brain atlases have been created for various species and image modalities (Toga and Thompson, 2009), and have been used as references to understand brain structures and functions, as well as to report scientific findings. In the neuroimaging community, the most widely used magnetic resonance image (MRI) modality that serves as a basis for the creation of a brain atlas is relaxation-based structural MRI (T1- or T2-weighted images). Other MRI including diffusion MRI, perfusion maps, functional activation maps, and quantitative susceptibility maps providing various contrasts have also been used. Other image modalities (e.g., histology images, computed tomography (CT), positron emission tomography, or single-photon emission CT) can be coregistered to the MRI atlas. The parcellation map is primarily created manually by experts in neuroanatomy and neuroradiology, based on their a priori knowledge about the relationships between image contrast and the biological properties of each anatomical structure. Although recent attempts have successfully parsed images based exclusively on image features, such as image contrast, the magnitude of brain activation, or neuronal connectivity among brain regions (Glasser et al., 2016; Kreilkamp et al., 2017; Gordon et al., 2016; Fan et al., 2016; Shi et al., 2017), we still depend on classical anatomical knowledge in brain parcellation due to the lack of a ground-truth based on which the human brain is parsed into a set of functional units sharing common anatomical and functional features. In the following sections, anatomical features and landmarks explicitly seen on structural or diffusion MRIs at a specific age-range during brain development, and developmental changes that need to be considered when brain images are parcellated, are reviewed.

Handbook of Pediatric Brain Imaging. https://doi.org/10.1016/B978-0-12-816633-8.00016-8

2. Anatomical features of the pediatric brain and the effect of image transformation

Atlas-based image analysis refers to a method in which each brain is parcellated based on its anatomical units in accordance with a brain atlas, followed by parcel-by-parcel statistics. This approach has been widely used in pediatric brain research to investigate chronological changes in morphology or signal intensity during normal development (Oishi et al., 2011; Akazawa et al., 2015; Chang et al., 2016a, b; Wu et al., 2017a, b; Rose et al., 2015, 2014a; Roze et al., 2015), as well as to identify the alterations seen in various diseases or conditions (Oishi et al., 2011; Chang et al., 2016a, b; Rose et al., 2014a, b; Pannek et al., 2013; He and Parikh, 2013; Kersbergen et al., 2014; Bai et al., 2012). Brain atlases play an essential role in atlas-based image analysis by providing a reference space and a set of parcels or regions of interest (ROI) that are used for image quantification (Fig. 1). To apply the parcellation map to target brains, a mathematical procedure, which is called image transformation, is used either by transforming an atlas to the target brains, or by transforming the target brains to the atlas. The image transformation is usually driven by the image contrast represented in anatomical MRI or by the directionality of the water diffusion measured by diffusion MRI: the transformation is the result of an effort to minimize mismatch in local image intensity or directionality between an atlas image and a target image. To achieve biologically appropriate image transformation, there are several prerequisites. First, both atlas and target images must have a set of identical anatomical structures. If a target image has structures or pathological changes that do not exist in an atlas image (e.g., white matter lesions or brain tumors), such structures are unable to be localized on an atlas space and therefore, interfere with biologically reasonable image transformation (Fig. 2). Similarly, if a target image lacks anatomical structures that exist on an

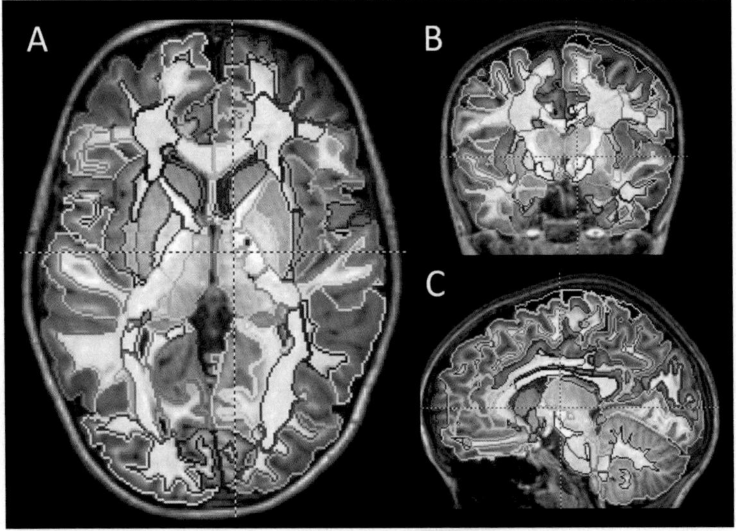

FIG. 1

Example of a pediatric brain atlas from the Johns Hopkins pediatric multiatlas library (Wu et al., 2016b). (A) axial view, (B) coronal view, and (C) sagittal view.

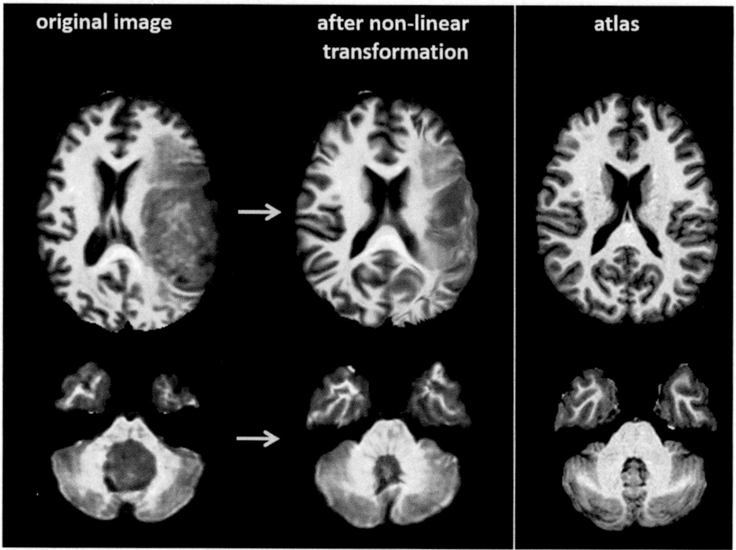

FIG. 2

Potential problem that occurs when transforming a brain MRI with a brain tumor to a normal brain atlas. The transformation algorithm relies on image contrast to coregister the anatomically identical areas of both images. In this case, the tumor in the left cerebrum was recognized as the cortical gray matter (upper row) and the tumor in the 4th ventricle was recognized as part of the ventricle and the cerebellar vermis (lower row). As the result, the transformation was biologically inappropriate.

atlas image, accurate image transformation is difficult to achieve. For example, it would be difficult to reasonably transform a target image without the corpus callosum due to a developmental malformation (agenesis of the corpus callosum) to an atlas with a normal corpus callosum. Second, the atlas and the target image need to be topologically identical. The topological mismatch is often seen in the lateral ventricle; even for normal brains, there are several variations in the shape of the lateral ventricle, such as an image with a single ventricular component, a closed ventricle, or a ventricle split into two unconnected compartments (Fig. 3). If the atlas and target ventricles are not topologically equivalent, the transformation between them fails (Djamanakova et al., 2013). Third, an atlas and the target images should be proportionally as similar as possible. If target brains are proportionally different from the atlas brain, the anatomical discrepancy between two images varies among brain locations and this variation can cause insufficient transformation in some brain areas and excess transformation in other brain areas.

Pediatric brains develop rapidly, which causes age-dependent variations in local brain volume and intensity. To account for the variations, particularly during early development (Feng et al., 2019; Zhan et al., 2013), pediatric brain atlases must be age-specific, since there are developmental stage-specific anatomical features that are not represented in brain atlases outside the target age-range (Feng et al., 2019; Hoeksma et al., 2005; Muzik et al., 2000; Wilke et al., 2002, 2003; Yoon et al., 2009; Murgasova et al., 2007). In the following sections, major anatomical features seen during brain development are discussed.

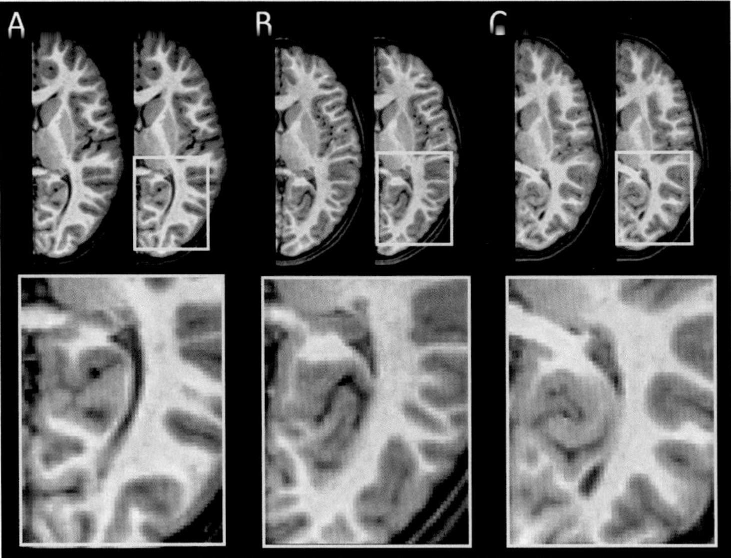

FIG. 3

Anatomical variations in the lateral ventricle, which are normally seen in healthy children. (A) a single ventricular component. (B) a closed ventricle. (C) a ventricle split into two unconnected compartments. The posterior horns of the left lateral ventricles are highlighted by red. Lower row: magnified view of the posterior horns.

3. Developmental change in image contrast

Image contrast has been used as one of the major clues to guide brain parcellation (Oishi et al., 2009; Tzourio-Mazoyer et al., 2002; Shattuck et al., 2008; Klein and Tourville, 2012; Desikan et al., 2006), particularly for the segmentation of each brain into three tissue compartments: gray and white matters; and cerebrospinal fluid (CSF) space. Although this compartmentation is simple for the adult brain, there are some issues with pediatric brains.

3.1 Rapid change in gray-white matter contrast

The gray-white matter separation is especially challenging for pediatric brains younger than 1 year of age, because of the limited contrasts between tissue types. For relaxation-based anatomical MRI contrasts, such as those seen on T1- and T2-weighted images, the relaxation property is affected by several factors, including the mobility of water molecules and the amount of paramagnetic content. Biological changes that occur during early brain development comprise proliferation and formation of oligodendroglial cells, synapses, and dendrites, as well as myelination, all of which result in increased signal intensity on T1-weighted images and decreased signal intensity on T2-weighted images. Time-dependent signal changes seen in white matter areas are mainly due to ongoing myelination (Barkovich et al., 1988; McArdle et al., 1987), which results in an increased amount of lipids that immobilize water molecules. T1-weighted images demonstrate the gray matter intensity brighter than

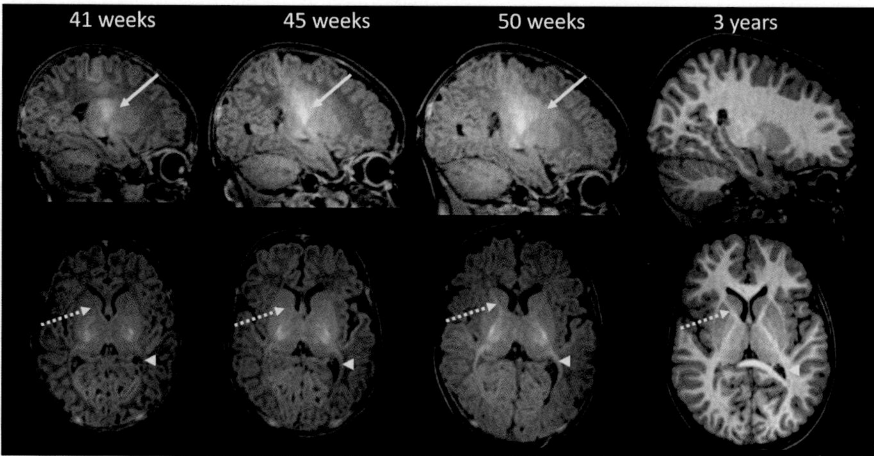

FIG. 4

Time-dependent signal changes observed in the white matter area on the T1-weighted image. The myelinated corticospinal tract is visualized as an area with high T1-weighted signal intensity at 41 weeks postmenstrual age. The high signal intensity area expands during development (*solid yellow arrows*). The unmyelinated anterior limb of the internal capsule (*dotted yellow arrows*) at 41 weeks postmenstrual age appears as a dark string between the caudate nucleus and the putamen. The intensity increases during development and appears as bright string at 50 weeks and after. The intensity of the posterior thalamic radiation (*yellow arrowheads*) is similar to that of the gray matter structures at 41 weeks postmenstrual age. The intensity increases due to ongoing myelination during development.

white matter at term, but active postnatal myelination causes the inversion of gray-white matter contrast that occurs during infancy. Notably, the timing and speed of myelination is structure-dependent, which causes co-existing myelinated and unmyelinated fibers during infancy (Fig. 4). Insufficient contrast between the gray and white matter structures hinder accurate tissue boundary definition, especially during 4–8 months of age, when many gray and white matter structures share similar intensities (Oishi et al., 2012). For the gray matter structures, high T1-weighted signal intensity is observed in the primary motor and sensory areas, such as the pre- and postcentral gyri, the pericalcarine cortex, and the transverse temporal gyrus (Heschl's gyrus), of the neonatal brain (Fig. 5). This hyperintensity is thought to be due to rapid glial proliferation and formation and synaptogenesis (Korogi et al., 1996). Transient T1-weighted signal hyperintensity seen in the subthalamic nucleus (Fig. 6) and globus pallidus in the neonatal brain (Counsell et al., 2002) is thought to be due to glial formation or reaction (Taoka et al., 2011), although the exact mechanism that causes the transient hyperintensity is unclear.

3.2 Effect of image contrast in the measurement of cortical thickness

Anatomical MRI has been used to quantify cortical thickness based on the gray-white matter contrast. Although there are some discrepancies among studies (Lyall et al., 2015; Schnack et al., 2015; Walhovd et al., 2017; Ducharme et al., 2016; Remer et al., 2017), MRI-based studies have observed that cortical thickness increases during infancy, reaches a plateau at some point, and decreases

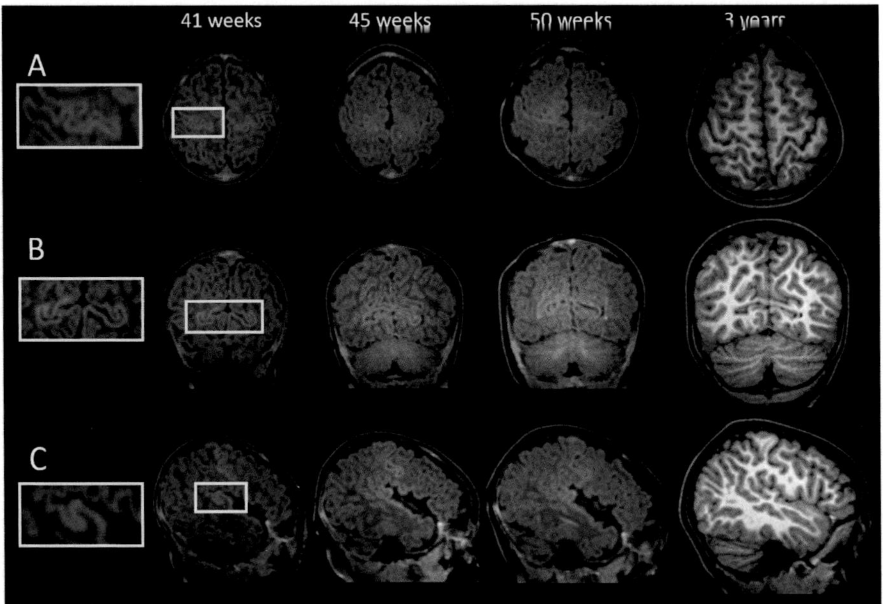

FIG. 5

High T1-weighted signal intensity that is observed in (A) the pre- and postcentral gyri, (B) the pericalcarine cortex, and (C) the transverse temporal gyrus, of the 41 weeks brain. The leftmost column demonstrates the magnified view.

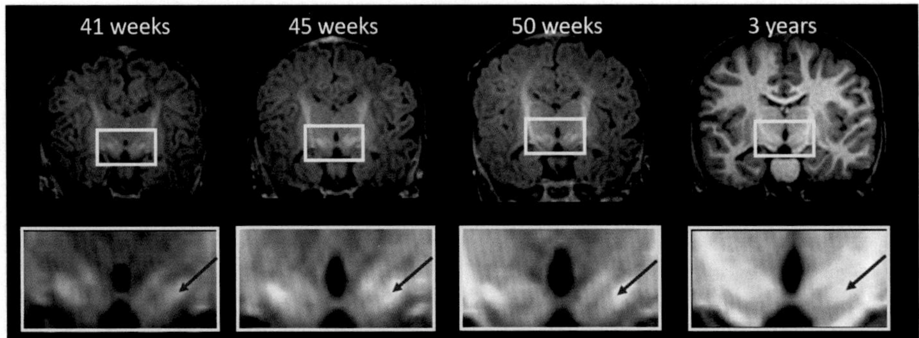

FIG. 6

High T1-weighted signal intensity that is observed in the subthalamic nuclei (*red arrow*). Lower row: magnified view.

thereafter. A longitudinal study reported that the whole-brain average cortical thickness reaches a plateau at about 14 months of age, although the age at the maximum cortical thickness varies depending on the brain area (Wang et al., 2019). However, whether the boundary between gray and white matter structures visible on anatomical MRI represents the boundary defined by the cytoarchitecture is yet to be investigated, particularly for still-developing brains. A study has demonstrated that increased myelin at the lateral ventral temporal cortex alters the gray-white matter contrast on MRI images, which, in turn, causes apparent cortical thinning, while cortical thinning seen on the medial ventral temporal cortex is related to cortical morphology (Natu et al., 2019). This finding suggests that the cortical thickening and thinning observed on anatomical MRI during development might be affected by various factors, including cortical morphology and ongoing myelination that occurs around the border of the gray and the white matters, and does not necessarily represent change in true cortical thickness that can be observed using histological specimens.

4. Proportion of the brain

At term, the total brain volume is one-third that of the adult brain and the growth rate is as fast as 1% per day. The growth rate gradually slows to 0.4% per day by the end of 3 months of age, when the brain reaches half the volume of the adult brain (Holland et al., 2014). Brain volume increases approximately 100% during the first year, then 15% during the second year (Knickmeyer et al., 2008), and reaches greater than 95% of that of the adult brain at around 5–6 years of age (Peterson et al., 2018). Notably, the shape of the brain, or a local brain volume in relation to other parts of the brain, which can be determined by the normalized structural volume (structural volume divided by the total brain volume), differs between neonatal and adult brains, and the growth rate varies depending on sex (boys grow faster than girls) and anatomical structures. The gray matter volume increases in a nonlinear manner, with region-specific growth patterns that peak at different ages: the frontal and parietal lobe at age 12; the temporal lobe at age 16; while, in the occipital lobe, the volume increases continuously through age 20 (Blakemore, 2012; Giedd et al., 1999). White matter volume linearly increases throughout adolescence (Giedd et al., 1999). The most striking difference between the neonatal and adult brain is seen in the cerebellum (Fig. 7). The growth rate of the cerebellum is more than 200% while the hippocampus grows only 47% during the first 3 months of life (Holland et al., 2014). The cerebellum volume increases 240% in the first year (Knickmeyer et al., 2008). The change in the local brain volume in relation to other parts of the brain necessitates the use of an age-specific brain atlas. For example, nonlinear transformation of a neonatal brain to an adult brain usually results in an insufficient coregistration of the cerebellum, because a strong mismatch in the initial location of the cerebellum disturbs biologically meaningful image transformation in which strong local deformation is required to coregister the cerebellum.

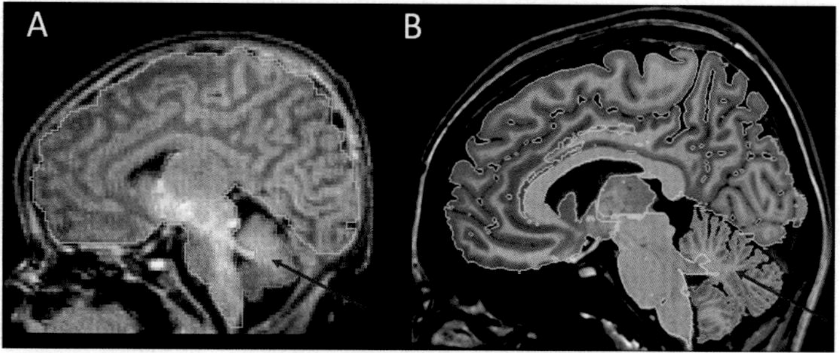

FIG. 7

Midsagittal slice of the T1-weighted images. The size of the cerebellum (*red arrows*) is smaller in the neonate (A) compared to that in the adult (B).

5. Surface of the brain

Developmental change can be observed on the surface of the brain, as increased surface areas and cortical folding (gyrification). Separation of the two cerebral hemispheres is completed around 9–10 gestational weeks (Paul et al., 2009). The basic four lobes (frontal, parietal, temporal, and occipital lobes) are formed by the end of the second trimester, with the formation of the lateral sulcus at 16 gestational weeks (clearly MRI-visible by the end of 23 gestational weeks), the parieto-occipital sulcus visible at 22 gestational weeks, and the central sulcus visible at 26 gestational weeks (Garel et al., 2012). Other sulci that are important to identify the cortical gyri also start to appear at the second trimester, and most of the major gyri seen in adult brains are visible at term. Gyrification continues until 2 years of age (Li et al., 2015).

Delineation of the brain surface is an initial step toward creating a brain atlas. T1-weighted contrast is typically employed to define the cortical surface for both the adult and the child brain. However, in brains younger than 3 years of age, the surface delineation is often difficult since the intensity of the structures that are attached to the surface of the brain, such as the dura mater and vascular structures, is almost identical to that of the cortical gray matter, and often with little to no cerebrospinal fluid space to separate them (Fig. 8A and B). For this reason, brain atlases for the early pediatric brain often employ T2-weighted contrast, which provides better contrast in delineating the cortical surface, and in defining the boundaries between the gray and white matter structures (Fig. 8C). Such atlases include the JHU-neonate-SS atlas (Oishi et al., 2011), the spatiotemporal atlas of the fetal brain (Habas et al., 2010), the dynamic 4D probabilistic atlas of the developing brain (Kuklisova-Murgasova et al., 2011), the multichannel 4D probabilistic atlas of the developing fetal brain (Serag et al., 2012), the consistent high-definition spatio-temporal neonatal brain atlas (Serag et al., 2012; Makropoulos et al., 2016), the UNC infant 0–1–2 atlases (Shi et al., 2011), the UNC detail-preserved longitudinal 0–3–6–9–12 months-old atlas (Zhang et al., 2016), the Edinburgh neonatal

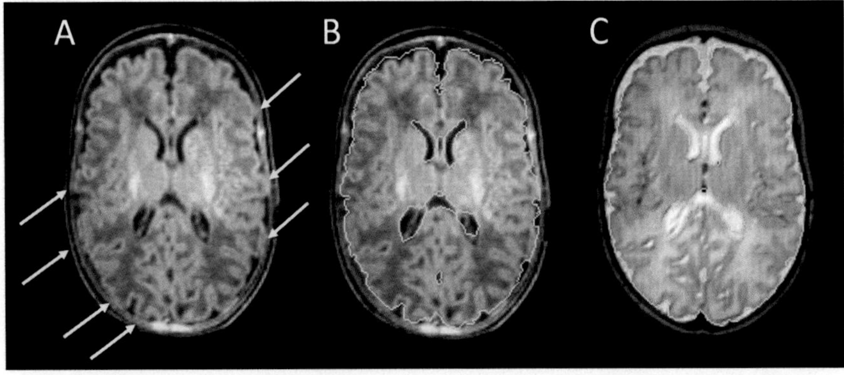

FIG. 8

T1-weighted (A and B) and T2-weighted (C) images of the infant brain. T1-weighted contrast is not ideal in defining cortical surface in multiple areas (indicated by *yellow arrows*). T2-weighted contrast provides better contrast in delineating the cortical surface (*cyan contour*). The surface drawn on the T2-weighed image can be overlaid on the coregistered T1-weighted image (B).

atlas (ENA33) (Blesa et al., 2016), and the M-CRIB atlas (Alexander et al., 2017). Atlases of the surface representation of the brain have provided the ability to capture the developmental changes seen in the brain, such as surface enlargement, gyrification, changes in cortical thickness, or myelination (Li et al., 2015; Van Essen and Drury, 1997; Van Essen, 2002).

6. Anatomical variation

Developmental variations in brain anatomy often cause topological changes that disturb the image transformation. Such variations are often seen in the cerebrospinal fluid areas. Three major variations are introduced below.

6.1 Cavum septum pellucidum

The cavum septum pellucidum is a cavity surrounded by a pair of thin membranes, the bilateral septum pellucidum, and filled with cerebrospinal fluid (Fig. 9). The posterior extension of this cavity (posterior to the fornices) is called the cavum Vergae. During normal brain development, the septum pellucidi gradually approach each other and finally attach and fuse at the mid-sagittal position to form a single membrane, when the cavum septum pellucidum disappears. Accordingly, the cavum septum pellucidum is seen in most fetuses, approximately 70% at 36 weeks, 35% at 40 weeks of gestation (Mott et al., 1992), 7% in children under 17 years of age (Pauling et al., 1998), and 1%–6% in the adult brain (Pauling et al., 1998; Gur et al., 2013; Chen et al., 2014; Macpherson and Teasdale, 1988). Notably, the volume of the cavum septum pellucidum and timing of the closure varies among children.

Transforming an image with the cavum septum pellucidum to an image without it is problematic because these two images are topologically different (Oishi et al., 2019). If an atlas with the cavum septum pellucidum is used as the reference to label a target brain without it, the topological difference causes confusion because the target brain lacks the label that exists in the atlas.

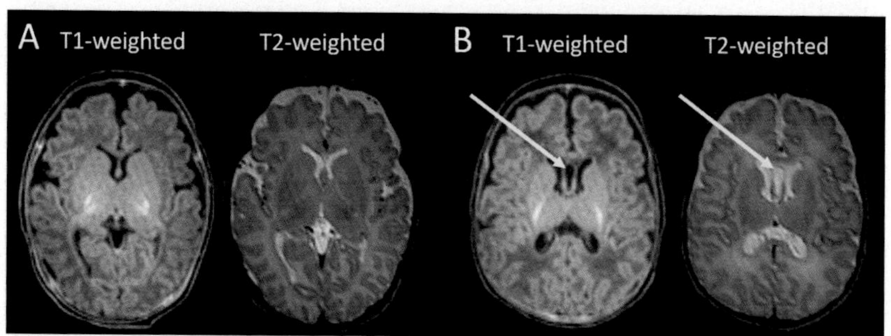

FIG. 9

T1- and T2-weighted images of neonates with (A) and without (B) the cavum septum pellucidum, which is indicated by *yellow arrows*.

Adapted from Oishi, K., Chang, L., Huang, H., 2018. Baby brain atlases. NeuroImage. 185, 865–80. Epub 2018/04/07. https://doi.org/10.1016/j.neuroimage.2018.04.003. 29625234; PMC6170732 with permission.

6.2 Frontal cerebrospinal fluid space

The external cerebrospinal fluid space is a space between the pia matter (surface of the brain) and the arachnoid layer of the meninges, and is filled with cerebrospinal fluid. The size of this space relative to the intracranial volume changes during brain development, and the time course of the relative volume varies among children (Fig. 10). The external cerebrospinal fluid space is often seen adjacent to a convexity of the frontal lobe (frontal cerebrospinal fluid space). This space is often prominent in infants with macrocephaly or low body weight at birth. The discrepancy between brain growth and skull growth is assumed to be the cause of the enlargement (Kawasaki et al., 2019). Image transformation between an image with and without prominent frontal cerebrospinal fluid spaces causes inaccurate image transformation, particularly in the frontal lobe.

6.3 Ventricular volume

The lateral ventricle is among the brain structures with the largest variations in volume (Fig. 11). Variations in the shape of the lateral ventricle, described in Section 2, Fig. 3, cause topological differences among images and cause inaccurate image transformation.

6.4 Multiatlas approach to account for anatomical variations

Anatomical variations seen during brain development cause inaccurate image transformation that results in anatomical mislabeling. To cover the entire landscape of anatomic variations, it is becoming a

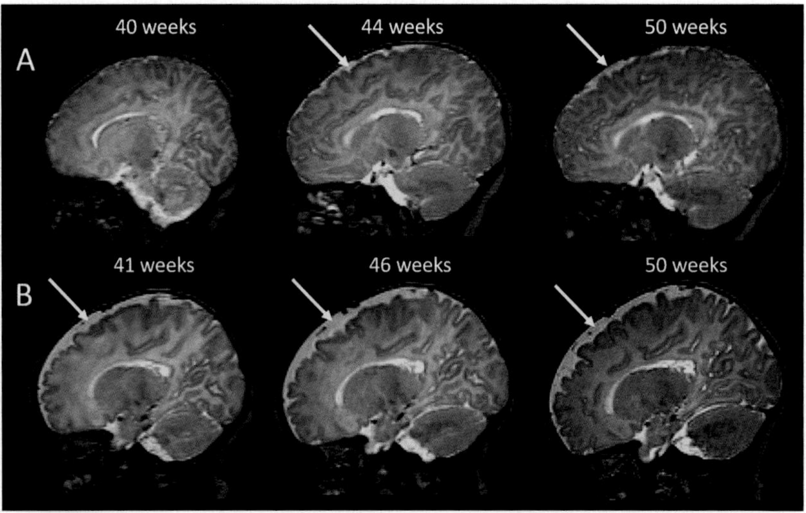

FIG. 10

Longitudinally scanned T1-weighted images from two healthy infants. The size of the frontal cerebrospinal fluid space (*yellow arrows*) changes during development. The size is larger in (B) compared to (A).

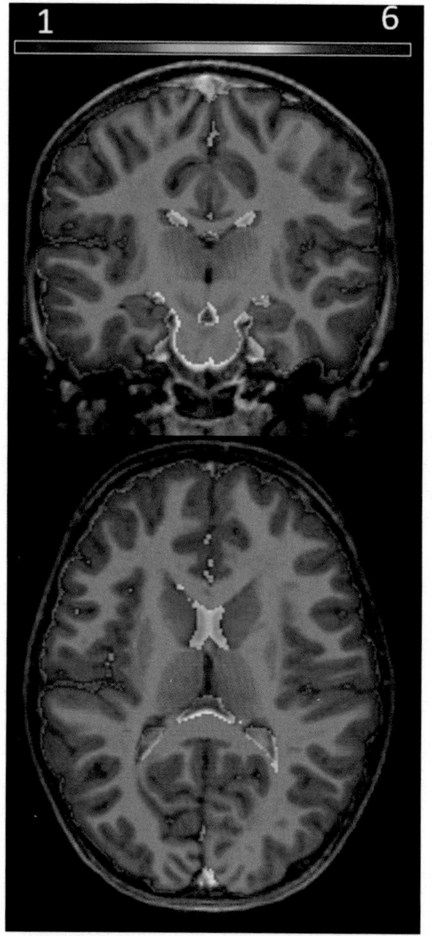

FIG. 11

Variations in local brain volume, color-coded by the coefficient of variation. The three-dimensional T1-weighted images obtained from normal children (4–8 year-olds, $n = 120$) were parcellated using the multiatlas label fusion method (Mori et al., 2016) with the JHU-pediatric multiatlas library (Wu et al., 2016b). The greatest variation is seen in the posterior horn of the lateral ventricle.

common practice to apply a set of multiple atlases, rather than using a group representative atlas. Such atlases include the label-based encephalic ROI template (ALBERT) (Gousias et al., 2012); Edinburgh neonatal atlas (ENA33) (Blesa et al., 2016); M-CRIB atlas (Alexander et al., 2017); and the MRICloud neonate and pediatric multiatlas repository (Otsuka et al., 2017). For example, the neonate multiatlas repository (Otsuka et al., 2017) includes a set of atlases with various sizes and shapes of the cavum septum pellucidum, frontal cerebrospinal fluid space, and the lateral ventricle to cover the major anatomical variations.

7. Age-specific anatomical structures

Fetal brains and preterm-born infant brains before their term-equivalent age (<40 postmenstrual weeks) are characterized by a transient anatomical status or structures (Ulfig et al., 2000) that lack a counterpart in the mature brain. These anatomical statuses and structures affect brain morphology and contrasts observed on structural MRI. Care should be taken when comparing prenatal and postnatal brain atlases since anatomical structures referenced in these atlases can be different.

7.1 Transient zones

The transient zones are a laminar organization of cellular compartments within the cerebral wall seen in the fetal brain (Paul et al., 2009). During the early phase of fetal development (12–15 postmenstrual weeks), the transient zones are MRI-visible as a three-layer formation, including the cortical plate, the intermediate zone, and the ventricular zone, in order from surface to deep seated (Rados et al., 2006). The transient zones develop during the mid-fetal phase (17–24 postmenstrual weeks) and form seven histologically-defined layers, including the marginal zone, cortical plate, subplate zone, intermediate zone, subventricular zone, periventricular zone, and ventricular zone, which are also clearly visible on conventional T1- and T2- weighted images, except for the marginal and periventricular zones (Rados et al., 2006; Kostovic et al., 2002). The transient zones gradually become less visible during the rest of the fetal period and disappear at term.

Since the anatomical features of the transient zones change rapidly from the early to the late fetal periods, a spatiotemporal atlas consisting of a set of age-specific template images and corresponding parcellation maps is necessary serving as the anatomical reference to analyze and interpret the brain images, particularly during the second trimester and early third trimester. There are brain MRI segmentation protocols (Corbett-Detig et al., 2011; Scott et al., 2011) to identify the subplate zone, the most prominent structure among the transient zones and reaching its developmental peak at 29–32 postmenstrual weeks (Paul et al., 2009). A protocol to identify intermediate and ventricular zones is elaborated and applied to create the spatiotemporal atlas of the fetal brain (Gholipour et al., 2017; Khan et al., 2019), which contains gestational week-specific atlases from 21 to 37 weeks of gestation (Fig. 12).

7.2 Germinal matrix

The germinal matrix is a structure with active cell proliferation seen in the periventricular area and is most prominent in the second trimester when neuronal and glial cells actively generate and proliferate. The germinal matrix appears as a structure with high T1-weighted signal intensity and low T2-weighted signal intensity. The dense cellular feature causes a low apparent diffusion coefficient and high signal intensity in the diffusion-weighted image (Huang et al., 2006, 2009) (Fig. 13). The germinal matrix becomes less visible after 30 gestational weeks and disappears at term. For quantification, atlases must include a parcellation map that contains a label for the germinal matrix. Such atlases include the spatiotemporal atlas of the fetal brain (University of Washington) (Habas et al., 2010), which was constructed from 40 fetal brains at 20.57–27.86 gestational weeks and the spatiotemporal atlas of the fetal brain (Boston Children's Hospital) (Gholipour et al., 2017) that covers 21–37 gestational weeks.

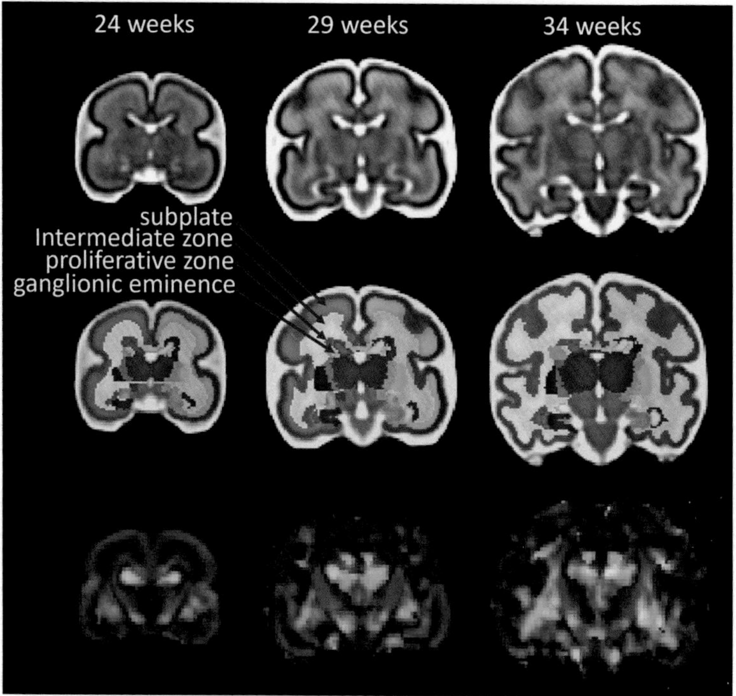

FIG. 12

T2-weighted (upper row) and DTI (lower row) atlas with the transient zones parcellated into the subplate, intermediate zone, proliferative zone, and the ganglionic eminence. The ventricular zone consists of the proliferative zone and the ganglionic eminence. The figure is provided courtesy of Dr. Ali Gholipour and Mr. Clemente Velasco-Annis, Harvard Medical School and Boston Children's Hospital.

7.3 Premyelination and myelination

The myelination process has been well studied in vivo using diffusion MRI (Wimberger et al., 1995). The initial phase is called premyelination (Huppi and Dubois, 2006) when an active proliferation of body and membranes of oligodendroglia occurs during 24–32 gestational weeks (Back et al., 2001; Kinney and Back, 1998). This cytological and histological change results in reduced water content and increased membrane density that leads to decreases in water diffusivity (Dubois et al., 2014). An increase in diffusion anisotropy is observed in the white matter area, probably due to an extension of oligodendroglial processes in the axonal direction (Zanin et al., 2011; Nossin-Manor et al., 2013). True myelination follows the premyelination, rapidly until 2 years of age, after which it continues slowly until adulthood (Lebel and Deoni, 2018). This phase is characterized by a tight ensheathment of oligodendroglial processes around the axons, which reduces the permeability of the cell membrane and the intermembrane space. For the white matter bundles where axonal fibers are well aligned toward a single direction, the myelination results in increased anisotropy and reduced radial diffusivity. This change in diffusion properties is complicated in areas where multiple fibers with different orientations

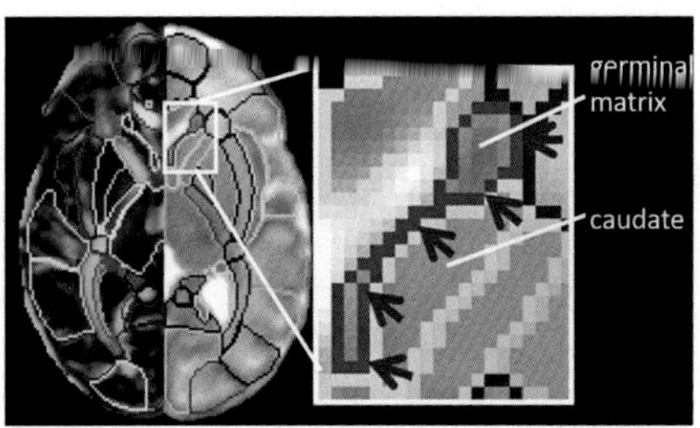

FIG. 13

Diffusion tensor atlas with the germinal matrix parcellation (*red arrow*).

Adapted from Feng, L., Li, H., Oishi, K., Mishra, V., Song, L., Peng, Q., Ouyang, M., Wang, J., Slinger, M., Jeon, T., Lee, L., Heyne, R., Chalak, L., Peng, Y., Liu, S., Huang, H., 2019. Age-specific gray and white matter DTI atlas for human brain at 33, 36 and 39 postmenstrual weeks. NeuroImage. 185, 685–98. Epub 2018/07/01. https://doi.org/10.1016/j.neuroimage.2018.06.069. 29959046; PMC6289605, with permission.

coexist. Suppose there are two fiber bundles crossing at a specific area and one fiber bundle becomes myelinated earlier than another: this might result in an initial increase followed by a decrease in anisotropy, and continuous reduction in mean diffusivity (Dubois et al., 2014).

The diffusion MRI atlas is often used to evaluate the myelination process during development. Such atlases include DTI templates accompanied by corresponding parcellation maps of the white matter areas or fibers. Age-specific DTI atlases of 33, 36, and 39 postmenstrual-week brains (Feng et al., 2019) are available for evaluation of infants born preterm, the ENA33 atlas (Blesa et al., 2016) for neonates, the JHU-neonate atlas (Oishi et al., 2011) for the initial 3 months of age, and the JHU-pediatric multiatlas repository (Tang et al., 2014) for 3–18 years of age.

8. Future directions

Any discussion of future directions must include the limitations of current MRI atlases of the human pediatric brain, as well as efforts to overcome the limitations.

8.1 Resolution

The voxel size of existing MRI atlases of the human pediatric brain is mostly defined by in vivo MRI acquisition protocols available to date, although continuing increase in image resolution is expected in the future. Technological advancement in both hardware and software is required to obtain pediatric images with a higher resolution and a signal-to-noise ratio that can serve as template images upon which to create atlases. Another approach in increasing resolution is the use of ex vivo images. Several ex vivo mesoscopic MRI atlases (Edlow et al., 2019; Oishi et al., 2020; Iglesias et al., 2018, 2015; Adler et al., 2018) have been generated and are available for adult brains, and such atlases are expected for pediatric brains.

8.2 Contrasts

While newer MRI contrasts are becoming available, atlases compatible with these contrasts are limited, particularly for pediatric brains. Three-dimensional digital atlases available to date for pediatric brains mostly include conventional T1- and T2-weighted contrasts or diffusion MRI-based contrasts or both. Some pediatric atlases are compatible with additional image contrasts, such as the pediatric template of brain perfusion (Avants et al., 2015), which includes resting-state functional connectivity and brain perfusion. More contrasts and modalities are expected to be included in the future.

8.3 Pathologies

Existing pediatric atlases have been generated from healthy individuals to provide anatomic or functional references. During the past decade, various types of pediatric brain atlases have been created based on accumulating knowledge about the image representation of the neuroanatomy and functions of developing brains. These atlases have been used to investigate normal developmental changes or the alterations caused by prenatal, perinatal, or postnatal events or neurodevelopmental diseases (Oishi et al., 2011; Chang et al., 2016a, b; Rose et al., 2014a, b; Pannek et al., 2013; He and Parikh, 2013; Kersbergen et al., 2014; Bai et al., 2012). Such application studies are expected to expand toward clinical applications, in which brain atlases will be used to quantify clinically indicated brain MRIs.

One of the biggest challenges in clinical applications is the heterogeneity of the clinical images, which depends on the type and severity of the various diseases. Clinical MRIs often include brains with a substantial amount of local volume changes (atrophy or edematous change), changes in intensity due to pathology, lesions that do not exist in reference atlases, geometrical distortion caused by lesions, or malformations that alter the topology of the brain. Atlases created based on the normal brains are not necessarily appropriate as references for the quantification and description of such pathological changes. To account for the clinical heterogeneity, atlases that cover the pathological features of the brain are required to serve as a reference (Fig. 14). Such a set of atlases must cover most of the pathological changes seen on clinical MRIs; therefore, these atlases must contain a huge number of pathological images with the associated clinical information. In addition to the traditional role of brain atlases as anatomical and functional references, the role of the atlas in this context expands to a clinical reference (Wu et al., 2016a; Qin et al., 2013). For example, an atlas repository that stores a set of pathological images containing the clinical features (diagnosis, prognosis, or response to treatment) works as a knowledge base, and can be used to identify a cluster of patients with similar neuroanatomical or clinical features (Oishi et al., 2019). Shared resources of clinical images with a wide variety of diagnoses are highly desirable to enable this concept.

9. Summary

Pediatric brains develop rapidly, which causes age-dependent variations in local brain volume and intensity, as well as developmental stage-specific anatomical features. To account for the variations in anatomical features, pediatric brain atlases must be age specific. The anatomical landmarks used for

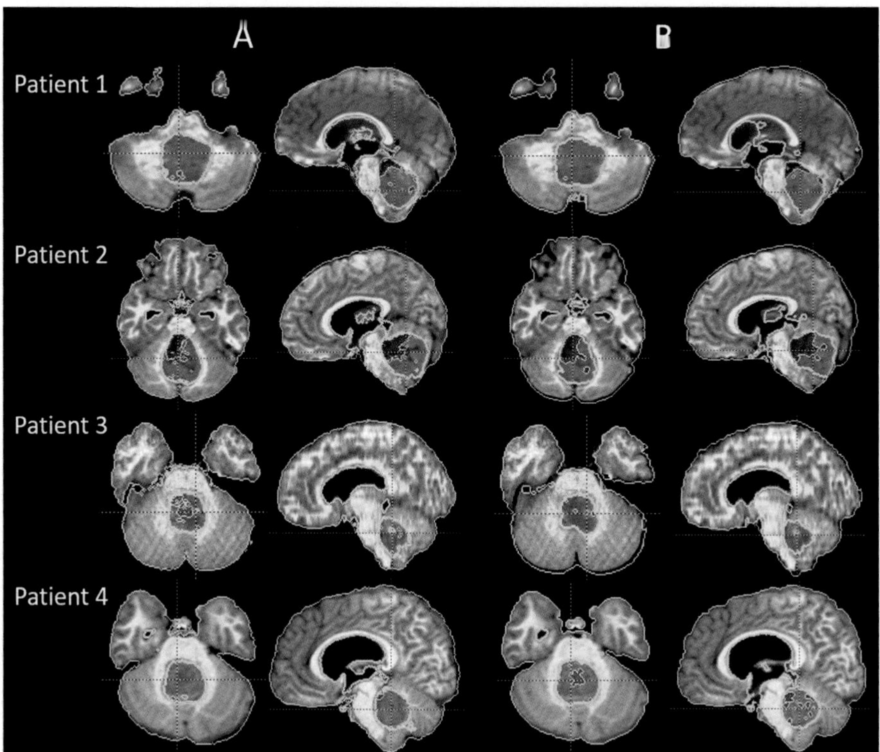

FIG. 14

Example of multiatlas label fusion approach based on an atlas repository that contained brain lesions. The labels consist of the brain parenchyma, the cerebrospinal fluid space, the isointense tumor area (intensity similar to that of the *gray matter*), and the low-intensity tumor area. The results of the multiatlas label fusion (A) are comparable to that of the manual parcellation (B).

pediatric brain image parcellation should have a focus on the developmental stage-dependent changes in image intensity, morphology, topology, and transient anatomical structures. Atlases with higher resolution and more contrasts are expected in the future. Shared clinical images with a wide variety of diagnoses, which can be used to create pathological brain atlases, are desired for the clinical application studies.

Acknowledgments

I would like to thank Dr. Linda Chang, Diagnostic Radiology and Nuclear Medicine and Neurology, University of Maryland School of Medicine, and Dr. Ali Gholipour and Mr. Clemente Velasco-Annis, Harvard Medical School and Boston Children's Hospital, for kindly allowing me to use their images.

References

Adler, D.H., Wisse, L.E.M., Ittyerah, R., Pluta, J.B., Ding, S.L., Xie, L., Wang, J., Kadivar, S., Robinson, J.L., Schuck, T., Trojanowski, J.Q., Grossman, M., Detre, J.A., Elliott, M.A., Toledo, J.B., Liu, W., Pickup, S., Miller, M.I., Das, S.R., Wolk, D.A., Yushkevich, P.A., 2018. Characterizing the human hippocampus in aging and Alzheimer's disease using a computational atlas derived from ex vivo MRI and histology. Proc. Natl. Acad. Sci. U. S. A. 115 (16), 4252–4257. Epub 2018/03/30. https://doi.org/10.1073/pnas.1801093115. 29592955. PMC5910869.

Akazawa, K., Chang, L., Yamakawa, R., Hayama, S., Buchthal, S., Alicata, D., Andres, T., Castillo, D., Oishi, K., Skranes, J., Ernst, T., Oishi, K., 2015. Probabilistic maps of the white matter tracts with known associated functions on the neonatal brain atlas: application to evaluate longitudinal developmental trajectories in term-born and preterm-born infants. NeuroImage 128, 167–179. Epub 2015/12/30. https://doi.org/10.1016/j.neuroimage.2015.12.026. 26712341.

Alexander, B., Murray, A.L., Loh, W.Y., Matthews, L.G., Adamson, C., Beare, R., Chen, J., Kelly, C.E., Rees, S., Warfield, S.K., Anderson, P.J., Doyle, L.W., Spittle, A.J., Cheong, J.L., Seal, M.L., Thompson, D.K., 2017. A new neonatal cortical and subcortical brain atlas: the Melbourne Children's regional infant brain (M-CRIB) atlas. NeuroImage 147, 841–851. Epub 2016/10/26. https://doi.org/10.1016/j.neuroimage.2016.09.068. 27725314.

Avants, B.B., Duda, J.T., Kilroy, E., Krasileva, K., Jann, K., Kandel, B.T., Tustison, N.J., Yan, L., Jog, M., Smith, R., Wang, Y., Dapretto, M., Wang, D.J., 2015. The pediatric template of brain perfusion. Sci. Data 2, 150003. Epub 2015/05/16. https://doi.org/10.1038/sdata.2015.3. 25977810. PMC4413243.

Back, S.A., Luo, N.L., Borenstein, N.S., Levine, J.M., Volpe, J.J., Kinney, H.C., 2001. Late oligodendrocyte progenitors coincide with the developmental window of vulnerability for human perinatal white matter injury. J. Neurosci. 21 (4), 1302–1312. 11160401.

Bai, J., Abdul-Rahman, M.F., Rifkin-Graboi, A., Chong, Y.S., Kwek, K., Saw, S.M., Godfrey, K.M., Gluckman, P. D., Fortier, M.V., Meaney, M.J., Qiu, A., 2012. Population differences in brain morphology and microstructure among Chinese, Malay, and Indian neonates. PLoS One 7 (10), e47816. Epub 2012/11/01. https://doi.org/10.1371/journal.pone.0047816. 23112850. 3480429.

Barkovich, A.J., Kjos, B.O., Jackson Jr., D.E., Norman, D., 1988. Normal maturation of the neonatal and infant brain: MR imaging at 1.5 T. Radiology 166 (1 Pt 1), 173–180. Epub 1988/01/01. 3336675.

Blakemore, S.J., 2012. Imaging brain development: the adolescent brain. NeuroImage 61 (2), 397–406. Epub 2011/12/20. https://doi.org/10.1016/j.neuroimage.2011.11.080. 22178817.

Blesa, M., Serag, A., Wilkinson, A.G., Anblagan, D., Telford, E.J., Pataky, R., Sparrow, S.A., Macnaught, G., Semple, S.I., Bastin, M.E., Boardman, J.P., 2016. Parcellation of the healthy neonatal brain into 107 regions using atlas propagation through intermediate time points in childhood. Front. Neurosci. 10, 220. Epub 2016/06/01. https://doi.org/10.3389/fnins.2016.00220. 27242423. 4871889..

Chang, L., Akazawa, K., Yamakawa, R., Hayama, S., Buchthal, S., Alicata, D., Andres, T., Castillo, D., Oishi, K., Skranes, J., Ernst, T., Oishi, K., 2016a. Delayed early developmental trajectories of white matter tracts of functional pathways in preterm-born infants: longitudinal diffusion tensor imaging data. Data Brief. https://doi.org/10.1016/j.dib.2016.01.064.

Chang, L., Oishi, K., Skranes, J., Buchthal, S., Cunningham, E., Yamakawa, R., Hayama, S., Jiang, C.S., Alicata, D., Hernandez, A., Cloak, C., Wright, T., Ernst, T., 2016b. Sex-specific alterations of white matter developmental trajectories in infants with prenatal exposure to methamphetamine and tobacco. JAMA Psychiatry 73 (12), 1217–1227. Epub 2016/11/10. https://doi.org/10.1001/jamapsychiatry.2016.2794. 27829078. PMC6467201..

Chen, J.J., Chen, C.J., Chang, H.F., Chen, D.L., Hsu, Y.C., Chang, T.P., 2014. Prevalence of cavum septum pellucidum and/or cavum Vergae in brain computed tomographies of Taiwanese. Acta Neurol. Taiwanica 23 (2), 49–54. Epub 2015/06/04. 26035920.

Corbett-Detig, J., Habas, P.A., Scott, J.A., Kim, K., Rajagopalan, V., McQuillen, P.S., Barkovich, A.J., Glenn, O. A., Studholme, C., 2011. 3D global and regional patterns of human fetal subplate growth determined in utero. Brain Struct. Funct. 215 ((3–4), 255–263. Epub 2010/11/04. https://doi.org/10.1007/s00429-010-0286-5. 21046152. PMC3041913.

Counsell, S.J., Maalouf, E.F., Fletcher, A.M., Duggan, P., Battin, M., Lewis, H.J., Herlihy, A.H., Edwards, A.D., Bydder, G.M., Rutherford, M.A., 2002. MR imaging assessment of myelination in the very preterm brain. AJNR Am. J. Neuroradiol. 23 (5), 872–881. Epub 2002/05/15 12006296.

Desikan, R.S., Segonne, F., Fischl, B., Quinn, B.T., Dickerson, B.C., Blacker, D., Buckner, R.L., Dale, A.M., Maguire, R.P., Hyman, B.T., Albert, M.S., Killiany, R.J., 2006. An automated labeling system for subdividing the human cerebral cortex on MRI scans into gyral based regions of interest. NeuroImage 31 (3), 968–980. Epub 2006/03/15. https://doi.org/10.1016/j.neuroimage.2006.01.021. 16530430.

Djamanakova, A., Faria, A.V., Hsu, J., Ceritoglu, C., Oishi, K., Miller, M.I., Hillis, A.E., Mori, S., 2013. Diffeomorphic brain mapping based on T1-weighted images: improvement of registration accuracy by multichannel mapping. J. Magn. Reson. Imaging 37 (1), 76–84. Epub 2012/09/14. https://doi.org/10.1002/jmri.23790. 22972747. 3525783.

Dubois, J., Dehaene-Lambertz, G., Kulikova, S., Poupon, C., Huppi, P.S., Hertz-Pannier, L., 2014. The early development of brain white matter: a review of imaging studies in fetuses, newborns and infants. Neuroscience 276, 48–71. Epub 2014/01/01. https://doi.org/10.1016/j.neuroscience.2013.12.044. 24378955.

Ducharme, S., Albaugh, M.D., Nguyen, T.V., Hudziak, J.J., Mateos-Perez, J.M., Labbe, A., Evans, A.C., Karama, S., Brain Development Cooperative, G., 2016. Trajectories of cortical thickness maturation in normal brain development—the importance of quality control procedures. NeuroImage 125, 267–279. Epub 2015/10/16. https://doi.org/10.1016/j.neuroimage.2015.10.010. 26463175. PMC4691414.

Edlow, B.L., Mareyam, A., Horn, A., Polimeni, J.R., Witzel, T., Tisdall, M.D., Augustinack, J.C., Stockmann, J.P., Diamond, B.R., Stevens, A., Tirrell, L.S., Folkerth, R.D., Wald, L.L., Fischl, B., van der Kouwe, A., 2019. 7 Tesla MRI of the ex vivo human brain at 100 micron resolution. Sci. Data 6 (1), 244. Epub 2019/11/02. https://doi.org/10.1038/s41597-019-0254-8. 31666530. PMC6821740.

Fan, L., Li, H., Zhuo, J., Zhang, Y., Wang, J., Chen, L., Yang, Z., Chu, C., Xie, S., Laird, A.R., Fox, P.T., Eickhoff, S.B., Yu, C., Jiang, T., 2016. The human brainnetome atlas: a new brain atlas based on connectional architecture. Cereb. Cortex 26 (8), 3508–3526. Epub 2016/05/28. https://doi.org/10.1093/cercor/bhw157. 27230218. 4961028.

Feng, L., Li, H., Oishi, K., Mishra, V., Song, L., Peng, Q., Ouyang, M., Wang, J., Slinger, M., Jeon, T., Lee, L., Heyne, R., Chalak, L., Peng, Y., Liu, S., Huang, H., 2019. Age-specific gray and white matter DTI atlas for human brain at 33, 36 and 39 postmenstrual weeks. NeuroImage 185, 685–698. Epub 2018/07/01. https://doi.org/10.1016/j.neuroimage.2018.06.069. 29959046. PMC6289605.

Garel, C., Delezoide, V., Delezoide, A.L., Guibaud, L., Sebag, G., Gressens, P., Elmaleh-Bergès, M., Hassan, M., Brisse, H., Chantrel, E., 2012. MRI of the Fetal Brain: Normal Development and Cerebral Pathologies. Springer, Berlin Heidelberg.

Gholipour, A., Rollins, C.K., Velasco-Annis, C., Ouaalam, A., Akhondi-Asl, A., Afacan, O., Ortinau, C.M., Clancy, S., Limperopoulos, C., Yang, E., Estroff, J.A., Warfield, S.K., 2017. A normative spatiotemporal MRI atlas of the fetal brain for automatic segmentation and analysis of early brain growth. Sci. Rep. 7 (1), 476. Epub 2017/03/30. https://doi.org/10.1038/s41598-017-00525-w. 28352082. 5428658.

Giedd, J.N., Blumenthal, J., Jeffries, N.O., Castellanos, F.X., Liu, H., Zijdenbos, A., Paus, T., Evans, A.C., Rapoport, J.L., 1999. Brain development during childhood and adolescence: a longitudinal MRI study. Nat. Neurosci. 2 (10), 861–863. Epub 1999/09/24. https://doi.org/10.1038/13158. 10491603.

Glasser, M.F., Coalson, T.S., Robinson, E.C., Hacker, C.D., Harwell, J., Yacoub, E., Ugurbil, K., Andersson, J., Beckmann, C.F., Jenkinson, M., Smith, S.M., Van Essen, D.C., 2016. A multi-modal parcellation of human cerebral cortex. Nature 536 (7615), 171–178. Epub 2016/07/21. https://doi.org/10.1038/nature18933. 27437579. 4990127.

Gordon, E.M., Laumann, T.O., Adeyemo, B., Huckins, J.F., Kelley, W.M., Petersen, S.E., 2016. Generation and evaluation of a cortical area parcellation from resting-state correlations. Cereb. Cortex 26 (1), 288–303. Epub 2014/10/16. https://doi.org/10.1093/cercor/bhu239. 25316338. 4677978.

Gousias, I.S., Edwards, A.D., Rutherford, M.A., Counsell, S.J., Hajnal, J.V., Rueckert, D., Hammers, A., 2012. Magnetic resonance imaging of the newborn brain: manual segmentation of labelled atlases in term-born and preterm infants. NeuroImage 62 (3), 1499–1509. Epub 2012/06/21. https://doi.org/10.1016/j.neuroimage.2012.05.083. 22713673.

Gur, R.E., Kaltman, D., Melhem, E.R., Ruparel, K., Prabhakaran, K., Riley, M., Yodh, E., Hakonarson, H., Satterthwaite, T., Gur, R.C., 2013. Incidental findings in youths volunteering for brain MRI research. AJNR Am. J. Neuroradiol. 34 (10), 2021–2025. Epub 2013/07/03. https://doi.org/10.3174/ajnr.A3525. 23811972.

Habas, P.A., Kim, K., Corbett-Detig, J.M., Rousseau, F., Glenn, O.A., Barkovich, A.J., Studholme, C., 2010. A spatiotemporal atlas of MR intensity, tissue probability and shape of the fetal brain with application to segmentation. NeuroImage 53 (2), 460–470. Epub 2010/07/06. https://doi.org/10.1016/j.neuroimage.2010.06.054. 20600970. 2930902.

He, L., Parikh, N.A., 2013. Atlas-guided quantification of white matter signal abnormalities on term-equivalent age MRI in very preterm infants: findings predict language and cognitive development at two years of age. PLoS One 8 (12), e85475. Epub 2014/01/07. https://doi.org/10.1371/journal.pone.0085475. 24392012. 3877364.

Hoeksma, M.R., Kenemans, J.L., Kemner, C., van Engeland, H., 2005. Variability in spatial normalization of pediatric and adult brain images. Clin. Neurophysiol. 116 (5), 1188–1194. Epub 2005/04/14. https://doi.org/10.1016/j.clinph.2004.12.021. 15826861.

Holland, D., Chang, L., Ernst, T.M., Curran, M., Buchthal, S.D., Alicata, D., Skranes, J., Johansen, H., Hernandez, A., Yamakawa, R., Kuperman, J.M., Dale, A.M., 2014. Structural growth trajectories and rates of change in the first 3 months of infant brain development. JAMA Neurol. 71 (10), 1266–1274. Epub 2014/08/12. https://doi.org/10.1001/jamaneurol.2014.1638. 25111045. 4940157.

Huang, H., Zhang, J., Wakana, S., Zhang, W., Ren, T., Richards, L.J., Yarowsky, P., Donohue, P., Graham, E., van Zijl, P.C., Mori, S., 2006. White and gray matter development in human fetal, newborn and pediatric brains. NeuroImage 33 (1), 27–38. 16905335.

Huang, H., Xue, R., Zhang, J., Ren, T., Richards, L.J., Yarowsky, P., Miller, M.I., Mori, S., 2009. Anatomical characterization of human fetal brain development with diffusion tensor magnetic resonance imaging. J. Neurosci. 29 (13), 4263–4273. Epub 2009/04/03. 29/13/4263 pii https://doi.org/10.1523/JNEUROSCI.2769-08.2009. 19339620. 2721010.

Huppi, P.S., Dubois, J., 2006. Diffusion tensor imaging of brain development. Semin. Fetal Neonatal Med. 11 (6), 489–497. Epub 2006/09/12. https://doi.org/10.1016/j.siny.2006.07.006. 16962837.

Iglesias, J.E., Augustinack, J.C., Nguyen, K., Player, C.M., Player, A., Wright, M., Roy, N., Frosch, M.P., McKee, A.C., Wald, L.L., Fischl, B., Van Leemput, K., Alzheimer's Disease Neuroimaging, I., 2015. A computational atlas of the hippocampal formation using ex vivo, ultra-high resolution MRI: application to adaptive segmentation of in vivo MRI. NeuroImage 115, 117–137. Epub 2015/05/06. https://doi.org/10.1016/j.neuroimage.2015.04.042. 25936807. PMC4461537.

Iglesias, J.E., Insausti, R., Lerma-Usabiaga, G., Bocchetta, M., Van Leemput, K., Greve, D.N., van der Kouwe, A., Alzheimer's Disease Neuroimaging, I., Fischl, B., Caballero-Gaudes, C., Paz-Alonso, P.M., 2018. A probabilistic atlas of the human thalamic nuclei combining ex vivo MRI and histology. NeuroImage 183, 314–326. Epub 2018/08/20. https://doi.org/10.1016/j.neuroimage.2018.08.012. 30121337. PMC6215335.

Kawasaki, Y., Yoshida, T., Matsui, M., Hiraiwa, A., Inomata, S., Tamura, K., Makimoto, M., Oishi, K., 2019. Clinical factors that affect the relationship between head circumference and brain volume in very-low-birth-weight infants. J. Neuroimaging 29 (1), 104–110. Epub 2018/09/28. https://doi.org/10.1111/jon.12558. 30260528.

Kersbergen, K.J., Leemans, A., Groenendaal, F., van der Aa, N.E., Viergever, M.A., de Vries, L.S., Benders, M.J., 2014. Microstructural brain development between 30 and 40weeks corrected age in a longitudinal cohort of extremely preterm infants. NeuroImage 103C, 214–224. Epub 2014/09/28. https://doi.org/10.1016/j.neuroimage.2014.09.039. 25261000.

Khan, S., et al., 2019. Fetal brain growth portrayed by a spatiotemporal diffusion tensor MRI atlas computed from in utero images. Neuroimage 185 (15), 593–608.

Kinney, H.C., Back, S.A., 1998. Human oligodendroglial development: relationship to periventricular leukomalacia. Semin. Pediatr. Neurol. 5 (3), 180–189. Epub 1998/10/20. https://doi.org/10.1016/s1071-9091(98)80033-8. 9777676.

Klein, A., Tourville, J., 2012. 101 labeled brain images and a consistent human cortical labeling protocol. Front. Neurosci. 6, 171. Epub 2012/12/12. https://doi.org/10.3389/fnins.2012.00171. 23227001. 3514540.

Knickmeyer, R.C., Gouttard, S., Kang, C., Evans, D., Wilber, K., Smith, J.K., Hamer, R.M., Lin, W., Gerig, G., Gilmore, J.H., 2008. A structural MRI study of human brain development from birth to 2 years. J. Neurosci. 28 (47), 12176–12182. Epub 2008/11/21. https://doi.org/10.1523/JNEUROSCI.3479-08.2008. 19020011. PMC2884385.

Korogi, Y., Takahashi, M., Sumi, M., Hirai, T., Sakamoto, Y., Ikushima, I., Miyayama, H., 1996. MR signal intensity of the perirolandic cortex in the neonate and infant. Neuroradiology 38 (6), 578–584. Epub 1996/08/01. https://doi.org/10.1007/BF00626104. 8880724.

Kostovic, I., Judas, M., Rados, M., Hrabac, P., 2002. Laminar organization of the human fetal cerebrum revealed by histochemical markers and magnetic resonance imaging. Cereb. Cortex 12 (5), 536–544. Epub 2002/04/16. https://doi.org/10.1093/cercor/12.5.536. 11950771.

Kreilkamp, B.A., Weber, B., Richardson, M.P., Keller, S.S., 2017. Automated tractography in patients with temporal lobe epilepsy using TRActs constrained by UnderLying Anatomy (TRACULA). NeuroImage Clin. 14, 67–76. Epub 2017/02/01. https://doi.org/10.1016/j.nicl.2017.01.003. 28138428. 5257189.

Kuklisova-Murgasova, M., Aljabar, P., Srinivasan, L., Counsell, S.J., Doria, V., Serag, A., Gousias, I.S., Boardman, J.P., Rutherford, M.A., Edwards, A.D., Hajnal, J.V., Rueckert, D., 2011. A dynamic 4D probabilistic atlas of the developing brain. NeuroImage 54 (4), 2750–2763. Epub 2010/10/26. https://doi.org/10.1016/j.neuroimage.2010.10.019. 20969966.

Lebel, C., Deoni, S., 2018. The development of brain white matter microstructure. NeuroImage 182, 207–218. Epub 2018/01/07. https://doi.org/10.1016/j.neuroimage.2017.12.097. 29305910. PMC6030512.

Li, G., Wang, L., Shi, F., Gilmore, J.H., Lin, W., Shen, D., 2015. Construction of 4D high-definition cortical surface atlases of infants: methods and applications. Med. Image Anal. 25 (1), 22–36. Epub 2015/05/20. https://doi.org/10.1016/j.media.2015.04.005. 25980388. 4540689.

Lyall, A.E., Shi, F., Geng, X., Woolson, S., Li, G., Wang, L., Hamer, R.M., Shen, D., Gilmore, J.H., 2015. Dynamic development of regional cortical thickness and surface area in early childhood. Cereb. Cortex 25 (8), 2204–2212. Epub 2014/03/05. https://doi.org/10.1093/cercor/bhu027. 24591525. PMC4506327.

Macpherson, P., Teasdale, E., 1988. CT demonstration of a 5th ventricle—a finding to KO boxers? Neuroradiology 30 (6), 506–510. Epub 1988/01/01 3265765.

Makropoulos, A., Aljabar, P., Wright, R., Huning, B., Merchant, N., Arichi, T., Tusor, N., Hajnal, J.V., Edwards, A.D., Counsell, S.J., Rueckert, D., 2016. Regional growth and atlasing of the developing human brain. NeuroImage 125, 456–478. Epub 2015/10/27. https://doi.org/10.1016/j.neuroimage.2015.10.047. 26499811. 4692521.

McArdle, C.B., Richardson, C.J., Nicholas, D.A., Mirfakhraee, M., Hayden, C.K., Amparo, E.G., 1987. Developmental features of the neonatal brain: MR imaging. Part I. Gray-white matter differentiation and myelination. Radiology 162 (1 Pt 1), 223–229. Epub 1987/01/01. https://doi.org/10.1148/radiology.162.1.3786767. 3786767.

Mori, S., Wu, D., Ceritoglu, C., Li, Y., Kolasny, A., Vaillant, M.A., Faria, A.V., Oishi, K., Miller, M.I., 2016. MRICloud: delivering high-throughput MRI neuroinformatics as cloud-based software as a service. Comput. Sci. Eng. 18 (5), 21–35. https://doi.org/10.1109/Mcse.2016.93. WOS:000382419700004.

Mott, S.H., Bodensteiner, J.B., Allan, W.C., 1992. The cavum septi pellucidi in term and preterm newborn infants. J. Child Neurol. 7 (1), 35–38. Epub 1992/01/01. https://doi.org/10.1177/088307389200700106. 1552150.

Murgasova, M., Dyet, L., Edwards, D., Rutherford, M., Hajnal, J., Rueckert, D., 2007. Segmentation of brain MRI in young children. Acad. Radiol. 14 (11), 1350–1366. Epub 2007/10/30. https://doi.org/10.1016/j.acra.2007.07.020. 17964459.

Muzik, O., Chugani, D.C., Juhasz, C., Shen, C., Chugani, H.T., 2000. Statistical parametric mapping: assessment of application in children. NeuroImage 12 (5), 538–549. Epub 2000/10/18. https://doi.org/10.1006/nimg.2000.0651. S1053-8119(00)90651-7 [pii] 11034861.

Natu, V.S., Gomez, J., Barnett, M., Jeska, B., Kirilina, E., Jaeger, C., Zhen, Z., Cox, S., Weiner, K.S., Weiskopf, N., Grill-Spector, K., 2019. Apparent thinning of human visual cortex during childhood is associated with myelination. Proc. Natl. Acad. Sci. U. S. A. 116 (41), 20750–20759. Epub 2019/09/25. https://doi.org/10.1073/pnas.1904931116. 31548375. PMC6789966.

Nossin-Manor, R., Card, D., Morris, D., Noormohamed, S., Shroff, M.M., Whyte, H.E., Taylor, M.J., Sled, J.G., 2013. Quantitative MRI in the very preterm brain: assessing tissue organization and myelination using magnetization transfer, diffusion tensor and T(1) imaging. NeuroImage 64, 505–516. Epub 2012/09/18. https://doi.org/10.1016/j.neuroimage.2012.08.086. 22982360.

Oishi, K., Faria, A., Jiang, H., Li, X., Akhter, K., Zhang, J., Hsu, J.T., Miller, M.I., van Zijl, P.C., Albert, M., Lyketsos, C.G., Woods, R., Toga, A.W., Pike, G.B., Rosa-Neto, P., Evans, A., Mazziotta, J., Mori, S., 2009. Atlas-based whole brain white matter analysis using large deformation diffeomorphic metric mapping: application to normal elderly and Alzheimer's disease participantstlas. NeuroImage 46 (2), 486–499. 19385016.

Oishi, K., Mori, S., Donohue, P.K., Ernst, T., Anderson, L., Buchthal, S., Faria, A., Jiang, H., Li, X., Miller, M.I., van Zijl, P.C., Chang, L., 2011. Multi-contrast human neonatal brain atlas: application to normal neonate development analysis. NeuroImage 56 (1), 8–20. Epub 2011/02/01. https://doi.org/10.1016/j.neuroimage.2011.01.051. 21276861. PMC3066278.

Oishi, K., Faria, A.V., Mori, S., 2012. Advanced neonatal NeuroMRI. Magn. Reson. Imaging Clin. N. Am. 20 (1), 81–91. Epub 2011/11/29. https://doi.org/10.1016/j.mric.2011.08.009. 1064-9689(11)00093-6 [pii] 22118594. 3256737.

Oishi, K., Chang, L., Huang, H., 2019. Baby brain atlases. NeuroImage 185, 865–880. Epub 2018/04/07. https://doi.org/10.1016/j.neuroimage.2018.04.003. 29625234. PMC6170732.

Oishi, K., Mori, S., Troncoso, J.C., Lenz, F.A., 2020. Mapping tracts in the human subthalamic area by 11.7T ex vivo diffusion tensor imaging. Brain Struct. Funct. https://doi.org/10.1007/s00429-020-02066-x. Epub 2020/04/19 32303844.

Otsuka, Y., Chang, L., Skranes, J., Ernst, T., Oishi, K. (Eds.), 2017. Neonatal brain MRI multi-atlas repository for automated image quantification. XXIII World Congress of Neurology, Kyoto, Japan.

Pannek, K., Hatzigeorgiou, X., Colditz, P.B., Rose, S., 2013. Assessment of structural connectivity in the preterm brain at term equivalent age using diffusion MRI and T2 relaxometry: a network-based analysis. PLoS One 8 (8), e68593. Epub 2013/08/21. https://doi.org/10.1371/journal.pone.0068593. 23950872. 3737239.

Paul, D., Griffiths, F., Janet Morris, M.S., Larroche, J.C., 2009. Michael Reeves F. Atlas of Fetal and Postnatal Brain MR. Elsevier Health Sciences.

Pauling, K.J., Bodensteiner, J.B., Hogg, J.P., Schaefer, G.B., 1998. Does selection bias determine the prevalence of the cavum septi pellucidi? Pediatr. Neurol. 19 (3), 195–198. Epub 1998/11/07 9806136.

Peterson, M., Warf, B.C., Schiff, S.J., 2018. Normative human brain volume growth. J. Neurosurg. Pediatr. 21 (5), 478–485. Epub 2018/03/03. https://doi.org/10.3171/2017.10.PEDS17141. 29498607. PMC6212293.

Qin, Y.Y., Hsu, J.T., Yoshida, S., Faria, A.V., Oishi, K., Unschuld, P.G., Redgrave, G.W., Ying, H.S., Ross, C.A., Van Zijl, P.C.M., Hillis, A.E., Albert, M.S., Lyketsos, C.G., Miller, M.I., Mori, S., Oishi, K., 2013. Gross feature recognition of Anatomical Images based on Atlas grid (GAIA): using the degree of local atlas-image segmentation disagreement to capture the features of anatomic brain MRI. NeuroImage Clin. 3, 202–211.

Rados, M., Judas, M., Kostovic, I., 2006. In vitro MRI of brain development. Eur. J. Radiol. 57 (2), 187–198. Epub 2006/01/28. https://doi.org/10.1016/j.ejrad.2005.11.019. 16439088.

Remer, J., Croteau-Chonka, E., Dean 3rd, D.C., D'Arpino, S., Dirks, H., Whiley, D., Deoni, S.C.L., 2017. Quantifying cortical development in typically developing toddlers and young children, 1–6 years of age. NeuroImage 153, 246–261. Epub 2017/04/11. https://doi.org/10.1016/j.neuroimage.2017.04.010. 28392489. PMC5460988.

Rose, J., Vassar, R., Cahill-Rowley, K., Guzman, X.S., Stevenson, D.K., Barnea-Goraly, N., 2014a. Brain microstructural development at near-term age in very-low-birth-weight preterm infants: an atlas-based diffusion imaging study. NeuroImage 86, 244–256. Epub 2013/10/05. https://doi.org/10.1016/j.neuroimage.2013.09.053. 24091089. 3985290.

Rose, J., Vassar, R., Cahill-Rowley, K., Stecher Guzman, X., Hintz, S.R., Stevenson, D.K., Barnea-Goraly, N., 2014b. Neonatal physiological correlates of near-term brain development on MRI and DTI in very-low-birth-weight preterm infants. NeuroImage Clin. 5, 169–177. Epub 2014/07/30. https://doi.org/10.1016/j.nicl.2014.05.013. 25068107. 4110350.

Rose, J., Cahill-Rowley, K., Vassar, R., Yeom, K.W., Stecher, X., Stevenson, D.K., Hintz, S.R., Barnea-Goraly, N., 2015. Neonatal brain microstructure correlates of neurodevelopment and gait in preterm children 18-22 mo of age: an MRI and DTI study. Pediatr. Res. 78 (6), 700–708. Epub 2015/09/01. https://doi.org/10.1038/pr.2015.157. 26322412.

Roze, E., Benders, M.J., Kersbergen, K.J., van der Aa, N.E., Groenendaal, F., van Haastert, I.C., Leemans, A., de Vries, L.S., 2015. Neonatal DTI early after birth predicts motor outcome in preterm infants with periventricular hemorrhagic infarction. Pediatr. Res. 78 (3), 298–303. Epub 2015/05/16. https://doi.org/10.1038/pr.2015.94. 25978802.

Schnack, H.G., van Haren, N.E., Brouwer, R.M., Evans, A., Durston, S., Boomsma, D.I., Kahn, R.S., Hulshoff Pol, H.E., 2015. Changes in thickness and surface area of the human cortex and their relationship with intelligence. Cereb. Cortex 25 (6), 1608–1617. Epub 2014/01/11. https://doi.org/10.1093/cercor/bht357. 24408955.

Scott, J.A., Habas, P.A., Kim, K., Rajagopalan, V., Hamzelou, K.S., Corbett-Detig, J.M., Barkovich, A.J., Glenn, O.A., Studholme, C., 2011. Growth trajectories of the human fetal brain tissues estimated from 3D reconstructed in utero MRI. Int. J. Dev. Neurosci. 29 (5), 529–536. Epub 2011/05/03. https://doi.org/10.1016/j.ijdevneu.2011.04.001. 21530634. PMC3315847.

Serag, A., Aljabar, P., Ball, G., Counsell, S.J., Boardman, J.P., Rutherford, M.A., Edwards, A.D., Hajnal, J.V., Rueckert, D., 2012. Construction of a consistent high-definition spatio-temporal atlas of the developing brain using adaptive kernel regression. NeuroImage 59 (3), 2255–2265. Epub 2011/10/12. https://doi.org/10.1016/j.neuroimage.2011.09.062. 21985910.

Shattuck, D.W., Mirza, M., Adisetiyo, V., Hojatkashani, C., Salamon, G., Narr, K.L., Poldrack, R.A., Bilder, R.M., Toga, A.W., 2008. Construction of a 3D probabilistic atlas of human cortical structures. NeuroImage 39 (3), 1064–1080. https://doi.org/10.1016/j.neuroimage.2007.09.031. 18037310. 2757616.

Shi, F., Yap, P.T., Wu, G., Jia, H., Gilmore, J.H., Lin, W., Shen, D., 2011. Infant brain atlases from neonates to 1- and 2-year-olds. PLoS One 6 (4), e18746. Epub 2011/05/03. https://doi.org/10.1371/journal.pone.0018746. 21533194. 3077403.

Shi, F., Salzwedel, A.P., Lin, W., Gilmore, J.H., Gao, W., 2017. Functional brain parcellations of the infant brain and the associated developmental trends. Cereb. Cortex, 1–11. Epub 2017/03/24. https://doi.org/10.1093/cercor/bhx062. 28334317.

Tang, X., Yoshida, S., Hsu, J., Huisman, T.A., Faria, A.V., Oishi, K., Kutten, K., Poretti, A., Li, Y., Miller, M. I., Mori, S., 2014. Multi-contrast multi-atlas parcellation of diffusion tensor imaging of the human brain. PLoS One 9 (5), e96985. Epub 2014/05/09. https://doi.org/10.1371/journal.pone.0096985. 24809486. PMC4014574.

Taoka, T., Aida, N., Ochi, T., Takahashi, Y., Akashi, T., Miyasaka, T., Iwamura, A., Sakamoto, M., Kichikawa, K., 2011. Transient hyperintensity in the subthalamic nucleus and globus pallidus of newborns on T1-weighted images. AJNR Am. J. Neuroradiol. 32 (6), 1130–1137. Epub 2011/04/23. https://doi.org/10.3174/ajnr.A2451. 21511869.

Toga, A.W., Thompson, P.M., 2009. Image registration and the construction of multidimensional brain atlases. In: Bankman, I.N. (Ed.), Handbook of Medical Image Processing and Analysis, second ed. Academic Press, pp. 707–724.

Tzourio-Mazoyer, N., Landeau, B., Papathanassiou, D., Crivello, F., Etard, O., Delcroix, N., Mazoyer, B., Joliot, M., 2002. Automated anatomical labeling of activations in SPM using a macroscopic anatomical parcellation of the MNI MRI single-subject brain. NeuroImage 15 (1), 273–289. Epub 2002/01/05. https://doi.org/10.1006/nimg.2001.0978. 11771995.

Ulfig, N., Neudorfer, F., Bohl, J., 2000. Transient structures of the human fetal brain: subplate, thalamic reticular complex, ganglionic eminence. Histol. Histopathol. 15 (3), 771–790. Epub 2000/08/30. 10.14670/HH-15.771. 10963122.

Van Essen, D.C., 2002. Surface-based atlases of cerebellar cortex in the human, macaque, and mouse. Ann. N. Y. Acad. Sci. 978, 468–479. 12582074.

Van Essen, D.C., Drury, H.A., 1997. Structural and functional analyses of human cerebral cortex using a surface-based atlas. J. Neurosci. 17 (18), 7079–7102. 9278543.

Walhovd, K.B., Fjell, A.M., Giedd, J., Dale, A.M., Brown, T.T., 2017. Through thick and thin: a need to reconcile contradictory results on trajectories in human cortical development. Cereb. Cortex 27 (2), 1472–1481. Epub 2017/04/04. https://doi.org/10.1093/cercor/bhv301. 28365755. PMC6075596.

Wang, F., Lian, C., Wu, Z., Zhang, H., Li, T., Meng, Y., Wang, L., Lin, W., Shen, D., Li, G., 2019. Developmental topography of cortical thickness during infancy. Proc. Natl. Acad. Sci. U. S. A. 116 (32), 15855–15860. Epub 2019/07/25. https://doi.org/10.1073/pnas.1821523116. 31332010. PMC6689940.

Wilke, M., Schmithorst, V.J., Holland, S.K., 2002. Assessment of spatial normalization of whole-brain magnetic resonance images in children. Hum. Brain Mapp. 17 (1), 48–60. Epub 2002/08/31. https://doi.org/10.1002/hbm.10053. 12203688.

Wilke, M., Schmithorst, V.J., Holland, S.K., 2003. Normative pediatric brain data for spatial normalization and segmentation differs from standard adult data. Magn. Reson. Med. 50 (4), 749–757. Epub 2003/10/03. https://doi.org/10.1002/mrm.10606. 14523961.

Wimberger, D.M., Roberts, T.P., Barkovich, A.J., Prayer, L.M., Moseley, M.E., Kucharczyk, J., 1995. Identification of "premyelination" by diffusion-weighted MRI. J. Comput. Assist. Tomogr. 19 (1), 28–33. Epub 1995/01/01. https://doi.org/10.1097/00004728-199501000-00005. 7529780.

Wu, D., Ceritoglu, C., Miller, M.I., Mori, S., 2016a. Direct estimation of patient attributes from anatomical MRI based on multi-atlas voting. NeuroImage Clin. 12, 570–581. Epub 2016/10/01. https://doi.org/10.1016/j.nicl.2016.09.008. 27689021. 5031476.

Wu, D., Ma, T., Ceritoglu, C., Li, Y., Chotiyanonta, J., Hou, Z., Hsu, J., Xu, X., Brown, T., Miller, M.I., Mori, S., 2016b. Resource atlases for multi-atlas brain segmentations with multiple ontology levels based on T1-weighted MRI. NeuroImage 125, 120–130. Epub 2015/10/27. https://doi.org/10.1016/j.neuroimage.2015.10.042. 26499813. PMC4691373.

Wu, D., Chang, L., Akazawa, K., Oishi, K., Skranes, J., Ernst, T., 2017a. Change-point analysis data of neonatal diffusion tensor MRI in preterm and term-born infants. Data Brief 12, 453–458. Epub 2017/05/19. https://doi.org/10.1016/j.dib.2017.04.020. 28516143. 5426014.

Wu, D., Chang, L., Akazawa, K., Oishi, K., Skranes, J., Ernst, T., 2017b. Mapping the critical gestational age at birth that alters brain development in preterm-born infants using multi-modal MRI. NeuroImage 149, 33–43. Epub 2017/01/24. https://doi.org/10.1016/j.neuroimage.2017.01.046. 28111189. 5367973.

Yoon, U., Fonov, V.S., Perusse, D., Evans, A.C., 2009. The effect of template choice on morphometric analysis of pediatric brain data. NeuroImage 45 (3), 769–777. 19167509.

Zanin, E., Ranjeva, J.P., Confort-Gouny, S., Guye, M., Denis, D., Cozzone, P.J., Girard, N., 2011. White matter maturation of normal human fetal brain. An in vivo diffusion tensor tractography study. Brain Behav. 1 (2), 95–108. Epub 2012/03/09. https://doi.org/10.1002/brb3.17. 22399089. PMC3236541.

Zhan, J., Dinov, I.D., Li, J., Zhang, Z., Hobel, S., Shi, Y., Lin, X., Zamanyan, A., Feng, L., Teng, G., Fang, F., Tang, Y., Zang, F., Toga, A.W., Liu, S., 2013. Spatial-temporal atlas of human fetal brain development during the early second trimester. NeuroImage 82, 115–126. Epub 2013/06/04. https://doi.org/10.1016/j.neuroimage.2013.05.063. 23727529. 3876574.

Zhang, Y., Shi, F., Wu, G., Wang, L., Yap, P.T., Shen, D., 2016. Consistent spatial-temporal longitudinal atlas construction for developing infant brains. IEEE Trans. Med. Imaging 35 (12), 2568–2577. Epub 2016/07/09. https://doi.org/10.1109/TMI.2016.2587628. 27392345.

CHAPTER

Segmentation with varying contrasts of pediatric MRI

12

Yue Sun[a], Gang Li[a], Zhengwang Wu[a], Kun Gao[a], Sijie Niu[a], Dinggang Shen[b], and Li Wang[a]

Department of Radiology and Biomedical Research Imaging Center, University of North Carolina at Chapel Hill, Chapel Hill, NC, United States[a] The Department of Research and Development, Shanghai United Imaging Intelligence Co., Ltd., Shanghai, China[b]

1. Introduction

Human brain growth in the first postnatal year is highly dynamic, involving the complicated development of brain structural and functional connectivity (Li et al., 2019), which likely plays an important role in later cognitive and behavioral outcomes and is critical for many neurodevelopment disorders (Knickmeyer et al., 2008). During this period, the total brain volume increases around 101%, driven mainly by gray matter growth in region-specific manners (Knickmeyer et al., 2008). To accurately characterize early brain development, one of the most critical steps is accurate segmentation of infant brain MR images into regions of interest, such as white matter (WM), gray matter (GM), and cerebrospinal fluid (CSF).

Fig. 1 shows T1-weighted (T1w) and T2-weighted (T2w) MR images of infant brains, scanned at 2 weeks, 3, 6, 9 and 12 months of age. In the first postnatal year, brain development can be divided into three distinct phases, i.e., infantile phase ($\leq$5 months), isointense phase (6–8 months), and early adult-like phase ($\geq$9 months). First, we can observe that brain volume increases rapidly from 2 weeks to 12 months. Second, during the infantile phase as shown in the first and second columns, the intensity of GM tissue is higher than that of WM in the T1w MR images; then with the myelination and maturation processes of the brain, the signal intensity of WM increases, which leads to an extremely low tissue contrast between WM and GM tissues during the isointense phase (the third column of Fig. 1); the last column is the early adult-like phase, where the intensity of GM is much lower than that of WM in T1w images, similar to the pattern of tissue contrast in the adult MR images. The corresponding tissue intensity distributions of these three phases are shown in the third row of Fig. 1, from which we can observe, in the isointense phase, the intensity distributions of voxels in GM and WM are largely overlapped, thus leading to the lowest tissue contrast and the most challenging task for tissue segmentation, in comparison to images at other phases of early brain development. Existing computational tools typically developed for processing and analyzing adult brain MRI (Xue et al., 2006), e.g., volBrain, SPM, FSL, BrainSuite, CIVET, FreeSurfer and HCP pipeline, often perform poorly on infant brain MRI (Wang et al., 2018a).

Many efforts have been devoted to infant brain segmentation and achieved encouraging results. An overview of the representative infant brain MRI segmentation techniques is summarized in Table 1.

Handbook of Pediatric Brain Imaging. https://doi.org/10.1016/B978-0-12-816633-8.00010-7

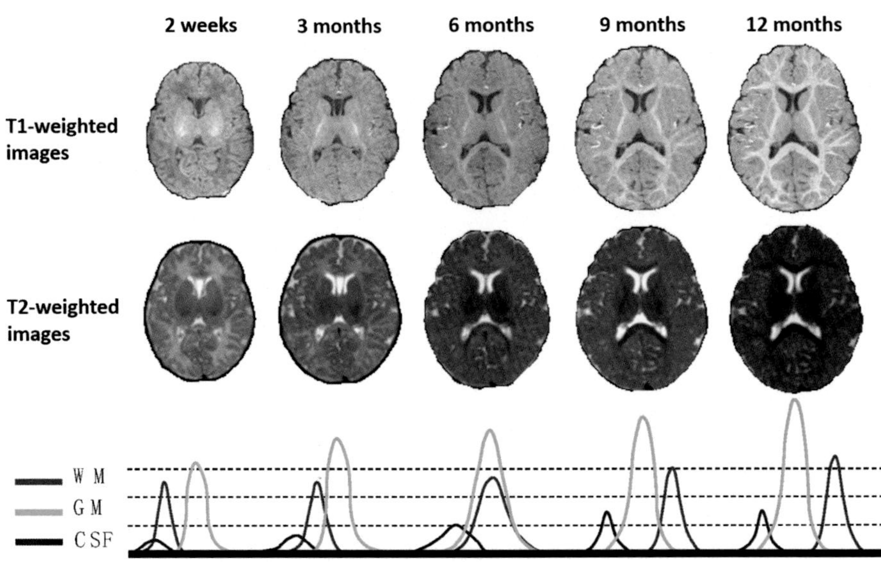

FIG. 1

T1w and T2w MR images of an infant scanned longitudinally at 2 weeks, 3, 6, 9 and 12 months of age. The corresponding tissue intensity distributions from T1w MR images are shown at the bottom row, where the WM and GM intensities are highly overlapped in the isointense phase.

Figure was adapted from Fig. 1 in Wang, L., Nie, D., Li, G., Dolz, P.É.J., Zhang, Q., Wang, F., Xia, J., Wu, Z., Chen, J., Thung, K., Bui, T. D., Shin, J., Zeng, G., Zheng, G., Fonov, V.S., Doyle, A., Xu, Y., Moeskops, P., Pluim, J.P.W., Desrosiers, C., Ayed, I.B., Sanroma, G., Benkarim, O.M., Casamitjana, A., Vilaplana, V., Lin, W., Li, G., Shen, D., 2019b. Benchmark on automatic six-month-old infant brain segmentation algorithms: the iSeg-2017 challenge. IEEE Trans. Med. Imaging. 38(9), 2219–2230. https://doi.org/10.1109/TMI.2019.2901712.

These pioneer methods are roughly divided into four categories: *atlas-based* (Prastawa et al., 2005; Xue et al., 2007; Weisenfeld and Warfield, 2009; Shi et al., 2010a, b, 2011a; Wang et al., 2014a), *deformable-surface-based* (Wang et al., 2011, 2014b), *learning-based* (Anbeek et al., 2013; Wang et al., 2015; Nie et al., 2016, 2017; Moeskops et al., 2016; Bui et al., 2020; Zhengyang Wang et al., 2020), and *hybrid approaches* (Gui et al., 2012; Beare et al., 2016). Meanwhile, the *atlas-based approaches* are further subdivided, based on the types of the atlases used, into population atlas-based and subject-specific atlas-based approaches. Similarly, learning-based approaches are subcategorized, based on the types of the features used, into hand-crafted features-based approaches and deep learning-based approaches. Table 1 illustrates that (1) the focus of infant brain segmentation has recently shifted from the infantile phase to the most challenging isointense phase; (2) deep learning-based methods have been widely employed for infant brain segmentation.

However, one major limitation of previous works is ignoring the prior anatomical knowledge of the brain structure, e.g., (1) tissue contrast between CSF and GM is higher than that between GM and WM in images; (2) the human cerebral cortex is a folded sheet of GM wrapping WM; (3) cortical thickness is within a certain range. For example, Wang et al. (Wang et al., 2015) developed a learning-based multi-source integration framework (namely LINKS) for tissue segmentation of 6-month infant brain images, where the random forest technique (Bosch et al., 2007) was employed to effectively integrate features

Table 1 Representative infant brain segmentation algorithms.

Study	Dataset	Modality	Tissues segmented	Atlas/features/ architecture	Method
(A.1) Atlas-based approaches—Population atlas-based approaches					
Prastawa et al. (2005)	50 Neonates	T1w, T2w	UWM, MWM, GM, CSF	Atlases built from 3 neonates	EM based framework for classification
Xue et al. (2007)	25 Neonates	T2w	UWM, GM, CSF	Age-specific templates from 27 to 45 gestational weeks	EM-Markov random field
Weisenfeld and Warfield, 2009)	23 Neonates	T1w, T2w	UWM, MWM, cGM, sGM, CSF	Atlases built from 15 newborns	Supervised classification, followed by iterative prototype editing
(A.2) Atlas-based approaches—Subject-specific atlas-based approaches					
Shi et al. (2010a)	10 Neonates	T2w	WM, GM, CSF	Atlases built from longitudinal scans	Probabilistic-atlas-based segmentation
Shi et al. (2010b)	10 Neonates	T2w	WM, GM, CSF	Atlases built by selection of similar exemplars	Multiregion-multireference framework
Shi et al. (2011a)	10 Neonates	T2w	WM, GM, CSF	Hybrid atlases built on subject-specific cortical structures, with population-based atlas	Use of phased array coil and creation of hybrid atlas
Wang et al. (2014a)	32 Infants at 6 months of age	T1w, T2w, FA	WM, GM, CSF	Subject-specific atlases built using multimodal sparse representation	Patch-based sparse representation of multimodal images + anatomical/topological constraints
(B) Deformable surface-based approaches					
Wang et al. (2011)	10 Neonates	T2w	WM, GM, CSF	Population atlas from (Shi et al., 2011b)	Coupled level sets with incorporation of atlas, local intensity, and cortical thickness
Wang et al. (2014b)	152 Neonates	T2w	WM, GM, CSF	Subject-specific atlases built by sparse representation	Patch-driven level set method

Continued

Table 1 Representative infant brain segmentation algorithms—cont'd

Study	Dataset	Modality	Tissues segmented	Atlas/features/ architecture	Method
(C.1) Learning-based approaches—Hand-crafted features-based approaches					
Anbeek et al. (2013)	7 Training +101 testing neonates	T1w, T2w	CB, MWM, UWM, BGT, BS, vCSF, eCSF, BGT	Intensity and spatial features	Supervised classification based on intensity and spatial values
Wang et al. (2015)	10 Training and 26, 22, 22, 23, and 26 testing subjects at 0, 3, 6, 9 and 12 months of age, respectively	T1w, T2w, FA	WM, GM, CSF	3D Harr-like features extracted from T1w, T2w, FA, and also the intermediate WM, GM, and CSF probability maps	Learning-based multisource integration framework (LINKS): Training a sequence of classifiers via random forest and auto-context model
(C.2) Learning-based approaches—Deep learning-based approaches					
Nie et al. (2016)	10 Infants at 6 months of age	T1w, T2w, FA	WM, GM, CSF	3 convolutional layers +2 deconvolutional layers	2D fully convolutional networks (FCN)
Moeskops et al. (2016)	22 Neonates	T2w	CB, MWM, UWM, BGT, BS, vCSF, eCSF, BGT	3 convolutional layers +1 fully connected layer in a multiscale fashion	2D multiscale CNN
Nie et al. (2017)	11 Infants at 6 months of age	T1w, T2w, FA	WM, GM, CSF	6 convolutional layers +6 deconvolutional layers	3D multimodal FCN
Bui et al. (2020)	60 Subjects at 6 months of age and 60 subjects at 24 months of age	T1w, T2w	WM, GM, CSF	2 generator networks+2 discriminator networks+2 segmentation networks	3D-cycleGAN-Seg architecture
Zhengyang Wang et al. (2020)	10 Subjects at 6 months of age	T1w, T2w	WM, GM, CSF	2 down-sampling blocks +2 up-sampling blocks residual connection+ global aggregation block	Nonlocal U-Net

Table 1 Representative infant brain segmentation algorithms—cont'd

Study	Dataset	Modality	Tissues segmented	Atlas/features/ architecture	Method
(D) Hybrid approaches					
Gui et al. (2012)	30 Neonates	T1w, T2w	CB, MWM, UWM, BGT, BS, CSF, eSF, BGT	Watershed + active contour model	Morphology-driven automatic segmentation
Beare et al. (2016)	41 Neonates	T2w	cGM, WM, sGM, CB, BS, CSF, amygdala, hippocampus	Unified segmentation with a population atlas, template adaptation and topological filtering	Morphological adaptation and unified segmentation

BG: *background;* BGT: *basal ganglia and thalami;* BS: *brainstem;* CB: *cerebellum;* **cGM**: *cortical gray matter;* CSF: *eCSF + vCSF;* **eCSF**: *cerebrospinal fluid in the extracerebral space;* GM: *cGM + sGM;* MWM: *myelinated white matter;* **sGM**: ***subcortical*** *gray matter;* UWM: *unmyelinated white matter;* **vCSF**: *cerebrospinal fluid in the ventricles;* WM: *MWM + UWM.*
Table was remade from table 1 in Li, G., Wang, L., Yap, P.-T., Wang, F., Wu, Z., Meng, Y., Dong, P., Kim, J., Shi, F., Rekik, I., Lin, W., Shen, D., 2019. Computational neuroanatomy of baby brains: A review (in eng). NeuroImage. 185, 906–925. https://doi.org/10.1016/j.neuroimage.2018.03.042.

from multimodal images together. Although LINKS achieves encouraging results, it did not leverage the guidance of the anatomy knowledge. For a better understanding of the importance of the anatomical guidance, we show a comparison of results from LINKS (without anatomical guidance) and the proposed method (Wang et al., 2018a) (with anatomical guidance) in Fig. 2. Herein, Fig. 2A–B show the representative examples of T1w and T2w images scanned at around 6 months of age. Due to the low contrast between WM and GM in the 6-month infant brain images, WM voxels may be under-segmented (as shown in Fig. 2C), resulting in a "U"-shape on the inner surface, as can be seen in Fig. 2D. The under-segmented WM usually results in increased cortical thickness, as shown in Fig. 2E. It is worth noting that the WM surface indicated in the red ellipse is topologically correct but anatomically incorrect (Yotter et al., 2011). In such a case, the automatic correction operation was not involved since it was already topologically correct. Therefore, it is necessary to incorporate prior anatomical knowledge for guiding tissue segmentation of infant brains.

In this study, we introduced an anatomy-guided joint tissue segmentation and topological correction framework for 6-month infant brain segmentation in MR images (Wang et al., 2018a, b), by using the above-mentioned anatomical knowledge. First, given the higher intensity contrast between CSF and GM than that between GM and WM in images, brain images were classified into two tissue classes, i.e., CSF and WM + GM (Fig. 3A–B). Second, based on the binary classification results, a signed distance map (i.e., level set function) with respect to the boundary of GM/CSF was constructed directly (Fig. 3C) as the anatomical guidance. It is worth noting that the definition of the signed distance map matches the brain anatomical knowledge: (1) the sign roughly constrained WM to be inside of WM + GM; and (2) the absolute distance value further constrained WM to keep the cortical thickness within a reasonable range.

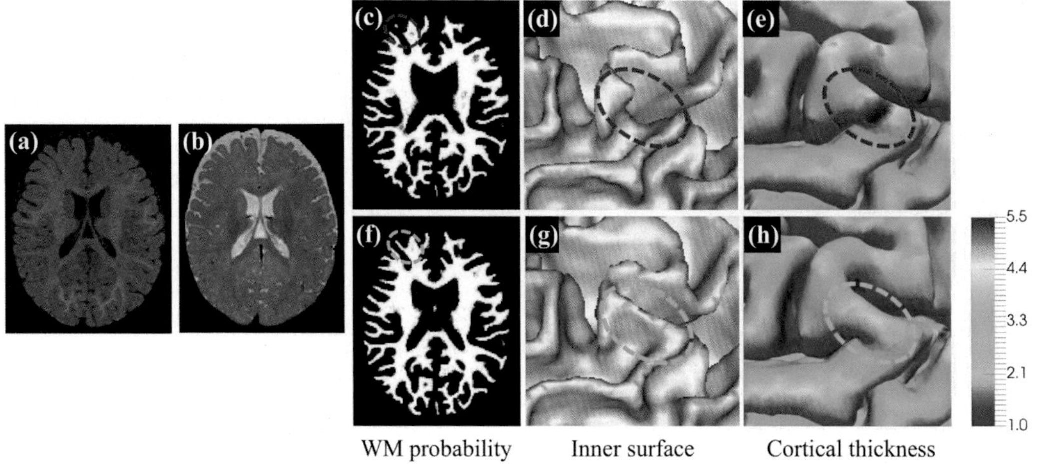

FIG. 2

The comparison of LINKS and the proposed method with anatomical guidance. (A) and (B) show T1w and T2w isointense infant brain images with extremely low tissue contrast. (C) and (F) are the WM probability maps estimated by LINKS (Wang et al., 2015) and the proposed work with anatomical guidance, respectively, with their corresponding inner surfaces shown in (D) and (G). In (D), the region indicated by the red ellipse is topologically correct, but anatomically incorrect, due to missing of a gyral region. Corresponding cortical thickness maps shown on the outer surfaces by LINKS and the proposed work are provided in (E) and (H), respectively.

Figure was adapted from fig. 1 in Wang, L., Li, G., Adeli, E., Liu, M., Wu, Z., Meng, Y., Lin, W., Shen, D., 2018a. Anatomy-guided joint tissue segmentation and topological correction for 6-month infant brain MRI with risk of autism. Hum. Brain Mapp. 39(6).

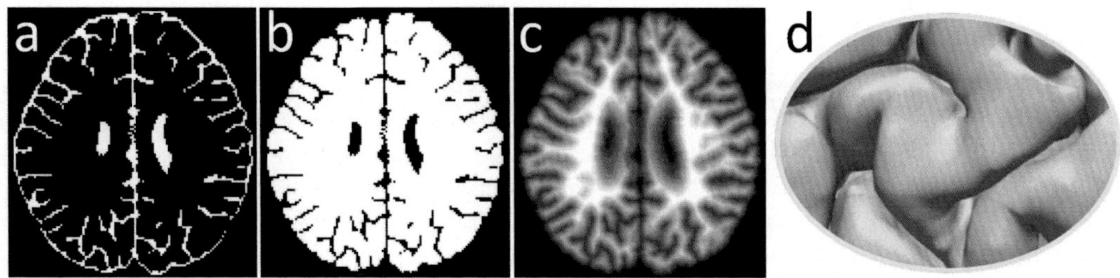

FIG. 3

(A) and (B) are CSF and GM + WM segmentation results, respectively, which are denoted by white color. (C) illustrates the signed distance function with respect to the outer surface shown in (D). In the signed distance map, the absolute value at each voxel is the shortest distance to its nearest point in the boundary of GM/CSF, and it takes positive values for voxels inside of WM + GM, while negative values outside of WM + GM.

Figure was adapted from fig. 3 in Wang, L., Li, G., Shi, F., Cao, X., Lian, C., Nie, D., Liu, M., Zhang, H., Li, G., Wu, Z., Lin, W., Shen, D., 2018b. Volume-based analysis of 6-month-old infant brain MRI for autism biomarker identification and early diagnosis. Med. Image Comput. Comput. Assist. Interv. 11072, 411–419. https://doi.org/10.1007/978-3-030-00931-1_47 (in English).

2. Dataset and image preprocessing

T1w and T2w infant brain MRIs were from the National Database for Autism Research (NDAR), which were acquired at around 6 months of age on Siemens 3 T scanners. During scanning, infants were naturally sleeping, fitted with ear protection, and their heads were secured in a vacuum-fixation device. T1w MR images were acquired with 160 sagittal slices using parameters: TR/TE = 2400/3.16 ms and voxel resolution = $1 \times 1 \times 1$ mm^3. T2w MR images were obtained with 160 sagittal slices using parameters: TR/TE = 3200/499 ms and voxel resolution = $1 \times 1 \times 1$ mm^3. Note that the imaging protocol has been optimized to maximize tissue contrast (Hazlett et al., 2012). In the preprocessing, T2w images were first linearly aligned onto the corresponding T1w images, and then skull stripping, intensity inhomogeneity correction, and histogram matching were performed for each MR modality by employing in-house tools (Shi et al., 2012; Tustison et al., 2010).

Accurate manual segmentation, providing labels for training, is of great importance for learning-based segmentation methods. Due to low contrast and huge number of voxels in brain images, manual segmentation is extremely time-consuming (de Macedo Rodrigues et al., 2015). Hence, to generate reliable manual segmentations, we first took advantage of longitudinal follow-up 24-month scans with high tissue contrast to generate an initial automatic segmentation for isointense subjects by using a publicly available software iBEAT V1.0 (http://www.nitrc.org/projects/ibeat/). This is based on the fact that, at term birth, the major sulci and gyri in the brain are already present, and are generally preserved but only fine-tuned during postnatal brain development (Chi et al., 1977). Therefore, we can utilize the longitudinal late-time-point images (e.g., 24-month), which can be segmented with a high accuracy by using existing segmentation tools, e.g., FreeSurfer (Fischl, 2012), to guide the segmentation of early-time-point (e.g., 6-month) infant images. Fig. 4 shows the automatic segmentation results by iBEAT on 4 representative subjects. Second, based on the segmentation results by iBEAT, manual editing was further performed by an experienced neuroradiologist. Details of the manual protocol are available in the (Wang et al., 2018a). The corresponding manual segmentation results are shown in the 4th column of Fig. 4, with their difference maps compared to iBEAT-based results shown in the last column. For each subject, it took almost a whole week (40 h) for manual segmentation, with around 26% of total brain voxels relabeled. In such a way, the issue of the potential bias from automatic segmentations can be largely minimized and the quality of manual segmentations can be ensured. Considering that there are thousands of MR images archived in NDAR, we believe it is worthwhile to make such a great manual annotation effort, which makes our learning algorithm more accurate and robust on this large dataset. Note that these follow-up scans were used only to generate manual segmentations for training. After training, segmentation was performed using only 6-month-old infant images, without reliance on any follow-up scans.

3. Methods

As discussed above, anatomical knowledge provides important guidance for brain tissue segmentation, especially for the isointense phase with large overlapping of GM and WM intensity distributions. In this section, we first introduced how to construct and employ the anatomical knowledge for infant brain segmentation in Section 3.1. Then, an anatomy-guided joint tissue segmentation and topological correction framework was developed for 6-month infant brain segmentation in MR images, which was implemented with random forest and deep neural network technologies (Wang et al., 2018a, b) in Sections 3.2 and 3.3, respectively.

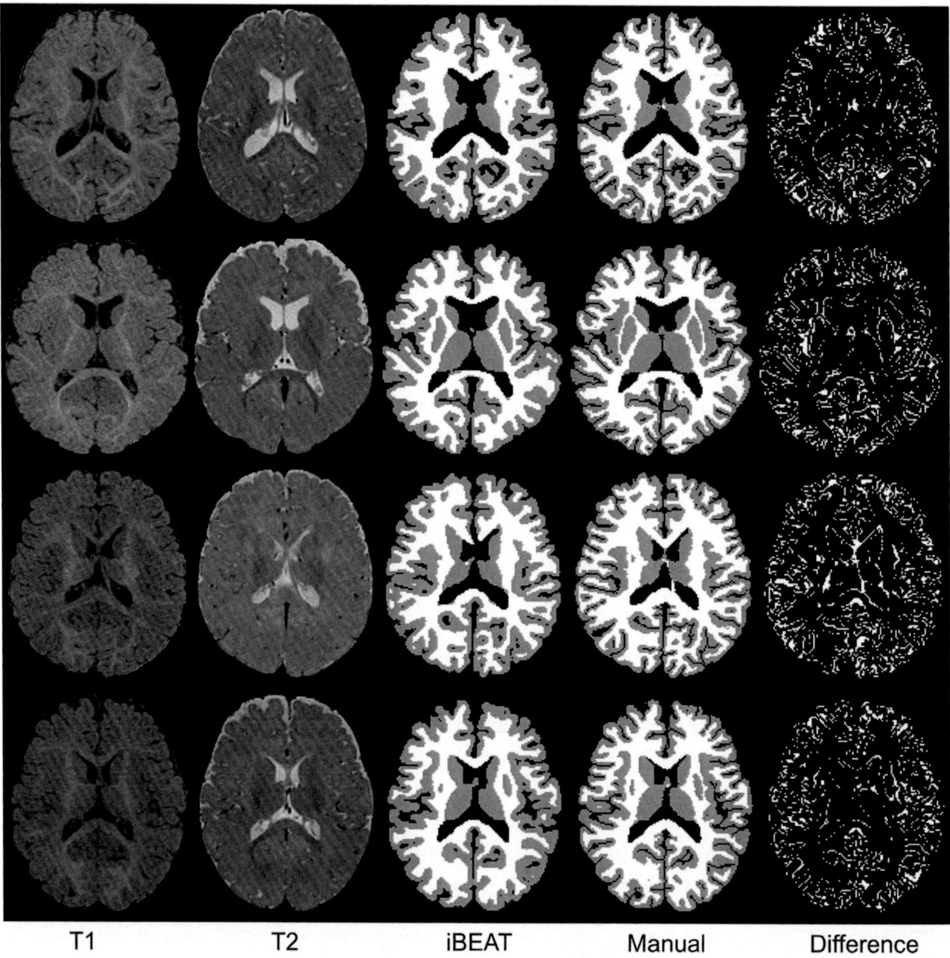

FIG. 4

The comparison of segmentations. The 1st and 2nd columns show the original T1w and T2w 6-month infant brain images, with the automatic segmentation results by iBEAT and the further manual corrections shown in the 3rd and 4th columns. The differences between iBEAT and manual correction results are also provided in the last column.

Figure was adapted from fig. 2 in Wang, L., Li, G., Adeli, E., Liu, M., Wu, Z., Meng, Y., Lin, W., Shen, D., 2018a. Anatomy-guided joint tissue segmentation and topological correction for 6-month infant brain MRI with risk of autism. Hum. Brain Mapp. 39(6).

3.1 Anatomical guidance

To derive anatomical guidance from the outer surface (i.e., GM/CSF boundary), we need to first classify brain images into two classes, i.e., CSF and WM + GM. Many classic methods can be employed for this binary classification problem. In this study, we first employ random forest (Wang et al., 2018a) to iteratively learn the probability maps of CSF and GM + WM from intensity images. Later, we further introduce more advanced deep learning technique (Wang et al., 2018b) to segment brain into CSF and GM + WM.

Based on the binary classification results, it is straightforward to construct a signed distance map (i.e., a level set function) with respect to the boundary of GM/CSF, as shown in Fig. 3C. Basically, the function value at each voxel is the shortest distance to its nearest point on the boundary of GM/CSF, and it takes positive values for voxels inside of WM + GM, while negative values outside of WM + GM. Therefore, the zero level set corresponds to the outer surface, as shown in Fig. 3D. It is worth noting that the definition of the signed distance map matches the brain anatomical knowledge: (1) the sign roughly constrained WM to be inside of WM + GM; and (2) the absolute distance value further constrained WM to keep the cortical thickness within a reasonable range.

3.2 Anatomy-guided random forest iterative learning (Wang et al., 2018a)

The random forest technique (Bosch et al., 2007) was used to implement the proposed framework. To derive anatomical guidance from the outer surface (i.e., GM/CSF boundary), the infant brain MR images are classified into two classes first. Similar to the previous work (Wang et al., 2015), we employ both intensity images and tentatively-estimated tissue probability maps to train a sequence of classifiers for CSF versus WM + GM classification. The flowchart is shown in Fig. 5, which contains three main components in the training stage. Specifically, (1) we use the appearance features extracted from intensity images, and employ random forests (Bosch et al., 2007) to train the first-layer classifiers. In details, 3D Haar-like features (Viola and Jones, 2004) are mainly used as the appearance features due to their computational efficiency. (2) Based on the trained first-layer classifiers, we can derive initial CSF and WM + GM probability maps. Inspired by the auto-context model (Tu and Bai, 2010; Loog and Ginneken, 2006), we then extract context features from the tentatively-estimated tissue probability maps, together with appearance features from original intensity images, to train the second-layer classifiers, for refining the segmentation results. (3) By iteratively training classifiers using both intensity images and the updated tissue probability maps, we can train a sequence of classifiers for segmentation. In the testing stage, the learned classifiers at each layer can be applied sequentially to iteratively refine the estimated probability maps for a new testing image.

Then, we further classify each WM + GM map into separate WM and GM maps by training another sequence of classifiers. It is worth noting that, besides using intensity images and tentatively-estimated

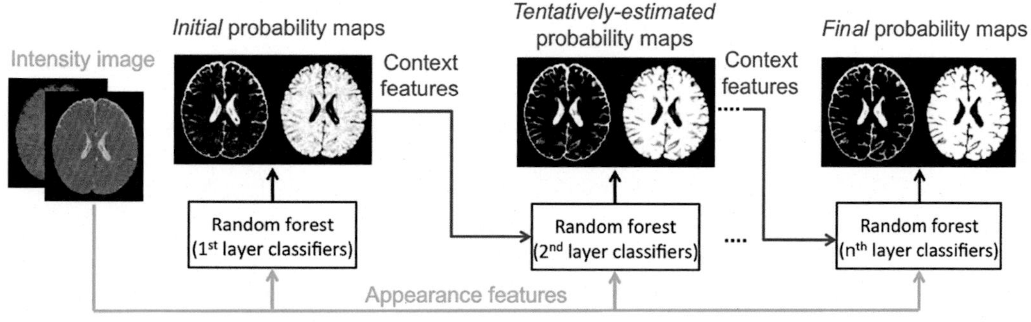

FIG. 5

The flowchart of training a sequence of classifiers for CSF versus WM + GM classification.

Figure was adapted from fig. 3 in Wang, L., Li, G., Adeli, E., Liu, M., Wu, Z., Meng, Y., Lin, W., Shen, D., 2018a. Anatomy-guided joint tissue segmentation and topological correction for 6-month infant brain MRI with risk of autism. Hum. Brain Mapp. 39(6).

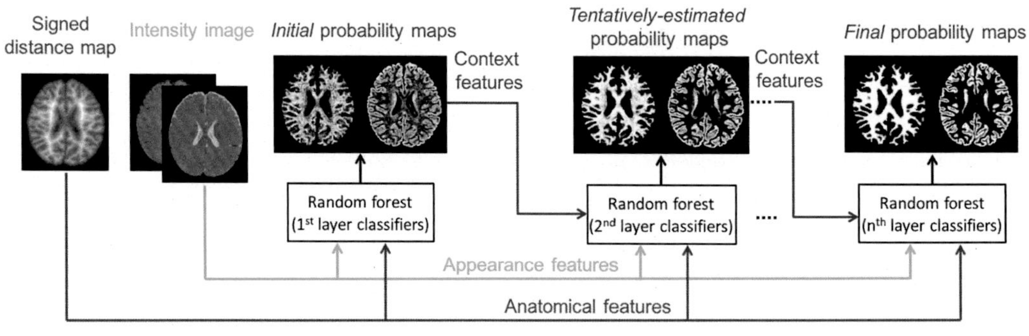

FIG. 6

The flowchart of training a sequence of classifiers for WM versus GM classification.

Figure was adapted from fig. 5 in Wang, L., Li, G., Adeli, E., Liu, M., Wu, Z., Meng, Y., Lin, W., Shen, D., 2018a. Anatomy-guided joint tissue segmentation and topological correction for 6-month infant brain MRI with risk of autism. Hum. Brain Mapp. 39(6).

tissue probabilities maps, the signed distance maps (used as anatomical guidance) was incorporated into the learning process. The flowchart for classifying WM and GM is shown in Fig. 6. Specifically, in the training stage, (1) we trained the first-layer of classifiers by extracting appearance features from intensity images along with the anatomical features from the signed distance map. (2) Based on the trained first-layer classifiers, we could derive initial WM and GM probability maps. Then, we extracted context features from the estimated tissue probability maps, together with appearance features from intensity images and anatomical features from the signed distance map, to train the second-layer classifiers. (3) By iteratively training classifiers with random forests on the intensity images, the signed distance map and the updated tissue probability maps, we could train a sequence of classifiers for classification. Note that, in our learning-based framework, the spatially varying cortical thickness (Fischl, 2012; Li et al., 2014) was implicitly and adaptively learned from the training images, instead of being explicitly defined in a constant range as in (Zeng et al., 1998).

In the testing stage, the learned classifiers were sequentially applied on each testing image to iteratively refine the estimated probability maps, steered by the anatomical guidance constructed in Section 3.1. Fig. 7 shows an example with the tentatively-estimated WM probability maps and the corresponding inner cortical surfaces (from left to right) estimated by the trained classifiers. With the anatomical guidance from the outer surface in the last column of Fig. 7, as indicated by the green ellipse, more WM voxels are expected to keep cortical thickness within a reasonable range. It can be observed that the WM probability in the green ellipse is gradually enhanced, and thus the missing gyrus is gradually recovered by the anatomical guidance, along which the cortical thickness (in the last row) is becoming reasonable. Similarly, the topological errors, e.g., holes or handles, causing abnormal cortical thickness, can also be corrected, with the results shown in the Section 4.2 (see Fig. 9).

3.3 Anatomy-guided densely-connected U-net (Wang et al., 2018b)

Although the random forest iterative learning in Section 3.2 can achieve encouraging results, the features are hand-crafted and predesigned, instead of being learned a data-driven fashion. To alleviate this problem, we leveraged convolutional neural networks, which can effectively and automatically learn

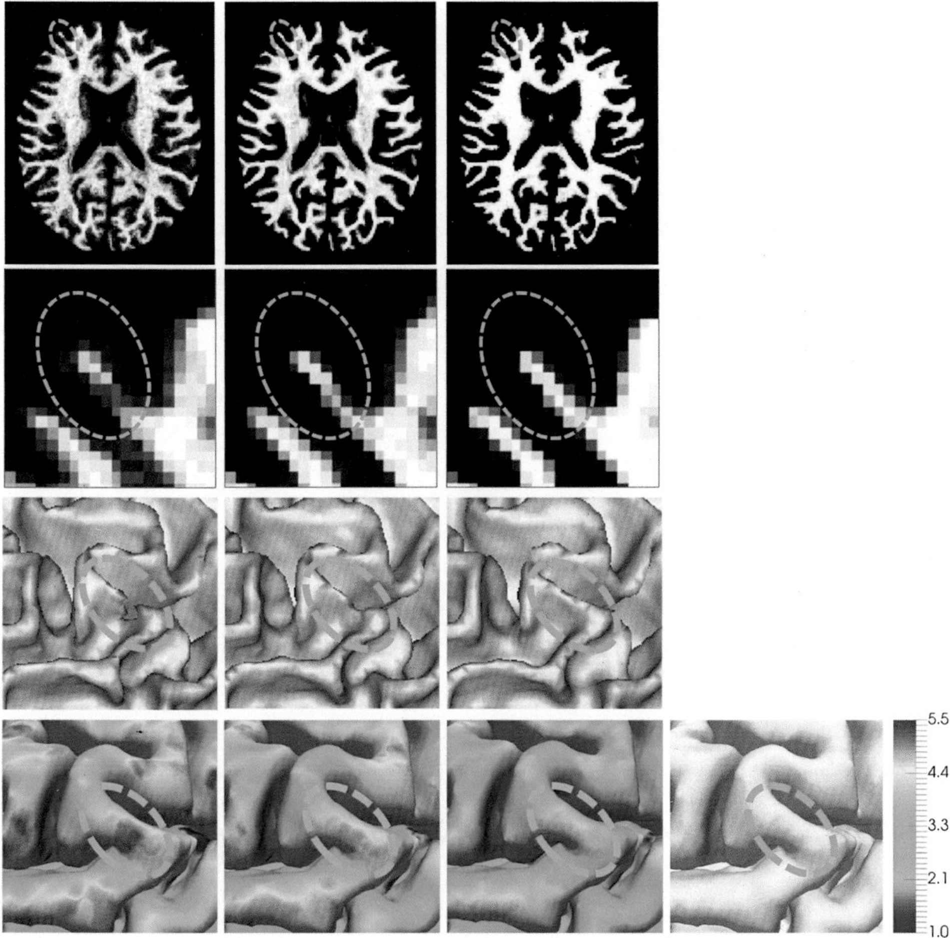

FIG. 7

The importance of using the anatomical guidance to correct errors. The 1st column shows the WM probabilities and their corresponding inner surfaces estimated without using anatomical guidance. The 2nd to 4th columns show the tentatively-estimated results of the proposed method. Steered by the anatomical guidance from the last column, the errors are gradually corrected.

Figure was adapted from fig. 6 in Wang, L., Li, G., Adeli, E., Liu, M., Wu, Z., Meng, Y., Lin, W., Shen, D., 2018a. Anatomy-guided joint tissue segmentation and topological correction for 6-month infant brain MRI with risk of autism. Hum. Brain Mapp. 39(6).

more representative and discriminative features. Inspired by the success of the U-Net architecture and the dense connection blocks, an Anatomy-guided Densely-connected U-Net (ADU-Net) was developed for brain image segmentation of 6-month infants.

The proposed network architecture is shown in Fig. 8, which includes a down-sampling path and an up-sampling path, going through seven dense blocks. Each dense block consists of three BN-ReLU-Conv-Dropout operations, in which each Conv includes 16 kernels and the dropout rate

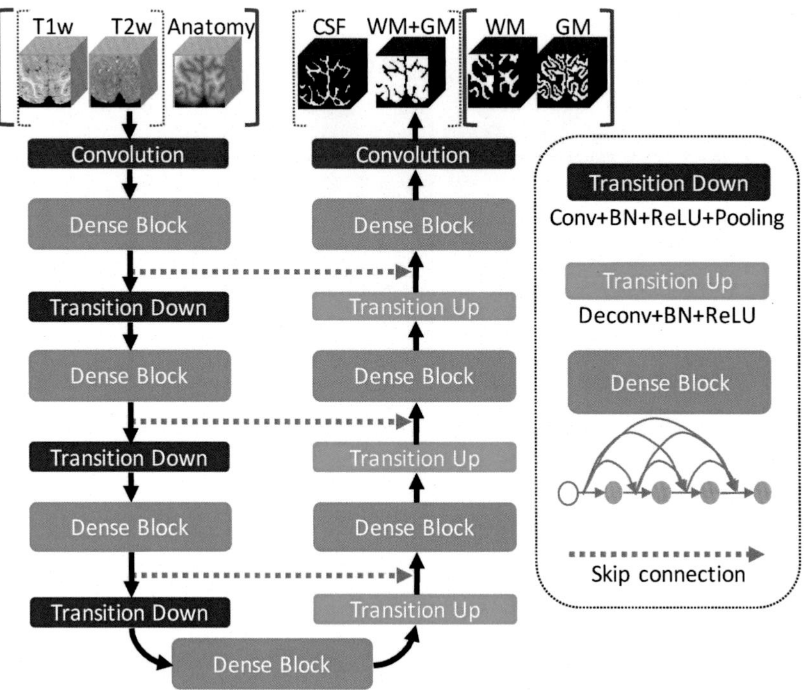

FIG. 8

The flowchart of ADU-Net architecture for infant brain segmentation. Input 1: T1w and T2w images for (CSF, WM + GM) segmentation to construct anatomy guidance; Input 2: T1w and T2w images and anatomical guidance for (WM, GM) segmentation.

Figure was adapted from fig. 2 in Wang, L., Li, G., Shi, F., Cao, X., Lian, C., Nie, D., Liu, M., Zhang, H., Li, G., Wu, Z., Lin, W., Shen, D., 2018b. Volume-based analysis of 6-month-old infant brain MRI for autism biomarker identification and early diagnosis. Med. Image Comput. Comput. Assist. Interv. 11072, 411–419. https://doi.org/10.1007/978-3-030-00931-1_47 (in English).

is 0.1. In the down-sampling path, between any two contiguous dense blocks, a transition down block (i.e., Conv-BN-ReLU followed by a max pooling layer) is included to reduce the feature map resolution and increase the receptive field. While in the up-sampling path, a transition up block, consisting of a transposed convolution, is included between any two contiguous dense blocks. It up-samples the feature maps from the preceding dense block. The up-sampled feature maps are then concatenated with the same level feature maps in the down-sampling path, and then input to the subsequent dense block. The final layer in the network is a convolution layer, followed by a softmax nonlinearity to provide the per-class probability at each voxel. For all the convolutional layers, the kernel size is $3 \times 3 \times 3$ with stride size 1 and 0-padding.

T1w and T2w MR images of training subjects and their corresponding manual segmentations are employed to train the network. To generate the anatomical guidance, as mentioned, we first train an initial ADU-Net to classify the brain images into two classes (i.e., CSF and WM + GM). Then, based on the segmentation results, it is straightforward to construct a signed distance function as shown in Fig. 3C. Finally, the intensity images, signed distance maps and annotations are input together to train another cascaded model for further separating GM and WM tissues.

4. Experiments

4.1 Quantitative evaluation metrics

Dice ratio (DR) and Modified (95th percentile) Hausdorff Distance (MHD) are used to evaluate the performance of automatic methods, which are defined as follows,

$$Dice = 2|A \cap B|/(|A| + |B|)$$

where A is the automated segmentation result, and B is the ground truth obtained by manual annotation.

$$MHD(A, B) = \max\left({}^{95}K^{th}_{\alpha \in surf(A)} d(\alpha, surf(B)), {}^{95}K^{th}_{\beta \in surf(B)} d(\beta, surf(A))\right)$$

where $surf(A)$ is the surface of segmentation A, ${}^{95}K^{th}_{\alpha \in surf(A)}$ represents the Kth ranked distance such that $K/|surf(A)| = 95\%$, and $d(\alpha, surf(B))$ is the nearest Euclidean distance from a surface point a to the surface B.

4.2 Evaluation on anatomy-guided random Forest iterative learning

The T1w and T2w MR images of 50 infants were chosen from NDAR dataset to train and validate the anatomy-guided random forest iterative learning method (Section 3.2). LINKS (Wang et al., 2015) and the infant-dedicated topological correction (TC) method (Hao et al., 2016) are compared with the proposed method. Fig. 9 further demonstrates the effectiveness of the anatomical guidance for topological correction. The 1st column shows the results without anatomical guidance, causing holes and handles. These holes and handles result in abnormal cortical thickness. The 2nd to 4th columns show the tentatively-estimated WM probability maps and the corresponding inner surfaces, steered by the anatomical guidance shown in the last column. It can be observed that these topological errors are gradually corrected by using the anatomical guidance.

In addition, during the image acquisition process, the motion of the infants is typical. We have to often repeat the acquisition when the acquired images are seriously affected by motion. However, there may still exist small motions. Therefore, a motion-robust segmentation method is highly desired. Fig. 10 shows an example of T1w and T2w images with motion effects. Existing work without considering anatomical knowledge, such as LINKS and TC method (Hao et al., 2016), cannot achieve reasonable results, as shown in (A) and (B), respectively. In contrast, the proposed work is robust to the motion and thus produces a more reasonable result (c), steered by anatomical guidance.

Furthermore, a quantitative analysis of the proposed method compared with LINKS and TC is illustrated in Table 2. To further compare significant difference among the three methods, a paired t-test on both Dice ratio and MHD is employed to calculate p-values. It can be seen from Table 2 that the proposed method achieves more accurate results in terms of both Dice ratio and MHD. It is worth noting that the Dice ratio of CSF is higher than that of WM or GM in all three methods, which is mainly due to the relatively high contrast between CSF and other tissues. That is also the reason that we use the outer surface (i.e., GM/CSF boundary) to guide the inner surface estimation.

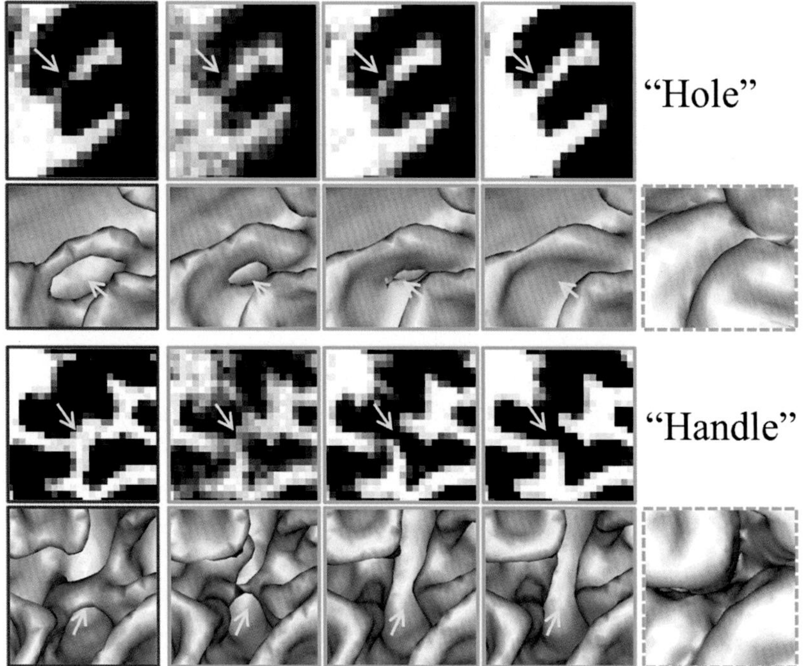

FIG. 9

The importance of using the anatomical guidance to correct topological errors. The 1st column shows the WM probabilities and their corresponding inner surfaces estimated without using anatomical guidance. The 2nd to 4th columns show the tentatively-estimated results of the proposed method. Steered by the anatomical guidance from the last column, the errors are gradually corrected.

Figure was adapted from fig. 7 in Wang, L., Li, G., Adeli, E., Liu, M., Wu, Z., Meng, Y., Lin, W., Shen, D., 2018a. Anatomy-guided joint tissue segmentation and topological correction for 6-month infant brain MRI with risk of autism. Hum. Brain Mapp. 39(6).

4.3 Evaluation on anatomy-guided densely-connected U-net

We further validated the proposed ADU-Net with other competitive deep learning-based methods, i.e., SegNet (Badrinarayanan et al., 2015), U-Net (Ronneberger et al., 2015) and Dense-Net (Bui et al., 2017). Particularly, the first competitive method has achieved promising results in natural images segmentation; the second one has achieved the best performance on ISBI 2012 EM challenge dataset, and the last one has won the first prize in iSeg-2017 (http://iseg2017.web.unc.edu/). The results on a testing subject by different methods are shown in Fig. 11. The estimated inner surface and cortical thickness by the proposed method are much more consistent with the ground truth from manual segmentation. We further quantitatively evaluate the results by using the Dice and MHD. As shown in Table 3, the proposed method achieves a significantly better performance in terms of Dice ratio on WM and GM, and MHD on WM.

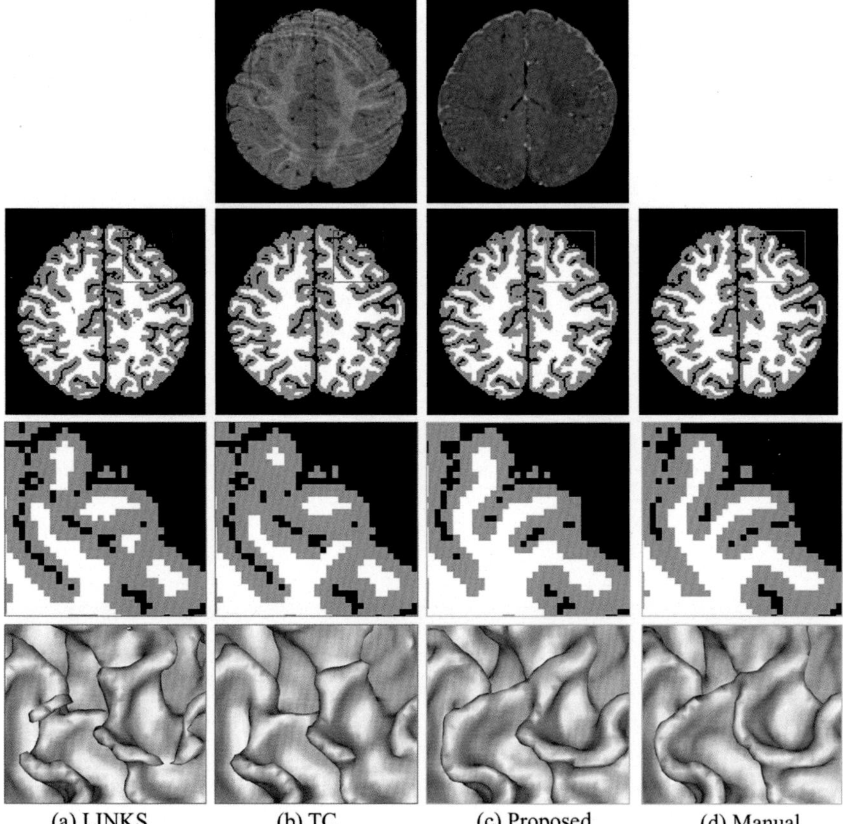

FIG. 10

Comparisons with learning-based segmentation method (LINKS) (Wang et al., 2015) and topological correction (TC) method (Hao et al., 2016) on a subject with motion. The 1st row shows T1w and T2w images with motion effects. Without anatomical guidance, LINKS (A) and TC (B) are sensitive to motion effect. By contrast, the proposed anatomy-guided framework achieves more reasonable results (C).

Figure was adapted from fig. 8 in Wang, L., Li, G., Adeli, E., Liu, M., Wu, Z., Meng, Y., Lin, W., Shen, D., 2018a. Anatomy-guided joint tissue segmentation and topological correction for 6-month infant brain MRI with risk of autism. Hum. Brain Mapp. 39(6).

4.4 Comparisons with Infant FreeSurfer

Recently, an automated segmentation and surface extraction pipeline designed to accommodate clinical MRI studies of infant brains in a population 0–2 year-old was proposed, named as *Infant FreeSurfer* (Zöllei et al., 2020) *Infant FreeSurfer* relies on a single channel of T1-weighted MR images to achieve automated segmentation of cortical and subcortical brain areas by the conventional multiatlas registration, producing volumes of subcortical structures and surface models of the cerebral cortex. To demonstrate the advantage of the proposed work, we have made a comparison with *Infant FreeSurfer on a* T1w neonatal brain images, as shown in Fig. 12. We can see our method produces a more

Table 2 Averaged Dice (%) and MHD (mm) of methods on 50 isointense infant images

Method		LINKS (Wang et al., 2015)	TC (Hao et al., 2016)	Proposed (Wang et al., 2018a)
Dice (%)	WM	87.1 ± 0.56 ($P = 0.0001$)	87.5 ± 0.45 ($P = 0.0001$)	**89.4 ± 0.31**
	GM	86.5 ± 0.78 ($P = 0.0003$)	87.2 ± 0.63 ($P = 0.0003$)	**90.5 ± 0.55**
	CSF	92.6 ± 0.29[a] ($P = 0.90$)	92.6 ± 0.29[a] ($P = 0.90$)	92.5 ± 0.31
MHD (mm)	WM/GM	1.50 ± 0.37 ($P = 0.0001$)	1.29 ± 0.25 ($P = 0.0001$)	**0.89 ± 0.11**

The bold indicates that the respective result is significantly better than others (P-value <0.005).
[a]*The symbol in the table indicates that the topological correction (TC) only corrects the inner cortical surface, and thus its accuracy on CSF segmentation is the same as the original LINKS (Wang et al., 2015).*
Table was copied from table 1 in Wang, L., Li, G., Adeli, E., Liu, M., Wu, Z., Meng, Y., Lin, W., Shen, D., 2018a. Anatomy-guided joint tissue segmentation and topological correction for 6-month infant brain MRI with risk of autism. Hum. Brain Mapp. 39(6).

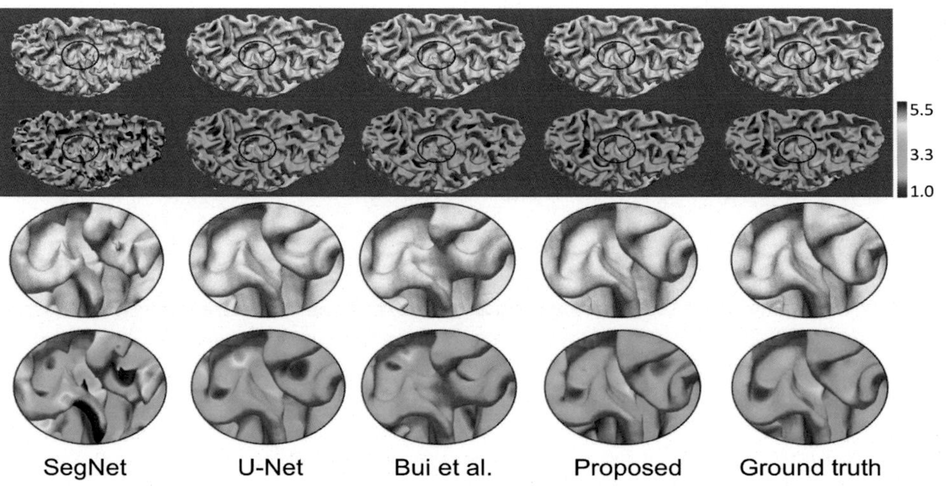

FIG. 11

Comparison with state-of-the-art methods on a 6-month-old infant subjects from iSeg-2017. The first and second rows show the inner surface and corresponding cortical thickness, respectively, with the zoomed views shown in the third and fourth rows. From left to right: results by SegNet (Badrinarayanan et al., 2015), U-Net (Ronneberger et al., 2015), Dense-Net (Bui et al., 2017), the proposed ADU-Net method (Wang et al., 2018b), and the ground truth from manual segmentation. Color bar indicates the thickness in mm.

Figure was adapted from fig. 4 in Wang, L., Li, G., Shi, F., Cao, X., Lian, C., Nie, D., Liu, M., Zhang, H., Li, G., Wu, Z., Lin, W., Shen, D., 2018b. Volume-based analysis of 6-month-old infant brain MRI for autism biomarker identification and early diagnosis. Med. Image Comput. Comput. Assist. Interv. 11072, 411–419. https://doi.org/10.1007/978-3-030-00931-1_47 (in English).

Table 3 Averaged DR (%) and MHD (mm) of methods on 6-month infant images from iSeg-2017.

	DR (%)			MHD (mm)		
Method	**CSF**	**GM**	**WM**	**CSF**	**GM**	**WM**
SegNet (Badrinarayanan et al., 2015)	89.5 ± 1.41	75.5 ± 0.96	80.6 ± 1.23	8.81 ± 1.11	7.80 ± 1.49	9.11 ± 1.10
U-Net (Ronneberger et al., 2015)	92.7 ± 0.89	89.0 ± 0.56	91.9 ± 0.43	6.68 ± 0.80	6.62 ± 0.74	6.79 ± 0.61
Dense-Net (Bui et al., 2017)	92.3 ± 0.85	88.5 ± 0.57	91.6 ± 0.44	6.59 ± 0.86	6.97 ± 1.22	8.08 ± 2.09
Proposed (Wang et al., 2018b)	95.8 ± 0.58	$\mathbf{92.3 \pm 0.54}$	$\mathbf{93.3 \pm 0.43}$	5.59 ± 0.72	5.84 ± 0.88	$\mathbf{5.05 \pm 1.10}$

The bold indicates that the respective result is significantly better than others (P-*value* <*0.005*).
Table copied from table 1 in Wang, L., Li, G., Shi, F., Cao, X., Lian, C., Nie, D., Liu, M., Zhang, H., Li, G., Wu, Z., Lin, W., Shen, D., 2018b. Volume-based analysis of 6-month-old infant brain MRI for autism biomarker identification and early diagnosis. Med. Image Comput. Comput. Assist. Interv. 11072, 411–419. doi: 10.1007/978-3-030-00931-1_47 (in English).

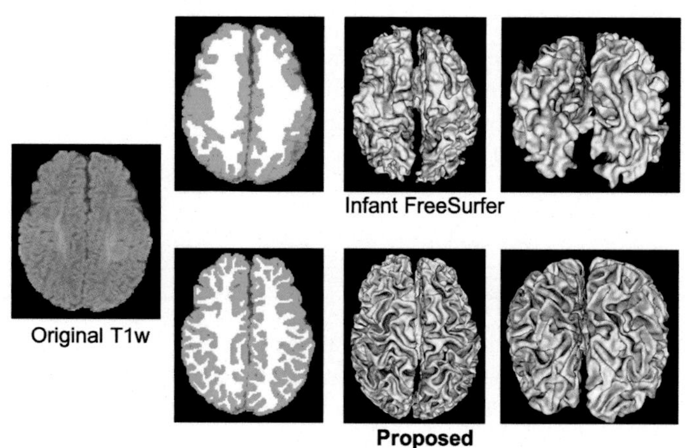

FIG. 12

Comparisons with *Infant FreeSurfer* (Zöllei et al., 2020) on a T1w neonatal brain image. Segmentation is overlaid on the intensity image.

anatomically reasonable result, especially from the overlaid segmentation and rendering WM surface. Fig. 13 further shows the comparisons on two infant subjects with moderate and severe motion artifacts. We can see our method is more robust to the motion, compared with *Infant FreeSurfer*. From Figs. 12 and 13, although we only perform visual comparisons with *Infant FreeSurfer*, it clearly demonstrates the advantage of our method in term of accuracy and robustness. For a quantitative

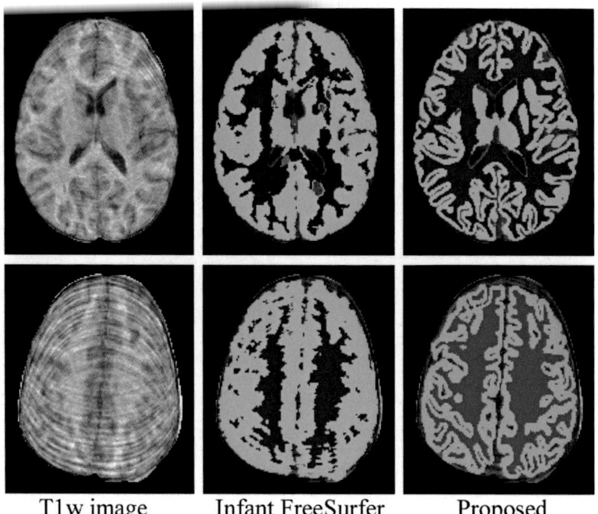

FIG. 13

Comparisons with *Infant FreeSurfer* (Zöllei et al., 2020) on two infant subjects with moderate (upper) and severe (lower) motion. Segmentation is overlaid on the intensity image.

comparison, *Infant FreeSurfer* reported its performance in terms of DR on iSeg-2017 training dataset, with 75%, 77%, and 73% for CSF, GM, and WM. However, they did not report the performance on the testing dataset. We could only make an indirect comparison with *Infant FreeSurfer* by referring to the performance on the testing dataset in Table 3.

5. Discussions and conclusion

To obtain reliable segmentation results of infant brain MR images at isointense phase, an anatomy-guided joint tissue segmentation and topological correction framework was presented by combining anatomical knowledge, which was implemented by two types of method (Wang et al., 2018a, b). During the isointense phase, due to the myelination and maturation process of the brain, the signal intensity of WM is increasing, which leads to a low intensity contrast between WM and GM regions, as shown in Fig. 1. Segmentation results obtained by previous works (Wang et al., 2015; Hao et al., 2016; Badrinarayanan et al., 2015; Ronneberger et al., 2015; Bui et al., 2017) are shown in Figs. 2, 9–11, with the corresponding quantitative analyses illustrated in Tables 2 and 3. We can conclude that theses competitive methods cannot achieve reasonable segmentations on 6-month brain MR images, i.e., with many anatomical and topological errors (e.g., "hole" or "handle" as shown in Fig. 8), and these methods are sensitive to the head motion. With the proposed work guided by the brain anatomy, the anatomical and topological errors in inner surfaces are corrected gradually, and the cortical thickness becomes more reasonable as shown in Fig. 7, which demonstrate the effectiveness of anatomical guidance. Based on the accurate tissue segmentation, cortical surface-based analysis of infant brains can be further performed to advance our understanding of normal and abnormal early brain development (Li et al., 2014, 2013; Wang et al., 2019).

Recently, datasets from multiple imaging sites poses another challenge for the infant brain image segmentation. For example, in 2019, we organized a MICCAI grand challenge on 6-month infant brain MRI segmentation from multiple sites: iSeg-2019, http://iseg2019.web.unc.edu. Usually, the trained model based on a single-site dataset often performs poorly on the dataset from other sites with different imaging protocols/scanners, which is known as multisite issue. A few researchers have addressed the multisite issue, e.g., few-shot learning (Motiian et al., 2017; Sun et al., 2019), domain adaption (Tzeng et al., 2015; Bousmalis et al., 2017; Mahmood et al., 2018), transfer or distributed transfer learning (Ganin et al., 2016; Sun et al., 2016; Kushibar et al., 2019; Long et al., 2016), and adversarial learning (Tzeng et al., 2017; Li et al., 2020). However, these methods still require either a small number of labels (or annotation) for fine-tuning or a large number of images for adaption, from other sites. Considering the fact that prior knowledge is site-independent/scanner-independent, incorporation of prior knowledge into the segmentation might be a promising direction to explore for better dealing with the multisite issue.

Our method is available in iBEAT V2.0 Cloud (http://www.ibeat.cloud), which is a toolbox for processing pediatric brain MR images, using multimodality (including T1w and T2w) or single-modality. The current functionality of iBEAT V2.0 Cloud includes: inhomogeneity correction, skull stripping and cerebellum removal, tissue segmentation, left/right hemisphere separation, topology correction, cortical surface reconstruction, quantitative cortical surface measurements computation, and cortical surface parcellation. Up to date, we have successfully processed 4100+ infant brain images with various protocols and scanners, from 60+ institutions including Harvard Medical School, Stanford University, Yale University, Princeton University, Emory University, Arkansas Children's Hospital, University of Tokyo, Loma Linda University, University of Houston, The University of Texas, and Vanderbilt University.

References

Anbeek, P., Isgum, I., van Kooij, B.J., Mol, C.P., Kersbergen, K.J., Groenendaal, F., Viergever, M.A., de Vries, L. S., Benders, M.J., 2013. Automatic segmentation of eight tissue classes in neonatal brain MRI. PLoS One 8 (12). https://doi.org/10.1371/journal.pone.0081895, e81895.

Badrinarayanan, V., Kendall, A., Cipolla, R., 2015. SegNet: A Deep Convolutional Encoder-Decoder Architecture for Image Segmentation. arXiv. 1511.00561.

Beare, R.J., Chen, J., Kelly, C.E., Alexopoulos, D., Smyser, C.D., Rogers, C.E., Loh, W.Y., Matthews, L.G., Cheong, J.L., Spittle, A.J., Anderson, P.J., 2016. Neonatal brain tissue classification with morphological adaptation and unified segmentation. Front. Neuroinform., 12. https://doi.org/10.3389/fninf.2016.00012.

Bosch, A., Zisserman, A., Munoz, X., 2007. Image classification using random forests and ferns. In: 2007 IEEE 11th International Conference on Computer Vision, 14–21 October 2007, pp. 1–8, https://doi.org/10.1109/ICCV.2007.4409066.

Bousmalis, K., Silberman, N., Dohan, D., Erhan, D., Krishnan, D., 2017. Unsupervised pixel-level domain adaptation with generative adversarial networks. In: Proceedings of the IEEE Conference on Computer Vision and Pattern Recognition, pp. 3722–3731.

Bui, T.D., Shin, J., Moon, T., 2017. 3D Densely Convolutional Networks for Volumetric Segmentation. arXiv. 1709.03199.

Bui, T.D., Wang, L., Lin, W., Li, G., Shen, D., 2020. 6-month infant brain Mri segmentation guided by 24-month data using cycle-consistent adversarial networks. In: 2020 IEEE 17th International Symposium on Biomedical Imaging (ISBI), 3–7 April 2020, pp. 359–362, https://doi.org/10.1109/ISBI45749.2020.9098515.

Chi, J., Dooling, E., Gilles, F., 1977. Gyral development of the human brain. Ann. Neurol. 1, 86–93.

de Macedo Rodrigues, K., Ben-Avi, E., Sliva, D.D., Choe, M.S., Drottar, M., Wang, R., Fischl, B., Grant, P.E., Zöllei, L., 2015. A FreeSurfer-compliant consistent manual segmentation of infant brains spanning the 0-2 year age range. Front. Hum. Neurosci. 9, 21. https://doi.org/10.3389/fnhum.2015.00021 (in English).

Fischl, B., 2012. FreeSurfer. NeuroImage 62 (2), 774–781. https://doi.org/10.1016/j.neuroimage.2012.01.021 (in English).

Ganin, Y., Ustinova, E., Ajakan, H., Germain, P., Larochelle, H., Laviolette, F., Marchand, M., Lempitsky, V., 2016. Domain-adversarial training of neural networks. J. Mach. Learn. Res. 17 (1), 2096.

Gui, L., Lisowski, R., Faundez, T., Hüppi, P.S., Lazeyras, F.O., Kocher, M., 2012. Morphology-driven automatic segmentation of MR images of the neonatal brain. Med. Image Anal. 16 (8), 1565–1579.

Hao, S., Li, G., Wang, L., Meng, Y., Shen, D., 2016. Learning-based topological correction for infant cortical surfaces. In: Presented at the MICCAI., https://doi.org/10.1007/978-3-319-46720-7_26. (Online). Available from:.

Hazlett, H.C., Gu, H., McKinstry, R.C., Shaw, D.W.W., Botteron, K.N., Dager, S., Styner, M., Vachet, C., Gerig, G., Paterson, S., Schultz, R.T., Estes, A.M., Evans, A.C., Piven, J., for the IBIS Network, 2012. Brain volume findings in six month old infants at high familial risk for autism. Am. J. Psychiatry 169 (6), 601–608. https://doi.org/10.1176/appi.ajp.2012.11091425.

Knickmeyer, R.C., Gouttard, S., Kang, C., Evans, D., Wilber, K., Smith, J.K., Hamer, R.M., Lin, W., Gerig, G., Gilmore, J.H., 2008. A structural MRI study of human brain development from birth to 2 years. J. Neurosci. 28 (47), 12176–12182. https://doi.org/10.1523/JNEUROSCI.3479-08.2008 (in English).

Kushibar, K., Valverde, S., González-Villà, S., Bernal, J., Cabezas, M., Oliver, A., Lladó, X., 2019. Supervised domain adaptation for automatic sub-cortical brain structure segmentation with minimal user interaction. Sci. Rep. 9 (1), 1–15.

Li, G., Nie, J., Wang, L., Shi, F., Lin, W., Gilmore, J.H., Shen, D., 2013. Mapping region-specific longitudinal cortical surface expansion from birth to 2 years of age. Cereb. Cortex 23 (11), 2724–2733. https://doi.org/10.1093/cercor/bhs265 (in English).

Li, G., Wang, L., Shi, F., Lyall, A.E., Lin, W., Gilmore, J.H., Shen, D., 2014. Mapping longitudinal development of local cortical gyrification in infants from birth to 2 years of age. J. Neurosci. 34 (12), 4228–4238. https://doi.org/10.1523/JNEUROSCI.3976-13.2014 (in English).

Li, G., Wang, L., Yap, P.-T., Wang, F., Wu, Z., Meng, Y., Dong, P., Kim, J., Shi, F., Rekik, I., Lin, W., Shen, D., 2019. Computational neuroanatomy of baby brains: a review. NeuroImage 185, 906–925. https://doi.org/10.1016/j.neuroimage.2018.03.042 (in English).

Li, H., Loehr, T., Wiestler, B., Zhang, J., Menze, B., 2020. E-UDA: Efficient Unsupervised Domain Adaptation for Cross-Site Medical Image Segmentation. arXiv preprint. arXiv:2001.09313.

Long, M., Zhu, H., Wang, J., Jordan, M.I., 2016. Unsupervised domain adaptation with residual transfer networks. Adv. Neural Inf. Proces. Syst., 136–144.

Loog, M., Ginneken, B., 2006. Segmentation of the posterior ribs in chest radiographs using iterated contextual pixel classification. IEEE Trans. Med. Imaging 25 (5), 602–611. https://doi.org/10.1109/tmi.2006.872747.

Mahmood, F., Chen, R., Durr, N.J., 2018. Unsupervised reverse domain adaptation for synthetic medical images via adversarial training. IEEE Trans. Med. Imaging 37 (12), 2572–2581.

Moeskops, P., Viergever, M.A., Mendrik, A.M., de Vries, L.S., Benders, M.J., Isgum, I., 2016. Automatic segmentation of MR brain images with a convolutional neural network. IEEE Trans. Med. Imaging 35 (5), 1252–1261. https://doi.org/10.1109/TMI.2016.2548501.

Motiian, S., Jones, Q., Iranmanesh, S., Doretto, G., 2017. Few-shot adversarial domain adaptation. Adv. Neural Inf. Process. Syst., 6670–6680.

Nie, D., Wang, L., Gao, Y., Sken, D., 2016. Fully convolutional networks for multi-modality isointense infant brain image segmentation. In: Biomedical Imaging (ISBI), 2016 IEEE 13th International Symposium on. IEEE, pp. 1342–1345.

Nie, D., Wang, L., Trullo, R., Adeli, E., Lin, W., Shen, D., 2017. Multi-modal isointense infant brain image segmentation with deep learning based methods. In: Presented at the ISMRM.

Prastawa, M., Gilmore, J.H., Lin, W., Gerig, G., 2005. Automatic segmentation of MR images of the developing newborn brain. Med. Image Anal. 9 (5), 457–466.

Ronneberger, O., Fischer, P., Brox, T., 2015. U-net: convolutional networks for biomedical image segmentation. In: Presented at the MICCAI.

Shi, F., Fan, Y., Tang, S., Gilmore, J.H., Lin, W., Shen, D., 2010a. Neonatal brain image segmentation in longitudinal MRI studies. NeuroImage 49 (1), 391–400.

Shi, F., Yap, P.-T., Fan, Y., Gilmore, J.H., Lin, W., Shen, D., 2010b. Construction of multi-region-multi-reference atlases for neonatal brain MRI segmentation. NeuroImage 51 (2), 684–693.

Shi, F., Shen, D., Yap, P., Fan, Y., Cheng, J., An, H., Wald, L.L., Gerig, G., Gilmore, J.H., Lin, W., 2011a. CENTS: cortical enhanced neonatal tissue segmentation. Hum. Brain Mapp. 32 (3), 382–396.

Shi, F., Yap, P.T., Wu, G., Jia, H., Gilmore, J.H., Lin, W., Shen, D., 2011b. Infant brain atlases from neonates to 1- and 2-year-olds. PLoS One 6 (4). https://doi.org/10.1371/journal.pone.0018746, e18746.

Shi, F., Wang, L., Dai, Y.K., Gilmore, J.H., Lin, W.L., Shen, D.G., 2012. LABEL: pediatric brain extraction using learning-based meta-algorithm. NeuroImage 62 (3), 1975–1986. https://doi.org/10.1016/j.neuroimage.2012.05.042 (in English).

Sun, B., Feng, J., Saenko, K., 2016. Return of frustratingly easy domain adaptation. In: Thirtieth AAAI Conference on Artificial Intelligence.

Sun, Q., Liu, Y., Chua, T.-S., Schiele, B., 2019. Meta-transfer learning for few-shot learning. In: Proceedings of the IEEE Conference on Computer Vision and Pattern Recognition, pp. 403–412.

Tu, Z., Bai, X., 2010. Auto-context and its application to high-level vision tasks and 3D brain image segmentation. IEEE Trans. Pattern Anal. Mach. Intell. 32 (10), 1744–1757. https://doi.org/10.1109/tpami.2009.186.

Tustison, N.J., Avants, B.B., Cook, P.A., Zheng, Y., Egan, A., Yushkevich, P.A., Gee, J.C., 2010. N4ITK: improved N3 bias correction. IEEE Trans. Med. Imaging 29 (6), 1310–1320. https://doi.org/10.1109/TMI.2010.2046908.

Tzeng, E., Hoffman, J., Darrell, T., Saenko, K., 2015. Simultaneous deep transfer across domains and tasks. In: Proceedings of the IEEE International Conference on Computer Vision, pp. 4068–4076.

Tzeng, E., Hoffman, J., Saenko, K., Darrell, T., 2017. Adversarial discriminative domain adaptation. In: Proceedings of the IEEE Conference on Computer Vision and Pattern Recognition, pp. 7167–7176.

Viola, P., Jones, M., 2004. Robust real-time face detection. Int. J. Comput. Vis. 57 (2), 137–154. 2004/05/01 https://doi.org/10.1023/B:VISI.0000013087.49260.fb. (in English).

Wang, L., Shi, F., Lin, W., Gilmore, J.H., Shen, D., 2011. Automatic segmentation of neonatal images using convex optimization and coupled level sets. NeuroImage 58 (3), 805–817.

Wang, L., Shi, F., Gao, Y., Li, G., Gilmore, J.H., Lin, W., Shen, D., 2014a. Integration of sparse multi-modality representation and anatomical constraint for isointense infant brain MR image segmentation. NeuroImage 89, 152–164. https://doi.org/10.1016/j.neuroimage.2013.11.040.

Wang, L., Shi, F., Li, G., Gao, Y., Lin, W., Gilmore, J.H., Shen, D., 2014b. Segmentation of neonatal brain MR images using patch-driven level sets. NeuroImage 84, 141–158.

Wang, L., Gao, Y., Shi, F., Li, G., Gilmore, J.H., Lin, W., Shen, D., 2015. LINKS: learning-based multi-source IntegratioN frameworK for segmentation of infant brain images. NeuroImage 108, 160–172. https://doi.org/10.1016/j.neuroimage.2014.12.042 (in English).

Wang, L., Li, G., Adeli, E., Liu, M., Wu, Z., Meng, Y., Lin, W., Shen, D., 2018a. Anatomy-guided joint tissue segmentation and topological correction for 6-month infant brain MRI with risk of autism. Hum. Brain Mapp. 39 (6), 2609–2623.

Wang, L., Li, G., Shi, F., Cao, X., Lian, C., Nie, D., Liu, M., Zhang, H., Li, G., Wu, Z., Lin, W., Shen, D., 2018b. Volume-based analysis of 6-month-old infant brain MRI for autism biomarker identification and early diagnosis. Med. Image Comput. Comput. Assist. Interv. 11072, 411–419. https://doi.org/10.1007/978-3-030-00931-1_47 (in English).

Wang, F., Lian, C., Wu, Z., Zhang, H., Li, T., Meng, Y., Wang, L., Lin, W., Shen, D., Li, G., 2019. Developmental topography of cortical thickness during infancy. Proc. Natl. Acad. Sci. 116 (32), 15855. https://doi.org/10.1073/pnas.1821523116.

Weisenfeld, N.I., Warfield, S.K., 2009. Automatic segmentation of newborn brain MRI. NeuroImage 47 (2), 564–572.

Xue, Z., Shen, D.G., Davatzikos, C., 2006. CLASSIC: consistent longitudinal alignment and segmentation for serial image computing. NeuroImage 30 (2), 388–399. https://doi.org/10.1016/j.neuroimage.2005.09.054 (in English).

Xue, H., Srinivasan, L., Jiang, S., Rutherford, M., Edwards, A.D., Rueckert, D., Hajnal, J.V., 2007. Automatic segmentation and reconstruction of the cortex from neonatal MRI. NeuroImage 38 (3), 461–477.

Yotter, R.A., Dahnke, R., Thompson, P.M., Gaser, C., 2011. Topological correction of brain surface meshes using spherical harmonics. Hum. Brain Mapp. 32 (7), 1109–1124. https://doi.org/10.1002/hbm.21095 (in English).

Zeng, X.L., Staib, L.H., Schultz, R.T., Duncan, J.S., 1998. Segmentation and measurement of the cortex from 3D MR images. In: Presented at the MICCAI 2013. Pt I.

Zhengyang Wang, N.Z., Shen, D., Ji, S., 2020. Non-local U-net for biomedical image segmentation. In: Proceedings of the AAAI Conference on Artificial Intelligence.

Zöllei, L., Iglesias, J.E., Ou, Y., Grant, P.E., Fischl, B., 2020. Infant FreeSurfer: an automated segmentation and surface extraction pipeline for T1-weighted neuroimaging data of infants 0–2 years. NeuroImage 218, 116946. 2020/09/01/ https://doi.org/10.1016/j.neuroimage.2020.116946.

CHAPTER

Surface-based analysis of the developing cerebral cortex 13

Zhengwang Wu*, Fenqiang Zhao*, Fan Wang*, Weili Lin, Li Wang, Dinggang Shen, and Gang Li
Department of Radiology and Biomedical Research Imaging Center, University of North Carolina at Chapel Hill, Chapel Hill, NC, United States

1. Introduction

The period of rapid brain development (Gilmore et al., 2018; Li et al., 2019) during early postnatal life is characterized by drastic cortical area expansion (Li et al., 2013), thickening/thinning (Li et al., 2015a), myelination, gyrification (Li et al., 2014a), etc., reflecting programmed underlying neurodevelopmental events (e.g., neurogenesis, cell death, myelination, pruning, synaptic plasticity, and glial development) (Power et al., 2010; Grayson and Fair, 2017). The recent advance in cortical surface-based neuroimaging analysis (Li et al., 2019; Glasser et al., 2013; Howell et al., 2019; Bozek et al., 2018; Batalle et al., 2017) unfolds a novel opportunity to more comprehensively characterize early brain development, which shows some important advantages over conventional volume-based analysis in multiple aspects. First, it helps more precisely measure multiple biologically distinct cortical properties, such as cortical thickness, surface area, myelin content, gyrification, diffusivity, and connectivity. Second, it respects the cortical geometry and provides an intuitive visualization of the highly convoluted cortical folds. Third, the surface-based cortical representation leads to more accurate intra-subject cortical registration, by taking the advantage of the spherical topology of the cerebral cortex, therefore facilitating the subsequent analysis. With increasing availability of multimodal MRI data of neonates, infants and toddlers (Howell et al., 2019; Hughes et al., 2017), surface-based analysis has become recognized as a critical way to accurately chart and understand the brain developmental patterns during early postnatal stages.

Typical steps involved in cortical surface-based analysis are summarized in Fig. 1, including intensity inhomogeneity correction, skull stripping, tissue segmentation, hemisphere separation, topology correction, surface reconstruction, cortical properties computation, spherical mapping, surface registration, and surface parcellation. However, due to dramatic differences in image contrast (Wang et al., 2019a), brain size, shape, and folding degree (Li et al., 2014a) between infants and adults, conventional tools for cortical surface-based analysis, which are mainly developed for adult brains, are not suitable for infant brains, especially for the rapidly developing infant brains, which typically exhibit extremely

*Equal contribution.

Handbook of Pediatric Brain Imaging. https://doi.org/10.1016/B978-0-12-816633-8.00024-7

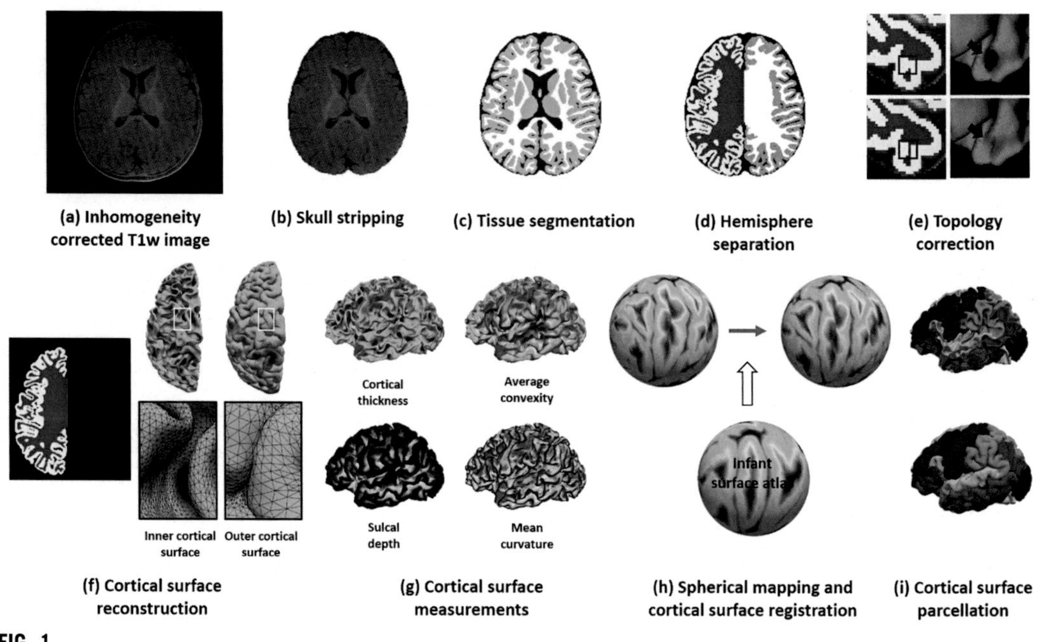

FIG. 1

Typical steps involved in cortical surface-based analysis of infant brains.

low tissue contrast. Therefore, it is crucial to develop tailored computational methods for cortical surface-based analysis of infant brains (Makropoulos et al., 2018; Li et al., 2015b; Hagler et al., 2019). As tissue segmentation methods for infant brains have been introduced in Chapter 12, in this chapter, we start from the tissue segmentation map and summarize the challenges and current solutions of the essential steps for cortical surface reconstruction, representation and analysis of infant brains. At the end of this chapter, we will introduce some publicly available tools and atlases for facilitating the cortical surface-based analysis of early brain development.

2. Cortical surface reconstruction, representation, and measurement

Anatomically, the human cerebral cortex is a thin and highly folded sheet composed of gray matter (GM) lying between white matter (WM) and cerebrospinal fluid (CSF). To study the cerebral cortex, researchers typically reconstruct two surfaces enclosing the cerebral cortex, i.e., the outer/pial surface (the interface between CSF and GM) and the inner/white surface (the interface between GM and WM) for each hemisphere, as shown in Fig. 3. In some applications, the middle/central cortical surface, which is defined as the geometric center of the outer and inner cortical surfaces, is also reconstructed for a more balanced representation of sulcal and gyral regions.

2.1 Cortical topology correction

After segmenting the infant brain into GM, WM, and CSF (Wang et al., 2019a), researchers typically first separate the brain into the left and right hemispheres and then fill in the subcortical regions with WM. This can be done by the registration of a template onto the infant brain. The template containing the labels of hemispheres and the subcortical regions can be propagated to the individual brain based on the registration. Although embedded in 3D space, the reconstructed cortical surfaces should be topologically equivalent to a sphere, i.e., a 2D closed surface in essence. However, due to low tissue contrast and dynamic imaging appearance in the infant brain images, some voxels would be incorrectly labeled in the segmentation map. This can cause two types of topological errors/defects on the inner surface, i.e., (1) holes in gyri; (2) bridges/handles in sulci, as shown in Fig. 2. Such errors will result in the topology of the reconstructed cortical surface no longer equivalent to a sphere, causing problems when inflating the cortical surfaces onto the sphere or flattening them into a plane and also leading to inaccurate geodesic, morphological and connectivity measurement on the cortical surfaces. Therefore, topological errors need to be corrected before reconstructing the cortical surfaces. Of note, generally we only need to correct the topology for the inner cortical surface, and then deform the inner surface to reconstruct the outer cortical surfaces. The outer surface typically cannot be directly reconstructed due to strong partial volume effects in deep tight opposing sulcal banks in infant images. This strategy will guarantee consistent topologies and vertex-to-vertex correspondences for inner, middle, and outer cortical surfaces.

Conventionally, to correct topological errors, firstly, we need to determine whether there are topological errors and locate where the errors are. The Euler number (Sossa-Azuela, 1996; Fischl et al., 2001) of the reconstructed cortical surface represented by a triangular mesh can be used to determine whether topological errors exist. However, the Euler number provides no spatial information of

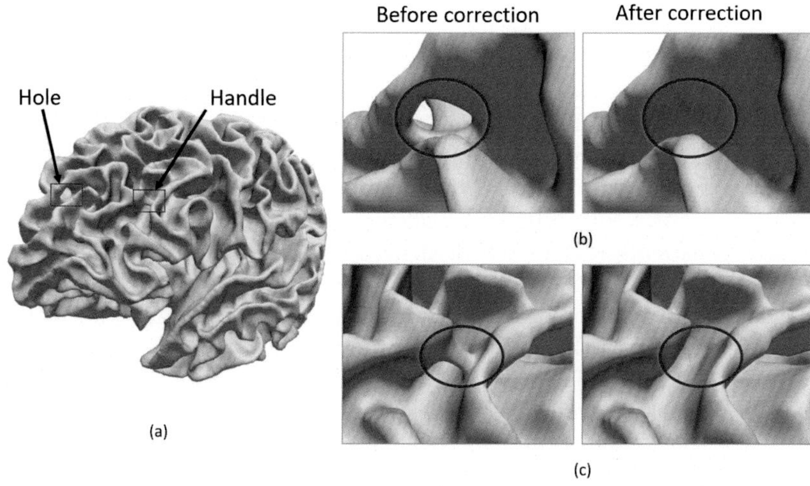

FIG. 2

(A) Typical topological errors on the inner surface. (B) Zoomed hole and corrected surface. (C) Zoomed handle and corrected surface.

topological errors. To locate topological errors, we can either search the circles in the WM volume graph (Shattuck and Leahy, 2001; Han et al., 2002) or locate the intersections when inflating the cortical surface onto a sphere (Fischl et al., 2001; Ségonne et al., 2007). Once the topological errors are located, two kinds of methods are frequently adopted to correct them. The first one is to directly correct the WM segmentation map. For example, a graph-based correction method (Shattuck and Leahy, 2001) can be used to remove topology defects by minimizing the modifications in the WM segmentation map. The second one is to correct topological errors on the reconstructed surface mesh. For example, in (Fischl et al., 2001), all edges are discarded in each topologically-defected region and then the local mesh is retessellated by gradually adding the removed edge back to the surface until the intersection is detected. In (Ségonne et al., 2007), a set of nonseparating loops are generated and selected to open and seal the reconstructed surface for correcting the defected regions.

As holes and handles on the cortical surface are typically difficult to distinguish solely relying on geometric and intensity information in these rule-based methods, we recently introduced a learning-based method to adaptively correct the detected topological errors. Specifically, for each hemisphere, we first deformed an initial surface with the sphere topology (i.e., an ellipsoid) to closely wrap the segmented WM volume, while preserving the initial topology, using a shrinking-wrapping topology-preserving level set (Han et al., 2003). Then, we identified the defect regions at the locations where the converged surface mismatches the original WM surface. To correct the identified defect regions, we learned the correction model from some training examples that have been manually edited by neuroscientists, and then adapted the learned model to new subjects. In (Sun et al., 2019), a deep convolutional neural network was leveraged to learn the strategy to correct labels in local image patches in defect regions. To correct large and complex handles or holes, we further enrolled the steps of defect localization and correction into an iterative framework.

2.2 Cortical surface reconstruction

After correction of topological errors, we can reconstruct the cortical surfaces and represent them using triangular meshes. This can be achieved by solving two sub-problems: i.e., reconstruction of the inner cortical surface and reconstruction of the middle and outer cortical surfaces. Reconstruction of the inner cortical surface is relatively easy. After topological correction, we can use a tessellation method, such as the marching cubes (Bazin and Pham, 2007), to represent the boundary of the corrected WM volume as a triangular surface mesh and further smooth and deform the surface mesh to obtain the inner cortical surface. Once the inner cortical surface is reconstructed, we can deform it toward the GM/CSF boundary to obtain the outer cortical surface. However, this deformation process needs to be defined with caution because of the following challenges. First, due to undergoing the myelination process, the infant brain has low tissue contrast, which means the boundaries between neighboring tissues are quite ambiguous. Second, due to the severe partial volume effects, especially at deep sulcal regions, the distance between opposing sulcal banks is often smaller than the MRI resolution and the cerebrospinal fluid can hardly be seen. Therefore, the outer surface reconstruction in the deep sulci can be very challenging. Third, the infant cerebral cortex expands rapidly even in a relatively small-time interval. Therefore, for the same infant, the reconstructed cortical surfaces at different time points are potentially inconsistent, resulting in temporally inconsistent and inaccurate measurement for the longitudinal brain development.

To address the low tissue contrast issue, instead of relying on the unreliable and noisy intensity gradient vector field to deform the inner cortical surface, we can derive the external force for driving surface deformation based on the Laplacian equation on the topology-corrected tissue map. This can generate more reliable driving force for surface deformation, as the topology-corrected tissue map is obtained not only based on the intensity gradient information, but also based on the informative contextual features and anatomical and topological priors. Besides the external force, we also need an internal force to keep the surface tight and smooth while deforming the surface. More details on the deformation strategy can be referenced in (Li et al., 2012).

To obtain the accurate outer cortical surface in the deep sulci, we can first recover the CSF in the deep sulci using the anatomically-consistent enhancement method (Han et al., 2004) to generate a no-more-than-one-voxel thick separation between opposite sulcal banks. Then, before entering the recovered CSF regions, the inner cortical surface is first deformed using both the internal and external forces. After entering the recovered regions, instead of using the external force based on tissue maps, we can use the local normal direction of the surface to help define the external force to make the opposing sulcal banks closely approaching each other. To ensure the spherical topology and avoid self-intersections on the outer surface, we need to check the possible triangle-triangle intersection (Möller, 1997) in each step of surface deformation and reduce the step size accordingly. Thus, the inner and outer surfaces have the same spherical topology and vertex-to-vertex correspondences. The middle surface can then be reconstructed as the average of inner and outer surfaces.

To further address the potential temporal inconsistency at different time points, we can deform the longitudinal surfaces of the same subject in a 4D (3D spatial and 1D temporal) manner, with an additional explicit force encouraging the temporal consistency (Li et al., 2014b). Fig. 3 shows the reconstructed inner and outer cortical surfaces (color-coded by cortical thickness) overlaying on the corresponding T1-weighted MR images at different time points. As can be seen, the reconstructed cortical surfaces are well aligned with the tissue boundaries.

2.3 Cortical surface-based measurement

Once cortical surfaces are reconstructed, we can compute multiple biologically distinct and meaningful cortical properties for each vertex based on structural MR images, e.g., cortical thickness, surface area, myelin content, sulcal depth, gyrification index, average convexity, and curvatures to comprehensively characterize the development of the cerebral cortex during infancy. Fig. 4 shows some typical cortical properties of a single subject at different time points. Specifically, cortical thickness is typically computed as the minimum distance between the inner surface and the outer surface (Fischl and Dale, 2000; Jones et al., 2000). The surface area is computed as one-third of the summed area of all triangles associated with a vertex on the middle cortical surface for a more balanced representation of sulci and gyri. Myelin content is computed as the T1w/T2w ratio on the middle cortical surface, reflecting the myeloarchitecture of the cortex (Glasser and Van Essen, 2011). Sulcal depth can be computed as the distance from the middle or outer surface to the nearest point on the cerebral hull surface tightly wrapping the brain, for characterizing both coarse and fine cortical shape information. Gyrification index is the areal ratio of the outer surface and the cerebral hull surface, and the local gyrification index is the areal ratio between a local region on the outer surface and the corresponding region on the cerebral hull surface. Note that the local gyrification index should be computed using an infant-tailored method to ensure a meaningful comparison and quantification during early brain development (Li et al., 2014a). Average convexity is the integrated normal movement of a vertex during inflation of the inner surface and mainly reflects the coarse-scale geometric information of cortical folding (Fischl et al., 1999a).

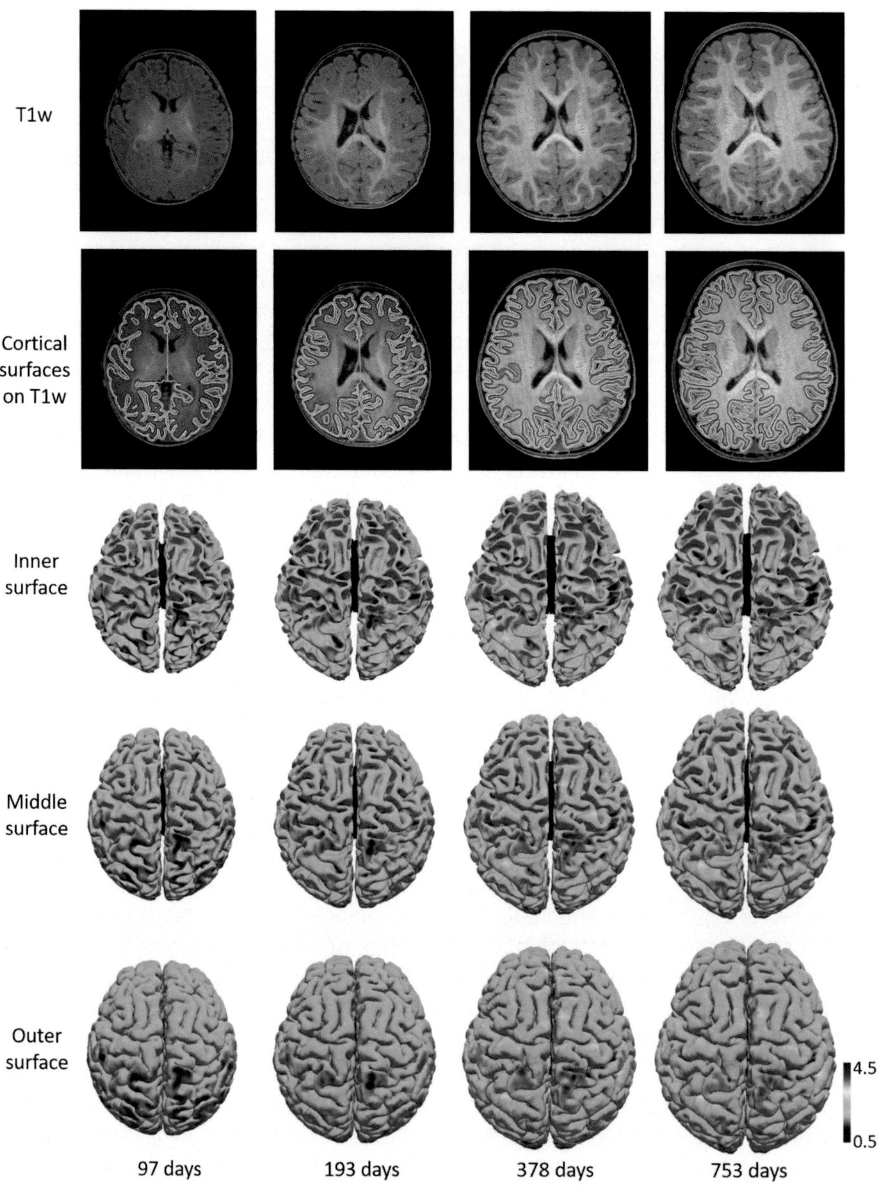

FIG. 3

T1w image, reconstructed inner, middle and outer cortical surfaces (color-coded by cortical thickness) from a single subject at different ages. *Red contours* indicate inner cortical surfaces, *yellow contours* indicate middle cortical surfaces, and *cyan contours* indicate outer cortical surfaces overlaid on the T1-weighted images.

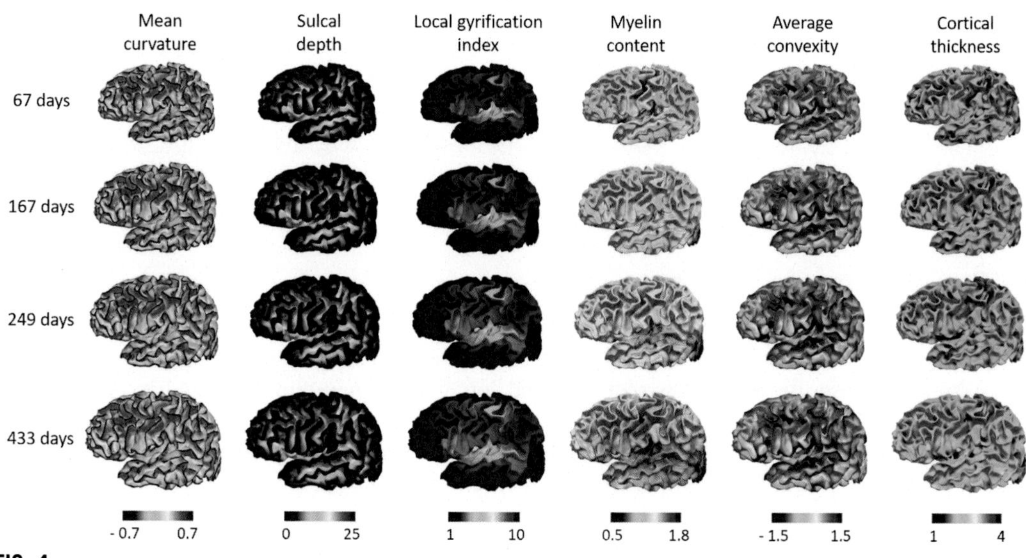

FIG. 4

Typical cortical property maps of a subject at different time points. Of note, sulcal depth and local gyrification index were computed based on the outer cortical surface, while the myelin content was computed based on the middle cortical surface. They were mapped to the inner cortical surface for visualization.

Mean curvature reflects the fine-scale local geometric information of cortical folding and is computed as the average of the minimum and maximum principal curvatures, which can also derive Gaussian curvature, shape index and curvedness for characterization of the local cortical folding (Duan et al., 2019; Nie et al., 2011). Meanwhile, based on sulcal depth and curvatures, we can also extract landmarks or curves for high-level representation of the cortical folding, such as sulcal pits (the points with the maximal sulcal depth in local neighborhoods), sulcal fundi (the curves connecting the bottom of sulci), and gyral crests (the curves connecting the ridges of gyri) (Li et al., 2009, 2010; Chen et al., 2017; Im and Grant, 2019; Meng et al., 2014).

Of note, the reconstructed cortical surfaces also provide us a framework for mapping and integration of the brain structural, functional and connectivity from multimodal images for better investigating early brain development. For example, in functional MRI, functional signals can be resampled on the middle cortical surface for studying functional connectivity, gradients and regional homogeneity. For diffusion MRI, diffusivity information can be mapped onto the middle cortical surface for studying cortical microstructure and white matter fibers can be mapped onto the inner surface for studying cortical structural connectivity.

3. Cortical surface registration, parcellation, modeling, and atlas construction

In the previous section, we have illustrated how to reconstruct cortical surfaces for individuals and how to compute cortical properties from these reconstructed surfaces. In this section, we mainly cover how to use them to conduct population-based analysis in four major topics, (1) cortical surface registration, which establishes the intra- and intersubject vertex-wise cortical correspondences; (2) cortical surface atlas construction, which constructs population-representative maps of cortical shape and functional properties for spatial normalization and analysis; (3) cortical surface parcellation, which parcellates the cerebral cortex into distinct biologically meaningful regions based on anatomical, functional and connectivity information; and (4) cortical surface based modeling and prediction, which models the dynamic development of the cerebral cortex and predicts its relationship with cognitive outcomes.

3.1 Cortical surface registration

Cortical surface registration aims to establish anatomically and functionally meaningful vertex-to-vertex correspondences across individuals and time points, and thus is a fundamental step in surface-based analysis for both cross-sectional and longitudinal neuroimaging studies of a cohort. To take advantage of the intrinsic spherical topology of the cortical surface for facilitating surface registration, a typical strategy is to first inflate and map each cortical surface onto a sphere using a homomorphic mapping with the minimal triangle area and angle distortion (Fischl et al., 1999a, b). Then, cortical surface registration can be conveniently performed based on the spherical surface representation (Yeo et al., 2009; Robinson et al., 2014). Herein, the cortical properties computed on the reconstructed cortical surfaces are mapped onto their corresponding spherical surfaces for driving the spherical surface registration. Essentially, surface registration estimates a smooth spherical deformation field to warp vertices and establish cortical correspondences across surfaces while ensuring no triangular mesh self-intersection (Möller, 1997). The correspondences are typically determined based on geometric features (e.g., mean curvature, average convexity and sulcal depth) to align the cortical folds (Yeo et al., 2009; Dale et al., 1999; Fischl et al., 1999b). However, due to the inconsistency between cortical folds and functional areas (Robinson et al., 2014), it is increasingly popular to add area-related features (e.g., myelin content, functional connectivity (Conroy et al., 2013) and fMRI activation (Robinson et al., 2014)) for better alignment of cortical functional areas.

Many spherical surface registration methods originally developed for adults have been successfully applied in infant cortical surfaces. These methods generally formulate registration as an optimization problem in spherical space to align the vertices with similar feature patterns, while enforcing smoothness on the deformation field. For example, the FreeSurfer (Fischl, 2012) registration algorithm calculates a dense displacement field for all the vertices by minimizing the mean squared distance between the source and target cortical geometric feature maps using a gradient descent algorithm. Spherical Demons (Yeo et al., 2009) uses the same similarity measurement as FreeSurfer, but utilizes Demons algorithm (Vercauteren et al., 2009) to greedily seek the local optimal displacement vectors on the tangent space by the Gauss-Newton method. The fast convergence rate of the Gauss-Newton method and effective extension of diffeomorphisms from Euclidean space to spherical space makes Spherical Demons fast and diffeomorphic. Alternatively, MSM (Robinson et al., 2014) solved a Markov Random Field (MRF) labeling model using discrete optimization for surface registration based on both geometric and functional features. Based on the rotation deformations, the regularization term in MSM penalizes the differences between adjacent vertices' rotation matrices and restricts the deformation size to ensure a topology-preserving registration. Recently, the deep learning-based registration has also been proposed (Zhao et al., 2021a), which leverages its strong mapping ability to directly learn the deformation field that can warp one cortical surface to another one.

As mentioned earlier, the resulting deformation field can warp a moving spherical surface to establish the correspondences with a target spherical surface, e.g., a surface atlas. As different surfaces have different numbers of vertices and triangular connections, to enable a direct comparison of cortical properties across surfaces, it is necessary to resample the registered spherical surface maps with a consistent discretized sphere. Typically, regular subdivisions of an icosahedron are used, as they are most closer to the sphere with relatively balanced samplings (Fischl, 2012). To have sufficient resolutions for cortical surfaces, 6th, or 7th level of subdivisions with 40,962 or 163,842 vertices are mostly used to resample the registered cortical surfaces in structural MRI analysis. In functional MRI analysis, the number of vertices can be further reduced to account for the relatively low spatial resolution of fMRI.

3.2 Surface atlas construction

In neuroimaging studies, cortical surface atlases play a fundamental role in normalizing, comparing, and analyzing brain structure and function across different individuals and studies (Oishi et al., 2019). Many cortical surface atlases have been constructed for adults, e.g., the FreeSurfer atlas (Fischl et al., 1999b), PALS atlas (Van Essen and Dierker, 2007; Van Essen, 2005), ICBM atlas (Lyttelton et al., 2007), HCP atlas (Glasser et al., 2016), etc. These cortical surface atlases, encoding either the geometric cortical properties (e.g., average convexity, sulcal depth, mean curvature, etc.) or other informative cortical properties (e.g., cortical thickness, myelin content, and functional connectivity), have been widely applied in human brain mapping. However, these atlases only encode the adult cortical properties, which cannot accurately characterize the rapidly developing cerebral cortex during infant stages. Therefore, we need to construct a set of age-specific cortical surface atlases, i.e., spatiotemporal atlases, with a high temporal resolution, for early brain development studies. For example, Fig. 5 shows spatiotemporal cortical surface atlases constructed at each week from 39 to 44 postmenstrual weeks from 764 neonatal brains, and Fig. 6 shows 4D infant cortical surface atlases constructed at 11 time points from 1 to 72 months of age. Notably, these cortical surface atlases have vertex-to-vertex cortical correspondence across all time points, thus allowing both cross-sectional and longitudinal analyses.

Generally, two steps are involved in construction of cortical surface atlases: (1) nonlinear registration of cortical surfaces from a group of subjects into the same common space for establishing the cortical correspondence across subjects; and (2) computation of the group-representative patterns of the warped cortical property maps. There are two key components that need to be specified for cortical surface registration during atlas construction, i.e., the cortical features for driving registration and the registration strategy. The cortical features for driving registration determine the criterion based on which the cortical surfaces are aligned together, and are related to the applications of surface atlases. In structural MRI studies, surface atlases are typically used for spatial normalization based on cortical folding patterns. Therefore, cortical geometric features that well characterize the cortical folding patterns, e.g., average convexity, mean curvature and sulcal depth, are frequently used in surface registration. In functional MRI studies, besides using the cortical geometric features, cortical area related properties, such as the myelin content, functional connectivity and functional gradient, would also be adopted for better driving the surface registration for functional alignment (Glasser et al., 2016). The registration strategy determines how the registration process will be conducted to co-register a group of surfaces into a common space. One popular strategy is to perform an unbiased group-wise registration of all cortical surfaces from a population. This strategy can mitigate the potential bias caused by the selection of any subject surface as the initial template and works well for the atlas construction in cross-

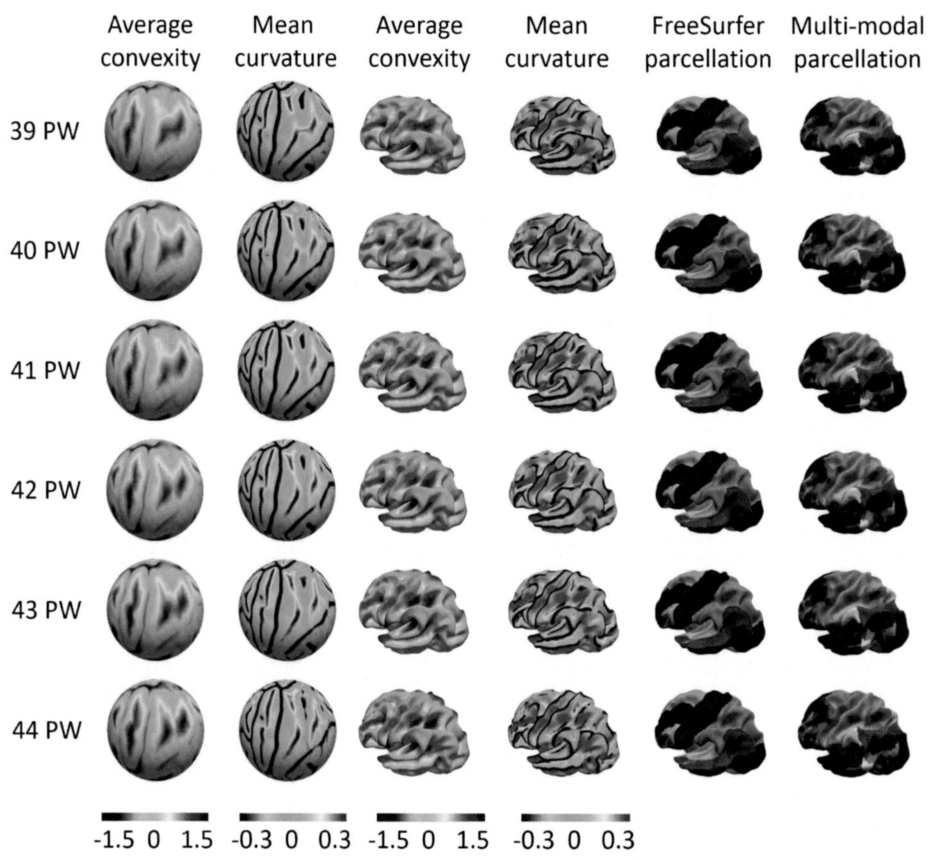

FIG. 5

UNC spatiotemporal neonatal cortical surface atlases with parcellation maps at 6 time points, i.e., 39, 40, 41, 42, 43, and 44 postmenstrual weeks (PW), publicly available at https://www.nitrc.org/projects/infantsurfatlas.

sectional studies. However, in the construction of spatiotemporal atlases involving longitudinal surfaces, this strategy ignores the within-subject longitudinal constraints and thus can lead to atlases without temporal correspondences and consistency, eventually resulting in inaccurate analysis. This is because group-wise surface registration involves highly complex nonlinear optimization and intersubject corresponding vertices established by group-wise registration at one time point might not be corresponding vertices at the other time points any more. To overcome this issue, we can adopt a two-stage group-wise cortical surface registration strategy (Wu et al., 2019a). Specifically, we can first conduct the within-subject group-wise registration to establish the longitudinal cortical correspondences to derive the within-subject mean surface maps at different time points. As all major cortical folds are present at term birth and are well preserved during postnatal development, each within-subject mean surface map well characterizes the subject-specific, spatially detailed information of cortical features. Then, we can conduct the intersubject group-wise registration to align all within-subject mean surface maps across different subjects. By concatenating the above two deformation fields for each surface, we

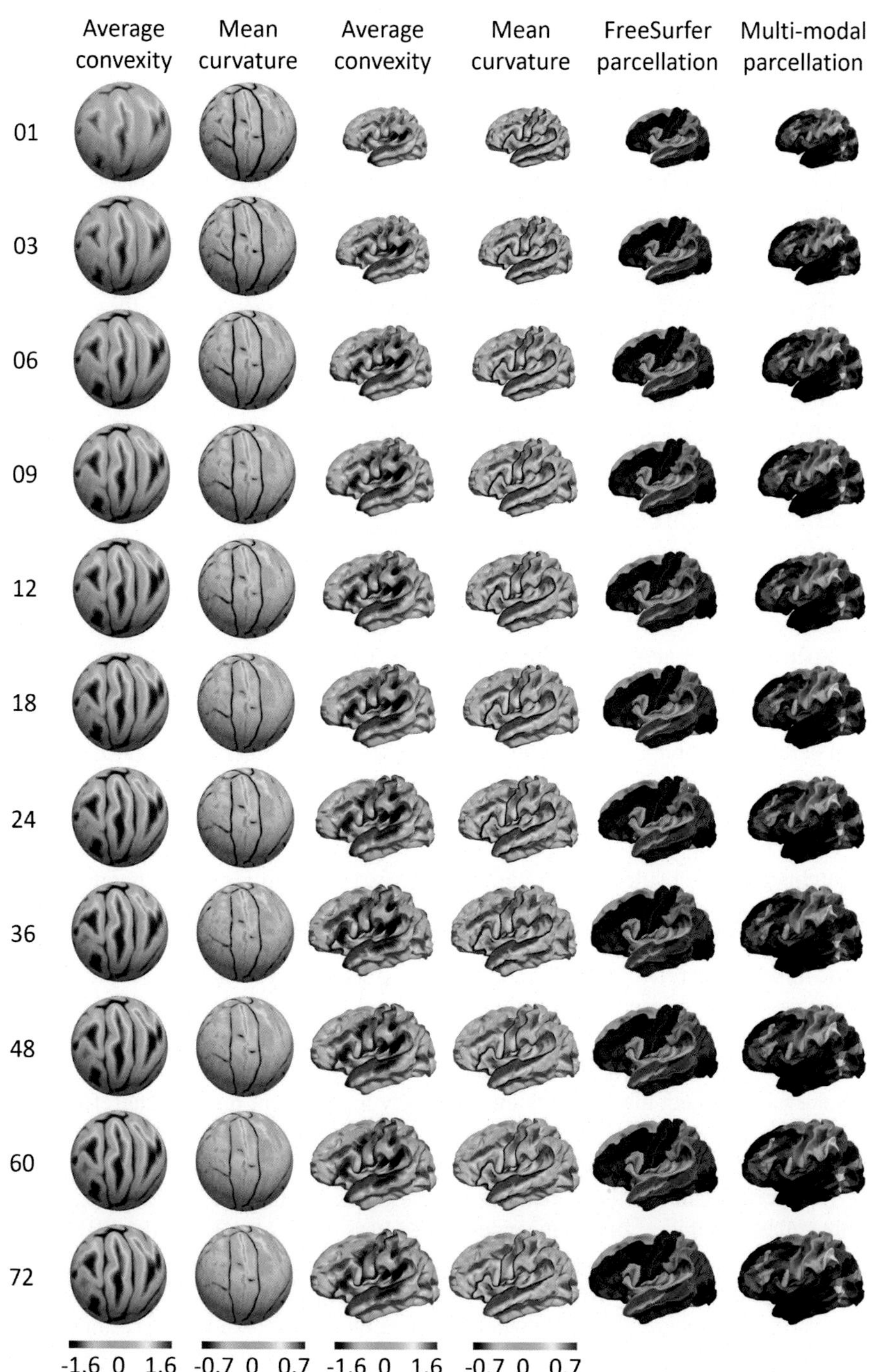

FIG. 6

UNC 4D infant cortical surface atlases with parcellation maps at 11 time points, i.e., 1, 3, 6, 9, 12, 18, 24, 36, 48, 60 and 72 months of age, publically-available at https://www.nitrc.org/projects/infantsurfatlas.

can warp cortical surfaces from different subjects and different time points into a common space in an unbiased and longitudinally consistent manner.

The next step is to compute the group-representative pattern of the cortical properties at each age group. The most straightforward strategy is to compute the average cortical property maps (Li et al., 2015b) based on the vertex-wise correspondence across subjects in the same age group. However, this may lead to over-smoothed cortical property patterns due to potential registration errors and large inter-subject variability. To overcome this issue, more advanced strategies can be adopted. For example, the sparse representation method for surface atlas construction computes the patch-wise average property pattern over the sparsely-selected patches from not only the correspondence patch but also neighboring patches (Wu et al., 2019a, 2018a, 2017). The recent Wasserstein average method for surface atlas construction (Chen et al., 2019) computes the meaningful Wasserstein barycenter of the cortical surface properties across subjects. The Wasserstein barycenter takes into account the alignment of spatial distribution of cortical property maps, and thus is more robust to potential registration errors during atlas building, thereby producing a geometrically more faithful population representation.

3.3 Cortical surface parcellation

Cortical surface parcellation is to divide the cerebral cortex into many distinct and neurobiologically meaningful regions, based on structural, functional and connectivity information from neuroimaging data. Defining a meaningful cortical parcellation is a prerequisite for many neuroimaging applications, e.g., region localization and node definition for network analysis, statistical sensitivity boosting, and feature reduction for brain disorder identification and prediction. According to the underlying features for defining the parcellation in infant brains, existing methods can be grouped into two categories: folding-based parcellation and growth-based parcellation. Of note, functional connectivity-based cortical parcellation is also emerging in infant brains, although this is popular in adult brains.

Folding-based parcellation: As early as 1905, researchers have parcellated the cerebral cortex into different regions according to the cytoarchitecture. Meanwhile, there is a high correlation between the cortical cytoarchitecture and sulcal-gyral folding patterns in certain regions. Therefore, sulcal-gyral patterns have been frequently used for cortical parcellation in both infant and adult neuroimaging studies. To this end, a set of cortical surfaces are first manually annotated by neuroscientists, based on cortical geometric information reflecting folding patterns, e.g., curvatures and sulcal depth. Based on these labeled surface maps and surface registration results, multiatlas label fusion and machine learning based methods are typically adopted for parcellation on the cortical surface (Yeo et al., 2009; Desikan et al., 2006). Note that, in longitudinal studies, independent parcellation of each cortical surface from the same subject may lead to longitudinally inconsistent results. Therefore, longitudinal constraints could be leveraged to improve the longitudinal consistency and accuracy (Li and Shen, 2011; Li et al., 2014c).

However, the performance of these methods largely relies on accurate cortical surface registration for establishing atlas-to-subject correspondences. To address this issue, Wu et al. (2018b) first applied the powerful deep Convolutional Neural Network (CNN) on cortical surface parcellation to directly learn the nonlinear mapping from cortical shape features to the parcellation labels without surface registration. They projected spherical surface patches into tangent spaces to form 2D image patches, and then the conventional CNN was employed to classify each patch. However, it treats each patch independently, thus leading to lots of redundancy due to patch overlapping. Also, there is a trade-off between prediction accuracy and patch size. To overcome these drawbacks, Zhao et al. (2021b) designed a 1-ring convolution kernel on the spherical surface so that the network can learn high level features from the hierarchical CNN architecture. Based on the 1-ring convolution kernel, they designed corresponding spherical convolution, pooling and upsampling operation and further constructed the Spherical U-Net architecture (Fig. 7). It has been successfully applied to infant cortical surface parcellation and achieved promising results. Recent advances in the graph convolutional network (GCN) have enabled direct parcellation on the original cortical surface before spherical mapping. In (Wu et al., 2019b), the convolution operation was extended to the surface manifold using a kernel strategy, which enabled learning parcellation map directly from the original cortical shapes with different vertex number and connections across subjects. This method thus not only avoided the time-consuming spherical mapping process, but also could deal with the impaired brains that violate spherical topology. Note that, in some sulci-based parcellation methods, cortical surfaces are divided as different regions using a data-driven method without surface registration, but these regions still need to be recognized and named using machine learning techniques (Li et al., 2009).

Growth-based Parcellation: Folding-based parcellations are mainly defined based on adult cortical properties, which are less applicable for infant studies, due to the following reasons. (1) There exist dramatic differences in cortical properties (e.g., cortical folding, cortical thickness, myelin content, functional connectivity) between adults and infants. Therefore, regions with distinct adult cortical properties may not correspond to the regions with distinct infant cortical properties. (2) These parcellations do not take advantage of the rich information in dynamic developmental patterns of cortical properties in infants. Essentially, these dynamic developmental patterns reflect rapid changes of underlying microstructures and their connectivity, and thus are highly useful for deriving distinct regions for infant brain studies.

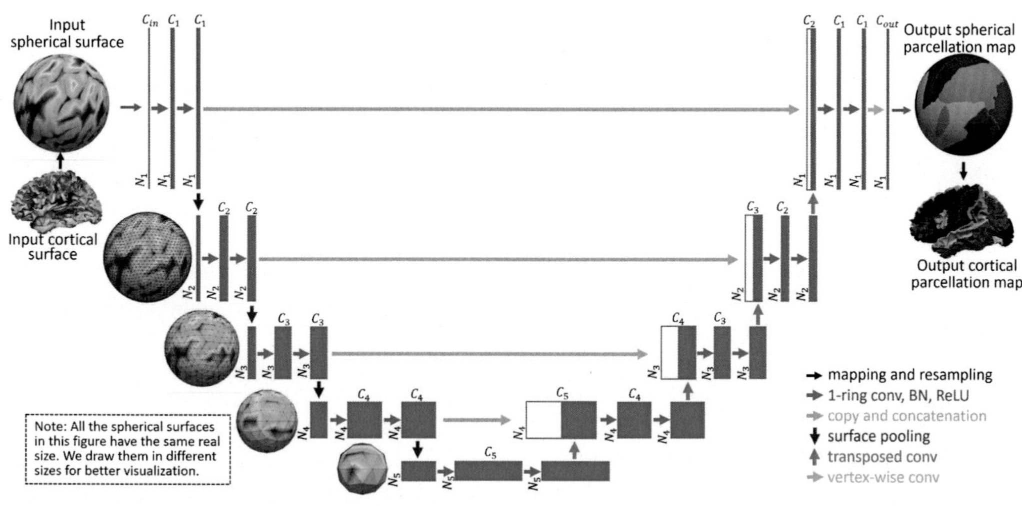

FIG. 7

Spherical U-Net architecture for cortical surface parcellation (Zhao et al., 2021b).

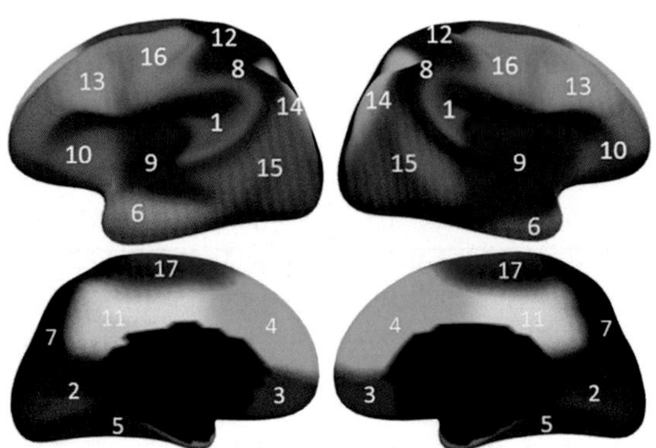

1) Perisylvian;
2) Medial occipital;
3) Medial orbitofrontal;
4) Medial prefrontal;
5) Medial temporal and fusiform;
6) Temporal pole;
7) Precuneus;
8) Inferior parietal;
9) Middle insula and anterior superior temporal;
10) Lateral orbitofrontal and anterior insula;
11) Middle and posterior cingulate;
12) Dorsal somatosensory;
13) Inferior frontal, triangularis and opercularis;
14) Superior parietal;
15) Posterior temporal and lateral occipital;
16) Sensorimotor;
17) Paracentral and superior frontal.

FIG. 8

Infant cortical parcellation based on growth patterns of cortical thickness (Wang et al., 2019b).

Accordingly, multiple studies have recently used data-driven methods to discover the cortical parcellation maps according to the growth pattern of cortical properties. For example, Li et al. (2015c) leveraged an infant cohort in which each subject has multiple longitudinal scans. Given the development trajectory of a cortical property (e.g., cortical thickness or vertex area), they first built the affinity matrix for each subject by correlating the growth trajectory of each vertex, and then fused the affinity matrices of all subjects. The fused affinity matrix was fed into a spectral clustering approach to generate the parcellation map. A similar method was implemented in fetuses (Xia et al., 2019) with modification due to the absence of longitudinal scan for ethnic reasons. As abovementioned approaches compute similarity using Pearson's correlation, which only captures the linear relationship between the growth trajectories of vertices. To address this issue, Wang et al. have proposed to discover the parcellation maps using nonnegative matrix factorization (NMF) (Wang et al., 2019b), without making any assumption on growth patterns. Specifically, the cortical thickness of each subject was organized in one column, forming a large data matrix by all subjects. This matrix was decomposed into a component matrix and a coefficient matrix, where each subject can be represented by a linear combination of all components. Intuitively, each component approximates a cortical parcel as it represents a group of vertices that are co-developing across subjects and time points. For example, Fig. 8 shows a cortical parcellation map based on growth patterns of cortical thickness during infancy. More recently, considering that different cortical properties have distinct growth patterns and reflect distinct biological mechanisms, Wang et al. (2019c) extended this work to multiple cortical properties by proposing a multiview scheme of NMF. These methods lead to population-level growth-based parcellation maps, which can be further propagated onto each individual surface.

3.4 Cortical surface-based prediction and modeling

Modeling and prediction of the dynamic and complicated cortical development during infancy, including cortical shape, size, and other properties, would help us better understand the normal brain developmental patterns and mechanisms, and provide important insights into early neurodevelopmental disorders. However, due to the difficulties in collecting longitudinal infant MRI data from birth, large intersubject variability and complicated growth patterns, predictive models capable of characterizing dynamic, regionally heterogeneous cortical development during infancy are still limited.

Conventional methods, prior to the recent deep learning models, generally simulate the development of brain multishape (cortical surface and white matter fibers) and cortical property map using meticulously designed model and hand-crafted features with elaborate mathematical representation. For example, some pioneering works (Nie et al., 2010, 2012) model the cerebral cortex as a deformable elastoplasticity surface to simulate the dynamic development of the cerebral cortex during the first year. Rekik et al. (2015) used a diffeomorphic surface regression model to predict the dynamic evolution of infant cortical surface shape solely from a single baseline cortical surface based on a spatio-temporal (4D) current-based learning approach. They have further advanced this model by using varifold metric (Rekik et al., 2016), a more robust and elegant shape representation, and extending it to jointly predict the development of cortical surface shape and underlying whiter matter fiber connectivity (Rekik et al., 2017). Meng et al. (2016) employed random forest for longitudinal prediction of infant cortical thickness using specific Haar-like features of cortical thickness and sulcal depth. While effective, these conventional methods are limited in the following ways: (1) they either require hand-crafted features or ad hoc models; (2) some of them need full longitudinal scans, which are not always available, while others propose specific strategies to use incomplete data but only for each time point independently, disregarding the temporal consistency.

To address these issues, recent works proposed to use deep CNNs for modeling cortical development, motivated by the strong learning ability of feature agnostic CNNs. Liu et al. (2019) introduced a method for longitudinal prediction of cortical surfaces using a spatial graph convolutional neural network (GCNN), which extends conventional CNNs from Euclidean space to surface manifolds. A GCNN model is designed to simulate the cortical growth trajectories and jointly predict inner and outer cortical surfaces at multiple time points. Zhao et al. (2021b) demonstrated that their Spherical U-Net architecture originally designed for cortical surface parcellation can also be applied to predict the development of the cortical property maps during infancy. They trained a Spherical U-Net model to predict cortical thickness map at the end of the first postnatal year using the cortical thickness and sulcal depth map at birth. The results showed that the task-agnostic and feature-agnostic Spherical U-Net still achieved better performance than the conventional random forest-based machine learning method, rendering the advantages of deep learning model for cortical properties prediction. These deep learning-based methods could be modified and improved for the prediction of cognitive outcomes (Adeli et al., 2019; Zhang et al., 2018) as well as risk and progression of neurodevelopmental disorders (Zhang et al., 2020; Hazlett et al., 2017).

4. Publicly available tools and atlases

Table 1 summarizes the representative, publicly available cortical surface-based computational tools and pipelines tailored for processing and analyzing brain MR images during early brain development. These pipelines contain many essential processing steps in surface-based analysis, e.g., skull stripping, cerebellum removal, tissue segmentation, cortical surface reconstruction, cortical surface parcellation and cortical surface measurements. However, users should carefully check the results generated by an infant pipeline, especially for tissue segmentation, surface reconstruction, parcellation and measurements, based on visual inspection and prior knowledge, e.g., examination of cortical surface folding,

Table 1 Representative cortical surface-based tools tailored for infant brain MR images.

Tool	Applicable subjects	Accepted modalities	Techniques	Links
iBEAT V2.0	Neonates, infants, toddlers, preschooler (0–6 years)	T1w and/ or T2w images	Deep learning-based skull stripping, tissue segmentation and parcellation; deformable surface	https://www.nitrc.org/projects/ibeat and http://www.ibeat.cloud/
dHCP Pipeline	Neonates	T1w and T2w images	Draw EM based segmentation; deformable surface	https://github.com/BioMedIA/dhcp-structural-pipeline
Infant FreeSurfer	Infants (0–2 years)	T1w images	Multiatlas based segmentation; deformable surface	https://surfer.nmr.mgh.harvard.edu/fswiki/infantFS

geometry, topology, and thickness maps. These tools were developed based on different techniques. Some tools may only be applicable to certain infant images and cannot generate reasonable results on other infant images, which may lead to suspicious conclusions. Of note, it is highly suggested to take the advantage of the complementary information of both T1w and T2w images for infant neuroimaging analysis, especially for images before 9 months of age. Besides the processing pipelines, cortical surface atlases also play an important role in surface-based analysis. Therefore, Table 2 summarizes the representative cortical surface atlases for early brain development studies. Notably, the UNC neonatal and infant cortical surface atlases have vertex-to-vertex cortical correspondence across all time points from birth to 72 months of age, allowing both cross-sectional and longitudinal analyses during early brain development.

5. Discussion and future directions

The surface-based analysis of the developing cerebral cortex is still a rapidly progressing field. With increasing the availability of large-scale infant neuroimaging datasets, several new research questions were raised. For example, it is necessary to identify poor-quality cortical surfaces generated by pipelines, as these poor-quality surfaces potentially degrade the performance of subsequent analysis and lead to suspicious results. Therefore, in these large-scale studies, it is highly desired to develop machine learning or deep learning techniques for automatic quality control of the results of cortical surface reconstruction, parcellation, registration and measurement, since manual quality control is tedious, time consuming and subject to interrater variability. Meanwhile, since large-scale datasets are typically acquired from multiple sites with remarkable differences of scanners in imaging protocol (e.g., field of view, resolution, etc.) and hardware (e.g., manufacturer, magnetic field strengths, coil channels, etc.), direct analyses of these multi-site data will unavoidably introduce data harmonization problem. Therefore, it is crucial to harmonize the multi-site cortical property maps, thus removing the effects of different data collection sites and meanwhile preserving the biological properties of developmental brain (Zhao et al., 2019b). In addition, the technique evolution especially the deep learning-based methods brings additional

Table 2 Representative cortical surface atlases constructed for infant brains.

Atlas	Applicable ages	Cortical properties	Cortical parcellations	Scan numbers	Links
PALS-term12	1 Template at 39 postmenstrual weeks	Sulcal depth	N/A	12	http://brainvis.wustl.edu/wiki/index.php/Caret:Atlases
UNC 4D infant surface atlas	11 Templates at 1, 3, 6, 9, 12, 18, 24, 36, 48, 60 and 72 months	Mean curvature, average convexity, sulcal depth, thickness, etc.	FreeSurfer Parcellation, HCP Multimodal Parcellation, Development-based parcellation	339	https://www.nitrc.org/projects/infantsurfatlas
UNC neonatal surface atlases	6 Templates from 39 to 44 postmenstrual weeks	Mean curvature, average convexity	FreeSurfer Parcellation, HCP Multimodal Parcellation, Development-based parcellation	764	https://www.nitrc.org/projects/infantsurfatlas
dHCP neonatal surface atlases	9 Templates from 36 to 44 postmenstrual weeks	Mean curvature, average convexity, myelin content	N/A	270	https://brain-development.org/brain-atlases/atlases-from-the-dhcp-project/cortical-surface-atlas-bozek/

opportunities to the surface-based analysis of the developing cerebral cortex. For example, the highly nonlinear representation ability of the deep neural networks would enable us to build more complex yet more accurate models for cortical segmentation, topology correction, surface reconstruction, registration, parcellation, modeling and prediction of cognitive outcomes and disease progression.

In this chapter, we have introduced the motivation, challenges, and essential steps in cortical surface-based analysis of the dynamic developing cerebral cortex of infant brains. We have provided details on how to reconstruct the topologically correct and geometrically accurate cortical surfaces and compute the biologically meaningful cortical measurements. We have also covered other important procedures, including cortical surface registration, cortical surface atlas construction, cortical surface parcellation, and cortical surface development prediction and modeling. To further facilitate the related studies, we have also summarized representative, publicly available tools and atlases for cortical surface-based mapping of dynamic and critical early brain development.

Acknowledgment

This work was partially supported by NIH grants (MH116225, MH117943, MH109773, and MH123202).

References

Adeli, E., Meng, Y., Li, G., Lin, W., Shen, D., 2019. Multi-task prediction of infant cognitive scores from longitudinal incomplete neuroimaging data. Neuroimage 185, 783–792.

Batalle, D., Hughes, E.J., Zhang, H., Tournier, J.-D., Tusor, N., Aljabar, P., et al., 2017. Early development of structural networks and the impact of prematurity on brain connectivity. Neuroimage 149, 379–392.

Bazin, P.-L., Pham, D.L., 2007. Topology correction of segmented medical images using a fast marching algorithm. Comput. Methods Programs Biomed. 88, 182–190.

Bozek, J., Makropoulos, A., Schuh, A., Fitzgibbon, S., Wright, R., Glasser, M.F., et al., 2018. Construction of a neonatal cortical surface atlas using multimodal surface matching in the developing human connectome project. Neuroimage 179, 11–29.

Chen, H., Li, Y., Ge, F., Li, G., Shen, D., Liu, T., 2017. Gyral net: a new representation of cortical folding organization. Med. Image Anal. 42, 14–25.

Chen, Z., Wu, Z., Sun, L., Wang, F., Wang, L., Zhao, F., et al., 2019. Construction of 4D neonatal cortical surface atlases using wasserstein distance. In: International Symposium on Biomedical Imaging, pp. 995–998.

Conroy, B.R., Singer, B.D., Guntupalli, J.S., Ramadge, P.J., Haxby, J.V., 2013. Intersubject alignment of human cortical anatomy using functional connectivity. Neuroimage 81, 400–411.

Dale, A.M., Fischl, B., Sereno, M.I., 1999. Cortical surface-based analysis: I. segmentation and surface reconstruction. Neuroimage 9, 179–194.

Desikan, R.S., Ségonne, F., Fischl, B., Quinn, B.T., Dickerson, B.C., Blacker, D., et al., 2006. An automated labeling system for subdividing the human cerebral cortex on MRI scans into gyral based regions of interest. Neuroimage 31, 968–980.

Duan, D., Xia, S., Rekik, I., Meng, Y., Wu, Z., Wang, L., et al., 2019. Exploring folding patterns of infant cerebral cortex based on multi-view curvature features: methods and applications. Neuroimage 185, 575–592.

Fischl, B., 2012. FreeSurfer. Neuroimage 62, 774–781.

Fischl, B., Dale, A.M., 2000. Measuring the thickness of the human cerebral cortex from magnetic resonance images. Proc. Natl. Acad. Sci. 97, 11050–11055.

Fischl, B., Sereno, M.I., Dale, A.M., 1999a. Cortical surface-based analysis: II: inflation, flattening, and a surface-based coordinate system. Neuroimage 9, 195–207.

Fischl, B., Sereno, M.I., Tootell, R.B., Dale, A.M., 1999b. High-resolution intersubject averaging and a coordinate system for the cortical surface. Hum. Brain Mapp. 8, 272–284.

Fischl, B., Liu, A., Dale, A.M., 2001. Automated manifold surgery: constructing geometrically accurate and topologically correct models of the human cerebral cortex. IEEE Trans. Med. Imaging 20, 70–80.

Gilmore, J.H., Knickmeyer, R.C., Gao, W., 2018. Imaging structural and functional brain development in early childhood. Nat. Rev. Neurosci. 19, 123–137.

Glasser, M.F., Van Essen, D.C., 2011. Mapping human cortical areas in vivo based on myelin content as revealed by T1-and T2-weighted MRI. J. Neurosci. 31, 11597–11616.

Glasser, M.F., Sotiropoulos, S.N., Wilson, J.A., Coalson, T.S., Fischl, B., Andersson, J.L., et al., 2013. The minimal preprocessing pipelines for the human connectome project. Neuroimage 80, 105–124.

Glasser, M.F., Coalson, T.S., Robinson, E.C., Hacker, C.D., Harwell, J., Yacoub, E., et al., 2016. A multi-modal parcellation of human cerebral cortex. Nature 536, 171–178.

Grayson, D.S., Fair, D.A., 2017. Development of large-scale functional networks from birth to adulthood: a guide to the neuroimaging literature. Neuroimage 160, 15–31.

Hagler Jr., D.J., Hatton, S., Cornejo, M.D., Makowski, C., Fair, D.A., Dick, A.S., et al., 2019. Image processing and analysis methods for the adolescent brain cognitive development study. Neuroimage 202, 116091.

Han, X., Xu, C., Braga-Neto, U., Prince, J.L., 2002. Topology correction in brain cortex segmentation using a multiscale, graph-based algorithm. IEEE Trans. Med. Imaging 21, 109–121.

Han, X., Xu, C., Prince, J.L., 2003. A topology preserving level set method for geometric deformable models. IEEE Trans. Pattern Anal. Mach. Intell. 25, 755–768.

Han, X., Pham, D.L., Tosun, D., Rettmann, M.E., Xu, C., Prince, J.L., 2004. CRUISE: cortical reconstruction using implicit surface evolution. Neuroimage 23, 997–1012.

Hazlett, H.C., Gu, H., Munsell, B.C., Kim, S.H., Styner, M., Wolff, J.J., et al., 2017. Early brain development in infants at high risk for autism spectrum disorder. Nature 542, 348–351.

Howell, B.R., Styner, M.A., Gao, W., Yap, P.-T., Wang, L., Baluyot, K., et al., 2019. The UNC/UMN baby connectome project (BCP): an overview of the study design and protocol development. Neuroimage 185, 891–905.

Hughes, E., Cordero-Grande, L., Murgasova, M., Hutter, J., Price, A., Gomes, A.D.S., et al., 2017. The Developing Human Connectome: announcing the first release of open access neonatal brain imaging. In: 23rd Annual Meeting of the Organization for Human Brain Mapping.

Im, K., Grant, P.E., 2019. Sulcal pits and patterns in developing human brains. Neuroimage 185, 881–890.

Jones, S.E., Buchbinder, B.R., Aharon, I., 2000. Three-dimensional mapping of cortical thickness using Laplace's equation. Hum. Brain Mapp. 11, 12–32.

Li, G., Shen, D., 2011. Consistent sulcal parcellation of longitudinal cortical surfaces. Neuroimage 57, 76–88.

Li, G., Guo, L., Nie, J., Liu, T., 2009. Automatic cortical sulcal parcellation based on surface principal direction flow field tracking. Neuroimage 46, 923–937.

Li, G., Guo, L., Nie, J., Liu, T., 2010. An automated pipeline for cortical sulcal fundi extraction. Med. Image Anal. 14, 343–359.

Li, G., Nie, J., Wu, G., Wang, Y., Shen, D., Alzheimer's Disease Neuroimaging Initiative, 2012. Consistent reconstruction of cortical surfaces from longitudinal brain MR images. Neuroimage 59, 3805–3820.

Li, G., Nie, J., Wang, L., Shi, F., Lin, W., Gilmore, J.H., et al., 2013. Mapping region-specific longitudinal cortical surface expansion from birth to 2 years of age. Cereb. Cortex 23, 2724–2733.

Li, G., Wang, L., Shi, F., Lyall, A.E., Lin, W., Gilmore, J.H., et al., 2014a. Mapping longitudinal development of local cortical gyrification in infants from birth to 2 years of age. J. Neurosci. 34, 4228–4238.

Li, G., Nie, J., Wang, L., Shi, F., Gilmore, J.H., Lin, W., et al., 2014b. Measuring the dynamic longitudinal cortex development in infants by reconstruction of temporally consistent cortical surfaces. Neuroimage 90, 266–279.

Li, G., Wang, L., Shi, F., Lin, W., Shen, D., 2014c. Simultaneous and consistent labeling of longitudinal dynamic developing cortical surfaces in infants. Med. Image Anal. 18, 1274–1289.

Li, G., Lin, W., Gilmore, J.H., Shen, D., 2015a. Spatial patterns, longitudinal development, and hemispheric asymmetries of cortical thickness in infants from birth to 2 years of age. J. Neurosci. 35, 9150–9162.

Li, G., Wang, L., Shi, F., Gilmore, J.H., Lin, W., Shen, D., 2015b. Construction of 4D high-definition cortical surface atlases of infants: methods and applications. Med. Image Anal. 25, 22–36.

Li, G., Wang, L., Gilmore, J.H., Lin, W., Shen, D., 2015c. Parcellation of infant surface atlas using developmental trajectories of multidimensional cortical attributes. In: International Conference on Medical Image Computing and Computer-Assisted Intervention, pp. 543–550.

Li, G., Wang, L., Yap, P.-T., Wang, F., Wu, Z., Meng, Y., et al., 2019. Computational neuroanatomy of baby brains: a review. Neuroimage 185, 906–925.

Liu, P., Wu, Z., Li, G., Yap, P.-T., Shen, D., 2019. Deep modeling of growth trajectories for longitudinal prediction of missing infant cortical surfaces. In: International Conference on Information Processing in Medical Imaging, pp. 277–288.

Lyttelton, O., Boucher, M., Robbins, S., Evans, A., 2007. An unbiased iterative group registration template for cortical surface analysis. Neuroimage 34, 1535–1544.

Makropoulos, A., Robinson, E.C., Schuh, A., Wright, R., Fitzgibbon, S., Bozek, J., et al., 2018. The developing human connectome project: a minimal processing pipeline for neonatal cortical surface reconstruction. Neuroimage 173, 88–112.

Meng, Y., Li, G., Lin, W., Gilmore, J.H., Shen, D., 2014. Spatial distribution and longitudinal development of deep cortical sulcal landmarks in infants. Neuroimage 100, 206–218.

Meng, Y., Li, G., Gao, Y., Lin, W., Shen, D., 2016. Learning-based subject-specific estimation of dynamic maps of cortical morphology at missing time points in longitudinal infant studies. Hum. Brain Mapp. 37, 4129–4147.

Möller, T., 1997. A fast triangle-triangle intersection test. J. Graph. Tools 2, 25–30.

Nie, J., Guo, L., Li, G., Faraco, C., Miller, L.S., Liu, T., 2010. A computational model of cerebral cortex folding. J. Theor. Biol. 264, 467–478.

Nie, J., Li, G., Wang, L., Gilmore, J.H., Lin, W., Shen, D., 2011. A computational growth model for measuring dynamic cortical development in the first year of life. Cereb. Cortex 22, 2272–2284.

Nie, J., Li, G., Wang, L., Gilmore, J.H., Lin, W., Shen, D., 2012. A computational growth model for measuring dynamic cortical development in the first year of life. Cereb. Cortex 22, 2272–2284.

Oishi, K., Chang, L., Huang, H., 2019. Baby brain atlases. Neuroimage 185, 865–880.

Power, J.D., Fair, D.A., Schlaggar, B.L., Petersen, S.E., 2010. The development of human functional brain networks. Neuron 67, 735–748.

Rekik, I., Li, G., Lin, W., Shen, D., 2015. Prediction of longitudinal development of infant cortical surface shape using a 4D current-based learning framework. In: International Conference on Information Processing in Medical Imaging, pp. 576–587.

Rekik, I., Li, G., Lin, W., Shen, D., 2016. Predicting infant cortical surface development using a 4D varifold-based learning framework and local topography-based shape morphing. Med. Image Anal. 28, 1–12.

Rekik, I., Li, G., Yap, P.-T., Chen, G., Lin, W., Shen, D., 2017. Joint prediction of longitudinal development of cortical surfaces and white matter fibers from neonatal MRI. Neuroimage 152, 411–424.

Robinson, E.C., Jbabdi, S., Glasser, M.F., Andersson, J., Burgess, G.C., Harms, M.P., et al., 2014. MSM: a new flexible framework for multimodal surface matching. Neuroimage 100, 414–426.

Ségonne, F., Pacheco, J., Fischl, B., 2007. Geometrically accurate topology-correction of cortical surfaces using nonseparating loops. IEEE Trans. Med. Imaging 26, 518–529.

Shattuck, D.W., Leahy, R.M., 2001. Automated graph-based analysis and correction of cortical volume topology. IEEE Trans. Med. Imaging 20, 1167–1177.

Sossa-Azuela, J.H., 1996. On the computation of the Euler number of a binary object. Pattern Recogn. 29, 471–476.

Sun, L., Zhang, D., Lian, C., Wang, L., Wu, Z., Shao, W., et al., 2019. Topological correction of infant white matter surfaces using anatomically constrained convolutional neural network. Neuroimage 198, 114–124.

Van Essen, D.C., 2005. A population-average, landmark-and surface-based (PALS) atlas of human cerebral cortex. Neuroimage 28, 635–662.

Van Essen, D.C., Dierker, D.L., 2007. Surface-based and probabilistic atlases of primate cerebral cortex. Neuron 56, 209–225.

Vercauteren, T., Pennec, X., Perchant, A., Ayache, N., 2009. Diffeomorphic demons: efficient non-parametric image registration. Neuroimage 45, S61–S72.

Wang, L., Nie, D., Li, G., Puybareau, É., Dolz, J., Zhang, Q., et al., 2019a. Benchmark on automatic six-month-old infant brain segmentation algorithms: the iSeg-2017 challenge. IEEE Trans. Med. Imaging 38, 2219–2230.

Wang, F., Lian, C., Wu, Z., Zhang, H., Li, T., Meng, Y., et al., 2019b. Developmental topography of cortical thickness during infancy. Proc. Natl. Acad. Sci. 116, 15855–15860.

Wang, F., Lian, C., Wu, Z., Wang, L., Lin, W., Gilmore, J.H., et al., 2019c. Revealing developmental regionalization of infant cerebral cortex based on multiple cortical properties. In: International Conference on Medical Image Computing and Computer-Assisted Intervention, pp. 841–849.

Wu, Z., Li, G., Meng, Y., Wang, L., Lin, W., Shen, D., 2017. 4D infant cortical surface atlas construction using spherical patch-based sparse representation. In: International Conference on Medical Image Computing and Computer-Assisted Intervention, pp. 57–65.

Wu, Z., Li, G., Wang, L., Lin, W., Gilmore, J.H., Shen, D., 2018a. Construction of spatiotemporal neonatal cortical surface atlases using a large-scale Dataset. In: IEEE International Symposium on Biomedical Imaging, pp. 1056–1059.

Wu, Z., Li, G., Wang, L., Shi, F., Lin, W., Gilmore, J.H., et al., 2018b. Registration-free infant cortical surface parcellation using deep convolutional neural networks. In: International Conference on Medical Image Computing and Computer-Assisted Intervention, pp. 672–680.

Wu, Z., Wang, L., Lin, W., Gilmore, J.H., Li, G., Shen, D., 2019a. Construction of 4D infant cortical surface atlases with sharp folding patterns via spherical patch-based group-wise sparse representation. Hum. Brain Mapp. 40, 3860–3880.

Wu, Z., Zhao, F., Xia, J., Wang, L., Lin, W., Gilmore, J.H., et al., 2019b. Intrinsic patch-based cortical anatomical parcellation using graph convolutional neural network on surface manifold. In: International Conference on Medical Image Computing and Computer-Assisted Intervention, pp. 492–500.

Xia, J., Wang, F., Benkarim, O.M., Sanroma, G., Piella, G., González Ballester, M.A., et al., 2019. Fetal cortical surface atlas parcellation based on growth patterns. Hum. Brain Mapp. 40, 3881–3899.

Yeo, B.T., Sabuncu, M.R., Vercauteren, T., Ayache, N., Fischl, B., Golland, P., 2009. Spherical demons: fast diffeomorphic landmark-free surface registration. IEEE Trans. Med. Imaging 29, 650–668.

Zhang, C., Adeli, E., Wu, Z., Li, G., Lin, W., Shen, D., 2018. Infant brain development prediction with latent partial multi-view representation learning. IEEE Trans. Med. Imaging 38, 909–918.

Zhang, X., Ding, X., Wu, Z., Xia, J., Ni, H., Xu, X., et al., 2020. Siamese verification framework for autism identification during infancy using cortical path signature features. In: 2020 IEEE 17th International Symposium on Biomedical Imaging (ISBI), pp. 1–4.

Zhao, F., Wu, Z., Wang, F., Lin, W., Xia, S., Shen, D., Wang, L., Li, G., 2021a. S3Reg: superfast spherical surface registration based on deep learning. IEEE Trans. Med. Imaging 40 (8), 1964–1976. https://doi.org/10.1109/TMI.2021.3069645.

Zhao, F., Wu, Z., Wang, L., Lin, W., Gilmore, J.H., Xia, S., Shen, D., Li, G., 2021b. Spherical deformable U-Net: application to cortical surface parcellation and development prediction. IEEE Trans. Med. Imaging 40 (5), 1217–1228. https://doi.org/10.1109/TMI.2021.3050072.

Zhao, F., Wu, Z., Wang, L., Lin, W., Xia, S., Shen, D., et al., 2019b. Harmonization of infant cortical thickness using surface-to-surface cycle-consistent adversarial networks. In: International Conference on Medical Image Computing and Computer-Assisted Intervention, pp. 475–483.

Connectome and graph analysis of the developing brain

Miao Cao[a,b] and Yong He[c,d,e]

Institute of Science and Technology for Brain-Inspired Intelligence, Fudan University, Shanghai, China[a] Key Laboratory of Computational Neuroscience and Brain-Inspired Intelligence, Fudan University, Ministry of Education, Shanghai, China[b] State Key Laboratory of Cognitive Neuroscience and Learning, Beijing Normal University, Beijing, China[c] Beijing Key Laboratory of Brain Imaging and Connectomics, Beijing Normal University, Beijing, China[d] IDG/McGovern Institute for Brain Research, Beijing Normal University, Beijing, China[e]

The newly emerging developmental connectomics framework together with advanced neuroimaging and neurophysiological techniques provide unprecedented opportunities to delineate how the human brain develops, from a circuitry or network perspective (Cao et al., 2017a; Zhao et al., 2019a). Specifically, the brain can be mapped as a complex network supporting global and local information communication at the macroscale level through noninvasively mapping structural and functional connectivity patterns based on multimodality imaging data (Cao et al., 2017a, 2016; Zhao et al., 2019a; Sporns et al., 2005; Kelly et al., 2012; Biswal et al., 2010; Sporns, 2011). Based on the constructed brain networks, the properties of nodes, edges and the entire network can be measured with respect to factors involving age, genes, and the environment (Fig. 1A). These advances have led to exciting new insights into the early development of the brain in both healthy and pathological populations and paved the way for a better understanding of how brain networks develop from infancy to early childhood as well as how it shapes the development of important cognitive and behavioral skills in later life.

1. Brain connectome and graph theory

In graph theory, a network can be mathematically modeled as a graph with a set of discrete elements (nodes or vertices) and their mutual relationships (edges or links), which can be summarized in the form of a connection matrix. In the context of brain networks, nodes usually represent imaging voxels, regions of interest, or sensors, while links represent structural, morphological, or functional connections, depending on the imaging modality considered (He and Evans, 2010; Bullmore and Sporns, 2012, 2009). In particular, structural connectivity can be obtained by reconstructing diffusion MRI (dMRI) traced white matter projections (Hagmann et al., 2007; Gong et al., 2009; Mori and van Zijl, 2002), or through computing the covariance of brain morphological features among regions (e.g., gray matter volume or cortical thickness) derived from structural MRI (sMRI) data (He et al., 2007; Lerch et al., 2006). Functional connectivity can be measured by examining synchronous neural activity over the distributed brain areas with functional MRI (fMRI), electroencephalography/

Handbook of Pediatric Brain Imaging. https://doi.org/10.1016/B978-0-12-816633-8.00021-1

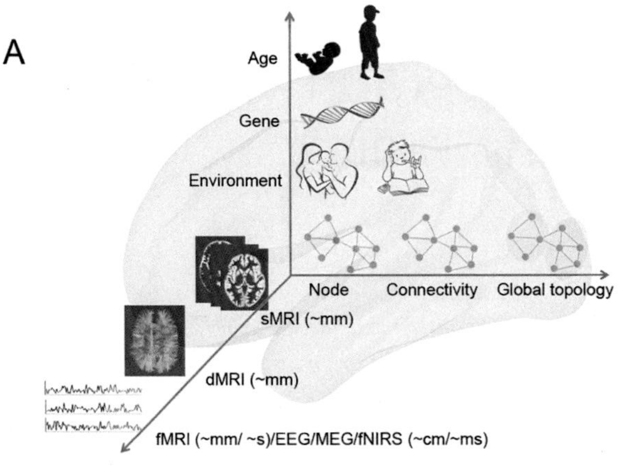

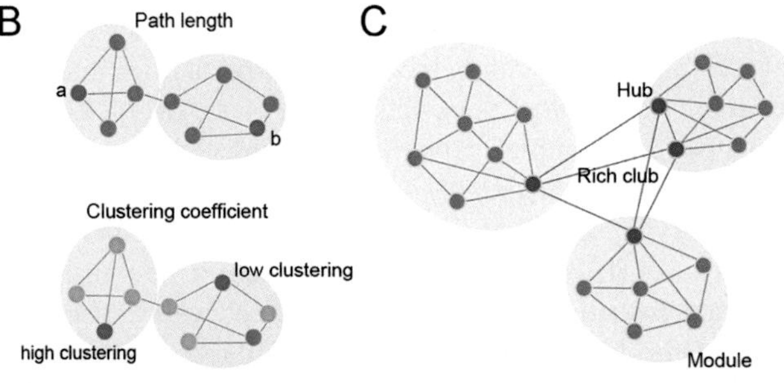

FIG. 1

Connectome construction and topological analyses of the brain.

Source: Adapted from Cao, M., Huang, H., He, Y., 2017a. Developmental connectomics from infancy through early childhood. Trends Neurosci. 40(8), 494–506; Cao, M., He, Y., Dai, Z., et al., 2017b. Early development of functional network segregation revealed by connectomic analysis of the preterm human brain. Cereb. Cortex. 27(3), 1949–63.

magnetoencephalography (EEG/MEG), or functional near-infrared spectroscopy (fNIRS) (Friston, 1994; Niu and He, 2014; Micheloyannis et al., 2006).

The examination of brain network topology using graph theory is a core element in the emerging field of connectomics. Network properties can be examined with various metrics based on network science on the topological organization principles (Rubinov and Sporns, 2010; Stam, 2010; Bullmore and Bassett, 2011). The topology of a brain network can be characterized in terms of its global, nodal, and connectional aspects. The global attributes measure the architecture of the whole network graph, whereas the nodal and connectional attributes measure topological features of a single node or connection. Below, we briefly introduce several key graph theory metrics from these aspects.

Global topological metrics can be classified according to their relationship with network segregation and integration processes. Topological segregation in the network's information processing refers to the neuronal processing carried out among spatially adjacent nodes with short-distance local connections which ensure functional specialization. There are two quantitative measurements of the segregation capacity of networks, the average *clustering coefficient* and *local efficiency* of a network across nodes (Fig. 1B). The clustering coefficient of a node is calculated by the existing edges among neighbors divided by the maximal number of possible edges, representing the density of local clusters. Another measurement, local efficiency, is similar to the clustering coefficient but can reflect the fault tolerance capacity of the network (Fig. 1B). A network possessing a high clustering coefficient or local efficiency indicates a high capacity for local information transfer and a high degree of network segregation. By contrast, global integration refers to the efficiency of global information communication or the ability to integrate distributed information in the network, which is usually measured by the characteristic *path length* or *global efficiency* of a network. The characteristic path length of a network is calculated by averaging the shortest path lengths between each pair of nodes in the network. Specifically, a path represents a route of edges that connect one node with others, wherein its length is defined as the sum of the number or weights of the edges, and the shortest route between two nodes refers to the shortest path length. The global efficiency of a network is the inverse of the average values of the shortest path length between any two nodes (Sporns, 2013). A network that possesses high global efficiency and low shortest path length has high global information transfer efficiency as well as a high degree of network integration. Notably, networks can be distinguished into different types based on perspectives of information segregation and integration, including regular, small-world and random networks. Regular network and random network correspond to the two extremes of segregation and integration, respectively. A *regular network* has a high clustering coefficient and long characteristic path length, while a *random network* has a low clustering coefficient and short characteristic path length. A *small-world network* has both high global and local information transformation capacities, which is characterized as a shorter characteristic path length than a regular network and a greater clustering coefficient than a random network. The optimized balance between segregation and integration of small-world structure is essential for high synchronizability and fast information transmission in a complex network (Watts and Strogatz, 1998; Latora and Marchiori, 2001).

Interestingly, small-world brain networks are generally supported by the presence of modules and hubs (Fig. 1C). Modules are sets of nodes that are highly interconnected but with relatively fewer connections to the others in different modules (Bullmore and Sporns, 2012). Modularity can be used to measure the existence of the modular structure of a network (Newman, 2006). Since the densely linked local clusters support the information specialization, connections linking within specific modules are usually considered intramodule connections and represent the network segregation abilities. In contrast, connections linking different modules may work as highways for the information integration among distinct local communities. These edges can be summarized as intermodule connections to represent network integration capacity. The nodal regions that are positioned to make strong contributions to global network communication in networks can be identified as hubs using numerous different graph measures (van den Heuvel and Sporns, 2013). The simplest graph measure used for identifying hubs is *degree centrality*, which evaluates the number of connections attached to a given node. Another measurement is *betweenness centrality*, defined as how many of the shortest paths between all other node pairs in the network pass through a given node, reflecting the ability of information transformation (Freedman, 1977). *Nodal efficiency* is also a frequently used measurement, which scales the average shortest path length between the given node and all the other nodes in the network (Achard and Bullmore, 2007). Importantly, these high-degree or high-central hubs strongly tend to be densely interconnected and form a rich-club structure, composing the critical backbone for efficient communication across the network (van den Heuvel and Sporns, 2011). These hubs and rich-clubs are found playing important roles in global information transformation, at the expense of relatively higher wiring and running costs and vulnerability (Bullmore and Sporns, 2012; van den Heuvel et al., 2012; Liang et al., 2013; Tomasi et al., 2013).

The connections are responsible for information transfer across regions or systems. Similarly, the topological roles of connections can be measured with different metrics regarding their contribution to whole network communication (Girvan and Newman, 2002; Zhou et al., 2016). Edge betweenness is a global centrality measurement that captures the influence of an edge over information flow between other nodes in the network. It is calculated as the number of shortest paths between any pairs of other nodes that pass through the edge. Another classification of connections is based on the hub members to further classify network edges into three types: rich-club connections, which link between rich-club nodes, feeder connections, which link between peripheral and core nodes, and local connections, which link between nonrich-club nodes (van den Heuvel and Sporns, 2011). After the detection of pivotal edges, the patterns of their utilization, namely their path motifs, could reflect the information transfer strategy of the network.

Human brain networks exhibit clusters with short-distance local connections between spatially adjacent nodes, which are often aggregated topologically and anatomically as modules/communities. Hub regions are usually highly connected or centralized and exhibit long-distance short-cuts linking different modules, which increase the efficiency of global information communication and the ability to integrate distributed information across the brain. Both brain functional and structural networks have been detected exhibiting rich-club and small-world organization (Sporns, 2013). Brain networks can therefore be said to exhibit an optimized balance between the global integration and local segregation of information transformation.

2. Maturation of structural brain connectome

During the early development period, the nontrivial small-world configuration has been consistently demonstrated in the baby brain networks, which is among one of the most influential findings regarding brain network development. Baby structural brain networks were identified to exhibit small-world organization early in postmortem fetuses at 20 postmenstrual weeks (PMW) (van den Heuvel et al., 2015; Cao et al., 2017b), and this architecture has been consistently observed in other studies of the preterm network (van den Heuvel et al., 2015; Batalle et al., 2017; Brown et al., 2014; Tymofiyeva et al., 2013).

In the prenatal stage, the shaping of the network seems to lean toward segregation enforcement which is proven by the increased normalized clustering coefficient (Batalle et al., 2017; Brown et al., 2014; Tymofiyeva et al., 2013) and stable normalized shortest path length (Brown et al., 2014; Tymofiyeva et al., 2013). The observation of increased small-worldness values during this period also confirmed this developmental bias (van den Heuvel et al., 2015; Batalle et al., 2017; Brown et al., 2014; Tymofiyeva et al., 2013). After birth, decreased characteristic path length in 6-month-old infants (Tymofiyeva et al., 2013) and increased global efficiency in 2-year-old toddlers were found compared with those in term neonates (Huang et al., 2015; Yap et al., 2011). Besides, the normalized clustering coefficient and small-worldness were found to decreased monotonically in term neonates, 2-year-old toddlers and adults (Tymofiyeva et al., 2013; Huang et al., 2015). These results indicate that during the early postnatal period, the structural segregation is decreasing while the structural integration is increasing with age. The growth of network integration during this period may be closely associated with the increasing proportion of long fiber connections linking distant areas (Tymofiyeva et al., 2013).

Additionally, the local efficiency of the structural network was found to be increased in 1-year-old and 2-year-old toddlers compared with that in neonates, indicating the improvement of the fault-tolerant ability of networks (Huang et al., 2015; Yap et al., 2011). Of note, the most rapid global and local reconfigurations occurred before 1-year of age (van den Heuvel et al., 2015; Cao et al., 2017b; Gao et al., 2011; Nie et al., 2014), with more stable changes taking place after that (Gao et al., 2011; Nie et al., 2014).

Modular organization was also detected already exist in the structural networks of approximately 30 PMW preterm babies (van den Heuvel et al., 2015; Ball et al., 2014). With development, an integrative evolution process occurred in the brain modular structure, with connectivity increasing within and across modules/communities. Specifically, the modularity continuously increased with age before birth, indicating the strengthening of modular specialization (van den Heuvel et al., 2015; Fan et al., 2011). After then, postnatal development experienced decreases in modularity, which were primarily driven by the enhancement of inter-module integration (Tymofiyeva et al., 2013; Hagmann et al., 2010).

In terms of the regional layout of the brain, the development of connections and brain regions is heterogeneous in the network. The degree distribution of the brain structural network nodes has been found to follow an exponentially truncated power law during the prenatal period (van den Heuvel et al., 2015; Brown et al., 2014; Ball et al., 2014), which guarantees the existence of highly efficient hubs but not huge hubs. Specifically, structural hubs emerged early within the dorsal medial frontal, parietal, and hippocampus regions, emulating an adult-like distribution pattern around birth (van den Heuvel et al., 2015) (Fig. 2A). These hub regions, together with precuneus/posterior cingulate cortex and insula, formed the rich-club architecture, which serves as the communication backbone of structural networks (Ball et al., 2014). During the third-trimester, short-range connections develop fast, with links between the primary sensorimotor cortex, occipital cortex and frontal cortex within the hemisphere (Ball et al., 2014; Zhao et al., 2019b). Dramatic development was also discovered in rich-club organization, including the principal proliferation of the feeder edges (Ball et al., 2014) and a gradual escalation, in which the connection strength increases in the local, feeder, and rich-club edges in the last stage before the birth stage (Zhao et al., 2019b). These changes highlight the centrality of the early-existed hub structures to make hubs more dominant among brain regions. Notably, the provincial hubs in charge of communication within specific modules develop more rapidly than the connector hubs, indicating a bias for network segregation during hub development (Zhao et al., 2019b). After birth, the brain network retains a degree distribution of truncated power law and demonstrates some refinements (Huang et al., 2015; Yap et al., 2011). The hub distribution identified by nodal efficiency still presents an adult-like pattern and primarily remains unchanged (Huang et al., 2015; Tymofiyeva et al., 2012), except for the left anterior cingulate gyrus and left superior occipital gyrus, which become hubs in toddler brains compared with neonate brains (Huang et al., 2015) (Fig. 2A). The nodal connectivity of all regions in the structural brain networks were reported to increase with postnatal development, with the most significant increases occurring in hubs located in the association regions, especially the precuneus (Huang et al., 2015). Toddlers exhibit age-dependent upgrades in network robustness against both random and targeted attacks compared with those in neonates (Huang et al., 2015). Notably, Yap et al. found that the topological roles of brain regions changed with age by accessing age-related classifications, according to their intramodular degree and participation coefficient (Yap et al., 2011). The centrality of the posterior-medial regions, such as the precuneus and cuneus, was also observed to be increased before preadolescence (Huang et al., 2015; Yap et al., 2011), while the importance of some brain regions, such

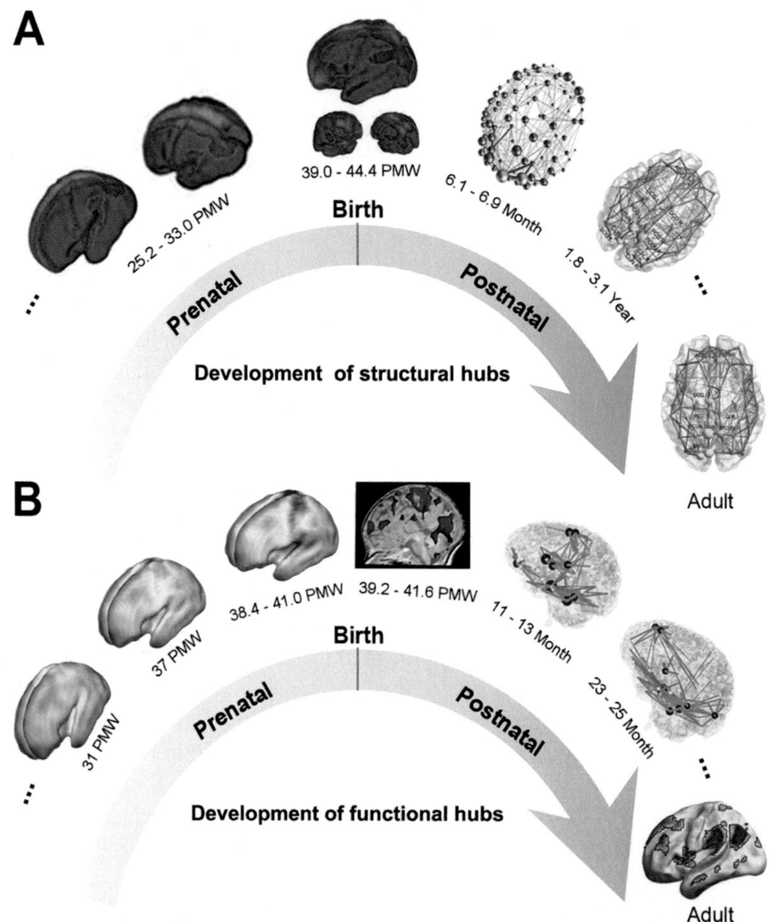

FIG. 2

The development of human brain hubs at the early stage of life. (A) Diffusion imaging findings about the development of structural hubs in the human cerebral cortex. The structural hubs are largely overlapped with those in adult at the time of birth, which include the superior and medial frontal, superior parietal, sensorimotor, posterior-medial cortices, insula regions, and inferior frontal cortex. (B) Resting-state functional imaging findings about the development of functional hubs in the human cerebral cortex. The functional hubs of infant brains are primarily located in the sensorimotor and visual cortices at birth and move toward the areas involved in high order cognitive functions, such as the medial superior frontal gyrus and some default mode network regions, which are still different from those in adults.

Source: Adapted from Zhao, T., Xu, Y., He, Y., 2019a. Graph theoretical modeling of baby brain networks. Neuroimage. 185, 711–27; Zhao, T., Mishra, V., Jeon, T., et al., 2019b. Structural network maturation of the preterm human brain. Neuroimage. 185, 699–710.

as the left Heschl's gyrus and bilateral precentral gyrus, are reduced with age due to their decreased normalized regional efficiency (Huang et al., 2015).

Morphological covariance network analyses revealed that the efficient small-world topology and nonrandom modular organization of brain connectome was established in infants ranging in age from 1 month to 2 years (Fan et al., 2011). The global efficiency, local efficiency, and modularity of the anatomical network all increased with age, demonstrating the increase of both network segregation and integration with development (Fan et al., 2011). However, another study using a cortical curvedness correlation network model has found increased local efficiency and decreased global efficiency from birth to 2 years of age (Nie et al., 2014), indicating a reinforcement of network segregation. Besides, while the primary visual and sensorimotor networks were more mature at birth, the default mode and dorsal attention network configuration remained immature by the age of 2 years (Geng et al., 2016). These inconsistent results may reflect different regional synchronized maturation in anatomy during cortex development.

3. Maturation of functional brain connectomes

For functional networks, the prominent small-world and rich-club structures were found at approximately 30 PMW in the brains of preterm babies (Cao et al., 2017b). Significant modular organization was observed at approximately 20 weeks in gestational age (GA) in fetal brains in utero (Thomason et al., 2014) and at 30 PMW in preterm brains (Cao et al., 2017b). Using minimum spanning tree graphs, an EEG study reported the early presence of an optimal hierarchical architecture over different frequency bands in infants at 36 weeks in GA (Toth et al., 2017). These results revealed that similar to structural network, the initial functional network also presents a highly efficient and organized topology.

With development, the clustering coefficient of the functional network increased significantly with age, indicating an enhanced segregation process (Cao et al., 2017b). This growth of the network segregation was also reflected by the deceased participation coefficient and deceased number of connectors with age in preterm brains (Cao et al., 2017b), resulting in separation of the modular system during the prenatal period. The EEG study found that the network topology was changing toward a less centralized and hierarchical organization with age in infants at the theta- and alpha-bands, which also indicates a segregation enhancement (Toth et al., 2017). The age-related decrease in global efficiency and increase in diameter (similar to the characteristic path length) were found in preterm and infant brains in the fMRI and EEG studies, revealing decreased network integration. However, some inconsistent results were also observed. Decreased modularity and increased intermodule connection strength with age were detected in the fetal fMRI study (Thomason et al., 2014), showing enhancement of the network integration process. Methodological differences, such as the choice of network thresholding method or brain node definition, may explain this discrepancy. After birth, the global efficiency and local efficiency of the brain functional network were found to increase in 1-year-old infants compared to neonates, while remaining stable during the second year of life (Gao et al., 2011). Among these changes, the increase of global efficiency was found mainly contributed by the development of long-distance connections. Another MEG study found marked increases of local efficiency and global efficiency of the sensorimotor network after the first year of life (Berchicci et al., 2015). These changes reveal an increase of both network segregation and integration processes during early postnatal development.

Notably, even though it exhibits prominent topological structure, the functional network of the brain is still in an incomplete state at the beginning of the third trimester. The intrinsic functional synchrony in fetuses were found to increase following the order of occipital (peak: 24.8 weeks), temporal (peak: 26 weeks), frontal (peak: 26.4 weeks), and parietal regions (peak: 27.5 weeks) (Jakab et al., 2014). By the time of birth, the evidence of sensorimotor, auditory/language, visual, cerebellar, thalamic, parietal, prefrontal, anterior cingulate as well as dorsal and ventral aspects of the default mode network, which are corresponding to the canonical resting state systems established in adults have been detected (Rajasilta et al., 2020). After birth, the primary sensorimotor and auditory networks matured first, which achieved matured network configurations both qualitatively and quantitatively by the time of birth. Then, the visual areas dramatically enhanced the connectivity during the first 3 month postnatally. The attention and default-mode regions matured next, in which dramatic increases in functional connectivity strength were observed across the first half year after birth. Finally, the executive control network matured, which continually developed during the first year with rapid changes between 9 and 12 months (Gao et al., 2015a, b). The important role of the thalamus in transforming the peripheral sensory information to the cortex as well as diversely associating with higher-order cognitive functions, has led to increasing interest in the development of thalamocortical connectivity. Specifically, thalamus-sensorimotor and thalamus-salience functional connectivity were already present in neonates, while specialized thalamus-medial visual and thalamus-default mode connectivity emerged later at 1 year of age (Alcauter et al., 2014). The modular structure was found reorganized from an anatomically local proximity-based pattern to a more functional distribution pattern over the early development period (Yap et al., 2011).

The functional hubs are also immature during the third trimester and largely confined to the primary regions, including the supplementary motor areas and visual regions (Cao et al., 2017b), which are distinctly different from adult brain hubs located in the superior parietal and superior frontal cortex and anterior and posterior cingulate gyrus, as well as insula regions (Liang et al., 2013) (Fig. 2B). With development, hubs spread into primary sensorimotor, visual regions and Wernicke's area in full-term neonates (Cao et al., 2017b; Fransson et al., 2011), and this growth is dominantly affected by the enhancement of short-to-middle range primary cortex connections (Cao et al., 2017b) (Fig. 2B). Meanwhile, the size of rich-club organization expands with age (Cao et al., 2017b). These regional changes suggest that the development of functional hubs during the prenatal period primarily concentrate on specific primary functional systems that may function as an urgent infrastructure to establish before birth. By the term age, the functional hubs of infant brains are primarily located in the sensorimotor and visual cortices (Gao et al., 2011; Fransson et al., 2011). After birth, the evolution of functional hub distribution continues through dynamic regional configurations. Nodal local efficiency was found to be increased in the temporal and occipital regions, as well as several subcortical regions, and decreased in the frontal regions during the first year of life. The increased nodal global efficiency was distributed in an extensive regional pattern during the first year and concentrated in the default mode network regions during the second year (Gao et al., 2011). Brain hubs moved toward the areas involved in high-order cognitive functions, such as the medial superior frontal gyrus and some default mode network regions, in 2 year olds (Gao et al., 2011) (Fig. 2B). Connection analyses also found that the anterior and posterior cortical regions are connected with each other through long functional connectivity by the age of two, while most primary sensorimotor regions are already functionally connected at birth (Gao et al., 2011; Fransson et al., 2007; Smyser et al., 2010). Task-based fNIRS brain connectivity analyses revealed that the adult-like neural activation in infants during object and socioemotional processing increase over the first year of life (Wilcox and Biondi, 2015). Together, these studies showed a clear evolution of brain hubs maturing from segregated primary regions to integrated higher-order function cortices, which is consistent with the behavior observed during this period (Gao et al., 2016). Additionally, although it has incomplete regional components, the functional network at birth is more resilient than simulated scale-free networks in targeted attacks (De Asis-Cruz et al., 2018). The early postnatal development of network integration through increased long-distance functional connections brings age-dependent improvements in network resilience in random and targeted attacks (Gao et al., 2011).

In summary, while the dramatic growth of the human brain occurs from infancy to early childhood, a strengthening global balance between local and global information processing have been detected that drives the brain networks toward an organized and optimized configuration with an efficient and hierarchical architecture (van den Heuvel et al., 2015; Cao et al., 2017b; Brown et al., 2014; Tymofiyeva et al., 2013; Huang et al., 2015; Gao et al., 2011; Nie et al., 2014; Fan et al., 2011; Hagmann et al., 2010) (Fig. 3A). Further empirical and computational modeling studies are needed to explore how the economic and efficient brain networks form and which factors drive this complex process. Besides, the developmental patterns of both the brain structure and function followed the rule that the primary cortex develops prior to higher-order regions (Fig. 3B). This particular principle is beneficial to focus prenatal resources on the regions/networks that are most important for early survival, while enabling the enriched development of higher-order association regions/networks through prolonged postnatal gene-by-environment interactions.

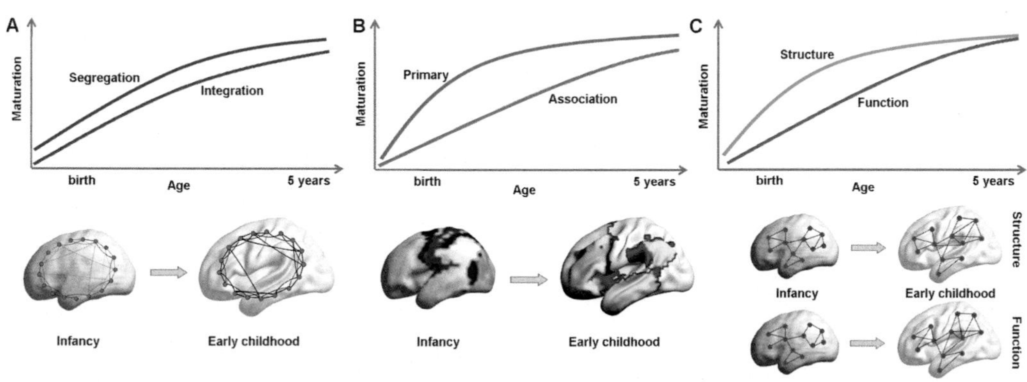

FIG. 3

Developmental network models of brain connectomes from infancy to early childhood. (A) The hypothetic developmental model of information segregation and integration in the brain networks. (B) The hypothetic developmental model of ordered maturation from primary to association regions. (C) The hypothetic developmental model of different maturation modes of structural and functional connectomes.

Source: Adapted from Cao, M., Huang, H., He, Y., 2017a. Developmental connectomics from infancy through early childhood. Trends Neurosci. 40(8), 494–506; Cao, M., He, Y., Dai, Z., et al., 2017b. Early development of functional network segregation revealed by connectomic analysis of the preterm human brain. Cereb. Cortex. 27(3), 1949–63

4. Maturation of the coupling between structural and functional connectomes

Although the developmental trends and orders are relatively consistent between the brain's structural and functional connectomes, they matured at different time points (Fig. 3C). The structural supports are far ahead of the functional emergences. The structural network has established pathways between high-order regions and forms adult-like hubs at the time of birth. While in functional networks, the configurations of hub and rich club organizations remained largely different from those in adult brains during infancy (Huang et al., 2015; Gao et al., 2011). The functional hubs were demonstrated to be largely confined to primary visual, auditory, and sensorimotor areas around the time of birth (Cao et al., 2017b; Fransson et al., 2011). By the age of 2, although bilateral superior medial frontal regions emerged as hubs, which may indicate a gradual shift of developmental focus to higher-order cognitive functions during this period, the functional hub distribution remained far from adult-like (Gao et al., 2011). Intriguingly, a relatively high metabolism was observed for these functional hub regions in infants, likely rendering them more vulnerable to deficits in energy consumption (Liang et al., 2013; Tomasi et al., 2013; Chugani, 1998).

While different developmental modes were observed for brain structure and function, empirical and computational modeling studies suggest that the functional network organization is sculpted by the underlying structural network but exhibits more diverse and flexible configurations in human adults (Wang et al., 2015; Kim et al., 2013). Studies on brain development reported that the coupling between structural and functional networks experienced continuous increases from 30 weeks of gestational age until approximately 20 years of age (van den Heuvel et al., 2015; Hagmann et al., 2010). This indicates that the non-parallel developmental patterns of structural and functional brain networks in infancy to early childhood merge to be in conformity in later life. The earlier maturing structural networks may serve as an initial foundation for the functional connections to develop diverse configurations. The continuous functional coactivation between different regions, either evoked or intrinsic, is important for the subsequent strengthening/weakening of existing structural connections in a Hebbian sense of plasticity (Song et al., 2000). Nevertheless, how exactly the development of structural networks tailors the functional network maturation, as well as how the changes in functional network further sculpt and reshape the underlying anatomical substrates, are of great importance and warrant intensive future research.

5. Maturation of the individual variability in brain connectomes

Although most studies have focused on demonstrating the general principles of brain development through group-level analysis, the importance of fully personalized investigations into this developmental phase has received considerable attention. Specifically, the structural and functional connectomes of the human brain vary across subjects, and these differences potentially underlie the individual differences in cognition and behavior (Mueller et al., 2013; Finn et al., 2015; Zhong et al., 2015).

Individual variability in the functional connectivity architecture of healthy adults showed heterogeneity across regions with significantly higher variability in the heteromodal association cortex and lower variability in the unimodal cortices, which was potentially rooted in evolution and predictive of individual cognitive differences (Mueller et al., 2013). Prenatal exploration showed that while the functional intersubject variability values were relatively high and homogeneous across regions at the age of 30 weeks, nonuniform decreases occurred with development as the adult-similar pattern appeared at approximately 37 weeks (Xu et al., 2019). After birth, the variability patterns remained relatively consistent, with the magnitude of variability values continually decreasing until 1 year and then increasing to 2 years old (Gao et al., 2014). The changing patterns in functional variability after birth were found to not be purely driven by genetic influences (Gao et al., 2014). However, genetic effects in neonates were detected in nearly all white matter tracts (Lee et al., 2015). Additionally, gender effects on white matter networks were explored, and males exhibited generally higher global and local efficiency compared with females from birth to 2 years old (Yap et al., 2011). These findings indicate that the brain maturation process is likely to experience a predominantly genetically determined growth first, in line with the diminishing intersubject variability during the first year of life, and is then followed by a more plastic gene-environment interaction period, enrooting to increasing intersubject differences during subsequent development.

Notably, the individual differences in the connectomic measurements of pediatric populations are predictive of behavioral performance and cognitive capacity in later life. In structural network studies, network integration and segregation measurements of the neonatal network, including global efficiency and the clustering coefficient, can serve as predictors of performance IQ and processing speed at 5 years of age (Keunen et al., 2017). The segregation capacity of information transformation in neonates' white matter networks significantly correlated with the behavior profiles assessed with the maternal reported internalizing and externalizing behaviors at 2 and 4 years old (Wee et al., 2016). The connection strength of preterm white matter pathways that run between the thalamus and the whole cortex could explain 11% of the variance in cognitive scores in 2-year-old children (Ball et al., 2015). The altered global and regional network topology observed in 1-year-old infants with intrauterine growth restriction was associated with abnormal performance in later neurodevelopmental abilities, such as socioemotional and adaptive behaviors, at 2 years of age (Batalle et al., 2012). For functional networks, the functional connectivity of the amygdala in new born babies was related to emerging fear and cognitive development (including emerging sensorimotor, attention and memory skills) at 6 months (Graham et al., 2016). Thalamo-salience network connectivity in 1-year olds was shown to be predictive for general cognitive development at 2 years of age (Alcauter et al., 2014) and the frequency profile of functional fluctuations in brain networks has also been linked to behavioral performances in 1 year-old infants (Alcauter et al., 2015). Additionally, electroencephalography coherence in the left hemisphere of infants was significantly correlated with epistemic language skills at 4 years old (Kuhn-Popp et al., 2016).

Collectively, identifying individual brain connectomic "fingerprints" during the early development is not only important for understanding cognitive development but also has potential implications for monitoring normal development in cognitive capacity and mental health.

6. Atypical early development of the brain connectomes

With rapid maturation, highly dynamic connectomic changes give the brain not only high plasticity but also vulnerability to risk factors leading to developmental problems and/or disorders. Simulation analysis revealed that the brain network robustness, which measures the capacity against attack, gradually increased with development but remained lower compared to that in adults, indicating the immature status of the human brain at the early stage of life (Huang et al., 2015; Gao et al., 2011).

The most common type of atypical growth in the early stage is preterm growth, which involves the sudden interruption of typical development processes as a result of complex genetic and environmental factors. Premature birth is an identifiable risk that has significant influences on brain development even in the absence of focal brain injury. While the overall layout of the brain network organizations, including small-world, modular, hubs and rich-club structures, remained similar, reduced local clustering and global network complexity were detected in both the structural and functional connectomes of preterm groups (Batalle et al., 2017; Ball et al., 2014; Thompson et al., 2016; Scheinost et al., 2016; Smyser et al., 2016). Reduced interhemispheric functional connectivity and impaired lateralization of language areas were also observed in preterm infants compared with healthy term controls (Kwon et al., 2015). Besides, accumulating literature converges on pervasively disrupted thalamocortical structural connectivity as a result of preterm birth in neonates and significant correlation with cognitive variances in later life (Ball et al., 2015, 2013). Moreover, preterm birth damage was noted to persist through childhood, leading to impaired global integration and segregation capacity, as well as impaired connectivity of hub regions in the brain networks of preadolescent populations, which were predictive of impaired intelligence quotient scores and motor performance (Thompson et al., 2016; Kim et al., 2014).

Another major threat is maternal substance exposure, which is a world-widely problem continuously on the rise. Specifically, maternal exposure to cocaine disrupts the amygdala-frontal and insula-sensorimotor functional circuits in infants (Salzwedel et al., 2015) as well as amygdala-frontal structural connectivity in adolescents (Li et al., 2013). Marijuana exposure was associated with disrupted functional connectivity of caudate and insula in neonates (Grewen et al., 2015). Interestingly, prenatal cortisol exposure exhibits sex-specific associations with network properties in children, which only impaired the network segregation of girls (Kim et al., 2016). This disrupted network connectivity is thought to play important roles in arousal regulation or reward processing, the alterations of which may lead to adverse developmental consequences such as drug abuse in later life. Other factors, such as early life stress, also have significant effects on brain connectome development. For instance, postnatal exposure to interparental conflict was significantly associated with higher integration among default mode regions in infants, potentially leading to higher negative infant emotionality (Graham et al., 2015a). Maternal depression significantly altered the functional connectivity of the amygdala in 6-month infants (Qiu et al., 2015) and of the frontal regions in 18 month infants (Soe et al., 2016).

Meanwhile, emerging data indicate that major psychiatric disorders have a prominent origin in early childhood development, such as in autism (onset of approximately 2 years old) (Di Martino et al., 2014). For instance, the crossed early developmental curves between autism (or autism-risk) populations and healthy controls were observed in both the structural and functional connectomes. Structural connectivity analysis with diffusion imaging data detected crossed developmental curves of autism subjects and healthy controls from 2 to 7 years old, with the crossed age at approximately 4 years (Ouyang et al., 2016). The white matter networks of autism subjects aged 2 years exhibited significantly decreased local and global network efficiencies compared with healthy babies (Lewis et al., 2014). Functional near-infrared spectroscopy study reported that infants at high risk for autism exhibited increased overall functional connectivity strength at 3 months old compared with subjects with low risk (Keehn et al., 2013). The differences diminished with development and reversed in the 12-month-old infants, i.e., the functional connectivity decreased in the high risk autism group compared with the low risk group (Keehn et al., 2013).

In summary, the effects of these risk factors on early brain development could be genetically programmed, epigenetically mediated, and environmentally influenced. Identifying the impairments of brain connectomics associated with these risks and disorders as early as possible is crucial for early identification and may provide the unique and important opportunity for early intervention and prevention.

7. Methodological issues

From a methodological viewpoint, there are still several issues that should be considered regarding baby brain connectome analysis (Cao et al., 2016; Di Martino et al., 2014; Shi et al., 2017; Xia and He, 2017). The definition of brain nodes and connections during network construction should be highlighted for exploring the baby brain in early development. In terms of node parcellation, adopting widely used adult brain atlases on baby data may induce methodological biases. As described in Chapter 11, the rapidly growing baby brain needs age-specific templates in fine age intervals which can offer an accurate reference for image registration and segmentation. Infant-specific brain parcellations are also needed to provide appropriate definitions of brain nodes in different developmental stages. In terms of the edge definition, dMRI-based tractography of infants is challenging because of the dynamic water content, low anisotropy, and increased risk of motion artifacts of neonatal brain imaging. Recent technical improvements about this issue have been introduced in Chapter 1. Additionally, the detection of potential white matter connections based on dMRI data in baby brain is also impeded by the low fractional anisotropy of the cortical regions and the dense axons running parallel to the cortical surface. This bias could be ameliorated by dilation of cortical gray matter atlases into white matter voxels when obtaining network connections. However, caveats should be kept in mind that the reconstructed fiber streamlines are highly dependent on the methodological parameters and may contain many invalid fiber bundles. For functional connections, several baby-specific issues also exist. The frequency profiles of functional bold signal fluctuations exhibit individual differences that are related to behavioral performance in 1-year-old infants (Alcauter et al., 2015). Meaningful functional connectivity patterns can be derived using frequency bands that are different from adults. Besides, the infant brain exhibits age-specific changes in neurovascular coupling. The detailed effects of these changes on the resting-state functional connectivity of the baby brain still require future studies (Graham et al., 2015b).

8. Concluding remarks

In this chapter, we emphasized developmental connectomics, which provides an unprecedented computational framework by effectively integrating multimodal and multiscale brain connectivity information. Connectomics significantly contributes to our understanding of early brain development. Notably, the study of baby brain network development is still in its infancy. Significant scientific challenges are to understand how the brain network organization formation of brain network organization; how the dynamic changes in brain networks, both structurally and functionally, reflect the underlying neural and metabolic developmental processes; how the changing patterns converge across different scales from the microscale of individual neurons to the macroscale of whole-brain recordings; and how the structural and functional networks interact with each other; as well as how the developmental connectomic changes interact with genetic and environmental factors to impact cognitive development, learning, and skill acquisition. Further elaboration of the principles of brain connectome development may significantly contribute to deeper understanding of cognitive and behavioral development in later life and the biological mechanisms of developmental disorders.

References

Achard, S., Bullmore, E., 2007. Efficiency and cost of economical brain functional networks. PLoS Comput. Biol. 3 (2), e17.

Alcauter, S., Lin, W., Smith, J.K., et al., 2014. Development of thalamocortical connectivity during infancy and its cognitive correlations. J. Neurosci. 34 (27), 9067–9075.

Alcauter, S., Lin, W., Smith, J.K., et al., 2015. Frequency of spontaneous BOLD signal shifts during infancy and correlates with cognitive performance. Dev. Cogn. Neurosci. 12, 40–50.

Ball, G., Boardman, J.P., Aljabar, P., et al., 2013. The influence of preterm birth on the developing thalamocortical connectome. Cortex 49 (6), 1711–1721.

Ball, G., Aljabar, P., Zebari, S., et al., 2014. Rich-club organization of the newborn human brain. Proc. Natl. Acad. Sci. U. S. A. 111 (20), 7456–7461.

Ball, G., Pazderova, L., Chew, A., et al., 2015. Thalamocortical connectivity predicts cognition in children born preterm. Cereb. Cortex 25 (11), 4310–4318.

Batalle, D., Eixarch, E., Figueras, F., et al., 2012. Altered small-world topology of structural brain networks in infants with intrauterine growth restriction and its association with later neurodevelopmental outcome. Neuroimage 60 (2), 1352–1366.

Batalle, D., Hughes, E.J., Zhang, H., et al., 2017. Early development of structural networks and the impact of prematurity on brain connectivity. Neuroimage 149, 379–392.

Berchicci, M., Tamburro, G., Comani, S., 2015. The intrahemispheric functional properties of the developing sensorimotor cortex are influenced by maturation. Front. Hum. Neurosci. 9, 39.

Biswal, B.B., Mennes, M., Zuo, X.N., et al., 2010. Toward discovery science of human brain function. Proc. Natl. Acad. Sci. U. S. A. 107 (10), 4734–4739.

Brown, C.J., Miller, S.P., Booth, B.G., et al., 2014. Structural network analysis of brain development in young preterm neonates. Neuroimage 101, 667–680.

Bullmore, E.T., Bassett, D.S., 2011. Brain graphs: graphical models of the human brain connectome. Annu. Rev. Clin. Psychol. 7, 113–140.

Bullmore, E., Sporns, O., 2009. Complex brain networks: graph theoretical analysis of structural and functional systems. Nat. Rev. Neurosci. 10 (3), 186–198.

Bullmore, E., Sporns, O., 2012. The economy of brain network organization. Nat. Rev. Neurosci. 13 (5), 336–349.

Cao, M., Huang, H., Peng, Y., Dong, Q., He, Y., 2016. Toward developmental connectomics of the human brain. Front. Neuroanat. 10, 25.

Cao, M., Huang, H., He, Y., 2017a. Developmental connectomics from infancy through early childhood. Trends Neurosci. 40 (8), 494–506.

Cao, M., He, Y., Dai, Z., et al., 2017b. Early development of functional network segregation revealed by connectomic analysis of the preterm human brain. Cereb. Cortex 27 (3), 1949–1963.

Chugani, H.T., 1998. A critical period of brain development: studies of cerebral glucose utilization with PET. Prev. Med. 27 (2), 184–188.

De Asis-Cruz, J., Donofrio, M.T., Vezina, G., Limperopoulos, C., 2018. Aberrant brain functional connectivity in newborns with congenital heart disease before cardiac surgery. Neuroimage Clin 17, 31–42.

Di Martino, A., Fair Damien, A., Kelly, C., et al., 2014. Unraveling the Miswired connectome: a developmental perspective. Neuron 83 (6), 1335–1353.

Fan, Y., Shi, F., Smith, J.K., Lin, W., Gilmore, J.H., Shen, D., 2011. Brain anatomical networks in early human brain development. Neuroimage 54 (3), 1862–1871.

Finn, E.S., Shen, X., Scheinost, D., et al., 2015. Functional connectome fingerprinting: identifying individuals using patterns of brain connectivity. Nat. Neurosci. 18 (11), 1664–1671.

Fransson, P., Skiold, B., Horsch, S., et al., 2007. Resting-state networks in the infant brain. Proc. Natl. Acad. Sci. U. S. A. 104 (39), 15531–15536.

Fransson, P., Aden, U., Blennow, M., Lagercrantz, H., 2011. The functional architecture of the infant brain as revealed by resting-state fMRI. Cereb. Cortex 21 (1), 145–154.

Freedman, L., 1977. A set of measures of centrality based on betweenness. Sociometry 40, 35–41.

Friston, K.J., 1994. Functional and effective connectivity in neuroimaging: a synthesis. Hum. Brain Mapp. 2 (1–2), 56–78.

Gao, W., Gilmore, J.H., Giovanello, K.S., et al., 2011. Temporal and spatial evolution of brain network topology during the first two years of life. PLoS One 6 (9), e25278.

Gao, W., Elton, A., Zhu, H., et al., 2014. Intersubject variability of and genetic effects on the brain's functional connectivity during infancy. J. Neurosci. 34 (34), 11288–11296.

Gao, W., Alcauter, S., Elton, A., et al., 2015a. Functional network development during the first year: relative sequence and socioeconomic correlations. Cereb. Cortex 25 (9), 2919–2928.

Gao, W., Alcauter, S., Smith, J.K., Gilmore, J.H., Lin, W., 2015b. Development of human brain cortical network architecture during infancy. Brain Struct. Funct. 220 (2), 1173–1186.

Gao, W., Lin, W., Grewen, K., Gilmore, J.H., 2016. Functional connectivity of the infant human brain: plastic and modifiable. Neuroscientist 23, 169–184.

Geng, X., Li, G., Lu, Z., et al., 2016. Structural and maturational covariance in early childhood brain development. Cereb. Cortex 27, 1795–1807.

Girvan, M., Newman, M.E., 2002. Community structure in social and biological networks. Proc. Natl. Acad. Sci. U. S. A. 99 (12), 7821–7826.

Gong, G., He, Y., Concha, L., et al., 2009. Mapping anatomical connectivity patterns of human cerebral cortex using in vivo diffusion tensor imaging tractography. Cereb. Cortex 19 (3), 524–536.

Graham, A.M., Pfeifer, J.H., Fisher, P.A., Carpenter, S., Fair, D.A., 2015a. Early life stress is associated with default system integrity and emotionality during infancy. J. Child Psychol. Psychiatry 56 (11), 1212–1222.

Graham, A.M., Pfeifer, J.H., Fisher, P.A., Lin, W., Gao, W., Fair, D.A., 2015b. The potential of infant fMRI research and the study of early life stress as a promising exemplar. Dev. Cogn. Neurosci. 12, 12–39.

Graham, A.M., Buss, C., Rasmussen, J.M., et al., 2016. Implications of newborn amygdala connectivity for fear and cognitive development at 6-months-of-age. Dev. Cogn. Neurosci. 18, 12–25.

Grewen, K., Salzwedel, A.P., Gao, W., 2015. Functional connectivity disruption in neonates with prenatal marijuana exposure. Front. Hum. Neurosci. 9, 601.

Hagmann, P., Kurant, M., Gigandet, X., et al., 2007. Mapping human whole-brain structural networks with diffusion MRI. PLoS One 2 (7), e597.

Hagmann, P., Sporns, O., Madan, N., et al., 2010. White matter maturation reshapes structural connectivity in the late developing human brain. Proc. Natl. Acad. Sci. U. S. A. 107 (44), 19067–19072.

He, Y., Evans, A., 2010. Graph theoretical modeling of brain connectivity. Curr. Opin. Neurol. 23 (4), 341–350.

He, Y., Chen, Z.J., Evans, A.C., 2007. Small-world anatomical networks in the human brain revealed by cortical thickness from MRI. Cereb. Cortex 17 (10), 2407–2419.

Huang, H., Shu, N., Mishra, V., et al., 2015. Development of human brain structural networks through infancy and childhood. Cereb. Cortex 25 (5), 1389–1404.

Jakab, A., Schwartz, E., Kasprian, G., et al., 2014. Fetal functional imaging portrays heterogeneous development of emerging human brain networks. Front. Hum. Neurosci. 8, 852.

Keehn, B., Wagner, J.B., Tager-Flusberg, H., Nelson, C.A., 2013. Functional connectivity in the first year of life in infants at-risk for autism: a preliminary near-infrared spectroscopy study. Front. Hum. Neurosci. 7, 444.

Kelly, C., Biswal, B.B., Craddock, R.C., Castellanos, F.X., Milham, M.P., 2012. Characterizing variation in the functional connectome: promise and pitfalls. Trends Cogn. Sci. 16 (3), 181–188.

Keunen, K., Counsell, S.J., Benders, M., 2017. The emergence of functional architecture during early brain development. Neuroimage 160, 2–14.

Kim, Y.D., Park, J.H., Yang, S.H., et al., 2013. Pain assessment in brain tumor patients after elective craniotomy. Brain Tumor. Res. Treat. 1 (1), 24–27.

Kim, D.J., Davis, E.P., Sandman, C.A., et al., 2014. Longer gestation is associated with more efficient brain networks in preadolescent children. Neuroimage 100, 619–627.

Kim, D.J., Davis, E.P., Sandman, C.A., et al., 2016. Prenatal maternal cortisol has sex-specific associations with child brain network properties. Cereb. Cortex 27, 5230–5241.

Kuhn-Popp, N., Kristen, S., Paulus, M., Meinhardt, J., Sodian, B., 2016. Left hemisphere EEG coherence in infancy predicts infant declarative pointing and preschool epistemic language. Soc. Neurosci. 11 (1), 49–59.

Kwon, S.H., Scheinost, D., Lacadie, C., et al., 2015. Adaptive mechanisms of developing brain: cerebral lateralization in the prematurely-born. Neuroimage 108, 144–150.

Latora, V., Marchiori, M., 2001. Efficient behavior of small-world networks. Phys. Rev. Lett. 87 (19), 198701.

Lee, S.J., Steiner, R.J., Luo, S., et al., 2015. Quantitative tract-based white matter heritability in twin neonates. Neuroimage 111, 123–135.

Lerch, J.P., Worsley, K., Shaw, W.P., et al., 2006. Mapping anatomical correlations across cerebral cortex (MACACC) using cortical thickness from MRI. Neuroimage 31 (3), 993–1003.

Lewis, J.D., Evans, A.C., Pruett, J.R., et al., 2014. Network inefficiencies in autism spectrum disorder at 24 months. Transl. Psychiatry 4, e388.

Li, Z., Santhanam, P., Coles, C.D., et al., 2013. Prenatal cocaine exposure alters functional activation in the ventral prefrontal cortex and its structural connectivity with the amygdala. Psychiatry Res. 213 (1), 47–55.

Liang, X., Zou, Q., He, Y., Yang, Y., 2013. Coupling of functional connectivity and regional cerebral blood flow reveals a physiological basis for network hubs of the human brain. Proc. Natl. Acad. Sci. U. S. A. 110 (5), 1929–1934.

Micheloyannis, S., Pachou, E., Stam, C.J., Vourkas, M., Erimaki, S., Tsirka, V., 2006. Using graph theoretical analysis of multi channel EEG to evaluate the neural efficiency hypothesis. Neurosci. Lett. 402 (3), 273–277.

Mori, S., van Zijl, P.C., 2002. Fiber tracking: principles and strategies—a technical review. NMR Biomed. 15 (7–8), 468–480.

Mueller, S., Wang, D., Fox, M.D., et al., 2013. Individual variability in functional connectivity architecture of the human brain. Neuron 77 (3), 586–595.

Newman, M.E., 2006. Modularity and community structure in networks. Proc. Natl. Acad. Sci. U. S. A. 103 (23), 8577–8582.

Nie, J., Li, G., Wang, L., et al., 2014. Longitudinal development of cortical thickness, folding, and fiber density networks in the first 2 years of life. Hum. Brain Mapp. 35 (8), 3726–3737.

Niu, H., He, Y., 2014. Resting-state functional brain connectivity: lessons from functional near-infrared spectroscopy. Neuroscientist 20 (2), 173–188.

Ouyang, M., Cheng, H., Mishra, V., et al., 2016. Atypical age-dependent effects of autism on white matter microstructure in children of 2-7 years. Hum. Brain Mapp. 37 (2), 819–832.

Qiu, A., Anh, T.T., Li, Y., et al., 2015. Prenatal maternal depression alters amygdala functional connectivity in 6-month-old infants. Transl. Psychiatry 5, e508.

Rajasilta, O., Tuulari, J.J., Bjornsdotter, M., et al., 2020. Resting-state networks of the neonate brain identified using independent component analysis. Dev. Neurobiol. 80 (3–4), 111–125.

Rubinov, M., Sporns, O., 2010. Complex network measures of brain connectivity: uses and interpretations. Neuroimage 52 (3), 1059–1069.

Salzwedel, A.P., Grewen, K.M., Vachet, C., Gerig, G., Lin, W., Gao, W., 2015. Prenatal drug exposure affects neonatal brain functional connectivity. J. Neurosci. 35 (14), 5860–5869.

Scheinost, D., Kwon, S.H., Shen, X., et al., 2016. Preterm birth alters neonatal, functional rich club organization. Brain Struct. Funct. 221 (6), 3211–3222.

Shi, F., Salzwedel, A.P., Lin, W., Gilmore, J.H., Gao, W., 2017. Functional brain parcellations of the infant brain and the associated developmental trends. Cereb. Cortex 28 (4), 1358–1368.

Smyser, C.D., Inder, T.E., Shimony, J.S., et al., 2010. Longitudinal analysis of neural network development in preterm infants. Cereb. Cortex 20 (12), 2852–2862.

Smyser, C.D., Snyder, A.Z., Shimony, J.S., Mitra, A., Inder, T.E., Neil, J.J., 2016. Resting-state network complexity and magnitude are reduced in prematurely born infants. Cereb. Cortex 26 (1), 322–333.

Soe, N.N., Wen, D.J., Poh, J.S., et al., 2016. Pre- and post-natal maternal depressive symptoms in relation with infant frontal function, connectivity, and behaviors. PLoS One 11 (4), e0152991.

Song, S., Miller, K.D., Abbott, L.F., 2000. Competitive Hebbian learning through spike-timing-dependent synaptic plasticity. Nat. Neurosci. 3 (9), 919–926.

Sporns, O., 2011. The human connectome: a complex network. Ann. N. Y. Acad. Sci. 1224, 109–125.

Sporns, O., 2013. Network attributes for segregation and integration in the human brain. Curr. Opin. Neurobiol. 23 (2), 162–171.

Sporns, O., Tononi, G., Kötter, R., 2005. The human connectome: a structural description of the human brain. PLoS Comput. Biol. 1 (4), e42.

Stam, C.J., 2010. Characterization of anatomical and functional connectivity in the brain: a complex networks perspective. Int. J. Psychophysiol. 77 (3), 186–194.

Thomason, M.E., Brown, J.A., Dassanayake, M.T., et al., 2014. Intrinsic functional brain architecture derived from graph theoretical analysis in the human fetus. PLoS One 9 (5), e94423.

Thompson, D.K., Chen, J., Beare, R., et al., 2016. Structural connectivity relates to perinatal factors and functional impairment at 7 years in children born very preterm. Neuroimage 134, 328–337.

Tomasi, D., Wang, G.J., Volkow, N.D., 2013. Energetic cost of brain functional connectivity. Proc. Natl. Acad. Sci. U. S. A. 110 (33), 13642–13647.

Toth, B., Urban, G., Haden, G.P., et al., 2017. Large-scale network organization of EEG functional connectivity in newborn infants. Hum. Brain Mapp. 38 (8), 4019–4033.

Tymofiyeva, O., Hess, C.P., Ziv, E., et al., 2012. Towards the "baby connectome": mapping the structural connectivity of the newborn brain. PLoS One 7 (2), e31029.

Tymofiyeva, O., Hess, C.P., Ziv, E., et al., 2013. A DTI-based template-free cortical connectome study of brain maturation. PLoS One 8 (5), e63310.

van den Heuvel, M.P., Sporns, O., 2011. Rich-club organization of the human connectome. J. Neurosci. 31 (44), 15775–15786.

van den Heuvel, M.P., Sporns, O., 2013. Network hubs in the human brain. Trends Cogn. Sci. 17 (12), 683–696.

van den Heuvel, M.P., Kahn, R.S., Goni, J., Sporns, O., 2012. High-cost, high-capacity backbone for global brain communication. Proc. Natl. Acad. Sci. U. S. A. 109 (28), 11372–11377.

van den Heuvel, M.P., Kersbergen, K.J., de Reus, M.A., et al., 2015. The neonatal connectome during preterm brain development. Cereb. Cortex 25 (9), 3000–3013.

Wang, Z., Dai, Z., Gong, G., Zhou, C., He, Y., 2015. Understanding structural-functional relationships in the human brain: a large-scale network perspective. Neuroscientist 21 (3), 290–305.

Watts, D.J., Strogatz, S.H., 1998. Collective dynamics of 'small-world' networks. Nature 393 (6684), 440–442.

Wee, C.Y., Tuan, T.A., Broekman, B.F., et al., 2016. Neonatal neural networks predict children behavioral profiles later in life. Hum. Brain Mapp. 38 (3), 1362–1373.

Wilcox, T., Biondi, M., 2015. fNIRS in the developmental sciences. Wiley Interdiscip. Rev. Cogn. Sci. 6 (3), 263–283.

Xia, M., He, Y., 2017. Functional connectomics from a "big data" perspective. Neuroimage 160, 152–167.

Xu, Y., Cao, M., Liao, X., et al., 2019. Development and emergence of individual variability in the functional connectivity architecture of the preterm human brain. Cereb. Cortex 29 (10), 4208–4222.

Yap, P.T., Fan, Y., Chen, Y., Gilmore, J.H., Lin, W., Shen, D., 2011. Development trends of white matter connectivity in the first years of life. PLoS One 6 (9), e24678.
Zhao, T., Xu, Y., He, Y., 2019a. Graph theoretical modeling of baby brain networks. Neuroimage 185, 711–727.
Zhao, T., Mishra, V., Jeon, T., et al., 2019b. Structural network maturation of the preterm human brain. Neuroimage 185, 699–710.
Zhong, S., He, Y., Gong, G., 2015. Convergence and divergence across construction methods for human brain white matter networks: an assessment based on individual differences. Hum. Brain Mapp. 36 (5), 1995–2013.
Zhou, S., Li, J., Gilroy, K.D., et al., 2016. Facile synthesis of silver nanocubes with sharp corners and edges in an aqueous solution. ACS Nano 10 (11), 9861–9870.

SECTION 3

Electrophysiology

CHAPTER

MEG systems for young children and recent developments of pediatric MEG

15

Christos Papadelis

Division of Newborn Medicine, Boston Children's Hospital, Harvard Medical School, Boston, MA, United States; Jane and John Justin Neurosciences Center, Cook Children's Health Care System, Fort Worth, TX, United States; School of Medicine, Texas Christian University and University of North Texas Health Science Center, Fort Worth, TX, United States; Department of Bioengineering, University of Texas at Arlington, Arlington, TX, United States

1. Introduction

Magnetoencephalography (MEG) is a neuroimaging technique that allows the noninvasive recording of the human brain's magnetic activity (Hämäläinen et al., 1993; Boto et al., 2018). Its principle is based on the phenomenon of electromagnetic induction, according to which every changing magnetic field generates, in a nearby coil, an electrical current (Ulaby, 2007). The amplitude of this current is instantaneously proportional to the magnetic induction. Several neurons, which are almost simultaneously active in a focal area of the brain, generate postsynaptic currents in the apical dendrites of the cortical pyramidal cells (Murakami and Okada, 2006). These currents generate a magnetic field that is measurable outside the human scalp. Recent studies have shown that action potentials can also contribute to the generation of the MEG signal (Kimura et al., 2008; Papadelis et al., 2012).

The magnetic activity generated by the human brain is weak: it is several magnitudes weaker than the ambient electromagnetic noise and weaker than the geomagnetic noise of the earth. The most traditional means to protect the MEG recordings from the ambient electromagnetic noise of the laboratory is by performing them inside protected environments, called Magnetically Shielded Rooms (MSR), which are made of different layers of mu-metal and aluminum. MEG recordings can either be performed in a seated or supine position. The subjects either sit comfortably in a specially designed armchair or lay down on a bed placing their heads inside the helmet that accommodates the inductions coils (either magnetometers or gradiometers) that measure the magnetic activity generated by the human brain. Yet, these coils (i.e., pick-up coils) are barely sensitive enough to measure the weak magnetic activity of the human brain. Superconducting quantum interference devices (SQUIDs), which are specially designed devices able to measure weak signals, are connected to the pick-up coils (Jaklevic et al., 1964). The SQUID devices must operate in temperatures close to absolute zero. For this reason, SQUIDs are placed inside a thermo-shielded tank that is filled with liquid helium. The liquid helium evaporates with time, so the MEG requires frequent refills (~100 L per week), though most modern MEG systems are nowadays equipped with closed-looped liquid helium recycling systems.

Handbook of Pediatric Brain Imaging. https://doi.org/10.1016/B978-0-12-816633-8.00003-X

MEG equipment has been exclusively designed for adult's use; several MEG studies have been done so far in pediatric cohorts, even infants, using adult MEG systems (for a review, see Chen et al., 2019). These recordings were performed by either placing the child's head at the center of an adult MEG helmet or in such a way that the brain area of interest was as close as possible to the MEG sensors. Yet, these strategies lead to nonoptimal or sometimes even inadequate MEG recordings, particularly for young children and infants, since the neural generators are far from the sensors and thus the MEG signal has low to signal-to-noise (SNR). To overcome this limitation, a few MEG systems especially designed for pediatric use became available in the last few years (Roberts et al., 2014; Okada et al., 2006, 2016; Johnson et al., 2010). Two of these systems, called BabySQUID and BabyMEG, have been accommodated at Boston Children's Hospital in the last few years. The systems were designed for children up to 3 years of age and were both used in clinical practice, mostly in the pre-surgical evaluation of young children with drug resistant epilepsy (DRE) undergoing surgery, as well as in research. Here, we will describe the operation of these facilities, present findings of the source localization of the epileptogenic zone in infants and young children with epilepsy and of mapping the eloquent motor cortex in typically developing (TD) children.

2. Pediatric MEG facilities

MEG recordings in children require children friendly environments. Our facilities are well-equipped and decorated to accommodate the needs of families with young children, our staff is well-trained to interact with children and their parents, and necessary toys and distraction tools are available in the facility.

2.1 BabySQUID

The BabySQUID system (Fig. 1A) is a partial coverage MEG system (Tristan Inc., San Diego, CA, USA) that accommodates 76 axial gradiometers within an oval region of interest (ROI) of 12–14 cm in diameter (Okada et al., 2006). This ROI is sufficient to fully cover one of the two hemispheres of an infant or a large portion of the frontal, temporal, and parietal areas in a child up to 4 years of age. In this system, the gap between the detection coils and the headrest, where the child's head is placed for testing, is just 7–10 mm, almost half the gap of an adult MEG system. Such a configuration increases the SNR of the MEG signal by a factor of ~4.

The system is installed into a one-layer MSR. During the recordings, the children lay down on a specially designed bed placing their head next to the headrest (Fig. 1B). The recordings are performed with a sampling rate of 1024 Hz. The coregistration between the locations of MEG sensors with respect to the child's head anatomy is performed using an in-house procedure that combines the use of a 6-degree-of-freedom commercial tracking device (FASTRAK, Polhemus Inc., USA) and an optical tracking system (Polaris, Northern Digital Inc., Canada). Together with MEG, we often record simultaneously electroencephalography (EEG), electrocardiography (ECG), and electromyography (EMG). The EEG signals are recorded either with gold-cap electrodes placed according to the 10–20 international system (Fig. 1B) or with a 128-channel EEG system (ANT-Neuro, Netherlands) using caps suitable for toddlers and children. The ECG and EMG recordings are performed with conventional bipolar leads, which are placed on the child's chest and chin respectively. ECG and EMG signals are used for

FIG. 1

BabySQUID facility. (A) The facility is equipped with toys and distraction tools for children. (B) The children lay down on a specially designed bed placing their head next to the MEG headrest. EEG recordings are often performed simultaneously with the MEG.

removing biological artifacts from the MEG and EEG recordings (Klados et al., 2011; Papadelis et al., 2018).

2.2 BabyMEG

The BabyMEG system (Fig. 2A) is a whole-head MEG system that accommodates an array of 375 magnetometers (Fig. 2B). The helmet has been designed for heads up to 95% of 36-month old boys in USA. The unique design of BabyMEG allows the magnetometers to be located as close as possible to the scalp maximizing the SNR of the MEG signal. The density array is the highest possible considering the diameter of detection coils and the limited space dictated by the small helmet size. Such a configuration maximizes the spatial resolution that can be achieved with infants and young children. More details about the hardware design of the BabyMEG system can be found elsewhere (Okada et al., 2016).

The BabyMEG is installed inside a two-layer MSR. The MSR is located in close proximity to the Neonatal Intensive Care Unit (NICU) in a facility that has been designed for studying both inpatients and outpatients as well as TD neonates, infants, and toddlers. The MSR is equipped with adjustable lighting and an audiovisual communication system that allows communication with the technical staff seated outside. During the recordings, the children lay down on a specially designed bed placing their head inside the MEG helmet (Fig. 2C). The recordings are performed using a sampling rate of 1024 Hz. The coregistration is performed using an in-house procedure that involves four head position indicator (HPI) coils and a laser scanner (Polaris, Northern Digital Inc., Canada) (Fig. 3). High-density EEG

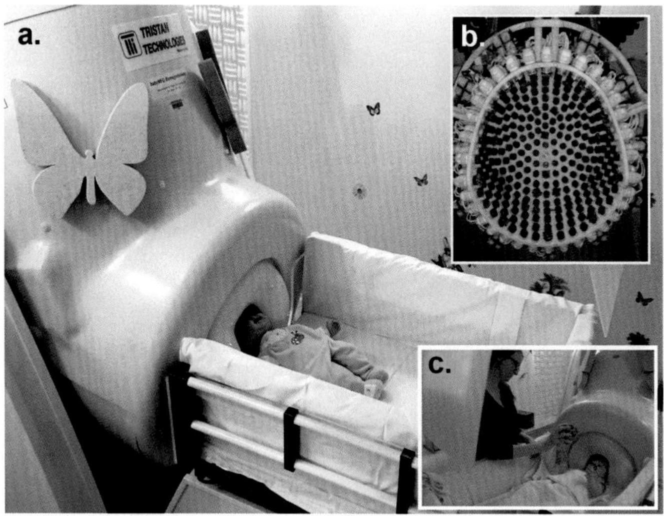

FIG. 2

The BabyMEG facility. (A) Children lay down on a specially designed bed and place their heads inside the BabyMEG helmet. (B) The BabyMEG sensor array that accommodates 375 magnetometers in a helmet designed for heads up to 95% of 36-month-old boys. (C) For distraction purposes, we display cartoon videos in a screen placed in front of the children while laying down on the bed.

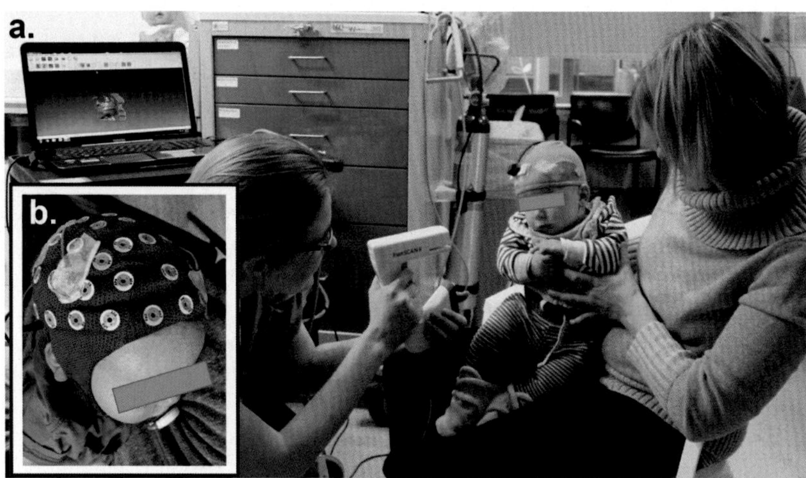

FIG. 3

Coregistration process. (A) The child's head shape is scanned with the FastScan near-infrared system. To avoid light absorption from child's hairs, we use a specially designed cap that has the ability to reflect the infrared spectrum light emitted from the FastScan system. At the upper left side on the computer screen, we see the reconstructed head surface of the child. (B) HD-EEG caps that accommodate 64 channels are placed on child's head. Conductivity between the child's head and EEG sensors is achieved by an electrolytes gel that is placed in each of these electrodes using a flat-tip syringe.

(HD-EEG) recordings are often performed simultaneously using a 64 channels eego™mylab EEG system (ANT-Neuro, Netherlands) with caps suitable for infants and toddlers (Fig. 3A).

3. Experimental procedures

Pediatric MEG recordings are challenging particularly for toddlers and young children. The challenges refer mostly to: (i) the ability of children to stay still for prolonged periods of time during the recordings; (ii) their limited span of attention to be engaged in active tasks; and (iii) the difficulty to follow instructions regarding the experimental procedures (e.g., coregistration process, placement of HD-EEG cap and electrodes for peripheral recordings, and claustrophobia in the MSR). From our own experience, school children and adolescents are usually able to follow instructions with the exception of children with mental or developmental disorders. MEG recordings performed in infants are relatively easy if the infant goes to sleep.

Our team follows a process that helps the infants to go to sleep during the recordings: we usually: (i) ask the parents to lightly sleep deprive their infant (i.e., waking up the infant earlier before their visit, not allowing sleeping in the car during the trip to the facility); (ii) we ask the parents to feed the infant just before the recording starts; (iii) we play relaxing music in the MSR; and (iv) we allow one parent to be inside the MSR during the recording to ease the infant. We usually perform the placement of HPI coils and HD-EEG cap while the infant is still awake. We then ask the parents to feed the baby. When the infant goes to sleep, we perform the co-registration, inject the conductive gel in all EEG electrodes (if simultaneous recordings are performed), place the infant's head inside the MEG helmet, and start the recordings.

By following this approach, we manage to collect sleep data for at least 30 min from each participant. Such recordings allow us to record interictal epileptiform discharges (IEDs) from children with epilepsy. We also record event-related cortical responses, more specifically somatosensory evoked fields (SEFs) and motor evoked fields (MEFs). For SEFs, we record the cortical activity in response to stimuli delivered through thin elastic membranes attached to the distal, volar parts of infant's digits. The membranes are inflated with compressed air pulses through rigid plastic tubes using the Somatosensory Stimulus Generator (4D NeuroImaging Inc., CA). The skin at the tip of fingers is gently tapped. The compressed air pulses are released with an interstimulus interval of 1.5 ± 0.5 s following a pseudorandom order. The pressure of the tactile stimulator rises to 0.10 bar overpressure in 10 ms. Each finger receives at least 200 stimuli in total to ensure high SNR evoked responses. For MEFs, we ask the children to press a button every time a cartoon picture appears in a screen in front of them. To ensure precise synchronization of motor responses in time, we collect EMG data from the abductor pollicis brevis or accelerometry data from a sensor attached to their index finger. We ask the child to perform this task till we manage to collect at least 100 trials with satisfactory SNR.

4. MEG data analysis

For MEG data analysis, we follow the guidelines of the International Federation of Clinical Neurophysiology (Hari et al., 2018). We perform all preprocessing and analysis of MEG and EEG data using Brainstorm (Tadel et al., 2011). In order to localize the irritative zone in children with DRE undergoing surgery, we filter the data in the frequency band of 1–70 Hz, remove the DC component, and apply a notch filter at 60 Hz. We then identify IEDs (i.e., spikes and sharp waves) on EEG and MEG sensors and mark them as events in Brainstorm. In cases of several underlying sources, we perform a classification of the events in different groups based on the electric and magnetic topographic maps. Magnetic source imaging (MSI) is performed by using either the equivalent current dipole (ECD) or a distributed source localization method [e.g., Minimum Norm Estimates (MNE), dynamic Statistical Parametric Mapping (dSPM), standardized Low Resolution Electromagnetic Tomography (sLORETA), or a beamformer]. For the forward model, we reconstruct a realistic head model with Boundary Element Model (BEM) using OpenMEEG (Gramfort et al., 2010). More details about the procedures we follow for MSI of epileptogenic activity can be found in our previous studies (Papadelis et al., 2013; Tamilia et al., 2019).

We also use MEG for the localization of the eloquent areas, particularly the primary somatosensory (Papadelis et al., 2014, 2017) and motor areas (Gaetz and Papadelis, 2020). For the SEF analysis, we filter the data in frequencies between 1 and 100 Hz, in addition to DC removal and notch filter at 60 Hz and perform MSI using MNE. For the MEF analysis, we filter the data between 1 and 100 Hz and estimate the time-frequency plots using Morlet transforms. Localization of the primary motor cortex is performed using a beamformer [i.e., Linear Constrained Minimum Variance (LCMV)].

5. Localization of the irritative zone in children with DRE

For children with DRE, MEG is predominantly used for the localization of the irritative zone, the brain area that generates the IEDs. The addition of MEG to the clinical evaluation of children with DRE can help to generate a hypothesis regarding the epileptogenic foci and may improve the postsurgical outcomes for these patients. Here, we present representative data from two young children with DRE undergoing presurgical evaluation at Boston Children's Hospital using the BabyMEG system. Fig. 4 shows the MEG recordings from a 2-year-old boy with focal cortical dysplasia (FCD) and DRE performed using the BabyMEG system. We observed frequent IEDs mostly in magnetometers covering the left frontal areas (Fig. 4). MSI performed with dSPM showed an epileptogenic focus laterally to the frontal horn of the left lateral ventricle (Fig. 5A). The focus was on the vicinity of focal cortical dysplasia in conjunction with noticeable hypometabolism observed with positron emission tomography (PET) (Fig. 5B). Epilepsy neurosurgery was performed guided by these findings and the child remains seizure free 1 year after surgery (Engel score: 1). Fig. 6 presents a portion of MEG recordings from a 9-month-old boy with DRE. We observed frequent IEDs at magnetometers covering areas of the right temporal cortex (highlighted magnetometers at inner upper right panel). The child had daily seizures of left arm elevation and shoulder twitch. MSI with ECD showed a tight cluster of dipoles with the same orientation located on the vicinity of a cortical dysplastic lesion at the right temporal lobe (Fig. 7).

6. Localization of somatosensory and motor areas in TD children

We record SEFs in a regular basis as part of the presurgical evaluation for children with DRE undergoing surgery. Fig. 8 presents the SEFs from a 5-year-old TD girl elicited by the stimulation of the right thumb with compressed air puffs. Recordings were performed while the child was sleeping. MSI at the

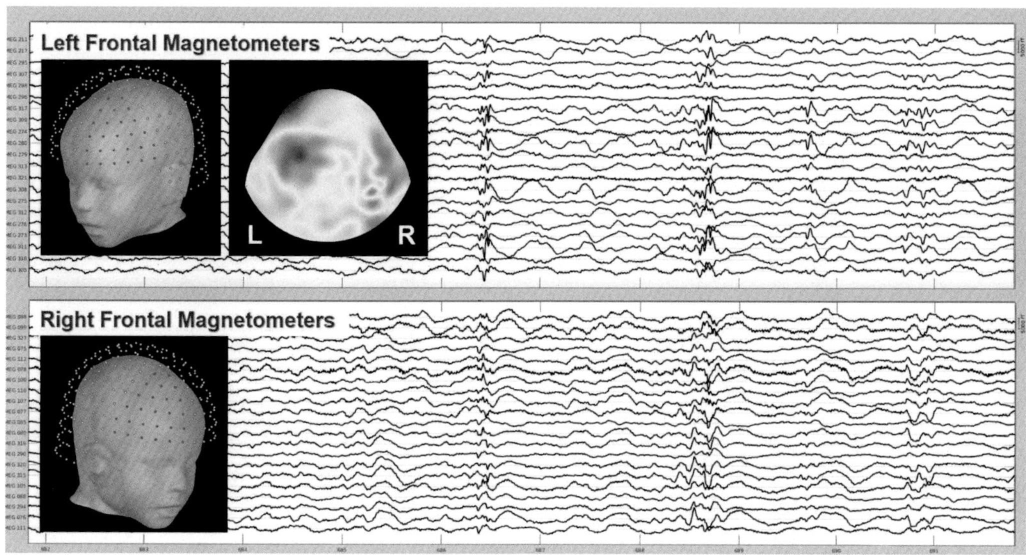

FIG. 4

MEG recordings with the BabyMEG system from a 2-year-old boy with DRE. Upper and lower panels show the signals (10 s) recorded from magnetometers covering the left and right frontal brain areas respectively. The relative locations of magnetometers with respect to the child's head anatomy are shown in the inner panels. Topographic mapping at the peak of the IEDs shows a clear change in the magnetic influx and outflux which indicates a possible underlying source at the left frontal areas.

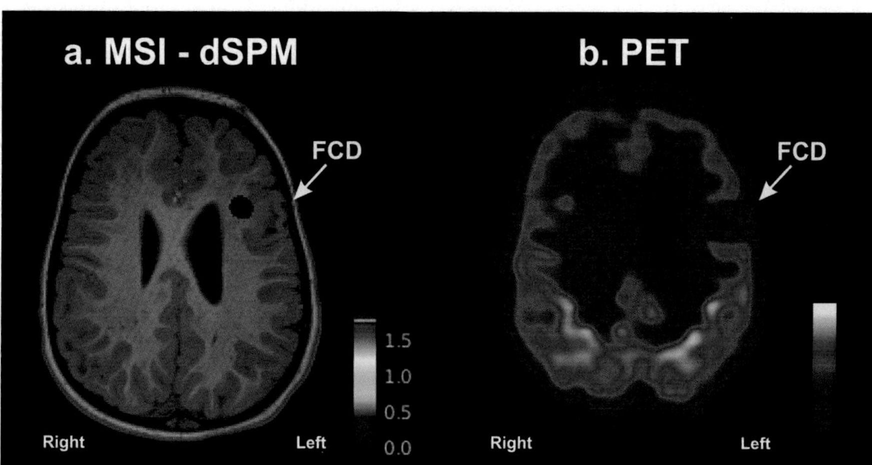

FIG. 5

MSI results for a 2-year-old boy with FCD. (A) MSI using dSPM thresholded at 2. FCD arrow indicates the location of the cortical lesion at the left frontal areas. (B) PET results for the same patient showing a hypometabolism at the same area where MEG indicates the location of the epileptogenic focus.

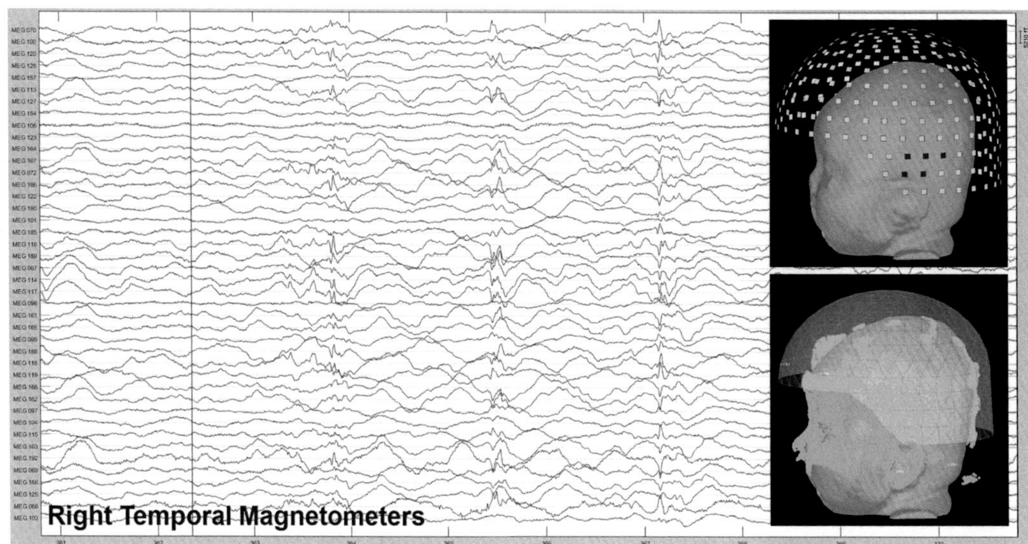

FIG. 6

MEG recordings from a 9-month-old boy with DRE. Recordings of magnetometers covering the right temporal areas are displayed (10 s). Upper inner panel shows the relative location of magnetometers with respect to the sensor array. Magnetometers with the highest rate of IEDs are highlighted (*red color*). Lower inner panel shows the co-registration results performed using the FastScan system.

peak of the first cortical response after the stimulus onset at ~60 ms revealed cortical activity located at the primary somatosensory cortex contralaterally to the stimulated hand (i.e., right thumb). These data indicate the feasibility of these recordings in young children and toddlers who are often uncooperative during neuroimaging studies. In contrast to the functional mapping of the somatosensory cortex, mapping of the primary motor cortex is more challenging since it involves repetitive active movements of extremities. Yet, with proper training of the research personnel and appropriate experimental designs, such recordings are possible in young children and toddlers. Fig. 9 shows the event-related desynchronization (ERD) of the mu-rhythm (8–13 Hz) from a 2-year-old TD boy due to finger movement. MSI with beamformer showed suppressed activity in the contralateral primary motor cortex starting 200 ms before the onset of the finger movement.

7. Discussion

Pediatric MEG is a promising noninvasive technology in clinical practice and research. MEG is being used increasingly in the preoperative evaluation of pediatric patients with MRE (Papadelis et al., 2013; Papadelis and Chen, 2020; Murakami et al., 2016; Pellegrino et al., 2018; Kim et al., 2016). Through the noninvasive detection of magnetic fields generated by abnormal interictal and ictal electromagnetic activity, MEG allows the accurate localization of the epileptogenic focus with MSI (Kim et al., 2016; Tamilia et al., 2019). MSI can thus obviate the need for invasive procedures in children with DRE or, in

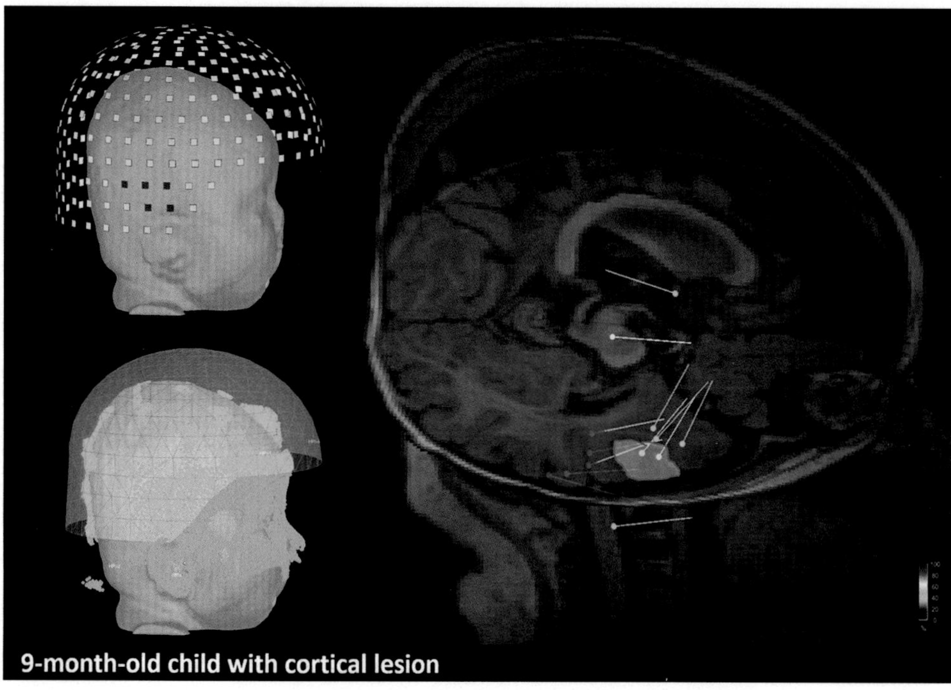

FIG. 7

MSI with ECDs on a 9-month-old child with DRE. ECD with a goodness-of-fit (GOF) >75% are overlayed on the child's T1 MRI. A cluster of dipoles is formulated on the vicinity of FCD highlighted with yellow.

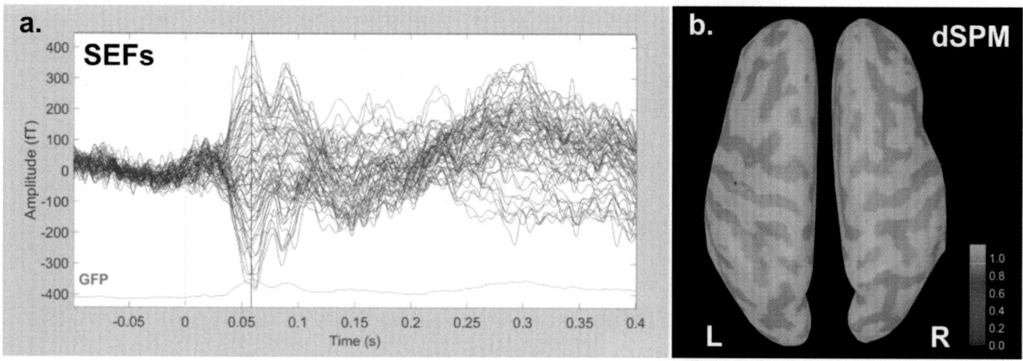

FIG. 8

SEFs from a 5-year-old TD girl. (A) SEFs elicited by the pneumatic stimulation of the right thumb (averaged signal of 200 trials). (B) MSI using dSPM at the peak of the first cortical response at 58.6 ms after the stimulus onset. MSI findings are overlaid on the cortical surface extracted from the child's head. L: left; R: Right.

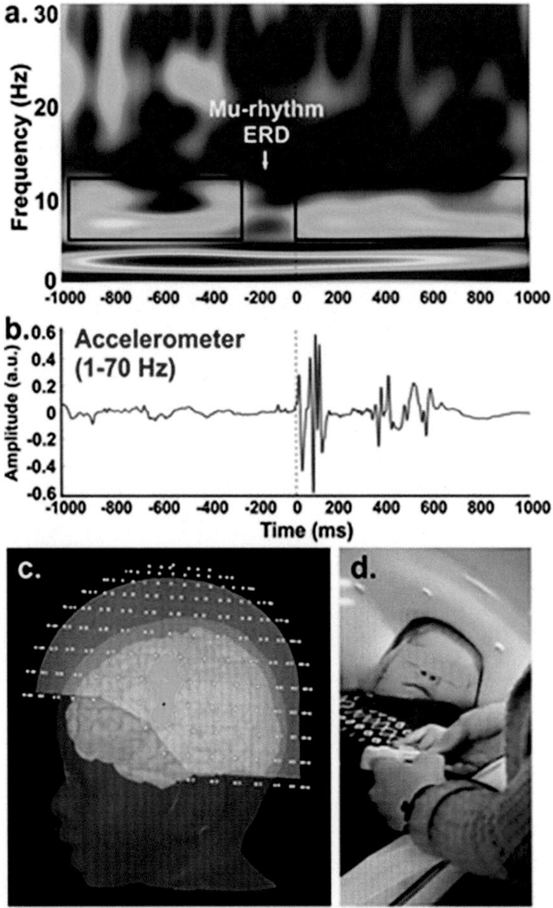

FIG. 9

Mu-rhythm suppression. (A) ERD of mu-rhythm (8–13 Hz) from a 2-year-old TD child before the movement onset. The ERD was estimated from a virtual channel placed on the contralateral primary motor cortex. The virtual channel was estimated using a beamformer (i.e., LCMV). (B) An accelerometer was connected on child's index finger in order to synchronize the onset of movements with millisecond precision. The signal is filtered in frequency band 1–70 Hz. (C) Localization of the virtual channel at the primary motor cortex contralateral to the stimulated right hand. (D) Experimental setup during which the child was pressing a button every time a cartoon picture was presented in a screen located in front of the child.

more complex clinical cases, can optimize their planning and potentially improve the surgical outcome for these patients (Rampp et al., 2019). MEG can be extremely useful in epilepsy patients with normal or inconclusive findings in their MRI scans (Ntolkeras et al., 2021; Ramachandran Nair et al., 2007); there is evidence that MEG can led to further reevaluation of MRI for undetected lesions after MEG data were considered in the interpretation of MRI findings (Moore et al., 2002). Several studies have also shown that MEG can detect and localize with high precision ictal activity from patients with DRE (Fujiwara et al., 2012; Alkawadri et al., 2018). Nevertheless, capturing ictal events with MEG can be difficult due to cooperation of the child, cost, and access to the facility. Although MEG is used more frequently in children with DRE undergoing surgery, a number of studies is increasing in patients with epilepsy not undergoing surgery. The goal of these studies is to identify the difference in function and basic patho-mechanism underlying the disease.

Pediatric MEG can be also useful in the presurgical mapping of eloquent areas (i.e., somatosensory, motor, auditory, visual, and language functional regions) for children undergoing brain surgery (e.g., children with DRE, children with low-grade brain tumors) or children with cerebral palsy (Papadelis et al., 2014, 2017). In these cases, eloquent areas may have migrated to other anatomical locations as a result of plasticity due to anatomical lesion or previous neurosurgery. Eloquent cortices should be protected to prevent paresis, aphasia, or visual loss and this becomes a critical issue if the epileptogenic zone is found close to these areas. Recent MEG studies have shown that MEG is also sensitive enough to detect more specific biomarkers of epilepsy, such as high frequency oscillations, though its use for this purpose in young children is still limited (Papadelis et al., 2016; Tamilia et al., 2017, 2020; Yin et al., 2019).

Based on recent advances in the field, we expect that the application of MEG in young children with epilepsy will accelerate during the coming years (Papadelis et al., 2015). Epilepsy surgery in young children with DRE is particularly important since it allows reversing psychological and social comorbidity responsible for dependence on family and society (Skirrow et al., 2011; Kossoff, 2011). Over the last decades, efficacy and safety of pediatric epilepsy surgery has been significantly improved (Widjaja et al., 2011); recent advances in pediatric MEG can significantly boost these efforts to increase the number of young children with DRE who are considered good candidates for epilepsy surgery.

MEG can also help studying infant and young children's brains offering complementary information for understanding the development of brain function beyond brain structure in pediatric populations. MEG has been so far used almost exclusively for assessing the brain activity of adults; few MEG studies have been used for studying the human brain development focusing mostly on examining the evolution of resting-state brain rhythms, as well as the auditory, somatosensory, and visual systems (for a review, see Chen et al., 2019; Papadelis and Chen, 2020). These studies can help expanding our understanding of human brain development during critical periods of time that happen early in life. Given the low success rate of neuroimaging studies in pediatric populations, MEG seems to be the most optimal neuroimaging technique for measuring whole-brain neural networks associated with basic and high-level neural networks in children.

Compared to other neuroimaging methods [i.e., high-density EEG (HD-EEG), functional MRI (fMRI), transcranial magnetic stimulation (TMS), and near infrared spectroscopy (fNIRS)], MEG presents a unique set of advantages which are significant in case of infants or young children: (i) MEG provides a direct measure of the neural activity (compared to fMRI or fNIRS that measure the brain's hemodynamic response); (ii) MEG does not apply any power into the brain (compared to fMRI or TMS that apply strong magnetic fields); (iii) MEG signals are reference free since they provide absolute measurements of the magnetic field produced by the brain, in contrast to EEG, which provides potential differences between two locations; (iv) MEG signals can be measured with a high density array of sensors (compared to HD-EEG that faces the problem of salt bridge between the electrodes); (v) MEG has a faster and easier preparation process; (vi) MEG is silent compared to fMRI providing an environment better suited for examining sensory, cognitive, and social processes; (vii) MEG measures the brain activity immediately after placing the child's head inside the special helmet, since there is no need to attach any sensors over the head like in EEG; (viii) MEG signals are not distorted by skull conductivity (Barth et al., 1986; Okada et al., 1999), like in EEG, and thus the MSI requires simpler head models; and (ix) MEG signals are less distorted than EEG by unfused regions of the cranial bone, such as fontanel or suture (Lew et al., 2013). Yet, MEG presents some limitations: (i) MEG recordings should be performed within an MSR limiting their duration in a clinical setup; (ii) MEG preferentially records activity from sources with tangential orientation (compared to EEG) while it is almost blind to deep thalamic sources or sources with radial orientation (Williamson and Kaufman, 1990); (iii) MEG is sensitive to electromagnetic noise from implanted devices (e.g., vagus nerve stimulation), metallic implants (e.g., shunt), and dental braces; and (iv) MEG is more expensive than EEG to setup and operate (the construction of MEG is ~50 times more expensive than the cost of setting up a HD-EEG facility).

In summary, MEG is a valuable modality with several advances compared to other neuroimaging techniques. MEG is particularly useful in the diagnosis and treatment of young children with epilepsy as well as in the study of normal human brain development. For children with DRE undergoing surgery, MEG can play critical role in the delineation of the irritative zone and eloquent cortex in lesional and nonlesional epilepsies. MEG findings could impact the patient's management in almost every single epilepsy case guiding the placement of intracranial EEG and potentially improving the surgical outcome of children with DRE. MEG can also increase the number of patients who can proceed to surgical treatment. The application of pediatric MEG would accelerate in the next few years as different types of pediatric systems are developed and more advanced data analysis methods would become available to clinicians and researchers.

References

Alkawadri, R., Burgess, R.C., Kakisaka, Y., Mosher, J.C., Alexopoulos, A.V., 2018. Assessment of the utility of ictal magnetoencephalography in the localization of the epileptic seizure onset zone. JAMA Neurol. 75 (10), 1264–1272.

Barth, D.S., Sutherling, W., Broffman, J., Beatty, J., 1986. Magnetic localization of a dipolar current source implanted in a sphere and a human cranium. Electroencephalogr. Clin. Neurophysiol. 63 (3), 260–273.

Boto, E., Holmes, N., Leggett, J., Roberts, G., Shah, V., Meyer, S.S., Muñoz, L.D., Mullinger, K.J., Tierney, T.M., Bestmann, S., Barnes, G.R., Bowtell, R., Brookes, M.J., 2018. Moving magnetoencephalography towards real-world applications with a wearable system. Nature 555 (7698), 657–661.

Chen, Y.H., Saby, J., Kuschner, E., Gaetz, W., Edgar, J.C., Roberts, T.P.L., 2019. Magnetoencephalography and the infant brain. Neuroimage 189, 445–458.

Fujiwara, H., Greiner, H.M., Hemasilpin, N., Lee, K.H., Holland-Bouley, K., Arthur, T., Morita, D., Jain, S.V., Mangano, F.T., Degrauw, T., Rose, D.F., 2012. Ictal MEG onset source localization compared to intracranial EEG and outcome: improved epilepsy presurgical evaluation in pediatrics. Epilepsy Res. 99 (3), 214–224.

Wilson, T.W., 2020. Clinical motor mapping with magnetoencephalography. In: Gaetz, W., Papadelis, C., Papanicolaou, A.C., TPL, R., Wheless, J.W. (Eds.), Fifty Years of Magnetoencephalography: Beginnings, Technical Advances, and Applications. Oxford University Press, p. 211.

Gramfort, A., Papadopoulo, T., Olivi, E., Clerc, M., 2010. OpenMEEG: opensource software for quasistatic bioelectromagnetics. Biomed. Eng. Online 45, 9.

Hämäläinen, M., Hari, R., Ilmoniemi, R.J., Knuutila, J., Lounasmaa, O.V., 1993. Magnetoencephalography—theory, instrumentation, and applications to noninvasive studies of the working human brain. Rev. Mod. Phys. 65 (2), 413–497.

Hari, R., Baillet, S., Barnes, G., Burgess, R., Forss, N., Gross, J., et al., 2018. IFCN-endorsed practical guidelines for clinical magnetoencephalography (MEG). Clin. Neurophysiol. 129 (8), 1720–1747.

Jaklevic, R.C., Lambe, J., Silver, A.H., Mercereau, J.E., 1964. Quantum interference effects in Josephson tunneling. Phys. Rev. Lett. 12, 159–160.

Johnson, B.W., Crain, S., Thornton, R., Tesan, G., Reid, M., 2010. Measurement of brain function in pre-school children using a custom sized whole-head MEG sensor array. Clin. Neurophysiol. 121, 340–349.

Kim, D., Joo, E.Y., Seo, D.W., Kim, M.Y., Lee, Y.H., Kwon, H.C., Kim, J.M., Hong, S.B., 2016. Accuracy of MEG in localizing irritative zone and seizure onset zone: quantitative comparison between MEG and intracranial EEG. Epilepsy Res. 127, 291–301.

Kimura, T., Ozaki, I., Hashimoto, I., 2008. Impulse propagation along thalamocortical fibers can be detected magnetically outside the human brain. J. Neurosci. 28 (47), 12535–12538.

Klados, M.A., Papadelis, C., Braun, C., Bamidis, P.D., 2011. REG-ICA: a hybrid methodology combining blind source separation and regression techniques for the rejection of ocular artifacts. Biomed. Signal Process. Control 6 (3), 291–300.

Kossoff, E., 2011. Temporal lobectomies in children: more than just for seizure control? Epilepsy Curr. 11 (6), 179–180.

Lew, S., Sliva, D.D., Choe, M.S., Grant, P.E., Okada, Y., Wolters, C.H., Hämäläinen, M.S., 2013. Effects of sutures and fontanels on MEG and EEG source analysis in a realistic infant head model. Neuroimage 76, 282–293.

Moore, K.R., Funke, M.E., Constantino, T., Katzman, G.L., Lewine, J.D., 2002. Magnetoencephalographically directed review of high-spatial-resolution surface-coil MR images improves lesion detection in patients with extratemporal epilepsy. Radiology 225, 880–887.

Murakami, S., Okada, Y., 2006. Contributions of principal neocortical neurons to magnetoencephalography and electroencephalography signals. J. Physiol. 575 (Pt 3), 925–936.

Murakami, H., Wang, Z.I., Marashly, A., Krishnan, B., Prayson, R.A., Kakisaka, Y., Mosher, J.C., Bulacio, J., Gonzalez-Martinez, J.A., Bingaman, W.E., Najm, I.M., Burgess, R.C., Alexopoulos, A.V., 2016. Correlating magnetoencephalography to stereo-electroencephalography in patients undergoing epilepsy surgery. Brain 139 (11), 2935–2947.

Ntolkeras, G., Tamilia, E., Alhilani, M., Bolton, J., Grant, P.E., Prabhu, S.P., Madsen, J.R., Stufflebeam, S.M., Pearl, P.L., Papadelis, C., 2021. Presurgical accuracy of dipole clustering in MRI-negative pediatric patients with epilepsy: validation against intracranial EEG and resection. Clin. Neurophysiol., S1388–2457–6. https://doi.org/10.1016/j.clinph.2021.01.036.

Okada, Y., Lahteenmäki, A., Xu, C., 1999. Experimental analysis of distortion of magnetoencephalography signals by the skull. Clin. Neurophysiol. 110 (2), 230–238.

Okada, Y., Pratt, K., Atwood, C., Mascarenas, A., Reineman, R., Nurminen, J., Paulson, D., 2006. BabySQUID: a mobile, high-resolution multichannel magnetoencephalography system for neonatal brain assessment. Rev. Sci. Instrum. 77, 024301.

Okada, Y., Hamalainen, M., Pratt, K., Mascarenas, A., Miller, P., Han, M., Robles, J., Cavallini, A., Power, B., Sieng, K., Sun, L., Lew, S., Doshi, C., Ahtam, B., Dinh, C., Esch, L., Grant, E., Nummenmaa, A., Paulson, D., 2016. BabyMEG: a whole-head pediatric magnetoencephalography system for human brain development research. Rev. Sci. Instrum. 87, 094301.

Papadelis, C., Chen, Y.H., 2020. Pediatric magnetoencephalography in clinical practice and research. Neuroimag. Clin. N Am. 30 (2), 239–248. https://doi.org/10.1016/j.nic.2020.02.002.

Papadelis, C., Leonardelli, E., Staudt, M., Braun, C., 2012. Can magnetoencephalography track the afferent information flow along white matter thalamo-cortical fibers? Neuroimage 60 (2), 1092–1105.

Papadelis, C., Harini, C., Ahtam, B., Doshi, C., Grant, E., Okada, Y., 2013. Current and emerging potential for magnetoencephalography in pediatric epilepsy. J. Pediatr. Epilepsy 2 (1), 73–85.

Papadelis, C., Ahtam, B., Nazarova, M., Nimec, D., Snyder, B., Grant, P.E., Okada, Y., 2014. Cortical somatosensory reorganization in children with spastic cerebral palsy: a multimodal neuroimaging study. Front. Hum. Neurosci. 8, 725.

Papadelis, C., Grant, P.E., Okada, Y., Preissl, H., 2015. Editorial on emerging neuroimaging tools for studying normal and abnormal human brain development. Front. Hum. Neurosci. 9, 127.

Papadelis, C., Tamilia, E., Stufflebeam, S., Grant, P.E., Madsen, J.R., Pearl, P.L., Tanaka, N., 2016. Interictal high frequency oscillations detected with simultaneous magnetoencephalography and electroencephalography as biomarker of pediatric epilepsy. J. Vis. Exp. (118), 54883.

Papadelis, C., Butler, E.E., Rubenstein, M., Sun, L., Zollei, L., Nimec, D., Snyder, B., Grant, P.E., 2017. Reorganization of the somatosensory cortex in hemiplegic cerebral palsy associated with impaired sensory tracts. Neuroimage Clin. 17, 198–212.

Papadelis, C., AlHilani, M., Pearl, P.L., November 21, 2018. Artifacts in pediatric and adult magnetoencephalography. In: Tatum, W. (Ed.), Atlas of Artifacts in Clinical Neurophysiology, first ed. Demos Medical, p. 183.

Pellegrino, G., Hedrich, T., Chowdhury, R.A., Hall, J.A., Dubeau, F., Lina, J.M., Kobayashi, E., Grova, C., 2018. Clinical yield of magnetoencephalography distributed source imaging in epilepsy: a comparison with equivalent current dipole method. Hum. Brain Mapp. 39 (1), 218–231.

Ramachandran Nair, R., Otsubo, H., Shroff, M.M., Ochi, A., Weiss, S.K., Rutka, J.T., et al., 2007. MEG predicts outcome following surgery for intractable epilepsy in children with normal or non-focal MRI findings. Epilepsia 48, 149–157.

Rampp, S., Stefan, H., Wu, X., Kaltenhäuser, M., Maess, B., Schmitt, F.C., Wolters, C.H., Hamer, H., Kasper, B.S., Schwab, S., Doerfler, A., Blümcke, I., Rössler, K., Buchfelder, M., 2019. Magnetoencephalography for epileptic focus localization in a series of 1000 cases. Brain 142 (10), 3059–3071.

Roberts, T.P., Paulson, D.N., Hirschkoff, E., Pratt, K., Mascarenas, A., Miller, P., Han, M., Caffrey, J., Kincade, C., Power, B., Murray, R., Chow, V., Fisk, C., Ku, M., Chudnovskaya, D., Dell, J., Golembski, R., Lam, P., Blaskey, L., Kuschner, E., Bloy, L., Gaetz, W., Edgar, J.C., 2014. Artemis 123: development of a whole-head infant and young child MEG system. Front. Hum. Neurosci. 8, 99.

Skirrow, C., Cross, J.H., Cormack, F., Harkness, W., Vargha-Khadem, F., Baldeweg, T., 2011. Long-term intellectual outcome after temporal lobe surgery in childhood. Neurology 76 (15), 1330–1337.

Tadel, F., Baillet, S., Mosher, J.C., Pantazis, D., Leahy, R.M., 2011. Brainstorm: a user-friendly application for MEG/EEG analysis. Comput. Intell. Neurosci. 2011, 8.

Tamilia, E., Madsen, J.R., Grant, P.E., Pearl, P.L., Papadelis, C., 2017. Current and emerging potential of magnetoencephalography in the detection and localization of high-frequency oscillations in epilepsy. Front. Neurol. 8, 14.

Tamilia, E., AlHilani, M., Tanaka, N., Tsuboyama, M., Peters, J.M., Grant, P.E., Madsen, J.R., Stufflebeam, S.M., Pearl, P.L., Papadelis, C., 2019. Assessing the localization accuracy and clinical utility of electric and magnetic source imaging in children with epilepsy. Clin. Neurophysiol. 130 (4), 491–504.

Tamilia, E., Dirodi, M., Alhilani, M., Grant, P.E., Madsen, J.R., Stufflebeam, S.M., Pearl, P.L., Papadelis, C., 2020. Scalp ripples as prognostic biomarkers of epileptogenicity in pediatric surgery. Ann. Clin. Transl. Neurol. 7 (3), 329–342.

Ulaby, F.T., 2007. Fundamentals of applied electromagnetics, fifth ed. Prentice Hall, Pearson, p. 255.

Widjaja, E., Li, B., Schinkel, C.D., Puchalski Ritchie, L., Weaver, J., Snead, O.C., Rutka, J.T., Coyte, P.C., 2011. Cost-effectiveness of pediatric epilepsy surgery compared to medical treatment in children with intractable epilepsy. Epilepsy Res. 94 (1–2), 61–68.

Williamson, J.S., Kaufman, L., 1990. Auditory evoked magnetic fields and electric potentials—Theory of neuromagnetic fields. In: Grandori, F., Hoke, M., Romani, G.L. (Eds.), Advances in Audiology. Karger, Basel, pp. 1–39.

Yin, C., Zhang, X., Chen, Z., Li, X., Wu, S., Lv, P., Wang, Y., 2019. Detection and localization of interictal ripples with magnetoencephalography in the presurgical evaluation of drug-resistant insular epilepsy. Brain Res. 1706, 147–156.

CHAPTER

MEG insights into brain development

16

Joni N. Saby and Heather L. Green
Department of Radiology, Children's Hospital of Philadelphia, Philadelphia, PA, United States

1. Introduction

Electrophysiological techniques, specifically electroencephalography (EEG) and magnetoencephalography (MEG), have been instrumental in advancing our understanding of the neural mechanisms of sensory and cognitive development. As described in previous chapters, an inherent advantage of electrophysiological methods lies in their temporal resolution, with the capacity to provide information about brain activation on a millisecond timescale. This contrasts with MR-based techniques, which provide excellent spatial resolution, but little to no information regarding the timing of neural activity.

The present chapter focuses specifically on MEG studies of brain development. While both MEG and EEG provide excellent temporal resolution, MEG is advantageous over EEG in the spatial domain considering that MEG signals are notably less sensitive than EEG signals to inaccurate estimates of tissue conductivity (Hämäläinen et al., 1993). For this reason, source localization is carried out more routinely for MEG studies, particularly for studies with infants given that immature skull features (fontanels and sutures) pose an additional challenge to models of signal conductivity (Lew et al., 2013).

The following sections will focus on four particular areas of research that have been advanced by MEG studies with infants and children: the development of cortical auditory processing, the development of speech and language processing, the development of cortical somatosensory processing, and the effects of preterm birth and other prenatal insults on the developing brain. The chapter will conclude with a discussion of how future MEG studies of brain development will be supported by the continuing development of dedicated MEG hardware for infants and young children (see Chapter 15). For other recent reviews of pediatric MEG studies, the reader is referred to Chen et al. (2019) as well as Chapter 15 and 17 of this volume.

2. Development of cortical auditory processing

A large proportion of the existing MEG literature with infants and children has focused on the development of cortical auditory processes. Early studies in this area focused on the feasibility of recording auditory evoked fields (AEFs) from infants and young children and localizing those responses to the auditory cortex (Cheour et al., 2004; Holst et al., 2005; Huotilainen et al., 2003; Lengle et al., 2001; Paetau et al., 1995). Following the success of these early studies, subsequent work has considered the

Handbook of Pediatric Brain Imaging. https://doi.org/10.1016/B978-0-12-816633-8.00001-6

development of AEFs over infancy and childhood. Generally, this line of research has established that cortical auditory responses as measured by MEG undergo a long developmental course, with adult-like responses not observed until late adolescence. The protracted developmental course of the AEF is consistent with findings from analogous EEG studies, which have reported a similar trajectory in the development of scalp-recorded auditory evoked potentials (Ohlrich et al., 1978; Ponton et al., 2000).

In infants, the AEF to simple tones is predominated by a single component, which peaks around 250 ms in term-age newborns (Huotilainen et al., 2003; Lengle et al., 2001; Lutter et al., 2006; Sambeth et al., 2009). The latency of this peak, typically referred to as the P250m or P1m component, declines rapidly over the first 6 months of life (Lutter et al., 2006) and then steadily over early childhood (see Fig. 1; Edgar et al., 2015b; Stephen et al. 2017). AEFs have also been studied in fetuses using a specialized system for fetal MEG recordings, the SQUID Array for Reproductive Assessment (SARA). Studies using the SARA system have shown the P250m/P1m can be detected in utero around the start of the third trimester of pregnancy (Draganova et al. 2007; Govindan et al. 2008), which corresponds to when fetuses begin to exhibit behavioral responses to voices and other sounds (Hepper and Shahidullah 1994).

The AEF in adults is characterized by two components that peak at approximately 50 (M50) and 100 ms (M100), respectively. Developmental studies have suggested that the infant P250m/P1m eventually becomes the M50 component of the adult response (Ceponiene et al. 2002; Paetau et al. 1995). The M100, in contrast, is not reliably detectable in most individuals until late adolescence. Prior to this point in development, the M50 continues to dominate the AEF waveform (Oram Cardy et al. 2004; Paetau et al. 1995).

A number of studies with children with autism spectrum disorder have indicated an atypical trajectory of AEF development in this population. Specifically, compared to typically developing peers, individuals with autism spectrum disorder demonstrate prolonged M50/M100 latencies (Edgar et al., 2015a; Matsuzaki et al. 2020; Roberts et al. 2010) and an abnormal decline in M50/M100 latency with age (Stephen et al. 2017). The magnitude of the delay in M50/M100 latency has been found to correlate

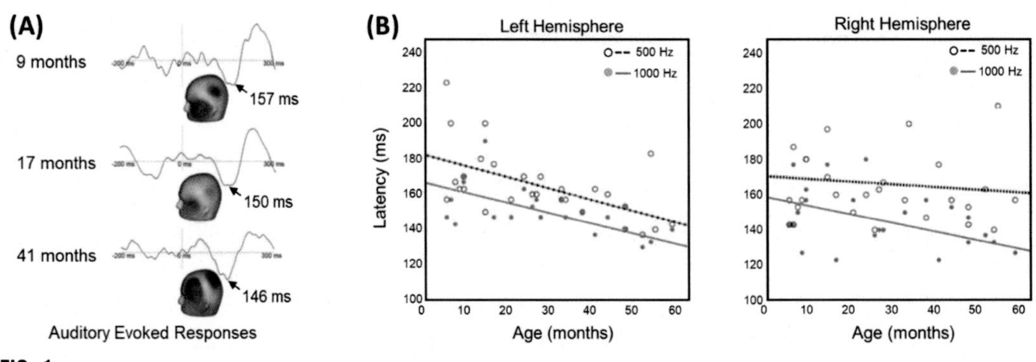

FIG. 1

Data from Edgar et al. (2015b) showing a decline in the latency of the P250m component of the auditory evoked response in children 6–59 months of age (referred to as P2m in this study). (A) Source-level waveforms and associated magnetic field patterns for the P2m in three representative subjects. (B) Scatterplots displaying the rate of change for P2m latency for 500 and 1000 Hz tones in the left and right hemispheres for all subjects.

with severity of the condition, with more pronounced delays in more affected individuals (Port et al. 2016; Roberts et al., 2019b). Ongoing research in this area is investigating the structural and/or neurochemical bases of the M50/M100 latency delay and its potential utility as a diagnostic, prognostic or stratification biomarker for children with autism spectrum disorder (Port et al. 2015; Roberts et al. 2013, 2019a, b).

In addition to examining responses to simple auditory stimuli, a number of the studies described above have additionally considered aspects of auditory change detection (i.e., how the brain responds to a change in auditory stimuli). Auditory change detection is typically studied using an "oddball" paradigm in which a deviant tone is presented at random among a string of more frequent, standard tones. The presentation of the deviant tone elicits an enhanced response in the resulting waveform, known as the mismatch negativity (MMN for EEG; MMNm for MEG). Compared to auditory evoked responses to basic tones, MMN/MMNm responses are thought to reflect higher-level, cognitive functions of the perceiver. Developmental MEG studies in this area have demonstrated that the MMNm can be reliably detected in newborns (Cheour et al. 2004; Huotilainen et al. 2003; Sambeth et al. 2006, 2009) as well as fetuses as young as 28 weeks gestational age (Draganova et al. 2007). The newborn/fetal MMNm is notably broader and later than the MMNm in children and adults. Nonetheless, the presence of MMNm responses in these groups demonstrates that infants are born with the capacity to discriminate sounds, an important prerequisite to the development of cognitive functions, including language.

3. Development of speech and language processing

MEG scientists have also utilized the oddball paradigm to examine developmental changes in infants' abilities to discriminate between speech sounds. These studies have shown that MMNm responses are reliably evoked in newborns following the presentation of a deviant vowel or syllable, indicating that infants are able to detect changes in speech stimuli from birth (Imada et al. 2006; Kujala et al. 2004; Pihko et al., 2004b). Studies with older infants have shown that this intrinsic ability to discriminate speech sounds becomes increasingly specific to the child's native language over the first year of life. Specifically, while 6-month-old infants demonstrate differential MEG responses for deviant versus standard speech sounds in their native as well as nonnative languages, 11- and 12-month-old infants only demonstrate differential MEG responses for contrasts within their own native language (Bosseler et al. 2013; Ferjan Ramirez et al. 2017; Kuhl et al. 2014). These findings are consistent with prior EEG and behavioral studies on phonological processing (Kuhl et al. 2008; Werker and Hensch 2015) and point to a perceptual narrowing of speech perception over the first year of life.

Capitalizing on the spatial precision afforded by MEG, Kuhl and colleagues have further examined how specific areas of the brain are differentially activated by speech sounds in infants of different ages. Imada et al. (2006) reported that listening to speech activates not only auditory areas, but also areas involved in speech production (specifically Broca's area) by 6 months of age. More recently, Kuhl et al. (2014) observed developmental differences in the activation of auditory cortex and Broca's area during the presentation of native and nonnative speech sounds in 7- and 11-month-old infants. In the younger age group, native and nonnative syllables were associated with similar levels of activation in auditory cortex and Broca's area. However, by 11 months of age, auditory areas were more strongly activated for native vs nonnative sounds, whereas motor areas were more strongly activated for nonnative vs native sounds. Together, these findings suggest that hearing speech throughout the first year of life increases infants' auditory as well as sensory-motor pairings of native speech sounds as perceived speech sounds are repeatedly linked to motor representations of sounds based on infants' own experience with speech production (e.g., babbling).

Other work by this group reported greater activation in prefrontal and orbitofrontal areas in bilingual (English-Spanish) compared to monolingual (English) 11-month-old infants during the passive presentation of English and Spanish syllables (Ferjan Ramirez et al. 2017). The finding of greater frontal activation to speech sounds in bilingual infants adds to a growing literature indicating that dual language exposure in infancy may promote the development of executive functioning skills (Bialystok 2015).

While most MEG studies of speech and language processing have focused on early changes in phonological perception, some work with older infants and children has considered the neural mechanisms of word learning. One study with 12- to 18-month-old infants reported that the presentation of familiar picture-word pairings was associated with activation of left frontotemporal cortices around 400 ms after word onset (Travis et al. 2011). This observed response was largely similar to the N400m response that characterizes word-object associations in adults, suggesting the mechanisms for linking lexico-semantic information are established in infancy and operate within similar brain regions throughout the lifespan. Other research on spoken word comprehension has highlighted important developmental differences in patterns of brain activation in children versus adults. Findings from these studies have pointed to greater neural plasticity for learning novel word forms in children compared to adults (Nora et al. 2017; Partanen et al. 2017), but greater neural efficiency for processing familiar words in adults compared to children (Dinga et al. 2018).

4. Development of cortical somatosensory processing

Next to auditory and speech processing, somatosensory processing has received the most attention from researchers employing MEG with pediatric groups. With few exceptions, these studies have used tactile stimulation, such as pneumatically driven taps, to elicit somatosensory evoked fields (SEFs). While responses to electrical stimulation (e.g., of the median or tibial nerve) are typically stronger than those obtained using tactile stimulation, tactile stimuli are more comfortable and unlike electrical stimuli, do not result in stimulus-related artifacts in the MEG recording.

Much like the newborn AEF, the newborn SEF is characterized by a broad deflection with a single peak. This peak occurs at around 60 ms following tactile stimulation of the fingertip (Nevalainen et al. 2008; Nevalainen et al. 2012; Pihko and Lauronen 2004; Pihko et al., 2004a) and slightly earlier for electrical stimulation of the median nerve (Pihko et al., 2005). Source analyses have shown that these responses originate from an anteriorly oriented dipolar source in primary somatosensory cortex. The relative simplicity of the newborn SEF contrasts with the response in adults, which is characterized by two distinct components from primary somatosensory cortex– an initial component with an anteriorly oriented dipolar source and a second, more prominent component with a posteriorly oriented dipolar source. The reason for the absence of a posteriorly oriented component in newborns is not clear, but it may reflect the immaturity of the inhibitory GABA system and/or immaturity of cortico-cortical connections in infants of this age (Nevalainen et al. 2014). Studies with older children have shown that the adult-like pattern is well established by school age, if not earlier (Gaetz et al., 2017; Marco et al., 2012;

Pihko et al., 2009). Taken together, these findings suggest that the SEF matures at a much faster rate than the AEF, which is not fully mature until late adolescence.

In addition to the initial response from the primary somatosensory cortex, SEFs in infants also contain later components, peaking at around 100 ms or later. Several studies have focused on these components as they are larger and more easily quantifiable compared to the earlier responses (Gondo et al. 2001; Meltzoff et al. 2018). Similar to the initial component in the SEF, these subsequent components also localize to the primary somatosensory cortex, although they likely have additional contributions from other sources, resulting in their comparatively larger amplitudes. A recent study with 7-month-old infants focused on two components in the SEF following tactile stimulation of the hands and feet, one around 100 ms and a second around 250 ms (Meltzoff et al. 2018). The source of the SEFs to hand stimulation were more lateral than the sources of SEFs for foot stimulation (see Fig. 2), indicating that the somatosensory cortex is organized in a somatotopic fashion in infants as it is in adults. Meltzoff and colleagues further reported that hand and foot areas of the infant somatosensory cortex were additionally activated when infants were simply observing another person's hand or foot being touched. The finding of vicarious activation of somatosensory cortex during the mere observation of touch in 7-month-old infants is consistent with the pattern observed in adults (Gillmeister et al. 2017; Keysers et al. 2010; Pihko et al. 2010) and implicates a role for the somatosensory cortex in early social-cognitive development.

Most MEG studies on somatosensory processes in infants have focused on neural activity from primary somatosensory cortex, however, a number of studies with newborns have also detected responses from secondary somatosensory cortex around 200 ms following the onset of tactile stimulation

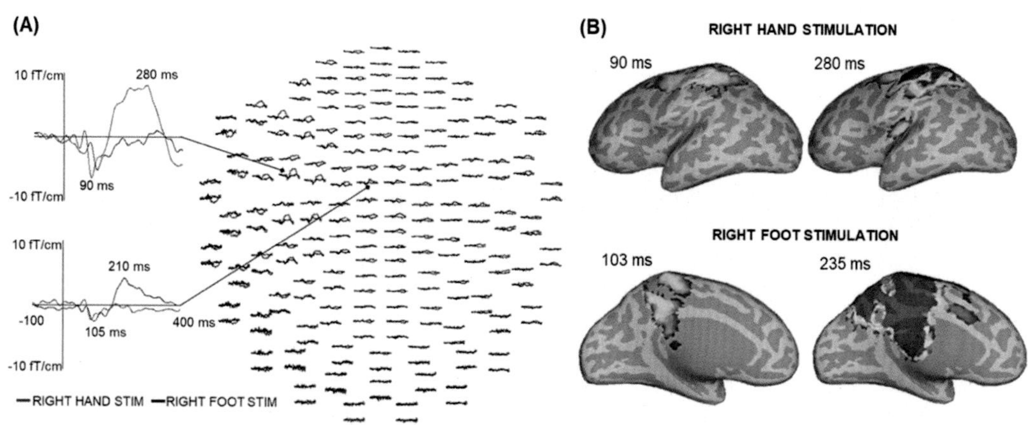

FIG. 2

(A) Data from Meltzoff et al. (2018) showing grand average waveforms for right hand (red) and right foot (black) tactile stimulation in 7-month-old infants. As expected based on the known somatotopic organization of the adult somatosensory cortex, hand stimulation was associated with activation over more lateral sensors compared to those for the foot. (B) Associated source maps for a representative subject showing activation in the expected (hand or foot) region of the somatosensory cortex during each peak of evoked response.

Adapted from Meltzoff, A.N., Ramirez, R.R., Saby, J.N., Larson, E., Taulu, S., Marshall, P.J., 2018. Infant brain responses to felt and observed touch of hands and feet: an MEG study. Dev. Sci. 21, e12651.

(Nevalainen et al. 2008, 2012). Similar to the secondary somatosensory response in adults (which peaks around 100 ms), the response in newborns is observed in both hemispheres and diminishes with a faster stimulus rate (Nevalainen et al. 2008). More recent findings from this group suggests that responses from secondary somatosensory cortex, in particular, may be useful as a prognostic biomarker for predicting long-term outcomes for infants at risk for neurological impairment (see following section, Nevalainen et al. 2015; Rahkonen et al. 2013). No studies to date have examined how secondary somatosensory responses develop beyond the neonatal period.

5. Effects of preterm birth and other prenatal insults on the developing brain

In addition to studies of typical brain development, MEG has also been used to characterize brain function in "at-risk" populations, including children born prematurely. Behaviorally, children born very preterm (<32 weeks gestational age) are known to demonstrate neurocognitive and behavioral deficits compared to children born at term age. A number of resting and task-based MEG studies have been conducted with school-age children to identify the neural mechanisms that may contribute to these behavioral differences. Studies of resting state data have routinely noted aberrations in resting connectivity as well as decreased spectral power among very preterm children compared to age-matched full-term controls (Doesburg et al. 2013; Doesburg et al., 2011a, b; Hunt et al. 2019; Kozhemiako et al. 2019; Ye et al. 2016). Studies utilizing task-based approaches, such as visual working memory tasks, have similarly reported differences in functional connectivity between task-relevant areas in very preterm children compared to controls (Barnes-Davis et al. 2018; Doesburg et al., 2011a, b; Moiseev et al. 2015; Sato et al. 2019). Some evidence has indicated that the aberrations in neural activity are greater for children who experienced a higher number of pain-provoking procedures in the NICU, pointing to a potential mediating role of early-life stress in atypical brain development among very preterm infants (Doesburg et al. 2013; Kozhemiako et al. 2019).

A separate line of research on prematurity has focused on the utility of somatosensory evoked fields as a prognostic tool for identifying preterm infants who are most at risk for poor developmental outcomes and thus, most in need of early intervention. In these studies, extremely preterm infants who lacked secondary somatosensory cortex responses (acquired at term age) were more likely to have unfavorable scores on standardized measures of neurodevelopment at two years of age compared to extremely preterm infants who had intact responses from secondary somatosensory cortex (Nevalainen et al. 2015; Rahkonen et al. 2013). Furthermore, the absence of a response from secondary somatosensory cortex was found to be more accurate in predicting unfavorable neurodevelopmental outcome than the evaluation of brain abnormalities based on MRI or cranial ultrasound (Rahkonen et al. 2013).

MEG has also been utilized to examine the effects of prenatal alcohol exposure on brain function across development. Studies of this type have reported differences in patterns of neural activation between adolescents with prenatal exposure to alcohol and age-matched controls. These differences include aberrations in interhemispheric connectivity (Gao et al. 2019), sensory evoked responses (Coffman et al. 2020, 2013) and task-modulated oscillatory power (Bolanos et al. 2017; Stephen et al. 2013). Although fewer studies have been conducted with younger children, existing work suggests that aberrations in neural activation among individuals with prenatal alcohol exposure are present early in life and persist into adolescence (Kabella et al. 2018; Stephen et al. 2018, 2012). Building on these findings with children and adolescence, a longitudinal study is now being conducted to determine if MEG parameters may be useful as an early marker of atypical brain development in infants at risk for fetal alcohol syndrome (Bakhireva et al. 2015).

6. Conclusion and future directions

As highlighted in this chapter, MEG has played an important role in advancing our understanding of typical and atypical brain development. We focused on four specific areas that have been particularly informed by MEG studies with infants and children: the development of cortical auditory processing, the development of speech and language processing, the development of cortical somatosensory processing, and the effects of preterm birth and other prenatal insults on the developing brain. MEG studies with pediatric groups have also considered other topics including visual/facial processing (He et al., 2015a, b; Taylor et al. 2011) and executive functioning (Mogadam et al. 2018; Taylor et al. 2012). However, these studies have thus far have been limited to older children, with future research needed to examine developmental changes in these areas from infancy.

The primary advantage of MEG for studying aspects of brain development is its capacity to provide precise information regarding the timing and location of neural activity within the brain. This contrasts with other brain imaging techniques (e.g., MRI, EEG), which provide excellent resolution in one domain but not the other. Despite its advantages, one challenge of MEG for pediatric research is its sensitivity to head positioning and the distance between the scalp and MEG sensors. With few exceptions, the studies reviewed here were conducted with conventional MEG systems designed for adults. Since the strength of MEG signals decreases with distance (Hämäläinen et al., 1993), the use of adult-sized systems results in a less than option signal-to-noise ratio for work with infants and children who have comparatively smaller heads (Gaetz et al. 2008). To circumvent this issue, a number of the studies described here positioned infants' heads directly against one side of the sensor array. Although this approach improves the signal-to-noise ratio, it only permits recording from one hemisphere at a time and thus limits possibilities for whole-brain analyses. In order to optimize MEG recordings with infants and young children, a small number of pediatric whole-head MEG systems have been developed (see Chapter 15 of this volume; Johnson et al. 2010; Okada et al. 2016; Roberts et al. 2014). Findings from research conducted with these systems thus far have demonstrated clear improvements in signal-to-noise ratios as a result of having the head closer to the MEG sensors (Edgar et al., 2015b; Johnson et al. 2010; Okada et al. 2016; Roberts et al. 2014). Although these systems are still extremely rare, the enhanced signal-to-noise ratio afforded by the use of pediatric MEG systems opens up possibilities for more complex whole-brain and connectivity analyses, including analyses of interactions between superficial and deeper regions of the brain. The improved signal-to-noise ratio is also likely to increase the sensitivity and specificity of MEG for stratification, prognostic, and diagnostic purposes (i.e., of infants at risk for neurodevelopmental adversity) and therefore facilitate the application of MEG to clinical pediatrics.

In recent years, there has also been substantial progress in the development of wearable MEG systems comprised of optically pumped magnetometers (OPMs; Boto et al. 2018; Boto et al. 2017). Similar to EEG caps, OPM systems sit on participants heads allowing them to move freely during data acquisition. Such a system is promising for work with pediatric populations, particularly infants and lower functioning children who struggle to remain still for prolonged periods of time. The portability of the OPM system could also provide opportunities to use MEG to characterize brain activity during more naturalistic behaviors, such as during motor tasks or social exchanges. Research in this area is still relatively new and a number of technical and practical challenges will need to be addressed before OPMs can be used with infants and young children. Despite these challenges, OPMs are a particularly promising technology for complementing conventional MEG research and advancing future MEG studies of brain development.

References

Bakhireva, L.N., Lowe, J.R., Gutierrez, H.L., Stephen, J.M., 2015. Ethanol, neurodevelopment, infant and child health (ENRICH) prospective cohort: study design considerations. Adv. Pediatr. Res. 2 (2015).

Barnes-Davis, M.E., Merhar, S.L., Holland, S.K., Kadis, D.S., 2018. Extremely preterm children exhibit increased interhemispheric connectivity for language: findings from fMRI-constrained MEG analysis. Dev. Sci. 21 (6), e12669.

Bialystok, E., 2015. Bilingualism and the development of executive function: the role of attention. Child Dev. Perspect. 9 (2), 117–121.

Bolanos, A.D., Coffman, B.A., Candelaria-Cook, F.T., Kodituwakku, P., Stephen, J.M., 2017. Altered neural oscillations during multisensory integration in adolescents with fetal alcohol Spectrum disorder. Alcohol. Clin. Exp. Res. 41 (12), 2173–2184.

Bosseler, A.N., Taulu, S., Pihko, E., Makela, J.P., Imada, T., Ahonen, A., Kuhl, P.K., 2013. Theta brain rhythms index perceptual narrowing in infant speech perception. Front. Psychol. 4, 690.

Boto, E., Meyer, S.S., Shah, V., Alem, O., Knappe, S., Kruger, P., Brookes, M.J., 2017. A new generation of magnetoencephalography: room temperature measurements using optically-pumped magnetometers. Neuroimage 149, 404–414.

Boto, E., Holmes, N., Leggett, J., Roberts, G., Shah, V., Meyer, S.S., Brookes, M.J., 2018. Moving magnetoencephalography towards real-world applications with a wearable system. Nature 555 (7698), 657–661.

Ceponiene, R., Rinne, T., Naatanen, R., 2002. Maturation of cortical sound processing as indexed by event-related potentials. Clin. Neurophysiol. 113 (6), 870–882.

Chen, Y.H., Saby, J., Kuschner, E., Gaetz, W., Edgar, J.C., Roberts, T.P.L., 2019. Magnetoencephalography and the infant brain. Neuroimage 189, 445–458.

Cheour, M., Imada, T., Taulu, S., Ahonen, A., Salonen, J., Kuhl, P., 2004. Magnetoencephalography is feasible for infant assessment of auditory discrimination. Exp. Neurol. 190 (Suppl 1), S44–S51.

Coffman, B.A., Kodituwakku, P., Kodituwakku, E.L., Romero, L., Sharadamma, N.M., Stone, D., Stephen, J.M., 2013. Primary visual response (M100) delays in adolescents with FASD as measured with MEG. Hum. Brain Mapp. 34 (11), 2852–2862.

Coffman, B.A., Candelaria-Cook, F.T., Stephen, J.M., 2020. Unisensory and multisensory responses in fetal alcohol Spectrum disorders (FASD): effects of spatial congruence. Neuroscience 430, 34–46.

Dinga, S., Wu, D., Huang, S., Wu, C., Wang, X., Shi, J., Xiang, J., 2018. Neuromagnetic correlates of audiovisual word processing in the developing brain. Int. J. Psychophysiol. 128, 7–21.

Doesburg, S.M., Ribary, U., Herdman, A.T., Miller, S.P., Poskitt, K.J., Moiseev, A., Grunau, R.E., 2011a. Altered long-range alpha-band synchronization during visual short-term memory retention in children born very preterm. Neuroimage 54 (3), 2330–2339.

Doesburg, S.M., Ribary, U., Herdman, A.T., Moiseev, A., Cheung, T., Miller, S.P., Grunau, R.E., 2011b. Magnetoencephalography reveals slowing of resting peak oscillatory frequency in children born very preterm. Pediatr. Res. 70 (2), 171–175.

Doesburg, S.M., Chau, C.M., Cheung, T.P., Moiseev, A., Ribary, U., Herdman, A.T., Grunau, R.E., 2013. Neonatal pain-related stress, functional cortical activity and visual-perceptual abilities in school-age children born at extremely low gestational age. Pain 154 (10), 1946–1952.

Draganova, R., Eswaran, H., Murphy, P., Lowery, C., Preissl, H., 2007. Serial magnetoencephalographic study of fetal and newborn auditory discriminative evoked responses. Early Hum. Dev. 83 (3), 199–207.

Edgar, J.C., Fisk Iv, C.L., Berman, J.I., Chudnovskaya, D., Liu, S., Pandey, J., Roberts, T.P., 2015a. Auditory encoding abnormalities in children with autism spectrum disorder suggest delayed development of auditory cortex. Mol. Autism. 6, 69.

Edgar, J.C., Murray, R.E., Kuschner, E., Pratt, K., Paulson, D., Dell, J., Golembski, R., Lam, P., Bloy, L., Gaetz, W., Roberts, T.P.L., 2015b. The maturation of auditory responses in infants and young children: a cross-sectional study from 6 to 59 Months. Front. Neuroanat. 9, 131.

Ferjan Ramirez, N., Ramirez, R.R., Clarke, M., Taulu, S., Kuhl, P.K., 2017. Speech discrimination in 11-month-old bilingual and monolingual infants: a magnetoencephalography study. Dev. Sci. 20 (1).

Gaetz, W., Otsubo, H., Pang, E.W., 2008. Magnetoencephalography for clinical pediatrics: the effect of head positioning on measurement of somatosensory-evoked fields. Clin. Neurophysiol. 119 (8), 1923–1933.

Gaetz, W., Jurkiewicz, M.T., Kessler, S.K., Blaskey, L., Schwartz, E.S., Roberts, T.P.L., 2017. Neuromagnetic responses to tactile stimulation of the fingers: evidence for reduced cortical inhibition for children with autism Spectrum disorder and children with epilepsy. Neuroimage Clin. 16, 624–633.

Gao, L., Grebogi, C., Lai, Y.C., Stephen, J., Zhang, T., Li, Y., Sommerlade, L., 2019. Quantitative assessment of cerebral connectivity deficiency and cognitive impairment in children with prenatal alcohol exposure. Chaos 29 (4), 041101.

Gillmeister, H., Bowling, N., Rigato, S., Banissy, M.J., 2017. Inter-individual differences in vicarious tactile perception: a view across the lifespan in typical and atypical populations. Multisens. Res. 30 (6), 485–508.

Gondo, K., Tobimatsu, S., Kira, R., Tokunaga, Y., Yamamoto, T., Hara, T., 2001. A magnetoencephalographic study on development of the somatosensory cortex in infants. Neuroreport 12 (15), 3227–3231.

Govindan, R.B., Wilson, J.D., Preissl, H., Murphy, P., Lowery, C.L., Eswaran, H., 2008. An objective assessment of fetal and neonatal auditory evoked responses. Neuroimage 43 (3), 521–527.

Hämäläinen, M., Hari, R., Ilmoniemi, R.J., Knuutila, J., Lounasmaa, O.V., 1993. Magnetoencephalography—theory, instrumentation, and applications to noninvasive studies of the working human brain. Rev. Mod. Phys. 65 (2), 413–497.

He, W., Brock, J., Johnson, B.W., 2015a. Face processing in the brains of pre-school aged children measured with MEG. Neuroimage 106, 317–327.

He, W., Garrido, M.I., Sowman, P.F., Brock, J., Johnson, B.W., 2015b. Development of effective connectivity in the core network for face perception. Hum. Brain Mapp. 36 (6), 2161–2173.

Hepper, P.G., Shahidullah, B.S., 1994. Development of fetal hearing. Arch. Dis. Child. Fetal Neonatal Ed. 71 (2), F81–F87.

Holst, M., Eswaran, H., Lowery, C., Murphy, P., Norton, J., Preissl, H., 2005. Development of auditory evoked fields in human fetuses and newborns: a longitudinal MEG study. Clin. Neurophysiol. 116 (8), 1949–1955.

Hunt, B.A.E., Scratch, S.E., Mossad, S.I., Emami, Z., Taylor, M.J., Dunkley, B.T., 2019. Disrupted visual cortex neurophysiology following very preterm birth. Biol. Psychiatry Cogn. Neurosci. Neuroimaging, 5, pp. 951–960.

Huotilainen, M., Kujala, A., Hotakainen, M., Shestakova, A., Kushnerenko, E., Parkkonen, L., Naatanen, R., 2003. Auditory magnetic responses of healthy newborns. Neuroreport 14 (14), 1871–1875.

Imada, T., Zhang, Y., Cheour, M., Taulu, S., Ahonen, A., Kuhl, P.K., 2006. Infant speech perception activates Broca's area: a developmental magnetoencephalography study. Neuroreport 17 (10), 957–962.

Johnson, B.W., Crain, S., Thornton, R., Tesan, G., Reid, M., 2010. Measurement of brain function in pre-school children using a custom sized whole-head MEG sensor array. Clin. Neurophysiol. 121 (3), 340–349.

Kabella, D.M., Flynn, L., Peters, A., Kodituwakku, P., Stephen, J.M., 2018. Amplitude by peak interaction but no evidence of auditory mismatch response deficits to frequency change in preschool-aged children with fetal alcohol spectrum disorders. Alcohol. Clin. Exp. Res. 42 (8), 1486–1492.

Keysers, C., Kaas, J.H., Gazzola, V., 2010. Somatosensation in social perception. Nat. Rev. Neurosci. 11 (6), 417–428.

Kozhemiako, N., Nunes, A., Vakorin, V.A., Chau, C.M.Y., Moiseev, A., Ribary, U., Doesburg, S.M., 2019. Atypical resting state neuromagnetic connectivity and spectral power in very preterm children. J. Child Psychol. Psychiatry 60 (9), 975–987.

Kuhl, P.K., Conboy, B.T., Coffey-Corina, S., Padden, D., Rivera-Gaxiola, M., Nelson, T., 2008. Phonetic learning as a pathway to language: new data and native language magnet theory expanded (NLM-e). Philos. Trans. R. Soc. Lond. B Biol. Sci. 363 (1493), 979–1000.

Kuhl, P.K., Ramirez, R.R., Bosseler, A., Lin, J.F., Imada, T., 2014. Infants' brain responses to speech suggest analysis by synthesis. Proc. Natl. Acad. Sci. U. S. A. 111 (31), 11238–11245.

Kujala, A., Huotilainen, M., Hotakainen, M., Lennes, M., Parkkonen, L., Fellman, V., Naatanen, R., 2004. Speech-sound discrimination in neonates as measured with MEG. Neuroreport 15 (13), 2089–2092.

Lengle, J.M., Chen, M., Wakai, R.T., 2001. Improved neuromagnetic detection of fetal and neonatal auditory evoked responses. Clin. Neurophysiol. 112 (5), 785–792.

Lew, S., Sliva, D.D., Choe, M.S., Grant, P.E., Okada, Y., Wolters, C.H., Hamalainen, M.S., 2013. Effects of sutures and fontanels on MEG and EEG source analysis in a realistic infant head model. Neuroimage 76, 282–293.

Lutter, W.J., Maier, M., Wakai, R.T., 2006. Development of MEG sleep patterns and magnetic auditory evoked responses during early infancy. Clin. Neurophysiol. 117 (3), 522–530.

Marco, E.J., Khatibi, K., Hill, S.S., Siegel, B., Arroyo, M.S., Dowling, A.F., Nagarajan, S.S., 2012. Children with autism show reduced somatosensory response: an MEG study. Autism Res. 5 (5), 340–351.

Matsuzaki, J., Ku, M., Dipiero, M., Chiang, T., Saby, J., Blaskey, L., Roberts, T.P.L., 2020. Delayed auditory evoked responses in autism Spectrum disorder across the life span. Dev. Neurosci. 41, 223–233.

Meltzoff, A.N., Ramirez, R.R., Saby, J.N., Larson, E., Taulu, S., Marshall, P.J., 2018. Infant brain responses to felt and observed touch of hands and feet: an MEG study. Dev. Sci. 21, e12651.

Mogadam, A., Keller, A.E., Taylor, M.J., Lerch, J.P., Anagnostou, E., Pang, E.W., 2018. Mental flexibility: an MEG investigation in typically developing children. Brain Cogn. 120, 58–66.

Moiseev, A., Doesburg, S.M., Herdman, A.T., Ribary, U., Grunau, R.E., 2015. Altered network oscillations and functional connectivity dynamics in children born very preterm. Brain Topogr. 28 (5), 726–745.

Nevalainen, P., Lauronen, L., Sambeth, A., Wikstrom, H., Okada, Y., Pihko, E., 2008. Somatosensory evoked magnetic fields from the primary and secondary somatosensory cortices in healthy newborns. Neuroimage 40 (2), 738–745.

Nevalainen, P., Pihko, E., Metsaranta, M., Sambeth, A., Wikstrom, H., Okada, Y., Lauronen, L., 2012. Evoked magnetic fields from primary and secondary somatosensory cortices: a reliable tool for assessment of cortical processing in the neonatal period. Clin. Neurophysiol. 123 (12), 2377–2383.

Nevalainen, P., Lauronen, L., Pihko, E., 2014. Development of human somatosensory cortical functions—what have we learned from magnetoencephalography: a review. Front. Hum. Neurosci. 8, 158.

Nevalainen, P., Rahkonen, P., Pihko, E., Lano, A., Vanhatalo, S., Andersson, S., Lauronen, L., 2015. Evaluation of somatosensory cortical processing in extremely preterm infants at term with MEG and EEG. Clin. Neurophysiol. 126 (2), 275–283.

Nora, A., Karvonen, L., Renvall, H., Parviainen, T., Kim, J.Y., Service, E., Salmelin, R., 2017. Children show right-lateralized effects of spoken word-form learning. PLoS One 12 (2), e0171034.

Ohlrich, E.S., Barnet, A.B., Weiss, I.P., Shanks, B.L., 1978. Auditory evoked potential development in early childhood: a longitudinal study. Electroencephalogr. Clin. Neurophysiol. 44 (4), 411–423.

Okada, Y., Hamalainen, M., Pratt, K., Mascarenas, A., Miller, P., Han, M., Paulson, D., 2016. BabyMEG: a whole-head pediatric magnetoencephalography system for human brain development research. Rev. Sci. Instrum. 87 (9), 094301.

Oram Cardy, J.E., Ferrari, P., Flagg, E.J., Roberts, W., Roberts, T.P., 2004. Prominence of M50 auditory evoked response over M100 in childhood and autism. Neuroreport 15 (12), 1867–1870.

Paetau, R., Ahonen, A., Salonen, O., Sams, M., 1995. Auditory evoked magnetic fields to tones and pseudowords in healthy children and adults. J. Clin. Neurophysiol. 12 (2), 177–185.

Partanen, E., Leminen, A., de Paoli, S., Bundgaard, A., Kingo, O.S., Krojgaard, P., Shtyrov, Y., 2017. Flexible, rapid and automatic neocortical word form acquisition mechanism in children as revealed by neuromagnetic brain response dynamics. Neuroimage 155, 450–459.

Pihko, E., Lauronen, L., 2004. Somatosensory processing in healthy newborns. Exp. Neurol. 190 (Suppl 1), S2–S7.

Pihko, E., Lauronen, L., Wikstrom, H., Taulu, S., Nurminen, J., Kivitie-Kallio, S., Okada, Y., 2004a. Somatosensory evoked potentials and magnetic fields elicited by tactile stimulation of the hand during active and quiet sleep in newborns. Clin. Neurophysiol. 115 (2), 448–455.

Pihko, E., Sambeth, A., Leppanen, P., Okada, Y., Lauronen, L., 2004b. Auditory evoked magnetic fields to speech stimuli in newborns—effect of sleep stages. Neurol. Clin. Neurophysiol. 6, 337–338.

Pihko, E., Lauronen, L., Wikstrom, H., Parkkonen, L., Okada, Y., 2005. Somatosensory evoked magnetic fields to median nerve stimulation in newborns. Int. Congr. Ser. 1278, 211–214.

Pihko, E., Nevalainen, P., Stephen, J., Okada, Y., Lauronen, L., 2009. Maturation of somatosensory cortical processing from birth to adulthood revealed by magnetoencephalography. Clin. Neurophysiol. 120 (8), 1552–1561.

Pihko, E., Nangini, C., Jousmaki, V., Hari, R., 2010. Observing touch activates human primary somatosensory cortex. Eur. J. Neurosci. 31 (10), 1836–1843.

Ponton, C.W., Eggermont, J.J., Kwong, B., Don, M., 2000. Maturation of human central auditory system activity: evidence from multi-channel evoked potentials. Clin. Neurophysiol. 111 (2), 220–236.

Port, R.G., Anwar, A.R., Ku, M., Carlson, G.C., Siegel, S.J., Roberts, T.P., 2015. Prospective MEG biomarkers in ASD: pre-clinical evidence and clinical promise of electrophysiological signatures. Yale J. Biol. Med. 88 (1), 25–36.

Port, R.G., Edgar, J.C., Ku, M., Bloy, L., Murray, R., Blaskey, L., Roberts, T.P.L., 2016. Maturation of auditory neural processes in autism spectrum disorder—a longitudinal MEG study. Neuroimage Clin. 11, 566–577.

Rahkonen, P., Nevalainen, P., Lauronen, L., Pihko, E., Lano, A., Vanhatalo, S., Metsaranta, M., 2013. Cortical somatosensory processing measured by magnetoencephalography predicts neurodevelopment in extremely low-gestational-age infants. Pediatr. Res. 73 (6), 763–771.

Roberts, T.P., Khan, S.Y., Rey, M., Monroe, J.F., Cannon, K., Blaskey, L., Edgar, J.C., 2010. MEG detection of delayed auditory evoked responses in autism spectrum disorders: towards an imaging biomarker for autism. Autism Res. 3 (1), 8–18.

Roberts, T.P., Lanza, M.R., Dell, J., Qasmieh, S., Hines, K., Blaskey, L., Berman, J.I., 2013. Maturational differences in thalamocortical white matter microstructure and auditory evoked response latencies in autism spectrum disorders. Brain Res. 1537, 79–85.

Roberts, T.P., Paulson, D.N., Hirschkoff, E., Pratt, K., Mascarenas, A., Miller, P., Edgar, J.C., 2014. Artemis 123: development of a whole-head infant and young child MEG system. Front. Hum. Neurosci. 8, 99.

Roberts, T.P.L., Bloy, L., Blaskey, L., Kuschner, E., Gaetz, L., Anwar, A., Edgar, J.C., 2019a. A MEG study of acute arbaclofen (STX-209) administration. Front. Integr. Neurosci. 13, 69.

Roberts, T.P.L., Matsuzaki, J., Blaskey, L., Bloy, L., Edgar, J.C., Kim, M., Embick, D., 2019b. Delayed M50/M100 evoked response component latency in minimally verbal/nonverbal children who have autism spectrum disorder. Mol. Autism. 10, 34.

Sambeth, A., Huotilainen, M., Kushnerenko, E., Fellman, V., Pihko, E., 2006. Newborns discriminate novel from harmonic sounds: a study using magnetoencephalography. Clin. Neurophysiol. 117 (3), 496–503.

Sambeth, A., Pakarinen, S., Ruohio, K., Fellman, V., van Zuijen, T.L., Huotilainen, M., 2009. Change detection in newborns using a multiple deviant paradigm: a study using magnetoencephalography. Clin. Neurophysiol. 120 (3), 530–538.

Sato, J., Mossad, S.I., Wong, S.M., Hunt, B.A.E., Dunkley, B.T., Urbain, C., Taylor, M.J., 2019. Spectral slowing is associated with working memory performance in children born very preterm. Sci. Rep. 9 (1), 15757.

Stephen, J.M., Kodituwakku, P.W., Kodituwakku, E.L., Romero, L., Peters, A.M., Sharadamma, N.M., Coffman, B.A., 2012. Delays in auditory processing identified in preschool children with FASD. Alcohol. Clin. Exp. Res. 36 (10), 1720–1727.

Stephen, J.M., Coffman, B.A., Stone, D.B., Kodituwakku, P., 2013. Differences in MEG gamma oscillatory power during performance of a prosaccade task in adolescents with FASD. Front. Hum. Neurosci. 7, 900.

Stephen, J.M., Hill, D.E., Peters, A., Flynn, L., Zhang, T., Okada, Y., 2017. Development of auditory evoked responses in normally developing preschool children and children with autism Spectrum disorder. Dev. Neurosci. 39 (5), 430–441.

Stephen, J.M., Flynn, L., Kabella, D., Schendel, M., Cano, S., Savage, D.D., Bakhireva, L.N., 2018. Hypersynchrony in MEG spectral amplitude in prospectively-identified 6-month-old infants prenatally exposed to alcohol. Neuroimage Clin. 17, 826–834.

Taylor, M.J., Mills, T., Pang, E.W., 2011. The development of face recognition; hippocampal and frontal lobe contributions determined with MEG. Brain Topogr. 24 (3–4), 261–270.

Taylor, M.J., Donner, E.J., Pang, E.W., 2012. fMRI and MEG in the study of typical and atypical cognitive development. Neurophysiol. Clin. 42 (1–2), 19–25.

Travis, K.E., Leonard, M.K., Brown, T.T., Hagler Jr., D.J., Curran, M., Dale, A.M., Halgren, E., 2011. Spatiotemporal neural dynamics of word understanding in 12- to 18-month-old-infants. Cereb. Cortex 21 (8), 1832–1839.

Werker, J.F., Hensch, T.K., 2015. Critical periods in speech perception: new directions. Annu. Rev. Psychol. 66, 173–196.

Ye, A.X., AuCoin-Power, M., Taylor, M.J., Doesburg, S.M., 2016. Disconnected neuromagnetic networks in children born very preterm: disconnected MEG networks in preterm children. Neuroimage Clin. 11, 376–384.

CHAPTER

MEG studies of children 17

Mitsuru Kikuchi and Yuko Yoshimura
Research Center for Child Mental Development, Kanazawa University, Kanazawa, Japan

1. Introduction

Magnetoencephalography (MEG) and electroencephalography (EEG) are noninvasive and high temporal resolution methods of recording neural activity. Unlike functional magnetic resonance imaging (fMRI), positron emission tomography (PET), and single-photon emission computed tomography (SPECT), MEG and EEG measure a direct consequence of the electrical activity of neurons. These two techniques have temporal resolution of approximately one millisecond, which is the typical resolution of measurable electrical phenomena in the brain. These two techniques have advantages over other neuroimaging techniques for use with young children, including improved safety, fewer constraints, and the absence of radiation and unpleasant sounds.

For epilepsy surgery in children (Velmurugan et al., 2019) as well as adults, MEG is approved for use as part of a non-invasive pre-surgical evaluation. In addition to filling its clinical role in epilepsy, MEG has emerged as an important investigatory tool in neurodevelopmental studies of young children irrespective of their typical (Zhang et al., 2009; Bosseler et al., 2013; Kuhl et al., 2014; Pihko et al., 2005, 2004a, b; Kikuchi et al., 2011; Yoshimura et al., 2012, 2014; Remijn et al., 2014) or atypical development. Conventional whole-head MEG systems have fixed sensor arrays designed to accommodate most adult heads. However, for research involving the markedly smaller heads of young children, sensor arrays optimized for adult brain measurements are not optimal. Therefore, until 2010, MEG studies of neurodevelopmental disorders rarely emphasized studies of children under 6 years old: a 6-year-old human head being too small for whole-head MEG systems. After development of a custom child-sized MEG in 2010 (Johnson et al., 2010), researchers were able to focus on brain activity in young children (e.g., 3–7 years old) (Kikuchi et al., 2011, 2013a, b; Yoshimura et al., 2012, 2014, 2013; Remijn et al., 2014). Furthermore, in 2014, a novel whole-head infant MEG system was developed (Roberts et al., 2014). This system was optimized for children 3 years of age and younger, allowing the helmet to be placed closer to the underlying neuronal sources, even in infants. Therefore, the time has come to use whole-head MEG systems for humans of all ages in furtherance of developmental brain research. The target ages of MEG studies for children are shown in Table 1.

Recent epidemiological reports have described high prevalence of some neurodevelopmental disorders such as autism spectrum disorder (ASD; 2.6%) (Kim et al., 2011) and attention deficit hyperactivity disorder (ADHD; 11.0%) (Visser et al., 2014) as well as language disorders (e.g., developmental dyslexia, 1–33% (Crystal, 1987); and specific language impairment (SLI), 7.4%

Handbook of Pediatric Brain Imaging. https://doi.org/10.1016/B978-0-12-816633-8.00008-9

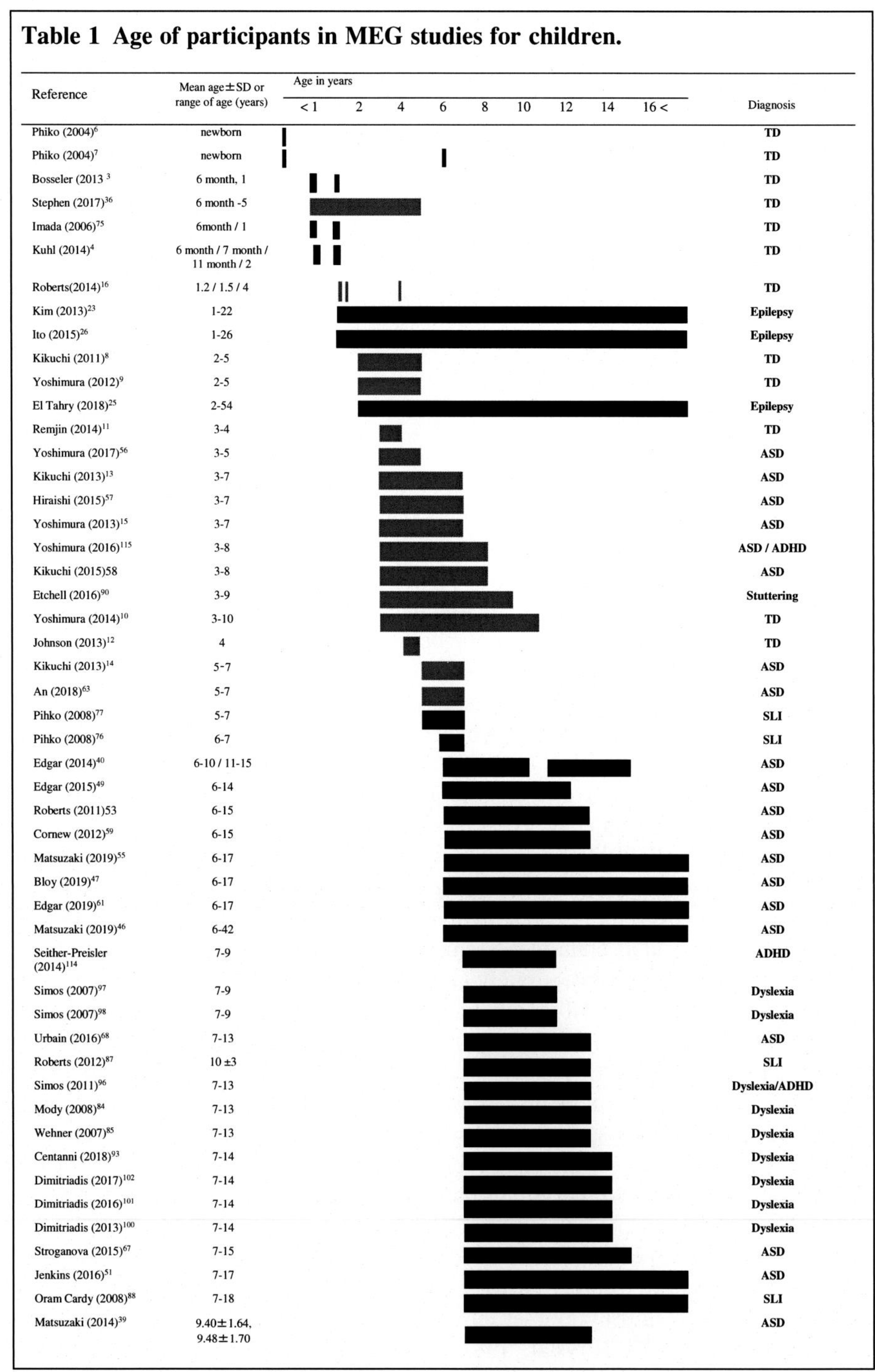

Table 1 Age of participants in MEG studies for children.

Reference	Mean age±SD or range of age (years)	Age in years: <1 2 4 6 8 10 12 14 16<	Diagnosis
Phiko (2004)[6]	newborn		TD
Phiko (2004)[7]	newborn		TD
Bosseler (2013 [3]	6 month, 1		TD
Stephen (2017)[36]	6 month -5		TD
Imada (2006)[75]	6month / 1		TD
Kuhl (2014)[4]	6 month / 7 month / 11 month / 2		TD
Roberts(2014)[16]	1.2 / 1.5 / 4		TD
Kim (2013)[23]	1-22		Epilepsy
Ito (2015)[26]	1-26		Epilepsy
Kikuchi (2011)[8]	2-5		TD
Yoshimura (2012)[9]	2-5		TD
El Tahry (2018)[25]	2-54		Epilepsy
Remjin (2014)[11]	3-4		TD
Yoshimura (2017)[56]	3-5		ASD
Kikuchi (2013)[13]	3-7		ASD
Hiraishi (2015)[57]	3-7		ASD
Yoshimura (2013)[15]	3-7		ASD
Yoshimura (2016)[115]	3-8		ASD / ADHD
Kikuchi (2015)58	3-8		ASD
Etchell (2016)[90]	3-9		Stuttering
Yoshimura (2014)[10]	3-10		TD
Johnson (2013)[12]	4		TD
Kikuchi (2013)[14]	5-7		ASD
An (2018)[63]	5-7		ASD
Pihko (2008)[77]	5-7		SLI
Pihko (2008)[76]	6-7		SLI
Edgar (2014)[40]	6-10 / 11-15		ASD
Edgar (2015)[49]	6-14		ASD
Roberts (2011)53	6-15		ASD
Cornew (2012)[59]	6-15		ASD
Matsuzaki (2019)[55]	6-17		ASD
Bloy (2019)[47]	6-17		ASD
Edgar (2019)[61]	6-17		ASD
Matsuzaki (2019)[46]	6-42		ASD
Seither-Preisler (2014)[114]	7-9		ADHD
Simos (2007)[97]	7-9		Dyslexia
Simos (2007)[98]	7-9		Dyslexia
Urbain (2016)[68]	7-13		ASD
Roberts (2012)[87]	10 ±3		SLI
Simos (2011)[96]	7-13		Dyslexia/ADHD
Mody (2008)[84]	7-13		Dyslexia
Wehner (2007)[85]	7-13		Dyslexia
Centanni (2018)[93]	7-14		Dyslexia
Dimitriadis (2017)[102]	7-14		Dyslexia
Dimitriadis (2016)[101]	7-14		Dyslexia
Dimitriadis (2013)[100]	7-14		Dyslexia
Stroganova (2015)[67]	7-15		ASD
Jenkins (2016)[51]	7-17		ASD
Oram Cardy (2008)[88]	7-18		SLI
Matsuzaki (2014)[39]	9.40±1.64, 9.48±1.70		ASD

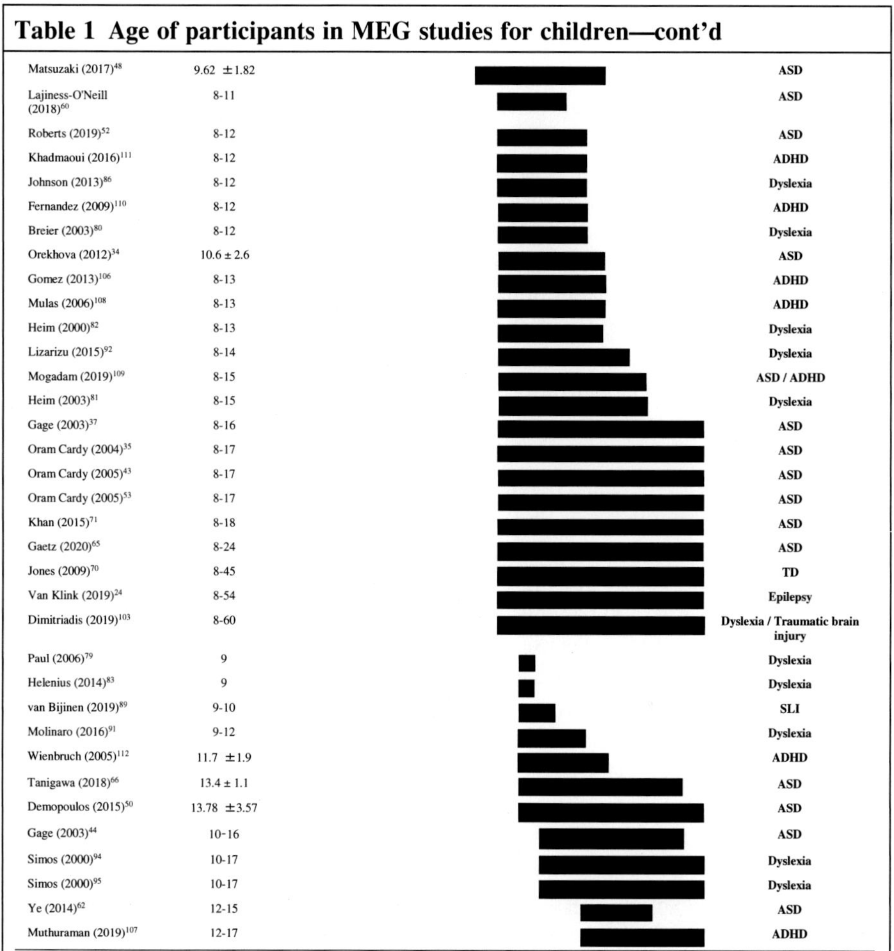

Table 1 Age of participants in MEG studies for children—cont'd

Study	Age	Disorder
Matsuzaki (2017)[48]	9.62 ±1.82	ASD
Lajiness-O'Neill (2018)[60]	8-11	ASD
Roberts (2019)[52]	8-12	ASD
Khadmaoui (2016)[111]	8-12	ADHD
Johnson (2013)[86]	8-12	Dyslexia
Fernandez (2009)[110]	8-12	ADHD
Breier (2003)[80]	8-12	Dyslexia
Orekhova (2012)[34]	10.6 ± 2.6	ASD
Gomez (2013)[106]	8-13	ADHD
Mulas (2006)[108]	8-13	ADHD
Heim (2000)[82]	8-13	Dyslexia
Lizarizu (2015)[92]	8-14	Dyslexia
Mogadam (2019)[109]	8-15	ASD / ADHD
Heim (2003)[81]	8-15	Dyslexia
Gage (2003)[37]	8-16	ASD
Oram Cardy (2004)[35]	8-17	ASD
Oram Cardy (2005)[43]	8-17	ASD
Oram Cardy (2005)[53]	8-17	ASD
Khan (2015)[71]	8-18	ASD
Gaetz (2020)[65]	8-24	ASD
Jones (2009)[70]	8-45	TD
Van Klink (2019)[24]	8-54	Epilepsy
Dimitriadis (2019)[103]	8-60	Dyslexia / Traumatic brain injury
Paul (2006)[79]	9	Dyslexia
Helenius (2014)[83]	9	Dyslexia
van Bijinen (2019)[89]	9-10	SLI
Molinaro (2016)[91]	9-12	Dyslexia
Wienbruch (2005)[112]	11.7 ±1.9	ADHD
Tanigawa (2018)[66]	13.4 ± 1.1	ASD
Demopoulos (2015)[50]	13.78 ±3.57	ASD
Gage (2003)[44]	10-16	ASD
Simos (2000)[94]	10-17	Dyslexia
Simos (2000)[95]	10-17	Dyslexia
Ye (2014)[62]	12-15	ASD
Muthuraman (2019)[107]	12-17	ADHD

ASD, autism spectrum disorder. ADHD, attention deficit hyper activity disorder. Reading difficulties and reading disorders are included in 'Dyslexia'. Red bar, range of age for custom child-sized / baby MEG. Black bar, range of age for conventional adult-sized MEG.

(Tomblin et al., 1997). These neurodevelopmental disorders appear in infancy and early childhood, possibly causing delays or impairments in social interaction, communication, and cognitive function. To gain insight into the development of these dysfunctions, their pathophysiology must be studied in young children. During the past decade, using conventional or custom child-sized MEG devices, researchers have strived to elucidate the neurophysiological mechanisms of these neurodevelopmental disorders in childhood. This review particularly describes MEG studies of children with these neurophysiological and neurodevelopmental disorders.

2. MEG studies of children with epilepsy

Epilepsy is a frequently occurring chronic neurological disorder. The prevalence of epilepsy is probably 0.8%–1.2%, of which 30%–40% are cases of drug-resistant epilepsy (i.e., seizures cannot be controlled with antiepileptic drugs). Epilepsy surgery has been reported as a valuable treatment option for 10%–50% of patients with drug-resistant epilepsy. Early surgery might improve cognitive development and quality of life in children. Pre-surgical assessment is recommended to be done as early as possible in appropriate surgical candidates. Epilepsy surgery involves two major objectives. The first is to control seizures by removing epileptogenic tissue. The other is to avoid neuropsychological and neurological deficits by sparing eloquent brain areas (Baumgartner et al., 2019; Ryvlin et al., 2014).

For pre-surgical evaluation of epilepsy, the most beneficial information has been provided by intracranial EEG, although it is an invasive method. Non-invasive MEG can localize inter-ictal spikes to a single area, but intracranial EEG localization is still recommended if MRI does not show lesions (Kim et al., 2013).

During the past couple of decades, non-invasive methods such as neurophysiological techniques (high-density EEG, MEG, electrical and magnetic source imaging), structural MRI, and functional imaging (positron emission tomography, PET, and single photon emission computed tomography, SPECT) have improved pre-surgical evaluation considerably. These methods have been used for consideration of epilepsy surgery before placing intracranial EEG. Moreover, the methods have presented the alternative of epilepsy surgery to patients who had not been previously considered as surgical candidates. In addition to structural MRI, the use of multimodal pre-surgical evaluations has been regarded as contributing to a good post-surgical prognosis (van Klink et al., 2019; El Tahry et al., 2018).

The epileptogenic zone has been defined as the "area of cortex that is necessary and sufficient for initiating seizures and the removal (or disconnection) of which is necessary for complete abolition of seizures." Identification of the epileptogenic zone is an important determinant of seizure control outcomes following surgical resection. Actually, MEG already plays an important role in pre-surgical evaluation to estimate the epileptogenic zone; e.g., MEG spike sources have been localized on MRI using a single dipole model to project equivalent current dipoles (Ito et al., 2015). In infants and in children of other ages, MEG can sensitively identify epileptogenic zones. It plays a fundamentally important role in pre-surgical evaluation of infants with refractory epilepsy (Garcia-Tarodo et al., 2018).

Recently interesting many epilepsy researchers are interictal high-frequency oscillations (HFOs), which are defined as spontaneous EEG events with frequencies of 80–500 Hz, consisting of at least four oscillations that stand out clearly from the background activity. Actually, HFOs recorded by intracranial EEG have provided important information for the effective surgical resection of epileptogenic zones (Cimbalnik et al., 2016). Furthermore, during the last 10 years, non-invasive measurements of HFOs have been applied for pre-surgery evaluation (Frauscher et al., 2017). According to the latest review published in 2019 (Velmurugan et al., 2019), HFOs recorded by MEG represent a promising non-invasive indicator for improvement of the pre-surgical assessment, and for post-surgical outcome prediction. Prospective multi-center trials conducted with large groups of children are anticipated for the wealth of information they will provide.

Epilepsy surgery has other important aspects aside from resection of an epileptogenic zone. Avoiding neuropsychological and other neurological deficits by identifying and preserving the eloquent (motor, language, and memory) cortex, which has important roles in daily life, is important. Identifying the language-dominant hemisphere and intra-hemispheric localization of this function are imperative for epilepsy surgery planning. With regard to the language-dominant hemisphere, high concordance between MEG and the intracarotid amobarbital (Wada) test has been reported. However, research for such brain functional mapping has been conducted predominantly for adults; the applicability of these techniques for pediatric epilepsy surgery is less established (Chou et al., 2018).

Even for children, epilepsy surgery is now recommended for drug-resistant epilepsy (Dwivedi et al., 2017). Although, additional data must be obtained from randomized trials with large samples of children, pre-surgical evaluation of brain function using MEG in young children is a promising method to identify the epileptogenic zone and to avoid neuropsychological and neurological deficits by sparing important brain areas.

3. MEG studies of children with ASD

Autism spectrum disorder (ASD), a spectrum of neurodevelopmental disorder characterized by social impairment and restricted or stereotyped behaviors, currently affect an estimated 1 in 59 children (Baio et al., 2018), or even more. Considerable interest has arisen in research efforts to elucidate abnormalities in neural activity and thereby clarify the pathophysiology of ASD. Evoked (or induced) responses to external stimuli (i.e., auditory, visual, or somatosensory stimuli) have often been used in MEG studies in young children. Auditory stimuli are suitable for young children who have difficulty controlling attention because they can elicit a brain response even when a child devotes no particular attention to stimuli. Therefore, common and reproducible electrophysiological findings in children with ASD are abnormal M50 and M100 responses to auditory stimuli. The M50 is the earliest cortical component of the auditory evoked magnetic field (AEF). It is a prominent component in 1–10-year-old children (Gilley et al., 2005). In MEG studies, this component has been alternatively labelled the P1m (Yoshimura et al., 2013), P50m (Yoshimura et al., 2012) or P100m (Orekhova et al., 2012). To avoid confusion, we designate this component as M50 for this report. According to Orekhova et al. (2012), the M50 component, which occurs approximately 100 ms after stimulation (in children), is the most prominent component of the auditory-evoked magnetic field response in children. The equivalent current dipoles (ECD) of the M50 have a predominantly anterosuperior orientation. The main sources of the M50 are the primary auditory cortex and association cortices. These brain areas are anatomically and functionally connected with language areas. Therefore, numerous earlier AEF studies have been related to language acquisition in children with ASD.

For instance, one earlier study of young children (3–7 years old) with ASD found less leftward lateralization in M50 magnitude than in typically developing children (Yoshimura et al., 2013), whereas another study of school-aged children with ASD demonstrated less rightward lateralization compared to typically developing children (Orekhova et al., 2012). One possible explanation for this discrepancy was that differences might arise in the developmental trajectory of M50 magnitude across preschool and school ages between children with ASD and typically developing control children. In fact, one earlier study specifically examined the developmental trajectory of M50 amplitude for voices in children aged 2–10 years. The results revealed that TD children showed an inverted U-shaped development peaking around 66 months, whereas children with ASD did not show the same growth pattern.

The second-earliest cortical component of the AEF is the M100. In earlier MEG studies, this component has been alternatively labelled as N1m or N100m. To avoid confusion, we designate this component as M100 in this report. It becomes a prominent component in school-aged children, whereas the magnitude of the M50 decreases in school-aged children. The ratio of M50/M100 magnitude has been reported to decrease with age in the left hemisphere in the same manner in both children with ASD and typically developing children (Oram Cardy et al., 2004). Similar to the M50, the M100 is probably a neurophysiological marker related to language acquisition. Because of the small magnitude of the M100 component, which gives a low signal/noise ratio in preschool-aged children, few reported studies to date have assessed M100 in preschool children. Only one study of young children with ASD (aged 2–5 years), specifically examined AEF including an M100-like component (Stephen et al., 2017). The results of this earlier study demonstrated delayed latency of AEF including the M100-like component in children with ASD (Stephen et al., 2017). With regard to school-aged children, numerous reports have described a deviant M100 component in ASD. In 2003, Gage and colleagues measured tone-evoked M100 response in bilateral hemispheres in school age children with ASD; the results revealed delayed M100 latency in children with ASD (Gage et al., 2003a). Since then, many studies have demonstrated delayed M100 latency in school-age children with ASD (Oram Cardy et al., 2004, 2005a; Gage et al., 2003a, b; Matsuzaki et al., 2012, 2014, 2019a, 2017; Edgar et al., 2014, 2015; Roberts et al., 2010; Schmidt et al., 2009; Tecchio et al., 2003; Bloy et al., 2019; Demopoulos et al., 2015; Jenkins et al., 2016). It is noteworthy that the AEF properties corresponding to the various phenotypes of ASD are reported. For example, delayed M50 and M100 latency were reported in ASD groups with severe speech impairment (Roberts et al., 2019) and in those with auditory hypersensitivity (Orekhova et al., 2012; Matsuzaki et al., 2012, 2014, 2017), which has been reported to have a frequency of over 40% in school-age children with ASD. Another study found that missing M100 responses were observed more frequently in children with ASD with language impairment than in TD children or children with ASD without language impairment (Edgar et al., 2014). In addition, Schmidt and colleagues specifically examined the spatial symmetry property of the M100 source in ASD. They demonstrated a greater symmetric property in children with ASD, whereas the M100 source in the control children tended to be located more anteriorly in the right hemisphere (i.e., more asymmetric). In addition, the degree of this asymmetry was associated with language ability across the two groups of children. These accumulated results of earlier studies suggest that MEG measurements of auditory cortical nerve activity might be an objective indicator corresponding to the various phenotypes of ASD.

The electrical mismatch negativity (MMN) and its magnetic analogue, the mismatch field (MMF), are of particular interest in assessing auditory discrimination. The MMN/MMF has been used as a neurophysiological index of auditory change detection that can be elicited in the absence of focused attention. The response is typically elicited using an auditory oddball paradigm, where listeners are presented a series of stimuli: some presented frequently and others infrequently. Relative to the response evoked by the standard stimuli, deviant stimuli evoke a pronounced response. In healthy populations, the time course of the MMN/MMF response has been used to probe speech discrimination. Atypical MMN/MMF responses have been reported in populations that have been adversely affected by developmental language disorders. Earlier studies of children with ASD have reported that the latency of MMF evoked by tones (Matsuzaki et al., 2019a; Roberts et al., 2011; Oram Cardy et al., 2005b) and vowels (Matsuzaki et al., 2019b) was prolonged significantly in children with ASD compared to typically developing children. Of particular note is one earlier study, which used child-customized MEG to investigate 3–5-year-old TD children and children with ASD (Yoshimura et al., 2017). Children with ASD were found to have significantly lower MMF amplitude in the left superior temporal gyrus than that of typically developing children. Classification of the children with ASD according to the developmental history of a speech onset delay (ASD with speech onset delay and ASD without speech onset delay, respectively) and comparison of them with typically developing children revealed that both ASD groups exhibited decreased activation in the left superior temporal gyrus. By contrast, the ASD with speech onset delay group exhibited increased activity in the left frontal cortex (i.e., pars orbitalis) compared with that of the other groups (Fig. 1). For all children with ASD, significant negative correlation was found between the MMF amplitude in the left pars orbitalis and language performance. These findings might reflect the diversity of brain function maturation associated with language development in ASD. Although randomized clinical studies are still necessary, using objective methods such as MMF to elucidate brain features corresponding to symptoms in young children can be expected to provide important information to support effective interventions from young childhood.

Brain spontaneous activity includes physiological oscillations that occur with or without an explicit task, such as sensory input. Brain spontaneous activity might be regarded as a disturbing factor (e.g., noise) if a researcher is interested in brain stimulus processing. However, spontaneous activity is informative of the current mental state (e.g., wakefulness or alertness). In addition, spontaneous activity is regarded as reflecting brain maturation during development, such as in network formation and synaptogenesis. Abnormalities in brain network during neural maturation attract many researchers: they are assumed to be related to the pathophysiology of ASD. Therefore, in recent years, many researchers have specifically studied spontaneous brain activity (i.e. resting-state (RS) neural rhythms) in children with ASD using MEG with higher temporal resolution. Preschool children are not usually able to tolerate the noises and narrow spaces of MRI recording. Therefore, it has been difficult to obtain structural brain information onto which researchers superimpose the coordinate systems of source-estimated

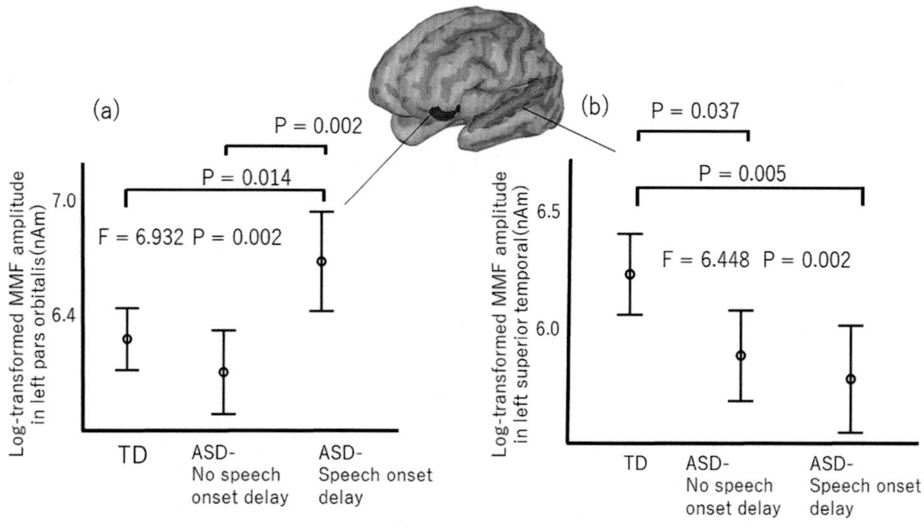

FIG. 1

Comparison of the voice-evoked MMF source amplitude among the three groups.

Modified from Yoshimura, Y., et al., 2017. Altered human voice processing in the frontal cortex and a developmental language delay in 3–5-year-old children with autism spectrum disorder. Sci. Rep. 7(1), 17116.

MEG signals. Therefore, to date, few studies have employed source-level analysis for spontaneous brain activity in preschool children. Instead, studies using sensor-level analysis have been reported for preschool-aged children (Kikuchi et al., 2013a, b, 2015; Hiraishi et al., 2015). Using a custom child-sized MEG system, one earlier study demonstrated significantly reduced long distance connectivity via theta oscillation in 3–7-year-old children with ASD. This reduced connectivity was correlated significantly with clinical severity (low sociability) in children with ASD (Kikuchi et al., 2015). Moreover, other studies have demonstrated rightward connectivity between the parietal and temporal regions in 3–7-year-old children with ASD via gamma-band oscillations (Kikuchi et al., 2013a). This rightward-lateralized connectivity is associated with preserved ability in a visual reasoning task in 5–7-year-old children with ASD (Kikuchi et al., 2013b). These findings indicate that children with ASD have inherently different neural connectivity, which is associated with their reduced social ability, but which might preserve the ability in visual tasks.

For children over 6 years old with ASD, some earlier studies of brain spontaneous activity have used source-level analysis with individual brain structures (Cornew et al., 2012; Lajiness-O'Neill et al., 2018; Edgar et al., 2019). Cornew and colleagues found elevated delta, theta, alpha, and high-frequency (20–120 Hz) powers in 6–15-year-old children with ASD. They found that increased temporal and parietal alpha power is associated with greater symptom severity (Cornew et al., 2012). Ye and colleagues found frequency-dependent alterations in functional connectivity in 12–15-year-old children with ASD (Ye et al., 2014). In this study, hyperconnectivity was observed among frontal, temporal, and sub-cortical regions in the beta and gamma frequency ranges, whereas parietal and occipital regions were hypoconnected to widespread brain regions in the theta and alpha bands in ASD. In addition, results from graphic analyses have confirmed that frequency-dependent alterations of network topology exist at both global and local levels. Furthermore, a study which specifically examined the peak alpha frequency (PAF) in children and adolescents with ASD demonstrated that the higher non-verbal IQ was associated with a higher PAF in ASD (older than 10 years old) (Edgar et al., 2019).

In neurophysiological studies, activities such as enhancement of the high-frequency component (gamma-oscillation) and attenuation of the low-frequency component power (alpha or beta) observed in the motor area have been reported in association with body movement. These dynamic changes in cortical oscillations are thought to reflect their local organized neural activities. Enhancement of a specific frequency oscillation because of the cortical activation is called event-related synchronization (ERS). The attenuation is called event-related desynchronization (ERD). Numerous studies have examined oscillation and ERS/ERD during psychological tasks. Aberrant ERS/ERD in children with ASD has been reported not only during motor tasks (An et al., 2018; Buard et al., 2018; Gaetz et al., 2020), but also during language processing task (Tanigawa et al., 2018), visual tasks (Stroganova et al., 2015), and working memory tasks (Urbain et al., 2016). In one recent study, Gaetz and colleagues examined motor cortical oscillation (mu 8–13 Hz, beta 15–30 Hz band) using button press tasks for 8–24-year-old people with ASD. They reported significant reduction in post-movement beta rebound power in the older cohort of children >13.2 years in ASD (Gaetz et al., 2020). In younger children of 5–7 years with ASD, another recent study revealed that the amplitude of motor-related gamma oscillations was significantly lower than that of control children (An et al., 2018). These aberrant dynamics of cortical oscillation might reflect the imbalance of cortical excitability and inhibition which is probably one aspect of the pathophysiology of ASD.

Recent development studies have devoted attention to phenomena caused by neural activities called cross-frequency coupling (CFC) and phase-amplitude coupling (PAC), in which different frequency components are mutually related. Actually, CFC is a phenomenon by which higher frequency signals are modulated or gated by lower frequency signals. One form of CFC, PAC, exhibits a phenomenon by which changes in the potential (amplitude) in high-frequency bands such as the gamma band are synchronized with changes in the phase of low-frequency components. Using this PAC analysis for MEG data, Port and colleagues investigated resting state brain activity in 119 4–16-year-old children with ASD. They demonstrated that children with ASD showed regionally specific abnormalities in alpha to low-gamma PAC, with increased alpha to low-gamma PAC for a central midline source and decreased PAC for lateral sources (Port et al., 2019). In addition, these results demonstrated that the lower temporal-posterior PAC estimates in the left hemisphere and the higher central midline PAC estimates were associated with greater autism severity (i.e. *t*-score of the social responsiveness scale).

Computational models have become an important tool for studying the nervous system. They are commonly used for the simulation of specific aspects of physiology and pathology at various levels. These computational models frame hypotheses that can be tested directly using biological or psychological experiments. Jones and colleagues proposed a biophysically realistic computational model for mu and alpha waves in the motor cortex using MEG (Jones et al., 2009). Using this computational model, Khan and colleagues evaluated functional connectivity in individuals with ASD aged 8–18 years old using MEG, which allowed them to resolve the directionality (feedforward versus feedback) of functional connectivity. The biophysically realistic computational model using data-driven feedforward and feedback parameters replicated the MEG data faithfully. The results suggest decreased nonlinearity (i.e., cortical feedback) alongside an increased veridical component of the cortical response (i.e., cortical feedforward) in ASD (Khan et al., 2015).

4. MEG studies in children with language disorders

Earlier reports of MEG studies have described children with dyslexia, specific language impairment (SLI), and stutterers. Many earlier studies have specifically examined the responses evoked (or induced) by external auditory stimuli (i.e., noise, tone, syllable or word), although some recent studies have emphasized the assessment of brain activity during listening, reading or speech tasks, or of spontaneous brain activity.

In typically developing children without any language disability, native-language phonetic perception has been assumed to represent a critically important step in initial language learning and in promoting language growth (Kuhl et al., 2006; Tsao et al., 2004; Kuhl, 2010). Brain responses to human voices have been examined as a physiological indicator of language acquisition (Kuhl et al., 2014; Yoshimura et al., 2012, 2014; Kuhl, 2010; Imada et al., 2006). Therefore, for children with language disorders, most earlier studies have also investigated brain responses to human voices. More specifically, many earlier studies have emphasized assessment of auditory brain response to syllables (Pihko et al., 2007, 2008; Paul et al., 2006a, b; Breier et al., 2003; Heim et al., 2003, 2000). Some earlier studies have emphasized responses to word stimuli (Helenius et al., 2014; Mody et al., 2008; Wehner et al., 2007), whereas some studies specifically addressed auditory-evoked responses to noise or tones (Oram Cardy et al., 2005a, 2008; Heim et al., 2000; Johnson et al., 2013; Roberts et al., 2012; van Bijnen et al., 2019). It is intriguing that, with improvement of data analyzing techniques such as envelope analysis, recent studies are specifically examining brain reactions when listening to continuous speech or rhythmic sounds (Etchell et al., 2016; Molinaro et al., 2016; Lizarazu et al., 2015; Centanni et al., 2018).

To assess brain responses to syllabic auditory stimuli, Pihko and colleagues demonstrated reduced M50 magnitude in both hemispheres (but no significant difference in the MMF component) of 5–7-year-old children with SLI (Pihko et al., 2008). It is intriguing that they also demonstrated that phonological intervention enhances M50 magnitude in both hemispheres and MMF magnitude in the left hemisphere in 6–7-year-old children with SLI (Pihko et al., 2007). In school-aged children with dyslexia, Heim and colleagues specifically investigated asymmetry of the auditory system and demonstrated reduced brain asymmetry in the location of the M50 (Heim et al., 2003) and N260m (Paul et al., 2006a) sources and aberrant location of the M210 source (Heim et al., 2000). Nevertheless, no significant differences were found in the MMF component (Paul et al., 2006b). Breier and colleagues reported the functional lateralization of the auditory system and demonstrated less left-dominant lateralization of brain activity corresponding to the M100 in school-aged children with dyslexia (Breier et al., 2003). With regard to the brain responses to auditory word stimuli, three earlier studies, one of children with SLI and two of children with dyslexia demonstrated aberrant brain activation in the left hemisphere during word perception (Helenius et al., 2014; Mody et al., 2008; Wehner et al., 2007).

To explore brain activity during reading or speech tasks, Simos and colleagues have emphasized the study of brain activity during reading. Based on those results, they have demonstrated reduced or aberrant activity in the left hemisphere in children and adolescents with dyslexia (Simos et al., 2000a, b, 2011). It is noteworthy that they also demonstrated that intensive phonological intervention induced normalizing (in the left hemisphere) or compensatory (in the right hemisphere) changes in 7–9-year-old children with dyslexia (Simos et al., 2007a, b).

With the recent development of analysis techniques, MEG studies in children with language disorders are examining brain wave entrainment to the human speech or rhythmic sounds. Brain wave entrainment is any procedure that causes one's brainwave frequencies to synchronize with a periodic stimulus (sound or light). Such entrainment is thought to reflect cognitive processing (Doelling and Poeppel, 2015). In one recent MEG study of young subjects aged 8–14 years with dyslexia, MEG signals were recorded while they were listening to continuously spoken sentences. The results demonstrated the reduced neural synchrony to speech oscillations in primary auditory regions in individuals with developmental dyslexia, which might hinder higher-order speech processing steps (Molinaro et al., 2016). Another recent study examined stuttering in children aged 3–9 years: MEG signals were recorded while they were listening to rhythmic sounds. The results suggest that stuttering might result from abnormalities in predictive brain responses that are reflected in abnormal entrainment of the beta band envelope to rhythmic sounds (Etchell et al., 2016). Although the exact aetiology of stuttering remains unknown, these results suggest that stuttering might result from abnormalities in predictive brain responses to rhythmic sounds.

Regarding the brain functional network, Dimitriadis and colleagues reported aberrant brain networks in young subjects with dyslexia using the weighted phase synchronization measure. They demonstrated reduced overall sensor-level network organization across all frequency bands and reduced temporal correlations between sensors covering the left temporoparietal region and the remaining sensors in the beta band (Dimitriadis et al., 2013). Furthermore, Dimitriadis and colleagues supported the aberrant brain network hypothesis using various analytical techniques; i.e., phase-to-amplitude coupling values (Dimitriadis et al., 2016), novel data-driven topological filtering technique based on orthogonal minimal spanning trees (Dimitriadis et al., 2017), graph modeling (Seither-Preisler et al., 2014), and dynamic functional connectivity (Dimitriadis et al., 2019).

5. MEG studies in children with ADHD

During the past three decades, EEG research has been undertaken to characterize and quantify the neurophysiology of ADHD, most consistently associating it with an increased theta/beta power ratio during resting conditions compared to non-ADHD controls (Loo and Makeig, 2012; Sangal and Sangal, 2014). In 2013, the US Food and Drug Administration (FDA) approved a medical device that uses this EEG theta/beta ratio to help assess ADHD in children and adolescents ages 6–17. This device, along with other clinical information, might help health care professionals to diagnose ADHD more accurately. However, with regard to MEG studies of children with ADHD, few studies have been reported.

As a diagnostic tool, two studies have demonstrated the usefulness of background MEG analysis. One fuzzy entropy method was used for 14 ADHD and 14 control children (Gomez et al., 2013). In the earlier study, using receiver operating characteristic (ROC) curves, the highest values of accuracy (82%) and the area under the ROC curve (0.9) were found using sensors located in anterior brain areas. The other study measured functional and effective connectivity using resting EEG and MEG data in 11 ADHD and 11 control children. High accuracy (98%) for the ADHD diagnosis was achieved using machine-learning algorithms (Muthuraman et al., 2019). However, because of the small sample sizes examined in these two earlier studies, additional studies must be conducted with larger sample sizes from a different cohort.

With regard to brain dysfunction in the frontal area, several earlier MEG studies have demonstrated aberrant frontal brain activity in school-aged children with ADHD using a set-shifting task (Mulas et al., 2006; Mogadam et al., 2019), complexity analysis during a resting condition (Fernandez et al., 2009), or connectivity analysis during a resting condition (Khadmaoui et al., 2016).

As a predictor of the clinical response to methylphenidate (MPH) treatment, one earlier study investigated the influence of MPH on the power spectrum of MEG activity during the resting state in children with ADHD (Wienbruch et al., 2005). This study demonstrated an increase of theta band power after administration of MPH. Moreover, it demonstrated that such an increase in the theta band over the left frontal region was associated with behavioral improvement.

In light of the close interdependence between auditory and attentional functions in humans (Riccio et al., 1994), one study specifically examined the size of Heschl's gyri and bilateral auditory evoked responses (M50) in musically trained children and children with ADHD. They demonstrated that children with ADHD showed smaller Heschl's gyri and bilaterally less synchronized auditory evoked responses (M50), which was the reverse of the pattern found for musically trained children (Seither-Preisler et al., 2014). It is intriguing that the results of one recent study suggest that bilaterally less synchronized auditory evoked responses (M50) are associated with ADHD-like symptoms in children with ASD (Yoshimura et al., 2016).

6. Points to consider for young children

Several crucially important points demand particular attention when researching the brain activity of children with neurodevelopmental disorders. Unlike psychiatric disorders in adulthood, neurodevelopmental disorders appear in early childhood (i.e., immature states of development). Given that children with neurodevelopmental disorders follow atypical developmental trajectories (e.g., linear, quadratic, or curvilinear) with respect to their brain maturation, fine-grained age-specific studies of children must be conducted over a wider age range. Otherwise, averaging over a wide age range might cancel out age-specific brain abnormalities in neurodevelopmental disorders. In addition, one must consider that sex, intelligence, and environmental issues (e.g., family income and education) might be confounding factors.

Furthermore, attention must be devoted to the heterogeneity of each disorder (i.e., ASD, ADHD and language disorders). In addition, some symptoms overlap among the different diagnoses. These disorders frequently co-occur. Therefore, further study of the physiological brain features corresponding to each symptom (in addition to diagnosis) is necessary to gain insight into the underlying pathophysiology of complex symptoms.

7. Conclusions

The history of epilepsy research with MEG has continued for more than 30 years. At present, MEG plays an important role in pre-surgical evaluation. In addition, for more than 10 years, MEG studies have contributed substantially to the understanding of brain function during both typical and atypical development in young children. Detailed findings from future studies provided using neuroimaging methods might aid clinical diagnosis and might even contribute to the refinement of diagnostic categories for neurodevelopmental disorders (e.g., ASD, ADHD, and language disorders). Although further MEG studies in young children, including infants (Roberts et al., 2014), and further technological innovation (Sander et al., 2012; Espy et al., 2013) are crucially important, MEG is a promising child-friendly method to address these goals.

References

An, K.M., et al., 2018. Altered gamma oscillations during motor control in children with autism Spectrum disorder. J. Neurosci. 38 (36), 7878–7886.

Baio, J., et al., 2018. Prevalence of autism Spectrum disorder among children aged 8 years - autism and developmental disabilities monitoring network, 11 sites, United States, 2014. MMWR Surveill. Summ. 67 (6), 1–23.

Baumgartner, C., et al., 2019. Presurgical epilepsy evaluation and epilepsy surgery. F1000Res 8. F1000 Faculty Rev-1818.

Bloy, L., et al., 2019. Auditory evoked response delays in children with 47, XYY syndrome. Neuroreport 30 (7), 504–509.

Bosseler, A.N., et al., 2013. Theta brain rhythms index perceptual narrowing in infant speech perception. Front. Psychol. 4, 690.

Breier, J.I., et al., 2003. Abnormal activation of temporoparietal language areas during phonetic analysis in children with dyslexia. Neuropsychology 17 (4), 610–621.

Buard, I., et al., 2018. Neuromagnetic beta-band oscillations during motor imitation in youth with autism. Autism Res. Treat. 2018, 9035793.

Centanni, T.M., et al., 2018. Increased variability of stimulus-driven cortical responses is associated with genetic variability in children with and without dyslexia. Dev. Cogn. Neurosci. 34, 7–17.

Chou, N., Serafini, S., Muh, C.R., 2018. Cortical language areas and plasticity in pediatric patients with epilepsy: a review. Pediatr. Neurol. 78, 3–12.

Cimbalnik, J., Kucewicz, M.T., Worrell, G., 2016. Interictal high-frequency oscillations in focal human epilepsy. Curr. Opin. Neurol. 29 (2), 175–181.

Cornew, L., et al., 2012. Resting-state oscillatory activity in autism spectrum disorders. J. Autism Dev. Disord. 42 (9), 1884–1894.

Crystal, D., 1987. The Cambridge Encyclopedia of Language. Cambridge University Press, Cambridge.

Demopoulos, C., et al., 2015. Deficits in auditory processing contribute to impairments in vocal affect recognition in autism spectrum disorders: a MEG study. Neuropsychology 29 (6), 895–908.

Dimitriadis, S.I., et al., 2013. Altered temporal correlations in resting-state connectivity fluctuations in children with reading difficulties detected via MEG. Neuroimage 83, 307–317.

Dimitriadis, S.I., et al., 2016. Greater repertoire and temporal variability of cross-frequency coupling (CFC) modes in resting-state neuromagnetic recordings among children with Reading difficulties. Front. Hum. Neurosci. 10, 163.

Dimitriadis, S.I., et al., 2017. Data-driven topological filtering based on orthogonal minimal spanning trees: application to multigroup magnetoencephalography resting-state connectivity. Brain Connect. 7 (10), 661–670.

Dimitriadis, S.I., et al., 2019. Typical and aberrant functional brain flexibility: lifespan development and aberrant organization in traumatic brain injury and dyslexia. Brain Sci. 9 (12), 380.

Doelling, K.B., Poeppel, D., 2015. Cortical entrainment to music and its modulation by expertise. Proc. Natl. Acad. Sci. U. S. A. 112 (45), E6233–E6242.

Dwivedi, R., et al., 2017. Surgery for drug-resistant epilepsy in children. N. Engl. J. Med. 377 (17), 1639–1647.

Edgar, J.C., et al., 2014. Missing and delayed auditory responses in young and older children with autism spectrum disorders. Front. Hum. Neurosci. 8, 417.

Edgar, J.C., et al., 2015. Auditory encoding abnormalities in children with autism spectrum disorder suggest delayed development of auditory cortex. Mol. Autism. 6, 69.

Edgar, J.C., et al., 2019. Abnormal maturation of the resting-state peak alpha frequency in children with autism spectrum disorder. Hum. Brain Mapp. 40 (11), 3288–3298.

El Tahry, R., et al., 2018. Magnetoencephalography and ictal SPECT in patients with failed epilepsy surgery. Clin. Neurophysiol. 129 (8), 1651–1657.

Espy, M., Matlashov, A., Volegov, P., 2013. SQUID-detected ultra-low field MRI. J. Magn. Reson. 229, 127–141.

Etchell, A.C., et al., 2016. Abnormal time course of low beta modulation in non-fluent preschool children: a magnetoencephalographic study of rhythm tracking. Neuroimage 125, 953–963.

Fernandez, A., et al., 2009. Complexity analysis of spontaneous brain activity in attention-deficit/hyperactivity disorder: diagnostic implications. Biol. Psychiatry 65 (7), 571–577.

Frauscher, B., et al., 2017. High-frequency oscillations: the state of clinical research. Epilepsia 58 (8), 1316–1329.

Gaetz, W., et al., 2020. Evaluating motor cortical oscillations and age-related change in autism spectrum disorder. Neuroimage 207, 116349.

Gage, N.M., Siegel, B., Roberts, T.P., 2003a. Cortical auditory system maturational abnormalities in children with autism disorder: an MEG investigation. Brain Res. Dev. Brain Res. 144 (2), 201–209.

Gage, N.M., et al., 2003b. Cortical sound processing in children with autism disorder: an MEG investigation. Neuroreport 14 (16), 2047–2051.

Garcia-Tarodo, S., et al., 2018. Magnetoencephalographic recordings in infants: a retrospective analysis of seizure-focus yield and postsurgical outcomes. J. Clin. Neurophysiol. 35 (6), 454–462.

Gilley, P.M., et al., 2005. Developmental changes in refractoriness of the cortical auditory evoked potential. Clin. Neurophysiol. 116 (3), 648–657.

Gomez, C., et al., 2013. Entropy analysis of MEG background activity in attention-deficit/hyperactivity disorder. Conf. Proc. IEEE Eng. Med. Biol. Soc. 2013, 5057–5060.

Heim, S., et al., 2000. Atypical organisation of the auditory cortex in dyslexia as revealed by MEG. Neuropsychologia 38 (13), 1749–1759.

Heim, S., Eulitz, C., Elbert, T., 2003. Altered hemispheric asymmetry of auditory P100m in dyslexia. Eur. J. Neurosci. 17 (8), 1715–1722.

Helenius, P., et al., 2014. Abnormal functioning of the left temporal lobe in language-impaired children. Brain Lang. 130, 11–18.

Hiraishi, H., et al., 2015. Unusual developmental pattern of brain lateralization in young boys with autism spectrum disorder: power analysis with child-sized magnetoencephalography. Psychiatry Clin. Neurosci. 69 (3), 153–160.

Imada, T., et al., 2006. Infant speech perception activates Broca's area: a developmental magnetoencephalography study. Neuroreport 17 (10), 957–962.

Ito, T., et al., 2015. Advantageous information provided by magnetoencephalography for patients with neocortical epilepsy. Brain Dev. 37 (2), 237–242.

Jenkins, J., et al., 2016. Auditory evoked M100 response latency is delayed in children with 16p11.2 deletion but not 16p11.2 duplication. Cereb. Cortex 26 (5), 1957–1964.

Johnson, B.W., et al., 2010. Measurement of brain function in pre-school children using a custom sized whole-head MEG sensor array. Clin. Neurophysiol. 121 (3), 340–349.

Johnson, B.W., et al., 2013. Lateralized auditory brain function in children with normal reading ability and in children with dyslexia. Neuropsychologia 51 (4), 633–641.

Jones, S.R., et al., 2009. Quantitative analysis and biophysically realistic neural modeling of the MEG mu rhythm: rhythmogenesis and modulation of sensory-evoked responses. J. Neurophysiol. 102 (6), 3554–3572.

Khadmaoui, A., et al., 2016. MEG analysis of neural interactions in attention-deficit/hyperactivity disorder. Comput. Intell. Neurosci. 2016, 8450241.

Khan, S., et al., 2015. Somatosensory cortex functional connectivity abnormalities in autism show opposite trends, depending on direction and spatial scale. Brain 138, 1394–1409.

Kikuchi, M., et al., 2011. Lateralized theta wave connectivity and language performance in 2- to 5-year-old children. J. Neurosci. 31 (42), 14984–14988.

Kikuchi, M., et al., 2013a. Altered brain connectivity in 3-to 7-year-old children with autism spectrum disorder. Neuroimage Clin. 2, 394–401.

Kikuchi, M., et al., 2013b. A custom magnetoencephalography device reveals brain connectivity and high reading/decoding ability in children with autism. Sci. Rep. 3, 1139.

Kikuchi, M., et al., 2015. Reduced long-range functional connectivity in young children with autism spectrum disorder. Soc. Cogn. Affect. Neurosci. 10 (2), 248–254.

Kim, Y.S., et al., 2011. Prevalence of autism spectrum disorders in a total population sample. Am. J. Psychiatry 168 (9), 904–912.

Kim, H., et al., 2013. Magnetic source imaging (MSI) in children with neocortical epilepsy: surgical outcome association with 3D post-resection analysis. Epilepsy Res. 106 (1–2), 164–172.

Kuhl, P.K., 2010. Brain mechanisms in early language acquisition. Neuron 67 (5), 713–727.

Kuhl, P.K., et al., 2006. Infants show a facilitation effect for native language phonetic perception between 6 and 12 months. Dev. Sci. 9 (2), F13–F21.

Kuhl, P.K., et al., 2014. Infants' brain responses to speech suggest analysis by synthesis. Proc. Natl. Acad. Sci. U. S. A. 111 (31), 11238–11245.

Lajiness-O'Neill, R., et al., 2018. Patterns of altered neural synchrony in the default mode network in autism spectrum disorder revealed with magnetoencephalography (MEG): relationship to clinical symptomatology. Autism Res. 11 (3), 434–449.

Lizarazu, M., et al., 2015. Developmental evaluation of atypical auditory sampling in dyslexia: functional and structural evidence. Hum. Brain Mapp. 36 (12), 4986–5002.

Loo, S.K., Makeig, S., 2012. Clinical utility of EEG in attention-deficit/hyperactivity disorder: a research update. Neurotherapeutics 9 (3), 569–587.

Matsuzaki, J., et al., 2012. Differential responses of primary auditory cortex in autistic spectrum disorder with auditory hypersensitivity. Neuroreport 23 (2), 113–118.

Matsuzaki, J., et al., 2014. Progressively increased M50 responses to repeated sounds in autism spectrum disorder with auditory hypersensitivity: a magnetoencephalographic study. PLoS One 9 (7), e102599.

Matsuzaki, J., et al., 2017. Delayed mismatch field latencies in autism Spectrum disorder with abnormal auditory sensitivity: a magnetoencephalographic study. Front. Hum. Neurosci. 11, 446.

Matsuzaki, J., et al., 2019a. Delayed auditory evoked responses in autism Spectrum disorder across the life span. Dev. Neurosci. 41 (3–4), 223–233.

Matsuzaki, J., et al., 2019b. Abnormal auditory mismatch fields in children and adolescents with 47, XYY Syndrome. Dev. Neurosci. 41 (1–2), 123–131.

Mody, M., Wehner, D.T., Ahlfors, S.P., 2008. Auditory word perception in sentence context in reading-disabled children. Neuroreport 19 (16), 1567–1571.

Mogadam, A., et al., 2019. Magnetoencephalographic (MEG) brain activity during a mental flexibility task suggests some shared neurobiology in children with neurodevelopmental disorders. J. Neurodev. Disord. 11 (1), 19.

Molinaro, N., et al., 2016. Out-of-synchrony speech entrainment in developmental dyslexia. Hum. Brain Mapp. 37 (8), 2767–2783.

Mulas, F., et al., 2006. Shifting-related brain magnetic activity in attention-deficit/hyperactivity disorder. Biol. Psychiatry 59 (4), 373–379.

Muthuraman, M., et al., 2019. Multimodal alterations of directed connectivity profiles in patients with attention-deficit/hyperactivity disorders. Sci. Rep. 9 (1), 20028.

Oram Cardy, J.E., et al., 2004. Prominence of M50 auditory evoked response over M100 in childhood and autism. Neuroreport 15 (12), 1867–1870.

Oram Cardy, J.E., et al., 2005a. Magnetoencephalography identifies rapid temporal processing deficit in autism and language impairment. Neuroreport 16 (4), 329–332.

Oram Cardy, J.E., et al., 2005b. Delayed mismatch field for speech and non-speech sounds in children with autism. Neuroreport 16 (5), 521–525.

Oram Cardy, J.E., et al., 2008. Auditory evoked fields predict language ability and impairment in children. Int. J. Psychophysiol. 68 (2), 170–175.

Orekhova, E.V., et al., 2012. Auditory cortex responses to clicks and sensory modulation difficulties in children with autism spectrum disorders (ASD). PLoS One 7 (6), e39906.

Paul, I., et al., 2006a. Reduced hemispheric asymmetry of the auditory N260m in dyslexia. Neuropsychologia 44 (5), 785–794.

Paul, I., et al., 2006b. Phonological but not auditory discrimination is impaired in dyslexia. Eur. J. Neurosci. 24 (10), 2945–2953.

Pihko, E., et al., 2004a. Somatosensory evoked potentials and magnetic fields elicited by tactile stimulation of the hand during active and quiet sleep in newborns. Clin. Neurophysiol. 115 (2), 448–455.

Pihko, E., et al., 2004b. Auditory evoked magnetic fields to speech stimuli in newborns—effect of sleep stages. Neurol. Clin. Neurophysiol. 2004, 6.

Pihko, E., et al., 2005. Magnetic fields evoked by speech sounds in preschool children. Clin. Neurophysiol. 116 (1), 112–119.

Pihko, E., et al., 2007. Group intervention changes brain activity in bilingual language-impaired children. Cereb. Cortex 17 (4), 849–858.

Pihko, E., et al., 2008. Language impairment is reflected in auditory evoked fields. Int. J. Psychophysiol. 68 (2), 161–169.

Port, R.G., et al., 2019. Children with autism Spectrum disorder demonstrate regionally specific altered resting-state phase-amplitude coupling. Brain Connect. 9 (5), 425–436.

Remijn, G.B., et al., 2014. Somatosensory evoked field in response to visuotactile stimulation in 3- to 4-year-old children. Front. Hum. Neurosci. 8, 170.

Riccio, C.A., et al., 1994. Comorbidity of central auditory processing disorder and attention-deficit hyperactivity disorder. J. Am. Acad. Child Adolesc. Psychiatry 33 (6), 849–857.
Roberts, T.P., et al., 2010. MEG detection of delayed auditory evoked responses in autism spectrum disorders: towards an imaging biomarker for autism. Autism Res. 3 (1), 8–18.
Roberts, T.P., et al., 2011. Auditory magnetic mismatch field latency: a biomarker for language impairment in autism. Biol Psychiatry 70 (3), 263–269.
Roberts, T.P., et al., 2012. Delayed magnetic mismatch negativity field, but not auditory M100 response, in specific language impairment. Neuroreport 23 (8), 463–468.
Roberts, T.P., et al., 2014. Artemis 123: development of a whole-head infant and young child MEG system. Front. Hum. Neurosci. 8, 99.
Roberts, T.P.L., et al., 2019. Delayed M50/M100 evoked response component latency in minimally verbal/nonverbal children who have autism spectrum disorder. Mol. Autism. 15 (10), 34.
Ryvlin, P., Cross, J.H., Rheims, S., 2014. Epilepsy surgery in children and adults. Lancet Neurol. 13 (11), 1114–1126.
Sander, T.H., et al., 2012. Magnetoencephalography with a chip-scale atomic magnetometer. Biomed. Opt. Express 3 (5), 981–990.
Sangal, R.B., Sangal, J.M., 2014. Use of EEG Beta-1 power and theta/beta ratio over Broca's area to confirm diagnosis of attention deficit/hyperactivity disorder in children. Clin. EEG Neurosci. 46 (3), 177–182.
Schmidt, G.L., et al., 2009. Absence of M100 source asymmetry in autism associated with language functioning. Neuroreport 20 (11), 1037–1041.
Seither-Preisler, A., Parncutt, R., Schneider, P., 2014. Size and synchronization of auditory cortex promotes musical, literacy, and attentional skills in children. J. Neurosci. 34 (33), 10937–10949.
Simos, P.G., et al., 2000a. Brain activation profiles in dyslexic children during non-word reading: a magnetic source imaging study. Neurosci. Lett. 290 (1), 61–65.
Simos, P.G., et al., 2000b. Cerebral mechanisms involved in word reading in dyslexic children: a magnetic source imaging approach. Cereb. Cortex 10 (8), 809–816.
Simos, P.G., et al., 2007a. Intensive instruction affects brain magnetic activity associated with oral word reading in children with persistent reading disabilities. J. Learn. Disabil. 40 (1), 37–48.
Simos, P.G., et al., 2007b. Altering the brain circuits for reading through intervention: a magnetic source imaging study. Neuropsychology 21 (4), 485–496.
Simos, P.G., et al., 2011. Functional disruption of the brain mechanism for reading: effects of comorbidity and task difficulty among children with developmental learning problems. Neuropsychology 25 (4), 520–534.
Stephen, J.M., et al., 2017. Development of auditory evoked responses in normally developing preschool children and children with autism Spectrum disorder. Dev. Neurosci. 39 (5), 430–441.
Stroganova, T.A., et al., 2015. Altered modulation of gamma oscillation frequency by speed of visual motion in children with autism spectrum disorders. J. Neurodev. Disord. 7 (1), 21.
Tanigawa, J., et al., 2018. Atypical auditory language processing in adolescents with autism spectrum disorder. Clin. Neurophysiol. 129 (9), 2029–2037.
Tecchio, F., et al., 2003. Auditory sensory processing in autism: a magnetoencephalographic study. Biol. Psychiatry 54 (6), 647–654.
Tomblin, J.B., et al., 1997. Prevalence of specific language impairment in kindergarten children. J. Speech Lang. Hear. Res. 40 (6), 1245–1260.
Tsao, F.M., Liu, H.M., Kuhl, P.K., 2004. Speech perception in infancy predicts language development in the second year of life: a longitudinal study. Child Dev. 75 (4), 1067–1084.
Urbain, C., et al., 2016. Desynchronization of fronto-temporal networks during working memory processing in autism. Hum. Brain Mapp. 37 (1), 153–164.
van Bijnen, S., et al., 2019. Left hemisphere enhancement of auditory activation in language impaired children. Sci. Rep. 9 (1), 9087.

van Klink, N., et al., 2019. Simultaneous MEG and EEG to detect ripples in people with focal epilepsy. Clin. Neurophysiol. 130 (7), 1175–1183.

Velmurugan, J., et al., 2019. Magnetoencephalography imaging of high frequency oscillations strengthens presurgical localization and outcome prediction. Brain 142 (11), 3514–3529.

Visser, S.N., et al., 2014. Trends in the parent-report of health care provider-diagnosed and medicated attention-deficit/hyperactivity disorder: United States, 2003-2011. J. Am. Acad. Child Adolesc. Psychiatry 53 (1), 34–46 (e2).

Wehner, D.T., Ahlfors, S.P., Mody, M., 2007. Effects of phonological contrast on auditory word discrimination in children with and without reading disability: a magnetoencephalography (MEG) study. Neuropsychologia 45 (14), 3251–3262.

Wienbruch, C., et al., 2005. The influence of methylphenidate on the power spectrum of ADHD children - an MEG study. BMC Psychiatry 5, 29.

Ye, A.X., et al., 2014. Atypical resting synchrony in autism spectrum disorder. Hum. Brain Mapp. 35 (12), 6049–6066.

Yoshimura, Y., et al., 2012. Language performance and auditory evoked fields in 2- to 5-year-old children. Eur. J. Neurosci. 35 (4), 644–650.

Yoshimura, Y., et al., 2013. Atypical brain lateralisation in the auditory cortex and language performance in 3- to 7-year-old children with high-functioning autism spectrum disorder: a child-customised magnetoencephalography (MEG) study. Mol. Autism. 4 (1), 38.

Yoshimura, Y., et al., 2014. A longitudinal study of auditory evoked field and language development in young children. Neuroimage 101, 440–447.

Yoshimura, Y., et al., 2016. Synchrony of auditory brain responses predicts behavioral ability to keep still in children with autism spectrum disorder: auditory-evoked response in children with autism spectrum disorder. Neuroimage Clin. 12, 300–305.

Yoshimura, Y., et al., 2017. Altered human voice processing in the frontal cortex and a developmental language delay in 3- to 5-year-old children with autism spectrum disorder. Sci. Rep. 7 (1), 17116.

Zhang, Y., et al., 2009. Neural signatures of phonetic learning in adulthood: a magnetoencephalography study. Neuroimage 46 (1), 226–240.

CHAPTER

A state-of-the-art methodological review of pediatric EEG

18

Wanze Xie[a,b] and Charles A. Nelson[c,d,e]

School of Psychological and Cognitive Sciences, Peking University, China[a] PKU-IDG/McGovern Institute for Brain Research, Peking University, China[b] Boston Children's Hospital, Boston, MA, United States[c] Harvard Medical School, Boston, MA, United States[d] Harvard Graduate School of Education, Cambridge, MA, United States[e]

1. Introduction to pediatric EEG

Electroencephalography (EEG) offers an easy-to-use tool to measure brain function in pediatric populations. It is often the method of choice when measuring brain activity in awake infants and children due to its superb temporal resolution, low-cost of recordings, and relatively higher tolerance to children's movements compared to other brain imaging methods, e.g., functional magnetic resonance imaging (fMRI). Using EEG allows researchers to monitor brain activity in young children during resting-state and cognitive tasks to understand the neurodevelopmental origin of human perception, cognition, and emotion.

Two widely adopted pediatric EEG measures are EEG power and event-related potential (ERP). The measure of EEG power in different frequency bands provides information regarding oscillatory activations in the brain at task and rest. ERP reflects time-locked changes in the brain's electrical activity in response to a perceptual or cognitive challenge. Both measures contribute to our understanding of the neural correlates of cognitive development in various domains, including attention (Richards, 2003a), face and emotion perception (de Haan and Nelson, 1997; Leppänen et al., 2007), action observation and execution (Marshall and Meltzoff, 2015), language acquisition (Kuhl, 2010), as well as memory and executive function (Wolfe and Bell, 2004). In addition, they are convenient and valid measurements to investigate the deviations from normative brain maturation in early experiences, e.g., adversities and neurodevelopmental disorders (Gabard-Durnam et al., 2019; Pierce et al., 2019; Wilkinson et al., 2019; Xie et al., 2019b). Articles and book series that offer comprehensive practical guides for using these two measures with pediatric populations are also available (Brooker et al., 2019; de Haan, 2007).

Although EEG power and ERP have contributed significantly to many aspects of our knowledge of early brain development, both tools provide limited information on the underlying neural generators (sources) nor the synchrony and connectivity among brain regions. To fill these gaps, recent advances have been made in adopting state-of-the-art techniques in pediatric EEG research, such as MRI-compatible EEG source localization and functional connectivity analysis. This chapter elaborates on these new techniques and their recent applications in the study of brain and cognitive development.

Handbook of Pediatric Brain Imaging. https://doi.org/10.1016/B978-0-12-816633-8.00014-4

Section 2 of the chapter gives an overview of MRI-compatible EEG source localization and introduces how it has been used along with conventional EEG power and ERP measures to inform neural mechanisms. Section 3 reviews cutting-edge methods to calculate the EEG functional connectivity and explains how they can be incorporated with EEG source localization to estimate connections between brain regions for pediatric participants.

There are two other characteristics of pediatric EEG/ERP: relatively low signal-to-noise ratio (SNR) and inconsistency in the selection of target ERP components, their time-window(s) and electrode location(s). While most researchers understand these are "naturally embedded features" in pediatric EEG studies, an alternative EEG approach, the *steady-state visual evoked potential* (ssVEP), has gained popularity among pediatric EEG researchers. This approach is purported to increase the SNR and allow researchers to objectively define the neural markers in their study (Rossion, 2014). Section 4 of this chapter will introduce the advantages and limitations of this method, as well as its recent applications in pediatric EEG studies.

2. MRI-compatible cortical source localization in pediatric EEG research

EEG signals recorded by electrodes placed on the scalp represent postsynaptic potentials generated by mass synchronized pyramidal neurons perpendicular to the cortical surface. Source localization or source analysis is the most often used method to identify underlying cortical generators (sources) of EEG potentials measured on the scalp. The sources of EEG signals can be modeled as electrical dipoles in the brain with three different features: position, directionality, and magnitude. The identification of the position of cortical sources is often obscured because the current generated by them spreads in all directions in the brain and gets smeared by the skull. To alleviate this problem, techniques to improve the spatial resolution of source localization have been constantly developed and refined. These efforts have made EEG a comprehensive and powerful brain imaging tool with reasonable spatial and superior temporal resolution (Michel and Murray, 2012).

Given the aforementioned advantages of using EEG with pediatric populations, MRI-compatible source localization with high-density EEG recordings has increasingly emerged as one of the top choices to investigate brain functioning in children. This section gives an overview of EEG source localization and the importance of using realistic head models in source localization for pediatric populations, followed by descriptions on recent studies using this technique as a neuroimaging tool to study brain functions and cognitive development in childhood.

2.1 EEG source localization

There are two major approaches to conduct source localization—equivalent current dipole (ECD) and distributed source modeling. ECD modeling uses a limited number of electrical dipoles or sources that are computed with a *forward model* to explain the distribution of the EEG on the scalp. A forward model is created with the locations of the electrodes on the scalp and a MRI head model that describes the tissues in the head and their conductivity values (Hallez et al., 2007). Distributed source modeling uses an *inverse model* along with the obtained EEG data to generate a large set of sources distributed across the brain. The inverse model is the "inverse" of the forward model and used to compute the position, directionality, and magnitude of the sources given the scalp EEG (He et al., 2018; Michel et al., 2004).

ECD source localization. ECD modeling assumes that the electrical potential over the entire scalp can be explained by a small set of dipoles (He et al., 1987). These hypothetical dipoles can vary in position, magnitude, and orientation in a 3D space. A forward model needs to be constructed to estimate the electrical activity over the scalp in ECD modeling. The forward model represents the head geometry and tissue conductivity and delineates how the activation generated by the dipoles propagates to the scalp; the so called "lead-field" matrix. The estimated electrical activity over the scalp is calculated by applying the forward model to the current dipoles with certain orientations and magnitudes (i.e., the forward solution). For ECD modeling, the output of this so-called forward solution can be compared to the actual electrical activity on the scalp, and thus the amount of variance explained by the selected current dipoles can be calculated (Richards, 2003b; Scherg, 1992). The optimal solution is gained through the iteration of the forward solution with different parameters (position, orientation, and magnitude) of the dipoles until the minimal residual variance is obtained (Scherg et al., 1999). Alternatively, a set of a priori fixed locations can be set based on theoretical specifications of the known effects, and thus only the parameters of orientation and magnitude are estimated. ECD models are generally overdetermined because the number of dipole parameters are significantly less than the number of surface sensors (electrodes, MEG positions) (Michel et al., 2004).

A practical concern associated with ECD modeling is the uncertainty about the number of dipoles and their locations to be tested by the forward solution. One solution to this problem is to make a priori assumptions of the number and location of dipoles based on a theoretical rationale from previous research using other neuroimaging tools, e.g., fMRI and positron emission tomography (PET) (Agam et al., 2011; Foxe et al., 2003; Gao et al., 2019).

Distributed source modeling. In distributed source models, cortical dipoles are distributed over the entire source space, each with a fixed position. The positions of the dipoles are called the *source space*. The source space can be gray matter (GM) voxels derived from a structural MRI, the surface of the brain, the inner compartment in boundary element methods, or the entire brain volume. A forward model is also needed for distributed source modeling. For distributed source modeling, the forward model is combined with the source space to estimate an inverse spatial filter (Grech et al., 2008). The inverse spatial filter, when multiplied by the observed scalp electrical current distribution, reconstructs the current density across the entire set of potential source positions.

The computation of the inverse spatial filter is problematic because the inverse of the lead-field matrix is "underdetermined" due to the number of sources being substantially larger than the number of surface electrodes. Thus, additional constraints must be imposed to obtain unique and well-posed linear inverse solutions (Grech et al., 2008; He et al., 2018). The solution to the underdetermined construction of the inverse spatial filter is to constrain the solution by some set of mathematical or quantitative procedures (Grech et al., 2008; Michel and He, 2012). There are a few widely adopted solutions in distributed source modeling, such as minimum norm estimation (MNE), standardized low-resolution electromagnetic tomography (sLORETA), exact low-resolution electromagnetic tomography (eLORETA), and beamforming techniques. Detailed description of these methods can be found elsewhere (Grech et al., 2008; Green and McDonald, 2009; Hallez et al., 2007; He et al., 2018).

2.2 Realistic head models for source localization in pediatric populations

The accuracy of source localization increases as the anatomical features of issues inside a head are more realistically represented and discriminated in the head model (Michel et al., 2004; Reynolds and Richards, 2009). Thus, using age-specific realistic head models for source localization is particularly important for pediatric populations, as there are substantial neuroanatomical changes of the tissues inside the head over childhood (e.g., synaptic pruning, myelination of axons and neurogenesis), and the structure of a child brain differs greatly from an adult brain (Phan et al., 2018; Reynolds and Richards, 2009; Richards and Xie, 2015). For example, the skull conductivity value and thickness are age dependent (Wendel et al., 2010), such that the skull conductivity value is much higher for infants than adults (Odabaee et al., 2014). Using adult skull conductivity values for infant EEG data may give rise to sources that are shallower in the cortex than where they should be.

A significant advance in cortical source analysis with pediatric participants is to use realistic head models created with individual MRIs or an age-appropriate MRI template (Guy et al., 2016; Hämäläinen et al., 2011; Ortiz-Mantilla et al., 2012; Xie et al., 2017). Although systematic estimation of skull conductivity for children at different ages has not been conducted, studies have tried to use higher skull conductivity values for source localization with pediatric EEG data (Hämäläinen et al., 2011; Ortiz-Mantilla et al., 2012; Xie et al., 2018a). There are now age-specific MRI templates available to the public for research purposes, which can be used to create realistic head models for children (e.g., the Neurodevelopment MRI Database) (Richards et al., 2016). Since the fontanels and unknitted skull sutures of an infant head may allow current flow to the scalp unimpeded by the skull, a future direction is to take these features into account when creating the realistic head models for infants.

2.3 Application of source localization in pediatric EEG research

Source localization of pediatric ERPs. Using cortical source localization techniques, researchers are able to identify the potential neural generators of ERP components in children. For example, the N290 ERP component is regarded as the precursor to the adult face-sensitive component, the N170 component (de Haan and Nelson, 1999; Halit et al., 2004). However, the cortical sources of this "infant face-sensitive component" remained unclear until two recent studies conducted source localization of the infant N290 component using the eLORETA method with realistic infant MRI models (Guy et al., 2016; Xie et al., 2019c). Both studies localized the infant N290 component to the fusiform face area (FFA) including the fusiform gyrus and inferior occipital gyrus, which is consistent with the cortical sources found for the adult N170 component (Gao et al., 2019). These studies also examined the cortical sources of two other frequently studied infant visual ERP components, the P400 and Nc components. These two components were predominantly localized to the posterior cingulate cortex (PCC) and precuneus regions, which highlights the important role that the P400 and Nc play in infant arousal and attention systems (Richards, 2003a; Xie and Richards, 2016). Source localization with age-appropriate head models has also been used to study the neural generators of infant auditory ERP components, such as ERPs in response to syllables and pitch changes (Hämäläinen et al., 2011; Ortiz-Mantilla et al., 2012), as well as well-studied visual evoked potentials (VEPs), e.g., the P1 and N1 (Jensen et al., 2019; Xie and Richards, 2017) (Fig. 1).

For older children and adolescents, the multimodal neuroimaging analysis could be conducted by a combination of MRI-constrained EEG source localization and fMRI techniques. This may provide convergent evidence on the underlying brain mechanisms of cognitive processes (Buzzell et al., 2017). A recent study examined the development of face-elicited brain activation in 9–12-year-old children using ERP source localization and fMRI measures (Liu et al., 2019). The authors found that the tomography of the ERP sources broadly corresponded with the fMRI activation evoked by the same facial

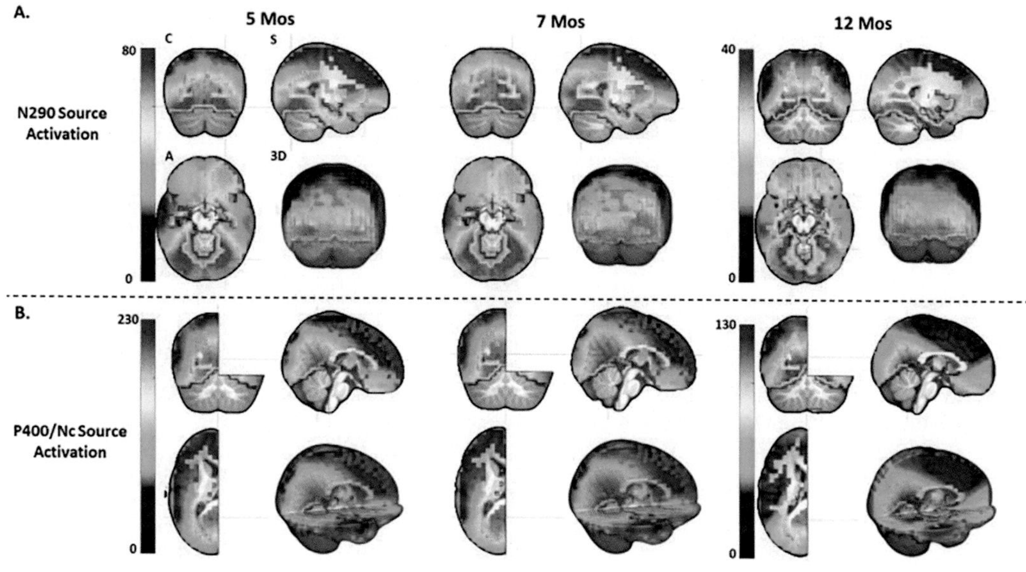

FIG. 1

Cortical source localization results of the infant N290, P400 and Nc components. Distributed source modeling was used with eLORETA method. The hot colors (*red and yellow*) in this figure represent brain regions showing greater activation in the time windows of the ERP components, which means they are more likely to be the cortical sources of the ERPs.

This figure is adopted from Xie, W., McCormick, S. A., Westerlund, A., Bowman, L. C., & Nelson, C. A., 2019c. Neural correlates of facial emotion processing in infancy. Dev. Sci. e12758. https://doi.org/10.1111/desc.12758.

stimuli, such that a core face-processing system including the inferior occipito-temporal and parietal regions was identified by both modalities.

Source localization of pediatric EEG rhythmic oscillations. EEG oscillations in different frequency bands have functional significances for cognitive development in various domains (Bell and Cuevas, 2012). Cortical source analysis of EEG rhythmic activation helps us to understand the neurodevelopmental origin of different cognitive processes. For instance, the mu rhythm (central alpha) is proposed to be associated with the human mirror neuron system (Marshall and Meltzoff, 2011). EEG source localization has been utilized to study the neurodevelopmental origin of the mirror neuron system in early childhood. A study by Thorpe and colleagues investigated the development of the mu activity during motor execution from childhood to adulthood (Thorpe et al., 2016). Distributed source analysis localized the mu activation to frontal and parietal regions, including the pre- and postcentral gyri, as well as the precuneus and inferior parietal lobule. The source locations of the mu rhythm were found to be consistent across 1- and 4-year-olds and adults. The finding of the posterior parietal regions being part of the sources generating the mu rhythm is reminiscent of two previous studies examining the infant mu rhythm using ECD models (Nystrom, 2008; Nystrom et al., 2011).

Prior studies have suggested that EEG rhythmic activity can be manipulated by infant visual attention. However, the cortical generators of brain rhythmic activity associated with infant attention remain unclear. To fill this knowledge gap, a recent study explored the complex patterns of EEG oscillations and their cortical sources observed during infant sustained attention (Xie et al., 2018b). Cortical source reconstruction of EEG power in different frequency bands was conducted with the eLORETA method and realistic head models created for each participant using individual MRIs. Infant sustained attention was found to be accompanied by increased theta power in the orbitofrontal and ventral temporal areas and decreased alpha power in brain regions within the default mode network (DMN). The relations between infant sustained attention and EEG power were not shown in infants at 6 and 8 months but emerged at 10 months and became well established by 12 months.

3. EEG functional connectivity and brain network measures for children

Progress made in developing novel neuroimaging tools in the past few decades makes it possible to investigate the dynamic interregional communications inside the brain and their development over childhood. Although fMRI is a frequently used neuroimaging to study the development of functional brain networks (Goldenberg and Galvan, 2015), the measure of EEG offers a comparatively inexpensive and easy-to-use alternative to achieve this research goal, particularly when dealing with pediatric populations (Boersma et al., 2013, 2011; Miskovic et al., 2015). The advantages stemming from the nature of EEG recording make it a more practical tool to estimate functional connectivity while young children are performing cognitive tasks or in rest-state while they are awake.

Construction of functional networks requires recording physiological or electrical signals from multiple spatial locations that can either be brain regions of interest (ROIs) or channels of EEG. Functional connectivity inside a network is typically estimated by analyzing the correlation or coherence between dynamic signals recorded at multiple locations. There are two widely used methods to define EEG functional networks—component analyses and seed-based connectivity maps. Component analysis, such as the independent and principle component analyses (ICA and PCA), highlights the brain networks (i.e., components) that share variance in EEG time series (Liu et al., 2017). Seed-based connectivity maps are comprised of predefined spatial locations (e.g., ROIs and electrodes) where EEG signals are synchronized with those in other seeds (Xie et al., 2018a, b). A broader view of EEG functional brain networks can be further pursued using graph theory measures to model the topology of networks and characterize their overall architecture (Rubinov and Sporns, 2010; Vertes and Bullmore, 2015).

The following paragraphs introduce methods that have been used to estimate the functional connectivity with EEG recordings. This is followed by a review on recent studies on EEG functional connectivity during task performance and the development of brain functional networks and using resting-state EEG recordings and graph theory measures. It should be noted that the combination of EEG source localization and functional connectivity analysis allows researchers to measure functional brain networks in the source-space (cortical level). Thus, this section also describes a few studies that have applied this technique to study source-space EEG functional connectivity in children.

3.1 Measures of EEG functional connectivity

A few methods have been developed to calculate functional connectivity among EEG signals. Frequently used methods in the field include coherence, phase-lock value, the imaginary part of the coherency (IC), phase lag index (PLI), weighted phase lag index (wPLI), and correlation between power envelope. The advantages and disadvantages of these methods have been discussed elsewhere (Bastos and Schoffelen, 2016). Here, we only briefly describe three of these methods, coherence, IC, and wPLI, and explain the volume conduction problem in EEG functional connectivity analysis.

$$C_{xy}(f) = \frac{|G_{xy}(f)|}{\sqrt{G_{xx}(f) * G_{xx}(f)}}.$$

Coherence (C_{xy}) between two signals x(t) and y(t) is defined by the equation above. "f" refers to the Fourier transformation of the signal in a certain time window. "Gxy" stands for the cross-spectral density (CSD) of the two signals "x" and "y" (e.g., two channels or brain regions) obtained from the Fourier frequency analysis. "Gxx" and "Gyy" represent the power-spectral density (PSD) for signals "x" and "y". It can be seen from the equation that coherence is a measure of the linear relationship between two signals and is an absolute value ranging between 0 and 1.

Coherence used to be a widely accepted method to estimate EEG functional connectivity and has been adopted in studies on EEG functional connectivity in pediatric populations (Cuevas et al., 2012; Thatcher et al., 1987). However, coherence between EEG electrodes can be easily contaminated by spurious or false positive connections due to the volume conduction or field spread problem (Nolte et al., 2004; Nunez et al., 1997). The volume conduction problem refers to the fact that the distance between source generators and EEG electrodes and the tissues that the currents flow through would lead to a mix of the currents generated by multiple sources. Additionally, there is spatial blurring effect of the skull on the distribution of EEG signals. Thus, rhythmic oscillations generated by a neuronal source may be picked up by multiple EEG sensors, particularly when they are close to each other, which in turn gives rise to unrealistically high coherence among these electrodes.

New methods have been developed to reduce the effects of volume conduction and the field spread on the estimation of functional connectivity between EEG sensors. The IC is one method that estimates the functional connectivity between two signals using the imaginary part of coherency (Nolte et al., 2004). Fourier transform of time series results in complex quantities that include a real part and an imaginary part. The imaginary part of coherency is only sensitive to the synchronization between two signals that are time-lagged to each other, i.e., it discards the contributions of 0° phase difference between the signals to their connectivity (Nolte et al., 2004). This is because there should be 0° phase difference (i.e., no time lag) between the spurious connections generated by the same sources, as electrical transmission in the brain is instantaneous. Thus, IC outperforms coherence in measuring the real interaction (connectivity) between two signals (Nolte et al., 2004).

wPLI is another recently developed method that is more resistant to the volume conduction problem than the measurement of coherence. wPLI is an extension of the PLI method. PLI estimates to what extent the phase leads or lags between two signals based on the imaginary part of the CSD of the two signals (Stam et al., 2007). A problem associated with PLI is that its estimation of the phase leads and lags can be impacted by noise perturbations in the signals that could possibly have near zero phase difference (Vinck et al., 2011). wPLI was designed to solve this issue by weighting the phase differences according to the magnitude of the leads and lags so that phase differences around zero would only have a marginal contribution to the wPLI value (Vinck et al., 2011).

Graph theory. Functional networks can be described as graphs that are composed of *nodes* and *edges*. The structure of a graph is typically described as a list of nodes and edges. This structure can be conveniently organized as a matrix termed as an *adjacency matrix*, which is generated with the outputs from EEG functional connectivity methods described mentioned above. An *adjacency matrix* is an $N \times N$ matrix representing the overall functional network with $N \times (N - 1)/2$ unique connections. Nodes are the components in the graph or matrix that represent the EEG electrodes or ROIs, while edges are the pairwise correlations/connectivity between the nodes in a functional network (i.e., graph; see (Bullmore and Sporns, 2009)).

The architecture (topology) of a functional brain network represented by the adjacency matrix can be qualified and quantified by graph theory measures. Widely used graph theory measures include but are not limited to path length, clustering coefficient, degree centrality, betweenness centrality, network hubs, and small-worldness. The definition of these graph theory measures can be found in Chapter 14 of this book and other review articles (Bullmore and Sporns, 2009; Chu-Shore et al., 2011; Power et al., 2010; Rubinov and Sporns, 2010).

3.2 EEG functional connectivity analysis in pediatric populations

Development of functional brain networks. There is growing interest in using EEG to examine the development of brain networks in pediatric populations because of the easy application of EEG and its tolerance to movement compared to fMRI (Boersma et al., 2011; Smit et al., 2011). The results from these EEG studies have shown comparable findings on the development of brain functional networks with those from fMRI studies. Overall, there were changes in both integration and segregation of information processing in children's resting-state functional networks measured with EEG recordings.

The examination of connectivity between EEG oscillations using graph theory provides insights into the changes in the electrophysiological dynamics within functional networks. A longitudinal study conducted by Boersma et al. (2011) recorded resting-state eyes-closed EEG oscillations from children at 5 and 7 years of age. Synchronization likelihood (SL) represents the co-oscillation between EEG signals. Boersma et al. (2011) calculated the SL in three frequency bands (theta: 4–6 Hz, alpha: 6–11 Hz, and beta: 11–25 Hz) between each pair of electrodes to obtain SL-weighted graphs. The mean SL over all pairs of electrodes was found to decrease from 5 to 7 years of age. Boersma et al. (2011) interpreted this finding as reflecting the pruning of unused synapses and the preservation of strong connections, which in turn might result in more cost-effective networks. To test this hypothesis, the authors calculated the mean normalized clustering coefficient and path length to characterize a network organization. They found that the average clustering coefficient increased from 5 to 7 years of age in the alpha rhythm and the path length increased during this age in all three frequency bands. These findings were interpreted as indicating a shift from random to more organized functional networks during the development of the brain. Evidence on brain network development also originates from other studies that have investigated the development of EEG functional connectivity and network topology throughout the lifespan (Miskovic et al., 2015; Smit et al., 2012, 2011).

Although the findings of functional connectivity between signals in EEG electrodes have shed light on the development of brain functional networks, limited information about the underlying connections between brain regions could be inferred from scalp recorded EEG data. The effects of volume conduction on spurious connections are reduced when analyzing the functional connectivity between reconstructed cortical source activities (Schoffelen and Gross, 2009). Functional connectivity between brain ROIs can be estimated after the source localization of EEG time-series in electrodes (Bathelt et al., 2013; Hillebrand et al., 2012; Xie et al., 2019a). The combination of EEG connectivity and source localization techniques provides a practical way to examine the development of cortical networks in pediatric populations.

Bathelt et al. (2013) conducted a cortical source analysis of EEG recordings with head models created from age-specific MRI templates, and then examined functional connectivity between localized activation in cortical regions. The authors found an increase of the node degree, clustering coefficient, and betweenness centrality of functional brain networks with age (Bathelt et al., 2013), which was in alignment with previous fMRI research (Power et al., 2010). Bathelt and colleagues also applied eigenvalue decomposition to obtain functional brain modules that are separate networks comprising nodes (i.e., ROIs) that are richly connected within than across the module. The connections within brain modules remain unchanged but the inter-hemispheric connections between modules increased between 2 and 6 years of age.

EEG functional connectivity during task performance in children. There is accumulating evidence supporting the idea that specific cognitive functions are likely to be carried out by multiple interacting brain areas, which highlights the need for understanding brain-behavior relations from a network perspective. EEG functional connectivity has been leveraged to investigate neural mechanisms underlying child behaviors in various cognitive tasks on attention (Xie et al., 2019a, b, c), error monitoring (Buzzell et al., 2019), action execution and observation (Debnath et al., 2019), etc. For example, a recent study examined EEG connectivity in the Mu rhythm during action execution and observation in 9-month-old infants' (Debnath et al., 2019). EEG functional connectivity in the mu (alpha) frequency band was estimated with wPLI and found to be elevated between the central and occipital electrodes during infants' observation of hand movements, which supports the hypothesis that a distinct functional connection between the mirror neuron and attention systems might emerge during infants' observation of human action.

Studying dynamic interregional communications during different attentional states is critical to understand infants' improved performance and elevated ERP responses in cognitive tasks observed during sustained attention (Xie and Richards, 2016, 2017). To investigate functional connectivity in brain networks of awake infants, a group of researchers has recently developed a pipeline to estimate functional connectivity in the cortical source space (Fig. 2; Xie et al., 2019a, b, c). This pipeline includes cortical source reconstruction of EEG recordings with age-appropriate MRIs, estimating brain functional connectivity between brain regions, and applying graph theory measures to examine the overall architecture of brain networks. Using this pipeline, the authors were able to study how functional connectivity in brain networks, such as the dorsal and ventral attention, default mode (DMN), and somatosensory networks, changes across different attentional states. Their results revealed that infant heart-rated defined sustained attention is associated with attenuated connectivity in the alpha band within the dorsal attention network and the DMN, as well as distinct network organization and efficiency indicated by graph theory measures (Xie et al., 2019a, b, c). These findings provide direct evidence for the important role that the dorsal attention network and the DMN have in infant visual attention.

EEG network analysis in children at-risk for atypical development. Understanding the patterns of functional connectivity in children at-risk for neurodevelopmental disorders carries important clinical potential and may inform how brain networks are disrupted among these children. For example, there is support for the proposal that there are disruptions in EEG functional connectivity in the alpha band in infancy that are associated with later diagnosis of autism spectrum disorder (ASD) (Haartsen et al., 2019; Orekhova et al., 2014). Both studies have shown that higher functional connectivity in the alpha band at 14 months is associated with greater severity of restricted and repetitive behaviors at 36 months in children who met criteria for ASD. EEG functional connectivity has also been regarded as a fruitful source of potential biomarkers for attention deficit hyperactivity disorder (ADHD). A recent study has found an altered thalamo-cortical EEG connectivity profile in children with ADHD compared to healthy controls in alpha, beta, and gamma frequency bands, and using these EEG connectivity features

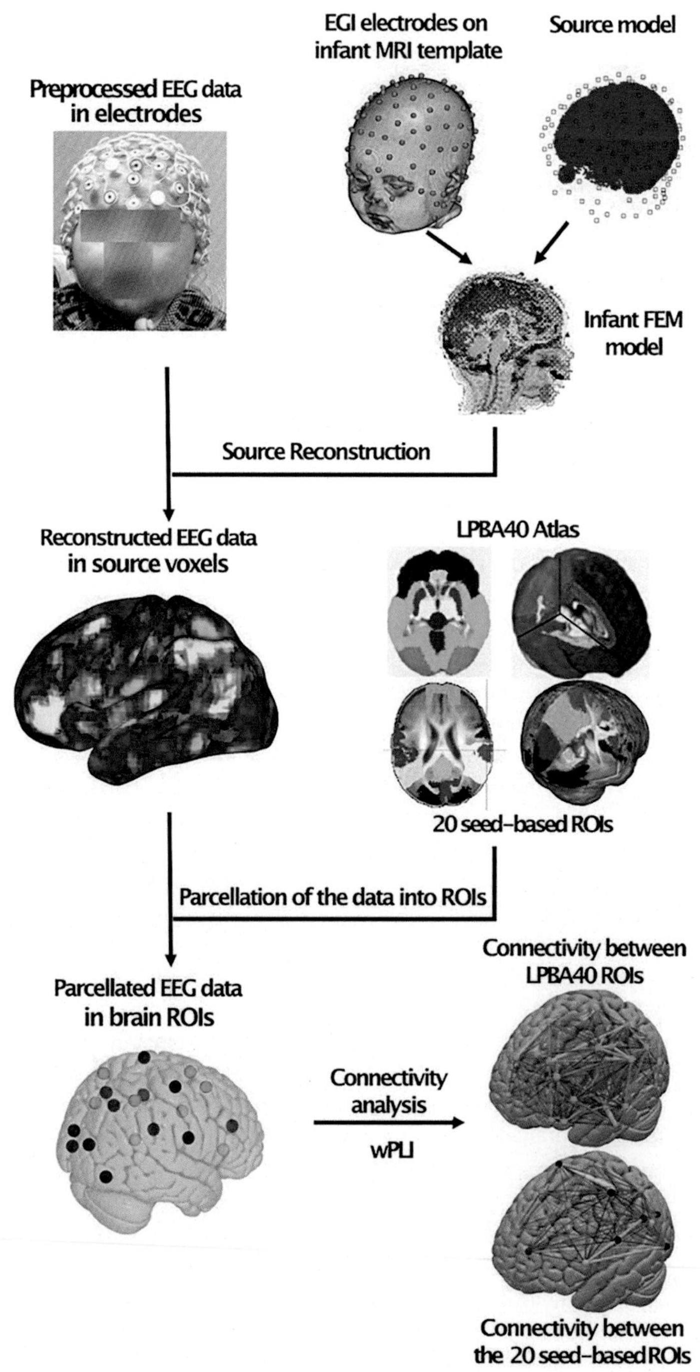

FIG. 2

A pipeline for EEG functional connectivity analysis in the source space. This pipeline was used in Xie et al. (2019a, b, c) with infants.

and machine learning techniques, the two groups can be classified/separated with high accuracy (Muthuraman et al., 2019). In another study, graph theory was applied to EEG connectivity matrices to determine whether network topology is different between ADHD children and typically developing controls (Ahmadlou et al., 2012). Decreased path length and increased clustering coefficient were found in children with ADHD compared to the control group. This atypical network topology might reflect more randomly organized brain networks with higher cost for functional connections in ADHD children.

The easy-to-use characteristic of EEG connectivity measures can also be harnessed to study how deviations in early experience, e.g., being exposed to early adversities, could shape brain networks, and affect neurocognitive outcomes in low-resource settings. To this end, a group of researchers have conducted a study examining the mechanistic pathways by which growth faltering in early childhood impacts future cognitive outcomes (Xie et al., 2019a). These investigators explored brain functional connectivity as a mediator of the effects of growth faltering on cognitive outcomes in a sample of impoverished, urban-dwelling, Bangladeshi children. This longitudinal study shows that whole-brain functional connectivity in the source space is associated with future cognitive function and, perhaps more importantly, that brain functional connectivity in theta and beta bands at 36 months mediates the relation between growth faltering and children's IQ 1 year later. These findings provide the first evidence of network connectivity as a neural pathway by which exposure to early adversity derails cognitive development in children living in low-resource settings. Another study using similar EEG connectivity and source localization methods examined the effect of prematurity (preterm birth) on early cortical network connectivity in newborns (Tokariev et al., 2019). The most prominent markers of prematurity, compared to healthy control infants, were found in functional connections involving the frontal regions, and these connections were correlated with newborn neurological performance.

4. ssVEP in pediatric EEG research

The steady-state visual evoked potential (ssVEP) is a type of evoked potential elicited by presenting a sequence of stimuli at a fixed rate, which can be obtained from scalp-recorded EEG signals. This approach has recently been adopted in studies on the neural bases of child visual perception. Compared to the conventional EEG and ERP measures, the major advantages of this approach include high SNR and objectively defined neural markers (frequencies) of interest (Rossion, 2014). These strengths have led to growing interest in using ssVEP to inform the neurodevelopmental origin of a few cognitive functions, such as visual attention (Christodoulou et al., 2018; Robertson et al., 2012) and face perception and recognition (de Heering and Rossion, 2015; Farzin et al., 2012). The current section gives a brief overview of the ssVEP approach, up-to-date examples on its application in children, as well as the limitations of this method in pediatric EEG research.

4.1 Introduction to ssVEP and its advantages

The ssVEPs are cortical responses generated at frequencies that are exact integer multiples of the stimulus presentation rate (Regan, 1989). The ssVEP method was developed by Regan (1966) in his study on human brain responses to low-level visual stimuli. In that study, Regan examined phase-locked neural responses to modulated light (luminance flicker) at different target frequency bins with respect to adjacencies frequencies (noise level). These steady-state or periodic brain responses to visual stimuli were identified predominately in central occipital electrodes and were found to be independent of the alpha activity that is a neural index of attention (Regan, 1966).

The frequency of stimulus presentation in an ssVEP paradigm is typically decided depending on the cognitive process of interest. There is a hypothesis that the stimulation frequency that generates the highest amplitude of the response is inversely related to the time needed for sufficiently processing the stimulus (Norcia et al., 2015). For instance, Regan (1966) found that the maximal brain response to the luminance flicker that evoked the process of low-level visual cues was at 10 Hz. However, a lower frequency (i.e., slower speed of presentation) may be needed for high-level cognitive processes (e.g., language processing and face perception). Indeed, a frequency rate of ~6 Hz for stimulus presentation has been used in studies on adult face perception (Rossion and Boremanse, 2011; Rossion et al., 2012), and presentation rate might need to be even slower for children (Farzin et al., 2012).

The ssVEP approach has a number of advantages compared to traditional ERP designs. One advantage of the ssVEP method is that this kind of frequency-tagging paradigm allows experimenters to objectively target the periodic visual response(s) of interest at a predefined frequency. For example, a 6 Hz stimulation sequence will provide a robust basic response at 6 Hz, and a target stimulus presented at the every 5th stimulation will elicit a distinct activation at 1.2 Hz (5/6 = 1.2). As a result, the basic and target responses are both confined to predefined frequencies of interest. A second advantage is that the fast-periodic stimulation sequence used in ssVEP experiments provides data with high SNR because a large number of stimuli can be presented in a relatively short period of time, e.g., 20–30 s. Moreover, noise in the data is distributed over the entire spectrum, and thus only a tiny fraction of the noise will be mixed with the target frequency bin of interest (Regan, 1989). These advantages make it possible to obtain a reliable periodic response at the individual level through only a few minutes of stimulus presentation. Therefore, the ssVEP approach has opened a new avenue for studying the neural correlates of cognitive processes in pediatric populations who have limited attention span.

4.2 Recent application of ssVEP

The ssVEP approach has been leveraged to study the neural correlates of face perception and categorization in childhood. Farzin et al. (2012) examined whether there was differential cortical activity underlying the structural encoding of human faces compared to objects in 4- and 6-month-old infants. The visual stimuli were presented at a frequency of 6 Hz (i.e., six images/s) and consisted of alternating scrambled and intact images (faces or objects) at a frequency of 3 Hz (i.e., three images/s for each category). This paradigm isolated brain responses to the structural differences between intact and scrambled images at the first harmonics (i.e., 3 Hz) from responses to the common local features in intact and scrambled images at the image update rate (i.e., 6 Hz). The authors found that infants showed significant ssVEP responses at 3 Hz for both faces and objects, meaning that they were able to detect the changes in the global structural information in these stimuli. Perhaps more importantly, the amplitude of the ssVEP response at 3 Hz was greater for faces than objects and the scalp distribution of this response was different between the two types of stimuli. These findings suggest that infants aged between 4 and 6 months already show more distinct neural responses to faces than objects, which is consistent with the existing infant ERP literature (de Haan and Nelson, 1999; Peykarjou and Hoehl, 2013; Xie and Richards, 2016).

de Heering and Rossion (2015) further investigated the rapid categorization of natural human faces from non-face objects in infants at this age (i.e., between 4 and 6 months) (de Heering and Rossion, 2015). During a stimulation train of 20 s, infants were presented with different images of objects at a fixed rate of 6 Hz, with face images varying in their size, viewpoint, luminance, gender, expression, and age, embedded at every fifth image (i.e., 1.2 Hz). The idea behind this paradigm is that if the infant's visual system discriminates between the two categories, their ssVEP response should be distinct at 1.2 Hz compared to the noise level. The response at 6 Hz and its harmonics was found to be located in the middle posterior regions, reflecting a general visual response to all stimuli (including faces), whereas the 1.2 Hz response was located in the occipito-temporal regions (de Heering and Rossion, 2015). This kind of ssVEP design was recently adopted by a study testing whether infants' ability to categorize faces from nonface objects could be boosted by their mother's odor (Leleu et al., 2019).

The strengths of the ssVEP approach also make it a useful tool for studying the development of attentional dynamics of visual search over childhood. Robertson et al. (2012) tested whether 12-week-old infants' ssVEP could be modulated by infant overt attention. Twelve-week-old infants were presented with a toy duck at the center of the screen in the first experiment. There were LED lights installed in the duck flicking at 8 Hz. The duck rotated back and forth for 2 s after infants fixated at it in the experimental condition, while it did not rotate in the control condition. The assumption was that rotating (moving) objects would increase infants' attention. The authors analyzed brain responses to the flicking duck at 8 Hz before and after the onset of its rotation and found that the ssVEP amplitude at 8 Hz increased significantly after the offset of the rotation in the experimental condition only, which indicates the effect of overt attention on infant ssVEPs. The effect of covert orienting on infant brain activation has also been studied using the ssVEP approach. In a recent experiment conducted by Christodoulou et al. (2018), 6×6 and 4×4 checkerboards were presented respectively in infants' peripheral fields (left and right) and an attractor was presented in the center. They were flicking at a frequency of 6 or 12 Hz. The 6×6 checkerboard is supposed to elicit more visual attention from young infants than the 4×4 checkerboard. Christodoulou et al. (2018) found that the amplitude of the ssVEP to the 6×6 checkerboard was greater than that to the 4×4 checkerboard regardless of the flicking frequency. This finding provides convergent evidence for the effect of covert orienting on infants' visual processing of a peripheral stimulus.

4.3 Limitations

Although the ssVEP approach has gradually become an alternative tool to investigate the neurodevelopmental origins of cognitive functions, a couple of limitations should be kept in mind. First, the frequency of stimulus presentation, i.e., how fast the stimulation sequence is presented, should be determined based on the age of participants and the cognitive functions examined. For example, a frequency rate of ~6 Hz for stimulus presentation has been adopted from studies on adult face perception in recent child ssVEP research; however, whether this rate is adequate for young children to process and discriminate different types of faces remains unclear given their low visual acuity and processing efficiency. Future research may consider testing a sweep ssVEP response to justify the presentation rate/speed for various kinds of visual stimuli and different age groups, as what has been done for adults (Alonso-Prieto et al., 2013).

The ssVEP approach is limited in offering precise temporal and spatial information of brain activation due to the periodic nature of steady-state stimuli, especially when they were presented at high rates (Norcia et al., 2015). The Fourier transform of EEG time series eliminates the temporal information of the cognitive processes triggered by the stimulation sequence. Although researchers have attempted to analyze the ERP components evoked by the fast and periodic stimulus presentation (Yan et al., 2019), directly relating results of ssVEP responses to the temporal evolution of ERPs is still challenging. The spatial resolution of ssVEP is also restricted due to the volume conduction issue. However, source localization of child ssVEP responses with age-appropriate MRIs should be advocated in future research, as the validity of source localization relies on the SNR in the EEG data. The high SNR in ssVEP offers an advantage of incorporating source localization into ssVEP analysis.

5. Conclusion

In this chapter, we reviewed recent progress made in pediatric EEG research and state-of-the-art EEG methods that have rendered EEG a top brain imaging tool to study the child brain. The straightforward compatibility of EEG with other brain imaging techniques, especially structural MRI, leads to the growing interest in using EEG source localization with age-appropriate MRI models to investigate the neural mechanisms underlying cognitive functions in children. Cutting-edge methods in EEG functional connectivity analysis now allow researchers to study the development of brain networks in infancy and how the trajectory could be derailed by neurodevelopmental disorders or exposure to early adversities. Moreover, alternative paradigms like ssVEP have recently been adopted to increase the SNR and objectively define neural markers of interests in pediatric EEG research. In spite of the many issues still to overcome in this filed, all the efforts and advances reviewed in this chapter have demonstrated how quickly the field is growing and the promising future of pediatric EEG research.

References

Agam, Y., Hamalainen, M.S., Lee, A.K., Dyckman, K.A., Friedman, J.S., Isom, M., Manoach, D.S., 2011. Multimodal neuroimaging dissociates hemodynamic and electrophysiological correlates of error processing. Proc. Natl. Acad. Sci. U. S. A. 108 (42), 17556–17561. https://doi.org/10.1073/pnas.1103475108.

Ahmadlou, M., Adeli, H., Adeli, A., 2012. Graph theoretical analysis of organization of functional brain networks in ADHD. Clin. EEG Neurosci. 43 (1), 5–13. https://doi.org/10.1177/1550059411428555.

Alonso-Prieto, E., Belle, G.V., Liu-Shuang, J., Norcia, A.M., Rossion, B., 2013. The 6 Hz fundamental stimulation frequency rate for individual face discrimination in the right occipito-temporal cortex. Neuropsychologia 51 (13), 2863–2875. https://doi.org/10.1016/j.neuropsychologia.2013.08.018.

Bastos, A.M., Schoffelen, J.M., 2016. A tutorial review of functional connectivity analysis methods and their interpretational pitfalls. Front. Syst. Neurosci. 9. https://doi.org/10.3389/Fnsys.2015.00175, 175.

Bathelt, J., O'Reilly, H., Clayden, J.D., Cross, J.H., de Haan, M., 2013. Functional brain network organisation of children between 2 and 5 years derived from reconstructed activity of cortical sources of high-density EEG recordings. NeuroImage 82, 595–604. https://doi.org/10.1016/j.neuroimage.2013.06.003.

Bell, M.A., Cuevas, K., 2012. Using EEG to study cognitive development: issues and practices. J. Cogn. Dev. 13 (3), 281–294. https://doi.org/10.1080/15248372.2012.691143.

Boersma, M., Smit, D.J., de Bie, H.M., Van Baal, G.C., Boomsma, D.I., de Geus, E.J., Stam, C.J., 2011. Network analysis of resting state EEG in the developing young brain: structure comes with maturation. Hum. Brain Mapp. 32 (3), 413–425. https://doi.org/10.1002/hbm.21030.

Boersma, M., Smit, D.J., Boomsma, D.I., De Geus, E.J., Delemarre-van de Waal, H.A., Stam, C.J., 2013. Growing trees in child brains: graph theoretical analysis of electroencephalography-derived minimum spanning tree in 5- and 7-year-old children reflects brain maturation. Brain Connect. 3 (1), 50–60. https://doi.org/10.1089/brain.2012.0106.

Brooker, R.J., Bates, J.E., Buss, K.A., Canen, M.J., Dennis-Tiwary, T.A., Gatzke-Kopp, L.M., Schmidt, L.A., 2019. Conducting event-related potential (ERP) research with young children. J. Psychophysiol., 1–22. https://doi.org/10.1027/0269-8803/a000243.

Bullmore, E., Sporns, O., 2009. Complex brain networks: graph theoretical analysis of structural and functional systems. Nat. Rev. Neurosci. 10 (3), 186–198. https://doi.org/10.1038/nrn2575.

Buzzell, G.A., Richards, J.E., White, L.K., Barker, T.V., Pine, D.S., Fox, N.A., 2017. Development of the error-monitoring system from ages 9-35: unique insight provided by MRI-constrained source localization of EEG. NeuroImage 157, 13–26. https://doi.org/10.1016/j.neuroimage.2017.05.045.

Buzzell, G.A., Barker, T.V., Troller-Renfree, S.V., Bernat, E.M., Bowers, M.E., Morales, S., Fox, N.A., 2019. Adolescent cognitive control, theta oscillations, and social observation. NeuroImage 198, 13–30. https://doi.org/10.1016/j.neuroimage.2019.04.077.

Christodoulou, J., Leland, D.S., Moore, D.S., 2018. Overt and covert attention in infants revealed using steady-state visually evoked potentials. Dev. Psychol. 54 (5), 803–815. https://doi.org/10.1037/dev0000486.

Chu-Shore, C.J., Kramer, M.A., Bianchi, M.T., Caviness, V.S., Cash, S.S., 2011. Network analysis: applications for the developing brain. J. Child Neurol. 26 (4), 488–500. https://doi.org/10.1177/0883073810385345.

Cuevas, K., Swingler, M.M., Bell, M.A., Marcovitch, S., Calkins, S.D., 2012. Measures of frontal functioning and the emergence of inhibitory control processes at 10 months of age. Dev. Cogn. Neurosci. 2 (2), 235–243. https://doi.org/10.1016/j.dcn.2012.01.002.

de Haan, M. (Ed.), 2007. Infant EEG and Event-Related Potentials. Psychological Press, New York.

de Haan, M., Nelson, C.A., 1997. Recognition of the mother's face by six-month-old infants: a neurobehavioral study. Child Dev. 68 (2), 187–210. https://doi.org/10.2307/1131845.

de Haan, M., Nelson, C.A., 1999. Brain activity differentiates face and object processing in 6-month-old infants. Dev. Psychol. 35 (4), 1113–1121.

de Heering, A., Rossion, B., 2015. Rapid categorization of natural face images in the infant right hemisphere. elife 4. https://doi.org/10.7554/eLife.06564, e06564.

Debnath, R., Salo, V.C., Buzzell, G.A., Yoo, K.H., Fox, N.A., 2019. Mu rhythm desynchronization is specific to action execution and observation: evidence from time-frequency and connectivity analysis. NeuroImage 184, 496–507. https://doi.org/10.1016/j.neuroimage.2018.09.053.

Farzin, F., Hou, C., Norcia, A.M., 2012. Piecing it together: infants' neural responses to face and object structure. J. Vis. 12 (13), 6. https://doi.org/10.1167/12.13.6.

Foxe, J.J., McCourt, M.E., Javitt, D.C., 2003. Right hemisphere control of visuospatial attention: line-bisection judgments evaluated with high-density electrical mapping and source analysis. NeuroImage 19 (3), 710–726.

Gabard-Durnam, L.J., Wilkinson, C., Kapur, K., Tager-Flusberg, H., Levin, A.R., Nelson, C.A., 2019. Longitudinal EEG power in the first postnatal year differentiates autism outcomes. Nat. Commun. 10 (1), 4188. https://doi.org/10.1038/s41467-019-12202-9.

Gao, C., Conte, S., Richards, J.E., Xie, W., Hanayik, T., 2019. The neural sources of N170: understanding timing of activation in face-selective areas. Psychophysiology. https://doi.org/10.1111/psyp.13336, e13336.

Goldenberg, D., Galvan, A., 2015. The use of functional and effective connectivity techniques to understand the developing brain. Dev. Cogn. Neurosci. 12, 155–164. https://doi.org/10.1016/j.dcn.2015.01.011.

Grech, R., Cassar, T., Muscat, J., Camilleri, K.P., Fabri, S.G., Zervakis, M., Vanrumste, B., 2008. Review on solving the inverse problem in EEG source analysis. J. Neuroeng. Rehabil. 5, 25. https://doi.org/10.1186/1743-0003-5-25.

Green, J.J., McDonald, J.J., 2009. A practical guide to beamformer source reconstruction for EEG. In: Handy, T.C. (Ed.), Brain Signal Analysis: Advances in Neuroelectric and Neuromagnetic Methods. The MIT Press, Cambridge, MA, pp. 76–98.

Guy, M.W., Zieber, N., Richards, J.E., 2016. The cortical development of specialized face processing in infancy. Child Dev. https://doi.org/10.1111/cdev.12543.

Haartsen, R., Jones, E.J.H., Orekhova, E.V., Charman, T., Johnson, M.H., Team, B., 2019. Functional EEG connectivity in infants associates with later restricted and repetitive behaviours in autism; a replication study. Transl. Psychiatry 9 (1), 66. https://doi.org/10.1038/s41398-019-0380-2.

Halit, H., Csibra, G., Volein, A., Johnson, M.H., 2004. Face-sensitive cortical processing in early infancy. J. Child Psychol. Psychiatry 45 (7), 1228–1234. https://doi.org/10.1111/j.1469-7610.2004.00321.x.

Hallez, H., Vanrumste, B., Grech, R., Muscat, J., De Clercq, W., Vergult, A., Lemahieu, I., 2007. Review on solving the forward problem in EEG source analysis. J. Neuroeng. Rehabil. 4, 46. https://doi.org/10.1186/1743-0003-4-46.

Hämäläinen, J.A., Ortiz-Mantilla, S., Benasich, A.A., 2011. Source localization of event-related potentials to pitch change mapped onto age-appropriate MRIs at 6 months of age. NeuroImage 54 (3), 1910–1918. https://doi.org/10.1016/j.neuroimage.2010.10.016.

He, B., Musha, T., Okamoto, Y., Homma, S., Nakajima, Y., Sato, T., 1987. Electric dipole tracing in the brain by means of the boundary element method and its accuracy. IEEE Trans. Biomed. Eng. 34 (6), 406–414.

He, B., Sohrabpour, A., Brown, E., Liu, Z., 2018. Electrophysiological source imaging: a noninvasive window to brain dynamics. Annu. Rev. Biomed. Eng. 20, 171–196. https://doi.org/10.1146/annurev-bioeng-062117-120853.

Hillebrand, A., Barnes, G.R., Bosboom, J.L., Berendse, H.W., Stam, C.J., 2012. Frequency-dependent functional connectivity within resting-state networks: an atlas-based MEG beamformer solution. NeuroImage 59 (4), 3909–3921. https://doi.org/10.1016/j.neuroimage.2011.11.005.

Jensen, S.K.G., Kumar, S., Xie, W., Tofail, F., Haque, R., Petri, W.A., Nelson, C.A., 2019. Neural correlates of early adversity among Bangladeshi infants. Sci. Rep. 9 (1), 3507. https://doi.org/10.1038/s41598-019-39242-x.

Kuhl, P.K., 2010. Brain mechanisms in early language acquisition. Neuron 67 (5), 713–727. https://doi.org/10.1016/j.neuron.2010.08.038.

Leleu, A., Rekow, D., Poncet, F., Schaal, B., Durand, K., Rossion, B., Baudouin, J.Y., 2019. Maternal odor shapes rapid face categorization in the infant brain. Dev. Sci. https://doi.org/10.1111/desc.12877, e12877.

Leppänen, J.M., Moulson, M.C., Vogel-Farley, V.K., Nelson, C.A., 2007. An ERP study of emotional face processing in the adult and infant brain. Child Dev. 78 (1), 232–245. https://doi.org/10.1111/j.1467-8624.2007.00994.x.

Liu, Q., Farahibozorg, S., Porcaro, C., Wenderoth, N., Mantini, D., 2017. Detecting large-scale networks in the human brain using high-density electroencephalography. Hum. Brain Mapp. https://doi.org/10.1002/hbm.23688.

Liu, P., Bai, X., Perez-Edgar, K.E., 2019. Integrating high-density ERP and fMRI measures of face-elicited brain activity in 9-12-year-old children: an ERP source localization study. NeuroImage 184, 599–608. https://doi.org/10.1016/j.neuroimage.2018.09.070.

Marshall, P.J., Meltzoff, A.N., 2011. Neural mirroring systems: exploring the EEG mu rhythm in human infancy. Dev. Cogn. Neurosci. 1 (2), 110–123. https://doi.org/10.1016/j.dcn.2010.09.001.

Marshall, P.J., Meltzoff, A.N., 2015. Body maps in the infant brain. Trends Cogn. Sci. 19 (9), 499–505. https://doi.org/10.1016/j.tics.2015.06.012.

Michel, C., He, B., 2012. EEG mapping and source imaging. In: Schomer, D., Lopes da Silva, F.H. (Eds.), Niedermeyer's Electroencephalography. Lippincott Williams & Wilkins, Philadelphia, PA, pp. 1179–1202.

Michel, C.M., Murray, M.M., 2012. Towards the utilization of EEG as a brain imaging tool. NeuroImage 61 (2), 371–385. https://doi.org/10.1016/j.neuroimage.2011.12.039.

Michel, C.M., Murray, M.M., Lantz, G., Gonzalez, S., Spinelli, L., Grave de Peralta, R., 2004. EEG source imaging. Clin. Neurophysiol. 115 (10), 2195–2222. https://doi.org/10.1016/j.clinph.2004.06.001.

Miskovic, V., Ma, X., Chou, C.A., Fan, M., Owens, M., Sayama, H., Gibb, B.E., 2015. Developmental changes in spontaneous electrocortical activity and network organization from early to late childhood. NeuroImage 118, 237–247. https://doi.org/10.1016/j.neuroimage.2015.06.013.

Muthuraman, M., Moliadze, V., Boecher, L., Siemann, J., Freitag, C.M., Groppa, S., Siniatchkin, M., 2019. Multimodal alterations of directed connectivity profiles in patients with attention-deficit/hyperactivity disorders. Sci. Rep. 9 (1), 20028. https://doi.org/10.1038/s41598-019-56398-8.

Nolte, G., Bai, O., Wheaton, L., Mari, Z., Vorbach, S., Hallett, M., 2004. Identifying true brain interaction from EEG data using the imaginary part of coherency. Clin. Neurophysiol. 115 (10), 2292–2307. https://doi.org/10.1016/j.clinph.2004.04.029.

Norcia, A.M., Appelbaum, L.G., Ales, J.M., Cottereau, B.R., Rossion, B., 2015. The steady-state visual evoked potential in vision research: a review. J. Vis. 15 (6), 4. https://doi.org/10.1167/15.6.4.

Nunez, P.L., Srinivasan, R., Westdorp, A.F., Wijesinghe, R.S., Tucker, D.M., Silberstein, R.B., Cadusch, P.J., 1997. EEG coherency. 1. Statistics, reference electrode, volume conduction, Laplacians, cortical imaging, and interpretation at multiple scales. Electroencephalogr. Clin. Neurophysiol. 103 (5), 499–515. https://doi.org/10.1016/S0013-4694(97)00066-7.

Nystrom, P., 2008. The infant mirror neuron system studied with high density EEG. Soc. Neurosci. 3 (3–4), 334–347. https://doi.org/10.1080/17470910701563665.

Nystrom, P., Ljunghammar, T., Rosander, K., von Hofsten, C., 2011. Using mu rhythm desynchronization to measure mirror neuron activity in infants. Dev. Sci. 14 (2), 327–335.

Odabaee, M., Tokariev, A., Layeghy, S., Mesbah, M., Colditz, P.B., Ramon, C., Vanhatalo, S., 2014. Neonatal EEG at scalp is focal and implies high skull conductivity in realistic neonatal head models. NeuroImage 96, 73–80. https://doi.org/10.1016/j.neuroimage.2014.04.007.

Orekhova, E.V., Elsabbagh, M., Jones, E.J., Dawson, G., Charman, T., Johnson, M.H., Team, B., 2014. EEG hyper-connectivity in high-risk infants is associated with later autism. J. Neurodev. Disord. 6 (1), 40. https://doi.org/10.1186/1866-1955-6-40.

Ortiz-Mantilla, S., Hamalainen, J.A., Benasich, A.A., 2012. Time course of ERP generators to syllables in infants: a source localization study using age-appropriate brain templates. NeuroImage 59 (4), 3275–3287. https://doi.org/10.1016/j.neuroimage.2011.11.048.

Peykarjou, S., Hoehl, S., 2013. Three-month-olds' brain responses to upright and inverted faces and cars. Dev. Neuropsychol. 38 (4), 272–280. https://doi.org/10.1080/87565641.2013.786719.

Phan, T.V., Smeets, D., Talcott, J.B., Vandermosten, M., 2018. Processing of structural neuroimaging data in young children: bridging the gap between current practice and state-of-the-art methods. Dev. Cogn. Neurosci. 33, 206–223. https://doi.org/10.1016/j.dcn.2017.08.009.

Pierce, L.J., Thompson, B.L., Gharib, A., Schlueter, L., Reilly, E., Valdes, V., Nelson, C.A., 2019. Association of perceived maternal stress during the perinatal period with electroencephalography patterns in 2-month-old infants. JAMA Pediatr. https://doi.org/10.1001/jamapediatrics.2019.0492.

Power, J.D., Fair, D.A., Schlaggar, B.L., Petersen, S.E., 2010. The development of human functional brain networks. Neuron 67 (5), 735–748. https://doi.org/10.1016/j.neuron.2010.08.017.

Regan, D., 1966. Some characteristics of average steady-state and transient responses evoked by modulated light. Electroencephalogr. Clin. Neurophysiol. 20, 238–248.

Regan, D., 1989. Human Brain Electrophysiology: Evoked Potentials and Evoked Magnetic Fields in Science and Medicine. Elsevier, Amsterdam.

Reynolds, G.D., Richards, J.E., 2009. Cortical source localization of infant cognition. Dev. Neuropsychol. 34 (3), 312–329. https://doi.org/10.1080/87565640902801890. PII 910996962.

Richards, J.E., 2003a. Attention affects the recognition of briefly presented visual stimuli in infants: an ERP study. Dev. Sci. 6 (3), 312–328. https://doi.org/10.1111/1467-7687.00287.

Richards, J.E., 2003b. Cortical sources of event-related potentials in the prosaccade and antisaccade task. Psychophysiology 40 (6), 878–894.

Richards, J.E., Xie, W., 2015. Brains for all the ages: structural neurodevelopment in infants and children from a life-span perspective. In: Benson, J. (Ed.), Advances in Child Development and Behavior. vol. 48. Elsevier, Philadephia, PA, pp. 1–52.

Richards, J.E., Sanchez, C., Phillips-Meek, M., Xie, W., 2016. A database of age-appropriate average MRI templates. NeuroImage 124, 1254–1259. https://doi.org/10.1016/j.neuroimage.2015.04.055.

Robertson, S.S., Watamura, S.E., Wilbourn, M.P., 2012. Attentional dynamics of infant visual foraging. Proc. Natl. Acad. Sci. U. S. A. 109 (28), 11460–11464. https://doi.org/10.1073/pnas.1203482109.

Rossion, B., 2014. Understanding face perception by means of human electrophysiology. Trends Cogn. Sci. 18 (6), 310–318. https://doi.org/10.1016/j.tics.2014.02.013.

Rossion, B., Boremanse, A., 2011. Robust sensitivity to facial identity in the right human occipito-temporal cortex as revealed by steady-state visual-evoked potentials. J. Vis. 11 (2). https://doi.org/10.1167/11.2.16.

Rossion, B., Prieto, E.A., Boremanse, A., Kuefner, D., Van Belle, G., 2012. A steady-state visual evoked potential approach to individual face perception: effect of inversion, contrast-reversal and temporal dynamics. NeuroImage 63 (3), 1585–1600. https://doi.org/10.1016/j.neuroimage.2012.08.033.

Rubinov, M., Sporns, O., 2010. Complex network measures of brain connectivity: uses and interpretations. NeuroImage 52 (3), 1059–1069. https://doi.org/10.1016/j.neuroimage.2009.10.003.

Scherg, M., 1992. Functional imaging and localization of electromagnetic brain activity. Brain Topogr. 5 (2), 103–111.

Scherg, M., Bast, T., Berg, P., 1999. Multiple source analysis of interictal spikes: goals, requirements, and clinical value. J. Clin. Neurophysiol. 16 (3), 214–224.

Schoffelen, J.M., Gross, J., 2009. Source connectivity analysis with MEG and EEG. Hum. Brain Mapp. 30 (6), 1857–1865. https://doi.org/10.1002/hbm.20745.

Smit, D.J., de Geus, E.J., van de Nieuwenhuijzen, M.E., van Beijsterveldt, C.E., van Baal, G.C., Mansvelder, H.D., Linkenkaer-Hansen, K., 2011. Scale-free modulation of resting-state neuronal oscillations reflects prolonged brain maturation in humans. J. Neurosci. 31 (37), 13128–13136. https://doi.org/10.1523/JNEUROSCI.1678-11.2011.

Smit, D.J., Boersma, M., Schnack, H.G., Micheloyannis, S., Boomsma, D.I., Hulshoff Pol, H.E., de Geus, E.J., 2012. The brain matures with stronger functional connectivity and decreased randomness of its network. PLoS One 7 (5). https://doi.org/10.1371/journal.pone.0036896, e36896.

Stam, C.J., Nolte, G., Daffertshofer, A., 2007. Phase lag index: assessment of functional connectivity from multi channel EEG and MEG with diminished bias from common sources. Hum. Brain Mapp. 28 (11), 1178–1193. https://doi.org/10.1002/hbm.20346.

Thatcher, R.W., Walker, R.A., Giudice, S., 1987. Human cerebral hemispheres develop at different rates and ages. Science 236 (4805), 1110–1113.

Thorpe, S.G., Cannon, E.N., Fox, N.A., 2016. Spectral and source structural development of mu and alpha rhythms from infancy through adulthood. Clin. Neurophysiol. 127 (1), 254–269. https://doi.org/10.1016/j.clinph.2015.03.004.

Tokariev, A., Roberts, J.A., Zalesky, A., Zhao, X., Vanhatalo, S., Breakspear, M., Cocchi, L., 2019. Large-scale brain modes reorganize between infant sleep states and carry prognostic information for preterms. Nat. Commun. 10 (1). https://doi.org/10.1038/s41467-019-10467-8.

Vertes, P.E., Bullmore, E.T., 2015. Annual research review: growth connectomics—the organization and reorganization of brain networks during normal and abnormal development. J. Child Psychol. Psychiatry 56 (3), 299–320. https://doi.org/10.1111/jcpp.12365.

Vinck, M., Oostenveld, R., van Wingerden, M., Battaglia, F., Pennartz, C.M., 2011. An improved index of phase-synchronization for electrophysiological data in the presence of volume-conduction, noise and sample-size bias. NeuroImage 55 (4), 1548–1565. https://doi.org/10.1016/j.neuroimage.2011.01.055.

Wendel, K., Vaisanen, J., Seemann, G., Hyttinen, J., Malmivuo, J., 2010. The influence of age and skull conductivity on surface and subdermal bipolar EEG leads. Comput. Intell. Neurosci. 2010, 397272. https://doi.org/10.1155/2010/397272.

Wilkinson, C.L., Levin, A.R., Gabard-Durnam, L.J., Tager-Flusberg, H., Nelson, C.A., 2019. Reduced frontal gamma power at 24 months is associated with better expressive language in toddlers at risk for autism. Autism Res. 12 (8), 1211–1224. https://doi.org/10.1002/aur.2131.

Wolfe, C.D., Bell, M.A., 2004. Working memory and inhibitory control in early childhood: contributions from physiology, temperament, and language. Dev. Psychobiol. 44 (1), 68–83. https://doi.org/10.1002/dev.10152.

Xie, W., Richards, J.E., 2016. Effects of interstimulus intervals on behavioral, heart rate, and event-related potential indices of infant engagement and sustained attention. Psychophysiology 53 (8), 1128–1142. https://doi.org/10.1111/psyp.12670.

Xie, W., Richards, J.E., 2017. The relation between infant covert orienting, sustained attention and brain activity. Brain Topogr. 30 (2), 198–219. https://doi.org/10.1007/s10548-016-0505-3.

Xie, W., Mallin, B.M., Richards, J.E., 2017. Development of infant sustained attention and its relation to EEG oscillations: an EEG and cortical source analysis study. Dev. Sci. https://doi.org/10.1111/desc.12562.

Xie, W., Jensen, K.G., Wade, M., Kumar, S., Westerlund, A., Kakon, S.H., Nelson, C.A., 2018a. Child growth predicts brain functional connectivity and future cognitive outcomes in urban Bangladeshi children exposed to early adversities. bioRxiv. https://doi.org/10.1101/447722, 447722.

Xie, W., Mallin, B.M., Richards, J.E., 2018b. Development of brain functional connectivity and its relation to infant sustained attention in the first year of life. Dev. Sci. https://doi.org/10.1111/desc.12703, e12703.

Xie, W., Jensen, S.K.G., Wade, M., Kumar, S., Westerlund, A., Kakon, S.H., Nelson, C.A., 2019a. Growth faltering is associated with altered brain functional connectivity and cognitive outcomes in urban Bangladeshi children exposed to early adversity. BMC Med. 17 (1), 199. https://doi.org/10.1186/s12916-019-1431-5.

Xie, W., Kumar, S., Kakon, S.H., Haque, R., Petri, W.A., Nelson, C.A., 2019b. Chronic inflammation is associated with neural responses to faces in Bangladeshi children. NeuroImage 202, 116110. https://doi.org/10.1016/j.neuroimage.2019.116110.

Xie, W., McCormick, S.A., Westerlund, A., Bowman, L.C., Nelson, C.A., 2019c. Neural correlates of facial emotion processing in infancy. Dev. Sci. https://doi.org/10.1111/desc.12758, e12758.

Yan, X., Liu-Shuang, J., Rossion, B., 2019. Effect of face-related task on rapid individual face discrimination. Neuropsychologia 129, 236–245. https://doi.org/10.1016/j.neuropsychologia.2019.04.002.

SECTION 4

Imaging development and disorders thereof

CHAPTER

Imaging early brain structural and functional development

19

Minhui Ouyang[a], Christopher D. Smyser[b,c,d,e], Jeffrey Neil[b,c,d,e], and Hao Huang[a,f]

Department of Radiology, Children's Hospital of Philadelphia, Philadelphia, PA, United States[a] Department of Neurology, Washington University School of Medicine, St. Louis, MO, United States[b] Department of Pediatrics, Washington University School of Medicine, St. Louis, MO, United States[c] Department of Radiology, Washington University School of Medicine, St. Louis, MO, United States[d] St. Louis Children's Hospital, St. Louis, MO, United States[e] Department of Radiology, Perelman School of Medicine, University of Pennsylvania, Philadelphia, PA, United States[f]

1. Introduction

Early brain developmental period, specifically from the mid-gestation to postnatal 2 years of age, is characterized by dramatic structural and functional changes. This period likely represents the most dynamic period of brain development across the entire lifespan. Immensely complicated yet precisely regulated, molecular and cellular processes (Silbereis et al., 2016), including neurogenesis and neuronal migration (Rakic, 1972, 1995; Sidman and Rakic, 1973), synapse formation (Huttenlocher, 1979; Huttenlocher and Dabholkar, 1997), dendritic arborization (Bystron et al., 2008; Sidman and Rakic, 1973), axonal growth, pruning (Innocenti and Price, 2005; Kostović and Jovanov-Milosević, 2006) and myelination (Miller et al., 2012; Yakovlev and Lecours, 1967), take place in the human brain during this period. These cellular and molecular processes shape the structural and functional architecture of the human brain and underlie varying maturational rates of functional systems in a specific developmental period.

As noted in histologic studies of brain development dating back more than 100 years ago (Brodmann, 1909), brain maturation is heterogeneous across brain regions, with primary motor and sensory regions maturing more quickly than association areas in the early developmental period (Sidman and Rakic, 1982). The spatiotemporal gradients underlying these major maturational events in the developing brain are described in Fig. 1. Synaptogenesis is a critical cortical developmental process. As shown in Fig. 1, synaptic density peaks early in life, after which it falls because of synaptic pruning associated with maturation. The rate of this developmental process varies by functional system. For example, synaptic density peaks during the 5th postnatal month in the primary visual cortex and much later in the frontal cortex (Huttenlocher and Dabholkar, 1997; Kwan et al., 2012) during the 15th postnatal month. Rates of myelination also vary by system, largely in synchrony with the development of the gray matter from which the white matter arises. For example, the corticospinal tract arising from primary motor cortex myelinates earlier (Brody et al., 1987; Kinney et al., 1988; Yakovlev and Lecours, 1967) than association tracts connecting to prefrontal cortex.

Handbook of Pediatric Brain Imaging. https://doi.org/10.1016/B978-0-12-816633-8.00018-1

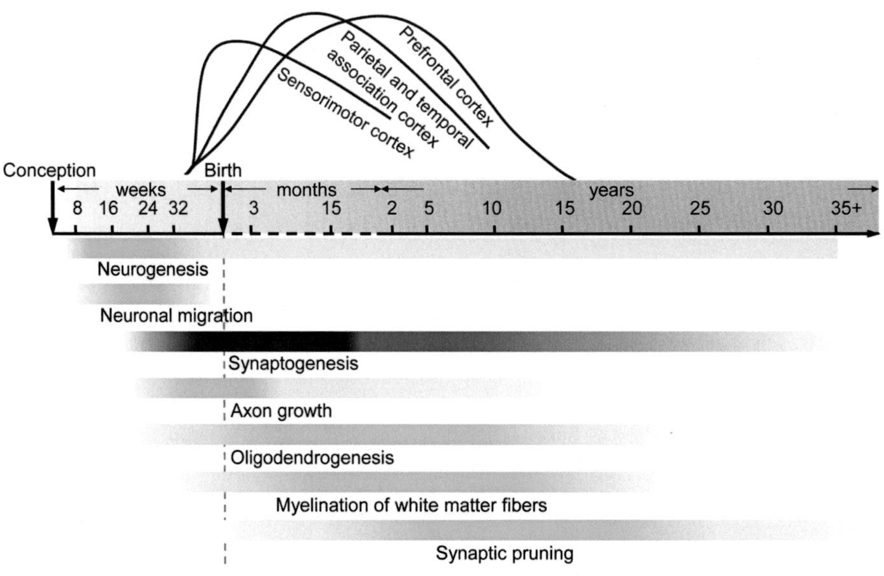

FIG. 1

Timeline of spatiotemporally distinctive human brain maturational processes, including neurogenesis, neuronal migration, synaptogenesis, axon growth, oligodendrogenesis, myelination of white matter fibers and synaptic pruning. Time axis is in postconceptional weeks (before birth), postnatal months (until 24 months), and postnatal years (after 2 years). The color intensity in each bar corresponds to the rate of developmental changes. The spatial progression across brain regions is illustrated using synaptogenesis (blue bar) as an example. Specifically, the spatial progression of synaptogenesis from primary sensorimotor cortex to higher-order prefrontal cortex is illustrated by the blue curves above the time axis.

This early developmental sequence may be disturbed in a number of major psychiatric disorders which have a prominent onset (e.g., Hazlett et al., 2017; Marín, 2016) in childhood. For example, in histological studies, it has been found that altered synaptic pruning is associated with autism, attention-deficit hyperactivity disorder, and schizophrenia (e.g., Feinberg, 1983; McGlashan and Hoffman, 2000; Tang et al., 2014). Thus, delineating structural and functional changes of the brain during early development provides new insights into the complicated processes of both typical neurodevelopment and the pathological mechanisms underlying various psychiatric and neurological disorders.

Contemporary magnetic resonance imaging (MRI), capable of surveying the entire brain routinely with a scan less than 1 h, has provided unprecedented opportunities to noninvasively quantify and map the early developmental changes at both whole brain and regional levels. MRI sequences, including structural T1- and T2-weighted images (T1w and T2w), diffusion (dMRI), functional (fMRI), and perfusion (pMRI) MRI, provide complementary information regarding typical brain changes as well as maturational processes across the cerebral cortex, subcortical gray matter and major white matter tracts in vivo. Herein, we review recent advances in understanding early structural and functional brain development during the second half of gestation and the first two postnatal years using modern MR techniques. First, we summarize early morphological and macrostructural findings in the brain using structural MRI. Next, we consolidate current understanding of the microstructural maturation of white matter tracts, as well as inhomogeneous cortical microstructural organization unique to fetuses and infants using MRI approaches, especially dMRI. Third, we review fMRI findings revealing functional organization and heterogeneous maturation patterns across the cortex and different brain networks. We also review physiological findings of early brain development using pMRI approaches, especially arterial spin labeling (ASL). Finally, we discuss issues and limitations of studying infant brain white and gray matter development using various MRI techniques and in clinical settings, and suggest avenues that could be explored for future research.

The terminology used to describe fetal and preterm brain age in postconceptional weeks (pcw), postmenstrual weeks (pmw), or weeks of gestation (wg) varies somewhat among publications. For the discussion below, these terms were taken directly from the reviewed studies without adaptation. The standard age terminology of fetal and infant brains can be found in the policy statement by American Academy of Pediatrics Committee (Engle and American Academy of Pediatrics Committee on Fetus and Newborn, 2004). Collectively, this chapter summarizes findings charting spatiotemporally heterogeneous gray and white matter structural and functional development. These developmental charts offer MRI-based biomarkers of typical brain development and set the stage for understanding aberrant brain development in neurological and psychiatric disorders described in followed chapters.

2. Early brain structural development

2.1 Morphological changes of brain structures with volumetric measures

The human brain is the most complex biological organ and is characterized by a long period of development that begins prenatally and continues for several decades after birth. It originates from the neural tube around the 4th pcw and develops into a highly complicated yet organized organ with adult-like architecture during early childhood (Huang and Vasung, 2014; Silbereis et al., 2016). It can be observed that remarkable morphological changes begin during the fetal stage and extend through the first 2 years of life using conventional structural MRI (e.g., T1- or T2-weighted images). During the 2nd trimester, MRI studies have shown that whole brain volumes increase more than 12-fold, from 2.5 mL at 13wg to 32 mL at 21wg (Huang et al., 2009). Volumes of the basal ganglia and ganglionic eminence increase in conjunction with the whole brain, while the relative size of the ventricles, a dominant brain structure at this fetal stage, decreases in the late 2nd trimester (Huang et al., 2009). Within a short period of the 3rd trimester, cortical gray matter volume increases more than fourfold (Hüppi et al., 1998a; Limperopoulos et al., 2005). In sum, from 19wg to term (~40wg), whole brain volumes increase almost 17-fold from 22 to 367 mL (Huang et al., 2006). Importantly, key brain structures develop disproportionately throughout this developmental period, with a reduction in the relative size of the ventricles and brainstem and an increase in the proportion of the cerebrum and cerebellum (Huang et al., 2006).

From birth to age 2 years, overall brain size continues to increase dramatically, reaching close to 90% of adult volume by age 2 (Pfefferbaum et al., 1994; Knickmeyer et al., 2008). Brain growth during this period is mainly the result of gray matter expansion (Gilmore et al., 2012; Knickmeyer et al., 2008), while white matter growth contributes more in the following years (Matsuzawa et al., 2001; Giedd and Rapoport, 2010). Specifically, gray matter volume increases ~106% in the first postnatal year and 18%

in the second year, whereas white matter volume increases ~11% in the first year and 19% in the second year (Knickmeyer et al., 2008). During this developmental period, cortical gray matter growth is more prominent in the frontal and parietal lobes compared with primary sensorimotor cortices (Gilmore et al., 2012), with cortical volumes reaching peak values at different times in late childhood and adolescence (Gogtay et al., 2004; Giedd and Rapoport, 2010).

2.2 Morphological changes of cortex with thickness, surface area and gyrification measures

Beyond the principal morphological index provided by volumetric measures, morphological changes of the cortex can also be quantified using measures of thickness, surface area and gyrification. At 13wg, the fetal brain surface is smooth except for the initial folding of the Sylvian fissure. The Sylvian fissure is more prominent by the end of the 2nd trimester with the temporal lobe becoming visible at 19–20wg (Huang et al., 2006, 2009). Sulcal formation and cortical gyrification become more pronounced after 24wg, as revealed by in utero structural MRI studies (Habas et al., 2012; Rajagopalan et al., 2011). Cortical folding demonstrates spatiotemporal differences in the preterm brain from 26 to 36 weeks (Dubois et al., 2008a). Sulcal formation starts in the central region, and first proceeds toward parietal, temporal and occipital regions, then toward frontal regions (Dubois et al., 2008a). At term, infant brains demonstrate similar patterns of cortical gyrification as those of adult brains, although their surface area is only one-third that of adults (Hill et al., 2010). Cortical volume is determined by both cortical thickness and surface area. Overall cortical thickness increases ~36% in the first 2 years of life, reaching 97% of adult value by age 2 years (Lyall et al., 2015). In contrast, cortical surface area expands 114% during this period, reaching 69% of adult values at age 2 years (Lyall et al., 2015). These increases in surface area and thickness during infancy are nonuniform across the cortex, with the lateral temporal, parietal, and frontal cortices growing faster than primary sensorimotor and occipital cortices (Li et al., 2013, 2015; Wang et al., 2019).

Brain tissue T1 and T2 relaxation time constants change markedly during the first year of life (Barkovich, 2000). Myelination leads to a large change of gray/white matter contrast in T1w and T2w images (Paus et al., 2001). Initially, unmyelinated white matter appears dark on T1w images and bright on T2w images. Once myelinated, white matter appears bright on T1w images and dark on T2w images, causing tissue gray/white contrast to flip. This transition takes place gradually. As can be appreciated from Penn-CHOP developmental connectome data (www.brainmrimap.org) shown in Fig. 2, gray/white matter contrast on T1w and T2w images steadily diminishes during the first months of life as myelination occurs, with white matter signal intensity on T1w images increasing and T2w images decreasing. Contrast is lowest at 6–8 postnatal months, when signal intensities from the white matter are similar to those of the gray matter on T1w and T2w images (Barkovich et al., 1992; van der Knaap and Valk, 1990; Paus et al., 2001). Thereafter, contrast steadily improves as myelination continues and image contrast takes on the appearance of the adult brain. Due to this varying contrast, tailored tools are needed to delineate cortical volume or thickness during the first 6 months of life, when image contrast is the reverse of that for adult brain. The factors above should be taken into consideration for measurement of morphological parameters across infant ages (Adamson et al., 2020; Dubois et al., 2014a; Zöllei et al., 2020).

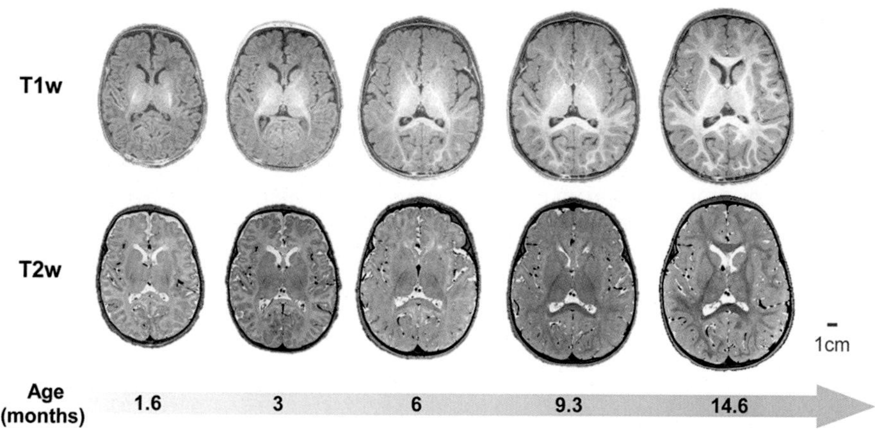

FIG. 2

High-resolution ($0.8 \times 0.8 \times 0.8 mm^3$) T1 weighted (T1w, top panel) and T2 weighted (T2w, bottom panel) images of the developing infant brain at the age of 1.6, 3, 6, 9.3, and 14.6 months. This figure is generated with the Penn-CHOP developmental connectome data (www.brainmrimap.org) from Huang lab.

3. Early brain development with diffusion MRI and beyond

Diffusion MRI (dMRI) provides unique imaging contrasts to delineate gray and white matter structures of the early developing human brain. Tractography based on dMRI sheds light on emergence of major long-range white matter tracts at the beginning of life and defining the maturational trajectories of white matter tracts in typical development (Dubois et al., 2006, 2008b; Huang et al., 2006, 2009; Hüppi et al., 1998b; Kasprian et al., 2008, 2013; Kolasinski et al., 2013; Miller et al., 2014; Neil et al., 1998; Partridge et al., 2004; Takahashi et al., 2011; Xu et al., 2012; Yu et al., 2020). Moreover, because of its sensitivity to the microstructural changes of organized cortical tissue unique in the fetal and infant brain, dMRI also offers insight into the development of cortical cytoarchitecture (Ball et al., 2013; DeIpolyi et al., 2005; Huang et al., 2009, 2013; Maas et al., 2004; McKinstry et al., 2002; Ouyang et al., 2019a, b; Yu et al., 2016).

3.1 Emergence of white matter tracts delineated with dMRI tractography

For several decades, the architecture of the white matter has been delineated using histological studies of postmortem brains. These labor-intensive histological delineations were complicated by the factors such as local coverage with small blocks and the challenges of three-dimensional reconstruction. In contrast, dMRI tractography enables noninvasive reconstruction of white matter tracts and sheds light on important questions such as when and how certain connections emerge at the beginning of life. The major long-range white matter tracts in the human brain can be categorized into five functional categories: limbic, commissural, projection, association and brainstem tract groups (Wakana et al., 2004, 2007). As in diffusion tensor imaging (DTI) based white matter atlases generated using adult data, high contrast from DTI-derived images (e.g., color-encoded orientation maps and fractional anisotropy maps) have been utilized to generate age-specific atlases for neonatal and infant brains (Oishi et al., 2011, 2019; Feng et al., 2019). Fig. 3A–E show the emergence of these five tract groups from the 2nd trimester to age 2 years based upon these results. Of note, since all tracts from Fig. 3 were reconstructed based on DTI tractography, the timeline demonstrated in this figure is restricted by the limitations of DTI tractography (see Jbabdi and Johansen-Berg, 2011 for review). For example, unmyelinated long tracts that have already emerged at certain developmental stages may not be successfully tracked using DTI tractography before they are myelinated because of their relatively low anisotropy. Thus, Fig. 3 may not reflect the exact emergence time of long-range white matter tracts.

Across fetal brain DTI studies (postmortem brain specimens in Huang et al., 2006, 2009; Ouyang et al., 2015; Song et al., 2017; Takahashi et al., 2011; in utero fetuses in Kasprian et al., 2008, 2013), a heterogeneous pattern of white matter development was observed across different tracts and tract groups. In the limbic tract group, the fornix (FX) emerges earlier than 13wg, and the cingulum bundle linking the cingulate gyrus (CGC) and hippocampus (CGH) appears around 19wg. In the commissural tract group, the body of the corpus callosum (BCC) emerges around 15wg, followed by the genu (GCC, before 19wg) and splenium (SCC, after 19wg) of the corpus callosum. In the projection fiber tracts, the anterior corona radiata (ACR) emerges before 13wg, followed by the superior portion (SCR) around 15wg and the posterior portion (PCR) after 19wg. In the association tract group, the external capsule (EC) emerges before 13wg, followed by the appearance of the uncinate fasciculus (UNC) around 15wg and the inferior longitudinal fasciculus (ILF) and inferior fronto-occipital fasciculus (IFO) around 19wg. The exact time for the emergence of the superior longitudinal fasciculus (SLF) is less clear. The observations from dMRI tractography suggest that the SLF may emerge during the 3rd trimester (Huang et al., 2006, 2009; Miller et al., 2014; Takahashi et al., 2011). Histological studies show such long-range cortico-cortical fibers emerge around 33-35pcw (Kostović and Jovanov-Milosević, 2006; Kostović and Rakic, 1990), although the SLF cannot be well traced even at birth using current dMRI-based tractography techniques. Across these studies, the white matter tracts emerging earlier (e.g., the brainstem tracts) play important roles in supporting the basic functions for life. Conversely, later emerging tracts, such as the SLF, may contribute to higher-level brain functions such as language (e.g., Zhang et al., 2007). Approximate emergence pattern of long-range white matter tracts from a suite of dMRI tractography studies (Huang et al., 2006, 2009; Kasprian et al., 2008, 2013; Kolasinski et al., 2013; Miller et al., 2014; Takahashi et al., 2011; Xu et al., 2012) and histological atlases (Bayer and Altman, 2004, 2005) is summarized in Fig. 3F.

Short-range white matter tracts, also known as U-fibers, connect adjacent gyri (Schüz and Braitenberg, 2002). There are relatively few studies of short-range tracts at all ages due to the challenges of reproducibly tracing them (Catani et al., 2012; Guevara et al., 2017; Ouyang et al., 2017a; Zhang et al., 2010). Our study found the ratio of the number of whole brain short-range fibers to the number of entire-brain cortico-cortical fibers demonstrated a U-shape development pattern from 2 to 25 years (Ouyang et al., 2016). It was also found that the regional ratio reaches its lowest value earlier in primary cortices and later in frontal cortex (Ouyang et al., 2016). However, short-range tracts have not been fully characterized in the early developing brain yet.

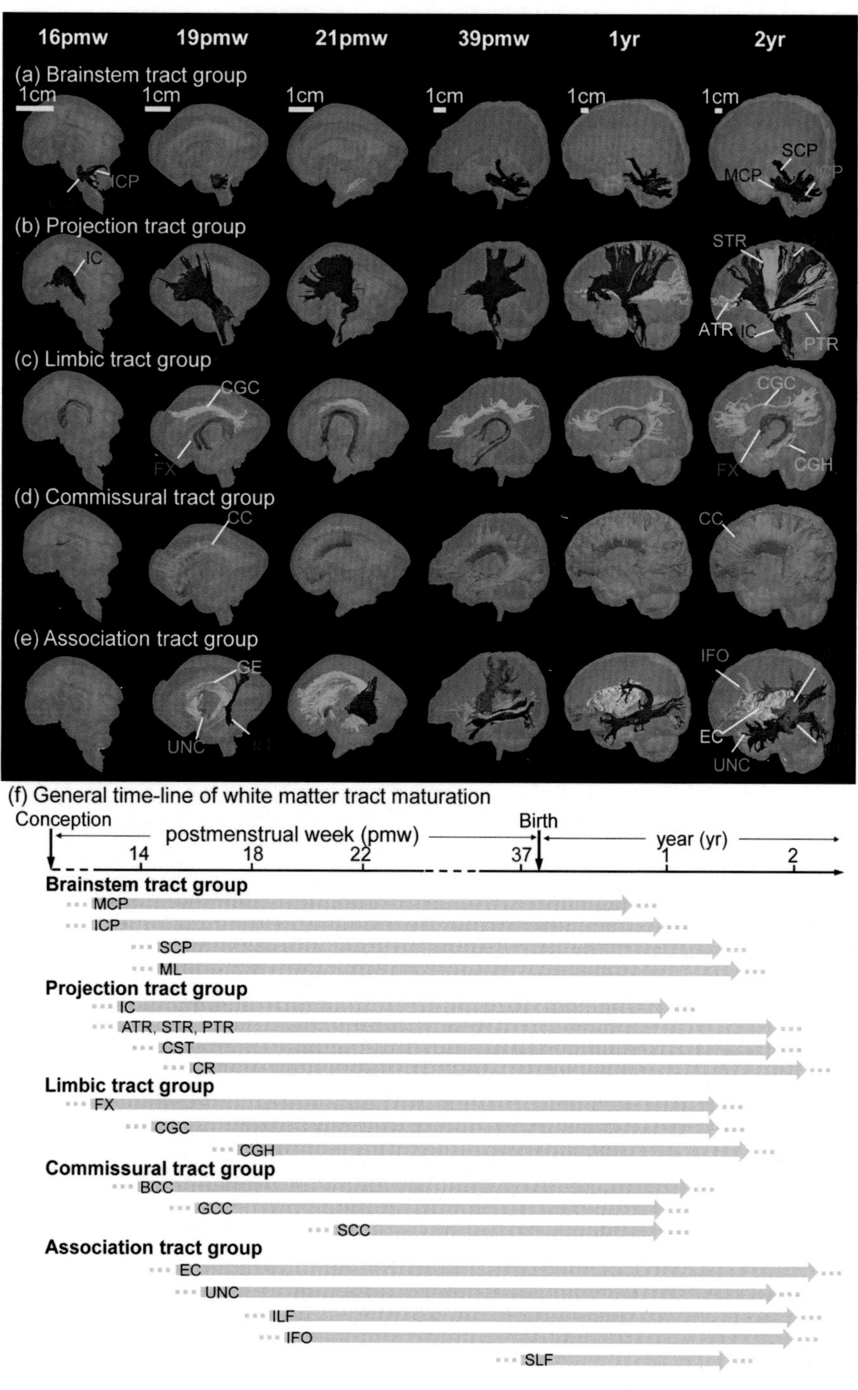

FIG. 3

See legend on next page

3.2 Microstructural changes of white matter with dMRI

Maturation processes of white matter tracts during fetal development (Kersbergen et al., 2014) and the first 2 years of life (Geng et al., 2012; Hermoye et al., 2006; Mishra et al., 2013; Mukherjee et al., 2001, 2002; Yu et al., 2014, 2020) have been elucidated with DTI-derived measurements. Fig. 4A shows DTI-derived maps of fetal and infant brains. A general pattern of age-dependent fractional anisotropy (FA) increase and diffusivity (i.e., mean/axial/radial diffusivity: MD/AD/RD) decrease has been found in most white matter tracts (e.g., Berman et al., 2005; Kersbergen et al., 2014; Dubois et al., 2008b; Geng et al., 2012; Yu et al., 2020). Besides this general pattern, the maturational rates of different white matter tracts and tract groups are spatiotemporally heterogeneous. Linear (Berman et al., 2005; Dubois et al., 2006, 2008b), exponential (Lebel et al., 2008; Mukherjee et al., 2001; Yu et al., 2020) and logarithmic (e.g., Yu et al., 2014) curves have been used to fit the age-dependent changes of DTI-derived metric measurements of white matter tracts based on the studied age range. Linear functions are generally sufficient for characterizing white matter microstructural changes in a relatively short period, while exponential or logarithmic functions are typically used for longer developmental periods. Schematic maturational curves of FA values for the five white matter tract groups from the 2nd trimester to age 2 years are illustrated in Fig. 4B (28–43wg in Berman et al., 2005; 30–40wg in Kersbergen et al., 2014; 1–4 month in Dubois et al., 2008b; 0–2 year in Gao et al., 2009a; Geng et al., 2012; Hermoye et al., 2006; Mukherjee et al., 2001, 2002; 0–8 year in Yu et al., 2020).

The increasing FA values in all tract groups likely indicate widespread myelination progressing across white matter regions, along with axon packing and reduction in partial volume effects elaborated below. In general, during the age from 20pmw to age 2 years, the FA values of commissural tracts are the highest among the five tract groups, while the association tracts are the lowest (Fig. 4B). These high FA values in commissural tracts could be due to the higher axonal density and lesser fiber orientation dispersion, while the lower FA values in association tracts may be related to lower axonal density and greater fiber orientation dispersion, as shown by neurite orientation dispersion and density imaging (NODDI) (Chang et al., 2015). These parameters may be affected by the presence of crossing fibers in these regions as well. Furthermore, developmental asynchrony across different white matter tracts has been suggested in the early developing brain through measurements of FA and diffusivity (Sadeghi

FIG. 3, CONT'D

Diffusion MRI tractography of the white matter tracts in developing fetal and infant brain from 16 postmenstrual weeks (pmw) to 2 years. (A) Brainstem tracts including inferior, middle, superior cerebellar peduncle (ICP, MCP, and SCP) and medial lemniscus (ML). (B) Projection tracts including interior capsule (IC), corona radiata (CR), corticospinal tract (CST), anterior, superior, and posterior thalamic radiation (ATR, STR, and PTR). (C) Limbic tracts including cingulum bundle in the cingulate cortex (CGC), cingulum bundle in the temporal cortex (CGH), and fornix (FX). (D) Commissural tracts including body, genu and splenium of corpus callosum (BCC, GCC, and SCC). (E) Association tracts including fibers in external capsule (EC), inferior longitudinal fasciculus (ILF), inferior occipitofrontal fasciculus (IFO), superior longitudinal fasciculus (SLF), and uncinate fasciculus (UNC). Ganglionic eminence (GE), a transient fetal brain structure and well traced with DTI tractography, is also included in this tract group. (F) General timeline of white matter maturation across different tracts and tract groups. Dotted lines indicate that white matter tracts emerge at these ages, though to a relatively minor degree, and arrows indicate that overall white matter tracts are formed with continuous maturational processes such as myelination and axonal packing thereafter. This figure is generated with the data from Huang lab.

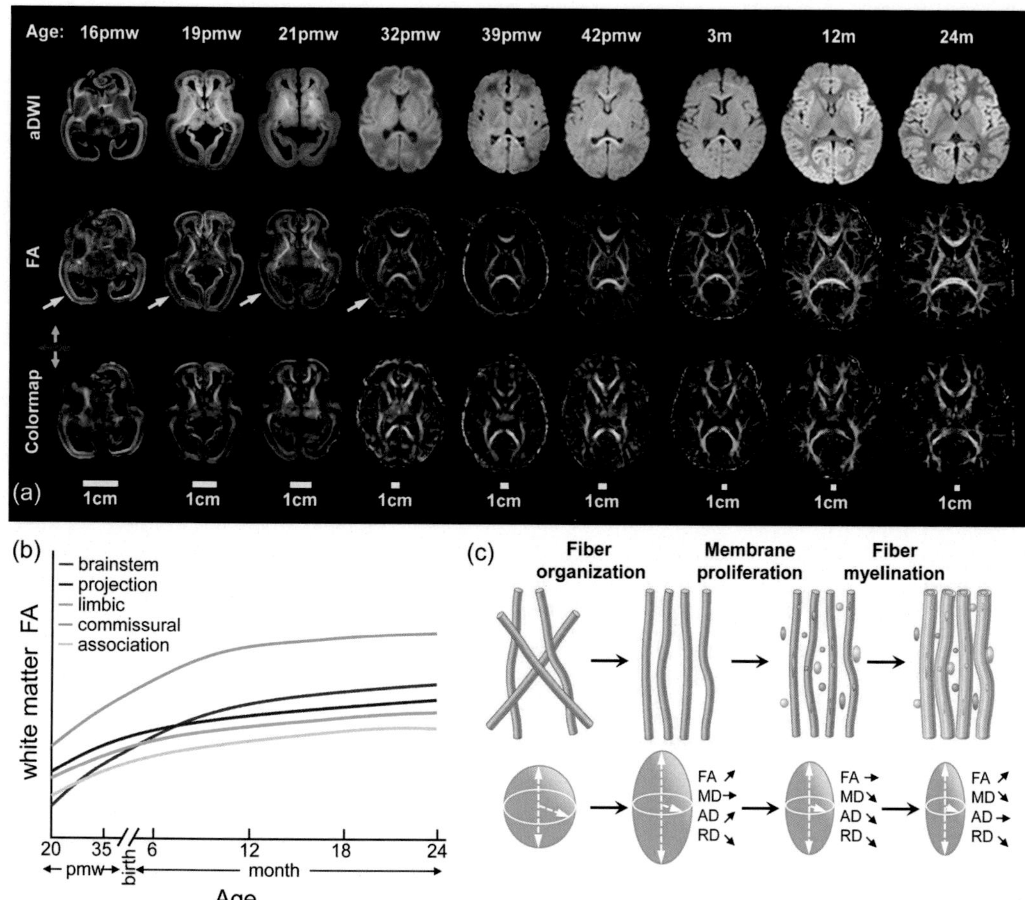

FIG. 4

Diffusion MRI contrast in the fetal and infant brain (A), developmental trajectories of fractional anisotropy (FA) across white matter tracts from the mid-fetal stage to 2 years (B) and the biophysical model of white matter maturation (C). In (A), from top to bottom, axial slices of the averaged diffusion weighted images (aDWI), FA maps and color-encoded diffusion orientation maps are shown. Yellow arrows indicate high FA values in the cortical plate, and red arrows indicate high FA values in the white matter regions during this early developing period. This panel was generated with the data from Huang lab (www.brainmrimap.org). In (B), sketch plots show age-dependent white matter FA changes in five tract groups, namely, brainstem, projection, limbic, commissural and association tract groups from 20 postmenstrual weeks (pmw) to 2 years. Time axis in (B) is in postmenstrual weeks (pmw) before birth and in postnatal months until 24 months. In (C), the biophysical model interprets the changes of DTI-derived metrics (i.e., FA, mean/axial/radial diffusivity: MD, AD, and RD).

Adapted with permission from Dubois, J., Dehaene-Lambertz, G., Perrin, M., Mangin, J.F., Cointepas, Y., Duchesnay, E., Le Bihan, D., Hertz-Pannier, L., 2008b. Asynchrony of the early maturation of white matter bundles in healthy infants: quantitative landmarks revealed noninvasively by diffusion tensor imaging. Hum. Brain Mapp. 29, 14–27.

et al., 2013; Yu et al., 2020). The percent increases in FA of the commissural and brainstem tract groups from 0 to 2 years were higher than those of the projection, limbic and association tract groups in the same developmental period (Fig. 4B). In addition, it was found that the association tract group is the last tract group to reach the plateau stage, suggesting the maturation of the association tracts continues for a longer time than other tract groups. Although DTI-derived measurements of white matter microstructure may offer significant information about brain development, caution needs to be taken when interpreting the results. FA and diffusivity measurements are affected by a number of factors including myelination (Beaulieu, 2002; Song et al., 2005), axon packing (Mädler et al., 2008) and axon density (Klawiter et al., 2011). For example, a high FA value in the unmyelinated corpus callosum of the preterm brain may reflect the higher levels of axonal packing than other white matter regions, and a low FA value in the EC may reflect its fanning geometry. Increased FA values are also associated with the reduction in partial volume effects, which artificially lower voxel FA values, as white matter tracts grow physically larger.

To better understand the cellular processes underlying white matter maturation in terms of axonal growth, organization and myelination, biophysical models have been proposed to link these cellular processes to the DTI-derived parameter changes observed during early brain development. For example, a model including different major maturational changes taking place in the tissue (fiber organization, membrane proliferation and myelination as shown in Fig. 4C) has been proposed as a biophysical interpretation for the changes of DTI-derived measurements during white matter development (see details in Dubois et al., 2008b; Nossin-Manor et al., 2015). In this model, the axonal or fiber organization stage is associated predominantly with an increase in AD without affecting RD, leading to an increase in both FA and MD. The membrane proliferation or "premyelination" stage, characterized by an expansion of immature oligodendroglia cells and their processes, is associated with a reduction in all three diffusivity indices due to the increased membrane density and the decreased water content in brain tissue. And FA would increase (Wimberger et al., 1995) in this stage. The third stage, myelination of white matter fibers, is associated with decreasing RD and little change in AD, also driving FA increases and MD decreases. In places where different tracts are crossing, the situation may require more complex interpretation if these tracts mature with different timelines (Dubois et al., 2014a). These DTI-based models could be tested with the newer multishell dMRI-based models (e.g., NODDI, diffusion kurtosis imaging, DKI; and diffusion spectrum imaging, DSI) that may measure free water content, axonal density, and fiber orientation dispersion.

3.3 Microstructural changes of gray matter with dMRI

With the spatiotemporal mapping of diffusion parameters of the cortical plate, dMRI also sheds light on the dynamics of neuronal processes across the early developing cerebral cortex. During cortical development, the majority of cortical neurons are generated near the cerebral ventricles and migrate toward the cortical surface along a radially arranged scaffolding of glial cells (Rakic, 1972, 1995; Sidman and Rakic, 1973). In this immature cortical plate, water molecules preferentially diffuse along the radial glial scaffold and radially oriented apical dendrites of pyramidal cells. Compared to the adult brain, the highly organized radial architecture of the immature cortical plate is characterized by high FA values (e.g., Ball et al., 2013; DeIpolyi et al., 2005; Huang et al., 2009, 2013; McKinstry et al., 2002; Maas et al., 2004; Ouyang et al., 2019a; Yu et al., 2016), as well as by an organized radial orientation of diffusion tensor primary eigenvectors (Huang et al., 2009; Huang, 2010; McKinstry et al., 2002; Deipolyi et al., 2005). Fig. 5A and B show the heterogeneous distribution of cortical FA maps

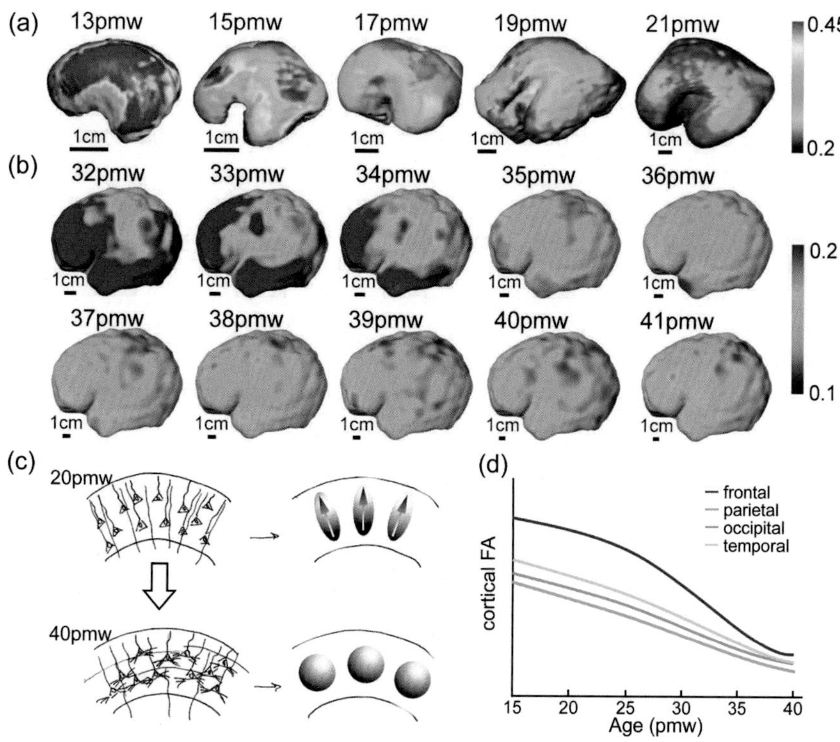

FIG. 5

Mapping of FA onto the cortical surface from 13 to 21 postmenstrual weeks (pmw) in the 2nd trimester (A) and mapping of the FA onto the cortical surface from 32 to 41pmw in the 3rd trimester (B). Biophysical model of disruption of radial glial scaffold and associated fractional anisotropy (FA) decrease (C) and distinctive spatiotemporal FA decreases across different cortical regions from 15 to 40 postmenstrual weeks (pmw) (D). In (C), upper left panel demonstrates highly organized radial glial fibers, pyramidal neurons with prominent, radially oriented apical dendrites in a 20pmw brain cortical plate, resulting in the diffusion ellipsoids with high FA values and the primary axes oriented radially (upper right panel); lower left panel demonstrates prominent basal dendrites for the pyramidal cells and thalamocortical afferents disrupting the organized radial organization in a 40pmw brain cortical plate, resulting in more round-shaped diffusion ellipsoids with low FA values.

(A) Adapted with permission from Huang, H., Jeon, T., Sedmak, G., Pletikos, M., Vasung, L., Xu, X., Yarowsky, P., Richards, L.J., Kostović, I., Šestan, N., Mori, S., 2013. Coupling diffusion imaging with histological and gene expression analysis to examine the dynamics of cortical areas across the fetal period of human brain development. Cereb. Cortex 23(11), 2620–2631. (B) Adapted with permission from Ouyang, M., Jeon, T., Sotiras, A., Peng, Q., Mishra, V., Halovanic, C., Chen, M., Chalak, L., Rollins, N., Roberts, T., Davatzikos, C., Huang, H., 2019a. Differential cortical microstructural maturation in the preterm human brain with diffusion kurtosis and tensor imaging. Proc. Natl. Acad. Sci. U. S. A. 116(10), 4681–4688. (C) Adapted with permission from McKinstry, R.C., Mathur, A., Miller, J.H., Ozcan, A., Snyder, A.Z., Schefft, G.L., Almli, C.R., Shiran, S.I., Conturo, T.E., Neil, J.J., 2002. Radial organization of developing preterm human cerebral cortex revealed by non-invasive water diffusion anisotropy MRI. Cereb. Cortex 12(12), 1237–1243.

during the 2nd (13–21pmw) and 3rd (32–41pmw) trimesters. A relatively high FA in the prefrontal cortex compared with primary sensorimotor cortex can be appreciated. This distribution (Ball et al., 2013; Huang et al., 2013; DeIpolyi et al., 2005; Kroenke et al., 2007, 2009; Yu et al., 2016; Ouyang et al., 2019a) confirms that the prefrontal cortex is relatively less mature, consistent with histological studies. While neuronal migration is essentially complete by 26pcw (Kostović et al., 2002; Sidman and Rakic, 1973), subsequent cortical maturation processes involving synaptogenesis and synapse pruning, dendritic arborization, myelination of intracortical white matter, and axonal growth (Bystron et al., 2008; Huttenlocher and Dabholkar, 1997; Kostović and Jovanov-Milosević, 2006; Marin-Padilla, 1992) disrupt the pronounced radial organization of radial glial scaffold and result in the FA decrease (Fig. 5C) (McKinstry et al., 2002). Note that steady reduction of FA in the maturing cortical plate is in contrast to increase of FA in maturing white matter.

Such cortical FA decreases have been reported in the developing human brain in the 2nd trimester using postmortem DTI (13-21wg in Huang et al., 2009, 2013) and 3rd trimester with in vivo DTI of preterm neonates (e.g., 27–38pcw in Ball et al., 2013; 25–38wg in Delpolyi et al., 2005; 27–42wg in Eaton-Rosen et al., 2017; 36wg in McKinstry et al., 2002; 26-40pmw in Smyser et al., 2016a, 20–35pmw and 35–40pmw in Yu et al., 2016; 31–42pmw in Ouyang et al., 2019a), as well as in the early developing animal brains (Huang et al., 2008; Kroenke et al., 2007, 2009; Mori et al., 2001; Sizonenko et al., 2007; Takahashi et al., 2010; Thornton et al., 1997). Although FA decreases globally during cortical maturation, the rate of maturation is asynchronous across cortical areas. Maturation of primary motor and sensory regions precedes that of the association and prefrontal areas, as summarized in the sketch plots in Fig. 5D. For slightly older neonates (38–45pcw in Ball et al., 2013; 36–41wg in McKinstry et al., 2002; 37–42pmw in Ouyang et al., 2019a), no significant FA changes were found in any cortical areas. Besides cortical FA, a continuous reduction of DTI-derived MD values was found in the cortical regions of neonates from 26–46pmw (27–46pcw in Ball et al., 2013; 26–40pmw in Smyser et al., 2016a; 31–42pmw in Ouyang et al., 2019a). The steady decrease of cortical MD could be associated with a dramatic decrease in water content of the cortex. More recently, age-related declines of the DKI-derived mean kurtosis (MK) measurement were overserved in developing cortex from 31 to 42pmw with multishell dMRI, even in cortical regions with no significant FA changes (Ouyang et al., 2019a). Reduced diffusion barriers reflected by decreased MK might be associated with the decrease in neuronal density caused by cell death, also known as apoptosis in the cortex (Chan and Yew, 1998). Beyond the prenatal and perinatal developmental period, cortical MK is more sensitive to certain underlying microstructural changes (e.g., neuronal density) (Zhu et al., 2020), that cannot be captured by DTI-derived FA measurements.

Marked microstructural changes are also observed in central gray nuclei throughout development. Pioneering DTI studies have shown that MD values strongly decrease in preterm infant brains between 30 and 40wg (Neil et al., 1998) and in infant brains from 1 day to 4 years (Mukherjee et al., 2001), while anisotropy in the central gray nuclei increases to a lesser extent than in white matter tracts (Mukherjee et al., 2001). Much like the cortical regions, the maturational pattern differs across nuclei (e.g., the caudate head and lentiform nucleus vs. the thalamus) (Mukherjee et al., 2001). In the thalamus, RD decreases with age in all substructures from 36 to 43pmw, while AD decreases in all except the right thalamo-postcentral and parietal and occipital substructures (Poh et al., 2015). In the basal ganglia (caudate, putamen, globus pallidus), AD and RD decrease while FA increases over the same period (Qiu et al., 2013).

3.4 Other quantitative MRI approaches to assess brain structural maturation

Other MRI-based techniques including relaxometry MRI and magnetization transfer imaging (MTI) have also been extensively used to study early brain structural development. A relaxometry MRI-based measurement, myelin water fraction (MWF), shows a strong increase during infancy (Kulikova et al.,

2016) followed by a nonlinear growth pattern until toddlerhood (Dean et al., 2014a; Deoni et al., 2011, 2012). The shortening of T1 or T2 relaxation time in brain tissues throughout development (Barkovich et al., 1988; Baumann and Pham-Dinh, 2001; Bültmann et al., 2018; Poduslo and Jang, 1984; Engelbrecht et al., 1998; Haselgrove et al., 2000; Leppert et al., 2009; Schneider et al., 2016), particularly in white matter, is related to decreases in brain water content (Matsumae et al., 2001) and increases in the concentration of macromolecules such as myelin (Barkovich et al., 1988; Kucharczyk et al., 1994). Magnetization transfer ratio (MTR), an index of MTI, has been used to characterize changes in brain tissue disorganization associated with axonal loss or demyelination. MTR increases during white matter maturation (Kucharczyk et al., 1994; Nossin-Manor et al., 2013, 2015) with an exponential time course (Engelbrecht et al., 1998; van Buchem et al., 2001). Differences in MTR were observed across regions, with a relatively mature stage at around 13 and 16 months in occipital and frontal white matter, and at 18 and 19 months in the splenium and genu of the corpus callosum (Xydis et al., 2006). Collectively, these MRI parameters provide complementary information regarding multiple maturational processes (Deoni et al., 2013; Lancaster et al., 2003). It is only by comparing these parameters that one can hope to outline comprehensive patterns of microstructural development (see Dubois et al., 2014a; Ouyang et al., 2019b for review). Thus, adopting these multiparametric approaches may help better disentangle microstructural processes and investigate maturational patterns across white matter, cortical and deep gray regions (Nossin-Manor et al., 2013, 2015; Melbourne et al., 2016).

4. Early brain functional development

Resting state (rs-fMRI) and task-based fMRI are complementary approaches enabling investigation of early functional brain development. rs-fMRI investigates the temporal correlations in low frequency (<0.1 Hz) fluctuations in blood oxygen level dependent (BOLD) signal that occur independent of task (Biswal et al., 1995; Fox et al., 2005; Lowe et al., 1998). These fluctuations represent the baseline variations in neuronal activity of the brain in the absence of goal-directed activity/stimulation and are used to identify resting state networks (RSNs) demonstrating synchronous, spontaneous neuronal activity (Fox and Raichle, 2007; Smith et al., 2009). Investigations applying this modality from the 2nd trimester of pregnancy through the first 2 years of life have consistently identified canonical RSNs throughout the brain incorporating cortical and subcortical areas known to be anatomically connected and coactivated by task performance. rs-fMRI methods afford many inherent advantages for studying brain function in infants (Smyser and Neil, 2015; Cao et al., 2017a). Most notably, functional networks throughout the brain can be assessed from an acquisition lasting minutes in duration. Further, these data can be acquired from subjects resting quietly, asleep, and even under anesthesia. In addition, analysis techniques for identifying and addressing common sources of colored noise due to nonneuronal signal in rs-fMRI data, such as that arising from atlas registration and subject motion, are now firmly established. Cumulatively, these benefits have served to expand use of this imaging modality across investigations beginning during the fetal period and extending through the first 2 years of life (Cao et al., 2017b; Doria et al., 2010; Fransson et al., 2007, 2009, 2011; Gao et al., 2013a, 2015a; Herzmann et al., 2019; Lin et al., 2008; Smyser et al., 2010, 2013, 2016b; Xu et al., 2019).

While these fetal and infant studies have included heterogeneous subject groups, implemented mixed study designs, and employed differing acquisition and analysis techniques, consistent patterns have emerged. Most notably, it has become increasingly evident that multiple canonical RSNs incorporating cortical and subcortical gray matter regions and the cerebellum are present during infancy. These include RSNs located in primary motor and sensory cortices (e.g., somatomotor [SMN], visual [VIS] and auditory networks) and those involving association cortices (e.g., default mode [DMN], frontoparietal control [FPC], dorsal attention [DAN] and ventral attention [VAN] networks). Through investigations in fetal and neonatal populations, the foundations of these networks are identifiable as early as 20 weeks' gestation (with corresponding studies in prematurely-born infants characterizing these RSNs as early as 26 weeks' postmenstrual age) (Blazejewska et al., 2017; Doria et al., 2010; Jakab et al., 2014; Schöpf et al., 2012; Thomason et al., 2014, 2015, 2017; Smyser et al., 2010). Many of these RSNs, particularly their early forms, consist of strong interhemispheric correlations between homotopic counterparts, with intra-hemispheric correlations present but quantifiably weaker. Early thalamocortical connectivity is also evident during this window (Alcauter et al., 2014; Doria et al., 2010; Smyser et al., 2010; Toulmin et al., 2015). The identified RSN topology is consistent with results obtained in adult and older pediatric populations, though the terminology used to describe group differences between infant and adult populations has varied across reports, using terms such as 'immature', 'proto', and 'precursor' (Cao et al., 2017b; Doria et al., 2010; Fransson et al., 2007, 2009; Smyser et al., 2010).

The rate at which correlations within and between RSNs develop differs by network (Doria et al., 2010; Gao et al., 2015b; Smyser et al., 2010, 2016b). Early RSN development is dependent upon establishment of structural connectivity as detailed previously (Mrzljak et al., 1992; Petanjek et al., 2008, 2011). RSNs incorporating primary motor and sensory areas, such as the SMN or VIS, are established by term (Fig. 6A), with topology and strength reflecting adult-like patterns and correlation values. Fig. 6B shows that functional connectivity strength (FCS) increased significantly in infants from 31 to 41 postmenstrual weeks in primary motor, somatosensory, visual, and auditory regions, but much less in high-order RSNs (Cao et al., 2017b). These RSNs with stronger FCS by term are located in cortical regions known to mature early, demonstrate less variability between subjects (Gao et al., 2014; Xu et al., 2019), and are less susceptible to pathology (Smyser et al., 2016b). In contrast, RSNs such as the DMN and DAN are typically identifiable in quantifiably weaker or topographically incomplete forms early in life (Doria et al., 2010; Fransson et al., 2007, 2009; Smyser et al., 2010). These RSNs mature nonlinearly over the first several years of life, showing greater increases in size and strength during specific developmental periods. They are typically located in association cortices known to mature relatively late. Relationships between RSNs gradually evolve, with correlation between RSN pairs assuming adult-like patterns during this period (Gao et al., 2013b, 2015b). This combination of results suggests RSN development is susceptible during critical developmental periods and/or to disruption of key structural processes.

In tandem with increasing application of fetal MRI across clinical settings, substantive advances have been achieved toward the application of fMRI to study functional brain development in utero (Blazejewska et al., 2017; Jakab et al., 2014; Schöpf et al., 2012; Thomason et al., 2014, 2015, 2017). These investigations initially centered upon addressing the numerous, unique technical challenges specific to this population (Afacan et al., 2019; Fulford et al., 2004; Jakab et al., 2014; Rutherford et al., 2008; Seshamani et al., 2014; Thomason et al., 2013; van den Heuvel and Thomason, 2016). With these methods now increasingly established, investigators have successfully studied fetuses both cross-sectionally and longitudinally during the 2nd and 3rd trimesters of pregnancy. Early results have reported findings in healthy fetuses are similar to those reported in infants studied at comparable ages, including initially incomplete forms of many RSNs which gradually mature during pregnancy (Schöpf et al., 2012; Thomason et al., 2013; van den Heuvel and Thomason,

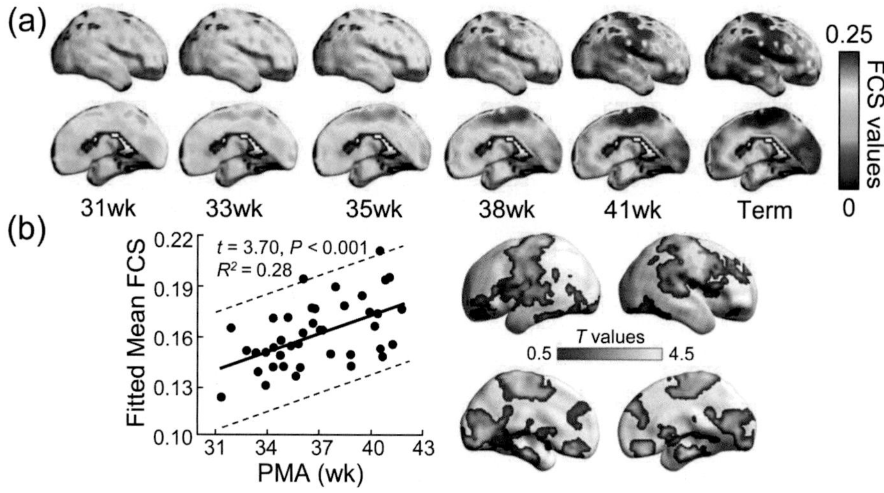

FIG. 6

Age-dependent changes in functional connectivity strength (FCS) from 31 to 41 postmenstrual age (PMA) in weeks. (A) Developing nodal FCS from 31 to 41 weeks demonstrating age-dependent gradual increase of nodal FCS. A map of FCS averaged from 10 term infants (>38.7 weeks at birth) was also presented as a reference. (B) The left panel shows fitted mean FCS changes with age; the right panel shows the distribution of brain regions with significant FCS increases. The regression line with 95% prediction error bounds is shown on the left panel.

Adapted with permission from Cao, M., He, Y., Dai, Z., Liao, X., Jeon, T., Ouyang, M., Chalak, L., Bi, Y., Rollins, N., Dong, Q., Huang, H., 2017b. Early development of functional network segregation revealed by connectomic analysis of the preterm human brain. Cereb. Cortex 27(3), 1949–1963.

2016). These RSNs initially demonstrate predominantly interhemispheric correlation between homotopic counterparts with increasing long-range connectivity with advancing gestational age (De Asis-Cruz et al., 2020; Jakab et al., 2014; Thomason et al., 2015; Turk et al., 2019). Recent investigations have also incorporated connectome-based analysis approaches to investigate the early organizational principles underlying functional brain development in utero (vida infra) (Thomason et al., 2014; Turk et al., 2019). As with investigations of infants, the acquisition, analysis, and interpretation techniques for use of fMRI in this population continue to rapidly evolve.

In tandem with this expanded utilization of rs-fMRI, neuroimaging assessments of cerebral function in fetuses and infants have also incorporated task-based investigations designed to define the anatomic localization of activations elicited by varied visual, auditory, olfactory, noxious, and motor stimuli (Arichi et al., 2010, 2013; Baxter et al., 2019; Born et al., 1998, 2000; Dall'Orso et al., 2018; Erberich et al., 2006; Heep et al., 2009; Lee et al., 2012; Perani et al., 2011; Scheef et al., 2017). Data from this approach complement that available through rs-fMRI, providing increasingly detailed information regarding the spatial localization and topographical integrity of functional networks and dynamic relationships within functional systems (Allievi et al., 2016; Dall'Orso et al., 2018). Many of these investigations utilized equipment custom-built for the study of infants, serving to optimize collection and improve data quality. Recent studies have expanded these lines of investigation, extending studies to incorporate prematurely-born infants studied as early as 31 weeks' postmenstrual age and developing age appropriate hemodynamic response function models in order to improve the accuracy of results across these investigations (Arichi et al., 2012). Efforts are ongoing to optimize the interrelationships between task-based and rs-fMRI approaches in this population, including how each modality can be most effectively employed to study and characterize early functional brain development.

5. Structural and functional connectome of early brain development

In addition to studies of structural and functional maturation across brain regions, it is important to understand the development of multiple interconnected brain systems. Connectomics, a framework to comprehensively map brain organization into a network, has been applied to study early brain development (e.g., Cao et al., 2017a). Exciting new advances in defining the developmental changes of whole-brain connectivity have been achieved by applying graph theory to diffusion tractography data for white matter, the "structural connectome," and resting state fMRI data for gray matter, the "functional connectome" (Bullmore and Sporns, 2009). In network analysis of the structural connectome, gray matter regions represent "nodes" and white matter connections between different nodes represent "edges."

It is beyond the scope of this chapter to comprehensively review this rapidly evolving field. Studies thus far demonstrate dramatic increases in the strength, efficiency and integration of the structural and functional brain networks during fetal (Jakab et al., 2014; Thomason et al., 2014, 2015; Schöpf et al., 2012; Song et al., 2017; van den Heuvel and Thomason, 2016) and neonatal (Ball et al., 2014; Brown et al., 2014; Cao et al., 2017b; Fransson et al., 2007; Huang et al., 2015; Smyser et al., 2010; Tymofiyeva et al., 2012, 2013; van den Heuvel et al., 2015; Zhao et al., 2019) development using traditional graph metrics, with both "small-world" and "rich club" organization already established at the earliest gestational ages investigated. The early developmental connectome is reconfigured through the integration and segregation processes (Cao et al., 2017b; Huang et al., 2015; Gao et al., 2009b; van den Heuvel and Thomason, 2016; Zhao et al., 2019), contributed to by increasing long-range connections and decreasing short-range connections, respectively (Cao et al., 2017a; Fair et al., 2009; Ouyang et al., 2017a). Prior studies have also highlighted a remarkable hierarchical order of connectome maturation from primary (e.g., sensorimotor and auditory) (Cao et al., 2017b; Fransson et al., 2007; Doria et al., 2010) to higher-order functional systems (e.g., DMN) (Gao et al., 2009b). The functional connectome information can also be leveraged to generate functionally parcellated brain regions in the early developing brain (Shi et al., 2018; Peng et al., 2020). Although nonparallel developmental patterns of structural and functional connectomes from infancy to early childhood have been suggested (Cao et al., 2017b; Fransson et al., 2007; Hagmann et al., 2010; Huang et al., 2015), the relationship between structural and functional connectomes remains an area for future investigation and new tools for empirical analyses of structure-function coupling are urgently needed (Van Essen, 2013).

6. Early brain metabolic and physiological development

Striking structural and functional changes in early brain development are underlined by associated physiological changes to meet metabolic requirement of these developmental processes. In human adults, the brain receives 15% of the cardiac output and accounts for 20% of total body energy consumption despite only representing 2% of body mass (Bouma and Muizelaar, 1990; Attwell and Laughlin, 2001). Notably, this proportion of energy consumption is even greater in the developing brain (Kennedy and Sokoloff, 1957). Brain energy is derived primarily from aerobic glycolysis and oxidative phosphorylation (Vaishnavi et al., 2010), for which glucose and oxygen are essential substrates. The cerebral metabolic rate for glucose (CMRGlc) and oxygen (CMRO2) are important indices directly related to brain metabolism and have been measured by positron emission tomography (PET) using ^{18}F-flurodeoxyglucose (FDG) and ^{15}O radiotracers, respectively.

Due to radiation concerns associated with the use of PET, there are limited studies on GMRGlc and CMRO2 during typical development of the healthy infant brain (Chugani and Phelps, 1986; Chugani et al., 1987; Chugani, 1998; Kinnala et al., 1996; Powers et al., 1998; Takahashi et al., 1999). In these studies, neonates demonstrated a remarkably different distribution pattern of regional CMRGlc from adults, with highest CMRGlc values found in primary sensorimotor cortex, thalamus, brainstem, and cerebellar vermis (Chugani and Phelps, 1986; Chugani et al., 1987; Kinnala et al., 1996). The glucose consumption rose rapidly from birth until 4 years of age, when CMRGlc values in children were approximately twice the adult value (Chugani and Phelps, 1986; Chugani et al., 1987). These PET studies revealed heterogeneous courses of metabolic maturation across the cortex, with increases in CMRGlc and CMRO2 first observed in parietal, temporal and primary visual cortices at 2–3 months of life, and then in frontal cortex at 6–12 months (Chugani and Phelps, 1986; Chugani et al., 1987; Kinnala et al., 1996; Takahashi et al., 1999). More recently, global CMRO2 was noninvasively quantified in the normal neonate brain using a novel T2 relaxation under spin tagging (TRUST) MRI technique, through which a significant increase in global CMRO2 was observed in neonates from 35 to 42 postmenstrual weeks (Liu et al., 2014; Liu et al., 2019a).

Both glucose and oxygen are delivered through blood flow. Cerebral blood flow (CBF) has been shown to be tightly coupled with regional metabolism (Fox and Raichle, 1986; Vaishnavi et al., 2010). With advances in perfusion MRI, global and regional CBF (rCBF) can be noninvasively measured by phase-contrast MRI (PC-MRI) and ASL MRI, respectively (Liu et al., 2014, 2019b; Miranda et al., 2006; Wang et al., 2008; Ouyang et al., 2017b). PC-MRI studies revealed an age-related increase in global CBF from 32 postmenstrual weeks to 18 months of age (Liu et al., 2014, 2019b; Ouyang et al., 2017b; Varela et al., 2012), with global CBF exceeding adult levels by 12 months (Liu et al., 2019b). At the regional level, rCBF distribution measured using an advanced 3D multishot stack-of-spirals ASL in early postnatal life (~2 months of age) demonstrated a similar pattern to that from PET studies, with higher values in primary auditory/sensorimotor cortices and deep gray matter shown in Fig. 7 (Ouyang et al., 2020a). Despite limited ASL studies in normal neonates and infants, the dynamic changes of rCBF during early development exhibited local differences across deep gray matter, primary cerebral cortex, and association areas (Jill et al., 2013; Miranda et al., 2006; Ouyang et al., 2017b; Wang et al., 2008). These findings are generally consistent with prior studies using PET. Taken together, these metabolic and physiological changes suggest a complex interplay between development and metabolic needs. Elucidating the spatiotemporal evolution of these changes during infancy could help advance our understanding on the physiological underpinnings of normal brain development.

7. Current issues and limitations

7.1 Challenges of imaging infant brains

There are several issues arising from studying the early brain structural and functional development across MRI modalities. First, motion-induced artifacts are prominent in neonatal and infant MRI. In certain clinical settings, this issue can sometimes be circumvented with sedation. However, sedation

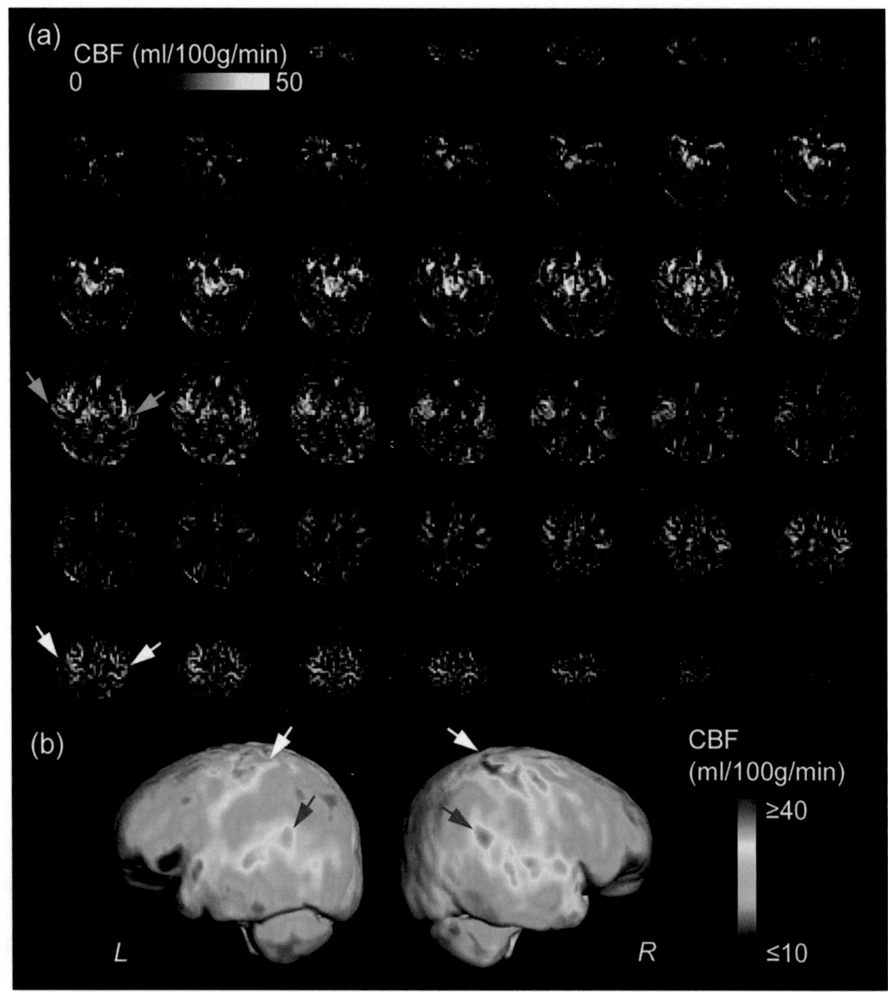

FIG. 7

(A) High-resolution ($2.5 \times 2.5 \times 2.5\ mm^3$) regional cerebral blood flow (rCBF) maps acquired with 3D multishot, stack-of-spirals pCASL from a representative infant aged 2 months and (B) rCBF maps projected to the 3D reconstructed surface. High rCBF values in the pre- and post-central gyri (primary sensorimotor cortex), and superior temporal gyrus (primary auditory cortex) are indicated by white and green arrows, respectively. R/L: right/left hemisphere.

This figure is adapted with permission from Ouyang, M., Detre, J., Lam, S., Edgar, J., and Huang, H., 2020a. High-resolution infant cerebral blood flow map measured with 3D multi-shot, stack-of-spirals pCASL. In: Proceedings of ISMRM. Abstract #0224.

is not desirable because of the associated clinical risk (Malviya et al., 2000), which is generally deemed unacceptable for most research studies. As a result, research subjects are usually scanned during natural sleep (Dean et al., 2014b; Howell et al., 2019). However, even small movements during sleep can make it challenging to acquire MR images without motion artifacts. A number of techniques (Gholipour et al., 2010; Kim et al., 2010; Dubois et al., 2014b; Cordero-Grande et al., 2018) have been developed to correct motion retrospectively based on postprocessing of the images. These can be augmented by prospective approaches to further improve motion correction. The prospective approaches include novel MR sequence improvements (e.g., self-navigated MR sequences, see Tisdall et al., 2012), acoustically derated sequences that limit sound profile of sequences, specific hardware devices (e.g., KinetiCor device for monitoring motion) and software suites (e.g., FIRMM for real-time feedback on data quality during acquisition, see Dosenbach et al., 2017). Second, given the smaller size of the infant brain, higher spatial resolution is needed to delineate brain structures with anatomical detail similar to that of the adult brains. This higher resolution imaging requires obtaining data with high signal-to-noise ratios (SNRs), making it difficult to reduce the scan time and thereby the likelihood of subject motion. Advances in data acquisition, such as simultaneous multiple-slice acquisition (Sotiropoulos et al., 2013) can dramatically speed up image acquisition. This permits greater signal averaging for a given scan time, and the associated improvement in SNR can be used to acquire data with higher spatial resolution—on the order of isotropic 1–1.5 mm in dMRI and 2 mm in fMRI. Third, dedicated infant brain MRI atlases and methodologies for postprocessing are needed (Barkovich et al., 2019; Feng et al., 2019; Li et al., 2019; Oishi et al., 2019). For instance, poor gray/white matter contrast in structural MRI makes it difficult to segment infant brains, but relatively few computational methods have been developed to tackle this challenge (Adamson et al., 2020; Wang et al., 2015; Zöllei et al., 2020).

In addition, we must keep in mind that MRI techniques are indirect approaches to exploring the underlying maturational processes of the human brain, and each technique has unique technical demands and intrinsic limitations. For example, in the case of dMRI, the advanced multishell sequences with many diffusion-encoded directions make it more difficult to reduce the scan time and minimize motion. Further, artifacts from dMRI acquisition (e.g., those related to magnetic gradient imperfections, eddy currents, etc.) must be considered. For data analysis, modeling of dMRI data has its own challenges. DTI-derived measurements can at best only infer the microstructure and do not directly quantify the axonal density, axonal packing or myelin level (Wheeler-Kingshott and Cercignani, 2009; Jones et al., 2013 for review). FA values can also be affected by crossing-fibers, even at an isotropic spatial resolution of 2 mm widely used in fetal and infant DTI research. This limitation directly affects the interpretation of the emergence of certain white matter tracts using tractography (Huang et al., 2009; Miller et al., 2014; Takahashi et al., 2011). Fortunately, a number of approaches have been developed to mitigate effects of crossing-fibers on FA measurements (e.g., Mishra et al., 2015). Also, when interpreting rs-fMRI based connectivity data, one should be aware of hemodynamic signals provide an indirect measure of neural activity. Nonneuronal factors such as systemic physiological changes can also drive changes in BOLD signal (Chen et al., 2020). Scientists investigating infant brain function may consider using an infant-specific hemodynamic response function for modeling the BOLD signal (Denisova, 2019). Despite these challenges, MRI techniques still offer great opportunities to noninvasively study early brain development in fetuses and infants.

7.2 Issues in clinical applications

The use of MRI of infants and fetuses in the clinical setting involves many same challenges as in the research setting. Advances developed for research studies, many of which are outlined above, are quite welcome as manufacturers incorporate them into clinical MRI systems. However, there are some issues of particular relevance for infant clinical studies. One is the efficiency of the radiofrequency (RF) coil used for image acquisition. While a number of factors affect coil efficiency, coil size is a major one, and smaller RF coils perform better than larger ones. This characteristic is related to the coil "filling factor," which can be visualized as the ratio of the volume of the sample to the volume of the coil (Doty et al., 1999). It is not uncommon for adult head coils with suboptimal filling factor to be used to image the infant brain. The sagittal scout image, which essentially shows the sensitive volume of the coil, can include not only the head but extend far enough inferiorly that the chest and abdomen are visible as well. This is evident in the scout images for smaller infants. Hence, the RF coil is much larger than it need be and the coil correspondingly inefficient. Acquiring images with a coil this size in an infant is tantamount to imaging an adult brain using the body coil, an approach that is patently unacceptable on the basis of SNR considerations. Thus, an infant-specific head coil should be used whenever possible (e.g., Keil et al., 2011). A second important detail is in regard to image acquisition parameters. The rapid changes in T1 and T2 relaxation time constants that occur during the first year of life detailed above require that image acquisition parameters be optimized on the basis of patient age in order to get the best possible contrast-to-noise ratio for structural images. However, in clinical settings, standardized acquisition parameters are typically utilized across wide age ranges, thereby limiting data quality in some populations. Finally, for system-based and clinical reasons, scan times are often designed to be as short as possible, particularly for ill and/or clinically labile infants. Subsequently, fast, motion-resistant pulse sequences should be used with optimized RF coils whenever available. However, this serves to both limit the quality of data collected (i.e., necessitating use of lower image spatial resolution) and mitigate the ability to utilize sequences more traditionally employed in research settings (e.g., dMRI with large numbers of directions and/or multiple b values, and fMRI).

8. Conclusions and future directions

We have consolidated the findings on early brain structural and functional development from fetuses to infants using MR imaging techniques. Specifically, the brain maturational process in the period from mid-gestation to age 2 years is characterized by emergence of white matter tracts and rapid increases of brain volume and FCS. By the time of birth, infant brains have very similar patterns of cortical gyrification and major white matter tracts as those of adult brains, and the primary sensorimotor functional system is well developed. The following 2 years of life is a period of continuous growth of gray matter, rapid myelination and axonal packing of white matter fiber bundles, and development of higher-order functional systems. The early development of white and gray matter is spatiotemporally heterogeneous. For example, myelination begins earlier in projection and commissural fiber tracts than in association fiber tracts. And the multimodal associative cortices (e.g., prefrontal regions) are shown to mature later than uni-modal associative cortices, which in turn mature later than primary sensory and motor cortices, consistent with past histologic studies.

Future research could include the development of novel MR imaging techniques in both data acquisition and postprocessing for motion correction in baby. More sophisticated diffusion models (e.g., DKI, NODDI) may overcome the limitations of the diffusion tensor model. After comprehensive validation of these models, they may provide information about microstructural changes in white matter and cortical regions in addition to those discovered through DTI. Further, complementary to current literature which mostly focuses on long-range white matter fiber development, more investigations are expected to improve our understanding of how short-range white matter fibers mature in this early brain developmental period (see, e.g., Ouyang et al., 2016, 2017b; Phillips et al., 2013 for review). Reliable methodologies are needed to perform the tractography of short-range white matter fibers or white matter bundles across different maturational stages (e.g., Dubois et al., 2016). By leveraging complementary information from various MRI approaches, multimodality studies will also be a promising direction to enhance our understanding on early brain development such as brain structure-function relationship. Another interesting direction for future research would be investigation of the relationships between brain and cognitive/behavioral development, which would particularly benefit from longitudinal studies that allow charting developmental trajectories. Establishing normative developmental charts of structure, function and behavior is not only essential for understanding the complicated and the rapid early development, but also critical for revealing alterations caused by neuropathology for early diagnosis and intervention. Moreover, developing machine learning techniques to predict cognitive abilities and behavior at the single-subject level based on rich information from neuroimaging is worth further attention. Such predictive modeling approaches may contribute to progress in both basic developmental neuroscience and personalized medicine (e.g., Hazlett et al., 2017; Ouyang et al., 2020b; Rosenberg et al., 2018; Smyser et al., 2016c). Finally, data sharing could significantly facilitate the understanding of the complicated structural and functional dynamics during the fetal and infant stages. Recent release of multimodality neonate and infant MRI from ERC-sponsored developing human connectome project (dHCP) (www.developingconnectome.org), NIH-sponsored fetal-neonate brain development (www.brainmrimap.org), and NIH-sponsored baby connectome project (BCP) (https://babyconnectomeproject.org/) could potentially expand our knowledge of early brain development.

Acknowledgments

The authors would like to acknowledge the National Institutes of Health (NIH) funding sources MH092535, MH092535-S1 and HD086984. These grants supported acquisition of the fetal, neonate and infant MRI data based on which figures of this chapter were created.

References

Adamson, C.L., Alexander, B., Ball, G., Beare, R., Cheong, J.L., Spittle, A.J., Doyle, L.W., Anderson, P.J., Seal, M.L., Thompson, D.K., 2020. Parcellation of the neonatal cortex using surface-based Melbourne Children's Regional Infant Brain atlases (M-CRIB-S). Sci. Rep. 10 (1), 1–11.

Afacan, O., Estroff, J.A., Yang, E., Barnewolt, C.E., Connolly, S.A., Parad, R.B., Mulkern, R.V., Warfield, S.K., Gholipour, A., 2019. Fetal echoplanar imaging: promises and challenges. Top. Magn. Reson. Imaging 28 (5), 245–254.

Alcauter, S., Lin, W., Smith, J.K., Short, S.J., Goldman, B.D., Reznick, J.S., Gilmore, J.H., Gao, W., 2014. Development of thalamocortical connectivity during infancy and its cognitive correlations. J. Neurosci. 34 (27), 9067–9075.

Allievi, A.G., Arichi, T., Tusor, N., Kimpton, J., Arulkumaran, S., Counsell, S.J., Edwards, A.D., Burdet, E., 2016. Maturation of sensori-motor functional responses in the preterm brain. Cereb. Cortex 26 (1), 402–413.

Arichi, T., Fagiolo, G., Varela, M., Melendez-Calderon, A., Allievi, A., Merchant, N., Tusor, N., Counsell, S.J., Burdet, E., Beckmann, C.F., Edwards, A.D., 2012. Development of BOLD signal hemodynamic responses in the human brain. NeuroImage 63 (2), 663–673.

Arichi, T., Gordon-Williams, R., Allievi, A., Groves, A.M., Burdet, E., Edwards, A.D., 2013. Computer-controlled stimulation for functional magnetic resonance imaging studies of the neonatal olfactory system. Acta Paediatr. 102 (9), 868–875.

Arichi, T., Moraux, A., Melendez, A., Doria, V., Groppo, M., Merchant, N., Combs, S., Burdet, E., Larkman, D.J., Counsell, S.J., Beckmann, C.F., 2010. Somatosensory cortical activation identified by functional MRI in preterm and term infants. NeuroImage 49 (3), 2063–2071.

Attwell, D., Laughlin, S.B., 2001. An energy budget for signaling in the grey matter of the brain. J. Cereb. Blood Flow Metab. 21 (10), 1133–1145.

Ball, G., Aljabar, P., Zebari, S., Tusor, N., Arichi, T., Merchant, N., Robinson, E.C., Ogundipe, E., Rueckert, D., Edwards, A.D., Counsell, S.J., 2014. Rich-club organization of the newborn human brain. Proc. Natl. Acad. Sci. U. S. A. 111 (20), 7456–7461.

Ball, G., Srinivasan, L., Aljabar, P., Counsell, S.J., Durighel, G., Hajnal, J.V., Rutherford, M.A., Edwards, A.D., 2013. Development of cortical microstructure in the preterm human brain. Proc. Natl. Acad. Sci. U. S. A. 110 (23), 9541–9546.

Barkovich, A.J., 2000. Concepts of myelin and myelination in neuroradiology. AJNR Am. J. Neuroradiol. 21 (6), 1099–1109.

Barkovich, A.J., Kjos, B.O., Jackson Jr., D.E., Norman, D., 1988. Normal maturation of the neonatal and infant brain: MR imaging at 1.5 T. Radiology 166 (1), 173–180.

Barkovich, A.J., Lyon, G., Evrard, P., 1992. Formation, maturation, and disorders of white matter. AJNR Am. J. Neuroradiol. 13 (2), 447–461.

Barkovich, M.J., Li, Y., Desikan, R.S., Barkovich, A.J., Xu, D., 2019. Challenges in pediatric neuroimaging. NeuroImage 185, 793–801.

Baumann, N., Pham-Dinh, D., 2001. Biology of oligodendrocyte and myelin in the mammalian central nervous system. Physiol. Rev. 81 (2), 871–927.

Baxter, L., Fitzgibbon, S., Moultrie, F., Goksan, S., Jenkinson, M., Smith, S., Andersson, J., Duff, E., Slater, R., 2019. Optimising neonatal fMRI data analysis: design and validation of an extended dHCP preprocessing pipeline to characterise noxious-evoked brain activity in infants. NeuroImage 186, 286–300.

Bayer, S.A., Altman, J., 2004. The Human Brain during the Third Trimester. CRC Press, Boca Raton, FL.

Bayer, S.A., Altman, J., 2005. The Human Brain During the Second Trimester. CRC Press, Boca Raton, FL.

Beaulieu, C., 2002. The basis of anisotropic water diffusion in the nervous system—a technical review. NMR Biomed. 15 (7–8), 435–455.

Berman, J.I., Mukherjee, P., Partridge, S.C., Miller, S.P., Ferriero, D.M., Barkovich, A.J., Vigneron, D.B., Henry, R.G., 2005. Quantitative diffusion tensor MRI fiber tractography of sensorimotor white matter development in premature infants. NeuroImage 27 (4), 862–871.

Biswal, B., Zerrin Yetkin, F., Haughton, V.M., Hyde, J.S., 1995. Functional connectivity in the motor cortex of resting human brain using echo-planar MRI. Magn. Reson. Med. 34 (4), 537–541.

Blazejewska, A.I., Seshamani, S., McKown, S.K., Caucutt, J.S., Dighe, M., Gatenby, C., Studholme, C., 2017. 3D in utero quantification of T2* relaxation times in human fetal brain tissues for age optimized structural and functional MRI. Magn. Reson. Med. 78 (3), 909–916.

Born, A.P., Miranda, M.J., Rostrup, E., Toft, P.B., Peitersen, B., Larsson, H.B.W., Lou, H.C., 2000. Functional magnetic resonance imaging of the normal and abnormal visual system in early life. Neuropediatrics 31 (01), 24–32.

Born, P., Leth, H., Miranda, M.J., Rostrup, E., Stensgaard, A., Peitersen, B., Larsson, H.B., Lou, H.C., 1998. Visual activation in infants and young children studied by functional magnetic resonance imaging. Pediatr. Res. 44 (4), 578–583.

Bouma, G.J., Muizelaar, J.P., 1990. Relationship between cardiac output and cerebral blood flow in patients with intact and with impaired autoregulation. J. Neurosurg. 73 (3), 368–374.

Brodmann, K., 1909. Vergleichende Lokalisationslehre der Grosshirnrinde in ihren Prinzipien dargestellt auf Grund des Zellenbaues. Barth.

Brody, B.A., Kinney, H.C., Kloman, A.S., Gilles, F.H., 1987. Sequence of central nervous system myelination in human infancy. I. An autopsy study of myelination. J. Neuropathol. Exp. Neurol. 46 (3), 283–301.

Brown, C.J., Miller, S.P., Booth, B.G., Andrews, S., Chau, V., Poskitt, K.J., Hamarneh, G., 2014. Structural network analysis of brain development in young preterm neonates. NeuroImage 101, 667–680.

Bullmore, E., Sporns, O., 2009. Complex brain networks: graph theoretical analysis of structural and functional systems. Nat. Rev. Neurosci. 10 (3), 86–198.

Bültmann, E., Spineli, L.M., Hartmann, H., Lanfermann, H., 2018. Measuring in vivo cerebral maturation using age-related T2 relaxation times at 3 T. Brain and Development 40 (2), 85–93.

Bystron, I., Blakemore, C., Rakic, P., 2008. Development of the human cerebral cortex: Boulder Committee revisited. Nat. Rev. Neurosci. 9, 110–122.

Cao, M., He, Y., Dai, Z., Liao, X., Jeon, T., Ouyang, M., Chalak, L., Bi, Y., Rollins, N., Dong, Q., Huang, H., 2017b. Early development of functional network segregation revealed by connectomic analysis of the preterm human brain. Cereb. Cortex 27 (3), 1949–1963.

Cao, M., Huang, H., He, Y., 2017a. Developmental connectomics from infancy through early childhood. Trends Neurosci. 40 (8), 494–506.

Catani, M., Dell'Acqua, F., Vergani, F., Malik, F., Hodge, H., Roy, P., Valabregue, R., de Schotten, M.T., 2012. Short frontal lobe connections of the human brain. Cortex 48 (2), 273–291.

Chan, W.Y., Yew, D.T., 1998. Apoptosis and Bcl-2 oncoprotein expression in the human fetal central nervous system. Anat. Rec. 252 (2), 165–175.

Chang, Y.S., Owen, J.P., Pojman, N.J., Thieu, T., Bukshpun, P., Wakahiro, M.L., Berman, J.I., Roberts, T.P., Nagarajan, S.S., Sherr, E.H., Mukherjee, P., 2015. White matter changes of neurite density and fiber orientation dispersion during human brain maturation. PLoS One 10 (6), e0123656.

Chen, J., Lewis, L., Chang, C., Tian, Q., Fultz, N., Ohringer, N., Rosen, B., Polimeni, J., 2020. Resting-state "physiological networks". NeuroImage 213, 116707.

Chugani, H.T., 1998. A critical period of brain development: studies of cerebral glucose utilization with PET. Prev. Med. 27 (2), 184–188.

Chugani, H.T., Phelps, M.E., 1986. Maturational changes in cerebral function in infants determined by 18FDG positron emission tomography. Science 231 (4740), 840–843.

Chugani, H.T., Phelps, M.E., Mazziotta, J.C., 1987. Positron emission tomography study of human brain functional development. Ann. Neurol. 22 (4), 487–497.

Cordero-Grande, L., Hughes, E.J., Hutter, J., Price, A.N., Hajnal, J.V., 2018. Three-dimensional motion corrected sensitivity encoding reconstruction for multi-shot multi-slice MRI: application to neonatal brain imaging. Magn. Reson. Med. 79 (3), 1365–1376.

Dall'Orso, S., Steinweg, J., Allievi, A.G., Edwards, A.D., Burdet, E., Arichi, T., 2018. Somatotopic mapping of the developing sensorimotor cortex in the preterm human brain. Cereb. Cortex 28 (7), 2507–2515.

De Asis-Cruz, J., Kapse, K., Basu, S.K., Said, M., Scheinost, D., Murnick, J., Chang, T., du Plessis, A., Limperopoulos, C., 2020. Functional brain connectivity in ex utero premature infants compared to in utero fetuses. NeuroImage 219, 117043.

Dean, D.C., Dirks, H., O'Muircheartaigh, J., Walker, L., Jerskey, B.A., Lehman, K., Han, M., Waskiewicz, N., Deoni, S.C., 2014b. Pediatric neuroimaging using magnetic resonance imaging during non-sedated sleep. Pediatr. Radiol. 44 (1), 64–72.

Dean, D.C., O'muircheartaigh, J., Dirks, H., Waskiewicz, N., Lehman, K., Walker, L., Han, M., Deoni, S.C., 2014a. Modeling healthy male white matter and myelin development: 3 through 60 months of age. NeuroImage 84, 742–752.

DeIpolyi, A.R., Mukherjee, P., Gill, K., Henry, R.G., Partridge, S.C., Veeraraghavan, S., Jin, H., Lu, Y., Miller, S.P., Ferriero, D.M., Vigneron, D.B., Barkovich, A.J., 2005. Comparing microstructural and macrostructural development of the cerebral cortex in premature newborns: diffusion tensor imaging versus cortical gyration. NeuroImage 27 (3), 579–586.

Denisova, K., 2019. Neurobiology, not artifacts: challenges and guidelines for imaging the high risk infant. NeuroImage 185, 624–640.

Deoni, S.C., Dean, D.C., O'muircheartaigh, J., Dirks, H., Jerskey, B.A., 2012. Investigating white matter development in infancy and early childhood using myelin water faction and relaxation time mapping. NeuroImage 63, 1038–1053.

Deoni, S.C., Matthews, L., Kolind, S.H., 2013. One component? Two components? Three? The effect of including a nonexchanging "free" water component in multicomponent driven equilibrium single pulse observation of T1 and T2. Magn. Reson. Med. 70 (1), 147–154.

Deoni, S.C., Mercure, E., Blasi, A., Gasston, D., Thomson, A., Johnson, M., Williams, S.C., Murphy, D.G., 2011. Mapping infant brain myelination with magnetic resonance imaging. J. Neurosci. 31 (2), 784–791.

Doria, V., Beckmann, C.F., Arichi, T., Merchant, N., Groppo, M., Turkheimer, F.E., Counsell, S.J., Murgasova, M., Aljabar, P., Nunes, R.G., Larkman, D.J., 2010. Emergence of resting state networks in the preterm human brain. Proc. Natl. Acad. Sci. U. S. A. 107 (46), 20015–20020.

Dosenbach, N.U., Koller, J.M., Earl, E.A., Miranda-Dominguez, O., Klein, R.L., Van, A.N., Snyder, A.Z., Nagel, B.J., Nigg, J.T., Nguyen, A.L., Wesevich, V., Greene, D.J., Fair, D.A., 2017. Real-time motion analytics during brain MRI improve data quality and reduce costs. NeuroImage 161, 80–93.

Doty, F.D., Entzminger Jr., G., Hauck, C.D., Staab, J.P., 1999. Practical aspects of birdcage coils. J. Magn. Reson. 138 (1), 144–154.

Dubois, J., Adibpour, P., Poupon, C., Hertz-Pannier, L., Dehaene-Lambertz, G., 2016. MRI and M/EEG studies of the white matter development in human fetuses and infants: review and opinion. Brain Plast. 2 (1), 49–69.

Dubois, J., Benders, M., Cachia, A., Lazeyras, F., Ha-Vinh Leuchter, R., Sizonenko, S.V., Borradori-Tolsa, C., Mangin, J.F., Hüppi, P.S., 2008a. Mapping the early cortical folding process in the preterm newborn brain. Cereb. Cortex 18 (6), 1444–1454.

Dubois, J., Dehaene-Lambertz, G., Kulikova, S., Poupon, C., Hüppi, P.S., Hertz-Pannier, L., 2014a. The early development of brain white matter: a review of imaging studies in fetuses, newborns and infants. Neuroscience 276, 48–71.

Dubois, J., Dehaene-Lambertz, G., Perrin, M., Mangin, J.F., Cointepas, Y., Duchesnay, E., Le Bihan, D., Hertz-Pannier, L., 2008b. Asynchrony of the early maturation of white matter bundles in healthy infants: quantitative landmarks revealed noninvasively by diffusion tensor imaging. Hum. Brain Mapp. 29, 14–27.

Dubois, J., Hertz-Pannier, L., Dehaene-Lambertz, G., Cointepas, Y., Le Bihan, D., 2006. Assessment of the early organization and maturation of infants' cerebral white matter fiber bundles: a feasibility study using quantitative diffusion tensor imaging and tractography. NeuroImage 30, 1121–1132.

Dubois, J., Kulikova, S., Hertz-Pannier, L., Mangin, J.F., Dehaene-Lambertz, G., Poupon, C., 2014b. Correction strategy for diffusion-weighted images corrupted with motion: application to the DTI evaluation of infants' white matter. Magn. Reson. Imaging 32 (8), 981–992.

Eaton-Rosen, Z., Scherrer, B., Melbourne, A., Ourselin, S., Neil, J.J., Warfield, S.K., 2017. Investigating the maturation of microstructure and radial orientation in the preterm human cortex with diffusion MRI. NeuroImage 162, 65–72.

Engelbrecht, V., Rassek, M., Preiss, S., Wald, C., Mödder, U., 1998. Age-dependent changes in magnetization transfer contrast of white matter in the pediatric brain. AJNR Am. J. Neruoradiol. 19 (10), 1923–1929.

Engle, W.A., American Academy of Pediatrics Committee on Fetus and Newborn, 2004. Age terminology during the perinatal period. Pediatrics 114, 1362–1364.

Erberich, S.G., Panigrahy, A., Friedlich, P., Seri, I., Nelson, M.D., Gilles, F., 2006. Somatosensory lateralization in the newborn brain. NeuroImage 29 (1), 155–161.

Fair, D.A., Cohen, A.L., Power, J.D., Dosenbach, N.U., Church, J.A., Miezin, F.M., Schlaggar, B.L., Petersen, S.E., 2009. Functional brain networks develop from a "local to distributed" organization. PLoS Comput. Biol. 5 (5), e1000381.

Feinberg, I., 1983. Schizophrenia: caused by a fault in programmed synaptic elimination during adolescence? J. Psychiatr. Res. 17, 319–334.

Feng, L., Li, H., Oishi, K., Mishra, V., Song, L., Peng, Q., Ouyang, M., Wang, J., Slinger, M., Jeon, T., Lee, L., 2019. Age-specific gray and white matter DTI atlas for human brain at 33, 36 and 39 postmenstrual weeks. NeuroImage 185, 685–698.

Fox, M.D., Raichle, M.E., 2007. Spontaneous fluctuations in brain activity observed with functional magnetic resonance imaging. Nat. Rev. Neurosci. 8 (9), 700–711.

Fox, M.D., Snyder, A.Z., Vincent, J.L., Corbetta, M., Van Essen, D.C., Raichle, M.E., 2005. The human brain is intrinsically organized into dynamic, anticorrelated functional networks. Proc. Natl. Acad. Sci. U. S. A. 102 (27), 9673–9678.

Fox, P.T., Raichle, M.E., 1986. Focal physiological uncoupling of cerebral blood flow and oxidative metabolism during somatosensory stimulation in human subjects. Proc. Natl. Acad. Sci. U. S. A. 83 (4), 1140–1144.

Fransson, P., Åden, U., Blennow, M., Lagercrantz, H., 2011. The functional architecture of the infant brain as revealed by resting-state fMRI. Cereb. Cortex 21 (1), 145–154.

Fransson, P., Skiöld, B., Engström, M., Hallberg, B., Mosskin, M., Åden, U., Lagercrantz, H., Blennow, M., 2009. Spontaneous brain activity in the newborn brain during natural sleep—an fMRI study in infants born at full term. Pediatr. Res. 66 (3), 301–305.

Fransson, P., Skiöld, B., Horsch, S., Nordell, A., Blennow, M., Lagercrantz, H., Aden, U., 2007. Resting-state networks in the infant brain. Proc. Natl. Acad. Sci. U. S. A. 104 (39), 15531–15536.

Fulford, J., Vadeyar, S.H., Dodampahala, S.H., Ong, S., Moore, R.J., Baker, P.N., James, D.K., Gowland, P., 2004. Fetal brain activity and hemodynamic response to a vibroacoustic stimulus. Hum. Brain Mapp. 22 (2), 116–121.

Gao, W., Alcauter, S., Elton, A., Hernandez-Castillo, C.R., Smith, J.K., Ramirez, J., Lin, W., 2015b. Functional network development during the first year: relative sequence and socioeconomic correlations. Cereb. Cortex 25 (9), 2919–2928.

Gao, W., Alcauter, S., Smith, J.K., Gilmore, J.H., Lin, W., 2015a. Development of human brain cortical network architecture during infancy. Brain Struct. Funct. 220 (2), 1173–1186.

Gao, W., Elton, A., Zhu, H., Alcauter, S., Smith, J.K., Gilmore, J.H., Lin, W., 2014. Intersubject variability of and genetic effects on the brain's functional connectivity during infancy. J. Neurosci. 34 (34), 11288–11296.

Gao, W., Gilmore, J.H., Alcauter, S., Lin, W., 2013b. The dynamic reorganization of the default-mode network during a visual classification task. Front. Syst. Neurosci. 7, 34.

Gao, W., Gilmore, J.H., Shen, D., Smith, J.K., Zhu, H., Lin, W., 2013a. The synchronization within and interaction between the default and dorsal attention networks in early infancy. Cereb. Cortex 23 (3), 594–603.

Gao, W., Lin, W., Chen, Y., Gerig, G., Smith, J., Jewells, V., Gilmore, J., 2009a. Temporal and spatial development of axonal maturation and myelination of white matter in the developing brain. AJNR Am. J. Neuroradiol. 30, 290–296.

Gao, W., Zhu, H., Giovanello, K.S., Smith, J.K., Shen, D., Gilmore, J.H., Lin, W., 2009b. Evidence on the mergence of the brain's default network from 2-week-old to 2-year-old healthy pediatric subjects. Proc. Natl. Acad. Sci. U. S. A. 106 (16), 6790–6795.

Geng, X., Gouttard, S., Sharma, A., Gu, H., Styner, M., Lin, W., Gerig, G., Gilmore, J.H., 2012. Quantitative tract-based white matter development from birth to age 2 years. NeuroImage 61, 542–557.

Gholipour, A., Estroff, J.A., Warfield, S.K., 2010. Robust super-resolution volume reconstruction from slice acquisitions: application to fetal brain MRI. IEEE Trans. Med. Imaging 29 (10), 1739–1758.

Giedd, J.N., Rapoport, J.L., 2010. Structural MRI of pediatric brain development: what have we learned and where are we going? Neuron 67 (5), 728–734.

Gilmore, J.H., Shi, F., Woolson, S.L., Knickmeyer, R.C., Short, S.J., Lin, W., Zhu, H., Hamer, R.M., Styner, M., Shen, D., 2012. Longitudinal development of cortical and subcortical gray matter from birth to 2 years. Cereb. Cortex 22 (11), 2478–2485.

Gogtay, N., Giedd, J.N., Lusk, L., Hayashi, K.M., Greenstein, D., Vaituzis, A.C., Nugent, T.F., Herman, D.H., Clasen, L.S., Toga, A.W., Rapoport, J.L., 2004. Dynamic mapping of human cortical development during childhood through early adulthood. Proc. Natl. Acad. Sci. U. S. A. 101 (21), 8174–8179.

Guevara, M., Román, C., Houenou, J., Duclap, D., Poupon, C., Mangin, J.F., Guevara, P., 2017. Reproducibility of superficial white matter tracts using diffusion-weighted imaging tractography. NeuroImage 147, 703–725.

Habas, P.A., Scott, J.A., Roosta, A., Rajagopalan, V., Kim, K., Rousseau, F., Barkovich, A.J., Glenn, O.A., Studholme, C., 2012. Early folding patterns and asymmetries of the normal human brain detected from in utero MRI. Cereb. Cortex 22 (1), 13–25.

Hagmann, P., Sporns, O., Madan, N., Cammoun, L., Pienaar, R., Wedeen, V.J., Meuli, R., Thiran, J.P., Grant, P.E., 2010. White matter maturation reshapes structural connectivity in the late developing human brain. Proc. Natl. Acad. Sci. U. S. A. 107 (44), 19067–19072.

Haselgrove, J., Moore, J., Wang, Z., Traipe, E., Bilaniuk, L., 2000. A method for fast multislice T1 measurement: feasibility studies on phantoms, young children, and children with Canavan's disease. J. Magn. Reson. Imaging 11 (4), 360–367.

Hazlett, H.C., Gu, H., Munsell, B.C., Kim, S.H., Styner, M., Wolff, J.J., Elison, J.T., Swanson, M.R., Zhu, H., Botteron, K.N., Collins, D.L., 2017. Early brain development in infants at high risk for autism spectrum disorder. Nature 542 (7641), 348–351.

Heep, A., Scheef, L., Jankowski, J., Born, M., Zimmermann, N., Sival, D., Bos, A., Gieseke, J., Bartmann, P., Schild, H., Boecker, H., 2009. Functional magnetic resonance imaging of the sensorimotor system in preterm infants. Pediatrics 123 (1), 294–300.

Hermoye, L., Saint-Martin, C., Cosnard, G., Lee, S.-K., Kim, J., Nassogne, M.-C., Menten, R., Clapuyt, P., Donohue, P.K., Hua, K., 2006. Pediatric diffusion tensor imaging: normal database and observation of the white matter maturation in early childhood. NeuroImage 29, 493–504.

Herzmann, C.S., Snyder, A.Z., Kenley, J.K., Rogers, C.E., Shimony, J.S., Smyser, C.D., 2019. Cerebellar functional connectivity in term- and very preterm-born infants. Cereb. Cortex 29 (3), 1174–1184.

Hill, J., Inder, T., Neil, J., Dierker, D., Harwell, J., Van Essen, D., 2010. Similar patterns of cortical expansion during human development and evolution. Proc. Natl. Acad. Sci. U. S. A. 107 (29), 13135–13140.

Howell, B.R., Styner, M.A., Gao, W., Yap, P.T., Wang, L., Baluyot, K., Yacoub, E., Chen, G., Potts, T., Salzwedel, A., Li, G., 2019. The UNC/UMN baby connectome project (BCP): an overview of the study design and protocol development. NeuroImage 185, 891–905.

Huang, H., 2010. Structure of the fetal brain: what we are learning from DTI. Neuroscientist 16, 634–649.

Huang, H., Jeon, T., Sedmak, G., Pletikos, M., Vasung, L., Xu, X., Yarowsky, P., Richards, L.J., Kostović, I., Šestan, N., Mori, S., 2013. Coupling diffusion imaging with histological and gene expression analysis to examine the dynamics of cortical areas across the fetal period of human brain development. Cereb. Cortex 23 (11), 2620–2631.

Huang, H., Shu, N., Mishra, V., Jeon, T., Chalak, L., Wang, Z.J., Rollins, N., Gong, G., Cheng, H., Peng, Y., Dong, Q., He, Y., 2015. Development of human brain structural networks through infancy and childhood. Cereb. Cortex 25 (5), 1389–1404.

Huang, H., Vasung, L., 2014. Gaining insight of fetal brain development with diffusion MRI and histology. Int. J. Dev. Neurosci. 32, 11–22.

Huang, H., Xue, R., Zhang, J., Ren, T., Richards, L.J., Yarowsky, P., Miller, M.I., Mori, S., 2009. Anatomical characterization of human fetal brain development with diffusion tensor magnetic resonance imaging. J. Neurosci. 29, 4263–4273.

Huang, H., Yamamoto, A., Hossain, M.A., Younes, L., Mori, S., 2008. Quantitative cortical mapping of fractional anisotropy in developing rat brains. J. Neurosci. 28 (6), 1427–1433.

Huang, H., Zhang, J., Wakana, S., Zhang, W., Ren, T., Richards, L.J., Yarowsky, P., Donohue, P., Graham, E., van Zijl, P.C., Mori, S., 2006. White and gray matter development in human fetal, newborn and pediatric brains. NeuroImage 33 (1), 27–38.

Hüppi, P.S., Maier, S.E., Peled, S., Zientara, G.P., Barnes, P.D., Jolesz, F.A., Volpe, J.J., 1998b. Microstructural development of human newborn cerebral white matter assessed in vivo by diffusion tensor magnetic resonance imaging. Pediatr. Res. 44 (4), 584–590.

Hüppi, P.S., Warfield, S., Kikinis, R., Barnes, P.D., Zientara, G.P., Jolesz, F.A., Tsuji, M.K., Volpe, J.J., 1998a. Quantitative magnetic resonance imaging of brain development in premature and mature newborns. Ann. Neurol. 43 (2), 224–235.

Huttenlocher, P.R., 1979. Synaptic density in human frontal cortex—developmental changes and effects of aging. Brain Res. 163, 195–205.

Huttenlocher, P.R., Dabholkar, A.S., 1997. Regional differences in synaptogenesis in human cerebral cortex. J. Comp. Neurol. 387, 167–178.

Innocenti, G.M., Price, D.J., 2005. Exuberance in the development of cortical networks. Nat. Rev. Neurosci. 6 (12), 955–965.

Jakab, A., Schwartz, E., Kasprian, G., Gruber, G.M., Prayer, D., Schöpf, V., Langs, G., 2014. Fetal functional imaging portrays heterogeneous development of emerging human brain networks. Front. Hum. Neurosci. 8, 852. https://doi.org/10.3389/fnhum.2014.00852.

Jbabdi, S., Johansen-Berg, H., 2011. Tractography: where do we go from here? Brain Connect. 1 (3), 169–183.

Jill, B., Petersen, E.T., De Vries, L.S., Groenendaal, F., Kersbergen, K.J., Alderliesten, T., Hendrikse, J., Benders, M.J., 2013. Regional changes in brain perfusion during brain maturation measured non-invasively with arterial spin labeling MRI in neonates. Eur. J. Radiol. 82 (3), 538–543.

Jones, D.K., Knösche, T.R., Turner, R., 2013. White matter integrity, fiber count, and other fallacies: the do's and don'ts of diffusion MRI. NeuroImage 73, 239–254.

Kasprian, G., Brugger, P.C., Schöpf, V., Mitter, C., Weber, M., Hainfellner, J.A., Prayer, D., 2013. Assessing prenatal white matter connectivity in commissural agenesis. Brain 136, 168–179.

Kasprian, G., Brugger, P.C., Weber, M., Krssák, M., Krampl, E., Herold, C., Prayer, D., 2008. In utero tractography of fetal white matter development. NeuroImage 43, 213–224.

Keil, B., Alagappan, V., Mareyam, A., McNab, J.A., Fujimoto, K., Tountcheva, V., Triantafyllou, C., Dilks, D.D., Kanwisher, N., Lin, W., Grant, P.E., 2011. Size-optimized 32-channel brain arrays for 3 T pediatric imaging. Magn. Reson. Med. 66 (6), 1777–1787.

Kennedy, C., Sokoloff, L., 1957. An adaptation of the nitrous oxide method to the study of the cerebral circulation in children; normal values for cerebral blood flow and cerebral metabolic rate in childhood. J. Clin. Invest. 36, 1130–1137.

Kersbergen, K.J., Leemans, A., Groenendaal, F., van der Aa, N.E., Viergever, M.A., de Vries, L.S., Benders, M.J., 2014. Microstructural brain development between 30 and 40 weeks corrected age in a longitudinal cohort of extremely preterm infants. NeuroImage 103, 214–224.

Kim, K., Habas, P.A., Rousseau, F., Glenn, O.A., Barkovich, A.J., Studholme, C., 2010. Intersection based motion correction of multislice MRI for 3-D in utero fetal brain image formation. IEEE Trans. Med. Imaging 29 (1), 146–158.

Kinnala, A., Suhonen-Polvi, H., Äärimaa, T., Kero, P., Korvenranta, H., Ruotsalainen, U., Bergman, J., Haaparanta, M., Solin, O., Nuutila, P., Wegelius, U., 1996. Cerebral metabolic rate for glucose during the first six months of life: an FDG positron emission tomography study. Arch. Dis. Child. Fetal Neonatal Ed. 74 (3), F153–F157.

Kinney, H.C., Brody, B.A., Kloman, A.S., Gilles, F.H., 1988. Sequence of central nervous system myelination in human infancy. J. Neuropathol. Exp. Neurol. 47, 217–234.

Klawiter, E.C., Schmidt, R.E., Trinkaus, K., Liang, H.F., Budde, M.D., Naismith, R.T., Song, S.K., Cross, A.H., Benzinger, T.L., 2011. Radial diffusivity predicts demyelination in ex vivo multiple sclerosis spinal cords. NeuroImage 55 (4), 1454–1460.

Knickmeyer, R.C., Gouttard, S., Kang, C., Evans, D., Wilber, K., Smith, J.K., Hamer, R.M., Lin, W., Gerig, G., Gilmore, J.H., 2008. A structural MRI study of human brain development from birth to 2 years. J. Neurosci. 28 (47), 12176–12182.

Kolasinski, J., Takahashi, E., Stevens, A.A., Benner, T., Fischl, B., Zöllei, L., Grant, P.E., 2013. Radial and tangential neuronal migration pathways in the human fetal brain: anatomically distinct patterns of diffusion MRI coherence. NeuroImage 79, 412–422.

Kostović, I., Jovanov-Milosević, N., 2006. The development of cerebral connections during the first 20-45 weeks' gestation. Semin. Fetal Neonatal Med. 11, 415–422.

Kostović, I., Judaš, M., Radoš, M., Hrabač, P., 2002. Laminar organization of the human fetal cerebrum revealed by histochemical markers and magnetic resonance imaging. Cereb. Cortex 12 (5), 536–544.

Kostović, I., Rakic, P., 1990. Developmental history of the transient subplate zone in the visual and somatosensory cortex of the macaque monkey and human brain. J. Comp. Neurol. 297 (3), 441–470.

Kroenke, C.D., Taber, E.N., Leigland, L.A., Knutsen, A.K., Bayly, P.V., 2009. Regional patterns of cerebral cortical differentiation determined by diffusion tensor MRI. Cereb. Cortex 19 (12), 2916–2929.

Kroenke, C.D., Van Essen, D.C., Inder, T.E., Rees, S., Bretthorst, G.L., Neil, J.J., 2007. Microstructural changes of the baboon cerebral cortex during gestational development reflected in magnetic resonance imaging diffusion anisotropy. J. Neurosci. 27 (46), 12506–12515.

Kucharczyk, W., Macdonald, P.M., Stanisz, G.J., Henkelman, R., 1994. Relaxivity and magnetization transfer of white matter lipids at MR imaging: importance of cerebrosides and pH. Radiology 192 (2), 521–529.

Kulikova, S., Hertz-Pannier, L., Dehaene-Lambertz, G., Poupon, C., Dubois, J., 2016. A new strategy for fast MRI-based quantification of the myelin water fraction: application to brain imaging in infants. PLoS One 11 (10). https://doi.org/10.1371/journal.pone.0163143, e0163143.

Kwan, K.Y., Šestan, N., Anton, E.S., 2012. Transcriptional co-regulation of neuronal migration and laminar identity in the neocortex. Development 139 (9), 1535–1546.

Lancaster, J.L., Andrews, T., Hardies, L.J., Dodd, S., Fox, P.T., 2003. Three-pool model of white matter. J. Magn. Reson. Imaging 17 (1), 1–10.

Lebel, C., Walker, L., Leemans, A., Phillips, L., Beaulieu, C., 2008. Microstructural maturation of the human brain from childhood to adulthood. NeuroImage 40, 1044–1055.

Lee, W., Donner, E.J., Nossin-Manor, R., Whyte, H.E., Sled, J.G., Taylor, M.J., 2012. Visual functional magnetic resonance imaging of preterm infants. Dev. Med. Child Neurol. 54 (8), 724–729.

Leppert, I.R., Almli, C.R., McKinstry, R.C., Mulkern, R.V., Pierpaoli, C., Rivkin, M.J., Pike, G.B., 2009. T2 relaxometry of normal pediatric brain development. J. Magn. Reson. Imaging 29 (2), 258–267.

Li, G., Lin, W., Gilmore, J.H., Shen, D., 2015. Spatial patterns, longitudinal development, and hemispheric asymmetries of cortical thickness in infants from birth to 2 years of age. J. Neurosci. 35 (24), 9150–9162.

Li, G., Nie, J., Wang, L., Shi, F., Lin, W., Gilmore, J.H., Shen, D., 2013. Mapping region-specific longitudinal cortical surface expansion from birth to 2 years of age. Cereb. Cortex 23 (11), 2724–2733.

Li, G., Wang, L., Yap, P., Wang, F., Wu, Z., Meng, Y., Dong, P., Kim, J., Shi, F., Rekik, I., Lin, W., Shen, D., 2019. Computational neuroanatomy of baby brains: a review. NeuroImage 185, 906–925.

Limperopoulos, C., Soul, J.S., Gauvreau, K., Huppi, P.S., Warfield, S.K., Bassan, H., Robertson, R.L., Volpe, J.J., du Plessis, A.J., 2005. Late gestation cerebellar growth is rapid and impeded by premature birth. Pediatrics 115 (3), 688–695.

Lin, W., Zhu, Q., Gao, W., Chen, Y., Toh, C.H., Styner, M., Gerig, G., Smith, J.K., Biswal, B., Gilmore, J.H., 2008. Functional connectivity MR imaging reveals cortical functional connectivity in the developing brain. AJNR Am. J. Neuroradiol. 29 (10), 1883–1889.

Liu, P., Huang, H., Rollins, N., Chalak, L.F., Jeon, T., Halovanic, C., Lu, H., 2014. Quantitative assessment of global cerebral metabolic rate of oxygen (CMRO2) in neonates using MRI. NMR Biomed. 27 (3), 332–340.

Liu, P., Parkinson, C., Jiang, D., Ouyang, M., De Vis, J.B., Northington, F.J., Tekes, A., Huang, H., Huisman, T.A., Golden, W.C., 2019a. Characterization of MRI techniques to assess neonatal brain oxygenation and blood flow. NMR Biomed. 32 (7), e4103.

Liu, P., Qi, Y., Lin, Z., Guo, Q., Wang, X., Lu, H., 2019b. Assessment of cerebral blood flow in neonates and infants: a phase-contrast MRI study. NeuroImage 185, 926–933.

Lowe, M.J., Mock, B.J., Sorenson, J.A., 1998. Functional connectivity in single and multislice echoplanar imaging using resting-state fluctuations. NeuroImage 7 (2), 119–132.

Lyall, A.E., Shi, F., Geng, X., Woolson, S., Li, G., Wang, L., Hamer, R.M., Shen, D., Gilmore, J.H., 2015. Dynamic development of regional cortical thickness and surface area in early childhood. Cereb. Cortex 25 (8), 2204–2212.

Maas, L.C., Mukherjee, P., Carballido-Gamio, J., Veeraraghavan, S., Miller, S.P., Partridge, S.C., Henry, R.G., Barkovich, A.J., Vigneron, D.B., 2004. Early laminar organization of the human cerebrum demonstrated with diffusion tensor imaging in extremely premature infants. NeuroImage 22 (3), 1134–1140.

Mädler, B., Drabycz, S.A., Kolind, S.H., Whittall, K.P., MacKay, A.L., 2008. Is diffusion anisotropy an accurate monitor of myelination?: correlation of multicomponent T2 relaxation and diffusion tensor anisotropy in human brain. Magn. Reson. Imaging 26, 874–888.

Malviya, S., Voepel-Lewis, T., Eldevik, O.P., Rockwell, D.T., Wong, J.H., Tait, A.R., 2000. Sedation and general anaesthesia in children undergoing MRI and CT: adverse events and outcomes. Br. J. Anaesth. 84 (6), 743–748.

Marín, O., 2016. Developmental timing and critical windows for the treatment of psychiatric disorders. Nat. Med. 22 (11), 1229–1238.

Marin-Padilla, M., 1992. Ontogenesis of the pyramidal cell of the mammalian neocortex and developmental cytoarchitectonics: a unifying theory. J. Comp. Neurol. 321, 223–240.

Matsumae, M., Kurita, D., Atsumi, H., Haida, M., Sato, O., Tsugane, R., 2001. Sequential changes in MR water proton relaxation time detect the process of rat brain myelination during maturation. Mech. Ageing Dev. 122 (12), 1281–1291.

Matsuzawa, J., Matsui, M., Konishi, T., Noguchi, K., Gur, R.C., Bilker, W., Miyawaki, T., 2001. Age-related volumetric changes of brain gray and white matter in healthy infants and children. Cereb. Cortex 11 (4), 335–342.

McGlashan, T.H., Hoffman, R.E., 2000. Schizophrenia as a disorder of developmentally reduced synaptic connectivity. JAMA Psychiatry 57 (7), 637–648.

McKinstry, R.C., Mathur, A., Miller, J.H., Ozcan, A., Snyder, A.Z., Schefft, G.L., Almli, C.R., Shiran, S.I., Conturo, T.E., Neil, J.J., 2002. Radial organization of developing preterm human cerebral cortex revealed by non-invasive water diffusion anisotropy MRI. Cereb. Cortex 12 (12), 1237–1243.

Melbourne, A., Eaton-Rosen, Z., Orasanu, E., Price, D., Bainbridge, A., Cardoso, M.J., Kendall, G.S., Robertson, N.J., Marlow, N., Ourselin, S., 2016. Longitudinal development in the preterm thalamus and posterior white matter: MRI correlations between diffusion weighted imaging and T2 relaxometry. Hum. Brain Mapp. 37 (7), 2479–2492.

Miller, D.J., Duka, T., Stimpson, C.D., Schapiro, S.J., Baze, W.B., McArthur, M.J., Fobbs, A.J., Sousa, A.M., Šestan, N., Wildman, D.E., Lipovich, L., 2012. Prolonged myelination in human neocortical evolution. Proc. Natl. Acad. Sci. U. S. A. 109, 16480–16485.

Miller, J.A., Ding, S.-L., Sunkin, S.M., Smith, K.A., Ng, L., Szafer, A., Ebbert, A., Riley, Z.L., Aiona, K., Arnold, J.M., 2014. Transcriptional landscape of the prenatal human brain. Nature 508, 199–206.

Miranda, M.J., Olofsson, K., Sidaros, K., 2006. Noninvasive measurements of regional cerebral perfusion in preterm and term neonates by magnetic resonance arterial spin labeling. Pediatr. Res. 60 (3), 359–363.

Mishra, V., Cheng, H., Gong, G., He, Y., Dong, Q., Huang, H., 2013. Differences of inter-tract correlations between neonates and children around puberty: a study based on microstructural measurements with DTI. Front. Hum. Neurosci. 7, 721. https://doi.org/10.3389/fnhum.2013.00721.

Mishra, V., Guo, X., Delgado, M.R., Huang, H., 2015. Toward tract-specific fractional anisotropy (TSFA) at crossing-fiber regions with clinical diffusion MRI. Magn. Reson. Med. 74 (6), 1768–1779.

Mori, S., Itoh, R., Zhang, J., Kaufmann, W.E., van Zijl, P., Solaiyappan, M., Yarowsky, P., 2001. Diffusion tensor imaging of the developing mouse brain. Magn. Reson. Med. 46 (1), 18–23.

Mrzljak, L., Uylings, H.B., Kostovic, I., van Eden, C.G., 1992. Prenatal development of neurons in the human prefrontal cortex. II. A quantitative Golgi study. J. Comp. Neurol. 316 (4), 485–496.

Mukherjee, P., Miller, J.H., Shimony, J.S., Conturo, T.E., Lee, B.C., Almli, C.R., McKinstry, R.C., 2001. Normal brain maturation during childhood: developmental trends characterized with diffusion-tensor MR imaging. Radiology 221, 349–358.

Mukherjee, P., Miller, J.H., Shimony, J.S., Philip, J.V., Nehra, D., Snyder, A.Z., Conturo, T.E., Neil, J.J., McKinstry, R.C., 2002. Diffusion-tensor MR imaging of gray and white matter development during normal human brain maturation. AJNR Am. J. Neuroradiol. 23 (9), 1445–1456.

Neil, J.J., Shiran, S.I., McKinstry, R.C., Schefft, G.L., Snyder, A.Z., Almli, C.R., Akbudak, E., Aronovitz, J.A., Miller, J.P., Lee, B.C., Conturo, T.E., 1998. Normal brain in human newborns: apparent diffusion coefficient and diffusion anisotropy measured by using diffusion tensor MR imaging. Radiology 209 (1), 57–66.

Nossin-Manor, R., Card, D., Morris, D., Noormohamed, S., Shroff, M.M., Whyte, H.E., Taylor, M.J., Sled, J.G., 2013. Quantitative MRI in the very preterm brain: assessing tissue organization and myelination using magnetization transfer, diffusion tensor and T1 imaging. NeuroImage 64, 505–516.

Nossin-Manor, R., Card, D., Raybaud, C., Taylor, M.J., Sled, J.G., 2015. Cerebral maturation in the early preterm period—a magnetization transfer and diffusion tensor imaging study using voxel-based analysis. NeuroImage 112, 30–42.

Oishi, K., Chang, L., Huang, H., 2019. Baby brain atlases. NeuroImage 185, 865–880.

Oishi, K., Mori, S., Donohue, P.K., Ernst, T., Anderson, L., Buchthal, S., Faria, A., Jiang, H., Li, X., Miller, M.I., van Zijl, P.C., Chang, L., 2011. Multi-contrast human neonatal brain atlas: application to normal neonate development analysis. NeuroImage 56 (1), 8–20.

Ouyang, A., Jeon, T., Sunkin, S.M., Pletikos, M., Sedmak, G., Sestan, N., Lein, E.S., Huang, H., 2015. Spatial mapping of structural and connectional imaging data for the developing human brain with diffusion tensor imaging. Methods 73, 27–37.

Ouyang, M., Detre, J., Lam, S., Edgar, J., Huang, H., 2020a. High-resolution infant cerebral blood flow map measured with 3D multi-shot, stack-of-spirals pCASL. In: Proceedings of ISMRM. Abstract #0224.

Ouyang, M., Dubois, J., Yu, Q., Mukherjee, P., Huang, H., 2019b. Delineation of early brain development from fetuses to infants with diffusion MRI and beyond. NeuroImage 185, 836–850.

Ouyang, M., Jeon, T., Mishra, V., Du, H., Wang, Y., Peng, Y., Huang, H., 2016. Global and regional cortical connectivity maturation index (CCMI) of developmental human brain with quantification of short-range association tracts. Proc. SPIE Int. Soc. Opt. Eng. 9788. https://doi.org/10.1117/12.2218029, 97881B.

Ouyang, M., Jeon, T., Sotiras, A., Peng, Q., Mishra, V., Halovanic, C., Chen, M., Chalak, L., Rollins, N., Roberts, T., Davatzikos, C., Huang, H., 2019a. Differential cortical microstructural maturation in the preterm human brain with diffusion kurtosis and tensor imaging. Proc. Natl. Acad. Sci. U. S. A. 116 (10), 4681–4688.

Ouyang, M., Kang, H., Detre, J.A., Roberts, T.P., Huang, H., 2017a. Short-range connections in the developmental connectome during typical and atypical brain maturation. Neurosci. Biobehav. Rev. 83, 109–122.

Ouyang, M., Liu, P., Jeon, T., Chalak, L., Heyne, R., Rollins, N.K., Licht, D.J., Detre, J.A., Roberts, T.P., Lu, H., Huang, H., 2017b. Heterogeneous increases of regional cerebral blood flow during preterm brain development: preliminary assessment with pseudo-continuous arterial spin labeled perfusion MRI. NeuroImage 147, 233–242.

Ouyang, M., Peng, Q., Jeon, T., Heyne, R., Chalak, L., Huang, H., 2020b. Diffusion-MRI-based regional cortical microstructure at birth for predicting neurodevelopmental outcomes of 2-year-olds. Elife 9, e58116.

Partridge, S.C., Mukherjee, P., Henry, R.G., Miller, S.P., Berman, J.I., Jin, H., Lu, Y., Glenn, O.A., Ferriero, D.M., Barkovich, A.J., 2004. Diffusion tensor imaging: serial quantitation of white matter tract maturity in premature newborns. NeuroImage 22, 1302–1314.

Paus, T., Collins, D.L., Evans, A.C., Leonard, G., Pike, B., Zijdenbos, A., 2001. Maturation of white matter in the human brain: a review of magnetic resonance studies. Brain Res. Bull. 54 (3), 255–266.

Peng, Q., Ouyang, M., Wang, J., Yu, Q., Zhao, C., Slinger, M., Li, H., Fan, Y., Hong, B., Huang, H., 2020. Regularized-Ncut: robust and homogeneous functional parcellation of neonate and adult brain networks. Artif. Intell. Med. 101872.

Perani, D., Saccuman, M.C., Scifo, P., Anwander, A., Spada, D., Baldoli, C., Poloniato, A., Lohmann, G., Friederici, A.D., 2011. Neural language networks at birth. Proc. Natl. Acad. Sci. U. S. A. 108 (38), 16056–16061.

Petanjek, Z., Judaš, M., Kostović, I., Uylings, H.B., 2008. Lifespan alterations of basal dendritic trees of pyramidal neurons in the human prefrontal cortex: a layer-specific pattern. Cereb. Cortex 18 (4), 915–929.

Petanjek, Z., Judaš, M., Šimić, G., Rašin, M.R., Uylings, H.B., Rakic, P., Kostović, I., 2011. Extraordinary neoteny of synaptic spines in the human prefrontal cortex. Proc. Natl. Acad. Sci. U. S. A. 108 (32), 13281–13286.

Pfefferbaum, A., Mathalon, D.H., Sullivan, E.V., Rawles, J.M., Zipursky, R.B., Lim, K.O., 1994. A quantitative magnetic resonance imaging study of changes in brain morphology from infancy to late adulthood. Arch. Neurol. 51 (9), 874–887.

Phillips, O.R., Clark, K.A., Luders, E., Azhir, R., Joshi, S.H., Woods, R.P., Mazziotta, J.C., Toga, A.W., Narr, K. L., 2013. Superficial white matter: effects of age, sex, and hemisphere. Brain Connect. 3 (2), 146–159. 86.

Poduslo, S.E., Jang, Y., 1984. Myelin development in infant brain. Neurochem. Res. 9 (11), 1615–1626.

Poh, J.S., Li, Y., Ratnarajah, N., Fortier, M.V., Chong, Y.S., Kwek, K., Saw, S.M., Gluckman, P.D., Meaney, M.J., Qiu, A., 2015. Developmental synchrony of thalamocortical circuits in the neonatal brain. NeuroImage 116, 168–176.

Powers, W.J., Rosenbaum, J.L., Dence, C.S., Markham, J., Videen, T.O., 1998. Cerebral glucose transport and metabolism in preterm human infants. J. Cereb. Blood Flow Metab. 18 (6), 632–638.

Qiu, A., Fortier, M.V., Bai, J., Zhang, X., Chong, Y.S., Kwek, K., Saw, S.M., Godfrey, K.M., Gluckman, P.D., Meaney, M.J., 2013. Morphology and microstructure of subcortical structures at birth: a large-scale Asian neonatal neuroimaging study. NeuroImage 65, 315–323.

Rajagopalan, V., Scott, J., Habas, P.A., Kim, K., Corbett-Detig, J., Rousseau, F., Barkovich, A.J., Glenn, O.A., Studholme, C., 2011. Local tissue growth patterns underlying normal fetal human brain gyrification quantified in utero. J. Neurosci. 31 (8), 2878–2887.

Rakic, P., 1972. Mode of cell migration to the superficial layers of fetal monkey neocortex. J. Comp. Neurol. 145, 61–83.

Rakic, P., 1995. Radial versus tangential migration of neuronal clones in the developing cerebral cortex. Proc. Natl. Acad. Sci. U. S. A. 92, 11323–11327.

Rosenberg, M.D., Casey, B.J., Holmes, A.J., 2018. Prediction complements explanation in understanding the developing brain. Nat. Commun. 9 (1), 589.

Rutherford, M., Jiang, S., Allsop, J., Perkins, L., Srinivasan, L., Hayat, T., Kumar, S., Hajnal, J., 2008. MR imaging methods for assessing fetal brain development. Dev. Neurobiol. 68 (6), 700–711.

Sadeghi, N., Prastawa, M., Fletcher, P.T., Wolff, J., Gilmore, J.H., Gerig, G., 2013. Regional characterization of longitudinal DT-MRI to study white matter maturation of the early developing brain. NeuroImage 68, 236–247.

Scheef, L., Nordmeyer-Massner, J.A., Smith-Collins, A.P., Müller, N., Stegmann-Woessner, G., Jankowski, J., Gieseke, J., Born, M., Seitz, H., Bartmann, P., Schild, H.H., 2017. Functional laterality of task-evoked activation in sensorimotor cortex of preterm infants: an optimized 3 T fMRI study employing a customized neonatal head coil. PLoS One 12 (1), e0169392.

Schneider, J., Kober, T., Graz, M.B., Meuli, R., Hüppi, P.S., Hagmann, P., Truttmann, A.C., 2016. Evolution of T1 relaxation, ADc, and fractional anisotropy during early brain maturation: a serial imaging study on preterm infants. AJNR Am. J. Neuroradiol. 37 (1), 155–162.

Schöpf, V., Kasprian, G., Brugger, P.C., Prayer, D., 2012. Watching the fetal brain at 'rest'. Int. J. Dev. Neurosci. 30 (1), 11–17.

Schüz, A., Braitenberg, V., 2002. The human cortical white matter: quantitative aspects of cortico-cortical long-range connectivity. In: Schüz, A., Miller, R. (Eds.), Cortical Areas: Unity and Diversity. CRC Press, London, pp. 377–385.

Seshamani, S., Cheng, X., Fogtmann, M., Thomason, M.E., Studholme, C., 2014. A method for handling intensity inhomogenieties in fMRI sequences of moving anatomy of the early developing brain. Med. Image Anal. 18 (2), 285–300.

Shi, F., Salzwedel, A.P., Lin, W., Gilmore, J.H., Gao, W., 2018. Functional brain parcellations of the infant brain and the associated developmental trends. Cereb. Cortex 28 (4), 1358–1368.

Sidman, R.L., Rakic, P., 1973. Neuronal migration, with special reference to developing human brain: a review. Brain Res. 62, 1–35.

Sidman, R.L., Rakic, P., 1982. Development of the human central nervous system. In: Haymaker, W., Adams, R.D. (Eds.), Histology and Histopathology of the Nervous System. C.C. Thomas, Springfield, pp. 3–145.

Silbereis, J.C., Pochareddy, S., Zhu, Y., Li, M., Sestan, N., 2016. The cellular and molecular landscapes of the developing human central nervous system. Neuron 89, 248–268.

Sizonenko, S.V., Camm, E.J., Garbow, J.R., Maier, S.E., Inder, T.E., Williams, C.E., Neil, J.J., Huppi, P.S., 2007. Developmental changes and injury induced disruption of the radial organization of the cortex in the immature rat brain revealed by in vivo diffusion tensor MRI. Cereb. Cortex 17 (11), 2609–2617.

Smith, S.M., Fox, P.T., Miller, K.L., Glahn, D.C., Fox, P.M., Mackay, C.E., Filippini, N., Watkins, K.E., Toro, R., Laird, A.R., Beckmann, C.F., 2009. Correspondence of the brain's functional architecture during activation and rest. Proc. Natl. Acad. Sci. U. S. A. 106 (31), 13040–13045.

Smyser, C.D., Dosenbach, N.U., Smyser, T.A., Snyder, A.Z., Rogers, C.E., Inder, T.E., Schlaggar, B.L., Neil, J.J., 2016c. Prediction of brain maturity in infants using machine-learning algorithms. NeuroImage 136, 1–9.

Smyser, C.D., Inder, T.E., Shimony, J.S., Hill, J.E., Degnan, A.J., Snyder, A.Z., Neil, J.J., 2010. Longitudinal analysis of neural network development in preterm infants. Cereb. Cortex 20 (12), 2852–2862.

Smyser, C.D., Neil, J.J., 2015. Use of resting-state functional MRI to study brain development and injury in neonates. Semin. Perinatol. 39 (2), 130–140.

Smyser, C.D., Snyder, A.Z., Shimony, J.S., Blazey, T.M., Inder, T.E., Neil, J.J., 2013. Effects of white matter injury on resting state fMRI measures in prematurely born infants. PLoS One 8 (7), e68098.

Smyser, C.D., Snyder, A.Z., Shimony, J.S., Mitra, A., Inder, T.E., Neil, J.J., 2016b. Resting-state network complexity and magnitude are reduced in prematurely born infants. Cereb. Cortex 26 (1), 322–333.

Smyser, T.A., Smyser, C.D., Rogers, C.E., Gillespie, S.K., Inder, T.E., Neil, J.J., 2016a. Cortical gray and adjacent white matter demonstrate synchronous maturation in very preterm infants. Cereb. Cortex 26 (8), 3370–3378.

Song, L., Mishra, V., Ouyang, M., Peng, Q., Slinger, M., Liu, S., Huang, H., 2017. Human fetal brain connectome: structural network development from middle fetal stage to birth. Front. Neurosci. 11. https://doi.org/10.3389/fnins.2017.00561, 561.

Song, S.K., Yoshino, J., Le, T.Q., Lin, S.J., Sun, S.W., Cross, A.H., Armstrong, R.C., 2005. Demyelination increases radial diffusivity in corpus callosum of mouse brain. NeuroImage 26, 132–140.

Sotiropoulos, S.N., Jbabdi, S., Xu, J., Andersson, J.L., Moeller, S., Auerbach, E.J., Glasser, M.F., Hernandez, M., Sapiro, G., Jenkinson, M., Feinberg, D.A., 2013. Advances in diffusion MRI acquisition and processing in the human connectome project. NeuroImage 80, 125–143.

Takahashi, E., Dai, G., Rosen, G.D., Wang, R., Ohki, K., Folkerth, R.D., Galaburda, A.M., Wedeen, V.J., Ellen Grant, P., 2010. Developing neocortex organization and connectivity in cats revealed by direct correlation of diffusion tractography and histology. Cereb. Cortex 21 (1), 200–211.

Takahashi, E., Folkerth, R.D., Galaburda, A.M., Grant, P.E., 2011. Emerging cerebral connectivity in the human fetal brain: an MR tractography study. Cereb. Cortex 22, 455–464.

Takahashi, T., Shirane, R., Sato, S., Yoshimoto, T., 1999. Developmental changes of cerebral blood flow and oxygen metabolism in children. AJNR Am. J. Neuroradiol. 20 (5), 917–922.

Tang, G., Gudsnuk, K., Kuo, S.H., Cotrina, M.L., Rosoklija, G., Sosunov, A., Sonders, M.S., Kanter, E., Castagna, C., Yamamoto, A., Yue, Z., 2014. Loss of mTOR-dependent macroautophagy causes autistic-like synaptic pruning deficits. Neuron 83 (5), 1131–1143.

Thomason, M.E., Brown, J.A., Dassanayake, M.T., Shastri, R., Marusak, H.A., Hernandez-Andrade, E., Yeo, L., Mody, S., Berman, S., Hassan, S.S., Romero, R., 2014. Intrinsic functional brain architecture derived from graph theoretical analysis in the human fetus. PLoS One 9 (5), e94423.

Thomason, M.E., Dassanayake, M.T., Shen, S., Katkuri, Y., Alexis, M., Anderson, A.L., Yeo, L., Mody, S., Hernandez-Andrade, E., Hassan, S.S., Studholme, C., 2013. Cross-hemispheric functional connectivity in the human fetal brain. Sci. Transl. Med. 5 (173). 173ra24.

Thomason, M.E., Grove, L.E., Lozon, T.A., Vila, A.M., Ye, Y., Nye, M.J., Manning, J.H., Pappas, A., Hernandez-Andrade, E., Yeo, L., Mody, S., 2015. Age-related increases in long-range connectivity in fetal functional neural connectivity networks in utero. Dev. Cogn. Neurosci. 11, 96–104.

Thomason, M.E., Scheinost, D., Manning, J.H., Grove, L.E., Hect, J., Marshall, N., Hernandez-Andrade, E., Berman, S., Pappas, A., Yeo, L., Hassan, S.S., 2017. Weak functional connectivity in the human fetal brain prior to preterm birth. Sci. Rep. 7 (1), 1–10.

Thornton, J.S., Ordidge, R.J., Penrice, J., Cady, E.B., Amess, P.N., Punwani, S., Clemence, M., Wyatt, J.S., 1997. Anisotropic water diffusion in white and gray matter of the neonatal piglet brain before and after transient hypoxia-ischaemia. Magn. Reson. Imaging 15 (4), 433–440.

Tisdall, M.D., Hess, A.T., Reuter, M., Meintjes, E.M., Fischl, B., van der Kouwe, A.J., 2012. Volumetric navigators for prospective motion correction and selective reacquisition in neuroanatomical MRI. Magn. Reson. Med. 68 (2), 389–399.

Toulmin, H., Beckmann, C.F., O'Muircheartaigh, J., Ball, G., Nongena, P., Makropoulos, A., Ederies, A., Counsell, S.J., Kennea, N., Arichi, T., Tusor, N., 2015. Specialization and integration of functional thalamocortical connectivity in the human infant. Proc. Natl. Acad. Sci. U. S. A. 112 (20), 6485–6490.

Turk, E., Van Den Heuvel, M.I., Benders, M.J., De Heus, R., Franx, A., Manning, J.H., Hect, J.L., Hernandez-Andrade, E., Hassan, S.S., Romero, R., Kahn, R.S., 2019. Functional connectome of the fetal brain. J. Neurosci. 39 (49), 9716–9724.

Tymofiyeva, O., Hess, C.P., Ziv, E., Lee, P.N., Glass, H.C., Ferriero, D.M., Barkovich, A.J., Xu, D., 2013. A DTI-based template-free cortical connectome study of brain maturation. PLoS One 8 (5), e63310.

Tymofiyeva, O., Hess, C.P., Ziv, E., Tian, N., Bonifacio, S.L., McQuillen, P.S., Ferriero, D.M., Barkovich, A.J., Xu, D., 2012. Towards the "baby connectome": mapping the structural connectivity of the newborn brain. PLoS One 7 (2), e31029.

Vaishnavi, S.N., Vlassenko, A.G., Rundle, M.M., Snyder, A.Z., Mintun, M.A., Raichle, M.E., 2010. Regional aerobic glycolysis in the human brain. Proc. Natl. Acad. Sci. U. S. A. 107 (41), 17757–17762.

van Buchem, M.A., Steens, S.C., Vrooman, H.A., Zwinderman, A.H., McGowan, J.C., Rassek, M., Engelbrecht, V., 2001. Global estimation of myelination in the developing brain on the basis of magnetization transfer imaging: a preliminary study. AJNR Am. J. Neuroradiol. 22 (4), 762–766.

van den Heuvel, M.I., Thomason, M.E., 2016. Functional connectivity of the human brain in utero. Trends Cogn. Sci. 20 (12), 931–939.

van den Heuvel, M.P., Kersbergen, K.J., de Reus, M.A., Keunen, K., Kahn, R.S., Groenendaal, F., de Vries, L.S., Benders, M.J., 2015. The neonatal connectome during preterm brain development. Cereb. Cortex 25 (9), 3000–3013.

van der Knaap, M.S., Valk, J., 1990. MR imaging of the various stages of normal myelination during the first year of life. Neuroradiology 31 (6), 459–470.

Van Essen, D.C., 2013. Cartography and connectomes. Neuron 80 (3), 775–790.

Varela, M., Groves, A.M., Arichi, T., Hajnal, J.V., 2012. Mean cerebral blood flow measurements using phase contrast MRI in the first year of life. NMR Biomed. 25 (9), 1063–1072.

Wakana, S., Caprihan, A., Panzenboeck, M.M., Fallon, J.H., Perry, M., Gollub, R.L., Hua, K., Zhang, J., Jiang, H., Dubey, P., 2007. Reproducibility of quantitative tractography methods applied to cerebral white matter. NeuroImage 36, 630–644.

Wakana, S., Jiang, H., Nagae-Poetscher, L.M., Van Zijl, P.C., Mori, S., 2004. Fiber tract-based atlas of human white matter anatomy. Radiology 230, 77–87.

Wang, F., Lian, C., Wu, Z., Zhang, H., Li, T., Meng, Y., Wang, L., Lin, W., Shen, D., Li, G., 2019. Developmental topography of cortical thickness during infancy. Proc. Natl. Acad. Sci. U. S. A. 116 (32), 15855–15860.

Wang, L., Gao, Y., Shi, F., Li, G., Gilmore, J.H., Lin, W., Shen, D., 2015. LINKS: learning-based multi-source IntegratioN frameworK for segmentation of infant brain images. NeuroImage 108, 160–172.

Wang, Z., Fernández-Seara, M., Alsop, D.C., Liu, W.C., Flax, J.F., Benasich, A.A., Detre, J.A., 2008. Assessment of functional development in normal infant brain using arterial spin labeled perfusion MRI. NeuroImage 39 (3), 973–978.

Wheeler-Kingshott, C.A., Cercignani, M., 2009. About 'axial' and 'radial' diffusivities. Magn. Reson. Med. 61 (5), 1255–1260.

Wimberger, D.M., Roberts, T.P., Barkovich, A.J., Prayer, L.M., Moseley, M.E., Kucharczyk, J., 1995. Identification of "premyelination" by diffusion-weighted MRI. J. Comput. Assist. Tomogr. 19 (1), 28–33.

Xu, G., Takahashi, E., Folkerth, R.D., Haynes, R.L., Volpe, J.J., Grant, P.E., Kinney, H.C., 2012. Radial coherence of diffusion tractography in the cerebral white matter of the human fetus: neuroanatomic insights. Cereb. Cortex 24, 579–592.

Xu, Y., Cao, M., Liao, X., Xia, M., Wang, X., Jeon, T., Ouyang, M., Chalak, L., Rollins, N., Huang, H., He, Y., 2019. Development and emergence of individual variability in the functional connectivity architecture of the preterm human brain. Cereb. Cortex 29 (10), 4208–4222.

Xydis, V., Astrakas, L., Zikou, A., Pantou, K., Andronikou, S., Argyropoulou, M.I., 2006. Magnetization transfer ratio in the brain of preterm subjects: age-related changes during the first 2 years of life. Eur. Radiol. 16 (1), 215–220.

Yakovlev, P.I., Lecours, A.R., 1967. The myelogenetic cycles of regional maturation of the brain. In: Minkowski, A. (Ed.), Regional Development of the Brain in Early Life. Blackwell Science, Oxford, pp. 3–70.

Yu, Q., Ouyang, A., Chalak, L., Jeon, T., Chia, J., Mishra, V., Sivarajan, M., Jackson, G., Rollins, N., Liu, S., Huang, H., 2016. Structural development of human fetal and preterm brain cortical plate based on population-averaged templates. Cereb. Cortex 26 (11), 4381–4391.

Yu, Q., Peng, Y., Kang, H., Peng, Q., Ouyang, M., Slinger, M., Hu, D., Shou, H., Fang, F., Huang, H., 2020. Differential white matter maturation from birth to 8 years of age. Cereb. Cortex 30 (4), 2674–2690.

Yu, Q., Peng, Y., Mishra, V., Ouyang, A., Li, H., Zhang, H., Chen, M., Liu, S., Huang, H., 2014. Microstructure, length, and connection of limbic tracts in normal human brain development. Front. Aging Neurosci. 6. https://doi.org/10.3389/fnagi.2014.00228, 228.

Zhang, J., Evans, A., Hermoye, L., Lee, S.K., Wakana, S., Zhang, W., Donohue, P., Miller, M.I., Huang, H., Wang, X., van Zijl, P.C., Mori, S., 2007. Evidence of slow maturation of the superior longitudinal fasciculus in early childhood by diffusion tensor imaging. NeuroImage 38 (2), 239–247.

Zhang, Y., Zhang, J., Oishi, K., Faria, A.V., Jiang, H., Li, X., Akhter, K., Rosa-Neto, P., Pike, G.B., Evans, A., Toga, A.W., Woods, R., Mazziotta, J.C., Miller, M.I., van Zijl, P.C.M., Mori, S., 2010. Atlas-guided tract reconstruction for automated and comprehensive examination of the white matter anatomy. NeuroImage 52 (4), 1289–1301.

Zhao, T., Mishra, V., Jeon, T., Ouyang, M., Peng, Q., Chalak, L., Wisnowski, J.L., Heyne, R., Rollins, N., Shu, N., Huang, H., 2019. Structural network maturation of the preterm human brain. NeuroImage 185, 699–710.

Zhu, T., Peng, Q., Ouyang, A., Huang, H., 2020. Neuroanatomical underpinning of diffusion kurtosis measurements in the cerebral cortex of healthy macaque brains. bioRxiv. https://doi.org/10.1101/2020.07.25.221093.

Zöllei, L., Iglesias, J.E., Ou, Y., Grant, P.E., Fischl, B., 2020. Infant FreeSurfer: an automated segmentation and surface extraction pipeline for T1-weighted neuroimaging data of infants 0–2 years. NeuroImage. https://doi.org/10.1016/j.neuroimage.2020.116946.

CHAPTER

Neuroimaging of *early brain development* and the consequences of preterm birth

20

Rachel E. Lean[a], Jeffrey J. Neil[b,c,d], and Christopher D. Smyser[b,c,d]

Department of Psychiatry, Washington University School of Medicine, St. Louis, MO, United States[a] Department of Neurology, Washington University School of Medicine, St. Louis, MO, United States[b] Department of Pediatrics, Washington University School of Medicine, St. Louis, MO, United States[c] Department of Radiology, Washington University School of Medicine, St. Louis, MO, United States[d]

1. Introduction

Throughout early development, the human brain presents a rapidly evolving target (Bystron et al., 2008). For the brain of an extremely preterm infant born at 22–24 weeks' gestation, neuronal migration is largely complete and elementary versions of the cortical layers are in place, yet the cortical surface is nearly completely smooth, with only the Sylvian fissures and broadly open central sulci serving as surface landmarks. Over the ensuing 4 months in which the infant reaches term-equivalent postmenstrual age (PMA; approximately 38–40 weeks), the brain undergoes significant structural changes during normative development. The cortical folds that form sulci and gyri are nearly fully developed; a myriad of synapses are added to form local and long-distance networks; thalamocortical afferents emerge and extend to the cortical plate; myelination begins in white matter pathways in the brainstem, corticospinal tracts and optic radiations; and neuronal firing patterns transition from spontaneous activity to firing with organized spatial and temporal patterns in response to external inputs. Critically, these processes proceed in an orderly and regionally specific manner. Given the remarkable complexity of these key elements of early brain development, it is not surprising that prematurely born infants who spend this critical period in the Neonatal Intensive Care Unit (NICU) are uniquely susceptible to the potentially harmful effects inherent to this environment and face high rates of neurodevelopmental impairment and psychopathology later in life. This sequence of developmental events also helps explain the role of the age at which brain injury occurs in determining outcome, as disrupting this process at differing stages will have varying neurodevelopmental and socio-emotional repercussions. Of course, brain development does not cease at term-equivalent PMA. Synaptic density continues to increase until approximately 2 years of age (Huttenlocher and Dabholkar, 1997) with the age at which the peak occurs varying regionally in accordance with the relative developmental rate of the system involved. This is followed by scheduled pruning of neuronal circuitry to achieve an organized and efficiently functioning brain. Finally, myelination continues at a rapid pace and is not fully complete until adolescence.

Handbook of Pediatric Brain Imaging. https://doi.org/10.1016/B978-0-12-816633-8.00022-3

One of the unique strengths of MRI among neuroimaging modalities is the plethora of image contrasts available, encompassing tissue macrostructure, microstructure, blood flow, metabolite levels, and level of activity. In this chapter, we will focus on the application of MRI to study these key elements of early brain development from mid-gestation through term-equivalent age, as well as the patterns and adverse consequences of prematurity and associated forms of brain injury. First, we describe the application of structural and functional imaging techniques (i.e., T_1-weighted, T_2-weighted, diffusion, resting state functional MRI) to the developing brain, both as it reflects the normative development and how it can be used to detect injury and aberrant development. We also cover the application of these imaging methods to volumetry and cortical cartography—two analysis approaches that have not yet found a significant clinical use. Next, we detail the results from investigations applying these imaging modalities to delineate the effects of prematurity, including forms of brain injury common in this population, on neurodevelopment and socio-emotional outcomes. In this context, we conclude by identifying existing unaddressed domains and key future investigational opportunities in this rapidly expanding field.

2. Neuroimaging methods for studying the early developing brain

2.1 T_1- and T_2-weighted imaging

In standard MRI, the image is constructed using signal from the ^1H nuclei in tissues. One reason for choosing this particular nucleus is that a substantial fraction of tissue is made up of water, which contains ^1H. Further, the concentration equivalent of ^1H nuclei in water is on the order of 110 M (~80 M in brain tissue). In comparison, other MR detectable nuclei, such as ^{23}Na and ^{31}P, are present in millimolar concentrations. Given that clinical MRI is based upon detection of ^1H in tissue water, one might ask how image contrast arises. In the case of T_1- and T_2-weighted imaging, hereafter referred to as "conventional imaging," the contrast is based on the physical relaxation time constants T_1 and T_2. These time constants vary with the local chemical environment. For ^1H_2O in cerebrospinal fluid (CSF), for example, the T_1 relaxation time constant for ^1H is relatively long, causing CSF to appear dark on T_1-weighted images, whereas for water in myelinated white matter, the T_1 relaxation time constant is relatively short, causing myelinated white matter to appear bright. Similarly, the T_2 relaxation time constants vary between tissues. Thus, conventional imaging provides a strong signal-to-noise ratio due to the high concentration of tissue water and excellent contrast between gray matter, white matter, and CSF because of differences in T_1 and T_2. The T_1 and T_2 relaxation time constants vary rapidly during early development. As a result, image acquisition parameters must be adjusted with age to obtain optimal tissue contrast.

From the standpoint of the developing brain, conventional imaging is useful for detecting myelination. Unmyelinated white matter is dark on T_1-weighted images and becomes brighter when it is myelinated. As can be seen in Fig. 1, the white matter of a newborn infant has only started to myelinate, and fiber tracts that myelinate early, such as the corticospinal tract, appear bright in comparison to the surrounding, unmyelinated white matter. By 1 year of age, though myelination is far from complete, essentially all white matter has some degree of myelin and appears bright on T_1-weighted images. Gray matter, in comparison, undergoes relatively little signal intensity change on T_1-weighted imaging during development (though there is some degree of brightening, which can be seen in the motor cortex of

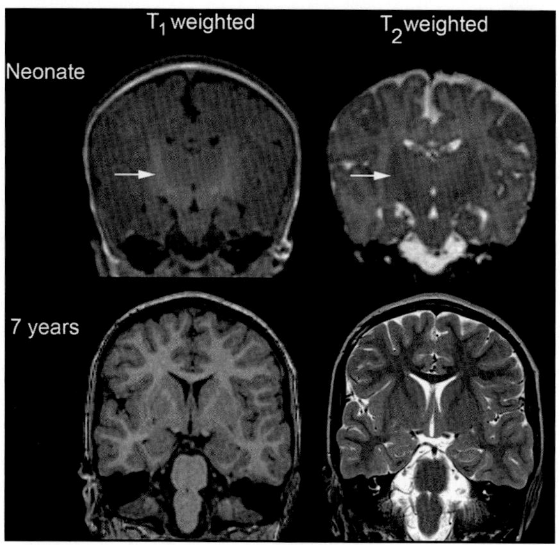

FIG. 1

T_1- and T_2-weighted images from newborn and 7-year-old subjects. Note the early myelination of the corticospinal tracts (arrow) on the images from the newborn, manifest as bright signal on T_1-weighted images and dark signal on T_2-weighted images. Note also the reversal of gray/white contrast by age 7 years, when all white matter has some degree of myelination, though myelination is still not yet complete.

term infants, that takes place as intracortical axons myelinate). Analogous changes in contrast occur for white matter in T_2-weighted images, which appears darker after myelination. This developmental progression of image contrast causes gray/white contrast to flip on T_1- and T_2-weighted images from infants in comparison to older children (Fig. 1). During the course of these white matter signal intensity changes, gray/white contrast reaches a minimum at approximately age 6 months. Contrast on T_1- and T_2-weighted images can be useful for tracking the course of myelination. In some instances, greater contrast between myelinated and unmyelinated white matter can be obtained by taking the ratio of T_1-weighted images, on which myelinated white matter is brighter than unmyelinated, to T_2-weighted images, on which myelinated white matter is darker than unmyelinated (Soun et al., 2017).

2.2 Volumetry

Volumetry involves measuring volumes of brain areas. MR images are obtained at a known spatial resolution, so the volume of each image element, or voxel, is known from the image acquisition parameters. To determine the volume of a given structure, it is necessary only to add up the number of voxels it occupies in the image. While total brain volume is of some interest, scientists are generally more interested in volumes broken down by tissue type, such as gray and white matter. This requires tissue segmentation, or the classification of the brain into tissue types for analysis, and it is common to separate gray matter, white matter, and CSF for volumetric analysis. Such classification relies on the image contrast between these tissues of interest. For images of the adult brain, T_1-weighted images are typically used, and segmentation is often achieved on the basis of image intensity (Fischl, 2012). For example, CSF appears dark on T_1-weighted images, so the voxels with the lowest signal intensity are assigned to that tissue class.

Segmentation of the newborn brain is more complicated, as tissue contrast is different because most white matter is not yet myelinated. Thus, in addition to the three classes listed above, white matter is typically divided into myelinated and unmyelinated. Since gray-white tissue contrast is mostly reversed, though CSF intensity is unchanged, the software developed for segmenting mature-appearing brains does not work effectively for infant brains. Further, T_2-weighted images tend to have better tissue contrast in infants than T_1-weighted images, and T_2-weighted images are the mainstay for tissue segmentation (though both T_1- and T_2-weighted images are often used together as well). In addition to the need for software that is specifically designed for the newborn brain, there are other technical issues that should be taken into account for volumetric analysis. For example, if the radiofrequency coil used for imaging has imperfections which cause the signal intensity to vary gradually across the image, signal intensity values for white and gray matter may overlap. While it is possible to filter this out to a degree, an additional approach is to use an already segmented model image as a starting point for the segmentation, assigning a baseline probability for each voxel in the image as belonging to each tissue class to inform an intensity-based segmentation (Avants et al., 2011; Adamson et al., 2020). It is important to bear in mind that the starting point for tissue classification varies with the age of the infant because contrast, myelination, and degree of cortical folding change as the brain matures. The relative signal intensity levels of different tissues also vary with the particular MRI pulse sequence used for data acquisition and the acquisition parameters chosen—mainly repetition and echo times. Thus, an analysis method optimized for one data set may well perform poorly on a seemingly similar different one. This becomes even more apparent if the MRI system is upgraded, not only for system hardware upgrades, but even for software updates to the pulse sequences and image reconstruction software. Overall, tissue classification is not yet routine in neonatal populations. It requires careful attention to detail and validation against time-consuming manual segmentations.

2.3 Cortical cartography

Cortical cartography refers to analysis of the cortical surface. Generating a surface map of the brain requires tissue segmentation into gray matter, white matter, and CSF as described above. The cortical "surface" used is usually not the actual pial surface of the brain. Instead, a surface running through the center of the gray matter, halfway between the pial surface and gray-white border (i.e., "mid-thickness"), is used. This approach avoids overestimating cortical curvature at the base of sulci and underestimating it at the edges of gyri. An important technical aspect of cartography concerns image spatial resolution. It is common in clinical imaging to obtain images in which the spatial resolution varies in space. For typical "two-dimensional" imaging, the time to acquire the image is proportional to the number of slices obtained. In an effort to employ relatively short imaging times, the image slices are relatively thick, on the order of 2–3 mm, so fewer slices can be used to cover the entire brain. Since obtaining resolution within the plane of the slice is relatively more time efficient, the "in-plane" spatial resolution is often higher, on the order $1 \times 1\ mm^2$, providing an overall spatial resolution of $1 \times 1 \times 2\ mm^3$. These images look appealing when viewed on a slice by slice basis but are unsuitable for cartography. When the slices are stacked and viewed from the side, step-offs are present where the relatively thick slices meet. These discontinuities make it difficult to generate a smooth brain surface along the axis orthogonal to the plane of the slices. For infants, spatial resolution of $1 \times 1 \times 1$ mm^3 (or better) is necessary to generate accurate cortical surfaces.

Several parameters are available once a surface has been generated. Among them are cortical surface area, sulcal depth, cortical curvature and gyrification index (Shimony et al., 2016). Characterizing the topography of the brain may sometimes involve dividing the cortical surface into areas with similar features based on histologic appearance [as was originally done by Brodmann (1909)], neurotransmitter receptor density, anatomic connections and/or function. As expected from the "classical" definition of cortical areas, the borders generated using these disparate measures often match, though this is not always the case (Van Essen, 2013; Eickhoff et al., 2018). Cartography and topography are related in that most of cortical cartography also involves an assessment of the functional consequences of the regions in which cartography shows abnormalities, which requires some knowledge of topography (Van Essen et al., 2006). Two mainstays of topography—anatomic connections and function—can be approached using the MRI methods of diffusion tractography and functional MRI. The combination of these methods provides the basis of the Human Connectome Project (Sporns et al., 2005) and other comparable studies.

2.4 Diffusion MRI

Diffusion imaging offers a number of parameters of interest (Neil, 2008) and is based upon water displacements in tissue. The locations of tissue water molecules are encoded early in the acquisition, and the distance the molecules have traveled is detected sometime later, typically on the order of 50 ms for clinical MRI systems. The water displacements under these conditions are on the order of 10 μm. It is impressive that this measurement works, considering the size of the displacements and the fact that they are measured in living, breathing subjects. Perhaps equally impressive is the amount of information available via these measurements. One parameter available is mean diffusivity (MD). MD values decrease within minutes of the onset of brain injury (Moseley et al., 1990) providing a means of early detection of brain injury that is in universal clinical use today.

A second commonly used parameter is diffusion anisotropy, often expressed as fractional anisotropy (FA). Anisotropy describes the characteristic of a measurement not being the same in all directions in space. In the case of diffusion, it is applied to diffusivity values, which vary directionally, particularly in white matter. To measure FA, water diffusion is measured a number of times on each brain slice, with each measurement done in such a fashion that diffusivity is measured along a different axis. These measurements can then be combined to generate a spatial profile of water displacements for each element, or voxel, in an image. The mathematical expression most commonly used to represent this profile is a tensor, hence the name diffusion tensor imaging (Basser and Pierpaoli, 2011). Conceptually, this tensor can be viewed as an ellipsoid. If diffusion is the same in all directions, such as in CSF where there are no boundaries to diffusion, the ellipsoid shape is a sphere and diffusion is isotropic. For white matter, where water displacements are smaller perpendicular to axon bundles than parallel to them, the shape is more like a cigar, with its long axis parallel to the axon bundles, and diffusion is anisotropic. FA values for isotropic diffusion are zero and become greater as the ellipsoid becomes a longer and thinner cigar. Generally speaking, higher FA values are taken as an indicator of white matter health, with greater FA values representing highly myelinated and well-packed axons. From a developmental standpoint, myelination leads to a large increase in diffusion anisotropy values. Since the principal axis of diffusion (the long axis of the ellipsoid) is parallel to axon bundles, this information can be used to track bundles through space, a method known as diffusion tractography. Diffusion tractography offers one means of measuring "structural connectivity" in the brain, in essence providing an indicator of the anisotropy and size of the tract connecting two brain areas. The other means of measuring connectivity, resting state functional MRI (vide infra), is considered a measure of "functional connectivity." These two methods are sometimes used together to perform "connectome-based" research (Sporns et al., 2005).

There are two additional measures that are often used to assess diffusion anisotropy in white matter—axial diffusivity (AD) and radial diffusivity (RD). AD refers to diffusivity parallel to axon bundles and is reduced following axon injury (Song et al., 2002, 2005). RD refers to diffusivity perpendicular to axons and is increased following myelin injury (Song et al., 2002, 2005). For isotropic diffusion, AD and RD are equal. As FA increases, AD and RD move further apart, with AD greater than RD by definition. In practice, if white matter FA values are low, AD and RD values are often assessed to see if the reduction is related to axonal injury (lower AD), myelin injury (higher RD), or some combination of the two. While this framework is not perfect, it may serve to a first approximation in many cases.

2.5 Resting state functional MRI (rs-fMRI)

Resting state (rs-fMRI) investigates the temporal correlations in low frequency (<0.1 Hz) fluctuations in blood oxygen level dependent (BOLD) signal that occur independent of task (Biswal et al., 1995; Fox et al., 2005; Lowe et al., 1998). These data are used to identify resting state networks (RSNs) which encompass regions located throughout the brain demonstrating synchronous, spontaneous neuronal activity. These RSNs represent the functional topography of the human brain, incorporating cortical, subcortical, and cerebellar regions responsible for cognitive, language, motor activity, sensation, memory, attention, and visual task performance (Smith et al., 2009; Fox and Raichle, 2007). From data sets routinely collected in 10–20 min, rs-fMRI data can be used to generate brain-wide measures of functional connectivity (i.e., correlations in spontaneous neuronal activity within and across regions of interest and/or RSNs). Application of this method has led to greater understanding of the brain's functional topography, aided evaluation of neuroanatomical models, and accounted for variability in human behavior across development and in health and disease. As detailed in Chapter 22, rs-fMRI methods afford many inherent advantages for studying brain function in neonates and infants, including enabling brain-wide assessments of functional connectivity from data sets collected in minutes, flexibility in data collection procedures (allowing data to be acquired from infants resting quietly, asleep, and even under anesthesia), and increasingly established, age-specific data collection and analysis approaches (Smyser and Neil, 2015). These attributes have led to expanded use of this imaging modality across investigations beginning during the fetal period and extending into childhood (Herzmann et al., 2018; Smyser et al., 2010, 2016a, b; Gao et al., 2015; Doria et al., 2010; Fransson et al., 2011; Gao et al., 2013).

Investigations applying rs-fMRI to neonatal and infant cohorts have consistently identified canonical RSNs incorporating distributed cortical, subcortical, and cerebellar regions throughout the brain. These include RSNs located in primary motor and sensory cortices (e.g., somatomotor [SMN], visual [VIS] and auditory networks) and those involving association cortices (e.g., default mode [DMN], frontoparietal control [FPC], dorsal attention [DAN], and ventral attention [VAN] networks). Many of these RSNs initially consist of strong interhemispheric correlations between homotopic counterparts, with thalamo-cortical and cortico-cerebellar connectivity also evident prior to term-equivalent PMA (Smyser et al., 2010; Doria et al., 2010; Alcauter et al., 2014). The topology within and across these RSNs is consistent with results obtained in older pediatric and adult populations, with networks demonstrating variable patterns of maturation (i.e., network strength and topology) consistent with known heterogeneity in rates of cortical maturation.

Functional connectivity is typically evaluated using approaches based upon either seed correlation analysis, which measures of the temporal correlation in BOLD signal between a priori defined regions of interest (i.e., spheres centered upon anatomic coordinates, cortical parcels), and/or independent component analysis, which relies upon statistical calculations to decompose data sets into maximally independent components based upon the signal intensity timecourse of spatial maps. Critically, while both of these analysis approaches possess relative strengths based upon the primary scientific question(s) of interest, comparable results have been generated in neonatal and pediatric populations using each technique. In addition, RSN composite correlation values can be used to simplify analyses in order to evaluate measures across networks and/or to streamline the number of connectivity measures evaluated in group comparisons. For example, for the DMN, which includes ROIs located in the medial prefrontal, posterior cingulate, lateral parietal, and lateral temporal cortices among other regions, the composite correlation value, C, for subject k is calculated as $C_k^{\mathrm{DMN}} = \langle Z_{ijk} \rangle_{i,\, j\, \in\, \mathrm{DMN}}$, where Z represents the correlation value (or, alternatively, a Fisher Z-transformed correlation coefficient value) between ROI pair i and j from a matrix which includes all ROIs within the RSN (Brier et al., 2012). As with diffusion MRI, rs-fMRI data can also be analyzed using technically sophisticated, matrix-based mathematical approaches, such as graph theory and/or machine learning, generating brain-wide and/or regional assessments of the organizational properties of the functional connectome. Importantly, each of these connectivity measures has been shown to be sensitive to aberrant development, adverse environmental exposures, and brain injury, commonly manifesting as reduced connectivity measures (either globally or regionally). Further, these connectivity measures have been increasingly linked to functional performance, highlighting their critical importance in neurodevelopmental and psychiatric outcomes.

3. Neuroimaging of early brain development in prematurely born infants

3.1 Volumetry

Volumetric MRI has proven useful for the assessment of structural changes in early brain development in preterm infants. Prematurity-related alterations in brain volumes have been observed for whole-brain gray and white matter volumes, as well as in specific brain structures of interest. For example, numerous structural MRI studies in very preterm (VPT, born <32 weeks gestational age) neonates scanned at term-equivalent age have consistently shown that VPT infants have smaller total and regional brain volumes (Bora et al., 2014; Inder et al., 2005; Limperopoulos et al., 2005) and corresponding increases in CSF (Bora et al., 2014; Inder et al., 2005) compared to full-term (FT) infants. Bora et al. (2014) highlighted specific cortical areas showing pronounced structural alterations, which included prefrontal, premotor, and sensorimotor regions. The impact of prematurity on temporal and parieto-occipital volumes was less pronounced. VPT infants have also been found to have reduced cerebellar volumes (Limperopoulos et al., 2005; Matthews et al., 2018) and smaller hippocampi (Strahle et al., 2019),

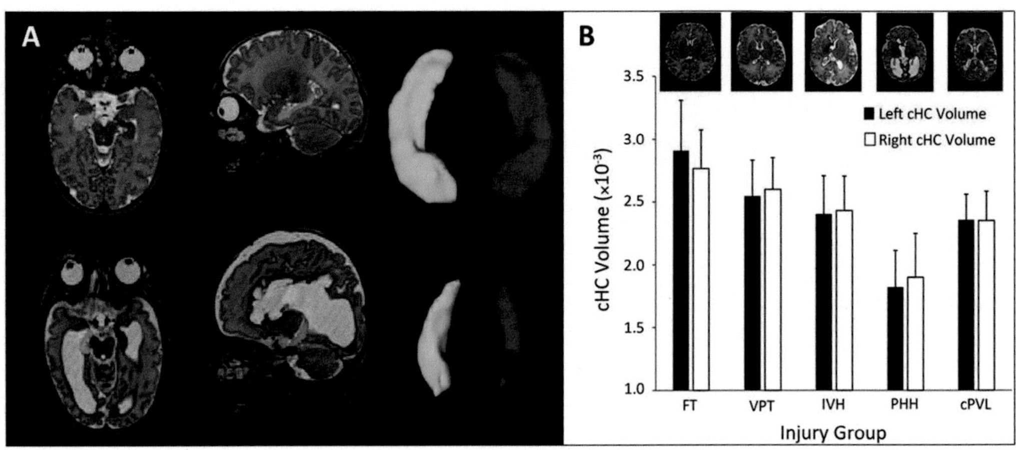

FIG. 2

Premature birth, perinatal high-grade brain injury, and hippocampal volume. (A) T2-weighted MRI images demonstrating axial and sagittal views and 3D volumetric reconstructions of segmented hippocampi bilaterally for a representative full-term infant (top images) and very preterm infant with post-hemorrhagic hydrocephalus (bottom images). Note the gross difference in hippocampal size between the control and injured infant. Blue = right and red = left hippocampus. (B) Plots demonstrating corrected hippocampal volumes (cHC) for infants by category, including full-term infants (FT), very preterm infants with no/mild brain injury (VPT), very preterm infants with grade III/IV intraventricular hemorrhage (IVH), very preterm infants with grade III/IV IVH and post-hemorrhagic hydrocephalus requiring neurosurgical intervention (PHH) and very preterm infants with cystic periventricular leukomalacia (cPVL). Overall, the PHH group had the smallest hippocampi. Black = left and white = right hippocampal volumes corrected by intracranial volume (ratios). Error bars represent one standard deviation.

Adapted with permission from Strahle, J.M., et al., 2019. NeuroImage Clin. 22, 101787.

amygdala (Cismaru et al., 2016), and thalami (Dewey et al., 2019; Makropoulos et al., 2016; Boardman et al., 2006). Furthermore, greater volumetric reductions in these regions have been associated with perinatal brain injury (Fig. 2) and supratentorial brain lesions (Strahle et al., 2019; Srinivasan et al., 2006). Complex epigenetic mechanisms may also underlie early alterations in structural brain development in preterm infants. Specifically, higher levels of infant stress in the NICU has been linked to greater SEL6A4 methylation at NICU discharge, and in turn, smaller anterior temporal lobe volume at term-equivalent age (Fumagalli et al., 2018).

Consistent with neonatal findings, structural MRI following NICU discharge has also shown that prematurity-related alterations in whole-brain and regional volumes persist into childhood and adolescence. Total gray matter volume is approximately 3.8%–8.8% smaller in VPT children and adolescents compared to their FT peers (Kesler et al., 2004; Nagy et al., 2009; Soria-Pastor et al., 2009). In addition to reduced total gray matter volume at school-age, there is also evidence of regional volumetric differences between VPT and FT children although findings are mixed. Some studies have reported reduced volume in temporal, parietal, prefrontal, and posterior-cingulate regions (Kesler et al., 2004, 2008; Lean et al., 2017a; Peterson, 2000), while others have reported increased volume in parietal and frontal regions (Kesler et al., 2004). Discrepancies in regional brain volume findings are likely attributable to study differences in variables including sample characteristics, age at assessment, and volumetric analysis methods. Nonetheless, the findings are more consistent regarding longer-term reductions in the subcortical gray matter, particularly in the thalamus and basal ganglia (Kesler et al., 2004, 2008; Lean et al., 2017a). VPT children also evidence reduced white matter volume in the cingulum bundles, corpus callosum, corticospinal tracts and longitudinal fasciculi (Ment et al., 2009; Thompson et al., 2015). Furthermore, longitudinal structural MRI studies now indicate that longer-term alterations in brain volumes may be explained by maturational delays in tissue growth and development. For example, Ment et al. (2009) found that both VPT and FT children showed decreased gray matter volume and increased white matter volume between the ages of eight and 12 years old, but that VPT children showed reduced rates of gray and white matter volume changes compared to FT children, especially in temporal gray and parietal white matter. A more recent study examining brain volume growth from term-equivalent age to age 7 years found that between-groups differences in cortical and subcortical volumes for VPT and FT children widened over time, highlighting the enduring and deleterious effects of preterm birth on longer-term brain growth (Monson et al., 2016). These longer-term structural alterations in the preterm brain are thought to reflect tissue growth failure associated with suboptimal or delayed myelination, poor axonal differentiation, and compromised synaptogenesis and pruning over time (Volpe, 2009).

3.2 Cortical cartography

Altered cortical development in VPT infants is evident both in terms of global measures of cortical surface area and gyrification (Shimony et al., 2016; Engelhardt et al., 2015), as well as regional alterations sulcal depth and shape (Engelhardt et al., 2015; Ajayi-Obe et al., 2000). For example, Engelhardt et al. found that VPT infants had smaller global cortical surface area and less complex cortical gyrification than FT infants at term-equivalent age. Furthermore, this study also demonstrated that preterm birth had the greatest impact on sulcal depth and cortical shape in the insula, superior temporal sulcus, and pre- and post-central sulci in both the left and right hemispheres (Engelhardt et al., 2015). Shape variations have also been reported for subcortical structures, including the hippocampus. For example, Thompson et al. (2013) found that VPT infants had straighter hippocampi than FT infants, with reduced curvature toward the midline and superior-inferiorly. Additionally, among VPT infants, reduced infolding and growth of the hippocampi were associated with white matter injury and postnatal corticosteroid administration (Strahle et al., 2019; Thompson et al., 2013). Longitudinal analyses in VPT infants, including incorporation of sophisticated mathematical modeling, have shown that cortical area expansion and regional folding are greatest in the lateral parietal-temporal-occipital and frontal regions between 30 and 40 weeks postmenstrual-age, with lower rates in medial and insular regions during this period (Garcia et al., 2018; Orasanu et al., 2016; Moeskops et al., 2015). Additionally, high-grade brain injury is associated with markedly reduced cortical growth in temporal and occipital regions from 30 to 34 weeks' postmenstrual-age, followed by improvements in cortical growth to age 38 weeks' PMA (Fig. 3) (Garcia et al., 2018).

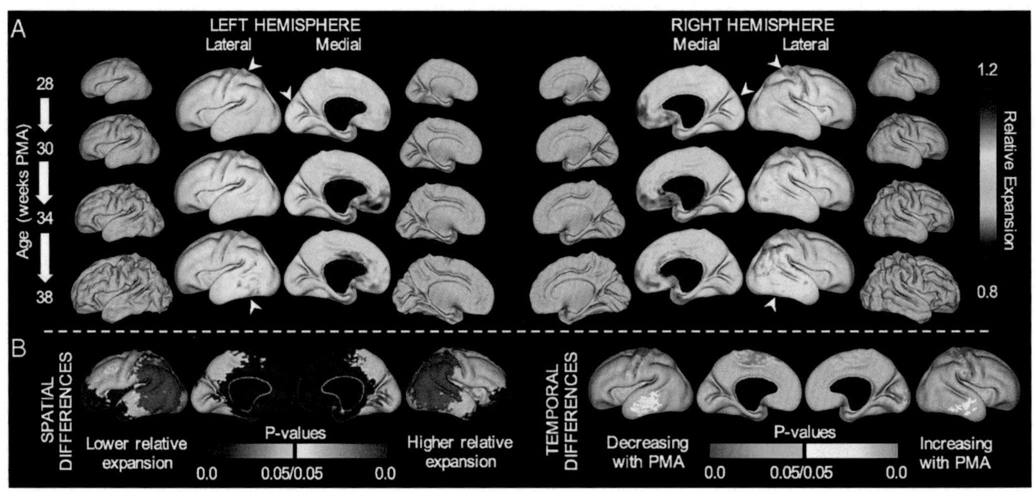

FIG. 3

Regions of highest cortical growth expansion over the third trimester. (A) Maps of average relative expansion are shown for specific windows of development, denoted on left. For very preterm infants in which three distinct periods of growth could be measured ($n = 4$), regions of maximum expansion (white arrowheads) appear to shift over time. For illustration, average midthickness surfaces are also shown to scale for each time point. (B) Regions of significant differences relative to global growth were observed based on 27 growth measurements (15 very preterm infants) over the third trimester equivalent (temporal resolution <6 weeks, mean postmenstrual age = 33 weeks). (B, Left) Relative expansion is higher in the lateral parietal, temporal, occipital, and frontal regions (red) and lower in the medial frontal and insular regions (blue). (B, Right) Relative expansion in the primary motor, sensory, and visual cortices, as well as in the insula, decreases over time (green). By contrast, relative expansion increases in the temporal lobe over time (yellow).

Reproduced with permission from Garcia, K.E., et al., 2018. Proc. Natl. Acad. Sci. 115(12), 3156–61.

3.3 Diffusion MRI

Diffusion MRI parameters change during normal development. In studies of preterm infants, MD values show a steady decrease with increasing PMA up to term, most likely as a result of decreasing brain water content during the first months of life (Hüppi et al., 1998; Neil et al., 1998). As water content falls, barriers to water diffusion move closer together, causing greater hindrance of diffusion and lower MD values. Hence, MD values are sometimes taken as an indicator of brain maturity. The changes in FA that accompany brain development are more complex. In white matter, the FA is strongly affected by myelination, but is affected by other factors as well. The parallel alignment of unmyelinated axons alone is sufficient to provide a degree of anisotropy. For example, the anterior limb of the internal capsule is unmyelinated at birth, yet still has higher anisotropy than surrounding gray matter. As white matter myelinates, anisotropy increases further in two steps. The first increase is associated with structural changes known as premyelination, and precedes the actual appearance of myelin (Wimberger et al., 1995). With the addition of myelin, there is a pronounced increase in FA. At term equivalent age, the unmyelinated anterior limb of the internal capsule has an FA value of 0.13, as compared with 0.21 for the myelinated posterior limb (Neil et al., 1998). The FA values for both white matter tracts will increase further after term equivalent as maturation continues.

While anisotropy is usually discussed in the context of white matter, the developing cortical plate also has changes in FA in association with myelination. In this case, the cortical plate has high FA values early in development that decrease with increasing PMA, which is opposite to the changes in white matter. Early in development, the microarchitecture of the cortical plate is dominated by the radially oriented apical dendrites of pyramidal cells and the presence of radial glia, which leads to greater MD values orthogonal to the cortical surface than parallel to it. As maturation progresses, processes such as the addition of basal dendrites to pyramidal cells and the arrival of afferent axons and interneurons lead to a loss of anisotropy, and this reduction in FA values takes place at varying rates in different areas, reflecting differences in regional cortical maturation (Kroenke, 2018). While FA values of cortex are essentially zero by term equivalent (McKinstry, 2002), FA values in the cortex of older children and even adults may still be informative with the application of more complex diffusion models to data obtained at high (submillimeter) spatial resolution (Dudink et al., 2015; Balasubramanian et al., 2021).

Brain injury in preterm infants is primarily manifest as white matter injury (with the caveat that all white matter is connected to gray matter), and FA is well-suited to evaluate this injury. This injury may be focal, as in periventricular leukomalacia, but more commonly is characterized by diffuse changes, or "diffuse periventricular leukomalacia."(Hüppi et al., 2001; Volpe et al., 2018) The nature of this injury has been defined histologically (Volpe, 2009), and diffusion imaging provides evidence supporting its presence via globally reduced white matter FA at term equivalent (Hüppi et al., 2001).

3.4 Resting state functional MRI (rs-fMRI)

As detailed above, rs-fMRI has been used to consistently identify and characterize RSNs encompassing the primary sensorimotor and association cortices, subcortical structures, and the cerebellum in neonates and infants across reports (Herzmann et al., 2018; Smyser et al., 2010, 2013, 2016a; Gao et al., 2015; Doria et al., 2010; Alcauter et al., 2014, 2015; Damaraju et al., 2010, 2014; Fransson et al., 2007, 2009, 2011; Gao et al., 2009; Lee et al., 2012; Lin et al., 2008; Perani et al., 2011). Early forms of these networks have been consistently identified in VPT infants as early 26 weeks PMA (and may be identifiable even earlier based upon fetal studies; see Chapter 22 for additional details). These RSNs gradually mature, including undergoing substantive development during the critical window of brain development when VPT infants are cared for in the NICU environment. Initially these networks predominantly demonstrate strong interhemispheric correlations between homotopic counterparts, with intrahemispheric, thalamocortical, and cortico-cerebellar correlations increasingly established with advancing PMA (Smyser et al., 2010). The rate at which the correlations within and between RSNs develop during this period differs by network and is assumed to be interrelated with the underlying establishment of structural connectivity (Smyser et al., 2010, 2016a; Gao et al., 2015; Doria et al., 2010; Mrzljak et al., 1992; Petanjek et al., 2008, 2011). The terminology used to describe these developing RSNs has varied across reports (e.g., "precursor," "proto," "immature"). Early developing RSNs in VPT infants are located in cortical regions known to mature early (i.e., areas radiating outward from the insula), demonstrate less variability between infants (Gao et al., 2014), and are less susceptible to neuropathology (Smyser et al., 2016a). In contrast, higher-order RSNs, including the DMN, FPC, and DAN, are predominantly identifiable in quantifiably weaker or topographically incomplete forms in

VPT infants at term-equivalent PMA (Smyser et al., 2010; Doria et al., 2010; Fransson et al., 2007, 2009).

Early reports employing conventional RSN mapping approaches demonstrated generally similar topography and qualitative measures between term and VPT infants scanned at comparable PMA. (Smyser et al., 2010; Doria et al., 2010; Fransson et al., 2007) Subsequent implementation of quantitative analysis approaches have demonstrated reductions in network amplitude and complexity in VPT infants compared to FT peers (Fig. 4) (Smyser et al., 2016a). The magnitude of these differences varies by RSN, and they are most prominent in networks located in the later developing higher-order association cortices (Smyser et al., 2010, 2016a; Toulmin et al., 2015). Thalamocortical connectivity also differs between these two groups (Smyser et al., 2010; Toulmin et al., 2015). More recent investigations employing state-of-the-art machine learning analyses have further demonstrated quantitative brain-wide differences in RSNs between these populations, including a robust ability to differentiate term and VPT infants scanned at term-equivalent PMA at both the group and individual-subject level (Smyser et al., 2016b; Ball et al., 2016). Similarly, graph theoretical analysis approaches have consistently demonstrated brain-wide differences in the functional organization properties of RSNs between these two populations (Gozdas et al., 2018; Bouyssi-Kobar et al., 2019). Further, VPT infants with forms of brain injury common in preterm populations (e.g., high-grade intraventricular hemorrhage [IVH], post-hemorrhagic hydrocephalus [PHH], cystic periventricular leukomalacia [cPVL]) demonstrate aberrant network development in a manner dependent upon the injury severity and proximity to the injury site (Smyser et al., 2013). In addition, RSN-specific reductions in correlation strength have been identified in prematurely born infants at term-equivalent PMA who have high exposure to stressful and/or painful procedures (Smith et al., 2011). Reports also suggest key clinical variables such as sex and socioeconomic status may affect the rate and patterns of RSN development in a network-specific manner (Gao et al., 2015). The impact of these and other potentially deleterious clinical features inherent to the NICU environment that have been previously linked to disruption of early cerebral development requires continued investigation (Ball et al., 2010; Chau et al., 2012; Padilla et al., 2015). Importantly, these disruptions in RSNs have been shown to persist into early childhood (Damaraju et al., 2010), adolescence (Constable et al., 2013; Myers et al., 2010), and even adulthood (White et al., 2014) across longitudinal cohorts. Further, recent reports suggest that VPT children and adolescents may rely upon an expanded, alternative set of brain-wide RSNs for domain-specific functions, though as detailed below, the role of these networks in adverse neurodevelopmental and psychiatric outcomes remains an area of ongoing investigation (Fig. 4).

4. Application of neuroimaging for neurodevelopmental and socio-emotional outcomes

In addition to characterizing prematurity-related alterations in early brain development, there is converging evidence across both conventional and advanced neuroimaging modalities that neonatal MRI is a useful tool for the prediction of later adverse developmental impairments that frequently burden this population. Extending early conventional MRI studies employing whole-brain volumetric MRI analysis methods, a growing number of investigative endeavors are now utilizing advanced MRI techniques to examine perturbations in neonatal brain structural and functional connectivity in relation to subsequent neurodevelopmental and psychiatric outcomes. Not only do these innovative studies

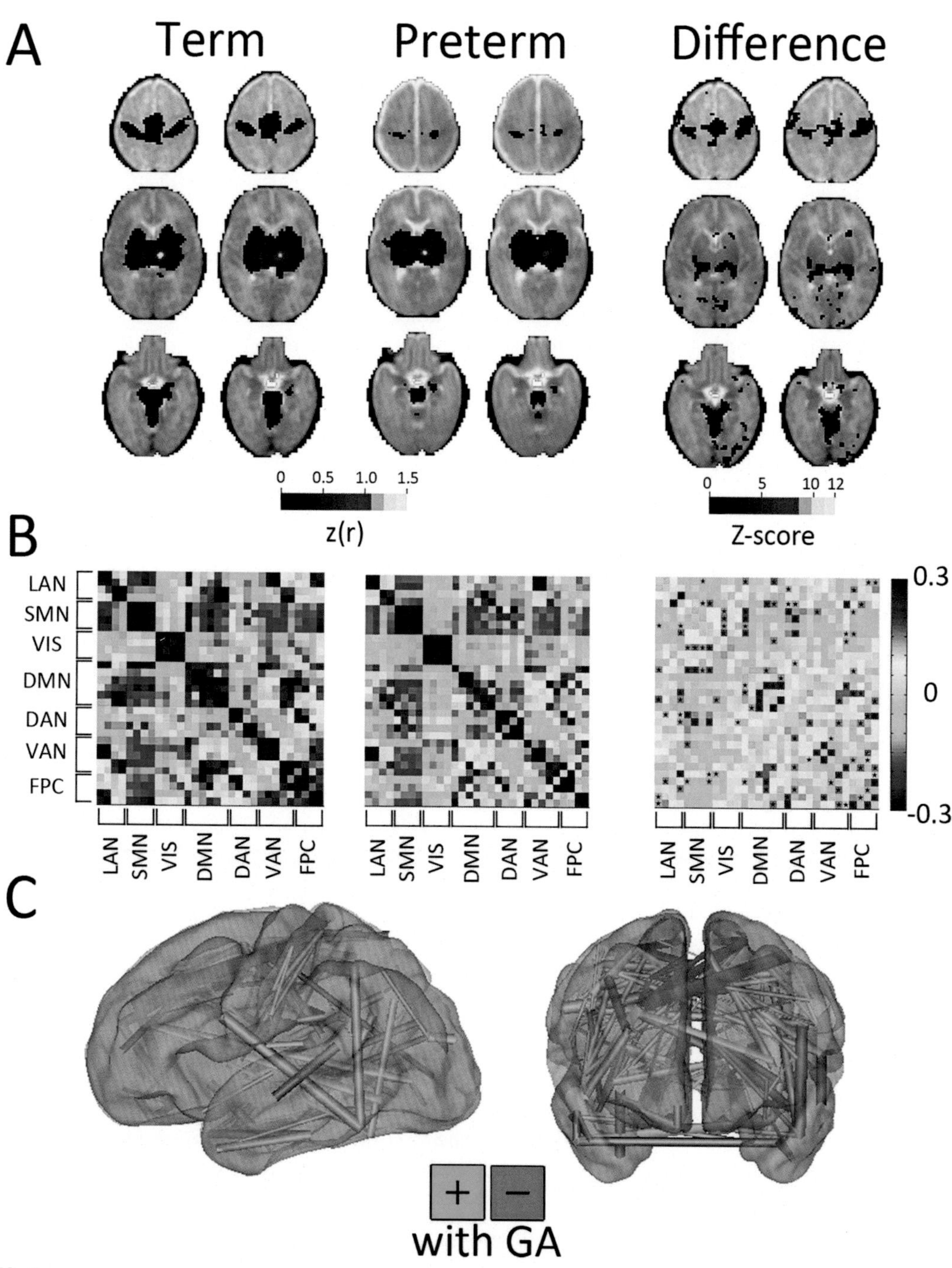

FIG. 4

See figure legend on next page.

Continued

provide insight into the neural mechanisms of impairment among preterm infants, they may also serve to identify which preterm infants will likely need longer-term developmental surveillance and timely referral to developmental and socio-emotional intervention services.

Most of our current understanding regarding the role that altered neonatal brain structure and function has in the developmental sequalae of prematurity is based on representative samples of VPT infants born less than 32 weeks' gestation and/or with very low birthweight (<1500 g). However, there is growing interest regarding the use of advanced MRI techniques to study the neural mechanisms of developmental impairment in selected groups of preterm infants who face even greater likelihoods of poor outcome, such as those with high-grade forms of perinatal brain injury common in this population, including IVH, PHH, and cPVL, which affect 4%–16% of VPT infants (Perlman, 1998; Kidokoro et al., 2014). These severe neurological complications carry a heavy neurodevelopmental toll, with 75%–85% of affected infants showing moderate to severe neurodevelopmental impairment and educational delays (Lean et al., 2019a; Luu et al., 2009a; Marret et al., 2013). While only a handful of brain-behavior studies have specifically focused on VPT infants with brain injury, they illustrate its deleterious impact on white matter microstructural and functional connectivity development, and in turn, adverse outcomes in childhood.

Against this general background, neonatal MRI provides an opportunity to examine the earliest changes in brain structure and function as neural precursors of neurodevelopmental impairment; working to identify biomarkers for poor outcome, improve early identification of high-risk preterm infants, and inform intervention efforts. The remainder of this chapter provides a brief overview of developmental follow-up research in preterm children and describes recent empirical findings linking neonatal MRI findings with variability in neurodevelopmental and socio-emotional outcomes. We also highlight the extent to which recent brain-behavior studies in higher-risk preterm infants inform the neuropathological mechanisms of brain injury and the effects of this injury on child development.

FIG. 4, cont'd Functional connectivity differences between term and very preterm infants. (A) Left: Group mean resting state-functional MRI correlation maps generated using a right thalamic seed for healthy, full-term and very preterm infants scanned at term equivalent postmenstrual age; Right: *Z*-scores demonstrating between group differences in connectivity obtained from voxel-wise *t*-test. Colored voxels denote areas with greater positive correlations in healthy, term infants. Results thresholded using $Z > 1.65$ (corresponding to $P < .05$). The right side of the image corresponds to the right side of the brain. (B) Left: Group mean matrices demonstrating covariance values within/across multiple canonical RSNs for healthy, full-term and very preterm infants at term equivalent postmenstrual age; Right: Difference between these two results (term minus preterm). Black stars denote cells with between group difference on two-tailed Mann-Whitney *U* test ($P < .05$; multiple comparisons uncorrected). (C) Functional connections important for differentiating healthy, full-term versus very preterm infants using support vector machine-multivariate pattern analysis to analyze data from 214 regions of interest located throughout the brain. Connections stronger in healthy, term infants are shown in green; those stronger in very preterm infants are in orange. The caliber of each connection is weighted by the between-group difference magnitude.

(A) Adapted with permission from Smyser, C.D., et al., 2010. Cerebral Cortex 20(12), 2852–2862. (B) Adapted with permission from Smyser, C.D., et al., 2016a. Cerebral Cortex 26(1), 322–333. (C) Adapted with permission from Smyser, C.D., et al., 2016b. NeuroImage 136, 1–9.

4.1 Neurodevelopmental and socio-emotional outcomes in infants born preterm

4.1.1 Neurodevelopmental outcomes in preterm children

Preterm birth is a major risk factor for a wide range of adverse neurodevelopmental and socio-emotional outcomes that emerge early in childhood and persist through to adulthood (O'Reilly et al., 2020; Walshe et al., 2008). Evidence from both cross-sectional and longitudinal follow-up studies suggests that VPT children experience substantive problems across multiple neurodevelopmental domains including cognitive, language, and motor function, and that these problems are often evident prior to school entry (Woodward et al., 2009; Pritchard et al., 2014).

VPT children typically obtain intelligence quotient scores around one standard deviation below FT children on standardized measures of general intellectual ability (Brydges et al., 2018; Lean et al., 2018; Wolke et al., 2008). Associations between preterm birth and cognitive impairment persist throughout childhood (Mangin et al., 2016). Not surprisingly, poorer cognitive ability among preterm children contributes to their high rates of academic underachievement (Aarnoudse-Moens et al., 2013; Johnson et al., 2009, 2011). VPT children also demonstrate more subtle cognitive problems in attention and executive function (EF) domains spanning planning, fluency, working memory, and inhibitory control (Lean et al., 2017a; Brydges et al., 2018; Aarnoudse-Moens et al., 2012; Anderson and Doyle, 2004; Woodward et al., 2011; Houdt et al., 2019). Compared to their FT peers, VPT children particularly struggle with the top-down control of attention necessary for effective goal-directed behavior and problem solving (Lean et al., 2017a; Murray et al., 2014; Delane et al., 2016). Longer-term intellectual and EF impairments place VPT individuals at increased likelihood of poorer life-course outcomes, including fewer years spent in educational settings, reduced occupational attainment, and poorer social functioning in adulthood (Kroll et al., 2017).

In terms of language development, VPT children perform less well on measures of expressive and receptive language ability than FT children (Foster-Cohen et al., 2010). Around one-third of VPT children obtain standardized expressive and receptive language scores in the delayed range on age-normed tests of language ability, with pronounced difficulties in semantics, grammar and phenome synthesis (Barre et al., 2011; Guarini et al., 2010). These rates of language delay are approximately two-to-three times higher than those of FT children (Lean et al., 2018; Foster-Cohen et al., 2010). Data pooled across three cohorts of VPT children has shown that the prevalence of severe cognitive/language impairment at age 2 years was disproportionately greater among preterm infants with IVH and PVL (Kidokoro et al., 2014). While some studies have shown that links between preterm birth and subsequent language delays persist throughout early childhood (Lean et al., 2018; Sansavini et al., 2014) and even into adulthood (O'Reilly et al., 2020), others have shown that language functioning may improve over time such that lower-risk VPT children perform as well as FT children on language tasks by late school-age and adolescence (Luu et al., 2009b, 2011).

In addition to cognitive and language impairments, a significant proportion of preterm children demonstrate impaired motor development in both fine and gross motor domains. Findings across multiple cohorts suggest that around 40% of preterm children have a mild to moderate motor impairment compared to around 7%–13% of term children (Lean et al., 2018; Williams et al., 2010; Griffiths et al., 2017; Spittle et al., 2018). Furthermore, recent longitudinal data has shown that early developing motor problems, particularly fine motor problems, worsen over early childhood (Lean et al., 2018; Sansavini et al., 2014). It is not surprising, therefore, that VPT children account for over half of all pediatric cerebral palsy diagnoses (Schieve et al., 2016). Perinatal high-grade brain injury, especially PVL and high-grade IVH, is tightly linked with motor impairment in childhood (Kidokoro et al., 2014; Lean et al., 2019a; Bolisetty et al., 2014).

4.1.2 Socioemotional outcomes in preterm children

Perinatal risk factors including younger gestational age at birth and lower birthweight have long been considered to play a causal role in the development of socio-emotional problems and psychiatric disorders in adolescents and adults (Batstra et al., 2006; Eaton et al., 2001; Lean et al., 2017b). Thus, considerable effort has been invested in understanding the nature and extent of psychiatric disorders (Johnson and Marlow, 2011), as well as the stability of psychiatric disorders (Yates et al., 2020; Linsell et al., 2018), for preterm children (Montagna and Nosarti, 2016). Neurobehavioral assessments conducted as early as term-equivalent age suggest that VPT neonates are characterized by higher levels of dysregulation (Lean et al., 2017b), and problems in regulatory abilities continue from infancy into early childhood (Clark et al., 2008; Wolf et al., 2002). VPT children are, therefore, at increased risk for later internalizing and externalizing impairments compared to FT children (Treyvaud et al., 2013; Rogers et al., 2013). For example data from a longitudinal study of VPT children assessed at ages 2, 4, and 9 years showed that VPT children had poorer levels of self-regulation at each time-point assessed by direct observation and/or parent-report. Poorer self-regulation earlier in childhood was, in turn, predictive of Attention Deficit Hyperactivity Disorder (ADHD), conduct disorder, and anxiety disorders at age 9 years. Importantly, temporal associations between early dysregulation and subsequent psychiatric disorders persisted after controlling for family social background characteristics (Woodward et al., 2017).

In addition to greater recognition of the link between preterm birth and childhood psychopathology, there is now converging evidence across a number of follow-up studies that preterm children evidence a specific pattern of psychiatric symptoms comprised of inattention, anxiety, and social-communication impairments (Yates et al., 2020; Brenner et al., 2020; Korzeniewski et al., 2017; Scott et al., 2012). These comorbid symptoms and the related disorders of ADHD, anxiety, and Autism Spectrum Disorder (ASD) are two to four times more common in preterm children than in FT children (Spittle et al., 2009; Johnson et al., 2010; Burnett et al., 2011; Shum et al., 2008; Indredavik et al., 2005; Hack et al., 2009; Elgen et al., 2002). In contrast, preterm birth confers little additional risk for conduct disorders (Treyvaud et al., 2013; Rogers et al., 2013; Johnson et al., 2010). Therefore, the constellation of ADHD, anxiety, and ASD frequently reported for VPT children has given rise to the Preterm Behavioral Phenotype (Johnson and Marlow, 2011). Preterm children born at younger gestational ages have a three- to four-fold increase in risk for ADHD, anxiety, and ASD relative to children born at older gestational ages (Johnson and Marlow, 2011). To date, few studies have examined the rates of these psychiatric disorders in preterm children with perinatal high-grade brain injury. One prospective study of low-birthweight infants who were systematically screened for the presence of perinatal brain injury in the first week of life and underwent evaluation for ASD at ages 16 and 21 years showed that perinatal high-grade brain injury was associated with a threefold increase in subsequent risk for ASD compared to low-birthweight infants without brain injury (Movsas et al., 2013). Additionally, risks of ASD were largely confined to those with ventricular enlargement (odds ratio 6.7), with little-to-no risk of ASD associated with parenchymal lesion without ventricular enlargement or with isolated germinal matrix and/or intraventricular hemorrhage. More recent work by Strahle et al. (2019) suggests that links between perinatal brain injury and impairments in socio-emotional functioning are observable even earlier in development. This study showed that perinatal brain injury was related to poorer social competency at age 2 years compared to both uninjured preterm and FT infants, with cPVL demonstrating the strongest association with social competency outcomes relative to the impact of IVH and PHH.

4.2 Neonatal MRI and neurodevelopmental and psychiatric outcomes

As detailed, infants born VPT, and particularly those with perinatal brain injury, demonstrate poorer neurodevelopmental and psychiatric outcomes compared to FT children. Investigative efforts that combine neonatal MRI with developmental follow-up assessments suggest that neonatal and longer-term alterations in brain structure and function may underlie the adverse neurodevelopmental and psychiatric outcomes common in this population.

4.2.1 Cognitive outcomes

Using both whole-brain and regional volumetric analysis, multiple studies have shown that altered cerebral growth and maturation in the neonatal period (Cheong et al., 2016; Haebich et al., 2020; Ullman et al., 2015) and childhood (Soria-Pastor et al., 2009; Peterson, 2000; Lemola et al., 2017) are associated with variability in general intellectual ability, inattention, and executive function. Collectively, these studies suggest that preterm birth is associated with regional reductions in white and gray matter volume, and in turn, poorer cognitive function (Cheong et al., 2016). For example, cross-sectional analyses in school-age preterm children has shown that smaller corpus callosum, hippocampus, and cerebellar volumes correlate with poorer cognitive, attention, and executive function skills (Thompson et al., 2013; Arhan et al., 2017; Nosarti et al., 2007). Furthermore, birth-group differences in performance on cognitive measures of selective, sustained, and executive attention have been found to be explained by reduced gray matter volume in cingulate, temporal, parietal, and occipital regions associated with prematurity (Lean et al., 2017a). Atypical increases in anterior cingulate and occipital volume have also been reported in relation to attentional functioning in VPT children (Lean et al., 2017a).

More recent studies utilizing advanced MRI suggest that alterations in cerebral white matter microstructure identified using dMRI have also been linked to adverse cognitive outcomes in preterm children (Murray et al., 2016; Thompson et al., 2016; Vollmer et al., 2017; Young et al., 2016). A recent prospective longitudinal study including serial dMRI scans in preterm infants at birth, term-equivalent PMA, and ages 2 and 4 years demonstrated that slower rates of change in MD of the internal and external capsules from birth to age 4 years, reflecting delayed and/or aberrant tract development, were associated with poorer intellectual ability at age 4 years (Young et al., 2016). In addition to these neonatal findings, reduced FA in the uncinate fasciculus, corticospinal tract, cingulum bundle, inferior frontal fasciculus, inferior frontal-occipital fasciculus, superior longitudinal fasciculus, and anterior thalamic radiations has also been associated with poorer cognitive and/or executive function skills in preterm children and adolescents (Murray et al., 2016; Vollmer et al., 2017). Reduced FA in the corticospinal tract, cingulum bundle (particularly the anterior region), superior longitudinal fasciculus (Wang et al., 2013), and thalamic radiations (Wang et al., 2013; Zubiaurre-Elorza et al., 2012) have also been implicated in severe cognitive impairment among preterm children with PVL.

There is an emerging body of work utilizing diffusion tractography analyzed with graph theory approaches to elucidate the *structural* connectivity of whole-brain white matter networks implicated in cognitive function. One such study has shown that VPT children with cognitive impairment demonstrate reduced connections in a diffuse white matter network including the thalamus, hippocampus, paracentral lobule, posterior cingulate, parietal, and occipital cortices, and frontal and temporal gyri compared to nonimpaired preterm children in a network-based analysis of white matter structural connectivity graphs (Thompson et al., 2016). In another recent study also using network-based analysis of white matter structural connectivity, Disselhoff and colleagues (Disselhoff et al., 2020) showed that FA was lower in a network comprising thalamo-frontal, thalamo-temporal, frontal, cerebellar, and intrahemispheric connections in preterm children compared to term children at ages 8–13 years. However, an alternative white matter network structure spanning the parietal, cerebellar, and subcortical connections was found to be related to inhibitory control abilities across both VPT and FT children, suggesting that the structural networks that correlate with components of EF may not overlap with the networks that differ between VPT and FT children. To date, few studies have examined measures of brain *functional* connectivity in relation to EF. While preterm infants have reduced functional connectivity in executive network regions (Gozdas et al., 2018), no study has yet linked neonatal functional connectivity alterations in executive networks to later attention and executive function impairments in preterm children.

4.2.2 Language outcomes

Converging lines of evidence suggests that neonatal MRI is a particularly useful tool for the prediction of language development in preterm children. Measures of neonatal brain morphometry, including cortical surface area and curvature, have been found to explain up to one-third of the variance in language development in preterm children at age 2 years (Kline et al., 2019; Kersbergen et al., 2016). Machine learning approaches have also shown that neonatal dMRI evaluating white matter microstructural abnormalities in preterm neonates demonstrates the strong predictive validity for both expressive and receptive language development by age 2 years (sensitivity $\geq$89%, specificity $\geq$86%) (Vassar et al., 2020). Multiple studies have also linked developmental changes in aberrant structural and functional cerebral development with poor language outcomes in preterm children. A serial MRI study reported that greater decreases in the rate of change in AD of the left posterior thalamic radiation from term-equivalent PMA to age 4 years was associated with poorer receptive and expressive language ability at age 4 years (Young et al., 2016). Higher MD in the centrum semiovale and left superior temporal gyrus has also been linked to poorer language outcomes in preterm children (Aeby et al., 2013; Pogribna et al., 2014). Consistent with these early childhood findings, alterations in the uncinate fasciculus, splenium of the corpus callosum, and anterior commissure explained up to 57% of the variability in language outcomes among preterm adolescents (Northam et al., 2012).

Recent rs-fMRI investigations have also shown that preterm children and adolescents demonstrate persisting alterations in language networks compared to FT peers (Choi et al., 2018; Wilke et al., 2014). One study examining the intrinsic language network connectivity in preterm and term children at age 4 years found that preterm children exhibited decreased functional connectivity in nearly all language regions, including Broca's area homologue and Wernicke's area, suggesting immature and altered language network function as a mechanism for language impairment (Choi et al., 2018). Others have found that VPT children demonstrate increased connectivity strength between the language network and other regions throughout the brain, with decreased right hemisphere lateralization (Kwon et al., 2014; Scheinost et al., 2015). These differences have been related to language performance, with VPT adolescents demonstrating weaker bilateral connectivity between left and right superior temporal regions also demonstrating poorer language ability at age 14–15 years (Northam et al., 2012; Wilke et al., 2014), with other regionally specific relationships also reported (Constable et al., 2013; White et al., 2014; Scheinost et al., 2012).

4.2.3 Motor outcomes

There now exists a robust body of literature linking preterm birth with reduced neonatal brain volumes and poorer motor development throughout childhood (Dewey et al., 2019; Cheong et al., 2016; Bolk et al., 2018; Keunen et al., 2016). For example, Loh et al. (2017) showed that VPT infants had smaller neonatal brain volumes in deep gray matter structures including the basal ganglia and the thalamus, which were, in turn, positively related to motor performance at age 7 years in both preterm and term children. Although there is consistent evidence prospectively linking reduced neonatal brain volumes with later motor impairment, one study has shown that the rate of brain volume growth from term-equivalent to age 7 years does not appear to relate to motor performance by age 7 years (Monson et al., 2016).

dMRI and rs-fMRI have been increasingly used to delineate alterations in key white matter tracts and the motor network in VPT infants and children. In a recent investigation, higher MD and RD within the splenium of the corpus callosum and lower FA in the left inferior temporal lobe in VPT infants, indicating delayed and/or aberrant tract development, were associated with worse motor functioning at age 2 years (Rogers et al., 2015; Thompson et al., 2012). Similar longitudinal relationships persist into later childhood, as VPT infants with decreased neonatal FA in inferior occipital and cerebellar regions demonstrated greater motor impairments at age 7 years (Thompson et al., 2014). Further, at age 7 years, VPT children with a higher degree of motor impairment demonstrated reduced structural connectivity within the precuneus, inferior parietal cortex, and temporal lobes in a network-based analysis (Thompson et al., 2016). Comparable patterns are present in adulthood, with VPT adults found to have lower FA in the corpus callosum, inferior longitudinal fasciculus, inferior fronto-occipital fasciculus, and external capsule demonstrating worse visual-motor integration and motor abilities (Sripada et al., 2015). Fewer studies have examined neonatal rs-fMRI measures in relation to motor outcome. Using resting state functional connectivity, Peyton et al. (2020) demonstrated that reduced functional connectivity between the basal ganglia and regions in parietal, frontotemporal, and visual lobes at term-equivalent age was associated with poorer motor development at age 12–15 weeks and at age 2 years. Reduced functional connectivity of the basal ganglia with the motor network, as well as thalamic-motor network connectivity, has also been linked to poorer motor performance in preterm children assessed at age 12 years (Wheelock et al., 2018).

Not surprisingly, white matter injury affects these brain-motor performance relationships. For example, motor-impaired VPT children with moderate-severe white matter injury have lower corpus callosum FA than VPT children with normal motor outcomes at age 7 years (Estep et al., 2014). Further, children with periventricular leukomalacia and gross motor impairment were found to have reduced corticospinal tract size (Rha et al., 2012) and decreased FA within the corticospinal tract and cerebellar peduncles (Wang et al., 2014). Using a region-of-interest diffusion approach, Lean et al. (2019a) found that preterm infants with high-grade perinatal brain injury had higher MD in the right optic radiation and lower FA in the right cingulum, PLIC, and corpus callosum at term-equivalent age compared to uninjured preterm infants, as well as poorer motor outcomes at age 2 years. Among VPT infants with brain injury, those with PHH or cPVL had the most significant microstructural alterations in the optic radiations (Fig. 5), left PLIC, and right caudate and worse motor outcomes. These findings suggest that VPT infants with brain injury are characterized by altered white and gray matter microstructure in regions affected by injury in a manner dependent upon injury type, and that the ensuring alterations in white and gray white matter microstructure have important clinical implications for motor

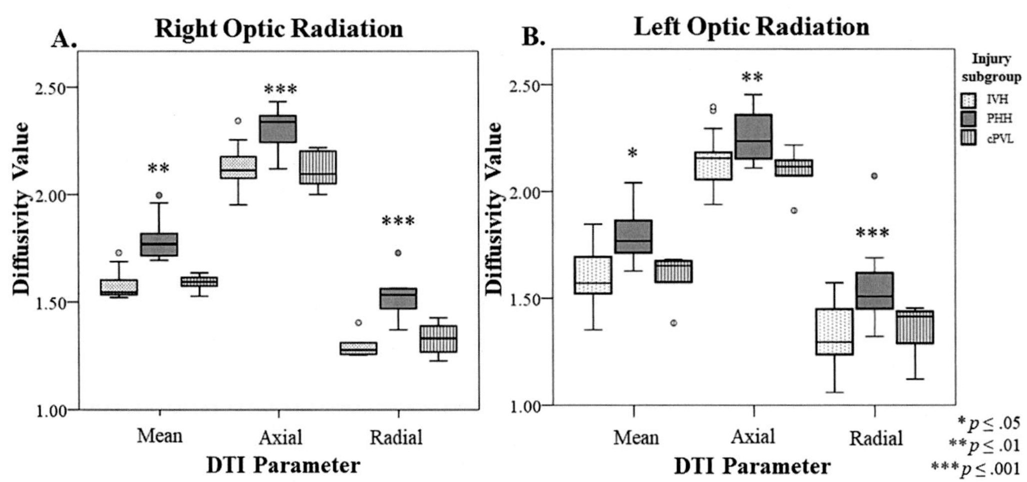

FIG. 5

Microstructural diffusivity in the optic radiations in very preterm infants with perinatal high-grade brain injury. Mean, axial, and radial diffusivity values (10^{-3} mm^2/s) for very preterm infants with grade III/IV intraventricular hemorrhage (IVH), post-hemorrhagic hydrocephalus (PHH), and cystic periventricular leukomalacia (cPVL) in the right (A) and left (B) optic radiation at term-equivalent postmenstrual age ($n = 32$). Higher mean, axial, and radial diffusivity was associated with the PHH group in both the right and left optic radiation, whereas differences were less pronounced between IVH and cPVL groups.

Reproduced with permission from Lean, R.E., et al., 2019. Pediatr. Res. 86(3), 365–374.

development. Similar findings have been reported using rs-fMRI, with investigations of prematurely born children, adolescents, and adults with spastic diplegic cerebral palsy due to PVL demonstrating aberrant motor network connectivity in relation to FT peers that correlated with severity of motor impairment (Lee et al., 2011; Burton et al., 2009).

4.2.4 Social-emotional outcomes

Neonatal reductions in brain tissue volumes, particularly in the dorsal prefrontal region, have been linked to persistent inattention/hyperactivity in a longitudinal study of VPT children assessed from ages 4 to 9 years (Bora et al., 2014). Others have shown that reduced gray matter volume in parietal, occipital, and thalamic regions may be related to symptoms of inattention relevant to ADHD (Lean et al., 2017a; Botellero et al., 2017). In additional to regional brain volume findings, altered neonatal structural and functional connectivity in key brain regions have been linked to symptoms of ADHD, as well as anxiety and ASD, which together comprise the Preterm Behavioral Phenotype (Castellanos and Proal, 2012; de Zeeuw et al., 2012; Wu et al., 2012; Casey et al., 2007; Koechlin et al., 2003; Cheon et al., 2011; Wolff et al., 2012; Dawson et al., 2012; Chevallier et al., 2012; Albaugh et al., 2016; Makris et al., 2008; Shukla et al., 2011; Billeci et al., 2012; Silk et al., 2009; Solso et al., 2016; Counsell et al., 2008; Roy et al., 2013; Qin et al., 2014; Maier et al., 2014; Rausch et al., 2016; Kim et al., 2011; Hamm et al., 2014; Andreescu et al., 2015). Links between preterm birth and increased risk for psychiatric disorders may be attributed to the role that infant stress during the NICU stay has on early hypothalamic-pituitary-adrenal axis function (Weinstock, 2008; Brummelte et al., 2015; Grunau et al., 2005; Provenzi et al., 2016) and brain connectivity (Smith et al., 2011; Scheinost et al., 2016). For example, the amygdala has been identified as a key glucocorticoid-rich subcortical structure(McEwen et al., 2016) implicated in the neural circuitry of emotion processing (LeDoux, 2003; Price, 2003; LeDoux, 2000) that is highly sensitive to the effects of prenatal stress in VPT infants (Scheinost et al., 2016). Indeed, multiple studies from our group have shown that neonatal rs-fMRI measures between the amygdala and regions of key cortical networks, including the DMN, FPN, and CO, are related to variability in anxiety symptoms in VPT infants at age 2 years (Fig. 6) (Rogers et al., 2017; Sylvester et al., 2017). Our body of work focusing on neonatal rs-fMRI has now been extended to include externalizing outcomes in preterm and term children at age 2 years. Specifically, Ramphal et al. (2020) showed that neonatal brain functional connectivity in the striatum with frontopolar and medial prefrontal cortex regions mediated the relationship between poverty and inhibition problems at age 2 years, whereas striatum-frontopolar connectivity mediated links between poverty and externalizing symptoms. Aberrant dMRI measures of white matter tracts related to ADHD, anxiety, and ASD symptoms, such as frontostriatal circuits and frontolimibic regions, including the

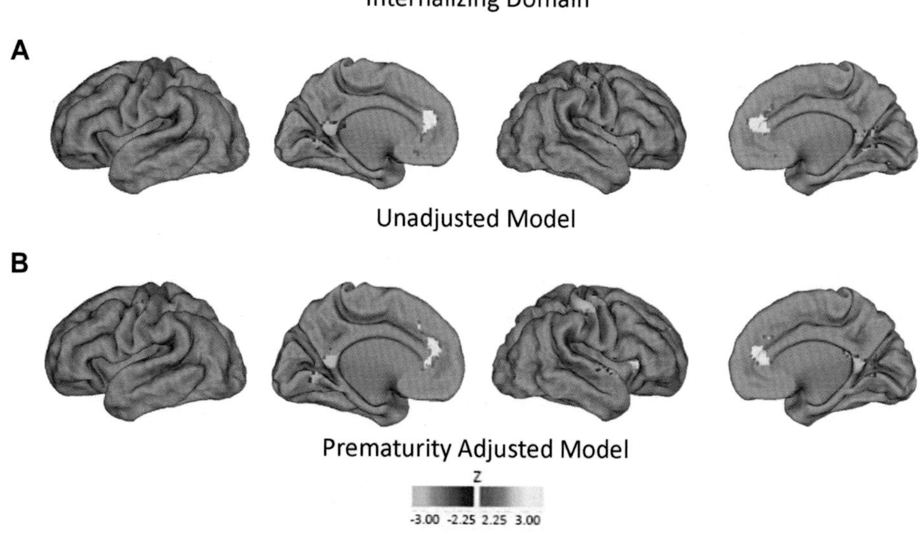

FIG. 6

Relationship between internalizing problems at age 2 years and neonatal functional connectivity of left amygdala. Whole-brain analyses correlating internalizing domain of the Infant Toddler Social Emotional Assessment at age 2 years with neonatal left amygdala resting state functional connectivity (rs-FC). (A) Unadjusted model demonstrating higher total internalizing domain scores were positively correlated with rs-FC between the left amygdala and the medial prefrontal cortex, right anterior insula, and superior frontal cortex. (B) Model adjusted for prematurity and interaction between prematurity and internalizing scores. Results thresholded using $|Z| > 2.25$ and 53 contiguous voxels, achieving whole-brain false-positive rate of 0.05.

Reproduced with permission from Rogers, C.E., et al., 2017. J. Am. Acad. Child Adolesc. Psychiatry 56(2), 157–166.

cingulum and uncinate (Makris et al., 2008; Shukla et al., 2011; Billeci et al., 2012; Silk et al., 2009; Solso et al., 2016; Counsell et al., 2008), have been associated with these same symptom domains in VPT children (Rogers et al., 2015, 2012; Fischi-Gómez et al., 2015). Recent findings from Brenner et al. (2020) highlight that altered neonatal white matter microstructure in the anterior portion of the cingulum bundle, which connects with subcortical structures in the limbic system implicated in socio-emotional development, may be especially important for subsequent Preterm Behavioral Phenotype symptoms at age 5 years (Fig. 7).

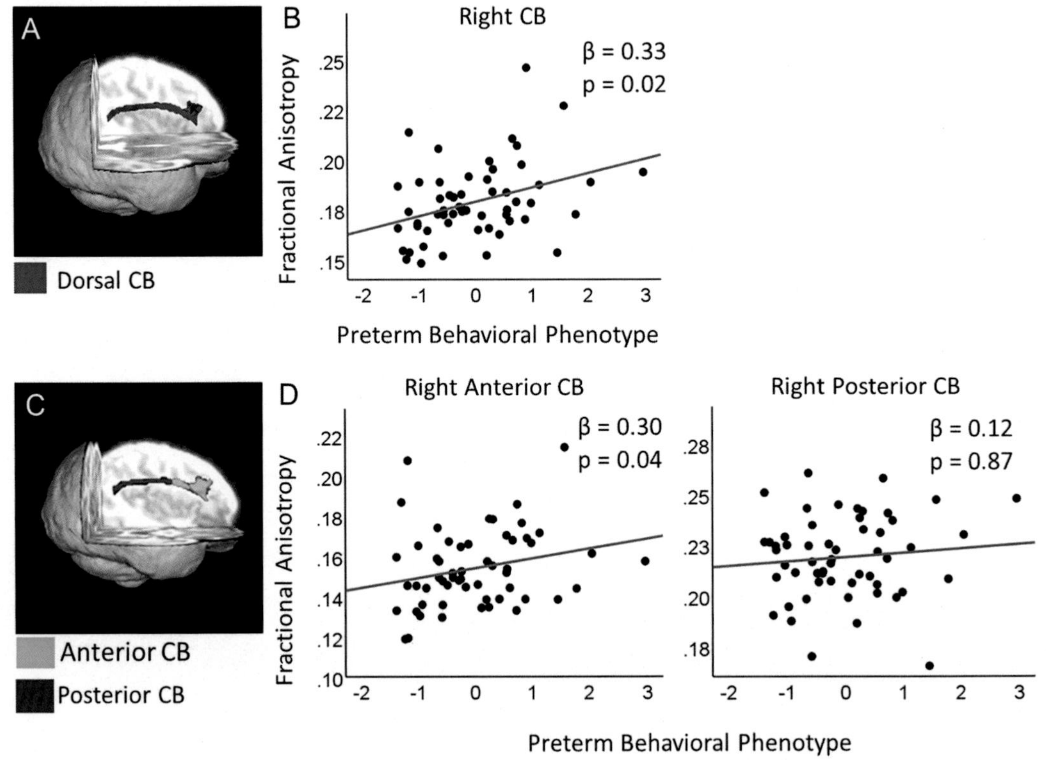

FIG. 7

Associations between neonatal white matter microstructure of the cingulum bundle and Preterm Behavioral Phenotype symptoms at age 5 years. (A) The dorsal cingulum bundle (CB) in a representative very preterm infant. (B) Neonatal fractional anisotropy of the right CB at term-equivalent age was associated with parent-rated Preterm Behavioral Phenotype symptoms in very preterm children at age 5 years. (C) The dorsal anterior and dorsal posterior portions of the CB in a representative very preterm infant. The anterior-posterior divide was placed at the intersection between the anterior limb of the internal capsule and the posterior limb of the internal capsule for each infant. (D) Neonatal fractional anisotropy of the right anterior CB at term-equivalent age was associated with parent-rated Preterm Behavioral Phenotype symptoms in very preterm children at age 5 years (left). There was no association for the right posterior CB (right).

Adapted with permission from Brenner, R.G., et al., 2020. Biol. Psychiatry; e-pub ahead of print.

4.3 Remaining considerations

Despite these advances, there are key remaining considerations within this line of research. First, the studies described above seek associations between imaging findings and outcome. While the identification of such associations may be useful to the clinician, their utility for understanding the mechanisms underlying the corresponding neurodevelopmental deficits is not clear because of the challenges of distinguishing between cause and effect versus association. It is difficult to tell if an identified structural/functional abnormality directly affects the relevant neural circuitry, thereby causing the abnormality, or instead involves unrelated neural circuitry and simply serves as a marker for injury to relevant circuitry elsewhere. Further, the neonatal MRI studies including longitudinal follow-up components published to date have been largely confined to short-term outcomes in early childhood, thus, the cascading effects of altered neonatal brain development on longer-term outcomes past school-age remain an area of ongoing investigation. Further, most of this research has focused on relating neonatal imaging to neurodevelopmental outcomes. However, fewer studies have examined neonatal MRI in relation to psychiatric outcomes; an important consideration given the high prevalence of these disorders in VPT children which persist into adolescence and have significant impact on life-course outcomes. These gaps are notably evident in studies of VPT infants with brain injury, where reported neurodevelopmental outcomes beyond age 2 years remain rare. In existing VPT-brain injury follow-up studies, most have focused on motor development followed by cognitive and language outcomes. The neural mechanisms of socio-emotional outcomes remain poorly understood in this population and further longer-term surveillance is needed.

Although findings across multiple studies have documented the adverse neurodevelopmental and psychiatric outcomes of VPT children, newer cluster-based analyses have elucidated a high degree of individual variability in neurodevelopmental and socio-emotional outcomes that may otherwise be obscured in group-level analyses (Lean et al., 2019b; Poehlmann-Tynan et al., 2015; Johnson et al., 2018; Heeren et al., 2017; Krasner et al., 2015; Ross et al., 2016; Lundequist et al., 2013). Interestingly, cluster-based analyses have shown that VPT children are a heterogeneous population with differentiated profiles of neurodevelopmental and/or socio-emotional problems, including resilient subgroups of VPT children with age-expected developmental and psychiatric functioning similar to their FT peers (Lean et al., 2019b; Poehlmann-Tynan et al., 2015; Johnson et al., 2018). The extent that early variability in neonatal structural and functional connectivity, as well as the socio-environmental exposures that shape brain connectivity during sensitive periods of brain plasticity (Poehlmann-Tynan et al., 2015), underlie heterogeneous patterns of neurodevelopmental and psychiatric outcomes in VPT children remains unknown. Relatedly, the degree to which maternal adversity during pregnancy (Sandman et al., 2011; Barrero-Castillero et al., 2019) may provide a foundation for altered neonatal structural and functional brain development in VPT infants remains largely unexplored. Maternal anxiety in pregnancy has been related to poorer neonatal neurobehavioral profiles in VPT infants (Hofheimer et al., 2020) and altered functional connectivity in regions of the DMN, CO and salience networks in FT infants (Sylvester et al., 2020). A recent study has also shown that prenatal exposure to poverty predicts altered neonatal striatum-ventrolateral prefrontal cortex functional connectivity in preterm and term neonates scanned at term-equivalent PMA (Ramphal et al., 2020). Investigation of these prenatal antecedents of neonatal MRI findings may underscore pregnancy as a particularly important window of opportunity to initiate psychosocial interventions for mothers with high levels of social adversity who are at risk for preterm delivery, and thus mitigate pathways to impairment for VPT infants early in this risk trajectory.

5. Conclusions

Over the last two decades, multiple MRI acquisition and analysis approaches have been successfully developed and employed in ground-breaking research which has delineated the interrelated macrostructural, microstructural, and functional changes underlying early brain development at an unparalleled scope and scale. Multiple investigations encompassing healthy, FT and VPT populations have defined both the orderly, regionally specific changes associated with typical early brain development and the deleterious impact of prematurity, including the effects of forms of brain injury common in this high-risk population. Most recently, technically sophisticated, connectome-based approaches, including machine learning and graph theory, have also been robustly applied in analyses of multimodality neonatal data sets to investigate these changes at both brain-wide and region/network-specific levels, further advancing this field. Importantly, neonatal neuroimaging measures across these complementary modalities have recently been linked to those from standardized assessments of childhood neurodevelopmental performance and psychiatric outcomes within longitudinal cohorts, with results indicating each of these neuroimaging approaches may provide key insights into brain-behavioral relationships at the group and individual-subject level. With this foundation now firmly established, additional expanded investigations employing multimodality neuroimaging and detailed serial neurodevelopmental assessments remain necessary to provide information critical for advancing our understanding of the modifiable risk factors underlying prematurity-related disorders and best practices for improving neurodevelopmental and mental health trajectories in this and other high-risk neonatal populations.

References

Aarnoudse-Moens, C., Weisglas-Kuperus, N., Duivenvoorden, H.J., van Goudoever, J.B., Oosterlaan, J., 2013. Executive function and IQ predict mathematical and attention problems in very preterm children. PLoS ONE 8 (2). https://doi.org/10.1371/journal.pone.0055994, e55994.

Aarnoudse-Moens, C.S.H., Duivenvoorden, H.J., Weisglas-Kuperus, N., Van Goudoever, J.B., Oosterlaan, J., 2012. The profile of executive function in very preterm children at 4 to 12 years. Dev. Med. Child Neurol. 54 (3), 247–253. https://doi.org/10.1111/j.1469-8749.2011.04150.x.

Adamson, C.L., Alexander, B., Ball, G., et al., 2020. Parcellation of the neonatal cortex using surface-based Melbourne Children's Regional Infant Brain atlases (M-CRIB-S). Sci. Rep. 10 (1), 4359. https://doi.org/10.1038/s41598-020-61326-2.

Aeby, A., De Tiège, X., Creuzil, M., et al., 2013. Language development at 2 years is correlated to brain microstructure in the left superior temporal gyrus at term equivalent age: a diffusion tensor imaging study. NeuroImage 78, 145–151. https://doi.org/10.1016/j.neuroimage.2013.03.076.

Ajayi-Obe, M., Saeed, N., Cowan, F., Rutherford, M., Edwards, A., 2000. Reduced development of cerebral cortex in extremely preterm infants. Lancet 356 (9236), 1162–1163. https://doi.org/10.1016/S0140-6736(00)02761-6.

Albaugh, M.D., Ducharme, S., Karama, S., et al., 2016. Anxious/depressed symptoms are related to microstructural maturation of white matter in typically developing youths. Dev. Psychopathol., 1–8. https://doi.org/10.1017/S0954579416000444. Published online June 14.

Alcauter, S., Lin, W., Keith Smith, J., Gilmore, J.H., Gao, W., 2015. Consistent anterior–posterior segregation of the insula during the first 2 years of life. Cereb. Cortex 25 (5), 1176–1187. https://doi.org/10.1093/cercor/bht312.

Alcauter, S., Lin, W., Smith, J.K., et al., 2014. Development of thalamocortical connectivity during infancy and its cognitive correlations. J. Neurosci. 34 (27), 9067–9075. https://doi.org/10.1523/JNEUROSCI.0796-14.2014.

Anderson, P.J., Doyle, L.W., 2004. Executive functioning in school-aged children who were born very preterm or with extremely low birth weight in the 1990s. Pediatrics 114 (1), 50–57.

Andreescu, C., Mennin, D., Tudorascu, D., et al., 2015. The many faces of anxiety-neurobiological correlates of anxiety phenotypes. Psychiatry Res. 234 (1), 96–105. https://doi.org/10.1016/j.pscychresns.2015.08.013.

Arhan, E., Gücüyener, K., Soysal, Ş., et al., 2017. Regional brain volume reduction and cognitive outcomes in preterm children at low risk at 9 years of age. Childs Nerv. Syst. 33 (8), 1317–1326. https://doi.org/10.1007/s00381-017-3421-2.

Avants, B.B., Tustison, N.J., Wu, J., Cook, P.A., Gee, J.C., 2011. An open source multivariate framework for n-tissue segmentation with evaluation on public data. Neuroinformatics 9 (4), 381–400. https://doi.org/10.1007/s12021-011-9109-y.

Balasubramanian, M., Mulkern, R.V., Neil, J.J., Maier, S.E., Polimeni, J.R., 2021. Probing in vivo cortical myeloarchitecture in humans via line-scan diffusion acquisitions at 7 T with 250-500 micron radial resolution. Magn. Reson. Med. https://doi.org/10.1002/mrm.28419.

Ball, G., Aljabar, P., Arichi, T., et al., 2016. Machine-learning to characterise neonatal functional connectivity in the preterm brain. NeuroImage 124, 267–275. https://doi.org/10.1016/j.neuroimage.2015.08.055.

Ball, G., Counsell, S.J., Anjari, M., et al., 2010. An optimised tract-based spatial statistics protocol for neonates: applications to prematurity and chronic lung disease. NeuroImage 53 (1), 94–102. https://doi.org/10.1016/j.neuroimage.2010.05.055.

Barre, N., Morgan, A., Doyle, L.W., Anderson, P.J., 2011. Language abilities in children who were very preterm and/or very low birth weight: a meta-analysis. J. Pediatr. 158 (5), 766–774.e1. https://doi.org/10.1016/j.jpeds.2010.10.032.

Barrero-Castillero, A., Morton, S.U., Nelson, C.A., Smith, V.C., 2019. Psychosocial stress and adversity: effects from the perinatal period to adulthood. NeoReviews 20 (12), e686–e696. https://doi.org/10.1542/neo.20-12-e686.

Basser, P.J., Pierpaoli, C., 2011. Microstructural and physiological features of tissues elucidated by quantitative-diffusion-tensor MRI. J. Magn. Reson. 213 (2), 560–570. https://doi.org/10.1016/j.jmr.2011.09.022.

Batstra, L., Neeleman, J., Elsinga, C., Hadders-Algra, M., 2006. Psychiatric morbidity is related to a chain of prenatal and perinatal adversities. Early Hum. Dev. 82 (11), 721–729. https://doi.org/10.1016/j.earlhumdev.2006.03.003.

Billeci, L., Calderoni, S., Tosetti, M., Catani, M., Muratori, F., 2012. White matter connectivity in children with autism spectrum disorders: a tract-based spatial statistics study. BMC Neurol. 12, 148. https://doi.org/10.1186/1471-2377-12-148.

Biswal, B., Yetkin, F.Z., Haughton, V.M., Hyde, J.S., 1995. Functional connectivity in the motor cortex of resting human brain using echo-planar MRI. Magn. Reson. Med. 34 (4), 537–541.

Boardman, J.P., Counsell, S.J., Rueckert, D., et al., 2006. Abnormal deep grey matter development following preterm birth detected using deformation-based morphometry. NeuroImage 32 (1), 70–78. https://doi.org/10.1016/j.neuroimage.2006.03.029.

Bolisetty, S., Dhawan, A., Abdel-Latif, M., et al., 2014. Intraventricular hemorrhage and neurodevelopmental outcomes in extreme preterm infants. Pediatrics 133 (1), 55–62. https://doi.org/10.1542/peds.2013-0372.

Bolk, J., Padilla, N., Forsman, L., Broström, L., Hellgren, K., Åden, U., 2018. Visual–motor integration and fine motor skills at 6½ years of age and associations with neonatal brain volumes in children born extremely preterm in Sweden: a population-based cohort study. BMJ Open 8 (2). https://doi.org/10.1136/bmjopen-2017-020478, e020478.

Bora, S., Pritchard, V.E., Chen, Z., Inder, T.E., Woodward, L.J., 2014. Neonatal cerebral morphometry and later risk of persistent inattention/hyperactivity in children born very preterm. J. Child Psychol. Psychiatry 55 (7), 828–838. https://doi.org/10.1111/jcpp.12200.

Botellero, V.L., Skranes, J., Bjuland, K.J., et al., 2017. A longitudinal study of associations between psychiatric symptoms and disorders and cerebral gray matter volumes in adolescents born very preterm. BMC Pediatr. 17 (1), 45. https://doi.org/10.1186/s12887-017-0793-0.

Bouyssi-Kobar, M., De Asis-Cruz, J., Murnick, J., Chang, T., Limperopoulos, C., 2019. Altered functional brain network integration, segregation, and modularity in infants born very preterm at term-equivalent age. J. Pediatr. 213, 13–21.e1. https://doi.org/10.1016/j.jpeds.2019.06.030.

Brenner, R.G., Smyser, C.D., Lean, R.E., et al., 2020. Microstructure of the dorsal anterior cingulum bundle in very preterm neonates predicts the 'Preterm Behavioral Phenotype' at 5 years. Biol. Psychiatry. https://doi.org/10.1016/j.biopsych.2020.06.015. Published online June.

Brier, M.R., Thomas, J.B., Snyder, A.Z., et al., 2012. Loss of intranetwork and internetwork resting state functional connections with Alzheimer's disease progression. J. Neurosci. 32 (26), 8890–8899. https://doi.org/10.1523/JNEUROSCI.5698-11.2012.

Brodmann, K., 1909. Vergleichende Lokalisationslehre der Grosshirnrinde in ihren Prinzipien dargestellt auf Grund des Zellenbaues. Johann Ambrosius Barth.

Brummelte, S., Chau, C.M.Y., Cepeda, I.L., et al., 2015. Cortisol levels in former preterm children at school age are predicted by neonatal procedural pain-related stress. Psychoneuroendocrinology 51, 151–163. https://doi.org/10.1016/j.psyneuen.2014.09.018.

Brydges, C.R., Landes, J.K., Reid, C.L., Campbell, C., French, N., Anderson, M., 2018. Cognitive outcomes in children and adolescents born very preterm: a meta-analysis. Dev. Med. Child Neurol. 60 (5), 452–468. https://doi.org/10.1111/dmcn.13685.

Burnett, A.C., Anderson, P.J., Cheong, J., Doyle, L.W., Davey, C.G., Wood, S.J., 2011. Prevalence of psychiatric diagnoses in preterm and full-term children, adolescents and young adults: a meta-analysis. Psychol. Med. 41 (12), 2463–2474. https://doi.org/10.1017/S003329171100081X.

Burton, H., Dixit, S., Litkowski, P., Wingert, J.R., 2009. Functional connectivity for somatosensory and motor cortex in spastic diplegia. Somatosens. Mot. Res. 26 (4), 90–104. https://doi.org/10.3109/08990220903335742.

Bystron, I., Blakemore, C., Rakic, P., 2008. Development of the human cerebral cortex: Boulder Committee revisited. Nat. Rev. Neurosci. 9 (2), 110–122. https://doi.org/10.1038/nrn2252.

Casey, B.J., Nigg, J.T., Durston, S., 2007. New potential leads in the biology and treatment of attention deficit-hyperactivity disorder. Curr. Opin. Neurol. 20 (2), 119–124. https://doi.org/10.1097/WCO.0b013e3280a02f78.

Castellanos, F.X., Proal, E., 2012. Large-scale brain systems in ADHD: beyond the prefrontal-striatal model. Trends Cogn. Sci. 16 (1), 17–26. https://doi.org/10.1016/j.tics.2011.11.007.

Chau, V., Brant, R., Poskitt, K.J., Tam, E.W.Y., Synnes, A., Miller, S.P., 2012. Postnatal infection is associated with widespread abnormalities of brain development in premature newborns. Pediatr. Res. 71 (3), 274–279. https://doi.org/10.1038/pr.2011.40.

Cheon, K.-A., Kim, Y.-S., Oh, S.-H., et al., 2011. Involvement of the anterior thalamic radiation in boys with high functioning autism spectrum disorders: a diffusion tensor imaging study. Brain Res. 1417, 77–86. https://doi.org/10.1016/j.brainres.2011.08.020.

Cheong, J.L.Y., Thompson, D.K., Spittle, A.J., et al., 2016. Brain volumes at term-equivalent age are associated with 2-year neurodevelopment in moderate and late preterm children. J. Pediatr. 174, 91–97.e1. https://doi.org/10.1016/j.jpeds.2016.04.002.

Chevallier, C., Kohls, G., Troiani, V., Brodkin, E.S., Schultz, R.T., 2012. The social motivation theory of autism. Trends Cogn. Sci. 16 (4), 231–239. https://doi.org/10.1016/j.tics.2012.02.007.

Choi, E.J., Vandewouw, M.M., Young, J.M., Taylor, M.J., 2018. Language network function in young children born very preterm. Front. Hum. Neurosci. 12. https://doi.org/10.3389/fnhum.2018.00512.

Cismaru, A.L., Gui, L., Vasung, L., et al., 2016. Altered amygdala development and fear processing in prematurely born infants. Front. Neuroanat. 10. https://doi.org/10.3389/fnana.2016.00055.

Clark, C.A.C., Woodward, L.J., Horwood, L.J., Moor, S., 2008. Development of emotional and Behavioral regulation in children born extremely preterm and very preterm: biological and social influences. Child Dev. 79 (5), 1444–1462. https://doi.org/10.1111/j.1467-8624.2008.01198.x.

Constable, R.T., Vohr, B.R., Scheinost, D., et al., 2013. A left cerebellar pathway mediates language in prematurely-born young adults. NeuroImage 64, 371–378. https://doi.org/10.1016/j.neuroimage.2012.09.008.

Counsell, S.J., Edwards, A.D., Chew, A.T.M., et al., 2008. Specific relations between neurodevelopmental abilities and white matter microstructure in children born preterm. Brain 131 (Pt 12), 3201–3208. https://doi.org/10.1093/brain/awn268.

Damaraju, E., Caprihan, A., Lowe, J.R., Allen, E.A., Calhoun, V.D., Phillips, J.P., 2014. Functional connectivity in the developing brain: a longitudinal study from 4 to 9months of age. NeuroImage 84, 169–180. https://doi.org/10.1016/j.neuroimage.2013.08.038.

Damaraju, E., Phillips, J., Lowe, J.R., Ohls, R., Calhoun, V.D., Caprihan, A., 2010. Resting-state functional connectivity differences in premature children. Front. Syst. Neurosci. 4. https://doi.org/10.3389/fnsys.2010.00023.

Dawson, G., Bernier, R., Ring, R.H., 2012. Social attention: a possible early indicator of efficacy in autism clinical trials. J. Neurodev. Disord. 4 (1), 11. https://doi.org/10.1186/1866-1955-4-11.

de Zeeuw, P., Mandl, R.C.W., Hulshoff Pol, H.E., van Engeland, H., Durston, S., 2012. Decreased frontostriatal microstructural organization in attention deficit/hyperactivity disorder. Hum. Brain Mapp. 33 (8), 1941–1951. https://doi.org/10.1002/hbm.21335.

Delane, L., Bayliss, D.M., Campbell, C., Reid, C., French, N., Anderson, M., 2016. Poor executive functioning in children born very preterm: using dual-task methodology to untangle alternative theoretical interpretations. J. Exp. Child Psychol. 152, 264–277. https://doi.org/10.1016/j.jecp.2016.08.002.

Dewey, D., Thompson, D.K., Kelly, C.E., et al., 2019. Very preterm children at risk for developmental coordination disorder have brain alterations in motor areas. Acta Paediatr. 108 (9), 1649–1660. https://doi.org/10.1111/apa.14786.

Disselhoff, V., Jakab, A., Schnider, B., Latal, B., Wehrle, F.M., Hagmann, C.F., 2020. Inhibition is associated with whole-brain structural brain connectivity on network level in school-aged children born very preterm and at term. NeuroImage 218, 116937. https://doi.org/10.1016/j.neuroimage.2020.116937.

Doria, V., Beckmann, C.F., Arichi, T., et al., 2010. Emergence of resting state networks in the preterm human brain. Proc. Natl. Acad. Sci. 107 (46), 20015–20020. https://doi.org/10.1073/pnas.1007921107.

Dudink, J., Pieterman, K., Leemans, A., Kleinnijenhuis, M., van Cappellen van Walsum, A.M., Hoebeek, F.E., 2015. Recent advancements in diffusion MRI for investigating cortical development after preterm birth—potential and pitfalls. Front. Hum. Neurosci. 8. https://doi.org/10.3389/fnhum.2014.01066.

Eaton, W.W., Mortensen, P.B., Thomsen, P.H., Frydenberg, M., 2001. Obstetric complications and risk for severe psychopathology in childhood. J. Autism Dev. Disord. 31 (3), 279–285. https://doi.org/10.1023/a:1010743203048.

Eickhoff, S.B., Constable, R.T., Yeo, B.T.T., 2018. Topographic organization of the cerebral cortex and brain cartography. NeuroImage 170, 332–347. https://doi.org/10.1016/j.neuroimage.2017.02.018.

Elgen, I., Sommerfelt, K., Markestad, T., 2002. Population based, controlled study of behavioural problems and psychiatric disorders in low birthweight children at 11 years of age. Arch. Dis. Child. Fetal Neonatal Ed. 87 (2), F128–F132.

Engelhardt, E., Inder, T.E., Alexopoulos, D., et al., 2015. Regional impairments of cortical folding in premature infants. Ann. Neurol. 77 (1), 154–162. https://doi.org/10.1002/ana.24313.

Estep, M.E., Smyser, C.D., Anderson, P.J., et al., 2014. Diffusion tractography and neuromotor outcome in very preterm children with white matter abnormalities. Pediatr. Res. 76 (1), 86–92. https://doi.org/10.1038/pr.2014.45.

Fischi-Gómez, E., Vasung, L., Meskaldji, D.-E., et al., 2015. Structural brain connectivity in school-age preterm infants provides evidence for impaired networks relevant for higher order cognitive skills and social cognition. Cereb. Cortex 25 (9), 2793–2805. https://doi.org/10.1093/cercor/bhu073.

Fischl, B., 2012. FreeSurfer. NeuroImage 62 (2), 774–781. https://doi.org/10.1016/j.neuroimage.2012.01.021.

Foster-Cohen, S.H., Friesen, M.D., Champion, P.R., Woodward, L.J., 2010. High prevalence/low severity language delay in preschool children born very preterm. J. Dev. Behav. Pediatr. 31 (8), 658–667.

Fox, M.D., Raichle, M.E., 2007. Spontaneous fluctuations in brain activity observed with functional magnetic resonance imaging. Nat. Rev. Neurosci. 8 (9), 700–711. https://doi.org/10.1038/nrn2201.

Fox, M.D., Snyder, A.Z., Vincent, J.L., Corbetta, M., Van Essen, D.C., Raichle, M.E., 2005. The human brain is intrinsically organized into dynamic, anticorrelated functional networks. Proc. Natl. Acad. Sci. U. S. A. 102 (27), 9673–9678.

Fransson, P., Aden, U., Blennow, M., Lagercrantz, H., 2011. The functional architecture of the infant brain as revealed by resting-state fMRI. Cereb. Cortex 21 (1), 145–154. https://doi.org/10.1093/cercor/bhq071.

Fransson, P., Skiöld, B., Engström, M., et al., 2009. Spontaneous brain activity in the newborn brain during natural sleep—an fMRI study in infants born at full term. Pediatr. Res. 66 (3), 301–305. https://doi.org/10.1203/PDR.0b013e3181b1bd84.

Fransson, P., Skiöld, B., Horsch, S., et al., 2007. Resting-state networks in the infant brain. PNAS 104 (39), 15531–15536. https://doi.org/10.1073/pnas.0704380104.

Fumagalli, M., Provenzi, L., Carli, P.D., et al., 2018. From early stress to 12-month development in very preterm infants: preliminary findings on epigenetic mechanisms and brain growth. PLoS One 13 (1). https://doi.org/10.1371/journal.pone.0190602, e0190602.

Gao, W., Alcauter, S., Elton, A., et al., 2015. Functional network development during the first year: relative sequence and socioeconomic correlations. Cereb. Cortex 25 (9), 2919–2928. https://doi.org/10.1093/cercor/bhu088.

Gao, W., Elton, A., Zhu, H., et al., 2014. Intersubject variability of and genetic effects on the brain's functional connectivity during infancy. J. Neurosci. 34 (34), 11288–11296. https://doi.org/10.1523/JNEUROSCI.5072-13.2014.

Gao, W., Gilmore, J.H., Shen, D., Smith, J.K., Zhu, H., Lin, W., 2013. The synchronization within and interaction between the default and dorsal attention networks in early infancy. Cereb. Cortex 23 (3), 594–603. https://doi.org/10.1093/cercor/bhs043.

Gao, W., Zhu, H., Giovanello, K.S., et al., 2009. Evidence on the emergence of the brain's default network from 2-week-old to 2-year-old healthy pediatric subjects. Proc. Natl. Acad. Sci. U. S. A. 106 (16), 6790–6795. https://doi.org/10.1073/pnas.0811221106.

Garcia, K.E., Robinson, E.C., Alexopoulos, D., et al., 2018. Dynamic patterns of cortical expansion during folding of the preterm human brain. Proc. Natl. Acad. Sci. 115 (12), 3156–3161. https://doi.org/10.1073/pnas.1715451115.

Gozdas, E., Parikh, N.A., Merhar, S.L., Tkach, J.A., He, L., Holland, S.K., 2018. Altered functional network connectivity in preterm infants: antecedents of cognitive and motor impairments? Brain Struct. Funct. 223 (8), 3665–3680. https://doi.org/10.1007/s00429-018-1707-0.

Griffiths, A., Morgan, P., Anderson, P.J., Doyle, L.W., Lee, K.J., Spittle, A.J., 2017. Predictive value of the movement assessment battery for children—second edition at 4 years, for motor impairment at 8 years in children born preterm. Dev. Med. Child Neurol. 59 (5), 490–496. https://doi.org/10.1111/dmcn.13367.

Grunau, R.E., Holsti, L., Haley, D.W., et al., 2005. Neonatal procedural pain exposure predicts lower cortisol and behavioral reactivity in preterm infants in the NICU. Pain 113 (3), 293–300. https://doi.org/10.1016/j.pain.2004.10.020.

Guarini, A., Sansavini, A., Fabbri, C., et al., 2010. Long-term effects of preterm birth on language and literacy at eight years. J. Child Lang. 37 (4), 865–885. https://doi.org/10.1017/S0305000909990109.

Hack, M., Taylor, H.G., Schluchter, M., Andreias, L., Drotar, D., Klein, N., 2009. Behavioral outcomes of extremely low birth weight children at age 8 years. J. Dev. Behav. Pediatr. 30 (2), 122–130. https://doi.org/10.1097/DBP.0b013e31819e6a16.

Haebich, K.M., Willmott, C., Scratch, S.E., et al., 2020. Neonatal brain abnormalities and brain volumes associated with goal setting outcomes in very preterm 13-year-olds. Brain Imaging Behav. 14 (4), 1062–1073. https://doi.org/10.1007/s11682-019-00039-1.

Hamm, L.L., Jacobs, R.H., Johnson, M.W., et al., 2014. Aberrant amygdala functional connectivity at rest in pediatric anxiety disorders. Biol. Mood Anxiety Disord. 4 (1), 15. https://doi.org/10.1186/s13587-014-0015-4.

Heeren, T., Joseph, R.M., Allred, E.N., O'Shea, T.M., Leviton, A., Kuban, K.C.K., 2017. Cognitive functioning at age 10 years among children born extremely preterm: a latent profile approach. Pediatr. Res. https://doi.org/10.1038/pr.2017.82. Published online June 5.

Herzmann, C.S., Snyder, A.Z., Kenley, J.K., Rogers, C.E., Shimony, J.S., Smyser, C.D., 2018. Cerebellar functional connectivity in term- and very preterm-born infants. Cereb. Cortex. https://doi.org/10.1093/cercor/bhy023. Published online 6 February.

Hofheimer, J.A., Smith, L.M., McGowan, E.C., et al., 2020. Psychosocial and medical adversity associated with neonatal neurobehavior in infants born before 30 weeks gestation. Pediatr. Res. 87 (4), 721–729. https://doi.org/10.1038/s41390-019-0607-1.

Houdt, C.A.V., Oosterlaan, J., Wassenaer-Leemhuis, A.G.V., Kaam, A.H.V., Aarnoudse-Moens, C.S.H., 2019. Executive function deficits in children born preterm or at low birthweight: a meta-analysis. Dev. Med. Child Neurol. 61 (9), 1015–1024. https://doi.org/10.1111/dmcn.14213.

Hüppi, P.S., Maier, S.E., Peled, S., et al., 1998. Microstructural development of human Newborn cerebral White matter assessed in vivo by diffusion tensor magnetic resonance imaging. Pediatr. Res. 44 (4), 584–590. https://doi.org/10.1203/00006450-199810000-00019.

Hüppi, P.S., Murphy, B., Maier, S.E., et al., 2001. Microstructural brain development after perinatal cerebral white matter injury assessed by diffusion tensor magnetic resonance imaging. Pediatrics 107 (3), 455–460. https://doi.org/10.1542/peds.107.3.455.

Huttenlocher, P.R., Dabholkar, A.S., 1997. Regional differences in synaptogenesis in human cerebral cortex. J. Comp. Neurol. 387 (2), 167–178. https://doi.org/10.1002/(sici)1096-9861(19971020)387:2<167::aid-cne1>3.0.co;2-z.

Inder, T.E., Warfield, S.K., Wang, H., Hüppi, P.S., Volpe, J.J., 2005. Abnormal cerebral structure is present at term in premature infants. Pediatrics 115 (2), 286–294. https://doi.org/10.1542/peds.2004-0326.

Indredavik, M.S., Vik, T., Heyerdahl, S., Kulseng, S., Brubakk, A.-M., 2005. Psychiatric symptoms in low birth weight adolescents, assessed by screening questionnaires. Eur. Child Adolesc. Psychiatry 14 (4), 226–236. https://doi.org/10.1007/s00787-005-0459-6.

Johnson, S., Hennessy, E., Smith, R., Trikic, R., Wolke, D., Marlow, N., 2009. Academic attainment and special educational needs in extremely preterm children at 11 years of age: the EPICure study. Arch. Dis. Child. Fetal Neonatal Ed. 94 (4), F283–F289. https://doi.org/10.1136/adc.2008.152793.

Johnson, S., Hollis, C., Kochhar, P., Hennessy, E., Wolke, D., Marlow, N., 2010. Psychiatric disorders in extremely preterm children: longitudinal finding at age 11 years in the EPICure study. J. Am. Acad. Child Adolesc. Psychiatry 49 (5), 453–463.e1.

Johnson, S., Marlow, N., 2011. Preterm birth and childhood psychiatric disorders. Pediatr. Res. 69 (5 Pt 2). https://doi.org/10.1203/PDR.0b013e318212faa0. 11R-8R.

Johnson, S., Waheed, G., Manktelow, B.N., et al., 2018. Differentiating the preterm phenotype: distinct profiles of cognitive and behavioral development following late and moderately preterm birth. J. Pediatr. 193, 85–92.e1. https://doi.org/10.1016/j.jpeds.2017.10.002.

Johnson, S., Wolke, D., Hennessy, E., Marlow, N., 2011. Educational outcomes in extremely preterm children: neuropsychological correlates and predictors of attainment. Dev. Neuropsychol. 36 (1), 74–95. https://doi.org/10.1080/87565641.2011.540541.

Kersbergen, K.J., Leroy, F., Išgum, I., et al., 2016. Relation between clinical risk factors, early cortical changes, and neurodevelopmental outcome in preterm infants. NeuroImage 142, 301–310. https://doi.org/10.1016/j.neuroimage.2016.07.010.

Kesler, S.R., Ment, L.R., Vohr, B., et al., 2004. Volumetric analysis of regional cerebral development in preterm children. Pediatr. Neurol. 31 (5), 318–325. https://doi.org/10.1016/j.pediatrneurol.2004.06.008.

Kesler, S.R., Reiss, A.L., Vohr, B., et al., 2008. Brain volume reductions within multiple cognitive systems in male preterm children at age twelve. J. Pediatr. 152 (4), 513–520.e1. https://doi.org/10.1016/j.jpeds.2007.08.009.

Keunen, K., Išgum, I., van Kooij, B.J.M., et al., 2016. Brain volumes at term-equivalent age in preterm infants: imaging biomarkers for neurodevelopmental outcome through early school age. J. Pediatr. 172, 88–95. https://doi.org/10.1016/j.jpeds.2015.12.023.

Kidokoro, H., Anderson, P.J., Doyle, L.W., Woodward, L.J., Neil, J.J., Inder, T.E., 2014. Brain injury and altered brain growth in preterm infants: predictors and prognosis. Pediatrics 134 (2), e444–e453. https://doi.org/10.1542/peds.2013-2336.

Kim, M.J., Gee, D.G., Loucks, R.A., Davis, F.C., Whalen, P.J., 2011. Anxiety dissociates dorsal and ventral medial prefrontal cortex functional connectivity with the amygdala at rest. Cereb. Cortex 21 (7), 1667–1673. https://doi.org/10.1093/cercor/bhq237.

Kline, J.E., Illapani, V.S.P., He, L., Altaye, M., Logan, J.W., Parikh, N.A., 2019. Early cortical maturation predicts neurodevelopment in very preterm infants. Arch. Dis. Child Fetal Neonatal Ed. https://doi.org/10.1136/archdischild-2019-317466. Published online November 8.

Koechlin, E., Ody, C., Kouneiher, F., 2003. The architecture of cognitive control in the human prefrontal cortex. Science 302 (5648), 1181–1185. https://doi.org/10.1126/science.1088545.

Korzeniewski, S.J., Joseph, R.M., Kim, S.H., et al., 2017. Social responsiveness scale assessment of the preterm behavioral phenotype in ten-year-olds born extremely preterm. J. Dev. Behav. Pediatr. 38 (9), 697–705. https://doi.org/10.1097/DBP.0000000000000485.

Krasner, A.J., Turner, J.B., Feldman, J.F., et al., 2015. ADHD symptoms in a non-referred low birthweight/preterm cohort: longitudinal profiles, outcomes, and associated features. J. Atten. Disord. https://doi.org/10.1177/1087054715617532. Published online December 23.

Kroenke, C.D., 2018. Using diffusion anisotropy to study cerebral cortical gray matter development. J. Magn. Reson. 292, 106–116. https://doi.org/10.1016/j.jmr.2018.04.011.

Kroll, J., Karolis, V., Brittain, P.J., et al., 2017. Real-life impact of executive function impairments in adults who were born very preterm. J. Int. Neuropsychol. Soc. 23 (5), 381–389. https://doi.org/10.1017/S1355617717000169.

Kwon, S.H., Vasung, L., Ment, L.R., Huppi, P.S., 2014. The role of neuroimaging in predicting neurodevelopmental outcomes of preterm neonates. Clin. Perinatol. 41 (1), 257–283. https://doi.org/10.1016/j.clp.2013.10.003.

Lean, R.E., Han, R.H., Smyser, T.A., et al., 2019a. Altered neonatal white and gray matter microstructure is associated with neurodevelopmental impairments in very preterm infants with high-grade brain injury. Pediatr. Res. 86 (3), 365–374. https://doi.org/10.1038/s41390-019-0461-1.

Lean, R.E., Lessov-Shlaggar, C., Gerstein, E.D., et al., 2019b. Maternal and family factors differentiate profiles of psychiatric impairments in very preterm children at age 5-years. J. Child Psychol. Psychiatry 61 (2), 157–166. https://doi.org/10.1111/jcpp.13116.

Lean, R.E., Melzer, T.R., Bora, S., Watts, R., Woodward, L.J., 2017a. Attention and regional gray matter development in very preterm children at age 12 years. J. Int. Neuropsychol. Soc. 23 (7), 539–550. https://doi.org/10.1017/S1355617717000388.

Lean, R.E., Paul, R.A., Smyser, T.A., Smyser, C.D., Rogers, C.E., 2018. Social adversity and cognitive, language, and motor development of very preterm children from 2 to 5 years of age. J. Pediatr. 203. https://doi.org/10.1016/j.jpeds.2018.07.110. 177-184.e1.

Lean, R.E., Smyser, C.D., Rogers, C.E., 2017b. Assessment: the newborn. Child Adolesc. Psychiatr. Clin. N. Am. 26 (3), 427–440. https://doi.org/10.1016/j.chc.2017.02.002.

LeDoux, J., 2003. The emotional brain, fear, and the amygdala. Cell. Mol. Neurobiol. 23 (4–5), 727–738.

LeDoux, J.E., 2000. Emotion circuits in the brain. Annu. Rev. Neurosci. 23, 155–184. https://doi.org/10.1146/annurev.neuro.23.1.155.

Lee, J.D., Park, H.-J., Park, E.S., et al., 2011. Motor pathway injury in patients with periventricular leucomalacia and spastic diplegia. Brain 134 (4), 1199–1210. https://doi.org/10.1093/brain/awr021.

Lee, W., Donner, E.J., Nossin-Manor, R., Whyte, H.E., Sled, J.G., Taylor, M.J., 2012. Visual functional magnetic resonance imaging of preterm infants. Dev. Med. Child Neurol. 54 (8), 724–729. https://doi.org/10.1111/j.1469-8749.2012.04342.x.

Lemola, S., Oser, N., Urfer-Maurer, N., et al., 2017. Effects of gestational age on brain volume and cognitive functions in generally healthy very preterm born children during school-age: a voxel-based morphometry study. PLoS One 12 (8). https://doi.org/10.1371/journal.pone.0183519, e0183519.

Limperopoulos, C., Soul, J.S., Gauvreau, K., et al., 2005. Late gestation cerebellar growth is rapid and impeded by premature birth. Pediatrics 115 (3), 688–695. https://doi.org/10.1542/peds.2004-1169.

Lin, W., Zhu, Q., Gao, W., et al., 2008. Functional connectivity MR imaging reveals cortical functional connectivity in the developing brain. AJNR Am. J. Neuroradiol. 29 (10), 1883–1889. https://doi.org/10.3174/ajnr.A1256.

Linsell, L., Johnson, S., Wolke, D., Morris, J., Kurinczuk, J.J., Marlow, N., 2018. Trajectories of behavior, attention, social and emotional problems from childhood to early adulthood following extremely preterm birth: a prospective cohort study. Eur. Child Adolesc. Psychiatry. https://doi.org/10.1007/s00787-018-1219-8. Published online 7 September.

Loh, W.Y., Anderson, P.J., Cheong, J.L.Y., et al., 2017. Neonatal basal ganglia and thalamic volumes: very preterm birth and 7-year neurodevelopmental outcomes. Pediatr. Res. 82 (6), 970–978. https://doi.org/10.1038/pr.2017.161.

Lowe, M.J., Mock, B.J., Sorenson, J.A., 1998. Functional connectivity in single and multislice echoplanar imaging using resting-state fluctuations. NeuroImage 7 (2), 119–132. https://doi.org/10.1006/nimg.1997.0315.

Lundequist, A., Böhm, B., Smedler, A.-C., 2013. Individual neuropsychological profiles at age 5½ years in children born preterm in relation to medical risk factors. Child Neuropsychol. 19 (3), 313–331. https://doi.org/10.1080/09297049.2011.653331.

Luu, T.M., Ment, L.R., Schneider, K.C., Katz, K.H., Allan, W.C., Vohr, B.R., 2009a. Lasting effects of preterm birth and neonatal brain hemorrhage at 12 years of age. Pediatrics 123 (3), 1037–1044. https://doi.org/10.1542/peds.2008-1162.

Luu, T.M., Vohr, B.R., Allan, W., Schneider, K.C., Ment, L.R., 2011. Evidence for catch-up in cognition and receptive vocabulary among adolescents born very preterm. Pediatrics 128 (2), 313–322. https://doi.org/10.1542/peds.2010-2655.

Luu, T.M., Vohr, B.R., Schneider, K.C., et al., 2009b. Trajectories of receptive language development from 3 to 12 years of age for very preterm children. Pediatrics 124 (1), 333–341. https://doi.org/10.1542/peds.2008-2587.

Maier, S.J., Szalkowski, A., Kamphausen, S., et al., 2014. Altered cingulate and amygdala response towards threat and safe cues in attention deficit hyperactivity disorder. Psychol. Med. 44 (1), 85–98. https://doi.org/10.1017/S0033291713000469.

Makris, N., Buka, S.L., Biederman, J., et al., 2008. Attention and executive systems abnormalities in adults with childhood ADHD: a DT-MRI study of connections. Cereb. Cortex 18 (5), 1210–1220. https://doi.org/10.1093/cercor/bhm156.

Makropoulos, A., Aljabar, P., Wright, R., et al., 2016. Regional growth and atlasing of the developing human brain. NeuroImage 125, 456–478. https://doi.org/10.1016/j.neuroimage.2015.10.047.

Mangin, K.S., Horwood, L.J., Woodward, L.J., 2016. Cognitive development trajectories of very preterm and typically developing children. Child Dev. https://doi.org/10.1111/cdev.12585. Published online 1 June.

Marret, S., Marchand-Martin, L., Picaud, J.-C., et al., 2013. Brain injury in very preterm children and neurosensory and cognitive disabilities during childhood: the EPIPAGE cohort study. PLoS One 8 (5). https://doi.org/10.1371/journal.pone.0062683, e62683.

Matthews, L.G., Inder, T.E., Pascoe, L., et al., 2018. Longitudinal preterm cerebellar volume: perinatal and neurodevelopmental outcome associations. Cerebellum 17 (5), 610–627. https://doi.org/10.1007/s12311-018-0946-1.

McEwen, B.S., Nasca, C., Gray, J.D., 2016. Stress effects on neuronal structure: hippocampus, amygdala, and prefrontal cortex. Neuropsychopharmacology 41 (1), 3–23. https://doi.org/10.1038/npp.2015.171.

McKinstry, R.C., 2002. Radial organization of developing preterm human cerebral cortex revealed by non-invasive water diffusion anisotropy MRI. Cereb. Cortex 12 (12), 1237–1243. https://doi.org/10.1093/cercor/12.12.1237.

Ment, L.R., Kesler, S., Vohr, B., et al., 2009. Longitudinal brain volume changes in preterm and term control subjects during late childhood and adolescence. Pediatrics 123 (2), 503–511. https://doi.org/10.1542/peds.2008-0025.

Moeskops, P., Benders, M.J.N.L., Kersbergen, K.J., et al., 2015. Development of cortical morphology evaluated with longitudinal MR brain images of preterm infants. PLoS One 10 (7). https://doi.org/10.1371/journal.pone.0131552, e0131552.

Monson, B.B., Anderson, P.J., Matthews, L.G., et al., 2016. Examination of the pattern of growth of cerebral tissue volumes from hospital discharge to early childhood in very preterm infants. JAMA Pediatr. 170 (8), 772–779. https://doi.org/10.1001/jamapediatrics.2016.0781.

Montagna, A., Nosarti, C., 2016. Socio-emotional development following very preterm birth: pathways to psychopathology. Front. Psychol. 7. https://doi.org/10.3389/fpsyg.2016.00080.

Moseley, M.E., Cohen, Y., Mintorovitch, J., et al., 1990. Early detection of regional cerebral ischemia in cats: comparison of diffusion- and T2-weighted MRI and spectroscopy. Magn. Reson. Med. 14 (2), 330–346. https://doi.org/10.1002/mrm.1910140218.

Movsas, T.Z., Pinto-Martin, J.A., Whitaker, A.H., et al., 2013. Autism spectrum disorder is associated with ventricular enlargement in a low birth weight population. J. Pediatr. 163 (1), 73–78. https://doi.org/10.1016/j.jpeds.2012.12.084.

Mrzljak, L., Uylings, H.B., Kostovic, I., van Eden, C.G., 1992. Prenatal development of neurons in the human prefrontal cortex. II. A quantitative Golgi study. J. Comp. Neurol. 316 (4), 485–496. https://doi.org/10.1002/cne.903160408.

Murray, A.L., Scratch, S.E., Thompson, D.K., et al., 2014. Neonatal brain pathology predicts adverse attention and processing speed outcomes in very preterm and/or very low birth weight children. Neuropsychology 28 (4), 552–562. https://doi.org/10.1037/neu0000071.

Murray, A.L., Thompson, D.K., Pascoe, L., et al., 2016. White matter abnormalities and impaired attention abilities in children born very preterm. NeuroImage 124, 75–84. https://doi.org/10.1016/j.neuroimage.2015.08.044.

Myers, E.H., Hampson, M., Vohr, B., et al., 2010. Functional connectivity to a right hemisphere language center in prematurely born adolescents. NeuroImage 51 (4), 1445–1452. https://doi.org/10.1016/j.neuroimage.2010.03.049.

Nagy, Z., Ashburner, J., Andersson, J., et al., 2009. Structural correlates of preterm birth in the adolescent brain. Pediatrics 124 (5), e964–e972. https://doi.org/10.1542/peds.2008-3801.

Neil, J.J., 2008. Diffusion imaging concepts for clinicians. J. Magn. Reson. Imaging 27 (1), 1–7. https://doi.org/10.1002/jmri.21087.

Neil, J.J., Shiran, S.I., McKinstry, R.C., et al., 1998. Normal brain in human newborns: apparent diffusion coefficient and diffusion anisotropy measured by using diffusion tensor MR imaging. Radiology 209 (1), 57–66. https://doi.org/10.1148/radiology.209.1.9769812.

Northam, G.B., Liégeois, F., Tournier, J.-D., et al., 2012. Interhemispheric temporal lobe connectivity predicts language impairment in adolescents born preterm. Brain 135 (Pt 12), 3781–3798. https://doi.org/10.1093/brain/aws276.

Nosarti, C., Giouroukou, E., Healy, E., et al., 2007. Grey and white matter distribution in very preterm adolescents mediates neurodevelopmental outcome. Brain. https://doi.org/10.1093/brain/awm282. Published online December 3.

O'Reilly, H., Johnson, S., Ni, Y., Wolke, D., Marlow, N., 2020. Neuropsychological outcomes at 19 years of age following extremely preterm birth. Pediatrics 145 (2). https://doi.org/10.1542/peds.2019-2087.

Orasanu, E., Melbourne, A., Cardoso, M.J., et al., 2016. Cortical folding of the preterm brain: a longitudinal analysis of extremely preterm born neonates using spectral matching. Brain Behav. 6 (8). https://doi.org/10.1002/brb3.488, e00488.

Padilla, N., Alexandrou, G., Blennow, M., Lagercrantz, H., Ådén, U., 2015. Brain growth gains and losses in extremely preterm infants at term. Cereb. Cortex 25 (7), 1897–1905. https://doi.org/10.1093/cercor/bht431.

Perani, D., Saccuman, M.C., Scifo, P., et al., 2011. Neural language networks at birth. Proc. Natl. Acad. Sci. U. S. A. 108 (38), 16056–16061. https://doi.org/10.1073/pnas.1102991108.

Perlman, J.M., 1998. White matter injury in the preterm infant: an important determination of abnormal neurodevelopment outcome. Early Hum. Dev. 53 (2), 99–120. https://doi.org/10.1016/S0378-3782(98)00037-1.

Petanjek, Z., Judas, M., Kostović, I., Uylings, H.B.M., 2008. Lifespan alterations of basal dendritic trees of pyramidal neurons in the human prefrontal cortex: a layer-specific pattern. Cereb. Cortex 18 (4), 915–929. https://doi.org/10.1093/cercor/bhm124.

Petanjek, Z., Judaš, M., Šimić, G., et al., 2011. Extraordinary neoteny of synaptic spines in the human prefrontal cortex. Proc. Natl. Acad. Sci. 108 (32), 13281–13286. https://doi.org/10.1073/pnas.1105108108.

Peterson, B.S., 2000. Regional brain volume abnormalities and long-term cognitive outcome in preterm infants. JAMA 284 (15), 1939. https://doi.org/10.1001/jama.284.15.1939.

Peyton, C., Einspieler, C., Fjørtoft, T., et al., 2020. Correlates of normal and abnormal general movements in infancy and long-term neurodevelopment of preterm infants: insights from functional connectivity studies at term equivalence. J. Clin. Med. 9 (3), 834. https://doi.org/10.3390/jcm9030834.

Poehlmann-Tynan, J., Gerstein, E., Burnson, C., et al., 2015. Risk and resilience in preterm children at age 6. Dev. Psychopathol. 27 (3), 843–858. https://doi.org/10.1017/S095457941400087X. .

Pogribna, U., Burson, K., Lasky, R.E., Narayana, P.A., Evans, P.W., Parikh, N.A., 2014. Role of diffusion tensor imaging as an independent predictor of cognitive and language development in extremely low-birth-weight infants. AJNR Am. J. Neuroradiol. 35 (4), 790–796. https://doi.org/10.3174/ajnr.A3725.

Price, J.L., 2003. Comparative aspects of amygdala connectivity. Ann. N. Y. Acad. Sci. 985, 50–58.

Pritchard, V.E., Bora, S., Austin, N.C., Levin, K.J., Woodward, L.J., 2014. Identifying very preterm children at educational risk using a school readiness framework. Pediatrics 134 (3), e825–e832. https://doi.org/10.1542/peds.2013-3865.

Provenzi, L., Giusti, L., Fumagalli, M., et al., 2016. Pain-related stress in the neonatal intensive care unit and salivary cortisol reactivity to socio-emotional stress in 3-month-old very preterm infants. Psychoneuroendocrinology 72, 161–165. https://doi.org/10.1016/j.psyneuen.2016.07.010.

Qin, S., Young, C.B., Duan, X., Chen, T., Supekar, K., Menon, V., 2014. Amygdala subregional structure and intrinsic functional connectivity predicts individual differences in anxiety during early childhood. Biol. Psychiatry 75 (11), 892–900. https://doi.org/10.1016/j.biopsych.2013.10.006.

Ramphal, B., Whalen, D.J., Kenley, J.K., et al., 2020. Brain connectivity and socioeconomic status at birth and externalizing symptoms at age 2 years. Dev. Cogn. Neurosci. https://doi.org/10.1016/j.dcn.2020.100811, 100811. Published online June 30.

Rausch, A., Zhang, W., Haak, K.V., et al., 2016. Altered functional connectivity of the amygdaloid input nuclei in adolescents and young adults with autism spectrum disorder: a resting state fMRI study. Mol. Autism 7, 13. https://doi.org/10.1186/s13229-015-0060-x.

Rha, D., Chang, W.H., Kim, J., Sim, E.G., Park, E.S., 2012. Comparing quantitative tractography metrics of motor and sensory pathways in children with periventricular leukomalacia and different levels of gross motor function. Neuroradiology 54 (6), 615–621. https://doi.org/10.1007/s00234-011-0996-2.

Rogers, C.E., Anderson, P.J., Thompson, D.K., et al., 2012. Regional cerebral development at term relates to school-age social-emotional development in very preterm children. J. Am. Acad. Child Adolesc. Psychiatry 51 (2), 181–191. https://doi.org/10.1016/j.jaac.2011.11.009.

Rogers, C.E., Lenze, S.N., Luby, J.L., 2013. Late preterm birth, maternal depression, and risk of preschool psychiatric disorders. J. Am. Acad. Child Adolesc. Psychiatry 52 (3), 309–318. https://doi.org/10.1016/j.jaac.2012.12.005.

Rogers, C.E., Smyser, T., Smyser, C.D., Shimony, J., Inder, T.E., Neil, J.J., 2015. Regional white matter development in very preterm infants: perinatal predictors and early developmental outcomes. Pediatr. Res. https://doi.org/10.1038/pr.2015.172. Published online September 15.

Rogers, C.E., Sylvester, C.M., Mintz, C., et al., 2017. Neonatal amygdala functional connectivity at rest in healthy and preterm infants and early internalizing symptoms. J. Am. Acad. Child Adolesc. Psychiatry 56 (2), 157–166. https://doi.org/10.1016/j.jaac.2016.11.005.

Ross, G.S., Foran, L.M., Barbot, B., Sossin, K.M., Perlman, J.M., 2016. Using cluster analysis to provide new insights into development of very low birthweight (VLBW) premature infants. Early Hum. Dev. 92, 45–49. https://doi.org/10.1016/j.earlhumdev.2015.11.005.

Roy, A.K., Fudge, J.L., Kelly, C., et al., 2013. Intrinsic functional connectivity of amygdala-based networks in adolescent generalized anxiety disorder. J. Am. Acad. Child Adolesc. Psychiatry 52 (3), 290–299.e2. https://doi.org/10.1016/j.jaac.2012.12.010.

Sandman, C.A., Davis, E.P., Buss, C., Glynn, L.M., 2011. Prenatal programming of human neurological function. Int. J. Pept. 2011, 1–9. https://doi.org/10.1155/2011/837596.

Sansavini, A., Pentimonti, J., Justice, L., et al., 2014. Language, motor and cognitive development of extremely preterm children: modeling individual growth trajectories over the first three years of life. J. Commun. Disord. 49, 55–68. https://doi.org/10.1016/j.jcomdis.2014.02.005.

Scheinost, D., Benjamin, J., Lacadie, C., et al., 2012. The intrinsic connectivity distribution: a novel contrast measure reflecting voxel level functional connectivity. NeuroImage 62 (3), 1510–1519. https://doi.org/10.1016/j.neuroimage.2012.05.073.

Scheinost, D., Kwon, S.H., Lacadie, C., et al., 2016. Prenatal stress alters amygdala functional connectivity in preterm neonates. NeuroImage 12, 381–388. https://doi.org/10.1016/j.nicl.2016.08.010.

Scheinost, D., Lacadie, C., Vohr, B.R., et al., 2015. Cerebral lateralization is protective in the very prematurely born. Cereb. Cortex 25 (7), 1858–1866. https://doi.org/10.1093/cercor/bht430.

Schieve, L.A., Tian, L.H., Rankin, K., et al., 2016. Population impact of preterm birth and low birth weight on developmental disabilities in US children. Ann. Epidemiol. 26 (4), 267–274. https://doi.org/10.1016/j.annepidem.2016.02.012.

Scott, M.N., Taylor, H.G., Fristad, M.A., et al., 2012. Behavior disorders in extremely preterm/extremely low birth weight children in kindergarten. J. Dev. Behav. Pediatr. 33 (3), 202–213. https://doi.org/10.1097/DBP.0b013e3182475287.

Shimony, J.S., Smyser, C.D., Wideman, G., et al., 2016. Comparison of cortical folding measures for evaluation of developing human brain. NeuroImage 125, 780–790. https://doi.org/10.1016/j.neuroimage.2015.11.001.

Shukla, D.K., Keehn, B., Müller, R.-A., 2011. Tract-specific analyses of diffusion tensor imaging show widespread white matter compromise in autism spectrum disorder. J. Child Psychol. Psychiatry 52 (3), 286–295. https://doi.org/10.1111/j.1469-7610.2010.02342.x.

Shum, D., Neulinger, K., O'Callaghan, M., Mohay, H., 2008. Attentional problems in children born very preterm or with extremely low birth weight at 7–9 years. Arch. Clin. Neuropsychol. 23 (1), 103–112. https://doi.org/10.1016/j.acn.2007.08.006.

Silk, T.J., Vance, A., Rinehart, N., Bradshaw, J.L., Cunnington, R., 2009. White-matter abnormalities in attention deficit hyperactivity disorder: a diffusion tensor imaging study. Hum. Brain Mapp. 30 (9), 2757–2765. https://doi.org/10.1002/hbm.20703.

Smith, G.C., Gutovich, J., Smyser, C., et al., 2011. Neonatal intensive care unit stress is associated with brain development in preterm infants. Ann. Neurol. 70 (4), 541–549. https://doi.org/10.1002/ana.22545.

Smith, S.M., Fox, P.T., Miller, K.L., et al., 2009. Correspondence of the brain's functional architecture during activation and rest. Proc. Natl. Acad. Sci. 106 (31), 13040–13045.

Smyser, C.D., Dosenbach, N.U.F., Smyser, T.A., et al., 2016b. Prediction of brain maturity in infants using machine-learning algorithms. NeuroImage 136, 1–9. https://doi.org/10.1016/j.neuroimage.2016.05.029.

Smyser, C.D., Inder, T.E., Shimony, J.S., et al., 2010. Longitudinal analysis of neural network development in preterm infants. Cereb. Cortex 20 (12), 2852–2862. https://doi.org/10.1093/cercor/bhq035.

Smyser, C.D., Neil, J.J., 2015. Use of resting-state functional MRI to study brain development and injury in neonates. Semin. Perinatol. 39 (2), 130–140. https://doi.org/10.1053/j.semperi.2015.01.006.

Smyser, C.D., Snyder, A.Z., Shimony, J.S., Blazey, T.M., Inder, T.E., Neil, J.J., 2013. Effects of white matter injury on resting state fMRI measures in prematurely born infants. PLoS ONE 8 (7). https://doi.org/10.1371/journal.pone.0068098, e68098.

Smyser, C.D., Snyder, A.Z., Shimony, J.S., Mitra, A., Inder, T.E., Neil, J.J., 2016a. Resting-state network complexity and magnitude are reduced in prematurely born infants. Cereb. Cortex 26 (1), 322–333. https://doi.org/10.1093/cercor/bhu251.

Solso, S., Xu, R., Proudfoot, J., et al., 2016. Diffusion tensor imaging provides evidence of possible axonal overconnectivity in frontal lobes in autism spectrum disorder toddlers. Biol. Psychiatry 79 (8), 676–684. https://doi.org/10.1016/j.biopsych.2015.06.029.

Song, S.-K., Sun, S.-W., Ramsbottom, M.J., Chang, C., Russell, J., Cross, A.H., 2002. Dysmyelination revealed through MRI as increased radial (but unchanged axial) diffusion of water. NeuroImage 17 (3), 1429–1436. https://doi.org/10.1006/nimg.2002.1267.

Song, S.-K., Yoshino, J., Le, T.Q., et al., 2005. Demyelination increases radial diffusivity in corpus callosum of mouse brain. NeuroImage 26 (1), 132–140. https://doi.org/10.1016/j.neuroimage.2005.01.028.

Soria-Pastor, S., Padilla, N., Zubiaurre-Elorza, L., et al., 2009. Decreased regional brain volume and cognitive impairment in preterm children at low risk. Pediatrics 124 (6), e1161–e1170. https://doi.org/10.1542/peds.2009-0244.

Soun, J.E., Liu, M.Z., Cauley, K.A., Grinband, J., 2017. Evaluation of neonatal brain myelination using the T1- and T2-weighted MRI ratio. J. Magn. Reson. Imaging 46 (3), 690–696. https://doi.org/10.1002/jmri.25570.

Spittle, A.J., Cameron, K., Doyle, L.W., Cheong, J.L., Group for the VICS, 2018. Motor impairment trends in extremely preterm children: 1991–2005. Pediatrics 141 (4). https://doi.org/10.1542/peds.2017-3410.

Spittle, A.J., Treyvaud, K., Doyle, L.W., et al., 2009. Early emergence of behavior and social-emotional problems in very preterm infants. J. Am. Acad. Child Adolesc. Psychiatry 48 (9), 909–918. https://doi.org/10.1097/CHI.0b013e3181af8235.

Sporns, O., Tononi, G., Kötter, R., 2005. The human connectome: a structural description of the human brain. PLoS Comput. Biol. 1 (4). https://doi.org/10.1371/journal.pcbi.0010042, e42.

Srinivasan, L., Allsop, J., Counsell, S.J., Boardman, J.P., Edwards, A.D., Rutherford, M., 2006. Smaller cerebellar volumes in very preterm infants at term-equivalent age are associated with the presence of supratentorial lesions. Am. J. Neuroradiol. 27 (3), 573–579.

Sripada, K., Løhaugen, G.C., Eikenes, L., et al., 2015. Visual-motor deficits relate to altered gray and white matter in young adults born preterm with very low birth weight. NeuroImage 109, 493–504. https://doi.org/10.1016/j.neuroimage.2015.01.019.

Strahle, J.M., Triplett, R.L., Alexopoulos, D., et al., 2019. Impaired hippocampal development and outcomes in very preterm infants with perinatal brain injury. Neuroimage Clin. 22, 101787. https://doi.org/10.1016/j.nicl.2019.101787.

Sylvester, C., Rogers, C., Pine, D., Petersen, S., Luby, J., Smyser, C., 2020. Maternal anxiety and neonatal brain response to novel sounds as measured with fMRI. Biol. Psychiatry 87 (9), S83. https://doi.org/10.1016/j.biopsych.2020.02.234.

Sylvester, C.M., Smyser, C.D., Smyser, T., et al., 2017. Cortical functional connectivity evident after birth and behavioral inhibition at age 2. Am. J. Psychiatry. https://doi.org/10.1176/appi.ajp.2017.17010018, appiajp201717010018. Published online August 4.

Thompson, D.K., Adamson, C., Roberts, G., et al., 2013. Hippocampal shape variations at term equivalent age in very preterm infants compared with term controls: perinatal predictors and functional significance at age 7. NeuroImage 70, 278–287. https://doi.org/10.1016/j.neuroimage.2012.12.053.

Thompson, D.K., Chen, J., Beare, R., et al., 2016. Structural connectivity relates to perinatal factors and functional impairment at 7 years in children born very preterm. NeuroImage 134, 328–337. https://doi.org/10.1016/j.neuroimage.2016.03.070.

Thompson, D.K., Inder, T.E., Faggian, N., et al., 2012. Corpus callosum alterations in very preterm infants: perinatal correlates and 2 year neurodevelopmental outcomes. NeuroImage 59 (4), 3571–3581. https://doi.org/10.1016/j.neuroimage.2011.11.057.

Thompson, D.K., Lee, K.J., Egan, G.F., et al., 2014. Regional white matter microstructure in very preterm infants: predictors and 7 year outcomes. Cortex 52, 60–74. https://doi.org/10.1016/j.cortex.2013.11.010.

Thompson, D.K., Lee, K.J., van Bijnen, L., et al., 2015. Accelerated corpus callosum development in prematurity predicts improved outcome: longitudinal corpus callosum development. Hum. Brain Mapp. 36 (10), 3733–3748. https://doi.org/10.1002/hbm.22874.

Toulmin, H., Beckmann, C.F., O'Muircheartaigh, J., et al., 2015. Specialization and integration of functional thalamocortical connectivity in the human infant. Proc. Natl. Acad. Sci. 112 (20), 6485–6490. https://doi.org/10.1073/pnas.1422638112.

Treyvaud, K., Ure, A., Doyle, L.W., et al., 2013. Psychiatric outcomes at age seven for very preterm children: rates and predictors: psychiatric outcome for very preterm children. J. Child Psychol. Psychiatry 54 (7), 772–779. https://doi.org/10.1111/jcpp.12040.

Ullman, H., Spencer-Smith, M., Thompson, D.K., et al., 2015. Neonatal MRI is associated with future cognition and academic achievement in preterm children. Brain 138 (11), 3251–3262. https://doi.org/10.1093/brain/awv244.

Van Essen, D.C., 2013. Cartography and connectomes. Neuron 80 (3), 775–790. https://doi.org/10.1016/j.neuron.2013.10.027.

Van Essen, D.C., Dierker, D., Snyder, A.Z., Raichle, M.E., Reiss, A.L., Korenberg, J., 2006. Symmetry of cortical folding abnormalities in Williams syndrome revealed by surface-based analyses. J. Neurosci. 26 (20), 5470–5483. https://doi.org/10.1523/JNEUROSCI.4154-05.2006.

Vassar, R., Schadl, K., Cahill-Rowley, K., Yeom, K., Stevenson, D., Rose, J., 2020. Neonatal brain microstructure and machine-learning-based prediction of early language development in children born very preterm. Pediatr. Neurol. 108, 86–92. https://doi.org/10.1016/j.pediatrneurol.2020.02.007.

Vollmer, B., Lundequist, A., Martensson, G., et al., 2017. Correlation between white matter microstructure and executive functions suggests early developmental influence on long fiber tracts in preterm born adolescents. PLoS One 12 (6). https://doi.org/10.1371/journal.pone.0178893, e0179993.

Volpe, J.J., 2009. Brain injury in premature infants: a complex amalgam of destructive and developmental disturbances. Lancet Neurol. 8 (1), 110–124. https://doi.org/10.1016/S1474-4422(08)70294-1.

Volpe, J.J., Inder, T.E., Darras, B.T., et al., 2018. Volpe's Neurology of the Newborn, sixth ed. Elsevier, https://doi.org/10.1016/C2010-0-68825-0.

Walshe, M., Rifkin, L., Rooney, M., et al., 2008. Psychiatric disorder in young adults born very preterm: role of family history. Eur. Psychiatry 23 (7), 527–531. https://doi.org/10.1016/j.eurpsy.2008.06.004.

Wang, S., Fan, G., Xu, K., Wang, C., 2013. Potential of diffusion tensor MR imaging in the assessment of cognitive impairments in children with periventricular leukomalacia born preterm. Eur. J. Radiol. 82 (1), 158–164. https://doi.org/10.1016/j.ejrad.2012.06.032.

Wang, S., Fan, G.G., Xu, K., Wang, C., 2014. Altered microstructural connectivity of the superior and middle cerebellar peduncles are related to motor dysfunction in children with diffuse periventricular leucomalacia born preterm: a DTI tractography study. Eur. J. Radiol. 83 (6), 997–1004. https://doi.org/10.1016/j.ejrad.2014.03.010.

Weinstock, M., 2008. The long-term behavioural consequences of prenatal stress. Neurosci. Biobehav. Rev. 32 (6), 1073–1086. https://doi.org/10.1016/j.neubiorev.2008.03.002.

Wheelock, M.D., Austin, N.C., Bora, S., et al., 2018. Altered functional network connectivity relates to motor development in children born very preterm. NeuroImage 183, 574–583. https://doi.org/10.1016/j.neuroimage.2018.08.051.

White, T.P., Symington, I., Castellanos, N.P., et al., 2014. Dysconnectivity of neurocognitive networks at rest in very-preterm born adults. Neuroimage Clin. 4, 352–365. https://doi.org/10.1016/j.nicl.2014.01.005.

Wilke, M., Hauser, T.-K., Krägeloh-Mann, I., Lidzba, K., 2014. Specific impairment of functional connectivity between language regions in former early preterms. Hum. Brain Mapp. 35 (7), 3372–3384. https://doi.org/10.1002/hbm.22408.

Williams, J., Lee, K.J., Anderson, P.J., 2010. Prevalence of motor-skill impairment in preterm children who do not develop cerebral palsy: a systematic review. Dev. Med. Child Neurol. 52 (3), 232–237. https://doi.org/10.1111/j.1469-8749.2009.03544.x.

Wimberger, D.M., Roberts, T.P., Barkovich, A.J., Prayer, L.M., Moseley, M.E., Kucharczyk, J., 1995. Identification of "premyelination" by diffusion-weighted MRI. J. Comput. Assist. Tomogr. 19 (1), 28–33. https://doi.org/10.1097/00004728-199501000-00005.

Wolf, M.J., Koldewijn, K., Beelen, A., Smit, B., Hedlund, R., de Groot, I.J.M., 2002. Neurobehavioral and developmental profile of very low birthweight preterm infants in early infancy. Acta Paediatr. 91 (8), 930–938.

Wolff, J.J., Gu, H., Gerig, G., et al., 2012. Differences in white matter fiber tract development present from 6 to 24 months in infants with autism. Am. J. Psychiatry 169 (6), 589–600. https://doi.org/10.1176/appi.ajp.2011.11091447.

Wolke, D., Samara, M., Bracewell, M., Marlow, N., 2008. Specific language difficulties and school achievement in children born at 25 weeks of gestation or less. J. Pediatr. 152 (2), 256–262.e1. https://doi.org/10.1016/j.jpeds.2007.06.043.

Woodward, L.J., Clark, C.A.C., Pritchard, V.E., Anderson, P.J., Inder, T.E., 2011. Neonatal White matter abnormalities predict global executive function impairment in children born very preterm. Dev. Neuropsychol. 36 (1), 22–41. https://doi.org/10.1080/87565641.2011.540530.

Woodward, L.J., Lu, Z., Morris, A.R., Healey, D.M., 2017. Preschool self regulation predicts later mental health and educational achievement in very preterm and typically developing children. Clin. Neuropsychol. 31 (2), 404–422. https://doi.org/10.1080/13854046.2016.1251614.

Woodward, L.J., Moor, S., Hood, K.M., et al., 2009. Very preterm children show impairments across multiple neurodevelopmental domains by age 4 years. Arch. Dis. Child. Fetal Neonatal Ed. 94 (5), F339–F344. https://doi.org/10.1136/adc.2008.146282.

Wu, Y.-H., Gau, S.S.-F., Lo, Y.-C., Tseng, W.-Y.I., 2012. White matter tract integrity of frontostriatal circuit in attention deficit hyperactivity disorder: association with attention performance and symptoms. Hum. Brain Mapp. https://doi.org/10.1002/hbm.22169. Published online 2012.

Yates, R., Treyvaud, K., Doyle, L.W., et al., 2020. Rates and stability of mental health disorders in children born very preterm at 7 and 13 years. Pediatrics 145 (5). https://doi.org/10.1542/peds.2019-2699, e20192699.

Young, J.M., Morgan, B.R., Whyte, H.E.A., et al., 2016. Longitudinal study of White matter development and outcomes in children born very preterm. Cereb. Cortex. https://doi.org/10.1093/cercor/bhw221. Published online 6 September.

Zubiaurre-Elorza, L., Soria-Pastor, S., Junqué, C., et al., 2012. Thalamic changes in a preterm sample with periventricular leukomalacia: correlation with white-matter integrity and cognitive outcome at school age. Pediatr. Res. 71, 354.

CHAPTER 21

Risk of abnormal outcomes based on basic and advanced MRI measurements

Banu Ahtam[a,b], Marina Solti[a,b], and P. Ellen Grant[a,b]

Department of Pediatrics, Harvard Medical School, Boston, MA, United States[a] Fetal-Neonatal Neuroimaging and Developmental Science Center, Division of Newborn Medicine, Boston Children's Hospital, Boston, MA, United States[b]

1. Introduction

Pre- and peri-natal conditions such as preterm birth, hypoxic-ischemic encephalopathy (HIE), perinatal stroke, and congenital heart disease (CHD), as well as neurodevelopmental disorders are highly associated with varying degrees of brain injury and/or structural abnormalities as well as adverse outcomes such as cognitive disabilities, behavioral problems, or psychomotor impairments (Rutherford et al., 2010c; Anderson et al., 2015; Groenendaal and de Vries, 2017; Mebius et al., 2017). Such neurodevelopmental delays and impairments affect the patient's quality of life by interfering with social and educational aspects of the child's life that persist into adulthood. Brain injuries can be difficult to assess, and some disorders may have delays between onset of symptoms and time of injury (Wolff et al., 2015; Rollins et al., 2017; Kuhl et al., 2020). Conditions that interfere with typical development should be closely monitored and therapeutic planning is essential in order to offer the best support possible to optimize neurodevelopmental outcomes (D'Mello et al., 2016).

In order to investigate brain abnormalities in newborns, especially preterm or unstable newborns, the standard of care has been cranial ultrasound (cUS) (Kwon et al., 2014; AIUM Practice Parameter for the Performance of Neurosonography in Neonates and Infants, 2020; Hand et al., 2020). This exam modality offers a quick, safe, readily available, and inexpensive bedside imaging tool to observe the neonate's brain, identifying lesions such as periventricular leukomalacia, intra or periventricular hemorrhage, and cerebellar injury. cUS is a good option for monitoring brain health within the first week of life, as it is easy to take multiple scans of the same patient at the bedside, with minimal disruption of their care in the intensive care unit (ICU) (van Wezel-Meijler et al., 2010). Despite its advantages, cUS has a significantly lower sensitivity for detecting acute ischemic injury and subtle or small abnormalities, when compared to Magnetic Resonance Imaging (MRI) (Leijser et al., 2010). Therefore, MRI has become the study of choice to fully document neonatal and infant brain abnormalities.

MRI is a noninvasive imaging modality that is used to acquire high-resolution images of brain structure and additional information with the use of specialized sequences and analysis techniques. This technique uses magnetic fields to evaluate the brain's structure without radiation. In clinical practice, it is the method of choice to evaluate a neonates' brain for injury or malformation (Barkovich and

Handbook of Pediatric Brain Imaging. https://doi.org/10.1016/B978-0-12-816633-8.00020-X

Raybaud, 2019). Furthermore, with good preparation and the close communication between the neonatal intensive care unit (NICU) and Radiology Departments, the transfer of the neonates from the NICU environment to the MRI scanner and scanning successfully without sedation is nowadays possible with success rates over 90% (Hüppi et al., 1998; Vigneron et al., 2001; Mathur et al., 2008; Haney et al., 2010; Neubauer et al., 2011; Smyser et al., 2012). Even imaging of young children up to 2 years of age and from 4 years old and up is often successful without sedation in many circumstances with appropriate preparation (Jaimes et al., 2020). Efforts to improve clinical MRI success across the ages, especially in those less than 3 years old, continue with motion mitigation strategies and child-friendly environments as repetitive sedation may have a negative impact on cognitive development and requires significant resources (Center for Drug Evaluation and Research, 2019; Frost et al., 2019).

Conventional T1-weighted and T2-weighted MRI sequences provide key information on brain structure and lack the sensitivity to detect acute ischemic injury and vacuolar change and for these purposes diffusion-weighted imaging is needed (Schaefer et al., 2000; Sagar and Grant, 2006; Rodrigues and Grant, 2011; Sakuma et al., 1991; Pannek et al., 2014). In addition to information on water compartmentalization, diffusion MRI (dMRI) offers insight into the microstructural organization of brain tissue. DTI tractography can generate 3D models and provide diffusivity measurements of white matter tracts that subserve different brain functions such as the corticospinal tract for motor and the arcuate fasciculus for language. DTI helps visualize the structural and functional integrity of the tracts and can be used in serial scans to compare the evolution of each one over time. Diffusivity metrics such as the Apparent Diffusion Coefficient (ADC) and Fractional Anisotropy (FA) obtained through dMRI help quantify changes with injury evolution due to underlying developmental disorders and with maturational change over time (Pannek et al., 2014; Plaisier et al., 2014). Proton MR spectroscopy is also routinely available, providing information on metabolites such as *N*-acetyl-aspartate (a marker of neuronal health and dendritic development) and detecting lactate (a marker of anaerobic metabolism seen with ischemic injuries and some metabolic disorders) (Groenendaal et al., 1994; Amess et al., 1999; Roelants-Van Rijn et al., 2001; Brissaud et al., 2005; L'Abee et al., 2005; Cheong et al., 2006; Shanmugalingam et al., 2006). Resting-state functional magnetic resonance imaging (rsfMRI) provides information on neurovascular health and functional localization and although a promising technique, it is yet uncommonly used in clinical practice.

This chapter will overview four principal neonatal conditions where there is a desire to use MRI modalities and measurements to provide risk assessments for altered neurodevelopmental outcomes namely, preterm birth, HIE, perinatal stroke, and CHD. In addition, as all of these medical conditions lead to increased risk of developmental disorders such as autism spectrum disorder (ASD) and language-based learning disabilities, we will also briefly discuss the role of MR imaging in providing risk assessments for ASD and developmental dyslexia.

2. Preterm birth

It is estimated that there are approximately 14.9 million preterm births per year worldwide (Blencowe et al., 2012), which represents 11.1% of all live births per year. Preterm birth has an increased risk of infant mortality and adverse neurodevelopmental outcomes (Pannek et al., 2014), and can be accompanied by subsequent brain injury (Saigal and Doyle, 2009; Plaisier et al., 2014). Physiological stress associated with preterm birth in or before the third-trimester affects regional brain maturation (Peterson et al., 2000). Even though advances in medicine to prevent adverse health outcomes have increased the survival rates among preterm infants, especially those with very low birth weight, the ones who do survive are at increased risk for neurodevelopmental disabilities (Bhutta et al., 2002; Marlow et al., 2005; Larroque et al., 2008; Saigal and Doyle, 2008; Williams et al., 2010; Plaisier et al., 2014). These neurodevelopmental disabilities include cognitive, language, behavioral, psychological, and neurosensory difficulties, motor impairments such as cerebral palsy and mild motor dysfunction, as well as higher rates of attention deficit hyperactivity disorder and ASD (Woodward et al., 2006; Institute of Medicine, Board on Health Sciences Policy and Committee on Understanding Premature Birth and Assuring Healthy Outcomes, 2007). Approximately 50% of extremely preterm infants receive a diagnosis of cognitive impairment by the time they reach 5 years old (Potharst et al., 2011). It has been shown that about 70% of children who were born extremely preterm (<32 weeks' gestational age) have at least one significant neurodevelopmental impairment by the time they are 8 years of age, while 50% of them have multiple impairments ($N=189$) (Hutchinson et al., 2013). The variability in the developmental outcome can be explained by many factors such as neurological abnormalities, neonatal medical complications, neonatal interventions, genetic and epigenetic factors, and environmental factors (Anderson et al., 2015, 2017). The wide spectrum of developmental impairments decreases the impacted individuals' quality of life through adulthood, can create an emotional burden on their families, and has important implications for society and the economy worldwide (Maunu et al., 2009; Hodek et al., 2011; Harvey et al., 2013; Kwon et al., 2014; Ullman et al., 2015). It has been shown that there are multiple perinatal risk factors, which as a result of cumulative exposure increase the risk of white matter injury and adverse neurodevelopmental outcome ($N=491$) (Barnett et al., 2018). MRI best documents the nature and timing of brain injury as well as altered brain development and these MRI findings should be integrated with information such as perinatal risk factors, genetic and epigenetic features, as well as distal and proximal social/environmental factors, in order to assess risk for cognitive and neurodevelopmental impairments, and in turn to guide early intervention studies (Keunen et al., 2012; Anderson et al., 2015).

Common findings of structural MRI in very preterm infants at term-equivalent age (TEA) include decreased size of the corpus callosum and ventriculomegaly with a scaphocephalic head shape which may be considered as a typical preterm brain phenotypic (Arulkumaran et al., 2020; Cooke and Abernethy, 1999; Stewart et al., 1999). Delayed myelination may be appreciated in the posterior limb internal capsule (PLIC) and gyrification may be delayed (Guit et al., 1990; Inder et al., 2003; Miller et al., 2005a; Anderson et al., 2017). Common lesions include germinal matrix hemorrhage which may be associated with intraventricular extension and posthemorrhagic ventricular dilatation (Fig. 1A–C). When a germinal matrix hemorrhage is large, it can result in a hemorrhagic parenchymal infarct (Fig. 1D), although this is rare. White matter injury in the form of periventricular leukomalacia is also now rare, however, punctate white matter lesions (Fig. 1E) and subependymal cysts are common (Dyet et al., 2006; He and Parikh, 2013; Arulkumaran et al., 2020). Cerebellar hemorrhages are increasingly being recognized (Fig. 1F) and are present in almost one-third of the preterm infants examined in this study (Arulkumaran et al., 2020). More detailed analyses can reveal reduced gray and white matter volume (Stewart et al., 1999; Boardman et al., 2010; Inder et al., 1999) which is associated with enlarged lateral ventricles (Stewart et al., 1999) and larger extracerebral space (Inder et al., 2003; Miller et al., 2005a; Anderson et al., 2017). Brain volume reductions are seen in both total and regional brain tissues; cortical gray matter volume including sensorimotor, premotor, parieto-occipital, mid temporal

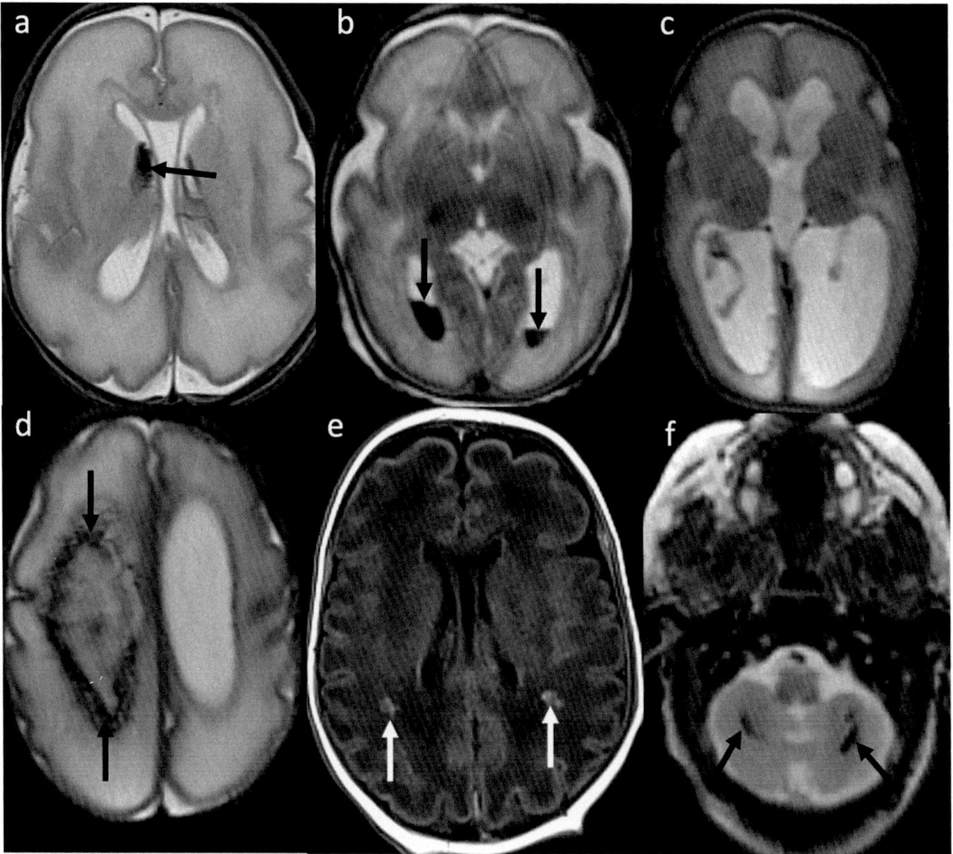

FIG. 1

Common lesions in preterm infants. (A) T2 TSE in preterm infant showing germinal matrix hemorrhage (arrow); (B) preterm infant with germinal matrix hemorrhage (not shown) and T2 TSE showing intraventricular extension (arrows show blood products layering in the occipital horns of the lateral ventricles); (C) T2 TSE in preterm infant showing post hemorrhagic ventricular dilatation with enlarged ventricles and compressed extra axial spaces secondary to germinal matrix hemorrhage (not shown); (D) T2 TSE in preterm infant showing hemorrhagic parenchymal infarct (arrows); (E) T1 image at term age in an infant born preterm shows punctate white matter injuries (arrows); (F) T2 TSE in preterm infant shows chronic cerebellar hemorrhages with hemosiderin in the bilateral cerebellar hemispheres (arrows).

cortices (Peterson et al., 2000; Young et al., 2015); subcortical gray matter volume including basal ganglia, amygdala, hippocampus, and thalamus (Peterson et al., 2000); myelinated white matter in the brainstem; unmyelinated white matter in central and orbitofrontal regions; internal capsule and cerebellar peduncles; and cerebellum (Cheong et al., 2016). Reductions in regional brain volume are more prominent for preterm infants who were born at earlier gestational ages (Inder, 2005; Limperopoulos et al., 2005; Boardman et al., 2006; Mewes et al., 2006; Srinivasan et al., 2006; Thompson et al., 2007; Keunen et al., 2012).

Some MRI findings at TEA are associated with adverse neurodevelopmental outcomes at later ages (Dyet et al., 2006; Woodward et al., 2006, 2012; Boardman et al., 2010; Iwata et al., 2012; Setänen et al., 2013; Arulkumaran et al., 2020). Decreased brain volumes have been shown to be associated with adverse neurodevelopmental and behavioral outcomes at eight years ($N = 25$) (Peterson et al., 2000). A longitudinal study of preterm infants showed that brain tissue volumes at birth and TEA are correlated with motor outcomes at 18–24 months ($N = 74$) and volumes at TEA and volume growth rates are correlated with cognitive scores at age 5 years ($N = 56$) (Gui et al., 2019). Another MRI study of preterm infants at TEA showed associations between ventricle volumes, unmyelinated white matter volume, cortical gray matter volume, cerebellar volume, and neurodevelopmental outcomes at ages 24 months, 3.5 years, and 5.5 years ($N = 112$) (Keunen et al., 2016). White matter volumes in the right hemispheric sensorimotor and mid temporal regions correlated strongly with measures of neurodevelopmental outcome, particularly with mental developmental indices at corrected ages 18–20 months ($N = 10$) (Peterson et al., 2003). An increased CSF volume and decreased total brain tissue volume at TEA are correlated with poorer cognitive performance at later ages from 1 to 5.5 years (Inder, 2005; Lind et al., 2011; Keunen et al., 2012); while increased volume of insula and putamen at TEA, are associated with better cognitive outcome, measured by performance in early mathematics at 5 and 7 years of age ($N = 195$) (Ullman et al., 2015). Increased total brain tissue, white matter, and cerebellar volumes at TEA are associated with better neurodevelopmental outcomes in late and preterm children at age 2 years ($N = 197$) (Cheong et al., 2016). Whereas increased global brain abnormalities at TEA were associated with lower cognitive, fine, and gross motor skills at 2 years corrected age ($N = 239$) (Brouwer et al., 2017). Similarly, diffuse white matter injury in preterm infants was associated with reduced developmental quotient at age 2 years ($N = 80$ and $N = 445$) (Boardman et al., 2010; Hintz et al., 2015) and later at 4 and 6 years ($N = 104$) (Woodward et al., 2012) Furthermore, the location and the extent of the white matter injury in very preterm infants are associated with cognitive and motor skills at 18 months of age ($N = 58$ and $N = 60$) (Guo et al., 2017; Cayam-Rand et al., 2019). In particular, injury of frontal areas were more associated with adverse cognitive outcomes which can be explained by altered connectivity in these regions which are responsible for cognition, learning, and memory (Guo et al., 2017; Cayam-Rand et al., 2019). In addition, white matter signal abnormalities on TEA MRI in preterm infants was associated with cognitive and language outcome at age 2 years ($N = 38$) (He and Parikh, 2013). A recent MRI study of preterm infants at TEA itemized types of brain injury and showed that 76% had acquired brain lesions with major lesions associated with a poor neurodevelopmental outcome at the 20 months of age ($N = 477$) (Arulkumaran et al., 2020). Diffusion MRI studies showed that the association between fractional anisotropy (FA) in a number of white matter pathways such as the genu of the corpus callosum and the corticospinal tracts and neurodevelopmental outcome gets stronger from earlier preterm to TEA scans and that FA can predict cognitive outcome at corrected age 18 months ($N = 166$) (Duerden et al., 2015). Other advanced MRI analysis techniques such as regional cortical curvature and surface area measures at TEA have also been shown to predict cognitive and language development at age 2 years ($N = 75$) (Kline et al., 2020). A multimodal imaging study showed that factors such as age, prematurity, intrauterine complications, and postnatal adversity, give rise to independent developmental trajectories ($N = 449$) (Ball et al., 2017).

Some MRI findings are also associated with Cerebral Palsy (CP), a condition in which there is motor impairment. Periventricular leukomalacia is among the strongest risk factors for CP ($N = 477$) (Arulkumaran et al., 2020). MRI scans performed on preterm infants between 1 and 12 months of age showed that those with higher T2-relaxation values in injured midbody periventricular WM, developed worse motor impairment between 12 and 50 months ($N = 38$) (Chen et al., 2018). Reduced volumes of total brain tissue, frontal lobes, basal ganglia and thalami, as well as cerebellum, together with neurological examination, were associated with motor outcomes and CP at age 11 years ($N = 98$) (Setänen et al., 2016). Interestingly, the presence of Punctate White Matter Lesions at TEA, in the absence of additional cerebral injuries, had a dose-dependent association with abnormal white matter microstructure and reduced thalamic volume, and worse motor outcome at 20 months of age ($N = 395$) (Tusor et al., 2017). In addition, lack of normal myelination in the PLIC at TEA has been correlated with an increased risk of motor impairment (de Vries et al., 2011; Arulkumaran et al., 2020). Similarly, low FA of the Posterior Limb of the Internal Capsule (PLIC) at 30 weeks postmenstrual age is correlated to poorer motor outcome at 2 years of age ($N = 24$) (Drobyshevsky et al., 2007). Almost all preterms without acquired focal lesions at TEA have a normal gross motor function at 20 months ($N = 477$) (Arulkumaran et al., 2020).

To better compare individual patients and outcomes, scoring systems have been developed to characterize the pattern and extent of brain injury (Kidokoro et al., 2013; Cohen et al., 2016). Many of the studies above used scoring systems to quantify white matter injury (Miller et al., 2002; Inder et al., 2003; Inder, 2005; Woodward et al., 2006, 2012; Drobyshevsky et al., 2007; Thompson et al., 2007; El-Dib et al., 2010; Leijser et al., 2010; Iwata et al., 2012; Duerden et al., 2015; Hintz et al., 2015; Ullman et al., 2015; Young et al., 2015; Keunen et al., 2016; Anderson et al., 2017; Brouwer et al., 2017; Guo et al., 2017; Cayam-Rand et al., 2019). However, these scoring systems are time-intensive, require neuroimaging expertise and efforts to calibrate each reader so similar scores are obtained on the same MRI scans. Thus although invaluable for research, these scoring systems are not in routine clinical use (Arulkumaran et al., 2020). However, a recent MRI study that simply itemized types of lesions, was also highly effective at determining the association between lesions types and outcomes ($N = 477$) (Arulkumaran et al., 2020).

To study the developing brain, there have been improvements in the last decade in MRI data acquisition quality and resolution (Ment et al., 2009) as well as the analysis techniques (for a review, see Batalle et al., 2017). Additionally, the MR sequences and head coils are optimized to provide better measurements for the neonates and infants (Hughes et al., 2017; Scheef et al., 2017). To deal with the motion, which can severely affect the image quality, MR sequences have been designed to be faster (Smith-Collins et al., 2015) or quieter (Solana et al., 2016). Furthermore, prospective (Kuperman et al., 2011) and retrospective (Cordero-Grande et al., 2016) methods for motion correction have become more common in use, increasing the quality of the data that is collected. The different tissue characteristics of the developing brain can also make image analysis challenging (Batalle et al., 2017). Age-appropriate brain templates and atlases have been created which helped follow brain development across different ages (Holland et al., 2014). Advanced diffusion data analysis allows the study of microstructural tissue characteristics of the white matter pathways, with measures such as fractional anisotropy (FA) and mean diffusivity (MD), or neurite density and orientation dispersion, as well as fiber density, which can be associated with developmental outcomes (Batalle et al., 2017). Functional MRI, both task-elicited/evoked and resting state, has been used to study the hemodynamic response function of the brain (Donaldson and Buckner, 2001) and the low frequency fluctuations (Biswal et al., 1995) to assess the functional connectivity of the developing brain. Since resting state fMRI can reflect the functional networks in the absence or stimulation (Smith et al., 2009), it has been chosen more for infant populations to study functional connectivity. Data analysis methods such as independent component analysis (ICA) or seed-based correlation approaches have been used to analyze rs-fMRI data of preterm and term infants (Doria et al., 2010). Network measures have been increasingly used in MRI data analysis where global organization of the brain can be studied using concepts such as network density, average strength, global efficiency, characteristic path length, local efficiency, and average clustering coefficient (Brown et al., 2014; van den Heuvel et al., 2015). Machine learning algorithms have been used with the rs-fMRI data of preterm infants to predict developmental outcome at 2 years of age, showing that functional brain connectome data could be a prognostic biomarker (Smyser et al., 2016; He et al., 2018, 2020). Such approaches have also been used with the DWI data of preterm neonates to identify brain regions that are most predictive of developmental outcome and classify high-risk infants for adverse outcome (Schadl et al., 2018).

3. Hypoxic ischemic encephalopathy/neonatal encephalopathy

Hypoxic ischemic encephalopathy (HIE), or neonatal encephalopathy, is a perinatal condition that results from the lack of blood flow and oxygen to the brain and can lead to significant neonatal brain injury. HIE typically occurs in term or near term neonates and has an estimated incidence rate of 1.5 per 1000 live births around the world (Kurinczuk et al., 2010) with about 27% of moderate and severely impacted newborns dying by 3 years of age (Ravichandran et al., 2020; Stoll and Kliegman, 2004). Clinical assessment of the degree of encephalopathy is routinely performed by a qualitative clinical exam with the most popular being the Sarnat score (Sarnat and Sarnat, 1976) modified to exclude EEG data, although other scoring systems exist (Garcia-Alix et al., 1994; Thompson et al., 1997; Amiel-Tison, 2002; Miller et al., 2004a). For patients with suspected HIE, therapeutic hypothermia (TH) is now the standard of care with a bedside ultrasound typically performed as soon as possible to rule out hemorrhage or other contraindications to TH. TH involves cooling the neonate to 33.5 degrees celsius beginning within the first 6 h of life and continuing for 72 h. TH has significantly improved outcomes; however, neurodevelopmental deficits, including permanent cognitive disabilities, behavioral problems, or psychomotor disabilities still occur in 40% of patients (Mwaniki et al., 2012; Cotten and Shankaran, 2010; Rogers et al., 2014; Aly et al., 2015; Shankaran et al., 2005; Gunn and Thoresen, 2019). The negative impact not only affects childhood but also extends into adolescence and beyond (Nagy et al., 2005). Thus, assessment of outcome risk in HIE is extremely important for therapeutic planning aimed at improving educational achievements and social interactions.

MRI examinations rarely play a role in decisions to perform TH as delays that might be required to obtain an MRI would impair access to the narrow time window for optimal care (Polat et al., 2013). However, to confirm the diagnosis and to document the type and extent of brain injury, an MRI is the exam of choice after completion of TH when neonates are stable to transport (Groenendaal and de Vries, 2017). HIE can be associated with different types of brain injuries that depend primarily on the severity and duration of the hypoxic ischemic insult (Cavalleri et al., 2014). However, in this era of TH, MRIs are interpreted as normal in up to 50% of cases (Rutherford et al., 2010a; Shankaran et al., 2015). The timing of the MRI is somewhat controversial as injuries evolve over time

(Barkovich et al., 2006), but should be performed within 2 weeks after birth, ideally within the first week when diffusion weighted imaging (DWI) is more sensitive ((Agut et al., 2014); (McKinstry et al., 2002; Rutherford et al., 2004)).

MRI studies of HIE infants with moderate to severe encephalopathy commonly showed signal intensity abnormalities in the posterior limb of internal capsule, ventral lateral (VL) thalamus, basal ganglia, as well as perirolandic cortex (Schneider et al., 2004; Malik et al., 2006; Logitharajah et al., 2009; Rutherford et al., 2010b; Polat et al., 2013; Shankaran et al., 2015; Mastrangelo et al., 2019). These regions are thought to be selectively vulnerable to an abrupt, severe loss in blood flow and oxygenation due to high metabolic demand (Barkovich and Raybaud, 2019). Brain injury can be seen on both conventional and DWI, but in the first week of life DWI is able to detect injury at earlier stages (Cavalleri et al., 2014; Groenendaal and de Vries, 2017; Mader et al., 2002; Ment et al., 2002; Rutherford et al., 2004; Barkovich et al., 2006; Alderliesten et al., 2011). DWI is less sensitive than conventional MRI after the first week of life since injuries evolve and no longer show decreased diffusion (McKinstry et al., 2002; Ment et al., 2002; Rutherford et al., 2004; Rutherford et al., 2010b). One study found that visually abnormal DWI studies in the first week of life, where punctate periventricular white matter injuries, single infarctions or abnormal signal in watershed zones were not included, was associated with death or major disability by 2 years ($N=32$ and $N=38$) (Cavalleri et al., 2014; Charon et al., 2016). DWI measurements such as apparent diffusion coefficient (ADC) and fractional anisotropy (FA) have been associated with later neurodevelopmental outcomes, however, it is important to note that ADC values evolve over time, so the threshold for increased or decreased values should be adapted for the timing of the exam (Groenendaal and de Vries, 2017). A DWI study conducted within the first 3 weeks after birth showed that children with HIE and unfavorable outcomes at the age of 24 months had lower FA in the corpus callosum, inferior longitudinal fasciculus, cingulum, centrum semiovale, anterior and posterior limbs of the internal capsule, external capsules, fornix, cerebral peduncles, and optic radiations when compared to the children who had favorable outcomes ($N=43$) (Tusor et al., 2012). Although conventional T1 and T2-weighted imaging may not be as sensitive in the first week, conventional MRI scans augmented with DWI in the first few days of life may offer better information on neurodevelopmental biomarkers (Twomey et al., 2010; Charon et al., 2016). A more recent study included assessment of both structural and diffusion MRI of neonates treated with TH, grading extent of brain injury grouped into deep gray matter, white matter/cortex and cerebellum, found that the deep gray matter involvement was an independent predictor of adverse outcome at 2 years and school age with white matter and cerebellar subscores not adding to the predictive value ($N=173$) (Weeke et al., 2018) (Fig. 2). Serial MRI studies are often conducted to improve predictions of neurodevelopmental outcome at 4 years of age with the MRI findings of the neonatal period shown to have the highest negative predictive value and the MRI findings at 4 months of age the highest predictive value for poor neurologic outcome ($N=21$) (Belet et al., 2004). Furthermore, in infants with HIE, volume in brain regions associated with language function measured at 6 months has been correlated with language skills at age 30 months ($N=32$) (Shapiro et al., 2017).

Advanced imaging techniques such as proton MR spectroscopy (^{1}H-MRS) have been used to predict neurodevelopmental outcomes in patients with HIE. One study found that myo-inositol/*N*-acetylaspartate peak height ratio was highly correlated with neurodevelopmental outcome at 2 years of age ($N=51$) (Barta et al., 2018). Others have also reported correlations with proton MRS of basal ganglia and thalamus with neurodevelopmental outcomes (Peden et al., 1993; Groenendaal et al., 1994; Thayyil et al., 2010; Lally et al., 2019). A proton MRS study of less than 1-week-old infants with HIE showed that gray matter choline levels were negatively correlated with gross motor skills and that

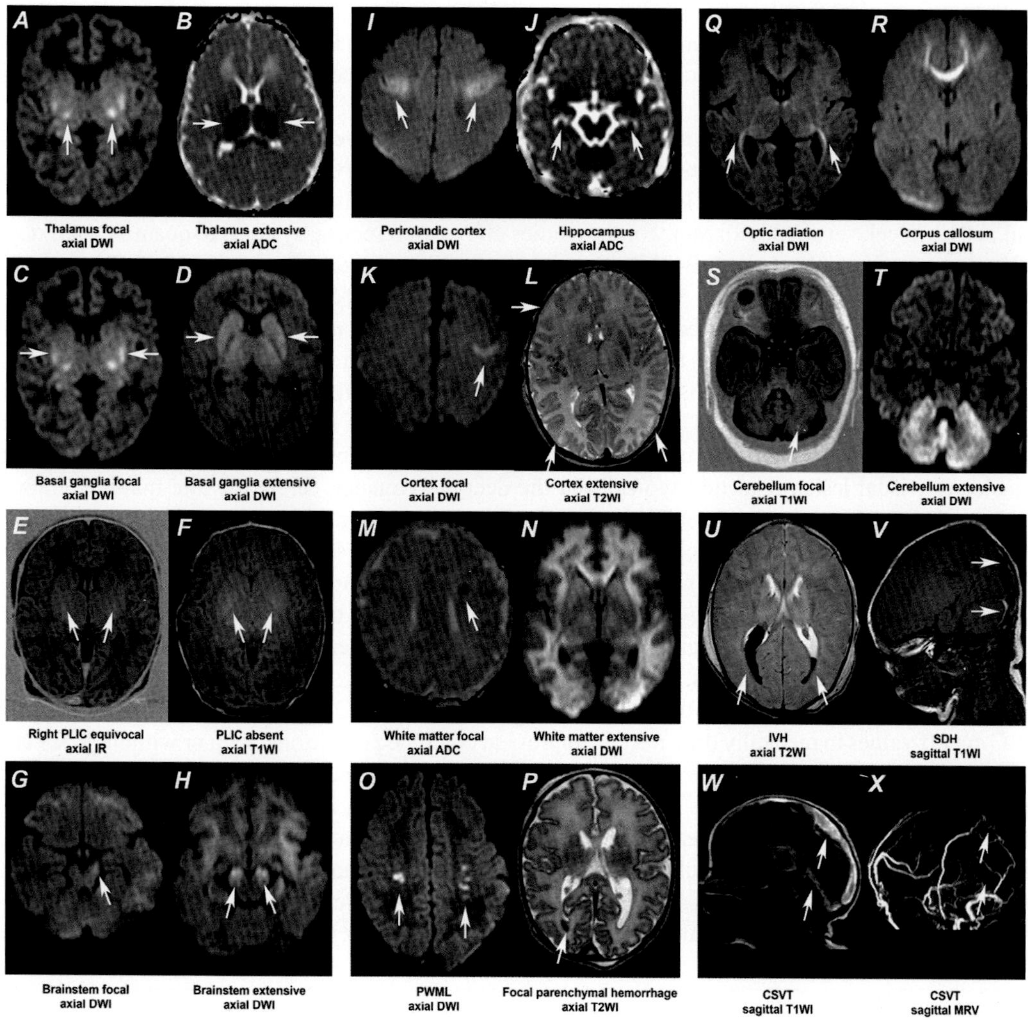

FIG. 2

MRI examples of all items to be scored with the novel MRI score. The abnormalities of interest are marked by the white arrows. (A) Focal bilateral thalamic lesions (high signal intensity [SI]) on an axial DWI. (B) Extensive bilateral thalamic lesions (low SI) on an axial ADC map. (C) Focal bilateral lesions (high SI) in the basal ganglia on an axial DWI. (D) Extensive bilateral lesions (high SI) in the basal ganglia on an axial DWI. (E) The posterior limb of the internal capsule (PLIC) is equivocal on both sides on an axial inversion recovery (IR) image. (F) Absent PLIC bilaterally seen as an inverted signal (low SI) on an axial T1-weighted image (T1WI). (G) Focal lesion (high SI) in the left cerebral peduncle on an axial DWI. (H) Extensive diffusion changes (high SI) in the cerebral peduncles bilaterally on an axial DWI. (I) Clear involvement (high SI) of the perirolandic gyrus bilaterally on an axial DWI. (J) Bilateral involvement (low SI) of the hippocampus on an axial ADC map. (K) Focal involvement (high SI) of the left cortex on an axial DWI.

(Continued)

white matter choline levels were negatively correlated with fine motor skills at 30 months of age ($N = 35$) (Sijens et al., 2017). Increased perfusion on arterial spin labelling (ASL) of basal ganglia and thalamus have also been associated with worse neurodevelopmental outcomes ($N = 28$) (de Vis et al., 2015; Wintermark, 2015) .

Scoring systems have been in use for assessing the nature and extent of brain injury on MRI in neonates with HIE and determining the relationship between injury score and outcome (Barkovich et al., 1998; Bonifacio et al., 2011; Rutherford et al., 2010a; Shankaran et al., 2012, 2016; Trivedi et al., 2017; Weeke et al., 2018). Many of the studies above used scoring systems to quantify the extent of brain injury (Kuenzle et al., 1994; Logitharajah et al., 2009; Alderliesten et al., 2011; Tusor et al., 2012; Polat et al., 2013; Cavalleri et al., 2014; Charon et al., 2016; Shapiro et al., 2017; Lally et al., 2019; Mastrangelo et al., 2019; Tharmapoopathy et al., 2020). The number of levels range from 6 in some of the earlier scoring systems to 57 in the most recent. As noted with preterm brain injury scoring above, these systems are time intensive and require neuroimaging expertise as well as efforts to ensure similar scoring among readers as agreement between scoring for neonates with HIE can be poor (Goergen et al., 2014). Therefore, such scoring systems are not used in routine clinical practice. Scoring depends on visual lesion detection typically in the deep gray nuclei, cerebral white matter, cerebral cortex and more recently, the cerebellum. The most recent study in 2018 explored the performance of the 57 point scoring system developed in one cohort provided the scoring system with an area under the curve (AUC) of 0.988 ($N = 97$) for determining abnormal outcomes at 2 years, but when applied to a second cohort ($N = 76$ where fewer died but more were impaired) the AUC dropped to 0.832. These findings show the potential of scoring systems but the need to use them with caution in patient populations with different characteristics.

Some have taken advantage of the quantitative nature of the ADC maps to explore the potential for ADC cut off values in manually drawn ROIs to provide outcome predictions, with or without MRS and MRI scoring systems (Alderliesten et al., 2011). These also show tremendous potential but need to be updated to include larger numbers of neonates who underwent TH. Recent atlasing approaches have characterized normal voxelwise mean ADC values and standard deviations (Ou et al., 2017). Using such normative atlases, z-score maps to characterize regional deviations can be created for individual cases to provide decision support when radiologists read the clinical studies (Jaimes et al., 2015) and can support machine learning approaches to automatically label injured regions on ADC maps (Ou et al., 2017).

FIG. 2, CONT'D (L) Extensive bilateral involvement of the cortex, seen as loss of the differentiation between the white matter and cortical gray matter in the occipital and frontal lobes bilaterally. (M) Focal unilateral abnormal signal (low SI) in the left periventricular white matter on an axial ADC map. (N) Extensive involvement of the white matter (high SI) on an axial DWI. (O) Bilateral punctate white matter lesions (PWML) seen as high SI on an axial DWI. (P) A small focal hemorrhage in the right occipital lobe (low SI) on an axial T2-weighted image (T2WI). (Q) Bilateral involvement of the optic radiation (high SI) on an axial DWI. (R) Involvement of the frontal part of the corpus callosum (high SI) on an axial DWI. (S) Focal lesion (high SI) in the left cerebellar hemisphere on an axial T1WI. (T) Extensive involvement of both cerebellar hemispheres (high SI) on an axial DWI. (U) Bilateral intraventricular hemorrhage (IVH) seen as low SI on an axial T2WI. (V) Subdural hemorrhage (SDH) supra- and infratentorial seen as high SI on a sagittal T1WI. (W) Cerebral sinovenous thrombosis (CSVT) seen as high SI at the location of the superior sagittal and straight sinus on a sagittal T1WI. (X) With corresponding lack flow (lack of high SI) in those veins on an MR venography (MRV) in sagittal view.

Reprinted from Weeke, L.C., et al., 2018. A novel magnetic resonance imaging score predicts neurodevelopmental outcome after perinatal asphyxia and therapeutic hypothermia. J. Pediatr. 33–40.e2. https://doi.org/10.1016/j.jpeds.2017.09.043 with permission.

Future approaches are likely to combine such automated lesion detection with information from EEG, vital monitors, and the electronic health care record to further improve individual outcome prediction.

4. Perinatal stroke

Perinatal arterial ischemic stroke leads to cognitive and motor neurodevelopmental impairments in about 40%–75% affected infants (Berfelo et al., 2010; Moharir et al., 2011; Fernández-López et al., 2014; Wagenaar et al., 2017). Arterial ischemic stroke has an estimated incidence rate of 1 in 2300–4000 live births (Lynch and Nelson, 2001; Kirton and deVeber, 2006). Stroke causes pronounced motor deficits in 30%–60% of affected patients, and can lead to cognitive impairment and cerebral palsy, which are of extreme importance for patient management (Wagenaar et al., 2018). With the increasing use of diffusion MRI, which is particularly helpful in detecting lesions, strokes in neonates are diagnosed as early as symptoms appear (Cowan et al., 1994; Krishnamoorthy et al., 2000; de Vries et al., 2005; Husson et al., 2010).

MRI studies point to certain findings that are associated with a risk of adverse motor outcomes in infants with perinatal arterial ischemic stroke, such as stroke size, injury to Broca's or Wernicke's areas, internal capsule, or basal ganglia (Lee et al., 2005). Early MRI results of infants with arterial ischemic stroke were helpful in predicting motor outcomes at the age of 2 years where infants with more than one type of infarct and involvement of the corticospinal tract were at high risk of developing hemiplegia compared to the infants who had isolated superficial middle cerebral artery (MCA) infarction ($N = 80$) (Husson et al., 2010). Another study of infants with cerebral infarction showed that the extent of the lesion was a better predictor for outcome than neonatal clinical examination, and that hemisphere, internal capsule, and basal ganglia involvement all together was associated with an adverse neuromotor outcome ($N = 24$) (Mercuri et al., 1999). Children with involvement of all these areas developed motor impairment, and were more likely to present with hemiplegia at follow up examinations after 15 months of age (Mercuri et al., 1999). In a later study by Mercuri and colleagues, MRI signs of internal capsule injury after neonatal stroke were once again correlated with adverse motor outcomes at school age ($N = 22$) (Mercuri et al., 2004). Additionally, infants with bilateral neonatal arterial ischemic stroke are more likely to have worse neurodevelopmental outcomes compared to infants with unilateral involvement ($N = 24$ and $N = 29$) (Mercuri et al., 1999; Jin et al., 2017). Conventional MRI at 1–14 weeks of age, was correlated with motor outcomes at age $\geq$12 months in infants with focal perinatal injury with diffusion MRI adding additional information in terms of the asymmetry of corticospinal tract involvement ($N = 20$) (Roze et al., 2012).

A diffusion MRI study of corticospinal tracts in infants with unilateral perinatal arterial ischemic stroke at 3 months of age demonstrated that higher FA and lower ADC were associated with motor deficits at 9–48 months of age ($N = 22$) (van der Aa et al., 2011). Another diffusion MRI study of infants with perinatal arterial ischemic stroke showed that lower FA measurements of optic radiations, corpus callosum, posterior and anterior limbs of the internal capsule, and posterior thalamic radiation at 3 months were associated with poorer visual, motor, and cognitive outcomes between 18 and 36 months of age ($N = 16$) (van der Aa et al., 2013a, 2013b). It has also been shown that in infants with arterial ischemic stroke, increased T2 signal intensity in the posterior limb of the internal capsule, cerebral peduncles and decreased ADC of the CST on neonatal DWI predicted poor motor ability outcome at 18 months ($N = 12$) (de Vries et al., 2005). Diffusion MRI results of infants with acute arterial ischemic stroke showed decreased ADC values in corticospinal tracts; furthermore, adverse motor outcome was associated with length and volume of corticospinal tracts in these patients ($N = 14$) (Kirton et al., 2007). Diffusion MRI data collected, within the first week after birth, from infants with perinatal arterial ischemic stroke, showed clearer patterns of signal intensity changes in the CST due to Wallarian degeneration in the second MRI which was 48 h within the onset of seizures, instead of the first MRI which was within 24 h ($N = 2$) (Wagenaar et al., 2017). Arterial Spin Labelling often shows hyperperfusion in acute arterial ischemic stroke due to either one or a combination of reperfusion, neuronal hyperexcitability, or associated seizure activity (Watson et al., 2016) (Fig. 3), but there is little data on relationship to outcome.

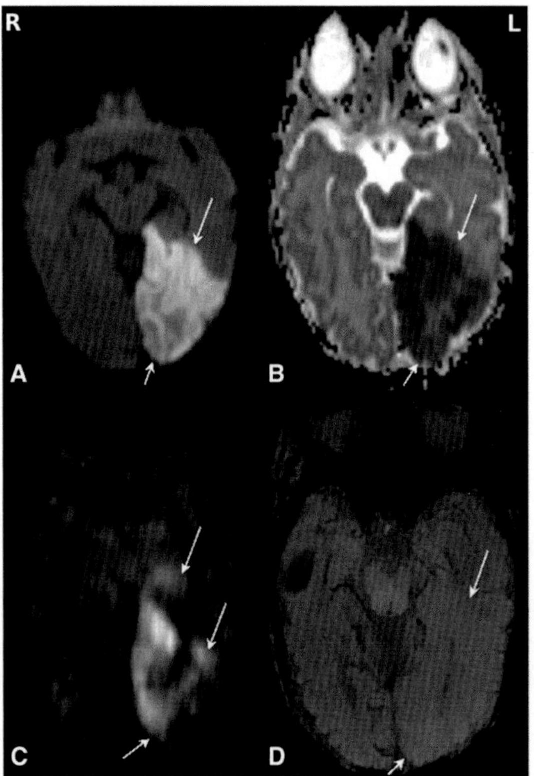

FIG. 3

Magnetic resonance imaging of a patient with arterial ischemic stroke and hyperperfusion on perfusion-weighted imaging (PWI). (A) Axial diffusion-weighted imaging (DWI) trace image; arrows show the edges of the diffusion abnormality. (B) Corresponding DWI apparent diffusion coefficient image to A; arrows show the edges of the diffusion abnormality. (C) Axial PWI image; arrows indicate edges of the perfusion abnormality. (D) Corresponding axial susceptibility-weighted imaging image; arrows show the edges of the signal wash-out area.

Reprinted from Watson, C.G., et al., 2016. Arterial spin labeling perfusion magnetic resonance imaging performed in acute perinatal stroke reveals hyperperfusion associated with ischemic injury. Stroke 47(6), 1514–1519 with permission.

The location of the arterial stroke is important for predicting outcome. The most commonly involved artery, with the worst adverse outcome, is the MCA, followed by its branches. Different types of lesions can be seen on MRI and DWI in the first week of life, and the areas of greatest concern are primary cortical motor area, PLIC, CST, cerebral peduncles, basal ganglia and thalamus (Wagenaar et al., 2018). For patients with non-MCA strokes, lesions to the basal ganglia and thalamus on neonatal MRI are associated with higher risk of cognitive deficit, behavioral problems, and cerebral palsy after 18 months of age. In this same group of patients, those with lesions in the cerebral peduncles had even higher risk of developing cerebral palsy (Wagenaar et al., 2018). In posterior cerebral artery (PCA) neonatal strokes, asymmetries in the optical radiations seen on MRI at 3 months, were associated with visual field deficit at later age (after 12 months) ($N = 16$) (van der Aa et al., 2013a, b).

5. Congenital heart disease

Approximately 8–10 in 1000 infants are born with severe congenital heart defects in the United States (Hoffman and Kaplan, 2002; Reller et al., 2008). About 50% of newborns with CHD require open heart surgery (Šamánek, 2000; Hoffman and Kaplan, 2002). Even though the survival rate of children with CHD who go through postnatal open heart surgery has increased over the years (Gilboa et al., 2010; Mazor Dray and Marelli, 2015; Claessens et al., 2018), pre- and postoperative brain injury is common in this patient group (Peyvandi et al., 2018). Detection of CHD in utero remains low (Quartermain et al., 2015) but infants who get diagnosed with CHD prenatally, compared to postnatally, have lower prevalence of preoperative brain injury and improved postnatal microstructural brain development (Peyvandi et al., 2016). Brain injury in CHD could be due to the decreased oxygen and nutrient amounts adversely affecting brain development causing delayed maturation and smaller brain volumes compared to typically developing infants (Limperopoulos et al., 2010; Donofrio et al., 2011; Sun et al., 2015; Kelly et al., 2017). It is also possible that during intrauterine life, the development of heart and brain shares common genetic pathways and a problem in one of these pathways could cause abnormal development in one or both of these two organs, leading to neurodevelopmental impairments (McQuillen et al., 2010; Mebius et al., 2017). In addition, the cardiac surgery itself might contribute to brain injury (Karl et al., 2004). About 50% of infants diagnosed with CHD, including ones who go through open-heart surgery, show long-term neurodevelopmental delays or deficits such as cognitive, behavioral, psychological, and motor problems (Marino et al., 2012; International Cardiac Collaborative on Neurodevelopment (ICCON) Investigators, 2016; Khalil et al., 2016; Mebius et al., 2017) that affect the overall life quality of these individuals (Walter, 1992; Schaefer et al., 2013; Werner et al., 2014). Different types of CHD diagnosis in infants with ventricular septal defect, tetralogy of Fallot, transposition of the great arteries, hypoplastic left heart syndrome, did not show significant differences in neurodevelopmental outcomes ($N = 178$) (Gaynor et al., 2010). Also, it has been shown that 5 year old children who went through different types of cardiac surgery during infancy did not differ significantly in terms of full-scale and verbal IQ scores, except for the children with chromosomal abnormalities who scored lower than the rest of the children with CHD (Creighton et al., 2007). However, infants with CHD who are also born preterm are at a higher risk for mortality and morbidity (Costello et al., 2010; Cnota et al., 2011). These infants also suffer from abnormalities in white matter and cortical development, leading to adverse neurodevelopmental outcomes (Inder et al., 1999; Miller et al., 2002, 2005a; Woodward et al., 2006). In fact, preterm infants (born <39 weeks) with CHD were shown to have worse neurodevelopmental outcomes at age 4 years compared to infants with CHD born at 39–40 weeks, after cardiac surgery during infancy ($N = 378$) (Goff et al., 2012).

MRI is the best technique for detecting brain injury in neonates, including those with multisystem conditions such as CHD. Neonatal MRI studies find that white matter injury and focal infarction are the most common types of brain injury observed in infants with CHD (Claessens et al., 2018; Peyvandi et al., 2018). Other common brain abnormalities observed in infants with CHD include gray matter injury; subdural hemorrhage; intraparenchymal hemorrhage; atrophy; watershed infarcts; gray matter focal infarctions; periventricular leukomalacia; reduced brain volume, reduced cortical folding, and delayed white matter maturation (Miller et al., 2007; Dimitropoulos et al., 2013; Algra et al., 2014; Peyvandi et al., 2016; Mebius et al., 2017; Mahle et al., 2002; Licht et al., 2009; Beca et al., 2013; McQuillen et al., 2006). The analysis of regional volumes in preoperative scans showed that infants with CHD have decreased frontal lobe and brainstem volumes, which correlated with delayed white matter microstructure development, in comparison to typically developing controls ($N = 67$) (Ortinau et al., 2012). A DWI study did not find any significant differences in the preoperative ADC values of infants diagnosed with different CHD types or in those with and without brain injury (Mulkey et al., 2013). However, lower FA was found for several white matter tracts, such as splenium of corpus callosum and corticospinal tracts, in infants with CHD who also had preoperative brain injury compared to infants with CHD who did not have preoperative brain injury, and both groups of infants with CHD had lower FA than the typically developing infants (Miller et al., 2007; Mulkey et al., 2014; Karmacharya et al., 2018). In a cohort of 167 infants with CHD, MRI detected preoperative brain injury in 26% of the infants while head ultrasound detected head injury in only 3% of the infants; moreover, 80% of the brain injuries detected by head ultrasound were false-positives suggesting that MRI should be the preferred method over head ultrasound when studying brain injury in infants with CHD (Rios et al., 2013). Multiple clinical factors have been associated with brain injury preoperatively (Mebius et al., 2017) including brain immaturity (Partridge et al., 2006; Andropoulos et al., 2010; Beca et al., 2013; Dimitropoulos et al., 2013), lower arterial oxygen saturation volumes (Miller et al., 2004b; Petit et al., 2009; Dimitropoulos et al., 2013; Bertholdt et al., 2014), lower Apgar scores at 5 min (McQuillen et al., 2007; Mulkey et al., 2013), longer time before surgery (Petit et al., 2009), presence of brain lactate (Mahle et al., 2002), and being male (Goff et al., 2014). In another cohort of 73 patients with CHD, 47% showed some kind of brain injury on preoperative MRI, with 26% presenting with multiple types of injury up to a maximum number of four different types of injury in a single child. The number of injury types increased on the postoperative MRI scan, from a maximum of 4 to 7 different injury types per child (McQuillen et al., 2006, 2007; Mulkey et al., 2013). Another study that compared preoperative and postoperative MRI results of infants diagnosed with CHD found that while moderate-severe white matter injury was observed in 12/34 infants preoperatively, this number increased to 21/24 postoperatively (Claessens et al., 2018).

Although initially research focused on the pre- and postoperative period for brain injury in infants with CHD; now there is evidence to show that many brain abnormalities already exist presurgery and even during the prenatal period (Mebius et al., 2017). For example, MRI studies of fetuses with CHD show brain abnormalities such as reduced brain growth with enlarged CSF spaces, ventriculomegaly, altered brain metabolism and blood flow, white-matter abnormalities, vermian hypoplasia, and altered brain maturation (Limperopoulos et al., 2010; Brossard-Racine et al., 2016; Khalil et al., 2016; Ortinau et al., 2018a; Claessens et al., 2019). An MRI study that collected data from the same children pre- and postnatally found that the brain abnormalities were detected in twice as many children postnatally when compared to the brain abnormalities detected prenatally (Brossard-Racine et al., 2016). A longitudinal study that examined brain growth from prenatally at 32 weeks gestation to 3 months of age showed that total brain volume was reduced in infants with CHD compared to typically developing infants (Mulkey et al., 2014; Ortinau et al., 2018b).

Despite the high number of MRI studies on infants with CHD, there are few studies that have examined the relationship between early MRI results and later neurodevelopmental outcomes (Peyvandi et al., 2019) (Fig. 4). MRI studies both before and after surgery show that delayed cerebral development was associated with a poor neurodevelopmental outcome at age 2 years ($N = 18$ and $N = 153$) (Beca et al., 2013; Clouchoux et al., 2013). Furthermore, preoperative brain injury was associated with decreased language and motor skills at 12 months of age ($N = 20$) (Andropoulos et al., 2012). It was shown that infants with CHD who had moderate to severe white matter injury during peri-operative MRI, had lower psychomotor development index scores at age 30 months compared to infants with CHD who had no or minimal white matter injury ($N = 70$) (Peyvandi et al., 2018). Additionally, for those infants with CHD who underwent cardiac surgery, the effect of perioperative higher anesthetic exposure was associated with lower neurodevelopmental outcomes scores at 12 months ($N = 59$) (Andropoulos et al., 2014). It has been shown that in infants with CHD, the postoperative width of the cerebellar inferior vermis was negatively correlated with expressive communication skills at age 9 to 36 months ($N = 9$) (Wong et al., 2017). Infants whose MRI at age 6 days showed global brain injury where the injury was more predominant at the basal ganglia and thalamus had adverse cognitive and motor outcome at the age of 30 months (Miller et al., 2005b). In a group of patients with biventricular CHD, brain volumes measured at age 12 months were positively correlated with language development at the same age ($N = 48$) (Rollins et al., 2017). More specifically, while cerebral white matter and brainstem volumes were correlated with development of phrases, vocabulary, and gestures, total brain, cerebral gray matter and subcortical gray matter volumes correlated with development of gestures (Rollins et al., 2017). In infants with CHD, white matter injury as measured with perioperative MRI was associated with lower cognitive scores at ages 2 and 6 years ($N = 30$) (Claessens et al., 2018). White matter microstructure disruption, with decreased FA values, was correlated with poorer cognition in adolescents who underwent surgery for CHD when infants ($N = 49$ and $N = 49$) (Rivkin et al., 2013; Rollins et al., 2014).

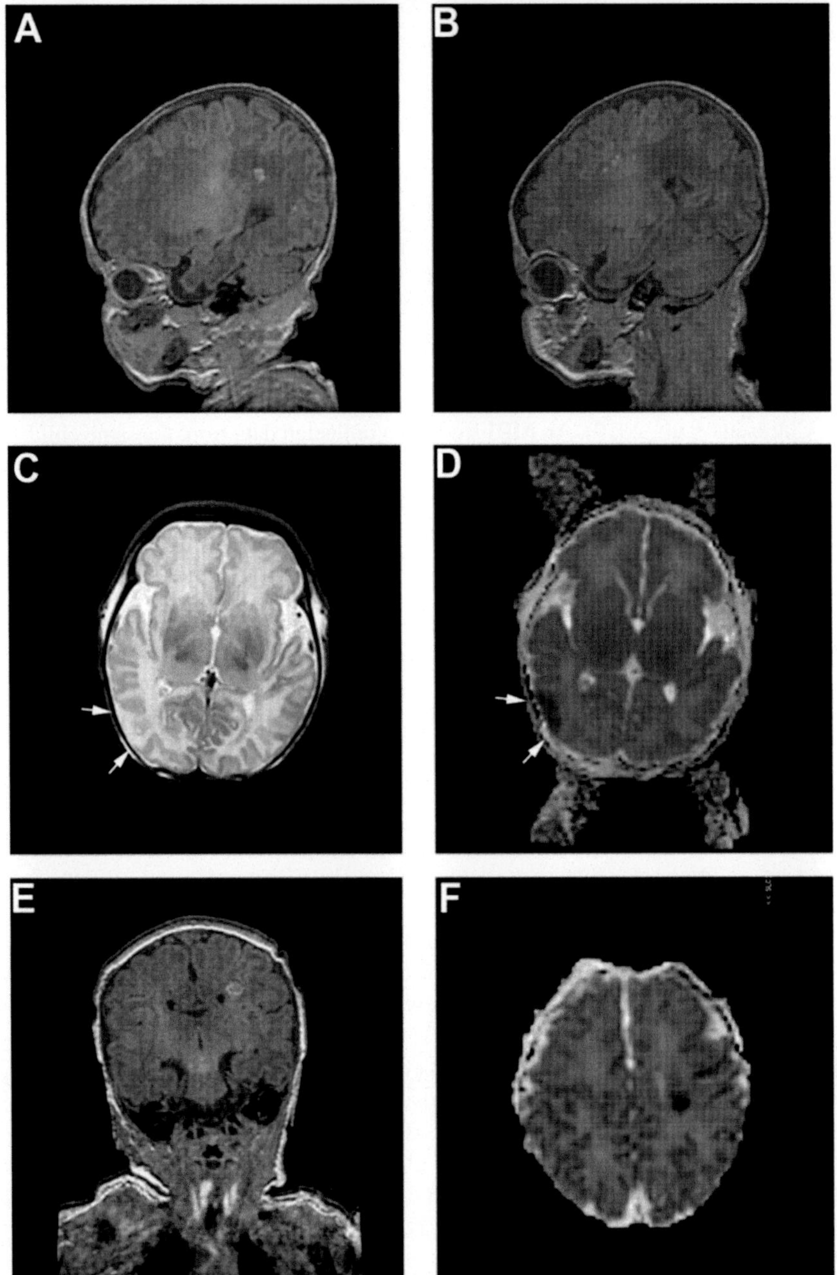

FIG. 4

MRI Patterns of Brain Injury in CHD. (A, B) Moderate white matter injury in a newborn with hypoplastic left heart syndrome is seen on sagittal T1 images in the postoperative scan. White matter injuries appear as small, focal areas of T1 hyperintensity (brightness). (C, D) Term newborn with hypoplastic left heart syndrome imaged postoperatively at day of life 17, after a modified Norwood procedure. A small middle cerebral artery distribution infarct is seen as cortical T2 hyperintensity [white arrows in (C)] and corresponding reduced diffusion [white arrows in (D)] in the right parietal-occipital lobe. (E, F) Term newborn with transposition of the great arteries imaged preoperatively after a balloon atrial septostomy. A single focus of T1 hyperintensity is seen in the periatrial white matter on the coronal SPGR sequence (E). This same focus has reduced water diffusivity on the average diffusivity (Dav) map (F, dark spot). This spot is larger than the typical solitary white matter lesion and may represent a small embolic stroke.

Reprinted from Peyvandi, S., et al., 2019. The neonatal brain in critical congenital heart disease: insights and future directions. NeuroImage 185, 776–782 with permission.

6. Neurodevelopmental disorders

6.1 Autism spectrum disorder

ASD is a multifactorial neurodevelopmental disorder, characterized by social and communication impairments, and the presence of restrictive and repetitive behaviors (American Psychiatric Association, 2000). The prevalence of ASD is 1 in 69 children among children aged 8 years in the USA (Christensen et al., 2016). Early diagnosis and intervention for individuals with ASD is very important to improve outcomes (Bradshaw et al., 2015; D'Mello et al., 2016) as this condition has life-long significant impacts on the affected individuals, their families, and the community (Ganz, 2007; Buescher et al., 2014). The diagnostic symptoms commonly appear at 2 years of age with early language delay being the most recognizable symptom (D'Mello et al., 2016).

Research on identifying early neural biomarkers for ASD benefits from studying infants who are defined as high-risk for ASD such as siblings of children with ASD, who are at up to 20 times higher risk to develop risk compared to low-risk infants (Spencer et al., 2011; Constantino et al., 2013). High-risk ASD infants were found to have larger cerebellar and subcortical volumes at age 4–6 months, compared to low-risk ASD infants, which were associated with increased repetitive behaviors at 36 months of age ($N = 24$) (Pote et al., 2019). Corpus callosum area and thickness were significantly increased in high-risk ASD group at 5 months of age, which was positively correlated with repetitive behaviors at age 2 years ($N = 378$) (Wolff et al., 2015). An MRI study of high-risk ASD infants between ages 6–9 months showed increased extra-axial fluid which was predictive of ASD diagnosis between ages 24 and 36 months ($N = 10$) (Shen et al., 2013). A deep-learning algorithm that used brain surface area in high-risk ASD infants at 6–12 months, was able to predict autism diagnosis at 24 months with 81% accuracy ($N = 435$) (Hazlett et al., 2017). A diffusion MRI study of high-risk ASD infants found brain differences as early as 6 months of age in infants who were later diagnosed with ASD, where the FA values for most white matter pathways differed between the high- and low-risk infant groups ($N = 92$) (Wolff et al., 2012). Network analysis of high risk ASD and low risk ASD infants at age 24 months showed decreased local and global efficiency over temporal, parietal, and occipital lobes in high risk ASD infants who received a diagnosis of ASD, in comparison to high risk infants who did not receive an ASD diagnosis and low risk ASD infants ($N = 113$) (Lewis et al., 2014). Furthermore, this network inefficiency was shown as early as at 6 months of age in high risk infants who do get a diagnosis of ASD at age 24 months ($N = 116$) (Lewis et al., 2017). A diffusion MRI study of high risk ASD infants showed microstructural abnormalities in the white matter pathways of language at age as early as 6 weeks old, which were associated with later language development at age 18 months and ASD symptomatology at age 36 months ($N = 19$) (Liu et al., 2019).

Patients with tuberous sclerosis complex (TSC) represent another cohort that is studied for identifying early neural biomarkers of ASD. The occurrence rate of ASD in TSC is about 40%–50% (Curatolo et al., 2010; Jeste et al., 2016; Torre-Ubieta et al., 2016; Capal et al., 2017). TSC can be diagnosed even prenatally or early in development, thus leading the way for identification of early neuroimaging markers of ASD before symptoms start to develop (Davis et al., 2015). A rs-fMRI study of infants with TSC at age 11.5 months found positive correlations between motor resting state networks and gross motor skills at age 18.5 months in TSC infants without ASD, but not in ones with ASD

($N = 34$) (Ahtam et al., 2019). A diffusion MRI study of infants with TSC at 12 months and 24 months of age found lower FA values for several white matter pathways such as the corpus callosum and arcuate fasciculus in infants with TSC who were later diagnosed with ASD compared to those who were not ($N = 23$) (McDonald et al., 2017). With developmental disorders, machine learning techniques are used for identifying biomarkers for early diagnosis, patient classification, prognosis prediction, and prediction of treatment response (Song et al., 2020). For example, machine learning approaches for ASD screening were shown to be effective with the use of rs-fMRI data from about 2200 children (Aghdam et al., 2019). Resting state functional brain connectivity measured in a high-risk ASD group of infants at 6 months of age showed potential to predict an ASD diagnosis at age 2 years using machine learning algorithms ($N = 59$) (Emerson et al., 2017) (Fig. 5).

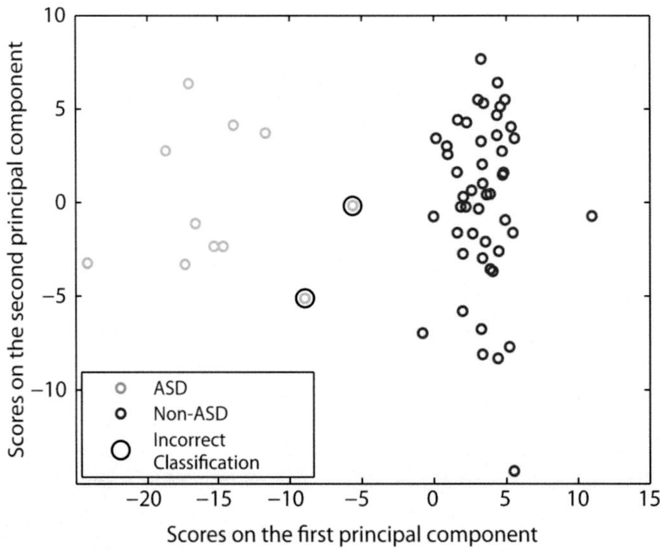

FIG. 5

Correct classification of 6-month-old infants at high familial risk for ASD using functional connectivity MRI. Functional connections were selected as those that showed a correlation with at least one of the 24-month ASD-related behaviors, which included measures of social behavior, language, motor development, and repetitive behavior. The top two principal components of the functional connections that showed a correlation with these behaviors are shown for both ASD (blue) and non-ASD (red) 6-month-old infants. The two participants that were incorrectly classified in the leave-one-out nested cross-validation analysis are circled; these two participants were diagnosed with ASD but were classified as non-ASD. Classification was correct for 96.6% of 6-month-old high-risk infants.

Reprinted from Emerson, R.W., et al., 2017. Functional neuroimaging of high-risk 6-month-old infants predicts a diagnosis of autism at 24 months of age. Sci. Transl. Med. 9(393). https://doi.org/10.1126/scitranslmed.aag2882 with permission.

6.2 Developmental dyslexia

Developmental dyslexia is a learning disorder characterized by poor reading and reading related skills such as spelling and written word comprehension, that is not due to low cognitive skills, poor hearing or vision, or lack of motivation (Moats and Dakin, 2008; Peterson and Pennington, 2012; Sanfilippo et al., 2020). It affects an estimated 5%–10% of school aged children (Shaywitz, 1998; Cortiella and Horowitz, 2014). The reading and related difficulties children with dyslexia face become an obstacle in their academic life, being one the most common learning disabilities (Shaywitz, 1998), and can lead to psychiatric comorbidities such as anxiety and depression (Sanfilippo et al., 2020). The deficit in fluent reading doesn't spontaneously resolve once the patient reaches adulthood; only one out of five children with developmental dyslexia are able to achieve good reading skills by adulthood (Hoeft et al., 2011).

The neurobiological substrate of dyslexia has been the subject of studies in order to provide an early diagnosis and potentially develop precise intervention therapies for patients. Neuroimaging has been widely used in that search, especially MRI. A longitudinal MRI study followed 32 children from pre literacy (age 4–5 years) to school age (8–9 years), and performed serial structural and functional MRI scans (Kuhl et al., 2020). MRI results of children who later got diagnosed with dyslexia, had higher gyrification in the primary auditory cortex (across all time points) and higher streamline density in the arcuate fasciculus (in the pre literacy phase) than the control group (Kuhl et al., 2020). These findings, also associated with poorer phonological processing skills, could be used as early biomarkers for children with high risk of developing dyslexia, before literacy age (Kuhl et al., 2020). A diffusion MRI study analyzed children before reading acquisition (age 5–6 years) and a follow-up 2 years after reading instruction, reporting that the left arcuate fasciculus was a good indicator of future reading ability and development of dyslexia for children with high familial risk. The left arcuate fasciculus was more precise in predicting outcomes of dyslexia than the high familial risk by itself ($N = 61$) (Vanderauwera et al., 2017). Another diffusion MRI study of infants with family history of developmental dyslexia aged 6–18 months found lower FA values in the left arcuate fasciculus compared to infants without a family history of dyslexia ($N = 32$) (Langer et al., 2017) (Fig. 6) suggesting that neonatal MRI has potential in identifying neonates at risk for language based learning disabilities.

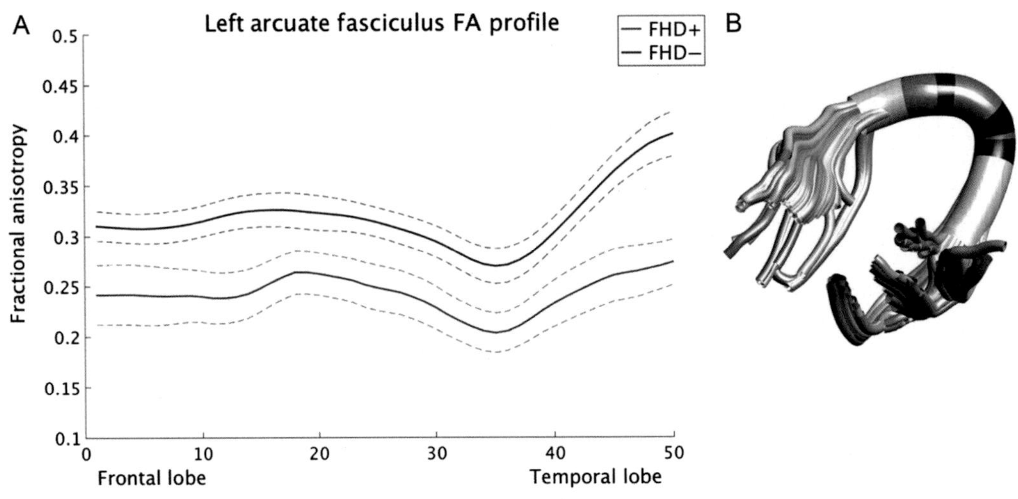

FIG. 6

Fractional anisotropy differences between infants with (FHD+) and without (FHD−) a familial risk for DD. (A) Tract profile of the left AF depicting FA values in FHD+ and FHD− infants at each of the 50 nodes. To illustrate the commonly reported dip in FA in the arc of the AF, we displayed the age-uncorrected FA values along the tract. However, the results for the age-corrected FA group differences look equivalent. The solid line represents the mean FA and the dashed line denotes one standard deviation. (B) Regions in which FHD+ infants exhibit significantly lower FA than FHD− infants are marked in red, and regions in which there are no significant differences between groups are marked in dark gray. Regions colored in white were not included in this specific analysis due to insignificant overlap between the infants.

Reprinted from Langer, N., et al., 2017. White matter alterations in infants at risk for developmental dyslexia. Cereb. Cortex 27(2), 1027–1036 with permission.

7. Conclusions

This chapter reviews the literature about key neurodevelopmental conditions and basic and advanced MRI methods commonly used in assessing risk for neurodevelopmental outcomes. Principal modalities of MRI covered in this chapter are T1 and T2-weighted, diffusion weighted and functional MRI. The timing of neonatal screening is very important in order to accurately investigate the condition of interest. Serial MRI scans follow the progression of cerebral lesions and can be used to correlate clinical presentation to the degree and pattern of injury. Despite the common use of head ultrasound and its importance as an early bedside screening exam, MRI has better resolution to detect subtle lesions, especially in the white matter, which is of great importance to normal cognitive development (Leijser et al., 2010; Rios et al., 2013). Conventional MRI can easily and readily assess structural damages and congenital or perinatal injuries (El-Dib et al., 2010; Kwon et al., 2014). Diffusion MRI is optimal to investigate white matter integrity and function, and its measurements are highly associated with neurodevelopmental outcomes (Pannek et al., 2014; Plaisier et al., 2014). Functional MRI assesses coherent functional activity possibly related to connectivity of tracts and is beginning to play a role in developmental disorders (Emerson et al., 2017; Kuhl et al., 2020).

It is important to note that currently MRI cannot predict individual outcomes, but provides the most accurate assessment of the character and extent of brain injury or alteration. However, the use of MRI during the neonatal period offers insight into the mechanisms of injury/dysfunction and risk for neurodevelopmental disabilities before the onset of symptoms that may impair the patient's quality of life. MRI biomarkers and evaluation of the brain's structure when combined with clinical information can help guide therapeutic planning decisions, especially in conditions where the early timing of interventions is associated with improved outcomes at later ages.

References

Aghdam, M.A., Sharifi, A., Pedram, M.M., 2019. Diagnosis of autism spectrum disorders in young children based on resting-state functional magnetic resonance imaging data using convolutional neural networks. J. Digit. Imaging 32 (6), 899–918.

Agut, T., et al., 2014. Early identification of brain injury in infants with hypoxic ischemic encephalopathy at high risk for severe impairments: accuracy of MRI performed in the first days of life. BMC Pediatr. 14, 177.

Ahtam, B., et al., 2019. Resting-state fMRI networks in children with tuberous sclerosis complex. J. Neuroimaging 29 (6), 750–759.

AIUM Practice parameter for the performance of neurosonography in neonates and infants, 2020. J. Ultrasound Med 39 (5), E57–E61.

Alderliesten, T., et al., 2011. MR imaging and outcome of term neonates with perinatal asphyxia: value of diffusion-weighted MR imaging and ^{1}H MR spectroscopy. Radiology 261 (1), 235–242.

Algra, S.O., et al., 2014. Neurological injury after neonatal cardiac surgery. Circulation, 224–233. https://doi.org/10.1161/circulationaha.113.003312.

Aly, H., et al., 2015. Melatonin use for neuroprotection in perinatal asphyxia: a randomized controlled pilot study. J. Perinatol. 35 (3), 186–191.

American Psychiatric Association, 2000. Diagnostic and Statistical Manual of Mental Disorders, fourth ed. American Psychiatric Association. Text Revision (DSM-IV-TR).

Amess, P.N., et al., 1999. Early brain proton magnetic resonance spectroscopy and neonatal neurology related to neurodevelopmental outcome at 1 year in term infants after presumed hypoxic-ischaemic brain injury. Dev. Med. Child Neurol., 436–445. https://doi.org/10.1017/s0012162299000973.

Amiel-Tison, C., 2002. Update of the Amiel-Tison neurologic assessment for the term neonate or at 40 weeks corrected age. Pediatr. Neurol. 27 (3), 196–212.

Anderson, P.J., Cheong, J.L.Y., Thompson, D.K., 2015. The predictive validity of neonatal MRI for neurodevelopmental outcome in very preterm children. Semin. Perinatol. 39 (2), 147–158.

Anderson, P.J., et al., 2017. Associations of Newborn brain magnetic resonance imaging with long-term neurodevelopmental impairments in very preterm children. J. Pediatr. 187, 58–65.e1.

Andropoulos, D.B., et al., 2010. Brain immaturity is associated with brain injury before and after neonatal cardiac surgery with high-flow bypass and cerebral oxygenation monitoring. J. Thorac. Cardiovasc. Surg., 543–556. https://doi.org/10.1016/j.jtcvs.2009.08.022.

Andropoulos, D.B., et al., 2012. Changing expectations for neurological outcomes after the neonatal arterial switch operation. Ann. Thorac. Surg., 1250–1256. https://doi.org/10.1016/j.athoracsur.2012.04.050.

Andropoulos, D.B., et al., 2014. The association between brain injury, perioperative anesthetic exposure, and 12-month neurodevelopmental outcomes after neonatal cardiac surgery: a retrospective cohort study. Paediatr. Anaesth. 24 (3), 266–274.

Arulkumaran, S., et al., 2020. MRI findings at term-corrected age and neurodevelopmental outcomes in a large cohort of very preterm infants. Am. J. Neuroradiol., 1509–1516. https://doi.org/10.3174/ajnr.a6666.

Ball, G., et al., 2017. Multimodal image analysis of clinical influences on preterm brain development. Ann. Neurol. 82 (2), 233–246.

Barkovich, A.J., Raybaud, C., 2019. Pediatric Neuroimaging, sixth ed. Lippincott Williams & Wilkins.

Barkovich, A.J., et al., 1998. Prediction of neuromotor outcome in perinatal asphyxia: evaluation of MR scoring systems. AJNR Am. J. Neuroradiol. 19 (1), 143–149.

Barkovich, A.J., et al., 2006. MR imaging, MR spectroscopy, and diffusion tensor imaging of sequential studies in neonates with encephalopathy. AJNR Am. J. Neuroradiol. 27 (3), 533–547.

Barnett, M.L., et al., 2018. Exploring the multiple-hit hypothesis of preterm white matter damage using diffusion MRI. Neuroimage Clin. 17, 596–606.

Barta, H., et al., 2018. Prognostic value of early, conventional proton magnetic resonance spectroscopy in cooled asphyxiated infants. BMC Pediatr. 18 (1), 302.

Batalle, D., et al., 2017. Early development of structural networks and the impact of prematurity on brain connectivity. NeuroImage 149, 379–392.

Beca, J., et al., 2013. New white matter brain injury after infant heart surgery is associated with diagnostic group and the use of circulatory arrest. Circulation 127 (9), 971–979.

Belet, N., et al., 2004. Hypoxic-ischemic encephalopathy: correlation of serial MRI and outcome. Pediatr. Neurol., 267–274. https://doi.org/10.1016/j.pediatrneurol.2004.04.011.

Berfelo, F.J., et al., 2010. Neonatal cerebral Sinovenous thrombosis from symptom to outcome. Stroke, 1382–1388. https://doi.org/10.1161/strokeaha.110.583542.

Bertholdt, S., et al., 2014. Cerebral lesions on magnetic resonance imaging correlate with preoperative neurological status in neonates undergoing cardiopulmonary bypass surgery. Eur. J. Cardiothorac. Surg., 625–632. https://doi.org/10.1093/ejcts/ezt422.

Bhutta, A.T., et al., 2002. Cognitive and behavioral outcomes of school-aged children who were born preterm: a meta-analysis. JAMA 288 (6), 728–737.

Biswal, B., et al., 1995. Functional connectivity in the motor cortex of resting human brain using echo-planar MRI. Magn. Reson. Med. 34 (4), 537–541.

Blencowe, H., et al., 2012. National, regional, and worldwide estimates of preterm birth rates in the year 2010 with time trends since 1990 for selected countries: a systematic analysis and implications. Lancet 379 (9832), 2162–2172.

Boardman, J.P., et al., 2006. Abnormal deep grey matter development following preterm birth detected using deformation-based morphometry. NeuroImage 32 (1), 70–78.

Boardman, J.P., et al., 2010. A common neonatal image phenotype predicts adverse neurodevelopmental outcome in children born preterm. NeuroImage 52 (2), 409–414.

Bonifacio, S.L., et al., 2011. Perinatal events and early magnetic resonance imaging in therapeutic hypothermia. J. Pediatr. 158 (3), 360–365. https://doi.org/10.1016/j.jpeds.2010.09.003.

Bradshaw, J., et al., 2015. Feasibility and effectiveness of very early intervention for infants at-risk for autism spectrum disorder: a systematic review. J. Autism Dev. Disord., 778–794. https://doi.org/10.1007/s10803-014-2235-2.

Brissaud, O., et al., 2005. Chemical shift imaging and localised magnetic resonance spectroscopy in full-term asphyxiated neonates. Pediatr. Radiol., 998–1005. https://doi.org/10.1007/s00247-005-1524-5.

Brossard-Racine, M., et al., 2016. Brain injury in neonates with complex congenital heart disease: what is the predictive value of MRI in the fetal period? AJNR Am. J. Neuroradiol. 37 (7), 1338–1346.

Brouwer, M.J., et al., 2017. Preterm brain injury on term-equivalent age MRI in relation to perinatal factors and neurodevelopmental outcome at two years. PLoS One 12 (5), e0177128.

Brown, C.J., et al., 2014. Structural network analysis of brain development in young preterm neonates. NeuroImage 101, 667–680.

Buescher, A.V.S., et al., 2014. Costs of autism spectrum disorders in the United Kingdom and the United States. JAMA Pediatr. 168 (8), 721–728.

Capal, J.K., et al., 2017. Utility of the autism observation scale for infants in early identification of autism in tuberous sclerosis complex. Pediatr. Neurol., 80–86. https://doi.org/10.1016/j.pediatrneurol.2017.06.010.

Cavalleri, F., et al., 2014. Prognostic value of diffusion-weighted imaging summation scores or apparent diffusion coefficient maps in newborns with hypoxic-ischemic encephalopathy. Pediatr. Radiol. 44 (9), 1141–1154.

Cayam-Rand, D., et al., 2019. Predicting developmental outcomes in preterm infants: a simple white matter injury imaging rule. Neurology 93 (13), e1231–e1240.

Center for Drug Evaluation and Research, 2019. FDA Drug Safety Communication. Available from: https://www.fda.gov/drugs/drug-safety-and-availability/fda-drug-safety-communication-fda-review-results-new-warnings-about-using-general-anesthetics-and. (Accessed 6 January 2021).

Charon, V., et al., 2016. Early MRI in neonatal hypoxic-ischaemic encephalopathy treated with hypothermia: prognostic role at 2-year follow-up. Eur. J. Radiol., 1366–1374. https://doi.org/10.1016/j.ejrad.2016.05.005.

Chen, L.-W., et al., 2018. T2 Relaxometry MRI predicts cerebral palsy in preterm infants. Am. J. Neuroradiol., 563–568. https://doi.org/10.3174/ajnr.a5501.

Cheong, J.L.Y., et al., 2006. Proton MR spectroscopy in neonates with perinatal cerebral hypoxic-ischemic injury: metabolite peak-area ratios, relaxation times, and absolute concentrations. AJNR Am. J. Neuroradiol. 27 (7), 1546–1554.

Cheong, J.L.Y., et al., 2016. Brain volumes at term-equivalent age are associated with 2-year neurodevelopment in moderate and late preterm children. J. Pediatr., 91–97.e1. https://doi.org/10.1016/j.jpeds.2016.04.002.

Christensen, D.L., et al., 2016. Prevalence and characteristics of autism Spectrum disorder among children aged 8 years—autism and developmental disabilities monitoring network, 11 sites, United States, 2012. MMWR Surveill. Summ., 1–23. https://doi.org/10.15585/mmwr.ss6503a1.

Claessens, N.H.P., et al., 2018. Perioperative neonatal brain injury is associated with worse school-age neurodevelopment in children with critical congenital heart disease. Dev. Med. Child Neurol. 60 (10), 1052–1058.

Claessens, N.H.P., et al., 2019. Brain and CSF volumes in fetuses and neonates with antenatal diagnosis of critical congenital heart disease: a longitudinal MRI study. AJNR Am. J. Neuroradiol. 40 (5), 885–891.

Clouchoux, C., et al., 2013. Delayed cortical development in fetuses with complex congenital heart disease. Cereb. Cortex, 2932–2943. https://doi.org/10.1093/cercor/bhs281.

Cnota, J.F., et al., 2011. Congenital heart disease infant death rates decrease as gestational age advances from 34 to 40 weeks. J. Pediatr., 761–765. https://doi.org/10.1016/j.jpeds.2011.04.020.

Cohen, J.F., et al., 2016. STARD 2015 guidelines for reporting diagnostic accuracy studies: explanation and elaboration. BMJ Open 6 (11), e012799.

Constantino, J.N., et al., 2013. Autism recurrence in half siblings: strong support for genetic mechanisms of transmission in ASD. Mol. Psychiatry, 137–138. https://doi.org/10.1038/mp.2012.9.

Cooke, R.W., Abernethy, L.J., 1999. Cranial magnetic resonance imaging and school performance in very low birth weight infants in adolescence. Arch. Dis. Child. Fetal Neonatal Ed. 81 (2), F116–F121.

Cordero-Grande, L., et al., 2016. Sensitivity encoding for aligned multishot magnetic resonance reconstruction. IEEE Trans. Comput. Imaging, 266–280. https://doi.org/10.1109/tci.2016.2557069.

Cortiella, C., Horowitz, S.H., 2014. The State of Learning Disabilities, third ed. vol. 25 National Center for Learning Disabilities, New York, pp. 2–45. Available from: https://www.ncld.org/wp-content/uploads/2014/11/2014-State-of-LD.pdf.

Costello, J.M., et al., 2010. Birth before 39 weeks' gestation is associated with worse outcomes in neonates with heart disease. Pediatrics, 277–284. https://doi.org/10.1542/peds.2009-3640.

Cotten, C.M., Shankaran, S., 2010. Hypothermia for hypoxic-ischemic encephalopathy. Expert Rev. Obstet. Gynecol. 5 (2), 227–239.

Cowan, F., et al., 1994. Early detection of cerebral infarction and hypoxic ischemic encephalopathy in neonates using diffusion-weighted magnetic resonance imaging. Neuropediatrics, 172–175. https://doi.org/10.1055/s-2008-1073018.

Creighton, D.E., et al., 2007. Neurocognitive, functional, and health outcomes at 5 years of age for children after complex cardiac surgery at 6 weeks of age or younger. Pediatrics, e478–e486. https://doi.org/10.1542/peds.2006-3250.

Curatolo, P., Napolioni, V., Moavero, R., 2010. Autism spectrum disorders in tuberous sclerosis: pathogenetic pathways and implications for treatment. J. Child Neurol. 25 (7), 873–880.

D'Mello, A.M., et al., 2016. Cerebellar gray matter differentiates children with early language delay in autism. Autism Res. 9 (11), 1191–1204.

Davis, P.E., et al., 2015. Tuberous sclerosis: a new frontier in targeted treatment of autism. Neurotherapeutics 12 (3), 572–583.

de Vis, J.B., et al., 2015. Arterial spin-labelling perfusion MRI and outcome in neonates with hypoxic-ischemic encephalopathy. Eur. Radiol. 25 (1), 113–121.

de Vries, L.S., et al., 2005. Prediction of outcome in new-born infants with arterial ischaemic stroke using diffusion-weighted magnetic resonance imaging. Neuropediatrics 36 (1), 12–20.

de Vries, L.S., et al., 2011. Myth: cerebral palsy cannot be predicted by neonatal brain imaging. Semin. Fetal Neonatal Med. 16 (5), 279–287.

Dimitropoulos, A., et al., 2013. Brain injury and development in newborns with critical congenital heart disease. Neurology, 241–248. https://doi.org/10.1212/wnl.0b013e31829bfdcf.

Donaldson, D.I., Buckner, R.L., 2001. Effective paradigm design. In: Matthews, P.M., Jezzard, P., Smith, S.M. (Eds.), Functional Magnetic Resonance Imaging: An Introduction to Methods. Oxford University Press., Oxford, pp. 178–197.

Donofrio, M.T., duPlessis, A.J., Limperopoulos, C., 2011. Impact of congenital heart disease on fetal brain development and injury. Curr. Opin. Pediatr., 502–511. https://doi.org/10.1097/mop.0b013e32834aa583.

Doria, V., et al., 2010. Emergence of resting state networks in the preterm human brain. Proc. Natl. Acad. Sci. U. S. A. 107 (46), 20015–20020.

Drobyshevsky, A., et al., 2007. Serial diffusion tensor imaging detects white matter changes that correlate with motor outcome in premature infants. Dev. Neurosci. 29 (4–5), 289–301.

Duerden, E.G., et al., 2015. Tract-based spatial statistics in preterm-born neonates predicts cognitive and motor outcomes at 18 months. AJNR Am. J. Neuroradiol. 36 (8), 1565–1571.

Dyet, L.E., et al., 2006. Natural history of brain lesions in extremely preterm infants studied with serial magnetic resonance imaging from birth and neurodevelopmental assessment. Pediatrics 118 (2), 536–548.

El-Dib, M., et al., 2010. Neuroimaging and neurodevelopmental outcome of premature infants. Am. J. Perinatol., 803–818. https://doi.org/10.1055/s-0030-1254550.

Emerson, R.W., et al., 2017. Functional neuroimaging of high-risk 6-month-old infants predicts a diagnosis of autism at 24 months of age. Sci. Transl. Med. 9 (393). https://doi.org/10.1126/scitranslmed.aag2882.

Fernández-López, D., et al., 2014. Mechanisms of perinatal arterial ischemic stroke. J. Cereb. Blood Flow Metab., 921–932. https://doi.org/10.1038/jcbfm.2014.41.

Frost, R., et al., 2019. Markerless high-frequency prospective motion correction for neuroanatomical MRI. Magn. Reson. Med. https://doi.org/10.1002/mrm.27705.

Ganz, M.L., 2007. The lifetime distribution of the incremental societal costs of autism. Arch. Pediatr. Adolesc. Med. 161 (4), 343–349.

Garcia-Alix, A., et al., 1994. Neuron-specific enolase and myelin basic protein: relationship of cerebrospinal fluid concentrations to the neurologic condition of asphyxiated full-term infants. Pediatrics 93 (2), 234–240.

Gaynor, J.W., et al., 2010. Is cardiac diagnosis a predictor of neurodevelopmental outcome after cardiac surgery in infancy? J. Thorac. Cardiovasc. Surg. 140 (6), 1230–1237.

Gilboa, S.M., et al., 2010. Mortality resulting from congenital heart disease among children and adults in the United States, 1999 to 2006. Circulation 122 (22), 2254–2263.

Goergen, S.K., et al., 2014. Early MRI in term infants with perinatal hypoxic-ischaemic brain injury: interobserver agreement and MRI predictors of outcome at 2 years. Clin. Radiol. 69 (1), 72–81.

Goff, D.A., et al., 2012. Younger gestational age is associated with worse neurodevelopmental outcomes after cardiac surgery in infancy. J. Thorac. Cardiovasc. Surg., 535–542. https://doi.org/10.1016/j.jtcvs.2011.11.029.

Goff, D.A., et al., 2014. Risk factors for preoperative periventricular leukomalacia in term neonates with hypoplastic left heart syndrome are patient related. J. Thorac. Cardiovasc. Surg., 1312–1318. https://doi.org/10.1016/j.jtcvs.2013.06.021.

Groenendaal, F., de Vries, L.S., 2017. Fifty years of brain imaging in neonatal encephalopathy following perinatal asphyxia. Pediatr. Res. 81 (1–2), 150–155.

Groenendaal, F., et al., 1994. Cerebral lactate and *N*-acetyl-aspartate/choline ratios in asphyxiated full-term neonates demonstrated in vivo using proton magnetic resonance spectroscopy. Pediatr. Res. 35 (2), 148–151.

Gui, L., et al., 2019. Longitudinal study of neonatal brain tissue volumes in preterm infants and their ability to predict neurodevelopmental outcome. NeuroImage 185, 728–741.

Guit, G.L., et al., 1990. Prediction of neurodevelopmental outcome in the preterm infant: MR-staged myelination compared with cranial US. Radiology 175 (1), 107–109.

Gunn, A.J., Thoresen, M., 2019. Neonatal encephalopathy and hypoxic-ischemic encephalopathy. Handb. Clin. Neurol. 162, 217–237.

Guo, T., et al., 2017. Quantitative assessment of white matter injury in preterm neonates. Neurology, 614–622. https://doi.org/10.1212/wnl.0000000000003606.

Hand, I.L., et al., 2020. Routine neuroimaging of the preterm brain. Pediatrics 146 (5). https://doi.org/10.1542/peds.2020-029082.

Haney, B., et al., 2010. Magnetic resonance imaging studies without sedation in the neonatal intensive care unit: safe and efficient. J. Perinat. Neonatal Nurs. 24 (3), 256–266.

Harvey, M.E., et al., 2013. Parents' experiences of information and communication in the neonatal unit about brain imaging and neurological prognosis: a qualitative study. Acta Paediatr., 360–365. https://doi.org/10.1111/apa.12154.

Hazlett, H.C., et al., 2017. Early brain development in infants at high risk for autism spectrum disorder. Nature 542 (7641), 348–351.

He, L., Parikh, N.A., 2013. Atlas-guided quantification of white matter signal abnormalities on term-equivalent age MRI in very preterm infants: findings predict language and cognitive development at two years of age. PLoS One 8 (12), e85475.

He, L., et al., 2018. Early prediction of cognitive deficits in very preterm infants using functional connectome data in an artificial neural network framework. Neuroimage Clin. 18, 290–297.

He, L., et al., 2020. A multi-task, multi-stage deep transfer learning model for early prediction of neurodevelopment in very preterm infants. Sci. Rep. 10 (1), 15072.

Hintz, S.R., et al., 2015. Neuroimaging and neurodevelopmental outcome in extremely preterm infants. Pediatrics 135 (1), e32–e42.

Hodek, J.-M., von der Schulenburg, J.-M., Mittendorf, T., 2011. Measuring economic consequences of preterm birth—methodological recommendations for the evaluation of personal burden on children and their caregivers. Heal. Econ. Rev. https://doi.org/10.1186/2191-1991-1-6.

Hoeft, F., et al., 2011. Neural systems predicting long-term outcome in dyslexia. Proc. Natl. Acad. Sci. U. S. A. 108 (1), 361–366.

Hoffman, J.I.E., Kaplan, S., 2002. The incidence of congenital heart disease. J. Am. Coll. Cardiol., 1890–1900. https://doi.org/10.1016/s0735-1097(02)01886-7.

Holland, D., et al., 2014. Structural growth trajectories and rates of change in the first 3 months of infant brain development. JAMA Neurol. 1266. https://doi.org/10.1001/jamaneurol.2014.1638.

Hughes, E.J., et al., 2017. A dedicated neonatal brain imaging system. Magn. Reson. Med. 78 (2), 794–804.

Hüppi, P.S., et al., 1998. Quantitative magnetic resonance imaging of brain development in premature and mature newborns. Ann. Neurol. 43 (2), 224–235.

Husson, B., et al., 2010. Motor outcomes after neonatal arterial ischemic stroke related to early MRI data in a prospective study. Pediatrics, e912–e918. https://doi.org/10.1542/peds.2009-3611.

Hutchinson, E.A., et al., 2013. School-age outcomes of extremely preterm or extremely low birth weight children. Pediatrics, e1053–e1061. https://doi.org/10.1542/peds.2012-2311.

Inder, T.E., 2005. Abnormal cerebral structure is present at term in premature infants. Pediatrics, 286–294. https://doi.org/10.1542/peds.2004-0326.

Inder, T.E., et al., 1999. Periventricular white matter injury in the premature infant is followed by reduced cerebral cortical gray matter volume at term. Ann. Neurol. 46 (5), 755–760.

Inder, T.E., et al., 2003. Defining the nature of the cerebral abnormalities in the premature infant: a qualitative magnetic resonance imaging study. J. Pediatr. 143 (2), 171–179.

Institute of Medicine, Board on Health Sciences Policy and Committee on Understanding Premature Birth and Assuring Healthy Outcomes, 2007. Preterm Birth: Causes, Consequences, and Prevention. National Academies Press.

International Cardiac Collaborative on Neurodevelopment (ICCON) Investigators, 2016. Impact of operative and postoperative factors on neurodevelopmental outcomes after cardiac operations. Ann. Thorac. Surg. 102 (3), 843–849.

Iwata, S., et al., 2012. Qualitative brain MRI at term and cognitive outcomes at 9 years after very preterm birth. Pediatrics 129 (5), e1138–e1147.

Jaimes, C., et al., 2020. Success of non-sedated neuroradiological MRI in children 1 to 7 years old. AJR Am. J. Roentgenol. https://doi.org/10.2214/AJR.20.23654.

Jaimes, C., Ou, Y., Shih, J., Bates, S., O'Reilly, D., Soul, J., Gollub, R., Grant, P.E., Zollei, L., 2015. Apparent diffusion coefficient Z-score maps compared to normative atlas in hypoxic ischemic encephalopathy. In: ASNR 53rd Annual Meeting & The Foundation of the ASNR Symposium.

Jeste, S.S., et al., 2016. Symptom profiles of autism spectrum disorder in tuberous sclerosis complex. Neurology 87 (8), 766–772.

Jin, J.H., et al., 2017. Abnormal neurodevelopmental outcomes are very likely in cases of bilateral neonatal arterial ischaemic stroke. Acta Paediatr. 106 (2), 229–235.

Karl, T.R., et al., 2004. Arterial switch with full-flow cardiopulmonary bypass and limited circulatory arrest: neurodevelopmental outcome. J. Thorac. Cardiovasc. Surg. 127 (1), 213–222.

Karmacharya, S., et al., 2018. Advanced diffusion imaging for assessing normal white matter development in neonates and characterizing aberrant development in congenital heart disease. Neuroimage Clin. 19, 360–373.

Kelly, C.J., et al., 2017. Impaired development of the cerebral cortex in infants with congenital heart disease is correlated to reduced cerebral oxygen delivery. Sci. Rep. https://doi.org/10.1038/s41598-017-14939-z.

Keunen, K., et al., 2012. Brain tissue volumes in preterm infants: prematurity, perinatal risk factors and neurodevelopmental outcome: a systematic review. J. Matern. Fetal Neonatal Med. 25 (Suppl 1), 89–100.

Keunen, K., et al., 2016. Brain volumes at term-equivalent age in preterm infants: imaging biomarkers for neurodevelopmental outcome through early school age. J. Pediatr. 172, 88–95.

Khalil, A., et al., 2016. Prevalence of prenatal brain abnormalities in fetuses with congenital heart disease: a systematic review. Ultrasound Obstet. Gynecol. 48 (3), 296–307.

Kidokoro, H., Neil, J.J., Inder, T.E., 2013. New MR imaging assessment tool to define brain abnormalities in very preterm infants at term. AJNR Am. J. Neuroradiol. 34 (11), 2208–2214.

Kirton, A., deVeber, G., 2006. Cerebral palsy secondary to perinatal ischemic stroke. Clin. Perinatol., 367–386. https://doi.org/10.1016/j.clp.2006.03.008.

Kirton, A., et al., 2007. Quantified corticospinal tract diffusion restriction predicts neonatal stroke outcome. Stroke 38 (3), 974–980.

Kline, J.E., et al., 2020. Early cortical maturation predicts neurodevelopment in very preterm infants. Arch. Dis. Child. Fetal Neonatal Ed. 105 (5), 460–465.

Krishnamoorthy, K.S., et al., 2000. Diffusion-weighted imaging in neonatal cerebral infarction: clinical utility and follow-up. J. Child Neurol., 592–602. https://doi.org/10.1177/088307380001500905.

Kuenzle, C., et al., 1994. Prognostic value of early MR imaging in term infants with severe perinatal asphyxia. Neuropediatrics, 191–200. https://doi.org/10.1055/s-2008-1073021.

Kuhl, U., et al., 2020. The emergence of dyslexia in the developing brain. NeuroImage 211, 116633.

Kuperman, J.M., et al., 2011. Prospective motion correction improves diagnostic utility of pediatric MRI scans. Pediatr. Radiol., 1578–1582. https://doi.org/10.1007/s00247-011-2205-1.

Kurinczuk, J.J., White-Koning, M., Badawi, N., 2010. Epidemiology of neonatal encephalopathy and hypoxic-ischaemic encephalopathy. Early Hum. Dev., 329–338. https://doi.org/10.1016/j.earlhumdev.2010.05.010.

Kwon, S.H., et al., 2014. The role of neuroimaging in predicting neurodevelopmental outcomes of preterm neonates. Clin. Perinatol. 41 (1), 257–283.

L'Abee, C., et al., 2005. Early diffusion-weighted MRI and ^{1}H-magnetic resonance spectroscopy in asphyxiated full-term neonates. Neonatology, 306–312. https://doi.org/10.1159/000087628.

Lally, P.J., et al., 2019. Magnetic resonance spectroscopy assessment of brain injury after moderate hypothermia in neonatal encephalopathy: a prospective multicentre cohort study. Lancet Neurol. 18 (1), 35–45.

Langer, N., et al., 2017. White matter alterations in infants at risk for developmental dyslexia. Cereb. Cortex 27 (2), 1027–1036.

Larroque, B., et al., 2008. Neurodevelopmental disabilities and special care of 5-year-old children born before 33 weeks of gestation (the EPIPAGE study): a longitudinal cohort study. Lancet 371 (9615), 813–820.

Lee, J., et al., 2005. Predictors of outcome in perinatal arterial stroke: a population-based study. Ann. Neurol. 58 (2), 303–308.

Leijser, L.M., et al., 2010. Is sequential cranial ultrasound reliable for detection of white matter injury in very preterm infants? Neuroradiology 52 (5), 397–406.

Lewis, J.D., et al., 2014. Network inefficiencies in autism spectrum disorder at 24 months. Transl. Psychiatry 4, e388.

Lewis, J.D., et al., 2017. The emergence of network inefficiencies in infants with autism spectrum disorder. Biol. Psychiatry 82 (3), 176–185.

Licht, D.J., et al., 2009. Brain maturation is delayed in infants with complex congenital heart defects. J. Thorac. Cardiovasc. Surg. 137 (3), 529–536 (discussion 536–7).

Limperopoulos, C., et al., 2005. Late gestation cerebellar growth is rapid and impeded by premature birth. Pediatrics 115 (3), 688–695.

Limperopoulos, C., et al., 2010. Brain volume and metabolism in fetuses with congenital heart disease. Circulation, 26–33. https://doi.org/10.1161/circulationaha.109.865568.

Lind, A., et al., 2011. Associations between regional brain volumes at term-equivalent age and development at 2 years of age in preterm children. Pediatr. Radiol. 41 (8), 953–961.

Liu, J., et al., 2019. Altered lateralization of dorsal language tracts in 6-week-old infants at risk for autism. Dev. Sci. 22 (3), e12768.

Logitharajah, P., Rutherford, M.A., Cowan, F.M., 2009. Hypoxic-ischemic encephalopathy in preterm infants: antecedent factors, brain imaging, and outcome. Pediatr. Res. 66 (2), 222–229.

Lynch, J.K., Nelson, K.B., 2001. Epidemiology of perinatal stroke. Curr. Opin. Pediatr., 499–505. https://doi.org/10.1097/00008480-200112000-00002.

Mader, I., et al., 2002. Neonatal cerebral infarction diagnosed by diffusion-weighted MRI. Stroke, 1142–1145. https://doi.org/10.1161/hs0402.105883.

Mahle, W.T., et al., 2002. An MRI study of neurological injury before and after congenital heart surgery. Circulation 106 (12 Suppl 1), I109–I114.
Malik, G.K., et al., 2006. Serial quantitative diffusion tensor MRI of the term neonates with hypoxic-ischemic encephalopathy (HIE). Neuropediatrics 37 (6), 337–343.
Marino, B.S., et al., 2012. Neurodevelopmental outcomes in children with congenital heart disease: evaluation and management. Circulation, 1143–1172. https://doi.org/10.1161/cir.0b013e318265ee8a.
Marlow, N., et al., 2005. Neurologic and developmental disability at six years of age after extremely preterm birth. N. Engl. J. Med. 352 (1), 9–19.
Mastrangelo, M., et al., 2019. Early post-cooling brain magnetic resonance for the prediction of neurodevelopmental outcome in newborns with hypoxic-ischemic encephalopathy. J. Pediatr. Neurosci. 191. https://doi.org/10.4103/jpn.jpn_25_19.
Mathur, A.M., et al., 2008. Transport, monitoring, and successful brain MR imaging in unsedated neonates. Pediatr. Radiol. 38 (3), 260–264.
Maunu, J., et al., 2009. Brain and ventricles in very low birth weight infants at term: a comparison among head circumference, ultrasound, and magnetic resonance imaging. Pediatrics, 617–626. https://doi.org/10.1542/peds.2007-3264.
Mazor Dray, E., Marelli, A.J., 2015. Adult congenital heart disease: scope of the problem. Cardiol. Clin. 33 (4), 503–512 (vii).
McDonald, N.M., et al., 2017. Early autism symptoms in infants with tuberous sclerosis complex. Autism Res., 1981–1990. https://doi.org/10.1002/aur.1846.
McKinstry, R.C., et al., 2002. A prospective, longitudinal diffusion tensor imaging study of brain injury in newborns. Neurology, 824–833. https://doi.org/10.1212/wnl.59.6.824.
McQuillen, P.S., Goff, D.A., Licht, D.J., 2010. Effects of congenital heart disease on brain development. Prog. Pediatr. Cardiol., 79–85. https://doi.org/10.1016/j.ppedcard.2010.06.011.
McQuillen, P.S., et al., 2006. Balloon atrial septostomy is associated with preoperative stroke in neonates with transposition of the great arteries. Circulation, 280–285. https://doi.org/10.1161/circulationaha.105.566752.
McQuillen, P.S., et al., 2007. Temporal and anatomic risk profile of brain injury with neonatal repair of congenital heart defects. Stroke, 736–741. https://doi.org/10.1161/01.str.0000247941.41234.90.
Mebius, M.J., et al., 2017. Brain injury and neurodevelopmental outcome in congenital heart disease: a systematic review. Pediatrics 140 (1). https://doi.org/10.1542/peds.2016-4055.
Ment, L.R., Hirtz, D., Hüppi, P.S., 2009. Imaging biomarkers of outcome in the developing preterm brain. Lancet Neurol. 8 (11), 1042–1055.
Ment, L.R., et al., 2002. Practice parameter: neuroimaging of the neonate: report of the quality standards Subcommittee of the American Academy of Neurology and the Practice Committee of the Child Neurology Society. Neurology 58 (12), 1726–1738.
Mercuri, E., et al., 1999. Early prognostic indicators of outcome in infants with neonatal cerebral infarction: a clinical, electroencephalogram, and magnetic resonance imaging study. Pediatrics 103 (1), 39–46.
Mercuri, E., et al., 2004. Neonatal cerebral infarction and neuromotor outcome at school age. Pediatrics 113 (1 Pt 1), 95–100.
Mewes, A.U.J., et al., 2006. Regional brain development in serial magnetic resonance imaging of low-risk preterm infants. Pediatrics 118 (1), 23–33.
Miller, S.P., Ferriero, D.M., et al., 2005a. Early brain injury in premature Newborns detected with magnetic resonance imaging is associated with adverse early neurodevelopmental outcome. J. Pediatr., 609–616. https://doi.org/10.1016/j.jpeds.2005.06.033.
Miller, S.P., Latal, B., et al., 2004a. Clinical signs predict 30-month neurodevelopmental outcome after neonatal encephalopathy. Am. J. Obstet. Gynecol., 93–99. https://doi.org/10.1016/s0002-9378(03)00908-6.

Miller, S.P., McQuillen, P.S., et al., 2004b. Preoperative brain injury in newborns with transposition of the great arteries. Ann. Thorac. Surg., 1698–1706. https://doi.org/10.1016/j.athoracsur.2003.10.084.

Miller, S.P., Ramaswamy, V., et al., 2005b. Patterns of brain injury in term neonatal encephalopathy. J. Pediatr. 146 (4), 453–460.

Miller, S.P., et al., 2002. Serial quantitative diffusion tensor MRI of the premature brain: development in newborns with and without injury. J. Magn. Reson. Imaging, 621–632. https://doi.org/10.1002/jmri.10205.

Miller, S.P., et al., 2007. Abnormal brain development in newborns with congenital heart disease. N. Engl. J. Med., 1928–1938. https://doi.org/10.1056/nejmoa067393.

Moats, L.C., Dakin, K., 2008. Basic Facts about Dyslexia & Other Reading Problems. International Dyslexia Association.

Moharir, M.D., et al., 2011. A prospective outcome study of neonatal cerebral sinovenous thrombosis. J. Child Neurol., 1137–1144. https://doi.org/10.1177/0883073811408094.

Mulkey, S.B., et al., 2013. Multi-tiered analysis of brain injury in neonates with congenital heart disease. Pediatr. Cardiol. 34 (8), 1772–1784.

Mulkey, S.B., et al., 2014. White matter injury in newborns with congenital heart disease: a diffusion tensor imaging study. Pediatr. Neurol. 51 (3), 377–383.

Mwaniki, M.K., et al., 2012. Long-term neurodevelopmental outcomes after intrauterine and neonatal insults: a systematic review. Lancet 379 (9814), 445–452.

Nagy, Z., et al., 2005. Diffusion tensor imaging on teenagers, born at term with moderate hypoxic-ischemic encephalopathy. Pediatr. Res. 58 (5), 936–940.

Neubauer, V., et al., 2011. Feasibility of cerebral MRI in non-sedated preterm-born infants at term-equivalent age: report of a single centre. Acta Paediatr. 100 (12), 1544–1547.

Ortinau, C., et al., 2012. Regional alterations in cerebral growth exist preoperatively in infants with congenital heart disease. J. Thorac. Cardiovasc. Surg. 143 (6), 1264–1270.

Ortinau, C.M., Mangin-Heimos, K., et al., 2018b. Prenatal to postnatal trajectory of brain growth in complex congenital heart disease. Neuroimage Clin. 20, 913–922.

Ortinau, C.M., Rollins, C.K., et al., 2018a. Early-emerging sulcal patterns are atypical in fetuses with congenital heart disease. Cereb. Cortex. https://doi.org/10.1093/cercor/bhy235.

Ou, Y., et al., 2017. Using clinically acquired MRI to construct age-specific ADC atlases: quantifying spatiotemporal ADC changes from birth to 6-year old. Hum. Brain Mapp. 38 (6), 3052–3068.

Pannek, K., et al., 2014. Magnetic resonance diffusion tractography of the preterm infant brain: a systematic review. Dev. Med. Child Neurol., 113–124. https://doi.org/10.1111/dmcn.12250.

Partridge, S.C., et al., 2006. Pyramidal tract maturation after brain injury in newborns with heart disease. Ann. Neurol., 640–651. https://doi.org/10.1002/ana.20772.

Peden, C.J., et al., 1993. Proton spectroscopy of the neonatal brain following hypoxic-ischaemic injury. Dev. Med. Child Neurol. 35 (6), 502–510.

Peterson, B.S., et al., 2000. Regional brain volume abnormalities and long-term cognitive outcome in preterm infants. JAMA 284 (15), 1939–1947.

Peterson, B.S., et al., 2003. Regional brain volumes and their later neurodevelopmental correlates in term and preterm infants. Pediatrics 111 (5 Pt 1), 939–948.

Peterson, R.L., Pennington, B.F., 2012. Developmental dyslexia. Lancet, 1997–2007. https://doi.org/10.1016/s0140-6736(12)60198-6.

Petit, C.J., et al., 2009. Preoperative brain injury in transposition of the great arteries is associated with oxygenation and time to surgery, not balloon atrial septostomy. Circulation, 709–716. https://doi.org/10.1161/circulationaha.107.760819.

Peyvandi, S., et al., 2016. Association of prenatal diagnosis of critical congenital heart disease with postnatal brain development and the risk of brain injury. JAMA Pediatr. 170 (4), e154450.

Peyvandi, S., et al., 2018. Neonatal brain injury and timing of neurodevelopmental assessment in patients with congenital heart disease. J. Am. Coll. Cardiol. 71 (18), 1986–1996.

Peyvandi, S., et al., 2019. The neonatal brain in critical congenital heart disease: insights and future directions. NeuroImage 185, 776–782.

Plaisier, A., et al., 2014. Optimal timing of cerebral MRI in preterm infants to predict long-term neurodevelopmental outcome: a systematic review. Am. J. Neuroradiol., 841–847. https://doi.org/10.3174/ajnr.a3513.

Polat, M., et al., 2013. Prediction of neurodevelopmental outcome in term neonates with hypoxic-ischemic encephalopathy. Eur. J. Paediatr. Neurol. 17 (3), 288–293.

Pote, I., et al., 2019. Familial risk of autism alters subcortical and cerebellar brain anatomy in infants and predicts the emergence of repetitive behaviors in early childhood. Autism Res. 12 (4), 614–627.

Potharst, E.S., et al., 2011. High incidence of multi-domain disabilities in very preterm children at five years of age. J. Pediatr. 159 (1), 79–85.

Quartermain, M.D., et al., 2015. Variation in prenatal diagnosis of congenital heart disease in infants. Pediatrics 136 (2), e378–e385.

Ravichandran, L., et al., 2020. Incidence, intrapartum risk factors, and prognosis of neonatal hypoxic-ischemic encephalopathy among infants born at 35 weeks gestation or more. J. Obstet. Gynaecol. Can. https://doi.org/10.1016/j.jogc.2020.04.020.

Reller, M.D., et al., 2008. Prevalence of congenital heart defects in metropolitan Atlanta, 1998–2005. J. Pediatr., 807–813. https://doi.org/10.1016/j.jpeds.2008.05.059.

Rios, D.R., et al., 2013. Usefulness of routine head ultrasound scans before surgery for congenital heart disease. Pediatrics 131 (6), e1765–e1770.

Rivkin, M.J., et al., 2013. Adolescents with D-transposition of the great arteries repaired in early infancy demonstrate reduced white matter microstructure associated with clinical risk factors. J. Thorac. Cardiovasc. Surg. 146 (3), 543–549.e1.

Rodrigues, K., Grant, P.E., 2011. Diffusion-weighted imaging in neonates. Neuroimaging Clin. N. Am. 21 (1), 127–151 (viii).

Roelants-Van Rijn, A.M., et al., 2001. Value of (1)H-MRS using different echo times in neonates with cerebral hypoxia-ischemia. Pediatr. Res. 49 (3), 356–362.

Rogers, E.E., et al., 2014. Erythropoietin and hypothermia for hypoxic-ischemic encephalopathy. Pediatr. Neurol. 51 (5), 657–662.

Rollins, C.K., et al., 2014. White matter microstructure and cognition in adolescents with congenital heart disease. J. Pediatr. 165 (5), 936–944.e1–2.

Rollins, C.K., et al., 2017. White matter volume predicts language development in congenital heart disease. J. Pediatr. 181, 42–48.e2.

Roze, E., et al., 2012. Tractography of the corticospinal tracts in infants with focal perinatal injury: comparison with normal controls and to motor development. Neuroradiology 54 (5), 507–516.

Rutherford, M., Biarge, M.M., et al., 2010c. MRI of perinatal brain injury. Pediatr. Radiol. 40 (6), 819–833.

Rutherford, M., Malamateniou, C., et al., 2010b. Magnetic resonance imaging in hypoxic-ischaemic encephalopathy. Early Hum. Dev. 86 (6), 351–360.

Rutherford, M., Ramenghi, L.A., et al., 2010a. Assessment of brain tissue injury after moderate hypothermia in neonates with hypoxic-ischaemic encephalopathy: a nested substudy of a randomised controlled trial. Lancet Neurol. 9 (1), 39–45.

Rutherford, M., et al., 2004. Diffusion-weighted magnetic resonance imaging in term perinatal brain injury: a comparison with site of lesion and time from birth. Pediatrics 114 (4), 1004–1014.

Sagar, P., Grant, P.E., 2006. Diffusion-weighted MR imaging: pediatric clinical applications. Neuroimaging Clin. N. Am. 16 (1), 45–74 (viii).

Saigal, S., Doyle, L.W., 2008. An overview of mortality and sequelae of preterm birth from infancy to adulthood. Lancet, 261–269. https://doi.org/10.1016/s0140-6736(08)60136-1.

Saigal, S., Doyle, L.W., 2009. Preterm birth 3: an overview of mortality and sequelae of preterm birth from infancy to adulthood. Obstet. Anesth. Dig., 8–9. https://doi.org/10.1097/01.aoa.0000344668.20582.5b.

Sakuma, H., et al., 1991. Adult and neonatal human brain: diffusional anisotropy and myelination with diffusion-weighted MR imaging. Radiology 180 (1), 229–233.

Šamánek, M., 2000. Congenital heart malformations: prevalence, severity, survival, and quality of life. Cardiol. Young, 179–185. https://doi.org/10.1017/s1047951100009082.

Sanfilippo, J., et al., 2020. Reintroducing dyslexia: early identification and implications for pediatric practice. Pediatrics 146 (1). https://doi.org/10.1542/peds.2019-3046.

Sarnat, H.B., Sarnat, M.S., 1976. Neonatal encephalopathy following fetal distress. A clinical and electroencephalographic study. Arch. Neurol. 33 (10), 696–705.

Schadl, K., et al., 2018. Prediction of cognitive and motor development in preterm children using exhaustive feature selection and cross-validation of near-term white matter microstructure. Neuroimage Clin. 17, 667–679.

Schaefer, C., et al., 2013. Neurodevelopmental outcome, psychological adjustment, and quality of life in adolescents with congenital heart disease. Dev. Med. Child Neurol. 55 (12), 1143–1149.

Schaefer, P.W., Ellen Grant, P., Gilberto Gonzalez, R., 2000. Diffusion-weighted MR imaging of the brain. Radiology, 331–345. https://doi.org/10.1148/radiology.217.2.r00nv24331.

Scheef, L., et al., 2017. Functional laterality of task-evoked activation in sensorimotor cortex of preterm infants: an optimized 3 T fMRI study employing a customized neonatal head coil. PLoS One. https://doi.org/10.1371/journal.pone.0169392, e0169392.

Schneider, J.F.L., et al., 2004. Fast quantitative diffusion-tensor imaging of cerebral white matter from the neonatal period to adolescence. Neuroradiology, 258–266. https://doi.org/10.1007/s00234-003-1154-2.

Setänen, S., et al., 2013. Predictive value of neonatal brain MRI on the neurodevelopmental outcome of preterm infants by 5 years of age. Acta Paediatr., 492–497. https://doi.org/10.1111/apa.12191.

Setänen, S., et al., 2016. Prediction of neuromotor outcome in infants born preterm at 11 years of age using volumetric neonatal magnetic resonance imaging and neurological examinations. Dev. Med. Child Neurol. 58 (7), 721–727.

Shankaran, S., et al., 2005. Whole-body hypothermia for neonates with hypoxic-ischemic encephalopathy. N. Engl. J. Med. 353 (15), 1574–1584.

Shankaran, S., et al., 2012. Brain injury following trial of hypothermia for neonatal hypoxic-ischaemic encephalopathy. Arch. Dis. Child. Fetal Neonatal Ed. 97 (6), F398–404. https://doi.org/10.1136/archdischild-2011-301524.

Shankaran, S., et al., 2015. Neonatal magnetic resonance imaging pattern of brain injury as a biomarker of childhood outcomes following a trial of hypothermia for neonatal hypoxic-ischemic encephalopathy. J. Pediatr. 167 (5), 987–993.e3.

Shankaran, S., et al., 2016. Hypothermia for neonatal hypoxic-ischemic encephalopathy: NICHD Neonatal Research Network contribution to the field. Semin. Perinatol. 40 (6), 385–390. https://doi.org/10.1053/j.semperi.2016.05.009.

Shanmugalingam, S., et al., 2006. Comparative prognostic utilities of early quantitative magnetic resonance imaging spin-spin relaxometry and proton magnetic resonance spectroscopy in neonatal encephalopathy. Pediatrics, 1467–1477. https://doi.org/10.1542/peds.2005-2976.

Shapiro, K.A., et al., 2017. Early changes in brain structure correlate with language outcomes in children with neonatal encephalopathy. Neuroimage Clin. 15, 572–580.

Shaywitz, S.E., 1998. Dyslexia. N. Engl. J. Med., 307–312. https://doi.org/10.1056/nejm199801293380507.

Shen, M.D., et al., 2013. Early brain enlargement and elevated extra-axial fluid in infants who develop autism spectrum disorder. Brain 136 (Pt 9), 2825–2835.

Sijens, P.E., Wischniowsky, K., Ter Horst, H.J., 2017. The prognostic value of proton magnetic resonance spectroscopy in term newborns treated with therapeutic hypothermia following asphyxia. Magn. Reson. Imaging 42, 82–87.

Smith, S.M., et al., 2009. Correspondence of the brain's functional architecture during activation and rest. Proc. Natl. Acad. Sci., 13040–13045. https://doi.org/10.1073/pnas.0905267106.

Smith-Collins, A.P.R., et al., 2015. High frequency functional brain networks in neonates revealed by rapid acquisition resting state fMRI. Hum. Brain Mapp., 2483–2494. https://doi.org/10.1002/hbm.22786.

Smyser, C.D., Kidokoro, H., Inder, T.E., 2012. Magnetic resonance imaging of the brain at term equivalent age in extremely premature neonates: to scan or not to scan? J. Paediatr. Child Health 48 (9), 794–800.

Smyser, C.D., et al., 2016. Prediction of brain maturity in infants using machine-learning algorithms. NeuroImage 136, 1–9.

Solana, A.B., et al., 2016. Quiet and distortion-free, whole brain BOLD fMRI using T2-prepared RUFIS. Magn. Reson. Med. 75 (4), 1402–1412.

Song, J.-W., et al., 2020. Neuroimaging-based deep learning in autism spectrum disorder and attention-deficit/hyperactivity disorder. J. Child Adolesc. Psychiatry 31 (3), 97–104.

Spencer, M.D., et al., 2011. A novel functional brain imaging endophenotype of autism: the neural response to facial expression of emotion. Transl. Psychiatry, e19. https://doi.org/10.1038/tp.2011.18.

Srinivasan, L., et al., 2006. Smaller cerebellar volumes in very preterm infants at term-equivalent age are associated with the presence of supratentorial lesions. AJNR Am. J. Neuroradiol. 27 (3), 573–579.

Stewart, A.L., et al., 1999. Brain structure and neurocognitive and behavioural function in adolescents who were born very preterm. Lancet, 1653–1657. https://doi.org/10.1016/s0140-6736(98)07130-x.

Stoll, B.J., Kliegman, R.M., 2004. Hypoxia-ischemia. In: Behrman, R.E., Kliegman, R.M. (Eds.), Nelson Textbook of Pediatrics. Saunders, Philadelphia, pp. 566–568.

Sun, L., et al., 2015. Reduced Fetal cerebral oxygen consumption is associated with smaller brain size in fetuses with congenital heart disease. Circulation, 1313–1323. https://doi.org/10.1161/circulationaha.114.013051.

Tharmapoopathy, P., et al., 2020. In clinical practice, cerebral MRI in newborns is highly predictive of neurodevelopmental outcome after therapeutic hypothermia. Eur. J. Paediatr. Neurol. 25, 127–133.

Thayyil, S., et al., 2010. Cerebral magnetic resonance biomarkers in neonatal encephalopathy: a meta-analysis. Pediatrics, e382–e395. https://doi.org/10.1542/peds.2009-1046.

Thompson, C.M., et al., 1997. The value of a scoring system for hypoxic ischaemic encephalopathy in predicting neurodevelopmental outcome. Acta Paediatr. 86 (7), 757–761.

Thompson, D.K., et al., 2007. Perinatal risk factors altering regional brain structure in the preterm infant. Brain 130 (Pt 3), 667–677.

Torre-Ubieta, L.D.L., et al., 2016. Advancing the understanding of autism disease mechanisms through genetics. Nat. Med., 345–361. https://doi.org/10.1038/nm.4071.

Trivedi, S.B., et al., 2017. A validated clinical MRI injury scoring system in neonatal hypoxic-ischemic encephalopathy. Pediatr. Radiol. 47 (11), 1491–1499. https://doi.org/10.1007/s00247-017-3893-y.

Tusor, N., et al., 2012. Prediction of neurodevelopmental outcome after hypoxic-ischemic encephalopathy treated with hypothermia by diffusion tensor imaging analyzed using tract-based spatial statistics. Pediatr. Res., 63–69. https://doi.org/10.1038/pr.2012.40.

Tusor, N., et al., 2017. Punctate White matter lesions associated with altered brain development and adverse motor outcome in preterm infants. Sci. Rep. 7 (1), 13250.

Twomey, E., et al., 2010. MR imaging of term infants with hypoxic-ischaemic encephalopathy as a predictor of neurodevelopmental outcome and late MRI appearances. Pediatr. Radiol. 40 (9), 1526–1535.

Ullman, H., et al., 2015. Neonatal MRI is associated with future cognition and academic achievement in preterm children. Brain 138 (Pt 11), 3251–3262.

van den Heuvel, M.P., et al., 2015. The neonatal connectome during preterm brain development. Cereb. Cortex 25 (9), 3000–3013.

van der Aa, N.E., et al., 2011. Does diffusion tensor imaging-based tractography at 3 months of age contribute to the prediction of motor outcome after perinatal arterial ischemic stroke? Stroke, 3410–3414. https://doi.org/10.1161/strokeaha.111.624858.

van der Aa, N.E., et al., 2013a. Neonatal posterior cerebral artery stroke: clinical presentation, MRI findings, and outcome. Dev. Med. Child Neurol. 55 (3), 283–290.

van der Aa, N.E., et al., 2013b. Quantification of white matter injury following neonatal stroke with serial DTI. Pediatr. Res., 756–762. https://doi.org/10.1038/pr.2013.45.

van Wezel-Meijler, G., Steggerda, S.J., Leijser, L.M., 2010. Cranial ultrasonography in neonates: role and limitations. Semin. Perinatol. 34 (1), 28–38.

Vanderauwera, J., et al., 2017. Early dynamics of white matter deficits in children developing dyslexia. Dev. Cogn. Neurosci. 27, 69–77.

Vigneron, D.B., et al., 2001. Three-dimensional proton MR spectroscopic imaging of premature and term neonates. AJNR Am. J. Neuroradiol. 22 (7), 1424–1433.

Wagenaar, N., et al., 2017. MR imaging for accurate prediction of outcome after perinatal arterial ischemic stroke: sooner not necessarily better. Eur. J. Paediatr. Neurol., 666–670. https://doi.org/10.1016/j.ejpn.2017.04.002.

Wagenaar, N., et al., 2018. Neurodevelopment after perinatal arterial ischemic stroke. Pediatrics 142 (3). https://doi.org/10.1542/peds.2017-4164.

Walter, P.J., 1992. Quality of Life after Open Heart Surgery. Springer Science & Business Media.

Watson, C.G., et al., 2016. Arterial spin labeling perfusion magnetic resonance imaging performed in acute perinatal stroke reveals hyperperfusion associated with ischemic injury. Stroke 47 (6), 1514–1519.

Weeke, L.C., et al., 2018. A novel magnetic resonance imaging score predicts neurodevelopmental outcome after perinatal asphyxia and therapeutic hypothermia. J. Pediatr. https://doi.org/10.1016/j.jpeds.2017.09.043. 33–40.e2.

Werner, H., et al., 2014. Health-related quality of life after open-heart surgery. J. Pediatr. https://doi.org/10.1016/j.jpeds.2013.10.022. 254–258.e1.

Williams, J., Lee, K.J., Anderson, P.J., 2010. Prevalence of motor-skill impairment in preterm children who do not develop cerebral palsy: a systematic review. Dev. Med. Child Neurol., 232–237. https://doi.org/10.1111/j.1469-8749.2009.03544.x.

Wintermark, P., 2015. Injury and repair in perinatal brain injury: insights from non-invasive MR perfusion imaging. Semin. Perinatol. 39 (2), 124–129.

Wolff, J.J., et al., 2012. Differences in white matter fiber tract development present from 6 to 24 months in infants with autism. Am. J. Psychiatry 169 (6), 589–600.

Wolff, J.J., et al., 2015. Altered corpus callosum morphology associated with autism over the first 2 years of life. Brain 138 (Pt 7), 2046–2058.

Wong, A., et al., 2017. Synchronous aberrant cerebellar and opercular development in fetuses and neonates with congenital heart disease: correlation with early communicative neurodevelopmental outcomes, initial experience. AJP Rep. 7 (1), e17–e27.

Woodward, L.J., et al., 2006. Neonatal MRI to predict neurodevelopmental outcomes in preterm infants. N. Engl. J. Med. 355 (7), 685–694.

Woodward, L.J., et al., 2012. Neonatal white matter abnormalities an important predictor of neurocognitive outcome for very preterm children. PLoS One 7 (12), e51879.

Young, J.M., et al., 2015. Deep grey matter growth predicts neurodevelopmental outcomes in very preterm children. NeuroImage 111, 360–368.

CHAPTER

Neuroimaging of perinatal brain disorders

22

Sandy Johng[a,b], Sara DeMauro[a,b], Daniel Licht[b,c], Scott Lorch[a,b], and Arastoo Vossough[b,d]

Division of Neonatology, Children's Hospital of Philadelphia, Philadelphia, PA, United States[a] University of Pennsylvania Perelman School of Medicine, Philadelphia, PA, United States[b] Divisions of Neurology and Pediatrics, Children's Hospital of Philadelphia, Philadelphia, PA, United States[c] Department of Radiology, Children's Hospital of Philadelphia, Philadelphia, PA, United States[d]

This chapter provides a systematic catalog of imaging findings in a broad array of perinatal brain disorders, documenting the relevant pathophysiological processes and noting the health significance in terms of incidence rates.

1. Congenital disorders of the central nervous system

1.1 Neural tube defects

1.1.1 Anencephaly

Incidence: 0.2–1:1000 births (Araujo Júnior et al., 2015; Brodsky and Martin, 2020).

Pathophysiology: Anencephaly is an open neural tube defect characterized by the absence of calvaria and brain tissue superior to the orbits (Araujo Júnior et al., 2015). Anencephaly is an early neurulation defect that occurs before 24 days of gestation and is due to failure of anterior neural tube closure (Gleason and Juul, 2018). Approximately 50% of cases will have associated anomalies such as a cleft palate, meningocele, meningomyelocele, or clubfoot (Martin et al., 2020; Pretorius et al., 1986). Most infants are stillborn, and if liveborn survive about 1–2 months, though longer survival is possible (Gleason and Juul, 2018).

Imaging: Anencephaly can be detected by first trimester ultrasound as early as 10 weeks, and becomes more distinctive as gestation continues (Martin et al., 2020). Diagnosis is made by appreciating an absence of normal cranial structures above the orbits (Fig. 1) (Araujo Júnior et al., 2015). There may be echogenic material superior to the orbits called angiomatous stroma, or area cerebrovasculosa, which represents vascularized and disorganized glial tissue (Gleason and Juul, 2018; Martin et al., 2020). When brain material appears flat, the term anencephaly is used. When brain material appears bulging and irregular, the term exencephaly may be used (Aubry et al., 2003). Exencephaly can eventually lead to anencephaly as brain tissue degrades in amniotic fluid (Gleason and Juul, 2018). During the second trimester, polyhydramnios may appear in 50% of cases (Martin et al., 2020).

1.1.2 Myelomeningocele

Incidence: 0.2–1:1000 live births (Brodsky and Martin, 2020).

Pathophysiology: Myelomeningocele is an open neural tube defect that occurs due to failure of posterior neural tube closure before 26 days of gestation (Gleason and Juul, 2018). The spinal cord, nerve

Handbook of Pediatric Brain Imaging. https://doi.org/10.1016/B978-0-12-816633-8.00012-0

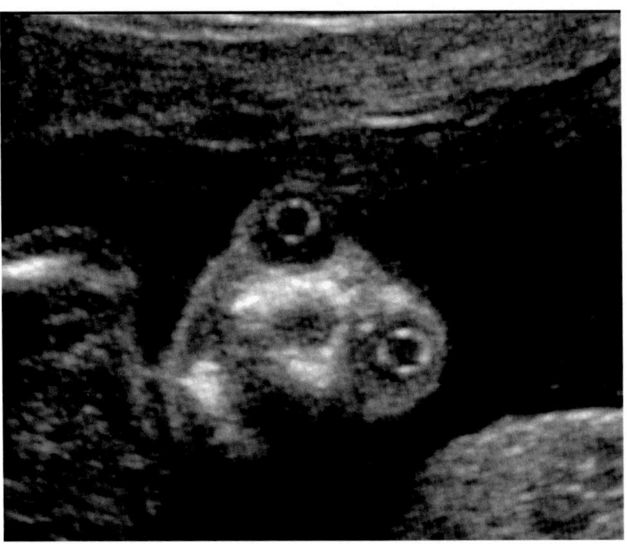

FIG. 1

Anencephaly. Fetal ultrasound at 20 weeks in the coronal plane shows absence of cephalic structures above the face.

roots, and meninges herniate through a defect in the spinal column, and are not covered by vertebrae or skin (Gleason and Juul, 2018). Most (about 75%) are thoracolumbar, lumbar, or lumbosacral (Martin et al., 2020). Prognosis improves when the defect occurs at a lower level of the spine, with the best prognosis occurring with sacral lesions (Brodsky and Martin, 2020).

Imaging: Myelomeningocele can be detected on second trimester ultrasound (Fig. 2). It may or may not have associated ventriculomegaly (Martin et al., 2020). Imaging findings may include the "lemon sign" indicating a skull deformity in which the calvarium is shaped like a lemon on axial view, which is best seen between 18 and 24 weeks. The "lemon sign," however, is not specific and may be seen in otherwise normal infants (Aubry et al., 2003; Martin et al., 2020). The "banana sign" refers to a cerebellum that has an abnormal crescent position around the brainstem (Aubry et al., 2003; Martin et al., 2020). Downward displacement of the cerebellar vermis, tonsils, medulla, and fourth ventricle into the spinal cord, as well as obliteration of the cisterna magna, are signs of a Type II Chiari malformation (Martin et al., 2020), which is often associated with myelomeningocele (Gleason and Juul, 2018). Hydrocephalus associated with Type II Chiari malformations is characterized by ventriculomegaly that is mild and asymmetric, and there is preferentially more dilation of the atria and occipital horns compared with the frontal horns (colpocephaly) (Pretorius et al., 1986).

1.1.3 Encephalocele

Incidence: 0.5–1.5:5000 live births (Araujo Júnior et al., 2015).

Pathophysiology: An encephalocele is a skin-covered herniation of brain tissue within the meningeal sac. It is thought to be a restricted defect of anterior neural tube closure that occurs before 26 days of gestation (Martin et al., 2020). The bony defect in the skull is due to failure of the surface ectoderm to

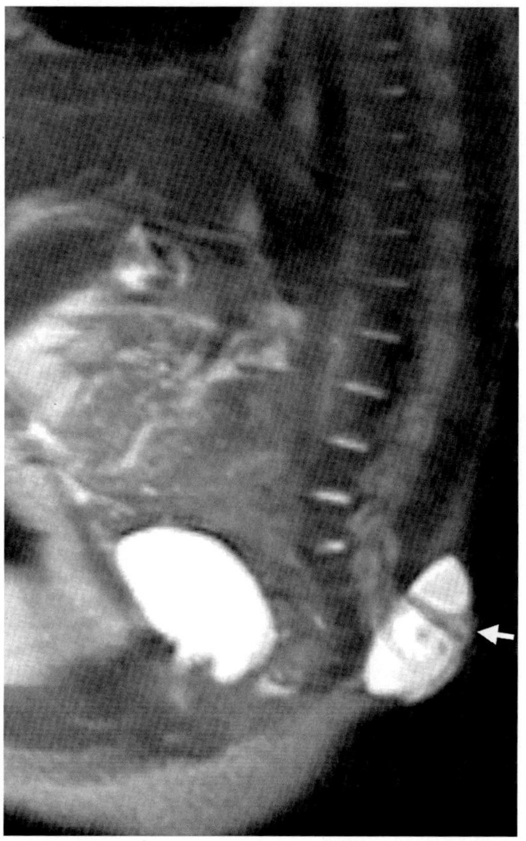

FIG. 2

Sagittal T2-weighted MRI shows a lumbosacral myelomeningocele with neural elements coursing into the sac toward the placode (*arrow*).

separate from the neuroectoderm (Pretorius et al., 1986). An encephalocele may occur in isolation, or in association with other abnormalities such as microcephaly, malformations of cortical development, craniosynostosis, dysgenesis of the corpus callosum, Chiari II malformation, hydrocephalus, arrhinencephaly, anophthalmia, cleft lip or palate, and amniotic band syndrome (Araujo Júnior et al., 2015; Gleason and Juul, 2018; Pretorius et al., 1986). Prognosis depends on whether the lesion is amenable to surgical repair. A palliative approach should be pursued for nonsurgical candidates. Outcome is also dependent on whether the encephalocele is associated with a chromosomal anomaly (i.e., trisomy 13 and 18) or other genetic syndrome (Gleason and Juul, 2018; Martin et al., 2020). In survivors, encephaloceles can be associated with medically intractable seizures and severe neurologic deficits (Brown and Sheridan-Pereira, 1992).

Imaging: An encephalocele can sometimes be detected on first trimester ultrasound, depending on location and size at the time of the scan. MRI is the study of choice, especially postnatally, to aid with surgical planning (Gleason and Juul, 2018). Findings include a calvarial defect, with herniation of a

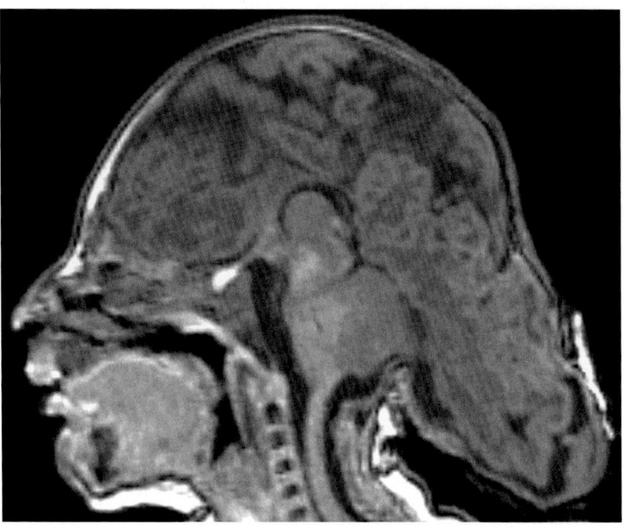

FIG. 3

Sagittal T1-weighted image shows a large occipital encephalocele, with posterior protrusion of the occipital lobes beyond the margins of the cranial vault. Presence of other malformations of the brain is associated with many of these cases.

cystic, solid, or combined cystic and solid mass (Araujo Júnior et al., 2015). The defect may be posterior (often between the lambdoid suture and foramen magnum; Fig. 3) or anterior (often between the bregma and the anterior margin of the ethmoid bone, and may involve nasal passages) (Araujo Júnior et al., 2015). The location of the encephalocele is less likely to be parietal or temporal (Martin et al., 2020). An occipital location is most common in Western populations, while a frontal location is most common in Southeast Asian populations and has a better prognosis (Gleason and Juul, 2018). When occipital and midline, the defect should be examined to ensure it is not soft tissue edema or a neck lymphangioma (Martin et al., 2020). A cranial meningocele is a type of cephalocele that contains meninges but not neural tissue (Gleason and Juul, 2018). There will often be associated polyhydramnios (Pretorius et al., 1986).

1.2 Disorders of prosencephalic development

1.2.1 Aprosencephaly and atelencephaly

Incidence: Very rare; case reports exist with no defined incidence (Nagaraj et al., 2016).

Pathophysiology: Aprosencephaly and atelencephaly are within a spectrum of disorders of forebrain development. The pathogenesis of these disorders is not entirely clear, but may be due to a disruptive mechanism that occurs very soon after neurulation. Cases may be sporadic, inherited in an autosomal recessive manner, or associated with abnormalities on chromosome 13 (Fallet-Bianco, 2018). Aprosencephaly is defined by absence of the prosencephalon, which is normally made up of the telencephalon (which gives rise to the cerebral hemispheres) and diencephalon (which gives rise to the thalami). In aprosencephaly, there still remains a cranial vault, which makes this entity distinct from anencephaly. Atelencephaly is characterized by the absence of the telencephalon, but with a retained rudimentary diencephalon. Aprosencephaly and atelencephaly are very severe and mostly lethal lesions (Nagaraj et al., 2016).

Imaging: Findings on prenatal ultrasound or MRI include an abnormal bilobed shaped skull, severe microcephaly, and a cranial protuberance that is covered by intact scalp. There will be no normal supratentorial cerebral structures. There may be only one or no orbits. The cerebellum may be normal or hypoplastic (Nagaraj et al., 2016).

1.2.2 Holoprosencephaly

Incidence: 0.5–1:10,000 live births (Kaliaperumal et al., 2016), increased in miscarried embryos and fetuses to up to 50:10,000 pregnancies (Gleason and Juul, 2018).

Pathophysiology: Holoprosencephaly represents a spectrum of defects due to absent or incomplete division of the prosencephalon between the diencephalon and the telencephalon, which would normally lead to two distinct cerebral hemispheres (Araujo Júnior et al., 2015). The defect occurs before day 33 of gestation (Martin et al., 2020). The types of holoprosencephaly, in order of mild to severe, are: Middle Interhemispheric Variant (MIHV) aka syntelencephaly, Lobar, Semilobar, and Alobar (Fig. 4) (Kaliaperumal et al., 2016). There are often extracranial cardiac, skeletal, gastrointestinal, and genitourinary malformations (Martin et al., 2020). Prognosis is extremely poor in the alobar form, unless the defect is very mild, however there are reports of some children who survive into adulthood (Kaliaperumal et al., 2016). Prognosis is improved when a holoprosencephaly diagnosis is made in isolation, and not related to a chromosomal or syndromic abnormality (Gleason and Juul, 2018).

Imaging: Holoprosencephaly can be detected on ultrasound, but false positives with ultrasound are common. Therefore, the imaging modality of choice is an MRI, which can better confirm the diagnosis, as well as characterize the severity of the defect. The "butterfly sign," or failure to identify a developing choroid plexus, may be a way to screen for holoprosencephaly in the first trimester (Kaliaperumal et al., 2016). To account for artifact from fetal movement with MRI, single-shot fast spin-echo (SS-FSE) techniques can be used. High-resolution imaging facilitates detection of more subtle forms of holoprosencephaly. Most forms of holoprosencephaly have an absent septum pellucidum and trigone, often with absent or hypoplastic olfactory bulbs and tracts (Martin et al., 2020). Note that the lobar, semilobar, and alobar forms are along a continuous spectrum of severity, with some overlapping features. *Middle Interhemispheric Variant (MIHV)*: MIHV involves fusion of the posterior frontal and parietal lobes, and variable fusion of the thalami (Kaliaperumal et al., 2016). MIHV may have associated hypotelorism and a single maxillary central incisor (Brodsky and Martin, 2020). *Lobar*: Lobar defects have nonseparation of the basal portion of typically hypoplastic frontal lobes, but the corpus callosum and third ventricle are present. There may be associated hypotelorism, single midline incisor, pyriform aperture stenosis, cleft lip and palate, colobomas, absent septum pellucidum, and nasal flattening (Brodsky and Martin, 2020; Pretorius et al., 1986). *Semilobar*: Semilobar defects have an interhemispheric fissure caudally, but at least 50% of the frontal lobes are fused, and thalami and hypothalamus may also be fused (Gleason and Juul, 2018). Semilobar defects have an absent anterior portion of the corpus callosum, and absent anterior horns of the lateral ventricles (Brodsky and Martin, 2020; Kaliaperumal et al., 2016). *Alobar*: Alobar defects have a complete lack of separation of the prosencephalon (no interhemispheric fissure), one common large central monoventricle with absence of the third ventricle, absence of the corpus callosum, fusion of thalami, basal ganglia, and hypothalamus, and optic nerve hypoplasia (Araujo Júnior et al., 2015; Kaliaperumal et al., 2016; Pretorius et al., 1986). An

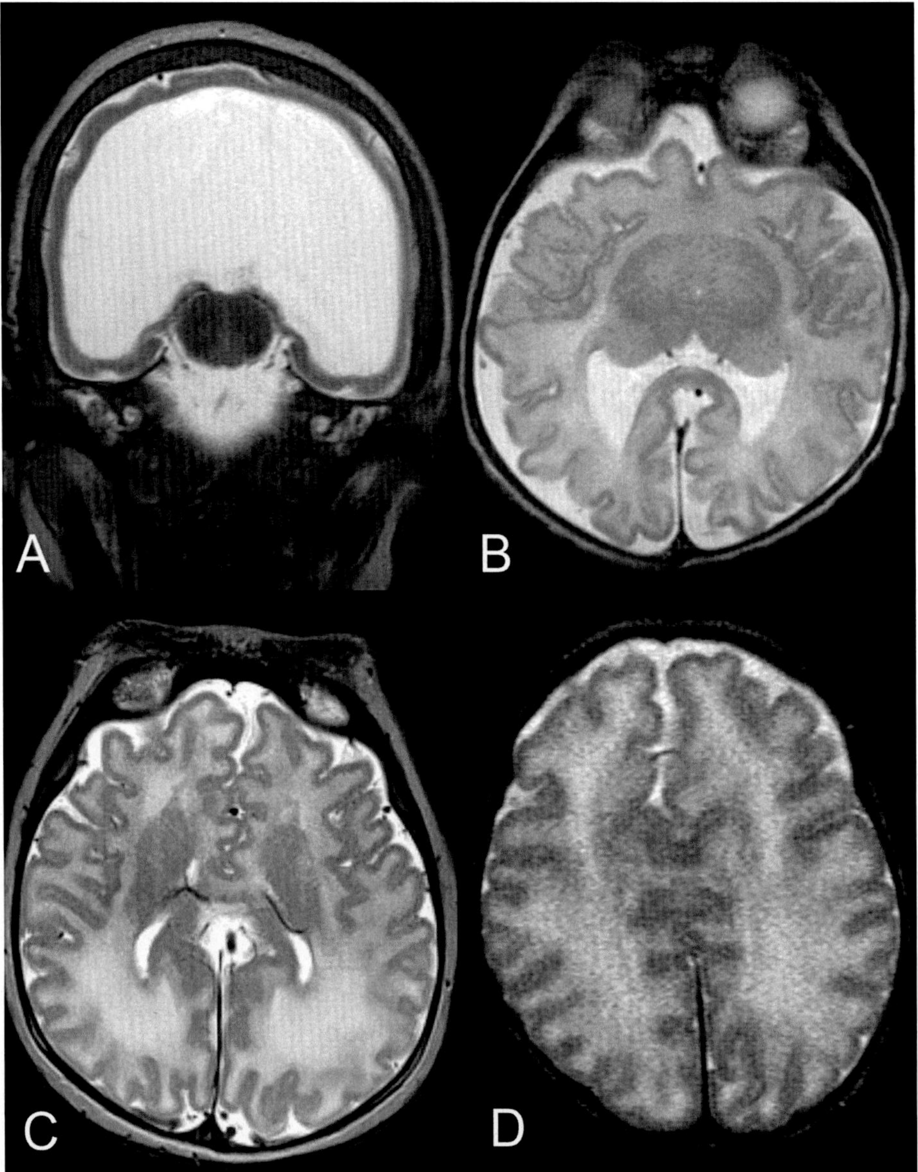

FIG. 4

(A) Alobar holoprosencephaly with midline fusion of the deep gray structures and a monoventricle. (B) Semilobar holoprosencephaly, with fusion of the deep gray nuclei, including the basal ganglia, partial ventricular fusion with absence of the septum pellucidum, and fusion of the frontal lobes. (C) Lobar holoprosencephaly with midline fusion of a part of the frontal lobes along the anterior interhemispheric fissure with absence of the genu of the corpus callosum and lightly abnormal medialization of the basal ganglia. (D) Middle interhemispheric variant holoprosencephaly (syntelencephaly) with midline fusion of a portion of the medial telencephalon along the expected location of the corpus callosum.

interhemispheric cyst may also be present in some cases. Alobar defects often have craniofacial features similar to the semilobar form and may even have cyclopia (Brodsky and Martin, 2020).

1.2.3 Agenesis of corpus callosum

Incidence: 0.5:10,000 in the general population (although true incidence is likely higher since it may be asymptomatic), 600:10,000 in children with neurologic disability (Gleason and Juul, 2018).

Pathophysiology: Agenesis of the corpus callosum (ACC) is a defect in midline development. Normally, the corpus callosum begins to form by 8 weeks, and by 12–13 weeks begins to grow caudally, typically the genu first, then the anterior body, posterior body, and splenium. This anterior-posterior development occurs over a 5–7-week period. The exception to anterior-posterior development is the rostrum, which develops later than other anterior structures, during 18–20 weeks of gestation (Barkovich and Norman, 1988). Myelination of the corpus callosum begins in the 20th week of gestation, and continues into adolescence (Davidson et al., 1985). ACC is associated with many other neuroimaging abnormalities including Dandy-Walker malformation, encephaloceles, holoprosencephaly, septo-optic dysplasia, microcephaly, cerebellar hypoplasia, polymicrogyria, simplified gyral patterns, heterotopia, hydrocephalus, and posterior fossa malformations (Barkovich and Norman, 1988; Gleason and Juul, 2018; Pretorius et al., 1986). Prognosis varies from normal development to having an increased risk for neurodevelopmental delay, particularly if associated with other malformations (Martin et al., 2020).

Imaging: The optimal timing of fetal MRI is at 20–22 weeks of gestation or later, in order to minimize the risk of false negatives with earlier scans, and to aid with pregnancy decision-making if the defect is severe (Gleason and Juul, 2018). Fetal imaging may miss a partial ACC, most commonly a dysgenetic anterior partial ACC. Ventriculomegaly may also obscure the posterior portions of the corpus callosum on MRI. Postnatal midline sagittal images are most useful in the diagnosis of ACC, in order to visualize the absence of a well-defined and myelinated cingulate gyrus (Fig. 5) (Barkovich and Norman, 1988). ACC is characterized by radial gyration medially in the bilateral hemispheres, due to the absence of the cingulate gyri, markedly separated frontal horns and bodies of the lateral ventricles, relative dilation of the occipital horns, and dilation of the third ventricle, also referred to as "colpocephaly" (Pretorius et al., 1986). Probst bundles are fiber bundles that run parallel to the interhemispheric fissure due to failure of these axonal bundles to cross midline, and are a classic finding of ACC that can be appreciated on axial or coronal imaging (Barkovich and Norman, 1988). Probst bundles may indent the superior-medial borders of the lateral ventricles, causing them to have a characteristic crescent shape (Barkovich and Norman, 1988). The medial cortex will curl away from the midline (rather than in normal development where the medial cortex curls toward the midline) (Gleason and Juul, 2018). There may be associated cysts and lipomas that can be appreciated on T1-weighted imaging (Gleason and Juul, 2018).

1.2.4 Absence of septum pellucidum

Incidence: 2–3:100,000 in the general population (Barkovich and Norman, 1989), but likely higher due to the large population of asymptomatic subjects.

Pathophysiology: Absence of the septum pellucidum may be an isolated finding, but may also be associated with an underlying brain malformation, such as holoprosencephaly, septo-optic dysplasia, agenesis of the corpus callosum, and Chiari II malformation (Barkovich and Norman, 1989). Prognosis is heavily dependent on whether there are associated CNS malformations, as isolated absence of the septum pellucidum may have normal development (Borkowski-Tillman et al., 2020). For this reason, if detected

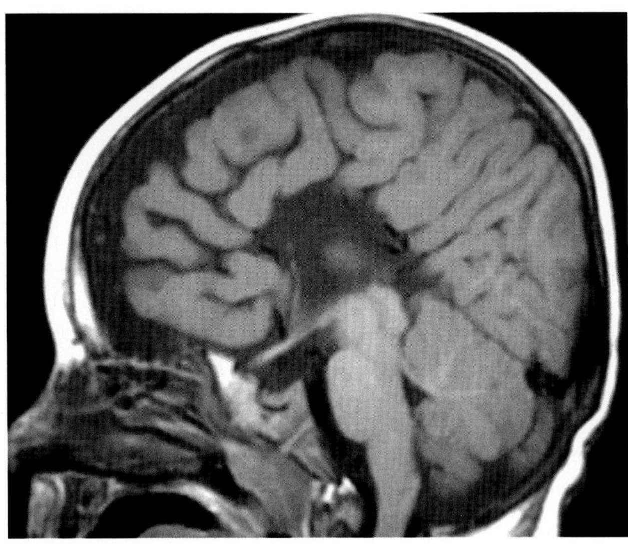

FIG. 5

Sagittal T1-weighted image of the brain shows absence of the corpus callosum.

on ultrasound, a follow-up fetal MRI is often recommended. Note that marked chronic hydrocephalus may also result in acquired tears and dissolution of the septum pellucidum, mimicking congenital absence.

Imaging: The septum pellucidum consists of two thin vertical membranes between the anterior horns of the lateral ventricles. The cavum septum pellucidum is the space between these two membranes (Brodsky and Martin, 2020). An absent septum pellucidum is often associated with a square-shaped appearance of the frontal horns of the lateral ventricles (Fig. 6) (Barkovich and Norman, 1989). The fornix may be in an abnormally low position, with a more caudal attachment to the splenium, thought to be due to a lack of tethering from the septum (Barkovich and Norman, 1989).

1.2.5 Septo-optic dysplasia

Incidence: 1:10,000 live births (Webb and Dattani, 2010).

Pathophysiology: Diagnosis of septo-optic dysplasia is made when at least two out of the three following criteria are met: optic nerve hypoplasia, absence of the septum pellucidum, and pituitary dysfunction. Approximately 30% of patients will have all three features, and 60% will have an absent septum pellucidum (Webb and Dattani, 2010). Septo-optic dysplasia may also be associated with schizencephaly in a minority of cases, which is an important distinction to make as it affects prognosis. The spectrum of disease ranges from diagnosis prenatally, diagnosis at birth due to the presence of multiple congenital anomalies, to diagnosis later in childhood secondary to growth failure and mild visual defects. Septo-optic dysplasia can be associated with cerebral palsy, developmental delay, and seizures (Webb and Dattani, 2010). Familial cases have been described and three genes (HESX1, OTX2, and SOX2) have been associated with the disorder, however the majority of cases do not have a recognized genetic mutation.

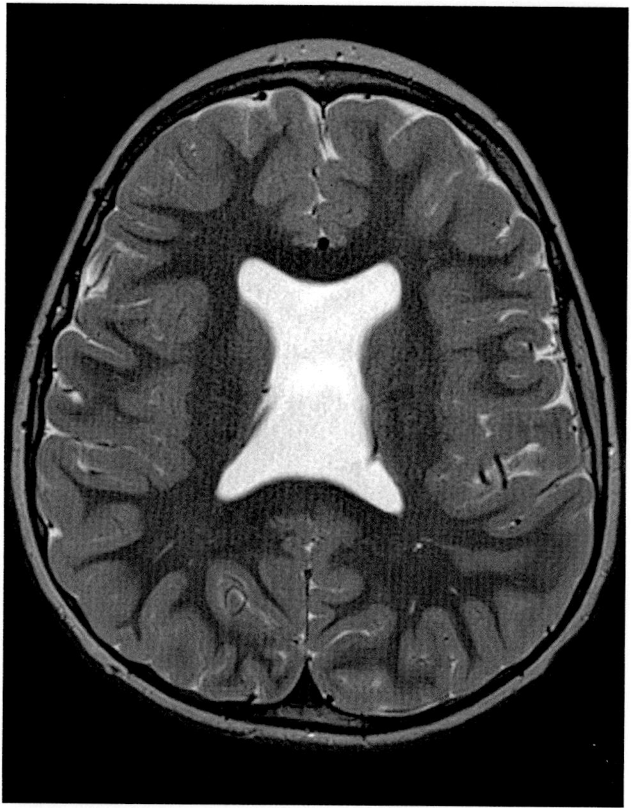

FIG. 6

Axial T2-weighted image shows absence of the septum pellucidum in the midline.

Imaging: Septo-optic dysplasia should be suspected prenatally with findings of absent septum pellucidum. Hypoplasia of the optic nerves may be unilateral or bilateral (Fig. 7). Postnatally, MRI should include dedicated pituitary images looking at the anterior pituitary size, presence and location of the posterior pituitary, and presence and caliber of the infundibulum (Webb and Dattani, 2010). Note that the vast majority of patients with absence of the septum pellucidum will not have discernible anatomic abnormalities on imaging.

1.3 Disorders of neuronal proliferation

1.3.1 Microcephaly

Incidence: Primary microcephaly is rare (<1:10,000) (Martin et al., 2020).

Pathophysiology: Primary microcephaly describes the failure of brain growth during pregnancy due to insufficient neurogenesis, while secondary microcephaly represents normal brain growth during pregnancy followed by abnormal brain growth postnatally. Primary microcephaly is likely on the same phenotypic continuum as microcephaly with simplified gyral pattern, of which there are two reported variants—normal/thin corpus callosum versus agenesis of the corpus callosum (Martin et al., 2020).

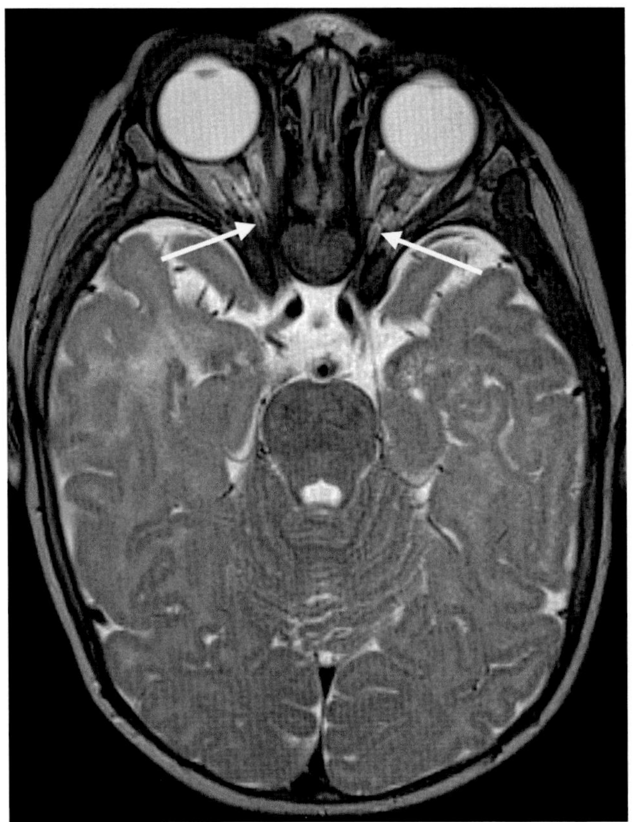

FIG. 7

Septo-optic dysplasia. Axial T2-weighted image through the level of the optic nerves shows abnormally thin optic nerves (*white arrows*) in a patient with absence of the septum pellucidum.

Primary microcephaly can also be seen as part of various genetic syndromes, and environmental factors including hypoxic ischemia, severe maternal malnutrition, and congenital infections (i.e., cytomegalovirus, *Toxoplasma gondii*, Rubella virus, and Zika virus) (Martin et al., 2020). The differential diagnosis for secondary microcephaly is very broad, and includes acquired etiologies and primary developmental microcephaly (Martin et al., 2020). Prognosis depends on associated conditions, as well as the severity of the microcephaly. Developmental delays are seen in approximately 80% of those with severe microcephaly (Gleason and Juul, 2018).

Imaging: Microcephaly diagnosis can be made on ultrasound, with measurement of a head circumference and biparietal diameter that is below two standard deviations for age and gender (Fig. 8). Severe microcephaly is defined as below three standard deviations for age and gender (Martin et al., 2020). Fetuses with microcephaly also have abdomen-head size discrepancy, given the head is smaller than expected, and serial ultrasounds demonstrate poor fetal brain growth (Pretorius et al., 1986). In cases where head circumference remains borderline and diagnosis is unclear, MRI can be used to help identify the presence of associated abnormalities (Aubry et al., 2003). Microcephaly may be associated with a variety of brain

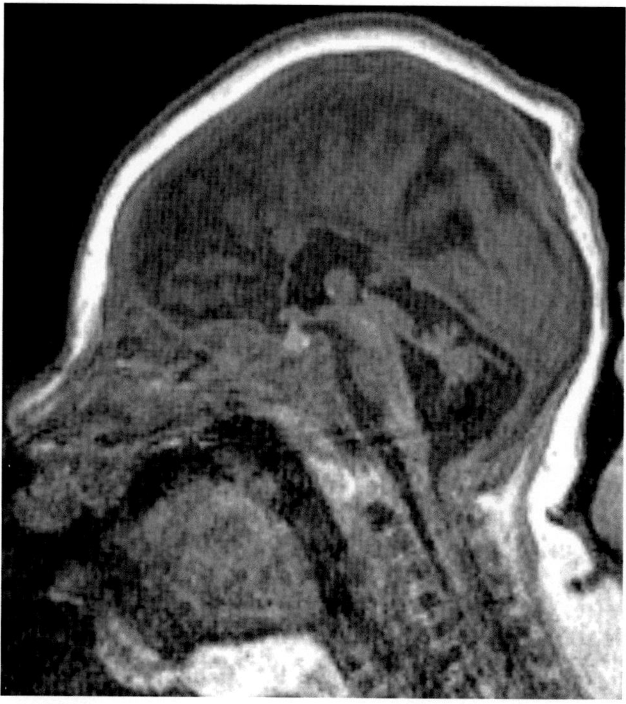

FIG. 8

Sagittal T1-weighted image of the brain shows abnormally small cranial vault and brain compared to the face in a patient with microcephaly. The cerebellum is also abnormal and small.

malformations, a simplified gyral pattern, with or without agenesis of the corpus callosum, other malformations of cortical development, or thinning of the corpus callosum. Brain parenchyma may be normal or, depending on the etiology, may appear disorganized, as with intrauterine infections (Martin et al., 2020).

1.3.2 Megalencephaly

Incidence: 2% of the general population is macrocephalic, and of those who are macrocephalic, 10%–30% have megalencephaly (Gooskens et al., 1988).

Pathophysiology: Megalencephaly is defined as an increase in brain size or weight greater than two standard deviations above the mean, and is due to an increased size and/or number of neurons and glia. This is in contrast to macrocephaly, which refers to an increase in head circumference for age, and may not be due to increase in brain size, but rather the size of the skull, ventricles, or collections of subdural fluid. Megalencephaly is often associated with developmental delay, behavioral problems, and epilepsy, whereas macrocephaly may be an isolated benign finding (Winden et al., 2015). Therefore, it is important to utilize neuroimaging in order to distinguish between megalencephaly and macrocephaly. Etiologies for megalencephaly are either metabolic (disorders that cause an abnormal accumulation of metabolites, i.e., organic acidurias, lysosomal storage disease, leukoencephalopathies, mucopolysaccharidosis) or anatomic (involving genetic mutations that affect neuronal growth, replication, and migration such as PIK3CA mutations (megalencephaly capillary malformation syndrome) and mTOR mutations)

(Gleason and Juul, 2018; Winden et al., 2015). Rarely, it may be part of a syndrome that includes other neuroimaging and anatomic abnormalities such as Megalencephaly, Polymicrogyria, Polydactyly, and Hydrocephalus (MPPH) syndrome (Gleason and Juul, 2018). The cortical malformation in MPPH syndrome consists of bilateral perisylvian polymicrogyria (Mirzaa, 1993). Megalencephaly may be unilateral (hemimegalencephaly) or bilateral (symmetric megalencephaly) (Martin et al., 2020).

Imaging: Diagnosis of macrocephaly can be made on ultrasound, by measuring a head circumference and biparietal diameter that is greater than two standard deviations above the mean (Gooskens et al., 1988). Once a diagnosis of macrocephaly is established, follow-up MRI can determine whether the etiology is increased growth of brain tissue, at which point a diagnosis of megalencephaly can be made. Symmetric megalencephaly may be associated with hydrocephalus or pachygyria (Martin et al., 2020). With hemimegalencephaly, the affected enlarged hemisphere is abnormal, with associated polymicrogyria, pachygyria, agyria, focal cortical dysplasia, gray matter heterotopia, and/or white matter signal changes (Fig. 9) (Martin et al., 2020; Santos et al., 2014). These associated abnormalities are best

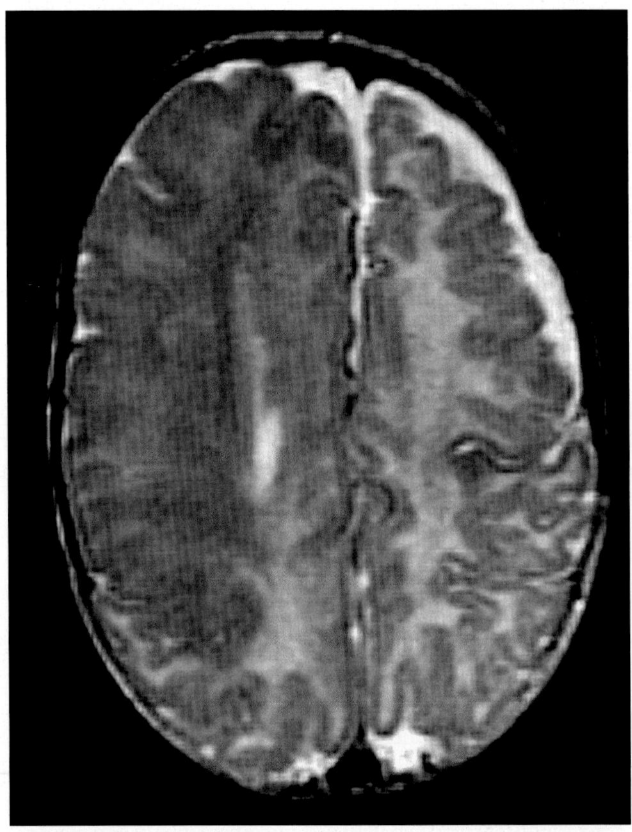

FIG. 9

Axial T2-weighted image shows an asymmetrically enlarged right cerebral hemisphere in a patient with hemimegalencephaly. The abnormal larger hemisphere demonstrates abnormal myelination and malformations of cortical development.

appreciated on MRI. Hemimegalencephaly can also be characterized into diffuse versus localized; the latter will refer to specific areas in which the abnormalities are concentrated, i.e., frontal-lobe-dominant type (in which frontal and temporal lobes are dominant) or occipital-lobe-dominant type (in which occipital and parietal lobes are dominant) (Nakahashi et al., 2009).

1.4 Disorders of neuronal migration

1.4.1 Schizencephaly

Incidence: Rare, around 1.5 per 100,000 births (Curry et al., 2005; Howe et al., 2012).

Pathophysiology: Schizencephaly is a congenital cleft in the cerebral hemisphere that is lined by abnormal cortical gray matter and may extend from the pial surface to the lateral ventricles (closed lip) or directly communicate into the ventricle (open lip) (Denis et al., 2000). Schizencephaly may be due to a variety of etiologies, including ischemia, vascular malformations, infection, or failure of neural migration during the second to fourth months of gestation (Denis et al., 2000; Gleason and Juul, 2018). A genetic etiology is possible as well, as familial cases of schizencephaly have been reported, and schizencephaly may be associated with septo-optic dysplasia syndrome (Denis et al., 2000). Clinical presentation is variable, and diagnosis may be made in utero, in infancy, or in adulthood (Denis et al., 2000). Presenting symptoms include asymmetric muscle tone (when unilateral), developmental delay (more likely when bilateral), or seizures (Denis et al., 2000).

Imaging: Diagnosis is best made by MRI, since it is the ideal imaging modality to distinguish gray matter and cortical abnormalities (Denis et al., 2000). Schizencephaly may be unilateral, bilateral, or multifocal, and can be open-lipped or closed-lipped (Martin et al., 2020). Close-lipped lesions do not have a cleft that communicates with the ventricles, have gray matter at its base, and cause dimpling of the ventricular wall (Denis et al., 2000). Open-lipped lesions have CSF within the cleft that extends from the lateral ventricles to the subarachnoid space (Fig. 10) (Denis et al., 2000). Severe lesions (bilateral open-lipped) typically have enlargement of the lateral ventricles (Gleason and Juul, 2018). Associated cerebral findings include an absent septum pellucidum, malformation of cortical development, agenesis or dysplasia of the corpus callosum, septo-optic dysplasia, arachnoid cysts, and optic nerve hypoplasia (Denis et al., 2000; Gleason and Juul, 2018).

1.4.2 Lissencephaly

Incidence: Rare, around 1 per 100,000 births (de Rijk-van Andel et al., 1991).

Pathophysiology: Lissencephaly is a spectrum of malformations due to an abnormality of normal neuronal migration outward from the ventricular zone near the lateral ventricles, which is associated with a thickened cortex with reduced folding (Fry et al., 2014). This leads to the absence of or reduced number of gyri, resulting in an abnormally smooth cortical surface (Fig. 11) (Gleason and Juul, 2018). Lissencephaly is associated with a number of genetic abnormalities, which may correlate with phenotypic neuroimaging findings described below under "Imaging." Lissencephaly is often diagnosed in utero in later pregnancy, or during infancy as symptoms of hypotonia, developmental delay, seizures, spasticity, and/or progressive microcephaly emerge (Gleason and Juul, 2018). The earliest radiologic findings appear around 23–26 weeks of gestation, which is why this diagnosis may be missed prenatally (Lerman-Sagie and Leibovitz, 2016).

Imaging: Mutations in the *LIS1* gene account for the majority of cases of classic lissencephaly, which fall within the classic lissencephaly/subcortical band heterotopia spectrum (also referred to as classical lissencephaly or type 1 lissencephaly) (Fry et al., 2014; Gleason and Juul, 2018). This form

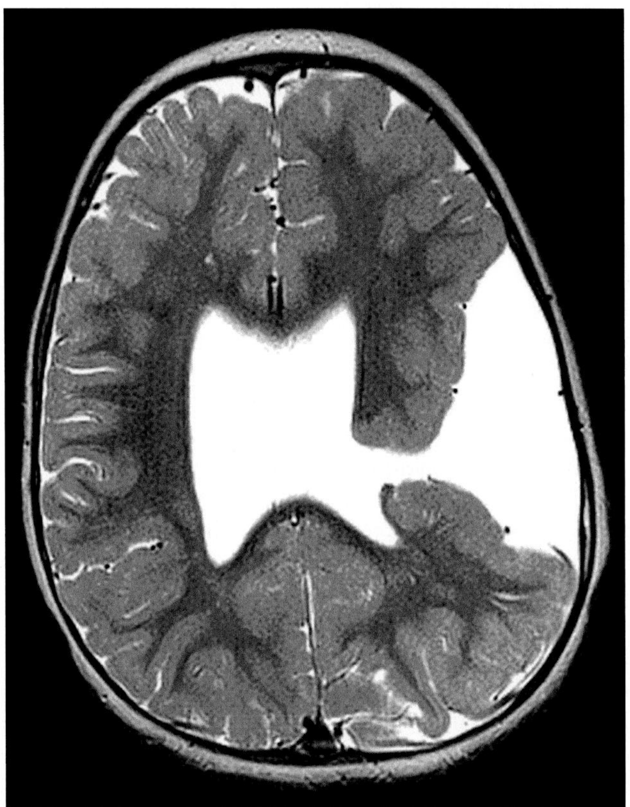

FIG. 10

Axial T2-weighted image of the brain shows an abnormal deep cleft in the left cerebral hemisphere communicating with the lateral ventricle (open lip schizencephaly). The cleft is lined by abnormal gray matter. There is a smaller closed lip cleft on the right.

of lissencephaly is distinguished by the presence of an abnormally thick cortex (12–20 mm compared with a normal thickness of 3–4 mm) separated from a deeper layer of neurons by a "cell sparse layer." There is a posterior-to-anterior severity gradient, in which posterior structures have more severe abnormalities (Fry et al., 2014; Lerman-Sagie and Leibovitz, 2016). There may be associated shallow Sylvian fissures, lateral ventriculomegaly, mild hypoplasia of the corpus callosum, and mild hypoplasia of the cerebellar vermis (Fry et al., 2014; Lerman-Sagie and Leibovitz, 2016). Classical lissencephaly is also associated with the *DCX* gene mutation, which causes 10% of isolated lissencephaly sequence (mostly males), 85% of sporadic subcortical band heterotopia in females, and 25% of sporadic subcortical band heterotopia in males. *DCX* mutations preferentially cause anterior rather than posterior abnormalities, ventricular dilation of the anterior horns, and mild hypoplasia of the corpus callosum (Fry et al., 2014). Mutations in tubulin genes can result in lissencephaly and are associated with cerebellar hypoplasia, a thin or absent corpus callosum, congenital microcephaly, and characteristic dysplasia of the basal ganglia and brainstem (Fry et al., 2014; Gleason and Juul, 2018). Mutations

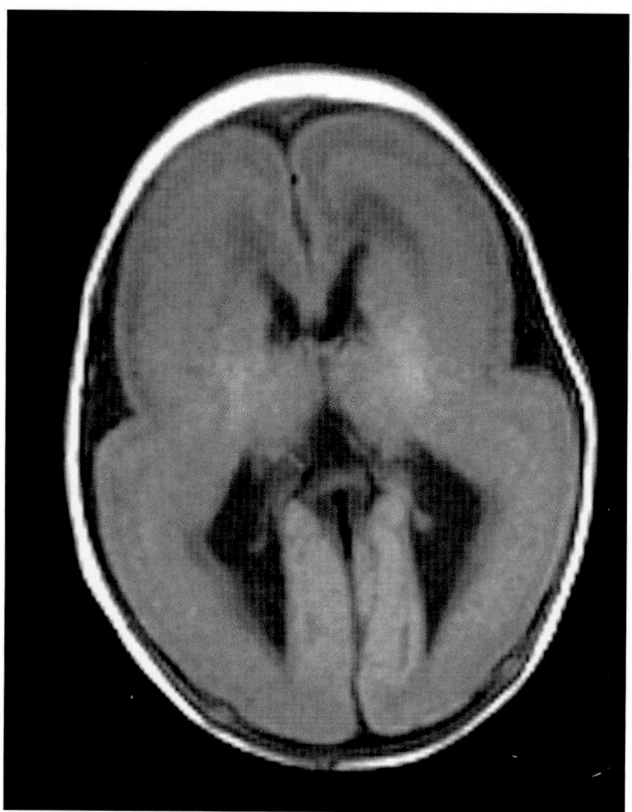

FIG. 11

Axial T1-weighted image of a brain with lissencephaly in a term infant showing abnormally smooth brain surface both anteriorly and posteriorly.

in the *ARX* gene cause an X-linked lissencephaly that has a slightly thicker cortex (i.e., 5–7 mm) and is more likely to have posterior abnormalities. This X-linked lissencephaly is associated with white matter immaturity, basal ganglia abnormalities, moderate dilation of the lateral ventricles, and an absent corpus callosum (Fry et al., 2014; Gleason and Juul, 2018). Homozygous mutations in the *RELN* gene result in an uncommon form of lissencephaly with severe cerebellar hypoplasia, abnormal brainstem, dysplastic hippocampus, and a thick cortex (Fry et al., 2014; Gleason and Juul, 2018). Homozygous mutations in the *NDE1* gene cause microlissencephaly, which is defined by lissencephaly in the presence of severe microcephaly (head circumference less than three standard deviations below the mean). Neuroradiological features of microlissencephaly include simplified gyration, agenesis of the corpus callosum, dilation of the lateral ventricles, and a small cerebellum and brainstem (Fry et al., 2014).

1.4.3 Polymicrogyria

Incidence: True incidence is unknown given the heterogeneity of this condition (Jansen and Andermann, 2005).

Pathophysiology: Polymicrogyria represents a spectrum of disorders of excessive gyration, due to abnormal development during late neuronal migration or early postmigration. There is overmigration beyond the limiting pial basement membrane. Etiology includes congenital infection, prenatal ischemia, metabolic disorders, as well as various genetic causes (Barkovich et al., 2005; Lerman-Sagie and Leibovitz, 2016). The appearance of polymicrogyria changes with increasing gestational age and may be very difficult or impossible to detect in the early stages of pregnancy, so serial images can be obtained throughout pregnancy after the suspicion of diagnosis, or in fetuses at risk. The extent of abnormal gyration determines the severity of clinical presentation. When polymicrogyria is bilateral or involves more than half of one hemisphere, there is a high risk of moderate-to-severe developmental delay (Barkovich et al., 2005).

Imaging: Polymicrogyria can occur anywhere in the cerebral cortex, but most commonly occurs around the Sylvian fissure, particularly the posterior aspect (Fig. 12). In addition to excessive cortical gyration, there may be apparent cortical thickening (particularly on lower resolution imaging or in

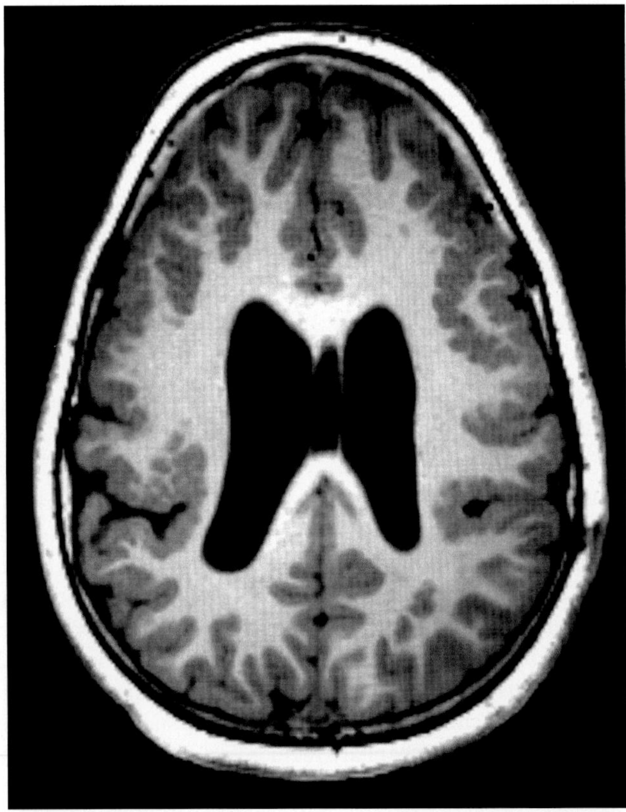

FIG. 12

Axial T1-weighted image of the brain shows abnormal small and serrated gyri in the bilateral frontal and perisylvian regions, in keeping with polymicrogyria.

unmyelinated brains), shallow sulci, and irregularity along the gray-white matter interface (Lerman-Sagie and Leibovitz, 2016).

1.5 Dandy-Walker malformation

Incidence: 1 in 5000 liveborn infants (Parisi and Dobyns, 2003).

Pathophysiology: The components of Dandy-Walker malformation include hypoplasia or aplasia of the cerebellar vermis, cystic dilation of the fourth ventricle, and elevation of the tentorium and torcular herophili (fed by the falcine sinus instead of the straight sinus), with or without obstructive hydrocephalus and enlarged lateral ventricles (Parisi and Dobyns, 2003). Approximately 10%–17% will have associated agenesis or dysgenesis of the corpus callosum. There are various etiologies for Dandy-Walker malformations, including environmental, vascular, and genetic factors. Given the low recurrence rate of 1%–3%, it is likely due to de novo mutations (Gleason and Juul, 2018). Presentation varies from prenatal diagnosis, to presenting in infancy or childhood (with macrocephaly, hydrocephalus, developmental delay, or ataxia), to presenting incidentally in asymptomatic adults (Parisi and Dobyns, 2003).

Imaging: Midsagittal MRI images of a Dandy-Walker malformation demonstrate an upwardly rotated hypoplastic or aplastic cerebellar vermis, and elevation of the torcular herophili (Fig. 13). Axial MR images can be used to visualize a large retrocerebellar space adjacent to the hypoplastic or aplastic vermis. Hydrocephalus will be present 50%–80% of the time. Midsagittal MRI images will demonstrate elevation of the torcula, or confluence of the sinuses, which is due to enlargement of the posterior fossa (Parisi and Dobyns, 2003).

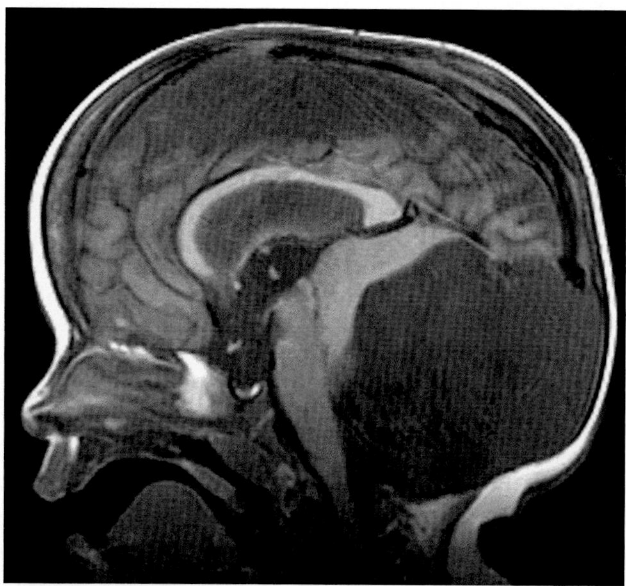

FIG. 13

Dandy-Walker malformation. Sagittal T1-weighted image of the brain shows a markedly expanded posterior fossa with a large cyst, abnormal development and displacement of the cerebellum, and elevated torcular herophili.

1.6 Fetal ventriculomegaly

Incidence: 2 in 1000 births (Pisapia et al., 2017).

Pathophysiology: Fetal ventriculomegaly involves enlargement of the lateral ventricles, and may or may not be associated with hydrocephalus, which indicates an increase in intracranial pressure (Pisapia et al., 2017). In most cases, there is isolated fetal ventriculomegaly, but there are a wide range of associated etiologies for fetal ventriculomegaly as well, including associated agenesis of the corpus callosum (colpocephaly), type II Chiari malformations, cerebral atrophy (due to infarction or metabolic, infectious, or hypoxic disorders), and obstruction to flow of cerebral spinal fluid (due to aqueductal stenosis from congenital malformations, infection, or hemorrhage) (Martin et al., 2020; Pisapia et al., 2017). When fetal ventriculomegaly is found in isolation, prognosis may be favorable. However, in the setting of associated cerebral anomalies or genetic disorders, patients may have significant neurodevelopmental delay (Winkler et al., 2018).

Imaging: Ventriculomegaly can be diagnosed on ultrasound and is defined as a single measurement over 10 mm at the level of the posterior atria of the lateral ventricles, at any stage of pregnancy. The atrium of the lateral ventricle is where the body, occipital horn, and temporal horn of the lateral ventricles converge. Atrial diameter is measured in the axial plane from the inner walls of the atria at the level of the glomus of the choroid plexus. Average atrial diameter values range from 6.2 ± 1.2 to 7.6 ± 0.6 mm, so a measurement over 10 mm is 3–4 standard deviations above the mean. A measurement of 10–12 mm is considered mild, 12–15 mm is intermediate, and >15 mm is considered to be severe (Pisapia et al., 2017). A combination of ultrasound and MRI imaging (Fig. 14) would be useful prenatally to assess for any other associated neuroimaging abnormalities, as the underlying cause of ventriculomegaly is much more indicative of future prognosis than simply the degree of ventriculomegaly (Pisapia et al., 2017).

2. Disorders related to prematurity

2.1 Intraventricular hemorrhage

Incidence: Incidence of severe intraventricular hemorrhage (IVH) (severe defined as grade 3 or grade 4 IVH) in all infants born at 22–28 weeks is 15%. The incidence of severe IVH increases with decreasing gestational age. At 22 weeks, the incidence of severe IVH is 39%, at 23 weeks it is 37%, at 24 weeks it is 24%, at 25 weeks it is 20%, at 26 weeks it is 12%, at 27 weeks it is 9%, and at 28 weeks it is 6% (Stoll et al., 2015).

Pathophysiology: The germinal matrix is a highly vascularized developmental structure along the caudo-thalamic groove. The germinal matrix is most prominent between 24 and 32 weeks' gestation along the lateral margins of the lateral ventricles, and often completely regresses by term gestation. Following preterm delivery, the germinal matrix vessels are highly vulnerable to rupture due to the inability to accommodate to variations in blood pressure and blood flow, thus predisposing these areas to hemorrhage. Grade 4 IVH, which is also referred to as periventricular hemorrhagic infarction (PVHI), was previously thought to be exclusively due to direct extension of IVH into the parenchyma, but is now thought to include secondary changes related to impaired venous drainage followed by venous infarction and hemorrhage. Of note, periventricular venous infarct with hemorrhage may not have a component of intraventricular hemorrhage, which would exclude it from being classified as an IVH

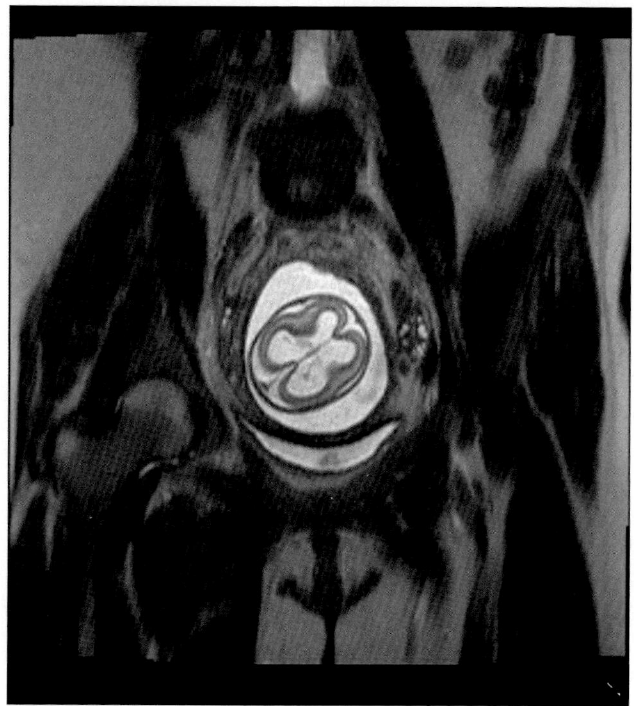

FIG. 14

Axial T2-weighted image in a 20-week-old fetus showing moderate ventriculomegaly.

grade. The majority of IVH will occur within the first week of life, and many of these will be within the first 48 h of life. About 10% will occur after the first week of life (Leijser and de Vries, 2019).

Imaging: Head ultrasounds are commonly used to screen for IVH in VLBW (<1500 g) and ELBW (<1000 g) infants <32 weeks of gestation. IVH is classified according to grades 1–4, grades 3 and 4 being considered severe IVH (Fig. 15). IVH grades 1–4 were initially described in CT scans, then were adopted to ultrasound (Papile et al., 1978). Grade 1 is a hemorrhage that is confined to the germinal matrix. Grade 2 describes IVH without ventricular dilation. Grade 3 involves IVH with ventricular dilation. Grade 4, or PVHI, describes venous infarction and hemorrhage in the parenchyma ipsilateral to the area of IVH (Dorner et al., 2018).

2.1.1 Short-term outcomes of IVH

Any degree of IVH, including mild IVH, has been associated with increased odds of moderate-severe neurodevelopmental impairment (NDI). The odds of moderate-severe NDI progressively increase with increased severity of IVH (Mukerji et al., 2015). Patients with parenchymal involvement as seen in grade 4 IVH are at particularly increased risk for cerebral palsy (Dorner et al., 2018). Please refer to Chapter 23 "Current status of neuroimaging of pediatric neurological disorders" for long-term outcomes.

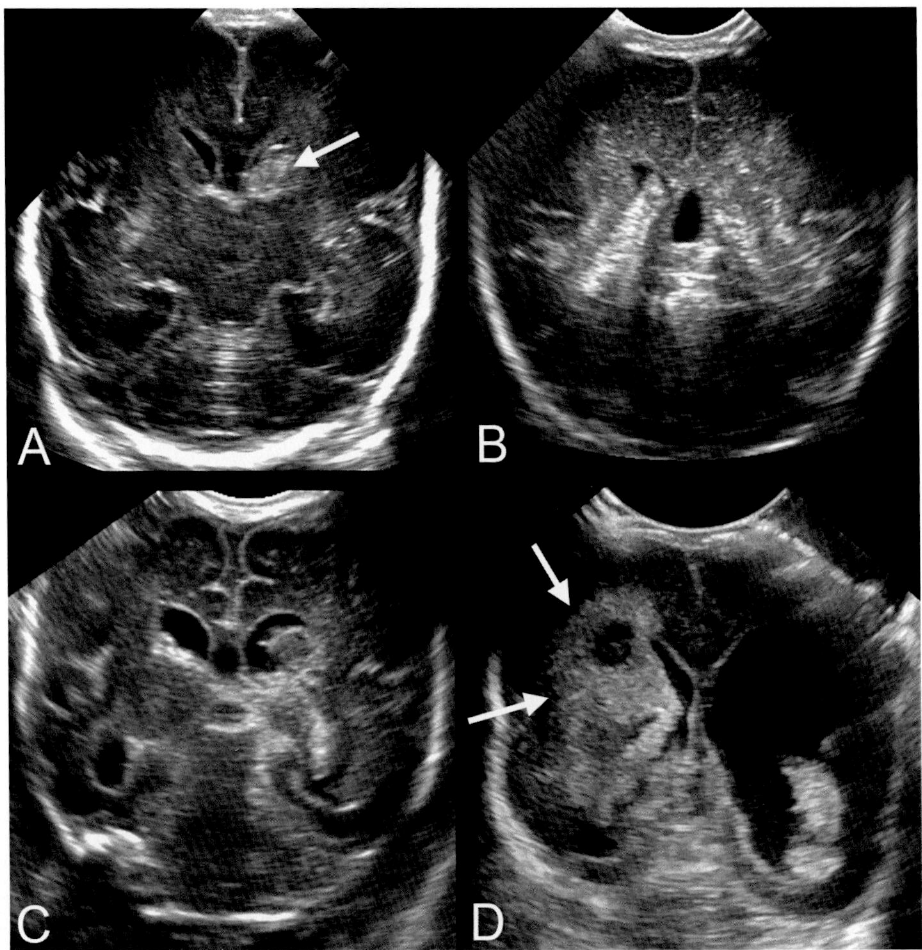

FIG. 15

Spectrum of intraventricular hemorrhage (IVH) on ultrasound. (A) Grade I IVH: On a coronal transfontanellar view, there is an echogenic focus in the left caudothalamic groove (*arrow*), in keeping with germinal matrix hemorrhage, with normal ventricular size. (B) Grade II IVH: There is intraventricular hemorrhage without lateral ventricle dilatation. (C) Grade III IVH: Coronal view shows intraventricular echogenicity in keeping with hemorrhage, with mild-to-moderate ventricular dilatation. (D) Grade IV IVH: Extensive hemorrhage bilaterally, right greater than left, with ventricular dilatation and involvement of the brain parenchyma (*arrows*).

2.1.2 Posthemorrhagic hydrocephalus

Incidence: 60% of patients with severe IVH (grade 3 or 4) progress to develop posthemorrhagic hydrocephalus (PHH) (Klebe et al., 2020).

Pathophysiology: Following IVH, disruption of the ventricular lining, meningeal fibrosis, subependymal gliosis, and periventricular inflammation prevent sufficient flow and resorption of cerebrospinal fluid, resulting in PHH (Leijser and de Vries, 2019). Other important contributors likely include an increase in parenchymal and perivascular deposition of extracellular matrix proteins (Cherian et al., 2004). PHH typically develops 1–3 weeks after IVH has occurred (Holt, 1989). It is possible to have posthemorrhagic ventricular dilatation (PHVD) without hydrocephalus. Once there are symptoms of increased intracranial pressure (including increased head circumference, splaying of sutures, and a bulging anterior fontanelle) with progressive ventricular dilation, the diagnosis of PHH may be made (Cherian et al., 2004; Holt, 1989).

Imaging: Head ultrasound is used in infants with IVH to screen for PHVD and PHH (Fig. 16) (Dorner et al., 2018). Serial ultrasounds are needed to distinguish between simple ventriculomegaly and progressive PHH (Holt, 1989). In coronal views, the biventricular-biparietal ratio (BV:BP) can be measured by dividing the ventricle width by the inner width of the skull. This is most reliably done at the level of the foramen of Monro. A normal ratio is 0.25, mild ventricular enlargement has a ratio of <0.4, moderate 0.4–0.6, and severe >0.6. On sagittal views, the ventricular diameter of the lateral ventricle can be obtained by measuring from the posterior edge of the thalamus at the 2 o'clock position and making a 45-degree angle line to the edge of the white matter in the parietal lobe. A normal ventricular diameter in >28 weeks' gestation is <5 mm. A ventricular diameter of 10–15 mm indicates mild ventricular enlargement, 15–20 mm is moderate, and >20 mm is severe (Holt, 1989).

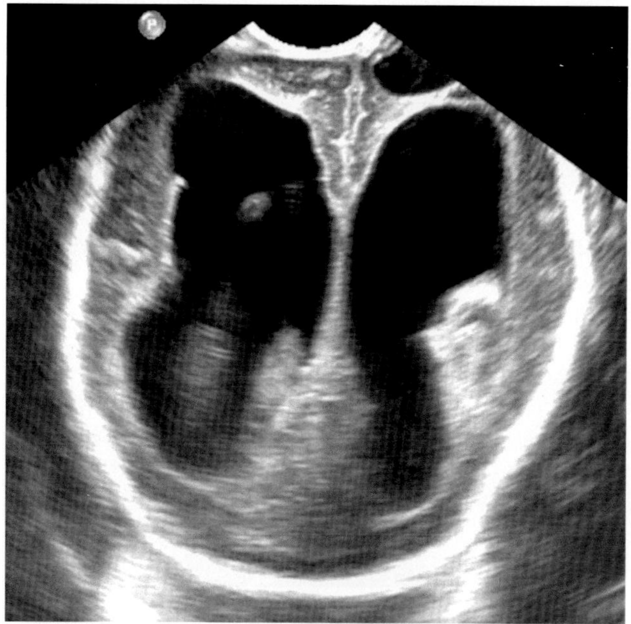

FIG. 16

Head ultrasound in a 4-week-old infant showing residual intraventricular hemorrhage and dilated ventricles, consistent with posthemorrhagic hydrocephalus.

2.2 Periventricular leukomalacia

Incidence: The incidence of periventricular leukomalacia (PVL) in infants born at 22–28 weeks' gestation is 4% (Stoll et al., 2015).

Pathophysiology: The pathophysiology of PVL is made up of two components—focal periventricular necrosis, and disturbance of preoligodendrocytes with associated astrogliosis and microgliosis, which leads to hypomyelination. The spectrum of PVL from least to greatest severity is as follows: microscopic focal necroses with focal gliosis, small macroscopic necroses with focal gliosis but no cystic change, and large macroscopic focal necroses with cystic change (Volpe, 2017). Punctate white matter injuries may also happen in term neonates, particularly in those with complex congenital heart disease.

Imaging: PVL can be detected on head ultrasound, and is characterized by intraparenchymal white matter lesions that appear as hyperechogenic regions and later become cystic (Fig. 17). Only once PVL becomes cystic can it be more easily detected on ultrasound, since ultrasound may not detect diffuse white

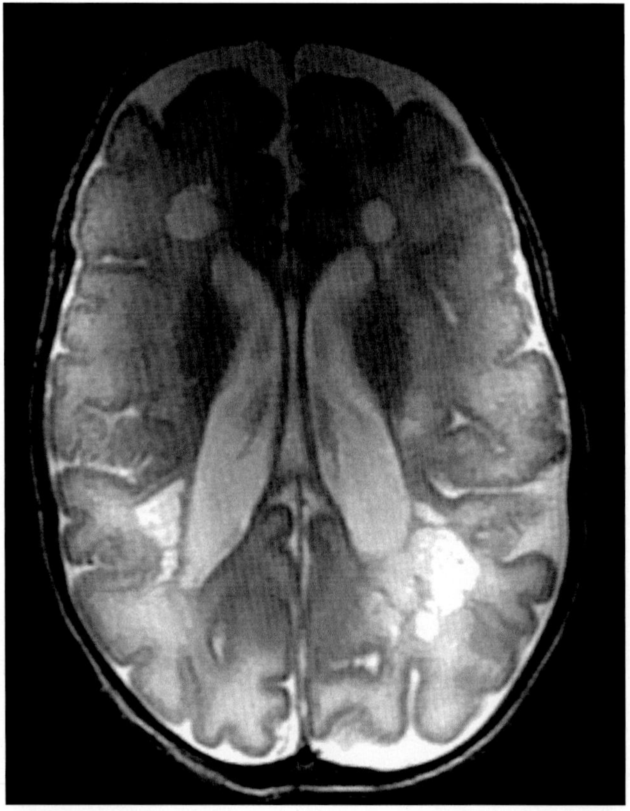

FIG. 17

Axial T2-weighted image shows multiple bilateral cystic areas in the white matter of the brain near the lateral ventricles, with mild prominence of the lateral ventricles. This is in keeping with cystic periventricular leukomalacia (cystic PVL).

matter gliosis, which is best detected on MRI. If the neonate has ventriculomegaly, PVL is often at the level of the frontal horns or the body of the lateral ventricle. One PVL classification system is as follows: Grade 1 involves periventricular echodensities; Grade 2 has periventricular echodensities evolving into localized frontoparietal cystic lesions; Grade 3 has extensive periventricular cystic lesions; and Grade 4 has cystic lesions that extend into the deep white matter and has subcortical cystic lesions (Dorner et al., 2018). Not all PVL or punctate white matter lesions become cystic on neuroimaging. Additionally, many cystic PVL lesions coalesce over time and may no longer be detected as cystic lesions, but rather as paucity of white matter and changes in the contour of the lateral ventricles. Of note, there are limitations of neuroimaging to detect cerebral white matter injury in preterm infants, as not all PVL, particularly microscopic necroses, may be detected by MRI (Volpe, 2017).

2.2.1 Short-term outcomes of PVL

Periventricular white matter injury affects cortical volume and can damage areas of the brain important for executive function, memory, and language. Cystic white matter injury has a strong association with motor delays, including quadriplegia, hemiplegia, and diplegia. Cystic lesions greater than or equal to 3 mm, particularly in the parieto-occipital periventricular white matter, have the highest risk for motor delay (Dorner et al., 2018). Please refer to Chapter 23 "Current status of neuroimaging of pediatric neurological disorders" for long-term outcomes.

3. Hypoxic-ischemic encephalopathy

Incidence: Incidence of peripartum asphyxia is 3–5 per 1000 live births in developed countries, and the incidence of moderate to severe hypoxic ischemic encephalopathy (HIE) is 0.5–1 per 1000 live births (Jacobs et al., 2013). There is a higher incidence of HIE in developing countries. HIE remains the leading cause of neonatal brain injury and mortality worldwide (Martin et al., 2020).

Pathophysiology: Hypoxic ischemic insult may result from a variety of etiologies. Maternal hypoxia (due to cardiac arrest, asphyxia, status epilepticus, or shock), placental derangements (such as placental abruption, cord prolapse, or uterine rupture), or fetal hypoxia (due to fetomaternal hemorrhage, twin-to-twin transfusion syndrome, or a cardiac defect) can all cause prenatal or peripartum hypoxic injury (Martin et al., 2020). Following a severe hypoxic insult, neuronal death occurs in two phases. First, there is a "primary neuronal death" as cells undergo primary energy failure. After at least 6 h, a second phase of "delayed neuronal death" occurs due to mitochondrial failure, toxin-mediated injury, free radical damage, and active cell death. This delayed phase is clinically associated with encephalopathy and seizure activity (Jacobs et al., 2013).

Imaging: MRI is the best modality to appreciate neuroimaging sequelae of hypoxic-ischemic injury. Perinatally acquired lesions are best appreciated around 1–2 weeks after delivery on conventional T1- and T2-weighted imaging. Diffusion-weighted imaging (DWI) allows for early (<1 week) detection of ischemic injury. However, DWI can underestimate the full injury, particularly in the basal ganglia and thalamus where injury is most likely to occur. Optimal timing of DWI is on day 3–4 after primary injury, due to pseudonormalization of diffusion that may occur in neonates after day 5. If this pseudonormalization does not occur, areas of injury visible on DWI may last for 7–10 days, by which time conventional imaging may become abnormal. T1 weighted sequence in the transverse plane is best for appreciating the basal ganglia and thalami, as well as the posterior limb of the internal capsule, which are important for predicting motor outcomes. T1 weighted sequence in the sagittal plane with volume acquisition may allow for thin slices that can be reformatted into any plane and used for quantification of different brain structures, although there is a different sensitivity depending on the type of T1 acquisitions. When there is a history of a sentinel event such as a uterine rupture or cord prolapse, typical areas of injury include the basal ganglia, thalamus, posterior limb of the internal capsule, and if severe, the brainstem, particularly dorsal brainstem. There may also be abnormal signal intensity around the central sulcus, interhemispheric fissure, and the insula as well as adjacent subcortical white matter. When there is no history of a sentinel event, basal ganglia and thalamus are still the most common areas of injury, with associated white matter injury. White matter injury alone in the absence of central gray matter injury is atypical (Rutherford et al., 2010), although the MRI appearance (central gray matter vs white matter) is highly dependent on the timing of imaging with respect to the event and severity of secondary injury (Fig. 18).

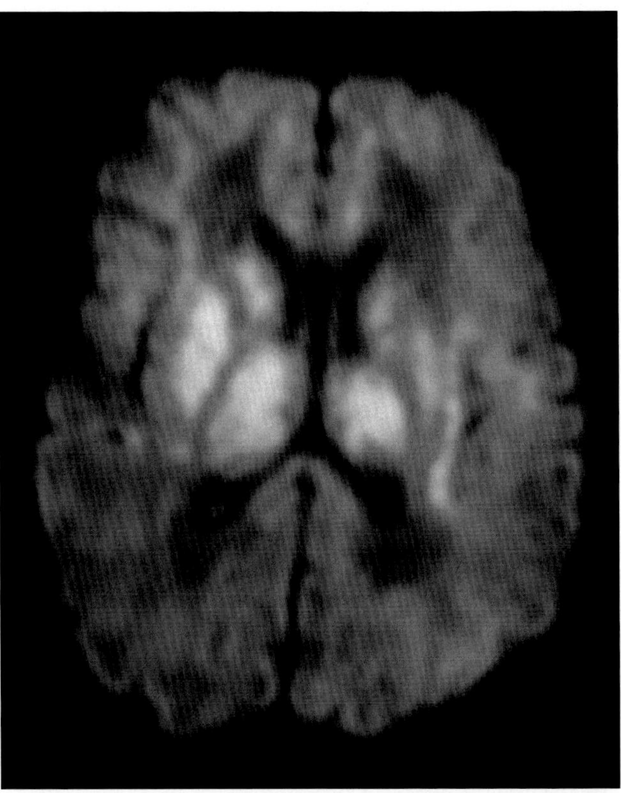

FIG. 18

Axial diffusion weighted image shows abnormal high signal that was consistent with restricted diffusion in the deep gray structures including the basal ganglia and thalami, in keeping with hypoxic-ischemic encephalopathy.

3.1 Short-term outcomes

The degree of severity of the secondary "delayed neuronal death" phase has been associated with mortality and neurodevelopmental impairment at 1 and 4 years of age. Therapeutic hypothermia initiated within 6 h after birth is neuroprotective, potentially by modifying cells that are otherwise programmed for apoptosis, as well as decreasing the cerebral metabolic rate and generation of toxic nitric oxide and free radicals (Jacobs et al., 2013). Therapeutic hypothermia significantly reduces mortality without increasing major disability in term and late preterm survivors of moderate-to-severe HIE. Therapeutic hypothermia has also been shown to improve neurodevelopmental outcomes at 18–24 months in patients with moderate-severe encephalopathy (Jacobs et al., 2013). Please refer to Chapter 23 "Current status of neuroimaging of pediatric neurological disorders" for long-term outcomes.

4. Total maturation score

An objective measure of brain maturation can aid in prognosis and provide a greater understanding of how a patient's overall physiology affects the developing brain. One method that has been developed to assess for brain maturation is the calculation of a fetal Total Maturation Score (fTMS) (Vossough et al., 2013). Fetal brain MR imaging is used to calculate six morphologic scores in the following domains: degree of insular sulcation, extent of visualization of the germinal matrix, extent of myelination, presence and depth of the superior temporal sulcus, and presence and depth of the inferior temporal sulcus. The sum of these scores equals the fTMS. Technical details of the MR imaging and subscore descriptions can be found in Vossough et al. (2013). The fTMS correlates with gestational age and fetal brain volumes. A Total Maturation Score (TMS) can also be used postnatally to evaluate the following four domains of maturity: myelination, cortical infolding, involution of glial cell migration bands, and presence of germinal matrix tissue (Childs et al., 2001). Postnatal TMS was found to be lower preoperatively in term neonates with critical congenital heart disease (hypoplastic left heart syndrome and transposition of the great arteries) (Licht et al., 2009). Therefore, TMS can be a useful tool to characterize brain maturation in infants at high risk for maturation delay and white matter injury.

References

Araujo Júnior, E., Rolo, L.C., Tonni, G., Haeri, S., Ruano, R., 2015. Assessment of fetal malformations in the first trimester of pregnancy by three-dimensional ultrasonography in the rendering mode. Pictorial essay. Med. Ultrason. 17 (1), 109–114.

Aubry, M.C., Aubry, J.P., Dommergues, M., 2003. Sonographic prenatal diagnosis of central nervous system abnormalities. Childs Nerv. Syst. 19 (7–8), 391–402.

Barkovich, A.J., Norman, D., 1988. Anomalies of the corpus callosum: correlation with further anomalies of the brain. Am. J. Roentgenol. 151 (1), 171–179.

Barkovich, A.J., Norman, D., 1989. Absence of the septum pellucidum: a useful sign in the diagnosis of congenital brain malformations. Am. J. Roentgenol. 152 (2), 353–360.

Barkovich, A.J., Kuzniecky, R.I., Jackson, G.D., Guerrini, R., Dobyns, W.B., 2005. A developmental and genetic classification for malformations of cortical development. Neurology 65 (12), 1873–1887.

Borkowski-Tillman, T., Garcia-Rodriguez, R., Viñals, F., et al., 2020. Agenesis of the septum pellucidum: prenatal diagnosis and outcome. Prenat. Diagn. 40 (6), 674–680.

Brodsky, D., Martin, C., 2020. Neonatology Review, third ed. vol. IV. Hanley & Belfus.
Brown, M.S., Sheridan-Pereira, M., 1992. Outlook for the child with a cephalocele. Pediatrics 90 (6), 914–919.
Cherian, S., Whitelaw, A., Thoresen, M., Love, S., 2004. The pathogenesis of neonatal post-hemorrhagic hydrocephalus. Brain Pathol. 14 (3), 305–311.
Childs, A.M., Ramenghi, L.A., Cornette, L., et al., 2001. Cerebral maturation in premature infants: quantitative assessment using MR imaging. Am. J. Neuroradiol. 22 (8), 1577–1582.
Curry, C.J., Lammer, E.J., Nelson, V., Shaw, G.M., 2005. Schizencephaly: heterogeneous etiologies in a population of 4 million California births. Am. J. Med. Genet. A 137 (2), 181–189.
Davidson, H.D., Abraham, R., Steiner, R.E., 1985. Agenesis of the corpus callosum: magnetic resonance imaging. Radiology 155 (2), 371–373.
de Rijk-van Andel, J.F., Arts, W.F., Hofman, A., Staal, A., Niermeijer, M.F., 1991. Epidemiology of lissencephaly type I. Neuroepidemiology 10 (4), 200–204.
Denis, D., Chateil, J.F., Brun, M., et al., 2000. Schizencephaly: clinical and imaging features in 30 infantile cases. Brain Dev. 22 (8), 475–483.
Dorner, R.A., Burton, V.J., Allen, M.C., Robinson, S., Soares, B.P., 2018. Preterm neuroimaging and neurodevelopmental outcome: a focus on intraventricular hemorrhage, post-hemorrhagic hydrocephalus, and associated brain injury. J. Perinatol. 38 (11), 1431–1443.
Fallet-Bianco, C., 2018. Neuropathology of holoprosencephaly. Am. J. Med. Genet. C Semin. Med. Genet. 178 (2), 214–228.
Fry, A.E., Cushion, T.D., Pilz, D.T., 2014. The genetics of lissencephaly. Am. J. Med. Genet. C Semin. Med. Genet. 166C (2), 198–210.
Gleason, C.A., Juul, S.E., 2018. Avery's Disease of the Newborn, 10th ed. Elsevier, Philadelphia.
Gooskens, R.H., Willemse, J., Bijlsma, J.B., Hanlo, P.W., 1988. Megalencephaly: definition and classification. Brain Dev. 10 (1), 1–7.
Holt, P.J., 1989. Posthemorrhagic hydrocephalus. J. Child Neurol. 4 (Suppl), S23–S31.
Howe, D.T., Rankin, J., Draper, E.S., 2012. Schizencephaly prevalence, prenatal diagnosis and clues to etiology: a register-based study. Ultrasound Obstet. Gynecol. 39 (1), 75–82.
Jacobs, S.E., Berg, M., Hunt, R., Tarnow-Mordi, W.O., Inder, T.E., Davis, P.G., 2013. Cooling for newborns with hypoxic ischaemic encephalopathy. Cochrane Database Syst. Rev.. (1), CD003311.
Jansen, A., Andermann, E., 2005. Genetics of the polymicrogyria syndromes. J. Med. Genet. 42 (5), 369–378.
Kaliaperumal, C., Ndoro, S., Mandiwanza, T., et al., 2016. Holoprosencephaly: antenatal and postnatal diagnosis and outcome. Childs Nerv. Syst. 32 (5), 801–809.
Klebe, D., McBride, D., Krafft, P.R., Flores, J.J., Tang, J., Zhang, J.H., 2020. Posthemorrhagic hydrocephalus development after germinal matrix hemorrhage: established mechanisms and proposed pathways. J. Neurosci. Res. 98 (1), 105–120.
Leijser, L.M., de Vries, L.S., 2019. Preterm brain injury: germinal matrix-intraventricular hemorrhage and post-hemorrhagic ventricular dilatation. Handb. Clin. Neurol. 162, 173–199.
Lerman-Sagie, T., Leibovitz, Z., 2016. Malformations of cortical development: from postnatal to fetal imaging. Can. J. Neurol. Sci. 43 (5), 611–618.
Licht, D.J., Shera, D.M., Clancy, R.R., et al., 2009. Brain maturation is delayed in infants with complex congenital heart defects. J. Thorac. Cardiovasc. Surg. 137 (3), 529–536 (discussion 536–537).
Martin, R.J., Fanaroff, A.A., Walsh, M.C., 2020. Fanaroff & Martin's Neonatal-Perinatal Medicine: Diseases of the Fetus and Infant, vol. I, 11th ed. Elsevier, Philadelphia.
Mirzaa, G., 1993. MPPH syndrome. In: Adam, M.P., Ardinger, H.H., Pagon, R.A. et al., (Eds.), GeneReviews®. University of Washington, Seattlehttp://www.ncbi.nlm.nih.gov/books/NBK396098/. Accessed 2 June 2020.
Mukerji, A., Shah, V., Shah, P.S., 2015. Periventricular/intraventricular hemorrhage and neurodevelopmental outcomes: a meta-analysis. Pediatrics 136 (6), 1132–1143.

Nagaraj, U.D., Lawrence, A., Vezina, L.G., Bulas, D.I., du Plessis, A.J., 2016. Prenatal evaluation of atelencephaly. Pediatr. Radiol. 46 (1), 145–147.

Nakahashi, M., Sato, N., Yagishita, A., et al., 2009. Clinical and imaging characteristics of localized megalencephaly: a retrospective comparison of diffuse hemimegalencephaly and multilobar cortical dysplasia. Neuroradiology 51 (12), 821–830.

Papile, L.A., Burstein, J., Burstein, R., Koffler, H., 1978. Incidence and evolution of subependymal and intraventricular hemorrhage: a study of infants with birth weights less than 1,500 gm. J. Pediatr. 92 (4), 529–534.

Parisi, M.A., Dobyns, W.B., 2003. Human malformations of the midbrain and hindbrain: review and proposed classification scheme. Mol. Genet. Metab. 80 (1–2), 36–53.

Pisapia, J.M., Sinha, S., Zarnow, D.M., Johnson, M.P., Heuer, G.G., 2017. Fetal ventriculomegaly: diagnosis, treatment, and future directions. Childs Nerv. Syst. 33 (7), 1113–1123.

Pretorius, D.H., Russ, P.D., Rumack, C.M., Manco-Johnson, M.L., 1986. Diagnosis of brain neuropathology in utero. Neuroradiology 28 (5–6), 386–397.

Rutherford, M., Malamateniou, C., McGuinness, A., Allsop, J., Biarge, M.M., Counsell, S., 2010. Magnetic resonance imaging in hypoxic-ischaemic encephalopathy. Early Hum. Dev. 86 (6), 351–360.

Santos, A.C., Escorsi-Rosset, S., Simao, G.N., et al., 2014. Hemispheric dysplasia and hemimegalencephaly: imaging definitions. Childs Nerv. Syst. 30 (11), 1813–1821.

Stoll, B.J., Hansen, N.I., Bell, E.F., et al., 2015. Trends in care practices, morbidity, and mortality of extremely preterm neonates, 1993-2012. JAMA 314 (10), 1039–1051.

Volpe, J.J., 2017. Confusions in nomenclature: "periventricular leukomalacia" and "white matter injury"-identical, distinct, or overlapping? Pediatr. Neurol. 73, 3–6.

Vossough, A., Limperopoulos, C., Putt, M.E., et al., 2013. Development and validation of a semiquantitative brain maturation score on fetal MR images: initial results. Radiology 268 (1), 200–207.

Webb, E.A., Dattani, M.T., 2010. Septo-optic dysplasia. Eur. J. Hum. Genet. 18 (4), 393–397.

Winden, K.D., Yuskaitis, C.J., Poduri, A., 2015. Megalencephaly and macrocephaly. Semin. Neurol. 35 (3), 277–287.

Winkler, A., Tölle, S., Natalucci, G., Plecko, B., Wisser, J., 2018. Prognostic features and long-term outcome in patients with isolated fetal ventriculomegaly. Fetal Diagn. Ther. 44 (3), 210–220. https://doi.org/10.1159/000480500.

CHAPTER

Current status of neuroimaging of pediatric neurological disorders 23

Susan Sotardi and Arastoo Vossough

Department of Radiology, Children's Hospital of Philadelphia, Philadelphia, PA, United States

1. Introduction

Our goal in this chapter is to review the current approaches for neuroimaging, in the context of the major intracranial neurological disorders of childhood. While a comprehensive overview of the neuroimaging of pediatric neurological disorders requires a more detailed discussion than can be provided in a single chapter, we outline several common diseases for which neuroimaging plays a critical role. These select disorders were chosen to serve as examples for which new and advanced neuroimaging techniques already contribute or have potential to impact on diagnosis and management. They include neuroimaging in brain tumors, headache/migraine disorders, hydrocephalus, epilepsy, inflammatory disorders of the white matter, cerebrovascular disorders, infection, and metabolic disorders. Other important disorders such as perinatal injury and neuropsychiatric illnesses have been previously discussed in prior chapters.

In the field of medicine, the initial presenting symptoms and signs often dictate the subsequent imaging evaluation. While the principal indication should reflect the primary clinical concern, the entire clinical picture must be assessed to provide context for the radiologist's interpretation of the images. Common indications for neuroimaging in the pediatric population include: headache, seizure, developmental delay or regression, sensory or motor changes, change in mental status, and the sequelae of trauma. Determining the underlying etiologies can be challenging in the pediatric population due to limitations in the clinical exam and patient histories. Once a diagnosis is established, many professional and pathology-specific organizations have guidelines for surveillance imaging for a number of diseases.

All imaging assessments require an understanding of the risks and benefits of the study. Concerns about radiation dose in the pediatric population require justification for the use of CT or formal angiography. Alternatively, concerns about pediatric sedation risks and gadolinium-based contrast agent exposure have led to modifications in the utilization of MR imaging. These concerns require a discussion with clinicians about the relative risks and benefits of specific imaging procedures, particularly with respect to the level of clinical concern and the role of imaging information in determining treatment options. Guidelines for the role of imaging in clinical practice are established and updated for many indications by the American College of Radiology and other clinical organizations, in order to provide clinicians with information toward imaging decision-making. Ultimately, however, imaging needs to be tailored to the individual patient and every imaging application may not be available at

Handbook of Pediatric Brain Imaging. https://doi.org/10.1016/B978-0-12-816633-8.00023-5

every institution. Therefore, the real and finite limitations of institutions also play a role in imaging strategy.

To discriminate pathology from the normal developing brain, the radiologist relies upon the patterns of tissue characteristics and the expected evolution of these properties by age and underlying disease. At our disposal are the myriad of imaging tools which we use to interrogate these properties in the hopes of finding distinguishing features of these diseases. While the correct imaging tool may elicit the necessary information to make this determination, radiologists are frequently confronted by the boundaries of our understanding of the disease pathology, stage of disease, and the distinguishing features. Additionally, the initial clinical presentation is often a single snapshot in time and may not accurately reflect the preceding or subsequent evolution of the disease. More refined diagnoses, therefore, require both an improved understanding of the discriminating features of these diseases, along with the prognostic implications of a given study.

CT and MR protocols are optimized at each institution based on the available technical features and radiologist preferences with input from clinical teams. Although there is no standard set of MR sequences required in an MR of the brain, most institutions have some degree of overlap in their protocols. Most noncontrast MR brain protocols include the following: T2 TSE, T2-FLAIR, diffusion-weighted, gradient echo and/or TSE T1 and sometimes T2*-weighted sequences. Post-contrast T1 weighted sequences often vary between institutions and may include a gradient echo T1, T1 TSE, or T1 FLAIR. Typically, the pre-contrast T1 sequence will match the post-contrast T1 sequence, to allow for the discrimination of intrinsically T1 weighted signal from post-contrast enhancement. T2-FLAIR weighted sequences have decreased utility in the neonatal and early nonmyelinated pediatric brain, due to differences in water content when compared with older children and adults. For vascular imaging, MR angiography comes in three main flavors, time-of-flight, phase contrast, and contrast-enhanced gradient echo sequences.

Additional advanced imaging techniques may be available, depending on the scanner and availability. Typically, these sequences include arterial spin labeling perfusion, contrast enhanced dynamic susceptibility MR perfusion, dynamic contrast enhanced permeability, susceptibility-weighted imaging, diffusion tensor imaging, steady-state free precession family of sequences, magnetization transfer imaging, and MR spectroscopy. In the clinical realm, functional MR imaging (fMRI) is almost exclusively used for presurgical assessment of eloquent brain functional localization, particularly in the setting of brain tumors or epilepsy. Additionally, magnetoencephalography may be used to assist in the localization of epileptogenic foci, particularly in the setting of refractory epilepsy, and again for preoperative functional localization.

Although many advanced MR techniques provide important clinical information, time constraints regarding scanner and sedation times may limit the use of additional sequences in clinical practice. While novel imaging sequences may be helpful in discriminating subtle characteristics of a given disease, in the current clinical landscape, the implementation of any new technology must justify the time and expense. In the United States in particular, billing codes are linked to ordering indications and usually determine insurance approval. In this manner, insurance authorization for a given study requires a justification of its utility. For example, MR spectroscopy has a unique billing code; however, only specific clinical indications may be covered by insurance and often require insurance preauthorization. Requests for insurance coverage are frequently rejected, thereby limiting the use of spectroscopy in the clinical realm.

In order to illustrate the role of neuroimaging in pediatric neurological diseases, we will consider the diagnostic and surveillance imaging of several common intracranial neurologic diseases, including: brain tumors, epilepsy, demyelinating disease, hydrocephalus, migraine, cerebrovascular disease, infections, and metabolic disorders.

2. Brain tumors

Brain tumors can occur at any age in the pediatric population. The patient's age at presentation, tumor location, and MR signal characteristics often play a significant role in the determination of pathology and prognosis. Supratentorial lesions, such as astrocytomas, embryonal tumors, and choroid plexus tumors are more common in children in the first 2 years of life; whereas, in children between 4 and 10 years old, infratentorial lesions, such as medulloblastoma and pilocytic astrocytoma are more common. Additional common areas for tumor localization include the brainstem, pineal, and suprasellar regions. The diagnosis of brainstem tumors relies heavily on imaging characterization, given the surgical difficulties associated with biopsies of the brainstem. Many of the higher-grade tumors may result in intrathecal (drop) metastases and often require spine imaging to assess for CSF seeding.

Imaging plays a significant role in evaluation, at presentation and follow-up, of brain tumors in the pediatric population. The MR features of tumors assist radiologists in developing an ordered list of possible diagnoses, known as a differential diagnosis. Imaging at the initial presentation is also important in the evaluation of local or distant metastatic disease, which may significantly alter the prognosis and treatment strategy. Follow-up MR imaging is important for assessing the therapy response and side effects of treatment.

Often pediatric MR imaging protocols for intracranial brain tumors include T1-weighted sequences, which may be volumetric 3D T1 gradient sequences and/or T1 TSE, before and after the administration of intravenous contrast. Volumetric T1 sequences are helpful in characterizing the anatomy of lesions and can be used for surgical navigation guidance; whereas, certain T1 TSE sequences may have better sensitivity for subtly enhancing lesions. Additional sequences, such as T2 TSE, T2-FLAIR, DWI, and sometimes T2* are typically included. If there is a high likelihood of the need for surgical intervention, volumetric surgical navigation guidance sequences are often added in order to be used for stereotactic guidance in the operating room. Evaluation of metastatic foci and dissemination is another critical role of imaging in pediatric brain tumors, both in close proximity to the lesion and in more distant regions, such as the spinal cord. Assessment of the subarachnoid spaces of the intracranial and spinal cord is often performed preoperatively. Postoperative spinal imaging may be performed in these cases as well, if there is no preoperative spinal imaging; however, evaluation of enhancing spinal lesions may be limited in the immediate postoperative period due to normal postoperative enhancement or early blood product contamination. Therefore, these exams may be done a few weeks after initial surgery and before the start of chemotherapy or radiation.

Advanced imaging techniques may aid in the initial characterization of brain tumors (Fig. 1). On proton spectroscopy, elevated choline and taurine levels have been found in several studies on medulloblastoma and may help differentiate medulloblastoma. However, taurine levels are low in some desmoplastic/nodular variants of medulloblastoma (Panigrahy et al., 2010). Quantitative high field MR spectroscopy may show may be better able to demonstrate metabolite changes than qualitative clinical MR spectroscopy. Some pilocytic astrocytomas demonstrate low creatine, myo-inositol, lipid and

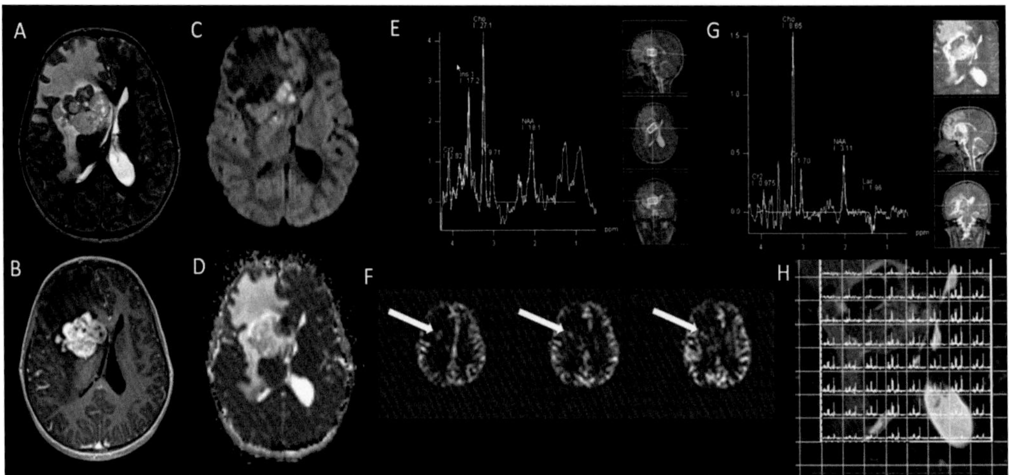

FIG. 1

A 7-year-old female with anaplastic ependymoma. (A) T2 TSE shows a heterogeneous mass with surrounding edema and extensive mass effect. (B) Postcontrast T1-weighted imaging shows avid heterogeneous enhancement of the mass, (C and D) Diffusion (trace) and ADC map show restricted diffusion within the medial aspect of the lesion. (E) Single voxel MR spectroscopy (MRS) technique through the right frontal lobe lesion (TR 1700 ms, TE 20 ms) shows decreased NAA and increased choline. (F) Arterial spin labeling with 2D PASL technique shows faint increased perfusion to the lesion (*arrow*). (G–H) 2D CSI MRS through the right frontal lobe lesion (TR 1700 ms, TE 135 ms) shows decreased NAA, increased choline, and some elevated lactate in keeping with a high-grade neoplasm.

choline concentrations, reflecting low cellularity (Panigrahy et al., 2010); however, the choline to creatine and choline to NAA ratios may still be elevated (Blüml and Panigrahy, 2012). High grade astrocytomas may demonstrate marked increased choline and elevated lactate, with decrease in NAA. Diffuse low grade astrocytomas often have elevated myo-inositol and ependymomas typically have higher myo-inositol than medulloblastoma or pilocytic astrocytoma. Choroid plexus papilloma characteristically demonstrate high myo-inositol peak which may differentiate them from other tumors, including choroid plexus carcinoma (Panigrahy et al., 2006). Some research suggests that arterial spin-labeling (ASL) can help in distinguishing high-grade and low-grade tumors, as cerebral blood flow is typically elevated in high-grade tumors (Narayanan et al., 2020). Nevertheless, the separation is rather imperfect. Additionally, perfusion imaging can assist in the selection of biopsy areas, since regions with higher perfusion may potentially result in more accurate pathology specimens. Functional MRI (fMRI) may play an important role in the preoperative planning and evaluation of eloquent cortex in tumors involving or adjacent to these areas, and as such may have an impact in assessing operative morbidity. Similarly, diffusion tensor imaging and tractography may play a role in the preoperative planning of select brain tumor cases, by delineating white matter tracts relevant to the surgical approach. Nevertheless, challenges remain in the accurate delineation of tracts using DTI and more advanced methods in the presence of tumor pathology and edema.

Intraoperative MR, either within the operating room or performed in the MR suite during a pause in the surgery, has increased in utilization in recent years. Intraoperative MR has been demonstrated to improve surgical outcomes (Choudhri et al., 2014). Typically, an abbreviated protocol is performed to answer the specific surgical question, which is most commonly assessment of possible residual tumor. Sequences are custom-tailored to mirror the tumor characteristics; for example, a tumor with nonenhancing T2 hyperintense signal characteristics would not require the administration of intravenous contrast for assessment of residual tumor.

Follow-up imaging of brain tumors is important for assessing therapy response and short- and long-term side effects of treatment. Common side effects of treatment include radiation necrosis, chemotherapy toxicity, and steroid-related complications (Shah et al., 2012; Vázquez et al., 2011; Dietrich et al., 2011). Occasionally, secondary tumors may result in areas of prior radiation. Intervals for posttreatment follow-up imaging are arranged by the surgical and oncology team. The role of advanced imaging in pediatric tumor surveillance is an active area of research. Perfusion imaging and MR spectroscopy have both been used in distinguishing treatment effects and recurrent brain tumors, although the evidence is much more limited in pediatric brain tumors compared to adults. FDG PET has also been reported to improve detection of residual or recurrent tumor in some tumors (Stanescu et al., 2013), and can also be used to differentiate radiation necrosis and recurrent tumor. There is a limitation imposed by normal high glucose uptake in the brain and for molecular and functional characterization of brain tumors and as such, newer non-FDG radiotracers have been developed, such markers of tumor amino acid transport and protein synthesis, markers of tumor proliferation rate, and markers of tumor oxygen metabolism. Although these novel radiotracers are being increasingly used in adults, there is a paucity of evidence in the pediatric brain tumor population. In summary, there are various potentially important roles for the use of multimodal new and advanced imaging techniques in various aspects of brain tumor diagnosis and management.

3. Headache/migraine

Headaches are a common cause of emergency room visits, as well as outpatient assessments. Neuroimaging is typically reserved for children with concerning features or an underlying disorder that predisposes to intracranial disease (Scagni and Pagliero, 2008; Lateef et al., 2009; Sheridan et al., 2013). Some common indications for neuroimaging in the setting of childhood headache are: neurologic deficits, mental status changes, decreased visual acuity or new findings on ophthalmologic exam, a history of nocturnal or early-morning headaches, headaches with nausea or vomiting, but without gastrointestinal complaints, concurrent signs of infection, less than 6 years of age with regression of milestones or learning difficulties. In the setting of isolated headache, neuroimaging is typically negative (Holle and Obermann, 2013). However, occasionally, an underlying process, such as intracranial hemorrhage, infection, or brain tumor can be diagnosed using standard imaging technique.

CT has a high sensitivity for intracranial hemorrhage and fractures, while adequately assessing ventricle size, large parenchymal lesions, and evidence of herniation. Whereas, MR imaging should be reserved for children with a specific clinical concern, while ensuring an imaging protocol and strategy that appropriately evaluates the clinical question. Advanced imaging techniques are not routinely utilized for the evaluation of migraine headaches, unless further indicated by an unexpected imaging finding. A rare particular subtype of complicated migraine, hemiplegic migraine, may present acutely with stroke like symptoms, among others. In these cases, arterial spin labeling perfusion MRI or susceptibility weighted imaging may show changes of hyperperfusion or hypoperfusion and associated changes in the vessels, depending on the stage of disease at the time of imaging.

4. Hydrocephalus

Hydrocephalus is a condition in which excess cerebral spinal fluid (CSF) accumulates in the ventricles and is the most common indication for cranial surgery in the pediatric population. As such, hydrocephalus poses a large public health burden, affecting 1 in 1000 children in the United States. Hydrocephalus results from obstruction to the flow of CSF, failure of CSF absorption, or overproduction of CSF. Noncommunicating hydrocephalus results from a focal mechanical obstruction, most commonly at the cerebral aqueduct or foramen of Monro. Common causes of noncommunicating hydrocephalus include congenital etiologies, tumors and adhesions resulting from prior infection, hemorrhage, or inflammation. Communicating hydrocephalus implies the absence of a focal obstruction to CSF flow within the ventricular system, and may result from either failure of re-absorption or overproduction of CSF.

Current imaging assessment of hydrocephalus may include either CT and MR. CT is often the utilized modality in the setting of concern for acute intracranial pressure and the need for urgent surgical intervention. Abbreviated, fast MR sequences for targeted evaluation of the ventricles may be helpful in an urgent setting, when there are no contraindications to MR and the child can tolerate the examination, particularly when prior MR examinations are available for comparison. However, CT is more readily available at most institutions and can usually be performed without the need for sedation; therefore, the urgency of intervention and the MR safety profile of the patient should determine the choice of CT versus MR. Additional high resolution sequences, such as steady state free precession sequences and 3D variable flip angle T2 sequences may be helpful for the evaluating the anatomy and patency of the cerebral aqueduct and third ventriculostomy, although they do significantly increase scan time. Phase contrast CSF flow studies may also be selectively used to assess CSF drainage disorders or evaluate the efficacy of treatment in select cases.

5. Epilepsy

Epilepsy is a common illness in the pediatric population, affecting approximately 1% of children. The etiologies responsible for the disease include: 42% cortical dysplasia, 19% tumors, 10% gliotic lesions (atrophy and stroke), 3% Rasmussen encephalitis, 3% Sturge Weber (Harvey et al., 2008). MRI plays a critical role in detection and characterization of the lesion, as well as lesion extent. Surgical outcomes are improved, when the underlying lesion is found and adequately assessed by MR.

The fundamental challenge in epilepsy imaging is determining the presence of subtle lesions. Even with large lesions, determining lesion extent and the involvement of nearby structures requires high resolution imaging. In order to improve the signal to noise ratio, MR imaging is ideally performed at high field, using thin, high resolution sequences while maintaining adequate tissue contrast. This imaging approach has been shown to improve detection of more subtle lesions and better characterize the extent of all lesions. If possible, a higher density multichannel head coil should be utilized to improve the signal to noise ratio, particularly at the cortical interfaces. 3D and multiplanar high resolution

2D sequences improve localization of lesions. Susceptibility weighted sequences may be helpful, particularly in the setting of trauma for assessment of prior injury as a cause for epilepsy.

Advanced imaging techniques may be helpful adjuncts for lesion detection. Arterial spin labeling sequences may improve localization of lesions in the post-ictal state. MR spectroscopy has been helpful in screening for metabolic derangements, lateralization of the occult epileptogenic nidus and possibly as an indicator of response to anti-epileptic drugs (Caruso et al., 2013), although it has not found widespread use beyond mass lesion characterization or detection of select metabolic disorders. FDG PET has been used in evaluation of epilepsy, including both temporal and extratemporal epilepsy, and which typically demonstrates hypometabolism during interictal PET and occasionally hypermetabolism during seizures (Stanescu et al., 2013). FDG PET may identify cortical regions with interictal hypometabolism that are difficult to detect with conventional MR imaging (Stanescu et al., 2013). As discussed in prior chapters, MEG data can also be helpful in the detection and characterization of lesions that are subtle or occult on standard imaging. Both MEG and FDG PET localizations may serve as clues for performing a "second look" at the MRI in the hopes of finding subtle abnormalities on anatomical imaging. MEG and fMRI are helpful in the determination of eloquent brain regions in preparation and planning for epilepsy surgery.

6. Inflammatory disorders of the white matter

The most common inflammatory disorders, predominantly involving the white matter, in the pediatric population are acute disseminated encephalomyelitis (ADEM), anti-myelin oligodendrocyte glycoprotein (MOG) associated encephalomyelitis, and multiple sclerosis (MS). ADEM is an autoimmune-mediated white matter disease, resulting in areas of demyelination within the brain and/or spinal cord, and typically occurs after a viral infection or recent vaccination. Diagnostic criteria were established in 2007 (Krupp et al., 2007), and the incidence of ADEM ranges from 0.64 to 4.1 per 100,000 (Marin and Callen, 2013).

MR imaging findings of ADEM include moderate to large areas of T2/FLAIR hyperintense signal abnormality within the supratentorial subcortical and deep white matter (Marin and Callen, 2013). The lesions are asymmetric in distribution, with variable patterns of involvement. Deep cerebral nuclei and infratentorial involvement, including the brainstem, spinal cord and cerebellar white matter may be seen in up to 50% patients (Dale et al., 2000; Baum et al., 1994; Murthy et al., 2002). The corpus callosum is less commonly involved in ADEM compared with MS. Varying patterns of enhancement and/or restricted diffusion may be seen in the acute and the subacute phases. Susceptibility-weighted images may be helpful in detecting foci of petechial hemorrhage within the lesions. Anti-MOG-associated encephalomyelitis is a more recently described disorder that has many features overlapping with ADEM, and may present with an ADEM like picture on MRI.

Advanced imaging techniques may be helpful for further characterization of lesions in the setting of suspected ADEM; however, many studies are small in scale and with nonspecific findings. MR spectroscopy has demonstrated a decrease in NAA/Cho ratios, (Balasubramanya et al., 2007) which is seen in many demyelinating processes. MR spectroscopy shows low NAA levels within lesions at the time of presentation; however, NAA typically normalizes with resolution of symptoms/MR abnormalities (Bizzi et al., 2001). Choline is believed to result from myelin breakdown and may be normal in the acute phase of ADEM, in contrast to MS. As the disease progresses, there may be an increase in choline

(Balasubramanya et al., 2007). Magnetization transfer ratio (MTR) imaging demonstrates normal values in normal-appearing white matter, unlike MS which demonstrates significantly lower MTR in the normal appearing white matter (Inglese et al., 2002). SPECT imaging with 99mTc-HMPAO (D,L-hexamethylpropylene amine oxime) has shown areas of hypoperfusion that appear larger than lesions identified on conventional MR neuroimaging (Broich et al., 1991).

Although the onset of multiple sclerosis more often occurs in early adulthood, childhood multiple sclerosis can occur in the pediatric population. Approximately 10% of patients with an eventual diagnosis of MS have an initial demyelinating event before the age of 18 years (Yeshokumar et al., 2017). The diagnosis may be made at the initial presentation using the 2017 revised McDonald criteria based on clinical and supporting MR imaging findings (Thompson et al., 2018). However, when criteria are not met at the time of the first event, repeat clinical evaluation and MR imaging may be needed to confirm the diagnosis of MS. The presence of optic nerve involvement indicates a higher likelihood of the diagnosis of pediatric multiple sclerosis (Yeshokumar et al., 2017) and orbital imaging should be obtained in any patients with referable ophthalmologic symptoms. However, despite revisions to diagnostic criteria, there are significant challenges in differentiating some cases of childhood multiple sclerosis from other forms of demyelinating and inflammatory disease. Up to 25% of children diagnosed with MS later in life initially presented with a diagnosis of ADEM (Callen et al., 2009), indicating overlap in the initial manifestations of these diseases in the pediatric age group.

The imaging findings of pediatric multiple sclerosis white matter lesions are often similar to those in adults, which typically demonstrate sharply demarcated T2/FLAIR signal abnormality without contrast enhancement in remote lesions and contrast enhancement and/or restricted diffusion in acute lesions. These lesions are typically located in the deep or juxta-cortical white matter, with periventricular locations being less common than in the adult population (Callen et al., 2009). Cortically-based lesions are often difficult to confirm on current imaging protocols, due to the small size and subtle differences in tissue contrast within the cortex. Standard MR imaging protocols for initial and symptomatic presentations of MS rely heavily upon T2/FLAIR and T1 postcontrast imaging, and typically include both high resolution 2D TSE and 3D acquisitions. The use of 3.0T magnet strength has been reported to increase the number of detected contrast-enhancing lesions and enhancing lesion volume, with approximately a 21% increase in number of lesions, compared with 1.5T imaging (Sicotte et al., 2003; Wattjes et al., 2006), although this is more reflective of the particular protocols used. Imaging performed for follow-up purposes and in the absence of clinical symptoms is increasingly performed without intravenous contrast, given the theoretical concerns associated with repeat exposure to intravenous contrast. Imaging of the orbits and spinal cord may be included based on referable symptoms or for differentiation and confirmation of disease.

Research on advanced imaging techniques, such as MR spectroscopy, PET/SPECT, ASL, magnetization transfer, diffusion tensor imaging, ultrahigh field imaging and quantitative MR volumetry have yielded important information about the imaging findings of the multiple sclerosis. However, in our experience, these findings support the diagnosis of multiple sclerosis and may be correlated to disease disability, but in a clinical diagnostic setting, are not able to reliably discriminate multiple sclerosis from other demyelinating diseases based on imaging criteria alone. On MR spectroscopy, short echo sequences may show elevated glutamate and glutamine in the lesions (Cianfoni et al., 2007). Elevated choline, lactate and lipid levels, along with decreased NAA are typical, albeit nonspecific, imaging findings of processes with a demyelinating component (Cianfoni et al., 2007).

Quantitative spectroscopy may aid in distinguishing different subsets of MS. For example, secondary progressive MS may show a decrease in NAA with otherwise normal-appearing gray matter, in contrast to relapsing-remitting MS (Adalsteinsson et al., 2003). Perfusion MR imaging may be helpful in determining tumefactive MS from some high-grade glial neoplasms, (Hourani et al., 2008); although there is limited utility with lower grade neoplasms, presumably due to overlap in the neuronal metabolic activity and vascularity (Blasel et al., 2011). Magnetization transfer imaging has been reported to better characterize the extent of MS lesions, with a decrease in MTR within MS lesions (Filippi et al., 2000).

7. Cerebrovascular disorders

Stroke is an important diagnosis in the pediatric population, and can be divided into perinatal/neonatal stroke (between late third trimester to 1 month old) and childhood stroke (>1 month of age). The incidence of stroke observed in the perinatal/neonatal period is between 1 per 1600 and 1 per 5000 live births (Lynch, 2009). In children, ages 30 days to 19 years, the overall incidence is approximately 2 per 100,000 (Fullerton et al., 2003). The clinical presentation typically guides the decision to obtain CT or MR imaging.

In the acute setting and before the initiation of anticoagulation or thrombectomy, CT is often utilized to specifically evaluate for intracranial hemorrhage, assessment of large vessel occlusion, parenchymal changes of acute stroke, or alternative diagnoses, such as hydrocephalus, or brain tumor, which may require a change in the treatment strategy. An abbreviated MR protocol may be helpful in the acute setting, for carefully selected patient groups; however, delays in patient treatment due to a prolonged process of obtaining an MR should be avoided. An abbreviated MR protocol typically involves a diffusion-weighted sequence, along with faster but low-resolution versions of standard FLAIR and T2* sequences. Addition of similar fast T1 and T2 images may further aid in the differential diagnosis of stroke. However, these sequences may have a low sensitivity for small, subtle lesions, and should only be utilized in urgent situations that require immediate decision making. Frequently, standard conventional MR imaging is necessary to confirm the presence or absence of subtle pathology. Various forms of perfusion imaging can be useful in the evaluation of perfusion deficits in the setting of pediatric stroke and cerebrovascular chronic steno-occlusive disease, as well as after revascularization (Narayanan et al., 2020). Perfusion methods, such as arterial spin labeling which does not use Gadolinium contrast may be helpful in the diagnosis of certain stroke mimics, such as hemiplegic migraine or occasionally in postictal states.

7.1 Arterial infarction

Imaging of stroke in the neonatal and childhood periods can be categorized into those of arterial and venous origins. In approximately 24% of childhood cases, the cause of arterial ischemic stroke (AIS) is not determined (Fullerton et al., 2007). The major sources of childhood AIS are arteriopathy, hypercoagulable states, and thromboembolism (Beslow and Jordan, 2010; Mackay et al., 2011). Clinical suspicion for trauma-related vascular injury, such as arterial dissection, often require the addition of vascular imaging. Either CT angiogram (with intravenous contrast) or MR angiogram (typically without intravenous contrast) may be helpful in characterizing vessel injury (Fig. 2). T1-weighted fat-

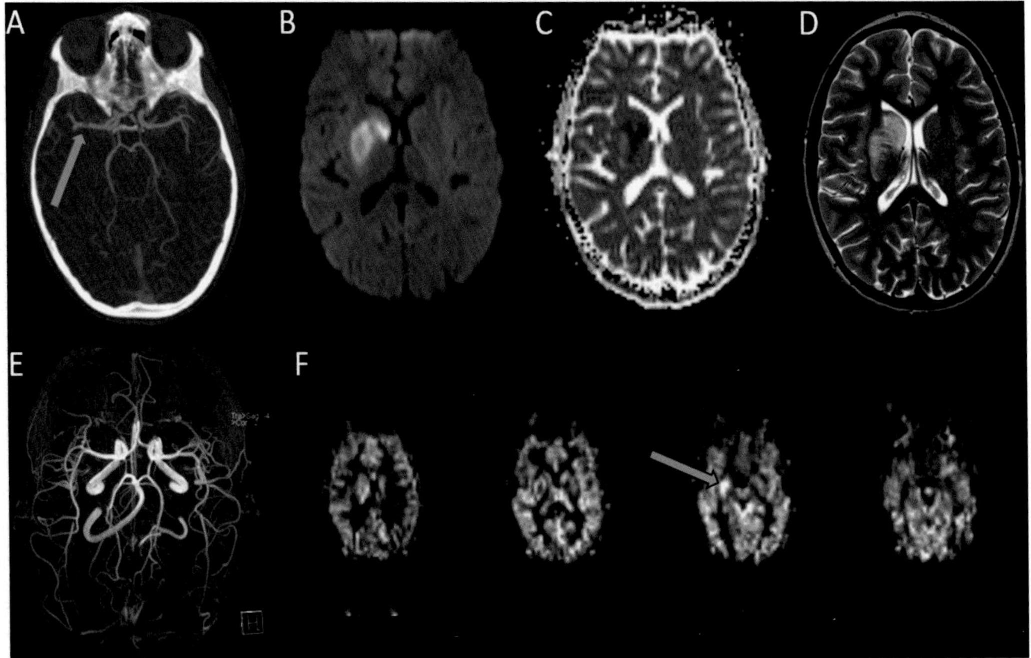

FIG. 2

A 14-year-old female with congenital heart disease status post Fontan procedure presented with light-headedness followed by dense left sided numbness and weakness. (A) CT angiogram (CTA) shows clot or narrowing (*arrow*) in the right middle cerebral artery (MCA); MR performed 3 days later shows: (B and C) DWI and ADC show acute infarct in the right putamen and caudate nucleus. (D) T2 TSE shows associated signal abnormality. (E) MR angiogram without contrast, time-of-flight technique shows improvement in the filling defect within the right MCA. (F) Arterial spin labeling performed with 2D PASL technique shows increased perfusion in the region of infarct (*arrow*) following reperfusion.

saturated sequences are performed to evaluate for T1 hyperintense signal along the vessel wall, indicating the subacute phase of blood products (methemoglobin) within an intramural hematoma. Thromboembolism is a common etiology for arterial stroke, and in the pediatric population, is often associated with congenital heart disease, intracardiac shunts, and cardiac procedures (Mackay et al., 2011).

Moyamoya syndrome is an arteriopathy associated with sickle cell disease, neurofibromatosis type 1, and trisomy 21 (Smith, 2015). MR findings of moyamoya syndrome typically include stenosis or absence of the distal carotid artery and proximal middle and anterior cerebral arteries, with formation of small serpiginous, collateral vessels. Slow flow within the distal sulcal vessels is observed as linear, sulcal FLAIR hyperintense signal.

Vasculitis is a common diagnosis in the pediatric population and may result in arterial infarction. Systemic diseases such as lupus, scleroderma, or polyarteritis nodosa, as well as primary CNS arteritides should be considered as etiologies (Twilt and Benseler, 2013). Vessel imaging in large vessel vasculitis, such as in post-varicella cerebral arteriopathy, may reveal wall thickening and enhancement due to inflammation, as well as unilateral or bilateral stenoses, with beading and irregularity. Small vessel vasculitides often have normal vessel imaging and may require a brain biopsy for diagnosis.

7.2 Venous stroke

In children, dural venous sinus thrombosis is the primary cause of venous stroke. The clinical and imaging diagnosis of venous sinus thrombosis can be challenging. Imaging of dural venous sinus thrombosis can be done with either CT or MRI. Often a noncontrast head CT demonstrates hyperdense material within the venous structures, suggesting thrombosis although assessment may be challenging in neonates due to the relative higher density of normal dural venous structures compared to the brain parenchyma. CT venography is sensitive for the evaluation of dural venous sinus thrombus, but may not be as sensitive as MRI for early parenchymal injury during the hyperacute and acute time periods. MRI with MRV, with the inclusion of contrast-enhanced MR can be considered for the evaluation of venous thrombosis in patients who can tolerate MR imaging. Several MR sequences are helpful for evaluation of sinovenous thrombosis and venous infarct, including DWI, GRE/SWI, T2, along with pre-contrast and post-contrast T1-weighted images, preferably 3D gradient echo T1-weighted imaging. DWI is important for the evaluation of associated parenchymal injury and infarction. GRE or SWI may be useful for demonstrating thrombus, which frequently "blooms" on these sequences. T2 weighted sequences may show the loss of a flow-void when filled with clot, although slow flow may mimic clot as well. Contrast-enhanced 3D T1-weighted images are reliable for delineation of filling defects in the venous system (Jackson et al., 2011). However, it is important to note that MR venograms, particularly the most common 2D time-of-flight acquisitions, may be prone to artifacts which may simulate clot. Therefore, noncontrast MRV should be interpreted in conjunction with other MRI sequences. MRV may also be helpful for follow-up imaging and assessment of recanalization, once the diagnosis of thrombosis is made on initial imaging.

8. Infections

Infections in the pediatric population can be separated into congenital and childhood time periods. Congenital infections are transmitted from the mother to the fetus and include toxoplasmosis, syphilis, human immunodeficiency virus, rubella, cytomegalovirus, Zika virus, and herpes simplex virus type 2. Infections within the early childhood period are most commonly related to bacterial or viral infections. However, the role of imaging in these patients is similar and typically involves the characterization of infections, the anatomical extent of disease and any associated complications, including hydrocephalus, empyema, abscess, ventriculitis, infarction and/or arteritis (Parmar and Ibrahim, 2012). Follow-up imaging to assess for progression or complications is often necessary. Due to the overlap in advanced imaging findings, imaging techniques such as MR spectroscopy and FDG PET, are not routinely utilized for the evaluation of common intracranial infections, unless further indicated by a specific imaging finding. ASL or DSC perfusion imaging may occasionally be helpful in the evaluation of perfusion abnormalities and extent of disease (Noguchi et al., 2016). Use of diffusion imaging and MRS has been reported to be able to distinguish bacterial tubercular, and fungal abscesses, but over between these types still exist (Luthra et al., 2007).

9. Metabolic disorders

A comprehensive discussion of metabolic disorders is beyond the scope of this text.

From an imaging perspective, we utilize conventional MR sequences to first distinguish whether the pattern of disease predominantly involves the white matter or gray matter, noting that some disorders involve both (Fig. 3) (Barkovich, 2007). Since many metabolic disorders are predisposed to involve specific brain regions, detailed assessment of each brain region may point the radiologist toward a particular diagnosis. For those with a specific interest in the characteristics of these diseases, we refer you to the definitive work by Van der Knaap MaV (2005). In summary, inborn errors of metabolism can be categorized by the metabolite or subcellular origin of the dysfunction. Currently, the list of these disorders can be roughly categorized as disease of: amino-acids, organic acids, urea synthesis, carbohydrates, glycosylation, lysosomal storage, mitochondria, peroxisomes, neurotransmitters, phakomatoses, vitamins, neuronal ceroid lipofuscinoses, and ion channels. As our understanding of cellular processes, and metabolic pathways, and genetic defects improves, this list will undoubtedly be refined.

MR spectroscopy (MRS) has utility in the evaluation of several metabolic disorders. Canavan's disease demonstrates a near-pathognomonic imaging appearance with markedly elevated NAA levels

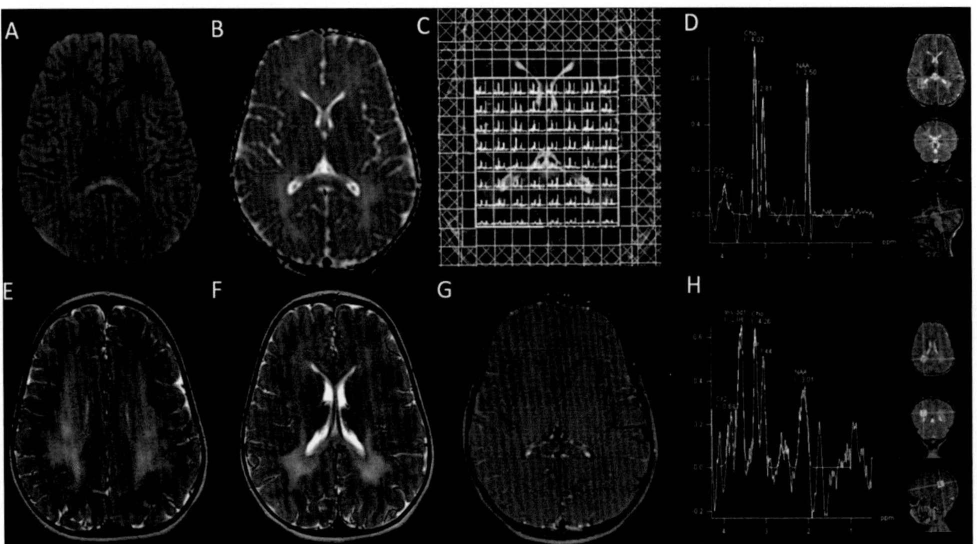

FIG. 3

A 2-year-old female with gait instability. (A and B) Diffusion (trace) and ADC map show areas of mild restricted diffusion within the splenium of the corpus callosum (C and D). 2D CSI MR spectroscopy (MRS) technique with TR 1690 ms and TE 135 ms shows slightly elevated choline (E and F). T2 TSE, shows symmetric T2 hyperintense signal within the white matter. (G) Postcontrast T1 TSE shows faint enhancement within the splenium (H). single voxel MRS was also performed through the right periatrial white matter with TR 1500 ms and TE 20 ms shows elevated myoinositol and decreased NAA. Overall, these findings are suggestive of Metachromatic Leukodystrophy, which was confirmed by laboratory and molecular investigation.

and consequently an elevated NAA-to-creatine ratio (Wittsack et al., 1996). In maple syrup urine disease, single-voxel proton MR spectroscopy may show branched-chain amino acids and branched-chain alpha-keto acids resonating at 0.9–1.0 ppm, particularly during a metabolic crisis (Jan et al., 2003). Urea cycle disorders include defects in ornithine carbamoyl transferase deficiency, carbamoyl phosphate synthetase deficiency, argininosuccinic aciduria, citrullinemia and hyperargininemia. MRS can sometimes detect elevated glutamine resulting from hyperammonemia in urea cycle disorders, and imaging findings may be reversed with treatment (Choi and Yoo, 2001). In pyruvate dehydrogenase complex deficiency, elevated pyruvate may be seen at 2.36 ppm (Zand et al., 2003). Spectroscopy can be helpful in the evaluation of mitochondrial disorders, since lactate peaks will be seen within many parts of the brain and CSF, in addition to areas of active injury (Bianchi et al., 2003). However, elevated lactate is not specific for mitochondrial disorders. In some rare instances, such as Creatine transporter disorders, MR spectroscopy may be the only modality showing the abnormality.

10. Summary

Pediatric neuroradiology is a dynamic, evolving field, which welcomes new imaging applications. Although prior research has demonstrated many important imaging features of pediatric neurological diseases, conventional imaging features frequently overlap. This fact underpins the critical need for improved methods to discriminate these diseases from one another, thereby assisting in clinical decision-making and treatment strategies.

References

Adalsteinsson, E., Langer-Gould, A., Homer, R.J., Rao, A., Sullivan, E.V., Lima, C.A., Pfefferbaum, A., Atlas, S. W., 2003. Gray matter N-acetyl aspartate deficits in secondary progressive but not relapsing-remitting multiple sclerosis. Am. J. Neuroradiol. 24 (10), 1941–1945. Epub 2003/11/20. 14625214.

Balasubramanya, K.S., Kovoor, J.M., Jayakumar, P.N., Ravishankar, S., Kamble, R.B., Panicker, J., Nagaraja, D., 2007. Diffusion-weighted imaging and proton MR spectroscopy in the characterization of acute disseminated encephalomyelitis. Neuroradiology 49 (2), 177–183. Epub 2006/11/30. https://doi.org/10.1007/s00234-006-0164-2. 17131116.

Barkovich, A.J., 2007. An approach to MRI of metabolic disorders in children. J. Neuroradiol. 34 (2), 75–88. Epub 2007/04/27. https://doi.org/10.1016/j.neurad.2007.01.125. 17459477.

Baum, P.A., Barkovich, A.J., Koch, T.K., Berg, B.O., 1994. Deep gray matter involvement in children with acute disseminated encephalomyelitis. Am. J. Neuroradiol. 15 (7), 1275–1283. Epub 1994/08/01. 7976938.

Beslow, L.A., Jordan, L.C., 2010. Pediatric stroke: the importance of cerebral arteriopathy and vascular malformations. Childs Nerv. Syst. 26 (10), 1263–1273. Epub 2010/07/14. https://doi.org/10.1007/s00381-010-1208-9. 20625743. PMC3061823.

Bianchi, M.C., Tosetti, M., Battini, R., Manca, M.L., Mancuso, M., Cioni, G., Canapicchi, R., Siciliano, G., 2003. Proton MR spectroscopy of mitochondrial diseases: analysis of brain metabolic abnormalities and their possible diagnostic relevance. Am. J. Neuroradiol. 24 (10), 1958–1966. Epub 2003/11/20. 14625217.

Bizzi, A., Uluğ, A.M., Crawford, T.O., Passe, T., Bugiani, M., Bryan, R.N., Barker, P.B., 2001. Quantitative proton MR spectroscopic imaging in acute disseminated encephalomyelitis. Am. J. Neuroradiol. 22 (6), 1125.

Blasel, S., Pfeilschifter, W., Jansen, V., Mueller, K., Zanella, F., Hattingen, E., 2011. Metabolism and regional cerebral blood volume in autoimmune inflammatory demyelinating lesions mimicking malignant gliomas. J. Neurol. 258 (1), 113–122. Epub 2010/08/31. https://doi.org/10.1007/s00415-010-5703-4. 20803026.

Blüml, S., Panigrahy, A., 2012. MR Spectroscopy of Pediatric Brain Disorders. Springer, New York.

Broich, K., Horwich, D., Alavi, A., 1991. HMPAO-SPECT and MRI in acute disseminated encephalomyelitis. J. Nucl. Med. 32 (10), 1897–1900. Epub 1991/10/01. 1919728.

Callen, D.J., Shroff, M.M., Branson, H.M., Lotze, T., Li, D.K., Stephens, D., Banwell, B.L., 2009. MRI in the diagnosis of pediatric multiple sclerosis. Neurology 72 (11), 961–967. Epub 2008/11/29. https://doi.org/10.1212/01.wnl.0000338629.01627.54. 19038852.

Caruso, P.A., Johnson, J., Thibert, R., Rapalino, O., Rincon, S., Ratai, E.M., 2013. The use of magnetic resonance spectroscopy in the evaluation of epilepsy. Neuroimaging Clin. N. Am. 23 (3), 407–424. Epub 2013/08/10. https://doi.org/10.1016/j.nic.2012.12.012. 23928197.

Choi, C.G., Yoo, H.W., 2001. Localized proton MR spectroscopy in infants with urea cycle defect. Am. J. Neuroradiol. 22 (5), 834–837. Epub 2001/05/05. 11337324.

Choudhri, A.F., Klimo Jr., P., Auschwitz, T.S., Whitehead, M.T., Boop, F.A., 2014. 3T intraoperative MRI for management of pediatric CNS neoplasms. Am. J. Neuroradiol. 35 (12), 2382–2387. Epub 2014/07/26. https://doi.org/10.3174/ajnr.A4040. 25059696.

Cianfoni, A., Niku, S., Imbesi, S.G., 2007. Metabolite findings in tumefactive demyelinating lesions utilizing short echo time proton magnetic resonance spectroscopy. Am. J. Neuroradiol. 28 (2), 272–277. Epub 2007/02/14. 17296993.

Dale, R.C., de Sousa, C., Chong, W.K., Cox, T.C., Harding, B., Neville, B.G., 2000. Acute disseminated encephalomyelitis, multiphasic disseminated encephalomyelitis and multiple sclerosis in children. Brain J. Neurol. 123 (Pt 12), 2407–2422. Epub 2000/12/02. https://doi.org/10.1093/brain/123.12.2407. 11099444.

Dietrich, J., Rao, K., Pastorino, S., Kesari, S., 2011. Corticosteroids in brain cancer patients: benefits and pitfalls. Expert. Rev. Clin. Pharmacol. 4 (2), 233–242. Epub 2011/06/15. https://doi.org/10.1586/ecp.11.1. 21666852. PMC3109638.

Filippi, M., Tortorella, C., Rovaris, M., Bozzali, M., Possa, F., Sormani, M.P., Iannucci, G., Comi, G., 2000. Changes in the normal appearing brain tissue and cognitive impairment in multiple sclerosis. J. Neurol. Neurosurg. Psychiatry 68 (2), 157–161. Epub 2000/01/25. https://doi.org/10.1136/jnnp.68.2.157. 10644780. PMC1736794.

Fullerton, H.J., Wu, Y.W., Zhao, S., Johnston, S.C., 2003. Risk of stroke in children: ethnic and gender disparities. Neurology 61 (2), 189–194. Epub 2003/07/23. https://doi.org/10.1212/01.wnl.0000078894.79866.95. 12874397.

Fullerton, H.J., Wu, Y.W., Sidney, S., Johnston, S.C., 2007. Risk of recurrent childhood arterial ischemic stroke in a population-based cohort: the importance of cerebrovascular imaging. Pediatrics 119 (3), 495–501. Epub 2007/03/03. https://doi.org/10.1542/peds.2006-2791. 17332202.

Harvey, A.S., Cross, J.H., Shinnar, S., Mathern, G.W., 2008. Taskforce tPESS. Defining the spectrum of international practice in pediatric epilepsy surgery patients. Epilepsia 49 (1), 146–155. https://doi.org/10.1111/j.1528-1167.2007.01421.x.

Holle, D., Obermann, M., 2013. The role of neuroimaging in the diagnosis of headache disorders. Ther. Adv. Neurol. Disord. 6 (6), 369–374. Epub 2013/11/15. https://doi.org/10.1177/1756285613489765. 24228072. PMC3825114.

Hourani, R., Brant, L.J., Rizk, T., Weingart, J.D., Barker, P.B., Horská, A., 2008. Can proton MR spectroscopic and perfusion imaging differentiate between neoplastic and nonneoplastic brain lesions in adults? Am. J. Neuroradiol. 29 (2), 366–372. Epub 2007/12/07. https://doi.org/10.3174/ajnr.A0810. 18055564. PMC2946840.

Inglese, M., Salvi, F., Iannucci, G., Mancardi, G.L., Mascalchi, M., Filippi, M., 2002. Magnetization transfer and diffusion tensor MR imaging of acute disseminated encephalomyelitis. Am. J. Neuroradiol. 23 (2), 267–272. Epub 2002/02/16. 11847052.

Jackson, B.F., Porcher, F.K., Zapton, D.T., Losek, J.D., 2011. Cerebral sinovenous thrombosis in children: diagnosis and treatment. Pediatr. Emerg. Care 27 (9), 874–880. quiz 81–83. Epub 2011/09/20. https://doi.org/10.1097/PEC.0b013e31822c9ccc. 21926891.

Jan, W., Zimmerman, R.A., Wang, Z.J., Berry, G.T., Kaplan, P.B., Kaye, E.M., 2003. MR diffusion imaging and MR spectroscopy of maple syrup urine disease during acute metabolic decompensation. Neuroradiology 45 (6), 393–399. Epub 2003/05/09. https://doi.org/10.1007/s00234-003-0955-7. 12736767.

Krupp, L.B., Banwell, B., Tenembaum, S., 2007. Consensus definitions proposed for pediatric multiple sclerosis and related disorders. Neurology 68 (16 Suppl 2), S7–12. Epub 2007/04/18. https://doi.org/10.1212/01.wnl.0000259422.44235.a8. 17438241.

Lateef, T.M., Grewal, M., McClintock, W., Chamberlain, J., Kaulas, H., Nelson, K.B., 2009. Headache in young children in the emergency department: use of computed tomography. Pediatrics 124 (1), e12–e17. Epub 2009/07/01. https://doi.org/10.1542/peds.2008-3150. 19564257.

Luthra, G., Parihar, A., Nath, K., Jaiswal, S., Prasad, K.N., Husain, N., Husain, M., Singh, S., Behari, S., Gupta, R.K., 2007. Comparative evaluation of fungal, tubercular, and pyogenic brain abscesses with conventional and diffusion MR imaging and proton MR spectroscopy. Am. J. Neuroradiol. 28 (7), 1332. https://doi.org/10.3174/ajnr.A0548.

Lynch, J.K., 2009. Epidemiology and classification of perinatal stroke. Semin. Fetal Neonatal Med. 14 (5), 245–249. Epub 2009/08/12. https://doi.org/10.1016/j.siny.2009.07.001. 19664976.

Mackay, M.T., Wiznitzer, M., Benedict, S.L., Lee, K.J., Deveber, G.A., Ganesan, V., 2011. Arterial ischemic stroke risk factors: the international pediatric stroke study. Ann. Neurol. 69 (1), 130–140. Epub 2011/02/01. https://doi.org/10.1002/ana.22224. 21280083.

Marin, S.E., Callen, D.J., 2013. The magnetic resonance imaging appearance of monophasic acute disseminated encephalomyelitis: an update post application of the 2007 consensus criteria. Neuroimaging Clin. N. Am. 23 (2), 245–266. Epub 2013/04/24. https://doi.org/10.1016/j.nic.2012.12.005. 23608688. PMC7111644.

Murthy, S.N., Faden, H.S., Cohen, M.E., Bakshi, R., 2002. Acute disseminated encephalomyelitis in children. Pediatrics 110 (2 Pt 1), e21. Epub 2002/08/08. https://doi.org/10.1542/peds.110.2.e21. 12165620.

Narayanan, S., Schmithorst, V., Panigrahy, A., 2020. Arterial spin labeling in pediatric neuroimaging. Semin. Pediatr. Neurol. 33, 100799. Epub 2020/04/26. https://doi.org/10.1016/j.spen.2020.100799. 32331614.

Noguchi, T., Yakushiji, Y., Nishihara, M., Togao, O., Yamashita, K., Kikuchi, K., Matsuo, M., Azama, S., Irie, H., 2016. Arterial spin-labeling in central nervous system infection. Magn. Reson. Med. Sci. 15 (4), 386–394. Epub 2016/03/24. https://doi.org/10.2463/mrms.mp.2015-0140. 27001393. PMC5608113.

Panigrahy, A., Krieger, M.D., Gonzalez-Gomez, I., Liu, X., McComb, J.G., Finlay, J.L., Nelson Jr., M.D., Gilles, F.H., Blüml, S., 2006. Quantitative short echo time 1H-MR spectroscopy of untreated pediatric brain tumors: preoperative diagnosis and characterization. Am. J. Neuroradiol. 27 (3), 560–572. Epub 2006/03/23. 16551993.

Panigrahy, A., Nelson Jr., M.D., Blüml, S., 2010. Magnetic resonance spectroscopy in pediatric neuroradiology: clinical and research applications. Pediatr. Radiol. 40 (1), 3–30. Epub 2009/11/26. https://doi.org/10.1007/s00247-009-1450-z. 19937238.

Parmar, H., Ibrahim, M., 2012. Pediatric intracranial infections. Neuroimaging Clin. N. Am. 22 (4), 707–725. Epub 2012/11/06. https://doi.org/10.1016/j.nic.2012.05.016. 23122263.

Scagni, P., Pagliero, R., 2008. Headache in an Italian pediatric emergency department. J. Headache Pain 9 (2), 83–87. Epub 2008/02/06. https://doi.org/10.1007/s10194-008-0014-1. 18250964. PMC3476181.

Shah, R., Vattoth, S., Jacob, R., Manzil, F.F., O'Malley, J.P., Borghei, P., Patel, B.N., Curé, J.K., 2012. Radiation necrosis in the brain: imaging features and differentiation from tumor recurrence. Radiographics 32 (5), 1343–1359. Epub 2012/09/15. https://doi.org/10.1148/rg.325125002. 22977022.

Sheridan, D.C., Meckler, G.D., Spiro, D.M., Koch, T.K., Hansen, M.L., 2013. Diagnostic testing and treatment of pediatric headache in the emergency department. J. Pediatr. 163 (6), 1634–1637. Epub 2013/08/24. https://doi.org/10.1016/j.jpeds.2013.07.006. 23968749.

Sicotte, N.L., Voskuhl, R.R., Bouvier, S., Klutch, R., Cohen, M.S., Mazziotta, J.C., 2003. Comparison of multiple sclerosis lesions at 1.5 and 3.0 Tesla. Investig. Radiol. 38 (7), 423–427. Epub 2003/06/25. https://doi.org/10.1097/01.RLI.0000065426.07178.f1. 12821856.

Smith, E.R., 2015. Structural causes of ischemic and hemorrhagic stroke in children: moyamoya and arteriovenous malformations. Curr. Opin. Pediatr. 27 (6), 706–711. Epub 2015/10/17. https://doi.org/10.1097/mop.0000000000000280. 26474344.

Stanescu, L., Ishak, G.E., Khanna, P.C., Biyyam, D.R., Shaw, D.W., Parisi, M.T., 2013. FDG PET of the brain in pediatric patients: imaging spectrum with MR imaging correlation. Radiographics 33 (5), 1279–1303. Epub 2013/09/13. https://doi.org/10.1148/rg.335125152. 24025925.

Thompson, A.J., Banwell, B.L., Barkhof, F., Carroll, W.M., Coetzee, T., Comi, G., Correale, J., Fazekas, F., Filippi, M., Freedman, M.S., Fujihara, K., Galetta, S.L., Hartung, H.P., Kappos, L., Lublin, F.D., Marrie, R.A., Miller, A.E., Miller, D.H., Montalban, X., Mowry, E.M., Sorensen, P.S., Tintoré, M., Traboulsee, A. L., Trojano, M., Uitdehaag, B.M.J., Vukusic, S., Waubant, E., Weinshenker, B.G., Reingold, S.C., Cohen, J.A., 2018. Diagnosis of multiple sclerosis: 2017 revisions of the McDonald criteria. Lancet Neurol. 17 (2), 162–173. Epub 2017/12/26. https://doi.org/10.1016/s1474-4422(17)30470-2. 29275977.

Twilt, M., Benseler, S.M., 2013. CNS vasculitis in children. Mult. Scler. Relat. Disord. 2 (3), 162–171. Epub 2013/07/01. https://doi.org/10.1016/j.msard.2012.11.002. 25877722.

Van der Knaap MaV, J., 2005. Magnetic Resonance of Myelination and Myelin Disorders, second ed. Springer, Berlin.

Vázquez, E., Delgado, I., Sánchez-Montañez, A., Barber, I., Sánchez-Toledo, J., Enríquez, G., 2011. Side effects of oncologic therapies in the pediatric central nervous system: update on neuroimaging findings. Radiographics 31 (4), 1123–1139. Epub 2011/07/20. https://doi.org/10.1148/rg.314105180. 21768243.

Wattjes, M.P., Harzheim, M., Kuhl, C.K., Gieseke, J., Schmidt, S., Klotz, L., Klockgether, T., Schild, H.H., Lutterbey, G.G., 2006. Does high-field MR imaging have an influence on the classification of patients with clinically isolated syndromes according to current diagnostic mr imaging criteria for multiple sclerosis? Am. J. Neuroradiol. 27 (8), 1794–1798. Epub 2006/09/15. 16971638.

Wittsack, H.-J., Kugel, H., Roth, B., Heindel, W., 1996. Quantitative measurements with localized 1H MR spectroscopy in children with Canavan's disease. J. Magn. Reson. Imaging 6 (6), 889–893. https://doi.org/10.1002/jmri.1880060609.

Yeshokumar, A.K., Narula, S., Banwell, B., 2017. Pediatric multiple sclerosis. Curr. Opin. Neurol. 30 (3), 216–221. Epub 2017/03/23. https://doi.org/10.1097/wco.0000000000000452. 28323645.

Zand, D.J., Simon, E.M., Pulitzer, S.B., Wang, D.J., Wang, Z.J., Rorke, L.B., Palmieri, M., Berry, G.T., 2003. In vivo pyruvate detected by MR spectroscopy in neonatal pyruvate dehydrogenase deficiency. Am. J. Neuroradiol. 24 (7), 1471–1474. Epub 2003/08/15. 12917150.

CHAPTER

24 Leveraging multi-modal neuroimaging for normal brain development and pediatric brain disorders

Hao Huang[a,b], Tianjia Zhu[b,c], and Timothy P.L. Roberts[a,b]

Department of Radiology, Children's Hospital of Philadelphia, Philadelphia, PA, United States[a] Department of Radiology, Perelman School of Medicine, University of Pennsylvania, Philadelphia, PA, United States[b] Department of Bioengineering, University of Pennsylvania, Philadelphia, PA, United States[c]

Along with multidimensional measures including biological, cognitive, behavioral, environmental, and social factors, neuroimaging offers unprecedented opportunities to delineate functional, structural, and physiological trajectories of typical brain maturation. Neuroimaging could also shed light on pathophysiological pathways in neurological or psychiatric disorders. In an atypically-developing brain, neuroimaging measurements can reveal deviations from typical brain developmental trajectories established with sufficient sample size; individual variability may help identity neuroimaging biomarkers, assist diagnosis of brain disorders, and help design individualized intervention. Covered in the chapters of this book, cutting-edge imaging techniques including functional, diffusion, structural and perfusion magnetic resonance imaging (MRI), magnetic resonance spectroscopy (MRS), electroencephalography (EEG), magnetoencephalography (MEG), along with state-of-the-art analytic approaches including motion correction, brain atlases, computational neuroanatomy, morphology, connectivity and graph-theory-based networks, have empowered recent investigations for generating new insights into pediatric brain structure, function, physiology, electrical and magnetic properties of brain circuits, and brain hemodynamics. Through in-depth and gradual introduction to each imaging modality, covering acquisition, preprocessing and post-processing techniques as well as the applications and challenges specific to fetuses, infants, and children, we hope this book will have helped prepare readers for solving the most pressing scientific and technical problems in multi-modal imaging of the pediatric brain.

Section 1 built the technical foundations for acquiring high-quality pediatric brain imaging data. Starting with data acquisition techniques specific to ages ranging from fetal to childhood, the section gradually built-up technical foundations for a variety of cutting-edge pediatric brain imaging modalities including diffusion, functional, perfusion, myelin water fraction (MWF), quantitative susceptibility mapping (QSM) MRI and magnetic resonance spectroscopy (MRS). The section ends with a chapter on preprocessing to remove distortion and motion artifacts. Chapter 1 provides strategies to resolve unique challenges in pediatric imaging, including optimized hardware and imaging sequences to achieve higher spatial resolution, motion control and correction techniques, and consciousness states during scanning. In Chapter 2, diffusion MRI (dMRI) is reviewed from basic concepts to advanced

Handbook of Pediatric Brain Imaging. https://doi.org/10.1016/B978-0-12-816633-8.00015-6

techniques and applications with a strong emphasis on the conceptual underpinnings of dMRI, its close connection to tissue microstructure, and its applications to the brain. Through advanced discussions of the theory and application, the chapter also promotes independent and creative thinking about future direction and new developments in the field. Building upon dMRI brain microstructure models like diffusion tensor imaging (DTI) from Chapter 2, Chapter 3 provides a comprehensive insight into dMRI based structural connectomics. Covered topics range from connectome creation with brain parcellation and tractography, connectome-derived metrics, to applications of structural connectome to studies on sex differences, brain injury and tumors, and developmental disorders. The chapter also offers perspectives on future breakthroughs possible with connectomes. Then, by delving into promises, developing robust methods, as well as challenges and limitations specific to resting-state functional MRI (rs-fMRI) in the pediatric population in both healthy conditions and brain disorders, Chapter 4 goes beyond a traditional introduction of rs-fMRI, functional connectome, and various brain networks and prepares readers to be at the forefront of the field. In a manner similar to Chapter 4, Chapter 5 not only articulates the basic concepts for Pseudo-Continuous Arterial Spin Labeling (pCASL) perfusion MRI, but also presents challenges specific to the pediatric population such as physiological parameter variations and new technical developments to tackle such challenges. Chapter 6 presents challenges such as fetal motion, poor contrast and resolution and long scan time, recent advances, and the high neuroscientific rewards of solving such pressing challenges in one of the most challenging imaging studies: fetal MRI imaging. Chapter 7 presents special MRI methods (MWF, QSM, etc.) sensitive to age, providing a thorough introduction of how multi-modal MRI contrasts and models are sensitive to developmental changes, Chapter 8 bridges the gap between multi-modal MRI techniques and discoveries in important pediatric brain maturational processes. Chapter 9 provides an overview of key topics for consideration for the immature brain such as magnetic field strength, pediatric sized head coils, water suppression techniques, localization pulse sequences, postprocessing methods, analysis, and interpretation. To ultimately synthesize the significance of pediatric proton MRS, a selection of interesting findings derived from clinical MRS is presented with suggestions for future MRS practice. Finally, with the understanding of unique challenges in multi-modal pediatric MR imaging gained from the first nine chapters, readers will find state-of-the-art pre-processing solutions for such challenges, specifically distortions and artifacts. Chapter 10 makes clear the necessity of considering the entirety of artifact sources to correct for consistent biases in quantitative analyses of neuroimaging data and presents an account of the most recent advances in correcting these artifacts. After reading Section 1, readers should be able to grasp the necessary technical background for acquiring and preprocessing high quality pediatric brain imaging data.

Section 2 introduces the major methods in post-processing pediatric MRI to enable regional and network-specific analysis. First, age-specific brain atlas and parcellation schemes, age-specific white matter tractography, and advanced gray/white matter segmentation for neonatal/infant brains are introduced to establish the foundation for regional, cortical, and brain network analysis. Network and graph analysis of the developing brain and surface-based analysis of the developing cerebral cortex were then discussed in-depth. The section ends with Chapter 15, introducing application of the advanced techniques to prediction of neurodevelopmental outcomes in the pediatric population. Chapter 11 discusses the anatomical landmarks used for pediatric brain atlas parcellation, with a focus on the developmental stage-dependent changes in image intensity, morphology, topology, and transient anatomical structures. Chapter 12 focuses on the challenges in segmenting the infant brain into gray matter, white matter, and cerebral spinal fluid, particularly in the isointense phase with poor contrast

(6–8 months). Major works in infant brain segmentation were surveyed, and a recent deep neural network model for segmenting infant brain in the isointense phase was introduced in detail. In Chapter 13, major challenges, available solutions, and key steps in cortical surface-based analysis of infant MR images were introduced. These steps include cortical topology correction, surface reconstruction, surface registration, surface parcellation, atlas construction, computation, and integration of biologically meaningful multimodal cortical properties. Chapter 14 comprehensively reviews recent neuroimaging and neurophysiological studies investigating connectome development. The chapter paves the way for a better understanding of how brain networks develop from infancy to early childhood as well as how it shapes the development of important cognitive and behavioral skills in later life. With the knowledge of various advanced MRI contrasts and metrics derived from postprocessing, Chapter 15 addresses how quantitative analysis could help clinical diagnosis through prediction of neurodevelopmental outcomes. The complex dynamics of disease or injury progression coupled with rapid brain development make accurately predicting developmental outcomes challenging; nonetheless novel methods can offer the most accurate assessment of the character and extent of brain injury and individual risks.

MEG and EEG represent powerful tools for studying brain development given the capacity of electrophysiological techniques to characterize brain function based on neural activity in both time and space and provides complementary electrophysiological information to structural and functional MRI. Section 3 focuses on the hardware, acquisition schemes, and processing of MEG specifically tailored for the pediatric population. Major brands of MEG systems were introduced through first-hand experiences, followed by well-rounded surveys on how MEG provides insights into brain development and recent MEG studies of children. State-of-the-art pediatric EEG and MRI-compatible EEG systems have also been introduced, providing a possibility for simultaneous multi-modal imaging that provides comprehensive and complementary information. Chapter 16 provides valuable first-hand experiences using two recently developed major pediatric MEG systems, the BabySQUID and the BabyMEG, in studying children with refractory epilepsy as well as typically developing infants and toddlers. Chapter 17 reviews existing MEG studies of functional brain development with a focus on four topics that have been particularly advanced by the use of MEG: the development of cortical auditory processing, the development of speech and language processing, the development of cortical somatosensory processing, and the effects of preterm birth and other prenatal insults on the developing brain. Chapter 18 reviews how MEG can contribute to the study of atypical brain development in children. Key MEG studies that focus on children with epilepsy, autism spectrum disorder (ASD), language disorders and attention deficit hyperactivity disorder (ADHD) were thoroughly surveyed. Offering complementing insights, Chapter 19 elaborates on both traditional techniques like EEG power and event-related potentials (ERP) and new techniques such as MRI-compatible EEG source localization and functional connectivity analysis and their recent applications in the study of brain and cognitive development.

Section 4 reviews recent advances in understanding infant brain development based on modern MR techniques. Chapter 20 reviews recent advances in early brain development during the second half of gestation and the first two postnatal years using modern MR techniques. The discussed imaging studies converge into typically developing brain structural and functional maturational curves that are distinct across brain regions, setting the stage for understanding aberrant brain development in neurological or neuropsychiatric disorders. Chapter 21 focuses more on unique methods and applications of T1-, T2-weighted, diffusion, and functional MRI in infants. Readers will understand how multimodal neuroimaging provides information critical for advancing understanding the modifiable risk factors underlying prematurity-related disorders and learn best practices for improving neurodevelopmental and mental health outcomes in preterm and other high-risk neonatal populations. Chapter 22 focuses on the perinatal period essential to disease diagnosis and treatment planning by outlining the incidence, pathophysiology, and neuroimaging findings in a variety of perinatal brain disorders. Chapter 23 reviews the current approaches for neuroimaging, in the context of the major intracranial neurological disorders of childhood and exemplifies how novel neuroimaging techniques already contribute or have potential to impact clinical diagnosis and management.

We hope the book has served as an informative and enriching textbook and handbook for imaging the pediatric brain, and the readers have set forth upon a fruitful and enjoyable journey in pediatric neuroimaging.

Index

Note: Page numbers followed by *f* indicate figures, and *t* indicate tables.

D

E

F

G

H

I

K

L

M

T

U

V

W

Y

Printed in the United States
by Baker & Taylor Publisher Services